Access 2024/Microsoft 365 Programming by Example

Julitta Korol

MERCURY LEARNING AND INFORMATION
Boston, Massachusetts

MERCURY LEARNING AND INFORMATION
121 High Street, 3rd Floor
Boston, MA 02110
info@merclearning.com

J. Korol. *Access 2024 / Microsoft 365 Programming by Example.*
ISBN: 978-1-50152-414-1

The publisher recognizes and respects all marks used by companies, manufacturers, and developers
as a means to distinguish their products. All brand names and product names mentioned in this
book are trademarks or service marks of their respective companies. Any omission or misuse (of any
kind) of service marks or trademarks, etc. is not an attempt to infringe on the property of others.

Library of Congress Control Number: 2025931802

242526321   This book is printed on acid-free paper in the United States of America.

Our titles are available for adoption, license, or bulk purchase by institutions, corporations, etc.

All of our titles are available in digital format at various digital vendors. All companion files for
this title are available by visiting the website for the book at *sciendo.com/book/9781501524141*
and by clicking on the "COMPANION FILES" tab. The sole obligation of Mercury Learning
and Information to the purchaser is to replace the files, based on defective materials or faulty
workmanship, but not based on the operation or functionality of the product.

Access 2024/Microsoft 365 Programming by Example

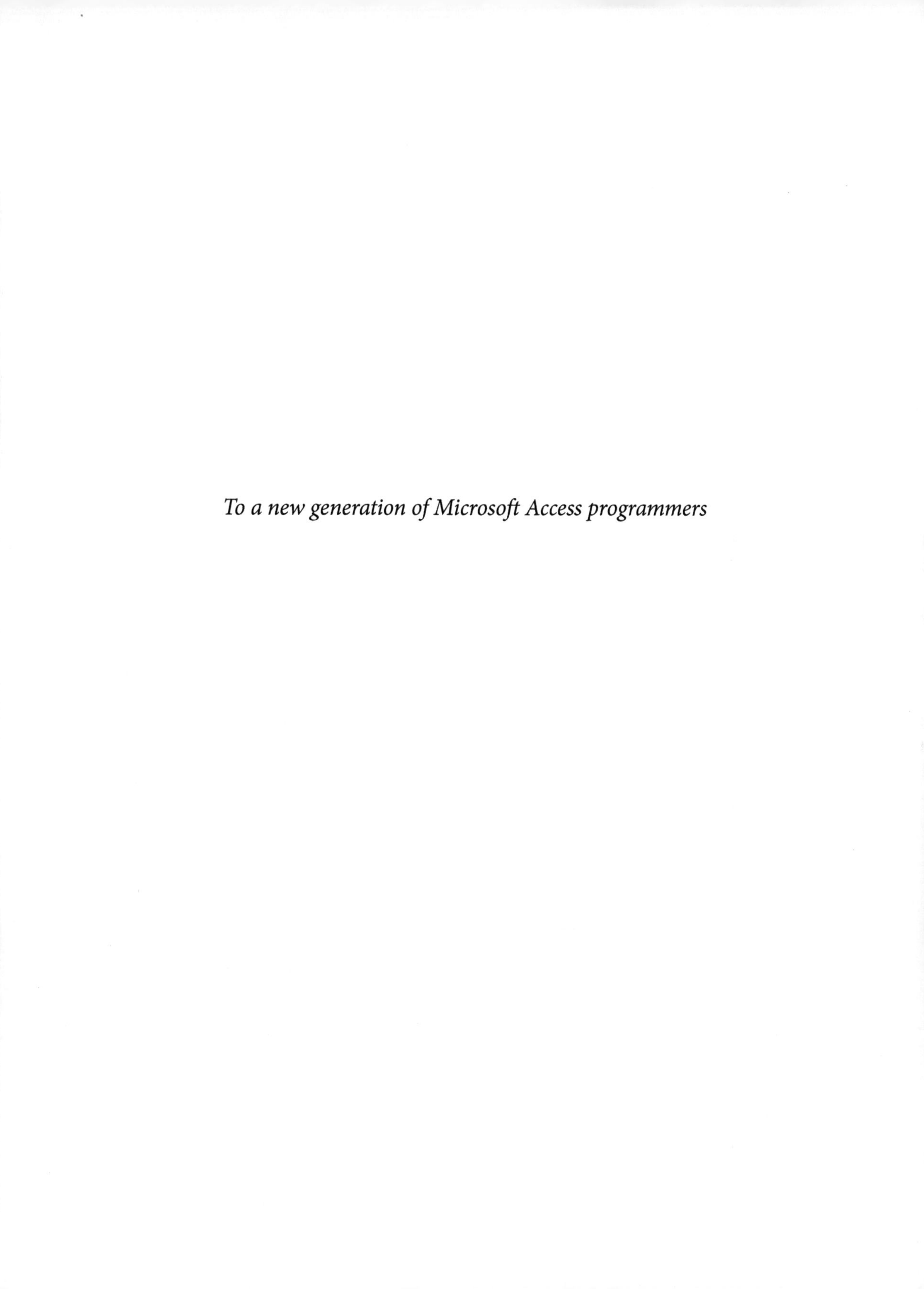

To a new generation of Microsoft Access programmers

CONTENTS

Acknowledgments..*xxvii*
Introduction..*xxix*
List of Figures..*xxxix*
List of Tables..*lxi*

PART I   ACCESS VBA PRIMER   1

Chapter 1   Introduction to VBA Programming 3

Statements, Commands, and Instructions....................................3
Procedures and Modules..4
   Module Types...5
   Procedure Types...6
Writing Procedures in a Module...10
Executing Your Procedures 13
Compiling and Saving Your Procedures....................................16
Placing a Database in a Trusted Location 18
VBA Data Types..22
Understanding and Using Variables 23
   Declaring Variables..24
   Specifying the Data Type of a Variable 28
      Using Data Type Declaration Characters 29
   Assigning Values to Variables 29
   Forcing Declaration of Variables 30
   Understanding the Scope of Variables 33
      Procedure-Level (Local) Variables 34
      Module-Level Variables...34
      Project-Level Variables..37
Understanding the Lifetime of Variables..................................38

Using Temporary Variables 38
    Creating a Temporary Variable with a TempVars
       Collection Object..39
    Retrieving Names and Values of TempVar Objects..........................40
    Using Temporary Global Variables in Expressions 41
    Removing a Temporary Variable from a TempVars Collection 41
Using Static Variables..42
Using Object Variables...44
    Disposing of Object Variables 47
Finding a Variable Definition 47
Determining the Data Type of a Variable...47
Using Constants 48
Using ChatGPT with Access...49
Summary 52

Chapter 2   Getting to Know Visual Basic Editor (VBE)...................53

Understanding the Project Explorer Window 53
Understanding the Properties Window..56
Understanding the Code Window...58
Other Windows in VBE 60
Assigning a Name to the VBA Project 61
Renaming a Module..62
Syntax and Programming Assistance...62
    List Properties/Methods 63
    Parameter Info 64
    List Constants...65
    Quick Info..66
    Complete Word...67
    Indent/Outdent..67
    Comment Block/Uncomment Block 68
Using the Object Browser 68
Using the VBA Object Library 71
Using the Immediate Window...72
Using ChatGPT with Access...75
Summary 76

Chapter 3   Access VBA Procedures and Functions 77

Writing Function Procedures...77
Running Function Procedures 78

Data Types and Functions 80
Passing Arguments (ByRef and ByVal)...82
Using Optional Arguments..83
VBA Built-In Functions for User Interaction 85
   Using the MsgBox Function..85
      Returning Values from the MsgBox Function 93
   Using the InputBox Function...95
Converting Data Types...97
Using ChatGPT with Access..99
Summary 100

Chapter 4   Adding Decisions to Your Access VBA Programs......101

Relational and Logical Operators...102
If...Then Statement 102
Multiline If...Then Statement 105
Decisions Based on More than One Condition 107
If...Then...Else Statement 109
If...Then...ElseIf Statement 112
Nested If...Then Statements...113
Select Case Statement 116
   Using Is with the Case Clause 119
   Specifying a Range of Values in a Case Clause 120
   Specifying Multiple Expressions in a Case Clause 122
Using ChatGPT with Access..123
Summary 123

Chapter 5   Adding Repeating Actions to Your
**   Access VBA Programs 125**

Using the Do...While Statement 125
   Another Approach to the Do...While Statement............................127
Using the Do...Until Statement...129
   Another Approach to the Do...Until Statement...........................130
Using the For...Next Statement...131
Using the For Each...Next Statement 134
Exiting Loops Early..135
Nested Loops...136
Using ChatGPT with Access..138
Summary 138

Chapter 6   Keeping Track of Multiple Values Using Arrays.........139

Understanding Arrays 139
  Declaring Arrays...141
  Array Upper and Lower Bounds 143
  Initializing and Filling an Array 143
    Filling an Array Using Individual Assignment Statements..............144
    Filling an Array Using the Array Function 144
    Filling an Array Using the For…Next Loop...............................144
Using a One-Dimensional Array 145
Arrays and Looping Statements 147
Using a Two-Dimensional Array..151
Static and Dynamic Arrays 152
Array Functions...155
  The Array Function..155
  The IsArray Function...156
  The Erase Function 157
  The LBound and UBound Functions 160
Errors in Arrays...161
Parameter Arrays...162
Passing Arrays to Function Procedures 163
Sorting an Array 165
Using ChatGPT with Access...166
Summary 167

Chapter 7   Keeping Track of Multiple Values
Using Collections 169

Creating Your Own Collection 170
  Adding Items to Your Collection......................................170
  Determine the Number of Items in Your Collection 172
  Accessing Items in a Collection 172
  Removing Items from a Collection 173
  Updating Items in a Collection...174
  Returning a Collection from a Function 176
Collections vs. Arrays 179
Watching the Execution of Your VBA Procedures....................180
Using ChatGPT with Access...186
Summary 189

Chapter 8   Getting to Know Built-In Tools for Testing and Debugging **191**

Syntax, Runtime, and Logic Errors 191
Stopping a Procedure 193
Using Breakpoints 194
  Removing Breakpoints 200
Using the Immediate Window in Break Mode 201
  Working in a Code Window in Break Mode 202
Using the Stop Statement 203
Using the Assert Statement 203
Using the Add Watch Window 205
  Removing Watch Expressions 207
Using Quick Watch 208
Using the Locals Window 209
Using the Call Stack Dialog Box 211
Stepping Through VBA Procedures 212
  Stepping over a Procedure 212
  Stepping out of a Procedure 213
  Running a Procedure to Cursor 214
  Setting the Next Statement 214
  Showing the Next Statement 214
Navigating with Bookmarks 215
Stopping and Resetting VBA Procedures 216
Trapping Errors 216
  Using the Err Object 217
  Procedure Testing 221
  Setting Error-Trapping Options 223
Using Toolbars in the VBE Window 224
Using ChatGPT with Access 225
Summary 226

PART II   ACCESS VBA PROGRAMMING WITH DAO AND ADO   **227**

Chapter 9   Data Access Technologies in Microsoft Access **229**

Introduction to Database Engines 230
  Types of Database Engines 231

Understanding Access Versions and File Formats.............................234
Understanding Library References...234
Overview of Object Libraries in Microsoft Access..........................237
   The VBA Object Library...237
   The Microsoft Access 16.0 Object Library...........................238
   OLE Automation..238
   The Microsoft Office 16.0 Access Database
      Engine Object Library...238
   The Microsoft DAO 3.6 Object Library...............................238
   The Microsoft ADO 6.1 Library...238
Creating a Reference to the ADO Library.....................................241
Understanding Connection Strings...242
   Using ODBC Connection Strings..244
   Creating and Using ODBC DSN Connections.......................245
   Creating and Using DSN-Less ODBC Connections................250
   ODBC Connection Strings for Common Data Sources...........250
   Using OLE DB Connection Strings.......................................251
   Connection Strings via a Data Link File...............................253
Using ChatGPT with Access..257
Summary..258

**Chapter 10   Creating and Manipulating
               Databases with DAO 259**

Setting Up Your Environment for DAO Programming......................259
Exploring the DAO Object Model..260
Creating a Database with DAO..261
Copying a Database...265
Opening Microsoft Access Databases..267
   Opening a Microsoft Jet Database in Read/Write Mode.........267
   Opening a Microsoft Access Database in Read-Only Mode......269
   Opening a Microsoft Jet Database Secured with a Password......269
Opening Other Files with DAO..271
Accessing Database Tables and Fields...273
   Creating an Access Table and Setting Field Properties...........274
   Defining Various Types of Fields in an Access Table..............280
   Removing a Field from a Table..289
   Retrieving Table Properties...291
   Linking a dBASE Table...292

Creating Indexes 292

    Adding a Multiple-Field Index to a Table................................294

Introduction to DAO Recordsets..295

    Opening a Recordset and Transferring Data 296

    Finding and Reading Records with DAO.................................300

    Counting Records and Retrieving Field Values.......................304

    Using the Seek Method to Find Records in a

    Table-Type Recordset..307

    Using the Find Methods to Find Records in

    Snapshots and Dynasets...308

    Adding a New Record to a Table 311

    Adding and Deleting Attachments..311

    Adding Values to Multvalue Lookup Fields 314

    Modifying a Record...318

    Deleting a Record 319

    Filtering Records...320

    Copying Records to an Excel Worksheet...............................321

Introduction to Queries..326

    Operators, Wildcards, and Predicates Used in Queries.........330

    Creating a Select Query with DAO 333

    Creating and Running a Parameter Query 334

    Creating and Running a Make-Table Query 337

    Creating and Running Update, Append, and Delete Queries ...338

    Creating and Running a Pass-Through Query........................341

    Performing Other Operations with Queries............................346

Transaction Processing 350

    Creating a Transaction with DAO...350

Using ChatGPT with Access..354

Summary 355

Chapter 11   Creating and Manipulating

                      Databases with ADO...**357**

Setting Up Your Environment for ADO Programming 358

Creating an Access Database with ADO...................................358

Copying a Database...360

    Copying a Database with FileSystemObject 360

More About Database Errors..361

Opening a Microsoft Jet Database in

Read/Write Mode 363

Connecting to the Current Access Database...366
Opening Other Databases, Spreadsheets,
  and Text Files..368
  Connecting to an SQL Server Database 368
  Opening a Microsoft Excel Workbook 368
  Opening a Text File 371
Creating a Microsoft Access Table and Setting
  Field Properties 372
Copying a Table...376
Deleting a Table...377
Adding New Fields to an Existing Table...377
Removing a Field from a Table 379
Retrieving Table and Field Properties...379
Linking a Microsoft Access Table..381
Linking a Microsoft Excel Worksheet...383
Listing Database Tables Using the Catalog Object..................................386
Listing Tables and Fields Using the OpenSchema Method.....................387
Listing Data Types...389
Retrieving the Value and the Increment of the
  AutoNumber Field 390
Creating a Primary Key Index..391
Creating a Single-Field Index 393
Listing Indexes in a Table...395
Deleting Table Indexes..396
Creating Table Relationships 398
Introduction to ADO Recordsets..400
  Cursor Types 402
  Lock Types...403
  Cursor Location 404
  The Options Parameter...405
  Opening a Recordset...409
    Opening a Recordset Based on a Table or Query...............................410
    Opening a Recordset Based on an SQL Statement.............................414
    Opening a Recordset Based on Criteria...415
  Moving Around in a Recordset...416
    Finding the Record Position...417
  Returning a Recordset as a String...418
  Finding Records Using the Find Method 421

Finding Records Using the Seek Method 422
Finding a Record Based on Multiple Conditions 424
Using Bookmarks 425
Using the GetRows Method to Fill the Recordset 429
Working with Records in ADO 430
Adding and Modifying Records 430
Editing Multiple Records...431
Deleting a Record 432
Copying Records to a Word Document 432
Copying Records to a Text File 434
Filtering and Sorting Records 436
Creating and Running Queries with ADO 438
Creating a Select Query with ADO 439
Executing an Existing Select Query with ADO..................................441
Modifying a Select Query..444
Creating and Running a Parameter Query 446
Executing an Update Query...449
Creating and Running a Pass-Through Query 452
Listing Database Queries 452
Deleting a Query...453
Using Advanced ADO Features...454
Fabricating a Recordset...455
Disconnected Recordsets...459
Saving a Recordset to Disk 461
Cloning a Recordset 478
Introduction to Data Shaping...483
Writing a Simple SHAPE Statement..485
Working with Data Shaping...485
Writing a Complex SHAPE Statement...489
Shaped Recordsets with Multiple
Children and Grandchildren 490
Connection Pooling..499
Transaction Processing 501
Creating a Transaction in ADO...501
Examining the References Collection...507
Using ChatGPT with Access..508
Summary 510

PART III   ACCESS STRUCTURED QUERY LANGUAGE (SQL)   511

Chapter 12   Understanding and Using SQL Within Microsoft Access...513

Overview of SQL and the Access SQL Dialect 513
   Key Differences Between SQL and Access SQL 514
   SQL Specification and Access SQL...515
   The Categories of SQL 517
Using Joins in Access SQL 518
   Types of Joins 518
Creating Tables..520
Deleting Tables 525
Using SQL Statements in the Query Design...526
Using DDL Statements with Tables...526
Modifying Tables with DDL...527
   Adding New Fields to a Table 527
   Changing the Data Type of a Table Column...............................529
   Changing the Size of a Text Column...530
   Deleting a Column from a Table 530
   Setting a Default Value for a Table Column................................530
   Changing the Seed and Increment Values of AutoNumber Columns...531
Working with Primary Keys and Indexes..533
   Adding a Primary Key to a Table..533
   Adding a Multiple-Field Index to a Table...................................535
   Deleting an Index and an Indexed Field......................................536
Creating Indexes with Restrictions...538
Understanding Table Constraints..541
   Using CHECK Constraints...542
Establishing Relationships Between Tables...546
Using the Data Definition Query Window 550
Creating and Using Views and Stored Procedures................................553
   Creating a View...553
   Enumerating Views 557
   Deleting a View...557
   Creating a Stored Procedure 558
   Creating a Parameterized Stored Procedure 559

Examining the Contents of a Stored Procedure 562
Executing a Parameterized Stored Procedure..563
Deleting a Stored Procedure..565
Changing Database Records with Stored Procedures............................566
Using ChatGPT with Access..567
Summary 568

PART IV IMPLEMENTING DATABASE SECURITY IN MICROSOFT ACCESS 571

Chapter 13 Security Measures in Access .accdb File Format Databases 573

Database Password Protection in Access .accdb Databases......................574
Setting a Database Password Manually..574
Using DAO to Set or Reset a Database Password....................................576
Using ADO to Set or Reset a Database Password 578
Removing a Database Password 579
Implementing Custom User Authentication with VBA............................580
Other Features for Enhanced Database Security 597
Using ChatGPT with Access..599
Summary 599

Chapter 14 Security Measures in Access .mdb File Format Databases 601

Setting a Database Password..602
Managing the Security and Permissions of
Your Access MDB Databases..604
Implementing User-Level Security..607
Understanding WIFs..607
Creating and Joining a WIF 610
Opening a Secured MDB Database..617
Managing User-Level Security with VBA..620
Managing User-Level Security with DAO..621
Creating a New User Account with DAO..621
Creating a New Group Account with DAO..623
Adding a User to a Group with DAO..624
Listing All Groups and Users with DAO 625
Deleting a User or Group Account or Users from Groups................627

Working with Object Permissions Using DAO 629
   Setting Permissions for an Object Using DAO 631
   Checking Object Permissions Using DAO 634
   Denying Object Permissions Using DAO 634
Managing User-Level Security with ADO (ADOX) 634
   Creating User and Group Accounts with ADO 634
   Deleting User and Group Accounts 638
   Listing User and Group Accounts Using ADO 640
   Listing Users in Groups Using ADO 642
   Setting and Retrieving User and Group
      Permissions Using ADOX 644
   Determining the Object Owner Using ADOX 644
   Setting User Permissions for an Object Using ADOX 645
   Setting User Permissions for a Database Using ADOX 647
   Setting User Permissions for a Container Using ADOX 647
   Checking Permissions for Objects Using ADOX 649
   Changing a User Password Using ADOX 649
Managing User-Level Security with SQL Commands 651
   SQL Commands for Managing User-Level Security 651
   Creating a User and Granting and Revoking
      Permissions to Objects 651
   Adding Users to Groups 653
   Removing a User from a Group 654
   Deleting a User Account 654
   Granting Permissions for an Object 654
   Revoking Security Permissions 655
   Deleting a Group Account 657
Correctly Opening a Secured Access
  MDB Database 657
Using ChatGPT with Access...657
Summary 658

**PART V   VBA PROGRAMMING IN ACCESS
FORMS AND REPORTS   659**

**Chapter 15   Using VBA to Interact with
Forms and Form Controls** **661**

Controlling Forms with Form Properties...662

Referring to Forms and Their Controls 682
Form Modules and Event Programming in Access................................685
Data Events 687
    The Current Event 687
    The BeforeInsert Event 688
    The AfterInsert Event..689
    The BeforeUpdate Event 690
    The AfterUpdate Event 691
    The Dirty Event..692
    The OnUndo Event 693
    The Delete Event...693
    The BeforeDelConfirm Event 694
    The AfterDelConfirm Event 694
Focus Events 695
    The Activate Event...695
    The Deactivate Event 696
    The GotFocus Event 696
    The LostFocus Event 696
Mouse Events 696
    The Click Event 697
    The DblClick Event 697
    The MouseDown Event 697
    The MouseMove Event 698
    The MouseUp Event 698
    The MouseWheel Event 698
Keyboard Events..699
    The KeyDown Event 699
    The KeyPress Event 701
    The KeyUp Event 701
Error Events 701
    The Error Event 702
Filter Events 703
    The Filter Event..703
    The ApplyFilter Event 704
Timing Events..705
    The Timer Event 705
Events Recognized by Form Sections...706
    The DblClick (Form Section) Event 706

Understanding and Using the OpenArgs Property....................................707
Using Images in Access Forms...713
Using the Attachments Control 714
Using the DoCmd Object with Access Forms...718
  Opening Forms 719
  Closing Forms 719
  Moving Between Records 720
  Saving Forms 720
  Using Requery with Forms and Controls..720
Forcing the Combo Box Dropdown on Form_Load................................721
Using ChatGPT with Access...723
Summary 724

**Chapter 16   Using VBA to Interact with Reports and
                Report Controls..727**

Creating Access Reports...728
Report Modules, Properties, and Event
Programming in Access Reports..737
  Report Properties...738
  Using Report Events 739
    Open 739
  Close...741
  Activate 741
  Deactivate 743
  NoData 743
  Page..743
  Error 745
  Events Recognized by Report Sections 746
    Format (Report Section Event) 746
    Print (Report Section Event) 749
    Retreat (Report Section Event) 753
Using the Report View 753
Sorting and Grouping Data 755
Saving Reports in .pdf or .xps File Format 757
Report Troubleshooting..757
Using the OpenArgs Property of the Report Object 758
Running Built-In Menu Commands from VBA.......................................761
Creating a Report with VBA...762

Using ChatGPT with Access...778
Summary 779

PART VI   ENHANCING THE USER EXPERIENCE   781

Chapter 17   Programming the Ribbon Interface
in Access...783

Understanding and Exploring the Ribbon Interface.............................784
Working with the Navigation Pane 786
Using VBA to Customize the Navigation Pane 791
Locking the Navigation Pane 791
Controlling the Display of Database Objects.................................791
Setting Displayed Categories...793
Saving and Loading the Configuration of the
Navigation Pane..794
A Quick Overview of the Access 2024
Ribbon Interface..796
Ribbon Programming with XML, VBA, and Macros 799
Tools for Ribbon Programming...800
Creating the Ribbon Customization XML Markup 800
Callback Procedures in Ribbon Programming...............................804
Loading Ribbon Customizations from an
External XML Document..805
Embedding Ribbon XML Markup in a VBA Procedure 812
Storing Ribbon Customization XML Markup in a
System Table...813
Assigning Ribbon Customizations to Forms and Reports.............819
Using Images in Ribbon Customizations 823
Requesting Images via the loadImage Callback 823
Requesting Images via the getImage Callback................................828
Understanding Attributes and Callbacks 833
Using Various Controls in Ribbon Customizations 834
Creating Toggle Buttons 834
Creating Split Buttons, Menus, and Submenus.............................836
Creating Checkboxes..838
Creating Edit Boxes 840
Creating Combo Boxes and Dropdowns..841
Creating a Gallery Control 843

Creating a Dialog Box Launcher 843
Disabling a Control 844
Repurposing a Built-In Control 845
Refreshing the Ribbon 846
The CommandBars Object and the Ribbon 849
Tab Activation and Group Auto-Scaling.......................................852
Customizing the Backstage View...853
Customizing the Quick Access Toolbar (QAT)............................857
Using ChatGPT with Access..859
Summary 859

PART VII   ADVANCED VBA PROGRAMMING CONCEPTS   861

Chapter 18   Creating Classes, Objects, Properties, Methods, and Events 863

Important Terminology 864
Creating Custom Objects in Class Modules...................................866
Creating a Class...867
Class Variables..868
Creating and Using Property Procedures 869
Immediate Exit from Property Procedures 871
Creating the Property Get and Property Let Procedures 871
Defining the Scope of Property Procedures............................872
Creating the Class Methods 873
Writing Event Procedures..878
Writing the Form_Load Event Procedure 878
Writing the lstMovies_AfterUpdate Event Procedure.......................881
Writing the btnClose_Click Event Procedure..........................883
Writing the btnUpdate_Click Event Procedure............................884
Writing the btnRemove_Click Event Procedure 887
Writing the btnAdd_Click and
btnSave_Click Event Procedures..888
Effective Code Analysis 893
Creating an Instance of a Class 893
Creating and Working with Collection Classes.............................894
The Collection Object..895
The Collection Class 896

Advanced Event Programming 900
   Sinking Events in Standalone Class Modules 902
   Writing Event Procedure Code in Two Places..........................909
   Responding to Control Events in a Class Module....................909
   Declaring and Raising Events 914
Using ChatGPT with Access..917
Summary 918

PART VIII   VBA AND MACROS   921

Chapter 19   Getting Comfortable with Access Macros and Templates 923

Macros or VBA? 924
Access 2024 Macro Security..925
Using the AutoExec Macro..928
Understanding Macro Actions, Arguments, and Program Flow..............929
Creating and Using Macros in Access 2024 932
   Creating Standalone Macros 932
   Running Standalone Macros...937
   Creating and Using Submacros...938
   Creating and Using Embedded Macros.......................................940
   Copying Embedded Macros...941
   Examining Shadow Properties...944
   Working in Sandbox Mode 946
   Generating Macros Using the Command Button Wizard.........947
   Understanding Data Macros 947
      Creating a Data Macro 948
      Creating a Named Data Macro 955
      Editing an Existing Named Data Macro............................958
      Calling a Named Data Macro from Another Macro.......958
      Using ReturnVars in Data Macros.....................................958
      Tracing Data Macro Execution Errors...............................960
   Copying Macros..962
   Error Handling in Macros 963
   Using Temporary Variables in Macros...966
Converting Macros to VBA Code...967
   Converting a Standalone Macro to VBA.....................................967
   Converting Embedded Macros to VBA..969

Access Templates 971
   Creating a Custom Blank Database Template.................................971
   Understanding the .accdt Template File Format 972
Using ChatGPT with Access..977
Summary 978

PART IX   WORKING TOGETHER: VBA, XML, AND REST API   979

Chapter 20   Using XML in Access 981

XML and Access..981
Structure of XML Documents 983
Exporting XML Data from Access..984
   Understanding the XML Data File...986
   Understanding the XML Schema File...988
   Understanding the XSL Transformation Files 990
Viewing XML Documents Formatted with Stylesheets....................994
Advanced XML Export Options 997
   Data Export Options...997
   Schema Export Options..999
   Presentation Export Options 1000
Applying XSLT Transforms to Exported Data 1006
Importing XML Data to Access 1013
   Importing a Schema File...1013
   Importing an XML File..1015
Using VBA to Export and Import XML Documents 1019
   Exporting to XML Using the ExportXML Method 1020
   Transforming XML Data with the
      TransformXML Method...1023
   Importing to XML Using the ImportXML Method.......................1031
Manipulating XML Documents Programmatically 1031
   Loading and Retrieving the Contents of an XML File..................1033
   Working with XML Document Nodes 1035
   Retrieving Information from Element Nodes..................................1036
   Retrieving Specific Information from Element Nodes....................1038
   Retrieving the First Matching Node...1040
Using ADO with XML..1040
   Saving an ADO Recordset as XML to Disk....................................1041

Attribute-Centric and Element-Centric XML 1044

Changing the Type of an XML File 1045

Applying an XSL Stylesheet..1046

Transforming Attribute-Centric XML Data into an
HTML Table 1049

Loading an XML Document in Excel 1053

Using ChatGPT with Access..1056

Summary 1056

Chapter 21   Access and REST API **1059**

Introduction to VBA Dictionary Objects 1059

Accessing the VBA Dictionary 1060

Adding a Reference to the Microsoft
Scripting Runtime Library 1060

Working with the Dictionary Object's
Properties and Methods 1061

Dictionary Versus Collection 1065

Introduction to Regular Expressions 1066

Character Matching in RegExp Patterns 1067

Quantifiers in RegExp Patterns 1068

Using the RegExp Object in VBA...1069

The RegExp Object Declaration 1070

RegExp Properties 1071

RegExp Methods 1071

Writing VBA Programs Using the RegExp Object 1071

Introduction to REST API 1075

Accessing REST APIs with VBA...1076

Methods and Properties of the XMLHTTPRequest Object 1077

Making a Basic GET Request..1081

Overview of JSON 1084

Loading JSON Data into Access 1086

Parsing JSON with Third-Party Libraries 1093

Using ChatGPT with Access..1093

Summary 1095

Appendix A   VBA Data Types..**1097**

Appendix B   Access 2007-2024 File Formats..............................**1101**

**Appendix C   Installing Internet Information
Services (IIS)** **1105**

Creating a Virtual Directory...1108
Setting ASP Configuration Properties...1110
Turning Off Friendly HTTP Error Messages...1111

Index **1115**

ACKNOWLEDGMENTS

First, I'd like to express my gratitude to the editorial team at DeGruyter and Mercury Learning and Information for working extremely hard to bring this book to print. A sincere thank-you to David Pallai for offering me the opportunity to update this book to the new 2024 version. We've been through so many versions together and I am so grateful for all his support and guidance during the past decade we've been working together on this and other titles. Together with Jennifer Blaney, David and I have kept this book updated for the new generation of Access power users and VBA developers. Jen continues to be my go-to person now at DeGruyter. She has numerous years of publishing expertise, and she's a great manager. With so many other staff members at the DeGruyter she tirelessly steered this book to publication from beginning to end. I also want to thank my copyeditor and compositor for their efforts in meticulous proofreading, manuscript editing and page layout.

Finally, I'd like to acknowledge readers like you who cared enough to post reviews of the previous editions of this book. Your invaluable feedback has helped me improve the quality of this work by including the material that matters to you most. Please continue to inspire me with your ideas and suggestions. And please forgive me if some of your suggestions didn't make it into this book. I simply ran out of pages!

Julitta Korol
April 2025

INTRODUCTION

This book, *Access 2024 / Microsoft 365 Programming by Example*, is not a reference manual but a step-by-step tutorial with selected topics that will teach you how to program in Access using its built-in language—Visual Basic for Applications (VBA). Unlike a detailed reference guide, this book takes you on a journey through the essentials, focusing on practical examples and hands-on exercises. Each chapter is designed to build on the last, gradually introducing more complex concepts and techniques as you progress.

The aim is to provide you with a solid foundation in VBA programming within the context of Access, covering the most critical and frequently used features. This book will not answer all questions about VBA programming but will equip you with the knowledge and skills to tackle common tasks and challenges. By the end of this tutorial, you'll have a robust understanding of how to use VBA to enhance and automate your Access databases, empowering you to develop more efficient and powerful applications.

Whether you're a beginner looking to get started or an experienced user wanting to refine your skills, this book offers a structured and approachable way to learn VBA programming in Access. While it won't cover every possible scenario or advanced topic, it provides a strong foundation and encourages further exploration and learning.

With the ChatGPT sections included in each chapter, you can gain additional insights and interactive support to enhance your learning experience. These sections provide on-the-spot explanations, code examples, and answers to frequently asked questions. By integrating this Artificial Intelligence (AI)-powered assistance, the book aims to make complex concepts more accessible and help you overcome common challenges more efficiently.

Each ChatGPT section is designed to complement the tutorial content, offering practical tips and real-world applications of the topics covered. You'll find interactive prompts that encourage you to experiment with the code, troubleshoot errors, and explore alternative solutions. This hands-on approach ensures that you not only understand the theory but also apply your knowledge in practical scenarios.

Furthermore, the ChatGPT sections serve as a valuable resource for continuous learning. Whenever you encounter a difficult concept or need clarification, you can refer to these sections and work with ChatGPT for immediate guidance. This integration of AI assistance helps bridge the gap between traditional learning methods and modern technology, making your journey through VBA programming in Access more engaging and effective.

In essence, the inclusion of ChatGPT sections transforms this book into an interactive learning companion, providing personalized support and enhancing your overall understanding of VBA programming in Access.

PREREQUISITES

Access 2024 / Microsoft 365 Programming by Example assumes that you already know how to manually design a Microsoft° Access database and perform various database tasks by creating and running queries. This book also assumes that you know how to create more complex forms with embedded subforms, combo boxes, and other built-in controls. If you don't have these skills, there are countless books on the market—including another of mine, *Access 365 Project Book (ISBN:978-1-68392-094-6)*—that can teach you, step by step, how to build simple databases. Trying to learn Access programming without existing Access skills can lead to confusion, frustration, and lack of progress, discouraging you from fully mastering Access. Without a solid understanding of the fundamental Access concepts and tools, you may find yourself overwhelmed by the complexity and breadth of Access' features. If you feel you are ready for the next step and are anxious to learn Access programming, you'll get the most out of this book by following its structured, step-by-step approach. This book is designed to guide you through Access programming, making it easier and more enjoyable. Instead of just reading about concepts, you'll be able to see them in action, performing them yourself and getting the confidence you need to tackle any future Access programming challenges on your own.

HOW THIS BOOK IS ORGANIZED

This book is divided into 9 parts (a total of 21 chapters) that progressively introduce you to programming Access databases.

PART I—ACCESS VBA PRIMER

Here, you are introduced to VBA—the programming language for Microsoft Access. In this part of the book, you acquire an understanding of the fundamentals of VBA that you will use repeatedly in building your own Access database applications.

Part I consists of eight chapters:
Chapter 1—Introduction to VBA Programming
In this chapter, you will learn about the types of Access procedures you can write and how and where they are written. This chapter also introduces basic VBA concepts that allow you to store various pieces of information for later use with different types of variables.

Chapter 2—Getting to Know Visual Basic Editor (VBE)
In this chapter, you will learn almost everything you need to know about working with the Visual Basic Editor window, commonly referred to as VBE. Some of the programming tools that are not covered here are discussed and used in Chapter 8.

Chapter 3—Access VBA Procedures and Functions
In this chapter, you will learn how to write and execute different types of VBA procedures and functions with and without arguments and explore data types.

Chapter 4—Adding Decisions to Your Access VBA Programs
In this chapter, you will learn how to control your program flow with several different decision-making statements.

Chapter 5—Adding Repeating Actions to Your Access VBA Programs
In this chapter, you will learn how to repeat the same actions in your VBA code by using looping structures.

Chapter 6—Keeping Track of Multiple Values Using Arrays
In this chapter, you will learn about static and dynamic arrays and how to use them to hold various values.

Chapter 7—Keeping Track of Multiple Values Using Collections
In this chapter, you will learn how you can maintain your items of data while your program is running by using a collection object.

Chapter 8—Getting to Know Built-In Tools for Testing and Debugging
In this chapter, you will begin using built-in debugging tools to test your programming code. You will also learn how to add effective error-handling code to your procedures.

The above eight chapters will equip you with the fundamental techniques and concepts you will need to continue on your Access VBA learning path. The skills obtained in the Access VBA Primer part are transferrable. They can be utilized in programming other Microsoft 365 applications that also use VBA as their native programming language, such as Excel, Word, PowerPoint, and Outlook.

PART II—ACCESS VBA PROGRAMMING WITH DAO AND ADO

In this part of the book, you are introduced to two sets of programming objects, known as Data Access Object (DAO) and ActiveX Data Object (ADO), that will enable you to access and manipulate data. You will learn how to use DAO and ADO objects in your VBA code to connect to a data source, as well as how to create, modify, and manipulate database objects.

Part II consists of three chapters:

Chapter 9—Data Access Technologies in Microsoft Access
In this chapter, you will get acquainted with several object libraries that provide objects, properties, and methods for your VBA procedures. You will also learn about types of database engines and connection strings.

Chapter 10—Creating and Manipulating Databases with DAO
This chapter demonstrates how to create, copy, link, and delete database tables programmatically by using objects from the DAO object library. Here, you will learn how to write code to add and delete fields, as well as creating listings of existing tables in a database and fields in a table. You will see how to add primary keys and indexes to your database tables and create relationships between your tables. After that, you will practice various methods of using programming code to open a set of database records, commonly referred to as a recordset. You will learn how to move around in a recordset and find, filter, and sort the required records, as well as reading their contents. You will then see how to perform essential database operations such as adding, updating, and deleting records. You will also learn how to render your database records in three popular file formats: Excel, Word, and a text file. Creating and running various types of database queries using VBA instead of the Query Design view is also covered in this chapter.

Chapter 11—Creating and Manipulating Databases with ADO
This chapter demonstrates how to create, copy, link, and delete database tables programmatically by using objects from the ADO object library. Here, you will learn

how to write code to add and delete fields, as well as creating listings of existing tables in a database and fields in a table. You will add primary keys and indexes to your database tables. You will also learn how to use objects from the ADOX library to create relationships between your tables. After that, you'll practice various methods of using programming code to open a set of database records, commonly referred to as a recordset. You will learn how to move around in a recordset and find, filter, and sort the required records, as well as reading their contents. You'll perform essential database operations such as adding, updating, and deleting records. You will also learn how to render your database records in three popular file formats: Excel, Word, and a text file. Creating and running various types of database queries using VBA instead of the query design view is also covered in this chapter. This chapter explains several advanced ADO features, such as how to disconnect a recordset from a database, save it in a disk file, clone it, and shape it. You will also learn about database transactions.

You will find the skills obtained in Part II of this book essential for accessing and manipulating Access databases.

PART III—ACCESS STRUCTURED QUERY LANGUAGE (SQL)

SQL, which stands for Structured Query Language, is a standard language designed to communicate with databases. It is used for querying, updating, and managing data. Access SQL is a variant of the SQL language specifically optimized for Microsoft Access databases. In this part of the book, you will learn how to use both basic and advanced components of Access SQL, which will allow you to efficiently interact with your Access database and perform complex data operations.

Chapter 12—Understanding and Using SQL Within Microsoft Access
In this chapter, you will learn about the key differences between SQL and Access SQL. You will learn SQL commands for creating a new Access database, as well as creating, modifying, and deleting tables. You will also learn commands for adding, modifying, and deleting fields and indexes and using and understanding table constraints and relationships. This chapter also introduces you to working with two powerful database objects, known as views and stored procedures.

The skills you learn in Part III of this book will allow you to create and manipulate your Access databases using SQL statements. Numerous Access SQL statements and concepts introduced here are important in laying the groundwork for moving into the client/server environment (porting your Microsoft Access database to SQL Server).

PART IV—IMPLEMENTING DATABASE SECURITY IN MICROSOFT ACCESS

In this part of the book, we focus on securing Access databases in the `.accdb` and `.mdb` file formats.

Part IV consists of two chapters

Chapter 13— Security Measures in Access .accdb File Format Databases
In this chapter, you will learn how to password-protect your `.accdb` databases using a manual method, as well as DAO and ADO programming methods. You will also learn how to implement custom user authentication with VBA.

Chapter 14—Security Measures in Access .mdb File Format Databases
In this chapter, you will learn about setting a database password and managing the security and permissions of your Access `.mdb` databases. We will walk through the implementation of user-level security and learn about creating and joining a workgroup information file. You will learn about managing security with DAO and ADOX objects and methods, as well as SQL commands.

The skills learned in Part IV will allow you to build more secure Access database applications that preserve and protect both data and the application itself. With the understanding of elements of security available in both file formats, you can create robust database solutions that will be less vulnerable to malicious attacks on your computers and entire networks.

PART V—VBA PROGRAMMING IN ACCESS FORMS AND REPORTS

Here, you will learn how to respond to events that occur in Access forms and reports. The behavior of Microsoft Access objects such as forms, reports, and controls can be modified by writing programming code known as an event procedure or an event handler. In this part of the book, you will learn how you can make your forms, reports, and controls perform useful actions by writing event procedures in form and report class modules.

Part V consists of two chapters:

Chapter 15—Using VBA to Interact with Forms and Form Controls
This chapter focuses on controlling Access forms with form properties, referring to forms and their controls, and working with form modules and various types of

form events. You will also learn how to use images and attachment controls on a form, how to use the `DoCmd` object to open, save, and close forms, and how to move between records.

Chapter 16—Using VBA to Interact with Reports and Report Controls
In this chapter, you will learn how to work with report modules, properties, and event programming in Access reports. You will learn how to use the report view, sort and group data, and create a report with VBA.

The skills acquired in Part V will help you create forms and reports that provide the desired functionality to your users thanks to the implementation of various events.

PART VI—ENHANCING THE USER EXPERIENCE

Since its 2007 release, Access, like other Microsoft 365 applications, has used the Ribbon interface for its menu system. Knowing how the Ribbon works and how you can modify it to customize your Access databases will enhance the experience of your database users. We will cover this topic in one big chapter with numerous illustrated hands-on examples and programming code written in VBA and Extensible Markup Language (XML).

Chapter 17—Programming the Ribbon Interface in Access
This chapter provides an overview of the programming elements available in the Ribbon and shows how you can customize the User Interface (UI) in your Access database applications. You will learn how to create XML Ribbon customization markup and load it into your database. You will also learn how to customize the backstage view and the Quick Access Toolbar, as well as assigning Ribbon customizations to forms or reports.

The skills acquired in Part VI of this book will allow you to enhance and alter the way users interact with your database application.

PART VII—ADVANCED VBA PROGRAMMING CONCEPTS

Microsoft Access offers numerous built-in objects that you can access from your VBA procedures to automate many aspects of your databases. You are not limited to just using these built-in objects, however. VBA allows you to create your own objects and collections of objects, complete with their own methods and properties. In this part of the book, you will learn how thinking in terms of objects can help you write reusable code that's easy to maintain.

Chapter 18—Creating Classes, Objects, Properties, Methods, and Events
In this chapter, you will work with advanced VBA concepts: VBA classes, class objects, collection objects, and events. You will learn how to create `Property Get` and `Property Let` procedures and custom methods for a custom `movie` and a `movieCollection` object defined in a class module. You will also learn how to respond to control events in a class module, as well as how to declare, raise, and sink custom events. This chapter has a long list of new terms you need to know to understand the concepts presented within.

The skills acquired in Part VII of this book will allow you to write VBA code that is more efficient, is much easier to read and maintain, and can be reused in many places.

PART VIII—VBA AND MACROS

Writing VBA code is not the only way to provide rich functionality to your Access database users. Macros have long been used to enhance the user experience without users having to write any VBA code. The Access Macro Builder allows you to include complex logic, business rules, and error handling in your macros. In this part of the book, you are introduced to three types of macros that you can create in Access. You will also learn how to convert macros into VBA and understand the inner workings of Access' built-in database templates that extensively use macros.

Chapter 19—Getting Comfortable with Access Macros and Templates
This chapter introduces you to using macros. We will take a detailed look at macro security, work with three types of macros (standalone, embedded, and data macros), see examples of using variables in macros, and examine error-handling actions in macros. We will also discuss working with the template format in Access 2024.

The skills acquired in Part VIII will allow you to correctly utilize many of the macros available in Microsoft-provided database templates in your own custom Access applications.

PART IX—WORKING TOGETHER: VBA, XML, AND REST API

XML has long been the standard format for sharing data regardless of the originating application or operating system. In this part of the book, you will learn how XML is used in Access to bring external data to your database, as well as providing your data to other applications. You will also learn about REST APIs, the newest and most flexible method of integrating applications. You will use your Access VBA and XML skills to make HTTP requests to a Web server to retrieve data and integrate it with Access. In this process, you are introduced to using JavaScript Object Notation (JSON), the most popular file format for storing and transporting data.

Part IX consists of the following two chapters:

Chapter 20—Using XML in Access
In this chapter, you will learn how to use XML in Access. You will learn how to export Access data manually and programmatically to XML files, as well as importing an XML file to Access and displaying its data in a table. You will also learn how to use stylesheets and transformations to present Access data to users in a desired format.

Chapter 21—Access and REST API
This chapter focuses on expanding your VBA skillset by covering topics such as working with a VBA Dictionary object, using regular expressions, and calling a new type of Web service, known as REST API.

The skills acquired in Part IX will make your Access applications ready to integrate with any operating system or Web-based platform.

Additionally, there are three Appendices.

Appendix A—VBA Data Types
Appendix B—Access 2007–2024 File Formats
Appendix C—Installing Internet Information Services (IIS)

This Appendix walks you through the installation of a Web server application that is used in the Chapter 20 hands-on projects.

HOW TO WORK WITH THIS BOOK

This book has been designed as a tutorial and should be followed chapter by chapter.

As you read each chapter, perform the tasks that are described. Be an active learner by getting involved in the book's hands-on exercises and custom projects. You learn faster by doing rather than studying. Do not move on to new information until you've fully grasped the current topic. Allow your brain to sort things out and put them in proper perspective before you move on. Take frequent breaks between your learning sessions, as some chapters in this book cover lots of material.

Do not try to do everything in one sitting. It's always better to divide the material into smaller units than attempt to master all there is to learn at once. Note, however, that you should never stop in the middle of a hands-on exercise; finish it before taking a break. After learning a particular technique or command, try to think of ways to apply it to your own work. As you work with this book, create small sample procedures for yourself based on what you've learned up to a particular point. These procedures will come in handy when you need to review the subject in the future or simply need to steal some ready-made code. Be sure to study the companion files with ChatGPT prompts and responses as they are designed to complement this tutorial content.

THE COMPANION FILES

The example files for all the hands-on activities in this book are available in the companion files included with this book. All companion files for this title are available by visiting the website for the book at *sciendo.com/book/9781501524141* and by clicking on the "COMPANION FILES" tab. Digital versions of this title are available at Amazon.com and other digital vendors.

LIST OF FIGURES

Chapter 1

Figure 1.1   An empty code module.

Figure 1.2   Message box coded in the ShowMessage3 procedure.

Figure 1.3   Message box generated by the DisplayResult procedure.

Figure 1.4   Creating a blank desktop Access database.

Figure 1.5   Activating a Visual Basic development environment.

Figure 1.6   Inserting a standard module.

Figure 1.7   Standard module with subprocedures and functions.

Figure 1.8   Running procedures and functions from the Immediate window.

Figure 1.9   Saving a VBA module.

Figure 1.10 Renaming a VBA module.

Figure 1.11 Saving a VBA module in an external file.

Figure 1.12 By default, Access does not trust any database that contains VBA code or macros and displays a security warning message when you open the database.

Figure 1.13 The Info tab with an explanation of the Security Warning message.

Figure 1.14 Working with the Trust Center (step 1).

Figure 1.15 Working with the Trust Center (step 2).

Figure 1.16 Working with the Trust Center (step 3).

Figure 1.17 Working with the Trust Center (step 4).

Figure 1.18 Fixing compilation errors in break mode.

Figure 1.19 The slsTax variable is declared as a module-level variable so it can be accessed by other procedures in the same module.

Figure 1.20 Learning VBA fundamentals with ChatGPT (example 1).

Figure 1.21 Dissecting VBA code with ChatGPT (example 2).

Chapter 2

Figure 2.1   The Project Explorer window provides easy access to your VBA procedure code.

Figure 2.2   Use the toolbar buttons to quickly access frequently used features in the VBE window.

Figure 2.3   The VBE Project Explorer window contains three buttons that allow you to view code or objects and toggle folders.

Figure 2.4   You can edit object properties in the Properties window, or you can edit them in the property sheet when a form or report is open in design view.

Figure 2.5   The Object drop-down box lists objects that are available in the module selected in the Project Explorer window. The code shown here is for the Form_frmOrderDetails form.

Figure 2.6   The Procedure drop-down box lists events to which the object selected in the Object drop-down box can respond. If the selected module contains events written for the highlighted object, the names of these events appear in bold type.

Figure 2.7   By splitting the Code window, you can view different sections of a long procedure or a different procedure in each windowpane.

Figure 2.8   You can use the Docking tab in the Options dialog box to control which windows are currently displayed in the Visual Basic programming environment.

Figure 2.9   You can use the Project Properties dialog box to rename the VBA project.

Figure 2.10   The Edit toolbar provides timesaving buttons while entering VBA code.

Figure 2.11   When Auto List Members is selected, Visual Basic suggests properties and methods that can be used with the object as you are entering the VBA instructions.

Figure 2.12   A tip window displays a list of arguments used by a VBA function or method.

Figure 2.13   The List Constants pop-up menu displays a list of constants that are valid for the property or method typed.

Figure 2.14   The Quick Info feature provides a list of function parameters, as well as constant values and VBA statement syntax.

Figure 2.15   The Options dialog box lists several features you can turn on and off to fit the VBA programming environment to your needs.

Figure 2.16   The Object Browser window allows you to browse through all the objects, properties, and methods available to the current VBA project.

Figure 2.17   Use the Immediate window to evaluate and try Visual Basic statements.

Figure 2.18   ChatGPT can help you review the material learned on any topic by generating review questions.

Chapter 3

Figure 3.1   To display a message to the user, place the text as the argument of the MsgBox function.

Figure 3.2   This long message will look more appealing to the user when you take care of the text formatting yourself.

Figure 3.3   You can break a long text string into several lines by using the Chr(13) function.

Figure 3.4   You can increase the readability of your message by increasing the spacing between selected text lines.

Figure 3.5   You can specify the number of buttons to include, their text, and an icon in the message box by using the optional buttons argument.

Figure 3.6   A dialog box generated by the Informant procedure.

Figure 3.7   To suggest that the user enter a specific type of data, you may want to provide a default value in the edit box.

Chapter 4

Figure 4.1   Placing text box controls on an Access form for Hands-On 4.5.

Figure 4.2   Setting the Name property of the text box control for Hands-On 4.5.

Figure 4.3   Setting the Command button properties for Hands-On 4.5.

Chapter 5

Figure 5.1   Data entry form created by Microsoft Access is shown in layout view.

Chapter 6

Figure 6.1   You can display the elements of a one-dimensional array with the MsgBox function.

Figure 6.2   The text displayed in the message box can be custom formatted. (Note that these are fictitious exchange rates for demonstration only.)

Figure 6.3   This run-time error was caused by an attempt to access a nonexistent array element.

Figure 6.4   The statement that triggered the error shown in Figure 6.3. is highlighted.

Figure 6.5   Calling the BubbleSort function procedure from the ManipulateArray procedure.

Chapter 7

Figure 7.1   A red circle in the margin indicates a breakpoint. The statement with a breakpoint is displayed as white text on a red background.

Figure 7.2   When Visual Basic encounters a breakpoint while running a procedure, it switches to the Code window and displays a yellow arrow in the margin to the left of the statement at which the procedure is suspended.

Figure 7.3   When you press the F8 key, you activate a step mode when each press of the key jumps to the next line of code, allowing you to step through the procedure.

Figure 7.4   The Function procedure asks for items separated by a comma. These items will be used to fill an array variable.

Figure 7.5   The Immediate window is populated with the data generated by the Debug Print statements.

Figure 7.6   Adding multiple breakpoints on important lines in VBA procedures allows you to better troubleshoot the code you've written or received from others.

Figure 7.7   Because there was a breakpoint on the line that calls the InputBox function, when this line executes, the yellow highlight is moved to the next statement in the function, indicating that this is the next statement to be executed.

Chapter 8

Figure 8.1   The Auto Syntax Check setting on the Editor tab of the Options dialog box helps you find typos in your VBA procedures.

Figure 8.2   This message appears after manually interrupting your procedure while it is running.

Figure 8.3   The combo box control shown on this form will be filled with the result of the ListEndDates function.

Figure 8.4   The line of code where the breakpoint is set is displayed in the color specified on the Editor Format tab in the Options dialog box.

Figure 8.5   Code window in break mode. Because the current statement also contains a breakpoint (indicated by a red circle), the margin displays both indicators overlapping one another (the circle and the arrow).

Figure 8.6   Code window in break mode with additional breakpoints to watch each procedure execution.

Figure 8.7   When code execution is suspended, you can check the current values of variables and expressions by entering appropriate

	statements in the Immediate window or resting the mouse pointer on the variable name.
Figure 8.8	When your procedure is suspended, you can access various options on the Debug menu.
Figure 8.9	You can insert a Stop statement anywhere in your VBA procedure code. The procedure will halt when it gets to the Stop statement, and the Code window will appear with the code line highlighted.
Figure 8.10	The Add Watch dialog box allows you to define conditions you want to monitor while a VBA procedure is running.
Figure 8.11	The content of the Watches window when our procedure is not in break Mode.
Figure 8.12	The Quick Watch dialog box shows the current value of a chosen expression in a VBA procedure.
Figure 8.13	The Locals window displays the current values of all the declared variables in the current VBA procedure.
Figure 8.14	The Call Stack dialog box displays a list of procedures that are started but not completed.
Figure 8.15	Using bookmarks, you can quickly jump between often-used sections of your procedures.
Figure 8.16	To test your error-handling code, use the Raise method of the Err object. This will generate a run-time error during the execution of your procedure.
Figure 8.17	Setting the error-trapping options in the Options dialog box will affect all instances of Visual Basic started after you change the setting.

Chapter 9

Figure 9.1	The default object libraries for Access 2024.
Figure 9.2	Object libraries can come in different versions.
Figure 9.3	Use the Object Browser to find the objects available in a specific library.
Figure 9.4	The ODBC Data Source Administrator allows you to set up appropriate connections with the required data provider via the user, system, or file DSN.
Figure 9.5	Creating a DSN to access a dBASE file.
Figure 9.6	The Data Link Properties dialog box appears after you launch the .udl file.
Figure 9.7	The Provider tab in the Data Link Properties dialog box lists the names of the ADO providers installed on your computer.

Figure 9.8   Use the Data Link Properties dialog box to define a data source name for the selected provider type. Be sure to enter .accdb as the extension for the NorthwindStarter database (the Data Source text box is too short to capture the entire path in this image).

Figure 9.9   You can obtain the connection string from the universal data link (.udl) file by opening the file in Windows Notepad.

Chapter 10

Figure 10.1   The Employees table created by using DAO objects in a VBA procedure.

Figure 10.2   The Employees table after modification. The Field Properties Lookup tab contains numerous properties that were set in the VBA procedure to tell Access how to display values in the Skills field.

Figure 10.3   The multivalue lookup field (Skills) created by the VBA procedure in Hands-On 10.7 displays a combo box with three skill choices.

Figure 10.4   The Employees table displaying the Expression property of the FullName calculated field and Expression Builder where the expression can be easily modified.

Figure 10.5   The Attachment field added with the VBA procedure in Hands-On 10.7 currently does not contain any attachments.

Figure 10.6   To collect history on a memo field, you must set the field's Append Only property to Yes.

Figure 10.7   The EmployeeBio field has its Text Format property set to Rich Text.

Figure 10.8   The Indexes window shows the PrimaryIndex settings for the EmployeeID field.

Figure 10.9   The Employees data was copied from another Access database using a VBA procedure.

Figure 10.10   The Employees table now shows data in the EmployeeBio field and the Notes field data was retrieved from the NothwindStarter database.

Figure 10.11   Attachment files can be added to records in an Access table manually using the Attachments dialog box or via VBA programming. You can view the attached file by double-clicking the attachment field.

Figure 10.12   The Multivalue Skills field has now additional entries.

Figure 10.13   Access records copied programmatically to Excel.

Figure 10.14   You can display an SQL statement underlying a query in a message box.

Figure 10.15   Data retrieved from an SQL Server database via a pass-through query.

Figure 10.16   An updatable query can contain one or more fields that cannot be edited.

Chapter 11

Figure 11.1   The table and field properties and their values are retrieved programmatically (see the VBA procedure in Hands-On 11.10).

Figure 11.2   The Access database Navigation Pane with two linked tables created by running procedures in this chapter.

Figure 11.3   The one-to-many relationship between the Publishers and Titles tables was created programmatically by accessing objects in the ADOX library (see the code in the CreateTblRelation procedure in Hands-On 11.22).

Figure 11.4   The Object Browser lists four predefined constants you can use to specify the cursor type to be retrieved.

Figure 11.5   The Object Browser lists four predefined constants that you can use to specify what type of locking ADO should use when you make a change to the data.

Figure 11.6   The CursorLocation parameter of the Recordset's Open method can be set by using the adUseClient or adUseServer constant.

Figure 11.7   The Options parameter of the Recordset's Open method is supplied by the constant values listed under the CommandType property of the Command object.

Figure 11.8   When updating remote tables from VBA procedures, there are many potential factors beyond your control that can lead to errors. In this example, the procedure code is correct, yet Access generates a run-time error. The error message indicates that a specific function used in a data macro is needed but is not available to our procedure.

Figure 11.9   This custom form is used to demonstrate how you can fill the combo box control with a disconnected recordset.

Figure 11.10   After opening the form prepared in Custom Project 11.1, the combo box is filled with the names of companies obtained via a persisted recordset.

Figure 11.11   This custom form is used to demonstrate the use of the saved recordset in an unbound form.

Figure 11.12   This custom form is used to demonstrate how the recordset cloning is used to read the contents of the previous record.

Figure 11.13   When you use SQL JOIN statements you get a flat recordset with a lot of duplicate information.

Figure 11.14   After running the ShapeDemo procedure in Hands-On 11.50, you can view the contents of the hierarchical recordset in the Immediate window.

Figure 11.15   Adding an ActiveX control to an Access form (step 1).

Figure 11.16   Adding an ActiveX control to an Access form (step 2).

Figure 11.17   The Microsoft TreeView control provides an excellent way to display shaped recordsets in an Access form.

Figure 11.18   A TreeView control after being placed and resized on the Access form.

Figure 11.19   You can set custom properties of the TreeView control in the Property Sheet of the TreeView control.

Figure 11.20   The TreeView control is filled with the data from the Northwind database when the user opens the form.

Figure 11.21   After running the procedure in Hands-On 11.51, a record for a new customer is added to the Customers, Orders, and OrderDetails tables.

Figure 11.22   You can retrieve the names of all references in your VBA project by calling upon the References collection in your VBA procedure.

Chapter 12

Figure 12.1   Use the Access Options window to set the ANSI 92 query mode for the current database or all new databases.

Figure 12.2   When you change the query mode to ANSI 92, Microsoft Access displays an informational message alerting you to possible problems.

Figure 12.3   The tblSchools table was generated by the CreateTable procedure in Hands-On 12.2 using the Microsoft Access SQL statement CREATE TABLE.

Figure 12.4   The tblSchools table shown here contains a primary key and a unique index based on two fields.

Figure 12.5   The index called idxSupplierCity does not allow Null values.

Figure 12.6   The index called idxSupplierPhone allows Null values in the SupplierPhone field. Records containing Null values, however, will be excluded from any searches that use that index.

Figure 12.7   This message appears when you attempt to enter a value in the YearsWorked column that is not within the range of values specified by the FromTo constraint.

Figure 12.8   When you attempt to enter a value that does not meet the validation rule, Access displays an error message.

Figure 12.9   If you try to manually delete a table referenced by the CHECK constraint, Access will display an error message.

Figure 12.10   To access the Relationships window, choose Database Tools | Relationships.

Figure 12.11   To access the Edit Relationships window, choose Relationships Design | Edit Relationships.

Figure 12.12   Using the Data Definition Query window to enter SQL statements.

Figure 12.13   Notice that the tables you created by running the DDL statements in steps 3 and 5 are joined on the ID column (see step 6).

Figure 12.14   You can edit relationships between tables via the Edit Relationships window.

Figure 12.15   When you double-click a stored procedure name in the database navigation pane of the Access database window, Access displays this message when the stored procedure expects parameters, and its SQL statement attempts to insert data into a table.

Figure 12.16   Because the stored procedure expects some input, you are prompted for the first parameter value.

Figure 12.17   Here you are prompted to enter the phone number for the second stored procedure parameter.

Figure 12.18   Once all input has been gathered via the parameters, Access informs you about the action that is to be performed. Click Yes to execute the stored procedure or No to cancel.

Figure 12.19   After clicking Yes, Access runs the Append query. To view the result of this operation, double-click the Shippers table in the Navigation Pane. Notice that a new record (Speedy Deliveries) was added to the Shippers table.

Figure 12.20   To view or modify the contents of a stored procedure, open it in design view.

Figure 12.21   The SQL view of the Query window displays the underlying SQL statement of the parameterized stored procedure.

Chapter 13

Figure 13.1   Encrypting a database with a password.

Figure 13.2   Opening a database in Exclusive mode.

Figure 13.3   When setting a database password, Access informs you that row-level locking will be ignored.

Figure 13.4   An Access login form created with VBA.

Figure 13.5   The main form with its Demo subform created entirely with the VBA code.
Figure 13.6   The Users table is populated with four user credentials.
Figure 13.7   After the successful login, the user is welcomed by their name.

Chapter 14

Figure 14.1   Built-in tools for managing security in an .mdb database.
Figure 14.2   The User and Group Accounts dialog box.
Figure 14.3   The User and Group Permissions dialog box.
Figure 14.4   Security Wizard (screen 1).
Figure 14.5   Security Wizard (screen 2). The WIF named Security.mdb will store user and group account information for the current database.
Figure 14.6   Security Wizard (screen 3).
Figure 14.7   Security Wizard (screen 4).
Figure 14.8   Security Wizard (screen 5).
Figure 14.9   Security Wizard (screen 6a).
Figure 14.10   Security Wizard (screen 6b).
Figure 14.11   Security Wizard (screen 6c).
Figure 14.12   Security Wizard (screen 7).
Figure 14.13   Security Wizard (screen 8).
Figure 14.14   Security Wizard (screen 9).
Figure 14.15   In Custom Project 14.1, while running the built-in user-level security wizard, we added the Developer user to the Admins group and removed the default Admin user from the Admins group.
Figure 14.16   Use the User and Group Permissions window to check current permissions for the users Admin and Developer after running the user-level security wizard in Custom Project 14.1.
Figure 14.17   The Developer user account is the object owner of the database (tables and queries that currently exist in the database).
Figure 14.18   Joining another WIF.
Figure 14.19   The Elite and Temps group accounts are created by running the procedure in Hands-On 14.8.
Figure 14.20   The names of existing security group and user accounts are written to the Immediate window by the procedure in Hands-On 14.10.
Figure 14.21   After running the procedure in Hands-On 14.11, security group account names and the corresponding user accounts are listed in the Immediate window.
Figure 14.22   The Object Browser displays the available constants for the Type parameter.

Figure 14.23   In ADOX, you can use many security constants for setting permissions to database objects.
Figure 14.24   Delete Data permission on new tables and queries was removed for the members of Masters.
Figure 14.25   This message is shown when you attempt to open a secured Access .mdb database and Access cannot find the WIF.

Chapter 15
Figure 15.1   The Order Details form in design view and its Property Sheet.
Figure 15.2   Custom form in design view as used in Custom Project 15.1.
Figure 15.3   Custom form in form view as used in Custom Project 15.1.
Figure 15.4   The completed FormInspector form provides easy access to the selected form properties and a mechanism to print the properties to a text file.
Figure 15.5   The selected form properties were saved to a text file.
Figure 15.6   The Form_AfterUpdate event procedure is used here to store information about newly added records in a text file.
Figure 15.7   Working with the OpenArgs demo (frmOpenArgs form).
Figure 15.8   After selecting the last value from the OpenArgs Demo drop-down list (see Figure 15.7), Access displays the Employee List form with changes made to the form caption (Employee List called from frmOpenArgs) and the Reports drop-down list.
Figure 15.9   You can tell Access how to store images in older versions of Access (2003 and earlier) by using the options under Picture Property Storage Format. The Access Options window can be accessed by clicking File | Options.
Figure 15.10   The picture is shown here using the Image control placed on an Access form.
Figure 15.11   The Access form uses the Attachments control to show images attached to a record.
Figure 15.12   Placing an unbound text box control on the form.
Figure 15.13   The Current File text box control added to the form provides information about the attachment filename currently displayed in the Attachments control.

Chapter 16
Figure 16.1   The Reports group on the Create Tab provides several tools for creating basic and advanced reports.
Figure 16.2   Detail report (source: Northwind.mdb).

Figure 16.3   Detail report design view (source: Northwind.mdb).

Figure 16.4   Summary report (source: Northwind 2007.accdb).

Figure 16.5   Summary report in design view (source: Northwind 2007.accdb).

Figure 16.6   Crosstab report (source: Northwind 2007.accdb).

Figure 16.7   Crosstab report in design view (source: Northwind 2007.accdb).

Figure 16.8   Report with a form (source: Northwind 2007.accdb).

Figure 16.9   Report with a form in design view (source: Northwind 2007. accdb).

Figure 16.10   Report with labels (source: Northwind.mdb).

Figure 16.11   Report with labels in design view (source: Northwind.mdb).

Figure 16.12   Report with a chart (source: Northwind.mdb).

Figure 16.13   Report with a chart in design view (source: Northwind.mdb).

Figure 16.14   The Report_Close event procedure is often used to close supporting forms.

Figure 16.15   You can frame your Access report pages with a red line by implementing the Report_Page event procedure shown in Hands-On 16.4.

Figure 16.16   This report displays the record range indicator at the bottom of the page (see Hands-On 16.8).

Figure 16.17   This report displays the first and last customer IDs for a specific page at the bottom of each printed page.

Figure 16.18   The Sales by Year report in the Northwind.mdb database uses the GroupFooter1_Retreat event procedure to control the printing of a page header.

Figure 16.19   Access reports can be displayed using four different views: Report View, Layout View, Design View, and Print Preview. The layout view may not be available for some reports.

Figure 16.20   The Group, Sort, and Total pane provides a quick way to group and sort data and add calculations in Access reports.

Figure 16.21   The Group, Sort, and Total pane indicates that the report is grouped on Country.

Figure 16.22   To save your report to .pdf or .xps file format, open it in design view and activate report view. With the report displayed on your screen, click File | Save As. Select Save Object As, select PDF or XPS, and click the Save As button. Access will display the Publish as PDF or XPS dialog box where you can specify the required file format, as well as the filename and destination folder.

Figure 16.23   The form used to filter the Employee Address Book report by City or Country/Region.

Figure 16.24   This report was filtered by using the value passed in the OpenArgs property.
Figure 16.25   Crosstab query design view.
Figure 16.26   Crosstab query in datasheet view.
Figure 16.27   Use the Query Parameter dialog box to define parameters for the crosstab query.
Figure 16.28   SQL statement for the completed crosstab query.
Figure 16.29   The Custom Demo Report in design view was generated using VBA code.
Figure 16.30   This custom form is used to provide the Year parameter for the report.
Figure 16.31   Resizing the form.
Figure 16.32   The Custom Demo Report shown in Print Preview.

Chapter 17
Figure 17.1   Accessing the QAT in Access 2024.
Figure 17.2   Accessing the Ribbon customization interface via a right-click menu.
Figure 17.3   Accessing the Ribbon customization interface via the Access Options dialog.
Figure 17.4   The database navigation pane in Access 2024 shows all available database objects organized into different categories. It can be hidden by clicking the Shutter Bar Open/Close button.
Figure 17.5   Grouping options in the database navigation pane.
Figure 17.6   Objects in the database navigation pane can be easily categorized, sorted, and filtered. Use the search bar to locate a hard-to-find object. Use the Navigation Options tool to create custom groups of objects.
Figure 17.7   The Navigation Options dialog box.
Figure 17.8   Creating custom groups in Navigation Options.
Figure 17.9   Displaying a custom group in the Navigation Pane.
Figure 17.10   The Navigation Pane with custom groupings.
Figure 17.11   Testing navigation statements in the Immediate window.
Figure 17.12   The current configuration of the Navigation Pane is saved in this XML file.
Figure 17.13   The Navigation Pane can be easily modified using the external XML file containing the custom configuration settings.
Figure 17.14   All Access commands related to creating various database objects are grouped on the Create tab.

Figure 17.15   Additional commands can be accessed by clicking on the down arrow to the right of the button control.

Figure 17.16   Clicking on the Application Parts button in the Template group of the Create tab displays a gallery of different types of blank form layouts.

Figure 17.17   The dialog box launcher button in the bottom-right corner of the Text Formatting group on the Home tab will display the Datasheet Formatting dialog box. The clipboard launcher button provides quick access to the contents of your Windows clipboard.

Figure 17.18   A contextual tab (Table Fields) in the Ribbon

Figure 17.19   This XML file defines a new tab with two groups for the existing Access 2024 Ribbon. See the output this file produces in Figure 17.20.

Figure 17.20   The custom Edu Systems tab is based on the XML markup file shown in Figure 17.19.

Figure 17.21   When you check Show add-in user interface errors, Access will notify you about any problems in the Ribbon XML.

Figure 17.22   To avoid compile errors, you must set library references as shown here.

Figure 17.23   To load a Ribbon customization in your Access database when the database is loaded, enter the custom LoadRibbon() function in the AutoExec macro.

Figure 17.24   Enabling a customized Ribbon in the current database.

Figure 17.25   Ribbon XML markup can be embedded inside the VBA procedure. To try this out, copy the EduSystems3.accdb database from the companion files to your VBAAccess2024_ByExample folder and then open the database. Opening the database directly from the companion files or another folder will generate an error.

Figure 17.26   USysRibbons is a special system table used for storing Ribbon customizations.

Figure 17.27   The USysRibbons table with a record defining Ribbon customization. To define multiple Ribbons in your application, simply add a new record to this table.

Figure 17.28   Creating the OpenStudentDetails submacro.

Figure 17.29   Creating the OpenStudentList submacro.

Figure 17.30   Upon loading the database, Access displays an error message if errors are found in the Ribbon customization markup.

Figure 17.31   Entering Ribbon customization for a report into the new record of the USysRibbons table.

Figure 17.32   Use the Ribbon Name property of the report to assign your Ribbon customization to the active report.

Figure 17.33   The custom Report Tools tab appears in the Access Ribbon when the Allergies and Medications report is opened.

Figure 17.34   Entering Ribbon customization for loading custom images. Notice that this is the third record in the USysRibbons table.

Figure 17.35   The Ribbon customization as defined in Custom Project 17.3 with two image buttons in the Special Features group of the Edu Systems tab.

Figure 17.36   Customized Ribbon with the gallery control.

Figure 17.37   The custom toggle button Student Questionnaire will become highlighted when pressed and will return to its normal state when clicked again.

Figure 17.38   Custom split button controls can use the built-in Office images. They can also contain menus and submenus consisting of checkboxes.

Figure 17.39   These checkbox controls are laid out horizontally.

Figure 17.40   An edit box control allows data entry directly on the Ribbon.

Figure 17.41   The Languages combo box and City Borough drop-down controls look the same on the Ribbon.

Figure 17.42   A dialog box launcher control on the Ribbon will display the Product License, Session ID, Third Party Notices, and Microsoft Software License Terms (not depicted in this image).

Figure 17.43   The built-in Database Documenter button has been repurposed and displays a different dialog box when the Student List form is open.

Figure 17.44   The Ribbon controls are shown here after the Ribbon refresh. The Health checkbox is enabled upon entry of text in the First and Last Name edit box and disabled when the entry is deleted. The first and last names now appear in uppercase letters.

Figure 17.45   Each time you apply a different Ribbon customization, you need to close and reopen the Access database. When the Ribbon customization requires VBA callbacks, you must exit Access and then reopen the database.

Figure 17.46   The custom button (Use Report Wizard) in the Special Features group of the Edu Systems tab uses a built-in image and runs a built-in Access feature based on the condition specified in the callback assigned to its onAction attribute. Notice the new database name is EduSystems_Local_Final, which is a copy of the EduSystems_

Local database and contains all the controls created so far in this chapter.

Figure 17.47   The commands in the Other Controls group of the Ribbon are automatically compressed to a single button when the Access application window is made smaller. To change the icon that appears when the group is compressed, assign an image to the group itself. When you set the autoScale attribute to true, the group of controls in Special Features will change its layout to best fit the resized window.

Figure 17.48   The backstage view is highly customizable. The Synchronize button and the Endless Possibilities tab were created by adding custom XML markup to the USysRibbons system table and the required VBA callbacks in a VBA module.

Figure 17.49   Customized QAT shown below the Ribbon displays two buttons: Calculator and Quick Print.

Chapter 18

Figure 18.1   Use the Name property in the Properties window to rename the Class module.

Figure 18.2   The Movies table design view.

Figure 18.3   The frmMovies form in the form design view.

Figure 18.4   The frmMovies Form displays the selected movie title details.

Figure 18.5   The frmMovies form prepared for data entry.

Figure 18.6   Class collection module named clsAssetCollection.

Figure 18.7   The enhanced frmMovies2 form contains additional controls and demonstrates the use of advanced event programming.

Figure 18.8   The enhanced clsMovieCollection class module contains additional code and declarations for handling MovieAdded and MovieRemoved events.

Figure 18.9   The Object drop-down list in the clsRecordLogger's Code window lists the m_frm object variable that was declared using the WithEvents keyword.

Figure 18.10   To sink form events in a custom class module, clsRecordLogger, you must enter VBA event procedures in the Form_frmMovies3 class module.

Figure 18.11   The frmMovies3 form in data entry mode is used for testing out the custom clsRecordLogger class.

Figure 18.12   The MyMovies.txt file is used by the clsRecordLogger custom class for tracking record additions.

Figure 18.13   The form class module shows code that instantiates and hooks up objects created in the clsRecordLogger and clsUCaseBox class modules with the form and a text box control.

Figure 18.14   The Genre text box control is driven by the events defined in the clsUCaseBox class module.

Figure 18.15   Creating user-defined, custom events in a class module requires the use of the Event statement.

Figure 18.16   To fire custom events, use write methods that use the RaiseEvent statement.

Figure 18.17   The form class module shows code that uses a custom object with its events.

Chapter 19

Figure 19.1   The Macro Settings options allow you to specify whether the macros should be disabled or allowed to run and whether you should see a notification when macros are disabled.

Figure 19.2   A security warning message appears on an attempt to load a database file containing content that could possibly harm your computer.

Figure 19.3   The Info tab in the backstage view displays information related to the security warning message and a brief description of the active content. By clicking on the Enable Content button, you can either enable all content in the current database or choose Advanced Options, which allows you to specify which active content should be enabled.

Figure 19.4   The Microsoft Office Security Options dialog box allows you to temporarily enable disabled programming content by selecting the Enable content for this session radio button.

Figure 19.5   The contents of the AutoExec macro in the NorthwindStarter 2 sample database.

Figure 19.6   The Action Catalog. A description of the selected macro action appears at the bottom of the window.

Figure 19.7   The AutoExec macro is shown here in edit mode.

Figure 19.8   Creating a standalone macro.

Figure 19.9   The initial Macro Design window.

Figure 19.10   The OpenTable macro action opens a table. You need to specify the required arguments: the name of the table to open, the type of view for the presentation of the data, and the data mode.

Figure 19.11   You can restrict the number of records in a table by using the SetFilter macro action.

Figure 19.12   Creating a macro expression using the Expression Builder.

Figure 19.13   Adding conditions to the macro.

Figure 19.14   Comments can be added anywhere within your macro code block.

Figure 19.15   The Suppliers macro in the sample Northwind.mdb database contains submacros that can be used in the Suppliers form.

Figure 19.16   Assigning an embedded macro to the event property of a form's command button in the Northwind 2007.accdb database.

Figure 19.17   Use the Property Sheet to change the Name and Caption properties of the Close command button.

Figure 19.18   When you copied the Home button, the new button inherited the embedded macro assigned to the On Click event property.

Figure 19.19   Examining an embedded macro after it's been copied from another event property.

Figure 19.20   Examining the Shadow property – OnClickMacro.

Figure 19.21   Creating a data macro from the table's datasheet view.

Figure 19.22   Macro Builder for writing data macros.

Figure 19.23   Adding an If block to the data macro.

Figure 19.24   Adding a local variable to your data macro.

Figure 19.25   Adding an action to look up a record in a table.

Figure 19.26   Storing data retrieved by the LookupRecord action in a local variable.

Figure 19.27   Adding a comment to a macro.

Figure 19.28   Adding a macro action to raise an error.

Figure 19.29   The highlighted Before Change button on the Ribbon indicates that there is a data macro attached to this event.

Figure 19.30   The error raised by the data macro assigned to the Before Change event.

Figure 19.31   Creating a named data macro.

Figure 19.32   The Macro Builder window for creating a named data macro.

Figure 19.33   Specifying parameters in the named data macro.

Figure 19.34   The completed named data macro.

Figure 19.35   If the table contains named data macros, the macro names are listed under the Edit Named Macro option.

Figure 19.36   Running named macros from the After Insert data macro in the Donations table.

Figure 19.37   The named data macro GetInventoryLevels located in the Inventory table of the Northwind Web database created from a template generated by an earlier version of Access demonstrates the use of return variables. You can open this database from the companion files.

Figure 19.38 Referencing return variables (ReturnVars) inside a macro attached to the After Update event of a control placed on a form. Notice that the value of the return variable is being retrieved into a local variable named varQtyBackOrdered.

Figure 19.39 Accessing the UsysApplicationLog table in the backstage view.

Figure 19.40 Viewing the contents of the UsysApplicationLog table.

Figure 19.41 Copying the macro content to a text file.

Figure 19.42 Error handling in an Access macro located in the Northwind 2007.accdb database (see the On Dbl Click event for the Order ID field in the Active Orders Subform for Home).

Figure 19.43 Debug your macros by selecting the Single Step option on the Ribbon and clicking the Run button.

Figure 19.44 Using temporary variables in an Access macro.

Figure 19.45 Click the Convert Macro to Visual Basic button to convert a standalone macro to VBA code.

Figure 19.46 Access displays this dialog box when you click the Convert Macros to Visual Basic button (see Figure 19.45).

Figure 19.47 This VBA code was generated by Access from a standalone macro.

Figure 19.48 Converting embedded macros to VBA using the Convert Form's Macros to Visual Basic button.

Figure 19.49 VBA code from a converted embedded macro.

Figure 19.50 Creating an Access database based on a specific template.

Figure 19.51 The MyLibrary database is based on the Lending Library template downloaded from the Microsoft Access online templates.

Figure 19.52 By adding the .zip file extension to the .accdt file format, you can turn it into a ZIP archive that you can examine and modify depending on your needs.

Figure 19.53 The directory structure of an Access template file.

Figure 19.54 The contents of the .rels .xml file in the _rels folder.

Figure 19.55 The contents of the core.xml file in the docProps folder.

Figure 19.56 The contents of the template folder and the Template.xml file.

Figure 19.57 The contents of the database folder.

Figure 19.58 Files in the objects folder contain information about different database objects in the template file as well as information about sample data and properties for each object included in the template.

Chapter 20

Figure 20.1   The Export XML dialog box displays three checkboxes; the first one is selected by default. The More Options button allows for more customizations.

Figure 20.2   After exporting the Products table to XML with all three checkboxes selected in the Export XML dialog box, Access creates four files.

Figure 20.3   The tree-like structure of the XML document.

Figure 20.4   The partial view of the schema file shown here defines the data in the Products.xml document.

Figure 20.5   The XSL stylesheet document is just another XML document that contains HTML formatting instructions and XSLT formatting elements for transforming raw XML data into HTML.

Figure 20.6   The XSLT formatting instructions in the Products.xsl file.

Figure 20.7   The VBScript functions were automatically added to the Products.xsl file.

Figure 20.8   Access-generated Products.htm file opened in Windows Notepad.

Figure 20.9   Access-generated Products.html file opened in the Microsoft Edge browser.

Figure 20.10   Use the Data tab in the Export XML window to set advanced data options.

Figure 20.11   Use the Schema tab in the Export XML dialog box to set advanced schema options.

Figure 20.12   Use the Presentation tab in the Export XML dialog box to set advanced presentation options.

Figure 20.13   The source code of the Customers_Server.asp file generated by Access.

Figure 20.14   Customers data is generated from Access by running an ASP that queries the data contained in an XML file and formats it with the stylesheet.

Figure 20.15   Use this window to indicate a transformation file (stylesheet) to be used after export.

Figure 20.16   To export XML data directly to the HTML file, you must choose the transformation file using the Transforms button and change the file extension from .xml to .html.

Figure 20.17   XML data can be formatted any way you like by applying a custom transformation.

Figure 20.18   When importing a schema file to an Access database, the Import XML dialog box displays the table name and its columns as defined in the schema.

Figure 20.19   The Products table was created by importing the Products.xsd schema file.

Figure 20.20   Applying a custom transform prior to XML data import will allow you to limit the number of imported columns.

Figure 20.21   Partial contents of the EmpExtensions.xml file.

Figure 20.22   The Extensions table after it was reformatted with another stylesheet.

Figure 20.23   To work with XML documents programmatically, you need to reference the Microsoft XML object type library.

Figure 20.24   To view objects, properties, and methods exposed by the XML DOM, open the Object Browser after setting up a reference to the Microsoft XML object type library (see Figure 20.22).

Figure 20.25   By using the XML property of the DOMDocument object, you can retrieve the raw data from an XML file.

Figure 20.26   Saving a recordset to an XML file with ADO produces an attribute-centric XML file.

Figure 20.27   This element-centric XML file is a result of applying a stylesheet to the attribute-centric ADO recordset that was saved to an XML file.

Figure 20.28   This table was imported to Access after conversion of an attribute-centric ADO recordset into an element-centric XML file.

Figure 20.29   You can apply a stylesheet to an XML document generated by ADO to display the data in a nicely formatted HTML table.

Figure 20.30   An ADO Recordset persisted to an XML file is now opened in Excel.

Chapter 21

Figure 21.1   Adding a reference to the Microsoft Scripting Runtime library.

Figure 21.2   Examining the contents of the Microsoft Scripting Runtime library.

Figure 21.3   This demo form employs the VBA Dictionary object for its order entry and lookup tasks.

Figure 21.4   Entering an order via the demo form.

Figure 21.5   Setting a reference to the Microsoft VBScript Regular Expressions 5.5 object library.

Figure 21.6   Regular expressions can be used via the VBScript Regular Expressions 5.5 library, displayed as VBScript_RegExp_55 in the Object Browser.

Figure 21.7   This VBA procedure uses the Replace method of the RegExp object to remove characters specified in the pattern from the searched string.
Figure 21.8   The Replace method of the RegExp object has successfully removed all occurrences of the { } "" characters from the original string.
Figure 21.9   Exploring the Microsoft XML vb.60 object library using the Object Browser.
Figure 21.10   The AllVehicleMakes table was created from the REST API response.
Figure 21.11   The Response table was created from the REST API response.
Figure 21.12   The XML data returned from the REST API.
Figure 21.13   Example of a JSON file format.
Figure 21.14   Access form used in the zip code demo REST API—JSON.
Figure 21.15   JSON structure returned from Zippopotam API.

Chapter 1

Table 1.1   Type Declaration Characters.
Table A.1   VBA Data Types (In Appendix A).
Table A.2   Values Returned by the VarType Function (In Appendix A).

Chapter 3

Table 3.1   The MsgBox buttons argument settings.
Table 3.2   Values Returned by the MsgBox Function.

Chapter 4

Table 4.1   Relational Operators in VBA.
Table 4.2   Logical Operators in VBA.
Table 4.3   The Weekday Function Values.

Chapter 8

Table 8.1   Error Message Box Buttons.
Table 8.2   Add Watch Dialog Box Sections.
Table 8.3   On Error Statement Options.

Chapter 9

Table 9.1   Database Engine Versions in Access 2024 and earlier.
Table 9.2   The Components of ADO.
Table 9.3   Common Data Providers used with ADO.
Table 9.4   ODBC Connection Strings for Common Data Sources.
Table 9.5   OLE DB Connection Strings for Common Data Sources.
Table 9.6.   Tabs in the Data Link Properties dialog box.

Chapter 10

Table 10.1.   Container objects.
Table 10.2.   Constants for the Type property in the DAO object library (DataTypeEnum enumeration).

Table 10.3   Data types used by multivalue lookup fields.
Table 10.4.   The DAO recordset types.
Table 10.5.   Constants used to specify the type of a DAO Recordset object.
Table 10.6.   Comparison operators used with the Seek method.
Table 10.7.   Find methods in a DAO recordset.
Table 10.8.   EditModeEnum constants used in the EditMode property of the DAO Recordset object.
Table 10.9.   Access Append Query SQL statement components.
Table 10.10.   Access Update Query SQL statement components.
Table 10.11.   Access Delete Query SQL statement components.
Table 10.12.   Operators commonly used in expressions.
Table 10.13.   Wildcard characters used in the LIKE operator patterns.
Table 10.14.   Commonly used predicates in SQL SELECT statements.
Table 10.15.   Access Make-Table Query SQL statement components.

Chapter 11

Table 11.1   Intrinsic Constants of the Connection Object's Mode Property.
Table 11.2   Intrinsic Constants of the Connection Object's State Property.
Table 11.3   The ADO Data Types versus Access Data Types.
Table 11.4   Spreadsheet Constants.
Table 11.5   Table Types in the ADOX Tables Collection.
Table 11.6   Intrinsic Constants for the IndexNulls Property of the ADOX Index Object (see the AllowNullsEnum in the ADOX Library).
Table 11.7   Seek Method Constants.
Table 11.8   The Enumerated Constants used with the UpdateBatch Method.
Table 11.9   The RecordStatusEnum Constants returned by the Status Property.

Chapter 12

Table 12.1   Table Design Data Types and their Access SQL Equivalents.
Table 12.2   The Table Constraints.

Chapter 14

Table 14.1   The Workgroup Information File in different versions of Access.
Table 14.2   Security Constants used in Access.
Table 14.3   GUIDs for Provider Objects.

Chapter 15

Table 15.1   Controls Used in the FormInspector Form.
Table 15.2   ApplyType Argument Constants.

Table 15.3   Parameters used with the OpenForm Method of the DoCmd Object.
Table 15.4.   Arguments of the OpenForm method of the DoCmd object.

Chapter 16
Table 16.1   CurrentView Property Constants.
Table 16.2   Effect of the Format Event on Report Sections.
Table 16.3   Effect of the Print Event on Report Sections.

Chapter 17
Table 17.1   Category and Group Arguments Used in the NavigateTo Method.

Chapter 18
Table 18.1   There are no tables in Chapter 18.

Chapter 19
Table 19.1   Data Macro Events.
Table 19.2   OnError Action Arguments.
Table 19.3   Buttons available in the Macro Single Step dialog box.

Chapter 20
Table 20.1   Arguments of the ImportXML Method (in order of appearance).

Chapter 21
Table 21.1.   Scripting.Dictionary's methods and properties.
Table 21.2.   Dictionary versus Collection.
Table 21.3.   Regular expression patterns.
Table 21.4.   Quantifiers in RegExp patterns.
Table 21.5.   The most common API headers.

Part I

ACCESS VBA PRIMER

The Visual Basic for Applications (VBA) programming language has a special development environment and offers a wide range of capabilities that you will need to learn before you can begin automating repetitive tasks and building custom user interfaces within your chosen Microsoft 365 applications, such as Access, Excel, Word, and Outlook. In the first eight chapters of this book, you will explore the integrated Visual Basic Editor (VBE) and get to know basic VBA programming concepts that will enable you to take further steps in programming your Access databases.

Chapter 1   Introduction to VBA Programming
Chapter 2   Getting to Know Visual Basic Editor (VBE)
Chapter 3   Access VBA Procedures and Functions
Chapter 4   Adding Decisions to Your Access VBA Programs
Chapter 5   Adding Repeating Actions to Your Access VBA Programs
Chapter 6   Keeping Track of Multiple Values Using Arrays
Chapter 7   Keeping Track of Multiple Values Using Collections
Chapter 8   Getting to Know Built-In Tools for Testing and Debugging

Chapter **1**

INTRODUCTION TO VBA PROGRAMMING

Visual Basic for Applications (VBA) is the programming language built into all Microsoft 365 applications, including Access. In this chapter, you will acquire an understanding of the fundamental features of VBA that you will use repeatedly in building real-world Access database applications. By learning how to program in VBA, you can write your own programming code that brings more customization and power to your Access databases. Programming code is simply special instructions, commands, or statements that you type in sheets called modules. Because VBA is a common programming language for all Microsoft 365 applications, many of the skills you learn in this chapter will apply to other applications, such as Excel, Word, Outlook, or PowerPoint.

STATEMENTS, COMMANDS, AND INSTRUCTIONS

Let's begin by exploring the distinction between statements, commands, and instructions that you will use in programming your applications. In VBA, *a statement* is a complete instruction that tells your computer what needs to be done. Each statement performs a specific action. Statements consist of certain elements, such as keywords (special reserved words), operators, variables, constants, and expressions. You will learn about these elements as we progress through the primer chapters. For example, you will write statements that assign a value to a variable so it can be used later in your program, or write a statement that displays a message to the user when the program has completed. The term *command* is often used interchangeably with *statement*. There is a subtle difference, however. Statements are individual lines of code that perform specific actions, while commands are used to refer to tasks and operations you want to accomplish. For example, when you want to perform the action that you have previously programmed, you must issue the command that will execute your program. In summary, commands are made of one or more statements that perform specific actions. Many commands include step-by-step details on how to perform specific tasks. These detailed steps are known as *instructions*.

PROCEDURES AND MODULES

A programmer's job boils down to writing various procedures that address specific problems. A *procedure* contains detailed instructions that allow you to accomplish certain tasks when your program runs. Although many tasks can be automated in Access by using macro actions, such as opening forms and reports, finding records, and executing queries, you will need VBA skills to perform advanced customizations in your Access databases.

Procedures are created and stored in modules. A *module* resembles a blank document in Microsoft Word. Each procedure in the same module must have a unique name; however, procedures in different modules can have the same name. Each module begins with a Declarations section that lists various settings and declarations that apply to every procedure in the module. Following the Declarations section is the procedure section, which holds the module's procedures. Each module can contain one or more procedures. Figure 1.1 shows an empty module inside the Microsoft VBA editor window. Notice that Access organizes standard modules into the Modules folder.

Microsoft Access adds a setting, Option Compare Database, at the top of VBA modules. This setting is included in the Declarations section and indicates that in string comparisons, Access will follow the sort order determined by the locale ID of the database.

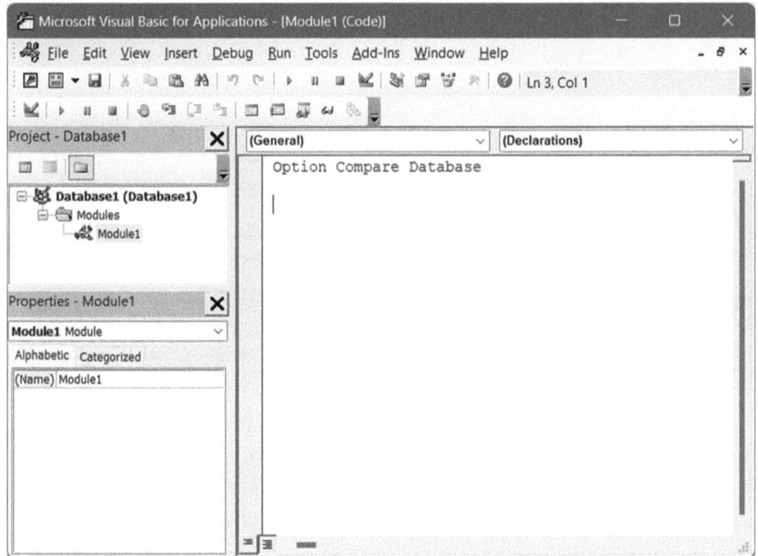

FIGURE 1.1.   An empty code module.

Module Types

There are two types of modules:

1. Standard Modules
A standard module is automatically assigned the name Module1 when created. You can see this module depicted in Figure 1.1 earlier. Standard modules are used to hold procedures that are not associated with any specific form, report, or object in your database. The procedures in a standard module can be accessed from anywhere in your Access application. It is a common location to place programming code that will be reused. The standard module can be added to your Access database project by choosing Insert | Module in the VBE window.

2. Class Modules
Class modules come in three varieties: *standalone class modules*, *form modules*, and *report modules*.

* Standalone Class Modules—These modules are used to create your own custom objects with their own properties and methods. You create a standalone class module by choosing Insert | Class Module in the Microsoft VBE window. Access will create a default class module named Class1

and will list it in the Class Modules folder in the Project Explorer window. You will work with standalone class modules later in this book.

- Form Modules—Each Access form can contain a form module, which is a special type of class module.
- Report Modules—Each Access report can contain a report module, which is a special type of class module.
- You will work with form and report modules when we learn how to customize forms and reports later in this book.

Procedure Types

Let's learn a bit about VBA procedure types so that you can quickly recognize them when you see them in books, magazine articles, or online. In VBA, you can write four types of procedures: *subroutine procedures, function procedures, event procedures,* and *property procedures.*

1. Subroutine procedures (also called subroutines or subprocedures) Subroutine procedures perform useful tasks but never return values. They begin with the keyword Sub and end with the keywords End Sub. *Keywords* are words that carry a special meaning in VBA. Let's look at the simple subroutine named ShowMessage that displays a message to the user:

```
Sub ShowMessage()
  MsgBox "This is a message box in VBA."
End Sub
```

Notice a pair of empty parentheses after the procedure name. The instruction that the procedure needs to execute is placed on a separate line between the Sub and End Sub keywords. Within a subroutine procedure, you may place one or more instructions and even complex control structures, which you will learn later. The ShowMessage procedure will always display the same message when executed. MsgBox is a built-in VBA function often used for programming user interactions (see Chapter 3, Access VBA Procedures and Functions, for more information on using, writing, and understanding functions).

If you'd like to write a more universal procedure that can display a different message each time the procedure is executed, you will need to write a subroutine that takes arguments. *Arguments* are values that are needed for a procedure to do something. Arguments are placed within the parentheses after the procedure name. Let's look at the following procedure, which also displays a message to the user; however, this time we can pass any text string to display:

```
Sub ShowMessage2(strMessage As String)
  MsgBox strMessage
End Sub
```

This subprocedure requires one text value before it can be run; `strMessage` is an arbitrary argument name. It can represent any text you want. Therefore, if you pass it the text `Today is Monday`, that is the text the user will see when the procedure is executed. If you don't pass the value to this procedure, VBA will display an error. Notice that following the argument name, we can also specify the data type for the argument. Data types are discussed later in this chapter. If the data type is not specified, Access will use its default data type (Variant) for this argument. The built-in `MsgBox` function requires that we pass to it a text string, so we can use the `String` data type for the `strMessage` argument.

If your subprocedure requires more than one argument, you must list the arguments within the parentheses and separate them with commas. For example, let's improve the preceding procedure by also passing it a text string containing a username:

```
Sub ShowMessage3(strMessage As String, strUserName as String)
  MsgBox strUserName & ", your message is: " & strMessage
End Sub
```

The *ampersand* (&) operator is used for concatenating (joining) text strings inside the VBA procedure. If we pass to the above subroutine the text "Keep on learning." as the `strMessage` argument and "John" as the `strUserName` argument, the procedure will display the following text in a message box (see Figure 1.2).

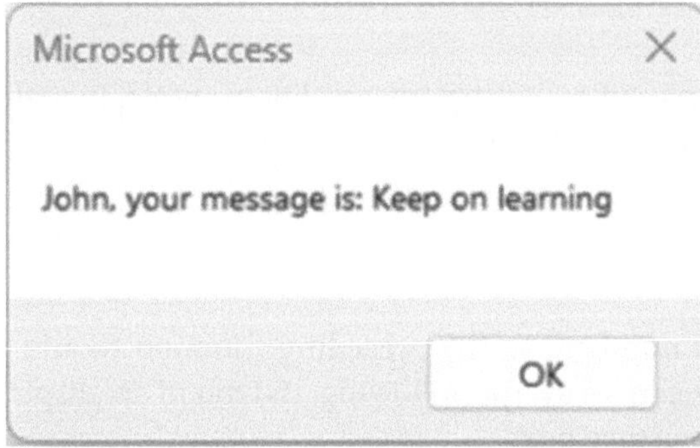

FIGURE 1.2.   Message box coded in the ShowMessage3 procedure.

2. Function Procedures (Functions)

Functions perform specific tasks and can return values. They begin with the keyword `Function` and end with the keywords `End Function`. Let's look at a simple function that adds two numbers:

```
Function addTwoNumbers()
   Dim num1 As Integer
   Dim num2 As Integer

   num1 = 3
   num2 = 2
   addTwoNumbers = num1 + num2
End Function
```

The preceding function procedure always returns the same result, which is the value 5. The `Dim` statements inside this function procedure are used to declare variables that the function will use. A *variable* is a name that is used to refer to an item of data. Because we want the function to perform a calculation, we specify that the variables named `num1` and `num2` will hold integer values, which is specified by the `Integer` data type. Variables and data types are covered in detail later in this chapter.

The variable definitions (the lines with the `Dim` statements) are followed by the variable assignment statements in which we assign specific numbers to the variables `num1` and `num2`. Finally, the calculation is performed by adding together the values held in both variables: `num1 + num2`. To return the result of our calculation, we set the function name to the value or the expression we want to return:

```
addTwoNumbers = num1 + num2
```

Although this function example returns a value, not all functions have to return values. Functions, like subroutines, can perform actions without returning any values.

Like procedures, functions can accept arguments. For example, to make our `addTwoNumbers` function more flexible, we can rewrite it as follows:

```
Function addTwoNumbers2(num1 As Integer, num2 As Integer)
   addTwoNumbers2 = num1 + num2
End Function
```

Now we can pass any two numbers to the preceding function to add them together. For example, we can write the following statement to display the result of the function in a message box:

```
Sub DisplayResult()
   MsgBox("Total=" & addTwoNumbers2(34,80))
End Sub
```

Notice that the procedure `DisplayResult` calls two functions: the built-in `MsgBox` function and your custom `addTwoNumbers2` function, which uses two numbers for the required two arguments. The result of the `addTwoNumbers2` function is concatenated to the `Total=114` string and then displayed to the user.

FIGURE 1.3.   Message box generated by the DisplayResult procedure.

3. Event Procedures

Event procedures are automatically executed in response to an event initiated by the user or program code or triggered by the system. Access provides numerous events that you can respond to, such as the click, double-click, open, load, and focus events. Events, event properties, and event procedures are introduced later in this book.

4. Property Procedures

Property procedures are used to get or set the values of custom properties for forms, reports, and class modules. The three types of property procedures (`Property Get`, `Property Let`, and `Property Set`) begin with the `Property` keyword followed by the property type (`Get`, `Let`, or `Set`), the property name, and a pair of empty parentheses, and end with the `End Property` keywords. Here's an example of a property procedure that retrieves the value of an author's royalty:

```
Property Get Royalty ()
  Royalty = (Sales * Percent) - Advance
End Property
```

Property procedures are an advanced feature in Access VBA programming and are covered in detail when we discuss creating classes later in this book.

WRITING PROCEDURES IN A MODULE

As mentioned earlier, general-use procedures that are not related to forms and reports are created and stored in standard modules. Because we already have a couple of procedures to try out, let's do a quick hands-on exercise to learn how to create a standard module, write procedures, and execute them.

NOTE	*All code files and figures for the hands-on projects may be found in the companion files.*

Hands-On 1.1   Working in a Standard Module

1. Create a folder on your hard drive named `C:\VBAAccess2024_ByExample`.
2. Open Access and click Blank database. Type `Chap01` in the File Name box and click the folder button to set the location for the database to the `C:\VBAAccess2024_ByExample` folder. Finally, click the Create button to create the specified database (see Figure 1.4). Access will create the database in its default `.accdb` format.

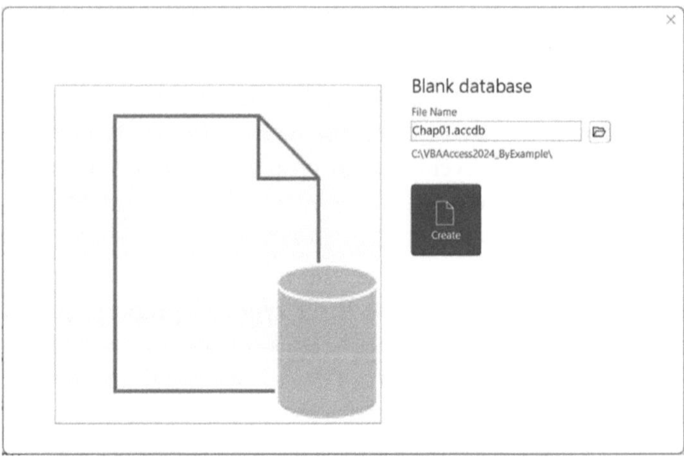

FIGURE 1.4.   Creating a blank desktop Access database.

Let's leave the standard Access application window to work in the programming environment.

3. To launch the programming environment, select the Database Tools tab and click Visual Basic (see Figure 1.5). Or you can press Alt+F11 to get to this screen.

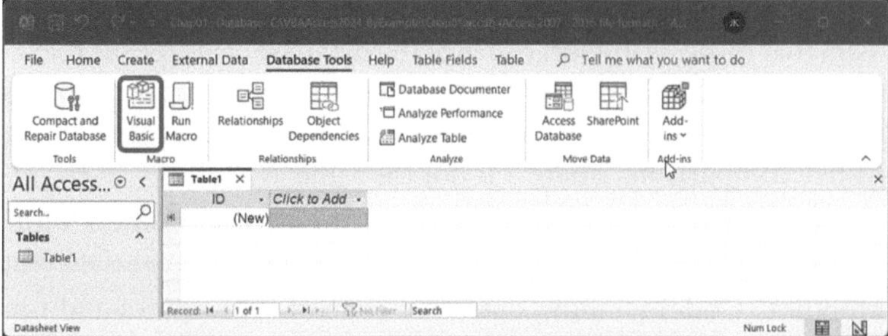

FIGURE 1.5.   Activating a Visual Basic development environment.

The screen that opens is your Visual Basic environment. All your coding will be performed on this screen. Before you can do your work here, you need to determine which module you need to work with. As mentioned earlier, we use a standard module for most general programming tasks. Initially, nothing is open, so let's add the first standard module.

4. Insert a standard module by choosing Module from the Insert menu (see Figure 1.6).

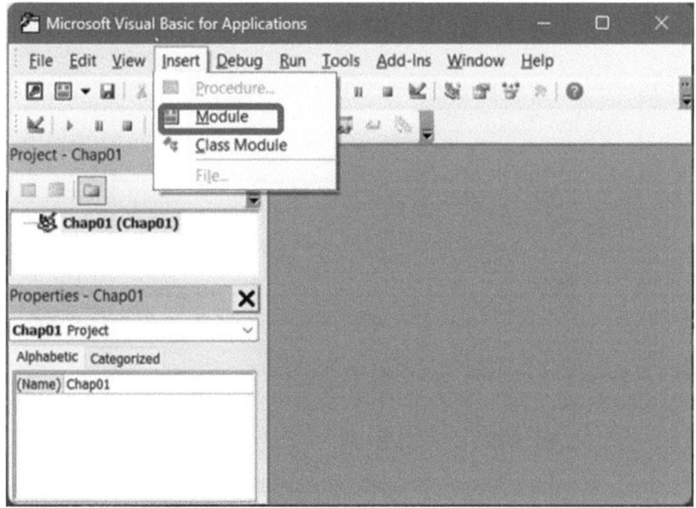

FIGURE 1.6.   Inserting a standard module.

As mentioned earlier, each module begins with a Declarations section that lists various settings and declarations that apply to every procedure in the module. As you saw earlier in Figure 1.1, the default declaration, `Option Compare Database`, specifies how string comparisons are evaluated in the module—

whether the comparison is case-sensitive or insensitive. This is a case-insensitive comparison that respects the sort order of the database. This means that `a` is the same as `A`. If you delete the `Option Compare Database` statement, the default string comparison setting for the module is `Option Compare Binary` (used for case-sensitive comparisons where `a` is not the same as `A`).

You can begin writing your procedures at the cursor position within the Module1 (Code) window below the `Option Compare Database` statement.

5. In the Module1 (Code) window, enter the code of subroutines and function procedures as shown in Figure 1.7. These are the same subprocedures and functions that we've discussed so far in this chapter. You can write procedures and functions in the same module, or you can keep them separate by adding another module to your VBA project.

Notice that Access inserts a horizontal line after each `End Sub` or `End Function` keyword to make it easier to identify each procedure. The Procedure drop-down box at the top-right corner of the Module1 (Code) window displays the name of the procedure in which the insertion point is currently located.

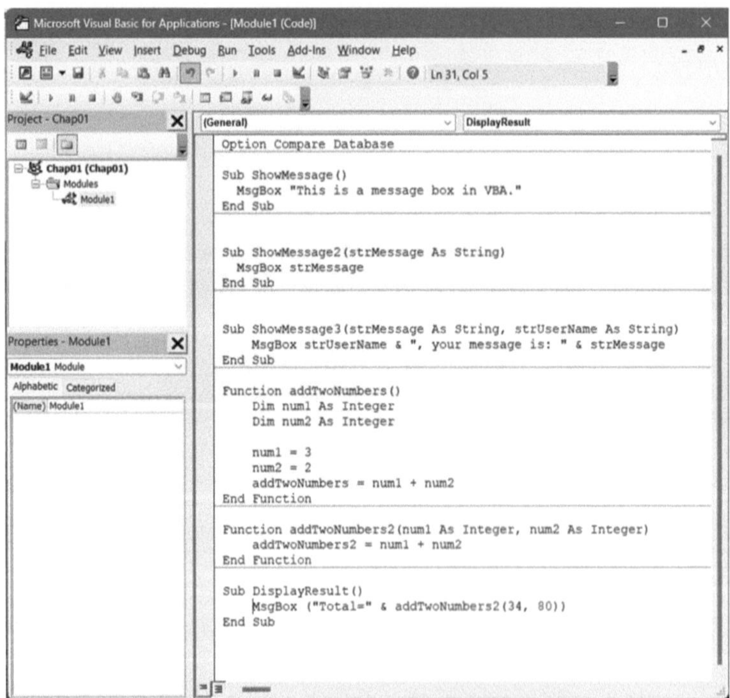

FIGURE 1.7. Standard module with subprocedures and functions.

You can move between the module procedures by selecting a procedure name from the Procedure box. You can also click around the module sheet to choose the procedure you want to run, as discussed in the next section. If you reposition the cursor to the declaration line, the Procedure box will display the text (Declarations).

EXECUTING YOUR PROCEDURES

Now that you've filled the standard module with procedures and functions, let's see how you can run them. There are many ways of running (executing) your code. In the next hands-on exercise, you will execute your code in four different ways, using the:

- Run menu (Run Sub/UserForm)
- Toolbar button (Run Sub/UserForm)
- Keyboard (F5)
- Immediate window

Hands-On 1.2   Running Procedures and Functions

1. Place the insertion point anywhere within the `ShowMessage` procedure. The procedure box should display ShowMessage.
2. Choose Run Sub/UserForm from the Run menu.
   Access runs the selected procedure and displays the message box with the text This is a message box in VBA. If you are using multiple monitors, this message may pop up on a different screen.
3. Now, you must click OK to close the message box before you can return to the VBE window.
4. Try running this procedure again, this time by pressing the F5 function key on the keyboard. If you are running Access on a laptop, you may need to hold another key to use the F5 function key. Again, click OK to close the message box. If the Access window seems stuck and you can't activate any menu option, this is often an indication that there is a message box open in the background. Access will not permit you to do any operation until you close the pop-up window.
5. Now, run this procedure for the third time, this time by clicking the Run Sub/UserForm button (▶) on the toolbar. This button has the same tooltip as the Run Sub/UserForm (F5) option on the Run menu.

NOTE	*Executing procedures that require arguments* *Procedures that require arguments cannot be executed directly using the methods you just learned. You need to type some input values for these procedures to run. A perfect place to do this is the Immediate window, which is covered in detail in Chapter 2, Getting to Know Visual Basic Editor (VBE). For now, let's open this window and see how you can use it to run VBA procedures with and without arguments.*

6. In the Microsoft VBE window, choose View | Immediate Window.

Notice you can also press Ctrl+G to open this window. Access opens a small window and places it just below the Module1 (Code) window. You can reposition this window as needed by dragging its title bar. You can then resize the window by dragging its corners or sides as you like. To quickly return the Immediate window to the default position at the bottom of the Module sheet, simply double-click its title bar.

7. Type the following command in the Immediate window and press Enter to execute.

```
ShowMessage2 "I'm learning VBA."
```

When you press the Enter key after typing a command in the Immediate window, Access executes the command. In this case, you should see a message box with the text I'm learning VBA. Click OK to close the message box. Notice that to execute the `ShowMessage2` procedure, you typed the procedure name (`ShowMessage2`), a space, and the text you wanted to display. The text string was surrounded by double quotation marks. In a similar way, you can execute the `ShowMessage3` procedure by providing two required text strings.

8. Click on a new line in the Immediate window, type the following statement, and press Enter to execute:

```
ShowMessage3 "Keep on learning.", "John"
```

When you press the Enter key, Access executes the `ShowMessage3` procedure and displays the message box as was shown earlier in Figure 1.2.

9. Click OK to close the message box.

<table>
<tr><td rowspan="2">NOTE</td><td>Using the <code>Call</code> statement in the Immediate window to execute a procedure
You can also use the <code>Call</code> statement to run a procedure in the Immediate window. When using this statement, if the procedure requires arguments, you must place their values within parentheses, as shown here:</td></tr>
<tr><td><code>Call ShowMessage3("Keep on learning.", "John")</code></td></tr>
</table>

Function procedures are executed using different methods. Step 10 demonstrates how to call the `addTwoNumbers` function.

10. On a new line in the Immediate window, type a question mark followed by the name of the function procedure and press Enter:

```
?addTwoNumbers
```

Access should display the result of this function (the number 5) on the next line in the Immediate window, as shown in Figure 1.8 at the end of this hands-on exercise.

11. Now run the `addTwoNumbers2` procedure by typing the following instruction in the Immediate window and pressing Enter:

```
?addTwoNumbers2(56, 24)
```

Access displays the result of adding these two numbers on the next line.

12. If you'd rather see the function result in a message box, type the following instruction in the Immediate window and press Enter:

```
MsgBox("Total=" & addTwoNumbers2(34,80))
```

Access displays a message box as shown earlier in Figure 1.3. Figure 1.8 shows all the commands that you entered in the Immediate window in this hands-on exercise.

```
Immediate                                                        ✕
ShowMessage2 "I'm learning VBA."
ShowMessage3 "Keep on learning.", "John"
Call ShowMessage3("Keep on learning.", "John")
?addTwoNumbers
 5
?addTwoNumbers2(56, 24)
 80
MsgBox("Total=" & addTwoNumbers2(34,80))
```

FIGURE 1.8.   Running procedures and functions from the Immediate window.

COMPILING AND SAVING YOUR PROCEDURES

The VBA code you write in the VBE Code window is automatically compiled by Access before you run it. Compilation is the process of converting a programming code you wrote into machine-executable code so that the computer can understand it and execute it. VBE checks your code for syntax errors to ensure that the code is error-free and ready for execution. If it discovers any issues with the code, such as typos, invalid constants or constructs, or missing references, Access will stop compiling the code and you will see a message box with a compile error. It will also highlight the line of code that contains the error. The compiling process can take from seconds to minutes or longer, depending on the number of procedures written and the number of modules used.

To ensure that your procedures have been compiled, you can explicitly compile them after you are done programming. You can do this by choosing Debug | Compile in the Visual Basic Editor window. If this menu option is grayed out, it indicates that the code has already been compiled. Access saves all the code in your database in its compiled form. Compiled code runs more quickly the next time you open it. You should always save your modules after you compile them. In Chapter 8, Getting to Know Built-In Tools for Testing and Debugging, you will learn how to test and troubleshoot your VBA procedures.

Now, let's find out how to save our VBA programming code so we can refer to it later. You can save your work with one of the following methods:

- Click the Save button on the toolbar. This button is represented by an image of a disc.
- Press the key combination Ctrl+S.
- Choose File | Save.

⊙ Hands-On 1.3　Saving, Printing, and Exporting Your VBA Modules

1. Choose File | Save Chap01.accdb
   Access displays the Save As dialog box listing Module1 as the module name.
2. In the Module Name text box, enter `SimpleProcedures`, as shown in Figure 1.9, and click OK.

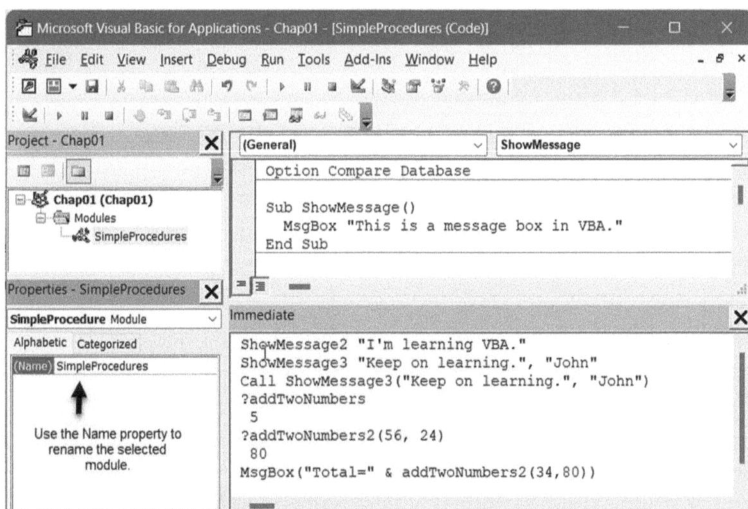

FIGURE 1.9.   Saving a VBA module.

Notice that in the Project window on the left-hand side of the Code window (Figure 1.10), in the Modules folder, Access has replaced Module1 with its new name (SimpleProcedures), and the Properties window now displays SimpleProcedures next to the Name property. If you need to change the name of the module, simply type a new name here.

FIGURE 1.10.   Renaming a VBA module.

If you have a printer available, you may print the module code by pressing Ctrl+P or choosing File | Print. Printing out your code can be very helpful for studying and analyzing the procedure syntax and locating logic errors.

3. To save the selected module in an external file so you can import it later into another Access database, choose File | Export File.

Access will open the Export File dialog, where you can choose the location for your exported file and assign a name to the file. VBA files are saved as the Basic Files type, recognized by the `.bas` file extension (see Figure 1.11).

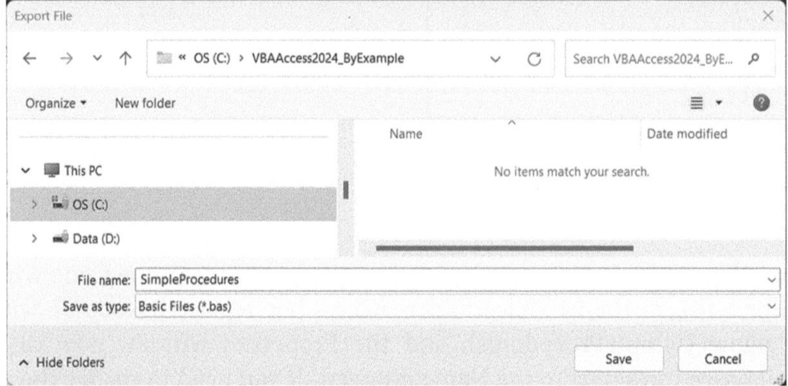

FIGURE 1.11.   Saving a VBA module in an external file.

Note that the File | Export File option will not be available if you have not selected the module in the Project window.

4. In the Export File dialog, click Save.
   You should now see the `SimpleProcedures.bas` file in the `VBAAccess2024_ByExample` folder. This is the working folder that we'll use while working on the examples in this book. This external code file can be imported to any Access database via the Import File option located on the File menu in the Visual Basic Editor window.

   Now let's close the Visual Basic Editor window and return to the Microsoft Access application window so we can set other options that will be helpful in your further programming endeavors.

5. Choose File | Close and Return to Microsoft Access, or press Alt+Q.
   This closes the VBE development environment and puts you back in the main Access window.

PLACING A DATABASE IN A TRUSTED LOCATION

By default, the security features built into Access disable the VBA code and macros when you open a database. If you close the `Chap01.accdb` database and then reopen it, Access will load the database with a security warning message, as shown in Figure 1.12.

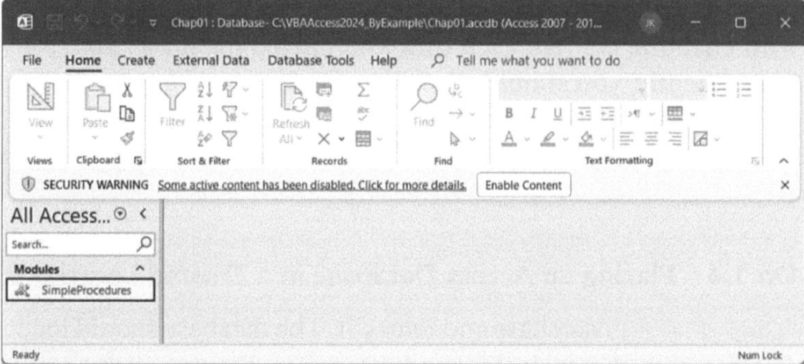

FIGURE 1.12.   By default, Access does not trust any database that contains VBA code or macros and displays a security warning message when you open the database.

If you trust the database, you can discard the message by clicking the Enable Content button in the SECURITY WARNING message bar. To find out more information about enabling content, you can click the provided text link in the message bar. Access will present you with the Info screen shown in Figure 1.13.

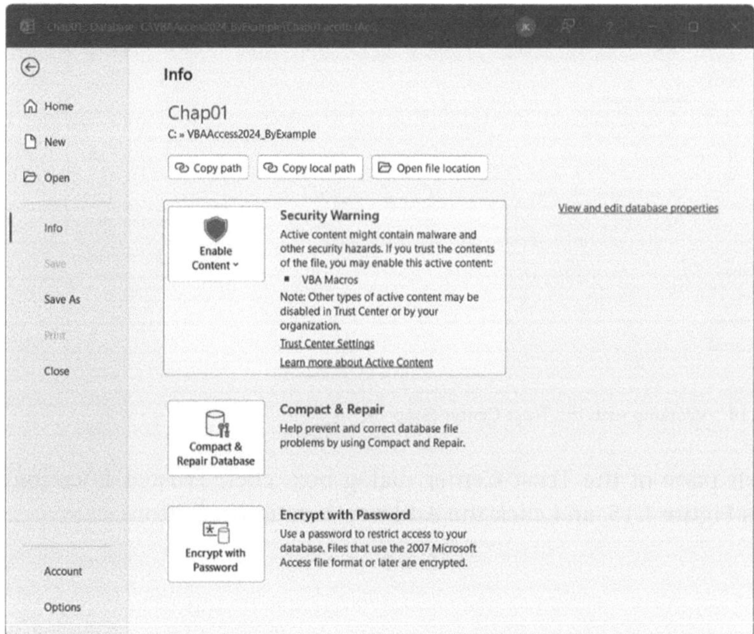

FIGURE 1.13.   The Info tab with an explanation of the Security Warning message.

To make it easy to work with Access databases in this book, you will not want to bother with enabling content each time you open a database. To trust your databases permanently, you should place them in a *trusted location*—a folder on your local or network drive that you mark as trusted. Hands-On 1.4 will take you through the process of setting up a trusted folder for your Access databases.

Hands-On 1.4   Placing an Access Database in a Trusted Location

1. Close the `Chap01.accdb` database and reload it. The database should load with the warning message shown in Figure 1.12 earlier. Do not click the Enable Content button.
2. Click the text link of the warning message. Access will activate the Info section of the File tab, as shown in Figure 1.13
3. On the same screen, in the left pane, click the Options button.
4. In the left pane of the Access Options dialog box, click Trust Center, and then click Trust Center Settings…, as shown in Figure 1.14.

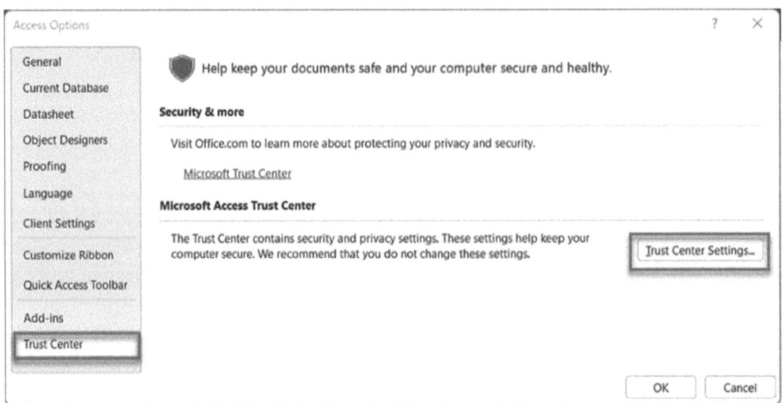

FIGURE 1.14   Working with the Trust Center (step 1).

5. In the left pane of the Trust Center dialog box, click Trusted Locations, as shown in Figure 1.15, and click the Add new location… button.

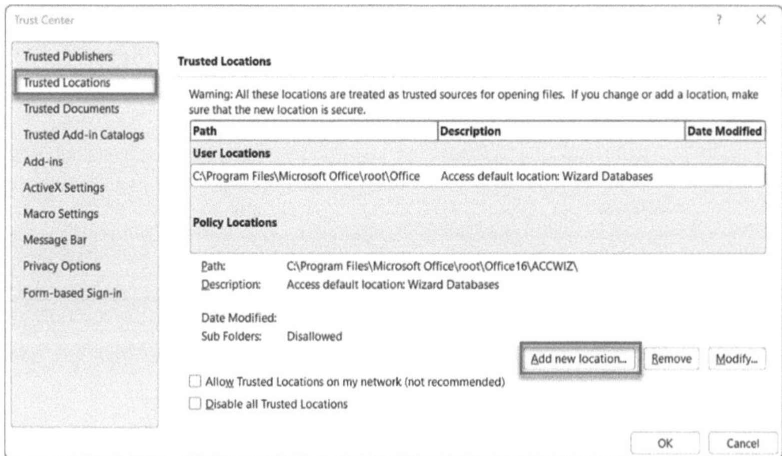

FIGURE 1.15.   Working with the Trust Center (step 2).

6. In the Path text box, type the path and folder name of the location on your local drive that you want to set up as a trusted source for opening files. Let's enter `C:\VBAAccess2024_ByExample` to designate this folder as a trusted location for all our VBA programming work (see Figure 1.16). Fill in the Description as shown.

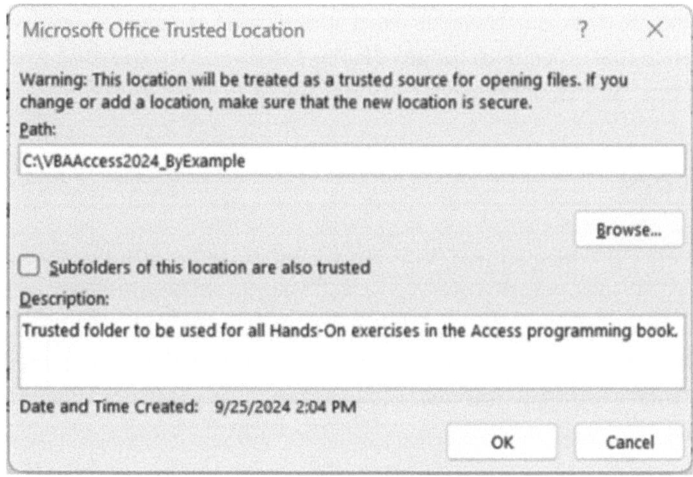

FIGURE 1.16.   Working with the Trust Center (step 3).

7. Click OK to close the Microsoft Office Trusted Location dialog box.

8. The Trusted Locations list in the Trust Center dialog box now includes the `C:\VBAAccess2024_ByExample` folder as a trusted source (see Figure 1.17). Files put in a trusted location can be opened without being checked by the Trust Center security feature.

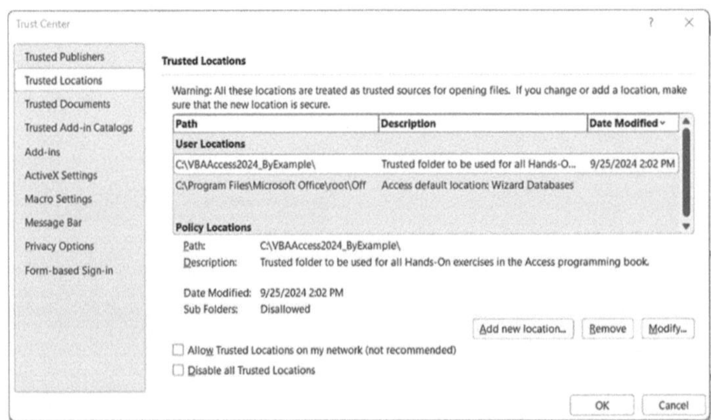

FIGURE 1.17.   Working with the Trust Center (step 4).

9. Click OK to close the Trust Center dialog box. Then, click OK to close the Access Options dialog box.
10. Close the `Chap01.accdb` database and exit Access.
11. Open the `Chap01.accdb` database file from your C:\VBAAccess2024_ByExample folder and notice that Access no longer displays the security warning message.
12. Close the `Chap01.accdb` database.

VBA DATA TYPES

When you create VBA procedures, you have a purpose in mind: you want to manipulate data. Because your procedures will handle different kinds of information, you should understand how VBA stores data.

A *data type* determines how the data is stored in the computer's memory. VBA provides many built-in (intrinsic) data types. The most popular of them are listed below:

- `Boolean`—Stores true or false values (2 bytes)
- `Byte`—Holds values from 0 to 255 (1 byte)
- `Decimal`—Provides high precision for decimal calculations (14 bytes)

- `Integer`—Ranges from -32,768 to 32,767 (2 bytes)
- `Long`—Spans from -2,147,483,648 to 2,147,483,647 (4 bytes)
- `Currency`—Used for financial calculations (8 bytes)
- `Date`—Represents dates and times (8 bytes)
- `Double`—Double-precision floating-point numbers (8 bytes)
- `Single`—Single-precision floating-point numbers (4 bytes)
- `String`—Variable-length text (up to approximately 2 billion characters)
- `Variant`—A versatile type that can hold various data types (16 bytes for numeric variants, 22 bytes for character variants).

The complete list of VBA data types can be found in Appendix A, Table A.1. You will use some data types from this extended list later in this book when we delve into more advanced programming topics.

In addition to the built-in data types, you can define your own custom data types using the Type keyword; these are known as *user-defined data types.* You will find an example of this data type in Appendix A, Table A.2.

Because data types take up different amounts of space in the computer's memory, some of them are more expensive than others. Therefore, to conserve memory and make your procedure run faster, you should select the data type that uses the fewest bytes but at the same time can handle the data that your procedure has to manipulate.

UNDERSTANDING AND USING VARIABLES

Earlier in this chapter, we wrote some procedures that used variables, and you learned that a *variable* is a name used to refer to an item of data. Understanding variables is crucial in your programming work. Each time you want to remember the result of a VBA instruction, think of a name that will represent it. For example, if you want to keep track of the number of controls on an Access form, you can make up a name such as `NumOfControls`, `TotalControls`, or `FormsControlCount`.

The names of variables that you create can contain characters, numbers, and punctuation marks except for the following:
, # $ % & @ !

It's important to note that the name of a variable cannot begin with a number or contain a space. If you want the name of the variable to include more than one word, use the underscore (_) as a separator. Although a variable name can contain as many as 254 characters, it's best to use short and simple names. Using short names will save you typing time when you need to reuse the variable in your VBA procedure. Visual Basic doesn't care whether you use uppercase or lowercase letters in variable names; however, most programmers use lowercase letters. When the variable name is composed of more than one word, most programmers use camel case; they capitalize the first letter of each word, as in the following: NumOfControls, First_Name.

Reserved Words Can't Be Used for Variable Names

You can use any label you want for a variable name except for the reserved words that VBA uses. Visual Basic function names and words that have a special meaning in VBA cannot be used as variable names. For example, words such as Name, Len, Empty, Local, Currency, and Exit will generate an error message if used as a variable name.

Give your variables names that can help you remember their roles. Some programmers use a prefix to identify the variable's type. For example, a variable name preceded by `str`, such as `strName`, can be quickly recognized within the procedure code as the variable holding the text string.

Declaring Variables

You can create a variable by declaring it with a special command or by just using it in a statement. When you declare your variable, you make Visual Basic aware of the variable's name and data type. This is called *explicit variable declaration*.

Advantages of Explicit Variable Declaration

❑ Speeds up the execution of your procedure. Since Visual Basic knows the data type, it reserves only as much memory as is necessary to store the data.

❑ Makes your code easier to read and understand because all the variables are listed at the very beginning of the procedure.

❑ Helps prevent errors caused by misspelling a variable name. Visual Basic automatically corrects the variable name based on the spelling used in the variable declaration.

If you don't let Visual Basic know about the variable prior to using it, you are implicitly telling VBA that you want to create this variable. *Implicit variables* are automatically assigned the `Variant` data type. Although implicit variable declaration is convenient (it allows you to create variables on the fly and assign values to them without knowing in advance the data type of the values being assigned), it can cause several problems.

Disadvantages of Implicit Variable Declaration

❑ If you misspell a variable name in your procedure, Visual Basic may display a runtime error or create a new variable. You are guaranteed to waste some time troubleshooting problems that could easily have been avoided had you declared your variable at the beginning of the procedure.

❑ Since Visual Basic does not know what type of data your variable will store, it assigns it the `Variant` data type. This causes your procedure to run slower because Visual Basic must check the data type every time it deals with your variable. Also, because `Variant` variables can store any type of data, Visual Basic must reserve more memory to store your data.

You declare a variable with the `Dim` keyword. `Dim` stands for *dimension*. The `Dim` keyword is followed by the variable's name and type.

Suppose you want your procedure to display the age of an employee. Before you can calculate the age, you must feed the procedure the employee's date of birth. To do this, you declare a variable called `dateOfBirth`, as follows:

```
Dim dateOfBirth As Date
```

Notice that the `Dim` keyword is followed by the name of the variable (`dateOf-Birth`). If you don't like this name, you are free to replace it with another word, provided your replacement word is not one of the VBA keywords. To specify the variable's data type, include the `As` keyword followed by the name of the data type. In our example, the `Date` data type tells Visual Basic that the variable `dateOfBirth` will store a date.

To store the employee's age, you can declare a variable as follows:

```
Dim intAge As Integer
```

The `intAge` variable will store the number of years between today's date and the employee's date of birth. Because age is displayed as a whole number, the `intAge` variable has been assigned the `Integer` data type. If you want your procedure to keep track of the employee's name, you can declare another variable to hold the employee's first and last name:

```
Dim strFullName As String
```

Because the word Name is on the VBA list of reserved words, using it in your VBA procedure would guarantee an error. To hold the employee's full name, we used the variable `strFullName` and declared it as the `String` data type because the data it will hold is text.

Declaring variables is regarded as good programming practice because it makes programs easier to read and helps prevent certain types of errors.

> ### Informal (Implicit) Variables
>
> Variables that are not explicitly declared with `Dim` statements are said to be implicitly declared. These variables are automatically assigned a data type called `Variant`. They can hold numbers, strings, and other types of information. You can create an informal variable by assigning some value to a variable name anywhere in your VBA procedure. For example, you implicitly declare a variable in the following way:
>
> ```
> intDaysLeft = 100
> ```

Now that you know how to declare variables, let's write a procedure that uses them.

(•) Hands-On 1.5   Using Variables

1. Start Access and open the `Chap01.accdb` database that you created earlier in this chapter.
2. Once the database is opened, press Alt+F11 to switch to the Visual Basic Editor window, or choose Database Tools | Visual Basic.
3. In the Visual Basic Applications window, choose Insert | Module to add a new standard module, and notice Module1 under the Modules folder in the Project Explorer window.
4. In the Module1 (Code) window, enter the following `AgeCalc` procedure.

```
Sub AgeCalc()
  ' variable declaration
  Dim strFullName As String
  Dim dateOfBirth As Date
  Dim intAge As Integer

  ' assign values to variables
  strFullName = "John Smith"
  dateOfBirth = #1/3/1967#

  ' calculate age
  IntAge = Year(Now()) - Year(dateOfBirth)
```

```
' print results to the Immediate window
  Debug.Print strFullName & " is " & intAge & " years old."
End Sub
```

Using Comments in Your Programming Code

The apostrophe placed at the beginning of a line of code denotes a comment. By default, all text in commented lines is colored in green. To change the comment color, select Tools | Options, and click the Editor Format tab to access the Comment Text color options. Besides the fact that comments make it easier to understand what the procedure does, comments are also very useful in testing and troubleshooting VBA procedures. For example, when you execute a procedure, it may not run as expected. Instead of deleting the lines of code that may be responsible for the problems encountered, you may want to skip the lines for now and return to them later. By placing an apostrophe at the beginning of the line you want to avoid, you can continue checking the other parts of your procedure. Commented lines are never executed when the procedure runs.

Notice that in the `AgeCalc` procedure, the variables are declared on separate lines at the beginning of the procedure. You can also declare several variables on the same line, separating each variable name with a comma, as shown here (be sure to enter this on one line):

```
Dim strFullName As String, dateOfBirth As Date,
intAge As Integer
```

When you list all your variables on one line, the `Dim` keyword appears only once at the beginning of the variable declaration line.

5. If the Immediate window is not open, press Ctrl+G or choose View | Immediate Window. Because the example procedure writes the results to the Immediate window, you should ensure that this window is open prior to executing step 6.

6. To run the `AgeCalc` procedure, click any line between the `Sub` and `End Sub` keywords and press F5.

7. Using the data supplied by the `dateOfBirth` variable, Visual Basic calculates the age of an employee and stores the result of the calculation in the variable called `intAge`. Then, the full name of the employee and the age are printed to the Immediate window using the built-in `Debug.Print` command.

What Is the Variable Type?

You can find out the type of a variable used in a VBA procedure by right-clicking the variable name and selecting Quick Info from the shortcut menu.

> ### Joining Text Strings in Your VBA Procedures
>
> You can combine two or more strings to form a new string. The joining operation is called *concatenation*. You saw an example of concatenated strings in the `AgeCalc` procedure. Concatenation is represented by an ampersand character (&). For instance, `"His name is" & strFirstName` will produce a string such as `His name is John` or `His name is Michael`. The name of the person will be determined by the contents of the `strFirstName` variable. Notice that there is an extra space between `is` and the ending quotation mark: `"His name is"`. Concatenation of strings can also be represented by a plus sign (+); however, many programmers prefer to restrict the plus sign to numerical operations to eliminate ambiguity.

Specifying the Data Type of a Variable

If you don't specify the variable's data type in the `Dim` statement, you end up with an *untyped* variable. Untyped variables in VBA are always assigned the `Variant` data type. `Variant` data types can hold all the other data types (except for user-defined data types). This feature makes `Variant` a very flexible and popular data type. Despite this flexibility, it is highly recommended that you create typed variables. When you declare a variable of a certain data type, your VBA procedure runs faster because Visual Basic does not have to stop to analyze the variable to determine its type.

Visual Basic can work with many types of numeric variables. Integer variables can hold only whole numbers from –32,768 to 32,767. Other types of numeric variables are `Long`, `Single`, `Double`, and `Currency`. Variables of the `Long` type can hold whole numbers in the range –2,147,483,648 to 2,147,483,647. As opposed to `Integer` and `Long` variables, `Single` and `Double` variables can hold decimals.

`String` variables are used to refer to text. When you declare a variable of the `String` data type, you can tell Visual Basic how long the string should be. For instance, `Dim strExtension As String * 3` declares a fixed-length `String` variable named `strExtension` that is three characters long. If you don't assign a specific length, the `String` variable will be *dynamic*. This means that Visual Basic will make enough space in computer memory to handle whatever text length is assigned to it.

After a variable is declared, it can store only the type of information that you stated in the declaration statement.

Assigning string values to numeric variables or numeric values to string variables results in the error message Type Mismatch or causes Visual Basic to modify the value. For example, if your variable was declared to hold whole numbers and your data uses decimals, Visual Basic will disregard the decimals and use only the whole part of the number.

Using Data Type Declaration Characters

If you don't declare a variable with a `Dim` statement, you can still designate a type for it by using a special character at the end of the variable name. For example, to declare the `FirstName` variable as `String`, you append the dollar sign to the variable name:

```
Dim FirstName$
```

This is the same as `Dim FirstName As String`. Other type declaration characters are shown in Table 1.1.. Notice that the data type declaration characters can be used only with six data types. To use it, append the character to the end of the variable name.

TABLE 1.1.   Type declaration characters.

Data Type	Character
Integer	%
Long	&
Single	!
Double	#
Currency	@
String	$

Declaring Typed Variables

The variable type can be indicated by the `As` keyword or by attaching a type symbol. If you don't add the data type character or the `As` keyword, VBA will default the variable to the `Variant` data type.

Assigning Values to Variables

When Visual Basic executes the variable declaration statements, it creates the variables with the specified names and reserves memory space to store their values. Then, specific values are assigned to these variables.

To assign a value to a variable, you begin with the variable name followed by an equal sign. The value entered to the right of the equal sign is the data you want to store in the variable. The data you enter here must be of the type stated in the variable declaration. Text data should be surrounded by quotation marks and for any dates, you use # characters, as was shown earlier in the `AgeCalc` procedure:

```
' assign values to variables
  strFullName = "John Smith"
  dateOfBirth = #1/3/1967#
```

> ### Variable Initialization
>
> Visual Basic automatically initializes a new variable to its default value when it is created. Numerical variables are set to zero (0), Boolean variables are initialized to `False`, string variables are set to an empty string (`""`), and date variables are set to `December 30, 1899`. For example, let's say in the `AgeCalc` procedure you forget to assign a value to the `strFullName` variable that was declared at the top of the procedure. When you run this procedure, VBA will use the initial value for the contents of the variable. Because the `strFullName` variable was declared as the `String` data type, and was not initialized by you, VBA will set it to an empty string, that is, a string that contains no characters. It is essentially a string with zero length—no letters, no spaces. When you encounter an empty string, it looks like this: `""`.
>
> Now, if you comment out the lines that assign the values to the `strFullName` and `dateOfBirth` variables and rerun the `AgeCalc` procedure, you can fully experience the effect of the default variable initialization.

Forcing Declaration of Variables

Visual Basic has an `Option Explicit` statement that you can use to automatically remind yourself to formally declare all your variables. This statement must be entered at the top of each of your modules. The `Option Explicit` statement will cause Visual Basic to generate an error message when you try to run a procedure that contains any undeclared variables.

◉ Hands-On 1.6   Forcing Declaration of Variables

1. Return to the Code window where you entered the `AgeCalc` procedure, and just below the last line of this procedure, enter the following code:

```
Sub CalcCost()

    slsPrice = 35
    slsTax = 0.085

    cost = Format(slsPrice + (slsPrice * slsTax), "0.00")
    strMsg = "The calculator total is $" & cost & "."
```

```
  MsgBox strMsg
End Sub
```

In the code above, we calculate the cost of the calculator. To display the cost with two decimal places, we can use the built-in VBA `Format` function, which allows us to change the format of data. This function has the following syntax:

```
Format(expression, format)
```

where `expression` is a value or variable you want to format (`slsPrice + (slsPrice * slsTax)`) and `format` is the type of format you want to apply (`"0.00"`).

Notice that the variables (`slsPrice`, `slsTax`) are not formally declared at the top of the procedure code. When you run this procedure, it will still be able to provide the correct result, as the variables were assigned initial values by the programmer. VBA, however, does not know what data type these variables are, which can lead to potential issues. When variables are not explicitly declared with a data type (such as `Integer`, `Double`, or `String`), VBA will try to infer their data type based on the assigned initial values. While this can work in some cases, it's generally better practice to declare variables explicitly. Explicitly declaring variables helps prevent unexpected behavior and ensures better code readability and maintainability.

2. At the top of the module window (just below the `Option Compare Database` statement), enter the following code and press Enter.

```
Option Explicit
```

   Visual Basic will display the statement in blue, adding it to the module's Declarations area.

3. Position the insertion point anywhere within the `CalcCost` procedure and press F5 to run it. Visual Basic now displays the error message Compile error: Variable not defined.

4. Click OK to exit the message box.

   As you can see in Figure 1.18, Visual Basic selects the name of the variable, `slsPrice`, and highlights in yellow the name of the procedure, `Sub CalcCost()`. The title bar displays Microsoft Visual Basic for Applications—Chap01 [break]—[Module1 (Code)]. The Visual Basic break mode allows you to correct the problem before you continue. Now you must formally declare the `slsPrice` variable.

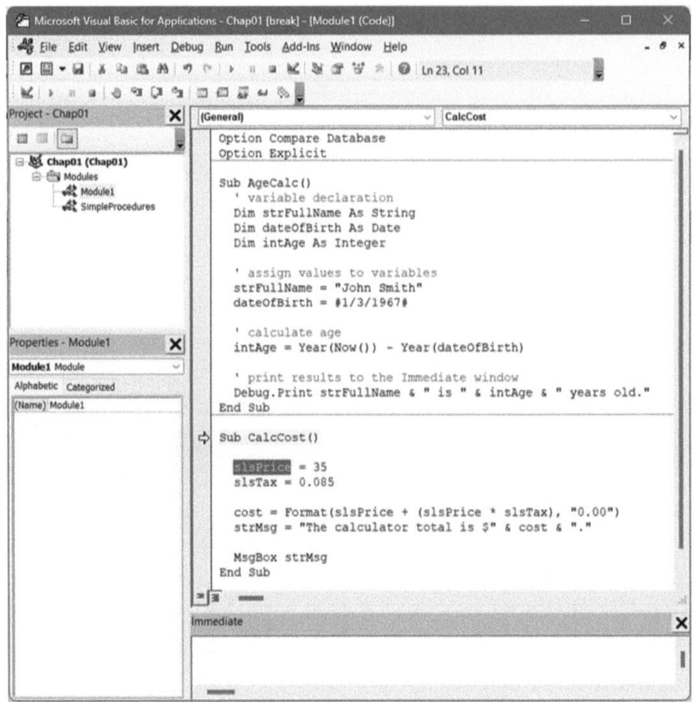

FIGURE 1.18.   Fixing compilation errors in break mode.

5. Enter the following declaration statement on a new line just below `Sub CalcCost()` and press F5 to continue.

```
Dim slsPrice As Currency
```

When you declare the `slsPrice` variable and rerun your procedure, Visual Basic again generates the same compile error because it encounters another variable name that was not declared. To fix the remaining problems with the variable declaration in this procedure, let's first exit break mode.

6. Click OK to dismiss the Compile Error message box and choose Run | Reset. Notice that you are no longer in break mode. You will work with break mode when we get to learn about the debugging techniques in Chapter 8.

7. Modify the `CalcCost` procedure by adding the missing variable declarations. The completed variable Declarations section should look as follows:

```
' declaration of variables
Dim slsPrice As Currency
Dim slsTax As Single
Dim cost As Currency
Dim strMsg As String
```

8. To run the procedure, click any line between the `Sub` and `End Sub` keywords and press F5 or choose Run | Run Sub/UserForm. You should no longer be interrupted by the compile error messages.

9. Press Ctrl+S to save your programming code. If you wish, you can rename Module1 in the Save As dialog, or you can do it later via the Properties window.

The `Option Explicit` statement you entered at the top of the module Code window forced you to declare variables. Because you must include the `Option Explicit` statement in each module where you want to require variable declaration, you can have Visual Basic enter this statement for you each time you insert a new module.

To automatically include `Option Explicit` in every new module you create, follow these steps:

1. Choose Tools | Options.
2. Ensure that the Require Variable Declaration checkbox is selected in the Options dialog box (Editor tab).
3. Choose OK to close the Options dialog box.

From now on, every new module you add to your database will have the `Option Explicit` statement. If you want to require variables to be explicitly declared in a module you created prior to enabling Require Variable Declaration in the Options dialog box, you must enter the `Option Explicit` statement manually by editing the module yourself.

More About Option Explicit

`Option Explicit` forces formal (explicit) declaration of all variables in a module. One big advantage of using `Option Explicit` is that misspellings of variable names will be detected at compile time (when Visual Basic attempts to translate the source code to machine-executable code). Note that the `Option Explicit` statement must appear in a module before any procedures.

Understanding the Scope of Variables

Variables can have different ranges of influence in a VBA procedure. Scope defines the availability of a variable to the same procedure or other procedures. Variables can have the following three levels of scope in VBA:

- Procedure-level scope
- Module-level scope
- Project-level scope

Procedure-Level (Local) Variables

From this chapter, you already know how to declare a variable using the `Dim` statement. The position of the `Dim` statement in the module determines the scope of a variable. Variables declared with the `Dim` statement within a VBA procedure have a *procedure-level* scope. Procedure-level variables can also be declared by using the `Static` statement (see Using Static Variables later in this chapter).

Procedure-level variables are frequently referred to as *local* variables, which can be used only in the procedure where they were declared. Undeclared variables always have a procedure-level scope.

Note that a variable's name must be unique within its scope. This means that you cannot declare two variables with the same name in the same procedure. You can, however, use the same variable name in different procedures. In other words, the `CalcCost` procedure can have the `slsTax` variable, and the `ExpenseRep` procedure in the same module can have its own variable called `slsTax`. Both variables are independent of each other.

Local Variables: With `Dim` or `Static`?

When you declare a local variable with the `Dim` statement, the value of the variable is preserved only while the procedure in which it is declared is running. As soon as the procedure ends, the variable dies. The next time you execute the procedure, the variable is reinitialized.

When you declare a local variable with the `Static` statement, the value of the variable is preserved after the procedure in which the variable was declared has finished running. Static variables are reset when you quit Access or when a runtime error occurs while the procedure is running.

Module-Level Variables

Sometimes you may want the variable to be available to other VBA procedures in the module after the procedure in which the variable was declared has finished running. This situation requires that you change the variable's scope to *module-level*.

Module-level variables are declared at the top of the module (above the first procedure definition) by using the `Dim` or `Private` statement. These variables are available to all the procedures in the module in which they were declared but are not available to procedures in other modules.

For instance, to make the `slsTax` variable available to any other procedure in the module, you could declare it by using the `Dim` or `Private` statement:

```
Option Explicit
Dim slsTax As Single

Sub CalcCost()
...Instructions of the procedure...
End Sub
```

Notice that the `slsTax` variable is declared at the top of the module, just below the `Option Explicit` statement and before the first procedure definition. You could also declare the `slsTax` variable like this:

```
Option Explicit
Private slsTax As Single

Sub CalcCost()
   ...Instructions of the procedure...
End Sub
```

Both the `Dim` and `Private` keywords allow you to declare variables that have a scope beyond just a single procedure. At the module level, however, using the `Private` keyword enhances code readability because it clearly communicates that the variable will be not accessible from other modules or projects.

Before you can see how module-level variables work, you need to create another procedure that also uses the `slsTax` variable.

⊚ Hands-On 1.7   Understanding Module-Level Variables

1. In the Code window, in the same module where you entered the `CalcCost` procedure, enter `Private slsTax As Single` at the top of the module sheet, just below the `Option Explicit` statement.
2. Comment out the declaration line `Dim slsTax As Single` inside the `CalcCost` procedure. Recall that to comment out the code line, you need to place an apostrophe at the beginning of the line.
3. In the same module, enter the following code of the `ExpenseRep` procedure (see Figure 1.19).

```
Sub ExpenseRep()
   Dim slsPrice As Currency
   Dim cost As Currency

   slsPrice = 55.99
   cost = slsPrice + (slsPrice * slsTax)
```

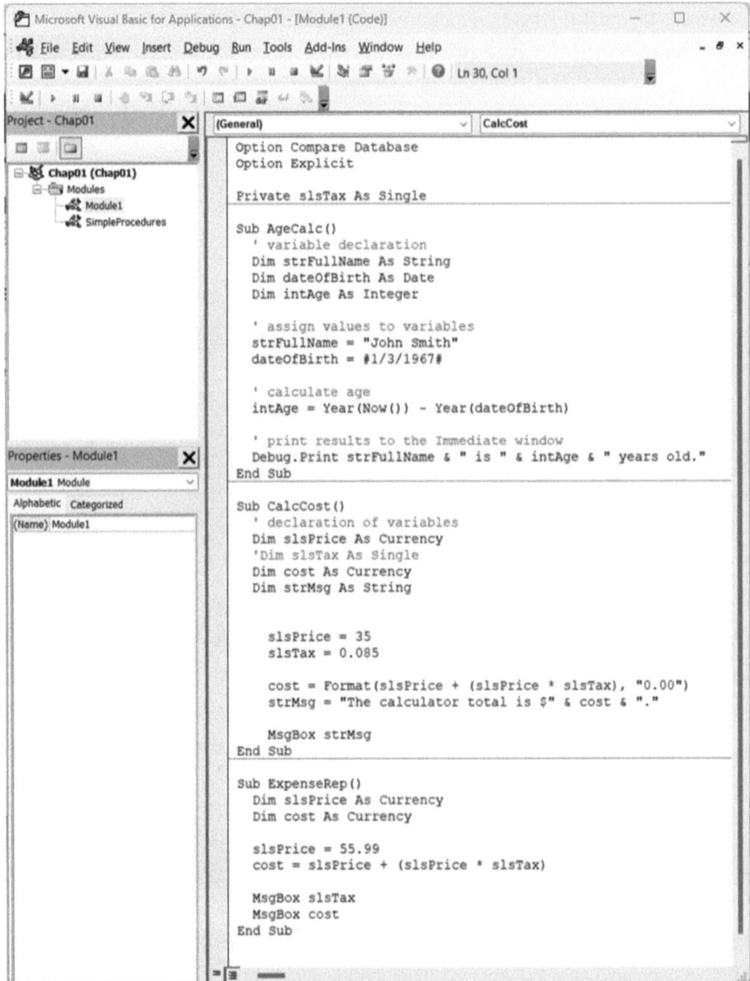

FIGURE 1.19.   The slsTax variable is declared as a module-level variable so it can be accessed by other procedures in the same module.

```
    MsgBox slsTax
    MsgBox cost
End Sub
```

Notice that the `ExpenseRep` procedure declares two local variables with the `Currency` data type: `slsPrice` and `cost`. The `slsPrice` variable is then assigned a value of `55.99`. This variable is independent of the `slsPrice` variable declared within the `CalcCost` procedure.

The `ExpenseRep` procedure calculates the cost of a purchase. The cost includes the sales tax provided by the `slsTax` variable that is declared at the top of the module. After Visual Basic executes the `CalcCost` procedure, the contents of the `slsTax` variable equals `0.085`. If `slsTax` were a local variable, the contents of this variable would be empty upon the termination of the `CalcCost` procedure. The `ExpenseRep` procedure ends by displaying the value of the `slsTax` and `cost` variables in two separate message boxes.

After running the `CalcCost` procedure, Visual Basic erases the contents of all the variables except for the `slsTax` variable, which was declared at the module level. As soon as you attempt to calculate the cost by running the `ExpenseRep` procedure, Visual Basic retrieves the value of the `slsTax` variable and uses it in the calculation.

4. Click anywhere inside the `CalcCost` procedure and press F5 to run it.
5. As soon as the `CalcCost` procedure finishes executing, run the `ExpenseRep` procedure.

Project-Level Variables

In the previous section, you learned that declaring a variable with the `Dim` or `Private` keyword at the top of the module makes it available to other procedures in that module. At the module level, you can also declare variables using the `Public` keyword. Such variables will have a project-level scope, meaning they can be used in any VBA module. When you want to work with a variable in all the procedures in all the open VBA projects, you must declare it with the `Public` keyword—for instance:

```
Option Explicit
Public gslsTax As Single

Sub CalcCost()
...Instructions of the procedure...
End Sub
```

Notice that the `gslsTax` variable declared at the top of the module with the `Public` keyword will now be available to any VBA modules that your code references. This type of variable is called a *global variable*. It is customary to use the prefix `g` to indicate its global scope.

When using global variables, it's important to keep in mind the following:

- The value of the global variable can be changed anywhere in your program. An unexpected change in the value of a variable is a common cause of problems. Be careful not to write a block of code that modifies a global variable. If you need to change the value of a variable within your application, make sure you are using a local variable.

- Values of all global variables declared with the `Public` keyword are cleared when Access encounters an error. Since the release of the Access 2007 database format (`.accdb`), you can use the `TempVars` collection for your global variable needs (see Using Temporary Variables later in this chapter).

- Don't put your global variable declaration in a form class module. Variables in the code module behind the form are never global even if you declare them as such. You must use a standard code module (Insert | Module) to declare variables to be available in all modules and forms. Variables declared in a standard module can be used in the code for any form.

- Use constants as much as possible whenever your application requires global variables. Constants are much more reliable because their values are static. Constants are covered later in this chapter.

Public Variables and the `Option Private Module` Statement

Variables declared using the `Public` keyword are available to all procedures in all modules across all applications. To restrict a public module-level variable to the current database, include the `Option Private Module` statement in the Declarations section of the standard or class module in which the variable is declared.

Understanding the Lifetime of Variables

In addition to scope, variables have a *lifetime*. The *lifetime* of a variable determines how long a variable retains its value. Module-level and project-level variables preserve their values as long as the project is open. Visual Basic, however, can reinitialize these variables if required by the program's logic. Local variables declared with the `Dim` statement lose their values when a procedure has finished. Local variables have a lifetime while a procedure is running, and they are reinitialized every time the program is run. Visual Basic allows you to extend the lifetime of a local variable by changing the way it is declared.

Using Temporary Variables

In the previous section, you learned that you could declare a global variable with the `Public` keyword and use it throughout your entire application. Global variables can be quite problematic, especially when you or another programmer accidentally change the value of the variable, or your application encounters an error and the values of the variables you have initially set for your application to use are completely wiped out. To avoid such problems, many programmers resort to using a separate global variables form to hold their global variables. If they need certain values to be available the next time the application starts, they create a separate database table to store these values. A *global variables form* is simply a blank Access form where you can place both bound and unbound controls. Bound controls are used to pull the data from the table where global variables have been stored. You can use unbound controls on a form to store values of global variables that are not stored in a separate table. Simply set the `ControlSource` property of the unbound control by typing a value in it or use a VBA procedure to set the value of the `ControlSource`. The form set up as a global variables form must be open while the application is running for the values of the bound and unbound controls to be available to other forms, reports, and queries in the database. A global variables form can be hidden if the values of the global variables are pulled from a database table or set using VBA procedures or macro actions.

If your database is in the `.accdb` format, instead of using a database table or global variables, you can use the `TempVars` collection to store the `Variant` values you want to reuse. `TempVars` stands for *temporary variables*. Temporary variables are global. You can refer to them in VBA modules, event procedures, queries, expressions, add-ins, and any referenced databases. Access `.accdb` databases allow you to define up to 255 temporary variables at one time. These variables remain in memory until you close the database (unless you remove them when you are finished working with them). Unlike public variables, temporary variable values are not cleared when an error occurs.

Creating a Temporary Variable with a TempVars Collection Object

Let's look at some examples of using the `TempVars` collection first introduced in Access 2007. Assume your application requires three global variables named `gtvUserName`, `gtvUserFolder`, and `gtvEndDate`.

To try this out, in the currently opened `Chap01.accdb` database file, in the VBE window, activate the Immediate window and type the following statements. The variable is created as soon as you press Enter after each statement.

```
TempVars("gtvUserName").Value = "John Smith"
```

```
TempVars("gtvUserFolder").Value = Environ("HOMEPATH")

TempVars("gtvEndDate").Value = Format(now(),"mm/dd/yyyy")
```

Notice that to create a temporary variable, all you must do is specify its value. If the variable does not already exist, Access adds it to the `TempVars` collection. If the variable exists, Access modifies its value.

You can explicitly add a global variable to the `TempVars` collection by using the `Add` method, like this:

```
TempVars.Add "gtvCompleted", "true"
```

Retrieving Names and Values of TempVar Objects

Each `TempVar` object in the `TempVars` collection has `Name` and `Value` properties that you can use to access the variable and read its value from any procedure. By default, the items in the collection are numbered from zero (`0`), with the first item being `0`, the second item being `1`, the third `2`, and so on. Therefore, to find the value of the second variable in the `TempVars`, you have entered (`gtvUser-Folder`) in the previous section, type the following statement in the Immediate window:

```
?TempVars(1).Value
```

When you press Enter, you will see the location of the user's private folder on the computer. In this case, it is your private folder. The folder information was returned by passing the `HOMEPATH` parameter to the built-in `Environ` function. Functions and parameter passing are covered in Chapter 3.

You can also retrieve the value of the variable from the `TempVars` collection by using its name, like this:

```
?TempVars("gtvUserFolder").Value
```

You can iterate through the `TempVars` collection to see the names and values of all global variables that you have placed in it. To do this from the Immediate window, you need to use the colon operator (`:`) to separate lines of code. Type the following statement all on one line to try this out:

```
For Each gtv in TempVars : Debug.Print gtv.Name & ":"
& gtv.Value : Next
```

When you press Enter, the `Debug.Print` statement will write to the Immediate window a name and value for each variable that is currently stored in the `TempVars` collection.

The `For Each...Next` statement, a popular VBA programming construct, is covered in detail in Chapter 5. The `gtv` is an object variable used as an iterator. An *iterator* allows you to traverse through all the elements of a collection. You can use any variable name as an iterator provided it is not a VBA keyword. Object variables are discussed later in this chapter. For more information on working with collections, see Chapter 7.

Using Temporary Global Variables in Expressions

You can use temporary global variables anywhere expressions can be used. For example, you can set the value of the unbound text box control on a form to display the value of your global variable. To do this, simply activate the form property sheet and type the following in the `ControlSource` property of the text box:

```
=[TempVars]![gtvCompleted]
```

You can also use a temporary variable to pass selection criteria to queries:

```
SELECT * FROM Orders WHERE Order_Date = TempVars!gtvEndDate
```

> ### **What Are Expressions?**
>
> An expression is a programming code that may include fixed values, such as numbers or text strings, variables and constants that hold values, and operators that perform operations on the values within the expression. In the `CalcCost` procedure, we wrote an expression that returned the total cost of the purchased calculator. An expression evaluates down to a single value of a specific data type. Expressions are used extensively in VBA calculations, conditional statements, arguments passed to functions, and so on.

Removing a Temporary Variable from a TempVars Collection

When you are done using a temporary variable, you can remove it from the `TempVars` collection with the `Remove` method, like this:

```
TempVars.Remove "gtvUserFolder"
```

To check the number of the `TempVar` objects in the `TempVars` collection, use the `Count` property in the Immediate window:

```
?TempVars.Count
```

Finally, to quickly remove all global variables (`TempVar` objects) from the `TempVars` collection, simply use the `RemoveAll` method, like this:

```
TempVars.RemoveAll
```

> ### The `TempVars` Collection Can Be Used in Access Macros
>
> The following three macros allow macro users to set and remove `TempVar` objects:
>
> ❏ `SetTempVar`—Sets a `TempVar` to a given value. You must specify the name of the temporary variable and the expression that will be used to set the value of this variable. Expressions must be entered without an equal sign (=).
>
> ❏ `RemoveTempVar`—Removes the `TempVar` from the `TempVars` collection. You must specify the name of the temporary variable you want to remove.
>
> ❏ `RemoveAllTempVars`—Clears the `TempVars` collection.
>
> The values of `TempVar` objects can be used in the arguments and the condition columns of macros. This book dedicates a separate chapter to understanding and working with macros.

Using Static Variables

A variable declared with the `Static` keyword is a special type of local variable. *Static variables* are declared at the procedure level. Unlike the local variables declared with the `Dim` keyword, static variables remain in existence and retain their values when the procedure in which they were declared ends. This can be useful for certain operations, but it also means that the value will remain in memory until the application is closed.

The `CostOfPurchase` procedure in the next hands-on exercise demonstrates the use of the static variable `allPurchase`. The purpose of this variable is to keep track of the running total.

◉ Hands-On 1.8   Using Static Variables

1. In the `Chap01` database, in the Visual Basic window, choose Insert | Module to add a new module. Access will insert `Module2` into the `Modules` folder.
2. Enter the following `CostOfPurchase` procedure code in the new module's Code window.

```
Sub CostOfPurchase()
  ' declare variables
  Static allPurchase As Single
  Dim newPurchase As String
  Dim purchCost As Single

  newPurchase = InputBox("Enter the cost of a purchase:")
  purchCost = CSng(newPurchase)
  allPurchase = allPurchase + purchCost

  ' display results
```

```
    MsgBox "The cost of a new purchase is: " & newPurchase
    MsgBox "The running cost is: " & allPurchase
End Sub
```

This procedure begins with declaring a static variable named `allPurchase` and two local variables named `newPurchase` and `purchCost`. The `InputBox` function is used to get a user's input while the procedure is running. As soon as the user inputs the value and clicks OK, Visual Basic assigns the value to the `newPurchase` variable. Because the result of the `InputBox` function is always a string, the `newPurchase` variable was declared as the `String` data type. You cannot use strings in mathematical calculations, so the next instruction uses a *type conversion* function (`CSng`) to translate the text value into a numeric value, which is stored as a `Single` data type in the variable `purchCost`. The `CSng` function requires only one argument: the value you want to translate. Refer to Chapter 3 for more information about converting data types.

The next instruction, `allPurchase = allPurchase + purchCost`, adds the new value supplied by the `InputBox` function to the current purchase value. When you run this procedure for the first time, the value of the `allPurchase` variable is the same as the value of the `purchCost` variable. During the second run, the value of the static variable is increased by the new value entered in the dialog box. You can run the `CostOfPurchase` procedure as many times as you want. The `allPurch` variable will keep the running total for as long as the project is open.

3. To run the procedure, position the insertion point anywhere within the `CostOfPurchase` procedure and press F5.
4. When the dialog box appears, enter a number. For example, type `100` and press Enter. Visual Basic displays the message The cost of a new purchase is: 100.
5. Click OK in the message box. Visual Basic displays the second message The running cost is: 100.
6. Rerun the same procedure.
7. When the input box appears, enter another number. For example, type `50` and press Enter. Visual Basic displays the message The cost of a new purchase is: 50.
8. Click OK in the message box. Visual Basic displays the second message The running cost is: 150.
9. Run the procedure a couple of times to see how Visual Basic keeps track of the running total.

Note that the `CostOfPurchase` procedure may fail as it doesn't perform any validation on the user input. It assumes that the user will always enter a valid numeric value. In Chapter 4, you will learn how to validate user input to handle cases where non-numeric or invalid values are entered.

> ### Type Conversion Functions
> To learn more about the `CSng` function, position the insertion point anywhere within the word `CSng` and press F1.

Using Object Variables

The variables we've introduced so far are used to store data, which is the main reason for using "normal" variables in your procedures. There are also special variables that refer to the Visual Basic objects. These variables are called *object variables*. Object variables don't store data; they store the location of the data. You can use them to reference databases, forms, and controls, as well as objects created in other applications. Object variables are declared in a similar way to the variables you've already seen. The only difference is that after the `As` keyword, you enter the type of object your variable will point to—for instance:

```
Dim myControl As Control
```

This statement declares the object variable called `myControl` of type `Control`.

Another statement, shown below, declares the object variable called `frm` of type `Form`.

```
Dim frm As Form
```

You can use object variables to refer to objects of a generic type, such as `Application`, `Control`, `Form`, or `Report`, or you can point your object variable to specific object types, such as `TextBox`, `ToggleButton`, `CheckBox`, `CommandButton`, `ListBox`, `OptionButton`, `Subform` or `Subreport`, `Label`, `BoundObjectFrame` or `UnboundObjectFrame`, and so on.

When you declare an object variable, you also must assign it a specific value before you can use it in your procedure. You assign a value to the object variable by using the `Set` keyword followed by the equal sign and the value that the variable refers to—for example:

```
Set myControl = Me!CompanyName
```

The preceding statement assigns a value to the object variable called `myControl`. This object variable will now point to the `CompanyName` control on the active form. If you omit the `Set` keyword, Visual Basic will display the error message Runtime error 91: Object variable or With block variable not set.

Again, it's time to walk through a practical example. The `HideControl` procedure in the next hands-on exercise demonstrates the use of two object variables, named `frm` and `myControl`.

⊙ Hands-On 1.9   Working with Object Variables

1. Close the Access database `Chap01.accdb`. When prompted to save changes in the modules, click `OK`. Save the modules with the suggested default names, `Module1` and `Module2`, or enter new names as you prefer.
2. Copy the `HandsOn_01_9.accdb` database from the companion files to your `C:\VBAAccess2024_ByExample` folder.
   This database contains a table, `Customer`, and a simple `Customer` form imported from the `Northwind.mdb` sample database that shipped with an earlier version of Access.
3. Open Access and load the `C:\VBAAccess2024_ByExample\HandsOn_01_9.accdb` database file.
4. Open the `Customers` form in form view and switch to the VBE window.
5. Choose Insert | Module to add a new module.
6. Enter the following `HideControl` procedure code in the new module's Code window.

```
Sub HideControl()
    Dim frm As Form
    Dim myControl As Control
    Dim strFormName As String

    strFormName = "Customers"

    'Open the specified form
    DoCmd.OpenForm strFormName, acNormal

    ' set an object variable pointing to the form
    Set frm = Forms!Customers
    ' set an object variable pointing to the CompanyName control
    Set myControl = frm.CompanyName

    ' manipulate the visibility of the form control
    myControl.Visible = False
End Sub
```

7. To run the procedure, click any line between the `Sub` and `End Sub` keywords and press F5, or choose Run | Run Sub/UserForm.

Notice that the procedure begins with the declaration of two object variables called `frm` and `myControl`. The object variable `frm` is set to reference the `Customers` form. For the procedure to work, the referenced form must be open. We can open the form using this statement:

```
DoCmd.OpenForm strFormName, acNormal
```

Next, the `myControl` object variable is set to point to the `CompanyName` control located on the `Customers` form.

Instead of using the object's entire address, you can use the shortcut—the name of the object variable. For example, the statement

```
Set myControl = frm.CompanyName
```

is the short version of

```
Set myControl = Forms!Customers.CompanyName
```

The purpose of this procedure is to hide the control referenced by the object variable `myControl`.

8. After running the `HideControl` procedure, switch to the Access window containing the open `Customers` form. The `CompanyName` control should not be visible on the form. In your VBA code, change the visibility of the control to bring it back. You can do this by changing the `Visible` property of the `myControl` object variable to `True`.

9. Rerun the `HideControl` procedure. Note that the `CompanyName` control is now visible on the `Customers` form.

10. Return to the VBE window and modify the `HideControl` procedure so it automatically closes the open form. You can do this by adding the following statement just before the `End Sub` keywords:

```
DoCmd.Close acForm, strFormName, acSaveYes
```

Note that the `DoCmd.Close` statement is used to close the specified object. For more details on using this statement, see the section "Using ChatGPT with Access".

Advantages of Using Object Variables

The advantages of object variables are:

❏ They can be used instead of the actual object.

❏ They are shorter and easier to remember than the actual values they point to.

❏ You can change their meaning while your procedure is running.

Disposing of Object Variables

When an object variable is no longer needed, you should assign `Nothing` to it. This frees up memory and system resources:

```
Set frm = Nothing
Set myControl = Nothing
```

NOTE	*You may add the above statements at the end of the* `HideControl` *procedure to ensure that the object variables are properly disposed of.*

Finding a Variable Definition

When you find an instruction that assigns a value to a variable in a VBA procedure, you can quickly locate the definition of the variable by selecting the variable name and pressing Shift+F2. Alternatively, you can choose View | Definition. Visual Basic will jump to the variable declaration line. To return your mouse pointer to its previous position, press Ctrl+Shift+F2 or choose View | Last Position.

Determining the Data Type of a Variable

Visual Basic has a built-in `VarType` function that returns an integer indicating the variable's type. You can try out this function in the Immediate window, like this:.

1. In the Immediate window, type the following statements that assign values to variables:

```
age = 28
birthdate = #1/1/1981#
firstName = "John"
```

2. Now, for each variable, ask Visual Basic what type of data it holds:

```
?varType(age)
```

When you press Enter, Visual Basic returns 2. The number 2 represents the `Integer` data type, as shown in Table A.2 in Appendix A.

```
?varType(birthdate)
```

Now Visual Basic returns 7 for `Date`. If you make a mistake in the variable name (suppose you type `birthday` instead of `birthdate`), Visual Basic returns zero (0).

```
?varType(firstName)
```

Visual Basic tells you that the value stored in the `firstName` variable is a `String` (8).

USING CONSTANTS

The value of a variable can change while your VBA procedure is executing. If your procedure needs to refer to unchanged values repeatedly, you should use constants. A *constant* is like a named variable that always refers to the same value. Visual Basic requires that you declare constants before you use them.

You declare constants by using the `Const` statement, as in the following examples:

```
Const dialogName = "Enter Data" As String
Const slsTax = 8.5
Const Discount = 0.5
Const ColorIdx = 3
```

A constant, like a variable, has a scope. To make a constant available within a single procedure, you declare it at the procedure level, just below the name of the procedure—for instance:

```
Sub WedAnniv()
  Const Age As Integer = 25
  ...instructions...
End Sub
```

If you want to use a constant in all the procedures of a module, use the `Private` keyword in front of the `Const` statement—for instance:

```
Private Const dsk = "D: " As String
```

The `Private` constant must be declared at the top of the module, just before the first `Sub` statement.

To make a constant available to all modules in your application, use the `Public` keyword in front of the `Const` statement—for instance:

```
Public Const NumOfChar As Integer = 255
```

The `Public` constant must be declared at the top of the module, just before the first `Sub` statement.

When declaring a constant, you can use any one of the following data types: `Boolean`, `Byte`, `Integer`, `Long`, `Currency`, `Single`, `Double`, `Date`, `String`, or `Variant`.

Like variables, constants can be declared on one line if separated by commas—for instance:

```
Const Age As Integer = 25, PayCheck As Currency = 350
```

Using constants makes your VBA procedures more readable and easier to maintain. For example, if you need to refer to a certain value several times in your procedure, use a constant instead of using a value. This way, if the value changes (e.g., the sales tax rate goes up), you can simply change the value in the declaration of the `Const` statement instead of tracking down every occurrence of the value.

What Are Intrinsic Constants?

Both Access and VBA have a long list of predefined (*intrinsic*) constants that do not need to be declared. These built-in constants can be looked up using the Object Browser window, which is discussed in Chapter 2.

USING ChatGPT WITH ACCESS

Since the introduction of ChatGPT (the Artificial Intelligence (AI) language model), we now have access to an incredibly powerful and user-friendly assistant that is integrated with various platforms and tools. There are many ways you can use Access and ChatGPT together. You can leverage ChatGPT's capabilities in Microsoft Access to enhance your database management and data analysis tasks, write and automate queries, design and generate forms and reports, as well as learn a great deal about basic and advanced VBA programming.

In this chapter, we will focus on ChatGPT's learning and training capabilities. We will ask it for help with different topics we have covered here. As ChatGPT's platform interfaces are constantly changing, your current ChatGPT tool and experience may be different from what I will be demonstrating here. I will, however, provide you with the most up-to-date information and guidance available. This way, you can adapt my instructions to your specific version and still achieve the desired results. I will be chatting with Microsoft Copilot, an AI-powered productivity tool embedded within the Microsoft 365 ecosystem. Copilot offers a simple chat-based interface, making it easy to interact with and get the needed help quickly.

To launch Copilot in Windows 11, click the Copilot icon on the taskbar or use the shortcut key Windows+C. You can also use the Copilot icon in the Microsoft Edge browser.

In this chapter, you spent a lot of time learning about variables. Let's ask ChatGPT the following question:

User Prompt: *In Access VBA, what are the common mistakes when using variables?*

Figure 1.20 displays the posed question and the generated response. This summarizes quite nicely what you've learned about variables and adds additional information to this topic. You can continue chatting by asking for detailed examples and learn even more.

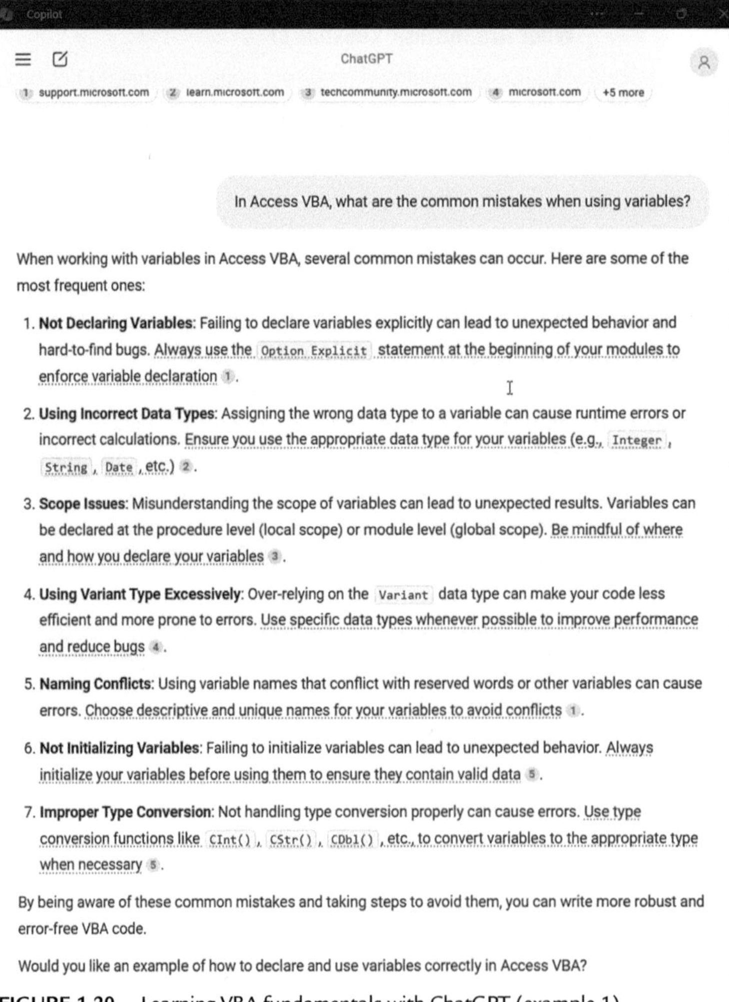

FIGURE 1.20.   Learning VBA fundamentals with ChatGPT (example 1).

In Hands-On 1.9, we wrote a procedure that hides a control on a form. Let's ask a coding question to better understand the statement that was used to close the form.

User Prompt: *Explain the following statement in Access VBA: DoCmd.Close acForm, strFormName, acSaveYes*

Figure 1.21 shows how ChatGPT breaks down the statement in easy-to-understand steps.

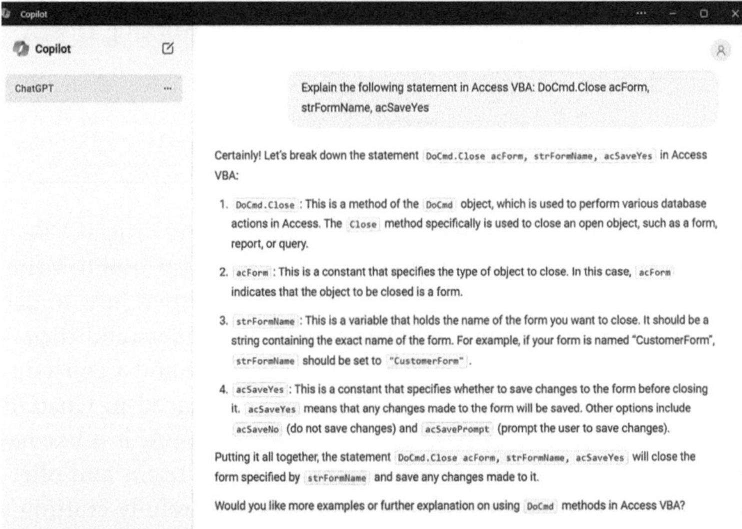

FIGURE 1.21.   Dissecting VBA code with ChatGPT (example 2).

As you can see, working with ChatGPT can quickly enhance your knowledge of VBA. Moreover, ChatGPT can speed up your work by writing the VBA code you need.

For instance, let's ask ChatGPT to write VBA code that closes an Access form. Here's the code and the explanations that you may get in response:

ChatGPT-Generated Code and Code Explanation

```
Private Sub CloseFormButton_Click()
    ' Replace "YourFormName" with the actual name of your form
    DoCmd.Close acForm, "YourFormName", acSaveYes
End Sub
```

In this example:

- Private Sub CloseFormButton_Click(): This defines a subroutine that runs when a button (named CloseFormButton) is clicked.
- DoCmd.Close acForm, "YourFormName", acSaveYes: This line closes the form named "YourFormName" and saves any changes made to it.

Make sure to replace "YourFormName" with the actual name of the form you want to close.

Each chapter of this book will have a section devoted to showing you how you can gain more knowledge on the topics covered by working closely with ChatGPT, the AI-powered tool.

SUMMARY

This chapter has introduced you to several fundamental and crucial VBA programming topics and definitions and showed you, step by step, how to write and execute your first VBA procedures and functions. You learned how to declare various types of variables, define their data types, and understand their various scopes. You also saw the difference between a variable and a constant and learned about VBA expressions. Finally, you were introduced to ChatGPT, a powerful AI tool that you can harness in learning Access VBA. It is like having a teacher who is always ready to explain a topic in simple terms and offer you suggestions. You can guide your teacher's responses by carefully crafting your prompts. A better prompt will lead to a clearer, more insightful response, and therefore will enhance the overall effectiveness and accuracy of your interaction with ChatGPT, making it easier to achieve your desired outcome.

This chapter has given you a glimpse of the Microsoft Visual Basic programming environment built into Access. The next chapter will take you deeper into this interface, showing you various windows and shortcuts that you can use to program faster and with fewer errors.

Chapter 2

GETTING TO KNOW VISUAL BASIC EDITOR (VBE)

Now that you know how to write procedures and functions in standard modules, we'll delve deeper into the VBE window to explore its various components, such as the Code, Project Explorer, and Properties windows. We'll also learn how to access various features from toolbars, customize the editor settings, and utilize the Immediate window for debugging and testing our VBA code.

You can enter the VBA programming environment in either of the following ways:

- In the main Access window, select the Database Tools tab, and click the Visual Basic button in the Ribbon's Macro group.
- Using the keyboard, press Alt+F11.

UNDERSTANDING THE PROJECT EXPLORER WINDOW

The Project Explorer window, located in the left pane of the VBE window, provides several types of folders that help organize your database objects and code (see Figure 2.1):

- The `Microsoft Access Class Objects` folder contains all the forms and all the reports in your database.

- The `Modules` folder holds all the standard modules with VBA code that isn't tied to a specific form or report.

- The `Class Modules` folder contains special types of modules that are used for defining custom objects, including their properties and methods.

Modules and procedures are fundamental components of VBA. Modules are containers that hold your VBA code. They can contain multiple procedures, functions, and declarations. Procedures are blocks of code within a module that perform a specific task.

Notice that Figure 2.1 shows various code modules that exist in the Northwind Starter database. This database was built by the Access team at Microsoft to showcase major Access features. Northwind is a fictitious trading company whose customers are independent grocery stores.

FIGURE 2.1. The Project Explorer window provides easy access to your VBA procedure code.

You can activate the Project Explorer window in one of three ways:

- From the View menu by selecting Project Explorer
- Using the keyboard by pressing Ctrl+R
- From the standard toolbar by clicking the Project Explorer button ( ),
  as shown in Figure 2.2.

NOTE	*If the Project Explorer window is visible but not active, activate it by clicking the Project Explorer title bar.*

The buttons on the standard toolbar (Figure 2.2) provide a quick way to access many Visual Basic features.

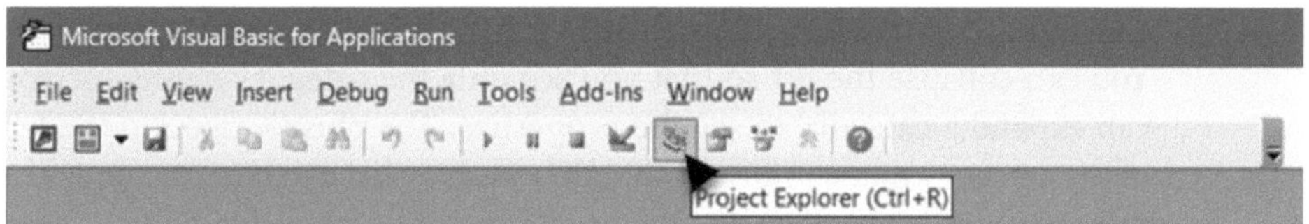

FIGURE 2.2.   Use the toolbar buttons to quickly access frequently used features in the VBE window.

The Project Explorer window (see Figure 2.3) contains three buttons:

- View Code—Displays the Code window for the selected module.
- View Object—Displays the selected form or report in the `Microsoft Access Class Objects` folder. This button is disabled when an object in the `Modules` or `Class Modules` folder is selected.
- Toggle Folders—Hides and unhides the display of folders in the Project Explorer window.

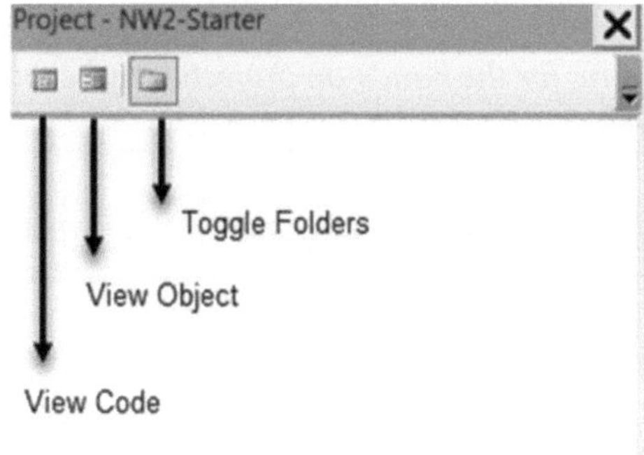

FIGURE 2.3.   The VBE Project Explorer window contains three buttons that allow you to view code or objects and toggle folders.

UNDERSTANDING THE PROPERTIES WINDOW

Properties are attributes that define the characteristics of an object, such as its name, size, color, and border. The Properties window is used to review and set properties for the currently selected Access class or module. For instance, if `modDAO` is selected under the `Modules` folder, the `modDAO` module will be shown just below the Properties window's title bar. Object properties can be viewed alphabetically or by category by clicking on the appropriate tab.

- Alphabetic Tab—Lists all properties for the selected object alphabetically. You can change the property setting by selecting the property name and then typing or selecting the new setting.

- Categorized Tab—Lists all properties for the selected object by category. You can collapse the list so that you see only the category names, or you can expand a category to see the properties. The plus (+) icon to the left of the category name indicates that the category list can be expanded. The minus (–) indicates that the category is currently expanded.

The Properties window can be accessed in the following ways:

- From the View menu by selecting Properties Window
- Using the keyboard by pressing F4
- From the standard toolbar by clicking the Properties Window button (▣) located to the right of the Project Explorer button on the toolbar shown in Figure 2.2.

Figure 2.4 displays the properties of the `txtStatusName` text box control located in the `Form_frmOrderDetails` form. To access properties for a specific form control, you need to perform the steps outlined in Hands-On 2.1.

NOTE	*All code files and figures for the hands-on projects may be found in the companion files.*

Hands-On 2.1   Using the Properties Window to View Control Properties

1. Copy the `NorthwindStarter` sample database from the companion files to your `C:\VBAAccess2024_ByExample` folder, then double-click the database to open it in Access.
2. Log in to the database as Andrew Cencini.
3. Activate the VBE window (choose Database Tools | Visual Basic).

4. In the Project Explorer window, click the Toggle Folders button ( ), double-click the name of the database (NW2-Starter (NorthwindStarter)), and open the `Microsoft Access Class Objects` folder. Click the `Form_frmOrderDetails` (Figure 2.4) and then click the View Object button ( ) located to the left of the Toggle Folders button. This will open the selected form in design view. Note that you must view the form in design view to access its properties in the VBA window.

5. Press Alt+F11 to return to VBE. The Properties window will be filled with the properties for the `Form_frmOrderDetails` form. To view the properties of the `txtStatusName` text box control on the form, select `txtStatusName` from the drop-down list located below the Properties window's title bar.

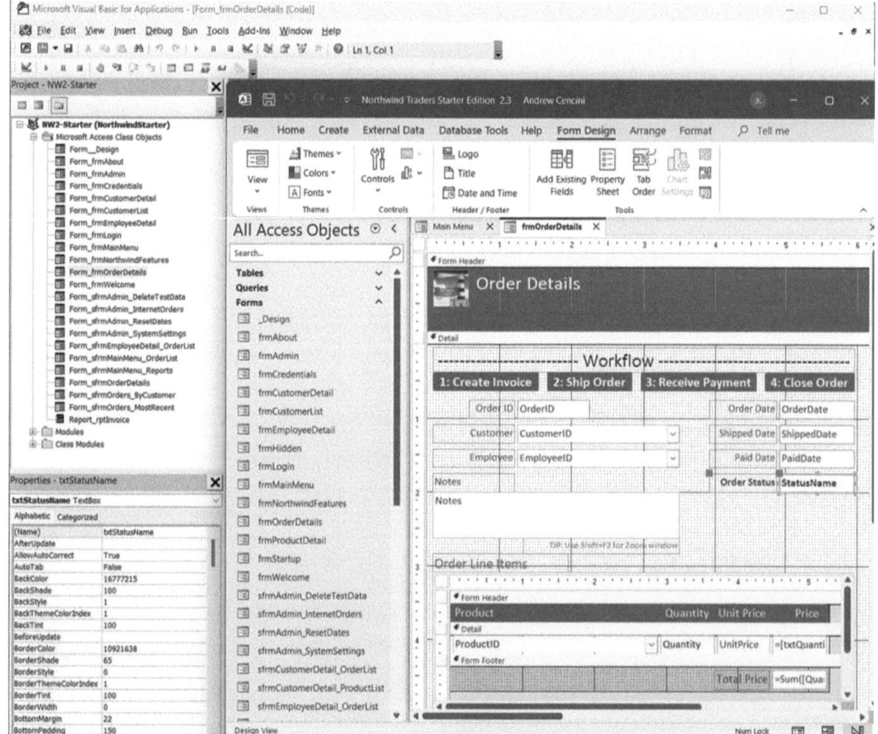

FIGURE 2.4. You can edit object properties in the Properties window, or you can edit them in the property sheet when a form or report is open in design view.

When you select a control from the Properties window's drop-down list, this control is automatically selected in the design view of the form. You can see this by positioning the Main Access window and the VBE window side by side or on different monitors.

UNDERSTANDING THE CODE WINDOW

The Code window is used for composing new VBA procedures, as well as for viewing and modifying existing procedures. Each VBA module can be opened in a separate Code window.

There are several ways to activate the Code window:

- From the Project Explorer window, choose the appropriate module and then click the View Code button (▣).
- From the Microsoft Visual Basic menu bar, choose View | Code.
- Using the keyboard, press F7.

At the top of the Code window, there are two drop-down list boxes that allow you to move quickly within the Visual Basic code. In the Object box on the left side of the Code window, you can select the object whose code you want to view, as shown in Figure 2.5. The Split Bar that is highlighted in this figure allows you to divide the Code window into two panes, as explained later and shown in Figure 2.7.

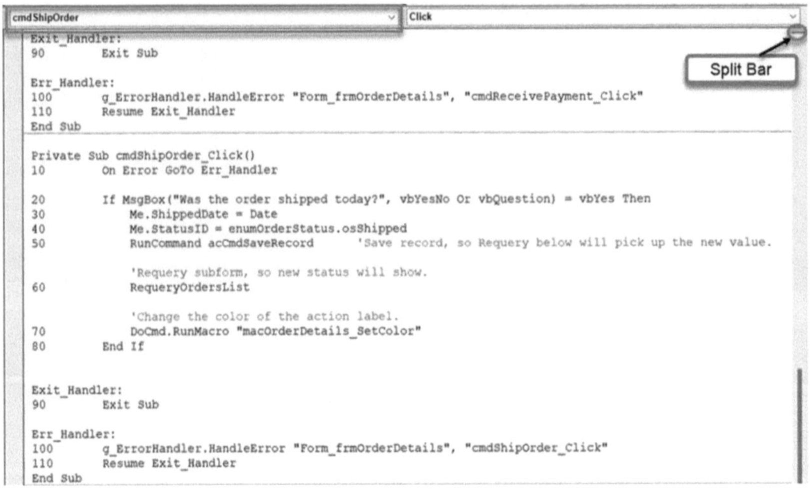

FIGURE 2.5.   The Object drop-down box lists objects that are available in the module selected in the Project Explorer window. The code shown here is for the Form_frmOrderDetails form.

The box on the right side of the Code window, above the split bar, is known as a Procedure box and allows you to select a procedure to view. When you click its down arrow, the names of all procedures located in a module will be listed alphabetically, as shown in Figure 2.6. When you make your selection, the cursor will jump to the first line of the selected procedure.

```
cmdShipOrder                                              ∨   Click                          ∨
        Exit_Handler:                                         Click
        90          Exit Sub                                  DblClick
                                                              Enter
        Err_Handler:                                          Exit
        100         g_ErrorHandler.HandleError "Form_frmOrderDe GotFocus
                                                              KeyDown
        110         Resume Exit_Handler                       KeyPress
        End Sub                                               KeyUp
                                                              LostFocus
        Private Sub cmdShipOrder_Click()                      MouseDown
        10          On Error GoTo Err_Handler                 MouseMove
                                                              MouseUp
        20          If MsgBox("Was the order shipped today?", vbYesNo Or vbQuestion) = vbYes Then
        30              Me.ShippedDate = Date
        40              Me.StatusID = enumOrderStatus.osShipped
        50              RunCommand acCmdSaveRecord      'Save record, so Requery below will pick up the new value.

                        'Requery subform, so new status will show.
        60              RequeryOrdersList

                        'Change the color of the action label.
        70              DoCmd.RunMacro "macOrderDetails_SetColor"
        80          End If


        Exit_Handler:
        90          Exit Sub

        Err_Handler:
        100         g_ErrorHandler.HandleError "Form_frmOrderDetails", "cmdShipOrder_Click"
        110         Resume Exit_Handler
        End Sub
```

FIGURE 2.6.   The Procedure drop-down box lists events to which the object selected in the Object drop-down box can respond. If the selected module contains events written for the highlighted object, the names of these events appear in bold type.

FIGURE 2.7.   By splitting the Code window, you can view different sections of a long procedure or a different procedure in each windowpane.

By choosing Window | Split or dragging the split bar (located at the top of the vertical scroll bar—see Figure 2.5) to a selected position in the Code window, you can divide the Code window into two panes, as shown in Figure 2.7.

Setting up the Code window for the two-pane display is useful for copying, cutting, and pasting sections of code between procedures in the same module. To return to a one-window display, drag the split bar all the way to the top of the Code window or choose Window | Split.

There are two icons at the bottom of the Code window (see Figure 2.7). The first one from the left is called Procedure View. When clicked, the Code window will show only one procedure. To select another procedure, you must use the Procedure drop-down box. The second icon activates full module view so you can see all the procedures in the selected module. Use the vertical scroll bar in the Code window to scroll through the module's code up and down. The gray bar to the left of the code window is the margin bar. It is used by VBE to display helpful indicators during editing and debugging.

OTHER WINDOWS IN VBE

In addition to the Code window, there are several other windows that are frequently used. They are the Immediate, Locals, Watch, Project Explorer, Properties, and Object Browser windows. The Docking tab in the Options dialog box, shown in Figure 2.8, displays a list of available windows and allows you to choose which windows you want to be dockable. To access this dialog box, select Tools | Options in the VBE window.

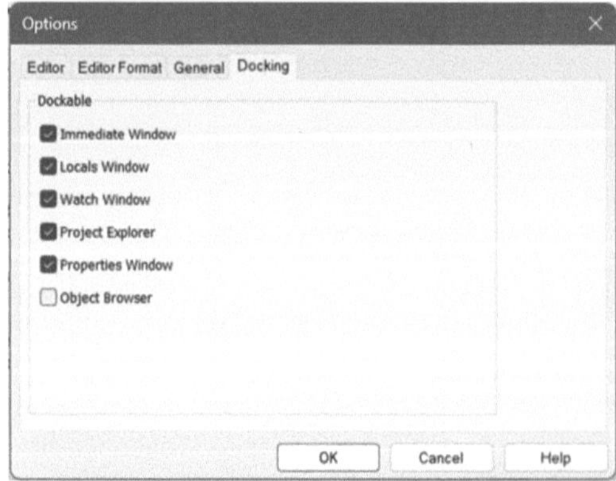

FIGURE 2.8.   You can use the Docking tab in the Options dialog box to control which windows are currently displayed in the Visual Basic programming environment.

ASSIGNING A NAME TO THE VBA PROJECT

A VBA project is a set of Microsoft Access objects, modules, forms, and references.

When you create a Microsoft Access database and later switch to the VBE window, you will see in the Project Explorer window that Access has automatically assigned the database name to the VBA project. For example, if your database is named `Chap01.accdb`, the Project Properties window displays `Chap01` `(Chap01)` where the first `Chap01` denotes the VBA project name and the `Chap01` in the parentheses is the name of the database. You can change the name of the VBA project in one of the following ways:

- Choose Tools | <database name> Properties, enter a new name in the Project Name box of the Project Properties window (see Figure 2.9), and click OK.

- In the Project Explorer window, right-click the name of the project and select <database name> Properties. Enter a new name in the Project Name box of the Project Properties window (see Figure 2.9) and click OK.

To avoid naming conflicts between projects, make sure that you give your projects unique names.

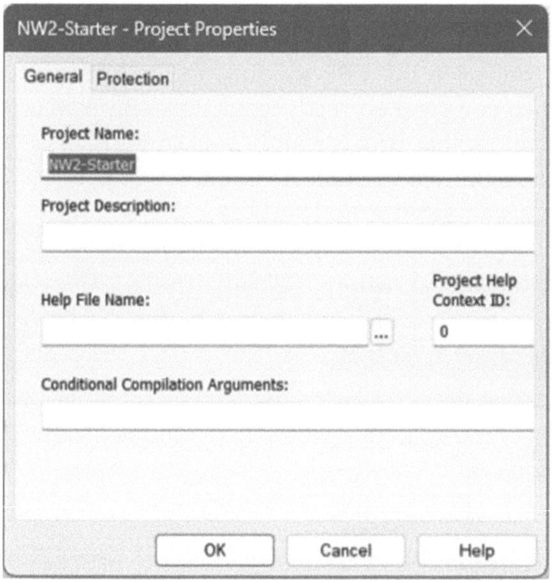

FIGURE 2.9.   You can use the Project Properties dialog box to rename the VBA project.

RENAMING A MODULE

As you've seen in Chapter 1, when you insert a new module into your VBA project, Access generates a default name for the module—`Module1`, `Module2`, and so on. You can rename your modules right after you insert them into the VBA project or when your project is being saved for the first time. In the latter case, Access will iterate through all the newly added (not saved) modules and prompt you with the Save As dialog box to accept or change the module name. You can change the module name at any time via the Properties window. Simply select the module name (e.g., Module1) in the Project Explorer window and click the Name property in the Properties window. Type the new name for the module and press Enter. The module name in the Project Explorer window should now reflect your change.

SYNTAX AND PROGRAMMING ASSISTANCE

Writing procedures in Visual Basic requires that you use hundreds of built-in instructions and functions. Because most people cannot memorize the correct syntax of all the instructions available in VBA, the IntelliSense® technology provides you with syntax and programming assistance on demand while you are entering your instructions. While working in the Code window, you can have special tools pop up and guide you through the process of creating correct VBA code. For instance, the Edit toolbar in the VBE window, shown in Figure 2.10, contains several buttons that let you enter correctly formatted VBA instructions with speed and ease. If the Edit toolbar isn't currently docked in the VBE window, you can turn it on by choosing View | Toolbars | Edit.

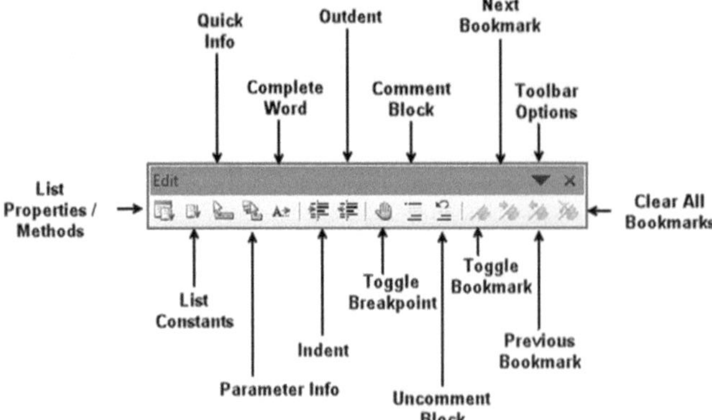

FIGURE 2.10.   The Edit toolbar provides timesaving buttons while entering VBA code.

List Properties/Methods

Each Access object can contain one or more properties and methods. As mentioned earlier, properties are attributes that define the characteristics of an object. Methods, on the other hand, are actions that can be performed on or by an object. For example, opening a form, closing a report, or running a query will require a method. The list of properties and methods will appear in a popup when you use the dot notation (for example, `DoCmd.`) in the VBA Editor (see Figure 2.11). This popup helps you quickly find and select the appropriate property or method for your object.

Dot Notation in VBA

In VBA, we use the concept of dot notation to refer to an object's properties and methods. For instance, the following procedure demonstrates how to set various properties of a form and its controls using dot notation.

```vba
Sub FormSetup()
    ' Set the caption of the form
    Forms!Form1.Caption = "Company Details"

    ' Make the form visible
    Forms!Form1.Visible = True

    ' Set the value of a text box control
    Forms!Form1!txtName.Value = "Big Enterprises Incorporated"

    ' Change the background color of a label
    Forms!Form1!lblTitle.BackColor = RGB(255, 255, 0)
End Sub
```

You can also use dot notation to call the methods of an object:

```vba
Sub RefreshForm()
    ' Requery the form to refresh its data
    Forms!Form1.Requery

    ' Set focus to a specific control
    Forms!Form1!txtName.SetFocus

    ' Repaint the form to update its display
    Forms!Form1.Repaint
End Sub
```

In the preceding examples, you will also notice the bang (!) operator, which is used to reference controls on forms and reports, or fields in recordsets. Recordsets are covered later in this book.

To ensure the popup is turned on, choose Tools | Options. In the Options dialog box, click the Editor tab, and check that the Auto List Members checkbox is selected.

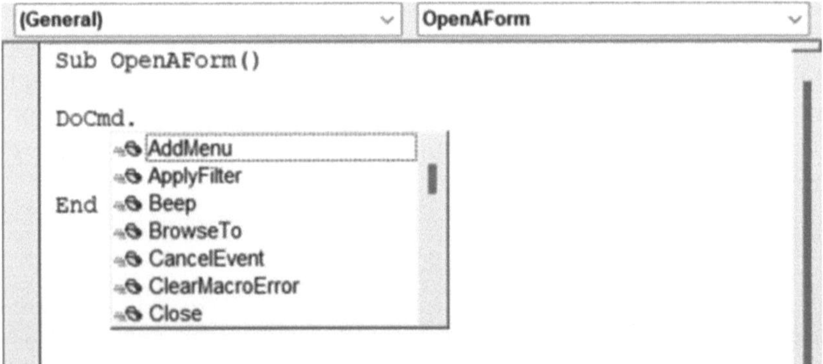

FIGURE 2.11.   When Auto List Members is selected, Visual Basic suggests properties and methods that can be used with the object as you are entering the VBA instructions.

To choose an item from the pop-up menu, start typing the name of the property or method you want to use. When the correct item name is highlighted, press Enter to insert the item into your code and start a new line, or press the Tab key to insert the item and continue writing instructions on the same line. You can also double-click the item to insert it into your code. To close the pop-up menu without inserting an item, press Esc. When you press Esc to remove the pop-up menu, Visual Basic will not display the menu for the same object again.

To display the Properties/Methods pop-up menu again, you can:

- Press Ctrl+J.
- Use the Backspace key to delete the period, and then type the period again.
- Right-click in the Code window and select List Properties/Methods from the shortcut menu.
- Choose Edit | List Properties/Methods.
- Click the List Properties/Methods button (⊡) on the Edit toolbar.

Parameter Info

Some VBA functions and methods can take one or more arguments (or parameters). If a VBA function or method requires an argument, you can see the names of required and optional arguments in a tip box that appears just below the cursor as soon as you type the open parenthesis or enter a space. The Parameter Info feature (see Figure 2.12) makes it easy for you to supply correct arguments to a VBA function or method. In addition, it reminds you of two other things that are very important for the function or method to work correctly: the order of the arguments and the required data type of each argument. For example, if you enter in the Code window the instruction `DoCmd.OpenForm` and type a space after the `OpenForm` method, a tip box appears just below the cursor. As soon as you supply the first argument and enter the comma, Visual Basic displays the next argument in bold. Optional arguments are surrounded by square brackets `[ ]`. To close the Parameter Info window, all you need to do is press the Esc key.

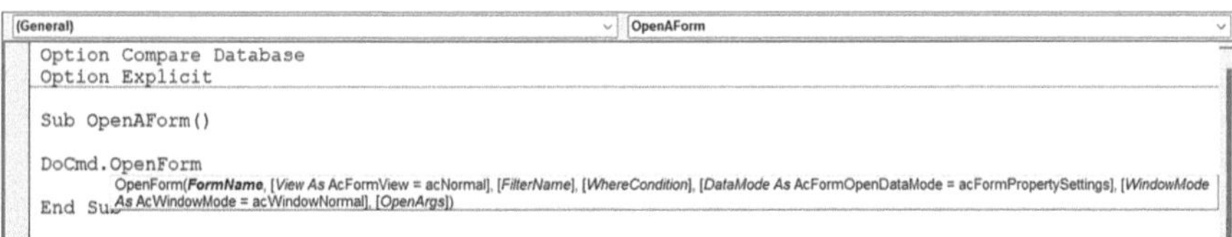

FIGURE 2.12.   A tip window displays a list of arguments used by a VBA function or method.

To open the tip box using the keyboard, enter the instruction or function, followed by the open parenthesis, and then press Ctrl+Shift+I. You can also click the Parameter Info button (🔳) on the Edit toolbar or choose Edit | Parameter Info from the menu bar.

You can display the Parameter Info box when entering a VBA function. To try this out quickly, choose View | Immediate Window, and then type the following in the Immediate window:

```
Mkdir(
```

You should see the MkDir(Path As String) tip box just below the cursor. Now, type `"C:\NewFolder"` followed by the ending parenthesis. When you press Enter, Visual Basic will create a folder named `NewFolder` in the root directory of your computer. Activate File Explorer and check it out!

List Constants

If there is a checkmark next to the Auto List Members setting in the Options dialog box (the Editor tab), Visual Basic displays a pop-up menu listing the constants that are valid for the property or method. A *constant* is a value that indicates a specific state or result. Access and other members of Microsoft 365 have numerous predefined, built-in constants.

Suppose you want to open a form in design view. In Access, a form can be viewed in design view (`acDesign`), datasheet view (`acFormDS`), PivotChart view (`acFormPivotChart`), PivotTable view (`acFormPivotTable`), form view (`acNormal`), and print preview (`acPreview`). Each of these options is represented by a built-in constant. Microsoft Access constant names begin with the letters `ac`. As soon as you enter a comma and a space following your instruction in the Code window (e.g., `DoCmd.OpenForm "Products"`), a pop-up menu will appear with the names of valid constants for the `OpenForm` method, as shown in Figure 2.13.

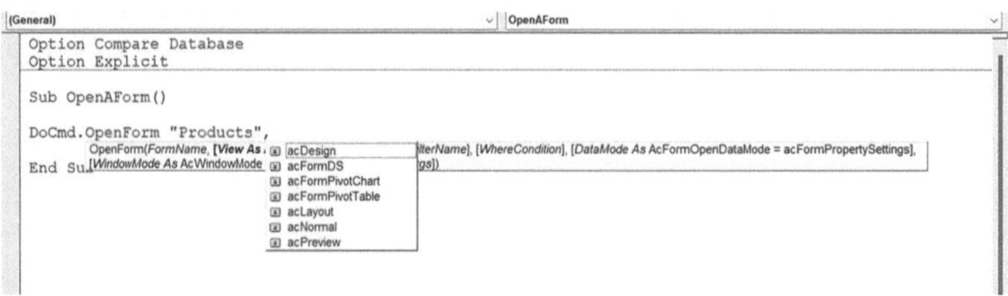

FIGURE 2.13. The List Constants pop-up menu displays a list of constants that are valid for the property or method typed.

The List Constants menu can be activated by pressing Ctrl+Shift+J or by clicking the List Constants button (⬇) on the Edit toolbar.

Quick Info

When you select an instruction, function, method, procedure name, or constant in the Code window and click the Quick Info button (🔍) on the Edit toolbar (or press Ctrl+I), Visual Basic displays the syntax of the highlighted item as well as the value of its constant (see Figure 2.14). The Quick Info feature can be turned on or off using the Options dialog box (Tools | Options). To use the feature, click the Editor tab in the Options dialog box, and make sure there is a checkmark in the box next to Auto Quick Info.

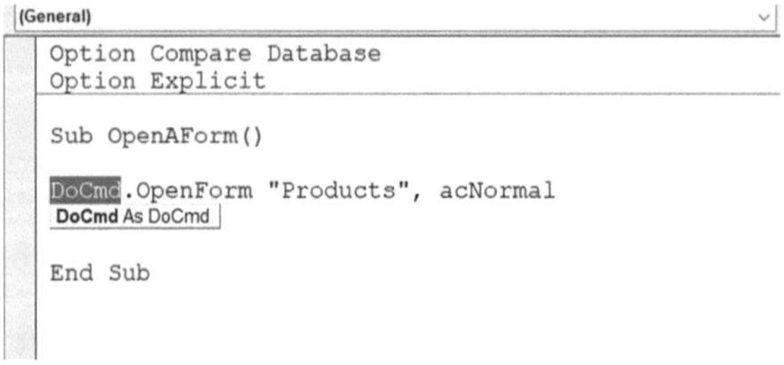

FIGURE 2.14. The Quick Info feature provides a list of function parameters, as well as constant values and VBA statement syntax.

Complete Word

Another way to increase the speed of writing VBA procedures in the Code window is with the Complete Word feature. As you enter the first few letters of a keyword and click the Complete Word button (A≥) on the Edit toolbar, Visual Basic will complete the keyword entry for you. For example, if you enter the first three letters of the keyword `DoCmd` (that is, `DoC`) in the Code window, and then click the Complete Word button on the Edit toolbar, Visual Basic will complete the rest of the command. In the place of `DoC`, you will see the entire instruction, `DoCmd`.

If there are several VBA keywords that begin with the same letters, when you click the Complete Word button on the Edit toolbar, Visual Basic will display a pop-up menu listing all of them. To try this, enter only the first three letters of the word `Application` (that is, `App`), and then press the Complete Word button on the toolbar. You can then select the appropriate word from the pop-up menu.

Indent/Outdent

The Editor tab in the Options dialog box, shown in Figure 2.15, contains many settings you can enable to make automated features available in the Code window. When the Auto Indent option is turned on, Visual Basic automatically indents the selected lines of code using the Tab Width value.

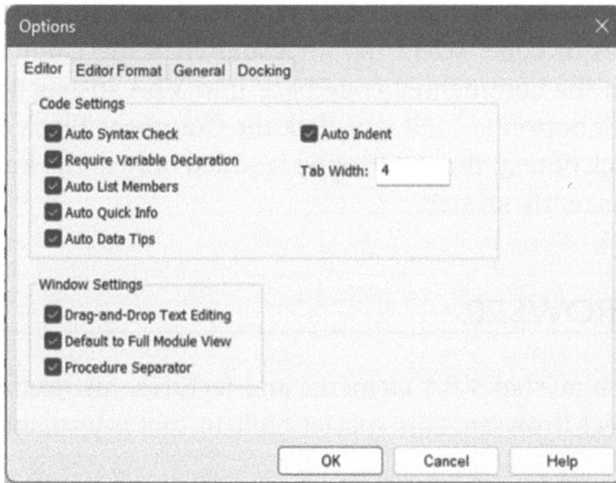

FIGURE 2.15.   The Options dialog box lists several features you can turn on and off to fit the VBA programming environment to your needs.

The default entry for Auto Indent is four characters. You can change the tab width by typing a new value in the text box. Indentation makes your VBA procedures more readable and easier to understand. Indenting is especially recommended for entering lines of code that make decisions or repeat actions. To indent a line of code in any VBA procedure, click the Indent button (⊞) on the Edit toolbar or press Tab on the keyboard. The selected block of code will move four spaces to the right. Click the Outdent button (⊞) on the Edit toolbar or press Shift+Tab to return the selected lines of code to the previous location in the Code window. You can indent or outdent blocks of code consisting of several lines of programming code by highlighting them prior to clicking Indent or Outdent.

Comment Block/Uncomment Block

The apostrophe placed at the beginning of a line of code denotes a comment. Besides the fact that comments make it easier to understand what the procedure does, comments are also very useful in testing and troubleshooting VBA procedures. For example, when you execute a procedure, it may not run as expected. Instead of deleting the lines of code that may be responsible for the problems encountered, you may want to skip the lines for now and return to them later. By placing an apostrophe at the beginning of the line you want to avoid, you can continue checking the other parts of your procedure. While commenting one line of code by typing an apostrophe works fine for most people, when it comes to turning entire blocks of code into comments, you'll find the Comment Block and Uncomment Block buttons on the Edit toolbar very handy and easy to use.

To comment a few lines of code, select the lines and click the Comment Block button (⊟). To turn the commented code back into VBA instructions, click the Uncomment Block button (⊟). If you click the Comment Block button without selecting a block of text, the apostrophe is added only to the line of code where the cursor is currently located.

USING THE OBJECT BROWSER

To move easily through the myriad VBA elements and features, just examine the capabilities of the Object Browser. This special built-in tool is available in the VBE window.

To access the Object Browser, use any of the following methods:

- Press F2.
- Choose View | Object Browser.
- Click the Object Browser button (⊞) on the toolbar.

The object Browser allows you to browse through the objects available to your VBA procedures, as well as view their properties, methods, and events. With the aid of the Object Browser, you can quickly move between procedures in your database application and search for objects and methods across various type libraries.

The Object Browser window, shown in Figure 2.16, is divided into several sections. The top of the window displays the Project/Library drop-down list box with the names of all currently available libraries and projects.

A *library* is a special file that contains information about the objects in an application. New libraries can be added via the References dialog box (select Tools | References). The entry for <All Libraries> lists the objects of all libraries installed on your computer. While the Access library contains objects specific to using Microsoft Access, the VBA library provides access to three objects (Debug, Err, and Collection), as well as several built-in functions and constants that give you flexibility in programming. You can send output to the Immediate window, get information about runtime errors, work with the Collection object, manage files, deal with text strings, convert data types, set the date and time, and perform mathematical operations.

Below the Project/Library drop-down list box is a search box (Search Text) that allows you to quickly find information in a library. This field remembers the last four items you searched for. To find only whole words, right-click anywhere in the Object Browser window, and then choose Find Whole Word Only from the shortcut menu. The Search Results section of the Object Browser displays the Library, Class, and Member elements that meet the criteria entered in the Search Text box. When you type the search text and click the Search button, Visual Basic expands the Object Browser window to show the search results. You can hide or show the Search Results section by clicking the button located to the right of the binoculars. In the lower section of the Object Browser window, the Classes list box displays the available object classes in the selected library. If you select the name of the open database (e.g., `Northwind`) in the Project/Library list box, the Classes list will display the objects as listed in the Explorer window.

In Figure 2.16, the `Form_frmCustomerList` object class is selected. When you highlight a class, the list on the right side (Members) shows the properties, methods, and events available for that class. By default, members are listed alphabetically. You can, however, organize the Members list by group type (properties, methods, or events) using the Group Members command from the Object Browser shortcut menu (right-click anywhere in the Object Browser window to display this menu).

The bottom of the Object Browser window displays a code template area with the definition of the selected member. Clicking the green hyperlink text in the code template lets you jump to the selected member's class or library in the Object Browser window. Text displayed in the code template area can be copied and pasted to a Code window. If the Code window is visible while the Object Browser window is open, you can save time by dragging the highlighted code template and dropping it into the Code window.

You can easily adjust the size of the various sections of the Object Browser window by dragging the dividing horizontal and vertical lines.

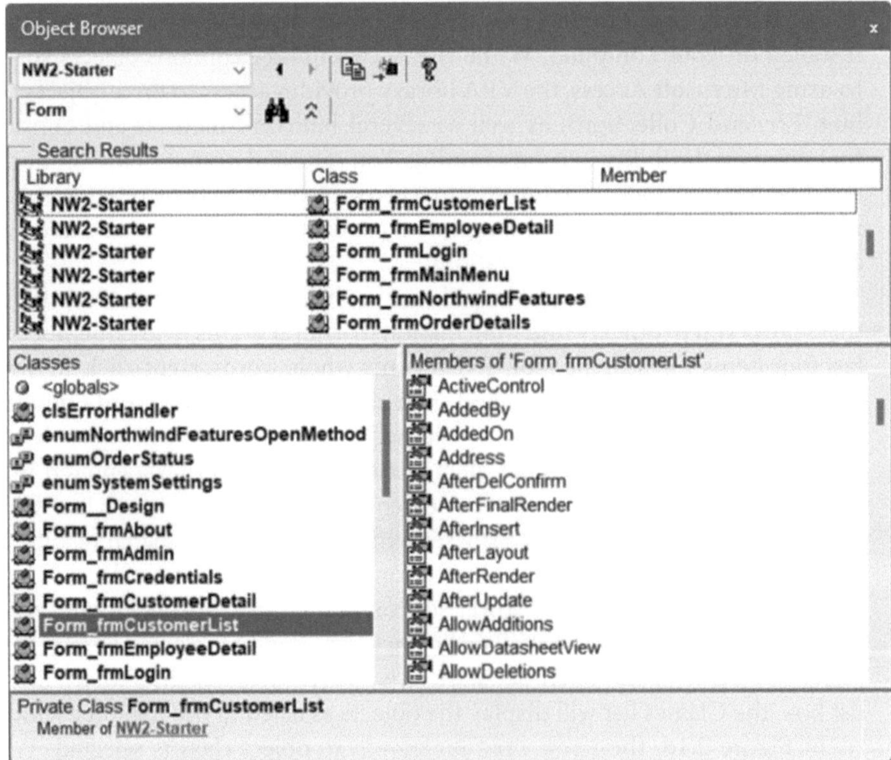

FIGURE 2.16. The Object Browser window allows you to browse through all the objects, properties, and methods available to the current VBA project.

Let's put the Object Browser to use in VBA programming. Assume that you want to write a VBA procedure to control a checkbox placed on a form and would like to see the list of properties and methods that are available for working with checkboxes.

⊙ Hands-On 2.2   Using the Object Browser

1. In the VBE window, press F2 to display the Object Browser.
2. In the Project/Library list box (see Figure 2.16), click the drop-down arrow and select the Access library.
3. Type `checkbox` in the Search Text box and click the Search button (🔍). Make sure you don't enter a space in the search string.
   Visual Basic begins to search the Access library and displays the search results. By analyzing the search results in the Object Browser window, you can find the appropriate VBA instructions for writing your VBA procedures. For example, looking at the Members list lets you determine that you can enable or disable a checkbox by setting the Enabled property. To get detailed information on any item found in the Object Browser, select the item and press F1 to activate the online help.

USING THE VBA OBJECT LIBRARY

While programming in Microsoft Access, you will need to rely on some functions that are general in nature. Functions that are available in the VBA object library will allow you to manage files and folders, set the date and time, interact with users, convert data types, deal with text strings, or perform mathematical calculations. In the following exercise, you will see how to use one of these functions to create a new subfolder without leaving Access.

⊙ Hands-On 2.3   Using Built-In VBA Functions

1. In the VBE window, with the `NorthwindStarter` database open, choose Insert | Module to create a new standard module.
2. In the Properties window, change the Name property of `Module1` to `VBA_Chap2`.
3. In the Code window, enter `Sub NewFolder()` as the name of the procedure and press Enter. Visual Basic will enter the ending keywords: `End Sub`.
4. Press F2 to display the Object Browser.
5. Click the drop-down arrow in the Project/Library list box and select VBA.
6. Enter `file` in the Search Text box and press Enter.
7. Scroll down in the Members list box and highlight the `MkDir` method.
8. Click the Copy button in the Object Browser window to copy the selected method name to the Windows clipboard.

9. Close the Object Browser and return to the Code window. Paste the copied instruction inside the `NewFolder` procedure.

10. Now, enter a space, followed by `"C:\Study"`. Be sure to enter the name of the entire path and the quotation marks. Your `NewFolder` procedure should look like the following:

```
Sub NewFolder()
   MkDir "C:\Study"
End Sub
```

11. Choose Run | Run Sub/UserForm to run the NewFolder procedure.
After you run the `NewFolder` procedure, Visual Basic creates a new folder on drive `C` called `Study`. To see the folder, activate File Explorer. After creating a new folder, you may realize that you don't need it after all. Although you could easily delete the folder while in File Explorer, how about getting rid of it programmatically?

The Object Browser contains many other methods that are useful for working with folders and files. The `RmDir` method is just as simple to use as the `MkDir` method. To remove the `Study` folder from your hard drive, replace the `MkDir` method with the `RmDir` method and rerun the `NewFolder` procedure. Alternatively, create a new procedure called `RemoveFolder`, as shown here:

```
Sub RemoveFolder()
   RmDir "C:\Study"
End Sub
```

When writing procedures from scratch, it's a good idea to consult the Object Browser for names of the built-in VBA functions.

USING THE IMMEDIATE WINDOW

The Immediate window is a sort of VBA programmer's scratch pad. Here, you can test VBA instructions before putting them to work in your VBA procedures. It is a great tool for experimenting with your new language. Use it to try out your statements. If the statement produces the expected result, you can copy the statement from the Immediate window into your procedure (or you can drag it right onto the Code window if the window is visible).

To activate the Immediate window, choose View | Immediate Window in VBE, or press Ctrl+G while in the VBE window.

The Immediate window can be moved anywhere on the VBE window, or it can be docked so that it always appears in the same area of the screen. The docking setting can be turned on and off from the Docking tab in the Options dialog box (Tools | Options).

To close the Immediate window, click the Close button in the top-right corner of the window.

The following hands-on exercise demonstrates how to use the Immediate window to check instructions and get answers.

Hands-On 2.4   Experiments in the Immediate Window

1. If you are not in the VBE window, press Alt+F11 to activate it.
2. Press Ctrl+G to activate the Immediate window or choose View | Immediate Window.
3. In the Immediate window, type the following instruction and press Enter:

```
DoCmd.OpenForm "frmOrderDetails"
```

4. If you entered the preceding VBA statement correctly, Visual Basic should open the Order Details form in the current database.
5. Enter the following instruction in the Immediate window:

```
Debug.Print Forms![frmOrderDetails].RecordSource
```

When you press Enter, Visual Basic indicates that `qryOrder` is the `RecordSource` for the Order Details form. Every time you type an instruction in the Immediate window and press Enter, Visual Basic executes the statement on the line where the insertion point is located. If you want to execute the same instruction again, click anywhere in the line containing the instruction and press Enter. For more practice, rerun the statements shown in Figure 2.17. Start from the instruction displayed in the first line of the Immediate window. Execute the instructions one by one by clicking in the appropriate line and pressing Enter.

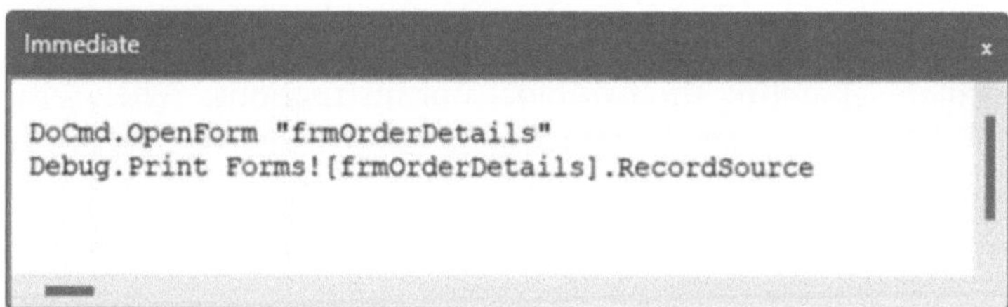

FIGURE 2.17.   Use the Immediate window to evaluate and try Visual Basic statements.

So far, you have used the Immediate window to perform some actions. The Immediate window also allows you to ask questions. Suppose you want to find out the answers to "How many controls are in the `frmOrderDetails` form?" or "What's the name of the current application?" When working in the Immediate window, you can easily get answers to these and other questions.

In the preceding exercise, you entered two instructions. Let's return to the Immediate window to ask some questions. Access remembers the instructions entered in the Immediate window even after you close this window. The contents of the Immediate window are automatically deleted when you exit Microsoft Access. You can also clear the Immediate window at any time by pressing Ctrl+A to select your entries and then pressing the Delete key.

⊙ Hands-On 2.5   Asking Questions in the Immediate Window

1. Click in a new line of the Immediate window and enter the following statement to find out the number of controls in the `frmOrderDetails` form:

```
? Forms![frmOrderDetails].Controls.Count
```

When you press Enter, Visual Basic enters the number of controls on a new line in the Immediate window.

2. Click in a new line of the Immediate window, and enter the following statement:

```
? Application.Name
```

When you press Enter, Visual Basic returns `Microsoft Access` as the name of the current application.

3. In a new line in the Immediate window, enter the following instruction:

```
? 12/3
```

When you press Enter, Visual Basic shows the result of the division on a new line. What if, however, you want to know the result of 3 + 2 and 12 * 8 right away? Instead of entering these instructions on separate lines, you can enter them on one line, as in the following example:

```
? 3+2:?12*8
```

Notice the colon separating the two blocks of instructions. When you press the Enter key, Visual Basic displays the results `5` and `96` on separate lines in the Immediate window.

Here are a couple of other statements you may want to try out on your own in the Immediate window:

```
? Application.GetOption("Default Database Directory")
? Application.CodeProject.Name
```

Instead of using the question mark, you may precede the statement typed in the Immediate window with the `Print` command, like this:

```
Print Application.CodeProject.Name
```

To delete the instructions from the Immediate window, highlight all the lines and press Delete.

4. In the VBE window, choose File | Close and return to Microsoft Access.
5. Close the `NorthwindStarter` database.

NOTE	*Recall that in Chapter 1, you also learned how to run subroutine procedures and functions from the Immediate window.*

USING ChatGPT WITH ACCESS

When you first use a database designed by someone else, it may be hard to find your way around it as objects that you can see listed in VBE's Project Explorer window might be hidden in the Navigation pane of the main Access application window. Even in matters like this, ChatGPT can give you the answer that solves your problem provided you enter a prompt that indicates what you want the AI to consider. The question you pose can be very simple. For instance, you can ask:

User Prompt: *In the Northwind Traders Starter Edition the forms don't appear in the Navigation pane. How can I access them?*

Make sure that the prompt only mentions the factors you want the AI to focus on. Giving it irrelevant details may confuse it. If your prompt fails to convey sufficient information, odds are that the AI will not be able to give you a good answer and you will need to rephrase your prompt. When composing your prompts, do not leave out any information that is essential to the question being asked.

So, how did the ChatGPT respond to the above question? It gave me a set of steps to follow to locate the missing forms. The last step, which resolved the issue, was to check the Filter by Object Type. At the top of the Navigation pane, there is a drop-down menu. Just make sure it is set to Object Type. The Forms category will now be available in the Navigation pane.

Now, let's ask ChatGPT to generate some review questions to check your knowledge gained from this chapter.

User Prompt: *Give me five review questions on the chapter about getting to know Visual Basic Editor in Microsoft Access.*

Figure 2.18 depicts the AI-generated response.

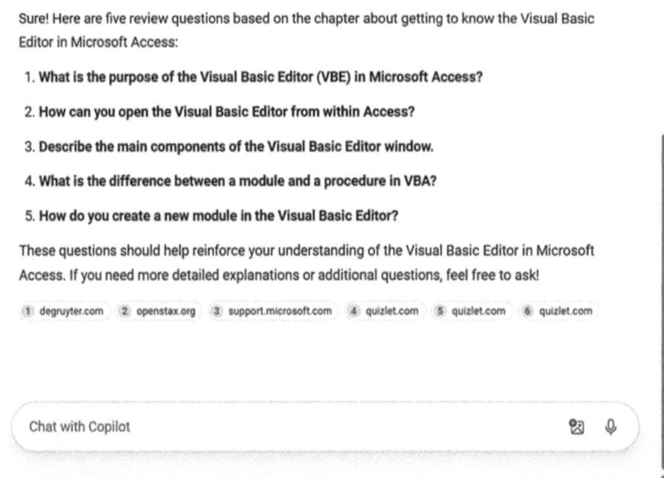

FIGURE 2.18.   ChatGPT can help you review the material learned on any topic by generating review questions.

SUMMARY

Programming in Access requires a working knowledge of various objects and collections of objects. In this chapter, you explored features of the VBE window that can assist you in writing VBA code. Here are some important points to remember:

- When in doubt about objects, properties, or methods in an existing VBA procedure, highlight the instruction in question and fire up the online help by pressing F1.

- When you need on-the-fly programming assistance while typing your VBA code, use the shortcut keys or buttons available on the Edit toolbar.

- If you need a quick listing of properties and methods for every available object or have trouble locating a hard-to-find procedure, go with the Object Browser.

- If you want to experiment with VBA and see the results of VBA commands immediately, use the Immediate window.

In the next chapter, you will expand your VBA knowledge by writing procedures and functions with arguments. In addition, you will learn how to use built-in functions that will allow your VBA procedures to interact with database users.

Chapter 3

ACCESS VBA PROCEDURES AND FUNCTIONS

As you already know from Chapter 1, VBA subroutines and function procedures often require arguments to perform certain tasks. In this chapter, you will learn various methods of passing arguments to procedures and functions.

WRITING FUNCTION PROCEDURES

Function procedures can perform calculations based on data received through arguments. When you declare a function procedure, you list the names of arguments inside a set of parentheses, as shown in Hands-On 3.1.

NOTE	*All code files and figures for the hands-on projects may be found in the companion files.*

⊙ Hands-On 3.1   Writing a Function Procedure with Arguments

1. Start Access and create a new database named `Chap03.accdb` in your `C:\VBAAccess2024_ByExample` folder.
2. Open the `Chap03` database and press Alt+F11 to switch to the VBE window.
3. Choose Insert | Module to add a new standard module and notice that `Module1` appears under the `Modules` folder in the Project Explorer window.

4. In the Module1 (Code) window, enter the code of the `JoinText` function procedure as shown here.

```
Function JoinText(k, o)
   JoinText = k + " " + o
End Function
```

Note that there is a space character in quotation marks concatenated between the two arguments of the `JoinText` function's result:

```
JoinText = k + " " + o.
```

A better way of adding a space is by using one of the following built-in functions:

```
JoinText = k + Space(1) + o
```

or:

```
JoinText = k + Chr(32) + o
```

The `Space` function returns a string of spaces as indicated by the number in the parentheses. The `Chr` function returns a string containing the character associated with the specified character code.

Other control characters you may need to use when writing your VBA procedures include:

Tab	`Chr(9)`
Linefeed	`Chr(10)`
Carriage Return	`Chr(13)`
Space	`Chr(32)`

RUNNING FUNCTION PROCEDURES

You can execute a function procedure from the Immediate window, or you can write a subroutine procedure to call the function. See Hands-On 3.2 and 3.3 for instructions on how to run the `JoinText` function procedure using these two methods.

Hands-On 3.2   Run a Function Procedure from the Immediate Window

This hands-on exercise requires prior completion of Hands-On 3.1.

1. Choose View | Immediate Window or press Ctrl+G, and enter the following statement:

```
?JoinText("function", "procedure")
```

Notice that as soon as you type the opening parenthesis, Visual Basic displays the arguments that the function expects. Type the value of the first argument, enter the comma, and supply the value of the second argument. Finish by entering the closing parenthesis.

2. Press Enter to execute this statement from the Immediate window. When you press Enter, the string `function procedure` appears in the Immediate window.

⊙ Hands-On 3.3   Executing a Function Procedure from a Subroutine

This hands-on exercise requires prior completion of Hands-On 3.1.

1. In the same module where you entered the `JoinText` function procedure, enter the following `EnterText` procedure:

```
Sub EnterText()
   Dim strFirst As String, strLast As String, strFull As String

   strFirst = InputBox("Enter your first name:")
   strLast = InputBox("Enter your last name:")
   strFull = JoinText(strFirst, strLast)

   MsgBox strFull
End Sub
```

2. Place the cursor anywhere inside the code of the `EnterText` procedure and press F5 to run it.

As Visual Basic executes the statements of the `EnterText` procedure, it uses the built-in VBA `InputBox` function to collect the data from the user, and then stores the data (the values of the first and last names) in the variables `strFirst` and `strLast`. These values are then passed to the `JoinText` function. Visual Basic substitutes the variables' contents for the arguments of the `JoinText` function and assigns the result to the name of the function (`JoinText`). When Visual Basic returns to the `EnterText` procedure, it stores the function's value in the `strFull` variable. The `MsgBox` function then displays the contents of the `strFull` variable in a message box. The result is the full name of the user (first and last names separated by a space).

> **More About Arguments**
>
> Argument names are like variables. Each argument name refers to whatever value you provide at the time the function or procedure is called. You write a subprocedure to call a function procedure. When a subprocedure calls a function procedure, the required arguments are passed to the procedure as variables. Once the function does something, the result is assigned to the function name. Notice that the function procedure's name is used as if it were a variable.

DATA TYPES AND FUNCTIONS

Like variables, functions can have types. The data type of your function's result can be a `String`, `Integer`, `Long`, and so forth. To specify the data type for your function's result, add the `As` keyword and the name of the desired data type to the end of the function declaration line—for example:

```
Function MultiplyIt(num1, num2) As Integer
```

If you don't specify the data type for a variable, constant, or function result, it defaults to the `Variant` data type. When you specify the data type for your function's result, you get the same advantages as when you specify the data type for your variables and constants—your procedure uses memory more efficiently, and therefore runs faster.

Let's look at an example of a function that returns an integer, even though the arguments passed to it are declared as `Single` in a calling subroutine.

⊙ Hands-On 3.4   Calling a Function from a Procedure

1. In the VBE window, choose Insert | Module to add a new module.
2. Enter the following `HowMuch` subroutine in the Code window:

```
Sub HowMuch()
  Dim num1 As Single
  Dim num2 As Single
  Dim result As Single

  num1 = 45.33
  num2 = 19.24
  result = MultiplyIt(num1, num2)

  MsgBox result
End Sub
```

3. Enter the following `MultiplyIt` function procedure in the Code window below the `HowMuch` subroutine:

```
Function MultiplyIt(num1, num2) As Integer
   MultiplyIt = num1 * num2
End Function
```

4. Click anywhere within the `HowMuch` procedure and press F5 to run it. Because the values stored in the variables `num1` and `num2` are not whole numbers, you may want to assign the `Integer` type to the result of the function to ensure that the result of the multiplication is a whole number. If you don't assign the data type to the `MultiplyIt` function's result, the `HowMuch` procedure will display the result in the data type specified in the declaration line of the `result` variable. Instead of `872`, the result of the multiplication will be `872.1492`.

To make the `MultiplyIt` function more useful, instead of hardcoding the values to be used in the multiplication, you can pass different values each time you run the procedure by using the `InputBox` function.

5. To pass a specific value from a function to a subroutine, assign the value to the function name. For example, the `NumOfDays` function shown here passes the value of `7` to the subroutine `DaysInAWeek`.

```
Function NumOfDays()
   NumOfDays = 7
End Function

Sub DaysInAWeek()
   MsgBox "There are " & NumOfDays & " days in a week."
End Sub
```

Subroutines (Subprocedures) or Functions: Which Should You Use?

The choice between using a subroutine (`Sub`) or a function in VBA depends on what you need your code to do:

Subroutines (`Sub`)

❏ Want to perform actions or execute a series of statements without needing a result

❏ Want to get input from the user

❏ Want to display a message on the screen

Functions:

❏ Want to perform actions and return a value

❏ Want to perform a simple calculation more than once

❏ Want to perform complex computations

❏ Want to call the same block of instructions more than once

❏ Want to check whether a certain expression is true or false

PASSING ARGUMENTS (BYRef AND BYVal)

In some procedures, when you pass arguments as variables, Visual Basic can suddenly change the value of the variables. To ensure that the called function procedure does not alter the value of the passed arguments, you should precede the name of the argument in the function's declaration line with the `ByVal` keyword. Let's see how this works in the following example.

Hands-On 3.5   Passing Arguments to Subroutines and Functions

1. In the VBE window, choose Insert | Module to add a new module.
2. In the Code window, type the following `ThreeNumbers` subroutine and the `MyAverage` function procedure:

```vba
Sub ThreeNumbers()
  Dim num1 As Integer, num2 As Integer, num3 As Integer
  num1 = 10
  num2 = 20
  num3 = 30

  MsgBox MyAverage(num1, num2, num3)
  MsgBox num1
  MsgBox num2
  MsgBox num3
End Sub

Function MyAverage(ByVal num1 As Integer, _
    ByVal num2 As Integer, ByVal  num3 As Integer) As Double
    num1 = num1 + 1
    MyAverage = (num1 + num2 + num3) / 3
End Function
```

3. Click anywhere within the `ThreeNumbers` procedure and press F5 to run it. The `ThreeNumbers` procedure initializes three integers and displays their average using the `MyAverage` function. It then displays the original values of num1, num2, and num3. The `MyAverage` function takes three integers as input, increments num1 by 1, and returns the average as a `Double`.

   By specifying data types for function parameters and return values, you can prevent errors and make the code more readable. To ensure that the original values of num1, num2, and num3 variables in the subprocedure are not altered by the function procedure, use the `ByVal` function.

Know Your Keywords: ByRef and ByVal

Because any of the variables passed to a function procedure (or a subroutine procedure) can be changed by the receiving procedure, it is important to know how to protect the original value of a variable. Visual Basic has two keywords that give or deny permission to change the contents of a variable: `ByRef` and `ByVal`.

By default, Visual Basic passes information to a function procedure (or a subroutine) by reference (the `ByRef` keyword), referring to the original data specified in the function's argument at the time the function is called. So, if the function alters the value of the argument, the original value is changed. You will get this result if you omit the `ByVal` keyword in front of the `num1` argument in the `MyAverage` function's declaration line. If you want the function procedure to change the original value, you don't need to explicitly insert the `ByRef` keyword because passed variables default to `ByRef`.

When you use the `ByVal` keyword in front of an argument name, Visual Basic passes the argument by value, which means that Visual Basic makes a copy of the original data. This copy is then passed to a function. If the function changes the value of an argument passed by value, the original data does not change—only the copy changes. That's why when the `MyAverage` function changed the value of the `num1` argument, the original value of the `num1` variable remained the same.

USING OPTIONAL ARGUMENTS

At times, you may want to supply an additional value to a function. Let's say you already have a function that calculates the price of a meal per person. Sometimes, however, you'd like the function to perform the same calculation for a group of two or more people. To indicate that a procedure argument isn't always required, precede the name of the argument with the `Optional` keyword. Arguments that are optional come at the end of the argument list, following the names of all the required arguments. Optional arguments must always be the `Variant` data type. This means that you can't specify the optional argument's type by using the `As` keyword.

In the preceding section, you created a function to calculate the average of three numbers. Suppose that sometimes you would like to use this function to calculate the average of two numbers. You could define the third argument of the `MyAverage` function as optional.

⊙ Hands-On 3.6   Using Optional Arguments

1. In the VBE window, choose Insert | Module to add a new module.
2. Type the following `Avg` function procedure in the Code window:

```
Function Avg(ByVal num1 As Integer, _
   ByVal num2 As Integer, Optional num3)   As Double
   Dim totalNums As Integer

   totalNums = 3
   If IsMissing(num3) Then
   num3 = 0
   totalNums = totalNums - 1
   End If
   Avg = (num1 + num2 + num3) / totalNums
End Function
```

3. Call this function from the Immediate window by entering the following instruction and pressing Enter:

```
? Avg(2, 3)
```

Visual Basic displays the result `2.5`.

4. Now, type the following instruction that passes the optional argument and press Enter:

```
?Avg(2, 3, 5)
```

This time, the result is `3.33333333333333`.

As you've seen, the `Avg` function is used to calculate the average of two or three numbers. You decide what values and how many values (two or three) you want to average. When you start typing the values for the function's arguments in the Immediate window, Visual Basic displays the name of the optional argument enclosed in square brackets:

```
Avg(ByVal num1 As Integer, ByVal num2 As Integer, [num3])
      As Double
```

Because the function must be capable of calculating an average of two or three numbers, the handy built-in function `IsMissing` is used here to check for the number of supplied arguments. This requires a decision-making statement that begins with `If` and ends with `End If`. You will learn about this statement in the next chapter. If the third (optional) argument is not supplied, the `IsMissing` function puts the value of `0` in its place and deducts the value of `1` from the value stored in the `totalNums` variable. Hence, if the optional argument is missing, `totalNums` is 2. The next statement calculates the average based on the supplied data, and the result is assigned to the name of the function.

VBA BUILT-IN FUNCTIONS FOR USER INTERACTION

VBA comes with numerous built-in functions that can be looked up in the Visual Basic online help. To access an alphabetical listing of all VBA functions in Access, use these links to the Microsoft documentation:

https://docs.microsoft.com/en-us/office/vba/access/concepts/criteria-expressions/functions-alphabetical-list

https://docs.microsoft.com/en-us/office/vba/Language/Reference/functions-visual-basic-for-applications

Each function is described in detail and is often illustrated with a code fragment or a complete function procedure that shows how to use it in a specific context. After completing this chapter, be sure to browse through the built-in functions to familiarize yourself with their names and usage.

One of the features of a good program is its interaction with the user. When you work with Access, you interact with the application by using various dialog boxes, such as message boxes and input boxes. When you write your own procedures, you can use the `MsgBox` function to inform users about an unexpected error or the result of a specific calculation. So far, you have seen a simple implementation of this function.

In the next section, you will learn how to control the appearance of your message.

Using the MsgBox Function

The `MsgBox` function you have used thus far was limited to displaying a message to the user in a simple, one-button dialog box. You close the message box by clicking the OK button or pressing the Enter key. You can create a simple message box by following the `MsgBox` function name with the text of the message enclosed in quotation marks. In other words, to display the message The procedure is complete. you use the following statement:

```
MsgBox "The procedure is complete."
```

You can try this instruction by entering it in the Immediate window. When you press Enter, Visual Basic displays the message box shown in Figure 3.1.

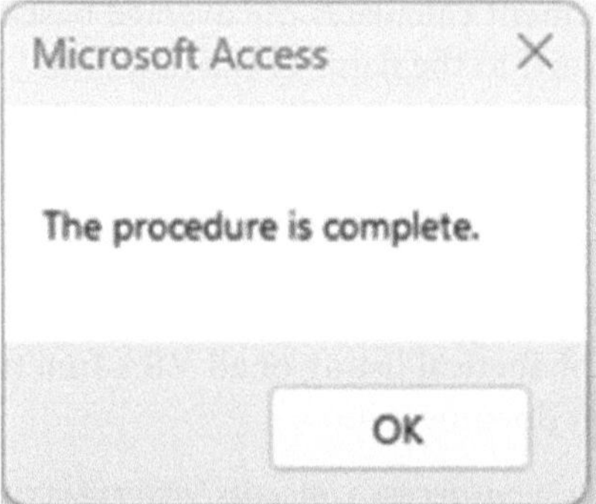

FIGURE 3.1.   To display a message to the user, place the text as the argument of the MsgBox function.

The `MsgBox` function allows you to use other arguments that make it possible to determine the number of buttons that should be available in the message box or to change the title of the message box from the default. You can also assign your own help topic. The syntax of the `MsgBox` function is shown here.

```
MsgBox (prompt [, buttons] [, title], [, helpfile, context])
```

Notice that while the `MsgBox` function has five arguments, only the first one, `prompt`, is required. The arguments listed in square brackets are optional.

When you enter a long text string for the `prompt` argument, Visual Basic decides how to break the text so it fits the message box. Let's use the Immediate window to learn various text formatting techniques.

Hands-On 3.7   Formatting Text in a Message Box

1. In the VBE window, activate the Immediate window and enter the following instruction. Be sure to enter the entire text string on one line, and then press Enter.

```
MsgBox "All done. Now open the File Explorer and locate ""Test.
doc"" document in your working folder."
```

When you press Enter, Visual Basic shows the resulting dialog box (see Figure 3.2). If you get a compile error, click OK. Then make sure that the name of the file is surrounded by double quotation marks (`""Test.doc""`).

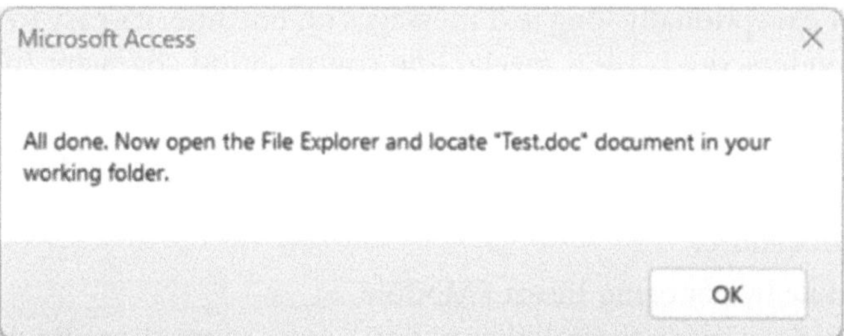

FIGURE 3.2. This long message will look more appealing to the user when you take care of the text formatting yourself.

When the text of your message is particularly long, you can break it into several lines using the VBA `Chr` function. The `Chr` function's argument is a number from 0 to 255, which returns a character represented by this number. For example, `Chr(13)` returns a carriage return character (this is the same as pressing the Enter key), and `Chr(10)` returns a linefeed character (this is useful for adding spacing between the text lines).

2. Modify the instruction entered in the previous step in the following way and make sure it stays on the same line in the Immediate window:

```
MsgBox "All done." & Chr(13) & "Now open the File Explorer" &
Chr(13) & "and locate ""Test.doc"" document" & Chr(13) & "in
your working folder."
```

Your result should look like Figure 3.3

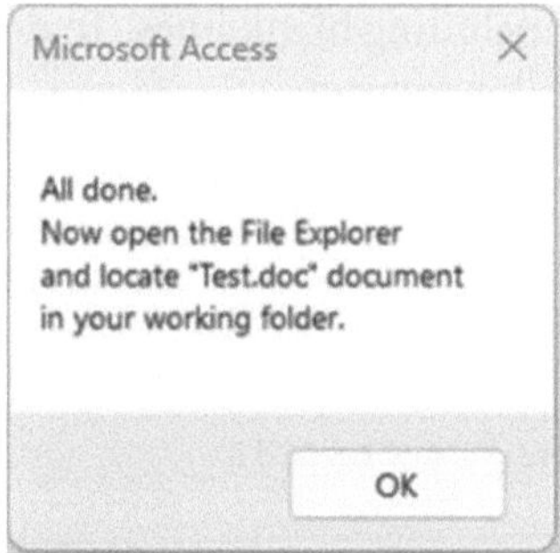

FIGURE 3.3. You can break a long text string into several lines by using the Chr(13) function.

You must surround each text fragment with quotation marks. Quoted text embedded in a text string requires an additional set of quotation marks, as in `""Test.doc""`. The `Chr(13)` function indicates a place where you'd like to start a new line. The concatenate character (`&`) is used to combine strings.

When you enter exceptionally long text messages on one line, it's easy to make a mistake. An underscore (_) is a special line continuation character in VBA that allows you to break a long VBA statement into several lines. Unfortunately, the line continuation character cannot be used in the Immediate window. A better place to try out formatting your long strings for the `MsgBox` function is within a VBA procedure.

3. Add a new module by choosing Insert | Module.

4. In the Code window, enter the following `MyMessage` subroutine. Be sure to precede each line continuation character (_) with a space.

```
Sub MyMessage()

MsgBox "All done." & Chr(13) _
    & "Now open the File Explorer" & Chr(13) _
    & "and locate ""Test.doc"" document" & Chr(13) _
    & "in your working folder."

End Sub
```

5. Position the insertion point within the code of the `MyMessage` procedure and press F5 to run it. Remember, you can also run a procedure by choosing Run | Run Sub\UserForm.

When you run the `MyMessage` procedure, Visual Basic displays the same message as the one illustrated earlier in Figure 3.3.

Notice that the text entered on several lines is more readable, and the code is easier to maintain. To improve the readability of your message, you may want to add more spacing between the text lines by including blank lines. To do this, use two `Chr(13)` functions, as shown in the following step.

6. Enter the following `MyMessage2` procedure:

```
Sub MyMessage2()

MsgBox "All done." & Chr(13) & Chr(13) _
    & "Now open the File Explorer" & Chr(13) _
    & "and locate ""Test.doc"" document" & Chr(13) _
    & "in your working folder."
End Sub
```

7. Run the `MyMessage2` procedure. The result should look as in Figure 3.4.

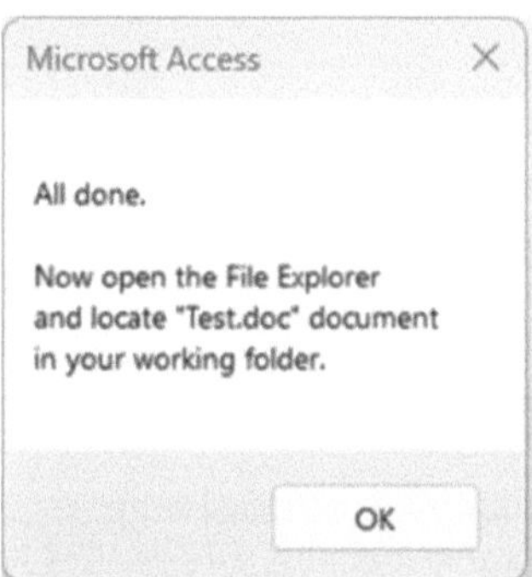

FIGURE 3.4.   You can increase the readability of your message by increasing the spacing between selected text lines.

Now let's take a closer look at the next argument of the `MsgBox` function. Although the `buttons` argument is optional, it is frequently used. The `buttons` argument specifies how many and what types of buttons you want to appear in the message box. This argument can be a constant or a number (see Table 3.1). If you omit it, the resulting message box contains only the default OK button, as you've seen in the preceding examples.

TABLE 3.1.   The MsgBox buttons argument settings.

Constant	Value	Description
Button settings		
vbOKOnly	0	Displays only an OK button. This is the default.
vbOKCancel	1	OK and Cancel buttons.
vbAbortRetryIgnore	2	Abort, Retry, and Ignore buttons.
vbYesNoCancel	3	Yes, No, and Cancel buttons.
vbYesNo	4	Yes and No buttons.
vbRetryCancel	5	Retry and Cancel buttons.
Icon settings		
vbCritical	16	Displays the Critical Message icon.
vbQuestion	32	Displays the Question Message icon.
vbExclamation	48	Displays the Warning Message icon.
vbInformation	64	Displays the Information Message icon.
Default button settings		
vbDefaultButton1	0	The first button is the default.

(Contd.)

Constant	Value	Description
vbDefaultButton2	256	The second button is the default.
vbDefaultButton3	512	The third button is the default.
vbDefaultButton4	768	The fourth button is the default.
Message box modality		
vbApplicationModal	0	The user must respond to the message before continuing to work in the current application.
vbSystemModal	4096	On Win16 systems, this constant is used to prevent the user from interacting with any other window until they dismiss the message box. On Win32 systems, this constant works like the vbApplicationModal constant with the following exception: the message box always remains on top of any other programs that may be running.
Other MsgBox display settings		
vbMsgBoxHelpButton	16384	Adds the Help button to the message box.
vbMsgBoxSetForeground	65536	Specifies the message box window as the foreground window.
vbMsgBoxRight	524288	Text is right aligned.
vbMsgBoxRtlReading	1048576	Text appears as right-to-left reading on Hebrew and Arabic systems.

When should you use the `buttons` argument? Suppose you want the user of your procedure to respond to a question with Yes or No. Your message box will then require two buttons. If a message box includes more than one button, one of them is considered a default button. When the user presses Enter, the default button is selected automatically.

Because you can display various types of messages (critical, warning, or information), you can visually indicate the importance of the message by including the graphical representation (icon). In addition to the type of message, the `buttons` argument can include a setting to determine whether the message box must be closed before the user switches to another application. It's quite possible that the user may want to switch to another program or perform another task before they respond to the question posed in your message box. If the message box is an application modal (`vbApplicationModal`), then the user must close the message box before continuing to use your application.

For example, consider the following message box:

```
MsgBox "How are you?", vbOKOnly + vbApplicationModal,
                        "Please Close Me"
```

If you type the preceding statement in the Immediate window and press Enter, a message box will pop up and you won't be able to work with your currently open Access database application until you respond to the message box.

On the other hand, if you want to keep the message box visible while the user works with other open applications, you must include the `vbSystemModal` setting in the `buttons` argument, like this:

```
MsgBox "How are you?", vbOKOnly + vbSystemModal, "System Modal"
```

> **NOTE** *Use the `vbSystemModal` constant when you want to ensure that your message box is always visible (not hidden behind other windows).*

The `buttons` argument settings are divided into five groups: button settings, icon settings, default button settings, message box modality, and other `MsgBox` display settings (see Table 3.1). Only one setting from each group can be included in the `buttons` argument. To create this argument, you can add up the values for each setting you want to include. For example, to display a message box with two buttons (Yes and No), the question mark icon, and the No button as the default button, look up the corresponding values in Table 3.1 and add them up. You should arrive at 292 (4 + 32 + 256).

To see the message box using the calculated message box argument, enter the following statement in the Immediate window:

```
MsgBox "Do you want to proceed?", 292
```

The resulting message box is shown in Figure 3.5.

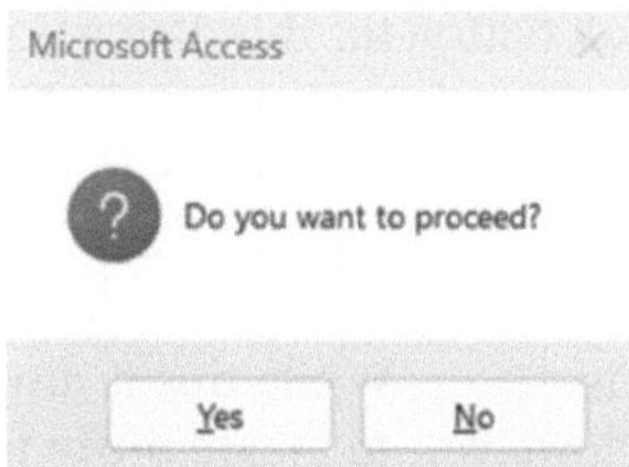

FIGURE 3.5. You can specify the number of buttons to include, their text, and an icon in the message box by using the optional buttons argument.

When you derive the `buttons` argument by adding up the constant values, your procedure becomes less readable. There's no reference table where you can check the hidden meaning of 292. To improve the readability of your `MsgBox` function, it's better to use constants instead of their values. For example, enter the following revised statement in the Immediate window:

```
MsgBox "Do you want to proceed?", vbYesNo + vbQuestion +
                                        vbDefaultButton2
```

The preceding statement produces the same result that is shown in Figure 3.5. Now let's use the `buttons` argument in the `MsgBox` function called from a Visual Basic procedure.

⊙ Hands-On 3.8   Using the MsgBox Function with Arguments

1. In the VBE window, choose Insert | Module to add a new module.
2. In the Code window, enter the `MsgYesNo` subroutine shown here:

```
Sub MsgYesNo()
   Dim question As String
   Dim myButtons As Integer

   question = "Do you want to open a new report?"
   myButtons = vbYesNo + vbQuestion + vbDefaultButton2
   MsgBox question, myButtons
End Sub
```

3. Run the `MsgYesNo` procedure by pressing F5.
   In this subroutine, the `question` variable stores the text of your message. The settings for the `buttons` argument are placed in the `myButtons` variable.

The `question` and `myButtons` variables are used as arguments for the `MsgBox` function. When you run the procedure, two buttons are displayed. Note that the No button is selected, indicating that it's the default button for this dialog box. If you press Enter, Visual Basic removes the message box from the screen. Nothing happens because your procedure does not have any instructions following the `MsgBox` function. To change the default button, use the `vbDefaultButton1` setting instead.

The third argument of the `MsgBox` function is `title`. While this is also an optional argument, it's very handy because it allows you to create procedures that don't provide visual clues to the fact that you programmed them with Access. Using this argument, you can set the title bar of your message box to any text you want.

Suppose you want the `MsgYesNo` procedure to display the text New report in its title. The following `MsgYesNo2` procedure includes the `title` argument.

```
Sub MsgYesNo2()
   Dim question As String
```

```
   Dim myButtons As Integer
   Dim myTitle As String

   question = "Do you want to open a new report?"
   myButtons = vbYesNo + vbQuestion + vbDefaultButton2
   myTitle = "New report"
   MsgBox question, myButtons, myTitle
End Sub
```

The text for the `title` argument is stored in the `myTitle` variable. If you don't specify the value for the `title` argument, Visual Basic displays the default text Microsoft Access in the message title bar. Notice that the arguments are listed in the order determined by the `MsgBox` function.

It is possible to list the arguments in any order, if you precede the value of each argument with the argument's name, as shown here:

```
MsgBox title:=myTitle, prompt:=question, buttons:=myButtons
```

The last two `MsgBox` arguments, `helpfile` and `context`, are used by advanced programmers who are experienced with using help files in the Windows environment. The `helpfile` argument indicates the name of a special help file that contains additional information you may want to display to your VBA application user. When you specify this argument, the Help button will be added to your message box. When you use the `helpfile` argument, you must also use the `context` argument. This argument indicates which help subject in the specified help file you want to display. Suppose `HelpX.hlp` is the help file you created and `55` is the context topic you want to use. To include this information in your `MsgBox` function, you would use the following instruction:

```
MsgBox title:=myTitle, _
   prompt:=question, _
   buttons:=myButtons, _
   helpfile:= "HelpX.hlp", _
   context:=55
```

The preceding is a single VBA statement broken down into several lines using the line continuation character.

Returning Values from the MsgBox Function

When you display a simple message box dialog with one button, clicking the OK button or pressing the Enter key removes the message box from the screen. When the message box has more than one button, however, your procedure should detect which button was pressed. To do this, you must save the result of the message box in a variable. Table 3.2 lists values that the `MsgBox` function returns, and the corresponding constants.

TABLE 3.2.   Values returned by the MsgBox function.

Button Selected	Constant	Value
OK	vbOK	1
Cancel	vbCancel	2
Abort	vbAbort	3
Retry	vbRetry	4
Ignore	vbIgnore	5
Yes	vbYes	6
No	vbNo	7

The MsgYesNo3 procedure in Hands-On 3.9 is a revised version of `MsgYesNo2` and it demonstrates how to store the user's response in a variable.

Hands-On 3.9   Returning Values from the MsgBox Function

1. In the VBE window, choose Insert | Module to add a new module.

2. In the Code window, enter the following code of the `MsgYesNo3` procedure:

```
Sub MsgYesNo3()
  Dim question As String
  Dim myButtons As Integer
  Dim myTitle As String
  Dim myChoice As Integer

  question = "Do you want to open a new report?"
  myButtons = vbYesNo + vbQuestion + vbDefaultButton2
  myTitle = "New report"
  myChoice = MsgBox(question, myButtons, myTitle)
  MsgBox myChoice
End Sub
```

3. Position the insertion point within the `MsgYesNo3` procedure and press F5 to run it.

In this procedure, you assigned the result of the `MsgBox` function to the variable `myChoice`. Notice that the arguments of the `MsgBox` function are now listed in parentheses:

```
myChoice = MsgBox(question, myButtons, myTitle)
```

When you run the `MsgYesNo3` procedure, a two-button message box is displayed. By clicking on the Yes button, the statement `MsgBox myChoice` displays the number 6. When you click the No button, the number 7 is displayed.

> ## MsgBox Function—With or Without Parentheses?
>
> Use parentheses around the `MsgBox` function argument list when you want to use the result returned by the `MsgBox` function. By listing the function's arguments without parentheses, you tell Visual Basic that you want to ignore the function's result. Most likely, you will want to use the function's result when the message box contains more than one button.

Using the InputBox Function

The `InputBox` function displays a dialog box with a message that prompts the user to enter data. This dialog box has two buttons: OK and Cancel. When you click OK, the `InputBox` function returns the information entered in the text box. When you select Cancel, the function returns the empty string (`""`). The syntax of the `InputBox` function is as follows:

```
InputBox(prompt [, title] [, default] [, xpos] [, ypos]
   [, helpfile, context])
```

The first argument, `prompt`, is the text message you want to display in the dialog box. Long text strings can be entered on several lines by using the `Chr(13)` or `Chr(10)` function (see examples of using the `MsgBox` function earlier in this chapter). All the remaining `InputBox` arguments are optional.

The second argument, `title`, allows you to change the default title of the dialog box. The default value is `Microsoft Access`.

The third argument of the `InputBox` function, `default`, allows the display of a default value in the text box. If you omit this argument, the empty text box is displayed.

The following two arguments, `xpos` and `ypos`, let you specify the exact position where the dialog box should appear on the screen. If you omit these arguments, the input box appears in the middle of the current window.

The `xpos` argument determines the horizontal position of the dialog box from the left edge of the screen. When omitted, the dialog box is centered horizontally.

The `ypos` argument determines the vertical position from the top of the screen. If you omit this argument, the dialog box is positioned vertically approximately one-third of the way down the screen. Both `xpos` and `ypos` are measured in special units called *twips*. One twip is the equivalent of approximately 0.0007 inches.

The last two arguments, `helpfile` and `context`, are used in the same way as the corresponding arguments of the `MsgBox` function discussed earlier in this chapter.

Now that you know the meaning of the `InputBox` arguments, let's see examples of using this function.

Hands-On 3.10   Using the InputBox Function

1. In the VBE window, choose Insert | Module to add a new module.
2. In the Code window, type the following `Informant` subroutine procedure:

```
Sub Informant()
   InputBox prompt:="Enter your place of birth:" & Chr(13) _
   & " (e.g., Boston, Great Falls, etc.)", title:="Birthplace"
End Sub
```

3. Position the insertion point within the `Informant` procedure and press F5 to run it.
   This procedure displays a dialog box with two buttons. The input prompt is displayed on two lines (see Figure 3.6). Like using the `MsgBox` function, you may want to store the result of the `InputBox` function in a variable.

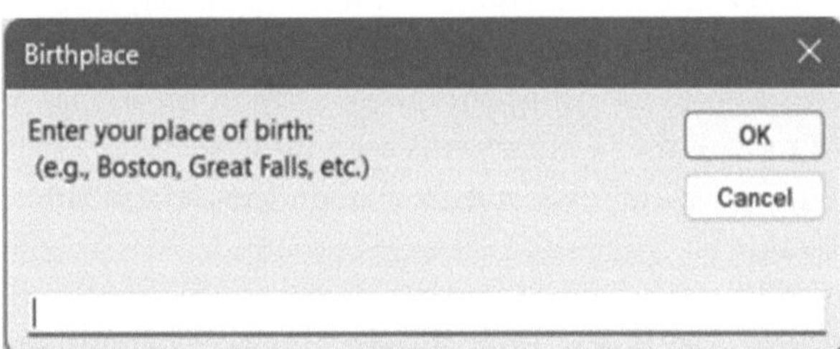

FIGURE 3.6.   A dialog box generated by the Informant procedure.

4. Now, in the same module, enter the following code of the `Informant2` procedure:

```
Sub Informant2()
   Dim myPrompt As String
   Dim town As String

   Const myTitle = "Enter data"
   myPrompt = "Enter your place of birth:" & Chr(13) _
   & " (e.g., Boston, Great Falls, etc.)"
   town = InputBox(myPrompt, myTitle)

   MsgBox "You were born in " & town & ".", , "Your response"

End Sub
```

5. Run the `Informant2` procedure.

   Notice that the `Informant2` procedure assigns the result of the `InputBox` function to the `town` variable. This time, the arguments of the `InputBox` function are listed in parentheses. Parentheses are required when you want to use the result of the `InputBox` function later in your procedure. The `Informant2` subroutine uses a constant to specify the text to appear in the title bar of the dialog box. Because the constant value remains the same throughout the execution of your procedure, you can declare the input box title as a constant. If, however, you'd rather use a variable, you still can.

   When you run a procedure using the `InputBox` function, the dialog box generated by this function always appears in the same area of the screen. To change the location of the dialog box, you must supply the `xpos` and `ypos` arguments, which were explained earlier.

6. To display the dialog box in the top left-hand corner of the screen, modify the `InputBox` function in the `Informant2` procedure as follows:

```
town = InputBox(myPrompt, myTitle, , 1, 200)
```

   Notice that the argument `myTitle` is followed by two commas. The second comma marks the position of the omitted `default` argument. The next two arguments determine the horizontal and vertical positions of the dialog box. If you omit the second comma after the `myTitle` argument, Visual Basic will use the number `1` as the value of the `default` argument. If you precede the values of arguments by their names (e.g., `prompt:=myPrompt, title:=myTitle, xpos:=1, ypos:=200`), you won't have to remember to insert a comma in the place of each omitted argument.

What happens if, instead of the name of a town, you enter a number? Because users often supply incorrect data in the input box, your VBA procedure must verify that the data the user entered can be used in further data calculations or manipulations. The `InputBox` function itself does not provide a facility for data validation. To validate user input, you must use other VBA statements, which are discussed in Chapter 4.

CONVERTING DATA TYPES

The result of the `InputBox` function is always a string. So, if a user enters a number, its *string* value must be converted to a *numeric* value before your procedure can use the number in mathematical computations. Visual Basic can automatically convert many values from one data type to another.

(•) Hands-On 3.11   Converting Data Types

1. In the VBE window, choose Insert | Module to add a new module.
2. In the Code window, enter the following `AddTwoNums` procedure:

```
Sub AddTwoNums()
   Dim myPrompt As String
   Dim value1 As String
   Dim mySum As Single

   Const myTitle = "Enter data"

   myPrompt = "Enter a number:"
   value1 = InputBox(myPrompt, myTitle, 0)
   If value1 = "" Then value1 = 0
   mySum = value1 + 2

   MsgBox mySum & " (" & value1 & " + 2)"
End Sub
```

3. Run the `AddTwoNums` procedure.

This procedure displays the dialog box shown in Figure 3.7. Instead of the default title Microsoft Access, the dialog box displays a text string as defined by the contents of the `myTitle` constant. The zero (0) entered as the default value in the edit box suggests to the user that they enter a number instead of text. Once the user provides the data and clicks OK, the input is assigned to the variable `value1`.

```
value1 = InputBox(myPrompt, myTitle, 0)
```

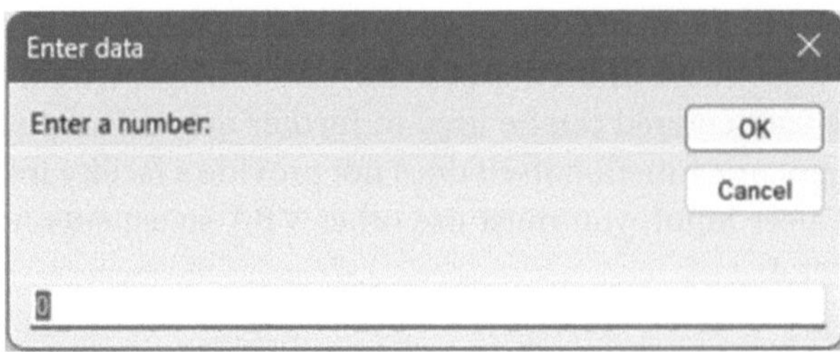

FIGURE 3.7.   To suggest that the user enter a specific type of data, you may want to provide a default value in the edit box.

The data type of the variable `value1` is `String`. You can check the data type easily if you follow the preceding instruction with this statement:

```
MsgBox varType(value1)
```

When Visual Basic runs this line, it will display a message box with the number 8, which represents the `String` data type. The next line:

```
mySum = value1 + 2
```

adds 2 to the user's input and assigns the result of the calculation to the variable `mySum`. Because the `value1` variable's data type is `String`, Visual Basic gets to work behind the scenes to perform the data type conversion. Visual Basic understands the need for data conversion. Without it, the two incompatible data types (text and number) would generate a `Type Mismatch` error. Also, if the user clicks Cancel without inputting a value, the same error will occur. To prevent this from happening, the procedure checks for the contents of the `value1` variable using the following decision statement:

```
If value1 = "" Then value1 = 0
```

The above statement will assign zero (0) to the `value1` variable if it is empty. We will discuss decision-making statements in the next chapter.

The procedure ends with the `MsgBox` function displaying the result of the calculation and showing the user how the total was derived.

4. Save all the modules created in this chapter.

> ### Define a Constant
>
> To ensure that all the title bars in a VBA procedure display the same text, assign the title text to a constant. By doing so, you will save yourself the time of typing the title text in more than one place.

USING ChatGPT WITH ACCESS

To reinforce your understanding of the user interaction functions discussed in this chapter, ask ChatGPT to perform the following tasks:

User Prompt: *Write an Access VBA procedure that uses both the MsgBox and InputBox functions.*

User Prompt: *Generate five questions about the built-in MsgBox and InputBox functions in Microsoft Access 2024 and provide answers to these questions.*

Review the AI-generated responses in the companion files—see the document `Chapter 3 - Using ChatGPT with Access`. Be sure to compare the chat answers with the answers you obtained from your personal interaction with ChatGPT.

SUMMARY

In this chapter, you learned the difference between subroutine procedures that perform actions and function procedures that return values. You saw examples of function procedures called from another Visual Basic procedure. You learned how to pass arguments to functions and how to determine the data type of a function's result. You increased your repertoire of VBA keywords with the `ByVal`, `ByRef`, and `Optional` keywords.

After working through this chapter, you should be able to create some custom functions of your own that are suited to your specific needs. You should also be able to interact easily with your users by employing the `MsgBox` and `InputBox` functions.

In the next chapter, you will learn how to introduce decisions into your VBA programs.

Chapter **4**

ADDING DECISIONS TO YOUR ACCESS VBA PROGRAMS

VBA offers special conditional statements (`If…Then…Else`), which you can use to execute different blocks of code based on specific conditions. In a conditional statement, a relational operator, a logical operator, or a combination of both is used to determine whether the statement is true or false. If the answer is true, the procedure executes a specified block of instructions. If the answer is false, the procedure either executes a different block of instructions or simply doesn't do anything. In this chapter, you will learn how conditional statements can alter the flow of your program.

RELATIONAL AND LOGICAL OPERATORS

To work with conditional statements in VBA, you need to know relational and logical operators (see Table 4.1 and Table 4.2).

TABLE 4.1. Relational operators in VBA.

Operator	Description
=	Equal to
<>	Not equal to
>	Greater than
<	Less than
>=	Greater than or equal to
<=	Less than or equal to

TABLE 4.2. Logical operators in VBA.

Operator	Description
AND	All conditions must be true before an action can be taken.
OR	At least one of the conditions must be true before an action can be taken.
NOT	If a condition is true, NOT makes it false. If a condition is false, NOT makes it true.

Boolean Expressions

Boolean expressions are the backbone of decision-making in programming. George Boole was a nineteenth-century British mathematician who made significant contributions to the evolution of computer programming. Boolean expressions evaluate to either true or false and are commonly used in conditional statements. For instance:

4 > 2	Evaluates to true
True And False	Evaluates to false
True Or False	Evaluates to true
Not True	Evaluates to false

Boolean expressions are essential for controlling the flow of your program by determining which code block should be executed.

IF...THEN STATEMENT

The simplest way to get some decision-making into your VBA procedure is by using the `If...Then` statement. Suppose you want to choose an action depending on a condition. You can use the following structure:

```
If condition Then statement
```

For example, a quiz procedure might ask the user to guess the number of weeks in a year. If the user's response is other than `52`, the procedure should display the message Try Again.

> **NOTE**   *All code files and figures for the hands-on projects may be found in the companion files.*

Hands-On 4.1   Using the If...Then Statement

1. Start Access and create a new database named `Chap04.accdb` in your `C:\ VBAAccess2024_ByExample` folder.
2. Choose Database Tools | Visual Basic or press Alt+F11 to switch to the VBE window.
3. Choose Insert | Module to add a new standard module.
   In the Module1 (Code) window, enter the following `SimpleIfThen` procedure:

```
Sub SimpleIfThen()
  Dim weeks As String

  weeks = InputBox("How many weeks are in a year:", "Quiz")
  If weeks <> 52 Then MsgBox "Try Again", , "Invalid Answer"
End Sub
```

The `SimpleIfThen` procedure stores the user's answer in the `weeks` variable. The variable's value is then compared with the number 52. If the result of the comparison is true (i.e., if the value stored in the variable `weeks` is not equal to `52`), Visual Basic will display the message Try Again.

4. Run the `SimpleIfThen` procedure and enter a number other than 52.
5. Rerun the `SimpleIfThen` procedure and enter the number `52`. When you enter the correct number of weeks, Visual Basic does nothing. The procedure ends. It would be nice to also display a message when the user guesses right.
6. Enter the following instruction on a separate line before the `End Sub` keywords:

```
If weeks = 52 Then MsgBox "Congratulations!", , "Good Guess"
```

7. Run the `SimpleIfThen` procedure again and enter the number `52`. When you enter the correct answer, Visual Basic does not execute the Try Again statement. When the procedure is executed, the statement to the right of the `Then` keyword is ignored if the result from evaluating the supplied condition is false.
   As you will recall, a VBA procedure can call another procedure. Let's see whether it can also call itself.

8. Modify the first `If` statement in the `SimpleIfThen` procedure as follows:

```
If weeks <> 52 Then MsgBox "Try Again", , _
    "Invalid Answer": SimpleIfThen
```

We added a colon and the name of the `SimpleIfThen` procedure to the end of the existing `If...Then` statement. If you enter the incorrect answer, you'll see a message. After clicking the OK button in the message box, you'll get another chance to supply the correct answer. You'll be able to keep on guessing for a long time. In fact, you won't be able to exit the procedure gracefully until you've supplied the correct answer. After clicking Cancel, you'll have to deal with the unfriendly Run-time error '13' - Type mismatch error message. For now (until you learn other ways of handling errors in VBA), let's create a revised procedure as follows:

```
Sub SimpleIfThen_Revised()
Dim weeks As String

On Error GoTo VeryEnd
weeks = InputBox("How many weeks are in a year:", "Quiz")
If weeks <> 52 Then MsgBox "Try Again", , _
    "Invalid Answer": SimpleIfThen_Revised
If weeks = 52 Then MsgBox "Congratulations!", , "Good Guess"

VeryEnd:
End Sub
```

The statement `On Error GoTo VeryEnd` sets up error handling to jump to the `VeryEnd` label if an error occurs. The `VeryEnd` label is a placeholder for any error-handling code, but in this case, it simply marks the end of the subroutine, so you don't get an error message when you press the Cancel button in the message box. Later in this chapter, you will find other examples of trapping errors in your VBA procedures.

Notice that the first `If` statement checks that the input (weeks) is not equal to `52`. If the condition is true (meaning the answer is wrong), it shows a message box with Try Again and Invalid Answer. Then, it recursively calls the `SimpleIfThen_Revised` procedure to prompt the user again. In other words, the code will keep prompting the user until they correctly answer that there are 52 weeks in a year.

Notice that the colon (:) is used here as a statement separator. This means that it allows multiple statements to be written on a single line. The two statements separated by a colon are:

```
MsgBox "Try Again", , "Invalid Answer"
SimpleIfThen_Revised
```

Instead of writing these statements on separate lines, the colon allows them to be written on the same line, making the code more compact. Please note that a multiline version of the If...Then statement, discussed in the next section, will be required if you'd like to keep these statements on separate lines.

The second If statement checks whether the input (weeks) is equal to 52. If the condition is true (meaning the answer is correct), it shows a message box with Congratulations and Good Guess.

9. Run the SimpleIfThen_Revised procedure a few times by supplying incorrect answers. The error trap that you added to your procedure will allow you to quit guessing without having to deal with the ugly error message.

MULTILINE IF...THEN STATEMENT

Sometimes you may want to perform several actions when the condition is true. Although you could add other statements on the same line by separating them with colons (as was demonstrated in the previous section), your code will look clearer if you use the multiline version of the If...Then statement, as shown here:

```
If condition Then
   statement1
   statement2
   statementN
End If
```

Let's create another version of the SimpleIfThen_Revised procedure to include additional statements.

Hands-On 4.2   Using the Multiline If...Then Statement

1. Insert a new module and enter the following SimpleIfThen_Revised2 procedure:

```
Sub SimpleIfThen_Revised2()
   Dim weeks As String
```

```
Dim response As String

On Error GoTo VeryEnd
weeks = InputBox("How many weeks are in a year?", "Quiz")
If weeks <> 52 Then
response = MsgBox("This is incorrect. Would you like " _
  & " to try again?", vbYesNo + vbInformation _
  + vbDefaultButton1, _
  "Continue Quiz?")
  If response = vbYes Then
    Call SimpleIfThen_Revised2
  End If
End If
If weeks = 52 Then MsgBox "Congratulations!", , "Good Guess"
VeryEnd:
End Sub
```

2. Run the `SimpleIfThen_Revised2` procedure and enter any number other than 52.

In this example, the statements between the first `Then` and first `End If` keywords don't get executed if the variable `weeks` is equal to 52. Notice that each multiline `If…Then` statement must end with the keywords `End If`. How does Visual Basic decide? Simply put, it evaluates the condition it finds between the `If…Then` keywords.

Notice that this procedure uses two conditions to handle the incorrect response. The initial condition checks that the variable `weeks` does not equal 52 and displays a message box with two buttons (Yes and No) for the user to respond. The user answer is stored in the `response` variable. The second condition checks which button was clicked. If the user clicked Yes (`vbYes`), the `SimpleIfThen_Revised2` subroutine is called using the VBA `Call` statement. The end of the conditional expression is marked by the `End If` keywords. The second `End If` ends the initial `If` condition.

Note that the last condition in this procedure, which checks whether the variable `weeks` is equal to 52, can also be written like this:

```
If weeks = 52 Then
    MsgBox "Congratulations!", , "Good Guess"
End If
```

Two Formats of the If...Then Statement

The `If...Then` statement has two formats: a single-line format and a multiline format. The short format is good for statements that fit on one line, like:

```
If secretCode <> "01W01" Then MsgBox "Access denied"
```

Or:

```
If secretCode = "01W01" Then alpha = True : beta = False
```

Notice that there is no `End If` clause in the above statements. In these examples, `secretCode`, `alpha`, and `beta` are the names of variables. In the first example, Visual Basic displays the message Access denied if the value of the `secretCode` variable is not equal to `01W01`. In the second example, Visual Basic will set the value of the variable `alpha` to `True` and the value of the variable `beta` to `False` when the `secretCode` value is equal to `01W01`. Notice that the second statement to be executed is separated from the first one by a colon.

The multiline `If...Then` statement is clearer when there are more statements to be executed when the condition is true, or when the statement to be executed is extremely long.

DECISIONS BASED ON MORE THAN ONE CONDITION

So far, we have only evaluated a single condition in the `If...Then` statement. This statement, however, can take more than one condition. To specify multiple conditions in an `If...Then` statement, you use the logical operators AND and OR (see Table 4.2 at the beginning of the chapter). Here is the syntax of the `If...Then` statement using the AND operator:

```
If condition1 AND condition2 Then statement
```

In this syntax, both `condition1` and `condition2` must be true for Visual Basic to execute the statement to the right of the `Then` keyword—for example:

```
If sales = 10000 AND salary < 45000 Then slsCom = sales * 0.07
```

In this example, `condition1` is `sales = 10000`, and `condition2` is `salary < 45000`.

When AND is used in the conditional expression, both conditions must be true before Visual Basic can calculate the sales commission (`slsCom`). If any of these conditions is false or both are false, Visual Basic ignores the statement after `Then`. When it's good enough to meet only one of the conditions, you should use the OR operator. Here is the syntax:

```
If condition1 OR condition2 Then statement
```

The OR operator is more flexible. Only one of the conditions must be true before Visual Basic can execute the statement following the Then keyword. Let's look at this example:

```
If dept = "S" OR dept = "M" Then bonus = 500
```

In this example, if at least one condition is true, Visual Basic assigns 500 to the bonus variable. If both conditions are false, Visual Basic ignores the rest of the line.

Now, let's look at a complete procedure example. Suppose you can get a 10% discount if you purchase 50 units of a product priced at $7.00. The IfThenAnd procedure demonstrates the use of the AND operator.

Hands-On 4.3   Using the If...Then...AND Statement

1. Insert a new module and enter the following IfThenAnd procedure in the module's Code window:

```
Sub IfThenAnd()
  Dim price As Single
  Dim units As Integer
  Dim rebate As Single

  Const strMsg1 = "To get a rebate, buy an additional "
  Const strMsg2 = "Price must equal $7.00"

  units = 234
  price = 7

  If price = 7 And units >= 50 Then
  rebate = (price * units) * 0.1
    MsgBox "The rebate is: $" & rebate
  End If

  If price = 7 And units < 50 Then
    MsgBox strMsg1 & "50 - units."
  End If

  If price <> 7 And units >= 50 Then
    MsgBox strMsg2
  End If

  If price <> 7 And units < 50 Then
    MsgBox "You didn't meet the criteria."
  End If
End Sub
```

2. Run the `IfThenAnd` procedure.

The `IfThenAnd` procedure has four `If...Then` statements that are used to evaluate the contents of two variables: `price` and `units`. The AND operator between the keywords `If...Then` allows more than one condition to be tested. With the AND operator, all conditions must be true for Visual Basic to run the statements between the `Then...End If` keywords.

Indenting If Block Instructions

To make the `If` blocks easier to read and understand, use indentation. Compare the following:

`If condition Then`
`action`
`End If`
	`If condition Then`
	`    action`
	`End If`

Looking at the block statement on the right side, you can easily see where the block begins and where it ends.

IF...THEN...ELSE STATEMENT

Now you know how to display a message or take an action when one or more conditions are true or false. What if your procedure needs to take one action when the condition is true and another action when the condition is false? By adding the `Else` clause to the simple `If...Then` statement, you can direct your procedure to the appropriate statement depending on the result of the test.

The `If...Then...Else` statement has two formats: single-line and multiline. The single-line format is as follows:

```
If condition Then statement1 Else statement2
```

The statement following the `Then` keyword is executed if the condition is true, and the statement following the `Else` clause is executed if the condition is false—for example:

```
If sales > 5000 Then Bonus = sales * 0.05 Else MsgBox "No Bonus"
```

If the value stored in the variable `sales` is greater than 5,000, Visual Basic will calculate the bonus using the following formula: `sales * 0.05`. If, however, the variable `sales` is not greater than 5,000, Visual Basic will display the message No Bonus.

The `If...Then...Else` statement should be used to decide which of two actions to perform. When you need to execute more statements when the condition is true or false, it's better to use the multiline format of the `If...Then...Else` statement:

```
If condition Then
    statements to be executed if condition is True
Else
    statements to be executed if condition is False
End If
```

Notice that the multiline (block) `If...Then...Else` statement ends with the `End If` keywords. Use the indentation as shown to make this block structure easier to read.

```
If Me.Dirty Then
  Me!btnUndo.Enabled = True
Else
  Me!btnUndo.Enabled = False
End If
```

In this example, if the condition (`Me.Dirty`) is true, Visual Basic will execute the statements between `Then` and `Else` and will ignore the statement between `Else` and `End If`. If the condition is false, Visual Basic will omit the statements between `Then` and `Else` and will execute the statement between `Else` and `End If`. The purpose of this procedure fragment is to enable the Undo button when the data on the form has changed and keep the Undo button disabled if the data has not changed. Let's look at a procedure example.

⊙ Hands-On 4.4   Using the If...Then...Else Statement

1. Insert a new module and enter the following `WhatTypeOfDay` procedure in the module's Code window:

```
Sub WhatTypeOfDay()
  Dim response As String
  Dim question As String
  Dim strMsg1 As String
  Dim strMsg2 As String
  Dim myDate As Date
  Dim strDay As String

  question = "Enter any date in the format mm/dd/yyyy:" _
    & Chr(13) & " (e.g., 07/06/2021)"
  strMsg1 = "weekday"
```

```
strMsg2 = "weekend"
response = InputBox(question)
myDate = Weekday(CDate(response))

    If myDate = 1 Then strDay = "Sunday"
    If myDate = 2 Then strDay = "Monday"
    If myDate = 3 Then strDay = "Tuesday"
    If myDate = 4 Then strDay = "Wednesday"
    If myDate = 5 Then strDay = "Thursday"
    If myDate = 6 Then strDay = "Friday"
    If myDate = 7 Then strDay = "Saturday"

  If myDate >= 2 And myDate <= 6 Then
    MsgBox strMsg1 & ":" & strDay
  Else
    MsgBox strMsg2 & ":" & strDay
  End If
End Sub
```

2. Run the `WhatTypeOfDay` procedure.
   This procedure asks the user to enter any date. The user-supplied string is then converted to the `Date` data type with the built-in `CDate` function. Finally, the `Weekday` function converts the date into an integer that indicates the day of the week (see Table 4.3). The integer is stored in the variable `myDate`. Several conditional tests are performed to check the value of the variable `myDate` and determine what day of the week it is. To determine whether it is a weekday or a weekend, we check whether the variable value is greater than or equal to 2 (>=2) and less than or equal to 6 (<=6). If the result of the test is true, the user is told that the supplied date is a weekday; otherwise, the program announces that it's a weekend.

3. Run the procedure a few more times, each time supplying a different date. Check the Visual Basic answers against your desktop or wall calendar.

TABLE 4.3.   The Weekday function values.

Constant	Value
vbSunday	1
vbMonday	2
vbTuesday	3
vbWednesday	4
vbThursday	5
vbFriday	6
vbSaturday	7

IF...THEN...ELSEIF STATEMENT

Quite often, you will need to check the results of several different conditions. To join a set of `If` conditions together, you can use the `ElseIf` clause. Using the `If...Then...ElseIf` statement, you can evaluate more conditions than is possible with the `If...Then...Else` statement that was the subject of the preceding section. Here is the syntax of the `If...Then...ElseIf` statement:

```
If condition1 Then
   statements to be executed if condition1 is True
ElseIf condition2 Then
   statements to be executed if condition2 is True
ElseIf condition3 Then
   statements to be executed if condition3 is True
ElseIf conditionN Then
   statements to be executed if conditionN is True
Else
   statements to be executed if all conditions are False
End If
```

The `Else` clause is optional; you can omit it if there are no actions to be executed when all conditions are false.

> ### ElseIf Clause
>
> Your procedure can include any number of `ElseIf` statements and conditions. The `ElseIf` clause always comes before the `Else` clause. The statements in the `ElseIf` clause are executed only if the condition in this clause is true.

Let's look at the following procedure fragment:

```
If myNumber = 0 Then
  MsgBox "You entered zero."
ElseIf myNumber > 0 Then
  MsgBox "You entered a positive number."
ElseIf myNumber < 0 Then
  MsgBox "You entered a negative number."
End If
```

This example checks the value of the number entered by the user and stored in the variable `myNumber`. Depending on the number entered, an appropriate message (zero, positive, or negative) is displayed. Notice that the `Else` clause is not used. If the result of the first condition (`myNumber = 0`) is false, Visual Basic jumps to the next `ElseIf` statement and evaluates its condition (`myNumber > 0`).

If the value is not greater than 0, Visual Basic skips to the next `ElseIf` and the condition `myNumber < 0` is evaluated.

NESTED IF...THEN STATEMENTS

You can make more complex decisions in your VBA procedures by placing an `If...Then` or `If...Then...Else` statement inside another `If...Then` or `If...Then...Else` statement. Structures in which an `If` statement is contained inside another `If` block are referred to as *nested* `If` statements. To understand how nested `If...Then` statements work, it's time for another hands-on exercise.

⊙ Hands-On 4.5   Using Nested If...Then Statements

1. In the main database window of `Chap04.accdb`, create a blank form by choosing Blank form in the Forms section of the Create tab.
2. When Access opens the new form in layout view, switch to design view.
3. Use the text box control in the Controls section of the Form Design tab to add two text boxes to the form (see Figure 4.1).

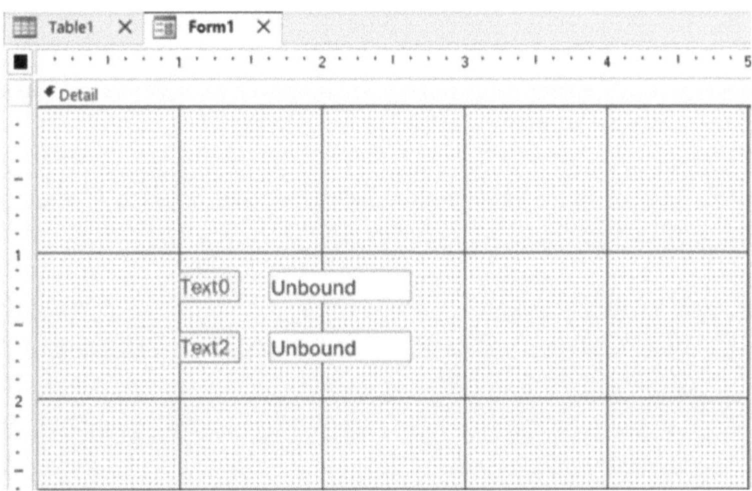

FIGURE 4.1.   Placing text box controls on an Access form for Hands-On 4.5.

4. Select the Text0 label and click the Property Sheet button in the Tools section of the Form Design tab.
5. In the property sheet, change the Caption property for the label to User.

6. In the property sheet, choose the second label from the dropdown and set its Caption property to Password. Change the Width property to `0.7"`.
7. Click the Unbound text box to the right of the User label. In the property sheet on the Other tab, set the Name property of this control to `txtUser`.
8. Click the Unbound text box to the right of the Password label. In the property sheet on the Other tab, set the Name property of this text box to `txtPwd` (see Figure 4.2).
9. In the property sheet on the Data tab, type `Password` next to the Input Mask property of the txtPwd text box control.
10. Click the Button (Form Control) in the Controls section of the Form Design tab and add a button to the form. When the Command Button Wizard dialog box appears, click Cancel. With the Command button selected, set the Caption and Name properties of this button by typing the following values in the property sheet next to the shown property name (see Figure 4.3):

    Name property: `cmdOK`

    Caption property: `OK`

11. Right-click the OK button and choose Build Event from the shortcut menu. In the Choose Builder dialog box, select Code Builder and click OK.
    Notice that Access inserts a Form code module (`Form_Form1`) in the `Microsoft Access Class Objects` folder. In the code section, Access also provides you with the structure for the procedure you need to write to handle the Click event for the OK button that was placed on the form.
12. Enter the following code for the `cmdOK_Click` event procedure. To make the procedure easier to understand, the conditional statements are shown with enhanced formatting (bold and underlined).

```
Private Sub cmdOK_Click()
  If txtPwd = "FOX" Then
    MsgBox "You're not authorized to run this report."
  ElseIf txtPwd = "DOG" Then
    If txtUser = "John" Then
      MsgBox "You're logged on with restricted privileges."
    ElseIf txtUser = "Mark" Then
      MsgBox "Contact the Admin now."
    ElseIf txtUser = "Anne" Then
      MsgBox "Go home."
    Else
      MsgBox "Incorrect user name."
    End If
  Else
```

```
    MsgBox "Incorrect password or user name"
  End If
  Me.txtUser.SetFocus
End Sub
```

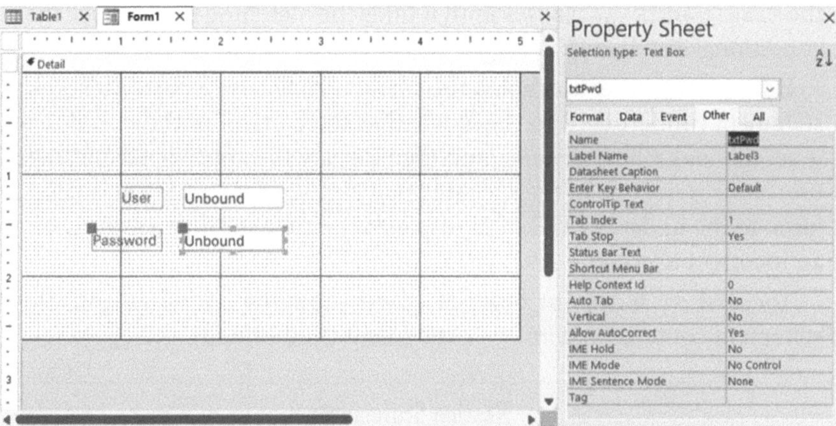

FIGURE 4.2.   Setting the Name property of the text box control for Hands-On 4.5.

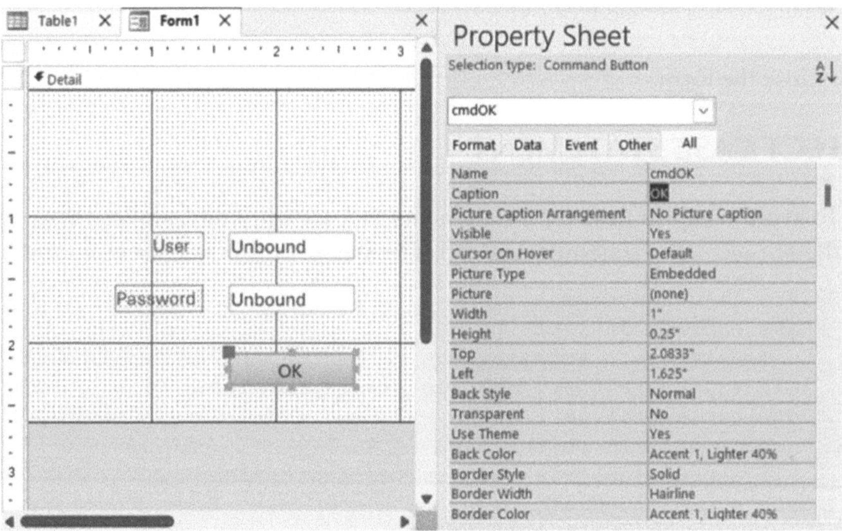

FIGURE 4.3.   Setting the Command button properties for Hands-On 4.5.

13. Choose File | Close and Return to Microsoft Access. Save your form as `frmTestNesting`. When prompted to save the standard modules you created in earlier exercises, save these objects with default names.

14. In the main Access window, switch to form view. Enter any data in the User
and Password text boxes, and then click OK.

The procedure checks whether the `txtPwd` text box on the form holds the text
string FOX. If this is true, the message is displayed, and Visual Basic skips over
the `ElseIf` and `Else` clauses until it finds the matching `End If` (see the bolded
conditional statement).

If the `txtPwd` text box holds the string DOG, we use a nested `If...Then...Else`
statement (underlined) to check whether the content of the `txtUser` text box
is set to `John`, `Mark`, or `Anne`, and then display the appropriate message. If the
username is not one of the specified names, then the condition is false, and we
jump to the underlined `Else` to display a message stating that the user entered
an incorrect username.

The first `If` block (in bold) is called the *outer* `If` statement. This outer
statement contains one *inner* `If` statement (underlined).

Nesting Statements

Nesting means placing one type of control structure inside another control structure. You
will see more nesting examples with the looping structures discussed in Chapter 5, Adding
Repeating Actions to Your Access VBA Programs.

---

15. Close the form.

SELECT CASE STATEMENT

To avoid complex nested `If` statements that are difficult to follow, you can use
the `Select Case` statement instead. The syntax of this statement is as follows:

```
Select Case testExpression
  Case expressionList1
    statements to be executed
    if expressionList1 matches testExpression
  Case expressionList2
    statements to be executed
    if expressionList2 matches testExpression
  Case expressionListN
    statements to be executed
    if expressionListN matches testExpression
  Case Else
    statements to be executed
    if no values match testExpression
End Select
```

You can place any number of cases to test between the keywords `Select Case` and `End Select`. The `Case Else` clause is optional. Use it when you expect that there may be conditional expressions that return `False`. In the `Select Case` statement, Visual Basic compares each `expressionList` with the value of `testExpression`.

Here's the logic behind the `Select Case` statement. When Visual Basic encounters the `Select Case` clause, it makes note of the value of `testExpression`. Then it proceeds to test the expression following the first `Case` clause. If the value of this expression (`expressionList1`) matches the value stored in `testExpression`, Visual Basic executes the statements until another `Case` clause is encountered, and then jumps to the `End Select` statement. If, however, the expression tested in the first `Case` clause does not match `testExpression`, Visual Basic checks the value of each `Case` clause until it finds a match. If none of the `Case` clauses contain the expression that matches the value stored in `testExpression`, Visual Basic jumps to the `Case Else` clause and executes the statements until it encounters the `End Select` keywords. Notice that the `Case Else` clause is optional. If your procedure does not use `Case Else`, and none of the `Case` clauses contain a value matching the value of `testExpression`, Visual Basic jumps to the statements following `End Select` and continues executing your procedure.

Let's look at an example of a procedure that uses the `Select Case` statement. As you already know, the `MsgBox` function allows you to display a message with one or more buttons. You also know that the result of the `MsgBox` function can be assigned to a variable. Using the `Select Case` statement, you can decide which action to take based on the button the user pressed in the message box.

Hands-On 4.6   Using the Select Case Statement

1. Press Alt+F11 to switch from the Access application window to the VBE window.
2. Insert a new module and enter the following `TestButtons` procedure in the module's Code window:

```
Sub TestButtons()
    Dim question As String
    Dim bts As Integer
    Dim myTitle As String
    Dim myButton As Integer

    question = "Do you want to preview the report now?"
```

```
bts = vbYesNoCancel + vbQuestion + vbDefaultButton1
myTitle = "Report"
myButton = MsgBox(prompt:=question, buttons:=bts, _
 Title:=myTitle)

Select Case myButton
  Case 6
    MsgBox "There are no reports to open."
  Case 7
    MsgBox "You can review the report later."
  Case Else
    MsgBox "You pressed Cancel."
End Select
End Sub
```

3. Run the `TestButtons` procedure three times, each time selecting a different button. (Because there is no `Sales by Year` report in the current database, an error message will pop up when you select Yes. Click End to exit the error message.)
The first part of the `TestButtons` procedure displays a message with three buttons: Yes, No, and Cancel. The value of the button selected by the user is assigned to the variable `myButton`.

If the user clicks Yes, the variable `myButton` is assigned the `vbYes` constant or its corresponding value 6. If the user selects No, the variable `myButton` is assigned the constant `vbNo` or its corresponding value 7. Lastly, if Cancel is pressed, the content of the variable `myButton` equals `vbCancel`, or 2.

The `Select Case` statement checks the values supplied after the `Case` clause against the value stored in the variable `myButton`. When there is a match, the appropriate `Case` statement is executed.

The `TestButtons` procedure will work the same if you use constants instead of button values:

```
Select Case myButton
  Case vbYes
    MsgBox "There are no reports to open."
  Case vbNo
    MsgBox "You can review the report later."
  Case Else
    MsgBox "You pressed Cancel."
End Select
```

You can omit the `Else` clause. Simply revise the `Select Case` statement as follows:

```
Select Case myButton
  Case vbYes
    MsgBox "There are no reports to open."
  Case vbNo
    MsgBox "You can review the report later."
  Case vbCancel
    MsgBox "You pressed Cancel."
End Select
```

> ### Capture Errors with Case Else
>
> Although using `Case Else` in the `Select Case` statement isn't required, it's always a good idea to include it just in case the variable you are testing has an unexpected value. The `Case Else` clause is a good place to put an error message.

Using Is with the Case Clause

Sometimes a decision is made based on whether the test expression uses the greater than, less than, equal to, or some other relational operator (see Table 4.1). The `Is` keyword lets you use a conditional expression in a `Case` clause. The syntax for the `Select Case` clause using the `Is` keyword is shown here:

```
Select Case testExpression
  Case Is condition1
    statements if condition1 is true
  Case Is condition2
    statements if condition2 is true
  Case Is conditionN
    statements if conditionN is true
End Select
```

Let's look at an example:

```
Select Case myNumber
  Case Is <= 10
    MsgBox "The number is less than or equal to 10."
  Case 11
    MsgBox "You entered 11."
  Case Is >= 100
    MsgBox "The number is greater than or equal to 100."
  Case Else
    MsgBox "The number is between 12 and 99."
End Select
```

If the variable `myNumber` holds `120`, the third `Case` clause is true, and the only statement executed is the one between `Case Is >= 100` and the `Case Else` clause.

Specifying a Range of Values in a Case Clause

In the preceding example, you saw a simple `Select Case` statement that uses one expression in each `Case` clause. Many times, however, you may want to specify a range of values in a `Case` clause. You do this by using the `To` keyword between the values of expressions, as in the following example:

```
Select Case unitsSold
  Case 1 To 100
    Discount = 0.05
  Case Is <= 500
    Discount = 0.1
  Case 501 To 1000
    Discount = 0.15
  Case Is >1000
    Discount = 0.2
End Select
```

Let's analyze this `Select Case` block with the assumption that the variable `unitsSold` currently has a value of `99`. Visual Basic compares the value of the variable `unitsSold` with the conditional expression in the `Case` clauses. The first and third `Case` clauses illustrate how to use a range of values in a conditional expression by using the `To` keyword.

Because `unitsSold` equals `99`, the condition in the first `Case` clause is true; thus, Visual Basic assigns the value `0.05` to the variable `Discount`. Well, how about the second `Case` clause, which is also true? Although it's obvious that 99 is less than or equal to 500, Visual Basic does not execute the associated statement `Discount = 0.1`. The reason for this is that once Visual Basic locates a `Case` clause with a true condition, it doesn't bother to look at the remaining `Case` clauses. It jumps over them and continues to execute the procedure with the instructions that may follow the `End Select` statement.

For more practice with the `Select Case` statement, let's use it in a function procedure. As you will recall from Chapter 3, function procedures allow you to return a result to a subroutine. Suppose a subroutine must display a discount based on the number of units sold. You can get the number of units from the user and then run a function to figure out which discount applies.

⊙ Hands-On 4.7   Using the Select Case Statement in a Function

1. Insert a new module and enter the following `DisplayDiscount` procedure in the Code window:

```vba
Sub DisplayDiscount()
  Dim unitsSold As Integer
  Dim myDiscount As Single
  Dim userInput As String

  On Error GoTo ErrorHandler

  userInput = InputBox("Units Sold:")
  If IsNumeric(userInput) And CInt(userInput) > 0 Then
    unitsSold = CInt(userInput)
    myDiscount = GetDiscount(unitsSold)
    MsgBox "Your discount is " & myDiscount * 100 & "%.", _
        vbInformation, "Discount"
  Else
    MsgBox "Please enter a valid positive number.", _
        vbExclamation, "Invalid input"
  End If

  Exit Sub

ErrorHandler:
    MsgBox "An error occurred. Please try again.", _
        vbCritical, "Error"
End Sub
```

2. In the same module, enter the following `GetDiscount` function procedure:

```vba
Function GetDiscount(unitsSold As Integer) As Single
  Select Case unitsSold
    Case 1 To 200
      GetDiscount = 0.05
    Case 201 To 500
      GetDiscount = 0.1
    Case 501 To 1000
      GetDiscount = 0.15
    Case Is > 1000
      GetDiscount = 0.2
    Case Else
      GetDiscount = 0
  End Select
End Function
```

3. Place the insertion point anywhere within the code of the `DisplayDiscount` procedure and press F5 to run it.

   The `DisplayDiscount` procedure prompts the user for a value and checks whether the user input is numeric and positive. `IsNumeric` and `CInt` are built-in VBA functions. The `IsNumeric` function checks whether an expression can be evaluated as a number and returns `True` if the expression is numeric and `False` otherwise. Use this function to validate user inputs to ensure they're numbers. The `CInt` function converts an expression into an `Integer`. It's used to ensure that a value is specifically treated as an integer, and if the expression cannot be converted, it throws an error. If the user input is numeric and positive, the `GetDiscount` function is called. The result of calling this function is saved in the `myDiscount` variable and used in the message box displayed to the user. If the input is incorrect, the user will see a custom error message. Notice that in this procedure, we added `ErrorHandler` code to catch any unexpected errors. This topic is covered in detail in Chapter 8. To ensure that the error-handler code is run only when an error occurs, you must use the `Exit Sub` keywords before the `ErrorHandler:` label.

   The `GetDiscount` function takes an integer (`unitsSold`) that returns a Single data type. Inside this function, we use a `Select Case` statement to determine the discount rate based on the `unitsSold`.

4. Choose File | Save Chap04 and click OK when prompted to save the changes to the modules you created during the hands-on exercises.
5. Choose File | Close and Return to Microsoft Access.
6. Close the `Chap04.accdb` database and exit Access.

Specifying Multiple Expressions in a Case Clause

You may specify multiple conditions within a single `Case` clause by separating each condition with a comma:

```
Select Case myMonth
  Case "January", "February", "March"
    Debug.Print myMonth & ": 1st Qtr."
  Case "April", "May", "June"
    Debug.Print myMonth & ": 2nd Qtr."
  Case "July", "August", "September"
    Debug.Print myMonth & ": 3rd Qtr."
  Case "October", "November", "December"
    Debug.Print myMonth & ": 4th Qtr."
End Select
```

> **Multiple Conditions Within a Case Clause**
>
> The commas used to separate conditions within a `Case` clause have the same meaning as the `OR` operator used in the `If` statement. The `Case` clause is true if at least one of the conditions is true.

USING ChatGPT WITH ACCESS

As you have seen in the earlier chapters, ChatGPT is an invaluable resource for asking questions that explain and clarify new concepts, as well as providing you with step-by-step guidance when writing or correcting your VBA code.

Before you move on to the next chapter, access ChatGPT's vast knowledge base to gather more information about the topics we discussed in this chapter. For instance, ask ChatGPT to rewrite the code of the `WhatTypeOfDay` procedure to use the `Select Case` statement, or do it on your own and ask ChatGPT to verify your code.

SUMMARY

Various conditional statements introduced in this chapter will allow you to control the flow of your VBA procedures. By testing the truth of a condition, you can decide which statements should be run and which should be skipped over. In other words, instead of running your procedure from top to bottom, line by line, you can execute only certain lines. Mastery of logical operators such as `AND`, `OR`, and `NOT` is also very important for constructing precise conditions within conditional statements.

Here are a few guidelines to help you determine which conditional statement you should use:

- If you want to supply only one condition, the simple `If...Then` statement is the best choice.
- If you need to decide which of two actions to perform, use the `If...Then... Else` statement.
- If your procedure requires two or more conditions, use the `If...Then... ElseIf` or `Select Case` statement.

- If your procedure has many conditions, use the `Select Case` statement. This statement is more flexible and easier to comprehend than the `If...Then...ElseIf` statement.

Knowing how to nest these conditional statements will allow you to create Access VBA applications with more advanced functionality.

Sometimes certain tasks must be repeated. The next chapter teaches you how your procedures can perform the same actions repeatedly.

Chapter **5**

ADDING REPEATING ACTIONS TO YOUR ACCESS VBA PROGRAMS

Now that you've learned how conditional statements can give your VBA procedures decision-making capabilities, it's time to get more involved. Not all decisions are easy. Sometimes you will need to perform a number of statements several times to arrive at a certain condition. On other occasions, however, after you've reached the decision, you may need to run the specified statements as long as a condition is true or until a condition becomes true. In programming, performing repetitive tasks is called *looping*. VBA has various looping statements that allow you to repeat a sequence of statements several times. In this chapter, you will learn how to loop through your code.

What Is a Loop?

A *loop* is a programming structure that causes a section of program code to execute repeatedly. VBA provides several structures to implement loops in your procedures: `Do...While`, `Do...Until`, `For...Next`, and `For Each...Next`.

USING THE DO...WHILE STATEMENT

Visual Basic has two types of `Do` loop statements that repeat a sequence of statements either as long as or until a certain condition is true: `Do...While` and `Do...Until`.

The `Do...While` statement lets you repeat an action as long as a condition is true. This statement has the following syntax:

```
Do While condition
   statement1
   statement2
   statementN
Loop
```

When Visual Basic encounters this loop, it first checks the truth value of the condition. If the condition is false, the statements inside the loop are not executed, and Visual Basic will continue to execute the program with the first statement after the `Loop` keyword or will exit the program if there are no more statements to execute. If the condition is true, the statements inside the loop are run one by one until the `Loop` statement is encountered. The `Loop` statement tells Visual Basic to repeat the entire process again as long as the testing of the condition in the `Do...While` statement is true.

Let's see how you can put the `Do...While` loop to good use in Access. You will write a procedure that continuously displays an input box until the user enters the correct password.

NOTE	*All code files and figures for the hands-on projects may be found in the companion files.*

⊙ Hands-On 5.1   Using the Do...While Statement

1. Start Access and create a new database named `Chap05.accdb` in your `C:\ VBAAccess2024_ByExample` folder.
2. Once your new database is opened, press Alt+F11 to switch to the VBE window.
3. Choose Insert | Module to add a new standard module.
4. In the Module1 (Code) window, enter the following `AskForPassword` procedure:

```
Sub AskForPassword()
   Dim pWord As String

   pWord = ""
   Do While pWord <> "DADA"
     pWord = InputBox("What is the report password?")
   Loop
   MsgBox "You entered the correct report password."
End Sub
```

5. Run the `AskForPassword` procedure.

In this procedure, the statement inside the `Do...While` loop is executed as long as the variable `pWord` is not equal to the string `DADA`. If the user enters the correct password (`DADA`), Visual Basic leaves the loop and executes the `MsgBox` statement after the `Loop` keyword.

To allow the user to exit the procedure gracefully and cancel out of the input box if they do not know the correct password, add the following statement on an empty line before the `Loop` keyword:

```
If pWord = "" Then Exit Do
```

The `Exit Do` statement tells Visual Basic to exit the `Do` loop if the variable `pWord` does not hold any value (please see the section titled Exiting Loops Early later in this chapter). Therefore, when the input box appears, the user can leave the text field empty and click OK or Cancel to stop the procedure. Without the `Exit Do` statement, the procedure will keep on asking the user to enter the password until the correct value is supplied.

To forgo displaying the informational message when the user has not provided the correct password, you may want to use the conditional statement `If...Then`, which you learned about in the previous chapter. Here is the revised `AskForPassword` procedure:

```
Sub AskForPassword_Revised() ' revised procedure
  Dim pWord As String

  pWord = ""
  Do While pWord <> "DADA"
    pWord = InputBox("What is the report password?")
    If pWord = "" Then
      MsgBox "You did not enter a password."
      Exit Do
    End If
  Loop
  If pWord <> "" Then
    MsgBox "You entered the correct report password."
  End If
End Sub
```

Another Approach to the Do...While Statement

The `Do...While` statement has another syntax that lets you test the condition at the bottom of the loop:

```
Do
    statement1
    statement2
```

```
      statementN
Loop While condition
```

When you test the condition at the bottom of the loop, the statements inside the loop are executed at least once. Let's try this in the next hands-on exercise.

Hands-On 5.2   Using the Do...While Statement with a Condition at the Bottom of the Loop

1. In the VBE window, insert a new module and enter the following `SignIn` procedure:

```
Sub SignIn()
  Dim secretCode As String

  Do
    secretCode = InputBox("Enter your secret code:")
    If secretCode = "sp1045" Then Exit Do
  Loop While secretCode <> "sp1045"
End Sub
```

2. Run the `SignIn` procedure.
   Notice that by the time the condition is evaluated, Visual Basic has already executed the statements one time. In addition to placing the condition at the end of the loop, the `SignIn` procedure shows again how to exit the loop when a condition is reached. When the `Exit Do` statement is encountered, the loop ends immediately.

   To exit the loop in the `SignIn` procedure without entering the password, you may revise it as follows:

```
Sub SignIn_Revised() 'revised procedure
  Dim secretCode As String

  Do
    secretCode = InputBox("Enter your secret code:")
    If secretCode = "sp1045" Or secretCode = "" Then
      Exit Do
    End If
  Loop While secretCode <> "sp1045"
End Sub
```

Avoid Infinite Loops

If you don't design your loop correctly, you can get an *infinite loop*—a loop that never ends. You will not be able to stop the procedure by using the Esc key. The following procedure causes the loop to execute endlessly because the programmer forgot to include the test condition:

```
Sub SayHello()
  Do
    MsgBox "Hello."
  Loop
End Sub
```

To stop the execution of the infinite loop, you must press Ctrl+Break. When Visual Basic displays the message box Code execution has been interrupted, click End to end the procedure.

USING THE DO...UNTIL STATEMENT

Another handy loop is Do...Until, which allows you to repeat one or more statements until a condition becomes true. In other words, Do...Until repeats a block of code as long as something is false. Here is the syntax:

```
Do Until condition
   statement1
   statement2
   statementN
Loop
```

Using the preceding syntax, you can now rewrite the AskForPassword procedure (written in Hands-On 5.1) as shown in the following hands-on exercise.

Hands-On 5.3   Using the Do...Until Statement

1. In the VBE window, insert a new module and type the AskForPassword2 procedure:

```
Sub AskForPassword2()
  Dim pWord As String

  pWord = ""

  Do Until pWord = "DADA"
    pWord = InputBox("What is the report password?")
  Loop
End Sub
```

2. Run the `AskForPassword2` procedure.

After the declaration and the initial assignment of the `pWord` variable, the first line of this procedure says: Perform the following statements until the variable `pWord` holds the value DADA. As a result, until the correct password is supplied, Visual Basic executes the `InputBox` statement inside the loop. This process continues as long as the condition `pWord = "DADA"` evaluates to false.

You could modify this procedure to allow the user to cancel the input box without supplying the password, as follows:

```
Sub AskForPassword_Revised() 'revised procedure
  Dim pWord As String

  pWord = ""
  Do Until pWord = "DADA"
    pWord = InputBox("What is the report password?")
    If pWord = "" Then Exit Do
  Loop
End Sub
```

Variables and Loops

All variables that appear in a loop should be assigned default values before the loop is entered.

Another Approach to the Do...Until Statement

Similar to the `Do...While` statement, the `Do...Until` statement has a second syntax that lets you test the condition at the bottom of the loop:

```
Do
   statement1
   statement2
   statementN
Loop Until condition
```

If you want the statements to execute at least once, no matter the value of the condition, place the condition on the line with the `Loop` statement. Let's try out the following example that prints 27 numbers to the Immediate window.

⊚ Hands-On 5.4   Using the Do...Until Statement with a Condition at the Bottom of the Loop

1. In the VBE window, insert a new module and type the `PrintNumbers` procedure shown here:

```
Sub PrintNumbers()
```

```
    Dim num As Integer

    num = 0
    Do
       num = num + 1
       Debug.Print num
    Loop Until num = 27
End Sub
```

2. Make sure the Immediate window is open in the VBE window (choose View |
   Immediate Window or press Ctrl+G).
3. Run the `PrintNumbers` procedure.
   The variable `num` is initialized at the beginning of the procedure to `0`. When
   Visual Basic enters the loop, the content of the variable `num` is increased by
   1, and the value is written to the Immediate window with the `Debug.Print`
   statement. Next, the condition tells Visual Basic that it should execute the
   statements inside the loop until the variable `num` equals `27`.
4. Return to the main Access application window by choosing File | Close and
   Return to Microsoft Access. When prompted, save the changes to all the
   modules.

What Are Counters?

A *counter* is a numeric variable that keeps track of the number of items that have been
processed. The preceding `PrintNumbers` procedure declares the variable `num` to keep
track of numbers that were printed. A counter variable should be initialized (assigned a
value) at the beginning of the program. This ensures that you always know the exact value
of the counter before you begin using it. A counter can be incremented or decremented by
a specified value.

USING THE FOR...NEXT STATEMENT

The `For...Next` statement is used when you know how many times you want to
repeat a group of statements. The syntax of a `For...Next` statement looks like this:

```
For counter = start To end [Step increment]
   statement1
   statement2
   statementN
Next [counter]
```

The code in the brackets is optional. `Counter` is a numeric variable that stores
the number of iterations. `Start` is the number at which you want to begin counting. `End` indicates how many times the loop should be executed. For example, if

you want to repeat the statements inside the loop five times, use the following `For` statement:

```
For counter = 1 To 5
   statements
Next
```

When Visual Basic encounters the `Next` statement, it will go back to the beginning of the loop and execute the statements inside the loop again, as long as the counter hasn't reached the end value. As soon as the value of `counter` is greater than the number entered after the `To` keyword, Visual Basic exits the loop. Because the variable `counter` automatically changes after each execution of the loop, sooner or later the value stored in the counter will exceed the value specified in `end`.

By default, every time Visual Basic executes the statements inside the loop, the value of the variable `counter` is increased by 1. You can change this default setting by using the `Step` clause. For example, to increase the variable `counter` by 3, use the following statement:

```
For counter = 1 To 5 Step 3
   statements
Next counter
```

When Visual Basic encounters this statement, it executes the statements inside the loop twice. The first time the loop runs, the counter equals `1`. The second time the loop runs, the counter equals `4` (1 + 3). The loop does not run a third time, because now the counter equals `7` (4 + 3), causing Visual Basic to exit the loop.

Note that the `Step` increment is optional. Optional statements are always shown in square brackets (see the syntax at the beginning of this section). The `Step` increment isn't specified unless it's a value other than 1. You can place a negative number after `Step` in order to subtract this value from the counter each time it encounters the `Next` statement. The name of the variable (`counter`) after the `Next` statement is also optional; however, it's good programming practice to make your `Next` statements explicit by including the `counter` variable's name.

How can you use the `For...Next` loop in Microsoft Access? Suppose you want to retrieve the names of the text boxes located on an active form. The procedure in the next hands-on exercise demonstrates how to determine whether a control is a text box and how to display its name if a text box is found.

⊙ Hands-On 5.5   Using the For...Next Statement

1. Close the `Table1` that Access created automatically when you created the `Chap5.accdb` database.
2. Make sure you have a copy of the `NorthwindStarter.accdb` database from the companion files in your `VBAAccess2024_ByExample` folder. You do not need to open this database.
3. Import the `Customers` table from the `NorthwindStarter.accdb` database to your `Chap5.accdb`. To do this, choose External Data | New Data Source | From Database | Access.
4. In the File name text box of the Get External Data dialog box, enter `C:\ VBAAccess2024_ByExample\NorthwindStarter.accdb` and click OK.
5. In the Import Objects dialog box, select the `Customers` table and click OK.
6. Click Close to exit the Get External Data dialog box. You should see the `Customers` table listed in the Database navigation pane in the Access application window.
7. Now, create a simple `Customers` form based on the imported `Customers` table. To do this, select the `Customers` table in the navigation pane by clicking on its name. Next, use the Form Wizard button in the Forms section of the Create tab. In the Form Wizard dialog box, click the >> button to add all the fields from the Available Fields box to the Selected Fields box and click Finish. Access creates a form as shown in Figure 5.1.

FIGURE 5.1.   Data entry form created by Microsoft Access is shown in layout view.

8. Press Alt+F11 to switch to the VBE window and insert a new module.

9. In the module's Code window, enter the following `GetTextBoxNames` procedure:

```vba
Sub GetTextBoxNames()
   Dim myForm As Form
   Dim myControl As Control
   Dim c As Integer

   Set myForm = Screen.ActiveForm
   Set myControl = Screen.ActiveControl

   For c = 0 To myForm.Count - 1
      If TypeOf myForm(c) Is TextBox Then
         Debug.Print myForm(c).Name
      End If
   Next c
End Sub
```

The conditional statement (`If…Then`) nested inside the `For…Next` loop tells Visual Basic to display the name of the active control only if it is a text box.

10. Run the `GetTextBoxNames` procedure and check all the entries that were written to the Immediate window.

Paired Statements

`For` and `Next` must be paired. If one is missing, Visual Basic generates the following error message: "For without Next."

USING THE FOR EACH...NEXT STATEMENT

When your procedure needs to loop through all the objects of a collection or all of the elements in an array (arrays are the subject of the next chapter), the `For Each…Next` statement should be used. This loop does not require a counter variable. Visual Basic can figure out on its own how many times the loop should execute. The `For Each…Next` statement looks like this:

```vba
For Each element In Group
   statement1
   statement2
   statementN
Next [element]
```

`Element` is a variable to which all the elements of an array or collection will be assigned. This variable must be of the `Variant` data type for an array and of the

`Object` data type for a collection. `Group` is the name of a collection or an array. Let's now see how to use the `For Each...Next` statement to print the names of the controls in the `Customers` form to the Immediate window.

Hands-On 5.6   Using the For Each...Next Statement

This hands-on exercise requires the completion of steps 1 and 2 of Hands-On 5.5.

1. In the VBE window, insert a new module and enter the `GetControls` procedure as shown here:

```
Sub GetControls()
    Dim myControl As Control
    Dim myForm As Form

    DoCmd.OpenForm "Customers"
    Set myForm = Screen.ActiveForm

    For Each myControl In myForm
        Debug.Print myControl.Name
    Next
End Sub
```

2. This code opens the `Customers` form, iterates through all the controls on that form, and prints each control's name. This can be useful for understanding the structure of your form.
3. Run the `GetControls` procedure.
   The results of the procedure you just executed will be displayed in the Immediate window. If the window is not visible, press Ctrl+G in the VBE window to open the Immediate window, or choose View | Immediate Window.

EXITING LOOPS EARLY

Sometimes you might not want to wait until the loop ends on its own. It's possible that a user will enter the wrong data, a procedure will encounter an error, or perhaps the task will complete and there's no need to do additional looping. You can leave the loop early without reaching the condition that normally terminates it. Visual Basic has two types of `Exit` statements:

- The `Exit For` statement is used to end either a `For...Next` or `For Each... Next` loop early.
- The `Exit Do` statement immediately exits any of the VBA `Do` loops.

The following hands-on exercise demonstrates how to use the `Exit For` statement to leave the `For Each...Next` loop early.

⊙ Hands-On 5.7   Early Exit from a Loop

1. In the VBE window, choose Insert | Module.
2. In the module's Code window, enter the following `GetControls2` procedure:

```
Sub GetControls2()
  Dim myControl As Control
  Dim myForm As Form

  DoCmd.OpenForm "Customers"
  Set myForm = Screen.ActiveForm

  For Each myControl In myForm
    Debug.Print myControl.Name
    If myControl.Name = "Address" Then
      Exit For
    End If
  Next
End Sub
```

3. Run the `GetControls2` procedure.
   The `GetControls2` procedure examines the names of the controls in the open `Customers` form. If Visual Basic encounters the control named `Address`, it exits the loop.
4. Return to the main Access application window by choosing File | Close and Return to Microsoft Access.

Early Exit from Subprocedures and Functions

If you want to exit a subroutine earlier than normal, use the `Exit Sub` statement. If the procedure is a function, use the `Exit Function` statement instead.

NESTED LOOPS

So far in this chapter, you have tried out various loops. Each procedure demonstrated the use of an individual looping structure. In programming practice, however, one loop is often placed inside another. Visual Basic allows you to "nest" various types of loops (`For` and `Do` loops) within the same procedure. When writing nested loops, you must make sure that each inner loop is completely contained inside the outer loop. Also, each loop must have a unique counter variable. When you use nesting loops, you can often execute specific tasks more effectively.

The `GetFormsAndControls` procedure shown in the following hands-on exercise illustrates how one `For Each...Next` loop is nested within another `For Each...Next` loop.

⦿ Hands-On 5.8   Using Nested Loops

1. Import the `Employees` table from the `NorthwindStarter.accdb` database located in your `VBAAccess2024_ByExample` folder (see Hands-On 5.5).
2. Use the Form Wizard to create a simple `Employees` form based on the `Employees` table.
3. Leave the `Employees` form in form view and press Alt+F11 to switch to the VBE window.
4. Choose Insert | Module to add a new module. In the module's Code window, enter the `GetFormsAndControls` procedure shown here:

```
Sub GetFormsAndControls()
   Dim accObj As AccessObject
   Dim myControl As Control

   For Each accObj In CurrentProject.AllForms
     Debug.Print accObj.Name & " Form"
     If Not accObj.IsLoaded Then
       DoCmd.OpenForm accObj.Name
     End If
     For Each myControl In Forms(accObj.Name).Controls
       Debug.Print Chr(9) & myControl.Name
     Next
     DoCmd.Close , , acSaveYes
   Next
End Sub
```

5. Run the `GetFormsAndControls` procedure.
   The `GetFormsAndControls` procedure uses two `For Each...Next` loops. It iterates through all forms in the current Access project, opens each form if it's not already open, and then lists all the controls on each form. To enumerate through the form's controls, the form must be fopen.

   `accObj` is declared to represent each form in the Access project. `myControl` is declared to represent each control on the forms. Notice the use of the Access built-in function `IsLoaded` to check that the form is not already open. The control names are indented in the Immediate window using the `Chr(9)` function. This is like pressing the Tab key once. To get the same result, you can replace `Chr(9)` with a VBA constant: `vbTab`. The next statement is used to proceed to the next form in the `AllForms` collection.

After reading the names of the controls, the form is closed, and the next form is processed in the same manner. The procedure ends when no more forms are found in the `AllForms` collection of `CurrentProject`.

6. Choose File | Save Chap05 to save changes to the modules.
7. Choose File | Close and Return to Microsoft Access.
8. Close the `Chap05.accdb` database.

USING ChatGPT WITH ACCESS

ChatGPT can be very helpful during the code-editing process, providing suggestions for revisions and improving your VBA code. Note, however, that you must carefully consider the AI recommendations and make adjustments based on your own judgment and expertise. As you gain more programming knowledge, you will find it easier to determine when to follow these suggestions directly and when to deviate from them based on the specific context of your project. This balance will allow you to harness the full potential of AI tools while still applying your personal understanding and creativity to achieve the best possible outcomes.

Before moving on to the next chapter, ask ChatGPT for a list of all the `Exit` statements that are used in Access VBA.

User Prompt: *Please provide a list of Exit statements used in Access VBA.*

ChatGPT/Microsoft Copilot's response can be found in the companion files— see the `Chapter 5 - Using ChatGPT with Access` document.

SUMMARY

In this chapter, you learned how to repeat certain groups of statements in VBA procedures by using loops. While working with several types of loops, you saw how each loop performs repetitions in a slightly different way. As you gain experience, you'll find it easier to choose the appropriate flow control structure for your task.

The next chapter shows you how to write procedures that require a large number of variables.

6

KEEPING TRACK OF MULTIPLE VALUES USING ARRAYS

In previous chapters, you worked with VBA procedures that used variables to hold specific information about an object, property, or value. For each single value you wanted your procedure to manipulate, you declared a variable. What if you have a series of values, though? If you had to write a VBA procedure to deal with larger amounts of data, you would have to create enough variables to handle all the data. Can you imagine the nightmare of storing currency exchange rates for all the countries in the world in your program? To create a table to hold the necessary data, you'd need at least three variables for each country: country name, currency name, and exchange rate. Fortunately, Visual Basic has a way to get around this problem. By clustering the related variables together, your VBA procedures can manage a large amount of data with ease. In this chapter, you'll learn how to manipulate lists and tables of data with arrays.

UNDERSTANDING ARRAYS

In Visual Basic, an *array* is a special type of variable that represents a group of similar values that are of the same data type (`String`, `Integer`, `Currency`, `Date`, etc.). The two most common types of arrays are one-dimensional arrays (lists) and two-dimensional arrays (tables).

A one-dimensional array is sometimes referred to as a *list*. A shopping list, a list of the days of the week, and an employee list are examples of one-dimensional arrays or, simply, numbered lists. Each element in the list has an index value that allows you to access that element. For example, in the following illustration, we have a one-dimensional array of six elements indexed from 0 to 5:

(0)	(1)	(2)	(3)	(4)	(5)

You can access the third element of this array by specifying index (2). By default, the first element of an array is indexed zero (0). You can change this behavior by using the `Option Base 1` statement or by explicitly coding the lower bound of your array, as explained later in this chapter.

All elements of the array should be of the same data type. In other words, if you declare an array to hold textual data, you cannot store in it both strings and integers. If you want to store values of *different* data types in the same array, you must declare the array as `Variant`, as discussed later. The following are two examples of one-dimensional arrays: an array named `cities` that is populated with text (`String` data type—$) and an array named `lotto` that contains six lottery numbers stored as integers (`Integer` data type—%).

A one-dimensional array: cities$		A one-dimensional array: lotto%	
cities(0)	Baltimore	lotto(0)	25
cities(1)	Atlanta	lotto(1)	4
cities(2)	Boston	lotto(2)	31
cities(3)	Washington	lotto(3)	22
cities(4)	New York	lotto(4)	11
cities(5)	Trenton	lotto(5)	5

As you can see, the data assigned to each array element matches the array type. Storing values of different data types in the same array requires that you declare the array as `Variant`. You will learn how to declare arrays in the next section.

A two-dimensional array may be thought of as a table or matrix. The position of each element in a table is determined by its row and column numbers. For example, an array that holds the yearly sales data for each product a fictitious company sells has two dimensions: the product name and the year. The following is a diagram of an empty two-dimensional array.

(0,0)	(0,1)	(0,2)	(0,3)	(0,4)	(0,5)
(1,0)	(1,1)	(1,2)	(1,3)	(1,4)	(1,5)
(2,0)	(2,1)	(2,2)	(2,3)	(2,4)	(2,5)
(3,0)	(3,1)	(3,2)	(3,3)	(3,4)	(3,5)
(4,0)	(4,1)	(4,2)	(4,3)	(4,4)	(4,5)
(5,0)	(5,1)	(5,2)	(5,3)	(5,4)	(5,5)

You can access the first element in the second row of this two-dimensional array by specifying indices (1, 0). The following are two examples of two-dimensional arrays: an array named `yearlyProductSales` that stores yearly product sales using the `Currency` data type (`@`) and an array named `exchange` (of the `Variant` data type) that stores the name of the country, its currency, and the U.S. dollar exchange rate.

A two-dimensional array: yearlyProductSales@

Walking Cane (0,0)	$25,023 (0,1)
Pill Crusher (1,0)	$64,085 (1,1)
Electric Wheelchair (2,0)	$345,016 (2,1)
Folding Walker (3,0)	$85,244 (3,1)

A two-dimensional array: exchange (not actual rates)

Japan (0,0)	Japanese Yen (0,1)	148.7163 (0,2)
Australia (1,0)	Australian Dollar (1,1)	1.466383 (1,2)
Canada (2,0)	Canadian Dollar (2,1)	1.357208 (2,2)
Norway (3,0)	Norwegian Krone (3,1)	10.654314 (3,2)
Europe (4,0)	Euro (4,1)	0.9106916 (4,2)

In these examples, the `yearlyProductSales` array can hold a maximum of 8 elements (4 rows * 2 columns = 8) and the `exchange` array will allow a maximum of 15 elements (5 rows * 3 columns = 15).

Although VBA arrays can have up to 60 dimensions, most people find it difficult to picture dimensions beyond 3D. A three-dimensional array is an array of two-dimensional arrays (tables) where each table has the same number of rows and columns. A three-dimensional array is identified by three indices: table, row, and column. The first element of a three-dimensional array is indexed (0, 0, 0).

Declaring Arrays

Because an array is a variable, you must declare it in a similar way that you declare other variables (by using the keyword `Dim`, `Private`, or `Public`). For fixed-length arrays, the array bounds are listed in parentheses following the variable name. The *bounds* of an array are its lowest and highest indices. If a variable-length, or dynamic, array is being declared, the variable name is followed by an empty pair of parentheses.

The last part of the array declaration is the definition of the data type that the array will hold. An array can hold any of the following data types: `Integer`, `Long`, `Single`, `Double`, `Variant`, `Currency`, `String`, `Boolean`, `Byte`, or `Date`. Let's look at some examples:

Array Declaration (one-dimensional)	Description
`Dim cities(5) As String`	Declares a six-element array, indexed 0 to 5
`Dim lotto(1 To 6) As String`	Declares a six-element array, indexed 1 to 6
`Dim supplies(2 To 11)`	Declares a 10-element array, indexed 2 to 11
`Dim myIntegers(-3 To 6)`	Declares a 10-element array, indexed –3 to 6
`Dim dynArray() As Integer`	Declares a variable-length array whose bounds will be determined at runtime (see examples later in this chapter)

Two-dimensional arrays are used for storing and manipulating data in a grid-like structure, similar to a table with rows and columns.

Array Declaration (two-dimensional)	Description
`Dim exchange(4,2) As Variant`	Declares a two-dimensional array (five rows by three columns)
`Dim yearlyProductSales(3, 1) As Currency`	Declares a two-dimensional array (four rows by two columns)
`Dim arr(1 To 3, 1 To 7) As Integer`	Declares a two-dimensional array (three rows indexed 1 to 3 by seven columns indexed 1 to 7)

When you declare an array, Visual Basic automatically reserves enough memory space for it. The amount of memory allocated depends on the array's size and data type. For a one-dimensional array with six elements, Visual Basic sets aside 12 bytes—2 bytes for each element of the array (recall that the size of the `Integer` data type is 2 bytes—hence 2 * 6 = 12). The larger the array, the more memory space is required to store the data. Because arrays can eat up a lot of memory and impact your computer's performance, it's recommended that you declare arrays with only as many elements as you think you'll use.

> ## What Is an Array Variable?
>
> An *array* is a group of variables that have a common name. While a typical variable can hold only one value, an *array variable* can store many individual values. You refer to a specific value in the array by using the array name and an index number.

> ## Subscripted Variables
>
> The numbers inside the parentheses of the array variables are called *subscripts*, and each individual variable is called a subscripted variable or element. For example, `cities(5)` is the sixth subscripted variable (element) of the array `cities()`.

Array Upper and Lower Bounds

By default, VBA assigns zero (`0`) to the first element of the array. Therefore, number `1` represents the second element of the array, number `2` represents the third, and so on. With numeric indexing starting at `0`, the one-dimensional array `cities(5)` contains six elements numbered from 0 to 5. If you'd rather start counting your array's elements from `1`, you can explicitly specify a lower bound of the array by using an `Option Base 1` statement. This instruction must be placed in the Declarations section at the top of a VBA module before any `Sub` statements. If you don't specify `Option Base 1` in a procedure that uses arrays, VBA assumes that the statement `Option Base 0` is to be used and begins indexing your array's elements at 0. If you'd rather not use the `Option Base 1` statement and still have the array indexing start at a number other than 0, you must specify the bounds of an array when declaring the array variable. As mentioned in the previous section, the *bounds* of an array are its lowest and highest indices. Let's look at the following example:

```
Dim cities(3 To 6) As Integer
```

This statement declares a one-dimensional array with four elements. The numbers enclosed in parentheses after the array name specify the lower (`3`) and upper (`6`) bounds of the array. The index of the first element of this array is `3`, the second `4`, the third `5`, and the fourth `6`. You must put the keyword `To` between the lower and upper indices.

Initializing and Filling an Array

After you declare an array, you must assign values to its elements. This is often referred to as "initializing an array," "filling an array," or "populating an array."

The three methods you can use to load data into an array are discussed in the following sections.

Filling an Array Using Individual Assignment Statements

Assume you want to store the names of your six favorite cities as a list. To do this, you can declare a one-dimensional array named `cities` using the `Dim` statement like this:

```
Dim cities(5) As String
```

Or:

```
Dim cities$(5)
```

Next, you can assign values to the `cities` array variable like this:

```
cities(0) = "Baltimore"
cities(1) = "Atlanta"
cities(2) = "Boston"
cities(3) = "San Diego"
cities(4) = "New York"
cities(5) = "Denver"
```

Filling an Array Using the Array Function

The `Array` function in VBA allows you to quickly create and fill an array with elements in a single line. This technique is often used for initializing arrays with predefined values like this:

```
Dim cities As Variant
cities = Array("London", "Tokyo", "New York")
```

In this example, the `cities` array is filled with the names of cities: `London`, `Tokyo`, and `New York`. You can then access these values using the appropriate index:

```
Debug.Print cities(0) ' prints London
Debug.Print cities(1) ' prints Tokyo
Debug.Print cities(2) ' prints New York
```

Filling an Array Using the For...Next Loop

The easiest way to learn how to use loops to populate an array is by writing a procedure that fills an array with a specific number of integer values. Let's look at the following example procedure that initializes an array with 10 random integers between 1 and 100 and prints these values to the Immediate window:

```
Sub LoadArrayWithIntegers()

  Dim myIntArray(1 To 10) As Integer
  Dim i As Integer

  ' Initialize random number generator
  Randomize

  ' Fill the array with 10 random numbers between 1 and 100
  For i = 1 To 10
    myIntArray(i) = Int((100 * Rnd) + 1)
  Next

  ' Print array values to the Immediate window
  For i = 1 To 10
    Debug.Print myIntArray(i)
  Next
End Sub
```

This procedure uses a `For…Next` loop to fill `myIntArray` with a random integer between 1 and 100. The second loop is used to print out the values from the array. The `Rnd` function is used to generate a random number between 0 and 1. `100 * Rnd` scales this number to between 0 and 100 and `Int((100*Rnd) + 1` converts this scaled number to an integer between 1 and 100. You can try the `Rnd` function from the Immediate window like this:

```
x=Rnd
?x
```

USING A ONE-DIMENSIONAL ARRAY

Having learned the basics of array variables, let's write a couple of VBA procedures to make arrays a part of your new skillset. The procedure in Hands-On 6.1 uses a one-dimensional array to programmatically display a list of six North American cities.

NOTE	*All code files and figures for the hands-on projects may be found in the companion files.*

◉ Hands-On 6.1   Using a One-Dimensional Array

1. Start Access and create a new database named `Chap06.accdb` in your `C:\VBAAccess2024_ByExample` folder.
2. Press Alt+F11 to switch to the VBE window.
3. Choose Insert | Module to add a new standard module.
4. In the Module1 (Code) window, enter the following `FavoriteCities` procedure. Be sure to enter the `Option Base 1` statement at the top of the module to ensure that the array numbering will begin from 1.

```
Option Base 1

Sub FavoriteCities()
  ' declare the array
  Dim cities(6) As String

  ' assign the values to array elements
  cities(1) = "Baltimore"
  cities(2) = "Atlanta"
  cities(3) = "Boston"
  cities(4) = "San Diego"
  cities(5) = "New York"
  cities(6) = "Denver"

  ' display the list of cities
  MsgBox cities(1) & Chr(13) & cities(2) & Chr(13) _
    & cities(3) & Chr(13) & cities(4) & Chr(13) _
    & cities(5) & Chr(13) & cities(6)
End Sub
```

5. Choose Run | Run Sub/UserForm to execute the `FavoriteCities` procedure. Before the `FavoriteCities` procedure begins, the default indexing for an array is changed. Notice the `Option Base 1` statement at the top of the module window before the `Sub` statement. This statement tells Visual Basic to assign the number 1 instead of the default 0 to the first element of the array. The array `cities` is declared with six elements of the `String` data type. Each element of the array is then assigned a value. The last statement in this procedure uses the `MsgBox` function to display the list of cities in a message box. When you run this procedure, each city name will appear on a separate line (see Figure 6.1). You can change the order of the displayed data by switching the index values.

FIGURE 6.1.   You can display the elements of a one-dimensional array with the MsgBox function.

6. Click OK to close the message box.

> ### The Range of the Array
>
> The spread of the elements specified by the `Dim` statement is called the *range* of the array—for example, `Dim mktgCodes(5 To 15)`.

ARRAYS AND LOOPING STATEMENTS

Several of the looping statements you learned about in Chapter 5 (`For...Next` and `For Each...Next`) will come in handy now that you're ready to perform tasks such as populating an array and displaying the elements of an array. It's time to combine the skills you've learned so far.

How can you rewrite the `FavoriteCities` procedure so each city name is shown in a separate message box?

⊚ Hands-On 6.2   Using the For Each...Next Statement to List the Array Elements

1. In the VBE window, insert a new module.
2. Enter the `FavoriteCities2` procedure in the Code window. Be sure to enter the `Option Base 1` statement at the top of the module.

```
Option Base 1

Sub FavoriteCities2()
    ' declare the array
```

```vba
    Dim cities(6) As String
    Dim city As Variant

    ' assign the values to array elements
    cities(1) = "Baltimore"
    cities(2) = "Atlanta"
    cities(3) = "Boston"
    cities(4) = "San Diego"
    cities(5) = "New York"
    cities(6) = "Denver"

    ' display the list of cities in separate messages
    For Each city In cities
      MsgBox city
    Next
End Sub
```

3. Choose Run | Run Sub/UserForm to execute the `FavoriteCities2` procedure. Notice that the `For Each...Next` loop uses the variable `city` of the `Variant` data type. As you will recall from the previous chapter, the `For Each...Next` loop allows you to loop through all the objects in a collection or all the elements of an array and perform the same action on each object or element. When you run the `FavoriteCities2` procedure, the loop will execute as many times as there are elements in the array.

In Chapter 3, you practiced passing arguments as variables to subroutines and functions. The `CityOperator` procedure in Hands-On 6.3 demonstrates how you can pass elements of an array to another procedure.

⊚ Hands-On 6.3   Passing Elements of an Array to Another Procedure

1. In the VBE window, insert a new module.
2. Enter the following two procedures (`CityOperator` and `Hello`) in the module's Code window. Be sure to enter the `Option Base 1` statement at the top of the module.

```vba
Option Base 1

Sub CityOperator()
  ' declare the array
  Dim cities(6) As String

  ' assign the values to array elements
  cities(1) = "Baltimore"
```

```vb
    cities(2) = "Atlanta"
    cities(3) = "Boston"
    cities(4) = "San Diego"
    cities(5) = "New York"
    cities(6) = "Denver"

    ' call another procedure and pass
    ' the cities array as an argument
    Hello cities()
End Sub

Sub Hello(cities() As String)
    Dim counter As Integer

    For counter = 1 To 6
        MsgBox "Hello, " & cities(counter) & "!"
    Next
End Sub
```

Notice that the last statement in the `CityOperator` procedure calls the `Hello` procedure and passes to it the array `cities()`, which holds the names of our favorite cities. Also notice that the declaration of the `Hello` procedure includes an array type argument—`cities()`—passed to this procedure as `String`. In order to iterate through the elements of an array, you need to know how many elements are included in the `cities` array. You can easily retrieve this information via two special array functions—`LBound` and `UBound`. These functions are discussed later in this chapter. In this procedure example, `LBound(cities())` will return `1` as the first element of the array, and `UBound(cities())` will return `6` as the last element of the `cities` array. Therefore, the statement `For counter = LBound(cities()) To UBound(cities())` will boil down to `For counter = 1 To 6`.

3. Run the `CityOperator` procedure.

Passing array elements from a subroutine to another subroutine or function procedure allows you to reuse the same array in many procedures without unnecessary duplication of the program code.

Here's how you can combine this newly acquired knowledge about arrays and loops in real life. If you're an avid lotto player who is getting tired of picking your own lucky numbers, you can have Visual Basic do the picking. The `Lotto` procedure in Hands-On 6.4 populates an array with 6 numbers from 1 to 54. You can adjust this procedure to pick numbers from any range.

⊙ Hands-On 6.4   Using Arrays and Loops in Real Life

1. In the VBE window, insert a new module.

2. Enter the following `Lotto` procedure in the module's Code window:

```
Sub Lotto()
  Const spins = 6
  Const minNum = 1
  Const maxNum = 54
  Dim t As Integer ' looping variable in outer loop
  Dim i As Integer ' looping variable in inner loop
  Dim myNumbers As String ' string to hold all picks
  Dim lucky(spins) As String ' array to hold generated picks

  myNumbers = ""
  For t = 1 To spins
    Randomize
    lucky(t) = Int((maxNum - minNum + 1) * Rnd) + minNum

    ' check if this number was picked before
    For i = 1 To (t - 1)
      If lucky(t) = lucky(i) Then
        lucky(t) = Int((maxNum - minNum + 1) * Rnd) + minNum
        i = 0
      End If
    Next i
      MsgBox "Lucky number is " & lucky(t), , "Lucky number " & t
      myNumbers = myNumbers & " -" & lucky(t)
  Next t
  MsgBox "Lucky numbers are " & myNumbers, , "6 Lucky Numbers"
End Sub
```

The `Randomize` statement initializes the random number generator. The instruction `Int((maxNum - minNum + 1) * Rnd + minNum)` uses the `Rnd` function to generate a random value from the specified `minNum` to `maxNum`. The `Int` function converts the resulting random number into an integer. Instead of assigning constant values for `minNum` and `maxNum`, you can use the `InputBox` function to get these values from the user.

The inner `For…Next` loop ensures that each picked number is unique—it may not be one of the previously picked numbers. If you omit the inner loop and run this procedure multiple times, you'll likely see some occurrences of duplicate numbers.

3. Execute the `Lotto` procedure to get your very own computer-generated lottery numbers.

Initial Value of an Array Element

Until a value is assigned to an element of an array, the element retains its default value. Numeric variables have a default value of zero (0), and string variables have a default value of empty string (`""`).

Passing Arrays Between Procedures

When an array is declared in a procedure, it is local to this procedure and unknown to other procedures. You can, however, pass the local array to another procedure by using the array's name followed by an empty set of parentheses as an argument in the calling statement. For example, the statement `Hello cities()` calls the procedure named `Hello` and passes to it the array `cities`.

USING A TWO-DIMENSIONAL ARRAY

Now that you know how to programmatically produce a list (a one-dimensional array), let's take a closer look at how you can work with tables of data. The following procedure creates a two-dimensional array that will hold the country name, currency name, and exchange rate for three countries.

⊙ Hands-On 6.5   Using a Two-Dimensional Array

1. In the VBE window, insert a new module.

2. Enter the `Exchange` procedure in the module's Code window:

```
Sub Exchange()
   Dim t As String
   Dim r As String
   Dim Ex(3, 3) As Variant

   t = Chr(9) & Chr(9) ' 2 Tabs
   r = Chr(13) ' Enter

   Ex(1, 1) = "Japan"
   Ex(1, 2) = "Yen"
   Ex(1, 3) = 148.7163
   Ex(2, 1) = "Europe"
```

```
Ex(2, 2) = "Euro"
Ex(2, 3) = 0.9106916
Ex(3, 1) = "Canada"
Ex(3, 2) = "Dollar"
Ex(3, 3) = 1.357208

MsgBox "Country " & t & "Currency" & t & _
  "1 USD" & r & r _
  & Ex(1, 1) & t & Ex(1, 2) & t & Ex(1, 3) & r _
  & Ex(2, 1) & t & Ex(2, 2) & t & Ex(2, 3) & r _
  & Ex(3, 1) & t & Ex(3, 2) & t & Ex(3, 3), , _
  "Exchange Rates"
End Sub
```

3. Run the `Exchange` procedure.
When you run the `Exchange` procedure, you will see a message box with the information presented in three columns, as shown in Figure 6.2.

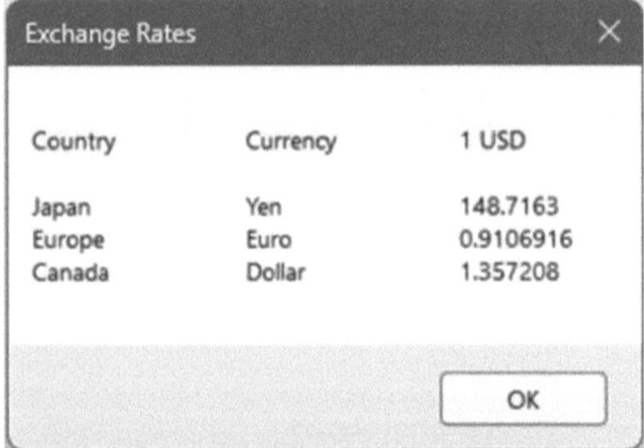

FIGURE 6.2. The text displayed in the message box can be custom formatted. (Note that these are fictitious exchange rates for demonstration only).

4. Click OK to close the message box.

STATIC AND DYNAMIC ARRAYS

The arrays introduced thus far are static. A *static array* is an array of a specific size. You use a static array when you know in advance how big the array should be. The size of the static array is specified in the array's declaration statement. For example, the statement `Dim Fruits(10) As String` declares a static array called `Fruits` that is made up of 10 elements.

What if you're not sure how many elements your array will contain, though? If your procedure depends on user input, the number of user-supplied elements might vary every time the procedure is executed. How can you ensure that the array you declare is not wasting memory?

You may recall that after you declare an array, VBA sets aside enough memory to accommodate the array. If you declare an array to hold more elements than what you need, you'll end up wasting valuable computer resources. The solution to this problem is making your arrays dynamic. A *dynamic array* is an array whose size can change. You use a dynamic array when the array size will be determined each time the procedure is run.

> ### Fixed-Dimension Arrays
>
> A static array contains a fixed number of elements. The number of elements in a static array will not change once it has been declared.

A dynamic array is declared by placing empty parentheses after the array name—for example:

```
Dim Fruits() As String
```

Before you use a dynamic array in your procedure, you must use the `ReDim` statement to dynamically set the lower and upper bounds of the array.

The `ReDim` statement *redimensions* arrays as the procedure code executes. The `ReDim` statement informs Visual Basic about the new size of the array. This statement can be used several times in the same procedure. Now let's write a procedure that demonstrates the use of a dynamic array.

⊙ Hands-On 6.6   Using a Dynamic Array

1. Insert a new module and enter the following `DynArray` procedure in the module's Code window:

```
Sub DynArray()
   Dim counter As Integer
   Dim myArray() As Integer ' declare a dynamic array
   ReDim myArray(5) ' specify the initial size of the array
   Dim myValues As String

   ' populate myArray with values
   For counter = 1 To 5
     myArray(counter) = counter + 1
     myValues = myValues & myArray(counter) & Chr(13)
```

```
  Next

   ' change the size of myArray to hold 10 elements
   ReDim Preserve myArray(10)

   ' add new values to myArray
   For counter = 6 To 10
     myArray(counter) = counter * counter
     myValues = myValues & myArray(counter) & Chr(13)
   Next counter

   MsgBox myValues
   For counter = 1 To 10
     Debug.Print myArray(counter)
   Next counter
End Sub
```

In the `DynArray` procedure, the statement `Dim myArray() As Integer` declares a dynamic array called `myArray`. Although this statement declares the array, it does not allocate any memory to the array. The first `ReDim` statement specifies the initial size of `myArray` and reserves for it 10 bytes of memory to hold its five elements. As you know, every `Integer` value requires 2 bytes of memory. The `For…Next` loop populates `myArray` with data and writes the array's elements to the variable `myValues`. The value of the variable `counter` equals `1` at the beginning of the loop.

The first statement in the loop (`myArray(counter) = counter +1`) assigns the value `2` to the first element of `myArray`. The second statement (`myValues = myValues & myArray(counter) & Chr(13)`) enters the current value of `myArray`'s element followed by a carriage return (`Chr(13)`) into the variable `myValues`. The statements inside the loop are executed five times. Visual Basic places each new value in the variable `myValues` and proceeds to the next statement: `ReDim Preserve myArray(10)`.

Normally, when you change the size of the array, you lose all the values that were in that array. When used alone, the `ReDim` statement reinitializes the array. You can, however, append new elements to an existing array by following the `ReDim` statement with the `Preserve` keyword. In other words, the `Preserve` keyword guarantees that the re-dimensioned array will not lose its existing data.

The second `For…Next` loop assigns values to the sixth through tenth elements of `myArray`. This time, the values of the array's elements are obtained by multiplication: `counter * counter`.

  2. Run the `DynArray` procedure.

> ### Dimensioning Arrays
>
> You can't assign a value to an array element until you have declared the array with the `Dim` or `ReDim` statement. (An exception to this is when you use the `Array` function, discussed in the next section.)

ARRAY FUNCTIONS

You can manipulate arrays with five built-in VBA functions: `Array`, `IsArray`, `Erase`, `LBound`, and `UBound`. The following sections demonstrate the use of each of these functions in VBA procedures.

The Array Function

The `Array` function allows you to create an array during code execution without having to first dimension it. This function always returns an array of `Variant` types. You can quickly place a series of values in a list by using the `Array` function.

The `CarInfo` procedure in the following hands-on exercise creates a fixed-size, one-dimensional, three-element array called `auto`.

◉ Hands-On 6.7   Using the Array Function

1. Insert a new module and enter the following `CarInfo` procedure in the module's Code window:

```
Option Base 1

Sub CarInfo()
  Dim auto As Variant

  auto = Array("Ford", "Black", "2021")
  MsgBox auto(2) & " " & auto(1) & ", " & auto(3)

  auto(2) = "4-door"
  MsgBox auto(2) & " " & auto(1) & ", " & auto(3)
End Sub
```

2. Run the `CarInfo` procedure and examine its results.
   When you run this procedure, you get two message boxes. The first one displays the following text: Black Ford, 2021. After changing the value of the second array element, the second message box will say 4-door Ford, 2021."

> **NOTE**
>
> *Be sure to enter* `Option Base 1` *at the top of the module before running the* `CarInfo` *procedure. If this statement is missing in your module, Visual Basic will display runtime error 9—"Subscript out of range."*

The IsArray Function

The `IsArray` function lets you test whether a variable is an array. The `IsArray` function returns `True` if the variable is an array or `False` if it is not an array. Let's do another hands-on exercise.

Hands-On 6.8   Using the IsArray Function

1. Insert a new module and enter the code of the `IsThisArray` procedure in the module's Code window:

```vba
Sub IsThisArray()
  ' declare a dynamic array
  Dim tblNames() As String
  Dim totalTables As Integer
  Dim counter As Integer
  Dim db As Database

  Set db = CurrentDb

  ' count the tables in the open database
  totalTables = db.TableDefs.Count

  ' specify the size of the array
  ReDim tblNames(1 To totalTables)

  ' enter and show the names of tables
  For counter = 1 To totalTables - 1
    tblNames(counter) = db.TableDefs(counter).Name
    Debug.Print tblNames(counter)
  Next counter

  ' check if this is indeed an array
  If IsArray(tblNames) Then
    MsgBox "The tblNames is an array."
  End If
End Sub
```

2. Run the `IsThisArray` procedure to examine its results.

When you run this procedure, the list of tables in the current database is written to the Immediate window. A message box tells us that the `tblNames` array is indeed an array.

The Erase Function

When you want to remove all data from an array, you should use the `Erase` function. This function deletes all the data held by static or dynamic arrays. In addition, the `Erase` function reallocates all the memory assigned to a dynamic array. If a procedure must use the dynamic array again, you must use the `ReDim` statement to specify the size of the array. The next hands-on exercise demonstrates how to erase the data from the array `cities`.

◉ Hands-On 6.9   Removing Data from an Array

1. Insert a new module and enter the code of the `FunCities` procedure in the module's Code window:

```
' start indexing array elements at 1
Option Base 1

Sub FunCities()
  ' declare the array
  Dim cities(1 To 5) As String

  ' assign the values to array elements
  cities(1) = "Las Vegas"
  cities(2) = "Orlando"
  cities(3) = "Atlantic City"
  cities(4) = "New York"
  cities(5) = "San Francisco"

  ' display the list of cities
  MsgBox cities(1) & Chr(13) & cities(2) & Chr(13) _
    & cities(3) & Chr(13) & cities(4) & Chr(13) _
    & cities(5)

  Erase cities

  ' check if contents of array were erased
  MsgBox cities(1) & Chr(13) & cities(2) & Chr(13) _
    & cities(3) & Chr(13) & cities(4) & Chr(13) _
    & cities(5)
End Sub
```

2. Run the `FunCities` procedure to examine its results.

3. Click OK to close the message box.
Visual Basic should now display an empty message box because all values were deleted from the array by the `Erase` function.

4. Click OK to close the empty message box.

You may be wondering whether there is a quicker and easier way to determine whether the array is empty or contains data. Instead of looping through the array elements, you can use the `Join` function to concatenate all elements of an array into a single string. Recall that you used this function earlier in the book to concatenate the first and last names. The syntax of the `Join` function is shown below:

```
Join (<source array>, [<Delimiter>])
```

The source array is the name of the array whose elements we need to join.

`Delimiter` is the character you'd like to use between the concatenated elements. This is an optional parameter and if it's not provided, a space will be used. If, instead, you provide a zero-length string (""), all elements will be joined without any extra characters in between. Let's see how to use the `Join` function with the `cities` array in the `FunCities_withJoinFunction` procedure.

```
Sub FunCities_withJoinFunction()
  ' declare the array
  Dim cities(1 To 5) As String
  Dim arrayContent As String
  Dim itm As Variant

  ' assign the values to array elements
  cities(1) = "Las Vegas"
  cities(2) = "Orlando"
  cities(3) = "Atlantic City"
  cities(4) = "New York"
  cities(5) = "San Francisco"

  ' display the list of cities
  MsgBox cities(1) & Chr(13) & cities(2) & Chr(13) _
    & cities(3) & Chr(13) & cities(4) & Chr(13) _
    & cities(5)

  ' another way to display the list of cities

    For Each itm In cities
        arrayContent = arrayContent & itm & vbCrLf
```

```
    Next

    MsgBox arrayContent

    ' print list of cities contained in cities array

    arrayContent = Join(cities, ", ")

    Debug.Print arrayContent

    ' erase all content from the cities array

   Erase cities

   arrayContent = Join(cities, "")

   Debug.Print arrayContent

  ' Check if cities array is empty

    If Len(arrayContent) = 0 Then

    Debug.Print "Array is Empty."
   Else
    Debug.Print "Array is not Empty."
    Debug.Print Len(arrayContent)
   End If

End Sub
```

When you run the above procedure, you should see the cities listed in the Immediate window like this:

```
Las Vegas, Orlando, Atlantic City, New York, San Francisco
```

The above string is generated via the following code snippet:

```
    ' print list of cities contained in cities array

    arrayContent = Join(cities, ", ")

    Debug.Print arrayContent
```

In the above code, the string variable `arrayContent` gets its value from the `Join` function, which concatenates the elements of the `cities` array with a comma and a space (", ").

After printing the contents of the `arrayContent` variable to the Immediate window, we call the `Erase` function to erase all the cities we entered in that array. To find out whether the array is indeed empty after we called `Erase`, we again fill the string variable `arrayContent` with the value returned from the `Join` function, but instead of a comma and a space, we use an empty string (`""`) as a delimiter:

```
arrayContent = Join(cities, "")

Debug.Print arrayContent
```

The result of the above is an empty line in the Immediate window. To confirm that the array is indeed empty, we can use the `Len` function to determine the size of the array:

```
' Check if cities array is empty
    If Len(arrayContent) = 0 Then
      Debug.Print "Array is Empty."
   Else
    Debug.Print "Array is not Empty."
    Debug.Print Len(arrayContent)
    End If
```

The LBound and UBound Functions

The `LBound` and `UBound` functions return whole numbers that indicate the lower-bound and upper-bound indices of an array.

Hands-On 6.10   Finding the Lower and Upper Bounds of an Array

1. Insert a new module and enter the code of the `FunCities2` procedure in the module's Code window:

```
Sub FunCities2()
  ' declare the array
  Dim cities(1 To 5) As String

  ' assign the values to array elements
  cities(1) = "Las Vegas"
  cities(2) = "Orlando"
  cities(3) = "Atlantic City"
  cities(4) = "New York"
  cities(5) = "San Francisco"

  ' display the list of cities
  MsgBox cities(1) & Chr(13) & cities(2) & Chr(13) _
    & cities(3) & Chr(13) & cities(4) & Chr(13) _
    & cities(5)
```

```
' display the array bounds
  MsgBox "The lower bound: " & LBound(cities) & Chr(13) _
    & "The upper bound: " & UBound(cities)
End Sub
```

2. Run the `FunCities2` procedure.

3. Click OK to close the message box that displays the favorite cities.

4. Click OK to close the message box that displays the lower- and upper-bound indices.

   To determine the upper and lower indices in a two-dimensional array, you may want to add the following statements at the end of the `Exchange` procedure that was prepared in Hands-On 6.5 (add these lines just before the `End Sub` keywords):

```
MsgBox "The lower bound (first dimension) is " & LBound(Ex, 1) & "."
MsgBox "The upper bound (first dimension) is " & UBound(Ex, 1) & "."
MsgBox "The lower bound (second dimension) is " & LBound(Ex, 2) & "."
MsgBox "The upper bound (second dimension) is " & UBound(Ex, 2) & "."
```

NOTE	*When determining the lower- and upper-bound indices of a two-dimensional array, you must specify the dimension number:* 1 *for the first dimension and* 2 *for the second dimension.*

ERRORS IN ARRAYS

When working with arrays, it's easy to make a mistake. If you try to assign more values than there are elements in the declared array, Visual Basic will display the error message Subscript out of range (see Figure 6.3).

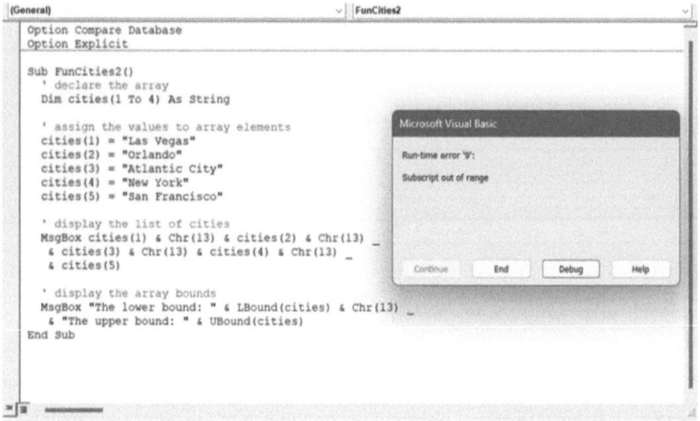

FIGURE 6.3.   This run-time error was caused by an attempt to access a nonexistent array element.

Suppose you declared a one-dimensional array that consists of four elements, and you are trying to assign a value to the fifth element. When you run the procedure, Visual Basic can't find the fifth element, so it displays the error message shown in Figure 6.3. If you click the Debug button, Visual Basic will highlight the line of code that caused the error (see Figure 6.4).

```
Option Compare Database
Option Explicit

Sub FunCities2()
  ' declare the array
  Dim cities(1 To 4) As String

  ' assign the values to array elements
  cities(1) = "Las Vegas"
  cities(2) = "Orlando"
  cities(3) = "Atlantic City"
  cities(4) = "New York"
  cities(5) = "San Francisco"

  ' display the list of cities
  MsgBox cities(1) & Chr(13) & cities(2) & Chr(13) _
    & cities(3) & Chr(13) & cities(4) & Chr(13) _
    & cities(5)

  ' display the array bounds
  MsgBox "The lower bound: " & LBound(cities) & Chr(13) _
    & "The upper bound: " & UBound(cities)
End Sub
```

FIGURE 6.4.   The statement that triggered the error shown in Figure 6.3. is highlighted.

Another frequent error you may encounter while working with arrays is a Type Mismatch error. To avoid this error, keep in mind that each element of an array must be of the same data type. Therefore, if you attempt to assign to an element of an array a value that conflicts with the data type of the array, you will get a Type Mismatch error during the code execution. If you need to hold values of different data types in an array, declare the array as `Variant`.

PARAMETER ARRAYS

In Chapter 3, you learned that values can be passed between subroutines or functions as either required or optional arguments. If the passed argument is not absolutely required for the procedure to execute, the argument's name is preceded by the keyword `Optional`. Sometimes, however, you don't know in advance how many arguments you want to pass. A classic example is addition. One time you may want to add 2 numbers together, while another time you may want to add 3, 10, or 15 numbers.

Using the keyword `ParamArray`, you can pass an array consisting of any number of elements to your subprocedures and functions. The following hands-on exercise uses the `AddMultipleArgs` function to add as many numbers as you may require. This function begins with the declaration of an array, `myNumbers`. Notice the use of the `ParamArray` keyword.

The array must be declared as the type Variant, and it must be the last argument in the procedure definition.

Hands-On 6.11   Working with Parameter Arrays

1. Insert a new module and enter the following `AddMultipleArgs` function procedure in the module's Code window:

```
Function AddMultipleArgs(ParamArray myNumbers() As Variant)
    Dim mySum As Single
    Dim myValue As Variant

    For Each myValue In myNumbers
    mySum = mySum + myValue
    Next
    AddMultipleArgs = mySum
End Function
```

2. Choose View | Immediate Window and type the following instruction, and then press Enter to execute it:

```
?AddMultipleArgs(1, 23.24, 3, 24, 8, 34)
```

When you press Enter, Visual Basic returns the total of all the numbers in the parentheses: `93.24`. You can supply an unlimited number of arguments. To add more values, enter additional values in the parentheses after the function name in the Immediate window, and then press Enter. Notice that each function argument must be separated by a comma.

PASSING ARRAYS TO FUNCTION PROCEDURES

You can pass an array to a function procedure and return an array from a function. For example, let's assume you have a list of countries. You want to convert the country names stored in your array to uppercase and keep the original array intact. You can delegate the conversion process to a function procedure. When the array is passed using the `ByVal` keyword, the function will work with the copy of the original array. Any modifications performed within the function will affect only the copy. Therefore, the array in the calling procedure will not be modified.

◉ Hands-On 6.12   Passing an Array to a Function Procedure

1. Insert a new module and enter the following procedure and function in the module's Code window:

```vba
Sub ManipulateArray()
  Dim countries(1 To 6) As Variant
  Dim countriesUCase As Variant
  Dim i As Integer

  ' assign the values to array elements
  countries(1) = "Bulgaria"
  countries(2) = "Argentina"
  countries(3) = "Brazil"
  countries(4) = "Sweden"
  countries(5) = "New Zealand"
  countries(6) = "Denmark"

  countriesUCase = ArrayToUCase(countries)

  For i = LBound(countriesUCase) To UBound(countriesUCase)
    Debug.Print countriesUCase(i)
    Debug.Print countries(i) & " (Original Entry)"
  Next i
End Sub

Public Function ArrayToUCase(ByVal myValues _
 As Variant) As String()
  Dim i As Integer
  Dim Temp() As String
  If IsArray(myValues) Then
    ReDim Temp(LBound(myValues) To UBound(myValues))
    For i = LBound(myValues) To UBound(myValues)
      Temp(i) = UCase(myValues(i))
    Next i
    ArrayToUCase = Temp
  End If
End Function
```

2. Run the `ManipulateArray` procedure and check its results in the Immediate window.

SORTING AN ARRAY

We all find it easier to work with sorted data. Some operations on arrays, such as finding maximum and minimum values, require that the array is sorted. Once it is sorted, you can find the maximum value by assigning the upper-bound index to the sorted array, as in the following:

```
y = myIntArray(UBound(myIntArray))
```

The minimum value can be obtained by reading the first value of the sorted array:

```
x = myIntArray(1)
```

So, how can you sort an array? Hands-On 6.13 demonstrates how to delegate the sorting task to a classic bubble sort routine. A *bubble sort* is a comparison sort. To create a sorted set, you step through the list to be sorted, compare each pair of adjacent items, and swap them if they are in the wrong order. As a result of this sorting algorithm, the smaller values "bubble" to the top of the list. In the next procedure, we will sort the list of countries alphabetically in ascending order.

Hands-On 6.13   Sorting an Array

This hands-on exercise requires prior completion of Hands-On 6.12.

1. In the same module where you entered the `ArrayToUCase` function procedure, enter the following `BubbleSort` function procedure:

```
Sub BubbleSort(myArray As Variant)
    Dim i As Integer
    Dim j As Integer
    Dim uBnd As Integer
    Dim Temp As Variant
    uBnd = UBound(myArray)
      For i = LBound(myArray) To uBnd - 1
        For j = i + 1 To uBnd
          If UCase(myArray(i)) > UCase(myArray(j)) Then
            Temp = myArray(j)
            myArray(j) = myArray(i)
            myArray(i) = Temp
          End If
        Next j
      Next i
End Sub
```

2. Add the following statements to the `ManipulateArray` procedure, placing them just above the `For...Next` statement block (see Figure 6.5):

```
' call function to sort the array
  BubbleSort countriesUCase
```

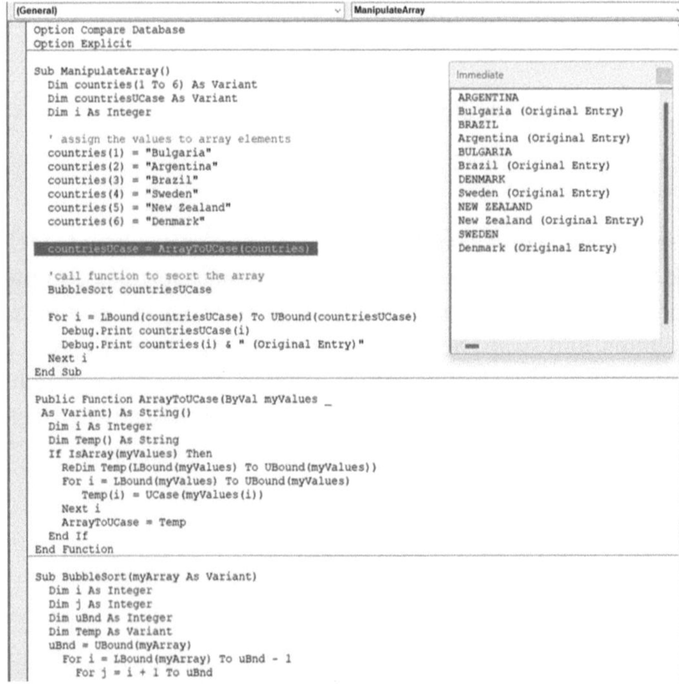

FIGURE 6.5.   Calling the BubbleSort function procedure from the ManipulateArray procedure.

3. Run the `ManipulateArray` procedure and check its results in the Immediate window. Notice that the countries that appear in uppercase letters are shown in alphabetic order.

4. Choose File | Save Chap06 and save the changes to the modules when prompted.

5. Choose File | Close and Return to Microsoft Access.

6. Close the `Chap06.accdb` database.

USING ChatGPT WITH ACCESS

Leveraging ChatGPT, or any other advanced AI tool, can significantly enhance your proficiency in using arrays in Access VBA programming. You can ask

ChatGPT to explain both basic and advanced concepts, such as dynamic arrays, multidimensional arrays, or array functions. Oftentimes, reading the same information from different sources reinforces our understanding of the topic we want to be proficient in.

For this exercise, ask ChatGPT to write a VBA procedure that declares, initializes, and manipulates arrays. Write your own procedures that use the built-in array functions and ask ChatGPT to offer improvements. Remember that you can share your own code with ChatGPT and get immediate feedback.

User Prompt: *Write a VBA procedure that declares, initializes, and manipulates arrays.*

ChatGPT/Microsoft Copilot's Response:
Here's a simple VBA procedure that demonstrates how to declare, initialize, and manipulate arrays. This procedure will declare a one-dimensional array, populate it with values, and then perform some basic manipulations like finding the maximum value and summing all the elements.

The complete chat is included in the companion files—see `Chapter 6 - Using ChatGPT with Access.`

SUMMARY

In this chapter, you learned how, by creating an array, you can write procedures that require a large number of variables. You worked with examples of procedures that demonstrated how to declare and use a one-dimensional array (list) and a two-dimensional array (table). You learned the difference between static and dynamic arrays. This chapter introduced you to five built-in VBA functions that are frequently used with arrays (`Array`, `IsArray`, `Erase`, `LBound`, and `UBound`), as well as the `ReDim` and `ParamArray` keywords. In addition, you learned how to use the `Join` and `Len` functions to determine whether the array contains any data. You also learned how to pass one array and return another array from a function procedure. Finally, you saw how to sort an array. You now know all the VBA control structures that can make your code more intelligent: conditional statements, loops, and arrays.

In the next chapter, you will learn how collections instead of arrays can be used to manipulate large amounts of data.

Chapter 7

KEEPING TRACK OF MULTIPLE VALUES USING COLLECTIONS

In the previous chapter, you learned how arrays are used to quickly and easily manipulate a large number of items. Instead of creating multiple variables to keep track of your data, you only need to declare an array. Using arrays instead of defining individual variables saves you from writing many lines of repetitive code. As you have seen so far, in programming, there are many ways of performing the same task. The method you use depends on your needs. So it is with storing multiple values. In addition to arrays, you can maintain your items of data while your program is running by using a special type of object—a collection. Like arrays, collections are used for grouping variables.

Because collections have built-in properties and methods that allow you to add, remove, access, and count their elements, they make working with multiple data items much easier than arrays. Collections can also be used to hold objects. This is a more advanced feature of object-oriented programming that we'll focus on later in this book. For now, let's learn the basic skills of using collections for tracking and maintaining data in your VBA procedures.

CREATING YOUR OWN COLLECTION

A collection is an object that represents a group of related items in VBA. It is a data type in VBA that allows you to store, manage, and manipulate a set of elements, such as numbers, strings, or other objects.

To create a collection, begin by declaring an object variable of the `Collection` data type. This variable is declared with the `New` keyword using the `Dim` statement, like this:

```
Dim CollectionName As New Collection
```

The `CollectionName` is the name of your collection. You can use any name so long as it is not one of the reserved words Access uses for its own collections or other internal operations. You can define more than one collection, but each collection you define should have a distinct name so you can easily reference it in your code. Collections can be defined at the top of the standard module or within a procedure. They can also be defined in `Class` modules. Notice that unlike arrays, collections do not require you to predefine their size. Once you define an object variable of the `Collection` type, you are ready to begin adding items to it.

Adding Items to Your Collection

You can insert new items into a collection by using the `Add` method. The items with which you populate your collection do not have to be of the same data type. The `Add` method looks as follows:

```
object.Add item[, key, before, after]
```

The `object` is the name you defined for your collection when you declared it. For example, if the name of your collection is `colFruits`, the following statements show how you can add several fruits to this collection:

```
colFruits.Add "Apple"
colFruits.Add "Pear"
colFruits.Add "Strawberry"
colFruits.Add "Blueberry"
colFruits.Add "Orange"
colFruits.Add "Peach"
```

Although the other arguments are optional, they are quite useful. It's important to understand that the items in a user-defined collection are automatically assigned numbers starting from 1. They can, however, also be assigned a unique key value. At the time an object is added to a collection, you can assign a key for that object. A key could be a text string or a number representing an ID of the item being added. For instance:

```
colFruits.Add "Apple", Key:= "frApe"
colFruits.Add "Pear", Key:= "frPer"
```

To identify an individual in a collection of students or employees, you could use their `EmployeeID` or `StudentID`. For example, here's how you can add `John Smith` to the `colPeople` collection, using his `EmployeeID` as a key:

```
Dim colPeople as New Collection
colPeople.Add "John Smith", Key:="123456"
```

If you need to specify the position of the object in the collection, you can use either the `Before` or `After` argument (but not both). The `Before` argument is the object before which the new object is added. The `After` argument is the object after which the new object is added. For example, to add `Kiwi` to the `colFruits` collection so that it appears after the second item, use the following statement:

```
colFruits.Add "Kiwi", , , 2
```

Or:

```
colFruits.Add "Kiwi", After:=2
```

Notice that if you are not using the named argument `After`, you must place a comma for each of the preceding optional arguments that you are not specifying.

To enter `Cherry` in the first position, use the named `Before` argument:

```
colFruits.Add "Cherry", Before:=1
```

By using the optional `Before` or `After` argument, you can easily add elements to your collection in any position.

Each element of a collection can be of a different data type. Please note that arrays can support different data types only if they are defined as `Variant` types. To store a date item in your collection, use the following statement:

```
colFruits.Add #12/10/2021#, Key:="InvoiceDate"
```

To store a number in your collection, the following statement can be used:

```
colFruits.Add 100.99, Key:="InvoiceTotal"
```

Determine the Number of Items in Your Collection

Use the `Count` property to find the number of items in your collection. To determine the current number of fruit items in `colFruits`, write the following statement:

```
Debug.Print colFruits.Count
```

Accessing Items in a Collection

To refer to a specific item in your collection, use its index or key value.

For example, to find out the name of the first collection item, use this statement:

```
Debug.Print colFruits.Item(1)
```

Because the `Item` method is a default method of the collection, you may omit it from the statement, as shown here:

```
Debug.Print colFruits(1)
```

If you know the item key, then you can quickly retrieve it like this:

```
Debug.Print colPeople("123456")
```

By using the key to access a collection item, you can go to it directly without the need to iterate through all the items. Access VBA does not provide a built-in method to check whether the key exists, but you can write your own function to return a Boolean value of `True` if the key exists. Here's how you would do it:

```
Function KeyExists(colName As Collection, _
        key As String) As Boolean
    On Error GoTo EndHere
    IsObject (colName.Item(key))
    KeyExists = True

EndHere:
End Function
```

See Hands-On 7.1 on how to call the `KeyExists` function from your procedure code. The `IsObject` is a built-in VBA function that returns `True` if the expression passed to it (i.e., the key name) represents an object variable. The statement `OnError GoTo EndHere` tells Access to jump to the line `EndHere:` if the result of the `IsObject` function is `False`. The error-handling statements introduced here are covered in detail in Chapter 8.

When using keys in your collection, keep in mind another caveat: you cannot update the value stored in the key unless the collection item was defined as an object. We focus on using objects in collections in the advanced chapters of this book.

Removing Items from a Collection

Removing an item from your custom collection is as easy as adding an item. To remove an item, use the `Remove` method in the following format:

```
object.Remove index
```

`object` is the name of the custom collection that contains the object you want to remove. `index` is an expression specifying the position of the object in the collection. To remove the third fruit item from `colFruits`, you simply write the following statement:

```
colFruits.Remove 3
```

Collections are reindexed automatically when an item is removed. Therefore, to remove all items from a custom collection, you can use 1 for the `Index` argument, as in the following example:

```
Do While colFruits.Count > 0
  colFruits.Remove Index:=1
Loop
```

Another way to remove all objects from your collection is by using the `For Each...Next` loop. For example, to remove all objects from `colFruits`, use the following looping structure:

```
Dim m As Variant


For Each m in colFruits
  colFruits.Remove 1
Next
```

Note that the control variable (`m`) used in the `For Each...Next` loop must be declared as the `Variant` or `Object` data type. Because collections are reindexed, the preceding statement will remove the first item of the collection on each iteration. After the loop completes, `colFruits` should have zero items. To be sure, however, use the `Count` property to find out.

```
Debug.Print colFruits.Count
```

You can also remove all items from a collection by setting the collection object variable to a new collection, like this:

```
Set colFruits = New Collection
```

Updating Items in a Collection

When you add an item to your collection that has a basic data type, such as `String`, `Integer`, `Long`, `Currency`, or `Date`, your collection will be read-only. This means you will not be able to change the value of the item. Access will display an error if you try to assign a value to an existing item in your collection:

```
' this statement will produce Run-time
' error 424 'Object required'
colFruits(4) = "Cranberry"
```

Therefore, if your procedure requires that the values be updated, you should group your items into an array. If you want to, stick with the collection to change an item, remove an item, and add a new one. The only time that a collection is updatable is when it references objects. You will use objects with collections in a later chapter.

Let's proceed to the first hands-on exercise in this chapter, where you will put all your knowledge about collections into a VBA procedure.

> **NOTE** *All code files and figures for the hands-on projects may be found in the companion files.*

◉ Hands-On 7.1   Creating and Manipulating a Custom Collection

1. Start Access and create a new database named `Chap07.accdb` in your `C:\VBAAccess2024_ByExample` folder.
2. Switch to the VBE window and insert a new standard module.
3. In the Module1 (Code) window, enter the following `WorkWith_Collection`, `Display_Items`, and `KeyExists` procedures.

```
Sub WorkWith_Collection()
    Dim colFruits As New Collection
    Dim itm As Variant
    Dim strColItems As String

    colFruits.Add "Apple"
    colFruits.Add "Pear"
    colFruits.Add "Strawberry"
    colFruits.Add "Blueberry"
```

```vba
colFruits.Add "Orange"
colFruits.Add "Peach"
colFruits.Add "Kiwi", , , 2
colFruits.Add "Mango", , 5
colFruits.Add "Cherry", Before:=1
colFruits.Add 100.99, Key:="InvoiceTotal"
colFruits.Add #12/10/2021#, Key:="InvoiceDate"

Debug.Print "Total Items in colFruits: " & colFruits.Count

'call a procedure to display all items in the collection
Display_Items colFruits, itm

colFruits.Remove 3
Debug.Print "New Total Items in colFruits: " & colFruits.Count

For Each itm In colFruits
    strColItems = strColItems & ", " & itm
Next

' remove a comma and a space from the beginning of
' the strColItems variable
strColItems = Mid(strColItems, 3, Len(strColItems))
Debug.Print strColItems

'Find if keys exist and if not display a message
'and go to the next line

If KeyExists(colFruits, "InvoiceDate") And _
    KeyExists(colFruits, "InvoiceTotal") Then
Debug.Print "Invoiced on: " & colFruits("InvoiceDate") & _
    vbCrLf & "Total: " & colFruits("InvoiceTotal")
Else
    MsgBox "Provided key(s) not found."
End If

' Remove all items from collection one by one
For Each itm In colFruits
    colFruits.Remove 1
Next
Debug.Print "Total Items in colFruits: " & colFruits.Count

End Sub


Sub Display_Items(col As Collection, myItm As Variant)

For Each myItm In col
```

```
        Debug.Print myItm
    Next
End Sub

Function KeyExists(colName As Collection, _
        key As String) As Boolean

    On Error GoTo EndHere

    IsObject (colName.Item(key))
    KeyExists = True

EndHere:
End Function
```

4. Choose **Run | Run Sub/UserForm** to execute the `WorkWith_Collection` procedure.
5. The `WorkWith_Collection` procedure performs various operations on the declared collection object variable, `colFruits`. Notice how this procedure uses the function procedure to check whether the specified key exists in the collection and how you can list all the items in your collection using a `For…Each` statement in a separate procedure.
6. The `WorkWith_Collection` procedure also uses two built-in VBA `String` functions—`Mid` and `Len`—to remove the first two characters from the `strColItems` string variable, leaving you with everything from the third character onward. The `Mid` function extracts a substring from `strColItems` starting at the third character position. The `Len` function returns the length of `strColItems`. Therefore, the substring starts at the third character and continues for the full length of `strColItems`. Use the `Mid` and `Len` functions together when you need to strip out a prefix or other leading characters from a string.
7. If you plan on using the same collection in other procedures in the same module, you will need to move its variable declaration statement to the top of the module.

Returning a Collection from a Function

Collections, like arrays, can be used as parameters or return values to functions or subroutine procedures. In Hands-On 7.2, you will collect entries from the user via the VBA `InputBox` function and store them in an array. After that, you will pass that array to a function and return a collection with the same items. Let's see how this is done.

Hands-On 7.2   Creating and Manipulating a Custom Collection

1. Choose Insert | Module to add a new standard module to the current VBA project.
2. In the Code window, enter the code as shown below and run the `ShowCollItems` procedure.
   Notice that the `allItems` variable is declared at the top of the module (above all the procedure code). This placement will make this variable available to all the procedures in this module.

```vba
Dim allItems As String

Sub ShowCollItems()
    Dim coll As Collection
    Dim myArray As Variant
    Dim itm As Variant

    ' get items from user input
    If AskForItems <> "" Then
        Debug.Print allItems
        ' extract items from the user input string (allItems)
        ' and place them in an array
        myArray = Split(allItems, ",")
        Debug.Print "Array has " & UBound(myArray) + 1 & " items."

        ' call function to create a collection from the array
        Set coll = CreateCollection(myArray)

        ' iterate through the collection to display each item
        For Each itm In coll
            Debug.Print itm
        Next
        Debug.Print "Total items in the collection: " & coll.Count
    End If
End Sub

Function AskForItems() As String
  allItems = InputBox("Enter your items separated by a comma", _
        "Demo - Get User Input", _
        "item1, item2")

  If allItems = "" Then
    AskForItems = ""
  Else
```

```vba
        AskForItems = allItems
    End If
End Function

Function CreateCollection(arrMyItems As Variant) As Collection
    Dim coll As New Collection
    Dim i As Integer
    For i = 0 To UBound(arrMyItems)
        coll.Add arrMyItems(i)
    Next i
    'Return a collection
    Set CreateCollection = coll
End Function
```

These three procedures work together to get user input, split it into an array, convert that array into a collection, and then display the collection items.

The module-level string variable `allItems` is declared to store user input.

The main procedure `ShowCollItems` declares three variables that we need for working with both the array and collection. The `If` block performs several tasks. First, we call the `AskForItems` function to get the user input. If the input is not empty, we print the user input to the Immediate window. In the `AskForItems` function, the user is prompted to enter items separated by commas. The user input is stored in the `allItems` variable. If no items are entered, the returned input will be an empty string, and the `ShowColItems` will not have any code to execute, therefore it will end.

Next, back in the `ShowColItems` procedure, we use the VBA built-in function `Split` to break the input string (`allItems`) into an array based on commas, and we store it in an array variable, `myArray`:

```vba
myArray = Split(allItems, ",")
```

After printing the number of items in the array, we call the `CreateCollection` function to convert the array into a collection:

```vba
Set coll = CreateCollection(myArray)
```

The declared object variable `coll` will be assigned a collection received from this function.

To do this, we set the `coll` variable to the result obtained from the `CreateCollection` function. We call the `CreateCollection` function and pass it to the `myArray` variable. Notice that `myArray` was declared as a `Variant` and the `CreateCollection` function was defined to expect a parameter of the `Variant` type.

Inside the `CreateCollection` function, we start by declaring the `coll` variable of the `Collection` type. We also need a counter (`i`) to loop through the items of the array variable that we passed to this function. Note that the parameter name that the `CreateCollection` function expects can be any name you define.

Using the `For…Next` loop, we loop through the items of the array, starting from 0, and add each array item to the collection. Once we are done looping, we pass the entire collection to the calling procedure `ShowCollItems`.

Note that `coll` is an object variable, so we need to use the Set keyword to return it from the function:

```
'Return a collection
Set CreateCollection = coll
```

Now we are back again in the `ShowCollItems` procedure, this time returning a collection. To view the collection items, we use the `For  Each…Next` loop to print each item to the Immediate window. Note that the `itm` iterator must be defined as `Variant`. The procedure ends by printing the total number of collection items.

The code in this hands-on exercise effectively demonstrated how you can collect user input, process it, and utilize arrays and collections to manage and display the data.

COLLECTIONS VS. ARRAYS

As you have seen so far, both collections and arrays provide a convenient way of storing and manipulating groups of similar items. Most people find collections easier to use and master than arrays. Before you decide which grouping structure to use for storing items in your program, however, ensure you examine your needs. Arrays are usually faster and more convenient to use if you know ahead of time the number of items you are going to store. If the number of elements varies and you often need to add and remove elements, collections may be more efficient to use.

Let's do a features comparison of collections versus arrays.

- Custom collections you create use 1 by default as the first element. Arrays by default are zero-based. You need to use the `Option Base 1` statement to force the numbering of array items to start at position 1.

- You don't need to specify the size of your collection upfront as collections are dynamically allocated. Arrays, on the other hand, require that you define their size, and if you need to change the array size further in your procedure, you must use the `ReDim` keyword. Each time you re-dimension the array, Access takes up more resources.

- It's easy to add or remove items from a collection with the `Add` and `Remove` methods. With arrays, before you can add or remove items, you need to find the size of the array by using its upper and lower bounds.

- You can add new items to a collection in any position. To perform the same task using arrays, you must write more code.

- Collections can store items of different data types. Arrays can only store items of different data types when they are declared as a `Variant`.

- You can use the `For` and `For Each` loops to access items in a collection, while with arrays, you must first set and verify the upper and lower bounds to iterate through the items.

- Collections allow you to use keys to access a particular item directly, while arrays don't provide this feature. If you want to access items using keys, use the `Dictionary` object instead of the `Collection` object. We will examine this object later in this book.

WATCHING THE EXECUTION OF YOUR VBA PROCEDURES

To help you understand what's going on when your code runs and how one procedure passes information to a function and receives back the function's result, let's walk through the `ShowCollItems` procedure you created in Hands-On 7.2. Treat this exercise as a brief introduction to the debugging techniques that are covered in detail in the next chapter.

Hands-On 7.3   Code Walkthrough

1. In the Module2 (Code) window, locate the `ShowCollItems` procedure.
2. Set a breakpoint by clicking in the left margin next to the following line of code, as shown in Figure 7.1:

```
If AskForItems <> "" Then
```

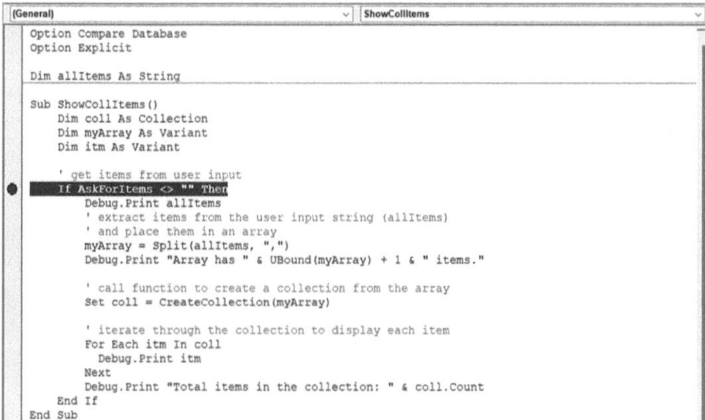

FIGURE 7.1.   A red circle in the margin indicates a breakpoint. The statement with a breakpoint is displayed as white text on a red background.

3. Choose View | Immediate Window and position the window next to the procedure, as shown in Figure 7.2.
4. Click anywhere within the code of the ShowCollItems procedure and press F5 or choose Run | Run Sub/User Form.
   Visual Basic should now jump to the line where you set a breakpoint (see Figures 7.1 and 7.2).

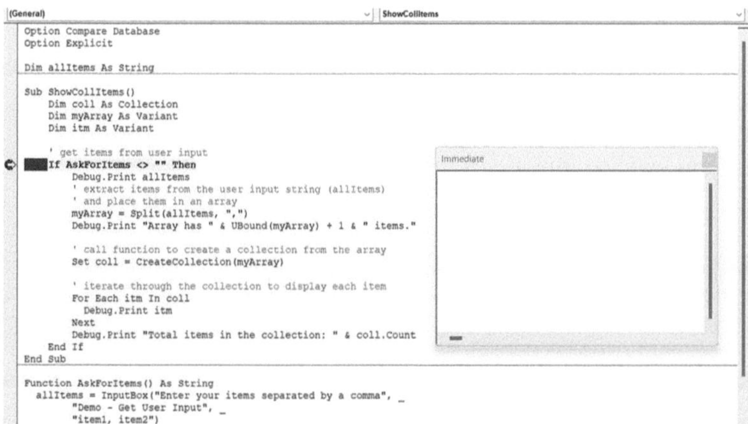

FIGURE 7.2.   When Visual Basic encounters a breakpoint while running a procedure, it switches to the Code window and displays a yellow arrow in the margin to the left of the statement at which the procedure is suspended.

5. Let's step through the code one statement at a time by pressing F8.
Visual Basic runs the current statement, which in this case is a call to the `AskForItems` function procedure. The yellow highlight moves to the line with the name of this function, as shown in Figure 7.3.

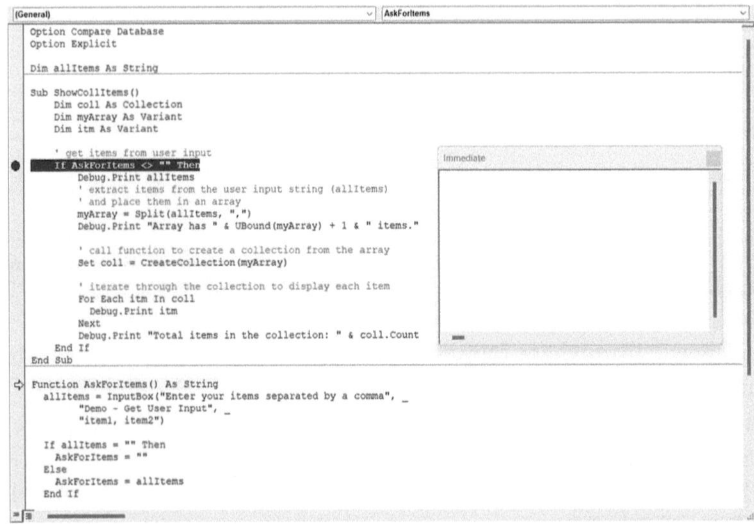

FIGURE 7.3.   When you press the F8 key, you activate a step mode when each press of the key jumps to the next line of code, allowing you to step through the procedure.

6. Press F8 again and the highlight should move to the first line of the function procedure. Press F8 again to execute this line.
You should now be presented with the Input box, where you need to enter the items you want to include in the array (see Figure 7.4). Notice that Access activates its main application window when you call the `InputBox` function.

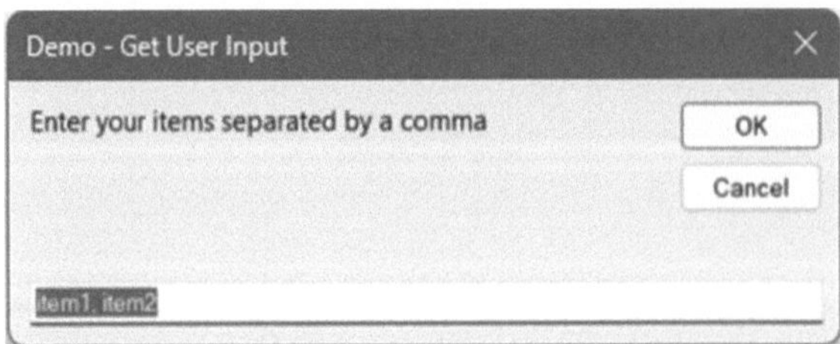

FIGURE 7.4.   The Function procedure asks for items separated by a comma. These items will be used to fill an array variable.

7. Enter four names of your best friends or family members, or any items you want, separated by a comma, and click OK. Clicking Cancel will terminate the procedure.

When you click OK, Access executes all the lines of the current function procedure and other code that was put in the `ShowCollItems` procedure and the `CreateCollection` function. You should see the Immediate window filled with the data you entered (see Figure 7.5).

All the `Debug` statements in your procedures wrote results to the Immediate window while the code was executing.

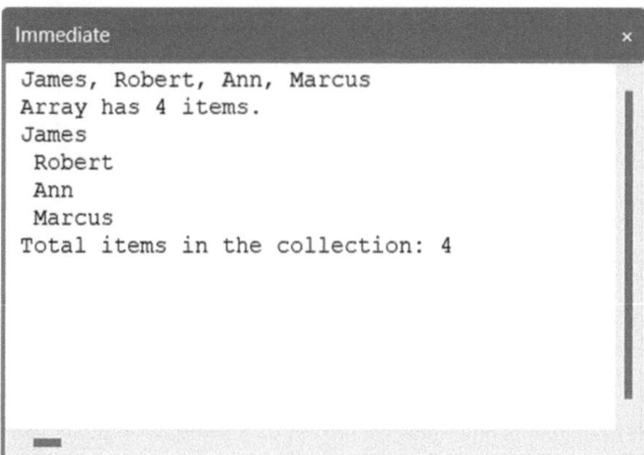

FIGURE 7.5.   The Immediate window is populated with the data generated by the Debug Print statements.

This was a quick runthrough of the VBA procedure. To go slower and gain more understanding of what's happening in the code, you need to put in more breakpoints next to the lines where you would like Visual Basic to temporarily stop the code execution.

8. Erase the data in the Immediate window by clicking anywhere within it, then press Ctrl+A, and then Delete.

Let's add more breakpoints and execute the procedure again.

9. Add the breakpoints as shown in Figure 7.6.

FIGURE 7.6.   Adding multiple breakpoints on important lines in VBA procedures allows you to better troubleshoot the code you've written or received from others.

10. Start from step 4 above to execute the procedure again. After you've entered your items in the Input box, you should be returned to the Code window with the yellow highlight positioned on the next statement in the `AskForItems` function procedure, as shown in Figure 7.7.

```
Function AskForItems() As String
    allItems = InputBox("Enter your items separated by a comma",
        "Demo - Get User Input",
        "item1, item2")

    If allItems = "" Then
      AskForItems = ""
    Else
      AskForItems = allItems
    End If
End Function
```

FIGURE 7.7.   Because there was a breakpoint on the line that calls the InputBox function, when this line executes, the yellow highlight is moved to the next statement in the function, indicating that this is the next statement to be executed.

While your procedure execution is in break mode with the yellow highlight on some code statement, you can use the Immediate window to find out the contents of your variables or issue other commands that will allow you to check the returned values. Let's find out what's in the `allItems` variable.

11. In the Immediate window, type the following and press Enter:

```
?allItems
```

You should see a list of the items as you entered them into the Input box. Here are my items:

```
Monday, Tuesday, Wednesday, Thursday
```

12. Keep pressing F8 to execute the function procedure step by step. The yellow highlight should eventually move to the line that tells Visual Basic to return the `allItems` variable from this function:

```
AskForItems = allItems
```

13. Press F8 until the execution moves to the `ShowAllItems` procedure. Press F8 and you should see the output of the `Debug.Print allItems` statement in the Immediate window.

14. Press F8 again when the yellow highlight reaches the line that uses the `Split` function to extract items from the `allItems` string variable into the `myArray` variable:

```
myArray = Split(allItems, ",")
```

15. Press F8 to fill the `myArray` variable.

16. Find the first element of the `myArray` variable by typing the following in the Immediate window and pressing Enter:

```
?myArray(0)
```

You should see the first item you entered.

17. Continue pressing the F8 key and examining each line of code until the execution moves to the `CreateCollection` function procedure.

18. Press F8 again to move to the `For Next` loop within the `CreateCollection` procedure. Let's use the Immediate window to find out what was passed to this function.

19. In the Immediate window, type `?Ubound(arrMyItems)` and press Enter. You should see the count of the total items you entered. Recall that arrays are zero-based by default, so the actual count is `?Ubound(arrMyItems) + 1`.

20. Press F8 until you are out of the loop that adds individual array items to the `coll` object variable.
21. When you reach the last statement of the `CreateCollection` procedure (`Set CreateCollection = coll`), type `?coll.count` to return the total number of items in your collection.
22. Press F8 to pass the collection back to the calling procedure (`ShowAllItems`) and exit the function by pressing F8 again.
    Now, you should be positioned on the next statement in the `ShowAllItems` procedure. This statement will loop through the collection as you continue pressing F8. All collection items and the total count will be written to the Immediate window.
23. Press F8 until you reach the end of the procedure. The code execution will stop. You can repeat this entire walkthrough for more practice before we clear the breakpoints in the next step.
24. Select Debug | Clear All Breakpoints.
25. Choose File | Close and Return to Microsoft Access.
26. Close the `Chap07.accdb` database and exit Access.

> ### VBA Debugging Tools
>
> Visual Basic provides many debugging tools to help you analyze how your application operates, as well as to locate the source of errors in your procedures. See the next chapter for details on working with these tools.

USING ChatGPT WITH ACCESS

In Access VBA, you can also write VBA programming code to accomplish tasks that are not directly related to Access or other Microsoft 365 applications. For instance, let's ask the ChatGPT assistant to write a procedure that accesses data outside of Access but is based on this chapter's topic. Think of what else you can store in a collection. How about getting a list of files from a specific folder on your computer and printing their names out to the Immediate window?

User Prompt: *How can I store a folder's files in a collection by using Access VBA?*

ChatGPT/Microsoft Copilot's Response:
Code Example

```
Sub StoreFilesInCollection()
```

```
Dim colFiles As New Collection
Dim strFolder As String
Dim strFile As String

' Specify the folder path
strFolder = "C:\YourFolderPath\"

' Get the first file in the folder
strFile = Dir(strFolder & "*.*")

' Loop through all files in the folder
Do While strFile <> ""
    ' Add the file to the collection
    colFiles.Add strFile

    ' Get the next file
    strFile = Dir
Loop

' Display the file names in the Immediate Window
Dim itm As Variant
For Each itm In colFiles
    Debug.Print itm
Next itm
End Sub
```

After reading a bunch of explanations about the provided code I was instructed to replace the folder path with the actual path of my folder and then I ran the procedure. It worked beautifully; all the `.mp3` files in my `AudioFiles` folder quickly showed up in the Immediate window. Then I thought, let's try another folder. As I'm writing this book, I have all my chapter files in a `2024 Access Programming Book` folder on my drive `D`. Well, the procedure did not work as I had spaces in the folder name. I created another prompt to share my problem with ChatGPT:

User Prompt: *The procedure you wrote does not work when the folder has spaces in the name.*

ChatGPT/Microsoft Copilot's Response:
Ah, got it. Let's tweak it to handle folder paths with spaces. The simplest way is to use double quotes around the folder path. Here's the updated procedure:
It gave me the same procedure in which the folder path was changed to:

```
strFolder = """C:\Your Folder Path With Spaces\"""
```

Now I ran the procedure with the name of my folder that contained spaces. Well, it still did not work. I told ChatGPT that I proceeded as instructed but now I got an *error 52, bad file name or number.*

The response was:
Ah, I see. The issue might not be with the spaces but with the way the folder path is being handled. Let's adjust it to ensure it works correctly, especially if the folder path contains spaces. Try this approach, using ChDir to change the directory and then listing the files.
    The same code was given, now with the extra statement on the line following the path assignment:

```
' Change to the target directory
    ChDir strFolder
```

I knew off the bat that this didn't seem like a good answer, but I gave it a try anyway. Of course, nothing happened; it did not work for me. So, going back to ChatGPT, frustrated, I entered this prompt:

User Prompt: *Think harder. None of this works. The folder name is "D:\2024 Access Programming Book\".*

The response seemed more promising:
    Alright, let's get this sorted. Sometimes paths with spaces and specific folder structures can trip up the Dir function. Let's use the FileSystemObject instead.
    This was followed by a modified procedure that now used the exact path of my folder:

```
Sub StoreFilesInCollection()
    Dim colFiles As New Collection
    Dim fso As Object
    Dim folder As Object
    Dim file As Object

    ' Create FileSystemObject
    Set fso = CreateObject("Scripting.FileSystemObject")

    ' Get the folder
    Set folder = fso.GetFolder("D:\2024 Access Programming Book\")

    ' Loop through each file in the folder
    For Each file In folder.Files
        colFiles.Add file.Name
    Next file
```

```
    ' Display the file names in the Immediate Window
    Dim itm As Variant
    For Each itm In colFiles
        Debug.Print itm
    Next itm
End Sub
```

I ran the modified procedure and, as in the first example with the `AudioFiles`, I was finally able to obtain the full list of my book files, and the folder name was no longer a problem.

The `FileSystemObject` is covered in detail later in this book as we proceed to more advanced topics.

As you can see from this chat, you can sharpen your VBA skills with these sorts of interactions with ChatGPT. Any challenge you face or curiosity you have—whether it's learning new concepts or code writing and troubleshooting—can be addressed by posing a specific question and persisting until the problem is fully resolved. Now, if you have time, convert the last procedure into a function so that you can run it to get files from any folder on your system. Do it on your own or dive into this topic with ChatGPT.

SUMMARY

This chapter covered quite a bit! It walked you through the process of building your own custom collection object that can be used to track and manipulate data in your VBA program. You also learned how to build an array and convert it into a collection. After making some comparisons between collections and arrays, you learned how to analyze your VBA procedures by stepping through the programming code using the F8 function key. You also saw how interacting with ChatGPT can assist you in writing better programming code and help you discover new functions that you can use to solve practical problems.

As your procedures become more complex, you will need to start using special tools for understanding programming logic and locating errors. These tools are the subject of the next chapter.

Chapter **8**

GETTING TO KNOW BUILT-IN TOOLS FOR TESTING AND DEBUGGING

You've probably heard more than once that computer programs are "full of bugs." In programming, errors are called bugs, and *debugging* is a process of eliminating errors from your programs. VBA provides a myriad of tools for tracking down and eliminating bugs. This chapter provides an overview of these tools that are at your fingertips when you work on the VBE screen.

SYNTAX, RUNTIME, AND LOGIC ERRORS

While writing or editing VBA procedures, no matter how careful you are, you're likely to make some mistakes. For example, you may misspell a variable name, misplace a comma or quotation mark, or forget a period or ending parenthesis. These kinds of mistakes are known as *syntax errors*. Fortunately, VBA is quite helpful in spotting these kinds of errors. To have VBA automatically check for correct syntax after you enter a line of code, choose Tools | Options in the VBE window. Make sure the Auto Syntax Check setting is selected on the Editor tab, as shown in Figure 8.1.

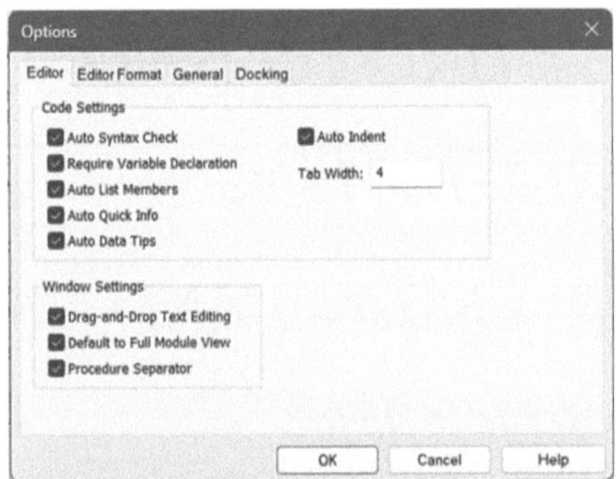

FIGURE 8.1.   The Auto Syntax Check setting on the Editor tab of the Options dialog box helps you find typos in your VBA procedures.

When VBA finds a syntax error, it displays an error message box and changes the color of the incorrect line of code to red or another color, as indicated on the Editor Format tab in the Options dialog box.

If the explanation of the error in the error message isn't clear, you can click the Help button for more help. If VBA cannot point you in the right direction, you must return to your procedure and carefully examine the offending instruction for missed letters, quotation marks, periods, colons, equal signs, and beginning and ending parentheses. Finding syntax errors can be aggravating and time-consuming. Certain syntax errors can be caught only during the execution of the procedure. While attempting to run your procedure, VBA can find errors that were caused by using invalid arguments or omitting instructions that are used in pairs, such as `If...End` statements and looping structures.

The first step in debugging a procedure is to correct all syntax errors. In addition to the syntax errors, there are two other types of errors: runtime and logic. *Run-time errors*, which occur while the procedure is running, are often caused by unexpected situations the programmer did not think of while writing the code. For example, the program may be trying to access a drive or a file that does not exist on the user's computer. Alternatively, it may be trying to copy a file to an external disk without first determining whether the user has connected the required media.

The third type of error, a *logic error*, often does not generate a specific error message. Even though the procedure has no flaws in its syntax and runs without errors, it produces incorrect results. *Logic errors* happen when your procedure simply does not do what you want it to do. Logic errors are usually very difficult to locate. Those that happen intermittently are sometimes so well concealed that you can spend long hours—even days—trying to locate the source of the error.

STOPPING A PROCEDURE

To understand what the VBA procedure is doing as it is being executed, you need to know how to put it in a state called "break mode." VBA offers four methods of stopping your procedure and entering into break mode:

- Manual interruption by pressing Ctrl+Break

  Note that the Break key, often labeled as Pause / Break, is typically located in the upper-right area of the keyboard, near the Scroll Lock key. Not all modern keyboards have it. If yours doesn't, you might need to use an alternative method of interrupting code in VBA. On my Dell laptop, the Break key is not present as a standalone key; to simulate it, I have to press Fn + Ctrl + B.

- Setting one or more breakpoints
- Inserting the `Stop` statement
- Adding a Watch expression

A break occurs when the execution of your VBA procedure is suspended. Visual Basic remembers the values of all variables and the statement from which the execution of the procedure should resume when you decide to continue.

You can resume a suspended procedure in one of the following ways:

- Click the Run Sub/UserForm button on the toolbar.
- Choose Run | Run Sub/UserForm from the menu bar.
- Click the Continue button in the error message box (see Figure 8.2).

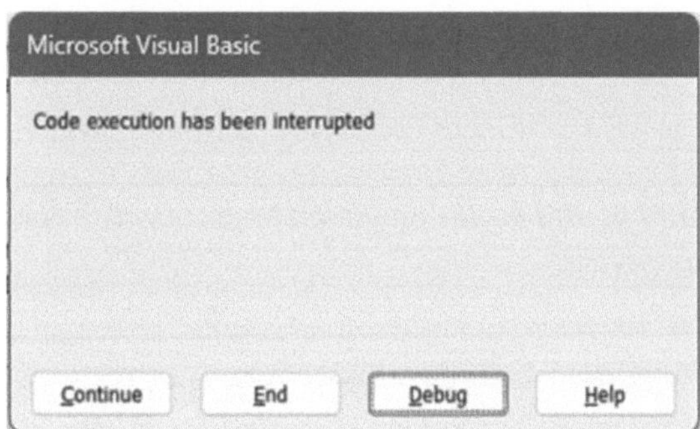

FIGURE 8.2.   This message appears after manually interrupting your procedure while it is running.

The error message box shown in Figure 8.2 informs you that the procedure was halted. A description of each button is provided in Table 8.1.

TABLE 8.1. Error message box buttons.

Button Name	Description
Continue	Click this button to resume code execution. This button will be grayed out if an error was encountered.
End	Click this button if you do not want to troubleshoot the procedure at this moment. VBA will stop code execution.
Debug	Click this button to enter break mode. The Code window will appear, and VBA will highlight the line at which the procedure execution was suspended. You can examine, debug, or step through the code.
Help	Click this button to view the online help that explains the cause of this error message.

USING BREAKPOINTS

If you know where there may be a problem in your procedure code, you should suspend code execution at that location (on a given line). Set a breakpoint by pressing F9 when the cursor is on the desired line of code. When VBA gets to that line while running your procedure, it will display the Code window immediately. At this point, you can step through the procedure code line by line by pressing F8 or choosing Debug | Step Into.

To see how this works, let's look at the following scenario. Assume that during the execution of the `LoadWeekEndingDates` function procedure (see Custom Project 8.1) you'd like to pause the procedure when it reaches the following line of code:

```
weekEndingDate = currDate + (7 - Weekday(currDate, vbMonday))
```

NOTE	*All code files and figures for the hands-on projects may be found in the companion files.*

⊙ Custom Project 8.1   Debugging a Function Procedure

1. Start Access and create a new database named `Chap08.accdb` in your `C:\ VBAAccess2024_ByExample` folder.
2. Create the form as shown in Figure 8.3.

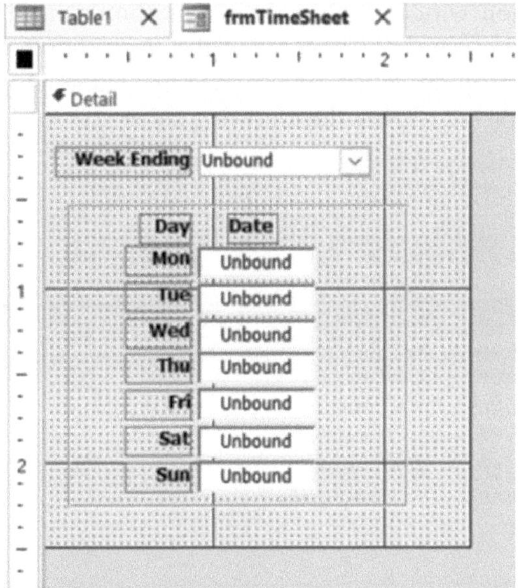

FIGURE 8.3. The combo box control shown on this form will be filled with the result of the ListEndDates function.

3. Use the property sheet to set the following control properties:

Control Name	Property Name	Property Setting
combo box	Name Row Source Type Column Count	cboEndDate Value List 1
text box controls	Name	txt1 txt2 txt3 txt4 txt5 txt6 txt7

4. Save the form as `frmTimeSheet`.
5. In the property sheet, select Form from the drop-down list box. Click the Event tab. Choose [Event Procedure] from the drop-down list next to the On Load property, and then click the Build button (…). Complete the following `Form_Load` procedure when the Code window appears:

```
Private Sub Form_Load()
    LoadWeekEndingDates Me.cboEndDate
End Sub
```

6. Back in the Access application window, select the combo box control (`cbo EndDate`) on the form. In the property sheet, click the Event tab. Choose [Event Procedure] from the drop-down list next to the On Change property, and then click the Build button (…). Enter the following code:

```
Private Sub cboEndDate_Change()
  Dim endDate As Date

  endDate = Me.cboEndDate.Value
  With Me
    .txt1 = Format(endDate - 6, "mm/dd")
    .txt2 = Format(endDate - 5, "mm/dd")
    .txt3 = Format(endDate - 4, "mm/dd")
    .txt4 = Format(endDate - 3, "mm/dd")
    .txt5 = Format(endDate - 2, "mm/dd")
    .txt6 = Format(endDate - 1, "mm/dd")
    .txt7 = Format(endDate - 0, "mm/dd")
  End With
End Sub
```

7. In the VBE window, choose Insert | Module to add a new standard module.

8. In the Properties window, change the `Name` property of `Module1` to `TimeSheetProc`.

9. Enter the `LoadWeekEndingDates` function procedure in the `TimeSheetProc` module:

```
Function LoadWeekEndingDates(cbo As ComboBox)
Dim i As Integer
Dim currDate As Date
Dim weekEndingDate As Date

currDate = Date
' Calculate the nearest Sunday
weekEndingDate = currDate + (7 - Weekday(currDate, vbMonday))

' Clear the combo box
cbo.RowSource = ""

' Add week-ending dates 6 weeks before
' the current week-ending date

' The RowSourceType property on the combo box Properties sheet
' must be set to 'Value List' to use this method
For i = 6 To 1 Step -1
    cbo.AddItem Format(weekEndingDate - (i * 7), "mm/dd/yyyy")
Next i
```

```vba
' Add the current week-ending date
cbo.AddItem Format(weekEndingDate, "mm/dd/yyyy")

' Add week-ending dates 6 weeks after
' the current week-ending date
For i = 1 To 6
    cbo.AddItem Format(weekEndingDate + (i * 7), "mm/dd/yyyy")
Next i
        End Function
```

10. In the `LoadWeekEndingDates` function procedure, click anywhere on the line containing the following statement:

```vba
weekEndingDate = currDate + (7 - Weekday(currDate, vbMonday))
```

11. Press F9 (or choose Debug | Toggle Breakpoint) to set a breakpoint on the line where the cursor is located.

When you set the breakpoint, Visual Basic displays a red dot in the margin. At the same time, the line that has the breakpoint will change to white text on a red background (see Figure 8.4). The color of the breakpoint can be changed on the Editor Format tab in the Options dialog box (choose Tools | Options).

Another way of setting a breakpoint is to click on the margin indicator to the left of the line on which you want to stop the procedure as we did in the previous chapter when walking through a procedure.

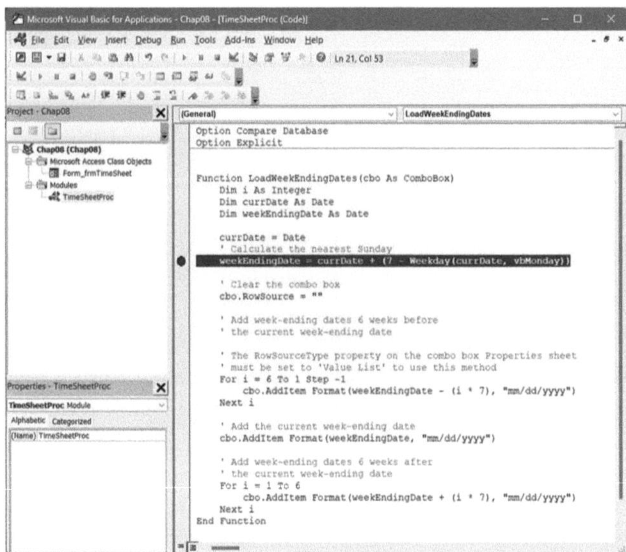

FIGURE 8.4.   The line of code where the breakpoint is set is displayed in the color specified on the Editor Format tab in the Options dialog box.

12. Leave the function procedure, as shown in Figure 8.4, and switch to the main Access application window.

13. Right-click the form `frmTimeSheet` tab and choose form view.

Now, the VBE screen should pop up. VBA will call the `LoadWeekEndingDates` function to fill the combo box, executing all the statements until it encounters the breakpoint. Your code execution will be suspended. You should see a yellow arrow in the margin to the left of the statement at which the procedure was suspended (Figure 8.5). At the same time, the statement appears inside a box with a yellow background. The arrow and the box indicate the current statement, or the statement that is about to be executed. If the current statement also contains a breakpoint, the margin displays both indicators overlapping one another (the circle and the arrow).

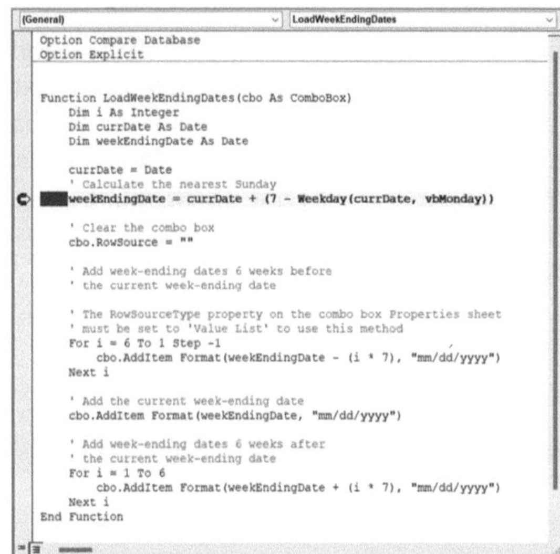


```
Option Compare Database
Option Explicit


Function LoadWeekEndingDates(cbo As ComboBox)
    Dim i As Integer
    Dim currDate As Date
    Dim weekEndingDate As Date

    currDate = Date
    ' Calculate the nearest Sunday
    weekEndingDate = currDate + (7 - Weekday(currDate, vbMonday))

    ' Clear the combo box
    cbo.RowSource = ""

    ' Add week-ending dates 6 weeks before
    ' the current week-ending date

    ' The RowSourceType property on the combo box Properties sheet
    ' must be set to 'Value List' to use this method
    For i = 6 To 1 Step -1
        cbo.AddItem Format(weekEndingDate - (i * 7), "mm/dd/yyyy")
    Next i

    ' Add the current week-ending date
    cbo.AddItem Format(weekEndingDate, "mm/dd/yyyy")

    ' Add week-ending dates 6 weeks after
    ' the current week-ending date
    For i = 1 To 6
        cbo.AddItem Format(weekEndingDate + (i * 7), "mm/dd/yyyy")
    Next i
End Function
```

FIGURE 8.5. Code window in break mode. Because the current statement also contains a breakpoint (indicated by a red circle), the margin displays both indicators overlapping one another (the circle and the arrow).

14. Click on the margin next to the highlighted line of code to remove the breakpoint. The selected line of code will stay highlighted in yellow.

15. Finish running the `ListEndDates` function procedure by pressing F5.

16. Now, return to your form and notice that the combo box is now populated with week-ending dates. When you choose a date from the combo box, Visual Basic will call the `cboEndDate_Change` event procedure located in the `Form_frmTimeSheet` class module.

17. In the `Form_frmTimeSheet` module, set the breakpoints as shown in Figure 8.6.

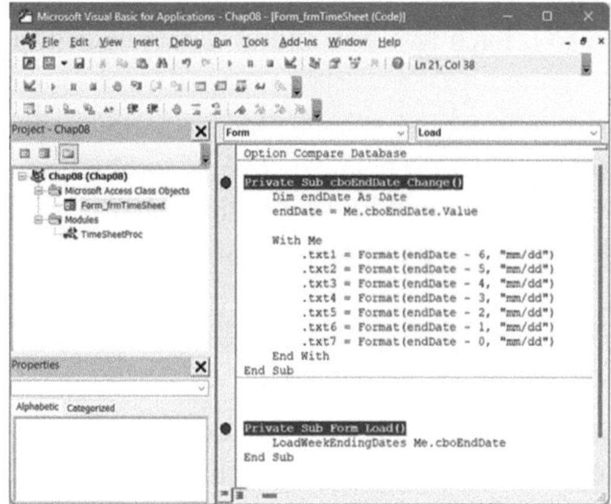


```vba
Option Compare Database

Private Sub cboEndDate_Change()
    Dim endDate As Date
    endDate = Me.cboEndDate.Value

    With Me
        .txt1 = Format(endDate - 6, "mm/dd")
        .txt2 = Format(endDate - 5, "mm/dd")
        .txt3 = Format(endDate - 4, "mm/dd")
        .txt4 = Format(endDate - 3, "mm/dd")
        .txt5 = Format(endDate - 2, "mm/dd")
        .txt6 = Format(endDate - 1, "mm/dd")
        .txt7 = Format(endDate - 0, "mm/dd")
    End With
End Sub

Private Sub Form_Load()
    LoadWeekEndingDates Me.cboEndDate
End Sub
```

FIGURE 8.6.   Code window in break mode with additional breakpoints to watch each procedure execution.

18. Switch to the Access application window and close the form. Save the changes when prompted.

19. Now, reopen the form in form view.
    Visual Basic will bring up the code window highlighting the beginning of the `Form_Load` event procedure that has a breakpoint. This procedure calls the `LoadWeekEndingDates` function procedure, passing it the combo box object (`cboEndDate`).

20. Press F5 to execute the `Form_Load` procedure code.
    When this procedure completes, you should see the `frmTimeSheet` form open in the Main Access application window.

21. Select any date from the combo box.
    Notice that now the highlight moves to the `cboEndDate_Change` procedure where you set the breakpoint.

22. Press F5 to execute all the lines in the `cboEndDate_Change` procedure.
    When this procedure completes, you should see the `frmTimeSheet` form open in the Main Access application window and all the text boxes filled in with the corresponding dates for the selected week ending date.

23. Select another date from the combo box and notice that Visual Basic jumps to the `cboEndDate_Change` procedure to load a new date value.

24. Press F5 to execute the procedure.
    As soon as the procedure finishes, you are returned to the form.

Note that the `cboEndDate_Change` procedure runs each time you make a selection from the combo box. It captures the selected date from `cboEndDate` and stores it in the `endDate` variable. The `With Me` block formats and assigns dates to text boxes (`txt1` to `txt7`). Each text box shows a date counting back from the selected `endDate`.

25. Click in the margin to remove the breakpoint from the `cboEndDate_Change` procedure and then make another selection from the form's combo box.
Notice that now you can work with the combo box without worrying about what's going on with the VBA code behind the scenes.

26. Close the form and reopen it.
There are still breakpoints left in the code, so Visual Basic jumps to the first procedure it needs to execute before the form is loaded.

Press F8 to step into the code of the procedure. If you continue pressing F8, Visual Basic will jump to the `LoadWeekEndingDates` function procedure as there is a breakpoint there.

Notice that this function takes a `ComboBox` object as an argument. There are three variable declarations. The variable `i` is declared as `Integer` and is used for the loop counters. The `currDate` variable is used to store the current date. The `weekEndingDate` will store the week-ending date. The VBA `Date` function is used to retrieve the current (today's) date from the system and store it in the `currDate` variable. Next, we calculate the next Sunday from the current date. The function `Weekday(currDate, vbMonday)` will return the weekday number with Monday as the start of the week, so `(7 - Weekday(currDate, vbMonday))` calculates how many days are left until the next Sunday. The next line, `cbo.RowSource = ""`, will clear the existing items in the combo box. The first `For...Next` loop adds week-ending dates 6 weeks before the current week-ending date to the combo box in the format mm/dd/yyyy. The `AddItem` method of the `ComboBox` object is used to add each new item to the list. The statement before the second `For...Next` loop will add the current week-ending date to the combo box. The loop at the end of the function procedure will run from 1 to 6 to add to the combo box the week-ending dates 6 weeks after the current week-ending date.

Removing Breakpoints

You can set any number of breakpoints in a VBA procedure. This way, you can suspend and continue the execution of your procedure as you please. As you have already seen, you can press F5 to quickly move between the breakpoints or use F8 to move line by line. You can analyze the code of your procedure and check the values of variables while code execution is suspended. You can also perform various tests by typing statements in the Immediate window. Consider setting a breakpoint if you suspect that your procedure never executes a certain block of code.

When you finish running the procedure in which you had set breakpoints, VBA does not automatically remove them. To remove the breakpoint, choose Debug | Clear All Breakpoints or press Ctrl+Shift+F9. All the breakpoints are removed. If you have set several breakpoints in a procedure and would like to remove only some of them, click on the line containing the breakpoint you want to remove and press F9 (or choose Debug | Clear Breakpoint). You should clear breakpoints when they are no longer needed. Breakpoints are automatically removed when you exit Access.

NOTE	*Remove the breakpoint you set in Custom Project 8.1.*

USING THE IMMEDIATE WINDOW IN BREAK MODE

When the procedure execution is suspended, the Code window appears in break mode. This is a good time to activate the Immediate window and type VBA

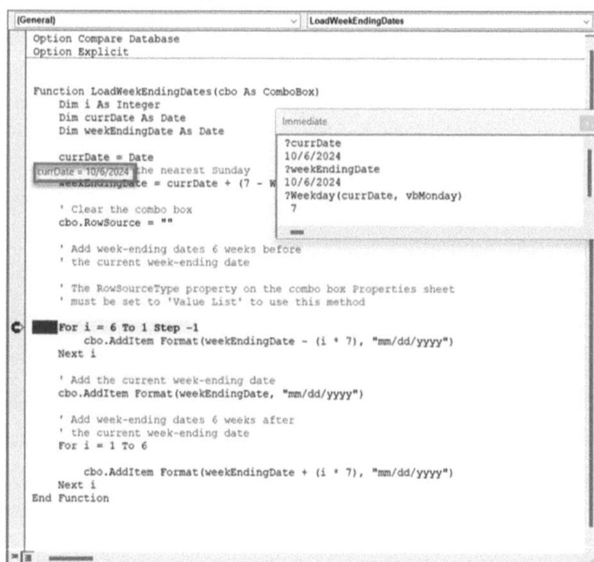

FIGURE 8.7. When code execution is suspended, you can check the current values of variables and expressions by entering appropriate statements in the Immediate window or resting the mouse pointer on the variable name.

instructions to find out, for instance, the name of the open form or the value of a certain control. You can also use the Immediate window to change the contents of variables to correct values that may be causing errors. By now, you should be an expert when it comes to working in the Immediate window. Figure 8.7 shows the suspended `LoadWeekEndingDates` function procedure with the Immediate window displaying the questions that were asked of VBA while in break mode.

In break mode, you can also hold the mouse pointer over any variable in a running procedure to see the variable's value. For example, in the `LoadWeek-EndingDates` function procedure shown in Figure 8.7, you can quickly find out the value of the `currDate` by resting the mouse pointer over its name. The name of the variable and its current value appear in a floating frame. To show the values of several variables used in a procedure, you should use the Locals window, which is discussed later in this chapter.

Working in a Code Window in Break Mode

While in break mode, you can change code, add new statements, execute the procedure one line at a time, skip lines, set the next statement, use the Immediate window, and more. When the procedure is in break mode, all the options on the Debug menu are available, as shown in Figure 8.8. If you change a line of code, VBA will prompt you to reset the project by displaying the message This action will reset your project, proceed anyway?. Click OK to stop the program's execution and proceed editing your code, or click Cancel to delete the new changes and continue running the code from the point where it was suspended. For example, try to change the variable declaration. As you press F5 to resume code execution, you'll be prompted to reset your project.

Debug	Run	Tools	Add-Ins	Window	
	Compile Chap08				
⌐	Step Into				F8
⌐	Step Over				Shift+F8
⌐	Step Out				Ctrl+Shift+F8
⌐	Run To Cursor				Ctrl+F8
	Add Watch...				
	Edit Watch...				Ctrl+W
6d	Quick Watch...				Shift+F9
⌐	Toggle Breakpoint				F9
	Clear All Breakpoints			Ctrl+Shift+F9	
⇨	Set Next Statement				Ctrl+F9
⌐	Show Next Statement				

FIGURE 8.8. When your procedure is suspended, you can access various options on the Debug menu.

USING THE STOP STATEMENT

Sometimes you won't be able to test your procedure right away. If you set up your breakpoints and then close the database file, the breakpoints will be removed; next time, when you are ready to test your procedure, you'll have to begin by setting up your breakpoints again. If you need to postpone the task of testing your procedure until later, you can take a different approach by inserting a `Stop` statement into your code wherever you want to halt a procedure.

Figure 8.9 shows the `Stop` statement before the `With…End With` construct. VBA will suspend the execution of the `cboEndDate_Change` event procedure when it encounters the `Stop` statement, and the screen will display the Code window in break mode. Although the `Stop` statement has the same effect as setting a breakpoint, it does have one disadvantage: all `Stop` statements stay in the procedure until you remove them. When you no longer need to stop your procedure, you must locate and remove all the `Stop` statements by deleting them. You can also comment them if you feel you may need them again.

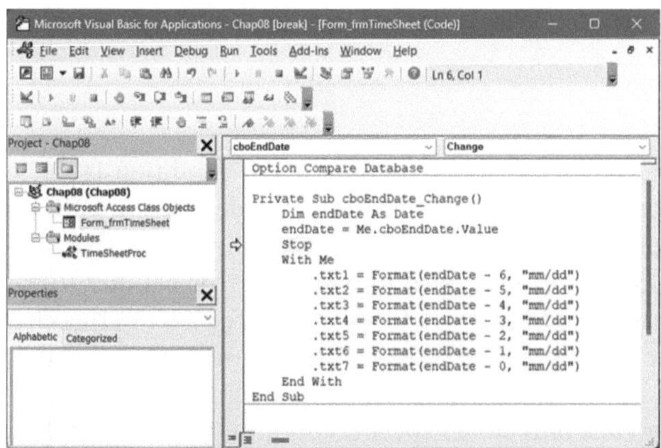

FIGURE 8.9. You can insert a Stop statement anywhere in your VBA procedure code. The procedure will halt when it gets to the Stop statement, and the Code window will appear with the code line highlighted.

USING THE ASSERT STATEMENT

A very powerful and easy-to-apply debugging technique is utilizing `Debug.Assert` statements. Assertions allow you to write code that checks itself while running. By including assertions in your programming code, you can verify that a particular condition or assumption is true. Assertions give you immediate feedback when an error occurs. They are great for detecting logic errors early in the development phase instead of hearing about them later from your end users. Just because your procedure ran on your system without generating an error, does not mean that there are no bugs in that procedure. Don't assume anything—always test for the validity of expressions and variables in your code. The `Debug.Assert` statement takes any expression that evaluates to `True` or `False` and activates break mode when that expression evaluates to `False`. The syntax for `Debug.Assert` is as follows:

```
Debug.Assert condition
```

where *condition* is some VBA code or expression that returns `True` or `False`. If *condition* evaluates to `False` or `0` (zero), VBA will enter break mode. For example, when running the following looping structure, the code will stop executing when the variable `i` equals 50:

```
Sub TestDebugAssert()
   Dim i As Integer
   For i = 1 To 100
       Debug.Assert i <> 50
   Next
End Sub
```

Keep in mind that `Debug.Assert` does nothing if the condition is `False` or zero (`0`). The execution simply stops on that line of code and the VBE screen opens with the line containing the false statement highlighted so that you can start debugging your code. You may need to write an error handler to handle the identified error. Error-handling procedures are covered later in this chapter. While you can stop the code execution by using the `Stop` statement (see the previous section), `Debug.Assert` differs from the `Stop` statement in its conditional aspect; it will stop your code only under specific conditions. Conditional breakpoints can also be set by using the Watches window (see the next section). After you have debugged and tested your code, comment out or remove the `Debug.Assert` statements from your final code. The easiest way to do this is to use Edit | Replace in the VBE editor screen:

- To comment out the `Debug.Assert` statements, in the Find What box, enter `Debug.Assert.` In the Replace With box, enter an apostrophe followed by `Debug.Assert.`

- To remove the `Debug.Assert` statements from your code, enter `Debug.Assert` in the Find What box. Leave the Replace With box empty but be sure to mark the Use Pattern Matching checkbox.

USING THE ADD WATCH WINDOW

Many errors in procedures are caused by variables that assume unexpected values. If a procedure uses a variable whose value changes in various locations, you may want to stop the procedure and check the current value of that variable. VBA offers a special Watches window that allows you to keep an eye on variables or expressions while your procedure is running. To add a watch expression to your procedure, select the variable whose value you want to monitor in the Code window, and then choose Debug | Add Watch. The screen will display the Add Watch dialog box, as shown in Figure 8.10.

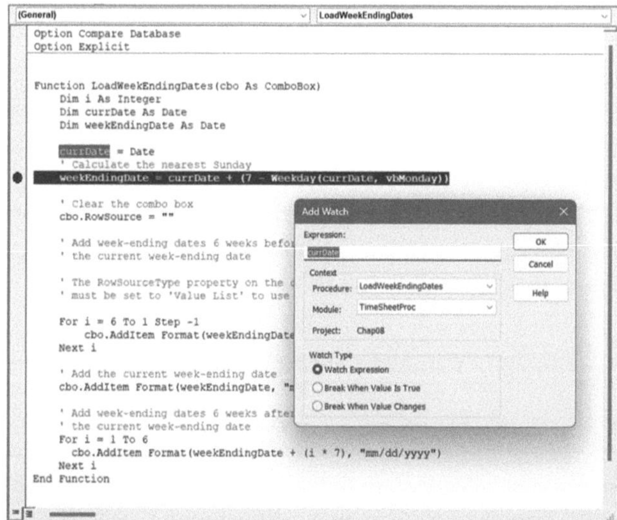

FIGURE 8.10.   The Add Watch dialog box allows you to define conditions you want to monitor while a VBA procedure is running.

The Add Watch dialog box contains three sections, which are described in Table 8.2.

TABLE 8.2.   Add Watch dialog box sections.

Section	Description
Expression	Displays the name of a variable you have highlighted in your procedure. If you opened the Add Watch dialog box without first selecting a variable name, type the name of the variable you want to monitor in the Expression text box.
Context	In this section, indicate the name of the procedure that contains the variable and the name of the module where this procedure is located.

(Contd.)

Section	Description
Watch Type	Specifies how to monitor the variable. If you choose: • The Watch Expression option button, you can read the value of the variable in the Add Watch window while in break mode. • Break When Value Is True, Visual Basic will automatically stop the procedure when the variable evaluates to True (nonzero). • Break When Value Changes, Visual Basic will automatically stop the procedure each time the value of the variable or expression changes.

You can add a watch expression before running a procedure or after suspending the execution of your procedure. The difference between a breakpoint and a watch expression is that the breakpoint always stops a procedure in a specified location, but the watch stops the procedure only when the specified condition (Break When Value Is True or Break When Value Changes) is met. Watches are extremely useful when you are not sure where the variable is being changed. Instead of stepping through many lines of code to find the location where the variable assumes the specified value, you can put a watch breakpoint on the variable and run your procedure as normal. Let's see how to monitor the values of variables in the `LoadWeekEndingDates` function we worked with earlier.

Hands-On 8.1 Watching the Values of VBA Expressions

NOTE	*Before working on this hands-on exercise, remove all the breakpoints that may be still set up in the VBE window. Choose Debug | Clear All Breakpoints. Also, make sure that the* `frmTimeSheet` *is closed.*

1. In the VBE window, activate the `TimeSheetProc` with the `LoadWeekEndingDates` function procedure.
2. Put a breakpoint on the line that calculates the nearest Sunday (see Figure 8.10).
3. Right-click the `currDate` variable and choose Add Watch. The Add Watch dialog box will appear on the screen. Make sure that it shows the same selections as shown in Figure 8.10, then click OK.
4. Apply Add Watch for the `weekEnding` variable. Right-click that variable name in the statement that calculates the nearest Sunday and choose Add Watch. In the Add Watch dialog box, make sure that Watch Type is set to Watch Expression (this is the default) and click OK.

5. Choose Debug | Add Watch, and in the expression text box, enter `weekEndingDate + (i + 7)` and select the Break When Value Changes option button in the Watch Type section. Then, click OK.

   You have now added three watch expressions that you will be monitoring as you step through the function procedure line by line. The watch expressions will be listed in the Watches window.

6. Choose View | Watch window to see all the watch expressions you have added. Figure 8.11 shows the contents of the Watches window when the procedure has finished running. You will see in the Value column an entry of <Out of context> instead of the variable value. In other words, when the watch expression is out of context, it does not have a value. When your procedure is running, however, you will see different values in the Value column.

Watches				
	Expression	Value	Type	Context
6d	currDate	<Out of context>	Empty	TimeSheetProc.LoadWeekEndingDates
6d	weekEndingDate	<Out of context>	Empty	TimeSheetProc.LoadWeekEndingDates
6d	weekEndingDate + (i * 7)	<Out of context>	Empty	TimeSheetProc.LoadWeekEndingDates

FIGURE 8.11.   The content of the Watches window when our procedure is not in break mode.

Recall that you must open the form to trigger the `LoadWeekEndingDates` function procedure.

7. In the Access application window, open the `frmTimeSheet` form.

   Visual Basic will go into break mode because it encounters the breakpoint that you set in step 2 of this hands-on exercise.

   Notice the values of the variables in the Watches window have now changed.

8. Keep on pressing F8 to execute the function procedure line by line and observe the values of the variables in the Watches window as the code executes.

   Using the Watches window in break mode can be very helpful when debugging your VBA code. It can give you a real-time insight into how variables are changing and help you pinpoint any discrepancies.

   When the function procedure ends, all the week-ending dates that were requested will be available in the form's combo box.

9. Close the `frmTimeSheet` form.

Removing Watch Expressions

To remove a watch expression, click on the expression you want to remove from the Watches window and press Delete. Now you can remove all the watch expressions you defined in the preceding hands-on exercise.

USING QUICK WATCH

To check the value of an expression not defined in the Watches window, use Quick Watch (see Figure 8.12).

To access the Quick Watch dialog box while in break mode, position the insertion point anywhere inside a variable name or an expression you want to watch and choose Debug | Quick Watch, or press Shift+F9.

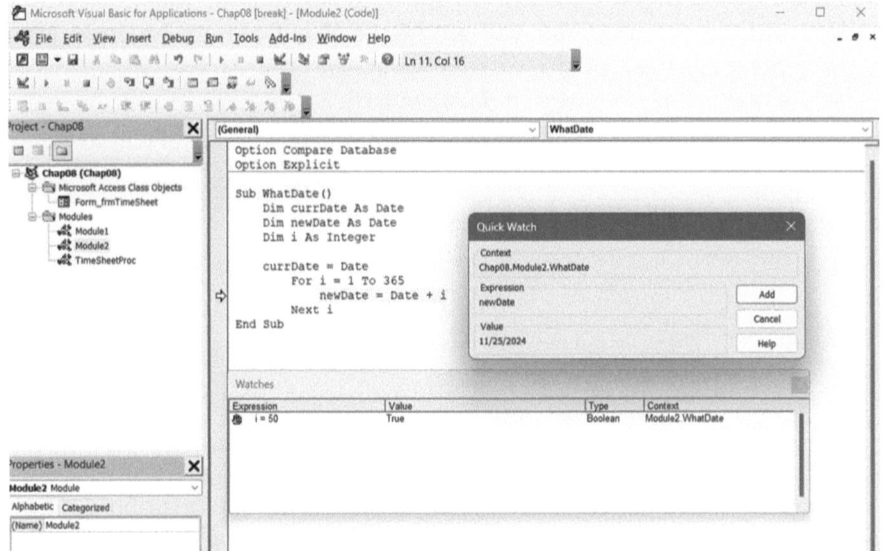

FIGURE 8.12.   The Quick Watch dialog box shows the current value of a chosen expression in a VBA procedure.

The Quick Watch dialog box contains an Add button that allows you to add the expression to the Watches window. Let's see how to take advantage of Quick Watch.

Hands-On 8.2   Using the Quick Watch Dialog Box

1. Insert a new module and enter the following procedure:

```
Sub WhatDate()
    Dim currDate As Date
    Dim newDate As Date
    Dim i As Integer

    currDate = Date
```

```
        For i = 1 To 365
            newDate = Date + i
        Next i
    End Sub
```

2. Position the insertion point within the code of the `WhatDate` procedure and press F8 to enter break mode.
3. Now, position the insertion point on the name of the variable `i`.
4. Choose Debug | Add Watch and enter the expression `i = 50`.
5. Choose the Break When Value Is True option button and click OK.
6. Run the `WhatDate` procedure.
   Visual Basic will suspend procedure execution when `i = 50`. Notice that the Watches window does not contain either the `newDate` or `currDate` variable. To check the values of these variables, you can position the mouse pointer over the appropriate variable name in the Code window, or you can invoke the Quick Watch dialog box.
7. In the Code window, position the mouse inside the `newDate` variable and press Shift+F9, or choose Debug | Quick Watch.
   The Quick Watch dialog box shows the name of the expression being watched and its current value (Figure 8.12).
8. Click Cancel to return to the Code window.
9. In the Code window, position the mouse inside the `currDate` variable and press Shift+F9, or choose Debug | Quick Watch.
   The Quick Watch dialog box now shows the value of the variable `currDate`.
10. Click Cancel to return to the Code window.
11. Press F5 to continue running the procedure.

USING THE LOCALS WINDOW

If you need to keep an eye on all the declared variables and their current values during the execution of a VBA procedure, choose View | Locals Window before you run your procedure. While in break mode, VBA will display a list of variables and their corresponding values in the Locals window (see Figure 8.13).

The Locals window contains three columns: Expression, Value, and Type.

The Expression column displays the names of variables that are declared in the current procedure. The first row displays the name of the module preceded by a plus sign. When you click the plus sign, you can check whether any variables have been declared at the module level. Here, the class module will show the system variable Me. In the Locals window, global variables and variables used by other projects aren't displayed.

The second column, Value, shows the current variable values. In this column, you can change the value of a variable by clicking on it and typing the new value. After changing the value, press Enter to register the change. You can also press Tab, Shift+Tab, or the up or down arrows, or click anywhere within the Locals window after you've changed the variable value.

The third column, named Type, displays the type of each declared variable.

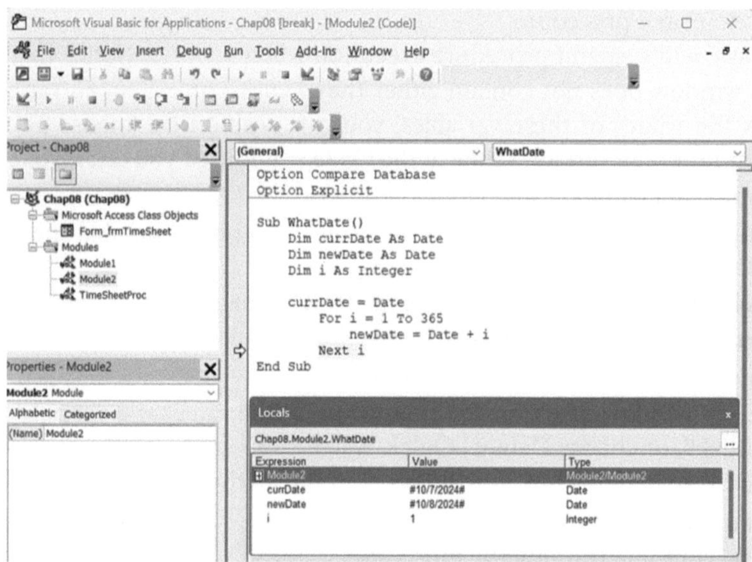

FIGURE 8.13.   The Locals window displays the current values of all the declared variables in the current VBA procedure.

To observe the variable values in the Locals window, let's proceed to the following hands-on exercise.

Hands-On 8.3   Using the Locals Window

1. Choose View | Locals Window.
2. Click anywhere inside the WhatDate procedure and press F8.
   Pressing F8 places the procedure in break mode. The Locals window displays the name of the current module, the local variables, and their beginning values.
3. Press F8 a few more times while keeping an eye on the Locals window.
4. Press F5 to continue running the procedure.

USING THE CALL STACK DIALOG BOX

Notice that the Locals window (Figure 8.13) contains a button with an ellipsis (…). This button opens the Call Stack dialog box (see Figure 8.14), which displays a list of all active procedure calls when you are in break mode. An *active procedure call* is a procedure that is started but not completed. You can also activate the Call Stack dialog box by choosing View | Call Stack. This option is only available in break mode.

The Call Stack dialog box is especially helpful for tracing nested procedures. A nested procedure is a procedure that is being called from within another procedure. If a procedure calls another, the name of the called procedure is automatically added to the calls list in the Call Stack dialog box. In Figure 8.14, the Call Stack dialog displays the name of the `LoadWeekEndingDates` function procedure that is called from the `Form_Load` event procedure. Both procedure names are therefore listed in the Call Stack dialog.

When VBA has finished executing the statements of the called procedure, the procedure name is automatically removed from the Call Stack dialog box. You can use the Show button in the Call Stack dialog box to display the statement that calls the next procedure listed in the Call Stack dialog box.

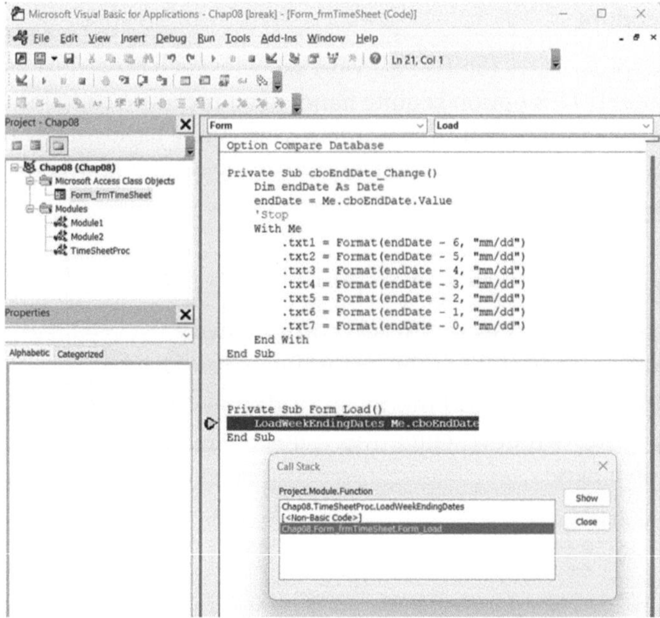

FIGURE 8.14.   The Call Stack dialog box displays a list of procedures that are started but not completed.

When the code must access external libraries to implement some functionality that VBA uses, you will see the [<Non-Basic-Code>] lines in the Call Stack dialog. This code cannot be debugged by you.

STEPPING THROUGH VBA PROCEDURES

Stepping through the code means running one statement at a time. This allows you to check every line in every procedure that is encountered. To start stepping through the procedure from the beginning, place the cursor anywhere inside the code of your procedure and choose Debug | Step Into, or press F8. The Debug menu contains several options that allow you to execute a procedure in step mode (see Figure 8.8 earlier in this chapter).

When you run a procedure one statement at a time, VBA executes each statement until it encounters the `End Sub` keywords. If you don't want to step through every statement, you can press F5 at any time to run the remaining code of the procedure without stepping through it.

You can also choose Run | Reset to stop the procedure at the current statement without executing the remaining statements.

Stepping over a Procedure

When you step over procedures (Shift+F8), VBA executes each procedure as if it were a single statement. This option is quite handy if a procedure contains calls to other procedures you don't want to step into because they have already been tested and debugged, or because you want to focus only on the new code that has not been debugged yet.

⊙ Hands-On 8.4   Stepping over a Procedure

This hands-on exercise refers to the Access form named `frmTimeSheet` that you created in Custom Project 8.1 at the beginning of this chapter.

1. In the VBE window, choose Insert | Module to add a new standard module.
2. In the module's Code window, enter the `MyProcedure` and `SpecialMsg` procedures as shown here:

```
Sub MyProcedure()
  Dim firstControlName As String
  Dim frm As Form

  Set frm = Forms("frmTimeSheet")
```

```vba
    firstControlName = frm.Controls(1).Name

    ' choose Step Over to avoid stepping through the
    ' lines of code in the called procedure - SpecialMsg
    SpecialMsg firstControlName, frm
End Sub

Sub SpecialMsg(controlName As String, myfrm As Form)
    Dim ctrl As Control

    Set ctrl = myfrm.Controls(controlName)
    If controlName = "Label1" Then
      MsgBox "The caption of " & controlName & _
        " is: " & ctrl.Caption
    End If
End Sub
```

3. Add a breakpoint within `MyProcedure` at the following statement:

```vba
SpecialMsg firstControlName, frm
```

4. Place the insertion point anywhere within the code of `MyProcedure` and press F5 to run it.
Visual Basic halts execution when it reaches the breakpoint.

5. Press Shift+F8 or choose Debug | Step Over.
Visual Basic runs the code of the `SpecialMsg` procedure and displays the message box. While the `SpecialMsg` procedure is being executed, VBA continues to display the current procedure in the Code window. When you click OK in the message box, the execution of the code advances to the statement immediately after the call to the `SpecialMsg` procedure (`End Sub`).

6. Press F5 to finish running the procedure.
Now suppose you want to execute `MyProcedure` to the line that calls the `SpecialMsg` procedure.

7. Click anywhere inside the statement `SpecialMsg firstControlName, frm`.

8. Choose Debug | Run to Cursor.
Visual Basic will stop the procedure when it reaches the specified line.

9. Press Shift+F8 to step over the `SpecialMsg` procedure.

10. Press F5 to execute the rest of the procedure without single stepping.

Stepping out of a Procedure

Another command on the Debug menu, Step Out (Ctrl+Shift+F8), is used when you step into a procedure and then decide that you don't want to step all the way through it. When you choose this option, Visual Basic will execute the remaining statements in this procedure in one step and proceed to activate the next statement in the calling procedure.

In the process of stepping through a procedure, you can switch between the Step Into, Step Over, and Step Out options. The option you select depends on which code fragment you wish to analyze at a given moment.

Running a Procedure to Cursor

The Debug menu Run to Cursor command (Ctrl+F8) lets you run your procedure until the line you have selected is encountered. This command is quite useful if you want to stop the execution before a large loop or intend to step over a called procedure.

Setting the Next Statement

At times, you may want to rerun previous lines of code in the procedure or skip over a section of code that is causing trouble. In each of these situations, you can use the Set Next Statement option on the Debug menu. When you halt the execution of a procedure, you can resume the procedure from any statement you want. VBA will skip execution of the statements between the selected statement and the statement where the execution was suspended.

> ### Skipping Lines of Code
>
> Although skipping lines of code can be very useful in the process of debugging your VBA procedures, it should be done with care. When you use the Next Statement option, you tell VBA that this is the line you want to execute next. All lines in between are ignored. This means that certain things you may have expected to occur don't happen, which can lead to unexpected errors.

Showing the Next Statement

If you are not sure where procedure execution will resume, you can choose Debug | Show Next Statement, and VBA will place the cursor on the line that will run next. This is particularly useful when you have been looking at other procedures and are not sure where execution will resume. The Show Next Statement option is available only in break mode.

NAVIGATING WITH BOOKMARKS

In the process of analyzing or reviewing your VBA procedures, you will often find yourself jumping to certain areas of code. Using the built-in bookmark feature, you can easily mark the spots you want to navigate between.

To set up a bookmark:

1. Click anywhere in the statement you want to define as a bookmark.
2. Choose Edit | Bookmarks | Toggle Bookmark (or click the Toggle Bookmark button on the Edit toolbar).

Visual Basic will place a blue, rounded rectangle in the left margin beside the statement, as shown in Figure 8.15.

Once you've set up two or more bookmarks, you can jump between the marked locations of your code by choosing Edit | Bookmarks | Next Bookmark or simply clicking the Next Bookmark button on the Edit toolbar. You may also right-click anywhere in the Code window and select Next Bookmark from the shortcut menu. To go to the previous bookmark, select Previous Bookmark. You can remove bookmarks at any time by choosing Edit | Bookmarks | Clear All or by clicking the Clear All Bookmarks button on the Edit toolbar. To remove a single bookmark, click anywhere in the bookmarked statement and choose Edit | Bookmarks | Toggle Bookmark, or click the Toggle Bookmark button on the Edit toolbar.

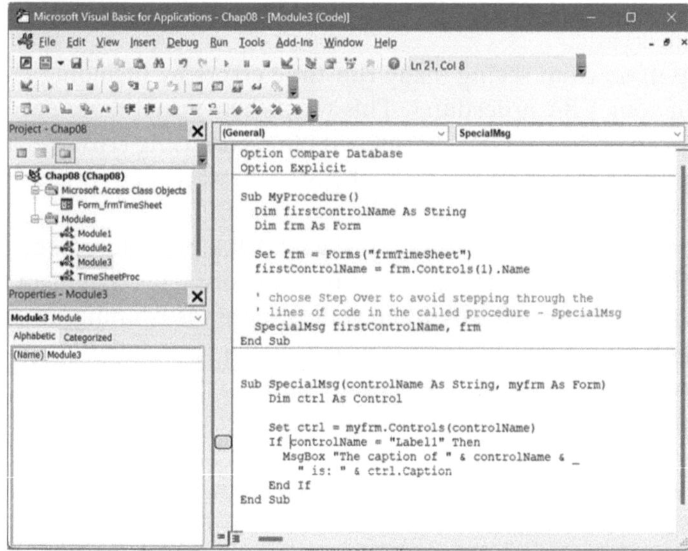

FIGURE 8.15. Using bookmarks, you can quickly jump between often-used sections of your procedures.

STOPPING AND RESETTING VBA PROCEDURES

At any time while stepping through the code of a procedure in the Code window, you can press F5 to execute the remaining instructions without stepping through them, or choose Run | Reset to finish the procedure without executing the remaining statements. When you reset your procedure, all the variables lose their current values. Numeric variables assume the initial value of zero (`0`), variable-length strings are initialized to a zero-length string (`""`), and fixed-length strings are filled with the character represented by the ASCII character code 0, or `Chr(0)`. `Variant` variables are initialized to `Empty`, and the value of `Object` variables is set to `Nothing`.

TRAPPING ERRORS

No one writes bug-free programs on the first try. For this reason, when you create VBA procedures, you have to determine how your program will respond to errors. Many unexpected errors happen at runtime. For example, your procedure may try to give a new file the same name as an open file.

Runtime errors are often discovered not by a programmer but by the user who attempts to do something that the programmer has not anticipated. If an error occurs when the procedure is running, Visual Basic displays an error message and the procedure is stopped. The error message that VBA displays to the user is often quite cryptic.

You can keep users from seeing many run-time errors by including error-handling code in your VBA procedures. This way, when Visual Basic encounters an error, instead of displaying a default and often confusing error message, it will show a much friendlier, more comprehensive message, perhaps advising the user on how to correct the error or whom to contact.

How do you implement error handling in your VBA procedure? The first step is to place the `On Error` statement in your procedure. This statement tells VBA what to do if an error happens while your program is running. In other words, VBA uses the `On Error` statement to activate an error-handling procedure that will trap run-time errors. Depending on the type of procedure, you can exit the error trap by using one of the following statements: `Exit Sub`, `Exit Function`, `Exit Property`, `End Sub`, `End Function`, or `End Property`.

You should write an error-handling routine for each procedure. Table 8.3 shows how the `On Error` statement can be used.

TABLE 8.3.   On Error statement options.

On Error Statement	Description
On Error GoTo Label	Specifies a label to jump to when an error occurs. This label marks the beginning of the error-handling routine. An *error handler* is a routine for trapping and responding to errors in your application. The label must appear in the same procedure as the On Error GoTo statement.
On Error Resume Next	When a run-time error occurs, Visual Basic ignores the line that caused the error and continues the procedure with the next line. An error message is not displayed.
On Error GoTo 0	Turns off error trapping in a procedure. When VBA runs this statement, errors are detected but not trapped within the procedure.

Is This an Error or a Mistake?

In programming, mistakes and errors are not the same thing. A mistake—such as a misspelled or missing statement, a misplaced quotation mark or comma, or the assignment of a value of one type to a variable of a different (and incompatible) type—can be removed from your program through proper testing and debugging. Note, however, that even though your code may be free of mistakes, errors can still occur. An *error* is the result of an event or operation that doesn't work as expected. For example, if your VBA procedure accesses a certain file on disk and someone deleted this file or moved it to another location, you'll get an error no matter what. An error prevents the procedure from carrying out a specific task.

Using the Err Object

Your error-handling code can utilize various properties and methods of the `Err` object. For example, to check which error occurred, check the value of `Err.Number`. The `Number` property of the `Err` object will tell you the value of the last error that occurred, and the `Description` property will return a description of the error. You can also find the name of the application that caused the error by using the `Source` property of the `Err` object (this is very helpful when your procedure launches other applications). After handling the error, use the `Err.Clear` statement to reset the error number. This will set `Err.Number` back to `0`.

To test your error-handling code you can use the `Raise` method of the `Err` object. For example, to raise the Disk not ready error, use the following statement:

```
Err.Raise 71
```

The following `OpenToRead` procedure demonstrates the use of the `On Error` statement and the `Err` object.

◉ Hands-On 8.6   Error-Trapping Techniques

1. Copy the `Vacation.txt` file from the companion files to your `VBAAccess2024_ByExample` folder.
2. In the VBE window in the `Chap08` database, insert a new module and rename it `ErrorTraps`.
3. In the Code window, enter the following `OpenToRead` procedure:

```
Sub OpenToRead()
  Dim strFile As String
  Dim strChar As String
  Dim strText As String
  Dim FileExists As Boolean

  FileExists = True

  On Error GoTo ErrorHandler

  strFile = InputBox("Enter the name of file to open:")
  Open strFile For Input As #1

  If FileExists Then
    Do While Not EOF(1) ' loop until the end of file
      strChar = Input(1, #1) ' get one character
      strText = strText + strChar
    Loop
    Debug.Print strText
    ' Close the file
    Close #1
  End If
  Exit Sub

ErrorHandler:
  FileExists = False
  Select Case Err.Number
    Case 71
      MsgBox "The CD/DVD drive is empty."
    Case 53
      MsgBox "This file can't be found on the specified drive."
    Case 76
      MsgBox "File Path was not found."
    Case Else
      MsgBox "Error " & Err.Number & " :" & Err.Description
      Exit Sub
  End Select
```

```
    Resume Next
End Sub
```

Before continuing with this hands-on, let's examine the code of the `OpenToRead` procedure. The purpose of this procedure is to read the contents of the user-supplied text file character by character. When the user enters a filename, various errors can occur. For example, the filename may be wrong, the user may attempt to open a file from a CD-ROM or DVD without placing the disc in the drive, or they may try to open a file that is already open. To trap these errors, the error-handling routine at the end of the `OpenToRead` procedure uses the `Number` property of the `Err` object. The `Err` object contains information about run-time errors. If an error occurs while the procedure is running, the statement `Err.Number` will return the error number.

If error `71`, `53`, or `76` occurs, Visual Basic will display the user-friendly messages given inside the `Select Case` block and then proceed to the `Resume Next` statement, which will send it to the line of code following the one that had caused the error. If another (unexpected) error occurs, Visual Basic will return its error code (`Err.Number`) and error description (`Err.Description`).

At the beginning of the procedure, the variable `FileExists` is set to `True`. If the program doesn't encounter an error, all the instructions inside the `If FileExists Then` block will be executed. If VBA encounters an error, however, the value of the `FileExists` variable will be set to `False` (see the first statement in the error-handling routine just below the `ErrorHandler` label).

If you comment the `Close #1` instruction, Visual Basic will encounter the error on the next attempt to open the same file. Notice the `Exit Sub` statement before the `ErrorHandler` block. Put the `Exit Sub` statement just above the error-handling routine. You don't want Visual Basic to carry out the error handling if there are no errors.

How does this procedure accomplish the read operation? The `Input` function allows you to return any character from a sequential file. *Sequential access files* are files where data is retrieved in the same order as it is stored, such as files stored in the CSV (comma-delimited text), TXT (text separated by tabs), or PRN format (text separated by spaces). Configuration files, error logs, HTML files, and all sorts of plain-text files are all sequential files. These files are stored on disk as a sequence of characters. The beginning of a new text line is indicated by two special characters: the carriage return and the linefeed. When you work with sequential files, start at the beginning of the file, and move forward character by character, line by line, until you encounter the end of the file. Sequential access files can be easily opened and manipulated by just about any text editor.

If you use the VBA function named LOF (length of file) as the first argument of the Input function, you can quickly read the contents of the sequential file without having to loop through the entire file.

For example, instead of the following Do...While loop statement block:

```
Do While Not EOF(1) ' loop until the end of file
  strChar = Input(1, #1) ' get one character
  strText = strText + strChar
Loop
```

you can simply write the following statement to get the contents of the file at once:

```
strText = Input(LOF(1), #1)
```

The LOF function returns the number of bytes in a file. Each byte corresponds to one character in a text file.

To read data from a file, you must first open the file with the Open statement using the following syntax:

```
Open pathname For mode[Access access][lock]
   As [#]filenumber _   [Len=reclength]
```

The Open statement has three required arguments: pathname, mode, and filenumber. The pathname is the name of the file you want to open. The filename may include the name of a drive and folder.

mode is a keyword that determines how the file was opened. Sequential files can be opened in one of the following modes: Input, Output, or Append. Use Input to read the file, Output to write to a file and overwrite any existing file, and Append to write to a file by adding to any existing information.

filenumber is a number from 1 to 511. This number is used to refer to the file in subsequent operations. You can obtain a unique file number using the VBA built-in FreeFile function.

The optional Access clause can be used to specify permissions for the file (Read, Write, or Read Write). The optional lock argument determines which file operations are allowed for other processes. For example, if a file is open in a network environment, lock determines how other people can access it. The following lock keywords can be used: Shared, Lock Read, Lock Write, or Lock Read Write. The last element of the Open statement, reclength, specifies the buffer size (total number of characters) for sequential files.

Therefore, to open a sequential file in order to read its data, the example procedure uses the following instruction:

```
Open strFile For Input As #1
```

To close the sequential file, the following statement is used:

```
Close #1
```

4. Click anywhere within the `OpenToRead` procedure and press F5 to run it. When prompted for the file to open, type `C:\VBAAccess2024_ByExample\Vacation.txt` in the input dialog box and click OK. The procedure reads the contents of the `Vacation.txt` file into the Immediate window.

5. Run the `OpenToRead` procedure again. When prompted for the file to open, type `D:\VBAAccess2024_ByExample\Vacation.txt` in the input dialog box and click OK. This time, Visual Basic cannot find the specified file, so it displays the message File Path was not found.

6. Run the `OpenToRead` procedure again. This time, when prompted for the filename, enter the name of any file that references your CD/DVD drive (when the drive slot is empty). This should trigger error `71` and result in the message The CD/DVD drive is empty. Skip this step if you don't have a CD/DVD drive.

7. Comment the `Close #1` statement and run `OpenToRead`. When prompted for the file, enter `C:\VBAAccess2024_ByExample\Vacation.txt` as the filename. Run the same procedure again, supplying the same filename. The second run will cause the statements within the `Case Else` block to run. You should get an error `55` File already open message because the text file will still be open in memory. To remove the file from memory, type `Close #1` in the Immediate window and press Enter. Next, uncomment the `Close #1` statement in the `OpenToRead` procedure to return it to the original state.

Procedure Testing

Remember that you are responsible for the code you write. Before you give your procedure to others to test, you should test it yourself. After all, you understand best how it is supposed to work. Some programmers think testing their own code is some sort of degrading activity, especially when they work in an organization that has a team devoted to testing. *Don't make this mistake.* The testing process at the programmer level is as important as the code development itself. After you've tested the procedure yourself, you should give it to the users to test. Users will provide you with answers to questions such as: Does the procedure produce the expected results? Is it easy and fun to use? Does it follow the standard conventions? Also, it is a good idea to give the entire application to someone who knows the least about using this type of application and ask them to play around with it and try to break it.

You can test the ways your program responds to run-time errors by causing them on purpose:

- Generate any built-in error by using the following syntax:

```
Error error_number
```

For example, to display the error message that occurs when you attempt to divide by zero (0), type the following statement in the Immediate window:

```
Error 11
```

When you press Enter, Visual Basic will display the error message saying, Run-time error 11. Division by zero. You can force this error also by entering in the Immediate window:

```
? 12/0
```

- To check the meaning of the generated error, use the following syntax:

```
Error(error_number)
```

For example, to find out what error number 7 means, type the following in the Immediate window:

```
?Error(7)
```

When you press Enter, Visual Basic returns the error description:

```
"Out of memory"
```

To generate the same error at runtime in the form of a message box like the one in Figure 8.16, enter the following in the Immediate window or in your procedure code:

```
Err.Raise 7
```

When you finish debugging your VBA procedures, make sure you remove all statements that raise errors.

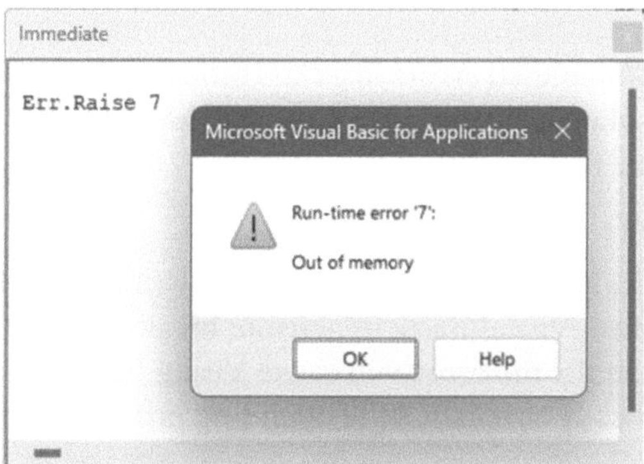

FIGURE 8.16.   To test your error-handling code, use the Raise method of the Err object. This will generate a run-time error during the execution of your procedure.

When testing your VBA procedure, use the following guidelines:

- If you want to analyze your procedure, step through your code one line at a time by pressing F8 or by choosing Debug | Step Into.

- If you suspect that an error may occur in a specific place in your procedure, use a breakpoint.

- If you want to monitor the value of a variable or expression used by your procedure, add a watch expression.

- If you are tired of scrolling through a long procedure to get to sections of code that interest you, set up a bookmark to quickly jump to the desired location.

Setting Error-Trapping Options

You can specify the error-handling settings for your current Visual Basic project by choosing Tools | Options and selecting the General tab (shown in Figure 8.17). The Error Trapping area located on the General tab determines how errors are handled in the Visual Basic environment. The following options are available:

- Break on All Errors

  This setting will cause Visual Basic to enter break mode on any error, no matter whether an error handler is active or whether the code is in a class module.

- Break in Class Module

  This setting will trap any unhandled errors in a class module. Visual Basic will activate break mode when an error occurs and will highlight the line of code in the class module that produced this error.

- Break on Unhandled Errors

  This setting will trap errors for which you have not written an error handler. The error will cause Visual Basic to activate break mode. If the error occurs in a class module, the error will cause Visual Basic to enter break mode on the line of code that called the offending procedure of the class.

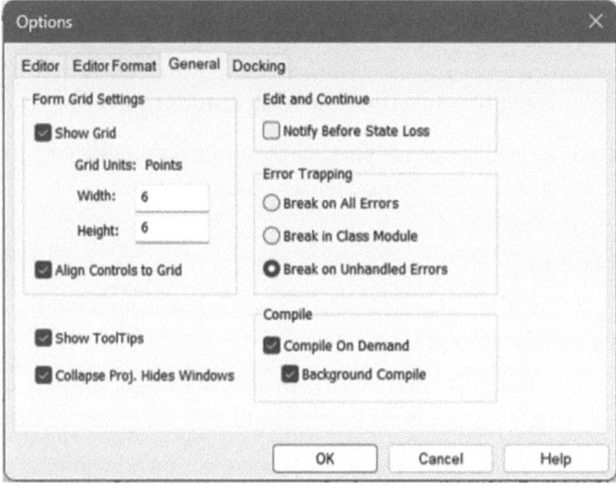

FIGURE 8.17.   Setting the error-trapping options in the Options dialog box will affect all instances of Visual Basic started after you change the setting.

USING TOOLBARS IN THE VBE WINDOW

In this chapter, you have accessed many debugging commands from the VBE main menu or a shortcut menu or used the recommended keyboard shortcuts. All the tools you have used so far can also be accessed via toolbar buttons. Using toolbars in the VBE window can streamline your coding process and make navigation easier. To turn toolbars on and off, use View | Toolbars. The Standard toolbar has buttons that make it easy to execute your code (Run), pause running code (Break), stop running code (Reset), or find and replace specific statements in the current procedure, current module, current project, or selected text block.

You can even insert a new module using a button on a Standard toolbar. Each button has a tooltip, so it is easy to identify it.

The Edit toolbar has buttons to manage your code snippets by giving you access to Cut/Copy/Paste. If these buttons are not available, they can be added by clicking the dropdown in the toolbar and choosing Add or Remove buttons | Customize. Using the Indent/Outdent button on the Edit toolbar, you can quickly adjust code indentation. You can also set or clear a breakpoint (Toggle Breakpoint), toggle bookmarks, and comment and uncomment selected lines or blocks of code.

The Debug toolbar can help you execute code line by line (Step Into (F8)), step over or out of procedures, and access other windows and tools introduced in this chapter.

It is very important that you familiarize yourself with various toolbar buttons and the corresponding keyboard shortcuts to become more efficient in the coding process. It is much quicker to click a toolbar button or press a key or a key combination to perform a specific action than it is to reach up and over to the main menu to access a specific feature. Also, toolbars can be dragged to whatever area on your screen is most convenient to you at a given moment, even outside of the VBE window.

USING ChatGPT WITH ACCESS

We all learn by trial and error. This principle extends to AI, such as ChatGPT, as well. Just as humans refine their understanding and skills through experiences and mistakes, AI systems improve by processing vast amounts of data, learning from patterns, and adjusting to provide more accurate responses. Both humans and AI evolve over time, continuously adapting and enhancing their capabilities through ongoing practice and feedback.

When enlisting the help of ChatGPT in your programming work, it's crucial to thoroughly test every bit of code it generates. Now, with the VBA debugging tools you learned about in this chapter, you should be able to debug any procedure or code snippet that comes your way. Thorough testing is vital because code behavior can vary based on context, dependencies, and specific configurations of your development environment. It is not unusual that a procedure or a function that works perfectly fine on one system fails on another.

In this section, you will work with ChatGPT on a special project that is outlined in the user prompt below:

User Prompt: *Write a real-world Access VBA procedure and function that uses loops, conditional statements, arrays, and collections and can handle errors.*

ChatGPT/Microsoft Copilot's response:

Sure! Let's say we have an Access form with a button that, when clicked, processes a list of sales transactions. Our goal is to categorize these transactions based on their amounts and then update a summary table. We'll use loops, conditional statements, arrays, collections, and error handling to achieve this.

The complete chat experience with the AI-generated VBA code can be accessed in the companion files—see `Chapter 8 - Using ChatGPT with Access`. Be sure to read the entire document first before entering any VBA procedures; it took multiple prompts to make ChatGPT remove unrelated content, correct the initial errors, and provide accurate guidance and responses. The completed project can be found in the companion files—see the `Chapter8_ChatGPT.accdb` database. Note that this project demonstrates how you can update an Access table using VBA programming code. You will be introduced here to the `Recordset` object and its various properties and methods. We will work with recordsets extensively in Part II of this book.

SUMMARY

In this chapter, you learned how to test your VBA procedures to make sure they perform as planned. You debugged your code by stepping through it using breakpoints and watches. You learned how to work with the Immediate window in break mode; you found out how the Locals window can help you monitor the values of variables; and you learned how the Call Stack dialog box can be helpful in keeping track of where you are in a complex program. You also learned how to mark your code with bookmarks so you can easily navigate between sections of your procedure. Additionally, this chapter showed you how to trap errors by including an error-handling routine inside your VBA procedure and how to use the VBA `Err` object.

By using the built-in debugging tools that you can access using various methods, you can quickly pinpoint the problem spots in your Access VBA procedures. Try to spend more time getting acquainted with the debugging tools discussed in this chapter. Mastering the art of debugging can save you hours of trial and error.

This chapter completes the fundamentals of VBA programming. With the basics mastered, you are now ready to delve into more advanced programming topics that will allow you to take full control of your Access database applications.

Access VBA
Programming with
DAO and ADO

Part **II**

There are two sets of programming objects, known as Data Access Object (DAO) and ActiveX Data Object (ADO), that enable Microsoft Access and other applications to access and manipulate data. You begin this part of the book by learning about database engines and their role in managing, storing, and retrieving data. You will learn about various libraries of objects that your VBA code can use, and then proceed to use DAO and ADO objects in your VBA procedures to connect to a data source; create, modify, and secure database objects; and read, add, update, and delete data.

Chapter 9   Data Access Technologies in Microsoft Access
Chapter 10   Creating and Manipulating Databases with DAO
Chapter 11   Creating and Manipulating Databases with ADO

DATA ACCESS TECHNOLOGIES IN MICROSOFT ACCESS

Database access is quite a complex task. Before you delve into more advanced VBA programming, you need to understand the choices that Access provides for accessing data programmatically. In this chapter, you will learn about two database engines that Access uses: the older Jet and the newer ACE. After that, we will look at versions and file formats supported by Access 2024 and discuss the importance of setting up various library references in your VBA modules. After reviewing various libraries that provide objects for your procedures, you will learn about connection strings. All this information is important, as you may need to access your database not only from Access itself but also from various external applications. Nothing great can be achieved until you are able to make a database connection.

INTRODUCTION TO DATABASE ENGINES

Database Management Systems (DBMSs) rely on special software components, known as *database engines*, to provide the functionality for managing, storing, and retrieving data in a database. The core functions of database engines are as follows:

- **Data Storage**

  Database engines ensure that the data is saved on disk in an organized, efficient, and easily accessible format.

- **Data Management**

  Database engines manage the relationships between different pieces of data. This includes enforcing data rules, constraints, and relationships, as well as indexing and cataloging data. Data management ensures integrity, consistency, and faster and more efficient access to data.

- **Data Retrieval**

  Database engines process queries written in languages such as SQL. These queries are used to retrieve the requested data. Database engines optimize this retrieval process to deliver results quickly even from large datasets.

- **Transaction Processing**

  Database engines ensure that multiple operations that must be performed together on the database, known as transactions, are executed reliably and adhere to the ACID (Atomicity, Consistency, Isolation, Durability) properties:
  - *Atomicity* ensures that each transaction is treated as a single unit; it will either completely succeed or completely fail. In a bank scenario, if you transfer money from one account to another, both the debit from one account and the credit to the other must succeed or both must fail.
  - *Consistency* ensures that a transaction takes the database from one valid state to another and all predefined rules, constraints, and triggers are followed. In a bank scenario, a transaction should not result in a negative balance if a database rule states that all account balances must be positive.
  - *Isolation* ensures that transactions are isolated from each other until they are completed so that concurrent transactions don't interfere with each other. In a bank scenario, if two customers both attempt to transfer

$500 from a joint account to their individual accounts at the same time, the system will lock the joint account's record, ensuring no other transaction can modify it until the first user's transaction completes and the joint account balance is updated. The second user's transaction will be processed next, but if there is insufficient balance in the joint account to complete the transfer, the transaction will be rejected or adjusted accordingly. Without isolation, this scenario could potentially lead to an incorrect balance and overdrawing of the account.

- *Durability* ensures that once a transaction is committed, it remains in the system even if there is a system failure, such as a power outage. In a bank scenario, if just after the transaction is completed and logged, the bank's server experiences a power outage and crashes, there will be no discrepancy or loss of data because the changes made by the transaction have been written to nonvolatile storage (a transaction log or a persistent database), and when the system is restored, the transaction log is checked to ensure that all committed transactions are reflected in the database.

- **Security and Access Control**

  Database engines control who can access and modify data and how user permissions and roles are managed to safeguard sensitive information. They protect data against unauthorized access and breaches.

- **Backup and Recovery**

  Database engines provide mechanisms to back up data and recover it in case of corruption, loss, or hardware failure.

In summary, database engines ensure that your data-driven applications are reliable and can run smoothly and efficiently.

Types of Database Engines

There exist different database engines, each having unique strengths and suited to different types of applications. Choosing the right engine depends on your specific needs; the size of the database, the number of concurrent users, security requirements, and technical environment. Here are the key database engines:

- **Microsoft Joint Engine Technology (Jet) Engine**

  Created in 1992, initially with Microsoft Access, to handle small to medium-sized database tasks, the Jet engine supports relational databases by allowing the definition of relationships between tables and enforcing data integrity. It also efficiently manages data with support for tables, queries, forms, and reports within Access databases. It provides support for SQL for querying and updating data. It supports various data types, such as text, number, date/time, and currency, and provides indexing capabilities to speed up data retrieval operations, as well as transactions, to ensure data integrity and consistency. While it provides basic security features, it lacks the advanced security capabilities that can be found in more powerful engines, such as Access Connectivity Engine (ACE) and SQL Server®. The Microsoft Jet engine has limited scalability, meaning that it cannot easily handle increasing amounts of data and concurrent users without compromising performance. It simply was not built to efficiently manage large volumes of transactions and data. As the amount of data increases, the query response times slow down, the database maintenance tasks take longer, and there is a higher risk of data corruption. Jet also struggles with high concurrency, meaning it is not able to handle well multiple operations simultaneously. If multiple staff members access and update records at the same time, the database may become slow or even crash.

The Microsoft Jet engine enables you to access data that resides in Microsoft Jet databases (`.mdb` files), external data sources such as Microsoft Excel spreadsheets, SharePoint lists, Microsoft Outlook folders, legacy dBASE files, text files, XML files, or HTML documents, as well as Open Database Connectivity (ODBC) data sources such as SQL Server and Oracle. To access external data via ODBC, you need a specific ODBC driver installed on the computer containing the data source (we look at ODBC later in this chapter). Different versions of Access use different versions of Jet (see Table 9.1). The main component of the Microsoft Jet database engine is a *dynamic-link library* file (`.dll`). On the Windows platform, DLLs are libraries of common code that can be used by more than one application.

- **ACE**

This is a database engine introduced with Access 2007, designed to succeed the Jet database engine. It offers enhanced data capacity, improved data types (e.g., multivalue fields and attachment data types), and enhanced security with encryption. It allows for more secure access control thanks to its integration with the Windows authentication system. ACE enhances SQL support by allowing you to create and run more complex queries, and even supports the execution of queries directly on external data sources, such as SQL Server. It supports larger databases and can accommodate up to 2 GB of data, which is double the capacity supported by earlier Jet versions. ACE is a powerful and flexible engine used for managing and interacting with Access databases (both `.accdb` and `.mdb` files). It allows you to integrate data from various data sources and is well suited for small to medium-size database applications running in desktop environments in single-user or small multiuser scenarios.

- **SQL Server**

This is a robust and secure database engine, released by Microsoft in 1989. It supports large-scale enterprise applications, offers advanced analytics, and handles complex queries and transaction processing. It is designed to scale efficiently and manage high levels of concurrent access with advanced locking mechanisms.

The SQL Server database engine can be used to overcome the limitations of Access' Jet and ACE engines. By using SQL Server as a back-end to Access, your database application can handle larger volumes of data and more simultaneous users efficiently. In Access, your user interface, forms, reports, and queries are known as a *front-end*. The *back-end* is the database that stores all your data. This can be another Access database or a more powerful system such as SQL Server. If your Access database begins to struggle with increased loads of data or multiple users, you can split it into a front-end and back-end to improve performance and manage more data. Splitting an Access database and the advantages of the back-end integration with SQL Server are covered in a later part of this book.

- **MySQL**

This is an open-source database engine, released in 1995, that is widely used in Web applications. It is a highly scalable database engine that supports complex queries and transaction processing.

- **Oracle Database**

Introduced by Oracle Corporation in 1977, this database engine can handle large datasets and supports complex queries, transactions, and database analytics. It is used in large enterprise environments to handle high transaction volumes.

- **PostgreSQL**

  This is an open-source database engine released in 1996. It supports advanced data types, indexes, and complex queries and is fully ACID-compliant. It is often used for applications requiring advanced data features.

- **SQLite**

  This is a lightweight serverless database engine released in 2000. It is suitable for small desktop applications, mobile apps, and embedded systems.

TABLE 9.1. Database engine versions in Access 2024 and earlier.

MS Access Version	Database Engine Used	Dynamic Link Library (DLL) File
Access 2007–2024	ACE 12	ace.dll
Access 2000–2003	Jet 4.0	msjet40.dll
Access 97	Jet 3.5	msjet35.dll

UNDERSTANDING ACCESS VERSIONS AND FILE FORMATS

In Access 2007–2024, the default file format is `.accdb`; however, you can still directly open and use Jet databases (`.mdb` files) created in Access 2000–2003. Jet databases created with Access 97 or earlier must be either enabled or converted for use in Access 2007–2024. When an older database is enabled, it is made compatible with Access so that you can make changes to the data. However, any design changes must be made in the version of Access that was used when the database was first created. When you opt to convert an Access 97 or earlier database into the `.accdb` file format, you must first convert it to Access 2000–2003.

Appendix B in the companion files shows various file formats that have been supported since the release of Access 2007.

UNDERSTANDING LIBRARY REFERENCES

A Microsoft Access database consists of various types of objects stored in different object libraries. *Libraries* are components that provide specific functionality. They contain classes, methods, and properties that you can call from your VBA code. They are listed in the References dialog box, shown in Figure 9.1, which can be opened from VBE by selecting Tools | References. When you create an

Access 2024 database in the default `.accdb` file format, you will see the following default references in the References dialog box:

- Visual Basic for Applications
- Microsoft Access 16.0 Object Library
- OLE Automation
- Microsoft Office 16.0 Access database engine Object Library

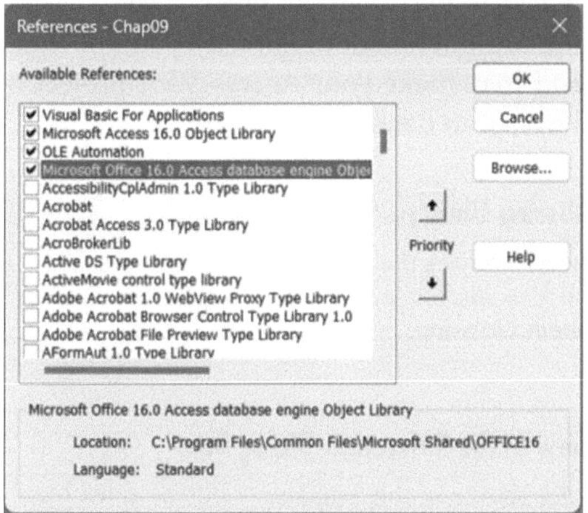

FIGURE 9.1.   The default object libraries for Access 2024.

The Visual Basic for Applications and Access libraries that appear at the top of the References dialog box are built in. Access will not allow you to remove them from the database. The library references that are checked are listed by priority. References that are not checked are listed alphabetically. When your VBA procedure references an object, Visual Basic searches each referenced object library in the order in which the libraries are displayed in the References dialog box. If the referenced libraries have objects with the same name, Visual Basic uses the object definition provided by the library listed higher in the Available References list. You can change the priority of an object library by selecting its name and clicking the up or down arrow button in the References dialog box. To help Visual Basic resolve library references, specify in your code the name of the library you intend to use. For example, to specify that the DAO recordset should be used, declare it like this:

```
Dim rst As DAO.Recordset
```

To use the ADO recordset, use the following declaration:

```
Dim rst As ADODB.Recordset
```

You can reference additional libraries in your Access database if your VBA application requires features that are not provided by the default libraries. For example, if your VBA procedures need to access files and folders on the computer, you may want to check the box next to Microsoft Scripting Runtime. To use Excel objects from your Access VBA procedures, for example, when automating the export of data from Access to Excel, check the box next to Microsoft Excel 16.0 Object Library. Do not add references to libraries you don't plan to use as they consume memory and may make your Access VBA project more time-consuming to compile and harder to debug.

Missing Library

If the library is marked as Missing in the References dialog box, click the Browse... button, and locate the correct library file. You can disable a missing reference by clearing the checkbox to the left of the reference labeled Missing.

Library Does Not Show in the References Dialog Box

If the library you want to reference is not shown in the Available References list box, you may need to unregister and reregister it with Windows.

To unregister a library (such as a DLL or OCX file) in Windows 11 or earlier, close Microsoft Access and follow these steps:

1. Open Command Prompt as Administrator.
   Press the Windows key, type `cmd`, right-click on Command Prompt, and select Run as administrator.
2. Navigate to the directory where the DLL or OCX file is located. For example, to unregister `msadox.dll`, use the `cd` command, type a space, and enter the path to your file:

```
cd C:\Program Files\Common Files\System\Ado
```

3. Unregister the file.
   Enter `regsvr32 /u` followed by a space and the name of the library file. For example, to unregister `msadox.dll`, enter the following:

```
regsvr32 /u msadox.dll
```

If the file has been unregistered successfully, you should see a confirmation message box.

To register a library, follow the same steps but without the `/u` switch. For example:

```
regsvr32 msadox.dll
```

The `regsvr32` command registers the DLL file whether it is 64-bit or 32-bit. When running 64-bit Windows, the 32-bit files are in the `Windows\SysWOW64` folder and the 64-bit DLL files are in the `Windows\System32` folder.

In 32-bit Windows, the DLL files are in the `Windows\System32` folder and there is no `SysWOW64` folder. These folder distinctions help Windows manage and differentiate seamlessly between 64-bit and 32-bit components.

If you run into any issues while using the `regsvr32` command, try to disable the User Account Control (UAC) in Windows, which may be preventing you from successfully registering the DLL file. Once you register a missing library, the library name should be listed in the References dialog box the next time you open Access.

NOTE	*If you move a library file from where it was originally installed, be sure to reregister it with the operating system or things may not work as expected.*

Because referencing a wrong library for the version of Access used can cause data corruption, it is important to know which library files were designed for a particular version of Access. The next section introduces you to library files that you will find useful in creating and manipulating databases in the `.mdb` and `.accdb` file formats using VBA code.

OVERVIEW OF OBJECT LIBRARIES IN MICROSOFT ACCESS

The object library contains information about its objects, properties, and methods. To work with the VBA programming examples included in this book, you will need to access objects from the libraries listed in the following subsections.

The VBA Object Library

Objects contained in this library allow you to access your computer's file system, work with date and time functions, perform mathematical and financial computations, interact with users, convert data, and read text files. The VBA library is stored in the `VBE7.DLL` file in the following folder:

```
C:\Program Files\Microsoft Office\root\vfs\ProgramFilesCom-
monX64\Microsoft Shared\VBA\VBA7.1
```

The Microsoft Access 16.0 Object Library

This library provides objects that are used to display data and work with the Microsoft Access application. In Access 2016–2024, the Access library is stored in the `MSACC.OLB` file in the following folder:

```
C:\Program Files\Microsoft Office\root\Office16
```

OLE Automation

The Object Linking and Embedding (OLE) library allows you to embed or link an object from another application. In Access 2016–2024, the library is stored in the `STDOLE2.TLB` file in the following folder:

```
C:\Windows\System32
```

The Microsoft Office 16.0 Access Database Engine Object Library

This library is an enhanced version of the DAO object library. It was built specifically for working with the ACE database engine. In Access 2016–2024, the library is stored in the `ACEDAO.DLL` file in the following folder:

```
C:\Program Files\Common Files\microsoft shared\OFFICE16
```

This library is used when you open an Access database in the default Access format (`.accdb`).

The Microsoft DAO 3.6 Object Library

This object library provides a set of objects and methods used to access and manipulate data stored in Microsoft Access databases. This library is stored in the `DAO360.DLL` file and is compatible with various versions of Microsoft Access for automating database tasks using VBA code. It allows developers to create, read, update, and delete records in a database. For example, you can set a reference to this library if you plan to write VBA code that will open a database, retrieve records from a table, and print the values to the Immediate window. You will work with DAO objects in Chapter 10.

The Microsoft ADO 6.1 Library

This library is stored in the `MSADO15.DLL` file. ADO objects that are provided by this library are used for accessing and manipulating data from a variety of sources, including SQL Server, Oracle, and ODBC-compliant databases. ADO works with the technology known as Object Linking and Embedding Database (OLE DB). This technology is object-based, but it is not limited to relational databases. OLE DB can access both relational and nonrelational data sources, such as directory services, mail stores, and multimedia and text files, as well as mainframe data (VSAM and MVS). You do not need any specific drivers installed on your computer to access external data with OLE DB because OLE DB does not use drivers; it uses data providers to communicate with data stores. *Data providers* are programs that enable access to data. OLE DB has many providers, such as Microsoft OLE DB for SQL Server and the OLE DB Provider for Microsoft Jet 4.0. There are also providers for Oracle, Active Directory˚, and ODBC.

If you scroll down the list of Available References (Figure 9.2), you may be confused to see several different versions of the Microsoft ADO library. Different versions of the ADO library correspond to updates and improvements made over time. Each new version is backward compatible with older ones, meaning newer versions can often handle code written for older versions. Always choose the version that matches your project requirements and ensures that you're leveraging the most recent advancements. For Windows 7 and above, use version 6.1.

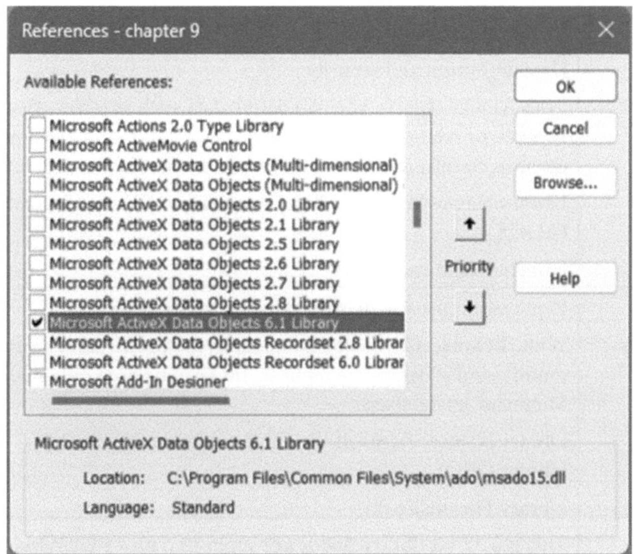

FIGURE 9.2.   Object libraries can come in different versions.

Similar to DAO, ADO objects make it possible to establish a connection with a data source in order to read, insert, modify, and delete data. ADO uses objects to represent data, connections, and commands and makes it easy to work with data programmatically. ADO offers programmers many advanced features that are not available in DAO. For example, the ADO `Connection` object's `State` property lets you determine whether the connection is closed (`adStateClosed`), open and ready (`adStateOpen`), still trying to connect (`adStateConnecting`), processing a command (`adStateExecuting`), or fetching data (`adStateFetching`). The ADO recordsets can be hierarchical, fabricated, disconnected, or persisted on disk.

ADO consists of three object models, each providing a different area of functionality (see Table 9.2). Because of this, only the objects necessary for a specific task need to be loaded at any given time.

TABLE 9.2. The components of ADO.

Object Model	What It's Used For
ADODB (ActiveX Data Object)	Data manipulation Access and manipulate data through an OLE DB provider. With ADO objects, you can connect to a data source and read, add, update, or delete data. Library Name: Microsoft ADO 6.1 Library Library File: msado15.dll
ADOX (ADO Extensions for DDL and Security)	Data definition and security With ADOX objects, you can define data such as tables, views, indexes, or relationships, as well as create and modify user and group accounts, and grant and revoke permissions on objects. Library Name: Microsoft ADO Ext. 6.0 for DDL and Security (ADOX) Library File: msadox.dll
JRO (Jet and Replication Objects)	Replication (used with .mdb databases only) With JRO objects, you can compact a Jet database, and create, modify, and synchronize replicas. JRO can be used only with Microsoft Jet databases. Library Name: Microsoft Jet and Replication Objects 2.6 Library (JRO) Library File: msjro.dll This is a 32-bit library that is not supported on 64-bit Windows systems.

You will work with ADO objects in Chapter 11.

NOTE	*Access 2000 was the first version to support ADO. In an attempt to promote universal data access, Microsoft made ADO the default library in Access 2000 and 2002. DAO was to be phased out and Access programmers were advised to move their application code from DAO to ADO. Since then, having found out that DAO still performed faster in most cases, was easier to use, and offered features that were specifically designed with Jet/ ODBC databases in mind, Microsoft has returned to DAO as the main data access layer. In Access 2007, DAO was enhanced to use the new data types and other improvements available in the* `.accdb` *format. This enhanced version of DAO was offered as the Microsoft Office 12.0 Access database engine object library. In Access 2016–2024, it is offered as the Microsoft Office 16.0 Access database engine object library.*

ADO Classic Versus ADO.NET

The classic ADO used in VBA in Microsoft Access and other Microsoft 365 applications is a completely different object model from ADO.NET used with the Microsoft .NET framework. ADO.NET is not built on ActiveX technology and its objects cannot be used directly in a VBA project.

CREATING A REFERENCE TO THE ADO LIBRARY

Prior to declaring variables as ADO objects in your VBA procedures, make sure that the reference to the library you intend to use is set in the References dialog box. Hands-On 9.1 demonstrates how to create a reference to the Microsoft ADO 6.1 object library.

NOTE	*All code files and figures for the hands-on projects may be found in the companion files.*

⊚ Hands-On 9.1   Setting Up a Reference to the ADO Object Library

1. Start Microsoft Access and create a new database named `Chap9.accdb` in your `C:\VBAAccess2024_ByExample` folder.
2. Press Alt+F11 to switch to the VBE window, and choose Tools | References.

3. Scroll down the list of available references until you locate the Microsoft ADO 6.1 library. Click the checkbox to the left of the name to select it (see Figure 9.2 in an earlier section).
4. Click OK to close the References dialog box.
   All libraries that are checked in the References dialog box can be browsed using the Object Browser. This is a good way to become familiar with the names of objects that are available in a specific library and their various properties and methods (see Figure 9.3).

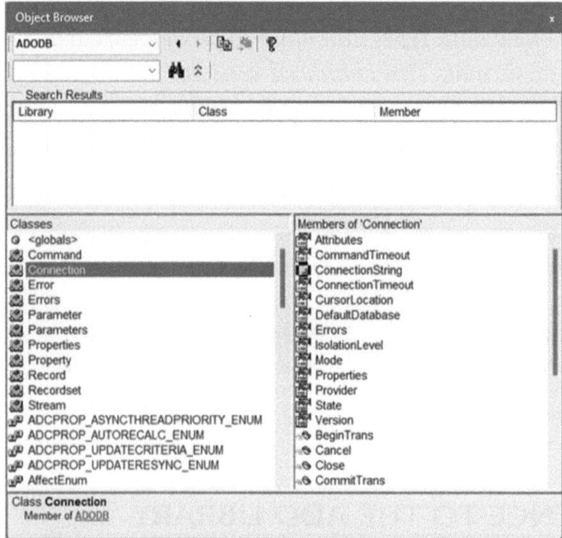

FIGURE 9.3.   Use the Object Browser to find the objects available in a specific library.

UNDERSTANDING CONNECTION STRINGS

Needless to say, to retrieve or write data to a database, you will need to open it first. There are many ways to connect to a database or an external data source from Microsoft Access. The first thing to know about establishing database connections from your VBA procedures is how to prepare and use connection strings.

A *connection string* is a string variable that tells your VBA application how to establish a connection to a data source. There are two types of connection strings:

- ODBC connection strings (used by ODBC drivers)
- OLE DB connection strings (used by the OLE DB provider)

The syntax of ODBC and OLE DB connection strings is very similar. The connection string consists of a series of keyword and value pairs separated by semicolons:

```
Keyword1=value; Keyword2=value
```

Please note that the connection string does not contain spaces before or after the equal sign (=). The parameters in the connection string may vary depending on the ODBC driver or OLE DB provider used and the data store that you are connecting to such as Microsoft Access, SQL Server, and so forth.

Let's examine the connection string you would need to connect to an older Microsoft Access database in the .mdb file format. In the examples that follow, we use the underscore (_) line continuation character to ensure that the connection string is easier to understand and the examples are more readable. The line continuation character allows us to break long lines of code into multiple shorter lines, enhancing clarity and making the code more manageable. By organizing the connection string this way, it becomes simpler to modify and debug, especially when dealing with complex connection parameters.

For the ODBC connection, the following connection string will allow you to connect to an Access database called Northwind.mdb:

```
"Driver={Microsoft Access Driver (*.mdb)};" & _
"DBQ=C:\VBAAccess2024_ByExample\Northwind.mdb;"
```

In the preceding connection string, Driver specifies what type of database you're using. DBQ is the physical path to the database. If the Northwind.mdb file is protected with a password, you must provide additional information in the connection string:

```
"Driver={Microsoft Access Driver (*.mdb)};" & _
"DBQ=C:\VBAAccess2024_ByExample\Northwind.mdb;" & _
"UID=admin;" & _
"PWD=secret;"
```

UID specifies the username. PWD specifies the user password.

To create an OLE DB connection to the same Northwind.mdb database that uses standard security, you will need to write the connection string as follows:

```
"Provider=Microsoft.Jet.OLEDB.4.0;" & _
"Data Source=C:\VBAAccess2024_ByExample\Northwind.mdb;" & _
"User ID=Admin;" & _
"Password=;"
```

Or:

```
"Provider=Microsoft.ACE.OLEDB.12.0;" & _
"Data Source=C:\VBAAccess2024_ByExample\Northwind.mdb;" & _
"User Id=Admin;" & _
"Password=;"
```

`Provider` identifies the OLE DB provider for your database; in this case, we want to use the Jet OLE DB provider or the ACE OLE DB provider. You should use the `Microsoft.ACE.OLEDB` provider if you are running Windows 64-bit and Office 64-bit.

`Data Source` specifies the full path and filename to the `Northwind.mdb` database file. `User ID` sets the user ID for the connection and `Password` is typically left empty for standard security.

To create an OLE DB connection to the SQL database called `Adventure-Works`, use the following connection string:

```
"Provider=SQLOLEDB;Data Source=(local);" & _
"Integrated Security=SSPI;Initial Catalog=AdventureWorks"
```

In this connection string, `SQLOLEDB` is the name of the OLE DB provider for SQL Server databases. The `Data Source` parameter specifies the name or address of the SQL Server. To connect with an SQL Server running on the same computer, use the keyword `(local)` for the `Data Source`. For a trusted connection (Microsoft Windows NT integrated security), set the `Integrated Security` parameter to `SSPI`. Use the `Initial Catalog` parameter to specify which database you want to connect to.

NOTE	*If the* `Provider` *keyword is not included in the connection string, the OLE DB provider for ODBC (`MSDASQL`) is the default value. This provides backward compatibility with ODBC connection strings that are discussed next.*

Using ODBC Connection Strings

ODBC is a standard Application Programming Interface (API) that allows Access to connect and interact with various database systems (such as SQL Server, MySQL, and Oracle).

When you choose to connect to a data source via ODBC, you must specify the connection information. You do this by creating a Data Source Name (DSN) or DSN-less connection. DSN connections store the connection information in the Windows Registry or in a `.dsn` file. In a *DSN-less* connection, all connection information is specified in the connection string. The following subsections explain each ODBC connection type in detail.

Creating and Using ODBC DSN Connections

Windows uses an ODBC Data Source Administrator (see Figure 9.4) to manage ODBC drivers and data sources available on your computer. You can access this tool by opening Control Panel | System and Security | Administrative Tools (in Windows 11, use Windows Tools) | ODBC Data Sources (32-bit) or ODBC Data Sources (64-bit).

The DSN contains information about database configuration, location, and user security. There are three types of DSNs:

- **User DSN**—A user DSN is stored locally in the Windows Registry and limits database connectivity to the user who creates it. In other words, if you create a user DSN under your user account, no other user will be able to see it or use it. Hands-On 9.2 demonstrates how to create this type of DSN so that you can run the example code on your computer.

- **System DSN**—A system DSN is stored locally in the Windows Registry and allows any logged-on user, process, and service to see and use it. Many organizations that run Web applications that rely on an SQL Server database for their data set up a system DSN to ensure that the application can connect to the database from any user account on the server.

- **File DSN**—A file DSN is a special type of file that stores all the connection settings. File DSNs are saved by default in the `Program Files\Common Files\Odbc\Data Sources` folder. Because the connection parameters and values are stored in a file, they can be easily shared with other

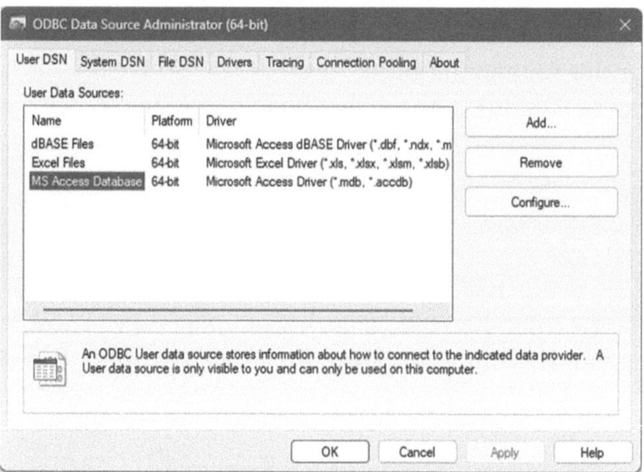

FIGURE 9.4. The ODBC Data Source Administrator allows you to set up appropriate connections with the required data provider via the user, system, or file DSN.

users. If other users require the same connection, simply send them the DSN file and you won't need to configure a DSN for each system.

Hands-On 9.2 will get you started with the ODBC Data Source Administrator by walking you through the creation of a user DSN named `MyDbaseFile` to access data in a legacy dBASE database file (`Customer.dbf`). You will then use this DSN to programmatically open a dBASE file with ADO using the ODBC DSN connection. If you don't have the dBASE driver on your newer Windows machine, you will need to download and install *Microsoft Access Database Engine 2016 Redistributable*, which contains a set of components used in data transfers between Microsoft Office system files and non-Microsoft Office applications. See the following site for the download:

https://www.microsoft.com/en-US/download/details.aspx?id=54920&form=MG0AV3

If the dBASE driver is already installed on your machine, you will be able to see the dBASE Files entry under User Data Sources in the ODBC Data Source Administrator (64-bit) dialog box (see Figure 9.4).

> **Hands-On 9.2 Creating and Using the ODBC DSN Connection to Read Data from a dBASE File**

The procedure code in this hands-on exercise relies on the reference to the ADO library that was set in Hands-On 9.1.

1. Copy the `Customer.dbf` file from the companion files to your `C:\VBAAccess2024_ByExample` folder.
2. Open the Control Panel, click System and Security | Windows Tools, and double-click ODBC Data Sources (64-bit).
   The ODBC Data Source Administrator dialog box appears, as shown earlier in Figure 9.4.
3. With the User DSN tab selected, click the Add button.
4. Select Microsoft Access dBASE driver (*.dbf, *ndx, *.mdx) and click Finish.
5. In the ODBC dBASE Setup dialog, enter `MyDbaseFile` as the DSN and choose dBASE 5.0 for the database version, as shown in Figure 9.5. Make sure you clear the Use Current Directory checkbox, then click the Select Directory button.

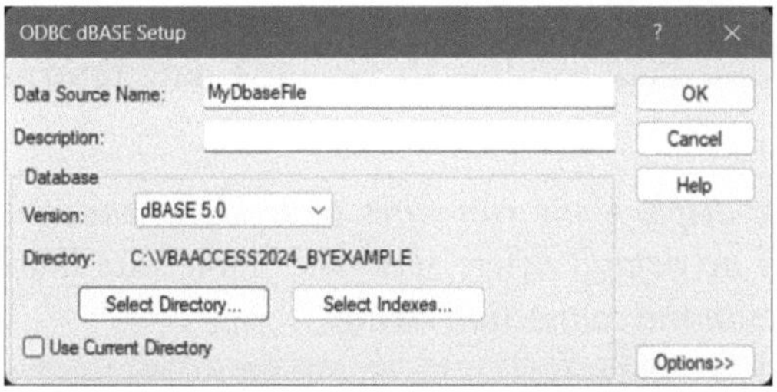

FIGURE 9.5.   Creating a DSN to access a dBASE file.

6. In the Select Directory dialog box, select the C:\VBAAccess2024_ByExample folder where the `Customer.dbf` file is located, and click the OK button.

7. Click OK to exit the ODBC dBASE Setup dialog box.
The `MyDbaseFile` data source now appears in the list of User Data Sources in the ODBC Data Source Administrator dialog box.

8. Click OK to close the ODBC Data Source Administrator dialog box.

9. In the `Chap09` database, activate the VBE window and choose Tools | References. Scroll down to find and check the Microsoft ADO 6.1 library, then click OK.

10. Choose Insert | Module, and in the module's Code window, enter the following `Open_AndRead_dBaseFile` procedure:

```
Sub Open_AndRead_dBaseFile()
   Dim conn As ADODB.Connection
   Dim rst As ADODB.Recordset

   Set conn = New ADODB.Connection
   conn.Open "Provider=MSDASQL;DSN=MyDbaseFile;"

   Debug.Print conn.ConnectionString

   Set rst = New ADODB.Recordset
   rst.Open "Customer.dbf", conn

   Do Until rst.EOF
     Debug.Print rst.Fields(1).Value
     rst.MoveNext
   Loop

   rst.Close
   Set rst = Nothing
   conn.Close
   Set conn = Nothing
End Sub
```

11. Choose Run | Run Sub/UserForm to execute the procedure.
12. Press Ctrl+G to open the Immediate window to view the data returned by the procedure.

<table>
<tr><td rowspan="2">NOTE</td><td>If Visual Basic displays the run-time error Data source name not found and no default driver specified, make sure there are no extra spaces in the connection string:

<code>conn.Open "Provider=MSDASQL;DSN=MyDbaseFile;"</code></td></tr>
<tr><td>This is a very common error and it's hard to trace because spaces are difficult to spot.</td></tr>
</table>

The `Open_AndRead_dBaseFile` procedure uses the ADO `Connection` object to establish a connection with the data source. Prior to using ADO objects in your VBA procedures, make sure that the References dialog box contains the reference to the ADO library. The procedure begins by declaring an object variable of the `Connection` type, like this:

```
Dim conn As ADODB.Connection
```

To handle data retrieval, an object variable of the `Recordset` type is also declared:

```
Dim rst As ADODB.Recordset
```

A recordset is a set of rows from a database table or the results of a query.

Before you can use the declared ADO `Connection` object, you must initialize the object variable by using the `Set` keyword:

```
Set conn = New ADODB.Connection
```

At this point, you can proceed to open the data source by using the ADO `Connection` object's `Open` method. The required database connection information is passed to the `Open` method in the connection string, like this:

```
conn.Open "Provider=MSDASQL;DSN=MyDbaseFile;"
```

`MSDASQL` is the Microsoft OLE DB provider for all ODBC data sources. The names of common data providers used with ADO are listed in Table 9.3. The `Provider` property of the ADO `Connection` object is used in the connection string as the provider name. DSN is the name of the data source that you specified for your connection settings in the ODBC Data Source Administrator dialog box. Since `MSDASQL` is the default provider for ODBC, it's also permitted to leave it off, like this:

```
conn.Open "DSN=MyDbaseFile;"
```

TABLE 9.3. Common data providers used with ADO.

Provider Name	Provider Property	Description
Microsoft ACE	Microsoft.ACE.OLEDB.12.0	Used by Access 2024–2010 databases in .accdb file format. By default, this provider opens databases in Read/Write mode.
Microsoft Jet	Microsoft.Jet.OLEDB.4.0	Used for Jet 4.0 databases (in .mdb file format). By default, this provider opens databases in Read/Write mode.
Microsoft SQL Server	SQLOLEDB	Used to access SQL Server databases.
Oracle	MSDAORA	Used to access Oracle databases.
ODBC	MSDASQL	Used to access ODBC data sources without a specific OLE DB provider. This is the default provider for ADO.
Active Directory Service	ADSDSOObject	Used to access Windows NT 4.0 directory services, Novell' directory services, and LDAP-compliant directory services.
Index Server	MSIDXS	Used for read-only access to Web data.

Once the connection to the dBASE database file is open, the procedure initializes the `rst` object variable using the `Set` keyword in order to gain access to its data:

```
Set rst = New ADODB.Recordset
```

The ADO `Recordset` object's `Open` method is used to open the `Customer.dbf` file, like this:

```
rst.Open "Customer.dbf", conn
```

The `Open` method can take several parameters. In this example, we are providing it with the connection information that is stored in the `conn` object variable. Once the recordset is open, you can start reading its data. The `Do Until` loop will iterate through the recordset until the `EOF` (end of file) is reached. Each time through the loop, VBA will write to the Immediate window the value of the second field (column) in the current record of the recordset. `Fields(0)` would retrieve data from the first field (column) as field indexing starts at zero (`0`). There are four fields in the `Customer.dbf` file. You can examine the data in the `Customer.dbf` file by bringing it to Access as a table. To do this, choose External Data | New Data Source | From Database | dBASE file.

When the procedure ends, you should see in the Immediate window the names of all customers from the `Customer.dbf` file.

When you are done reading the records, the procedure uses the `Close` method to close the recordset and destroy the `rst` object variable by setting it to `Nothing`:

```
rst.Close
Set rst = Nothing
```

This statement completely releases the resources used by the `Recordset` object. The same should be done with the `Connection` object variable (`conn`) when it is no longer needed:

```
conn.Close
Set conn = Nothing
```

Creating and Using DSN-Less ODBC Connections

It is possible that your VBA application that relies on database access via an ODBC DSN may suddenly fail because the DSN was modified or deleted. Therefore, it may be a better idea to use another type of connection known as a DSN-less connection. Instead of setting up a DSN as you did in Hands-On 9.2, specify your ODBC driver name and all driver-specific information in your connection string. Different types of databases can require that you specify different parameters. Because the ODBC DSN setup using the ODBC Administrator dialog is not required, this type of connection is called "DSN-less."

Additional Code in the Companion Files

You can rewrite the procedure in Hands-On 9.2 to use a DSN-less ODBC connection. See `HandsOn9.2_Supplement.txt` in the companion files.

ODBC Connection Strings for Common Data Sources

Table 9.4 shows examples of ODBC connection strings that cover a range of data sources that you can use from your Access VBA code. You should customize the paths and parameters according to your specific setup and data requirements.

TABLE 9.4. ODBC connection strings for common data sources.

Data Source	ODBC Connection String (Used in DSN-Less Connections)
Microsoft Access 1997–2003 (accessing .mdb files)	"Driver={Microsoft Access Driver (*.mdb)}; Dbq=C:\path\to\YourDatabase.mdb;"
Microsoft Access 2007–2024 (accessing .mdb or .accdb files)	"Driver={Microsoft Access Driver (*.mdb, *.accdb)}; Dbq=C:\path\to\YourDatabase.accdb;"

Data Source	ODBC Connection String (Used in DSN-Less Connections)
Microsoft Excel 1997–2003 (accessing .xls files)	"Driver={Microsoft Excel Driver (*.xls)}; Dbq=C:\path\to\YourFile.xls;"
Microsoft Excel 2007 and later (accessing .xls, .xlsx, .xlsm, and .xlsb files)	"Driver={Microsoft Excel Driver (*.xls, *.xlsx, *.xlsm, *.xlsb)}; Dbq=C:\path\to\YourFile.xls /.xlsx/.xlsm/.xlsb; Extended Properties=""Excel 12.0;HDR=YES;IMEX=1"";"
Text Files (accessing CSV and TXT files)	"Driver={Microsoft Access Text Driver (*.txt, *.csv)}; Dbq=C:\path\to\your\directory\;Extensions=txt,csv;HDR=YES;"
SQL Server	"Driver={SQL Server}; Server=YourServerName;Database=YourDatabaseName; Uid=YourUsername;Pwd=YourPassword;"
Oracle	"Driver={Oracle in XE ODBC Driver}; Dbq=YourServerName;Uid=YourUsername;Pwd=YourPassword;"
MySQL	"Driver={MySQL ODBC 8.0 Unicode Driver}; Server=YourServerName;Database=YourDatabaseName; Uid=YourUsername;Pwd=YourPassword;"
dBASE	"Driver={Microsoft Access dBASE Driver (*.dbf, *.ndx, *.mdx)}; DBQ= C:\path\to\your\directory;" (do not specify the file name)

As you can see from Table 9.4, ODBC connection strings typically include the `Driver`, `Server`, `Database`, `UID` (user ID), and `PWD` (password).

Using OLE DB Connection Strings

Before we delve into the topic of this section, you need to understand what COM is and how it relates to OLDE DB. COM (which stands for *Component Object Model*) is a Microsoft technology that allows software components to communicate and interact with one another, regardless of the language they are written in or the platform they are running on. For example, the `IDBInitialize` interface is used to set up the connection to the data source and the `IDBCreateSession` interface creates a session to manage interactions with the data source. Other COM interfaces are used to create commands for executing queries and perform updates, retrieve data from the data source in the form of rows, or handle transactions to ensure that all changes are properly committed or rolled back.

OLE DB uses these COM-based interfaces to access data from various sources, whether it's a relational database, a spreadsheet, or another type of data store. Thanks to these interfaces, OLE DB can interact with data in a consistent, efficient, and uniform manner.

In the previous section, you learned how ODBC is used to connect to different data sources. While ODBC uses drivers to connect to databases, OLE DB uses providers. See Table 9.3 earlier in this chapter for the names of common OLE DB providers used with ADO. The choice between using ODBC or OLE DB for your database connectivity depends on your specific needs. OLE DB is considered more flexible because it can connect not only to relational databases but also to other types of data stores, such as spreadsheets and text files. It provides more detailed control over how data is accessed and manipulated. In contrast, ODBC is simpler and widely compatible with various database systems.

Table 9.5 shows examples of OLE DB connection strings for common data sources. You will learn how to use them in VBA procedures in the next chapters.

TABLE 9.5.   OLE DB connection strings for common data sources.

Data Source	OLE DB Connection String
Access 2003 and Earlier (.mdb)	"Provider=Microsoft.Jet.OLEDB.4.0; Data Source=C:\path\to\your\database.mdb; User Id=admin;Password=;"
Access 2007 and Later (.accdb)	"Provider=Microsoft.ACE.OLEDB.12.0; Data Source=C:\path\to\your\database.accdb; Persist Security Info=False;"
Excel 97–2003 (.xls)	"Provider=Microsoft.Jet.OLEDB.4.0; Data Source=C:\path\to\your\file.xls; Extended Properties="Excel 8.0;HDR=YES;IMEX=1";"
Excel 2007 and Later (.xlsx)	"Provider=Microsoft.ACE.OLEDB.12.0; Data Source=C:\path\to\your\file.xlsx; Extended Properties="Excel 12.0 Xml;HDR=YES;IMEX=1";"
Microsoft SQL Server	"Provider=SQLOLEDB;Data Source=YourServerName; Initial Catalog=YourDatabaseName; User ID=YourUsername;Password=YourPassword;"
Oracle	"Provider=OraOLEDB.Oracle;Data Source=YourOracleSID; User Id=YourUsername;Password=YourPassword;"

As you can see from Table 9.5, OLE DB connection strings typically include the `Provider`, `Data Source`, `Initial Catalog` (database), `User ID`, and `Pass-`

word. These connection strings should help you connect to various data sources using OLE DB. Be sure to customize the paths and parameters according to your data requirements.

Connection Strings via a Data Link File

If you are using the Windows operating system and are looking for an easy way to create and test a connection string that uses an ODBC driver or OLE DB provider, you may want to use the Data Link Properties dialog box, which is shown in Figure 9.6.

A universal data link file (`.udl`) is a text file containing the connection information. Hands-On 9.3 demonstrates how to create the `.udl` file to connect to an Access database. You can use the same technique to create a valid connection string to other external data sources as long as the ADO provider is installed on your computer.

Hands-On 9.3   Creating and Using a Universal Data Link File

1. In Windows File Explorer, select the `C:\VBAAccess2024_ByExample` folder. Make sure that the option to show filename extensions is selected in the View dropdown.
2. Choose New | Text Document to create a new text document in the `C:\VBAAccess2024_ByExample` folder.
3. A new file named `New Text Document.txt` appears in the `VBAAccess2021_ByExample` folder. Rename this file `ConnectToAccdb.udl`.
   When changing the filename, be sure to type the new extension (`.udl`) as indicated.

   Windows will display a warning message that changing the file extension can cause the file to become unusable. Ignore this message and click OK.

   Windows creates an empty universal data link file. Notice that the file size is 0 KB.
4. Double-click the ConnectToAccdb.udl file to open the Data Link Properties dialog. Windows opens the Data Link Properties dialog box (Figure 9.6), which contains the following four tabs:

TABLE 9.6. Tabs in the Data Link Properties dialog box

Data Link Tab	Description
Provider	Lists the names of the ADO providers installed on your computer. The provider name you select must be appropriate for the data source you want to use. For example, if you select the Microsoft Jet 4.0 OLE DB provider, you must select an Access database in .mdb format.
Connection	Allows you to define a DSN for the selected provider type. The entries shown here are specific to the provider type selected via the Provider tab. The Connection tab is active by default when you activate the Data Link Properties dialog box.
Advanced	Allows you to view and set other initialization properties for your data connection.
All	Allows you to review and edit all OLE DB initialization properties available for the selected OLE DB provider.

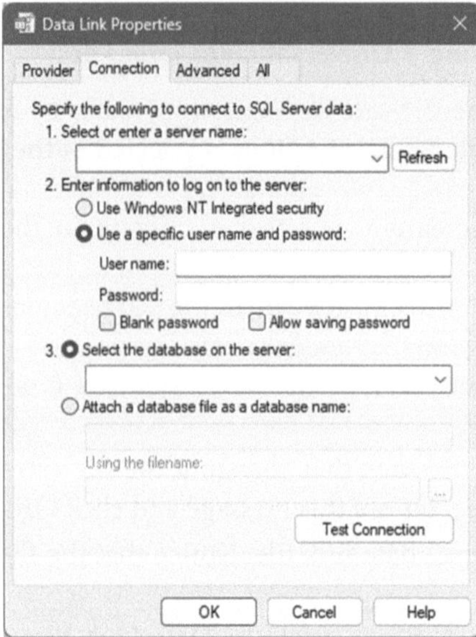

FIGURE 9.6. The Data Link Properties dialog box appears after you launch the .udl file.

5. Click the Provider tab and select Microsoft Office 16.0 Access Database Engine OLE DB Provider, as shown in Figure 9.7.

> **NOTE**
>
> *If you don't see the above-mentioned data provider, you can try using the Office 12.0 provider. If neither of these providers is available, you will need to download and install the Microsoft Access Database Engine 2016 Redistributable from Microsoft.*

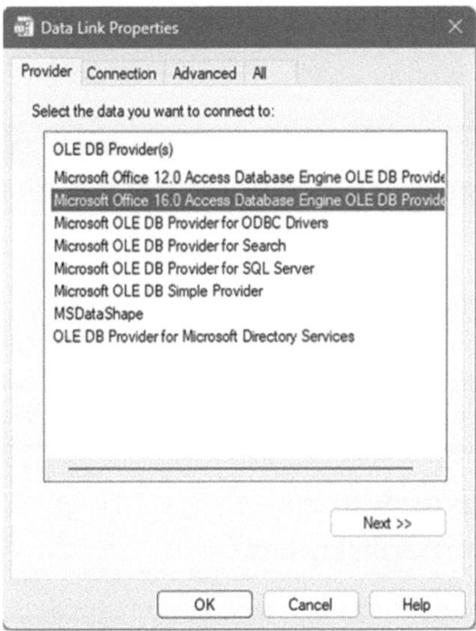

FIGURE 9.7.   The Provider tab in the Data Link Properties dialog box lists the names of the ADO providers installed on your computer.

6. Click the Next button or activate the Connection tab.
    The entries shown on the Connection tab are related to the type of provider you selected in step 5.

7. In the Data Source box, type the location and filename of the database you want to connect to: `C:\VBAAccess2024_ByExample\NorthwindStarter.accdb` (see Figure 9.8).

8. Click the Test Connection button to test whether you can connect to the specified database using the chosen data provider.

9. Click OK on the message box Test connection succeeded.
    If you misspelled a filename or Windows cannot locate the file in the specified folder, you will get an error.

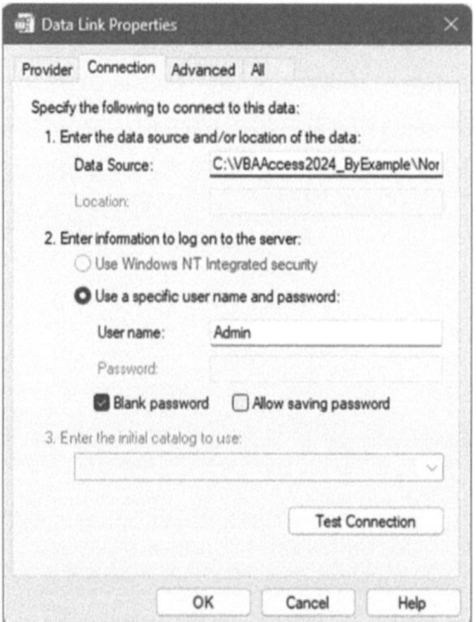

FIGURE 9.8.   Use the Data Link Properties dialog box to define a DSN for the selected provider type. Be sure to enter .accdb as the extension for the NorthwindStarter database (the Data Source text box is too short to capture the entire path in this image).

At this point, your connection string is ready to use.

10. Click OK to close the Data Link Properties dialog box.

When writing a VBA procedure to connect to the `NorthwindStarter.accdb` database, you can simply pass the `.udl` filename to the `Connection` object's `Open` method:

```
Dim conn As ADODB.Connection
Set conn As New ADODB.Connection
```

```
conn.Open "File Name=C:\VBAAccess2024_ByExample\ConnectToAccdb.udl;"
```

When you use `.udl` files to store connection information, it is very easy to switch your procedure's data source without having to make changes to your code. Simply double-click the `.udl` file and make the desired modifications in the Data Link Properties dialog box.

If you'd rather use the connection string in your VBA procedure, then go ahead and copy the string from the `.udl` file. You can open this file in Notepad in one of the following ways:

- Right-click the `.udl` filename and choose Open With, then select Notepad.

  If Notepad is not available in the shortcut menu, select Choose Program (or choose another app), then select Notepad, and click OK.

- Make a copy of the `.udl` file. Change the `.udl` extension of the created copy to `.txt`. Double-click the file to open it in Notepad.

The connection string is shown in Figure 9.9.

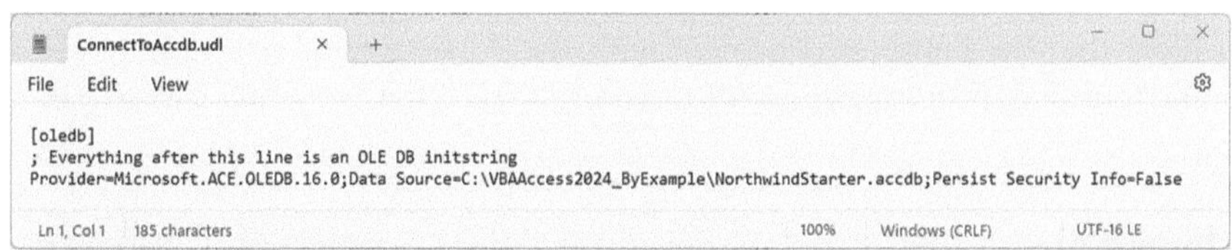

FIGURE 9.9. You can obtain the connection string from the universal data link (.udl) file by opening the file in Windows Notepad.

USING ChatGPT WITH ACCESS

How can you use ChatGPT to significantly enhance the material presented in this chapter? I'm sure by now you have many ideas of your own that you can't wait to try out. Let me suggest that you start with something that will allow you to gain additional coding skills. VBA offers hundreds of objects that can be used in different parts of your Access applications, but you may not know how these objects are named and used. ChatGPT can point you to these objects when you ask it to solve a specific problem providing you with code examples and detailed explanations.

To expand on this chapter content, we will ask ChatGPT to write a procedure in Access VBA that retrieves the names of installed libraries, the ones that are selected in the References dialog box (see Figure 9.1). This request will introduce you to the Microsoft Visual Basic for Applications Extensibility 5.3 library, which must be referenced to work with the Visual Basic Integrated Development Environment (VBIDE) object library. This is the library you need to reference if your application needs to interact with and manipulate the VBA environment programmatically.

The complete chat experience with the AI-generated VBA code can be accessed in the companion files—see the document `Chapter 9 - Using Chat-GPT with Access`. Be sure to read the entire document first before entering any VBA procedures. When testing out code written by someone else or an AI tool, remember to run it first line by line using the Step Into button on the Debug toolbar or the F8 function key. This will ensure that you thoroughly understand how each part of the code works and can catch any potential issues early. Stepping through the code allows you to observe the flow of execution, see how variables change, and identify where things might be going wrong. This approach not only helps in debugging but also deepens your comprehension of the code, ensuring that you can confidently modify or extend it as needed. By taking the time to step through the code, you reduce the risk of unexpected errors and enhance the overall quality and reliability of your application.

Note that the completed project with the AI-generated example procedures can be found in the companion files—see `Module 3` in the `Chap9.accdb` database.

SUMMARY

In this chapter, you were introduced to various types of database engines, including Access' own Jet and ACE engines. You explored several libraries that you can call in your VBA programs to extend their capabilities and perform complex tasks. These libraries provide a wealth of predefined functions and objects that will make your programming easier and more efficient. For instance, the DAO 3.6 object library allows you to interact with Access databases, performing operations such as data retrieval and manipulation with ease. You will get a chance to see how this works in practice in the next chapter. Additionally, you learned how to explore these libraries using the Object Browser. You also learned how to set up references to these libraries in the VBA editor so their objects, properties, and methods can be used in your code. Finally, you were introduced to the various types of connection strings, including ODBC and OLE DB. This exploration provided you with a solid understanding of how to establish and manage connections to different data sources. You learned how by utilizing the ODBC Data Source Administrator, you can easily set up DSNs, configure the required drivers, and manage database connections with ease. This tool simplifies the process of linking your applications to databases such as SQL Server, Oracle, MySQL, and even a legacy database such as dBASE. You learned that OLE DB connection strings provide a more flexible and powerful means of connecting to data sources not limited to relational databases. You can configure and test your OLE DB connections through the Universal Data Link (UDL) Properties dialog. By mastering the tools and concepts presented in this chapter, you are now ready to dive deeper into the fascinating world of Access database management and manipulation.

In the next chapter, you will learn how to create and manipulate databases using objects from the DAO object library. This will involve understanding the DAO architecture, creating Access databases programmatically, managing tables, executing queries, and handling data. Let's take your skills to the next level with DAO programming!

Chapter 10

CREATING AND MANIPULATING DATABASES WITH DAO

The DAO library is a powerful tool for managing and interacting with Access databases. DAO is optimized for Jet databases, the underlying database engine for Access, providing you with a rich set of objects and methods that you can use to create, read, and update databases. Because DAO was specifically designed for Access, it offers better performance and is easier to use within an Access environment than the ADO library, which will be covered in the next chapter. The following sections of this chapter will get you started with using DAO objects and methods to perform various database tasks.

SETTING UP YOUR ENVIRONMENT FOR DAO PROGRAMMING

Before you can interact with the DAO objects and methods in your VBA code, you must set up a reference to the Microsoft DAO 3.6 object library:

1. Press Alt+F11 or use choose Database Tools | Visual Basic to open the VBA editor in Access.
2. In the VBA editor, choose Tools | References.
3. Scroll through the list of available references and check the box next to Microsoft DAO 3.6 Object Library.
4. Click OK to close the References dialog box.

EXPLORING THE DAO OBJECT MODEL

An *object model* is a structured framework that represents the components of a software system and their relationships. In Microsoft Access, the DAO object model defines how the different elements of your database, such as tables, queries, forms, and reports, interact with each other programmatically through VBA. For example, using the DAO object model, you can write VBA code to create a new table with various types of fields, or create and run a query that retrieves data and displays the results in an Access form. In the following sections of this chapter, you will work with several key DAO objects, which are briefly introduced below.

- `Database` Object
  The `Database` object represents the entire Access database and is used to create new databases, open existing databases, and manage database properties.

- `TableDef` Object
  The `TableDef` object represents a table in a database. It is used for creating new tables, modifying existing tables, and managing table properties.

- `Field` Object
  The `Field` object represents a field (column) in a table, and it allows you to define the data type, size, and other properties of a field.

- `QueryDef` Object
  The `QueryDef` object represents a saved query in the database. It is used to create, modify, and run queries.

- `Recordset` Object
  The `Recordset` object represents a set of records from a table or the results of a query. It is used for navigating, reading, and updating data.

As you can see, the DAO object model is very intuitive as it mirrors exactly the structure of a typical Access database. Of course, there are a great number of other DAO objects that you will need to learn to efficiently manage and manipulate databases using DAO, but starting with core objects such as `Database`, `TableDef`, `Field`, `QueryDef`, and `Recordset` sets a solid foundation. With these objects, you will be able to perform a wide array of tasks from creating databases and tables to executing complex queries. Going deeper into DAO programming, we will cover additional objects that will allow you to create, design, and manage user interfaces such as forms and reports. Other objects, such as `Index` and `Relation`, will allow you to optimize your database, enforce data integrity, and set up relationships between tables. Moreover, you will learn how to use the `Workspace` object to manage multiple transactions and handle multiple concurrent users in a database environment.

Each of these DAO objects comes with a number of methods and properties that are designed to give you precise control over your database operations.

CREATING A DATABASE WITH DAO

While the Access interface provides a very easy way to create a new database, the knowledge of creating a database programmatically using DAO is particularly useful when you need to set up multiple databases with similar structures, or you need to integrate the database creation process into a larger-scale database project.

In DAO, to interact with databases programmatically, you need to initialize the `DBEngine` object. This involves declaring an object variable that will hold the `DBEngine` object, which is responsible for managing database workspaces and opening databases. A *workspace* is an environment within which you can perform database operations. A workspace provides isolation for transactions, enabling concurrent users to interact with the database without conflicting with each other. You will learn more about workspaces when we cover DAO transactions at the end of this chapter.

The `Workspace` object has several useful methods; the most frequently used are `CreateDatabase` (for creating a new database) and `OpenDatabase` (for opening an existing database). The `CreateDatabase` method requires that you specify the name and path of your database, as well as the built-in constant indicating a collating order for creating the database. Use the built-in constant `dbLangGeneral` for English, German, French, Portuguese, Italian, and Modern Spanish.

The procedure in Hands-On 10.1 creates a new Access database using DAO. It then adds a table named `Employees` and defines fields for that table. Note that when creating a database, Access will automatically create a number of system tables for its own use.

<table>
<tr><td>NOTE</td><td>All code files and figures for the hands-on projects may be found in the companion files.</td></tr>
</table>

(◉) Hands-On 10.1   Creating a Database and a Table Using DAO

1. Start Access and create a new database named `Chap10.accdb` in your `C:\ VBAAccess2024_ByExample` folder.
2. In the VBE window, choose Insert | Module.
3. In the module's Code window, type the following `CreateNewDB_DAO` procedure:

```vba
Sub CreateNewDatabase_DAO()
    Dim dbEngine As DAO.dbEngine
    Dim db As DAO.Database
    Dim tdf As DAO.TableDef
    Dim fld As DAO.Field
    Dim tbl As Variant
    Dim dbName As String
    Dim strMsg As String


    dbName = "C:\VBAAccess2024_ByExample\DAODatabase.accdb"
    strMsg = "The database was created successfully! It contains"

    On Error GoTo ErrorHandler

    ' Initialize the DAO DBEngine
    Set dbEngine = New DAO.dbEngine

    ' Create a new database
    Set db = dbEngine.CreateDatabase(dbName, dbLangGeneral)

    ' Create a new table definition
    Set tdf = db.CreateTableDef("Employees")

    ' Add fields to the table
    Set fld = tdf.CreateField("EmployeeID", dbLong)
    tdf.Fields.Append fld
    Set fld = tdf.CreateField("FirstName", dbText, 50)
    tdf.Fields.Append fld
    Set fld = tdf.CreateField("LastName", dbText, 50)
    tdf.Fields.Append fld
    Set fld = tdf.CreateField("HiredOn", dbDate)
    tdf.Fields.Append fld

    ' Append the new table to the database
    db.TableDefs.Append tdf
```

```
    ' List table names in the Immediate window
    For Each tbl In db.TableDefs
        Debug.Print tbl.Name
    Next

    MsgBox strMsg & db.TableDefs.Count & " tables.", _
        vbInformation, "New Database Name: " & db.Name
    ' Clean up
    Set fld = Nothing
    Set tdf = Nothing
    Set db = Nothing
    Set dbEngine = Nothing

    Exit Sub
ErrorHandler:
' Handle any errors

    MsgBox "Error " & Err.Number & ":" & _
        Err.Description, vbCritical, "Error"
    If Not fld Is Nothing Then Set fld = Nothing
    If Not tdf Is Nothing Then Set tdf = Nothing
    If Not db Is Nothing Then Set db = Nothing
    If Not dbEngine Is Nothing Then Set dbEngine = Nothing
End Sub
```

4. Choose Run | Run Sub/UserForm to execute the procedure.
Notice that the procedure begins by declaring and initializing the DBEngine
object:

```
' declaration of the DBEngine object
Dim dbEngine As DAO.DBEngine
' Initialization of the DEBEngine object
Set dbEngine = new DAO.DBEngine
```

With the DBEngine object declared and initialized, you gain access to this
object's methods and properties and you can proceed to program subsequent
DAO operations. The CreateDatabase method of the DBEngine object is used
to create a new Access database file. This method requires that you specify the
name and path of your database, as well as the built-in constant indicating
the language and regional settings for the database. Use the built-in constant
dbLangGeneral for English, German, French, Portuguese, Italian, and Modern
Spanish.

To add your own table to the database, use the CreateTableDef method of
the DBEngine object. This method requires that you specify a string or string

variable to hold the name of the new `TableDef` object. Each saved table in an Access database is an object called a `TableDef` object. The `TableDef` object has a number of properties that characterize it, such as `Name`, `RecordCount`, `DateCreated`, and `DateUpdated`. The `TableDef` object also has methods that act on the object. For example, the `CreateField` method creates a new field for the `TableDef` object.

Because a table must have at least one field, the next step in the table creation process is to use the `CreateField` method of the `TableDef` object to create the fields we need. For instance, in the following statement:

```
Set fld = tdf.CreateField("FirstName", dbText, 50)
```

- `tdf` is a table definition variable.
- `"FirstName"` is a string specifying the name of the new `Field` object.
- `dbText` is a constant that determines the data type of the new `Field` object.
- `50` is an integer indicating the maximum size in bytes for a text field. Text fields can hold from 1 to 255 bytes. This argument is ignored for other types of fields.

In Access, all database tables are stored in the `TableDefs` collection. Therefore, when we are done defining the fields for our new table, we need to append the finished table to the database's `TableDefs` collection:

```
' Append the new table to the database
  db.TableDefs.Append tdf
```

At this point, the database and the table are ready and we can proceed to release all the resources we used by setting object variables to `Nothing`. Before doing so, however, we can also craft some informational messages. In this case, we use the `For Each...Next` loop to iterate through the database tables and print table names to the Immediate window. Next, we display a message about successful database creation and specify the number of tables in the new database. Our new database contains six tables; five of them are system tables that Access creates for its own use.

As with any VBA procedure you write, the added error-handling code will ensure that the procedure knows how to exit gracefully. Notice how the statement `On Error GoTo ErrorHandler` at the beginning of the procedure directs the code to the `ErrorHandler:` label at the end of the procedure in case an error occurs. The `ErrorHandler` is a block of code that actually handles errors. Here, you can display an error message using the `MsgBox` function and the `Number` and `Description` properties of the VBA `Err` object that you learned about in Chapter 8. Also, this is the place where you should perform the necessary cleanup of object variables to ensure that the resources are properly released. This is very important in environments where memory management is critical as it helps to prevent memory leaks. Correct resource management will make your database applications stable and reliable. In our procedure, each line of the `ErrorHandler` code that begins with `If Not` checks that the specified object is not already set to `Nothing`. If the object was already set to `Nothing`, then there is no need to set it again. Remember to use the `Exit Sub` statement on a line preceding the `ErrorHandler:` label so that the error-handling code is executed only if an error occurs.

5. Run the procedure again to ensure that the error-handling code is working properly. You should see a message that the database already exists.

COPYING A DATABASE

At times, you may want to duplicate your database programmatically. This can be easily done in DAO with the `DBEngine` object's `CompactDatabase` method.

Before using the `CompactDatabase` method, make sure the source database is closed and there is enough disk space to create a duplicate copy. Creating a copy of your database using this method requires that you define two string variables: one to hold the name of the source database and the other to specify the name for the duplicate version. Access will compact and copy the entire database, ensuring that the target database is an exact copy of the source and is also optimized.

Hands-On 10.2 shows how to use the `CompactDatabase` method to copy a database.

(◉) Hands-On 10.2   Copying a Database

This hands-on exercise makes a copy of the `DAODatabase.accdb` file created in Hands-On 10.01.

1. In the VBE window, choose Insert | Module.
2. In the module's Code window, type the following `CopyDB_DAO` procedure:

```
Sub CopyDB_DAO()
    Dim sourceDbPath As String
```

```vba
    Dim targetDbPath As String

    On Error GoTo ErrorHandler

    sourceDbPath = "C:\VBAAccess2024_ByExample\DAODatabase.accdb"
    targetDbPath = "C:\VBAAccess2024_ByExample\Copy_DAODatabase.accdb"

    'Compact and copy the database into a new file
    dbEngine.CompactDatabase sourceDbPath, targetDbPath

    MsgBox "Database was copied successfully", vbInformation
    Exit Sub
ErrorHandler:
'Handle any errors
    Dim strResponse As Integer

    If Err.Number = 3204 Then
    strResponse = MsgBox(Err.Description & vbCrLf & _
    "Do you want to delete " & targetDbPath & "?", _
      vbYesNo, "File Exists")
      If strResponse = vbYes Then
          Kill targetDbPath
          If Dir(targetDbPath) = "" Then
              MsgBox "The existing database was deleted."
              ' resume the execution to retry the compact operation
              Resume
          End If
      Else
          Exit Sub
      End If
    Else
      MsgBox "Error " & Err.Number & ": " & _
      Err.Description, vbCritical, "Error"
    End If
End Sub
```

3. Choose Run | Run Sub/UserForm to execute the procedure.
   In this procedure, we added the `ErrorHandler` section to check for errors. Error 3204 indicates that the target file already exists. When this is true (`Err.Number = 3204`), we prompt the user to delete the existing file. If the user chooses `Yes` (`vbYes`), the existing target file will be deleted using a `Kill` statement. Because the database cannot be deleted programmatically using DAO, the VBA `Kill` statement is used to perform the deletion. If there is no file in the directory (`Dir(targetDbPath) = ""`), we confirm that the file was deleted.

The VBA `Dir` function is used to check for the existence of the database with the specified name. The `Resume` statement that comes next retries the compact operation after deleting the existing file. If you step through the procedure code, you will notice that when Visual Basic encounters the `Resume` statement, it will jump up to the `dbEngine.CompactDatabase` statement. Finally, if the error is not related to the file already existing, we will capture the error and display it in a message box.

Note that you can also copy an Access database programmatically with DAO by opening the source database, creating a new target database, and copying all Access objects from the source to the target. This will require that you iterate through the `TableDefs`, `QueryDefs`, `Relations`, and other collections of objects that exist in the source database in order to duplicate them.

OPENING MICROSOFT ACCESS DATABASES

In this section, we will focus on using DAO to open existing Access databases in `.accdb` and `.mdb` format. These databases may be opened in read/write mode or in read-only mode, and some of them may be protected with database passwords or user-level security.

Opening a Microsoft Jet Database in Read/Write Mode

The easiest way of opening an existing Access database from a VBA procedure is by using the database engine's `OpenDatabase` method. This method requires that you provide at least one parameter—the name of the existing database. When you open the database with the `OpenDatabase` method, always remember to close it using the `Close` method.

The next hands-on example will list containers and documents in the open database. Each database object has a `Containers` collection that consists of built-in `Container` objects. The `Containers` collection is used for storing Microsoft Access' own objects. The Jet engine creates the following `Container` objects: `Databases`, `Tables`, and `Relations`. Other `Container` objects are created by Access (`Forms`, `Reports`, `Macros`, and `Modules`).

Table 10.1 lists the `Container` objects and the type of information they contain.

TABLE 10.1.   Container objects.

Container Name	Type of Information Stored
Databases	Saved databases
Tables	Saved tables and queries
Relations	Saved relationships
Forms	Saved forms
Modules	Saved modules
Reports	Saved reports
Scripts	Saved scripts

Each `Container` object contains a `Documents` collection. Each document in this collection represents an object that can be found in an Access database. For example, the `Forms` container stores a list of all saved forms in a database, and each form is represented by a `Document` object. You cannot create new `Container` and `Document` objects; you can only retrieve the information about them.

⊙ Hands-On 10.3   Opening a Database in Read/Write Mode

1. In the `Chap10.accdb` database that you created in Hands-On 10.1, switch to the VBE window and choose Insert | Module to add a new module to the current VBA project.

2. In the module's Code window, type the following `openDB_DAO` procedure:

```
Sub openDB_DAO()
   Dim db As DAO.Database
   Dim dbName As String
   Dim c As Container
   Dim doc As Document

   dbName = InputBox("Enter a name of an existing database:", _
    "Database Name")

   If dbName = "" Then Exit Sub
   If Dir(dbName) = "" Then
     MsgBox dbName & " was not found."
     Exit Sub
   End If

   Set db = OpenDatabase(dbName)
   With db
     ' list the names of the Container objects
     For Each c In .Containers
```

```
    Debug.Print c.Name & " container:" & _
     c.Documents.Count
    ' list the document names
    ' in the specified Container
    If c.Documents.Count > 0 Then
      For Each doc In c.Documents
        Debug.Print vbTab & doc.Name
      Next doc
    End If
  Next c
  .Close
 End With
End Sub
```

This procedure uses the `OpenDatabase` method of the `DBEngine` object to open the specified database in the default workspace. The database is opened as shared with read/write access. By supplying additional arguments to the `OpenDatabase` method, you could open the database exclusively (a database opened exclusively can be accessed by a single user at a time) or as read-only.

The `openDB_DAO` procedure uses a `For Each...Next` loop to retrieve the names of all the `Container` objects in the opened database. If the specified container is not empty, the inner `For Each...Next` loop will print the name of each `Document` object in the Immediate window.

3. Position the insertion point anywhere within the code of `openDB_DAO` and press F5 or choose Run | Run Sub/UserForm to execute the procedure.
   When you run this procedure, you are prompted to enter the name of the Access database.

4. Enter `C:\VBAAccess2024_ByExample\NorthwindStarter.accdb` and press OK. Check the procedure output in the Immediate window.

Opening a Microsoft Access Database in Read-Only Mode

You can open an Access database in read-only mode by providing settings for optional arguments in the `OpenDatabase` method.

Additional code is available in the companion files.
File Name: `openDB_DAOReadOnly.txt`
Description: `Open a database for shared, read-only access using DAO`

Opening a Microsoft Jet Database Secured with a Password

Using passwords to secure the database or objects in the database is known as *share-level security*. When you set a password on the database, users will be required to enter a password to gain access to the data and database objects. Keep in mind that passwords are case-sensitive. When using DAO to change the password of an existing Access database in a VBA procedure, follow these steps:

1. Open the database in exclusive mode by setting the second argument of the `OpenDatabase` method to `True`.
2. To set a database password, use the `NewPassword` property of the `Database` object. This property requires that you first specify the old password and the new one. Passwords can be up to 20 characters long and can include any characters except the ASCII character `0` (null). To specify that the database does not have a password, use a zero-length string (`""`) in the first parameter of the `NewPassword` property. To clear the password, use the zero-length string for the second parameter of the `NewPassword` property.

To open a password-protected database using DAO, you must specify the database password in the `Connect` parameter of the `OpenDatabase` method, as shown in Hands-On 10.4.

Hands-On 10.4 Setting a Database Password and Opening a Password-Protected Database

1. In the VBE window, choose Insert | Module to add a new module to the currently open `Chap10.accdb` database.
2. In the module's Code window, type the `setPass_AndOpenDB_withDAO` procedure shown here:

```
Sub setPass_AndOpenDB_withDAO()
    Dim db As DAO.Database
    Dim strDb As String

    strDb = "C:\VBAAccess2024_ByExample\NorthwindStarter.accdb"

    ' open the database in exclusive mode
    ' to set database password
    Set db = DBEngine.OpenDatabase(strDb, True)
    db.NewPassword "", "secret"
    MsgBox "Access Database version: " & Int(db.Version)
    db.Close

    ' open password-protected database
    Set db = DBEngine.OpenDatabase(Name:=strDb, _
     Options:=False, _
     ReadOnly:=False, _
     Connect:=";PWD=secret")
```

```
MsgBox "Successfully opened a password-protected database."
db.Close
MsgBox "Password-protected database was closed."

' remove password protection from the database
Set db = DBEngine.OpenDatabase(Name:=strDb, _
 Options:=True, _
 ReadOnly:=False, _
 Connect:=";PWD=secret")
 db.NewPassword "secret", ""

MsgBox "Password protection was removed."
db.Close
End Sub
```

3. Position the insertion point anywhere within the code of the `setPass_AndOpenDB_withDAO` procedure and press F5 or choose Run | Run Sub/ UserForm to execute the procedure.

   When you run this procedure, Access displays the version number of the Access database engine using the `Version` property of `DBEngine`. The version number consists of the version number, a period, and the release number. The procedure uses the VBA `Int` function to display only the integer portion of the number. Access 2024 uses the Microsoft Access 14.0 database engine.

<table>
<tr><td rowspan="2">NOTE</td><td>If a VBA procedure uses a method or a property that requires two or more parameters, you can make the procedure more readable by specifying the names of the parameters like this:</td></tr>
<tr><td>

```
Set db = DBEngine.OpenDatabase(Name:=strDb, _
   Options:=False, _
   ReadOnly:=False, _
   Connect:=";PWD=secret")
```

</td></tr>
</table>

Use the Microsoft Visual Basic online help or ChatGPT's assistance to find the names of methods and properties and the names of the required and optional parameters.

OPENING OTHER FILES WITH DAO

By using the `OpenDatabase` method in DAO, you can also open other types of data sources from your Access VBA procedures and perform the required operations as needed. Hands-On 10.5 demonstrates how to use DAO to open an Excel workbook.

⊚ Hands-On 10.5   Opening an Excel Workbook

1. Copy the `Report2024.xlsx` and `Report.xls` workbook files from the companion files to your `C:\VBAAccess2024_ByExample` folder.
2. In the VBE window, choose Insert | Module.
3. In the module's Code window, type the following `Open_Excel_DAO` procedure:

```
Sub Open_Excel_DAO(strFileName)
  Dim db As DAO.Database
  Dim rst As DAO.Recordset
  Dim strHeader As String
  Dim strValues As String
  Dim fld As Variant

  strHeader = ""
  strValues = ""

  If Right(strFileName, 1) = "x" Then
    Set db = OpenDatabase(CurrentProject.Path & _
      "\Report2024.xlsx", False, True, _
      "Excel 12.0; HDR=YES;")
  Else
    Set db = OpenDatabase(CurrentProject.Path & _
      "\Report.xls", False, True, _
      "Excel 8.0; HDR=YES;")
  End If

  Set rst = db.OpenRecordset("Sheet1$")

  ' get column names
  For Each fld In rst.Fields
    strHeader = strHeader & fld.Name & vbTab
  Next

  Debug.Print strHeader

  ' get cell values
  Do Until rst.EOF
    For Each fld In rst.Fields
      strValues = strValues & fld.Value & _
        vbTab & vbTab
    Next
    Debug.Print strValues
```

```
        strValues = ""
        rst.MoveNext
    Loop

    rst.Close
    Set rst = Nothing
    db.Close
    Set db = Nothing
End Sub
```

4. In the VBE window, press Ctrl+G to open the Immediate window or choose View | Immediate Window.

5. To run the `Open_Excel_DAO` procedure, type `Open_Excel_DAO  "Report.xls"` in the Immediate window and press Enter.

6. Run the procedure again, supplying `Report2024.xlsx` as the parameter.

   To run the `Open_Excel_DAO` procedure, you must provide the name of the workbook file to open. If the last character in the file extension is `x` (this is determined with the VBA `Right` function), then the procedure uses the connection string designed for opening Excel 2007–2024 files. After making a connection to the Excel file, the procedure goes on to retrieve information stored in the desired worksheet. Using DAO's `OpenRecordset` method, we can access the data on the `Sheet1` worksheet. Notice the dollar sign (`$`) appended to the sheet name. You must use the dollar sign syntax, `Sheet1$`, to refer to a sheet. The procedure uses the `For  Each...Next` loop to obtain the names of all worksheet columns. The heading string is then written to the Immediate window. Next, the `Do  Until...Loop` block loops through the records until the end of file (`EOF`) is reached. Cell values from each worksheet row are written to the `strValues` variable and then to the Immediate window. Once the data retrieval is completed, the `Recordset` is closed and its variable is destroyed. The same is done with the `Connection` object. You will get more hands-on experience with recordsets as you progress through this chapter.

ACCESSING DATABASE TABLES AND FIELDS

Previously in this chapter, you wrote VBA code that created an Access database and defined a new table. There are many operations that you may want to programmatically perform on database tables and fields. These include:

- Duplicating or deleting a table
- Listing table properties

- Adding or deleting table fields
- Setting and changing field properties
- Changing the `AutoNumber`
- Listing data types
- Linking a table to a database
- Listing tables in a database

In the following sections, you will write VBA procedures that use DAO objects to perform these database tasks.

Creating an Access Table and Setting Field Properties

In Hands-On 10.1, you learned how to programmatically create a table in an Access database using the `TableDef` object and its `CreateTableDef` method. You also used the `CreateField` method of the `Field` object to add new fields to a table. This enabled you to define the basic structure of your database tables. In this section, you will enhance your understanding by learning how to add and manage table and field properties. Properties define the characteristics and behaviors of tables and fields, such as data types, field sizes, default values, and validation rules. By setting these properties, you can ensure data integrity, provide a more robust database structure, and optimize performance. Here, we will explore how you can customize table-level settings to control behavior and performance. You will also learn how to define the attributes of each table field, such as data type, size, default values, and validation rules, to ensure data entered into the table meets specific criteria.

In the next hands-on exercise, you will create another version of the `Employ-ees` table, but this time in the current database, and you will learn how to set up various table and field properties.

Hands-On 10.6   Creating a Table and Setting Table and Field Properties

1. Insert a new module in `Chap10.accdb`, and in the module's Code window, type the following `CreateTableWithProperties` procedure:

```
Sub CreateTableWithProperties()
    Dim db As DAO.Database
    Dim tdf As DAO.TableDef
    Dim fld As DAO.Field
    Dim idx As DAO.Index
    Dim prp As DAO.Property
```

```
' Open the current database
Set db = CurrentDb()

' Create a new table definition
Set tdf = db.CreateTableDef("Employees")

' Add fields to the table with properties
Set fld = tdf.CreateField("EmployeeID", dbLong)
fld.Attributes = dbAutoIncrField ' AutoNumber field
tdf.Fields.Append fld

Set fld = tdf.CreateField("FirstName", dbText, 50)
fld.AllowZeroLength = False ' Disallow zero-length strings
tdf.Fields.Append fld

Set fld = tdf.CreateField("LastName", dbText, 50)
fld.AllowZeroLength = False ' Disallow zero-length strings
tdf.Fields.Append fld

Set fld = tdf.CreateField("HireDate", dbDate)
fld.Required = True ' This field must have a value
tdf.Fields.Append fld

Set fld = tdf.CreateField("DateOfBirth", dbDate)
fld.Required = True
fld.ValidationRule = "<= Date()"
fld.ValidationText = "Date of Birth cannot be a future date."
tdf.Fields.Append fld

Set fld = tdf.CreateField("Country", dbText, 20)
fld.DefaultValue = "USA" 'This field will have a default value
tdf.Fields.Append fld

' Add a primary key index to the table
Set idx = tdf.CreateIndex("PrimaryKey")
Set fld = idx.CreateField("EmployeeID")
idx.Fields.Append fld
idx.Primary = True ' Set index as primary key
tdf.Indexes.Append idx

' Append the new table to the database
db.TableDefs.Append tdf


' Set the Caption property for the DateOfBirth field
Set prp = tdf.Fields("DateOfBirth").CreateProperty("Caption")
```

```
    prp.Type = dbText
    prp.Value = "Date of Birth"
    tdf.Fields("DateOfBirth").Properties.Append prp


    Set prp = tdf.CreateProperty("Description")
    prp.Type = dbText
    prp.Value = "Sample table created with DAO code"
    tdf.Properties.Append prp


    ' Clean up
    Set prp = Nothing
    Set idx = Nothing
    Set fld = Nothing
    Set tdf = Nothing
    Set db = Nothing

    MsgBox "New table 'Employees' created with field " & _
        "properties and table-level settings!"
End Sub
```

2. Choose Run | Run Sub/UserForm to execute the `CreateTableWithProperties` procedure.

3. Choose File | Save and click OK to save the module when prompted. This will ensure that Access refreshes the application window and makes the newly created table visible in the navigation bar.

   The `CreateTableWithProperties` procedure uses the `CurrentDb` method to define an object variable (`db`) to point to the database that is currently open in the Microsoft Access window. This method allows you to access the current database from Visual Basic without having to know the database name. Next, a table is created using the `CreateTableDef` method of a DAO database object. This method requires that you specify a string or string variable to hold the name of the new `TableDef` object. Because a table must have at least one field, the next step in the table creation process is to use the `CreateField` method of the `TableDef` object to create fields. Here, you must provide the name of the field, the field data type, and its size if the field is to hold string data. Table 10.2 lists constants that you can use for different data types in DAO programming.

TABLE 10.2. Constants for the Type property in the DAO object library (DataTypeEnum enumeration).

Data Type Name	Value	Description
dbAttachment	101	Attachment data
dbBigInt	16	Big integer data
dbBinary	9	Binary data
dbBoolean	1	Boolean (true/false) data
dbByte	2	Byte (8-bit) data
dbChar	18	Text data (fixed width)
dbComplexByte	102	Multivalue byte data
dbComplexDecimal	108	Multivalue decimal data
dbComplexDouble	106	Multivalue double-precision floating-point data
dbComplexGUID	107	Multivalue GUID data
dbComplexInteger	103	Multivalue integer data
dbComplexLong	104	Multivalue long integer data
dbComplexSingle	105	Multivalue single-precision floating-point data
dbComplexText	109	Multivalue text data (variable width)
dbCurrency	5	Currency data
dbDate	8	Date value data
dbDecimal	20	Decimal data (ODBCDirect only)
dbDouble	7	Double-precision floating-point data
dbFloat	21	Floating-point data (ODBCDirect only)
dbGUID	15	GUID data
dbInteger	3	Integer data
dbLong	4	Long integer data
dbLongBinary	11	Binary data (bitmap)
dbMemo	12	Memo data (extended text)
dbNumeric	19	Numeric data (ODBCDirect only)
dbSingle	6	Single-precision floating-point data
dbText	10	Text data (variable width)
dbTime	22	Data in time format (ODBCDirect only)
dbTimeStamp	23	Data in time and date format (ODBCDirect only)
dbVarBinary	17	Variable binary data (ODBCDirect only)

When creating fields for your table, you may want to set certain field properties, such as `Validation Rule`, `Validation Text`, `Default Value`, and `Required`.

The `Validation Rule` property is a text string that describes the rule for valida-tion. In the `CreateTableWithProperties` procedure, we require that `Date of Birth` cannot be a future date. The `Validation Text` property is a string that is displayed to the user when the validation fails; that is, when the user attempts to enter data that does not comply with the specific validation rule.

The `DefaultValue` property sets or returns the default value of a `Field` ob-ject. In this example procedure, we make the data entry easier for the user by specifying USA as the default value in the `Country` field. Each new record will automatically have an entry of USA in the `Country` field. Because certain fields should not be left blank, you can ensure that the user enters data in a particular field by setting the `Required` property of that field to `True`.

Notice that the procedure includes setting a primary key for the table, which is an essential table-level property for ensuring data integrity and optimizing queries. The `CreateIndex` method of the `TableDef` object is used to create a new index named `PrimaryKey`. The `CreateField` method is then used to add the `EmployeeID` field to the index. The statement that follows sets the index as the primary key for the table. Finally, the statement `tdf.Indexes.Append idx` appends the primary key index to the table.

In addition to the built-in properties of an object, there are two other types of properties:

- Application-defined properties
- User-defined properties

The application-defined property is created only if you assign a value to that property. A classic example of such a property is the `Description` property of the `TableDef` object. To set the `Description` property of a table in the Access user interface, simply right-click on the table name and choose Table Proper-ties, then type the text you want in the Description field. Access will create a `Description` property for the table and append it automatically to the `Proper-ties` collection for that `TableDef` object. If you do not type a description in the Description field, Access will not create a `Description` property. Therefore, if you use the `Description` property in your code in this case, Access will display an error. For this reason, it is a good idea to check beforehand whether a refer-enced property exists. Users may create their own properties to hold additional information about an object.

The `CreateTableWithProperties` procedure demonstrates how to use the `CreateProperty` method of the `TableDef` object to create application-defined or user-defined properties. To create a property you will need to supply the name of the property, the property type, and the property value. For example, here's how to use the `CreateProperty` method to create a `Caption` property for the `DateOfBirth` field in the newly created table `Employees`:

```
Set prp = tdf.Fields("DateOfBirth").CreateProperty("Caption")
```

Next, the data type of the `Property` object is defined:

```
prp.Type = dbText
```

See Table 10.2 for the names of the `Type` property constants in VBA.

Finally, a value is assigned to the new property:

```
prp.Value = "Date of Birth"
```

Instead of writing three separate lines of code, you can create a new property of an object with the following line:

```
Set prp = tdf.Fields("DateOfBirth"). _
CreateProperty("Caption", dbText, "Date of Birth")
```

A user-defined property must be appended to the `Properties` collection of the corresponding object. In this example procedure, the `Caption` property is appended to the `Properties` collection of the `Field` object, and the `Description` property is appended to the `Properties` collection of the `TableDef` object.

After creating a field and setting its built-in, application-defined, or user-defined properties, the `Append` method is used to add the field to the `Fields` collection, as in the following example:

```
tdf.Fields.Append fld
```

Once all the fields have been created and appended to the `Fields` collection, remember to append the new table to the `TableDefs` collection, as in the following example:

```
db.TableDefs.Append tdf
```

You can delete user-defined properties from the `Properties` collection, but you can't delete built-in properties. If you set a property in the user interface, you don't need to create and append the property in code because the property is automatically included in the `Properties` collection.

After running the procedure code, a new table named `Employees` appears in the Microsoft Access window. To check the value of the `Description` property for the `Employees` table that was set as a result of running the example procedure, right-click the `Employees` table in the database window and choose Table Properties from the shortcut menu.

To check the properties that were set and defined in this procedure, activate the `Employees` table in Design view, click the field name for which you set or created a custom property in the code, and examine the corresponding field properties. Figure 10.1 shows the current settings of the `Validation Rule` and `Validation Text` properties for the `DateOfBirth` field.

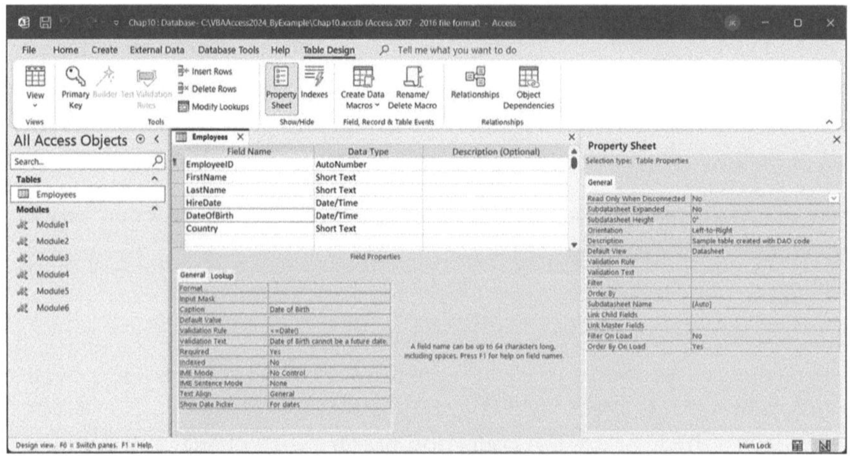

FIGURE 10.1. The Employees table created by using DAO objects in a VBA procedure.

Defining Various Types of Fields in an Access Table

As you know, an Access table can contain a variety of field types, each designed to hold a specific kind of data. In this section, you will create a new VBA procedure that will modify the `Employees` table created in the previous hands-on exercise. So far, the table `Employees` contains simple text and date fields. While the `ShortText` data type is ideal for names, addresses, and other short strings, sometimes you will need to store long entries such as descriptions or notes. The `LongText (Memo)` field can store up to 64,000 characters and also allows you to richly format your text with bold, italics, and different font colors. The tables you create in Access may require that you attach files to records, such as images, documents, and spreadsheets. To meet this need, Access provides the `Attachment` data type. Other times, you will need to have a designated field to store the result of a calculation obtained via an expression. Again, Access provides a way to do this by means of the `Calculated` data type. If you need to select multiple values from a list or keep a history of changes made to the field, the multivalue lookup fields and append-only memo fields can easily be added to your table.

Let's write a VBA procedure that modifies the `Employees` table to add the following types of fields and set their properties:

- Multivalue lookup field
- Calculated field
- Attachment field
- Append-only memo field
- Rich text field

⊙ Hands-On 10.7   Adding Specialized Types of Fields to a Table

1. In the VBE window, choose Insert | Module.
2. In the module's Code window, type the following `ModifyEmployeesTable` procedure:

```
Sub ModifyEmployeesTable()
    Dim db As DAO.Database
    Dim tdf As DAO.TableDef
    Dim fld As DAO.Field2
    Dim prop As DAO.Property

    On Error GoTo ErrorHandler
    ' Open the current database
    Set db = CurrentDb()
    Set tdf = db.TableDefs("Employees")

    ' Add Multi-Value Lookup Field (e.g., Skills)
    Set fld = tdf.CreateField("Skills", dbComplexText)
    tdf.Fields.Append fld
    With fld
        .Properties.Append .CreateProperty( _
            "DisplayControl", dbInteger, acComboBox)
        .Properties.Append .CreateProperty( _
            "RowSourceType", dbText, "Value List")
        .Properties.Append .CreateProperty( _
            "RowSource", dbText, "Skill1;Skill2;Skill3")
        .Properties.Append .CreateProperty( _
            "ListWidth", dbText, "1.5")
        .Properties.Append .CreateProperty( _
            "AllowMultipleValues", dbBoolean, True)
        .Properties.Append .CreateProperty( _
            "AllowValueListEdits", dbBoolean, True)
    End With
```

```vba
    ' Add Calculated Field (e.g., FullName)

    Set fld = tdf.CreateField("FullName", dbText, 50)
    fld.Expression = "[FirstName] & "" "" & [LastName]"
    tdf.Fields.Append fld


    ' Add Attachment Field (e.g., EmployeeAttachments)
    Set fld = tdf.CreateField("EmployeeAttachments", dbAttachment)
    tdf.Fields.Append fld

    ' Add Append Only Memo Field (e.g., Notes)
    Set fld = tdf.CreateField("Notes", dbMemo)

    tdf.Fields.Append fld
    fld.AppendOnly = True

    ' Add Rich Text Field (e.g., EmployeeBio)
    Set fld = tdf.CreateField("EmployeeBio", dbMemo)

    tdf.Fields.Append fld
    fld.Properties.Append fld.CreateProperty("TextFormat", dbByte, 1)


    MsgBox "Employees table was modified successfully!"
ExitHere:
    ' Clean up
    Set fld = Nothing
    Set tdf = Nothing
    Set db = Nothing
    Exit Sub

ErrorHandler:
  MsgBox Err.Number & ": " & Err.Description
  Resume ExitHere
End Sub
```

3. Choose Run | Run Sub/UserForm to run the `ModifyEmployeesTable` procedure and check in the main Access window that the `Employees` table now contains the fields shown in Figure 10.2.

> ### DAO Objects for Fields
>
> The DAO library includes two different objects for fields: `DAO.Field` and `DAO.Field2`. The standard `DAO.Field` object is used to define fields in DAO, as you've seen in earlier examples in this chapter. It is used for basic field operations such as creating, modifying, and accessing field properties in tables. The `DAO.Field2` object that we are using in Hands-On 10.7 is an extended version of the `DAO.Field` object that provides additional properties and methods that are not available in `DAO.Field`. You can use the `DAO.Field2` object when working with more advanced data types introduced in later versions of Access, such as multivalue fields, attachments fields, or properties that are specific to newer versions of Access, such as `AppendOnly`, `MultiValued`, and `ComplexType`.

Now that we know why we are suddenly using the `DAO.Field2` object in our VBA code, let's examine different sections of this procedure.

Procedure Section: Adding a Multivalue Lookup Field (e.g., Skills)

After setting a reference to the current database and its `Employees` table, we start by adding the `Skills` field, which we define as a multivalue lookup field. Recall that to create a new field in a table, we use the `CreateField` method of the `TableDef` object. Before we can set up various properties for this lookup field, we append the newly created `Skills` field to the table's `Fields` collection. Next, we use the `With...End With` construct to quickly add specific properties (`DisplayControl`, `RowSourceType`, `ListWidth`, `AllowMultipleValues`, and `AllowValueListEdits`) that we want to set to the `Properties` collection of the `Field2` object. These properties are shown in the Field Properties section in the lower part of Figure 10.2.

To create and set a property for a field, you use the `CreateProperty` method of the `Field2` object, specifying the name of the property, its data type, and its value. For example, the following statement will set the Display Control (`DisplayControl`) property to Combo Box for the current field (`Skills`):

```
fld.Properties.Append fld.CreateProperty("DisplayControl",
                                    dbInteger, acComboBox)
```

Note that when using the `With...End With` construct, we can omit typing the `fld` object variable:

```
With fld
  .Properties.Append .CreateProperty("DisplayControl",
dbInteger, acComboBox)
End With
```

Be sure to include a space between the `Append` method and the dot operator in front of the `CreateProperty` method. Using the `With...End With` construct makes the code both clearer and faster to execute.

Employees ✕

Field Name	Data Type	Description (Optional)
EmployeeID	AutoNumber	
FirstName	Short Text	
LastName	Short Text	
HireDate	Date/Time	
DateOfBirth	Date/Time	
Country	Short Text	
Skills	Short Text	
FullName	Calculated	
EmployeeAttachments	Attachment	
Notes	Long Text	
EmployeeBio	Long Text	

Field Properties

General Lookup

Display Control	Combo Box
Row Source Type	Value List
Row Source	Skill1;Skill2;Skill3
Bound Column	1
Column Count	1
Column Heads	No
Column Widths	
List Rows	16
List Width	1.5"
Limit To List	No
Allow Multiple Values	Yes
Allow Value List Edits	Yes
List Items Edit Form	
Show Only Row Source Value	No

A field name can be up to 64 characters long, including spaces. Press F1 for help on field names.

Property Sheet ✕

Selection type: Table Properties

General

Read Only When Disconnected	No
Subdatasheet Expanded	No
Subdatasheet Height	0"
Orientation	Left-to-Right
Description	Sample table created with DAO code
Default View	Datasheet
Validation Rule	
Validation Text	
Filter	
Order By	
Subdatasheet Name	[Auto]
Link Child Fields	
Link Master Fields	
Filter On Load	No
Order By On Load	Yes

FIGURE 10.2. The Employees table after modification. The Field Properties Lookup tab contains numerous properties that were set in the VBA procedure to tell Access how to display values in the Skills field.

Using the multivalue lookup fields, Access table columns can store more than one value. Anyone can create a lookup field without having to know much about setting table relationships. Access will automatically store the values entered in multivalue fields in hidden system tables and create proper table relationships if necessary. The source data for a multivalue field can be one of the following: value list, field list, or table/query. When modifying a table manually, you can have Access guide you in the creation of a multivalue field, by choosing Lookup Wizard in the Data Type column of the table's design view.

Multivalue lookup fields are often referred to as complex fields because they use data types that begin with `dbComplex` (see Table 10.3).

TABLE 10.3. Data types used by multivalue lookup fields.

Data Type	Value	Description
dbComplexByte	102	Multivalue byte data
dbComplexDecimal	108	Multivalue decimal data
dbComplexDouble	106	Multivalue double-precision floating-point data
dbComplexGUID	107	Multivalue GUID data

Data Type	Value	Description
dbComplexInteger	103	Multivalue integer data
dbComplexLong	104	Multivalue long integer data
dbComplexSingle	105	Multivalue single-precision floating-point data
dbComplexText	109	Multivalue text data (variable width)

When you open the `Employees` table in the datasheet view and click the Skills column, you will notice a list of choices to select for this field (see Figure 10.3).

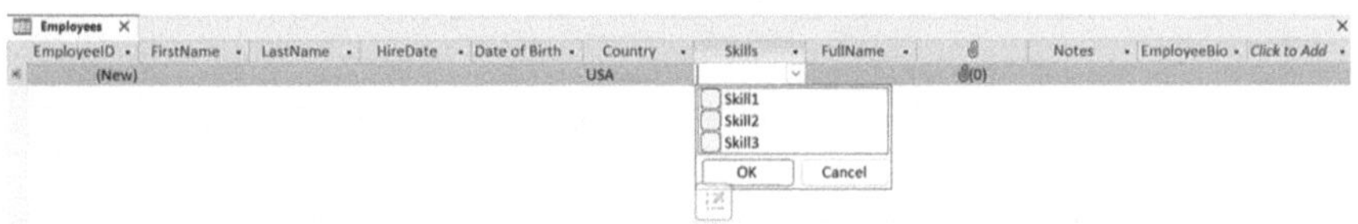

FIGURE 10.3.   The multivalue lookup field (Skills) created by the VBA procedure in Hands-On 10.7 displays a combo box with three skill choices.

Procedure Section: Adding a Calculated Field (e.g., FullName)

The next field we create is called `FullName` and it is used only to demonstrate how you can add a calculated field to your table. Since Access 2010, you can define an expression for the calculation in the calculated field and Access will store the calculated value in the table. With this feature, there is no need to calculate the person's full name in multiple locations in your Access application. When the underlying values change (for example, a female employee gets married and the last name field used in the expression is updated), the expression will automatically update the value that is stored in the calculated field. Calculated columns can be added to Access tables manually or with VBA.

NOTE	*Certain calculations should not be stored in a calculated field within a table. For instance, expressions based on date and time functions, like* `Date()` *and* `Now()`, *return different values with each call and should therefore be left in queries. Similarly, expressions using domain aggregate functions (such as* `DCount()`, `DSum()`, *and* `DAvg()`) *are also unsuitable for calculated fields, as checking changes in underlying functions can negatively impact database performance.*

To create a calculated field in DAO, you will need to set the `Expression` property of the `DAO.Field2` object to the expression you'd like to use for the calculated field:

```
fld.Expression = "[FirstName] & "" "" & [LastName]"
```

Before creating a calculated field, make sure that the fields the calculation is based upon are present in the table.

Figure 10.4 shows the `Employees` table in design view displaying the properties of the `FullName` calculated field. To manually change the calculation expression, you can click the ellipsis button to the right of the `Expression` property to bring up the Expression Builder dialog.

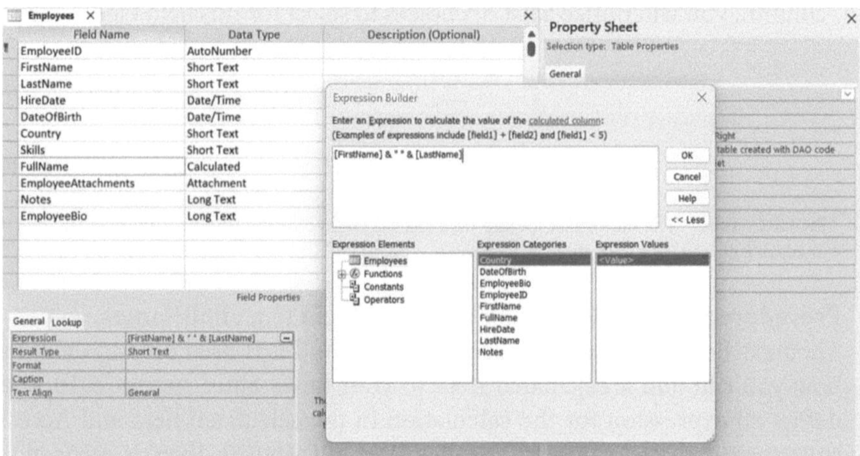

FIGURE 10.4.   The Employees table displaying the Expression property of the FullName calculated field and Expression Builder where the expression can be easily modified.

Procedure Section: Adding an Attachment Field (e.g., Employee Attachments)

The `Attachment` data type makes it possible to store various types of external files directly in the database. This data type is only available in Access databases created in the `.accdb` file format in Access 2007–2024. Earlier versions of Access used the OLE `Object` data type for embedding external files within MDB databases, and this format continues to be available in Access 2024 for backward compatibility. The `Attachment` data type eliminates the bloating issues that plagued Access MDB databases whenever the OLE `Object` data type was used. To keep `.accdb` files as small as possible, Access compresses the uncompressed files in the attachments before storing them in a database.

The `Attachment` data type allows you to add multiple attachments to a single record. Keep in mind, however, that the size of an attached data file cannot exceed 256 MB (megabytes). You can store as many external files as you want as long as you stay within 2 GB (gigabytes) of data, which is the maximum size of an Access database. You cannot restrict how many attachments are allowed in a database field. Also, some attachment file types are not supported.

You can work with attachments manually via the Attachments dialog box or programmatically using the `Attachment` object.

In the Hands-On 10.7 procedure, we added the `EmployeeAttachments` field to the `Employees` table using the `CreateField` method. When you open the `Employees` table in the datasheet view, you will notice that the attachment field is denoted by the paper clip. To add attachments manually, double-click the `@(0)` in the record to bring up the Attachments dialog box (see Figure 10.5). Find out how to add and manipulate attachments programmatically in Custom Project 10.1 later in this chapter.

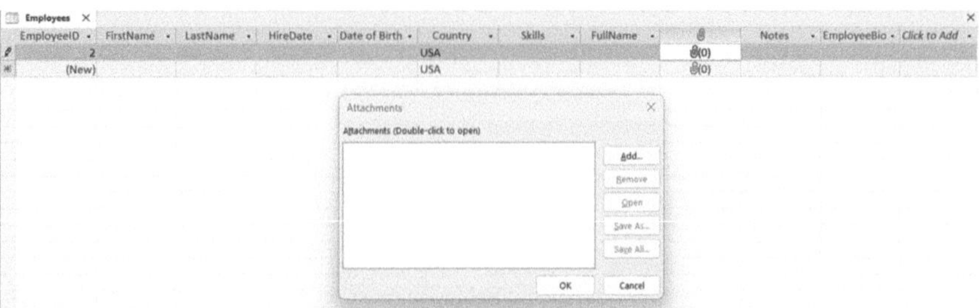

FIGURE 10.5.   The Attachment field added with the VBA procedure in Hands-On 10.7 currently does not contain any attachments.

Procedure Section: Adding an Append-Only Memo Field (e.g., Notes)

Another type of complex multivalue field available in the `.accdb` file format is the append-only memo field (see Figure 10.6). When the Append Only property is set to Yes, you can append data to the field, but you are not allowed to change the data that has been previously entered into this field. This feature is useful for keeping track of the changes made to the field.

Notice that after creating the Notes memo field, the `AppendOnly` property of this field is set to `True` to ensure that Access keeps the history of changes for this field.

Every time you edit the data in the append-only memo field, the date and timestamp and your changes are automatically saved to the version history of the field.

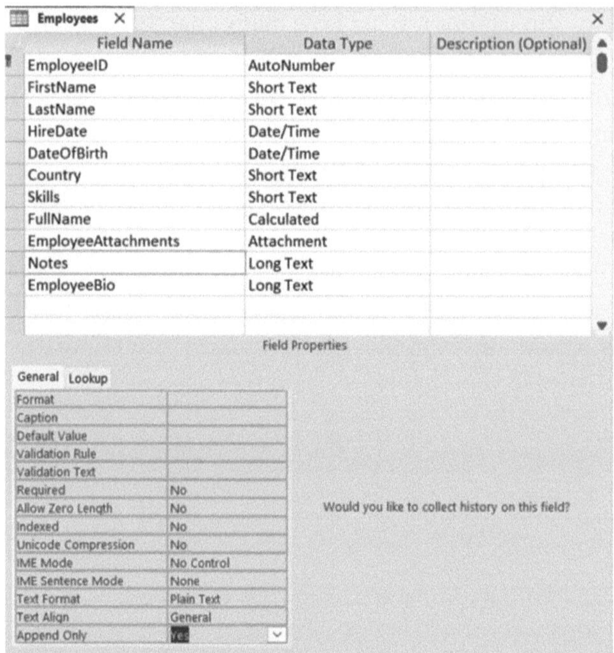

FIGURE 10.6. To collect history on a memo field, you must set the field's Append Only property to Yes.

> | | |
> |---|---|
> | **NOTE** | *Beginning with Access 2013, there is no "memo" data type in the Data Type list. The `Long Text` data type has replaced the memo data type found in prior versions of Access. The `Long Text` data type is used for longer text fields (see the Notes field in Figure 10.6) and the `Short Text` data type is used for storing up to 255 characters.* |

Procedure Section: Adding a Rich Text Field (e.g., EmployeeBio)

The last specialty field in our `ModifyEmployees` table procedure is the `EmployeeBio` field, which is set as a rich text memo field. The Rich Text feature allows you to format your memo fields in a datasheet with the bold, italics, underline, and other formatting options that are available via the Ribbon. The same `CreateField` method is used to create the Rich Text Data field. Once the field is appended to the `TableDefs` collection of the `Employees` table, we set its `TextFormat` property to Rich Text. This is achieved via the following statement:

```
fld.Properties.Append fld.CreateProperty("TextFormat", dbByte, 1)
```

In this statement, 1 denotes the Rich Text setting. The default value of the `TextFormat` property is 0 (Plain Text). Figure 10.7 displays the `EmployeeBio` field with its Text Format set to Rich Text.

When you use the Rich Text feature in a memo field, Access will store the data in the HTML format.

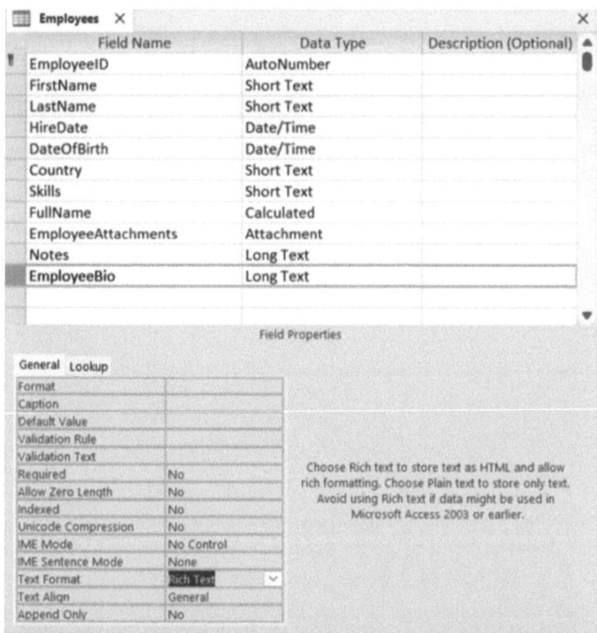

FIGURE 10.7.   The EmployeeBio field has its Text Format property set to Rich Text.

Removing a Field from a Table

You may remove any field from an existing table, whether or not this field contains data. You can't, however, delete a field after you have created an index that references that field. You must first delete the index.

In DAO, use the `Fields` collection's `Delete` method to remove a field from a table. In the following hands-on exercise, we will delete the `HiredOn` field from the `Employees` table located in the `DAODatabase.accdb` file that you created at the beginning of this chapter.

⊙ Hands-On 10.8   Removing a Field from a Table

1. In the VBE window in the current `Chap10` database, choose Insert | Module.
2. In the module's Code window, type the following `DeleteFields_DAO` procedure:

```vba
Sub DeleteFields_DAO()
   Dim db As DAO.Database
   Dim tdf As DAO.TableDef
   Dim strDBName As String
   Dim strTblName As String
   Dim strFolder As String
   Dim strfldName As String

   On Error GoTo ErrorHandler

   strFolder = "C:\VBAAccess2024_ByExample\"
   strDBName = "DAODatabase.accdb"
   strTblName = "Employees"
   strfldName = "HiredOn"

   Set db = OpenDatabase(strFolder & strDBName)
   Set tdf = db.TableDefs(strTblName)

   MsgBox "Number of fields in the table: " & _
    db.TableDefs(strTblName).Fields.Count

 ' Check if the field exists
     If FieldExists(tdf, strfldName) Then
         ' Delete the field
         tdf.Fields.Delete strfldName
         MsgBox "Field '" & strfldName & _
           "' deleted successfully.", vbInformation
         MsgBox "Current number of fields in the table: " & _
             db.TableDefs(strTblName).Fields.Count

     Else
         MsgBox "Field '" & strfldName & _
         "' does not exist in the Employees table.", vbInformation
     End If

 ' Clean up
   Set tdf = Nothing
   Set db = Nothing
   Exit Sub
```

```
ErrorHandler:
  MsgBox Err.Number & ": " & Err.Description, vbCritical, "Error"
   Resume Next
End Sub



' Function to check if a field exists in a table
Function FieldExists(tdf As DAO.TableDef, fieldName As String)
As Boolean
    Dim fld As DAO.Field
    FieldExists = False
    For Each fld In tdf.Fields
        If fld.Name = fieldName Then
            FieldExists = True
            Exit Function
        End If
    Next fld
End Function
```

3. Choose Run | Run Sub/UserForm to execute the procedure.
   Notice that before the field is deleted, the `DeleteFields_DAO` procedure checks whether the field exists in the `Employees` table. This check is performed by calling the `FieldExists` subprocedure and passing to it the `TableDef` object and the name of the field to delete. If the function returns `True` (meaning the field exists), the `Delete` method of the `Fields` collection is used to delete the specified field. The `ErrorHandler` that is included in the main procedure ensures that potential issues encountered during the procedure execution are handled properly.

   Run the `DeleteField_DAO` procedure again and notice how errors are handled.

Retrieving Table Properties

You can use the `Properties` collection of the DAO `TableDef` object to list properties of the `Employees` table in the `Chap10.accdb` database, as demonstrated in the procedure available in the companion files.

Additional code is available in the companion files.
File Name: `ListTableProperties_DAO.txt`
Description: `Listing Table Properties`

Linking a dBASE Table

In DAO, to link a table to an Access database, use the `CreateTableDef` method to create a new table:

```
Set myTable = db.CreateTableDef("TableDBASE")
```

Next, specify the `Connect` property of the `TableDef` object. For example, the following statement specifies the connect string:

```
myTable.Connect = "dBase 5.0;Database=C:\VBAAccess2024_ByExample"
```

Next, specify the `SourceTableName` property of the `TableDef` object to indicate the actual name of the table in the source database:

```
myTable.SourceTableName = "Customer.dbf"
```

Finally, use the `Append` method to append the `TableDef` object to the `TableDefs` collection:

```
db.TableDefs.Append myTable
```

Additional code is available in the companion files.
File Name: `LinkDBaseTable_DAO.txt`
Description: `Linking a dBASE table to the current database`

Creating Indexes

Earlier in this chapter, in the `CreateTableWithProperties` procedure, we created the `PrimaryKey` index on the `EmployeeID` field. In DAO, indexes are created using the `CreateIndex` method for a `TableDef` object. The following statement creates an index named `PrimaryKey`:

```
Set idx = tdf.CreateIndex("PrimaryKey")
```

To ensure that the correct type of index is created, you need to set the index properties. For example, the `Primary` property of an index indicates that the index fields constitute the primary key for the table:

```
idx.Primary = True
```

Use the `Unique` property to specify whether the values in an index must be unique:

```
idx.Unique = True
```

The `Required` property indicates whether the index can accept `Null` values. When you set this property to `True`, nulls will not be accepted:

```
idx.Required = True
```

Use the `IgnoreNulls` property to determine whether a record with a `Null` value in the index fields should be included in the index:

```
idx.IgnoreNulls = False
```

To actually index a table, you must use the `CreateField` method on the `Index` object to create a `Field` object for each field you want to include in the index:

```
Set fld = idx.CreateField("EmployeeID")
```

Once the `Field` object is created, you need to append it to the `Fields` collection:

```
idx.Fields.Append fld
```

The last step in index creation is appending the `Index` object to the `Indexes` collection:

```
tdf.Indexes.Append idx
```

To verify that the index was created, open the `Employees` table in the `Chap10.accdb` database. Activate the design view and click the Indexes button on the Ribbon. The Indexes dialog is shown in Figure 10.8.

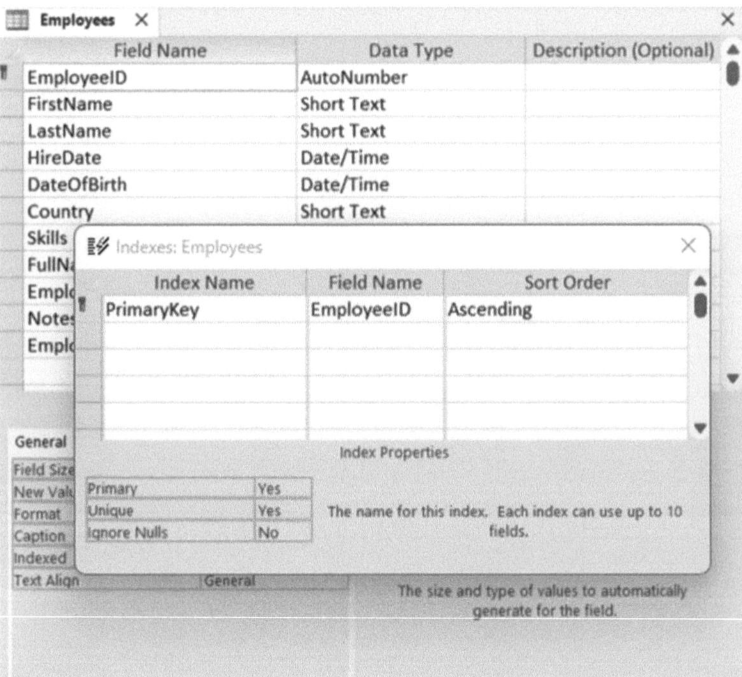

FIGURE 10.8.   The Indexes window shows the PrimaryIndex settings for the EmployeeID field.

Adding a Multiple-Field Index to a Table

You can use DAO code to add a multiple-field index to your `Employees` table. For example, by adding an index that includes both the `LastName` and `First-Name` fields, you can greatly optimize searches and sorting operations based on `LastName` and `FirstName`.

⊙ Hands-On 10.9   Adding a Multiple-Field Index to an Existing Table

1. In the VBE window, choose Insert | Module.
2. In the module's Code window, type the `Add_MultiFieldIndex` procedure shown here:

```
Sub Add_MultiFieldIndex()
    Dim db As DAO.Database
    Dim tdf As DAO.TableDef
    Dim idx As DAO.Index
    Dim fld As DAO.Field

    On Error GoTo ErrorHandler

    ' Open the current database
    Set db = CurrentDb()
    Set tdf = db.TableDefs("Employees")

    ' Create a new index object
    Set idx = tdf.CreateIndex("LastNameFirstNameIndex")

    ' Add fields to the index
    Set fld = idx.CreateField("LastName")
    idx.Fields.Append fld
    Set fld = idx.CreateField("FirstName")
    idx.Fields.Append fld

    ' Append the index to the table
    tdf.Indexes.Append idx

    ' Clean up
    Set fld = Nothing
    Set idx = Nothing
    Set tdf = Nothing
    Set db = Nothing

    MsgBox "Multiple field index " _
        & "'LastNameFirstNameIndex' was added!", vbInformation
```

```
    Exit Sub
ErrorHandler:
    ' Handle any errors
    MsgBox "Error " & Err.Number & ": " & _
      Err.Description, vbCritical, "Error"
    Resume Next
End Sub
```

3. Choose Run | Run Sub/UserForm to execute the procedure.

The `Add_MultiFieldIndex` procedure creates a two-field index in the `Employees` table. To create an index, use the `CreateIndex` method on a `TableDef` object. Next, use the `CreateField` method on the `Index` object to create the first field to be included in the index, and then append this field to the `Fields` collection. Repeat the same steps for the second field you want to include in the index. It is important to remember that the order in which the fields are appended has an effect on the index order. The last step in the multiple-field index creation process is to ensure that the new index is appended to the `Employees` table. If you open the Indexes window after running this procedure, you will be able to review the index that was created using the above procedure code.

INTRODUCTION TO DAO RECORDSETS

To successfully work with data, you need to learn about the `Recordset` object. The `Recordset` object represents a set of records in a table or a set of records returned by executing a stored query or an SQL statement. Each column of a recordset represents a field, and each row represents a record. The `Recordset` is a temporary object and is not saved in the database. All `Recordset` objects cease to exist after the procedure ends. All open `Recordset` objects are contained in the `Recordsets` collection. Creating and using the `Recordset` objects depends on the type of object library (DAO/ADO) that you've selected for your programming task.

In DAO, there are five types of `Recordset` objects:

- Table type
- Dynaset type
- Snapshot type
- Forward-only type
- Dynamic type

Each of these recordsets offers a different functionality (see Table 10.4).

You create a `Recordset` object using the `OpenRecordset` method. The type of the recordset is specified by the `type` argument of the `OpenRecordset` method. If the recordset's type is not specified, DAO will attempt to create a table-type recordset. If this type isn't available, attempts are made to create a dynaset-, snapshot-, or forward-only-type recordset object.

TABLE 10.4.   The DAO recordset types.

Recordset Type	Description
Table type	Used to access records in a table stored in an Access database. You can retrieve, add, update, and delete records in a single table.
Dynaset type	Used to retrieve, add, update, and delete records from one or more tables in a database, as well as any table that is linked to the Access database.
Snapshot type	Used to access records from a local table stored in an Access database, as well as any linked table or query. Snapshot recordsets contain a copy of the records in RAM (*random-access memory*) and provide no direct access to the underlying data. They are used for reading data only—you can't use them to add, update, or delete records. It does not reflect changes made by other users.
Forward-only type	This is a special type of snapshot recordset that only allows you to scroll forward through the records. It provides the fastest access when you want to make a single pass through the data. It's very efficient for read-only operations.
Dynamic type	This recordset is generated by a query based on one or more tables. It allows you to add, change, or delete records from a row-returning query. In addition, it includes the records that other users may have added, modified, or deleted.

In the following sections of this chapter, you will learn how to open the `Recordset` object and loop through its records. You will also find out how to navigate in the recordset, and how to find, filter, read, and count the records. Only DAO recordsets will be covered here. Refer to the next chapter if you require the use of ADO recordsets.

Opening a Recordset and Transferring Data

So far in this chapter, you have created a table and defined its structure by adding various types of fields. An empty table, however, is not very useful; it's time to populate it with some data. We could do this manually by entering data for each field in the table datasheet view, but this is a very tedious process, especially when you need lots of data right away. Also, we need the data quickly, so we can learn how to manipulate it. Therefore, let's get the data programmatically from another database.

⊙ Hands-On 10.10   Populating the Employees Table with Data

NOTE	*This hands-on exercise assumes you are still working within the* Chap10.accdb *database file and your* VBAAccess2024_ByExample *folder contains the copy of the* Northwind.mdb *database from the companion files.*

1. In the VBE window, choose Insert | Module.
In the module's Code window, type the PopulateEmployeesFromNorthwindMdb
procedure shown here:

```
Sub PopulateEmployeesFromNorthwindMdb()
    Dim dbSource As DAO.Database
    Dim dbTarget As DAO.Database
    Dim rsSource As DAO.Recordset
    Dim rsTarget As DAO.Recordset
    Dim srcPath As String

    On Error GoTo ErrorHandler

    ' Specify the path to the Northwind database
    srcPath = "C:\VBAAccess2024_ByExample\Northwind.mdb"

    ' Open the current database
    Set dbTarget = CurrentDb()

    ' Open the Northwind database
    Set dbSource = dbEngine.Workspaces(0).OpenDatabase(srcPath)

    ' Open the source and target recordsets
    Set rsSource = dbSource.OpenRecordset("Employees",
                                    dbOpenSnapshot)
    Set rsTarget = dbTarget.OpenRecordset("Employees",
                                    dbOpenDynaset)

    ' Loop through the source recordset
    ' and add records to the target recordset
    Do While Not rsSource.EOF
        rsTarget.AddNew
        rsTarget!EmployeeID = rsSource!EmployeeID
        rsTarget!FirstName = rsSource!FirstName
        rsTarget!LastName = rsSource!LastName
        rsTarget!DateOfBirth = rsSource!BirthDate
        rsTarget!HireDate = rsSource!HireDate
```

```
                rsTarget!Country = rsSource!Country
                rsTarget!Notes = rsSource!Notes
                rsTarget.Update
                rsSource.MoveNext
        Loop
        ' Clean up
        rsSource.Close
        rsTarget.Close
        dbSource.Close
        Set rsSource = Nothing
        Set rsTarget = Nothing
        Set dbSource = Nothing
        Set dbTarget = Nothing

      MsgBox "Employees table populated successfully!", vbInformation
        Exit Sub
    ErrorHandler:
        ' Handle any errors
        MsgBox "Error " & Err.Number & ": " & _
          Err.Description, vbCritical, "Error"
        Resume Next
    End Sub
```

2. Run the `PopulateEmployeesFromNorthwindMdb` procedure.
3. When the procedure finishes, switch to the main Access application window and open the `Employees` table. The table should now contain nine employee records, as shown in Figure 10.9.

EmployeeID	FirstName	LastName	HireDate	Date of Birth	Country	Skills	FullName	📎	Notes	EmployeeBio	Click to Add
1	Nancy	Davolio	5/1/1992	12/8/1968	USA		Nancy Davolio	📎(0)	Education inclu		
2	Andrew	Fuller	8/14/1992	2/19/1952	USA		Andrew Fuller	📎(0)	Andrew receive		
3	Janet	Leverling	4/1/1992	8/30/1963	USA		Janet Leverling	📎(0)	Janet has a BS d		
4	Margaret	Peacock	5/3/1993	9/19/1958	USA		Margaret Peacock	📎(0)	Margaret holds		
5	Steven	Buchanan	10/17/1993	3/4/1955	UK		Steven Buchanan	📎(0)	Steven Buchana		
6	Michael	Suyama	10/17/1993	7/2/1963	UK		Michael Suyama	📎(0)	Michael is a gra		
7	Robert	King	1/2/1994	5/29/1960	UK		Robert King	📎(0)	Robert King ser		
8	Laura	Callahan	3/5/1994	1/9/1958	USA		Laura Callahan	📎(0)	Laura received i		
9	Anne	Dodsworth	11/15/1994	7/2/1969	UK		Anne Dodsworth	📎(0)	Anne has a BA d		
(New)					USA			📎(0)			

FIGURE 10.9.   The Employees data was copied from another Access database using a VBA procedure.

Let's analyze the procedure code so we understand what it does. To perform the data transfer operation, we declared variables to represent both the current database and the `Northwind` database, along with their respective recordsets. Since we are dealing with two databases, we need to open both the current database and the `Northwind` database before accessing their `Employees` data.

Once the databases are open, we proceed to open their tables. Notice that `rsSource` opens a `Snapshot Recordset` on the `Northwind Employees` table.

Use the `OpenRecordset` method to create or open a recordset. For example:

```
Set rsSource = dbSource.OpenRecordset("Employees",
                                        dbOpenSnapshot)
```

Notice that the second argument in the `OpenRecordset` method specifies the type of recordset. The `RecordsetTypeEnum` constants (shown in Table 10.5) can be used here. The `OpenRecordset` method opens a new recordset for reading, adding, updating, or deleting records from a database.

TABLE 10.5.   Constants used to specify the type of a DAO Recordset object.

Type Constant	Value	Description
dbOpenTable	1	Opens a table-type recordset
dbOpenDynaset	2	Opens a dynaset-type recordset
dbOpenSnapshot	4	Opens a snapshot-type recordset
dbOpenForwardOnly	8	Opens a forward-only-type recordset
dbOpenDynamic	16	Opens a dynamic-type recordset

We only need to read from this table, so the snapshot recordsets will give us the best performance because they provide a static copy of the data. To copy data into the current database, we open a dynaset recordset on the current database's `Employees` table. This allows us to read and write to the table.

Next, we loop through each record in the source recordset to copy data from the corresponding fields. Looping continues until the `EOF` is reached, indicating there are no more records to process in the source table `Employees`. Inside the loop, we use the `AddNew` method to add a new record to the target recordset (the current database's `Employees` table).

We then map the fields by matching the names of fields in both recordsets so that we can copy their field values accurately. Notice, in VBA, the exclamation mark (`!`) I used as a shorthand for accessing members of a collection, such as fields in a recordset or controls on the form. It is often used to simplify the syntax when working with objects such as `Recordset`, `Form`, or `Report`. For example:

```
rsTarget!EmployeeID = rsSource!EmployeeID
```

This code assigns the value of the `EmployeesID` field from the source recordset to the `EmployeeID` field in the target recordset. You could also use a longer syntax, such as this:

```
rsTarget.Fields("EmployeeID") = rsSource.Fields("EmployeeID")
```

Using the exclamation mark (!), however, makes the code shorter and more readable.

Once we have copied all the field values for the current record, we commit this record to the target recordset using the Update method. After updating, we move to the next record in the source recordset using the MoveNext method. This process repeats until there are no more records in the source table.

After processing all the records, we close both recordsets and release the resources to ensure memory is freed. We also close the source database. The procedure includes the error-handling code to manage any issues that may arise during code execution, displaying an error message with the error number and description.

Finding and Reading Records with DAO

To find and read database records, you must understand how to navigate through the recordset. When you open a Recordset object, the first record is the current record. All recordsets have a current record.

- To move to subsequent records, use the MoveNext method.
- To move to the previous record, use the MovePrevious method.
- The MoveFirst and MoveLast methods move the cursor to the first and last records, respectively.
- If you call the MoveNext method when the cursor is already pointing to the last record, the cursor will move off the last record to the area known as End of File (EOF), and the EOF property will be set to True.
- If you call the MoveNext method when the EOF property is True, an error is generated because you cannot move past the end of the file. Similarly, by calling the MovePrevious method when the cursor is pointing to the first record, you will move the cursor to the area known as Beginning of File (BOF). This will set the BOF property to True. When the BOF property is True and you call the MovePrevious method, an error will be generated.
- You can also move forward or backward n positions using the Move method followed by a space and the number indicating the position you desire to move to.
- For example, Move 5 will move the record pointer to the fifth record in the recordset. Recordsets are zero-based, so this statement actually moves to the sixth record. If you attempt to move beyond the bounds of the recordset, an error will occur.

When navigating through a recordset, you may want to mark a specific record in order to return to it at a later time. You can use the `Bookmark` property to obtain a unique identification for a specific record.

The `Recordset` object has numerous properties and methods. We will discuss only those properties and methods that are required for performing a specific task, as demonstrated in the example procedures.

If you examine closely the `Employees` table data, you will notice that the data in the Notes field really belongs in the `EmployeeBio` field. How can we move existing data from one field to another? This is the topic of our next hands-on exercise. In addition to that, we will also update the Notes field with new data from another database.

 **Hands-On 10.11   Finding and Moving Data Using the Recordset**

<table>
<tr><td>

____

NOTE</td><td>This hands-on exercise assumes you are still working within the Chap10.accdb database file and your VBAAccess2024_ByExample folder contains the copy of the NorthwindStarter. accdb database from the companion files. It also assumes you have successfully completed the previous hands-on exercise.</td></tr>
</table>

1. In the VBE window, choose Insert | Module.
2. In the module's Code window, type the `UpdateEmployeeFields` procedure shown here:

```vba
Sub UpdateEmployeeFields()
    Dim db As DAO.Database
    Dim sourceDb As DAO.Database
    Dim rs As DAO.Recordset
    Dim rsSource As DAO.Recordset
    Dim srcPath As String

    On Error GoTo ErrorHandler

    ' Specify the path to the Northwind database
    srcPath = "C:\VBAAccess2024_ByExample\NorthwindStarter.accdb"

    ' Open the current database
    Set db = CurrentDb()

    ' Open the Northwind database
    Set sourceDb = dbEngine.Workspaces(0).OpenDatabase(srcPath)
```

```vba
    ' Open the Employees table in the current database
    Set rs = db.OpenRecordset("Employees", dbOpenDynaset)

    ' Move data from Notes to EmployeeBio in the current database
    Do While Not rs.EOF
        rs.Edit
        rs!EmployeeBio = rs!Notes
        rs!Notes = Null ' Clear the Notes field after moving data
        rs.Update
        rs.MoveNext
    Loop
    ' Open the Employees table in the Northwind database
    Set rsSource = sourceDb.OpenRecordset("Employees", dbOpenSnapshot)

    ' Copy data from Northwind Notes to
    ' current database Notes for matching employees
    Do While Not rsSource.EOF
        rs.MoveFirst ' Reset current recordset to start search
        rs.FindFirst "EmployeeID = " & rsSource!EmployeeID
        If Not rs.NoMatch Then
            rs.Edit
            rs!Notes = rsSource!Notes
            rs.Update
        End If
        rsSource.MoveNext
    Loop

    ' Clean up
    rs.Close
    rsSource.Close
    sourceDb.Close
    Set rs = Nothing
    Set rsSource = Nothing
    Set sourceDb = Nothing
    Set db = Nothing

    MsgBox "Employee fields updated successfully!", vbInformation
    Exit Sub
ErrorHandler:
    ' Handle any errors
    MsgBox "Error " & Err.Number & ": " & _
Err.Description, vbCritical, "Error"
    Resume Next
End Sub
```

3. Run the `UpdateEmployeeFields` procedure.

4. When the procedure finishes, switch to the main Access application window and open the `Employees` table. The table should now contain nine employee records, as shown in Figure 10.10.

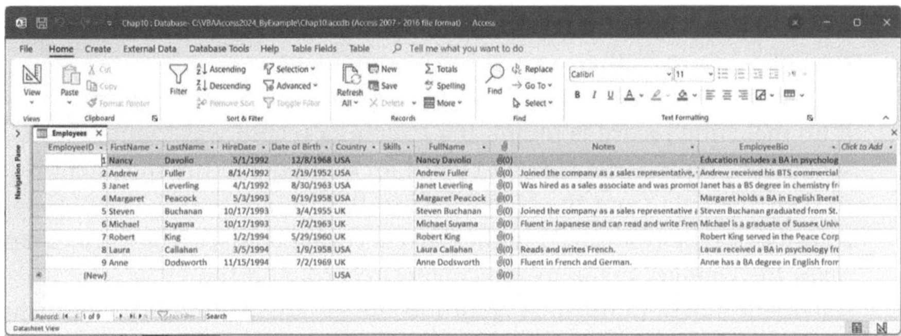

FIGURE 10.10.   The Employees table now shows data in the EmployeeBio field and the Notes field data was retrieved from the NothwindStarter database.

Notice that our procedure contains several sections that you are already familiar with: Variable Declarations, Error Handling Setup, and Opening Databases.

Let's focus on the section that moves data from `Notes` to `EmployeeBio`. Moving data requires that you first open a dynaset recordset on the `Employees` table in the current database. Next, you loop through each employee record to move data. Notice the use of the `Do While Not rs.EOF` statement. This loop continues as long as the `EOF` property of the `rs` recordset is `False`. The `EOF` property is `True` when the recordset pointer reaches the end of the recordset. So, this loop processes each record until all records are processed. The `rs.Edit` statement prepares the current record for editing. The `Edit` method is necessary to modify the field in the recordset. The next statement moves the data from the Notes field to the `EmployeeBio` field. After the data has been moved, the Notes field is cleared using the following statement:

```
rs!Notes = Null
```

After that, the changes made to the current record are saved using the `Update` method of the `Recordset` object. To process the next record in the loop, be sure to call the `rs.MoveNext` to ensure that the loop processes each record sequentially.

The next `While… Loop` is used to bring data from the Notes field in the `Employees` table in the `NorthwindStarter` database to the Notes field in the current database's `Employees` table. Again, we continue looping through the records as long as the `EOF` property of the `rs` recordset is `False`. It is necessary that we start the search for each matching employee from the beginning of the current database. To do this, we use the `rs.MoveFirst` statement. Next, we attempt to locate a specific record based on a condition. The `FindFirst` method allows us to find the first record in `rs` where the `EmployeeID` matches the `EmployeeID` in the `rsSource`. The statement `If Not rs.NoMatch Then` checks whether a matching record was found. The `NoMatch` property is `True` if no matching record is found. If a matching record was found, the `rs.Edit` statement prepares the current record for editing and the statement is issued to copy the data from the Notes field in the `NorthwindStarter (rsSource)` recordset to the Notes field in the current (`rs`) recordset. The `rs.Update` then saves the changes made to the current record, and the `rsSource.MoveNext` statement moves to the next record in the `rsSource` recordset, ensuring that each record is processed sequentially.

This procedure demonstrated how you can use various `Recordset` methods—`Edit`, `Update`, `MoveFirst`, and `MoveNext`—to navigate and modify records within the recordsets and transfer data between the fields for corresponding or matching records.

Counting Records and Retrieving Field Values

When you want to search tables or queries to retrieve data, you will get the fastest results by opening a snapshot-type recordset. A snapshot is simply a non-updatable set of records that contain fields from one or more tables or queries. At times, you may see code in which the type of recordset is not specified. When you open a recordset without explicitly specifying the type in DAO, it defaults to a dynaset type (see the example code below).

To retrieve the contents of fields in a recordset, you can use the `DAO.Recordset` object. The `RecordCount` property of the `Recordset` object will get you the count of the number of records in the table.

For example, the following procedure opens a dynaset recordset for a table named `Employees` and stores the values from the `LastName` field into a collection, and then prints the contents of the collection. Note that when adding values to a collection, you must use the `Value` property to avoid a No current record error when retrieving values from the collection.

(◉) Hands-On 10.12   Counting Records and Retrieving Field Values

1. Add the following procedure code in a new module of the current VBA project
   and then run it.

```vba
Sub RetrieveAllFieldValues()
    Dim db As DAO.Database
    Dim rst As DAO.Recordset
    Dim fieldValues As Collection
    Dim i As Integer

    Set db = CurrentDb()
    Set rst = db.OpenRecordset("Employees") ' defaults to Dynaset
    Set fieldValues = New Collection

    Debug.Print "Number of records: " & rst.RecordCount

    ' Get values from LastName field
    If Not rst.EOF Then
        rst.MoveFirst
        Do While Not rst.EOF
            fieldValues.Add rst!LastName.Value
            rst.MoveNext
        Loop
    End If

    ' Print out all values
    For i = 1 To fieldValues.Count
        Debug.Print "Value " & i & ": " & fieldValues(i)
    Next i

    rst.Close
    Set rst = Nothing
    Set db = Nothing

    SendKeys "^g"
End Sub
```

2. In the procedure code, explicitly define the type of the recordset as snapshot
   (`dbOpenSnapshot`) and rerun the procedure.
   If you change the type of the recordset to snapshot and rerun this procedure,
   the count of records will be incorrect. To get an accurate count with a snapshot
   recordset, you need to start from the last record to ensure that Access retrieves
   all records.

3. Modify the procedure as follows and rerun it to view the results.

```
' Move to the last record to get the correct count
If Not rst.BOF And Not rst.EOF Then
    rst.MoveLast
    Debug.Print "Number of records: " & rst.RecordCount
Else
    Debug.Print "No records found."
End If
```

At times, you may need to know where you are in a recordset. There are two properties that can be used to determine your position in the recordset:

- The `AbsolutePosition` property allows you to position the current record pointer at a specific record based on its ordinal position in a dynaset- or snapshot-type recordset object. This property lets you determine the current record number. Zero (`0`) refers to the first record in the `Record-set` object. If there is no current record, the `AbsolutePosition` property returns `-1`. Because the position of a record changes when the preceding records are deleted, however, you should rely more on bookmarks to position the current record. The `AbsolutePosition` property can be used only with dynasets and snapshots. Because the `AbsolutePosition` property value is zero-based, `1` is added to the `AbsolutePosition` value to display the current record information:

  ```
  MsgBox "Current record: " & rst.AbsolutePosition + 1
  ```

- The `PercentPosition` property shows the current position relative to the number of records that have been accessed. Both `AbsolutePosition` and `PercentPosition` are not accurate until you move to the last record.

Let's see how the `AbsolutePosition` property can be used in our procedure.

4. Modify the section of the `RetrieveAllFieldValues` procedure that retrieves values from the `LastName` field:

```
' Get values from LastName field
If Not rst.EOF Then
    rst.MoveFirst
    Do While Not rst.EOF
        If rst.AbsolutePosition + 1 = 5 Then
            fieldValues.Add rst!FirstName.Value & _
              " " & rst!LastName.Value
        Else
          fieldValues.Add rst!LastName.Value
```

```
        End If
        rst.MoveNext
    Loop
End If
```

5. Run the modified procedure.

   Notice that the Immediate window now shows the last names of all employees except for the fifth employee, whose first and last name is printed out: `Steven Buchanan`.

Using the Seek Method to Find Records in a Table-Type Recordset

While the `Move` methods are convenient for looping through records in a record-set, you should use the `Seek` or `Find` method to look for specific records.

When you know exactly which record you want to find in a table-type re-cordset and the field you are searching is indexed, the quickest way to find that record is to use the `Seek` method.

One thing to remember with the `Seek` method is that the table must contain an index. The `Index` property must be set before the `Seek` method can be used. If you try to use the `Seek` method on a table-type recordset without first set-ting the current index, a run-time error will occur. The `Seek` method searches through the recordset and locates the first matching record. Once the record is found, it is made the current record and the `NoMatch` property is set to `False`. If the record is not found, the `NoMatch` property is set to `True` and the current record is undefined. Table 10.6 lists comparison operators that you can use with the `Seek` method.

TABLE 10.6. Comparison operators used with the Seek method.

Operator	Description
"="	Finds the first record whose indexed field is equal to the specified value
">="	Finds the first record whose indexed field is greater than or equal to the specified value
">"	Finds the first record whose indexed field is greater than the specified value
"<="	Finds the first record whose indexed field is less than or equal to the specified value
"<"	Finds the first record whose indexed field is less than the specified value

The comparison operator used with the `Seek` method must be enclosed in quotes. If there are several records that match your criteria, the `Seek` method returns the first record it finds. The `Seek` method cannot be used to search for records in a linked table. You must use the `Find` methods (see the next section) for locating specific records in linked tables, as well as dynaset- and snapshot-type recordsets.

The procedure in Hands-On 10.13 searches for an employee whose last name begins with the letter K.

⊙ Hands-On 10.13   Finding records in a table-type recordset

1. In the VBE window, choose Insert | Module.

2. In the module's Code window, type the following `FindRecordsInTable` procedure:

```
Sub FindRecordsInTable()
   Dim db As DAO.Database
   Dim tblRst As DAO.Recordset


   Set db = CurrentDb

   Set tblRst = db.OpenRecordset("Employees", dbOpenTable)
   ' find the first employee in the table whose
   ' name begins with the letter "K"

   tblRst.Index = "LastNameFirstNameIndex"
   tblRst.Seek ">=", "K"

   If Not tblRst.NoMatch Then
     MsgBox "Found the following employee: " & _
        tblRst![LastName]
   Else
     MsgBox "There is no employee with such a name."
   End If

   tblRst.Close
   Set tblRst = Nothing
   db.Close
   Set db = Nothing
End Sub
```

3. Choose Run | Run Sub/UserForm to execute the procedure.

Using the Find Methods to Find Records in Snapshots and Dynasets

Use the `Find` methods to search for a record in dynaset-type and snapshot-type recordsets. Table 10.7 lists the available `Find` methods.

TABLE 10.7. Find methods in a DAO recordset.

Method Name	Description
FindFirst	Finds the first matching record in the recordset
FindNext	Finds the next matching record, starting at the current record
FindPrevious	Finds the previous matching record, starting at the current record
FindLast	Finds the last matching record in the recordset

If a record is not found for the given criteria, the NoMatch property of the Recordset object is set to True. Before searching for records, set a bookmark at the current record. If the search fails, you will be able to use the bookmark to return to the current record; otherwise, you will get the error No current record. Each record in a Recordset object has a unique bookmark that you can use to locate that record. To get the current record's bookmark, move the cursor to that record and assign the value of the Bookmark property of the Recordset object to a Variant variable:

```
Dim mySpot As Variant
mySpot = dynaRst.Bookmark
```

In Hands-On 10.14, the bookmark is set on the first record of a dynaset-type recordset. The procedure then searches for employees whose name ends with the string er. The asterisk (*) in the search string is a wildcard character representing any number of letters (*er).

To return to the bookmarked record, set the Bookmark property to the value held by the Variant variable:

```
dynaRst.Bookmark = mySpot
```

While recordsets based on local Access tables support bookmarks, non-Access databases may not support them. To determine whether a Recordset object supports bookmarks, you can check the Bookmarkable property. Bookmarks are supported if this property is True.

```
If dynaRst.Bookmarkable Then
mySpot = dynaRst.Bookmark
End If
```

If the Recordset object does not support bookmarks, an error occurs. You can set as many bookmarks as you wish. Bookmarks can be created for a record other than the current record by moving to the desired record and assigning the value of the Bookmark property to a String variable that identifies that record.

⦿ Hands-On 10.14   Finding a Record in a Dynaset-Type Recordset

1. In the VBE window, choose Insert | Module.

2. In the module's Code window, type the following `FindRecInDynaset` procedure:

```
Sub FindRecInDynaset()
    Dim db As DAO.Database
    Dim dynaRst As DAO.Recordset
    Dim mySpot As Variant
    Dim strFound As String


    Set db = CurrentDb
    Set dynaRst = db.OpenRecordset("Employees", dbOpenDynaset)

    MsgBox "Current employee: " & dynaRst![LastName]
    mySpot = dynaRst.Bookmark

    ' find clients whose name ends
    ' with the string "an"
    dynaRst.FindFirst "[LastName] Like '*an'"

    Do While Not dynaRst.NoMatch
      strFound = strFound & dynaRst![LastName] & ","
      dynaRst.FindNext "[LastName] Like '*an'"
    Loop
    MsgBox "Found: " & Mid(strFound, 1, Len(strFound) - 1)

    dynaRst.Bookmark = mySpot
    MsgBox "Back to: " & dynaRst![LastName]
    dynaRst.Close

    Set dynaRst = Nothing
    db.Close
    Set db = Nothing
    SendKeys "^g"
End Sub
```

3. Choose Run | Run Sub/UserForm to execute the procedure.
The names of all employees that match the search criteria are shown in a message box.

Adding a New Record to a Table

Earlier in this chapter, you saw how you can add new records to a table using the `AddNew` method. Once you have a blank record, you may set values for all or some of the fields in the new record. You must set the field's value if the `Required` property of a field is set to `True`. In the Access user interface, in table design view, there will be a `Yes` entry next to the `Required` property if the entry in the selected field is required. Here are some examples of setting field values in code:

```
rst.Fields("LastName").Value = "Smith"
rst.Fields("Country").Value = "Canada"
```

Note that because `Value` is the default property of a `Field` object, the use of this keyword is optional, so it can be omitted in your VBA code. After filling in the field values, you need to use the `Update` method on the `Recordset` object to ensure that the newly added record is saved:

```
rst.Update
```

In a table-type recordset, the new record is placed in the order identified by the table's index. In a dynaset-type recordset, the new record is added at the end of the recordset.

When you add a new record to a table, the new record does not become the current record. The record that was current prior to adding the new record remains current. In other words, while a new record is being added to the end of the table, the cursor remains in the record that was selected prior to adding a new record. You can, however, make the newly added record current by using the `Bookmark` and `LastModified` properties, like this:

```
rst.Bookmark = rst.LastModified
```

Adding and Deleting Attachments

In this section, you will take care of the empty attachment field in the `Employees` table. Our objective is the transfer of employee photos stored in the attachments field of the `Employees` table in the `NorthwindStarter` database to the same table in our current database, using VBA code. Custom Project 10.1 below involves the following steps to meet this objective.

1. Access the Source and Destination Database
   The source is `NorthwindStarter.accdb` and the destination is the current database (`Chap10.accdb`).

2. Retrieve Images from the Source Database
   You will need to start by opening a recordset to fetch the records from the `Employees` table in the `NorthwindStarter` database. Next, you will need to access the attachments field to get the employee photos.

3. Save Retrieved Images to a Local Directory
   You can store the image files permanently or temporarily using an appropriate filename. In this case, we will use the employee's first name for the name.

4. Attach Retrieved Images to Records in the Destination Database
   You will need to open a recordset to update the `Employees` table in the current database. Next, you will load the saved images into the attachment field of the corresponding records in the current database's `Employees` table.

5. Clean Up
   Delete the image files from the hard drive after they have been successfully added to the destination database. If you decide to keep the files, simply comment out the `Kill` statement that is used to delete files.

   You must also close all opened recordsets and databases to free up resources.

NOTE	*The VBA programming code for Custom Project 10.1 is included in the companion files.*

Custom Project 10.1 Transfer Images to the EmployeeAttachments Field

1. In the VBE window, choose Insert | Module.
2. Copy the procedure code from the `CustomProject 10.1 Image Transfer.txt` file in the companion files and paste it into the module's code window.
3. Analyze the procedure code. Check all the references, making sure that the `NorthwindStarter` database is in the specified location. Notice the Variable Declarations section contains a number of declared variables of different data types:

   - `dbSource` and `dbDest` are references to the source and destination databases.

   - `rsSource`, `rsAttachSource`, `rsDest`, and `rsAttachDest` are recordsets that we need to read and manipulate data in the `Employees` tables of both databases.

   - `fldSoure` and `fldDest` are fields in the `Employees` tables and are defined as `DAO.Filed2` objects of the `Recordset` as the `Field2` object supports working with attachments.

- `rsSourceQry` is a string variable specifying fields that we want to include in the source recordset.
- `strFilePath`, `employeeName`, and `fileExtension` are used for saving and naming the image files.

The code is commented and it should be easy to follow. One thing that may be unfamiliar at this point in your learning is the SQL query. We will cover it in detail later in this chapter. Because we are only interested in data in the limited number of columns (fields) in the source table, instead of opening the recordset for the entire `Employees` table, we can use the `Select` statement to specify which columns from the `Employees` table we want to choose:

```
rsSourceQry = "SELECT EmployeeID, FirstName,Attachments
               FROM Employees"
Set rsSource = dbSource.OpenRecordset(rsSourceQry,
                                 dbOpenDynaset)
```

Note that in the `NorthwindStarter` database, the attachment field in the `Employees` table stores the `.jpg` images as binary data directly within the table itself. These images are not stored as separate files on the file system but are embedded within the records in the `Employees` table. Inside the statement:

```
rsAttachSource.Fields("FileData").SaveToFile strFilePath
```

`rsAttachSource` is a recordset that contains the attachments. `Fields ("FileData")` refers to the field within that recordset that holds the actual binary data of the attached file.

`SaveToFile` is a method to save the contents of the field (the binary data) to a specified file on your disk (`strFilePath`).

To add a file to the attachment field, use the `LoadFromFile` method like this:

```
rsAttachDest.Fields("FileData").LoadFromFile strFilePath
```

4. Execute the `TransferImages` procedure in debug mode, stepping through the code line by line.
5. When the procedure completes, verify that the `Employees` table now contains the employee images in the `EmployeeAttachments` field (see Figure 10.11).

FIGURE 10.11. Attachment files can be added to records in an Access table manually using the Attachments dialog box or via VBA programming. You can view the attached file by double-clicking the attachment field.

Attachments can be deleted from table records using the `Delete` method of the `Recordset2` object. You will need to use a recordset to find the specific record and then access the attachment field to remove the desired file.

Additional code in companion files.

See the `DeleteRobertAttachment.txt` file in the companion file for the complete procedure code that deletes the `Robert.jpg` attachment file from the `Employees` table. This procedure also shows how to reliably check whether a table is open or closed.

Adding Values to Multvalue Lookup Fields

Earlier in this chapter, you used DAO to create a multivalue lookup field called `Skills`. A multivalue lookup field allows you to store multiple values in a single field. To add values to the Skills lookup field in the `Employees` table, you need to use DAO to manipulate the recordsets. Start by declaring and initializing the variables. Next, write code to find the employee by `EmployeeID`. Once the employee is found, enter edit mode and write code to access and update the multivalue lookup field. Finish the procedure by including the cleanup and error-handling code.

1. In the VBE window, choose Insert | Module.
2. In the module's Code window, type the following `AddSkillsToEmployee` procedure:

```
Sub AddSkillsToEmployee(employeeID As Long, _
  ParamArray skills() As Variant)
    Dim db As DAO.Database
    Dim rs As DAO.Recordset
    Dim rsMultiValue As DAO.Recordset
    Dim fld As DAO.Field2
    Dim skill As Variant
    Dim skillExists As Boolean
    Dim skillsAdded As Boolean

    On Error GoTo ErrorHandler

    ' Initialize database
    Set db = CurrentDb()

    ' Open the Employees table
    Set rs = db.OpenRecordset("Employees", dbOpenDynaset)

    ' Find the employee by EmployeeID
    rs.FindFirst "EmployeeID = " & employeeID
    If rs.NoMatch Then
        MsgBox "Employee not found."
        GoTo CleanUp
    End If

    ' Enter edit mode
    If rs.EditMode Then
        rs.Update ' Commit any changes if already in Edit Mode
    End If
    rs.Edit

    ' Access the Skills multi-value lookup field
    Set fld = rs.Fields("Skills")
    Set rsMultiValue = fld.Value

    skillsAdded = False

    ' Add each skill to the Skills field
    ' if it does not already exist
```

```vba
For Each skill In skills
    skillExists = False
    ' before attempting to move to the first record,
    ' check if there are any records in rsMultiValue to
    ' avoid the "No current record" error

    If Not rsMultiValue.BOF And Not rsMultiValue.EOF Then
        rsMultiValue.MoveFirst
    End If
    Do While Not rsMultiValue.EOF
        If rsMultiValue.Fields("Value") = skill Then
            skillExists = True
            Exit Do
        End If
        rsMultiValue.MoveNext
    Loop
    If Not skillExists Then
        rsMultiValue.AddNew
        rsMultiValue.Fields("Value") = skill
        rsMultiValue.Update
        skillsAdded = True
    End If
Next skill

' Save the changes
rs.Update ' Commit any changes if already in edit mode

If skillsAdded Then
    MsgBox "Skills added successfully."
Else
    MsgBox "No skills were added as they were all duplicates."
End If
CleanUp:
    ' Close recordsets and clean up
    On Error Resume Next
    If Not rsMultiValue Is Nothing Then
        rsMultiValue.Close
        Set rsMultiValue = Nothing
    End If
    If Not rs Is Nothing Then
        rs.Close
        Set rs = Nothing
    End If
    If Not db Is Nothing Then
        Set db = Nothing
    End If
```

```
On Error GoTo 0

Exit Sub

ErrorHandler:
    MsgBox "An error occurred: " & Err.Description
    Resume CleanUp
End Sub
```

This procedure takes two arguments: `employeeID` and `ParamArray skills()`. The first argument identifies the specific employee to whom the skills will be added. It is necessary to find the correct employee record in the `Employees` table. Each employee has a unique `EmployeeID`. The second argument is `ParamArray skills()`. This is the parameter array we introduced in Chapter 6. It allows us to pass a variable number of skill entries to the procedure. Each skill is added as an item in the multivalue lookup field (Skills).

The multivalue lookup fields do not allow duplicate entries. Because we only want to have unique values in the multivalue lookup field, we need to check each skill value being passed to the procedure.

3. Run the `AddSkillsToEmployee` procedure by typing the following statement in the Immediate window and pressing Enter to execute:

`AddSkillsToEmployee 2, "French", "German", "Italian"`

4. Run the `AddSkillsToEmployee` procedure again to ensure that it handles the duplicates correctly.

5. Run the `AddSkillsToEmployee` procedure again by typing the following statement in the Immediate window and pressing Enter to execute:

`AddSkillsToEmployee 3, "Chemistry"`

6. Open the `Employees` table in the `Chap10.accdb` database and take a look at the drop-down list in the Skills field for the second and third employees. In addition to the initial values added when we created the table, you should see the entries that were added by the VBA code (see Figure 10.12).

7. Close the `Employees` table.

EmployeeID	FirstName	LastName	HireDate	Date of Birth	Country	Skills	FullName	
1	Nancy	Davolio	5/1/1992	12/8/1968	USA		Nancy Davolio	(1)
2	Andrew	Fuller	8/14/1992	2/19/1952	USA	French, German, Italian	Andrew Fuller	(1)
3	Janet	Leverling	4/1/1992	8/30/1963	USA	Chemistry	Janet Leverling	(1)
4	Margaret	Peacock	5/3/1993	9/19/1958	USA	☐ Skill1	Margaret Peacock	(1)
5	Steven	Buchanan	10/17/1993	3/4/1955	UK	☐ Skill2	Steven Buchanan	(1)
6	Michael	Suyama	10/17/1993	7/2/1963	UK	☐ Skill3	Michael Suyama	(1)
7	Robert	King	1/2/1994	5/29/1960	UK	☑ Chemistry	Robert King	(1)
8	Laura	Callahan	3/5/1994	1/9/1958	USA	OK Cancel	Laura Callahan	(1)
9	Anne	Dodsworth	11/15/1994	7/2/1969	UK		Anne Dodsworth	(1)
*	(New)				USA			(0)

FIGURE 10.12.   The Multivalue Skills field has now additional entries.

Modifying a Record

To edit an existing record, use the `OpenRecordset` method to open the `Recordset` object. Next, locate the record you want to modify. In a table-type recordset, you can use the `Seek` method and a table index to find a record that meets your criteria.

In dynaset-type and snapshot-type recordsets, you can use any of the `Find` methods (`FindFirst`, `FindNext`, `FindPrevious`, and `FindLast`) to locate the appropriate record. Recall, however, that you can edit data only in table-type or dynaset-type recordsets (snapshots are used for retrieving data only). Once you've located the record, use the `Edit` method of the recordset object and proceed to change field values. When you are done with the record modification, invoke the `Update` method for the `Recordset` object.

The `EditMode` property of the `Recordset` object is used to determine whether the edit operation is in progress. The `EditModeEnum` constants, which are shown in Table 10.8, indicate the state of editing for the current record.

Assume that you just called the `Edit` method of the `Recordset` object (`rst.Edit`). The following code checks whether the edit operation is in progress, and the user is asked to verify whether the changes should be saved or canceled. If the `Yes` button is selected in the message box, the recordset's `Update` method is called; otherwise, the `CancelUpdate` method of the `Recordset` object will discard the changes made to the current record.

```
If rst.EditMode = dbEditInProgress Then
  intResult = MsgBox("Do you want to save the " & _
    "changes to this record?", vbYesNo, _
    "Save or Cancel Changes?")
End If
If intResult = 6 Then ' Save changes
  rst.Update
ElseIf intResult = 7 Then ' Cancel changes
  rst.CancelUpdate
End If
```

To cancel any pending updates to the data, call the `CancelUpdate` method of the DAO `Recordset` object. This method aborts any changes you've made to the current row. You can use the `CancelUpdate` method to cancel any changes made after the `Edit` or `AddNew` method was invoked. You can check whether there is a pending operation that can be canceled by using the `EditMode` property of the `Recordset` object.

TABLE 10.8. EditModeEnum constants used in the EditMode property of the DAO Recordset object.

Constant Name	Value	Description
dbEditNone	0	Edit method not invoked
dbEditInProgress	1	Edit method invoked
dbEditAdd	2	AddNew method invoked

Deleting a Record

To delete an existing record, open the `Recordset` object by calling the `Open-Recordset` method, then locate the record you want to delete. In a table-type recordset, you can use the `Seek` method and a table index to find a record that meets your criteria. In a dynaset-type recordset, you can use any of the find methods (`FindFirst`, `FindNext`, `FindPrevious`, and `FindLast`) to locate the appropriate record. Next, use the `Delete` method on the `Recordset` object to perform the deletion. Before using the `Delete` method, it is a good idea to write code to ask the user to confirm or cancel the deletion. Immediately after a record is deleted, there is no current record. Use the `MoveNext` method to move the record pointer to an existing record. The following procedure demonstrates how to delete all employees that were hired in 1994.

```
Sub DeleteEmployeesHiredIn1994()
    Dim db As DAO.Database
    Dim rs As DAO.Recordset
    Dim strQry As String

    On Error GoTo ErrorHandler

    ' Initialize database
    Set db = CurrentDb()

    strQry = "SELECT * FROM Employees WHERE Year([HireDate]) = 1994"

    ' Open the Employees table based on a query
    Set rs = db.OpenRecordset(strQry, dbOpenDynaset)

    ' Loop through and delete records
    If Not rs.BOF And Not rs.EOF Then
        rs.MoveFirst
        Do While Not rs.EOF
            rs.Delete
            rs.MoveNext
        Loop
        MsgBox "Employees hired in 1994 deleted successfully."
```

```
    Else
        MsgBox "No employees hired in 1994 found."
    End If

    ' Clean up
    rs.Close
    Set rs = Nothing
    Set db = Nothing
    Exit Sub
ErrorHandler:
    MsgBox "An error occurred: " & Err.Description
    If Not rs Is Nothing Then rs.Close
    Set rs = Nothing
    Set db = Nothing
End Sub
```

The `Year` function is used to extract the year portion from the `HireDate` field. The recordset is open based on a query that only selects those employees where the year part of the `HireDate` is `1994`. The asterisk (`*`) is a wildcard character that tells Access to include all columns in the results. If the recordset is not empty, the procedure loops through each record and deletes it. By using a query with the correctly defined condition, you can ensure that only employees hired in 1994 are targeted for deletion.

NOTE	*Need to Perform Deletions? Proceed with Caution!*

Please note that once records are deleted, this action cannot be reversed. The deletion process is permanent, meaning the information will be irretrievably lost and cannot be restored at a later time unless you have backed up your data first and know how to put it back. It is crucial to ensure that you have confirmed the accuracy and necessity of this deletion before proceeding, as any data removed will be gone forever. Take extra care to verify your decision to avoid any unintended loss of valuable information.

Filtering Records

Filtering records in DAO allows you to work with a subset of data from your database tables or queries. This can be very useful for focusing on specific records based on certain criteria, improving efficiency, and reducing the amount of data processed in your code. In the previous section, we used the WHERE clause of the SQL query statement to select all employees hired in 1994. You can also use the `Filter` property of a recordset to obtain a set of records that meet specific criteria. For example, the following procedure finds all products with a product name that begins with the letter P and prints the product names to the Immediate window.

```vba
Sub FilterRecords_DAO()
  Dim db As DAO.Database
  Dim rst As DAO.Recordset
  Dim filterRst As DAO.Recordset
  Dim strDb As String
  Dim strPath As String

  strPath = "C:\VBAAccess2024_ByExample\"
  strDb = "NorthwindStarter.accdb"

  Set db = OpenDatabase(strPath & strDb)
  Set rst = db.OpenRecordset("Products", _
    dbOpenDynaset)
  rst.Filter = "ProductName like 'P*'"
  Set filterRst = rst.OpenRecordset()

  Do Until filterRst.EOF
    Debug.Print filterRst.Fields _
        ("ProductName").Value
    filterRst.MoveNext
  Loop
  filterRst.Close
  Set filterRst = Nothing
  rst.Close
  Set rst = Nothing
  db.Close
  Set db = Nothing
End Sub
```

Copying Records to an Excel Worksheet

Many users like to view data in Excel worksheets. You can copy the contents of a DAO `Recordset` object directly to an Excel worksheet or a worksheet range by using the Workbook `Range` object's `CopyFromRecordset` method.

- To copy all the records in the Recordset object to a worksheet range starting at cell A1, use the following statement:

  ```vba
  Set rng = objSheet.Cells(2, 1)
  rng.CopyFromRecordset rst
  ```

  The `rst` following the name of the method is an object variable representing a `Recordset` object.

- To copy five records to a worksheet range, use the following statement:

```
Set rng = objSheet.Cells(2, 1)
rng.CopyFromRecordset rst, 5
```

- To copy five records and four fields to a worksheet range, use the following statement:

```
Set rng = objSheet.Cells(2, 1)
rng.CopyFromRecordset rst, 5, 4
```

You can also specify the number of records (rows) and fields to be copied using variables:

```
Set rng = objSheet.Cells(2, 1)
rng.CopyFromRecordset rst, myRows, myColumns
```

The procedure in Hands-On 10.16 uses the `CopyFromRecordset` method to copy data from the `Employees` table to an Excel worksheet (see Figure 10.16).

Hands-On 10.16   Copying Records to an Excel Worksheet

1. In the VBE window, choose Insert | Module.
2. In the module's Code window, type the following `ExportToExcel_DAO` procedure:

```
Sub ExportToExcel_DAO()
  Dim db As DAO.Database
  Dim rst As DAO.Recordset
  Dim xlApp As Object
  Dim wkb As Object
  Dim objSheet As Object
  Dim rng As Object
  Dim strExcelFile As String
  Dim count As Integer
  Dim iCol As Integer
  Dim rowsToReturn As Integer

  On Error GoTo ErrorHandler

  strExcelFile = CurrentProject.Path & _
    "\ExcelFromAccess.xlsx"


  ' If Excel file already exists, delete it
  If Dir(strExcelFile) <> "" Then Kill strExcelFile
```

```
Set db = CurrentDb
Set rst = db.OpenRecordset("Employees", dbOpenDynaset)

' get the number of records from the recordset
rst.MoveLast
count = rst.RecordCount

rowsToReturn = CInt(InputBox _
  ("How many records to copy?"))

  If rowsToReturn > count Then
      MsgBox "Specify a number less than " & count + 1 & "."
      If Not rst Is Nothing Then rst.Close
      If Not db Is Nothing Then Set db = Nothing
      Exit Sub
  Else
      rst.MoveFirst

      ' set the reference to Excel and make
      ' Excel visible
      Set xlApp = CreateObject("Excel.Application")
      xlApp.Application.Visible = True

      ' set references to the Excel workbook
      ' and worksheet
      Set wkb = xlApp.Workbooks.Add
      Set objSheet = xlApp.ActiveWorkbook.sheets(1)
      objSheet.Activate

      ' write column names to the first
      ' worksheet row
      For iCol = 0 To rst.Fields.count - 1
        objSheet.Cells(1, iCol + 1).Value = rst.Fields(iCol).Name
      Next

      ' specify the cell range that will receive the data
      Set rng = objSheet.Cells(2, 1)

      ' copy the specified number of records
      ' to the worksheet
      rng.CopyFromRecordset rst, rowsToReturn

      ' autofit the columns to make the data fit
      objSheet.columns.AutoFit
```

```
        ' save and close the workbook
        wkb.SaveAs fileName:=strExcelFile

        ' Note:
        ' to save it in Excel 97-2003 file format
        ' wkb.SaveAs fileName:=strExcelFile, FileFormat:=56
        ' also replace extension in the file name with .xls

        wkb.Close
        ' quit Excel and release object variables
        xlApp.Quit
        Set objSheet = Nothing
        Set wkb = Nothing
        Set xlApp = Nothing
        rst.Close
        Set rst = Nothing
        Set db = Nothing
        Exit Sub
    End If
ErrorHandler:
    MsgBox "An error occurred: " & Err.Description
    If Not rst Is Nothing Then rst.Close
    If Not db Is Nothing Then Set db = Nothing
    If Not wkb Is Nothing Then
        If Not wkb Is Nothing Then wkb.Close
        Set wkb = Nothing
    End If
    If Not xlApp Is Nothing Then
        If Not xlApp Is Nothing Then xlApp.Quit
        Set xlApp = Nothing
    End If
End Sub
```

3. Position the insertion point anywhere within the procedure code and choose
   Debug | Step Into to execute the procedure one line at a time.
   This procedure creates a recordset based on the `Employees` table and stores
   the total number of records in the `count` variable. The user is asked to specify
   the number of records to copy to Excel. If the specified number is less than
   or equal to the total number of records in the recordset, the code proceeds to
   copy the records to Excel using the `CopyFromRecordset` method. Notice that
   the procedure uses the `As Object` clause to declare object variables that will
   contain references to Excel objects when the procedure is run.

   When you define an object variable as `Object`, the variable is late bound.
   This means that VBA does not know what type of object the variable references

until the program is run. To set a reference to Excel, it is necessary to use the `CreateObject` function. Once the object is created (`Excel.Application`), it is referenced with the object variable (`xlApp`). The `CreateObject` function will create a new instance of the Excel application.

To use the current instance, or to start Excel and load a specific file while Excel is already running, use the `GetObject` function. To view what's going on while the procedure is running, we set the `Visible` property of the Microsoft Excel application to `True`. Then, if you run the `ExportToExcel_DAO` procedure in step mode, you can check the contents of the Excel window as you execute each statement.

Before you can copy Access data to an Excel worksheet, you must set references to the `Workbook`, `Worksheet`, and `Range` objects. Once these references are defined, the procedure uses the `Add` method to add a new Excel workbook and then activates the first worksheet. The recordset fields' names are written as column names to the first worksheet row. Next, the reference is set to the `Range` object that will receive the data from the recordset. The `CopyFromRecordset` method is used to copy the specified number of records to the worksheet. Once data is placed in the worksheet, it is fit into the columns with the `AutoFit` property. The Excel worksheet is then saved in the file format compatible with the current version of Excel. The `FileFormat` parameter of the workbook's `SaveAs` method specifies the file format for the workbook.

The following file formats are used in Excel. Please note that Excel uses specific numeric codes for different formats:

- 50 (`xlExcel12`)—Excel binary workbook with or without macros (`.xlsb`)
- 52 (`xlOpenXMLWorkbookMacroEnabled`)—`.xml` file format with or without macros (`.xlsm`)
- 51 (`xlOpenXMLWorkbook`)—`.xml` file format without macros (`.xlsx`)
- 56 (`xlExcel8`)—97–2003 format (`.xls`)

After saving the workbook, the procedure uses the workbook `Close` method to close the Excel workbook. The Excel `Application` object's `Quit` method is used to close the Excel application.

Figure 10.13 displays five employee records from the `Employees` table that were copied to Excel.

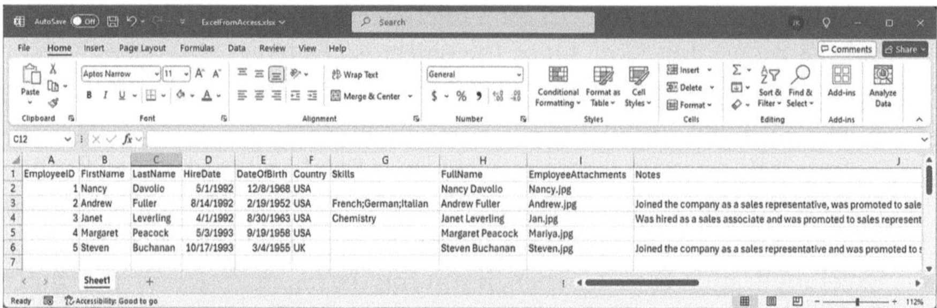

FIGURE 10.13.   Access records copied programmatically to Excel.

INTRODUCTION TO QUERIES

Having worked with Access for a while, you already know how to retrieve relevant information from your database and perform data-oriented tasks. You can do even more with queries. *Queries* are SQL statements that are saved in the database and can be run at any time. SQL is a programming language used to perform various operations on the data within the database. In Microsoft Access, SQL is used to create and execute queries that interact with the database. Access supports several types of queries.

- **Select Queries**
  Allow you to retrieve a set of records from one or more tables. For example:

  ```
  SELECT FirstName, LastName, Country
  FROM Employees
  SELECT * FROM Employees;
  ```

  Select queries are easily recognized by the SELECT and FROM keywords in their syntax. They either list the fields you want to select or use the asterisk (*) to denote that all fields should be selected.
  You can also select data from more than one table at a time by writing more complex select queries that use various SQL JOIN statements.

- **Action Queries**
  Allow you to perform actions on the data such as insert (append query), update (update query), or delete (delete query).
  - Append Query
    Use this query to insert data. For example:

    ```
    INSERT INTO EmployeesBackup (FirstName, LastName, HireDate)
    SELECT FirstName, LastName, HireDate
    ```

```
FROM Employees
WHERE Year(HireDate) = 1994;
```

The above `INSERT INTO` statement will insert values from the fields specified by the select statement into specific columns of the `EmployeeBackup` table. The `WHERE` clause is used with select queries to specify criteria that determine which records the query will affect. The above example uses the `WHERE` clause to restrict records to employees hired in 1994.

Access SQL Append Query SQL statement includes different components as shown in Table 10.9.

TABLE 10.9.   Access Append Query SQL statement components.

INSERT INTO target [(Field1, Field2)]	The name of the table or query to which records are appended. You may indicate the names of the fields to which data is appended.
SELECT fieldName(s)	The names of fields from which data is obtained.
FROM tableName or expression	The name of the table or tables from which records are inserted, the name of a saved query, or a SELECT statement.
WHERE condition	Criteria/limit operation to desired rows.

- **Update Query**

  Use this query to update values in specified fields. For example:

```
UPDATE Employees
SET Country = 'Canada'
WHERE Country = 'USA';
```

  The `UPDATE` statement components are shown in Table 10.10.

  TABLE 10.10.   Access Update Query SQL statement components.

UPDATE	TableName or QueryName
SET	Expression/operation to perform
WHERE	Criteria/limit operation to desired rows

- **Delete Query**

  Use this query to delete records. For example, the following query deletes records from the `Employees` table for employees that were hired in 1994.

```
DELETE FROM Employees
WHERE Year(HireDate) = 1994;
```

  The `DELETE` statement used to delete rows from a table consists of the following three components which are shown in Table 10.11.

TABLE 10.11.　Access Delete Query SQL statement components.

DELETE	
FROM	Table name
WHERE	Criteria/limit operation to desired rows

- **Make Table Queries**

  A make table query creates a new table out of records from one or more tables or queries. Make table queries are often used to preserve data as it existed at a particular time or to create a backup copy of a table without backing up the entire database. Use the `SELECT INTO` statement to create a make table query. For example, the following SQL statement creates a table named `UK_Employees` with the names of employees who have `'UK'` in the `Country` field:

```
SELECT FirstName, LastName
INTO UK_Employees
FROM Employees
WHERE Country='UK';
```

  Note that multivalue fields are not allowed in `SELECT INTO` statements.

- **Parameter Queries**

  These are special types of `Select` queries that are used to prompt the user for the input. For example:

```
PARAMETERS [Enter LastName:] Text;
SELECT FirstName, LastName, Country
FROM Employees
WHERE LastName = [Enter LastName:];
```

- **Aggregate Queries**

  These are special types of `Select` queries that perform calculations on data such as sums, averages, counts, minimums, maximums, etc. They are often used with the `GROUP BY` clause to group rows that have the same values in specified columns into summary rows. For example, the following SQL statement is an aggregate query that lists the number of employees in each country.

```
SELECT Country, COUNT(*) AS NumberOfEmployees
FROM Employees GROUP BY Country;
```

  The `COUNT(*)` function counts the number of all rows that match the criteria.

You can find the `LatestHireDate` with the MAX function, like this:

```
SELECT MAX(HireDate) AS LatestHireDate
FROM Employees;
```

Replace the MAX with `Min` to find the `EarliestHireDate`.

o Cross-tab Queries
These are special aggregate queries that aggregate data by two sets of values – one displayed down the left side of the datasheet and another across the top.

- **Union, Pass-Through, and Data Definition Queries**

These are advanced types of queries in Access. Each of these queries serves a unique purpose and can be useful for managing and manipulating data in specific ways.

o Union Queries
These queries are used to combine the results of two or more `Select` queries into a single result set. The queries combined with a UNION clause must have the same number of columns in the result set with similar data types. For example, this query combines the `FirstName`, `LastName`, and `HireDate` from the `UK_Employees` table with the `FirstName`, `LastName`, and `DateHired` (renamed as `HireDate`) from the `USA_Employees` table:

```
SELECT FirstName, LastName, HireDate
FROM UK_Employees
UNION
SELECT FirstName, LastName, DateHired AS HireDate
FROM USA_Employees;
```

o Pass-Through Queries
These queries allow you to send SQL commands directly to an external database server. This is extremely useful when working with linked tables from external databases such as SQL Server, Oracle, or MySQL, where you want to leverage the server's processing power. You will find an example of creating and running a pass-through query later in this chapter.

o Data Definition Queries
Also known as DDL, or data definition language, queries, these are used to create, alter, and delete database objects such as tables, indexes, and relationships. They allow you to modify the structure of the database itself. The data definition query language is the topic of Part III of this book.

Operators, Wildcards, and Predicates Used in Queries

You can use expressions in WHERE clauses to qualify SQL statements. An SQL expression is a string that is used in SQL statements. Expressions can contain literal values, constants, field names, operators, and functions. Several operators that are often used in expressions are shown in Table 10.12. Table 10.13 shows wildcard characters used in the LIKE operator patterns.

TABLE 10.12.   Operators commonly used in expressions.

Operator Name	Description/Usage
IN	The IN operator is used to determine whether the value of an expression is equal to any of several values in a specified list. If the expression is found in the list of values, the IN operator returns True; otherwise, it returns False. You can include the NOT logical operator to determine whether the expression is not in the list of values.
	For example, you can use NOT IN to determine which employees don't live in Redmond or London:
	SELECT * FROM Employees WHERE City NOT IN ('Redmond', 'London');
LIKE	The LIKE operator compares a string expression to a pattern in an SQL expression. For a pattern, you specify the complete value (for example, LIKE 'Buchanan, Steven'), or you can use wildcard characters to find a range of values (for example, LIKE 'B*'). You can use a number of wildcard characters in the LIKE operator pattern (see Table 10.13).
BETWEEN... AND	The BETWEEN...AND operator is used to determine whether the value of an expression falls within a specified range of values. If the value of the expression is between value1 and value2 (inclusive), the BETWEEN...AND operator returns True; otherwise, it returns False. You can include the NOT logical operator to evaluate the opposite condition, that is, whether the expression falls outside the range defined by value1 and value2.
	For example, you can select all products with the amount in the UnitPrice field less than $10 and greater than $25:
	SELECT * FROM Products WHERE UnitPrice NOT BETWEEN 10 AND 25;
IS NULL	The IS NULL operator is used to determine whether the expression value is equal to the Null value. A Null value indicates missing or unknown data. You can include the NOT logical operator to return only records that have values in the specified field.
	For example, you can extract only the employee records that have a value in the Notes field. Records where the Notes field is blank will not be included:
	SELECT * FROM Employees WHERE Notes IS NOT NULL;

TABLE 10.13.   Wildcard characters used in the LIKE operator patterns.

Wildcard	Description
* (asterisk)	Matches any number of characters.
? (question mark)	Matches any single character.
% (percent sign)	Matches any number of characters (used only with the ADO and Jet OLE DB provider, not in the Access user interface).
_ (underscore)	Matches any single character (used only with the ADO and Jet OLE DB provider, not in the Access user interface).
# (number sign)	Matches any single digit.
[] (square brackets)	Matches any single character within the list of characters enclosed in brackets.
! (exclamation point)	Matches any single character that is not found in the list enclosed in the square brackets.
- (hyphen)	Matches any one of the range of characters enclosed in the square brackets.

In addition to the WHERE clause, you can use predicates to further restrict the set of records to be retrieved. A *predicate* is an SQL statement that qualifies the SELECT statement, similar to the WHERE clause; however, the predicate must be placed before the column list. Several popular predicates are shown in Table 10.14.

TABLE 10.14.   Commonly used predicates in SQL SELECT statements.

Predicate Name	Description/Usage
ALL	The ALL keyword is the default keyword and is used when no predicate is declared in the SQL statement. The following two examples are equivalent and return all records from the Employees table: SELECT ALL * FROM Employees ORDER BY EmployeeID; SELECT * FROM Employees ORDER BY EmployeeID;
DISTINCT	The DISTINCT keyword eliminates duplicate values from the returned set of records. The values for each field listed in the SELECT statement must be unique. For example, to return a list of nonduplicate (unique) countries from the Employees table, you can write the following SELECT statement: SELECT DISTINCT Country FROM Employees;

(Contd.)

Predicate Name	Description/Usage
	NOTE: The output of a query that uses DISTINCT isn't updatable (it's read-only).
DISTINCTROW	While the DISTINCT keyword is based on duplicate fields, the DISTINC-TROW keyword is based on entire rows. It is used only with multiple tables. For example, if you join the Customers and Orders tables on the CustomerID field, you can find customers that have at least one order. The Customers table contains no duplicate CustomerID fields, but the Orders table does because each customer can have many orders. SELECT DISTINCTROW CompanyName FROM Customers, Orders WHERE Customers.CustomerID = Orders.CustomerID ORDER BY CompanyName; *NOTE:* If you omit DISTINCTROW, this SELECT statement will produce multiple rows for each company that has more than one order. DISTINC-TROW has an effect only when you select fields from some, but not all, of the tables used in the query. DISTINCTROW is ignored if your query includes only one table or if you output fields from all tables.
TOP or PERCENT	The TOP keyword returns a certain number of records that fall at the top or bottom of a range specified by an ORDER BY clause. For example, suppose you want to select the five most expensive products: SELECT TOP 5 * FROM Products ORDER BY UnitPrice DESC; The TOP predicate doesn't choose between equal values. If there are equal values present, the TOP keyword will return all rows that have the equal value. You can also use the PERCENT keyword to return a percentage of records that fall at the top or bottom of a range specified by an ORDER BY clause. For example, to return the lowest 10 percent priced products, you can write the following statement: SELECT TOP 10 PERCENT * FROM Products ORDER BY UnitPrice ASC; *NOTE:* If you don't include the ORDER BY clause, the SELECT TOP statement will return a random set of rows.

If you'd like to sort records returned by the SELECT statement, use the ORDER BY clause with the ASC (ascending sort) or DESC (descending sort) keyword, as shown in the following example:

```
SELECT * FROM Employees ORDER BY Country DESC;
```

The above will select all records from the Employees table and arrange them in descending order based on the Country field. If no order is specified, the order is ascending (ASC) by default.

By default, records are sorted in ascending order (ASC). The fields you want to sort by do not need to be enumerated in the SELECT statement's field list. Instead of sorting by field name, you can sort by field position. For example, the following statement will sort the records in ascending order by the second field:

```
SELECT * FROM EMPLOYEES ORDER BY 2;
```

Creating a Select Query with DAO

In DAO, the QueryDef object represents a saved query in a database. All QueryDef objects are contained in the QueryDefs collection. You can read and set the SQL definition of a query object using the SQL property. To create a query in code, use the CreateQueryDef method.

For example, to create a select query named FrenchSpeakers, the following statement is used:

```
Set qdf = db.CreateQueryDef("FrenchSpeakers", strSQL)
```

When you specify the name for your query, the new QueryDef object is automatically appended to the QueryDefs collection when it is created. The second argument of the CreateQueryDef method is a string variable that holds a valid Access SQL statement. Prior to using this variable, you must assign to it a string expression:

```
strSQL = "SELECT * FROM Employees WHERE Notes LIKE '*French*'; "
```

The WHERE clause is used with select queries to specify criteria that determine which records the query will affect. The procedure in Hands-On 10.17 selects from the Employees table all records that have the string French mentioned anywhere within the Notes field of the NorthwindStarter database.

When creating queries in code, be sure to include an error handler. The query you are trying to create may already exist, or an unexpected error could occur.

⊙ Hands-On 10.17   Creating a Select Query

1. In the VBE window, choose Insert | Module.
2. In the module's Code window, type the Create_SelectQuery_DAO procedure shown here:

```
Sub Create_SelectQuery_DAO()
    Dim db As DAO.Database
```

```
Dim qdf As DAO.QueryDef
Dim strSQL As String
Dim strDb As String

strDb = "C:\VBAAccess2024_ByExample\NorthwindStarter.accdb"

On Error GoTo Err_SelectQuery

strSQL = "SELECT * FROM Employees "
strSQL = strSQL & "WHERE Notes LIKE '*French*';"
Set db = OpenDatabase(strDb)
Set qdf = db.CreateQueryDef("FrenchSpeakers", strSQL)
ExitHere:
  Set qdf = Nothing
  db.Close
  Set db = Nothing
  Exit Sub
Err_SelectQuery:
  If Err.Number = 3012 Then
    MsgBox "Query with this name already exists."
  Else
    MsgBox Err.Description
  End If
  Resume ExitHere
End Sub
```

3. Choose Run | Run Sub/UserForm to execute the procedure.

When you run the `Create_SelectQuery_DAO` procedure, the next time you open the `NorthwindStarter` database, you should see the query named `FrenchSpeakers` in the list of stored queries in the Access window.

Temporary Queries

Instead of a query that is saved in the database for future use, it is possible to create a temporary query by setting the `QueryDefName` property to a zero-length string (`""`), as in the following example:

```
Set qdf = db.CreateQueryDef("", strSQL)
```

The advantage of temporary queries is that they don't clutter the Access Application window.

Creating and Running a Parameter Query

A special type of a select query is known as a *parameter* query. Instead of retrieving the same records each time a query is run, a user can enter the search criteria in a special dialog box at runtime. In DAO, the parameters of a parameter query are represented by `Parameter` objects. The `QueryDef` object contains a `Param-eters` collection. Parameter objects represent existing parameters.

To create a parameter query, create a query string that includes the PARAM-ETERS keyword:

```
strSQL = "PARAMETERS [Enter Country] Text;" & _
 "SELECT * FROM CUSTOMERS WHERE Country = [Enter Country];"
```

Before executing an existing parameter query, assign a value to the parameter, then open a recordset based on the query.

The next hands-on exercise demonstrates how to create and run a parameter query to retrieve the names of employees in the specified country.

⊙ Hands-On 10.18   Creating a Parameter Query

1. In the VBE window, choose Insert | Module.
2. In the module's Code window, type the following `CreateRun_ParameterQuery_DAO` procedure:

```
Sub CreateRun_ParameterQuery_DAO()
    Dim db As DAO.Database
    Dim qdf As DAO.QueryDef
    Dim rst As DAO.Recordset
    Dim strQryName As String
    Dim strSQL As String

    On Error GoTo Err_Handler

    strQryName = "myParamQuery"
    strSQL = "PARAMETERS [Enter Country] Text; " & _
      "SELECT * FROM Employees WHERE " & _
      "Country = [Enter Country];"

    Set db = CurrentDb
    Set qdf = db.CreateQueryDef(strQryName, strSQL)

RunQuery:
    ' specify the parameter
    qdf.Parameters("Enter Country") = _
     InputBox("Enter the country name:", _
     "Which Country?", "Germany")

    If IsNull(qdf.Parameters("Enter Country").Value) _
     Then GoTo ExitHere
```

```
' open a recordset based on the specified query
Set rst = qdf.OpenRecordset(dbOpenDynaset)
rst.MoveLast
MsgBox "Number of records: " & rst.RecordCount

' write the contents of the second field
' to the Immediate window
rst.MoveFirst
Do Until rst.EOF
  Debug.Print rst(1)
  rst.MoveNext
Loop

ExitHere:
If Not rst Is Nothing Then
  rst.Close
  Set rst = Nothing
End If
Set qdf = Nothing
db.Close
Set db = Nothing
Exit Sub

Err_Handler:
If Err.Number = 3012 Then
  MsgBox "This query already exists."
  Set qdf = db.QueryDefs(strQryName)
  Resume RunQuery
ElseIf Err.Number = 3021 Then
  MsgBox "There are no employees for the specified country."
End If
Resume ExitHere
End Sub
```

3. Choose Run | Run Sub/UserForm to execute the procedure.

   This procedure defines a parameter query that contains one parameter named `Enter Country`. Prior to running this query, the procedure retrieves the name of the country from the user via the VBA `InputBox` method. While the suggested default country name is `Germany`, the user can supply the name of another country. The supplied value is then used as the value of the `Enter Country` parameter. Next, the recordset is opened based on the specified query, and the number of records for the specified country is retrieved via the `RecordCount` property of the `Recordset` object. To get the correct record count, you must move to the end of the recordset, using the `MoveLast` method to access all records. The procedure ends by retrieving to the Immediate window the names of employees in the specified country. The procedure contains several labels, such as `RunQuery`, `ExitHere`, and `Err_Handler`, which are used in error trapping and ensuring that certain code lines are run only when required. For example, when you execute this procedure again, the statement that attempts to create a query will fail and VBA will generate error `3012`. At this point, we want to run the existing query, so we must set the `qdf` object variable with the following statement:

```
Set qdf = db.QueryDefs(strQryName)
```

Then we can safely resume running the code from the label `RunQuery`.

Creating and Running a Make-Table Query

A make-table query creates a new table out of records from one or more tables or queries. Use the `SELECT  INTO` statement to create a make-table query as shown in Table 10.15.

TABLE 10.15.   Access Make-Table Query SQL statement components.

SELECT fieldname	Field name (use * for all fields)
INTO newTableName	Name of the new table
FROM table/queryName	Name of a table or query from which data is taken
WHERE condition	Criteria/limit operation to desired rows (optional)
ORDER BY fieldname	Order of the records in the new table (optional)

The procedure in the next hands-on exercise creates a table of the employees in the U.S.

Hands-On 10.19   Creating and Running a Make-Table Query

1. In the VBE window, choose Insert | Module.
2. In the module's Code window, type the following `MakeATableQuery_DAO` procedure:

```
Sub MakeATableQuery_DAO()
   Dim db As DAO.Database
   Dim qdf As DAO.QueryDef
   Dim strSelect As String
   Dim strWhere As String
   Dim strSQL As String

   On Error GoTo Err_Handler
```

```
  strSelect = "SELECT EmployeeID, FirstName, "
  strSelect = strSelect & "LastName, DateOfBirth, HireDate"
  strWhere = "FROM Employees WHERE Country='USA';"
  strSQL = strSelect & " INTO USA_Employees " & strWhere

Debug.Print strSQL

  Set db = CurrentDb
  Set qdf = db.CreateQueryDef("", strSQL)
  qdf.Execute
  Application.RefreshDatabaseWindow

ExitHere:
  Set qdf = Nothing
  db.Close
  Set db = Nothing
  Exit Sub
Err_Handler:
  MsgBox Err.Description
  Resume ExitHere
End Sub
```

3. Choose Run | Run Sub/UserForm to execute the procedure.
The SELECT INTO statement in the MakeATableQuery_DAO procedure is used
to make and populate a new table named USA_Employees with the specified
fields. Notice that by not assigning a name to the query, we create a make-table
query that is temporary (not stored in the Access window):

```
Set qdf = db.CreateQueryDef("", strSQL)
```

When tables are created or modified programmatically in Access, you
sometimes need to refresh the Navigation Pane to display the changes:

```
Application.RefreshDatabaseWindow
```

Notice that the MakeATableQuery_DAO procedure demonstrates how you can
break long SQL statements into smaller parts that are easier to understand and
debug.

Creating and Running Update, Append, and Delete Queries

In this section, we'll create a VBA procedure that demonstrates the use of
update, append, and delete queries using DAO with the Employees table. We'll
include all three types of queries in one procedure to showcase how each can be
used effectively.

(◉) Custom Project 10.2   Creating and Running Action Queries

1. Review the action queries topic in the Introduction to Queries section earlier in this chapter.
2. Create a backup of the `Employees` table.
   a. In the Database Navigation pane of the Access Application window, right-click the Employees table and choose Export | Access.
   b. When you are prompted to select the destination for the data you want to export, enter the name of the current database, `C:\VBAAccess2024_ByExample\Chap10.accdb`, and click OK.
   c. In the Export dialog box, enter `BackupTable_Employees`. Ensure that the Definition and Data option button is selected in the Export Tables and click OK.
   d. Click Close to exit the Export – Access Database window.
3. In the VBE window, choose Insert | Module.
4. Enter the following procedure code in the module's Code window:

```
Sub ManageEmployeesData()
    Dim db As DAO.Database
    Dim qdf As DAO.QueryDef
    Dim strSQL As String

    On Error GoTo ErrorHandler

    ' Initialize database
    Set db = CurrentDb()

    ' Update Query: Update Employee's DateOfBirth based on a condition
    strSQL = "UPDATE Employees SET DateOfBirth = '9/30/1963'"
    strSQL = strSQL & " WHERE EmployeeID = 3;"

    Debug.Print strSQL
    Set qdf = db.CreateQueryDef("", strSQL)
    qdf.Execute dbFailOnError
    qdf.Close
    Set qdf = Nothing
    MsgBox "Employee DateOfBirth was corrected."

    ' Append Query: Insert new records into Employees table
    strSQL = "INSERT INTO [Employees] " & _
    "( FirstName, LastName, Country, HireDate, DateOfBirth )" & _
    " Values (""Mary"", ""Doe"", ""Canada"", #11/02/2022#, #01/15/2002#);"
```

```vba
    Debug.Print strSQL
    Set qdf = db.CreateQueryDef("", strSQL)
    qdf.Execute dbFailOnError
    qdf.Close
    Set qdf = Nothing
    MsgBox "Append Query executed: New employee added."

    ' Delete Query: Remove employees who were hired in 1994
    strSQL = "DELETE FROM Employees WHERE Year([HireDate]) = 1994"
    strSQL = strSQL & " AND Country = 'UK';"

    Debug.Print strSQL
    Set qdf = db.CreateQueryDef("", strSQL)

    ' Chr(13) & Chr(13) is a double carriage return
    If (MsgBox("Do you want to: " & Chr(13) & Chr(13) _
        & qdf.SQL, vbYesNo + vbDefaultButton2, _
        "SQL Expression")) = vbYes Then

        qdf.Execute dbFailOnError
    End If

    MsgBox "Deleted: " & qdf.RecordsAffected & " record(s)"

    qdf.Close
    Set qdf = Nothing
CleanUp:
    Set qdf = Nothing
    Set db = Nothing
    Exit Sub
ErrorHandler:
    MsgBox "An error occurred: " & Err.Description
    Resume CleanUp
End Sub
```

5. Run the `ManageEmployeesData` procedure.

The `Execute` method of the `QueryDef` object is used to run action queries or execute an SQL statement. This method can take optional arguments. For example, in the statement:

```vba
qdf.Execute dbFailOnError
```

the constant `dbFailOnError` will generate a run-time error if an error occurs, and any updates or deletions will be rolled back. Use the `RecordsAffected` property of the `QueryDef` object to determine the number of records affected by the most recent `Execute` method. For example, the following statement displays the number of records that were deleted:

```
MsgBox "Deleted: " & qdf.RecordsAffected & " record(s)"
```

The `ManageEmployeesData` procedure executes the delete query if the user responds positively to the message shown in Figure 10.14.

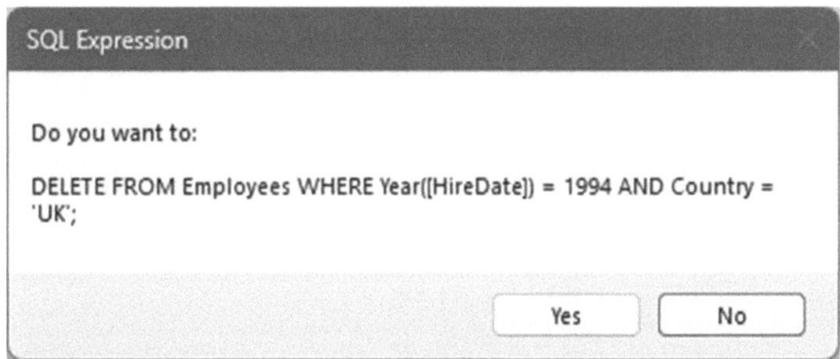

FIGURE 10.14.   You can display an SQL statement underlying a query in a message box.

To delete all the rows from the `Employees` table, the following statement can be executed:

```
DELETE FROM Employees
```

You cannot reverse the operation performed by the `DELETE` statement. Always make a backup copy of your table prior to running a delete query. It is a good idea to create and run a select query before using `DELETE` to see which rows will be affected by the delete operation.

Creating and Running a Pass-Through Query

A *pass-through query* works directly with an external ODBC data source, such as SQL Server. Unlike traditional Access queries that work with linked tables, pass-through queries bypass Access' query processing engine, sending the SQL code directly to the external database server. This allows you to execute complex queries and operations directly on the server where the data resides, leveraging the server's processing power and capabilities.

Since pass-through queries work with external data sources, you must have access to the ODBC data source configured and connected. This could mean having access to an SQL Server database, for example. To try out the examples, you would need to install:

- SQL Server 2022 Developer Edition—A full-featured, free edition of SQL Server for development and testing
    - o Download from the official Microsoft Web site.

- o Follow the installation instructions to set up SQL Server on your machine.

- SQL Server Management Studio (SSMS)—A tool for managing SQL Server databases
  - o Download SSMS from the Microsoft Web site.
  - o Follow the installation instructions.

- AdventureWorks2022 Database—A sample database provided by Microsoft, useful for learning and experimentation
  - o Obtain the AdventureWorks2022 database from the Microsoft Web site or other sources.
  - o Restore the database in your SQL Server instance using Restore Database in SSMS.

Once everything is installed and configured, you can create a pass-through query in Access, connecting to SQL Server and pulling data from the `Production.Product` table, which is used in this section's examples. To create a pass-through query manually in Access, follow these steps:

1. In the Access application window, choose Create | Query Design.
2. Close the Add Tables pane and click Query Design | Pass-Through.
   This will change the query to a Pass-Through query.
3. Name your query (for example, `GetProducts_SQLServ`) and click OK.
   This will bring up a query window where you can type your SQL statement.
4. In the Query Design window, write the SQL query statement as described below:
   For example, the following statement, typed in the SQL view of the pass-through query window, retrieves all fields from the `Production.Product` table in the SQL Server `AdventureWorks2022` database:

```
SELECT * FROM Production.Product;
```

   The SQL statement must be in the format understood by the external data source from which you are retrieving or manipulating data. Pass-through queries can be used in lieu of action queries when you need to bulk append, update, or delete data in remote databases.
5. Find the `ODBC Connect Str` property in the Query Properties window and enter the ODBC connection string for your SQL Server. Here's an example connection string:

```
ODBC;Driver={SQL Server};
```

```
Server=YourServerName;
Database=AdventureWorks2022;
Trusted_Connection=Yes;
```

The entire connection string must be written on one line in the Properties sheet. Be sure to replace `YourServerName` with the actual name of your SQL Server.

6. Save your pass-through query by clicking the Save button.
   The saved query should appear with a globe icon in the Queries section of the Database pane.

7. While still in the SQL view, click the Run button (red exclamation mark) to execute the query and see the results.
   If you configured and followed these steps, you should see a datasheet filled with 504 records from the `AdventureWorks2022` database's `Production.Product` table (see Figure 10.15).

ProductID	Name	ProductNumber	MakeFlag	FinishedGoc	Color	SafetyStockLevel	ReorderPoir	StandardCost	ListPrice
1	Adjustable Race	AR-5381	0	0		1000	750	$0.00	$0.00
2	Bearing Ball	BA-8327	0	0		1000	750	$0.00	$0.00
3	BB Ball Bearing	BE-2349	-1	0		800	600	$0.00	$0.00
4	Headset Ball Bearings	BE-2908	0	0		800	600	$0.00	$0.00
316	Blade	BL-2036	-1	0		800	600	$0.00	$0.00
317	LL Crankarm	CA-5965	0	0	Black	500	375	$0.00	$0.00
318	ML Crankarm	CA-6738	0	0	Black	500	375	$0.00	$0.00
319	HL Crankarm	CA-7457	0	0	Black	500	375	$0.00	$0.00
320	Chainring Bolts	CB-2903	0	0	Silver	1000	750	$0.00	$0.00
321	Chainring Nut	CN-6137	0	0	Silver	1000	750	$0.00	$0.00
322	Chainring	CR-7833	0	0	Black	1000	750	$0.00	$0.00
323	Crown Race	CR-9981	0	0		1000	750	$0.00	$0.00
324	Chain Stays	CS-2812	-1	0		1000	750	$0.00	$0.00
325	Decal 1	DC-8732	0	0		1000	750	$0.00	$0.00
326	Decal 2	DC-9824	0	0		1000	750	$0.00	$0.00
327	Down Tube	DT-2377	-1	0		800	600	$0.00	$0.00

Record: I◄ ◄ 504 of 504 ► ►I ► No Filter | Search

FIGURE 10.15.   Data retrieved from an SQL Server database via a pass-through query.

Once you retrieve data using a pass-through query in Access, you can copy it to another table within Access. You can do this by creating a destination table. This can be a new table or an existing table in Access. Earlier, you learned about make-table queries. This type of query can be easily used for creating a local table and populating it with remote data using the pass-through query. Simply follow these steps:

1. Choose Create | Query Design.
   You should see an empty Query Design window and the Add Tables pane with different tabs: Tables, Links, Queries, and All. If the Add Tables pane is not visible, click the Table Names button on the Query Design toolbar.

2. Drag the `GetProducts_SQLServ` query to the Query Design window or select this query and click the Add Selected Tables button.
The Query Design grid now shows a visual representation of the pass-through query with all the available fields.

3. Select all the fields by double-clicking the GetProducts_SQLServ heading in the Query Design window.

4. Drag and drop all the selected fields in the Field row (column 1) of the Query Design grid.
So far, we have made a select query, indicating what data we want to pull. Now, let's turn this into a table.

5. In the Query Design tab, click the make-table query (with the exclamation mark).
Access displays a Make Query dialog box with the Current Database option button selected.

6. Type `LocalProduct` for the table name and click OK.
Access dismisses the dialog box and creates the make-table query. The make-table button should be selected on the Query Design toolbar.

7. Click the Run button (with the exclamation mark) to execute the query.
Access displays a message that you are about to paste 504 row(s) into a new table.

8. Click Yes to have Access create a new table with the selected records.
Access gets to work. Your Query Design screen remains unchanged, but you may notice a new table (`LocalProduct`) was added to the Database Navigation pane.

9. Click the Save button and save your make-table query as `CreateTable_LocalProduct`.

10. Close the query window and open the `LocalProduct` table in design view.
Notice that Access created all the fields for this table with the equivalent data types. The datasheet view should also list all the data from the remote `Production.Product` table.

Getting back to DAO programming, pass-through queries can be created and executed programmatically from your VBA procedures. Use the `CreateQueryDef` to create a new query definition and its `Connect` property to set the connection string and SQL statement for the query definition. If you don't specify a connection string in the `Connect` property, Access will ask you for the connection information every time you run the pass-through query. In the following procedure, we create the `GetProducts_DAO` pass-through query to pull data from the `Production.Product` table in the `AdventureWorks2022` database.

```
Sub CreatePassThroughQuery()
    Dim db As DAO.Database
    Dim qdf As DAO.QueryDef
    Dim strConnect As String
    Dim strSQL As String

    On Error GoTo ErrorHandler

    ' Set up the ODBC connection string
    strConnect = "ODBC;Driver={SQL Server};" & _
    "Server=VOSTJKLap;Database=AdventureWorks2022;" & _
    "Trusted_Connection=Yes;"

    ' SQL statement to pull data from Production.Product
    strSQL = "SELECT * FROM Production.Product;"

    ' Initialize the database
    Set db = CurrentDb()

    ' Create a new query definition
    Set qdf = db.CreateQueryDef("GetProducts_DAO")

    ' Set the connection string and the SQL statement
    qdf.Connect = strConnect
    qdf.sql = strSQL
    qdf.ReturnsRecords = True

    ' Save the query
    qdf.Close
    Set qdf = Nothing
    Set db = Nothing

    MsgBox "Pass-Through Query created successfully."
CleanUp:
    Exit Sub
ErrorHandler:
    MsgBox "An error occurred: " & Err.Description
    Resume CleanUp
End Sub
```

The `ReturnsRecords` property is used with DAO `QueryDef` objects, particularly with pass-through queries. This property indicates whether the query returns records when executed. When the `ReturnsRecords` property is set to `True`, the query is expected to return records, such as a SELECT statement. If your query does return records, set the ReturnsRecords property to False (used with the INSERT, UPDATE, or DELETE statement).

If you have an existing pass-through query and you want to read the remote data using the VBA code, use the OpenRecordset method on the existing pass-through query:

```vba
Sub PrintProductsFromPassThroughQuery()
    Dim db As DAO.Database
    Dim rst As DAO.Recordset
    Dim counter As Integer

    On Error GoTo ErrorHandler

    ' Initialize the database
    Set db = CurrentDb()
    ' Open the recordset using the existing Pass-Through Query
    Set rst = db.OpenRecordset("GetProducts_DAO")

    ' Print the first 15 records to the Immediate Window
    counter = 0
    Do While Not rst.EOF And counter < 15
        Debug.Print "ProductID: " & rst!ProductID & _
        ", Name: " & rst!Name & ", ProductNumber: " & _
        rst!ProductNumber
        rst.MoveNext
        counter = counter + 1
    Loop
    MsgBox "15 records printed to the Immediate Window."
    SendKeys "^g"
CleanUp:
    ' Clean up
    If Not rst Is Nothing Then rst.Close
    Set rst = Nothing
    Set db = Nothing
    Exit Sub
ErrorHandler:
    MsgBox "An error occurred: " & Err.Description
    Resume CleanUp
End Sub
```

Performing Other Operations with Queries

You can use VBA to perform other operations related to queries, such as retrieving a list of queries and their properties, deleting a query, and determining whether a query is updatable.

To obtain the listing of all queries in a database, use the `For...Each..Next` loop to enumerate the `QueryDefs` collection of the DAO `QueryDef` object.

Just like tables and other database objects, queries have properties. To generate a list of properties for a specific query, use the `For Each...Next` looping structure to iterate through the `Properties` collection of the DAO `QueryDef` object.

To remove a DAO `QueryDef` object from a `QueryDefs` collection, use the `Delete` method:

```
db.QueryDefs.Delete "YourQueryName"
```

The DAO `QueryDef` object has an `Updatable` property that you can use in your VBA code to find out whether the query definition can be updated. An *updatable* query allows you to modify the data directly in the query results. This means you can add, edit, or delete records directly from the query datasheet. Your changes are automatically reflected in the underlying tables.

Usually, a query is updatable when it is based on a single table. The underlying table or tables used in a query must have a primary key. If the query uses joins, they must be on key fields and cannot result in ambiguous or non-updatable joins. One-to-one or one-to-many joins are typically updatable. To be updatable, a query must not include aggregate functions, such as SUM, AVG, MIN, MAX, or COUNT, that produce summary results. When a query includes these functions, it typically summarizes data across multiple rows, making individual rows ambiguous or noneditable.

Union queries and queries that use GROUP BY or TOTALS are not updatable. Other queries that are not updatable are those that use the DISTINCT keyword and calculated fields that are generated by an expression.

The following procedure will list all the queries in the current database along with their properties and indicate whether each query is updatable. The information will be printed to the Immediate window.

```
Sub ListQueriesAndProperties()
    Dim db As DAO.Database
    Dim qdf As DAO.QueryDef
    Dim prop As DAO.Property
    Dim rst As DAO.Recordset
    Dim updatable As String

    ' Initialize database
    Set db = CurrentDb()

    ' Print header
    Debug.Print "Query Name", "Updatable", "Properties"
```

```vba
    ' Loop through all QueryDefs in the database
    For Each qdf In db.QueryDefs
        ' Check if the query is updatable
        On Error Resume Next
        Set rst = qdf.OpenRecordset(dbOpenDynaset)
        If Err.Number = 0 Then
            If rst.updatable Then
                updatable = "Yes"
            Else
                updatable = "No"
            End If
            rst.Close
        Else
            updatable = "N/A"
        End If
        On Error GoTo 0

        ' Print query name and updatable status
        Debug.Print qdf.Name, updatable;

        ' Loop through all properties of the query
        For Each prop In qdf.Properties
            On Error Resume Next
            Debug.Print , , prop.Name & ": " & prop.Value
            On Error GoTo 0
        Next prop
    Next qdf
    ' Clean up
    Set rst = Nothing
    Set qdf = Nothing
    Set db = Nothing

    MsgBox "Check out the Immediate Window."
End Sub
```

When writing VBA code, to determine whether a recordset can be updated, you must use the Updatable property of the DAO Recordset object. If the Recordset object cannot be edited, the value of the Updatable property is False. The Updatable property of the DAO snapshot-type and forward-only-type Recordset objects is always False. The same is true if the Recordset object contains read-only fields. When one or more fields are updatable, however, the property's value is True.

Because a recordset can contain fields that can't be updated, you may want to check the DataUpdatable property of each field in the Fields collection of the

`Recordset` object before attempting to edit a record. The following procedure checks whether records returned by two queries in the legacy `Northwind.mdb` database can be edited.

```vba
Sub IsQryUpdatable_DAO()
  Dim db As DAO.Database
  Dim rst As DAO.Recordset
  Dim fld As DAO.Field
  Dim strDb As String
  Dim strQryName1 As String
  Dim strQryName2 As String
  Dim strPath As String

  strPath = "C:\VBAAccess2024_ByExample\"
  strDb = "Northwind.mdb"
  strQryName1 = "Order Subtotals"
  strQryName2 = "Invoices"


  Set db = OpenDatabase(strPath & strDb)

  Set rst = db.OpenRecordset(strQryName1)
  Debug.Print strQryName1 & _
   ": Updatable=" & rst.updatable
  Set rst = db.OpenRecordset(strQryName2)
  Debug.Print strQryName2 & _
   ": Updatable=" & rst.updatable
  For Each fld In rst.Fields
    If Not fld.DataUpdatable Then
      Debug.Print fld.Name & " cannot be edited."
    End If
  Next

  rst.Close
  Set rst = Nothing
  db.Close
  Set db = Nothing
End Sub
```

When you run this procedure, the `Updatable` property returns `True` for the `Invoices` query and `False` for the `Order Subtotals` query. The `OpenRecordset` method is used to open each of these queries. The `Order Subtotals` query is not updatable because its SQL statement contains a `GROUP BY` clause. While the `Invoices` query is updatable, not all fields in the resulting recordset can be edited (see Figure 10.16).

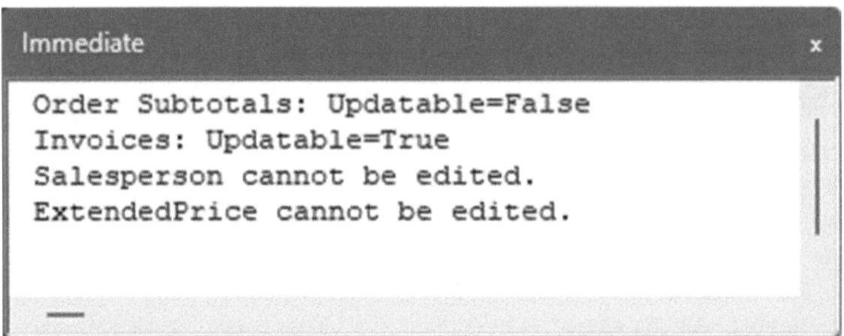

FIGURE 10.16.   An updatable query can contain one or more fields that cannot be edited.

TRANSACTION PROCESSING

To improve your application's performance and ensure that database activities can be recovered in case an unexpected hardware or software error occurs, consider grouping sets of database activities into a transaction. A *transaction* is a set of operations that are performed together as a single unit.

If you have used an Automated Teller Machine (ATM), you are already familiar with transaction processing. When you go to the bank to get cash, your account must be debited. In other words, the cash withdrawal must be deducted from your savings or checking account. A transaction is a two-sided operation. If anything goes wrong during the transaction, the entire transaction is canceled. If both operations succeed, that is, you get the cash and the bank debits your account, the transaction's work is saved (or committed).

Database transactions often involve modifications and additions of one or more records in a single table or several tables. When a transaction has to be undone or canceled, the transaction is rolled back. Often, when you perform batch updates to database tables and an error occurs, updates to all tables must be canceled or the database could be left in an inconsistent state, resulting in not only the loss of important information but also a number of other headaches.

Transactions are extremely important for maintaining data integrity and consistency.

Creating a Transaction with DAO

The DAO object model supports transactions through the `BeginTrans`, `CommitTrans`, and `Rollback` methods of the `Workspace` and `DBEngine` objects. When you use these transaction methods with the `DBEngine` object, the transaction is applied to the default workspace—`DBEngine.Workspaces(0)`. If you need to manage transactions or connections to multiple databases, use the `Workspace` object. A `Workspace` object represents a user's session. A transaction on a workspace will affect all data modifications made within the workspace. You can manage transactions independently across `Database` objects by creating additional `Workspace` objects.

Use the `BeginTrans` method to specify the beginning of a transaction, the `CommitTrans` method to save the changes, and `Rollback` to cancel the transaction.

`BeginTrans` and `CommitTrans` are used in pairs. The data-modifying instructions you place between these keywords are stored in memory until VBA encounters the `CommitTrans` statement. After reaching `CommitTrans`, Access writes to the disk the changes that have occurred since the `BeginTrans` statement; therefore, any changes you've made in the tables become permanent.

If an error is generated during the transaction process, the `Rollback` statement placed further down in your procedure will undo all changes made since the `BeginTrans` statement, which ensures that the data is returned to the state it was in before you started the transaction.

Transaction processing should be used for archiving historical data. For instance, the procedure in Hands-On 10.20 selects all orders placed in 1997 and appends them to an archive table in the current database. Then, the records are deleted from the source table.

Hands-On 10.20   Using a Database Transaction to Archive Records

1. In the main Access window of the `Chap10.accdb` database, choose External Data | New Data Source | From Database | Access.
2. In the File name box of the Get External Data dialog box, enter `C:\VBAAccess2024_ByExample\Northwind.mdb`, and then click OK.
3. In the Import Objects window, select the Orders table and click OK.
4. Click Close to exit the Get External Data dialog box.
5. In the VBE window, choose Insert | Module.
6. In the module's Code window, enter the `OrdersArchive1997_DAO` procedure shown here:

```vba
Sub OrdersArchive1997_DAO()
    Dim db As DAO.Database
    Dim wrk As Workspace
    Dim blnTrans As Boolean
    Dim strSQL As String
    Dim strPath As String
```

```vba
Dim strDb As String
Dim strDateCriteria As String

On Error GoTo ErrorHandler

strPath = "C:\VBAAccess2024_ByExample\"
strDb = "Chap10.accdb"
strDateCriteria = "BETWEEN #1/1/1997# AND #12/31/1997#;"

Set wrk = dbEngine(0)
Set db = CurrentDb()

'begin transaction

blnTrans = True
wrk.BeginTrans

' create an archive table on the fly
' and fill it with records

strSQL = _
"SELECT * INTO OrdersArchive1997 IN " & _
 Chr(34) & strPath & strDb & Chr(34) & _
 " FROM Orders WHERE Orders.OrderDate " & _
 strDateCriteria

db.Execute strSQL, dbFailOnError

' delete records from the source table
If db.RecordsAffected <> 0 Then
  strSQL = "DELETE FROM Orders " & _
  "WHERE Orders.OrderDate " & strDateCriteria

  db.Execute strSQL, dbFailOnError

' ask user if OK to commit changes
  If MsgBox("Click OK if you want to archive " _
  & db.RecordsAffected & " records.", _
  vbOKCancel + vbQuestion + vbDefaultButton2, _
  "Proceed?") = vbOK Then
      dbEngine.CommitTrans
  Else
    If blnTrans Then dbEngine.Rollback
  End If
Else
  dbEngine.Rollback
```

```
      MsgBox "No records to archive " & _
        "with the specified criteria.", _
        vbInformation + vbOKOnly, "Records not found"
    End If
Cleanup:
  Set db = Nothing
  Exit Sub
ErrorHandler:
  If Err.Number = 3010 Then
  ' hardcoding path and filename for
  ' demonstration only
    strSQL = "INSERT INTO OrdersArchive1997 IN " & _
    """C:\VBAAccess2024_ByExample\Chap10.accdb""" & _
    " SELECT * FROM Orders WHERE Orders.OrderDate " & _
    strDateCriteria
    Resume 0
  Else
    If blnTrans Then dbEngine.Rollback
      MsgBox Err.Description
      Resume Cleanup
  End If
End Sub
```

7. Choose Run | Run Sub/UserForm to execute the procedure.

Because transactions exist in a `Workspace` object, we define an object variable, `wrk`, and set its value to `DBEngine(0)`, which stands for the default workspace. Before we begin the transaction with the `BeginTrans` method of the `Workspace` object, we set the transaction flag to `True` (`blnTrans`) to indicate that the transaction is active. We also set the `Database` object variable (`db`) to point to the current database. The first data operation in this transaction requires that we create a table to store the selected records from the `Orders` table. In the Access user interface, we would simply create a make-table query; in VBA programming, we can use the SQL SELECT...INTO statement. The first part of this statement specifies the fields we want to select; in this case, we use a wildcard (*) to denote that all fields should be copied into the new table. This is followed by the INTO clause and the name of the table to be created. The path and database name must be surrounded by quotation marks. You can use the `Chr(34)` function to prepend and append double quotes to strings.

If the table already exists, then the SELECT...INTO statement will fail and VBA will respond with error 3010. We must set an error trap (see the `ErrorHandlerAttach` code). To add the data to the existing table, we must use the SQL INSERT INTO statement. The name of the table in the SELECT...INTO statement is followed by the IN clause and the name of the database into which data is to be inserted. Again, you need to specify the full path to the target database file. Here, the path and database name are hardcoded for you to see another way of building an SQL insert statement string.

The name of the database is followed by the `FROM` clause and the name of the existing table from which records are selected. You may select data from more than one table. You may also specify selection criteria following the `WHERE` clause. After creating the SQL statement, we execute it using the `Execute` method of the `Database` object.

Notice the use of the `dbFailOnError` option with the `Execute` method. If the statement fails, `dbFailOnError` will generate an error message we can trap. Without it, we are not notified of any errors, and the entire procedure may not produce the intended results. You can see how the error trap works by running the procedure more than once. If the `Execute` statement succeeds, we proceed to delete records from the source table. We don't, however, want to execute the delete code if the `SELECT` statement returns no records. After the `Execute` command is run, we use the `RecordsAffected` property of the `Database` object to obtain the number of records affected by the most recent `Execute` command.

If we have more than one record, we specify the records to delete using the SQL `DELETE` statement, and then carry out the delete operation by calling the `Execute` method of the `Database` object. If `dbFailOnError` did not notify us of any errors, we assume that the `Execute` statement succeeded and we can commit the transaction. Before carrying out this operation, we ask the user to confirm or cancel the transaction. If the user chooses not to go ahead with the changes, we roll back the transaction. We also withdraw changes to the records if there were no records to archive.

It is important to keep in mind that in case of an error, you must roll back the transaction. Always check whether the transaction is still active by using a flag. Rolling back the transaction will ensure that the transaction doesn't stay active after your VBA procedure has ended.

8. Run the procedure once again in step mode (using F8) to walk through the error code.

USING ChatGPT WITH ACCESS

Welcome to the fun part of your learning journey! Here, you have the unique opportunity to interact with Copilot and deepen your understanding of the topics covered in this chapter. Whether you're tackling a specific challenge that requires DAO programming or you are simply curious about a DAO concept, you can feel free to describe your problem and ask for guidance. The best part of this interaction is the judgment-free environment—you can ask any question, no matter how simple, and receive the help you need to succeed.

To get started, let's ask ChatGPT the following questions:

User Prompt: *Can you provide me with an example that demonstrates the most useful DAO feature?*

User Prompt: *How can I optimize my DAO queries for better performance?*

User Prompt: *How can I automate repetitive database tasks using DAO?*

The `Chapter 10 - Using ChatGPT with Access` document in the companion files provides ChatGPT's responses to these prompts. Keep in mind that any VBA code provided in the ChatGPT responses has to be double-checked for accuracy before it can be adapted to your specific needs. My advice is to step through the code from the beginning of the VBA procedure and, if you get stuck, share the offending statement or error code with Copilot and ask for the fix or improvement.

SUMMARY

This chapter covered some basic and more advanced DAO material that you should find useful in developing professional applications in Access. You started by learning how to create and open databases using DAO methods. You learned how to create tables, add and modify their properties, and work with various types of fields, keys, and indexes. After that, you spent a great deal of time learning and working with the `Recordset` object. With this object now pretty much mastered, you should have no trouble working with data.

This chapter also showed you how you can create and run queries in your VBA procedures. Finally, you learned how transactions are used to ensure that certain database operations are always performed as a single unit.

In the next chapter, we will focus on writing VBA procedures that handle the same types of topics that we covered in this chapter by using the ADO library. We will also cover features that can only be accomplished by using ADO.

Chapter **11**

CREATING AND MANIPULATING DATABASES WITH ADO

In Chapter 10, we focused on performing various database tasks using the Data Access Objects library, commonly referred to as DAO. In this chapter, you will learn how to create and manipulate databases using another data access library—ActiveX Data Objects, or ADO.

While DAO is primarily designed for working with Microsoft Access databases and is optimized for the Access environment, ADO is a more general-purpose data access technology that can connect to various data sources, including SQL Server, Oracle, and other ODBC-compliant databases. ADO supports a broader range of data operations and environments compared to DAO. It also allows for disconnected recordsets, batch updates, and parameterized queries.

When developing Access database applications, you must understand the differences between the DAO and ADO libraries so that you can choose the right technology for your specific needs and the context of your project.

For example, ADO is the preferred choice if:

- You are developing an application that needs to access data from both an Access database and an SQL Server database and your application must handle complex queries and batch updates, and perhaps require offline data manipulation and robust transaction processing.

- You are developing Internet/Intranet applications that require data access over the Web. Here, ADO would be the preferred choice due to its support for Internet protocols and its ability to handle disconnected recordsets.
- You are developing an application that needs to connect to different types of databases (SQL Server, Oracle, MySQL, etc.). ADO is a better choice because it provides universal data access through OLE DB or ODBC providers, and using ADO objects, you can better leverage the processing power of an external database server, resulting in better performance.

We will spend quite a bit of time in this chapter learning about the ADO object model so that you can gain a thorough understanding of its structure and capabilities. By delving into the various components of ADO, you will be ready to use them effectively in your own database applications.

SETTING UP YOUR ENVIRONMENT FOR ADO PROGRAMMING

Before you can interact with the ADO objects and methods in your VBA code, you must set up a reference to the Microsoft ActiveX Data Objects library:

1. Press Alt+F11, or choose Database Tools | Visual Basic, to open the VBA editor in Access.
2. In the VBA editor, choose Tools | References.
3. Scroll through the list of available references and check the box next to Microsoft ActiveX Data Objects Library (for ADO 6.1) or Microsoft ActiveX Data Objects 2.x Library (for older versions of ADO).
4. Click OK to close the References dialog box.

CREATING AN ACCESS DATABASE WITH ADO

To create a new Access database using ADO, you must use the ActiveX Data Objects Ext. 6.0 for DDL and Security (ADOX) `Catalog` object's `Create` method. ADOX is an extension of the core ADO library. The ADOX library provides additional objects for creating, modifying, and deleting tables, procedures, and other database objects. It also includes security objects to manage users and groups, and to grant and revoke permissions on these objects (see Chapter 17). The `Create` method creates and opens a new ADO connection to the data source. An error will occur if the provider does not support creating new catalogs.

The procedure in Hands-On 11.1 creates a new blank database named `LearnADO.accdb` in your `C:\VBAAccess2024_ByExample` folder. The error trap ensures that the procedure works correctly even if the specified file already exists. When error `-2147217897` occurs, the procedure deletes the database file using the VBA `Kill` statement and returns to the statement that caused the error.

> **NOTE** — *All code files and figures for the hands-on projects may be found in the companion files.*

(●) Hands-On 11.1   Creating a Database

1. Open Access and create a new database called `Chap11.accdb` in your `C:\VBAAccess2024_ByExample` folder.
2. In the VBE window, choose Tools | References. In the References dialog box, click the checkbox next to Microsoft ADO Ext. 6.0 for DDL and Security Object Library and click OK.
3. Add a new standard module and enter the `CreateNewDB_ADO` procedure shown here:

```vba
Sub CreateNewDB_ADO()
    ' you must make sure that a reference to
    ' Microsoft ADO Ext. 6.0 for DDL and Security
    ' Object Library is set in the References dialog box

    Dim cat As ADOX.Catalog
    Dim strDb As String

    Set cat = New ADOX.Catalog
    strDb = "C:\VBAAccess2024_ByExample\LearnADO.accdb"

    On Error GoTo ErrorHandler
    cat.Create "Provider=Microsoft.ACE.OLEDB.12.0;" & _
      "Data Source=" & strDb
    MsgBox "The database was created (" & strDb & ")."
    Set cat = Nothing
    Exit Sub

ErrorHandler:
    If Err.Number = -2147217897 Then
        Kill strDb
        Resume 0
```

```
    Else
       MsgBox Err.Number & ": " & Err.Description
    End If
End Sub
```

4. Choose Run | Run Sub/UserForm to execute the procedure.
When you open the newly created database, it will be completely blank. It won't contain even a single table. You will learn how to use ADO to add tables to this database in a later section.

COPYING A DATABASE

At times, you may want to duplicate your database programmatically. This can be easily done in DAO with the `DBEngine` object's `CompactDatabase` method. ADO does not have a special method for copying files. You can, however, set up a reference to the File Scripting object (the Microsoft Scripting Runtime library) to gain access to your computer file system, or use the `CreateObject` function to access this library without setting up a reference.

Copying a Database with FileSystemObject

You can use the `CopyFile` method of the `FileSystemObject` from the Microsoft Scripting Runtime library to copy any file. This method allows you to copy one or more files and requires that you specify the source and destination files. The source is the name of the file you want to copy or the file specification. For example, to copy all your databases located in a specific directory, you can include wildcard characters to specify the source like this: `C:\VBAAccess2024_ByExample*.accdb`. The destination is the string specifying where the file or files are to be copied. The third argument of the `CopyFile` method is optional. It indicates whether existing files in the destination are to be overwritten. If `True`, files are overwritten; if `False`, they are not. The default is `True`.

Hands-On 11.2 demonstrates how to copy a file from one directory to another using this method.

⊙ Hands-On 11.2   Copying a File Using FileSystemObject

This hands-on exercise makes a copy of the `LearnADO.accdb` database created in Hands-On 11.1.

1. In the VBE window, choose Insert | Module.

2. In the module's Code window, type the following procedures:

```
Sub Copy_AnyFile(strFileName As String)
  Dim fso As Object
  Dim strSourceFolder As String
  Dim strDestFolder As String
  Dim strDb As String

  On Error GoTo ErrorHandler
  strSourceFolder = "C:\VBAAccess2024_ByExample\"
  strDestFolder = strSourceFolder & "TestFolder"
  strDb = strSourceFolder & strFileName

  Set fso = CreateObject("Scripting.FileSystemObject")
  fso.CreateFolder strDestFolder
  fso.CopyFile strDb, strDestFolder & "\" & strFileName

  Set fso = Nothing
  Exit Sub
ErrorHandler:
  MsgBox Err.Number & ":" & Err.Description
End Sub

Sub Execute_Copy_AnyFile()
    Copy_AnyFile "LearnADO.accdb"
End Sub
```

3. Run the `Execute_Copy_Any_File` procedure.
The `CreateObject` method is used to return a reference to a `FileSystemObject` from the Microsoft Scripting Runtime library. The `CreateFolder` method of the `FileSystemObject` is used to create a new subfolder named `TestFolder`. The `CopyFile` method of the `FileSystemObject` is then used to copy the specified database to the newly created folder.

MORE ABOUT DATABASE ERRORS

So far in this book, you've seen several procedures that incorporate error handling. You already know that an *error handler* is a block of code that is executed when a run-time error occurs. The procedure execution is transferred to error-handling code via the `On Error GoTo <Label>` statement.

In Chapter 8, you learned that VBA has a built-in `Err` object that has several properties useful for determining the type of error that occurred. You can use the `Err` object's `Number` property to determine the error number. The `Description` property contains the text description of the error. You can also find out the source of an error by using the `Source` property.

When using ADO to access data, you can get information about the errors from both the VBA `Err` object and the ADO `Error` object. When an error occurs in an application that uses the ADO object model, an `Error` object is appended to the ADO `Errors` collection of the `Connection` object, and you are advised about the error via a message box.

While the VBA `Err` object holds information only about the most recent error, the ADO `Errors` collection can contain several entries regarding the last ADO error. You can count the errors caused by an invalid operation by using the `Count` property of the `Errors` collection. By checking the contents of the `Errors` collection, you can learn more information about the nature of the error. The `Errors` collection is available only from the `Connection` object. Errors that occur in ADO itself are reported to the VBA `Err` object. Errors that are provider-specific are appended to the `Errors` collection of the ADO `Connection` object. These errors are reported by the specific OLE DB provider when ADO objects are being used to access data.

The `DBError2` procedure in Hands-On 11.3 attempts to open a nonexistent database to demonstrate the capabilities of the VBA `Err` object and the ADO `Errors` collection.

Hands-On 11.3   Using the VBA Err Object and ADO Errors Collection

1. In the VBE window, choose Insert | Module.
2. Open Tools | References and set the reference to the Microsoft ActiveX 6.1 Object Library.
3. In the module's Code window, type the following `DBError2` procedure:

```vba
Sub DBError2()
  Dim conn As New ADODB.Connection
  Dim errADO As ADODB.Error

  On Error GoTo CheckErrors
  conn.Open "Provider=Microsoft.ACE.OLEDB.12.0;" _
    & "Data Source=" & CurrentProject.Path & "\myDB.accdb"
  Debug.Print CurrentProject.Path
CheckErrors:
  Debug.Print "Listed below is information " _
    & "regarding this error " & vbCrLf _
    & "contained in the ADO Errors collection."
  For Each errADO In conn.Errors
    Debug.Print vbTab & _
      "Error Number: " & errADO.Number
```

```
      Debug.Print vbTab & _
        "Error Description: " & errADO.Description
      Debug.Print vbTab & _
        "Jet Error Number: " & errADO.SQLState
      Debug.Print vbTab & _
        "Native Error Number: " & errADO.NativeError
      Debug.Print vbTab & _
        "Source: " & errADO.Source
      Debug.Print vbTab & _
        "Help Context: " & errADO.HelpContext
      Debug.Print vbTab & _
        "Help File: " & errADO.HelpFile
   Next
   MsgBox "Errors were written to the Immediate window."
   SendKeys "^g"
End Sub
```

4. Choose Run | Run Sub/UserForm to execute the procedure.

In this procedure, an error is encountered when VBA attempts to open a database file that does not exist in the specified directory. The `On Error GoTo CheckErrors` statement tells VBA to jump to the line labeled `CheckErrors`. The line that prints the current project path is never executed. The `CheckErrors` handler reads the content of the VBA `Err` object and prints the error number and its description to the Immediate window. After that, we retrieve more information about the encountered errors by looping through the ADO `Errors` collection. Here's the output from running the procedure in this hands-on exercise:

```
Listed below is information regarding this error
contained in the ADO Errors collection.
    Error Number: -2147467259
    Error Description: Could not find file 'C:\myDB.accdb'.
    Jet Error Number: 3024
    Native Error Number: -534578963
    Source: Microsoft Access Database Engine
    Help Context: 5003024
    Help File:
```

OPENING A MICROSOFT JET DATABASE IN READ/WRITE MODE

You can use ADO to open an Access database for shared access (read/write). The names of common data providers used with ADO are listed in Chapter 9 (see Table 9.3).

To specify the data source name, use the `Connection` object's `Connection-String` property. As you will recall from an earlier discussion, connection strings describe how to access data. Here's a code fragment that specifies the minimum required connection information:

```
With conn
    .Provider = "Microsoft.ACE.OLEDB.12.0;"
    .ConnectionString = "Data Source=" & CurrentProject.Path & _
    "\NorthwindStarter.accdb"
End With
```

The data source includes the full path to the database file you are going to open. Once you've specified the minimum connection information, you may proceed to open the database. Use the `Connection` object's `Open` method to open the connection to a data source:

```
conn.Open
```

ADO syntax is quite flexible. A connection to a database can also be opened like this:

```
conn.Open "Provider = Microsoft.ACE.OLEDB.12.0;Data Source=" & _
  CurrentProject.Path & "\NorthwindStarter.accdb"
```

As you can see in the preceding code fragment, the `Provider` name and the data source (in this example, the path to the database) are supplied as arguments when you call a `Connection` object's `Open` method.

Alternatively, you could open the database connection like this:

```
With conn
    .Provider = "Microsoft.ACE.OLEDB.12.0;"
    .Mode = adModeReadWrite
    .ConnectionString = "Data Source=" & CurrentProject.Path & _
    "\NorthwindStarter.accdb"
    .Open
End With
```

By default, the `Connection` object's `Open` method opens a database for shared access. You can use the `Connection` object's `Mode` property to explicitly specify the type of access to a database. The `Mode` property must be set prior to opening the connection because it is read-only once the connection is open. Connections can be set to read-only, write-only, or read/write. You can also specify whether other applications should be prevented from opening a connection. The value for the `Mode` property can be one of the constants/values specified in Table 11.1.

TABLE 11.1. Intrinsic constants of the Connection object's Mode property.

Constant Name	Value	Type of Permission
adModeUnknown	0	Permissions have not been set yet or cannot be determined. This is the default setting.
adModeRead	1	Read-only permissions.
adModeWrite	2	Write-only permissions.
adModeReadWrite	3	Read/write permissions.
adModeShareDenyRead	4	Prevents others from opening the connection with read permissions.
adModeShareDenyWrite	8	Prevents others from opening the connection with write permissions.
adModeShareExclusive	12	Prevents others from opening the connection.
adModeShareDenyNone	16	Prevents others from opening the connection with any permissions.

Hands-On 11.4 demonstrates how to use ADO to open an Access database for shared access (read/write).

Hands-On 11.4   Opening a Database with ADO in Read/Write Mode

1. In the VBE window, choose Insert | Module to add a new module to the currently open `Chap11.accdb` database.
2. In the module's Code window, type the following `openDB_ADO` procedure:

```
Sub openDB_ADO()
    Dim conn As ADODB.Connection
    Dim strDb As String

    On Error GoTo ErrorHandler

    strDb = CurrentProject.Path & "\NorthwindStarter.accdb"
    Set conn = New ADODB.Connection

    With conn
        .Provider = "Microsoft.ACE.OLEDB.12.0;"
        .Mode = adModeReadWrite
        .ConnectionString = "Data Source=" & strDb
        .Open
    End With

    If conn.State = adStateOpen Then
        MsgBox "Connection was opened."
    End If
```

```
   conn.Close
   Set conn = Nothing
   MsgBox "Connection was closed."
   Exit Sub
ErrorHandler:
   MsgBox Err.Number & ": " & Err.Description
End Sub
```

3. Position the insertion point anywhere within the code of the `openDB_ADO` procedure and press F5 or choose Run | Run Sub/UserForm to execute the procedure.

The ADO Connection object's `State` property returns a value that describes whether the connection is open, closed, connecting, executing, or retrieving data (see Table 11.2).

TABLE 11.2.   Intrinsic constants of the Connection object's State property.

Constant	Value	Description
adStateClosed	0	Connection is closed.
adStateOpen	1	Connection is open.
adStateConnecting	2	Connection is connecting.
adStateExecuting	4	Connection is executing a command.
adStateFetching	8	Connection is retrieving data.

CONNECTING TO THE CURRENT ACCESS DATABASE

Microsoft Access provides a quick way to access the current DAO database by using the `CurrentDb` method. This method returns an object variable of type `Database` that represents the database currently open in the main Access window. In ADO, however, you must use the `CurrentProject.Connection` statement to access the currently open database. The `CurrentProject` object refers to the project for the current Access database. These statements work only in VBA procedures created in Access. If you'd like to reuse your VBA procedures in other Microsoft 365 Visual Basic applications, you will be better off creating a connection via an appropriate OLE DB provider.

The procedure in Hands-On 11.5 uses the `CurrentProject.Connection` statement to return a reference to the current database. Once the connection to the current database is established, the example procedure loops through the `Properties` collection of the `Connection` object to retrieve its property names and settings. The results are written both to the Immediate window and to a text file named `C:\VBAAccess2024_ByExample\Propfile.txt`.

 **Hands-On 11.5   Establishing a Connection to the Current Access Database**

1. In the VBE window, choose Insert | Module.
2. In the module's Code window, type the `Connect_ToCurrentDB` procedure shown here:

```
Sub Connect_ToCurrentDB()
    Dim conn As ADODB.Connection
    Dim fs As Object
    Dim txtfile As Object
    Dim i As Integer
    Dim strFileName As String

    strFileName = "C:\VBAAccess2024_ByExample\Propfile.txt"

    Set conn = CurrentProject.Connection
    Set fs = CreateObject("Scripting.FileSystemObject")
    Set txtfile = fs.CreateTextFile(strFileName, True)

    For i = 0 To conn.Properties.Count - 1
      Debug.Print conn.Properties(i).Name & "=" & _
        conn.Properties(i).Value
      txtfile.WriteLine (conn.Properties(i).Name & _
        "=" & conn.Properties(i).Value)
    Next i
    MsgBox "Please check results in the " & _
      "Immediate window." & vbCrLf _
      & "The results have also been written to the " _
      & Chr(13) & strFileName & " file."

    txtfile.Close

    Set fs = Nothing
    conn.Close
    Set conn = Nothing
End Sub
```

3. Choose Run | Run Sub/UserForm to execute the procedure.
   To create a text file from a VBA procedure, the `CreateObject` function is used to access the `Scripting.FileSystemObject`. This function returns the `FileSystemObject` (fs). The `CreateTextFile` method of the `FileSystemObject` creates the `TextStream` object that represents a text file (`txtfile`). The `WriteLine` method writes each property and the corresponding setting to the newly created text file (`Propfile.txt`). Finally, the `Close` method closes the text file.

OPENING OTHER DATABASES, SPREADSHEETS, AND TEXT FILES

The Microsoft Access Jet/ACE database engine can be used to access other databases, spreadsheets, and text files. The following subsections of this chapter demonstrate how to connect to SQL Server, Excel spreadsheets, and text files.

Connecting to an SQL Server Database

ADO provides a number of ways of connecting to an SQL Server database. To access data residing on Microsoft SQL Server, use SQLOLEDB, which is the native Microsoft OLE DB provider for SQL. You can also connect to an SQL database using the MSDASQL provider. This provider allows you to access any existing ODBC data sources.

You can open a connection to SQL Server by using an ODBC DSN or an ODBC DSN-less connection. Both of these connection types were discussed in Chapter 9. The following code snippet opens and then closes a connection with the SQL Server database based on a DSN named Works.

```
With conn
  .Open "Provider=MSDASQL;DSN=Works"
  Debug.Print .Provider
  .Close
End With
```

Recall that you can skip setting the Provider property because MSDASQL is the default provider for ODBC. All you really need to establish a connection in this case is a DSN.

Additional code in the companion files.
File Name: SQLOLEDB_Provider.txt
Description: Connecting to an SQL Server Database Using SQLOLEDB Provider

Opening a Microsoft Excel Workbook

To open Excel 2007–2024 workbook files with the .xlsx file format using ADO, use the Microsoft ACE OLE DB 12.0 provider and use the Extended Properties of the ADO Connection object to pass the connection string like this:

```
Dim conn As ADODB.Connection
Set conn = New ADODB.Connection
conn.Open "Provider=Microsoft.ACE.OLEDB.12.0;" & _
  "Data Source=C:\VBAAccess2024_ByExample\" & _
```

```
"Report2024.xlsx;" & _
"Extended Properties=""Excel 12.0;HDR=YES"";"
```

To open workbook files created in Excel 2000–2003, use the OLE DB Provider
for Microsoft Jet 4.0 and Excel 8.0 in the `Extended Properties`:

```
Dim conn As ADODB.Connection
conn.Open "Provider=Microsoft.Jet.OLEDB.4.0;" & _
  "Data Source=C:\VBAAccess2024_ByExample\Report.xls;" & _
  "Extended Properties=""Excel 8.0;HDR=YES"";"
```

Hands-On 11.6 demonstrates how to open an Excel workbook with ADO and
modify its data.

Hands-On 11.6   Opening an Excel Workbook

1. In the standard module, enter the following procedures:

```
Sub Open_Excel_ADO(strFileName As String)
   Dim conn As ADODB.Connection
   Dim rst As ADODB.Recordset
   Dim strFindWhat As String

   Set conn = New ADODB.Connection

     With conn
       .Provider = "Microsoft.ACE.OLEDB.12.0;"
       .ConnectionString = "Data Source=" & _
        CurrentProject.Path & "\" & strFileName & _
        ";Extended Properties=""Excel 12.0;HDR=Yes;IMEX=0"";"""
       .Open
     End With

   Set rst = New ADODB.Recordset
   rst.Open "SELECT * FROM [Sheet1$]", conn, _
     adOpenStatic, adLockOptimistic

   strFindWhat = "[Excel Version] = 'Excel 2021'"
   rst.Find strFindWhat
   rst(1).Value = "1500"
   rst.Update
   rst.Close
   Set rst = Nothing
   MsgBox "Excel workbook was opened and updated."

   conn.Close
```

```
    Set conn = Nothing
End Sub

Sub Execute_Open_Excel_ADO()
    Call Open_Excel_ADO("Report2024.xlsx")
End Sub
```

2. Run the `Execute_Open_Excel_ADO` procedure.

Notice how the `Open_Excel_ADO` procedures passed the connection string to the ADO `Connection` object's `Open` method. The `Provider` property is set to Microsoft ACE OLE DB 12.0 for the current version of an Excel file (`*.xlsx`), and `Extended Properties` is set to use Excel 12.0. Notice that the `IMEX` option, which stands for import/export mode, is set to zero (`IMEX=0`). This setting will allow the data in the worksheet to be updatable. When `IMEX=1`, the file becomes read-only, and you'll get an error on attempting to update the recordset. Once the connection to the workbook file is open, a recordset is opened. We instruct the procedure to select all data from the `Sheet1` worksheet using the following SQL statement:

```
"SELECT * FROM [Sheet1$]"
```

In the `SELECT` statement, the sheet name must be enclosed in square brackets and have a dollar sign (`$`) appended to it. The recordset is opened using the open connection (`conn`). The procedure uses the ADO constants `adOpenStatic` (the `Cursor Type` parameter) and `adLockOptimistic` (the `Lock Type` parameter) to ensure that the recordset is updatable. ADO recordsets are discussed in detail later in this chapter.

Before you can modify data in a worksheet, you must find it. The search criteria string is defined in the `strFindWhat` variable. To find the data, the procedure uses the `Find` method of the ADO `Recordset` object. Once the searched data is located, we simply assign a new value to the recordset field using the `Value` property:

```
rst(1).Value = "1500"
```

The ADO `Recordset` fields are counted beginning with zero (`0`). Therefore, the preceding statement sets the value in the second column in the worksheet. To save the changes to the file, call the `Update` method, like this:

```
rst.Update
```

The remaining code in this procedure performs the standard cleanup: closing the objects and releasing the memory used by the object variables (`rst`, `conn`).

Opening a Text File

There are several ways to open text files programmatically. This section demonstrates how to gain access to a text file by using the *Microsoft Access Text driver*. Notice that this is a DSN-less connection (as explained in Chapter 9). Hands-On 11.7 demonstrates how to open a recordset based on a comma-separated file format and write the file contents to the Immediate window.

(•) Hands-On 11.7   Opening a Text File

1. Copy the `Employees.txt` file from the companion files to your `C:\VBAAccess2024_ByExample` folder, or prepare the text file from scratch by typing the following in Notepad and saving the file as `Employees.txt`:

```
"Last Name", "First Name", "Birthdate", "Years Worked"
        "Krawiec","Bogdan",#1963-01-02#,3
        "Gorecka","Jadwiga",#1948-05-12#,1
        "Olszewski","Stefan",#1957-04-07#,0
```

2. In the VBE window, choose Insert | Module.
3. In the module's Code window, type the following `Open_TextFile` procedure:

```vba
Sub Open_TextFile()
  Dim conn As ADODB.Connection
  Dim rst As ADODB.Recordset
  Dim fld As ADODB.Field

  Set conn = New ADODB.Connection
  conn.Open "DRIVER={Microsoft Access & _
    Text Driver (*.txt, *.csv)};" & _
    "DBQ=" & CurrentProject.Path & "\"

  Debug.Print conn.ConnectionString

  Set rst = New ADODB.Recordset
  rst.Open "SELECT * FROM [Employees.txt]", conn, adOpenStatic, _
    adLockReadOnly, adCmdText
  Do Until rst.EOF
    Debug.Print "*****************************"
    For Each fld In rst.Fields
      Debug.Print fld.Name & "=" & fld.Value
    Next fld
    rst.MoveNext
  Loop
```

```
   rst.Close
   Set rst = Nothing

   conn.Close
   Set conn = Nothing
   MsgBox "Open the Immediate window to view the data."
End Sub
```

4. Make sure the `C:\VBAAccess2024_ByExample\Employees.txt` file is closed and choose Run | Run Sub/UserForm to execute the procedure.

<table>
<tr><td>

NOTE

</td><td>If you are getting an error while running this procedure, check that the driver is spelled out exactly as it appears on the Drivers tab in the ODBC Data Source Administrator (64-bit). If you are running on a 32-bit system, you should change the ODBC Driver name to <code>Microsoft Text Driver (*.txt, *.csv)</code>.</td></tr>
</table>

If you worked through the previous exercises in this chapter, you should have no problem following the code of the `Open_TextFile` procedure. To read records, you can open the recordset using the `adOpenStatic` and `adLockReadOnly` ADO constants. Notice that the ADO constant `adCmdText` is used as the last parameter of the recordset's `Open` method:

```
rst.Open "SELECT * FROM [Employees.txt]", conn, adOpenStatic, _
    adLockReadOnly, adCmdText
```

The last parameter in the preceding statement can be any valid option. You can indicate the type of source you are using with the `adCmdText` constant (for an SQL statement), `adCmdTable` (to retrieve all the rows in a table), or `adCmdStoredProc` (to get records via a stored procedure). If you do not specify the type of source, `adCmdUnknown` is used as the default.

CREATING A MICROSOFT ACCESS TABLE AND SETTING FIELD PROPERTIES

It's time to add a table to the database we created earlier. Many of the database objects are created, modified, or deleted using the ADOX library. To use ADOX in your VBA procedures, choose Tools | References from your VBE window and select Microsoft ADO Ext. 6.0 for DDL and Security. The most important ADOX object is called `Catalog`. It represents an entire database and contains database tables, columns, indexes, groups, users, procedures, and views. You will use the ADOX `Catalog` object in your VBA procedures to create a table.

The following steps outline the process of creating a new Access table using ADOX:

1. Declare the variables representing the `Connection`, `Catalog`, and `Table` objects:

```
Dim conn As ADODB.Connection
Dim cat As ADOX.Catalog
Dim tbl As ADOX.Table
```

2. Open the connection to your database:

```
Set conn = New ADODB.Connection
conn.Open "Provider=Microsoft.ACE.OLEDB.12.0;" & _
  "Data Source=C:\VBAAccess2024_ByExample\LearnADO.accdb"
```

3. Supply the open connection to the `ActiveConnection` property of the ADOX `Catalog` object:

```
Set cat = New ADOX.Catalog
Set cat.ActiveConnection = conn
```

4. Create a new `Table` object:

```
Set tbl = New ADOX.Table
```

5. Provide the name for your table:

```
tbl.Name = "tblAssets"
```

The `Table` object is a member of the `Tables` collection, which in turn is a member of the `Catalog` object. Each `Table` object has a `Name` property and a `Type` property. The `Type` property specifies whether a `Table` object is a standard Access table, a linked table, a system table, or a view.

Append the `Table` object to the `Catalog` object's `Tables` collection:

```
cat.Tables.Append tbl
```

At this point, your table is empty.

6. Add new fields (columns) to your new table:

```
With tbl.Columns
   .Append "SiteID", adVarWChar, 10
   .Append "Category", adSmallInt
   .Append "InstallDate", adDate
End With
```

The preceding code fragment creates three fields, named `SiteID`, `Category`, and `InstallDate`. You can create new fields in a table by passing the `Column` object's `Name`, `Type`, and `DefinedSize` properties as arguments of the `Columns` collection's `Append` method. Notice that ADOX uses different data types than those used in the Access user interface (see Table 11.3 for a comparison of the data types).

<table>
<tr><td rowspan="3">

NOTE

</td><td>

The `Table` *object contains the* `Columns` *collection, which contains* `Column` *objects. To add a new field to a table, you could create a* `Column` *object and write the code like this:*

```
Dim col As ADOX.Column
set col = New ADOX.Column
With col
    .Name = "SiteID"
    .DefinedSize = 10
End With
tbl.Columns.Append col
```

The last statement in the preceding example appends the new `Column` *object (field) to the* `Columns` *collection of a table. The* `Name` *property specifies the name of the column. The* `Defined-Size` *property designates the maximum size of an entry in the column. To create another field, you would have to create a new* `Column` *object and set its properties. Creating fields in this manner takes longer and is less efficient than using the method demonstrated earlier.*

</td></tr>
</table>

The complete procedure is shown here:

```
Sub CreateTableADO()
    Dim conn As ADODB.Connection
    Dim cat As ADOX.Catalog
    Dim tbl As ADOX.Table

    ' make sure to set up a reference to
    ' the Microsoft ActiveX Data Objects 6.1 Library
    ' and ADO Ext. 6.0 for DDL and Security

    Set conn = New ADODB.Connection
    conn.Open "Provider=Microsoft.ACE.OLEDB.12.0;" & _
      "Data Source=C:\VBAAccess2024_ByExample\LearnADO.accdb"

    Set cat = New ADOX.Catalog
```

```
    Set cat.ActiveConnection = conn

    Set tbl = New ADOX.Table
    tbl.Name = "tblAssets"

    cat.Tables.Append tbl

    With tbl.Columns
        .Append "SiteID", adVarWChar, 10
        .Append "Category", adSmallInt
        .Append "InstallDate", adDate
    End With

    Set cat = Nothing
    conn.Close
    Set conn = Nothing
End Sub
```

TABLE 11.3. ADO data types versus Access data types.

ADO Data Type	Corresponding Data Type in Access
adBoolean	Yes/No
adUnsignedTinyInt	Number (FieldSize = Byte)
adSmallIInt	Number (FieldSize = Integer)
adSingle	Number (FieldSize = Single)
adDouble	Number (FieldSize = Double)
adDecimal	Number (FieldSize = Decimal)
adInteger	Number (FieldSize = LongInteger) AutoNumber
adCurrency	Currency
adVarWChar	Text
adDate	Date/Time
adLongVarBinary	OLE object
adLongVarWChar	Memo
adLongVarWChar	Hyperlink

NOTE	*ADO does not support the Attachment data type, multiselect lookup fields, or the append-only and rich text memo fields. To programmatically access these features in Access 2007–2024, you must rely on the DAO object library (see the example procedures in Chapter 10).*

COPYING A TABLE

The procedure in Hands-On 11.8 uses the SQL SELECT...INTO statement to select all records from the Customers table in the NorthwindStarter database and place them into a new table called CustomersCopy. The SELECT...INTO statement is equivalent to a MakeTable query in the Access user interface. This statement creates a new table and inserts data from other tables. To copy a table, the SQL statement is passed as the first argument of the Execute method of the ADO Connection object. Note that the copied table will not have the indexes that may exist in the original table.

⊙ Hands-On 11.8   Making a Copy of a Table

1. Use Copy/Paste in the File Explorer to create a backup copy of the NorthwindStarter.accdb file. Save it as NorthwindStarter_Backup.accdb in your working folder.
2. In the VBE window, choose Insert | Module.
3. In the module's Code window, type the following Copy_Table procedure:

```
' make sure to set up a reference to
' the Microsoft ActiveX Data Objects 6.1 Library

Sub Copy_Table()
  Dim conn As ADODB.Connection
  Dim strTable As String
  Dim strSQL As String

  On Error GoTo ErrorHandler

  strTable = "Customers"

  strSQL = "SELECT " & strTable & ".* INTO "
  strSQL = strSQL & strTable & "Copy "
  strSQL = strSQL & "FROM " & strTable

  Debug.Print strSQL

  Set conn = New ADODB.Connection
  conn.Open "Provider=Microsoft.ACE.OLEDB.12.0;" & _
    "Data Source=" & CurrentProject.Path & _
      "\NorthwindStarter.accdb"

  conn.Execute strSQL
  conn.Close
```

```
    Set conn = Nothing
    MsgBox "The " & strTable & " table was copied."
    Exit Sub

ErrorHandler:
  If Err.Number = -2147217900 Then
    conn.Execute "DROP Table " & strTable
    Resume
  Else
    MsgBox Err.Number & ": " & Err.Description
  End If
End Sub
```

4. Choose Run | Run Sub/UserForm to execute the procedure.
When you run this procedure, Access creates a copy of the `Customers` table named `CustomersCopy` in the `NorthwindStarter.accdb` database.

DELETING A TABLE

You can use ADO to delete a table programmatically by opening the ADOX `Catalog` object, accessing its `Tables` collection, and calling the `Delete` method. The following code snippet demonstrates how to delete the specified table:

```
Set cat = New ADOX.Catalog

cat.ActiveConnection = conn

cat.Tables.Delete strTblName
```


ADDING NEW FIELDS TO AN EXISTING TABLE

At times, you may want to programmatically add a new field to an existing table. The procedure in Hands-On 11.9 adds a new text field called `MyNewField` to a table located in the `LearnADO.accdb` database.

Hands-On 11.9   Adding a New Field to a Table

The procedure demonstrated in this hands-on exercise uses the `CustomersCopy` table in the `Northwind` database.

1. In the VBE window, choose Insert | Module.

2. In the module's Code window, type the following `Add_NewFields` procedure:

```
Sub Add_NewFields()
   Dim conn As ADODB.Connection
   Dim cat As New ADOX.Catalog

   ' Initialize the connection
   Set conn = New ADODB.Connection
   conn.Open "Provider=Microsoft.ACE.OLEDB.12.0;" & _
     "Data Source=" & CurrentProject.Path & _
     "\LearnADO.accdb"

  ' Initialize the catalog
   Set cat = New ADOX.Catalog
   cat.ActiveConnection = conn

   ' Add the field to the table
   cat.Tables("tblAssets").Columns.Append _
     "MyNewField", adVarWChar, 15

   ' Clean up
   Set cat = Nothing
   conn.Close
   Set conn = Nothing
End Sub
```

3. Choose Run | Run Sub/UserForm to run the `Add_NewFields` procedure.
4. Open the `LearnADO.accdb` database to ensure that the added field appears in the table `tblAssets`.
5. Close the `LearnADO` database and run the `Add_NewFields` procedure again. Microsoft Visual Basic should display the run-time error Cannot define field more than once. Therefore, before adding a new field, it is always a good idea to check whether the field already exists in the table.
6. On your own, rewrite the `Add_NewFields` procedure to check for the existence of the specified field prior to adding it to the table.

Additional Code in the companion files.

The revised `Add_NewFields` procedure can be found in the companion files. See the file `FieldExists.txt`.

REMOVING A FIELD FROM A TABLE

You may remove any field from an existing table, whether or not this field contains data. You can't, however, delete a field after you have created an index that references that field. You must first delete the index.

The following code snippet illustrates how to access the ADOX `Columns` collection of a `Table` object and use the `Columns` collection's `Delete` method to remove a field from a table:

```
cat.Tables("tblAssets").Columns.Delete  "MyNewField"
```

RETRIEVING TABLE AND FIELD PROPERTIES

You can set or retrieve table properties using the `Properties` collection of an ADOX `Table` object. The `Properties` collection exposes standard ADO properties as well as properties specific to the data provider. You can iterate through all of the properties of an object using the `For Each...Next` programming structure.

The following procedure retrieves the properties of the `Customers` table and its fields in the `NorthwindStarter` database. This procedure will print the table and field properties to the Immediate window (see Figure 11.1).

Hands-On 11.10   Listing Table and Field Properties

1. In the VBE window, choose Insert | Module.
2. In the module's Code window, type the following `List_TableProperties` procedure:

```
Sub RetrieveTableAndFieldPropertiesADO()
    Dim conn As ADODB.Connection
    Dim cat As ADOX.Catalog
    Dim tbl As ADOX.Table
    Dim col As ADOX.Column
    Dim prop As ADOX.Property

    On Error GoTo ErrorHandler

    ' Create a new ADO Connection object
    Set conn = CreateObject("ADODB.Connection")

    ' Open the connection
```

```vba
    conn.Open "Provider=Microsoft.ACE.OLEDB.12.0;" & _
    "Data Source=" & CurrentProject.Path & "\NorthwindStarter.accdb"

    ' Create a new ADOX Catalog object
    Set cat = CreateObject("ADOX.Catalog")
    Set cat.ActiveConnection = conn

    ' Get the table definition for the Customers table
    Set tbl = cat.Tables("Customers")

    ' Print table properties
    Debug.Print "Table: " & tbl.Name
    Debug.Print "---------------------------"
    For Each prop In tbl.Properties
        On Error Resume Next
        Debug.Print "Table Property: " & _
            prop.Name & " = " & prop.Value
        On Error GoTo 0
    Next prop
    Debug.Print "---------------------------"

    ' Loop through each field in the table
    For Each col In tbl.Columns
        ' Print field properties
        Debug.Print "Field: " & col.Name
        Debug.Print "---------------------------"
        For Each prop In col.Properties
            On Error Resume Next
            Debug.Print "  Field Property: " & _
                prop.Name & " = " & prop.Value
            On Error GoTo 0
        Next prop
        Debug.Print "---------------------------"
    Next col

    ' Clean up
    Set prop = Nothing
    Set col = Nothing
    Set tbl = Nothing
    Set cat = Nothing
    conn.Close
    Set conn = Nothing

    MsgBox "Table and field properties retrieved successfully. " & _
        "Check it out in the Immediate Window."
CleanUp:
```

```
    Exit Sub
ErrorHandler:
    MsgBox "An error occurred: " & Err.Description
    Resume CleanUp
End Sub
```

3. Choose Run | Run Sub/UserForm to execute the procedure.

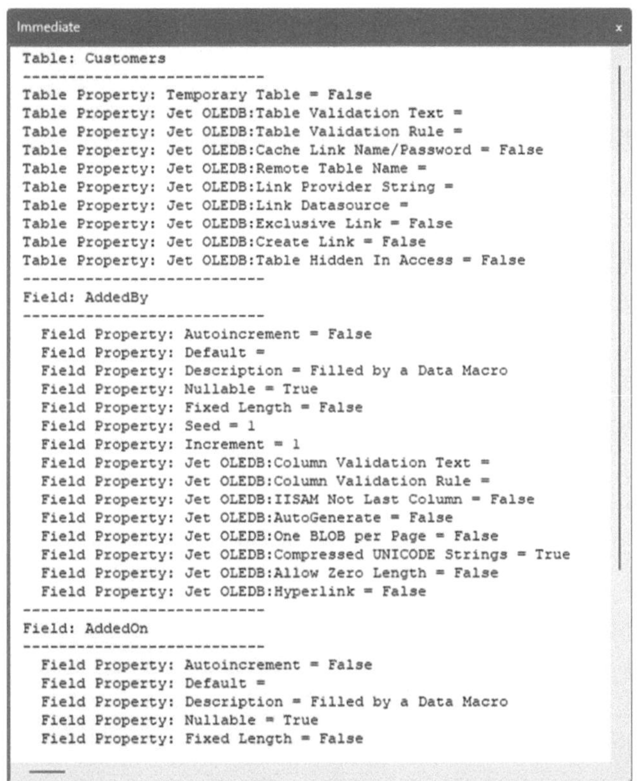

FIGURE 11.1.   The table and field properties and their values are retrieved programmatically (see the VBA procedure in Hands-On 11.10).

LINKING A MICROSOFT ACCESS TABLE

Linked tables in Microsoft Access allow you to connect to and use tables stored in external databases without having to import the data into your Access database. This provides the convenience of working with external data while keeping your Access database lightweight. Linked tables appear in your Access database just like local tables, and you can query them using SQL and interact with them through the Access interface. To create a linked Access table, you must set the following table properties:

```
Jet OLEDB:LinkDatasource
Jet OLEDB:Remote Table Name
Jet OLEDB:CreateLink
```

The procedure in Hands-On 11.11 demonstrates how to establish a link to the `Customers` table located in the `NorthwindStarter` database.

(◉) Hands-On 11.11   Linking a Microsoft Access Table

1. In the VBE window, choose Insert | Module.
2. In the module's Code window, type the `Link_JetTable` procedure, as shown below.

```
Sub Link_JetTable()
   Dim cat As ADOX.Catalog
   Dim lnkTbl As ADOX.Table
   Dim strDb As String
   Dim strTable As String

   On Error GoTo ErrorHandler

   strDb = CurrentProject.Path & "\NorthwindStarter.accdb"
   strTable = "Customers"
   Set cat = New ADOX.Catalog
   cat.ActiveConnection = CurrentProject.Connection

   Set lnkTbl = New ADOX.Table
   With lnkTbl
      ' Name the new Table and set its ParentCatalog property
      ' to the open Catalog to allow access
      ' to the Properties collection.

      .Name = strTable
      Set .ParentCatalog = cat

     ' Set the properties to create the link
      .Properties("Jet OLEDB:Create Link") = True
      .Properties("Jet OLEDB:Link Datasource") = strDb
      .Properties("Jet OLEDB:Remote Table Name") = strTable
   End With

   ' Append the table to the Tables collection
   cat.Tables.Append lnkTbl
```

```
    Set cat = Nothing
    MsgBox "The current database contains a linked " & _
      "table named " & strTable
    Exit Sub

ErrorHandler:
    MsgBox Err.Number & ": " & Err.Description
End Sub
```

3. Choose Run | Run Sub/UserForm to execute the procedure.
To access the linked `Customers` table after running this procedure, be sure to refresh the Access application window.

LINKING A MICROSOFT EXCEL WORKSHEET

You can link an Excel worksheet to an Access database by using the `TransferSpreadsheet` method of the `DoCmd` object, as shown in Hands-On 11.12. Note, however, that neither the `DoCmd` object nor its `TransferSpreadsheet` method are members of the ADO object model. The `DoCmd` object is built into the Microsoft Access library.

Hands-On 11.12   Linking an Excel Worksheet

This hands-on exercise uses the `Regions.xlsx` workbook file provided in the companion files. You can revise the procedure code to use any workbook file that you have available; however, you must match the name of the spreadsheet constant with the Excel version. Table 11.4 shows the constant names and values if you need a different format.

TABLE 11.4.   Spreadsheet constants.

Constant	Value	Description
acSpreadsheetTypeExcel3	0	Microsoft Excel 3.0 format
acSpreadsheetTypeExcel4	6	Microsoft Excel 4.0 format
acSpreadsheetTypeExcel5	5	Microsoft Excel 5.0 format
acSpreadsheetTypeExcel7	5	Microsoft Excel 95 format
acSpreadsheetTypeExcel8	8	Microsoft Excel 97 format
acSpreadsheetTypeExcel9	8	Microsoft Excel 2000–2003 format
acSpreadsheetTypeExcel12	9	Microsoft Excel 2007–2010 format (.xls)
acSpreadsheetTypeExcel12Xml	10	Microsoft Excel 2007–2024 format (.xml)

1. Copy the `Regions.xlsx` workbook from the companion files to your `C:\ VBAAccess2024_ByExample` folder.
2. In the VBE window, choose Insert | Module.
3. In the module's Code window, type the following `Link_ExcelSheet` procedure:

```vba
Sub Link_ExcelSheet()
    Dim rst As ADODB.Recordset

    DoCmd.TransferSpreadsheet acLink, _
      acSpreadsheetTypeExcel12, _
      "mySheet", _
      CurrentProject.Path & "\Regions.xlsx", _
      -1, "Regions!A1:B15"

    Set rst = New ADODB.Recordset
    With rst
      .ActiveConnection = CurrentProject.Connection
      .CursorType = adOpenKeyset
      .LockType = adLockOptimistic
      .Open "mySheet", , , , adCmdTable
    End With

    Do Until rst.EOF
      Debug.Print rst.Fields(0).Value, _
                  rst.Fields(1).Value
      rst.MoveNext
    Loop
    rst.Close
    Set rst = Nothing
End Sub
```

4. Choose Run | Run Sub/UserForm to execute the procedure.
   The current database navigation pane should now show the `mySheet` linked table that displays data from an Excel worksheet (Figure 11.2).

   The `Link_ExcelSheet` procedure begins by creating a linked table named `mySheet` from the specified range of cells (A1:B15) in the `Regions` worksheet in the `Regions.xlsx` file. The first argument in the `DoCmd` statement indicates that the first row of the spreadsheet contains column headings. Next, the procedure uses the ADO `Recordset` object to retrieve the data from the `mySheet` table into the Immediate window. Notice that prior to opening the recordset, several properties of the `Recordset` object must be set:

   - The `ActiveConnection` property sets the reference to the current database.

- The `CursorType` property specifies how the `Recordset` object should interact with the data source:
  - The `adOpenKeyset` setting tells Visual Basic that instead of retrieving all the records from the data source, only the keys are to be retrieved. The data for these keys is retrieved only as you scroll through the recordset. This guarantees better performance than retrieving big chunks of data at once.
- The `LockType` property determines how to lock the data while it is being manipulated:
  - The `adLockOptimistic` setting locks the record only when you attempt to save it.
- Opening the `Recordset` object also requires that you specify the data source. The data source in this procedure is the linked table named `mySheet`. The parameter passed depends on the source type used.
- The `adCmdTable` setting indicates that all rows from the source table should be included.

You could also open the `Recordset` object by passing all the required parameters at once, as follows:

```
rst.Open "mySheet", _
CurrentProject.Connection, adOpenKeyset, adLockOptimistic, _
adCmdTable
```

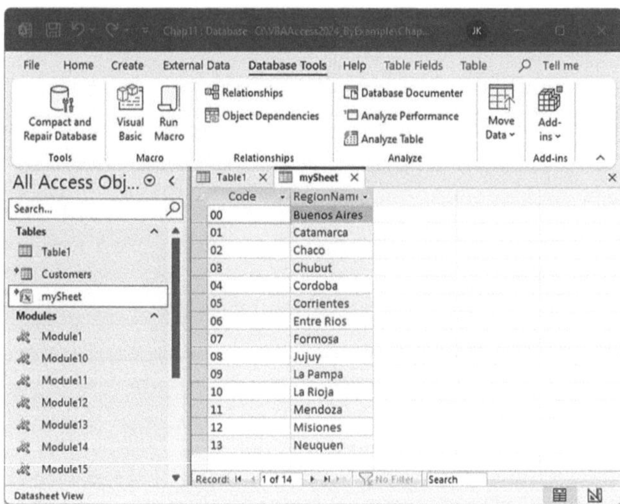

FIGURE 11.2.   The Access database Navigation Pane with two linked tables created by running procedures in this chapter.

LISTING DATABASE TABLES USING THE CATALOG OBJECT

The procedure in Hands-On 11.13 generates a list of tables in the `Northwind-Starter.accdb` database. It uses the ADOX `Catalog` object to gain access to the database, then iterates through the `Tables` collection to retrieve the names of Access tables, system tables, and views. The ADOX `Tables` collection stores various types of `Table` objects, as shown in Table 11.5.

TABLE 11.5. Table types in the ADOX tables collection.

Name	Description
ACCESS TABLE	An Access system table
LINK	A linked table from a non-ODBC data source
PASS-THROUGH	A linked table from an ODBC data source
SYSTEM TABLE	A Microsoft Jet system table
TABLE	A Microsoft Access table
VIEW	A table from a row-returning, nonparameterized query

⊙ Hands-On 11.13 Creating a List of Database Tables

1. In the VBE window, choose Insert | Module.
2. In the module's Code window, type the following `ListTbls` procedure:

```vba
Sub ListTbls()
    Dim cat As ADOX.Catalog
    Dim tbl As ADOX.Table

    Set cat = New ADOX.Catalog
    cat.ActiveConnection = _
      "Provider=Microsoft.ACE.OLEDB.12.0;" & _
      "Data Source=" & CurrentProject.Path & _
      "\NorthwindStarter.accdb"

    For Each tbl In cat.Tables
      If tbl.Type <> "VIEW" And _
        tbl.Type <> "SYSTEM TABLE" And _
        tbl.Type <> "ACCESS TABLE" Then
          Debug.Print tbl.Name
      End If
    Next tbl
    Set cat = Nothing
```

```
      MsgBox "View the list of tables in " & _
             "the Immediate window."
   End Sub
```

3. Choose Run | Run Sub/UserForm to execute the procedure.

LISTING TABLES AND FIELDS USING THE OPENSCHEMA METHOD

In the previous section, you learned how to enumerate tables in the `Northwind-Starter` database by accessing the `Tables` collection of the ADOX `Catalog` object. The procedures in Hands-On 11.14 and Hands-On 11.15 demonstrate how to use the `OpenSchema` method of the ADO `Connection` object to obtain more information about a database table and its fields.

Hands-On 11.14   Using the OpenSchema Method to List Database Tables

1. In the VBE window, choose Insert | Module.

2. In the module's Code window, type the following `ListTbls2` procedure:

```
Sub ListTbls2()
   ' This procedure lists database tables using
   ' the OpenSchema method
   Dim rst As ADODB.Recordset
   Set rst = CurrentProject.Connection.OpenSchema _
             (adSchemaTables)

   Do Until rst.EOF
     Debug.Print rst.Fields("TABLE_TYPE") & " ->" _
     & rst.Fields("TABLE_NAME")
     rst.MoveNext
   Loop
End Sub
```

3. Choose Run | Run Sub/UserForm to execute the procedure.

The output of the `ListTbls2` procedure is shown below:

```
LINK ->Customers
ACCESS TABLE ->MSysAccessStorage
SYSTEM TABLE ->MSysACEs
SYSTEM TABLE ->MSysComplexColumns
ACCESS TABLE ->MSysNameMap
```

```
ACCESS TABLE ->MSysNavPaneGroupCategories
ACCESS TABLE ->MSysNavPaneGroups
ACCESS TABLE ->MSysNavPaneGroupToObjects
ACCESS TABLE ->MSysNavPaneObjectIDs
SYSTEM TABLE ->MSysObjects
SYSTEM TABLE ->MSysQueries
SYSTEM TABLE ->MSysRelationships
ACCESS TABLE ->MSysResources
LINK ->mySheet
```

To obtain the names of table fields, use `adSchemaColumns` as the parameter for the `OpenSchema` method. The `ListTblsAndFields` procedure in Hands-On 11.15 retrieves the names of fields in each table of the `NorthwindStarter.accdb` database.

⊙ Hands-On 11.15   Listing Tables and Their Fields Using the OpenSchema Method

1. In the VBE's Code window, type the following `ListTblsAndFields` procedure:

```vba
Sub ListTblsAndFields()
  Dim conn As ADODB.Connection
  Dim rst As ADODB.Recordset
  Dim curTable As String
  Dim newTable As String
  Dim counter As Integer

  Set conn = New ADODB.Connection
  conn.Open "Provider=Microsoft.ACE.OLEDB.12.0;" _
   & "Data Source=" & CurrentProject.Path & _
   "\NorthwindStarter.accdb"

  Set rst = conn.OpenSchema(adSchemaColumns)
  curTable = ""
  newTable = ""
  counter = 1
  Do Until rst.EOF
    curTable = rst!table_Name
    If (curTable <> newTable) Then
      newTable = rst!table_Name
      Debug.Print "Table: " & rst!table_Name
      counter = 1
    End If
    Debug.Print "Field" & counter & ": " & _
        rst!Column_Name
```

```
            counter = counter + 1
            rst.MoveNext
    Loop
    rst.Close
    conn.Close
    Set rst = Nothing
    Set conn = Nothing
End Sub
```

2. Open the Immediate window and run the procedure in the Step mode to view the results as they are being generated.

LISTING DATA TYPES

The `ListDataTypes` procedure in Hands-On 11.16 uses the `adSchemaProvider-Types` parameter of the ADO `Connection` object's `OpenSchema` method to list the data types supported by the Microsoft ACE OLE DB 12.0 provider.

(⦿) Hands-On 11.16   Listing Supported Data Types

1. In VBE's Code window, type the `ListDataTypes` procedure shown below.

```
Sub ListDataTypes()
  Dim conn As ADODB.Connection
  Dim rst As ADODB.Recordset

  Set conn=New ADODB.Connection
  conn.Open "Provider=Microsoft.ACE.OLEDB.12.0;" _
   & "Data Source=" & CurrentProject.Path & _
   "\NorthwindStarter.accdb"
  Set rst=conn.OpenSchema(adSchemaProviderTypes)
  Do Until rst.EOF
    Debug.Print rst!Type_Name & vbTab _
    & "Size: " & rst!Column_Size
    rst.MoveNext
  Loop

  rst.Close
  conn.Close
  Set rst = Nothing
  Set conn = Nothing
End Sub
```

2. Choose Run | Run Sub/UserForm to execute the procedure.
The `ListDataTypes` procedure generates the following output:

```
Short Size: 5
Long Size: 10
Single Size: 7
Double Size: 15
Currency Size: 19
DateTime Size: 8
Bit Size: 2
Byte Size: 3
GUID Size: 16
BigBinary Size: 4000
LongBinary Size: 1073741823
VarBinary Size: 510
LongText Size: 536870910
VarChar Size: 255
Decimal Size: 28
```

RETRIEVING THE VALUE AND THE INCREMENT OF THE AUTONUMBER FIELD

When you create a table in an Access database, you can assign an `AutoNumber` data type to a primary key field manually using the Access user interface. The `AutoNumber` is a unique sequential number (incremented by 1) or a random number assigned by Access whenever a new record is added to a table. The procedure in Hands-On 11.17 opens the ADO `Recordset` object based on the `Customers` table in the `NorthwindStarter.accdb` database, retrieves the last used `AutoNumber` value, and determines the current step (increment) value in effect.

Hands-On 11.17   Inspecting the Last Used AutoNumber Value

1. In the VBE window, choose Insert | Module.
2. In the module's Code window, type the `ChangeAutoNumber` procedure shown here:

```
Sub RetrieveLastAutoNumber()
    Dim conn As ADODB.Connection
    Dim rst As ADODB.Recordset
    Dim strSQL As String
    Dim beginNum As Integer
    Dim stepNum As Integer
```

```
Set conn = New ADODB.Connection
conn.Open "Provider = Microsoft.ACE.OLEDB.12.0;" & _
  "Data Source=" & CurrentProject.Path & _
  "\NorthwindStarter.accdb"

Set rst = New ADODB.Recordset
With rst
   .CursorType = adOpenKeyset
   .LockType = adLockReadOnly
   .Open "Customers", conn
   .MoveLast
End With
beginNum = rst(0)
rst.MovePrevious
stepNum = beginNum - rst(0)

MsgBox "Last Auto Number Value = " & _
   beginNum & vbCr & _
  "Current Step Value = " & stepNum, _
  vbInformation, _
  "AutoNumber"

rst.Close
conn.Close
Set conn = Nothing
End Sub
```

3. Choose Run | Run Sub/UserForm to execute the procedure.

The following sections of this chapter focus on the ADOX objects that are designed to work with primary keys, indexes, and relationships between tables.

CREATING A PRIMARY KEY INDEX

Indexes determine the order in which records are accessed from database tables and whether or not duplicate records are accepted. While indexes can speed up access to specific records in large tables, too many indexes can also slow down updates to the database. Each table in your database should include a field (or set of fields) that uniquely identifies each individual record in a table. Such a field or set of fields is called a *primary key*. A primary key is an index with its Unique and Primary properties set to True. There can be only one primary key per table.

In ADO, indexes are created using the `Key` object from the ADOX library. The `Type` property of the `Key` object allows you to determine whether the key is primary, foreign, or unique. For example, to create a primary key, set the `Key` object's `Type` property to `adKeyPrimary`.

The procedure in Hands-On 11.18 demonstrates how to add a primary key to the `tblFilters` table.

Hands-On 11.18   Creating a Primary Key

1. In the VBE window, choose Insert | Module.
2. In the module's Code window, type the following `Create_PrimaryKey` procedure:

```
' make sure to set up a reference to
' the Microsoft ActiveX Data Objects 6.1
' and Microsoft ADO Ext. 6.0 for DDL and Security

Sub Create_PrimaryKey()
Dim cat As ADOX.Catalog
   Dim tbl As ADOX.Table
   Dim pKey As ADOX.Key

   On Error GoTo ErrorHandler

   Set cat = New ADOX.Catalog
   cat.ActiveConnection = CurrentProject.Connection

   Set tbl = New ADOX.Table
   tbl.Name = "tblFilters"

   cat.Tables.Append tbl

   With tbl.Columns
      .Append "ID", adVarWChar, 10
      .Append "Description", adVarWChar, 255
      .Append "Type", adInteger
   End With

   SetKey:
   Set pKey = New ADOX.Key
   With pKey
      .Name = "PrimaryKey"
      .Type = adKeyPrimary
   End With
```

```
pKey.Columns.Append "ID"
tbl.Keys.Append pKey

Set cat = Nothing
Exit Sub

ErrorHandler:
  If Err.Number = -2147217856 Then
    MsgBox "The " & tbl.Name & " is open.", _
      vbCritical, "Please close the table"
  ElseIf Err.Number = -2147217857 Then
    MsgBox Err.Description
    Set tbl = cat.Tables(tbl.Name)
    Resume SetKey
  ElseIf Err.Number = -2147217767 Then
    tbl.Keys.Delete pKey.Name
    Resume
  Else
    MsgBox Err.Number & ": " & Err.Description
  End If
End Sub
```

3. Choose Run | Run Sub/UserForm to execute the procedure.

The `Create_PrimaryKey` procedure begins by creating a table named `tblFilters` in the currently open database and proceeds to set the primary key index on the `ID` field. If the `tblFilters` table already exists, the error-handler code displays the error message and sets an object variable (`tbl`) to point to this table. The `Resume SetKey` statement refers the procedure execution to the label `SetKey`. The code that follows that label defines the primary key using the `Name` and `Type` properties of the `Key` object. Next, the procedure appends the `ID` column to the `Columns` collection of the `Key` object, and the `Key` object itself is appended to the `Keys` collection of the table. Because errors could occur if a table is open or it already contains the primary key, the error handler is included to ensure that the procedure runs as expected.

4. Run this procedure again by stepping through its code line by line (press F8).

CREATING A SINGLE-FIELD INDEX

In ADO, you can add an index to a table by using the ADOX `Index` object. Before creating an index, make sure the table is not open and that it does not already contain an index with the same name. To define an index, perform the following:

1. Append one or more columns to the index by using the `Append` method.
2. Set the `Name` property of the `Index` object and define other index properties, if necessary.
3. Use the `Append` method to add the `Index` object to the table's `Indexes` collection.

You can use the `Unique` property of the `Index` object to specify whether the index keys must be unique. The default value of the `Unique` property is `False`. Another property, `IndexNulls`, lets you specify whether `Null` values are allowed in the index. This property can be set to one of the constants shown in Table 11.6.

TABLE 11.6.　Intrinsic constants for the IndexNulls property of the ADOX index object (see the AllowNullsEnum in the ADOX library).

Constant Name	Description
adIndexNullsAllow	You can create an index if there is a Null value in the index field (an error will not occur).
adIndexNullsDisallow (This is the default value)	You cannot create an index if there is a Null value in the index field for the column (an error will occur).
adIndexNullsIgnore	You can create an index if there is a Null value in the index field (an error will not occur). The Ignore Nulls property in the Indexes window in the user interface will be set to Yes.
adIndexNullsIgnoreAny (This value is not supported by the Microsoft Jet provider)	You can create an index if there is a Null value in the index field. The Ignore Nulls property in the Indexes window in the user interface will be set to No.

The `Add_SingleFieldIndex` procedure in Hands-On 11.19 demonstrates how to add a single-field index called `idxDescription` to the table `tblFilters`.

◉ Hands-On 11.19　Adding a Single-Field Index to an Existing Table

This procedure uses the `tblFilters` table created in Hands-On 11.18.

1. In the module's Code window, type the following `Add_SingleFieldIndex` procedure:

```
Sub Add_SingleFieldIndex()
   Dim cat As New ADOX.Catalog
   Dim myTbl As New ADOX.Table
```

```
Dim myIdx As New ADOX.Index
Dim strTblName As String

On Error GoTo ErrorHandler

strTblName = "tblFilters"
cat.ActiveConnection = CurrentProject.Connection
Set myTbl = cat.Tables(strTblName)

With myIdx
  .Name = "idxDescription"
  .Unique = False
  .IndexNulls = adIndexNullsIgnore
  .Columns.Append "Description"
  .Columns(0).SortOrder = adSortAscending
End With
myTbl.Indexes.Append myIdx

  Set cat = Nothing
  Exit Sub
ErrorHandler:
  If Err.Number = -2147217856 Then
    MsgBox strTblName & " will be closed.", _
      vbCritical, "Warning: Table is Open"
    DoCmd.Close acTable, strTblName, acSaveYes
    Resume
  ElseIf Err.Number = -2147217868 Then
    myTbl.Indexes.Delete myIdx.Name
    Resume
  Else
    MsgBox Err.Number & ": " & Err.Description
  End If
End Sub
```

2. Choose Run | Run Sub/UserForm to execute the procedure.
   After the index properties are set, the `Description` column is appended to the
   index, and the index sort order is set to the default (`adSortAscending`). To set
   the index field's sort order to descending, use the `adSortDescending` constant.
   Next, the index is appended to the `Indexes` collection of the `Table` object.

LISTING INDEXES IN A TABLE

The ADO `Indexes` collection contains all `Index` objects of a table. You can
retrieve all the index names from the `Indexes` collection. The procedure in the

next hands-on exercise demonstrates how to list the names of indexes available in the `NorthwindStarter.accdb` database's `Customers` table in the Immediate window.

(⊙) Hands-On 11.20   Listing Indexes in a Table

1. In the module's Code window, type the following `List_Indexes` procedure:

```
Sub List_Indexes()
  Dim conn As New ADODB.Connection
  Dim cat As New ADOX.Catalog
  Dim tbl As New ADOX.Table
  Dim idx As New ADOX.Index

  With conn
    .Provider = "Microsoft.ACE.OLEDB.12.0"
    .Open "Data Source=" & CurrentProject.Path & _
     "\NorthwindStarter.accdb"
  End With
  cat.ActiveConnection = conn
  Set tbl = cat.Tables("Customers")

  For Each idx In tbl.Indexes
    Debug.Print idx.Name
  Next idx

  conn.Close
  Set conn = Nothing
  MsgBox "Indexes are listed in the Immediate window."
End Sub
```

2. Choose Run | Run Sub/UserForm to execute the procedure and check the procedure output in the Immediate window.

DELETING TABLE INDEXES

Although you can delete unwanted or obsolete indexes from the Indexes window in the Access user interface, it is much faster to remove them programmatically. The procedure in Hands-On 11.21 illustrates how to delete all but the primary key index from the `Customers` table located in the `Northwind-Starter.accdb` database.

(•) Hands-On 11.21   Deleting Indexes from a Table

1. In the module's Code window, type the following `Delete_Indexes` procedure:

```vba
Sub Delete_Indexes()
  ' This procedure deletes all but the primary
  ' key index from the Customers table

  Dim conn As New ADODB.Connection
  Dim cat As New ADOX.Catalog
  Dim tbl As New ADOX.Table
  Dim idx As New ADOX.Index
  Dim count As Integer

  With conn
    .Provider = "Microsoft.ACE.OLEDB.12.0"
    .Open "Data Source=" & CurrentProject.Path & _
      "\NorthwindStarter.accdb"
  End With

  cat.ActiveConnection = conn
Setup:
  Set tbl = cat.Tables("Customers")

  Debug.Print tbl.Indexes.count
  For Each idx In tbl.Indexes
    If idx.PrimaryKey <> True Then
      tbl.Indexes.Delete (idx.Name)
      GoTo Setup
    End If
  Next idx

  conn.Close
  Set conn = Nothing
End Sub
```

2. Choose Run | Run Sub/UserForm to execute the procedure.
Each time you delete an index from the table's `Indexes` collection, you must set the reference to the table because the current settings are lost when an index is deleted. Hence, the `GoTo Setup` statement sends Visual Basic to the `Setup` label to get the new reference to the `Table` object.

3. Run the procedure in Hands-On 11.20 to list the indexes in the `Customers` table. There should be only one index (`PrimaryKey`) left.

CREATING TABLE RELATIONSHIPS

This section demonstrates how you can relate two tables using VBA code. We will establish the most common relationship, known as a *parent-child relationship*. In database terms, this relationship is also called a *one-to-many relationship*. We will create a `Publishers` table as a parent table and a `Titles` table as a child table. Then, we will link them by a parent-child relationship. In this type of relationship, a record in the parent table can have multiple child records in the other table. In other words, when the term *one-to-many* is used, the parent is the *one* (single record) and *many* represents the children (multiple child records) in the other table.

In ADO, to establish a one-to-many relationship between tables, you'll need to perform the following steps:

1. Use the ADOX `Key` object to create a foreign key and set the `Type` property of the `Key` object to `adKeyForeign`. A *foreign key* consists of one or more fields in a foreign table that uniquely identify all rows in a primary table.
2. Use the `RelatedTable` property to specify the name of the related table.
3. Use the `Append` method to add appropriate columns in the foreign table to the foreign key. A foreign table is usually located on the "many" side of a one-to-many relationship and provides a foreign key to another table in a database.
4. Set the `RelatedColumn` property to the name of the corresponding column in the primary table.
5. Use the `Append` method to add the foreign key to the `Keys` collection of the table containing the primary key.

The procedure in Hands-On 11.22 illustrates how to create a one-to-many relationship between two tables: `Titles` and `Publishers`.

(⊙) Hands-On 11.22   Creating a One-to-Many Relationship

1. In the current database (`Chap11.accdb`), create the `Titles` and `Publishers` tables with the fields shown in the following table:

Table Name	Field Name	Data Type	Size
Titles	TitleID	Number	
Titles	PubID	Number	
Titles	Title	Short Text	100
Titles	Price	Currency	
Publishers	PubID	Number	

Table Name	Field Name	Data Type	Size
Publishers	PubName	Short Text	40
Publishers	City	Short Text	25
Publishers	Country	Short Text	25

Hint: Instead of creating these tables manually, write procedures that perform these tasks programmatically (see Hands-On 11.18 for an example).

2. Make `TitleID` the primary key for the `Titles` table and `PubID` the primary key for the `Publishers` table.

3. In the VBE window, choose Insert | Module.

4. In the module's Code window, type the `CreateTblRelation` procedure shown here:

```
Sub CreateTblRelation()
    Dim cat As New ADOX.Catalog
    Dim fKey As New ADOX.Key

    On Error GoTo ErrorHandler

    cat.ActiveConnection = CurrentProject.Connection

    With fKey
       .Name = "fkPubID"
       .Type = adKeyForeign
       .RelatedTable = "Publishers"
       .Columns.Append "PubID"
       .Columns("PubID").RelatedColumn = "PubID"
    End With
    cat.Tables("Titles").Keys.Append fKey
    MsgBox "Relationship was created."

    Set cat = Nothing
    Exit Sub

ErrorHandler:
    cat.Tables("Titles").Keys.Delete "fkPubID"
    Resume
End Sub
```

5. Choose Run | Run Sub/UserForm to execute the procedure.
    If you receive an error while running this procedure, make sure that both tables are closed.

    You can view the relationship between the `Publishers` and `Titles` tables that was created by the `CreateTblRelation` procedure in the Relationships window. To activate this window, switch to the Access application window and choose Database Tools | Relationships. You should see the `Publishers` and `Titles` tables in the Relationships window linked with a one-to-many relationship (see Figure 11.3).

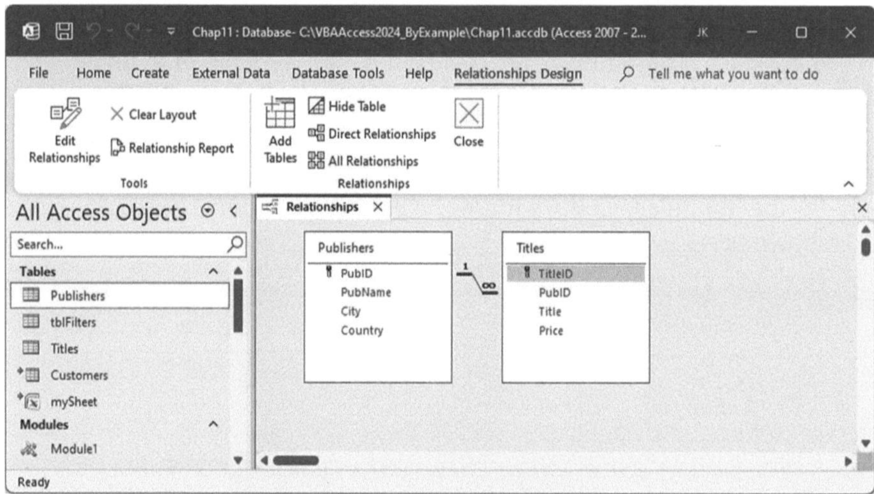

FIGURE 11.3.   The one-to-many relationship between the Publishers and Titles tables was created programmatically by accessing objects in the ADOX library (see the code in the CreateTblRelation procedure in Hands-On 11.22).

INTRODUCTION TO ADO RECORDSETS

The `Recordset` object is one of the three most-used ADO objects (the other two are `Connection` and `Command`). You can open an ADO recordset by using the `Recordset` object's `Open` method. The information needed to open a recordset can be provided by first setting properties and then calling the `Open` method, or by using the `Open` method's parameters like this:

```
rst.Open [Source], [ActiveConnection], [CursorType], [LockType],
[CursorLocation], [Options]
```

Notice that all the parameters are optional (they appear in square brackets). If you decide that you don't want to pass parameters, then use a different syntax to open a recordset. For example, examine the following code block:

```
With rst
  .Source = strSQL
```

```
   .ActiveConnection = strConnect
   .CursorType = adOpenStatic
   .LockType = adLockOptimistic
   .CursorLocation = adUseClient
   .Open Options := adCmdText
End with
```

The preceding code segment opens a recordset by first setting the properties of the `Recordset` object, and then calling its `Open` method. Notice that the names of the required `Recordset` properties are equivalent to the parameter names listed earlier. The values assigned to each property are discussed later. You will become familiar with both methods of opening a recordset as you work with the example procedures that follow.

Let's return to the syntax of the recordset's `Open` method, which specifies the parameters. Needless to say, you need to know what each parameter is and how it is used. The `Source` parameter determines where you want your records to come from. The data source can be an SQL string, a table, a query, a stored procedure or view, a saved file, or a reference to a `Command` object. Later in this chapter, you will learn how to open a recordset based on a table, a query, and an SQL statement.

The `ActiveConnection` parameter can be an SQL string that specifies the connection string or a reference to a `Connection` object. This parameter tells where to find the database as well as what security credentials to use.

Before we discuss the next three parameters, you need to know that the ADO recordsets are controlled by a cursor. The *cursor* determines whether the recordset is scrollable (backward and forward or forward only), whether it is read-only or updatable, and whether changes made to the data are visible to other users.

The ADO cursors have three functions, specified by the following parameters:

- `CursorType`
- `LockType`
- `CursorLocation`

Before you choose the cursor, you need to think of how your application will use the data. Some cursors yield better performance than others. It's important to determine where the cursor will reside and whether changes made while the cursor is open need to be visible immediately. The following subsection should assist you in choosing the correct cursor.

Cursor Types

The `CursorType` parameter specifies how the recordset interacts with the data source and what is allowed or not allowed when it comes to data changes or movement within the recordset. This parameter can take one of four constants: `adOpenForwardOnly` (0), `adOpenKeyset` (1), `adOpenDynamic` (2), and `adOpenStatic` (3).

You can find out the types of cursors that are available by using the Object Browser. Before proceeding, check that the database file you are working with has a reference to the ActiveX Data Objects library. Set this reference by switching to the VBE window and choosing Tools | References. Find and select Microsoft ActiveX Data Objects 6.1 Library in the References dialog box and click OK. Next, activate the Object Browser window by pressing F2 or choose View | Object Browser. Select ADODB from the Project/Library drop-down list box, type `CursorType` in the Search text box, and press Enter (see Figure 11.4).

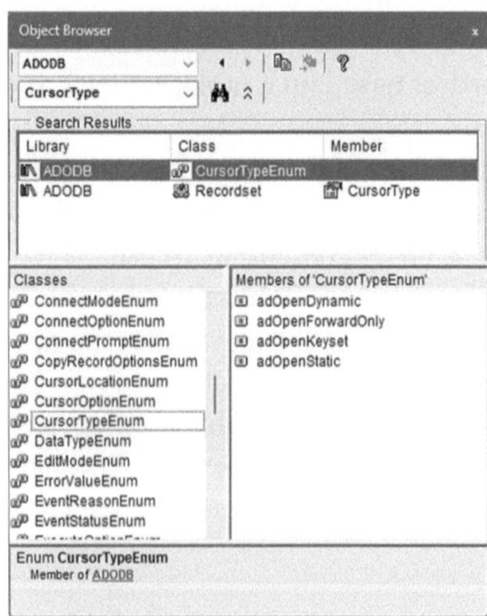

FIGURE 11.4.   The Object Browser lists four predefined constants you can use to specify the cursor type to be retrieved.

- When the cursor type is dynamic (`adOpenDynamic`), users are allowed to view changes other users made to the database. The dynamic cursor is not supported by the Jet 4.0 engine in Microsoft Access. To use this cursor, you must use other OLE DB providers, such as `MSDASQL` or `SQLOLEDB`. When you use the dynamic cursor, you can move back and forth in the recordset.

- When the cursor type is forward-only (`adOpenForwardOnly`), additions, changes, or deletions made by other users are not visible. This is both the default and the fastest cursor because it only allows you to scroll forward in the recordset.

- When the cursor type is keyset-driven (`adOpenKeyset`), you can scroll back and forth in the recordset; however, you cannot view records added or deleted by other users. Use the recordset's `Requery` method to overcome this limitation.

- When the cursor type is static (`adOpenStatic`), all the data is retrieved as it was at a point in time. This cursor is desirable when you need to find data or generate a report. You can scroll back and forth within a recordset, but additions, changes, or deletions by other users are not visible. Use this cursor to retrieve an accurate record count.

You must set the `CursorType` before opening the recordset with the `Open` method. Otherwise, Access will create a forward-only recordset. You may use a constant name or its value in your VBA procedures.

Lock Types

After you choose the cursor type, it is important to specify how ADO should lock the row when you make a change. The `LockType` specifies whether the recordset is updatable. The default setting for `LockType` is read-only. The `LockType` predefined constants are listed in the Object Browser, as shown in Figure 11.5.

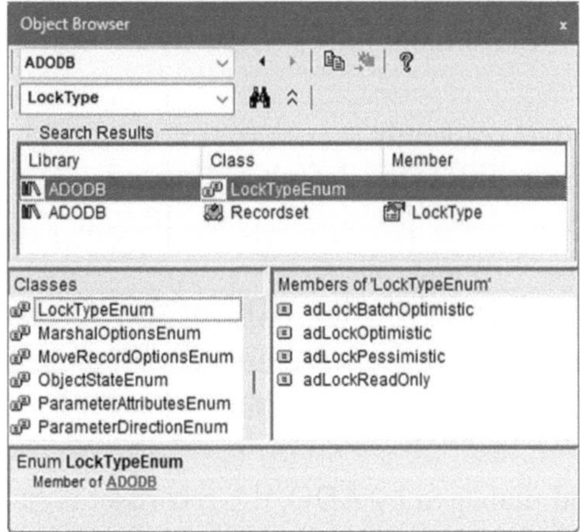

FIGURE 11.5.   The Object Browser lists four predefined constants that you can use to specify what type of locking ADO should use when you make a change to the data.

- When the `LockType` property is batch optimistic (`adLockBatchOptimis-tic`), batch updates made to the data are stored locally until the `Update-Batch` method is called, during which all pending updates are committed all at once. Until the `UpdateBatch` method is called, no locks are placed on edited data. Batch-optimistic locking eliminates network roundtrips that normally occur with optimistic locking (`adLockOptimistic`) when users make changes to one record and move to another. With batch-optimistic locking, a user can make all the changes to all the records and then submit them as a single operation.

- When the `LockType` property is optimistic (`adLockOptimistic = 3`), no locks are placed on the data until you attempt to save a row. Records are locked only when you call the `Update` method, and the lock is released as soon as the save operation is completed. Two users are allowed to update a record at the same time. Optimistic locking allows you to work with one row at a time. If you need to make multiple updates, it's better to save them all at once by using batch-optimistic locking.

- When the `LockType` property is pessimistic (`adLockPessimistic = 2`), all the records are locked as soon as you begin editing a record. The record remains locked until the edit is committed or canceled. This type of lock guarantees that two users will not make changes to the same record. If you use pessimistic locking, ensure that your code does not require any input from the users. You certainly don't want a scenario where a user opens a record and makes a change, then leaves for lunch without saving the record. In that case, the record is locked until the user comes back and saves or discards the edit. In this situation, it is better to use optimistic locking.

- When the `LockType` property is read-only (`adLockReadOnly = 1`), you will not be able to alter any data. This is the default setting.

Cursor Location

The `CursorLocation` parameter determines whether ADO or the SQL Server database engine manages the cursor. *Cursors* use temporary resources to hold the data. These resources can be memory, a disk paging file, temporary disk files, or even temporary storage in the database.

- When a cursor is created and managed by ADO, the recordset is said to be using a *client-side cursor* (`adUseClient`). With the client-side cursor, all the data is retrieved from the server in one operation and is placed on the client computer. Because all the requested data is available locally, the connection to the database can be closed and reopened only when another set of data is needed. Since the entire result set has been downloaded to the client computer, browsing through the rows of data is very fast.

- When a cursor is managed by a database engine, the recordset is said to be using a *server-side cursor* (`adUseServer`). With the server-side cursor, all the data is stored on the server and only the requested data is sent over the network to the user's computer. This type of cursor can provide better performance than the client-side cursor when excessive network traffic is an issue. It's important to point out, however, that a server-side cursor consumes server resources for every active client and, because it provides only single-row access to the data, it can be quite slow.

It is recommended that you use the server-side cursor when working with local Access databases, and the client-side cursor when working with remote Access databases or SQL Server databases.

The `CursorLocation` predefined constants are listed in the Object Browser, as shown in Figure 11.6.

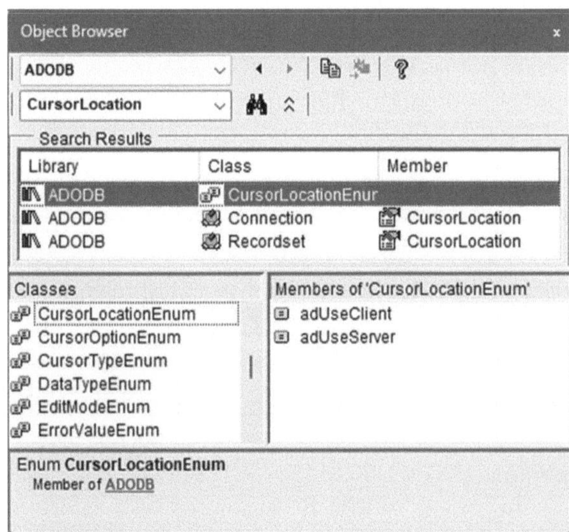

FIGURE 11.6.   The CursorLocation parameter of the Recordset's Open method can be set by using the adUseClient or adUseServer constant.

The Options Parameter

The `Options` parameter specifies the data source type being used. Similar to the parameters related to cursors, the `Options` parameter can take one of many values, as shown in Figure 11.7.

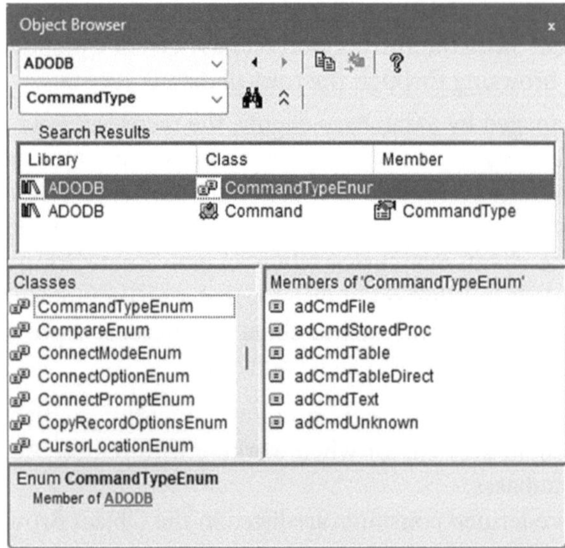

FIGURE 11.7.   The Options parameter of the Recordset's Open method is supplied by the constant values listed under the CommandType property of the Command object.

- When the `Options` parameter is set to `adCmdFile` (256), it tells ADO that the source of the recordset is a path or filename. ADO can open recordsets based on files in different formats.

- When the `Options` parameter is set to `adCmdStoredProc` (4), it tells ADO that the source of the recordset is a stored procedure or parameterized query.

- When the `Options` parameter is set to `adCmdTable` (2), it tells ADO that the source of the recordset is a table or view. The `adCmdTable` constant will cause the provider to generate an SQL query to return all rows from a table or view by prepending `SELECT * FROM` in front of the specified table or view name.

- When the `Options` parameter is set to `adCmdTableDirect` (512), it tells ADO that the `Source` argument should be evaluated as a table name. How does this constant differ from `adCmdTable`? The `adCmdTableDirect` constant is used by OLE DB providers that support opening tables directly by name, using an interface called `IOpenRowset` instead of an ADO `Command` object. Since the `IOpenRowset` method does not need to build and execute a `Command` object, its use results in increased performance and functionality.

- When the `Options` parameter is set to `adCmdText` (1), it tells ADO that you are using an SQL statement to open the recordset.

- When the `Options` parameter is set to `adCmdUnknown` (8), it tells ADO that the command type in the `Source` argument is unknown. This is the default, which is used if you don't specify any other option. By using the `adCmdUnknown` constant, or not specifying any constant at all for the `Options` parameter, you force ADO to make an extra roundtrip to the server to determine the source type. As you would expect, this will decrease your VBA procedure's performance; therefore, you should use `adCmdUnknown` only if you don't know what type of information the `Source` parameter will contain.

> **NOTE**
> *Not all options are supported by all data providers. For example, the OLE DB Provider for Microsoft Jet does not support the* `adCmdTableDirect` *cursors.*

In addition to specifying the type of `CommandType` in the `Options` parameter (see Figure 11.7), you can pass additional information in the `Options` parameter. For example, you can tell ADO how to execute the command by specifying whether ADO should wait while all the records are being retrieved or should continue asynchronously.

Asynchronous Record Fetching

Asynchronous fetching is an ADO feature that allows some records to be downloaded to the client while the remaining records are still being fetched from the database. As soon as the user sees some records, they can begin paging through them. The user does not know that only a few records have been returned. As they page through the rows backward and forward, a new connection is made to the server and more records are fetched and passed to the client's computer. Once all records have been returned, paging is very quick because all records are on the client. Asynchronous fetching makes it seem to the user that the data retrieval is pretty fast. The downside is that records cannot be sorted until they have all been downloaded.

Additional `Options` parameters are described in the following list. Note that only the first three constants (`adAsyncExecute`, `adAsyncFetch`, and `adAsyncFetch-NonBlocking`) can be used with the recordset's `Open` method. Other constants are used with the `Command` or `Connection` object's `Execute` method.

- `adAsyncExecute` (16)—This tells ADO to execute the command asynchronously, meaning that all requested rows are retrieved as soon as they are available. Using `adAsyncExecute` enables the application to perform other tasks while waiting for the cursor to populate.

- o Note that the adAsyncExecute constant cannot be used with `adCmdTableDirect`.
- `adAsyncFetch` (32)—Using this constant requires that you specify a value greater than 1 for the recordset's `CacheSize` property. The `CacheSize` property is used to determine the number of records ADO will hold in local memory. For example, if the cache size is `100`, the provider will retrieve the first 100 records after first opening the `Recordset` object. The `adAsyncFetch` constant tells ADO that the rows remaining after the initial quantity specified in the `CacheSize` property should be retrieved asynchronously.
- `adAsyncFetchNonBlocking` (64)—This option tells ADO that it should never wait for a row to be fetched. The application will continue execution while records are being continuously extracted from a very large data file. If the requested recordset row has not been retrieved yet, the current row automatically moves to the end of the file (causing the recordset's `EOF` property to become `True`). In other words, the data retrieval process will not block other processes.
  - o Note that `adAsynchFetchNonBlocking` has no effect when the `adCmdTableDirect` option is used to open the recordset. Also, `adAsyncFetchNonBlocking` is not supported with a server cursor (`adUseServer`) when you use the ODBC provider (`MSDASQL`).
- `adExecuteNoRecords` (128)—This option tells ADO not to expect any records when the command is executed. Use this option for commands that do not return records, such as INSERT, UPDATE, or DELETE. Use the `adExecuteNoRecords` constant with `adCmdText` to improve the performance of your application. When this option is specified, ADO does not create a `Recordset` object and does not set any cursor properties.
  - o Note that `adExecuteNoRecords` can only be passed as an optional parameter to the `Command` or `Connection` object's `Execute` method and cannot be used when opening a recordset.
- `adExecuteStream` (256)—Indicates that the results of a `Command` execution should be returned as a stream. The `adExecuteStream` constant can only be passed as an optional parameter to the `Command` or `Connection` object's `Execute` method and it cannot be used when opening a recordset.

- adExecuteRecord (512)—Indicates that the value of the CommandText property is a command or stored procedure that returns a single row as a Record object (a Record object represents one row of data).

- adOptionUnspecified (-1)—Indicates that the command is unspecified. This is the default option.

- Note that similar to adExecuteNoRecords, adExecuteStream, and adExecuteRecord, this constant can only be passed as an optional parameter to the Command or Connection object's Execute method and cannot be used when opening a recordset.

Opening a Recordset

ADO offers numerous ways of opening a Recordset object. To begin with, you can create ADO recordsets from scratch without going through any other object. Suppose you want to retrieve all the records from the Employees table. The code you need to write is very simple. Let's try this out in Hands-On 11.23.

Hands-On 11.23   Opening a Recordset

1. In the VBE window, choose Insert | Module.
2. In the module's Code window, type the following OpenADORst procedure:

```
' make sure to set up a reference to
' the Microsoft ActiveX Data Objects 6.1 Library

Sub OpenADORst()
  Dim conn As ADODB.Connection
  Dim rst As ADODB.Recordset

  Set conn = New ADODB.Connection
  With conn
    .Provider = "Microsoft.ACE.OLEDB.12.0"
    .Open "Data Source=" & CurrentProject.Path & _
      "\NorthwindStarter.accdb"
  End With

  Set rst = New ADODB.Recordset
  With rst
    .Source = "SELECT * FROM Employees"
    .ActiveConnection = conn
    .Open
    Debug.Print rst.Fields.Count
```

```
      .Close
   End With

   Set rst = Nothing
   conn.Close
   Set conn = Nothing
End Sub
```

3. Choose Run | Run Sub/UserForm to execute the procedure.

In the preceding code example, we first define and open a connection to the database. Next, we declare a `Recordset` object and create a new instance of it. The `Recordset` object's `Source` property specifies the data you want to retrieve. The source can be a table, query, stored procedure, view, saved file, or `Command` object. The SQL `SELECT` statement tells VBA to select all the data from the `Employees` table. Next, the `ActiveConnection` property specifies how to connect to the data. We set the `ActiveConnection` property to the object variable (`conn`) that holds the connection information. Finally, the `Open` method retrieves the specified records into the recordset. Before we close the recordset using the recordset's `Close` method, we retrieve the number of fields in the open recordset by examining the recordset's `Fields` collection and write the result to the Immediate window.

Opening a Recordset Based on a Table or Query

A recordset can be based on a table, view, SQL statement, or command that returns rows. It can be opened via a `Connection` or `Command` object's `Execute` method or a recordset's `Open` method (see the following example procedures).

- Using the `Execute` method of the `Connection` object:

```
Sub ConnectAndExec()
   Dim conn As ADODB.Connection
   Dim rst As ADODB.Recordset
   Dim fld As Variant

   Set conn = New ADODB.Connection
   conn.Open "Provider=Microsoft.ACE.OLEDB.12.0;" & _
     "Data Source=" & CurrentProject.Path & _
     "\NorthwindStarter.accdb"
   Set rst = conn.Execute("SELECT * FROM Employees")
   Debug.Print rst.Source
   Do Until rst.EOF
     Debug.Print "\\\\\\\\\\\\\\\\\\\\\\\\\\\\\\\"
     For Each fld In rst.Fields
```

```
        Debug.Print fld.Name & "=" & fld.Value
    Next
    'Debug.Print "---new record ---"
    rst.MoveNext
Loop
'Debug.Print rst.Fields(1).Value
rst.Close
Set rst = Nothing
conn.Close
Set conn = Nothing

End Sub
```

Once you open the recordset, you can perform the required operation on its data. In this example, we use the recordset's `Source` property to write to the Immediate window the SQL command on which the recordset is based. Next, we loop through the recordset to retrieve the contents of each field in every record.

- Using the `Execute` method of the `Command` object:

```
Sub CommandAndExec()
    Dim conn As ADODB.Connection
    Dim cmd As ADODB.Command
    Dim rst As ADODB.Recordset

    Set conn = New ADODB.Connection
    With conn
        .ConnectionString = _
            "Provider=Microsoft.ACE.OLEDB.12.0;" & _
            "Data Source=" & CurrentProject.Path & _
            "\NorthwindStarter.accdb"
        .Open
    End With

    Set cmd = New ADODB.Command
    With cmd
        .ActiveConnection = conn
        .CommandText = "SELECT * FROM Customers"
    End With

    Set rst = cmd.Execute

    MsgBox rst.Fields(1).Value

    rst.Close
```

```
    Set rst = Nothing
    conn.Close
    Set conn = Nothing
End Sub
```

Once you open the recordset, you can perform the required operation on its data. In this example, we display a message with the name of the first customer.

- Using the `Open` method of the `Recordset` object:

```
Sub RecSetOpen()
    Dim rst As ADODB.Recordset
    Dim strConnection As String

    strConnection = _
      "Provider=Microsoft.ACE.OLEDB.12.0;" & _
      "Data Source=" & CurrentProject.Path & _
      "\NorthwindStarter.accdb"

    Set rst = New ADODB.Recordset
    With rst
      .Open "SELECT * FROM Customers", _
       strConnection, adOpenForwardOnly
      .Save CurrentProject.Path & "\MyRst.dat"
      .Close
    End With
    Set rst = Nothing
End Sub
```

NOTE	*Once you open the recordset, you can perform the required operation on its data. In this example, we save the entire recordset to a disk file named* MyRst.dat. *Later in this chapter, you will learn how to work with records that have been saved in a file like that.*

The procedure in Hands-On 11.24 illustrates how to open a recordset based on a table or query.

⊙ Hands-On 11.24   Opening a Recordset Based on a Table or Query

1. In the VBE window, choose Insert | Module.
2. In the module's Code window, type the following `OpenRst_TableOrQuery` procedure:

```
Sub OpenRst_TableOrQuery()
    Dim conn As ADODB.Connection
```

```vba
Dim rst As ADODB.Recordset

Set conn = New ADODB.Connection
With conn
  .Provider = "Microsoft.ACE.OLEDB.12.0"
  .Open "Data Source=" & CurrentProject.Path & _
  "\NorthwindStarter.accdb"
End With

Set rst = New ADODB.Recordset
rst.Open "Employees", conn

Debug.Print "CursorType: " & _
  rst.CursorType & vbCr _
  & "LockType: " & rst.LockType & vbCr _
& "Cursor Location: " & rst.CursorLocation

Do Until rst.EOF
  Debug.Print rst.Fields(2)
  rst.MoveNext
Loop

rst.Close
Set rst = Nothing
conn.Close
Set conn = Nothing
End Sub
```

3. Choose Run | Run Sub/UserForm to execute the procedure.

After opening the recordset, it's a good idea to check what type of recordset was created. Notice that this procedure uses the `CursorType`, `LockType`, and `CursorLocation` properties to retrieve this information to the Immediate window. Because we did not specify any parameters in the recordset's `Open` method, we obtained a default recordset. This recordset is forward-only (0), read-only (1), and server-side (2).

To create a different type of recordset, pass the appropriate parameters to the recordset's `Open` method. For example, if you open your recordset like this:

```vba
rst.Open "Employees", conn, adUseClient, adLockReadOnly
```

you will get the static (3), read-only (1), and client-side (3) recordset. In this recordset, you can easily find out the number of records by using the recordset's `RecordCount` property:

```vba
Debug.Print rst.RecordCount
```

Counting Records

Use the `Recordset` object's `RecordCount` property to determine the number of records in a recordset. If the number of records cannot be determined, this property will return −1. The `RecordCount` property setting depends on the cursor type and the capabilities of the provider. To get the actual count of records, open the recordset with the static (`adOpenStatic`) or dynamic (`adOpenDynamic`) cursor.

Is This Recordset Empty?

A recordset may be empty. To check whether your recordset has any records in it, use the `Recordset` object's `BOF` and `EOF` properties. The `BOF` property stands for "beginning of file," and `EOF` indicates "end of file."

❑ If you open a `Recordset` object that contains no records, the `BOF` and `EOF` properties are both set to `True`.

❑ If you open a `Recordset` object that contains at least one record, the `BOF` and `EOF` properties are `False` and the first record is the current record.

You can use the following conditional statement to test whether there are any records:

```
If rst.BOF and rst.EOF Then
  MsgBox "This recordset contains no records"
End If
```

To open a recordset based on a saved query, replace the table name with your query name.

Opening a Recordset Based on an SQL Statement

The procedure in Hands-On 11.25 demonstrates how to use the `Connection` object's `Execute` method to open a recordset based on an SQL statement that selects all the employees from the `Employees` table. Only the name of the first employee is written to the Immediate window. As in the preceding example, the resulting recordset is forward-only and read-only.

◉ Hands-On 11.25 Opening a Recordset Based on an SQL Statement

1. In the VBE window, choose Insert | Module.
2. In the module's Code window, type the CreateRst_WithSQL procedure shown here:

```
Sub CreateRst_WithSQL()
  Dim conn As ADODB.Connection
```

```
Dim rst As ADODB.Recordset
Dim strConn As String

strConn = _
  "Provider = Microsoft.ACE.OLEDB.12.0;" & _
  "Data Source=" & CurrentProject.Path & _
  "\NorthwindStarter.accdb"

Set conn = New ADODB.Connection
conn.Open strConn

Set rst = conn.Execute _
  ("SELECT * FROM Employees")
Debug.Print rst("LastName") & _
  ", " & rst("FirstName")

rst.Close
Set rst = Nothing
conn.Close
Set conn = Nothing
End Sub
```

3. Choose Run | Run Sub/UserForm to execute the procedure.

Opening a Recordset Based on Criteria

Instead of retrieving all the records from a specific table or query, you can use the SQL WHERE clause to get only those records that meet certain criteria. The procedure in Hands-On 11.26 calls the recordset's Open method to create a forward-only and read-only recordset populated with employees who are sales representatives.

Hands-On 11.26   Opening a Recordset Based on Criteria

1. In the VBE window, choose Insert | Module.
2. In the module's Code window, type the following OpenRst_WithCriteria procedure:

```
Sub OpenRst_WithCriteria()
    Dim conn As ADODB.Connection
    Dim rst As ADODB.Recordset
    Dim strSQL As String

    On Error GoTo ErrorHandler
```

```vba
    ' Initialize and open the connection
    Set conn = New ADODB.Connection
    conn.Open "Provider=Microsoft.ACE.OLEDB.12.0;" & _
              "Data Source=" & CurrentProject.Path & _
              "\NorthwindStarter.accdb;"

    ' Define the SQL query
    strSQL = "SELECT * FROM Employees where [JobTitle] = "
    strSQL = strSQL & "'Sales Representative'"

    Debug.Print strSQL

    ' Initialize the recordset
    Set rst = New ADODB.Recordset

    ' Open the recordset
      rst.Open strSQL, conn, adOpenForwardOnly, adLockReadOnly

    ' Process the recordset
    Do While Not rst.EOF
        Debug.Print rst.Fields(1) & " " & rst.Fields(2).Value
        rst.MoveNext
    Loop

    ' Clean up
    rst.Close
    conn.Close
    Set rst = Nothing
    Set conn = Nothing

    MsgBox "Check the Immediate Window for results."

CleanUp:
    Exit Sub

ErrorHandler:
    MsgBox "An error occurred: " & Err.Description
    Resume CleanUp
End Sub
```

3. Choose Run | Run Sub/UserForm to execute the procedure.

Moving Around in a Recordset

You can navigate an ADO recordset by using the following five methods: `Move-First`, `MoveLast`, `MoveNext`, `MovePrevious`, and `Move`. The procedure in the previous hands-on exercise uses the `MoveNext` method to move around in a recordset and retrieve the values from the specified fields.

Finding the Record Position

Use the `AbosolutePosition` property of the `Recordset` object to determine the current record number. This property specifies the relative position of a record in an ADO recordset. The procedure in Hands-On 11.27 opens a recordset filled with employee records from the `Employees` table and uses the `AbsolutePosition` property to return the record number three times during the procedure execution.

Hands-On 11.27   Finding the Record Position

1. In the VBE window, choose Insert | Module.
2. In the module's Code window, type the following `FindRecordPosition` procedure:

```
Sub FindRecordPosition()
   Dim conn As ADODB.Connection
   Dim rst As ADODB.Recordset
   Dim strConn As String

   strConn = _
     "Provider=Microsoft.ACE.OLEDB.12.0;" & _
     "Data Source=" & CurrentProject.Path & _
     "\NorthwindStarter.accdb"

   Set conn = New ADODB.Connection
   conn.Open strConn

   Set rst = New ADODB.Recordset
   With rst
     .Open "SELECT * FROM Employees", _
         conn, adOpenKeyset, _
         adLockOptimistic, adCmdText
     Debug.Print .AbsolutePosition
     .Move 3 ' move forward 3 records
     Debug.Print .AbsolutePosition
     .MoveLast ' move to the last record
     Debug.Print .AbsolutePosition
     Debug.Print .RecordCount
     .Close
   End With
```

```
    Set rst = Nothing
    conn.Close
    Set conn = Nothing
End Sub
```

3. Choose Run | Run Sub/UserForm to execute the procedure.
Notice that at the beginning of the recordset, the record number is 1. Next, the `FindRecordPosition` procedure uses the `Move` method to move the cursor three rows forward, after which the `AbsolutePosition` property returns 4 (1 + 3) as the current record position. Finally, the `MoveLast` method is used to move the cursor to the end of the recordset. The `AbsolutePosition` property now determines that this is the eleventh record. The `RecordCount` property of the `Recordset` object returns the total number of records.

Returning a Recordset as a String

Instead of using a loop to read the values of fields in all rows of the open record-set, you can use the `Recordset` object's `GetString` method to get the desired data in one step. The `GetString` method returns a recordset as a string-valued `Variant`. This method has the following syntax:

```
Variant = Recordset.GetString(StringFormat, NumRows, _
    ColumnDelimiter, RowDelimiter, NullExpr)
```

- The first argument (`StringFormat`) determines the format for representing the recordset as a string. Use the `adAddClipString` constant as the value for this argument.

- The second argument (`NumRows`) specifies the number of recordset rows to return. If blank, `GetString` will return all the rows.

- The third argument (`ColumnDelimiter`) specifies the delimiter for the columns within the row (the default column delimiter is tab (`vbTab`)).

- The fourth argument (`RowDelimiter`) specifies a row delimiter (the default is carriage return (`vbCrLf`)).

- The fifth argument (`NullExpr`) specifies an expression to represent `Null` values (the default is an empty string (`""`)).

⊙ Hands-On 11.28   Converting the Recordset into a String

1. In the VBE window, choose Insert | Module.

2. In the module's Code window, type the `GetRecords_AsString` procedure shown here:

```vb
Sub GetRecords_AsString()
    Dim conn As ADODB.Connection
    Dim rst As ADODB.Recordset
    Dim varRst As Variant
    Dim fso As Object
    Dim myFile As Object
    Dim strSQL As String

    Set conn = New ADODB.Connection
    With conn
      .Provider = "Microsoft.ACE.OLEDB.12.0"
      .Open "Data Source=" & _
      CurrentProject.Path & _
        "\NorthwindStarter.accdb"
    End With

    Set rst = New ADODB.Recordset

    strSQL = "SELECT EmployeeId, "
    strSQL = strSQL & "LastName & "" "" & FirstName "
    strSQL = strSQL & "AS FullName "
    strSQL = strSQL & "From Employees"

    rst.Open strSQL, conn, adOpenForwardOnly, _
     adLockReadOnly, adCmdText

    If Not rst.EOF Then
    ' Return all rows as a formatted string with
    ' columns delimited by Tabs, and rows
    ' delimited by carriage returns

      varRst = rst.GetString(adClipString, , _
      vbTab, vbCrLf)
      Debug.Print varRst
    End If

    ' save the recordset string to a text file
    Set fso = CreateObject _
          ("Scripting.FileSystemObject")
    Set myFile = fso.CreateTextFile _
          (CurrentProject.Path & _
          "\RstString.txt", True)
    myFile.WriteLine varRst
```

```
   myFile.Close

   Set fso = Nothing
   rst.Close
   Set rst = Nothing
   conn.Close
   Set conn = Nothing
End Sub
```

3. Choose Run | Run Sub/UserForm to execute the procedure.

4. In the File Explorer open and review the `RstString.txt` file created by this procedure.

The `GetRecords_AsString` procedure demonstrates how you can transform a recordset into a tab-delimited list of values using the `Recordset` object's `GetString` method. You can use any characters you want to separate columns and rows. This procedure uses the following statement to convert a recordset into a string:

```
varRst = rst.GetString(adClipString, , vbTab, vbCrLf)
```

Notice that the second argument is omitted. This indicates that we want to obtain all the records. To convert only three records to a string, you could write the following line of code:

```
varRst = rst.GetString(adClipString, 3, vbTab, vbCrLf)
```

The `vbTab` and `vbCrLf` arguments are VBA constants that denote the Tab and carriage return characters.

Because `adClipString`, `vbTab`, and `vbCrLf` are default values for the `GetString` method's arguments, you can skip them altogether. Therefore, to put all of the records in this recordset into a string, you can simply use the `GetString` method without arguments, like this:

```
varRst = rst.GetString
```

Sometimes you may want to save your recordset string to a file. To gain access to a computer's filesystem, the procedure uses the `CreateObject` function to access the `FileSystemObject` from the Microsoft Scripting Runtime library. You can easily create a `File` object by using the `CreateTextFile` method of this object. Notice that the second argument of the `CreateTextFile` method (`True`) indicates that the file should be overwritten if it already exists. Once you have defined your file, you can use the `WriteLine` method of the `File` object to write the text to the file. In this example, your text is the variable holding the contents of a recordset converted to a string.

Finding Records Using the Find Method

The ADO object model provides you with two methods for locating records: Find and Seek. This section demonstrates how to use the ADO Find method to locate all the employee records based on a condition. ADO has a single Find method. The search always begins from the current record or an offset from it. The search direction and the offset from the current record are passed as parameters to the Find method. The SearchDirection parameter can be either adSearchForward or adSearchBackward.

⊙ Hands-On 11.29   Finding Records Using the Find Method

1. In the VBE window, choose Insert | Module.
2. In the module's Code window, type the following Find_WithFind procedure:

```
Sub Find_WithFind()
  Dim conn As ADODB.Connection
  Dim rst As ADODB.Recordset

  Set conn = New ADODB.Connection
  conn.Open _
    "Provider=Microsoft.ACE.OLEDB.12.0;" & _
    "Data Source=" & CurrentProject.Path & _
    "\NorthwindStarter.accdb"

  Set rst = New ADODB.Recordset
  rst.Open "Employees", conn, _
        adOpenKeyset, adLockOptimistic

  ' find the first record matching
  ' the criteria
  rst.Find "Title ='Ms.'"
  Do Until rst.EOF
    Debug.Print rst.Fields("Title") & rst.Fields("LastName").Value
    ' search forward starting from the next record
    rst.Find "Title='Ms.'", _
        SkipRecords:=1, _
        SearchDirection:=adSearchForward
  Loop

  rst.Close
  Set rst = Nothing
  conn.Close
  Set conn = Nothing
End Sub
```

3. Choose Run | Run Sub/UserForm to execute the procedure.

To find the last record, call the `MoveLast` method before using `Find`. If none of the records meets the criteria, the current record is positioned before the beginning of the recordset (if searching forward) or after the end of the recordset (if searching backward). You can use the `EOF` or `BOF` property of the `Recordset` object to determine whether a matching record was found.

<table>
<tr><td rowspan="2">

____

NOTE

____</td><td>The ADO `Find` method does not support the `Is` operator. To locate a record that has a `Null` value, use the equal sign (=). For example:</td></tr>
<tr><td>

```
' find records that do not have an entry in the
  Title field

rst.Find "Title = Null"


' find records that have data in the Title field

rst.Find "Title <> Null"
```

</td></tr>
</table>

To find records based on more than one condition, use the `Filter` property of the `Recordset` object, as shown later in this chapter.

Finding Records Using the Seek Method

You can use the `Recordset` object's `Seek` method to locate a record based on an index. If you don't specify the index before searching, the primary key will be used. If the record is found, the current row position is changed to that row. The syntax of the `Seek` method looks like this:

```
recordset.Seek KeyValues, SeekOption
```

The first argument of the `Seek` method specifies the key values you want to find. The second argument specifies the type of comparison to be made between the columns of the index and the corresponding `KeyValues`.

The procedure in Hands-On 11.30 uses the `Seek` method to find the first company with an entry in the `Region` field equal to `"SP"`:

```
rst.Seek "SP", adSeekFirstEQ
```

To find the last record that meets the same condition, use the following statement:

```
rst.Seek "SP", adSeekLastEQ
```

The type of `Seek` to execute is specified by the constants shown in Table 11.7.

TABLE 11.7.   Seek method constants.

Constant	Value	Description
adSeekFirstEQ	1	Seeks the first key equal to KeyValues
adSeekLastEQ	2	Seeks the last key equal to KeyValues
adSeekAfterEQ	4	Seeks a key either equal to KeyValues or just after where that match would have occurred
adSeekAfter	8	Seeks a key just after where a match with KeyValues would have occurred
adSeekBeforeEQ	16	Seeks a key either equal to KeyValues or just before where that match would have occurred
adSeekBefore	32	Seeks a key just before where a match with KeyValues would have occurred

The `Seek` method is recognized only by the Microsoft Jet 4.0/ACE 12.0 databases. To determine whether the `Seek` method can be used to locate a row in a recordset, use the `Recordset` object's `Supports` method. This method determines whether a specified `Recordset` object supports a particular type of feature. The Boolean value of `True` indicates that the feature is supported; `False` indicates that it is not.

```
' find out if the recordset supports the Seek method

MsgBox rst.Supports(adSeek)
```

(◉) Hands-On 11.30   Finding Records Using the Seek Method

1. In the VBE window, choose Insert | Module.
2. In the module's Code window, type the following `Find_WithSeek` procedure:

```
Sub Find_WithSeek(ProductName As String)
    Dim conn As ADODB.Connection
    Dim rst As ADODB.Recordset

    Set conn = New ADODB.Connection
    conn.Open _
      "Provider=Microsoft.ACE.OLEDB.12.0;" & _
      "Data Source=" & CurrentProject.Path & _
      "\NorthwindStarter.accdb"

    Set rst = New ADODB.Recordset
    With rst
      .Index = "ProductName"
      .Open "Products", conn, adOpenKeyset, _
```

```
    adLockOptimistic, adCmdTableDirect

  ' find out if this recordset
  ' supports the Seek method
  MsgBox rst.Supports(adSeek)
  .Seek ProductName, adSeekFirstEQ
End With

If Not rst.EOF Then
  Debug.Print rst.Fields _
      ("ProductCode").Value
End If

rst.Close
Set rst = Nothing
conn.Close
Set conn = Nothing
End Sub
```

3. Execute the procedure from the Immediate window by typing `Find_WithSeek` `"Granola"` and pressing Enter.

   If the `Seek` method is based on a multifield index, use the VBA `Array` function to specify values for the `KeyValues` parameter. For example, the `Orders` table in the `NorthwindStarter` database uses a multifield index as the `PrimaryKey`. This index is a combination of the `OrderID` and `StatusID` fields. To find the order in which `OrderID` = 18 and `StatusID` = 1, use the following statement:

```
rst.Seek Array(18, 1), adSeekFirstEQ
```

Finding a Record Based on Multiple Conditions

ADO's `Find` method does not allow you to find records based on more than one condition. The workaround is using the `Recordset` object's `Filter` property to create a view of the recordset that contains only those records that match the specified criteria. The procedure in Hands-On 11.31 uses the `Filter` property to find the Senior Buyer customers who do not live in Atlanta.

Hands-On 11.31   Finding a Record Based on Multiple Criteria

1. In the VBE window, choose Insert | Module.
2. In the module's Code window, type the `Find_WithFilter` procedure shown here:

```
Sub Find_WithFilter()
```

```vba
Dim conn As ADODB.Connection
Dim rst As ADODB.Recordset

Set conn = New ADODB.Connection
conn.Open _
  "Provider=Microsoft.ACE.OLEDB.12.0;" & _
  "Data Source=" & CurrentProject.Path & _
  "\NorthwindStarter.accdb"

Set rst = New ADODB.Recordset
rst.Open "Customers", conn, adOpenKeyset, adLockOptimistic
rst.Filter = "PrimaryContactJobTitle='Senior Buyer' And " & _
             "City <> 'Atlanta'"
Do Until rst.EOF
  Debug.Print rst!CustomerName.Value & "-->" & _
      rst!PrimaryContactFirstName & " " & _
      rst!PrimaryContactLastName
  rst.MoveNext
Loop

rst.Close
Set rst = Nothing
conn.Close
Set conn = Nothing
End Sub
```

3. Choose Run | Run Sub/UserForm to execute the procedure.

Using Bookmarks

When you work with database records, you must keep in mind that the actual number of records in a recordset can change at any time as new records are added or others are deleted. Therefore, you cannot save a record number to return to it later. Because records change all the time, the record numbers cannot be trusted. Programmers, however, often need to save the position of a record after they've moved to it or found it based on certain criteria. Instead of scrolling through every record in a recordset comparing the values, you can move directly to a specific record by using a bookmark. A *bookmark* is a value that uniquely identifies a row in a recordset.

Use the `Bookmark` property of the `Recordset` object to mark the record so you can return to it later. The `Bookmark` property is read/write, which means that you can get a bookmark for a record or set the current record in a `Recordset` object to the record identified by a valid bookmark. The recordset's

`Bookmark` property always represents the current row. Therefore, if you need to mark more than one row for later retrieval, you may want to use an array to store multiple bookmarks.

A single bookmark can be stored in a `Variant` variable. For example, when you get to a particular row in a recordset and decide that you'd like to save its location, store the recordset's bookmark in a variable, like this:

```
varMyBkmrk = rst.Bookmark
```

`varMyBkmrk` is the name of a `Variant` variable declared with the following statement:

```
Dim varMyBkmrk As Variant
```

To retrieve the bookmark, move to another row, then use the saved bookmark to move back to the original row, like this:

```
rst.Bookmark = varMyBkmrk
```

Because not all ADO recordsets support the `Bookmark` property, you should use the `Supports` method to determine whether the recordset does. Here's how:

```
If rst.Supports(adBookmark) then
  MsgBox "Bookmarks are supported."
Else
  MsgBox "Sorry, can't use bookmarks!"
End If
```

Recordsets defined with a `Static` or `Keyset` cursor always support bookmarks. If you remove the `adOpenKeyset` intrinsic constant from the code used in the next procedure (Hands-On 11.32), the default cursor (`adOpenForwardOnly`) will be used, and you'll get an error because this cursor does not support bookmarks.

Another precaution to keep in mind is that there is no valid bookmark when the current row is positioned at the new row in a recordset. For example, if you add a new record with the following statement:

```
rst.AddNew
```

and then attempt to mark this record with a bookmark:

```
varMyBkmrk = rst.Bookmark
```

you will get an error.

When you close the recordset, bookmarks you've saved become invalid. Also, bookmarks are unique to the recordset in which they were created. This means that you cannot use a bookmark created in one recordset to move to the same record in another recordset. If you clone a recordset (that is, you create a duplicate `Recordset` object), however, a `Bookmark` object from one `Recordset` object will refer to the same record in its clone.

(◉) Hands-On 11.32   Marking Records with a Bookmark

1. In the VBE window, choose Insert | Module.

2. In the module's Code window, type the following `TestBookmark` procedure:

```vba
Sub TestBookmark()
    Dim conn As ADODB.Connection
    Dim rst As ADODB.Recordset
    Dim varMyBkmrk As Variant

    Set conn = New ADODB.Connection
    conn.Open _
        "Provider=Microsoft.ACE.OLEDB.12.0;" & _
        "Data Source=" & CurrentProject.Path & _
        "\NorthwindStarter.accdb"

    Set rst = New ADODB.Recordset
    rst.Open "Employees", conn, adOpenKeyset

    If Not rst.Supports(adBookmark) Then
        MsgBox "This recordset does not " & _
        "support bookmarks!"
        Exit Sub
    End If

    varMyBkmrk = rst.Bookmark
    Debug.Print rst.Fields(1).Value

    ' Move to the 7th row
    rst.AbsolutePosition = 7
    Debug.Print rst.Fields(1).Value

    ' move back to the first row
    ' using bookmark
    rst.Bookmark = varMyBkmrk
    Debug.Print rst.Fields(1).Value
    rst.Close
    Set rst = Nothing
End Sub
```

3. Choose Run | Run Sub/UserForm to execute the procedure.
Notice that this procedure uses the `AbsolutePosition` property of the `Recordset` object. The absolute position isn't the same as the record number. This property can change if a record with a lower number is deleted.

Bookmarks provide the fastest way of moving through rows. You can also use them to filter a recordset, as shown below:

```
Sub Filter_WithBookmark()
   Dim rst As ADODB.Recordset
   Dim varMyBkmrk() As Variant
   Dim strConn As String
   Dim i As Integer
   Dim strCountry As String
   Dim strCity As String

   i = 0
   strCountry = "France"
   strCity = "Paris"

   strConn = _
     "Provider=Microsoft.ACE.OLEDB.12.0;" & _
     "Data Source=" & CurrentProject.Path & _
     "\Northwind.mdb"

   Set rst = New ADODB.Recordset
   rst.Open "Customers", strConn, adOpenKeyset

   If Not rst.Supports(adBookmark) Then
     MsgBox "This recordset does not " & _
     "support bookmarks!"
     Exit Sub
   End If

   Do While Not rst.EOF
     If rst.Fields("Country") = strCountry And _
       rst.Fields("City") = strCity Then
       ReDim Preserve varMyBkmrk(i)
       varMyBkmrk(i) = rst.Bookmark
       i = i + 1
     End If
     rst.MoveNext
   Loop

   rst.Filter = varMyBkmrk()
```

```
  rst.MoveFirst
  Do While Not rst.EOF
    Debug.Print rst("CustomerId") & _
     " - " & rst("CompanyName")
    rst.MoveNext
  Loop
  rst.Close
  Set rst = Nothing
End Sub
```

Using the GetRows Method to Fill the Recordset

To retrieve multiple rows from a recordset, use the `GetRows` method, which
returns a two-dimensional array. Recall that using arrays in VBA procedures
was the main focus of Chapter 6. To find out how many rows were retrieved,
use VBA's `UBound` function, as illustrated in Hands-On 11.33. Because arrays are
zero-based by default, you must add 1 to the result of the `UBound` function to get
the correct record count.

(⊙) Hands-On 11.33   Counting the Number of Returned Records

1. In the VBE window, choose Insert | Module.

2. In the module's Code window, type the following `CountRecords` procedure:

```
Sub CountRecords()
    Dim conn As ADODB.Connection
    Dim rst As ADODB.Recordset
    Dim myarray As Variant
    Dim returnedRows As Integer
    Dim r As Integer ' record counter
    Dim f As Integer ' field counter

    Set conn = New ADODB.Connection
    conn.Open _
      "Provider=Microsoft.ACE.OLEDB.12.0;" & _
      "Data Source=" & CurrentProject.Path & _
      "\NorthwindStarter.accdb"

    Set rst = New ADODB.Recordset
    rst.Open "SELECT * FROM Employees", _
     conn, adOpenForwardOnly, _
          adLockReadOnly, _
          adCmdText

    ' Return all rows into array
```

```
myarray = rst.GetRows()
returnedRows = UBound(myarray, 2) + 1

MsgBox "Total number of records: " & _
        returnedRows

' Find upper bound of second dimension
For r = 0 To UBound(myarray, 2)
   Debug.Print "Record " & r + 1
   ' Find upper bound of first dimension
   For f = 0 To UBound(myarray, 1)
      ' Print data from each row in array
      Debug.Print Tab; _
      rst.Fields(f).Name & " = " & myarray(f, r)
   Next f
Next r

rst.Close
Set rst = Nothing
conn.Close
Set conn = Nothing
End Sub
```

3. Choose Run | Run Sub/UserForm to execute the procedure.
Notice how the `CountRecords` procedure prints the contents of the array to
the Immediate window by using a nested loop.

WORKING WITH RECORDS IN ADO

Now that you've familiarized yourself with various methods of opening, moving
around in a recordset, finding records, and reading the contents of a recordset,
let's look at ADO techniques for adding, modifying, copying, deleting, and sorting records.

Adding and Modifying Records

To add a new record, use the ADO recordset's `AddNew` method. Use the `Update`
method if you are not going to add any more records. In ADO, it is not necessary to call the `Update` method if you are moving to the next record. Calling
the `Move` method implicitly calls the `Update` method before moving to the new
record. Look at the following statements:

```
rst![Last Name] = "Roberts"
rst.MoveNext
```

In this code fragment, the `Update` method is automatically called when you move to the next record.

To modify data in a specific field, find the record and set the `Value` property of the required field to a new value, for example:

```
With rst
   .Open "SELECT * FROM Employees WHERE " _
    & "[Last Name] = 'Roberts'", _
   strConn, adOpenKeyset, adLockOptimistic
   .Fields("City").Value = "Redmond"
   .Fields("State/Province").Value = "WA"
   .Fields("Country/Region").Value = "USA"
   .Update
   .Close
End With
```

Always call the `Update` method if you are not planning to edit any more records. If you modify a row and then try to close the recordset without calling the `Update` method first, ADO will trigger a run-time error.

When adding or modifying records, you can set the record's field values in one of the following ways:

```
rst.Fields("FirstName").Value = "Paul"
```

or

```
rst![First Name] = "Paul"
```

You can modify several fields in a specific record by calling the `Update` method and passing it two arrays. The first array should specify the field names, and the second one should list the new values to be entered. For example, the following statement updates the data in the `City`, `State/Province`, and `Country/Region` fields with the corresponding values:

```
rst.Update Array("City", "State/Province", "Country/Region"),
Array("Redmond", "WA", "USA")
```

Additional code in companion files
File Name: `AddModifyRecords_ADO.txt`

Editing Multiple Records

ADO has the ability to perform batch updates using the `Recordset` object's `UpdateBatch` method. This means that you can edit multiple records and send them to the data provider in a single operation. To take advantage of batch updates, you must use the `Keyset` or `Static` cursor (see the Introduction to

ADO Recordsets section earlier in this chapter for more information about cursors).

Additional code in companion files

File Name: `BatchUpdate_Employee.txt`

Updating Data: Differences Between ADO and DAO

ADO differs from DAO in the way update and delete operations are performed. In DAO, you are required to use the `Edit` method of the `Recordset` object prior to making any changes to your data. ADO does not require you to do this; consequently, there is no `Edit` method in ADO. Also, in ADO, your changes are automatically saved when you modify a record. In DAO, leaving a row without first calling the `Update` method of the `Recordset` object will automatically discard your changes. DAO does not have an `UpdateBatch` method. The `UpdateBatch` method is specific to ADO, which is designed for different types of database operations, including batch updates.

Deleting a Record

To delete a record, find the record you want to delete and call the `Delete` method. After you delete a record, it's still the current record. You must use the `MoveNext` method to move to the next row if you are planning to perform additional operations with your records. An attempt to do anything with the row that has just been deleted will generate a run-time error.

Copying Records to a Word Document

There are several techniques for placing Microsoft Access data in a Microsoft Word document. The procedure in Hands-On 11.34 demonstrates how to use the recordset's `GetString` method to insert invoice data into a newly created Word document.

⊙ Hands-On 11.34   Copying Records to a Word Document

1. Choose Tools | References in the VBE window. Scroll down to locate the Microsoft Word 16 Object Library, click the checkbox next to it, and then click OK to exit.
2. In the VBE window, choose Insert | Module.
3. In the module's Code window, type the following `SendToWord_ADO` procedure:

```
' be sure to select Microsoft Word 16 Object Library
' in the References dialog box
```

```vba
Public myWord As Word.Application

Sub SendToWord_ADO()
  Dim conn As ADODB.Connection
  Dim rst As ADODB.Recordset
  Dim doc As Word.Document
  Dim strSQL As String
  Dim varRst As Variant
  Dim f As Variant
  Dim strHead As String

  Set conn = New ADODB.Connection
  Set rst = New ADODB.Recordset

  conn.Provider = "Microsoft.ACE.OLEDB.12.0;" & _
   "Data Source=" & CurrentProject.Path & _
   "\NorthwindStarter.accdb"

  strSQL = "SELECT * FROM [qryInvoice] WHERE EmployeeID = 10;"

  conn.Open
  rst.Open strSQL, conn, adOpenForwardOnly, _
   adLockReadOnly, adCmdText

  ' retrieve data and table headings into variables
  If Not rst.EOF Then
    varRst = rst.GetString(adClipString, , vbTab, vbCrLf)
    For Each f In rst.Fields
      strHead = strHead & f.Name & vbTab
    Next
  End If

  ' notice that Word application is declared
  ' at the top of the module
  Set myWord = New Word.Application

  ' create a new Word document
  Set doc = myWord.Documents.Add
  myWord.Visible = True

  ' paste contents of variables into
  ' Word document
  doc.Paragraphs(1).Range.Text = strHead & vbCrLf
  doc.Paragraphs(2).Range.Text = varRst
```

```
    On Error GoTo ErrorHandler
    doc.Close SaveChanges:=wdPromptToSaveChanges
EndProc:
    myWord.Quit
    Set myWord = Nothing
    Exit Sub
ErrorHandler:
    If Err = 4198 Then
      MsgBox "You refused to save this document."
    End If
    Resume EndProc
End Sub
```

4. Choose Run | Run Sub/UserForm to execute the procedure.

   The `Recordset` object's `GetString` method is used here to return recordset data as a string-valued `Variant` (see the Returning a Recordset as a String section earlier in this chapter). Prior to running this procedure, you must set a reference to the Microsoft Word 16 object library. This reference allows the procedure to access the Word application objects, properties, and methods via its own library. The top of the module contains the declaration of the `myWord` object variable that will point to the Word application. Notice that this variable is declared with the `Public` scope; therefore, it can be accessed by other procedures in the current VBA project. To launch Word and create a new document, set the `Application` object to a new instance of `Word.Application` using the `New` keyword, like this:

```
Set myWord = New Word.Application
```

   To work with a Word document, the `Add` method of the Word `Documents` collection is used to create a blank document. The reference to this document is then stored in the `doc` object variable. To enable the user to see what's going on while the procedure is running, the `Visible` property of the Word application is set to `True`. Next, the contents of the recordset that we previously saved in the string variable is written to the Word document using the `Document` object's `Paragraphs` property. The procedure ends by prompting the user to save changes to the Word document. If the user does not opt to save the document, error `4198` is triggered.

Copying Records to a Text File

The procedure in Hands-On 11.35 demonstrates how to write the records from the `OrderStatus` table in the `NorthwindStarter.accdb` database to a text file named `OrderStatus`.

◉ Hands-On 11.35   Copying Records to a Text File

1. In the VBE window, choose Insert | Module.
2. In the module's Code window, type the following `WriteToFile` procedure:

```
Sub WriteToFile()
  Dim conn As ADODB.Connection
  Dim rst As ADODB.Recordset
  Dim fld As ADODB.Field
  Dim fso As Object
  Dim txtfile As Object
  Dim strFileName As String

  Set conn = New ADODB.Connection
  conn.Open "Provider=Microsoft.ACE.OLEDB.12.0;" & _
   "Data Source=" & CurrentProject.Path & _
   "\NorthwindStarter.accdb"

  strFileName = CurrentProject.Path & "\OrderStatus.txt"

  Set fso = CreateObject("Scripting.FileSystemObject")
  Set txtfile = fso.CreateTextFile(strFileName, True)

  Set rst = New ADODB.Recordset
  rst.Open "[OrderStatus]", conn, adOpenForwardOnly, adLockReadOnly

  With rst
    For Each fld In .Fields
      ' Write field name to the text file
      txtfile.Write (fld.Name)
      txtfile.Write vbTab
    Next

    ' move to a new line
    txtfile.WriteLine

    ' write out all the records to the text file
    txtfile.Write rst.GetString(adClipString)

    .Close
  End With

  txtfile.Close
  Set rst = Nothing
  conn.Close
```

```
  Set conn = Nothing
End Sub
```

3. Choose Run | Run Sub/UserForm to execute the procedure.
This procedure uses the `CreateObject` function to access the `FileSystemObject`. The `File` object is created using the `FileSystemObject`'s `CreateTextFile` method. The first argument of this method specifies the name of the file to create, and the second argument (`True`) indicates that the file should be overwritten if it already exists. Next, the procedure iterates through the recordset based on the `OrderStatus` table and writes field names to the text file using the `Write` method of the `File` object. The data from the recordset is converted into a string using the `GetString` method of the `Recordset` object and then written to the text file using the `File` object's `Write` method. The text file is then closed with the `Close` method.

Filtering and Sorting Records

To filter records in an ADO recordset, you can use the `Filter` property. This allows you to specify criteria to restrict the view of data to only those records that meet the specified condition.

If the specific set of records you want to obtain is located on SQL Server, however, you should use stored procedures instead of the `Filter` property.

To remove the filter, set the `Filter` property to `adFilterNone`.

The following procedure creates a filtered view of customers who are located in the state of Washington (`WA`).

```
Sub FilterRecords_ADO()
    Dim conn As ADODB.Connection
    Dim rst As ADODB.Recordset
    Dim strConn As String

    ' Define connection string
    strConn = "Provider=Microsoft.ACE.OLEDB.12.0;" & _
    "Data Source=" & CurrentProject.Path & _
    "\NorthwindStarter.accdb"

    ' Initialize and open the connection
    Set conn = New ADODB.Connection
    conn.Open strConn

    ' Initialize and open the recordset
    Set rst = New ADODB.Recordset
    rst.CursorLocation = adUseClient
```

```
    rst.LockType = adLockOptimistic
    rst.CursorType = adOpenKeyset
    rst.Source = "SELECT * FROM Customers"
    rst.ActiveConnection = conn
    rst.Open

    ' Apply a filter to the recordset
    rst.Filter = "State = 'WA'"

    ' Process the filtered records
    Do While Not rst.EOF
        Debug.Print rst("CustomerName"), rst("State")
        rst.MoveNext
    Loop

    ' Clean up
    rst.Close
    Set rst = Nothing
    conn.Close
    Set conn = Nothing
End Sub
```

Use the `Recordset` object's `Sort` property to change the order in which records are displayed. The `Sort` property does not physically rearrange the records; it merely displays the records in the order specified by the index. If you are sorting on nonindexed fields, a temporary index is created for each field specified in the index. This index is removed automatically when you set the `Sort` property to an empty string. In ADO, you can only use `Sort` on client-side cursors. If you use the server-side cursor, you will receive this error The operation requested by the application is not supported by the provider.

The default sort order is ascending. To order a recordset by country in ascending order, then by city in descending order, you would use the following statement:

```
rst.Sort = "Country ASC, City DESC"
```

Although you can use the `Sort` property to sort your data, you will most likely get better performance by specifying an SQL ORDER BY clause in the SQL statement or query used to open the recordset.

The procedure in Hands-On 11.36 displays customer records in ascending order by `State`.

⊙ Hands-On 11.36 Sorting Records

1. In the VBE window, choose Insert | Module.

2. In the module's Code window, type the following `SortRecords_ADO` procedure:

```vba
Sub SortRecords_ADO()
  Dim conn As ADODB.Connection
  Dim rst As ADODB.Recordset

  Set conn = New ADODB.Connection
  conn.Open "Provider=Microsoft.ACE.OLEDB.12.0;" & _
    "Data Source=" & CurrentProject.Path & _
    "\NorthwindStarter.accdb"

  Set rst = New ADODB.Recordset

  ' Apply a sort order to the recordset
  With rst
    .CursorLocation = adUseClient
    .Open "Customers", conn, adOpenKeyset, _
       adLockOptimistic
    .Sort = "State"
    Do Until .EOF
      Debug.Print !CustomerName & ": " & !State
    .MoveNext
    Loop
  End With

  Set rst = Nothing
  conn.Close
  Set conn = Nothing
End Sub
```

3. Choose Run | Run Sub/UserForm to execute the procedure.

Note that to efficiently manage and manipulate data in your recordsets, you can combine filtering and sorting in the same VBA procedure. Start by applying a filter to the recordset using the `Filter` property, and then apply a sort order to the filtered recordset using the `Sort` property.

CREATING AND RUNNING QUERIES WITH ADO

By now, you should feel comfortable handling ADO recordsets. In the following sections of this chapter, we will focus on creating and running Access queries from your VBA procedures.

Creating a Select Query with ADO

In ADO, queries, SQL statements, views, and stored procedures are represented by the `Command` object. This object is part of the ADOX object model. The `Command` object has many properties and methods that will allow you to return records or execute changes to your data (inserts, updates, and deletes). In the following example procedures, you will become acquainted with the properties of the `Command` object, including `ActiveConnection`, `CommandText`, and `CommandType`. These properties will be discussed as they appear in the code examples. You will also learn how to use the `Command` object's `Execute` method to run your queries.

The procedure in Hands-On 11.37 demonstrates how to create and save a select query using ADO.

Hands-On 11.37   Creating a Select Query

1. In the VBE window of the `Chap15.accdb` database, choose Insert | Module.
2. Ensure that the following object libraries are selected in the References dialog box:
   - ADO Ext. 6.0 for DDL and Security Object Library
   - Microsoft ActiveX Data Objects 6.1 Object Library
3. In the module's Code window, type the following `Create_SelectQuery_ADO` procedure:

```
Sub Create_SelectQuery_ADO()
   Dim cat As ADOX.Catalog
   Dim cmd As ADODB.Command
   Dim strPath As String
   Dim strSQL As String
   Dim strQryName As String

   On Error GoTo ErrorHandler

   ' assign values to string variables
   strPath = CurrentProject.Path & _
      "\NorthwindStarter.accdb"
   strSQL = "SELECT Customers.* "
   strSQL = strSQL & "FROM Customers WHERE "
   strSQL = strSQL & "City='Atlanta';"

   strQryName = "Atlanta Customers"
```

```
    ' open the Catalog
    Set cat = New ADOX.Catalog
    cat.ActiveConnection = _
      "Provider=Microsoft.ACE.OLEDB.12.0;" & _
      "Data Source=" & strPath

    ' create a query based on the specified
    ' SELECT statement
    Set cmd = New ADODB.Command
    cmd.CommandText = strSQL

    ' add the new query to the database
    cat.Views.Append strQryName, cmd

    MsgBox "Operation completed successfully.", _
      vbInformation, "Create Select Query"
ExitHere:
    Set cmd = Nothing
    Set cat = Nothing
    Exit Sub

ErrorHandler:
    If InStr(Err.Description, _
      "already exists") Then
          cat.Views.Delete strQryName
      Resume
    Else
      MsgBox Err.Number & ": " & Err.Description
      Resume ExitHere
    End If
End Sub
```

4. Choose Run | Run Sub/UserForm to execute the procedure.

   The `Create_SelectQuery_ADO` procedure opens the `Catalog` object and sets its `ActiveConnection` property:

```
Set cat = New ADOX.Catalog
cat.ActiveConnection="Provider=Microsoft.ACE.OLEDB.12.0;" & _
  "Data Source=" & strPath
```

As you may recall from an earlier discussion, the `Catalog` object represents an entire database. It contains objects that represent all the elements of the database: tables, stored procedures, views, columns of tables, and indexes. The `ActiveConnection` property of the `Catalog` object indicates the ADO `Connection` object the `Catalog` belongs to. The value of this property can be a reference to the `Connection` object or a connection string containing the definition for a connection. Next, the procedure defines a `Command` object and uses its `CommandText` property to set the SQL statement for the query:

```
Set cmd = New ADODB.Command
cmd.CommandText = strSQL
```

The `CommandText` property contains the text of a command you want to issue against a provider. In this procedure, we assigned the string variable's value (`strSQL`) to the `CommandText` property.

The ADO `Command` object always creates a temporary query. So, to create a stored (saved) query in a database, the procedure must append the `Command` object to the ADOX `Views` collection, like this:

```
cat.Views.Append strQryName, cmd
```

When you open the `NorthwindStarter.accdb` database after running this procedure, you will find the `Atlanta Customers` query in the Access window.

Row-Returning, Nonparameterized Queries

Queries that return records, such as select queries, are known as row-returning, *nonparameterized* queries. In ADO, use the `View` object to work with queries that return records and do not take parameters. All `View` objects are contained in the `Views` collection of the ADOX `Catalog` object. To save these queries in a database, append the ADO `Command` object to the ADOX `Views` collection.

Executing an Existing Select Query with ADO

There's more than one way of executing a row-returning query with ADO. This section demonstrates two procedures that run the `qryProducts` query located in the `NorthwindStarter` database. The procedure in Hands-On 11.38 uses the `Command` and `Recordset` objects to perform this task.

⦿ Hands-On 11.38   Executing a Select Query with a Command Object

1. In the VBE window, choose Insert | Module.
2. In the module's Code window, type the `Execute_SelectQuery_ADO` procedure shown here:

```
Sub Execute_SelectQuery_ADO()
    Dim cmd As ADODB.Command
    Dim rst As ADODB.Recordset
```

```
Dim strPath As String

strPath = CurrentProject.Path & _
   "\NorthwindStarter.accdb"

Set cmd = New ADODB.Command
With cmd
   .ActiveConnection = _
        "Provider=Microsoft.ACE.OLEDB.12.0;" & _
     "Data Source=" & strPath
   .CommandText = "qryProducts"
   .CommandType = adCmdTable
End With

Set rst = cmd.Execute
Debug.Print rst.GetString

rst.Close
Set rst = Nothing
Set cmd = Nothing
MsgBox "View results in the Immediate window."
End Sub
```

3. Choose Run | Run Sub/UserForm to execute the procedure.

Notice how the `Command` object's `CommandText` property specifies the name of the query you want to run. You must place square brackets around the query's name when it contains spaces. The query type is determined by setting the `CommandType` property of the `Command` object. Use the `adCmdTable` or `adCmdStoredProc` constants if the query string in the `CommandText` property is a query name. Finally, use the `Execute` method of the `Command` object to run the query. The resulting recordset is passed to the recordset object variable so that you can access the records retrieved by the query. Instead of looping through the records to read the returned records, the procedure uses the `Recordset` object's `GetString` method to print all the recordset rows to the Immediate window. The `GetString` method returns the recordset as a string.

In addition to the ADO `Command` and `Recordset` objects, you can use the ADOX `Catalog` object to run a row-returning query with ADO.

⊚ **Hands-On 11.39   Executing a Select Query with a Catalog Object**

1. In the VBE window, choose Insert | Module.

2. In the module's Code window, type the following `Execute_SelectQuery2_ADO` procedure:

```vba
Sub Execute_SelectQuery2_ADO()
    Dim cat As ADOX.Catalog
    Dim cmd As ADODB.Command
    Dim rst As ADODB.Recordset
    Dim strPath As String

    strPath = CurrentProject.Path & _
        "\NorthwindStarter.accdb"

    Set cat = New ADOX.Catalog
    cat.ActiveConnection = _
        "Provider=Microsoft.ACE.OLEDB.12.0;" & _
      "Data Source=" & strPath

    Set cmd = cat.Views("qryProducts").Command

    Set rst = New ADODB.Recordset
    rst.Open cmd, , adOpenStatic, _
        adLockReadOnly, adCmdTable

    Debug.Print rst.GetString
    MsgBox "The query returned " & _
        rst.RecordCount & vbCr & _
      " records to the Immediate window."
    rst.Close
    Set rst = Nothing
    Set cmd = Nothing
    Set cat = Nothing
End Sub
```

3. Choose Run | Run Sub/UserForm to execute the procedure.
In this procedure, the following line of code is used to indicate the name of the query to be executed:

```vba
Set cmd = cat.Views("Products by Category").Command
```

This statement sets the `cmd` object variable to the desired query stored in the `Views` collection of the ADOX `Catalog` object. Next, the `Open` method of the `Recordset` object is used to open the recordset based on the specified query:

```vba
rst.Open cmd, , adOpenStatic, adLockReadOnly, adCmdTable
```

Notice that several optional arguments of the `Open` method are used to specify the data source: `cmd`, `ActiveConnection` (a comma appears in this spot because the existing connection is being used), `CursorType` (`adOpenStatic`), `LockType` (`adLockReadOnly`), and `Options` (`adCmdTable`). Refer to an earlier section of this chapter for information about using these ADO constants. Next, the procedure dumps the contents of the records into the Immediate window by using the recordset's `GetString` method. The `MsgBox` function contains a string that includes the information about the number of records retrieved. The `RecordCount` property of the `Recordset` object is used to get the record count. To get the correct record count, you must set the `CursorType` argument of the recordset's `Open` method to `adOpenStatic`. If you set this argument to `adOpenDynamic` or `adOpenForwardOnly`, the `RecordCount` property will return -1.

Modifying a Select Query

If you'd like to modify an existing query, follow these steps:

1. Retrieve the query from the `Views` or `Procedures` collection of the `Catalog` object.
2. Set the `CommandText` property of the `Command` object to the new SQL statement.
3. Save the changes by setting the `Procedure` or `View` object's `Command` property to the modified `Command` object.

Earlier in this chapter, you learned how to create a select query named `Atlanta Customers` by using ADO. The following hands-on exercise modifies this query so that customer records are ordered by customer name.

(◉) Hands-On 11.40   Modifying a Select Query

1. In the VBE window, choose Insert | Module.
2. In the module's Code window, type the following `Modify_Query_ADO` procedure:

```
Sub Modify_Query_ADO()
    Dim cat As ADOX.Catalog
    Dim cmd As ADODB.Command
    Dim strPath As String
    Dim newStrSQL As String
    Dim oldStrSQL As String
    Dim strQryName As String
```

```
    strPath = CurrentProject.Path & _
        "\NorthwindStarter.accdb"

    newStrSQL = "SELECT Customers.* FROM " & _
      "Customers WHERE City='Atlanta'" & _
      " ORDER BY [CustomerName];"

    strQryName = "Atlanta Customers"

    Set cat = New ADOX.Catalog
    cat.ActiveConnection = _
      "Provider=Microsoft.ACE.OLEDB.12.0;" & _
      "Data Source=" & strPath

    'Set cmd = New ADODB.Command
    Set cmd = cat.Views(strQryName).Command

    ' get the current SQL statement for this query
    oldStrSQL = cmd.CommandText

    MsgBox oldStrSQL, vbInformation, _
      "Current SQL Statement"

    ' now update the query's SQL statement
    cmd.CommandText = newStrSQL
    MsgBox newStrSQL, vbInformation, _
      "New SQL Statement"

    ' save the modified query
    Set cat.Views(strQryName).Command = cmd

    Set cmd = Nothing
    Set cat = Nothing
End Sub
```

3. Choose Run | Run Sub/UserForm to execute the procedure.
When you run this procedure the `Atlanta Customers` query created in
Hands-On 11.37 is modified from the following SQL statement:

```
SELECT Customers.*
FROM Customers
WHERE City='Atlanta';
```

to:

```
SELECT Customers.*
```

```
FROM Customers
WHERE City='Atlanta' ORDER BY [CustomerName];
```

Creating and Running a Parameter Query

In ADO, to create a row-returning, parameterized query, simply add the parameters to the query's SQL string. The parameters must be defined by using the PARAMETERS keyword, as in the following:

```
strSQL = "PARAMETERS [City] Text;" & _
 "SELECT Customers.* FROM Customers WHERE " _
 & "City=[Type City Name];"
```

The preceding SQL statement begins by defining one parameter called City. This parameter will be able to accept text entries. The second part of the SQL statement selects all the records from the Customers table that have an entry in the City field equal to the provided parameter value. The complete procedure is shown in Hands-On 11.41.

Hands-On 11.41   Creating a Parameter Query

1. In the VBE window, choose Insert | Module.
2. In the module's Code window, type the following Create_ParameterQuery_ADO procedure:

```
Sub Create_ParameterQuery_ADO()
    Dim cat As ADOX.Catalog
    Dim cmd As ADODB.Command
    Dim strPath As String
    Dim strSQL As String
    Dim strQryName As String

    On Error GoTo ErrorHandler

    strPath = CurrentProject.Path & "\NorthwindStarter.accdb"

    strSQL = "PARAMETERS [City Name] Text;" & _
      "SELECT Customers.* FROM Customers WHERE " _
       & "Customers.City=[City Name];"

    strQryName = "Customers by City"

    Set cat = New ADOX.Catalog
    cat.ActiveConnection = _
      "Provider=Microsoft.ACE.OLEDB.12.0;" & _
```

```
    "Data Source=" & strPath

  Set cmd = New ADODB.Command
  cmd.CommandText = strSQL

  cat.Procedures.Append strQryName, cmd
  Set cmd = Nothing
  Set cat = Nothing

  MsgBox "The procedure completed.", _
  vbInformation, "Create Parameter Query"
  Exit Sub

ErrorHandler:
  If InStr(Err.Description, "already exists") Then
    cat.Procedures.Delete strQryName
    Resume
  Else
    MsgBox Err.Number & ": " & Err.Description
  End If
End Sub
```

3. Choose Run | Run Sub/UserForm to execute the procedure.

This procedure creates a simple parameter query with one parameter. Because the ADO `Command` object always creates a temporary query, you must append the `Command` object to the ADOX `Procedures` collection in order to save a parameterized query in a database.

Row-Returning, Parameterized Queries

Queries that return records and take parameters are known as row-returning, parameterized queries. In ADO, use the ADOX `Procedure` object to work with queries that return records and take parameters. All `Procedure` objects are contained in the `Procedures` collection of the ADOX `Catalog` object. To save these queries in a database, append the ADO `Command` object to the ADOX `Procedures` collection.

To execute a parameter query, you must specify the parameter value using the `Parameters` collection of the `Command` object, like this:

```
cmd.Parameters("City Name") = "Atlanta"
```

The procedure in Hands-On 11.42 shows how to run the parameter query created by the procedure in Hands-On 11.41.

◉ Hands-On 11.42 Executing a Parameter Query

1. In the VBE window, choose Insert | Module.
2. In the module's Code window, type the following `Execute_ParamQuery_ADO` procedure:

```
Sub Execute_ParamQuery_ADO(strSearch As String)
    Dim cat As ADOX.Catalog
    Dim cmd As ADODB.Command
    Dim rst As ADODB.Recordset
    Dim strQryName As String
    Dim strPath As String

    strQryName = "Customers by City"
    strPath = CurrentProject.Path & "\NorthwindStarter.accdb"

    Set cat = New ADOX.Catalog
    cat.ActiveConnection = _
      "Provider=Microsoft.ACE.OLEDB.12.0;" & _
      "Data Source=" & strPath

    Set cmd = cat.Procedures(strQryName).Command

    ' specify a parameter value
    cmd.Parameters("[City Name]") = strSearch

    ' use the Execute method of the Command
    ' object to open the recordset
    Set rst = cmd.Execute

    ' return company names to the Immediate window
    Do Until rst.EOF
      Debug.Print rst(1)
      rst.MoveNext
    Loop

    rst.Close
    Set rst = Nothing
    Set cmd = Nothing
    Set cat = Nothing
End Sub
```

3. Execute this procedure from the Immediate window by typing the following statement and pressing Enter:

```
Execute_ParamQuery_ADO "Richmond"
```

Instead of specifying the parameter values before the recordset is open, you can use the `Parameters` argument of the `Command` object's `Execute` method to pass the parameter value, as follows:

```
Set rst = cmd.Execute(Parameters:=strSearch)
```

Executing an Update Query

Executing bulk queries that update data is quite easy with ADO. You can use the `Execute` method of the `Connection` or `Command` object. The procedure in Hands-On 11.43 uses the `Connection` object's `Execute` method to update records in the `Products` table of the `Northwind.mdb` database, where `CategoryId` is equal to `8`. The `UnitPrice` of the records that match this condition will be increased by 1 dollar. Note that the number of updated records is returned by the `Execute` method in the `NumOfRec` variable.

(⦿) Hands-On 11.43   Executing an Update Query

1. In the VBE window, choose Insert | Module.
2. In the module's Code window, type the following `Execute_UpdateQuery_ADO` procedure:

```
Sub Execute_UpdateQuery_ADO(intProductID As Integer)
    Dim conn As ADODB.Connection
    Dim NumOfRec As Integer
    Dim strPath As String

    strPath = CurrentProject.Path & "\NorthwindStarter.accdb"

    Set conn = New ADODB.Connection

    conn.Open "Provider=Microsoft.ACE.OLEDB.12.0;" & _
      "Data Source=" & strPath

    conn.Execute "UPDATE Products " & _
      "SET UnitPrice = UnitPrice + 1" & _
      " WHERE ProductID = " & intProductID, _
      NumOfRec, adExecuteNoRecords

    MsgBox NumOfRec & " records were updated."
    conn.Close
    Set conn = Nothing
End Sub
```

The `Execute_UpdateQuery_ADO` procedure uses the Data Manipulation Language (DML) `UPDATE` statement to make a change in the `UnitPrice` field of the `Products` table. The `Execute` method of the `Connection` object allows the provider to return the number of records that were affected via the `RecordsAffected` parameter. This parameter applies only to action queries or stored procedures. To get the number of records returned by a result-returning query or stored procedure, you must use the `RecordCount` property. In the `Execute_UpdateQuery_ADO` procedure, we store the number of records affected in the string variable `NumOfRec`. Note that when a command does not return a recordset, you should include the constant `adExecuteNoRecords`. This constant can only be passed as an optional parameter to the `Command` or `Connection` object's `Execute` method.

3. Set the breakpoint on the first code line in the `Execute_UpdateQuery_ADO` procedure.
4. Run the procedure from the Immediate window by entering and executing the following statement:

```
Execute_UpdateQuery_ADO 25
```

   Note that the number `25` is the `ProductID` for almonds in the `Products` table.
5. When Access generates the error shown in Figure 11.8, click the Debug button. At this point, Access will highlight in yellow the statement it can't execute.
6. Drag the yellow arrow in the margin area to the `conn.close` line and press F5 to complete the procedure.

   Please note that data macros are covered in detail in a separate chapter of this book devoted to macros. In the `NorthwindStarter` database, data macros are used to help maintain audit fields, such as tracking who created or modified a record, by automatically populating these fields with the user's information. To run your procedure error-free, you must set up a reference to the `NorthwindStarter` database so Access can find and run the function code used in the data macro expression.
7. In the VBE window, choose Tools | References, and click the Browse button.
8. In the Add Reference dialog, choose Microsoft Access Databases (*.accdb) from the drop-down list located to the right of the File name text box, select NorthwindStarter.accdb and click Open.

   You should see the NW2-Starter reference added to the Available References list.
9. Click OK to close the References dialog box.

   The Project window on the VBE screen should display the referenced database's objects and code modules.

10. Rerun the statement you typed earlier in the Immediate window (see step 4 above).

Access should now run the update statement without any issues as it can easily locate and execute the required VBA function.

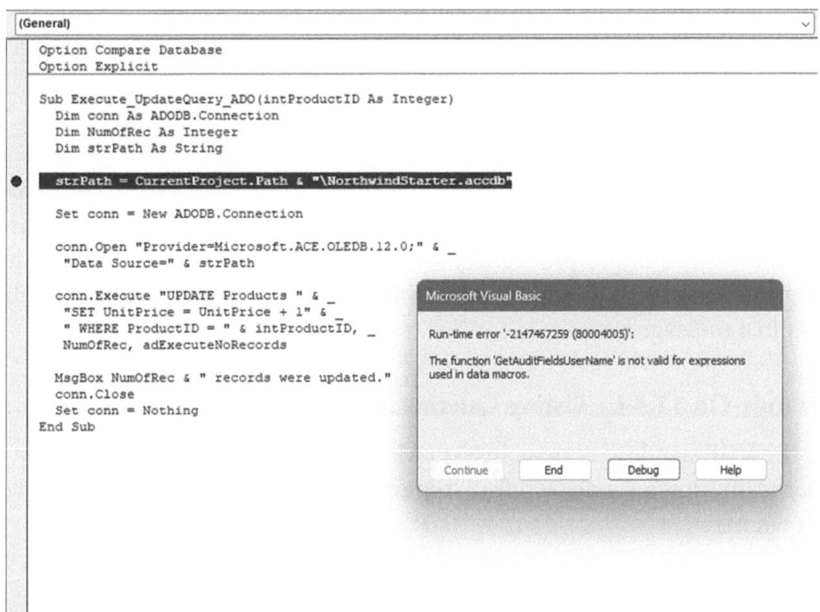

FIGURE 11.8.   When updating remote tables from VBA procedures, there are many potential factors beyond your control that can lead to errors. In this example, the procedure code is correct, yet Access generates a run-time error. The error message indicates that a specific function used in a data macro is needed but is not available to our procedure.

Non-Row-Returning Queries

Queries that do not return records, such as action queries or DDL queries, are known as non-row-returning queries.

❏ Action queries are DML queries that perform bulk operations on a set of records. They allow you to add, update, or delete records.

❏ DDL queries are used for creating database objects and altering the structure of a database.

❏ Use the ADOX `Procedure` object to work with queries that don't return records. All `Procedure` objects are contained in the `Procedures` collection of the ADOX `Catalog` object. To save these types of queries in a database, append the ADO `Command` object to the ADOX `Procedures` collection.

Creating and Running a Pass-Through Query

As mentioned in the previous chapter, SQL pass-through queries are SQL statements that are sent directly to the database server for processing. In ADO, you can use Microsoft OLE DB Provider for SQL Server to directly access SQL Server. For this reason, you do not need to create pass-through queries, and if needed, the typical approach for creating pass-through queries in Access is using DAO.

Listing Database Queries

Retrieving the names of all saved queries in a specific database can be extremely useful for various reasons, especially when managing or auditing databases. In the following example procedure, we retrieve the names of all saved queries using the `Catalog` and `Views` objects in the ADOX object library and display them in a message box.

⦿ Hands-On 11.44   Listing Queries in a Database

1. In the VBE window, choose Insert | Module.
2. In the module's Code window, type the `List_AllQueries_ADO` procedure shown here:

```vba
' you must set up a reference to the ADOX Object Library
'(Microsoft ADO Ext. 6.0 for DDL and Security)

Sub ListAllQueries_ADOX()
    Dim cat As ADOX.Catalog
    Dim view As ADOX.view
    Dim conn As ADODB.Connection
    Dim strConn As String
    Dim strQueryList As String

    On Error GoTo ErrorHandler

    ' Define the connection string to the Access database
    strConn = "Provider=Microsoft.ACE.OLEDB.12.0;" _
        Data Source=" & _
        CurrentProject.Path & "\NorthwindStarter.accdb;"

    ' Initialize and open the ADO connection
    Set conn = New ADODB.Connection
    conn.Open strConn
```

```
    ' Initialize the ADOX Catalog object
    Set cat = New ADOX.Catalog
    Set cat.ActiveConnection = conn

    ' Loop through the Views collection to retrieve query names
    For Each view In cat.Views
        strQueryList = strQueryList & view.Name & vbCrLf
    Next view

    ' Display the list of query names
    MsgBox "Saved Queries in the Database:" & vbCrLf & strQueryList

    ' Clean up
CleanUp:
    conn.Close
    Set cat = Nothing
    Set conn = Nothing

    Exit Sub

ErrorHandler:
    MsgBox "An error occurred: " & Err.Description
    Resume CleanUp
End Sub
```

3. Choose Run | Run Sub/UserForm to execute the procedure.

Deleting a Query

To delete a query in ADO, use the `Delete` method of the `Procedures` or `Views` collection. Let's delete the `Atlanta Customers` query created in Hands-On 11.37.

Hands-On 11.45   Deleting a Query from a Database

1. In the VBE window, choose Insert | Module.
2. In the module's Code window, type the following `DeleteAQuery_ADO` procedure:

```
Sub DeleteAQuery_ADO()
    Dim cat As New ADOX.Catalog
    Dim strPath As String

    On Error GoTo ErrorHandler
```

```
  strPath = _
   CurrentProject.Path & "\NorthwindStarter.accdb"
  cat.ActiveConnection = _
   "Provider=Microsoft.ACE.OLEDB.12.0;" & _
   "Data Source= " & strPath

  cat.Views.Delete "Atlanta Customers"

ExitHere:
  Set cat = Nothing
  Exit Sub
ErrorHandler:
  If Err.Number = 3265 Then
    MsgBox "Query does not exist."
  Else
    MsgBox Err.Number & ": " & Err.Description
  End If
  Resume ExitHere
End Sub
```

3. Choose Run | Run Sub/UserForm to execute the procedure.

In the preceding sections of this chapter, you learned how to use ADO objects to perform the most frequent database operations: create, run, and modify various types of queries. In the remaining sections of this chapter, we focus on using more advanced features of the ADO object model.

USING ADVANCED ADO FEATURES

At this point, you should feel comfortable using ADO in most of your Access programming endeavors. By using the knowledge you've acquired in this chapter, you can basically switch to any other Microsoft 365 application (Excel, Word, PowerPoint, or Outlook) and start programming. Because you already know the ADO methods of accessing databases and manipulating records, all you need to learn is the object model that the specific application is using. Learning a new type library is not very difficult. Recall that VBA offers the Object Browser, which lists all the application's objects, properties, methods, and intrinsic constants that you may need for writing code. If you'd like to accomplish more with ADO, however, the following sections of this chapter will introduce you to a couple of more advanced ADO features that will set you apart from beginner programmers. You will learn about fabricating, persisting, disconnecting, cloning, and shaping recordsets. You will also learn how to process data modifications and additions by using ADO transactions.

Fabricating a Recordset

Until now, you've worked with recordsets that were created from data that came from an Access database, a text or a dBASE file, or an Excel spreadsheet. You may have also practiced working with a recordset generated from an SQL Server database. In each of these circumstances, to get the necessary data, you needed to establish a connection to the appropriate data source. In other words, you worked with recordsets that had a live connection to the data source. These connected recordsets obtained their structure and data from a query to a data source to which they were connected. What if you need to create a recordset with data that does not come from a data source? As you may recall from Chapter 9, Data Access Technologies in Microsoft Access, the ADO object model allows you to work with both relational and nonrelational data stores.

To store nonrelational data in an ADO recordset, you can create your recordset from scratch. This recordset will be defined programmatically in memory and will not be connected to any data source. For example, you can easily fabricate a custom recordset that holds nonrelational data, such as the information about the files located in one of your hard drive's directories.

When you create your own recordset from scratch, you define the types of fields in the recordset and then populate the recordset with the information you want. The fields are defined using the `Fields` collection's `Append` method. You must specify the field name and the data type. The syntax for the `Append` method looks like this:

```
Fields.Append Name, DataType[, FieldSize], [Attribute]
```

The arguments in square brackets are optional. `FieldSize` specifies the size in characters or bytes. `Attribute` specifies characteristics such as whether the field enables `Null` values or whether it is a primary key or an identity column.

Once you have defined the structure of your recordset, simply open it and populate it with the desired data. You can add data to your custom recordset in the same way you add data to a connected recordset: by using the `Recordset` object's `AddNew` method.

The procedures in Hands-On 11.46 demonstrate creating an empty recordset containing three fields (`Name`, `Size`, and `Modified`), populating it with files located in a user-specified file folder, and generating a text file showing the directory listing.

⊙ Hands-On 11.46   Creating a Custom Recordset

1. In the database window, press Alt+F11 to switch to the VBE window.
2. In the VBE window, choose Insert | Module.
3. In the module's Code window, type the following procedures:

```
Sub Custom_Recordset()
  Dim rst As ADODB.Recordset
  Dim strFile As String
  Dim strPath As String
  Dim strFolder As String
  Dim heading As Variant
  Dim listing As String

  Const MyFolder = "C:\VBAAccess2024_ByExample"

  heading = Array("Name", "Size", "Modified")

  strPath = InputBox("Enter pathname, e.g., " & MyFolder, _
   "Enter the Folder Name", MyFolder)

  If Right(strPath, 1) <> "\" Then strPath = strPath & "\"

  strFolder = strPath
  strFile = Dir(strPath & "*.*")

  If strFile = "" Then
    MsgBox "This folder does not contain files."
    Exit Sub
  End If

  Set rst = New ADODB.Recordset
  ' Create an empty recordset with 3 fields
  With rst
    Set .ActiveConnection = Nothing
    .CursorLocation = adUseClient
    With .Fields
      .Append "Name", adVarChar, 255
      .Append "Size", adDouble
      .Append "Modified", adDBTimeStamp
    End With
    .Open
    Do While strFile <> ""
      If strFile = "" Then Exit Do
      ' Add a new record to the recordset
```

```vba
        .AddNew heading, _
         Array(strFile, FileLen(strFolder & strFile), _
         FileDateTime(strFolder & strFile))
        ' get the name of the next file in folder
         strFile = Dir
      Loop
      .MoveFirst
      listing = rst.GetString(adClipString)
      .Close
   End With

   Set rst = Nothing
   'create a text file with directory listing
   CreateTxtFile heading, listing

End Sub


Sub CreateTxtFile(heading As Variant, rst As String)
   Dim fso As Object
   Dim txtfile As Object
   Dim strFileName As String

   strFileName = CurrentProject.Path & "\DirectoryListing.txt"

   Set fso = CreateObject("Scripting.FileSystemObject")
   Set txtfile = fso.CreateTextFile(strFileName, True)

   With txtfile
     ' Write field names to the text file
      .Write heading(0)
      .Write Chr(9)   ' Tab
      .Write heading(1)
      .Write Chr(9)
      .Write heading(2)

      ' move to a new line
      .WriteLine

      ' write out all the records to the text file
      .Write rst

      ' close the text file
      .Close
   End With

End Sub
```

4. Execute the `Custom_Recordset` procedure.
   In the `Custom_Recordset` procedure, we start by creating a `Recordset` object
   variable. To tell ADO that our recordset is not connected to any database, we
   set the `ActiveConnection` property of the `Recordset` object to `Nothing`. We
   also set the `CursorLocation` property to `adUseClient` to indicate that the
   processing will occur on the client machine as opposed to the database server.
   Next, we determine what columns the recordset should contain and add these
   columns to the recordset's `Fields` collection by using the `Append` method.
   Once the structure of your recordset is defined, you can call the `Open` method
   to actually open your custom recordset. Now you can populate the recordset
   with the data you want. We obtain the data by looping through the folder the
   user specified in the input box and reading the information about each file.
   The VBA `Dir` function is used to obtain the filename in the specified path.
   The `FileLen` function is used to retrieve the size of a file in bytes. Another
   VBA function, `FileDateTime`, is used to retrieve the date and time a file was
   last modified. To retrieve the date and time separately, use the `FileDateTime`
   function as an argument of the `DateValue` or `TimeValue` functions.

   For each found file, we use the recordset `AddNew` method to create a new
record. The syntax of the `AddNew` method is shown below:

```
Recordset.AddNew FieldList, Values
```

The `FieldList` can be a single name, or an array of names. In our procedure,
we use the heading array to specify the field names. Because the `FieldList`
is specified as an array, the `Values` must also be specified as an array with the
same number of members. The order of fields must match the order of filed
values in each array. Here's how we do it:

```
.AddNew heading, _
    Array(strFile, FileLen(strFolder & strFile), _
    FileDateTime(strFolder & strFile))
```

The `strFile` will provide the value for the `Name` column, the `FileLen` function
specifies the value for the `Size` column, and the `FileDateTime` function will
populate the `Modified Date` column.

   Once the recordset is fabricated and populated with the required data, you
can save it to a string variable using the `GetString` function and push the data
to another application. In this case, we call the `CreateTxtFile` procedure that
creates a text file with a directory listing based on the passed parameters.

Disconnected Recordsets

In the previous section, you learned how to create a recordset from scratch. This recordset had a structure custom-defined by you and was populated with data that did not come from a database. In other words, it was a disconnected recordset that was defined on the fly. A *disconnected recordset* is a recordset that is not connected to a data source. A disconnected recordset can be defined programmatically (as you saw in Hands-On 11.46) or it can get its information from the data source (as shown in Hands-On 11.47).

Using disconnected recordsets allows you to connect to a database, retrieve some records, return the records to the client, and then disconnect from the database. By keeping your connection to a database open just long enough to obtain the required data, you can help conserve valuable server resources. You can work with the disconnected recordset offline and then connect to the database again to add your changes.

To get started with using disconnected recordsets, perform Hands-On 11.47. The example procedure retrieves some data from the Orders table in the NorthwindStarter database and then disconnects from the database. While disconnected from the database, you can manipulate and examine the content of the retrieved recordset.

Hands-On 11.47   Creating a Disconnected Recordset

1. In the VBE window, choose Insert | Module.
2. In the module's Code window, type the following Rst_Disconnected procedure:

```
Sub Rst_Disconnected()
    Dim conn As ADODB.Connection
    Dim rst As ADODB.Recordset
    Dim strConn As String
    Dim strSQL As String
    Dim strRst As String
    Dim strFilePath As String
    Dim strFile As String
    Dim strPath As String

    strPath = "C:\VBAAccess2024_ByExample\"
    strFile = "NorthwindStarter.accdb"
    strSQL = "SELECT * FROM Customers WHERE " & _
            "State = 'WA'"
    strFilePath = strPath & strFile
```

```vba
strConn = "Provider=Microsoft.ACE.OLEDB.12.0;"
strConn = strConn & "Data Source = " & strFilePath
Set conn = New ADODB.Connection
conn.ConnectionString = strConn
conn.Open

Set rst = New ADODB.Recordset
Set rst.ActiveConnection = conn

' retrieve the data
rst.CursorLocation = adUseClient
rst.LockType = adLockBatchOptimistic
rst.CursorType = adOpenStatic
rst.Open strSQL, , , , adCmdText

' disconnect the recordset
Set rst.ActiveConnection = Nothing

' change the CustomerID in the first
' record to 'OCEAN'
rst.MoveFirst
Debug.Print "Job Title before change: " _
   & rst.Fields("PrimaryContactJobTitle").Value
rst.Fields("PrimaryContactJobTitle").Value = "Unknown"
rst.Update

' stream out the recordset as
' a comma-delimited string
strRst = rst.GetString(adClipString, , ",")
Debug.Print strRst
End Sub
```

3. Choose Run | Run Sub/UserForm to execute the procedure.

To create a disconnected recordset that gets its data from a data source, you need to set the `CursorLocation`, `LockType`, and `CursorType` properties of the `Recordset` object. `CursorLocation` should be set to `adUseClient`. This setting indicates that the cursor will reside on the client computer that is creating the recordset. Set `LockType` to `adLockBatchOptimistic` to enable multiple records to be updated. Finally, set `CursorType` to `adOpenStatic` to retrieve a snapshot of the data.

To disconnect a recordset, you must set the `Recordset` object's `ActiveConnection` property to `Nothing` after you've called the recordset's `Open` method.

When the recordset is disconnected from the database, you can freely manipulate its data or pass it to another application or process. In this example procedure, we manipulate our recordset by changing the value of the `PrimaryContactJobTitle` field in the first retrieved record from `Senior Buyer` to `Unknown`. Then, we create a comma-delimited string using the `Recordset` object's `GetString` method. The content of the disconnected recordset is then printed out to the Immediate window.

Saving a Recordset to Disk

The ADO object library has a `Save` method that allows you to save a recordset to disk and work with it from your VBA application. This method takes two parameters. You must specify a filename and one of the following two data formats:

- `adPersistADTG`—Advanced Data TableGram
- `adPersistXML`—Extensible Markup Language

A *saved* (or *persisted*) *recordset* is a recordset that is saved to a file. This file can later be reopened without an active connection.

In this section, you will persist a recordset into a file using the `adPersistADTG` format. You will work with the `adPersistXML` format in Chapter 20 - Using XML in Access.

To save a recordset in a file, you must first open it. When you have applied a filter to a recordset and then decide to save that recordset, only the filtered records will be saved. Using the `Save` method does not close the recordset. You can continue to work with the recordset after it has been saved. Always remember, however, to close the recordset when you are done working with it.

The procedure in Hands-On 11.48 opens the recordset based on the `Customers` table. Once the recordset is open, the `Save` method is called to persist the customer records into a file.

(⦿) Hands-On 11.48   Saving Records to a Disk File

1. In the VBE window, choose Insert | Module.
2. In the module's Code window, type the following `SaveRecordsToDisk` procedure:

```
Sub SaveRecordsToDisk()
   Dim conn As ADODB.Connection
   Dim rst As ADODB.Recordset
```

```vba
    Dim strFileName As String
    Dim strNorthPath As String

    strFileName = CurrentProject.Path & "\Companies.rst"
    strNorthPath = CurrentProject.Path & "\NorthwindStarter.accdb"

    On Error GoTo ErrorHandler

    Set conn = New ADODB.Connection

    With conn
      .Provider = "Microsoft.ACE.OLEDB.12.0"
      .ConnectionString = "Data Source = " & strNorthPath
      .Mode = adModeReadWrite
      .Open
    End With

    Set rst = New ADODB.Recordset
    With rst
      .CursorLocation = adUseClient
      ' Retrieve the data
      .Open "Customers", conn, _
      adOpenKeyset, adLockBatchOptimistic, adCmdTable

      ' Disconnect the recordset
      .ActiveConnection = Nothing

      ' Save the recordset to disk
      .Save strFileName, adPersistADTG
      .Close
    End With

    MsgBox "Records were saved in " & strFileName & "."
ExitHere:
    ' Cleanup
    Set rst = Nothing
Exit Sub
ErrorHandler:
    If Not IsEmpty(Dir(strFileName)) Then
      Kill strFileName
      Resume
    Else
      MsgBox Err.Number & ": " & Err.Description
      Resume ExitHere
    End If
End Sub
```

3. Choose Run | Run Sub/UserForm to execute the procedure.
   This procedure saves all the data located in the `Customers` table to a file with a `.rst` extension. We named this file `Companies.rst`, but you are free to choose any filename and extension when saving your recordset.

Persisted recordsets are very useful for populating combo boxes or list boxes, especially when the data is located on a server and does not change too often. You can update your data as needed by running a procedure that creates a new dump of the required records and deletes the old disk file. This way, your Access application can display the most recent data without having to connect to a database. Let's look at how you can fill a combo box with a saved recordset by working with Custom Project 11.1.

Custom Project 11.1   Filling a Combo Box with a Disconnected Recordset

NOTE	*This custom project requires that you complete Hands-On 11.48.*

1. In the current database (`Chap11.accdb`), choose Create | Form Design and create an Access form, as shown in Figure 11.9.
2. Use the Ribbon to locate the combo box control and place it on the form.
3. Cancel out of the Combo box wizard.
4. Click the Property Sheet button on the Ribbon.
5. Change the Name property of the unbound Combo0 control to cboCompany.
6. Click the Combo0 label on the form and in the Property Sheet and set the Caption property of the label control to `Company`.
7. Resize the Label and the combo box controls, as shown in Figure 11.9.

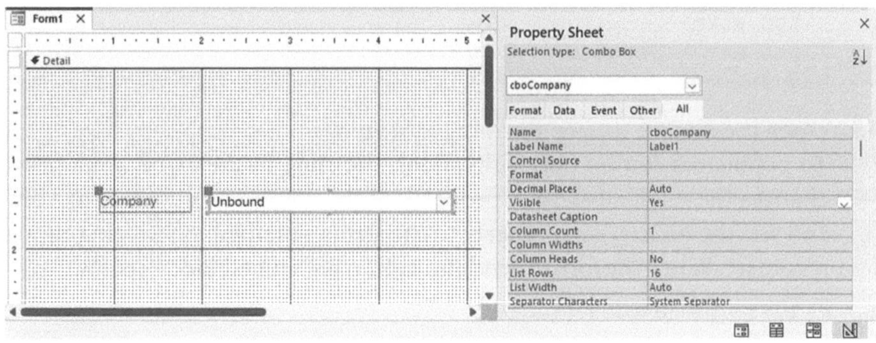

FIGURE 11.9.   This custom form is used to demonstrate how you can fill the combo box control with a disconnected recordset.

8. In the Property Sheet, choose Form from the drop-down box and set the form's Caption property to `DisconnectedCombo`.
9. Set the Form's Record Selectors property to No.
10. Save the form as `frmFillCombo`.
11. In the form's Property Sheet, activate the Event tab, click next to the On Load event name, and click the ellipsis button. In the Choose Builder dialog box, select Code Builder and click OK.
12. Complete the `Form_Load` procedure as shown here:

```vba
Private Sub Form_Load()
    Dim rst As ADODB.Recordset
    Dim strRowSource As String
    Dim strName As String

    strName = CurrentProject.Path & "\Companies.rst"

    Set rst = New ADODB.Recordset
    With rst
      .CursorLocation = adUseClient
      .Open strName, , , , adCmdFile
      Do Until .EOF
       strRowSource = strRowSource & rst!CompanyName & ";"
       .MoveNext
      Loop
      With Me.cboCompany
       .RowSourceType = "Value List"
       .RowSource = strRowSource
       .SetFocus
      End With

      .Close
    End With
    Set rst = Nothing
End Sub
```

13. Open the `frmFillCombo` form in form view.
    To populate a combo box with values, the code in the `Form_Load` procedure changes the `RowSourceType` property of the combo box control to Value List and sets the `RowSource` property to the string obtained by iterating though the recordset. When the form opens, its caption is changed to `DisconnectedCombo`, as shown in Figure 11.10.
14. Close the `DisconnectedCombo` (`frmFillCombo`) form.

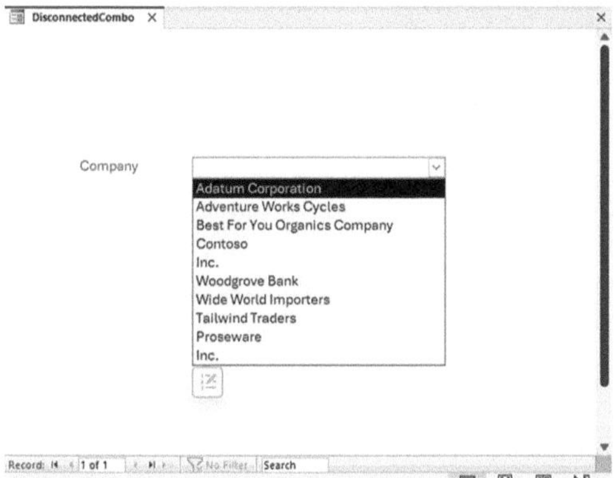

FIGURE 11.10.   After opening the form prepared in Custom Project 11.1, the combo box is filled with the names of companies obtained via a persisted recordset.

Persisted recordsets are especially handy when you need to support disconnected users or when you want to take data on the road with you. You can save the required set of records to a disk file, send it to your users in remote locations, or take it with you. While disconnected from the database, you or your users can view or modify the records. The next time you connect to the database, you can update the original data with your changes using the `BatchUpdate` method. Custom Project 11.2 demonstrates this scenario.

Custom Project 11.2   Taking Persisted Data on the Road

NOTE	*This custom project requires that you complete Hands-On 11.48.*

Part 1: Saving a Recordset to Disk

Before you can take a recordset on the road with you, you must save the records to a disk file. To create the data for this project, prepare and run the procedure in Hands-On 11.48. You should have the `Companies.rst` file available in your `C:\VBAAccess2024_ByExample` folder before you proceed to Part 2.

Part 2: Creating an Unbound Access Form to View and Modify Data

Once you've saved the recordset to a disk file, the recordset becomes portable. You can take the file with you on the road or send it to someone else. Before you or another user can view the data and modify it, however, you need some sort of user interface. In this part, like in Custom Project 11.1, you will create an unbound Access form that will enable you to work with the file that contains the saved recordset.

1. Create a form as shown in Figure 11.11.
   Notice that this form contains only a couple of fields from the Customers table. This form serves only as an example. You can use as many fields as you have saved in the disk file.

2. Add three text boxes and five command buttons to the form.
   Set the following properties for the form's text box controls:

Object	Property	Setting
First unbound text box label	Caption	Company Name:
First unbound text box	Name	txtCompany
Second unbound text box label	Caption	Address:
Second unbound text box	Name Back Color	txtAddress Accent 6
Third unbound text box label	Caption	City:
Third unbound text box	Name	txtCity
Command button 1	Name Caption	cmdFirst First
Command button 2	Name Caption	cmdPrevious Previous
Command button 3	Name Caption	cmdNext Next
Command button 4	Name Caption	cmdLast Last
Command button 5	Name Caption	cmdClose Close Form

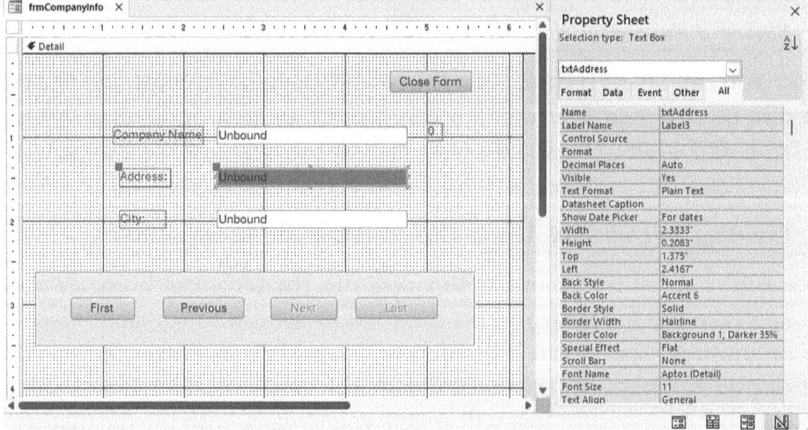

FIGURE 11.11. This custom form is used to demonstrate the use of the saved recordset in an unbound form.

> **NOTE**
>
> *We have set the Back Color property of the* txtCity *text box in the example application to visually indicate that the user can update only this field's data. You can select any color you like.*

3. To visually match the form in Figure 11.11, draw a rectangle control over the command buttons and set its Back Color property to any color you like. Select the rectangle and choose Arrange | Send to Back to move the rectangle behind the command buttons.

4. Add a label control to the right of the first text box (txtCompany) and set its Name property to lblRecordNo and its Caption property to 0.

   In the property sheet, select Form from the drop-down list and activate the Format tab. Set the following properties for the form:

   - Scroll Bars: Neither

   - Record Selectors: No

   - Navigation Buttons: No

5. Save the form as frmCompanyInfo.

Part 3: Writing Procedures to Control the Form and Its Data

The form is now ready and now you need to write a couple of VBA procedures. The first procedure you'll write is an event procedure for the Form_Load event. This procedure will load the form with data from the persisted file. You will start by declaring a module-level Recordset object variable called rst and a module-level Integer variable called counter. You will also write click procedures for all the command buttons and a procedure to fill the text boxes with the data from the current record in the recordset. Let's get started!

1. In the form's property sheet, ensure that the form is selected from the dropdown.
2. Activate the Event tab and click next to the On Load event name.
3. Click the ellipsis button and select Code Builder, then click OK.
4. Enter the code for the Form_Load event procedure, as shown here, starting with the declaration of module-level variables above the procedure:

```
Dim rst As ADODB.Recordset
Dim counter As Integer

Private Sub Form_Load()
  Dim strFileName As String

  strFileName = CurrentProject.Path & "\Companies.rst"
  On Error GoTo ErrorHandler
```

```
Set rst = New ADODB.Recordset
With rst
  .CursorLocation = adUseClient
  .Open strFileName, , adOpenKeyset, _
   adLockBatchOptimistic, adCmdFile
End With

counter = 1
Call FillTxtBoxes(rst, Me)

With Me
  .txtCompany.SetFocus
  .cmdFirst.Enabled = False
  .cmdPrevious.Enabled = False
  .cmdLast.Enabled = True
  .cmdNext.Enabled = True
  .lbRecordNo.Caption = counter
End With
ExitHere:
  Exit Sub
ErrorHandler:
  MsgBox Err.Number & ": " & Err.Description
  If InStr(1, Err.Description, "cannot be found") > 0 Then
    Call SaveRecordsToDisk
  Resume 0
  End If
  Resume ExitHere
End Sub
```

The `Form_Load` event procedure loads `Companies.rst` from a disk file. To fill the text boxes with the data from the current record in the recordset, you need to write the following code:

```
With Me
  .txtCompany = rst!CompanyName
  .txtAddress = rst!Address
  .txtCity = rst!City
End With
```

Because the preceding code will need to be entered in several procedures in this application, you can save yourself a great deal of typing by placing this code in a subroutine and calling it like this:

```
Call FillTxtBoxes(rst, Me)
```

This statement calls the subroutine named `FillTxtBoxes` and passes it two arguments: the `Recordset` object variable and the reference to the current form. The `FillTxtBoxes` procedure (see step 3) is entered in a standard module and contains the code shown in the next step.

The `counter` variable, which was declared at the module level, is initialized to the value of `1`. We will use this variable to control the display of command buttons on the form. The `Form_Load` event procedure ends by setting the focus to the first text box (`txtCompany`) and disabling the first two command buttons. These buttons will not be required when the form first opens on the first record.

5. In the VBE Code window, choose Insert | Module and type the code of the following `FillTxtBoxes` procedure:

```
Sub FillTxtBoxes(ByVal rst As ADODB.Recordset, frm As Form)
   With frm
      .txtCompany = rst!CustomerName
      .txtAddress = rst!Address
      .txtCity = rst!City
   End With
End Sub
```

This procedure fills the three text boxes on the form with the data from the current record in the recordset. This procedure is called from the `Form_Load` event procedure and the click event procedures for each command button. Be sure to double-check the names of the fields in your disconnected recordset as they may be different from the names used for the form's text fields.

6. In the `Form_frmCompanyInfo` Code window, type the following click event procedure for the First command button:

```
Private Sub cmdFirst_Click()
   On Error GoTo Err_cmdFirst_Click

   If rst.Fields("Address").OriginalValue <> Me.txtAddress Then
      rst.Update "Address", Me.txtAddress
   End If
   rst.MoveFirst

   Call FillTxtBoxes(rst, Me)

   With Me
      .txtCompany.SetFocus
      .cmdFirst.Enabled = False
      .cmdLast.Enabled = True
      .cmdPrevious.Enabled = False
      .cmdNext.Enabled = True
```

```
      counter = 1
      .lbRecordNo.Caption = counter
   End With
Exit_cmdFirst_Click:
   Exit Sub
Err_cmdFirst_Click:
   MsgBox Err.Description
   Resume Exit_cmdFirst_Click
End Sub
```

7. In the `Form_frmCompanyInfo` Code window, type the following click event procedure for the Next command button:

```
Private Sub cmdNext_Click()
   On Error GoTo Err_cmdNext_Click

   If rst.Fields("Address").OriginalValue <> Me.txtAddress Then
     rst.Update "Address", Me.txtAddress
   End If
   rst.MoveNext
   counter = counter + 1


   Call FillTxtBoxes(rst, Me)
   Me.cmdFirst.Enabled = True

   Me.cmdPrevious.Enabled = True
   Me.lbRecordNo.Caption = counter
   Me.txtCompany.SetFocus
   If counter = rst.RecordCount Then
     Me.cmdNext.Enabled = False
     Me.cmdLast.Enabled = False
   End If

Exit_cmdNext_Click:
   Exit Sub
Err_cmdNext_Click:
   MsgBox Err.Description
   Resume Exit_cmdNext_Click
End Sub
```

8. In the `Form_frmCompanyInfo` Code window, type the following click event procedure for the Previous command button:

```
Private Sub cmdPrevious_Click()
   On Error GoTo Err_cmdPrevious_Click
```

```
If rst.Fields("Address").OriginalValue <> Me.txtAddress Then
  rst.Update "Address", Me.txtAddress
End If
rst.MovePrevious
counter = counter - 1

Call FillTxtBoxes(rst, Me)

With Me
  .txtCompany.SetFocus
  .cmdLast.Enabled = True
  .cmdNext.Enabled = True
  .lbRecordNo.Caption = counter
End With
If counter = 1 Then
  Me.cmdFirst.Enabled = False
  Me.cmdPrevious.Enabled = False
End If

Exit_cmdPrevious_Click:
  Exit Sub
Err_cmdPrevious_Click:
  MsgBox Err.Description
  Resume Exit_cmdPrevious_Click
End Sub
```

9. In the `Form_frmCompanyInfo` Code window, type the following click event procedure for the Last command button:

```
Private Sub cmdLast_Click()
  On Error GoTo Err_cmdLast_Click

  If rst.Fields("Address").OriginalValue <> Me.txtAddress Then
    rst.Update "Address", Me.txtAddress
  End If
  rst.MoveLast

  Call FillTxtBoxes(rst, Me)

  With Me
    .txtCompany.SetFocus
    .cmdFirst.Enabled = True
    .cmdPrevious.Enabled = True
    .cmdLast.Enabled = False
    .cmdNext.Enabled = False
  End With
```

```
  counter = rst.RecordCount
  Me.lbRecordNo.Caption = counter
Exit_cmdLast_Click:
  Exit Sub
Err_cmdLast_Click:
  MsgBox Err.Description
  Resume Exit_cmdLast_Click
End Sub
```

10. In the `Form_frmCompanyInfo` Code window, type the following click event procedure for the Close Form command button:

```
Private Sub cmdClose_Click()
    DoCmd.Close acForm, "frmCompanyInfo", acSaveYes
End Sub
```

When the Close Form button is clicked, Access will execute the code in the `cmdClose_Click` procedure and proceed to call the code in the `Form_Unload` event procedure shown in step 9.

Notice that all the click event procedures you prepared in steps 4–7 contain the following statement:

```
If rst.Fields("Address").OriginalValue <> Me.txtAddress Then
  rst.Update "Address", Me.txtAddress
End If
```

This statement updates the value of the Address field in the recordset with the current value found in the `txtAddress` text box on the form whenever you make a change to the Address field as you move through the records. Although the user can enter data in other text boxes, all modifications are ignored as there is no code in the click event procedures that will allow changes to fields other than Address. Of course, you can easily change this behavior by adding the necessary lines of code. Depending on which button was clicked, certain command buttons are disabled, and others are enabled. This gives the user a visual clue of what actions are allowed at a particular moment.

To make the form work, we need to write one more event procedure. Before closing the form, we must make sure that the changes to the Address field in the current record are saved and all changes in the Address field we made while working with the form data are written back to the disk file. In other words, we must replace the `Companies.rst` disk file with a new file. This is done in the `Form_Unload` event procedure, as shown in the next step.

11. In the `Form_frmCompanyInfo` Code window, type the code of the `Form_Unload` event procedure, as shown here:

```
Private Sub Form_Unload(Cancel As Integer)
  If rst.Fields("Address").OriginalValue <> Me.txtAddress Then
    rst.Update "Address", Me.txtAddress
  End If
  rst.Save CurrentProject.Path & "\Companies.rst", _
  adPersistADTG
End Sub
```

ADO recordsets have a special property called `OriginalValue`, which is used for storing original values that were retrieved from a database. These original values are left unchanged while you edit the recordset offline. Any changes to the data made locally are recorded using the `Value` property of the `Recordset` object. The `OriginalValue` property is updated with the values changed locally when you reconnect to the database and perform an `UpdateBatch` operation (see part 5 in this custom project).

The `Form_Unload` event occurs when you attempt to close a form but before the form is removed from the screen. This is a good place to perform those operations that must be executed before the form is closed. In the `Form_Unload` procedure, we use the recordset's `OriginalValue` property to check whether changes were made to the content of the `Address` field in the current record. If `OriginalValue` is different from the value found in the current record's `txtAddress` text box, we want to save the record by using the `Update` method of the recordset. Next, we save the current recordset to a file with the same name.

Part 4: Viewing and Editing Data Offline

All the procedures we need for this custom project are now ready, so let's test it out.

1. Open the `frmCompanyInfo` form in form view.

2. In the first record, enter `100 Oak Street` in the Address text box.

3. Click the Last button, then change the street number to `999`.

4. Click the First button and notice that the value of Address matches what you entered in step 2.

5. Use the Next button until you reach the fourth record and enter a new street address of your choice.

6. Click the Close Form button to close the form.

7. Reopen the form and check whether the values in the Address text box in the first, fourth, and last records match your previous entries.
8. Close the `frmCompanyInfo` form.

Part 5: Connecting to a Database to Update the Original Data

After you've made changes to the data by using the custom form, you can send the file with the modified recordset to any of your database administrators so that they can update the underlying database with your changes. Let's write a procedure that will take care of the update.

NOTE	*The procedure that you are about to write will modify the* `Customers` *table in the* `NorthwindStarter` *database. I recommend that you take a few minutes now and create a copy of this database so that you can restore the original data later if necessary.*

1. In the VBE window of the `Chap11.accdb` database, choose Insert | Module.
2. In the module's Code window, type the following `UpdateDb` procedure:

```vba
Sub UpdateDb()
    Dim conn As ADODB.Connection
    Dim rst As ADODB.Recordset
    Dim strNorthPath As String
    Dim strRecStat As String

    On Error GoTo ErrorHandler
    strNorthPath = CurrentProject.Path & "\NorthwindStarter.accdb"

    ' Open the connection to the database
    Set conn = New ADODB.Connection
    With conn
        .Provider = "Microsoft.ACE.OLEDB.12.0"
        .ConnectionString = "Data Source = " & strNorthPath
        .Mode = adModeReadWrite
        .Open
    End With

    ' Open the recordset from the local file
    ' that was persisted to the hard drive
    ' and update the data source with the changes
    Set rst = New ADODB.Recordset
    With rst
        .CursorLocation = adUseClient
```

```
      .Open CurrentProject.Path & "\Companies.rst", conn, _
          adOpenKeyset, adLockBatchOptimistic, adCmdFile
      .UpdateBatch adAffectAll

      ' Check if there were records with conflicts
      ' during the update
      .Filter = adFilterAffectedRecords
      Do Until .EOF

      If !Address.Status = adRecOK Then
          Debug.Print !CustomerID & _
            " address was successfully updated to " & _
            !Address & "." & vbCrLf
      End If

      strRecStat = strRecStat & !CustomerID & "->" & _
          !Address & ":" & !Address.Status & vbCrLf
      .MoveNext
      Loop
      .Close
      If strRecStat <> "" Then
          Debug.Print strRecStat
      Else
          Debug.Print "The Recordset was not changed."
      End If
   End With

ExitHere:
   Set rst = Nothing
   Set conn = Nothing
      ' Generate a new Companies.rst file with
      ' the updated recorset so it is available
      ' the next time you want to work with the form
      Call SaveRecordsToDisk

   Exit Sub
ErrorHandler:
   MsgBox Err.Number & ": " & Err.Description
   Resume ExitHere
End Sub
```

3. Choose Run | Run Sub/UserForm to execute the procedure.

In the `UpdateDb` procedure, we used the `UpdateBatch` method of the ADO `Recordset` object to update the underlying database with the changes we made to the data while working with it offline using the `frmCompanyInfo` form. The `UpdateBatch` method takes an optional parameter that determines how many records will be affected by the update. This parameter can be one of the constants shown in Table 11.8.

TABLE 11.8. The enumerated constants used with the UpdateBatch method.

Constant	Value	Description
adAffectCurrent	1	Pending changes will be written only for the current record.
adAffectGroup	2	Pending changes will be written for the records that satisfy the current filter.
adAffectAll	3	Pending changes will be written for all the records in the recordset. This is the default.

When you update the data, your changes are compared with values that are currently in the database table. The update will fail if the record was deleted or updated in the underlying database since the recordset was saved to disk. Therefore, after calling the `UpdateBatch` method, you should check the status of the records to locate records with conflicts. To do this, we must filter the recordset to see only the affected records:

```
rst.Filter = adFilterAffectedRecords
```

Next, we loop through the recordset and check the `Status` property of each record. This property can return different values, as shown in Table 11.9. You can locate these values in the Object Browser by typing `RecordStatusEnum` in the search box.

TABLE 11.9. The RecordStatusEnum constants returned by the Status property.

Constant	Value	Description
adRecCanceled	256	The record was not saved because the operation was canceled.
adRecCantRelease	1024	The new record was not saved because the existing record was locked.
adRecConcurrencyViolation	2048	The record was not saved because optimistic concurrency was in use.
adRecDBDeleted	262144	The record has already been deleted from the data source.
adRecDeleted	4	The record was deleted.
adRecIntegrityViolation	4096	The record was not saved because the user violated integrity constraints.
adRecInvalid	16	The record was not saved because its bookmark is invalid.

Constant	Value	Description
adRecMaxChangesExceeded	8192	The record was not saved because there were too many pending changes.
adRecModified	2	The record was modified.
adRecMultipleChanges	64	The record was not saved because it would have affected multiple records.
adRecNew	1	The record is new.
adRecObjectOpen	16384	The record was not saved because of a conflict with an open storage object.
adRecOK	0	The record was successfully updated.
adRecOutOfMemory	32768	The record was not saved because the computer has run out of memory.
adRecPendingChanges	128	The record was not saved because it refers to a pending insert.
adRecPermissionDenied	65536	The record was not saved because the user has insufficient permissions.
adRecSchemaViolation	131072	The record was not saved because it violates the structure of the underlying database.
adRecUnmodified	8	The record was not modified.

If the record was successfully updated, then its `Status` property is `adRecOK` (see Table 11.9 above) and we print a message to the Immediate window. We also collect all the information about the updates in the `strRecStat` variable and print it to the Immediate window.

While iterating through the recordset, you can add additional code to resolve any encountered conflicts or check, for example, the original value and the updated value of the fields in updated records. As mentioned earlier, the `OriginalValue` property returns the field value that existed prior to any changes (since the last `Update` method was called). You can cancel all pending updates by using the `CancelBatch` method.

When you execute the `UpdateDb` procedure, your changes are written to the database. At the end of the procedure, we call the `SaveRecordsToDisk` procedure to generate the updated disconnected recordset.

4. Open the `NorthwindStarter` database and review the content of the Address field in the `Customers` table. You should see the changes you made in the first, fourth, and last records. The same changes should be visible in the linked `Customers` table in the current `Chap11.accdb` database.

5. Close the `NorthwindStarter.accdb` database and the Access window in which it was displayed. Do not close the `Chap11.accdb` database.

This completes Custom Project 11.2 in which you learned how to:

- Save the recordset to disk with the `Save` method.
- Create a custom form to view and edit the recordset data in the disk file.
- Open the recordset from disk with the `Open` method.
- Work with the recordset offline (view and edit data).
- Reopen the connection to the original database and write your changes with the `UpdateBatch` method.

Cloning a Recordset

Sometimes you may want to manipulate a recordset without losing the current position in the recordset. You can do this by *cloning* your original recordset. Use the ADO `Clone` method to create a recordset that is a copy of another recordset. You can create a recordset clone like this:

```
Dim rstOrg As ADODB.Recordset  ' your original recordset
Dim rstClone As ADODB.Recordset      ' cloned recordset

Set rstClone = rstOrg.Clone
```

As you can see from the assignment statement, the `rstClone` object variable contains a reference to the original recordset. After you've used the `Clone` method, you end up with two copies of the recordset that contain the same records but can be filtered and manipulated separately. You can create more than one clone of the original recordset.

Use the `Clone` method when you want to perform an operation on a recordset that requires multiple current records. The `Clone` object and the original `Recordset` object each have their own current records; therefore, the record pointers in the original and cloned recordsets can move independently of one another. Also, because the clone points to the same set of data as the original, any changes made using either the original recordset or any of its clones will be visible in the original and its clones. The original recordset and its clones can, however, get out of sync if you requery the original recordset against the database. When you close the original recordset, the clones remain open until you close them. Closing any of the clones does not close the original recordset.

Because the `Clone` method does not create another copy of the data (it only points to the data), cloning a recordset is faster and more efficient than opening a second recordset based on the same criteria. A recordset created by a method other than cloning will have a different set of bookmarks than the original re-cordset, even when it is based on the same SQL statement.

You can make a clone read-only by using an optional parameter like this:

```
Set rstClone = rstOrg.Clone(adLockReadOnly)
```

It's worth mentioning that you can only clone bookmarkable recordsets. Use the `Recordset` object's `Supports` method to find out whether the recordset supports bookmarks (see the Using Bookmarks section in this chapter). If you try to clone a non-bookmarkable recordset, you will receive a run-time error. The clone and the original recordset have the same bookmarks, which you can share. A bookmark reference from one `Recordset` object refers to the same record in any of its clones.

Custom Project 11.3 demonstrates how the `Clone` method can be used to create a single form for displaying the current and previous records side by side (see Figure 11.12).

Custom Project 11.3   Displaying the Contents of the Current and Previous Records by Using the Clone Method

1. In the main Access window of the `Chap11.accdb` database, make sure that you have a table called `Customers`. If this table is missing, choose External Data | Access.

2. In the File name box of the Get External Data dialog box, enter `C:\ VBAAccess2024_ByExample\NorthwindStarter`, and then click OK. In the Import Objects window, select the Customers table and click OK. Click Close to exit the Get External Data dialog box.

3. Choose Create | Form Design and create a form like the one depicted in Figure 11.12. The following steps will help you set up the form and various control properties.

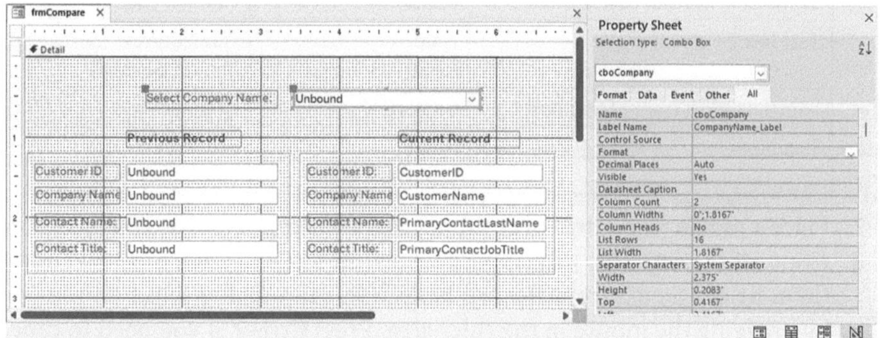

FIGURE 11.12.   This custom form is used to demonstrate how the recordset cloning is used to read the contents of the previous record.

4. In the Controls area of the Form Design tab, click the Combo Box control and click inside the form area to position it at the upper right, as shown in Figure 11.12. In the Combo Box Wizard's first screen, choose the option button labeled I want the combo box to look up the values in a table or query. Click Next. Make sure the Customers table is selected and click Next. The fields available in the `Customers` table should appear. Move CustomerID and CompanyName from the Available Fields box to the Selected Fields box and then click Next. Specify CompanyName as the Ascending sort order for your combo box and then click Next. In the next wizard dialog, adjust the width of the combo box column to fit the longest company name and click Finish. Now you should see the combo box placed on your form. Choose the Property Sheet in the Tools group of the Form Design Ribbon and set the Caption property of `CompanyName_Label` to Select Company Name. Set the Tag property of this label control to `cbo`. Set the Name property of the Company combo (unbound) to `cboCompany` and its Tag property to `cbo`.

5. Place two label controls on the form. Set the Caption property of the first one to `Previous Record` and the second one to `Current Record`. Adjust the size of both label controls so the captions are fully visible.

6. Place four text boxes below the Previous Record label and set their properties as shown below:

Object	Property	Setting
First label in front of text box 1	Caption	Customer ID:
Text box 1	Name Control Source	CustIDPrev should be blank
Second label in front of text box 2	Caption	Company Name:
Text box 2	Name Control Source	CompanyPrev Should be blank
Third label in front of text box 3	Caption	Contact Name:
Text box 3	Name Control Source	ContactPrev Should be blank
Fourth label in front of text box 4	Caption	Contact Title:
Text box 4	Name Control Source	TitlePrev Should be blank

7. Place a rectangle control over the set of four text boxes that you have created.

8. Copy all the controls that appear below the Previous Record label and paste them below the Current Record label. You can quickly select all the controls by dragging the mouse in the ruler area. Press Ctrl+Z if you need to cancel the action and try again.

9. Set the properties of the pasted text box controls as shown below:

Customer ID text box	Name	CustomerID
	Control Source	CustomerID
Company Name text box	Name	CompanyName
	Control Source	CustomerName
Contact Name text box	Name	ContactName
	Control Source	PrimaryContactLastName
Contact Title text box	Name	ContactTitle
	Control Source	PrimaryContactJobTitle

10. In the property sheet, select Form from the drop-down box and set the following form properties:

Property Name	Setting
Record Source	Customers
Caption	Record Comparison
Scroll Bars	Neither
Record Selectors	No
Navigation Buttons	No

Notice that the Record Source property of the form is set to the `Customers` table. If the Record Source is left empty, you will get error `91`: *Object variable or With block variable not set.*

11. Save the form as `frmCompare`.

12. Click the combo box control on the form to select it. Activate the Event tab in the property sheet and click to the right of the AfterUpdate event name. Select [Event Procedure] from the drop-down box, and then click the Build button (...) to activate the Code window. Complete the `cboCompany_AfterUpdate` procedure shown here:

```
Private Sub cboCompany_AfterUpdate()
    Dim rs As Object
    Dim c As Control

    On Error GoTo ErrHandle

    Set rs = Me.Recordset.Clone
    ' Find the record that matches the combo box selection
    rs.FindFirst "[CustomerID] = " & Me![cboCompany]

    If Not rs.EOF Then
        Me.Bookmark = rs.Bookmark
```

```
    ' Always display current record's data
    For Each c In Me.Controls
        c.Visible = True
    Next

    ' Check if the current record is the first record
    If rs.AbsolutePosition = 0 Then
    ' Clear previous record controls
    ' since no previous record exists
        Me.CustIDPrev = Null
        Me.CompanyPrev = Null
        Me.ContactPrev = Null
        Me.TitlePrev = Null
    Else
        ' Move to the previous record in the clone
        rs.MovePrevious
        If Not rs.BOF Then
            With Me
                .CustIDPrev = rs.Fields(0)
                .CompanyPrev = rs.Fields(1)
                .ContactPrev = rs.Fields(2)
                .TitlePrev = rs.Fields(4)
            End With
        End If
    End If

ExitHere:
    Exit Sub

ErrHandle:
    MsgBox Err.Number & ": " & Err.Description
    Resume ExitHere
End Sub
```

Notice that the `cboCompany_AfterUpdate` event procedure begins by creating a clone of the form's recordset. Next, the `FindFirst` method is used to locate the customer record based on the entry selected in the combo box. To ensure that the form's record is in sync with the entry selected in the combo box, the following line of code moves the form's bookmark to the same location as the recordset clone's bookmark if we are not at EOF:

```
If Not rs.EOF Then Me.Bookmark = rs.Bookmark
```

13. Press Ctrl+S to save the current changes.

14. Test your form by opening it in form view. Selecting a company name from the combo box should fill the text boxes under the Current Record label with the selected company's data. The boxes under the Previous Record label should pull company data from the previous record if such a record is available.

Before we start working with this custom project, let's write a `Form_Load` event procedure to ensure that only the combo box and its label are visible when the form is opened.

15. In the Code window where you have written the `cboCompany_AfterUp-date` event procedure, select Form from the object drop-down box in the top-left corner. Select Load from the procedure drop-down box on the right. Complete the code for the `Form_Load` event procedure as shown here:

```
Private Sub Form_Load()
   Dim c As Control

   For Each c In Me.Controls
     If c.Tag <> "cbo" Then
       c.Visible = False
     End If
   Next
End Sub
```

16. Make sure there are no errors in your code by choosing Debug | Compile Chap11.

17. Save and close your form.

18. Open the `frmCompare` form in form view and test it by choosing different company names from the combo box.

19. Close the form.

Think of ways to improve this form. For example, add a set of controls and write additional code to display the next record.

INTRODUCTION TO DATA SHAPING

Designing database applications often requires that you pull information from multiple tables. For instance, to obtain a listing of customers and their orders, you must link the required tables with SQL JOIN statements, as shown here:

```
SELECT Customers.CustomerID AS [Cust Id],
   Customers.CustomerName,
   Orders.OrderDate,
```

```
   [OrderDetails].OrderID,
   Products.ProductName,
   [OrderDetails].UnitPrice,
   CCur([OrderDetails].[UnitPrice]*[Quantity])
      AS [Extended Price]
FROM Products
   INNER JOIN ((Customers
   INNER JOIN Orders ON Customers.CustomerID = Orders.CustomerID)
   INNER JOIN [OrderDetails]
   ON Orders.OrderID = [OrderDetails].OrderID)
   ON Products.ProductID = [OrderDetails].ProductID
   ORDER BY Customers.CustomerID, Orders.OrderDate DESC;
```

When you execute this SQL statement in the `NorthwindStarter` database, your output will match Figure 11.13.

Cust Id	Customer Name	Order Date	OrderID	Product Name	UnitPrice	Extended Price
1	Adatum Corporation	10/7/2023 12:28:00 PM	28	Almonds	$10.00	$110.00
1	Adatum Corporation	10/3/2023 12:21:00 PM	21	Beer	$14.00	$140.00
1	Adatum Corporation	9/25/2023 12:05:00 PM	5	Syrup	$10.00	$220.00
1	Adatum Corporation	9/25/2023 12:05:00 PM	5	Chai	$18.00	$18.00
2	Adventure Works Cycles	10/31/2023 1:05:00 PM	65	Walnuts	$23.25	$813.75
2	Adventure Works Cycles	10/31/2023 1:05:00 PM	65	Coffee	$46.00	$1,058.00
2	Adventure Works Cycles	10/31/2023 1:05:00 PM	65	Clam Chowder	$9.65	$67.55
2	Adventure Works Cycles	10/27/2023 1:00:00 PM	60	Coffee	$46.00	$1,058.00
2	Adventure Works Cycles	10/27/2023 1:00:00 PM	60	Clam Chowder	$9.65	$67.55
2	Adventure Works Cycles	10/23/2023 12:55:00 PM	55	Coffee	$46.00	$1,058.00
2	Adventure Works Cycles	10/23/2023 12:55:00 PM	55	Clam Chowder	$9.65	$67.55
2	Adventure Works Cycles	10/19/2023 12:50:00 PM	50	Clam Chowder	$9.65	$67.55
2	Adventure Works Cycles	10/19/2023 12:50:00 PM	50	Coffee	$46.00	$1,058.00
2	Adventure Works Cycles	10/11/2023 12:33:00 PM	33	Almonds	$10.00	$220.00
2	Adventure Works Cycles	10/11/2023 12:33:00 PM	33	Boysenberry Spread	$25.00	$825.00
2	Adventure Works Cycles	10/11/2023 12:33:00 PM	33	Cajun Seasoning	$22.00	$1,210.00
2	Adventure Works Cycles	10/11/2023 12:33:00 PM	33	Chocolate	$12.75	$420.75
2	Adventure Works Cycles	10/7/2023 12:26:00 PM	26	Dried Plums	$3.50	$35.00
2	Adventure Works Cycles	10/7/2023 12:26:00 PM	26	Brownie Mix	$12.49	$74.94
2	Adventure Works Cycles	10/7/2023 12:26:00 PM	26	Boysenberry Spread	$25.00	$1,050.00
2	Adventure Works Cycles	10/7/2023 12:26:00 PM	26	Clam Chowder	$9.65	$221.95
2	Adventure Works Cycles	10/7/2023 12:26:00 PM	26	Crab Meat	$18.40	$128.80
2	Adventure Works Cycles	10/3/2023 12:18:00 PM	18	Almonds	$10.00	$20.00
5	Woodgrove Bank	11/2/2023 1:07:00 PM	67	Clam Chowder	$9.65	$453.55
5	Woodgrove Bank	11/2/2023 1:07:00 PM	67	Green Beans	$1.20	$26.40
5	Woodgrove Bank	10/31/2023 1:06:00 PM	66	Chocolate Biscuits Mix	$9.20	$294.40

Record: H ◄ 5 of 72 ► H ►▪ No Filter Search

FIGURE 11.13.   When you use SQL JOIN statements you get a flat recordset with a lot of duplicate information.

When you output your data in a standard way by using the SQL JOIN syntax, you get a lot of duplicate information. You can eliminate this redundant information by using an advanced feature of ADO known as a *shaped* (or *hierarchical*) recordset.

Data shaping allows you to create recordsets within recordsets with a single ADO object. This sort of hierarchical data arrangement is often seen as a *parent-child relationship.* The parent recordset contains the child recordset. A child recordset can contain another child recordset, which is a grandchild of the original recordset. A parent-child relationship can be placed in an easy-to-read tree structure. You will produce such a structure in Custom Project 11.4 later in this chapter. For now, let's focus on learning some new concepts that will enable you to present your data in a format that's easy to view and navigate.

Writing a Simple SHAPE Statement

You can easily create a hierarchy of data by using a data-shaping language. All you need to know is how to use the following three commands: SHAPE, APPEND, and RELATE. The basic syntax looks like this:

```
SHAPE {parent-command}
 APPEND ({child-command} [[AS] table-alias]
  RELATE (parent-column TO child-column)
```

parent-command and child-command are often SQL SELECT statements that pull the data from the required tables. Let's look at the following example that uses the preceding syntax:

```
SHAPE {SELECT CustomerID AS [Cust ID],
                              CustomerName FROM Customers}
 APPEND ({SELECT OrderID, CustomerID, OrderDate FROM Orders}
                              AS custOrders
  RELATE (Cust ID TO CustomerID)
```

The preceding statement is a shaped recordset. This statement selects two fields from the Customers table and three fields from the Orders table. By using this SHAPE statement, you can list all orders for each of the customers in the Customers table without returning any redundant information.

Notice that there are two SELECT statements in this shaped recordset:

- The first SELECT statement is the parent recordset. This recordset retrieves the data from the Customers table. Notice this SELECT statement is surrounded by curly braces and preceded by the SHAPE command, which defines a recordset.
- The second SELECT statement is the child recordset. It gets the data from the Orders table. This SELECT statement is also surrounded by curly braces; however, it is preceded by the APPEND clause and an opening parenthesis. The APPEND clause will add the child recordset to the parent recordset.
- The RELATE keyword establishes the relationship between the parent and child recordset. Always specify the name of the parent column first.

Working with Data Shaping

To work with data shaping in your VBA procedure, you need two providers: one for the data-shaping functionality and the other for the data itself. Therefore, before you can create shaped (hierarchical) recordsets in your procedures, you will need to specify:

- **The Name of a Service Provider**

  The data-shaping functionality is provided by the data-shaping service for OLE DB. The name of this service provider is `MSDataShape` and it is specified as the value of the `Connection` object's `Provider` property like this:

  ```
  conn.Provider = "MSDataShape"
  ```

  Or it can be a connection string like this:

  ```
  "Provider=MSDataShape"
  ```

- **The Name of a Data Provider**

  Because a shaped recordset needs to be populated with rows of data, you must specify the name of a data provider as the value of the `DataProvider` property of the `Connection` object:

  ```
  conn.DataProvider = "Microsoft.ACE.OLEDB.12.0;"
  ```

  Or in the connection string like this:

  ```
  "Data Provider=Microsoft.ACE.OLEDB.12.0;"
  ```

The data-shaping service creates a shaped (hierarchical) recordset from any data supplied by a data provider. In order to provide shaped data from a database other than Access, let's say, an SQL Server database, a connection string might look like this:

```
Dim conn As ADODB.Connection
Set conn = New ADODB.Connection

conn.Open = "Provider=MSDataShape;" & _
  "Data Provider=SQLOLEDB;" & _
  "Server=YourServerName;" & _
  "Initial Catalog=AdventureWorks2022;" & _
  "Integrated Security=SSPI;"
```

In Hands-On 11.50, you will create a shaped recordset in a VBA procedure and display hierarchical data in the Immediate window (see Figure 11.14).

⊙ Hands-On 11.50   Creating a Shaped Recordset

1. In the VBE window of the `Chap11.accdb` database, choose Insert | Module.
2. In the module's Code window, enter the `ShapeData` procedure shown here:

```vba
Sub ShapeData()
    Dim conn As ADODB.Connection
    Dim rs As ADODB.Recordset
    Dim rsChild As ADODB.Recordset
    Dim strConn As String
    Dim strShape As String

    On Error Resume Next

' define database connection string
 strConn = "Data Provider=Microsoft.ACE.OLEDB.12.0;"
 strConn = strConn & "Data Source = " & _
  "C:\VBAAccess2024_ByExample\NorthwindStarter.accdb"

 ' specify Data Shaping provider
 ' and open connection to the database
 Set conn = New ADODB.Connection
 With conn
    .ConnectionString = strConn
    .Provider = "MSDataShape"
    .Open
 End With

 ' Create the shaping command
 strShape = "SHAPE {SELECT CustomerID as [Cust ID], " & _
            "CustomerName FROM Customers} " & _
            "APPEND ({SELECT OrderID, CustomerID, OrderDate " & _
            "FROM Orders} as custOrders " & _
            "RELATE [Cust ID] TO CustomerID)"

 ' Open the hierarchical Recordset
 Set rs = New ADODB.Recordset
 rs.Open strShape, conn, adOpenStatic, adLockReadOnly

 ' Navigate through the hierarchical Recordset
 Do Until rs.EOF
     Debug.Print "Cust#: " & rs![Cust ID] & Space(2) & _
         rs!CustomerName & vbCrLf
     Set rsChild = rs("custOrders").Value
     rsChild.MoveFirst
```

```
        If rsChild.RecordCount <> 0 Then
            Debug.Print vbTab & "Order #" & vbTab & "OrderDate"
        Else
            Debug.Print "No orders exist."
        End If
        Do Until rsChild.EOF
            Debug.Print vbTab & rsChild!OrderID & vbTab & vbTab & _
                Format(rsChild!OrderDate, "mm/dd/yyyy")
            rsChild.MoveNext
        Loop
        Debug.Print vbCrLf
        rs.MoveNext
    Loop

    ' Clean up
    rs.Close
    Set rs = Nothing
    conn.Close
    Set conn = Nothing
End Sub
```

3. Choose Run | Run Sub/UserForm to execute the procedure.

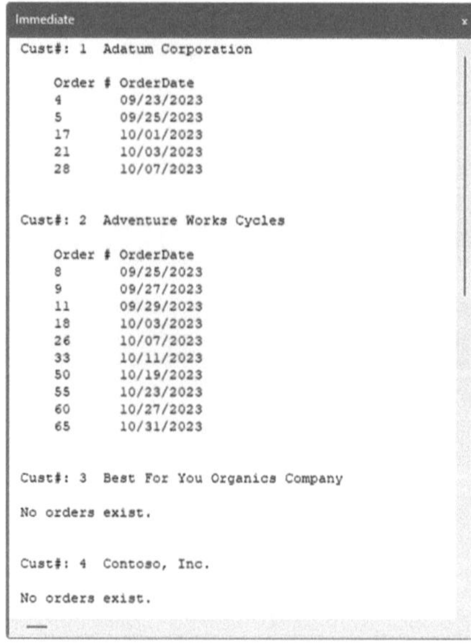

FIGURE 11.14.　After running the ShapeDemo procedure in Hands-On 11.50, you can view the contents of the hierarchical recordset in the Immediate window.

How to Determine Whether a Recordset
Contains a Field Pointing to Another Recordset

To find out whether a certain recordset contains another recordset, let's examine the following code snippet:

```vb
Dim rst As New ADODB.Recordset
Dim rstChild As ADODB.Recordset

Do Until rs.EOF
Debug.Print "Customer: " & rs!CustomerName

' check if the custOrders field is a chapter (child Recordset)
If rst.Fields("custOrders").Type = adChapter then
    Debug.Print "This is a child recordset"

    Set rstChild = rst("custOrders").Value

' Navigate through the child recordset
    Do Until rstChild.EOF
      Debug.Print " Order: " & _
  rstChild!OrderID & _
  "Date: " & rstChild!OrderDate
    rstChild.MoveNext
    Loop
End If
rst.MoveNext
Loop
```

A *chapter* in ADO is a way to represent hierarchical data structures within a recordset. The `adChapter` data type in ADO is used to denote a hierarchical or child recordset within a parent recordset. When a field in a parent recordset is of type `adChapter`, it denotes that this field holds another recordset, which represents related child records. In other words, when you encounter a field of type `adChapter`, it means that this field does not contain scalar data (such as a string or a number), but rather another recordset. Chapters make is easier to work with complex data relationships.

Writing a Complex SHAPE Statement

In the previous section, you worked with a simple SHAPE statement that displayed order information for each customer. In the following sections, you will write more complex SHAPE statements that include multiple child and grandchild recordsets.

Shaped Recordsets with Multiple Children and Grandchildren

Data shaping does not limit you to having just one child recordset within a parent recordset. You can specify as many children as you want. For example, to display a parent with two children, use the following syntax:

```
SHAPE {SELECT * FROM Parent}
APPEND ({SELECT * FROM Child1}
RELATE parent-column TO child1-column) AS child1-alias,
({SELECT * FROM Child2}
RELATE parent-column TO child2-column) AS child2-alias
```

In addition to the parent recordset having multiple children, the child recordset can contain a child of its own. Simply put, your hierarchical recordset can contain grandchildren. Creating such a hierarchy is a bit harder, but it can be tackled in no time if you take a step-by-step approach. The SHAPE syntax that includes grandchildren looks like this:

```
SHAPE {SELECT * FROM Parent}
APPEND ((SHAPE {SELECT * FROM Child}
APPEND ({SELECT * FROM Grandchild}
RELATE child-column TO grandchild-column) AS grandchild-alias)
RELATE parent-column TO child-column) as child-alias
```

Notice that when grandchildren are present, the child recordset is appended with another SHAPE command. Although you can have as many children or grandchildren as you want, it will be more difficult to write a SHAPE statement that uses more than three or four levels.

In Custom Project 11.4, you create a shaped recordset that contains both children and grandchildren. Next, you display this recordset on the Access form in the ActiveX TreeView control (see Figure 11.20 for the final output). This project will also introduce you to using aggregate functions within your shaped recordsets.

 ## Custom Project 11.4 Using Hierarchical Recordsets

Part 1: Creating a Form with a TreeView Control

1. In the Access window of the `Chap11.accdb` database, choose Create | Form Design. The Form design window opens.
2. In the Controls area of the Form Design tab, click the More button in the Scroll area, and choose ActiveX Controls (see Figures 11.15 and 11.16).

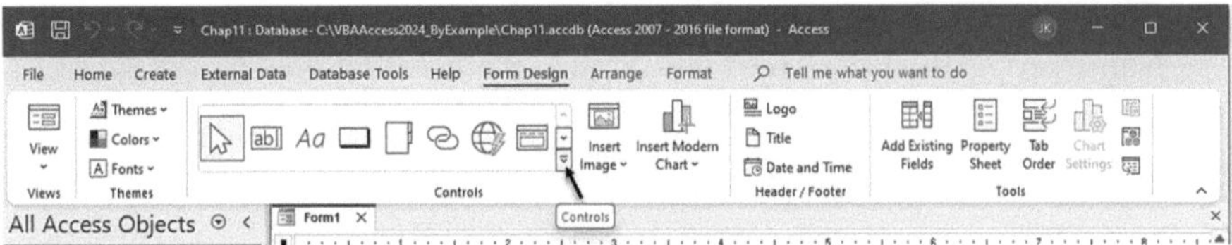

FIGURE 11.15.   Adding an ActiveX control to an Access form (step 1).

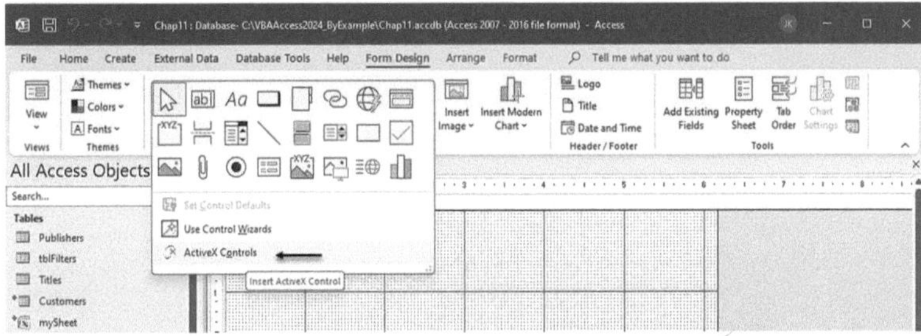

FIGURE 11.16.   Adding an ActiveX control to an Access form (step 2).

3. In the Insert ActiveX Control window, choose Microsoft TreeView Control, version 6.0, as shown in Figure 11.17, and click OK to place a TreeView control on the form.

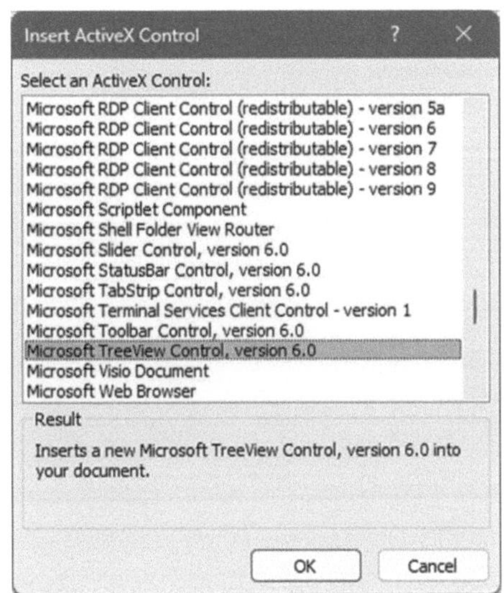

FIGURE 11.17.   The Microsoft TreeView control provides an excellent way to display shaped recordsets in an Access form.

4. Resize the TreeView control and the form to match Figure 11.18.

5. Click the TreeView control to select it. In the property sheet, change the Name property of the TreeView control from `TreeView0` to `myTreeCtrl`.

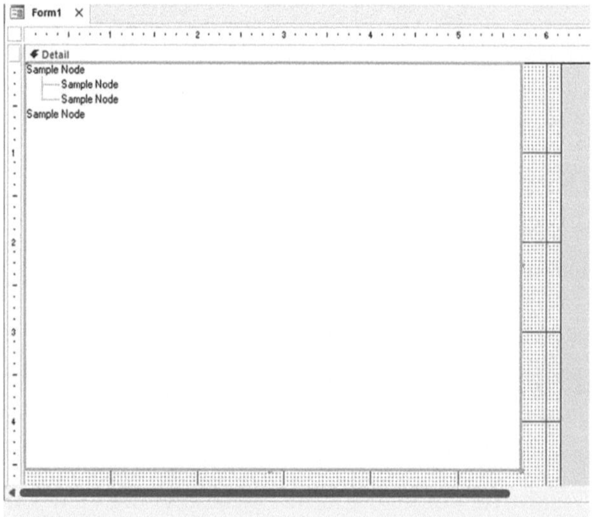

FIGURE 11.18. A TreeView control after being placed and resized on the Access form.

You can use the Property Sheet to adjust various properties of the TreeView control (Figure 11.19).

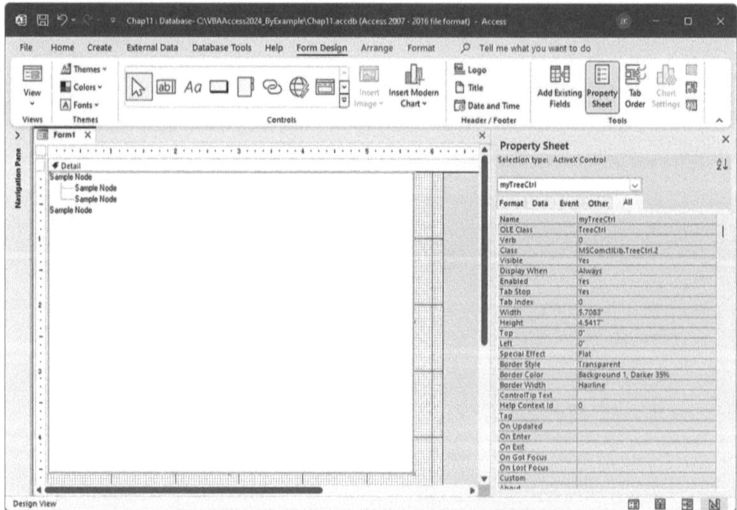

FIGURE 11.19. You can set custom properties of the TreeView control in the Property Sheet of the TreeView control.

6. Save the form as `frmOrders`.

Part 2: Writing an Event Procedure for the Form Load Event

1. In the property sheet, select Form from the drop-down box and click the Event tab for the selected form.
2. Click the Build button (…) next to the On Load event name to display the Choose builder dialog box.
3. In the Choose Builder dialog box, select Code Builder and click OK. The form module window appears with the following `Form_Load` event procedure stub:

```
Private Sub Form_Load()

End Sub
```

4. Type the code for the `Form_Load` event procedure shown here, or copy the procedure code from `Chap11.txt` in the companion files:

```
Private Sub Form_Load()
    Dim conn As ADODB.Connection
    Dim rstCustomers As ADODB.Recordset
    Dim rstOrders As ADODB.Recordset
    Dim rstOrderDetails As ADODB.Recordset
    Dim fld As Field
    Dim objNode1 As Node
    Dim objNode2 As Node
    Dim strConn As String
    Dim strSQL As String
    Dim strSQLCustomers As String
    Dim strSQLOrders As String
    Dim strSQLOrderDetails As String
    Dim strSQLRelParentToChild As String
    Dim strSQLRelGParentToParent As String

    ' Create the ADO Connection object
    Set conn = New ADODB.Connection

    ' Specify a valid connection string
    strConn = "Data Provider=Microsoft.ACE.OLEDB.12.0;"
    strConn = strConn & "Data Source = " & _
      "C:\VBAAccess2024_ByExample\NorthwindStarter.accdb"

    conn.ConnectionString = strConn

    ' Specify the Data Shaping provider
    conn.Provider = "MSDataShape"
```

```
' Open the connection
conn.Open

' Specify SELECT statement for the Grandparent
strSQLCustomers = "SELECT CustomerID " & _
  "AS [Cust #], CustomerName AS [Customer] " & _
  "FROM Customers"

' Specify SELECT statement for the Parent
strSQLOrders = "SELECT OrderID AS [Order #]," & _
  "Format(OrderDate, 'mm/dd/yyyy') AS [Order Date]," & _
  "Orders.CustomerID AS [Cust #] " & _
  "FROM Orders ORDER BY OrderDate DESC"

' Specify SELECT statement for the Child
strSQLOrderDetails = _
  "SELECT od.OrderID AS [Order #], od.ProductID," & _
  "p.ProductName AS [Product], od.Quantity," & _
  "od.UnitPrice AS [Unit Price]," & _
  "(od.UnitPrice * od.Quantity) " & _
  "AS [Extended Price] FROM [OrderDetails] od " & _
  "INNER JOIN Products p " & _
  "ON od.ProductID = p.ProductID " & _
  "ORDER BY od.OrderID, p.ProductName"


' Specify RELATE clause to link Parent to Child
strSQLRelParentToChild = "RELATE [Order #] TO [Order #]"

' Specify RELATE clause to link Grandparent to Parent
strSQLRelGParentToParent = "RELATE [Cust #] TO [Cust #]"

' Build complete SQL statement for the shaped
' recordset adding aggregate functions for
' the Grandparent and Parent
strSQL = "SHAPE(SHAPE{" & strSQLCustomers & "}"
strSQL = strSQL & " APPEND((SHAPE{" & strSQLOrders & "} "
strSQL = strSQL & _
  " APPEND({" & strSQLOrderDetails & "} "
strSQL = strSQL & _
  strSQLRelParentToChild & ") AS rstOrderDetails,"
strSQL = strSQL & " COUNT(rstOrderDetails.Product) "
strSQL = strSQL & " AS [Items On Order],"
strSQL = strSQL & _
  "SUM(rstOrderDetails.[Extended Price]) "
strSQL = strSQL & " AS [Order Total])"
```

```
strSQL = strSQL & _
  strSQLRelGParentToParent & ") AS [rstOrders],"
strSQL = strSQL & " SUM(rstOrders.[Order Total]) "
strSQL = strSQL & " AS [Cust Grand Total]"
strSQL = strSQL & ") AS rstCustomers"

' Create and open the Grandparent recordset
Set rstCustomers = New ADODB.Recordset
rstCustomers.Open strSQL, conn

' Fill the TreeView control
Do While Not rstCustomers.EOF
  Set objNode1 = myTreeCtrl.Nodes.Add _
    (Text:=rstCustomers.Fields(0) & _
    "   " & rstCustomers.Fields(1) & _
    "   ($ " & rstCustomers.Fields(3) & ")")
  Set rstOrders = _
    rstCustomers.Fields("rstOrders").Value
      Do While Not rstOrders.EOF
        Set objNode2 = myTreeCtrl.Nodes.Add _
        (relative:=objNode1.Index, _
        relationship:=tvwChild, _
        Text:=rstOrders.Fields(0) & _
        "   " & rstOrders.Fields(1) & _
        "   " & rstOrders.Fields(4) & " (items)" & _
        "    $" & rstOrders.Fields(5) & _
        " (Order Total)")
        Set rstOrderDetails = _
        rstOrders.Fields("rstOrderDetails").Value
        Do While Not rstOrderDetails.EOF
          myTreeCtrl.Nodes.Add _
            relative:=objNode2.Index, _
            relationship:=tvwChild, _
            Text:=rstOrderDetails!Quantity & _
            "   " & rstOrderDetails!Product & _
            "   $" & rstOrderDetails![Extended Price] & _
            "   (" & rstOrderDetails!Quantity & _
            " x $" & rstOrderDetails![Unit Price] & ")"
          rstOrderDetails.MoveNext
        Loop
        rstOrders.MoveNext
    Loop
    rstCustomers.MoveNext
Loop

' Cleanup
rstCustomers.Close
```

```
      Set rstCustomers = Nothing
      Set conn = Nothing
End Sub
```

5. Choose Tools | References and set the reference to the Microsoft Windows Common Controls 6.0 (SP6). If this reference is not listed in the Available References list box, click the Browse button. In the Add Reference dialog box, switch to the Windows\System 32 or Windows\SysWOW64 folder and select ActiveX Controls (*.ocx) in the file type drop-down box. Scroll down to locate and select `MSCOMCTL.OCX`. Click the Open button to confirm your selection, and then click OK to exit the References window.

6. Return to the Access application window and open `frmOrders` in form view.

When you open the `frmOrders` form, the `Form_Load` procedure populates the TreeView control with the data from the `NorthwindStarter` database. As you can see in Figure 11.20, the results are quite impressive. Double-clicking on the nodes in the TreeView control expands and collapses the details underneath those nodes.

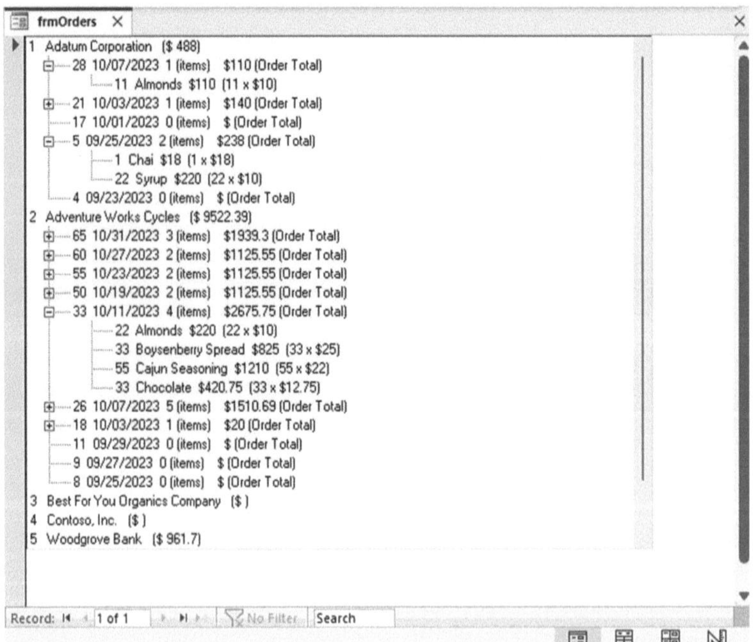

FIGURE 11.20. The TreeView control is filled with the data from the Northwind database when the user opens the form.

Because a TreeView control displays data as a hierarchy, we need to build a complex SQL statement using the SHAPE syntax we learned about in preceding sections. To make things easier for ourselves, we start by defining SQL statements with fields we want to display for grandchild, parent, and child recordsets. Notice that we renamed some fields using the AS clause. We also defined separate statements to allow us to link grandparent to parent and parent to child.

After defining the relationship and the fields for our data hierarchy, we used the SHAPE commands to build the complete SHAPE statement. While creating the SHAPE statement, we added additional calculated fields using the aggregate functions. For instance, in the parent recordset (rstOrders), we calculated the number of items ordered using the COUNT function. We also used the SUM function to obtain the total amount of the order. In the grandparent recordset (rstCustomers), we used the SUM function to calculate the total amount owed by a customer.

Notice that the SHAPE statement we built contains standard fields pulled from the database tables and child recordsets (rstOrders, rstOrderDetails), as well as calculated columns.

The rstOrders recordset is a field in the rstCustomers recordset. This field contains order information for a customer.

rstOrderDetails is a field within the rstOrders recordset. This field contains the order details information for a customer's order.

Now that we've completed the SHAPE statement, we can open the grandparent recordset and begin populating the TreeView control with our data.

A TreeView control consists of Node objects, which you can expand or collapse to display or hide child nodes. Nodes that have child nodes are referred to as *parent* nodes. The nodes located at the top of the tree control are referred to as *root* nodes. Root nodes can have *sibling* nodes that are located on the same level. For example, customer Adatum Corporation (see Figure 11.20) is a root node, and so is the customer Adventure Works Cycles, and so on. They are also siblings of one another.

To populate a TreeView control, we used the Add method of the Nodes collection. objNode1 is an object variable representing the Node object. The first node added to a TreeView is a root node. The Add method of the Nodes collection uses the following syntax:

```
object.Add([relative,] [relationship,] [key], text[, image,]
[selectedimage])
```

The only required arguments in the syntax are `object` and `text`. The object is the object variable (`myTreeCtrl`) representing the TreeView control. The text is a string that appears in the node.

<table>
<tr><td>

NOTE

</td><td>

When a `Node` object is created, it is automatically assigned an index number. This number is stored in the `Node` object's `Index` property.

</td></tr>
</table>

Now that we've taken care of the root node, we go on to add children and grandchildren. A child node has a relationship to a parent node that has already been added. To define a child node, in addition to the required `text` argument, we used two optional arguments of the `Add` method, as follows:

- `relative`—This is the index number or key of a preexisting `Node` object. In our example, we used the index of the parent node that we just created (`relative:=objNode1.Index`).

- `relationship`—Specifies the type of relationship you are creating. Use the `tvwChild` setting to create a child node of the node named in the `relative` argument. The statement that creates a child node looks like this:

```
Set objNode2 = myTreeCtrl.Nodes.Add _
  (relative:=objNode1.Index, _
  relationship:=tvwChild, _
  Text:=rstOrders.Fields(0) & _
  "  " & rstOrders.Fields(1) & _
  "  " & rstOrders.Fields(4) & " (items)" & _
  "  $" & rstOrders.Fields(5) & _
  " (Order Total)")
```

The preceding statement displays order information for a customer. The child node `text` argument is set to display:

```
Order # (rstOrders.Fields(0))
Order Date (rstOrders.Fields(1))
Items On Order (rstOrders.Fields(4))
Order Total (rstOrders.Fields(5))
```

Because this statement appears inside a looping structure, the TreeView control will display the order information for each customer. Finally, we add grandchildren using the following statement:

```
myTreeCtrl.Nodes.Add _
  relative:=objNode2.Index, _
  relationship:=tvwChild, _
  Text:=rstOrderDetails!Quantity & _
```

```
"   " & rstOrderDetails!Product & _
"   $" & rstOrderDetails![Extended Price] & _
"   (" & rstOrderDetails!Quantity & _
" x $" & rstOrderDetails![Unit Price] & ")"
```

This statement displays order details for a customer's order. Notice that this `Node` object references the index number of the child object that has just been added (`relative:=objNode2.Index`). Notice two different ways you can access the fields in your recordsets.

The looping structure ensures that the order details are listed for all customers' orders.

Now that you are done with this custom project, you should be able to provide your own hierarchical data in a pretty neat user interface.

CONNECTION POOLING

Another advanced feature of ADO is called *connection pooling*. This feature allows developers to efficiently manage connections by reusing existing connections and therefore reducing the overhead of establishing new connections. Connecting to a database can be resource-intensive. Connection pooling maintains a pool of database connections in memory, ready to reuse. When an application needs to establish a database connection, it simply retrieves one from the pool, and when the connection is no longer needed, it returns it to the pool instead of being closed. Therefore, connection pooling limits the number of active connections, preventing resource exhaustion and ensuring efficient resource utilization.

In ADO, connection pooling is enabled by default for OLE DB providers that support it, for example, Microsoft OLE DB Provider for SQL Server. Connection pooling can be controlled via a connection string parameter, as shown in the following example procedure that connects to the SQL Server `Adventure-Works2022` database.

```
Sub UseConnectionPooling()
    Dim conn As ADODB.Connection
    Dim rs As ADODB.Recordset
    Dim strConn As String

    strConn = "Provider=SQLOLEDB;Data Source=YourSQLServer;" & _
    "Initial Catalog=AdventureWorks2022;" & _
    "Integrated Security=SSPI;" & _
```

```vba
    "Pooling=True;Min Pool Size=5;Max Pool Size=50;"

    ' Open the connection
    Set conn = New ADODB.Connection
    conn.Open strConn

    ' Use the connection
    Set rs = New ADODB.Recordset
    rs.Open "SELECT * FROM Production.Product", _
        conn, adOpenStatic, adLockReadOnly

    ' Process the results
    Do Until rs.EOF
        Debug.Print rs("Name")
        rs.MoveNext
    Loop
    ' Close the recordset and connection
    rs.Close
    Set rs = Nothing
    conn.Close
    Set conn = Nothing
End Sub
```

With the connection pooling enabled via the specific parameters in the connection string, when the connection is closed, it returns to the pool rather than being destroyed.

To enable connection pooling, set the `Pooling` parameter to `True`: `Pooling = True`.

When connection pooling is enabled (`True`), connections to the database are reused rather than created and destroyed each time a connection is requested.

The next parameter, `Min Pool Size = 5`, sets the minimum number of connections that the pool maintains.

When the connection pool is created, it will automatically create this number of connections to ensure that there are always a few connections ready to use. This reduces wait times for initial connection requests.

The parameter `Max Pool Size = 50` sets the maximum number of connections that the pool can maintain.

If all connections in the pool are in use and a new connection request is made, the pool will create a new connection, provided that the total number of connections does not exceed this limit.

You can optimize the performance and resource usage of your application by tuning these parameters.

TRANSACTION PROCESSING

To improve your application's performance and ensure that database activities can be recovered in case an unexpected hardware or software error occurs, consider grouping sets of database activities into a transaction. A *transaction* is a set of operations that are performed together as a single unit. Recall that we already discussed transactions in Chapter 10 when we covered the DAO object library. There we used the transaction methods of the `Workspace` or `DBEngine` object: `BeginTrans`, `CommitTrans`, and `Rollback`.

In ADO, the `Connection` object offers three methods (`BeginTrans`, `CommitTrans`, and `RollbackTrans`) for managing transaction processing. You should use these methods to save or cancel a series of changes made to the data as a single unit.

- `BeginTrans`—Begins a new transaction
- `CommitTrans`—Saves any changes and ends the current transaction
- `RollbackTrans`—Cancels any changes made during the current transaction and ends the transaction

Please note that in ADO, a transaction is limited to one database because the `Connection` object can only point to one database.

Creating a Transaction in ADO

Use the `BeginTrans` method to specify the beginning of a transaction and the `CommitTrans` method to save the changes. `BeginTrans` and `CommitTrans` are used in pairs. The data-modifying instructions you place between these keywords are stored in memory until VBA encounters the `CommitTrans` statement. After reaching `CommitTrans`, Access writes to the disk the changes that have occurred since the `BeginTrans` statement; therefore, any changes you've made in the tables become permanent.

If an error is generated during the transaction process, the `RollbackTrans` statement placed further down in your procedure will undo all changes made since the `BeginTrans` statement. The rollback ensures that the data is returned to the state it was in before you started the transaction.

Using transaction processing helps improve database performance because the operations carried out during a transaction are run in memory. If the transaction succeeds, the results are written to the disk in a single operation. If any operation included in a transaction fails, the transaction is simply aborted and no changes are written to the database. If you don't use transactions, the results of each operation must be written to the disk separately—a process that consumes more database resources.

The procedure in Hands-On 11.51 assumes that you want to enter an order for a new customer. Because this customer does not exist in the database, you will use a transaction to ensure that the new order is entered only after the customer record has been created in the Customers table. The result is shown in Figure 11.21.

Hands-On 11.51   Using a Database Transaction to Insert Records

1. In the VBE window, choose Insert | Module.
2. In the module's Code window, enter the AddNewCustomerWithOrder procedure as shown here:

```
Sub AddNewCustomerWithOrder()
    Dim conn As ADODB.Connection
    Dim cmd As ADODB.Command
    Dim rs As ADODB.Recordset
    Dim strConn As String
    Dim customerID As String
    Dim newCustomerID As String
    Dim newOrderID As Long
    Dim newProductID As Long
    Dim newQuantity As Integer
    Dim newUnitPrice As Currency
    Dim newStatusID As Integer
    Dim strSQL As String


    ' Define connection string
    strConn = "Provider=Microsoft.ACE.OLEDB.12.0;" & _
    "Data Source=" & _
    "C:\VBAAccess2024_ByExample\NorthwindStarter.accdb"

    ' Initialize connection
    Set conn = New ADODB.Connection
    conn.ConnectionString = strConn

    On Error GoTo ErrorHandler

    ' Open connection and begin transaction
    conn.Open
    conn.BeginTrans
```

```vb
' Insert a new customer
Set cmd = New ADODB.Command
strSQL = "INSERT INTO Customers (" & _
"CustomerName, PrimaryContactLastName, & _
"PrimaryContactFirstName," & _
"PrimaryContactJobTitle, Address," & _
"City, State, Zip, Notes)" & _
" VALUES (?, ?, ?, ?, ?, ?, ?, ?, ?)"

With cmd
    .ActiveConnection = conn
    .CommandText = strSQL
    .Parameters.Append .CreateParameter(, adVarChar, _
        adParamInput, 50, "Advantage Solutions Partners")
    .Parameters.Append .CreateParameter(, adVarChar, _
        adParamInput, 50, "Garnia")
    .Parameters.Append .CreateParameter(, adVarChar, _
        adParamInput, 50, "Martin")
    .Parameters.Append .CreateParameter(, adVarChar, _
        adParamInput, 50, "Sales Manager")
    .Parameters.Append .CreateParameter(, adVarChar, _
        adParamInput, 100, "123 New Street")
    .Parameters.Append .CreateParameter(, adVarChar, _
        adParamInput, 50, "Melville")
    .Parameters.Append .CreateParameter(, adVarChar, _
        adParamInput, 50, "NY")
    .Parameters.Append .CreateParameter(, adVarChar, _
        adParamInput, 10, "11746")
    .Parameters.Append .CreateParameter(, adVarChar, _
        adParamInput, 50, "Customer created by an
                        ADO procedure.")
    .Execute
End With

' Retrieve the new CustomerID
' (assuming it's an AutoNumber field)
Set rs = conn.Execute("SELECT @@IDENTITY AS NewCustomerID")
If Not rs.EOF Then
    newCustomerID = rs!newCustomerID
End If
rs.Close


' Define SQL query to retrieve the last identity
' value from OrderID field
```

```vba
strSQL = "SELECT MAX(OrderID) AS LastOrderID FROM Orders2"

Dim LastOrderID As Integer
' Execute the query and retrieve the result
Set rs = conn.Execute(strSQL)
If Not rs.EOF Then
    LastOrderID = rs!LastOrderID
End If

newOrderID = LastOrderID + 1
newStatusID = 3 ' new order

' Insert a new order for the new customer
Set cmd = New ADODB.Command

strSQL = "INSERT INTO Orders (" & _
 "OrderID, EmployeeID, CustomerID, OrderDate, StatusID)" & _
  "VALUES (?, ?, ?, ?, ?)"

With cmd
    .ActiveConnection = conn
    .CommandText = strSQL
    .Parameters.Append .CreateParameter(, adInteger, _
        adParamInput, , newOrderID)
    .Parameters.Append .CreateParameter(, adInteger, _
        adParamInput, , 8)
    .Parameters.Append .CreateParameter(, adVarChar, _
        adParamInput, 5, newCustomerID)
    .Parameters.Append .CreateParameter(, adDate, _
        adParamInput, , Date)
    .Parameters.Append .CreateParameter(, adDate, _
        adParamInput, , newStatusID)
    .Execute
End With

' Insert order details for the new order
newProductID = 21 ' ProductID for Ravioli
newQuantity = 10
newUnitPrice = 20.5
Set cmd = New ADODB.Command

'Define SQL query to insert the Order into OrderDetails table
strSQL = "INSERT INTO OrderDetails (" & _
    "OrderID, ProductID, Quantity, UnitPrice) " & _
    "VALUES (?, ?, ?, ?)"
```

```
With cmd
    .ActiveConnection = conn
    .CommandText = strSQL
    .Parameters.Append .CreateParameter(, adInteger, _
        adParamInput, , newOrderID)
    .Parameters.Append .CreateParameter(, adInteger, _
        adParamInput, , newProductID)
    .Parameters.Append .CreateParameter(, adInteger, _
        adParamInput, , newQuantity)
    .Parameters.Append .CreateParameter(, adCurrency, _
        adParamInput, , newUnitPrice)
    .Execute
End With

' Commit the transaction
conn.CommitTrans

MsgBox "New customer and order added successfully.", _
    vbInformation

Exit Sub

ErrorHandler:
    ' Rollback the transaction in case of error
    conn.RollbackTrans
    MsgBox "An error occurred: " & Err.Description, vbCritical

    ' Clean up
    On Error Resume Next
    If Not rs Is Nothing Then rs.Close
    If Not conn Is Nothing Then conn.Close
End Sub
```

3. Choose Run | Run Sub/UserForm to execute the procedure.

NOTE	*For this procedure to execute successfully, you must have a reference to the* `NorthwindStarter` *database (*`NW2-Starter`*) in the References dialog box. For details, see the section named Executing an Update Query (Hands-On 11.43).*

The `AddNewCustomerWithOrder` procedure demonstrates how to use transaction processing in ADO to insert a new customer into the `Customers` table and add a new order with details for this customer in the `Order` and `OrderDetails` tables. The procedure uses transactions to ensure that all related operations are completed successfully or none are applied in case of an error, ensuring data integrity.

Let's examine `AddNewCustomerWithOrder` procedure in detail.

After opening a database connection, we start a new transaction. Notice that all subsequent operations are part of this transaction. To add a new customer to the `Customers` table, we create and execute an `SQL INSERT INTO` command. We use the `ADODB.Command` object to execute a command on the data source. The `CommandText` property of the `Command` object contains the SQL statement to be executed. This statement specifies the fields where we want to insert the data, and the `Values` clause lists the values for each field. The question marks (`?`) are placeholders for the actual values that will be inserted into the database and they are used for parameterized queries. This helps prevent SQL injection attacks, which are a common security threat. By using placeholders, the values are treated as parameters rather than part of the SQL command, making it hard for malicious code to be executed. Parameters are passed separately from the SQL statement, reducing the risk of SQL injection. For each placeholder (`?`), you must create and append a parameter. The `CreateParameter` method of the `ADODB.Command` object is used to create a new `Parameter` object with specified properties.

```
.Parameters.Append .CreateParameter(, adVarChar, _
          adParamInput, 50, "Advantage Solutions Partners")
```

Parameters specify the data type (`adVarChar`), direction (`adParamInput`), size (e.g., 50 characters), and value (e.g., `"Advantage Solutions Partners"`).

The comma in the first position of the `CreateParameter` method's arguments is a placeholder for the optional `Name` argument that specifies the name of the parameter. It is often left blank, hence the comma at the start.

The parameters must specify the data type. For example, `adVarChar`, `adInteger`, `adDate`, `adCurrency`, etc. The direction parameter indicates whether the parameter is input (`adParamInput`), output (`adParamOutput`), or both (`adParamInputOutput`). The size defines the maximum size of the parameter value and is particularly relevant for variable-length data types, such as `adVarChar`. The value is the actual value to be passed to the parameter and its type should match the specified data type of the parameter.

The `Execute` command executes the SQL command with the provided parameters. If any parameter is missing, an error will occur and the transaction will be rolled back.

Once the customer record is added to the `Customers` table, we need to retrieve the last-inserted identity value for `CustomerID`. This is done by running an SQL query. The `@@IDENITY` is an SQL function that returns the last-inserted identity value. We hold this value in the `newCustomerID` variable so we can use it in the following code segment that inserts data into the `Orders` table. Here, we use the same `INSERT INTO` statement and define appropriate parameters and values. Before inserting data into the `Orders` table, we retrieve the last identity value from the `OrderID` field using the `MAX` function. If we forget anything in this process, an error will occur and the transaction will be rolled back. Next, we proceed to insert order details for the new order into the `OrderDetails` table. If all goes well, we commit the transaction using the `conn.CommitTrans` statement and display a success message. The procedure has simple error-handling code that manages errors by rolling back the transaction and displaying an error message.

This procedure demonstrates how you can maintain data integrity with transactions. If any part of the operation fails, all changes are automatically rolled back.

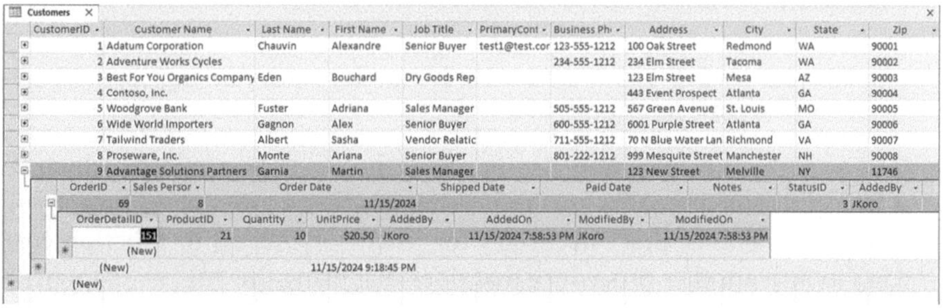

FIGURE 11.21. After running the procedure in Hands-On 11.51, a record for a new customer is added to the Customers, Orders, and OrderDetails tables.

EXAMINING THE REFERENCES COLLECTION

As you have seen in this chapter, your programming code may require the presence of certain libraries that provide the required objects, properties, and methods. Access provides you with the `References` collection, which you can use to examine which references are set for the current application. The following `ShowProjReferences` procedure iterates through the references set in the `Chap11.accdb` database and prints the reference name and its path to the Immediate window.

```
Sub ShowProjReferences()

Dim intRef As Integer

    For intRef = 1 To References.count
        Debug.Print "Reference Name:" & _
            References(intRef).Name & _
            "(" & References(intRef).FullPath & ")"

    Next
End Sub
```

After running the above procedure, the following list of references is pulled from the current VBA project, as shown in Figure 11.22.

```
Immediate                                                                      x
Reference Name:VBA(C:\Program Files\Common Files\Microsoft Shared\VBA\VBA7.1\VBE7.DLL)
Reference Name:Access(C:\Program Files\Microsoft Office\root\Office16\MSACC.OLB)
Reference Name:stdole(C:\Windows\System32\stdole2.tlb)
Reference Name:DAO(C:\Program Files\Common Files\Microsoft Shared\OFFICE16\ACEDAO.DLL)
Reference Name:ADOX(C:\Program Files\Common Files\System\ado\msadox.dll)
Reference Name:ADODB(C:\Program Files\Common Files\System\ado\msado15.dll)
Reference Name:Word(C:\Program Files\Microsoft Office\root\Office16\MSWORD.OLB)
Reference Name:NW2-Starter(C:\VBAAccess2024_ByExample\NorthwindStarter.accdb)
Reference Name:MSComctlLib(C:\WINDOWS\system32\MSCOMCTL.OCX)
```

FIGURE 11.22.   You can retrieve the names of all references in your VBA project by calling upon the References collection in your VBA procedure.

The `References` collection also provides the `BuiltIn` property, which returns a Boolean value (`True`/`False`) indicating whether a `Reference` object points to a default reference that's necessary for Microsoft Access to function correctly. Let's look at another procedure that does that using the `For Each` loop:

```
Sub IsBuiltInReference()
 Dim ref As Reference

 For Each ref In References
  If ref.BuiltIn = True Then
    Debug.Print ref.Name
  End If
 Next ref
End Sub
```

USING ChatGPT WITH ACCESS

You've now learned many terms and concepts that form the foundation of working with Access VBA and ADO, which should enable you to efficiently interact with databases, ensuring data integrity and optimized performance. If you need more specific details on any of the topics introduced here, feel free to explore more with the help of your always-ready assistant—ChatGPT.

In this section, we will ask ChatGPT for help with our Access VBA project. While working with this chapter's hands-on exercises, you were instructed to create many modules that you may have saved with the default names (`Module1`, `Module2`, etc.). I currently have 51 modules with such names and it's getting extremely difficult to know what's available in those modules. Renaming the modules one by one will take too much effort, so let's delegate this task to Chat-GPT. I gave it the following prompt:

User Prompt: *In an Access VBA project, there are numerous standard modules named Module1, Module2, etc. Each module contains one or more procedures. Write a VBA procedure that will rename each module with the name of the first procedure found in a module.*

Within a few seconds, a response came in with ready-to-use VBA code. The `Chapter 11 - Using ChatGPT with Access` document in the companion files provides AI-generated responses to the prompts defined in this section.

When I attempted to run the procedure that I got from the chat, I was informed that the variable `vbext_ct_StdModule` was not defined. I knew that the problem had to do with the missing references. While in the initial response to my prompt I was told that my request would need to leverage the VBA Extensibility library, ChatGPT did not tell me the exact name of this library. As you know, there are lots of libraries in the References dialog box, and finding the one you need can be hard, if you don't know its name. So, I went back to the chat window and wrote another prompt:

User Prompt: *Variable vbext_ct_StdModule not defined.*

This time, the response included a step-by-step process of enabling the *Microsoft VBA Extensibility 5.3* library. I was also given a revised procedure where the definition of the `vbext_ct_StdModule` constant was included. I was now ready to try out the revised procedure. The code ran smoothly until it encountered a blank module. Most of my modules now had meaningful names. I went back to ChatGPT to let it know that I got an error:

User Prompt: *Some modules were not renamed due to the error "Application object defined error".*

ChatGPT came back with the refined procedure code and added more robust error handling to ensure that all modules could be processed correctly. I gave it another try, and all went well. I was just left with one module with the default name. I went back to ChatGPT and wrote the following prompt:

User Prompt: *The problem was resolved. Only the module with no code is left with a default module name. This module was a reason why the previous code failed to rename the remaining modules.*

ChatGPT was happy that everything fell into place, and it said that "indeed, a module without any code can cause issues."

Well, here you go. Working with ChatGPT can be a learning experience for everyone involved. Find something in this chapter that interests you the most and get your answers.

SUMMARY

This marathon chapter covered quite a bit of simple and advanced ADO material that you will find useful in developing professional applications in Access. You started by learning how to create and manipulate a database with ADO objects. You worked with tables, table relationships, and queries, and learned about ADO recordsets and their methods. You created your own recordset from scratch and used it for storing nonrelational data. Next, you learned how to disconnect a recordset from a database and work with it offline. You also learned that a recordset can be saved to a disk file and later reopened without an active connection to the database. After that, you discovered how you can use the `Clone` method of the recordset to create a recordset that is a copy of another recordset. Finally, you familiarized yourself with the concepts of data shaping and learned statements that make it possible to create impressive hierarchical views of your data. You also learned about connection pooling and saw how transactions are used to ensure that certain database operations are always performed as a single unit. In addition, you found out how you can discover the references set in a VBA project without opening the References dialog box.

Access provides different techniques for performing similar database tasks. In the next chapter, which begins Part III of this book, you will be introduced to Access SQL. You will learn special DDL commands for creating a new Access database, as well as creating, modifying, and deleting tables. You will also learn how you can add, modify, and delete fields and indexes using DDL.

Part  # Access Structured Query Language (SQL)

SQL, which stands for Structured Query Language, is a standard language designed to communicate with databases. It is used for querying, updating, and managing data. Access SQL is a variant of the SQL language specifically optimized for Microsoft Access databases. In this part of the book, you will learn how to use both basic and advanced components of Access SQL, which will allow you to efficiently interact with your Access database and perform complex data operations.

Chapter 12   Understanding and Using SQL Within Microsoft Access

12

Understanding and Using SQL Within Microsoft Access

In Part II of this book, you tried out different methods that are available in Access for creating and manipulating databases via VBA programming code using the DAO and ADO object models. In particular, you learned how to create new databases from scratch, add tables and indexes, and create and execute various types of queries. In some of the procedures, we used SQL statements to perform specific tasks. In this chapter, we will delve deeper into the essential topics of the SQL language and see numerous examples of its use within Microsoft Access.

OVERVIEW OF SQL AND THE ACCESS SQL DIALECT

SQL is a widely used language for data retrieval and the manipulation of relational databases. Access SQL is a variant of SQL used in Microsoft Access. The primary functions of SQL are:

- **The Creation and Modification of Database Structures**

  SQL statements such as `CREATE TABLE`, `ALTER TABLE`, `DROP TABLE`, `ADD COLUMN`, `ALTER COLUMN`, `DROP COLUMN`, `CREATE INDEX`, and `DROP INDEX` allow you to define or alter the database schema (tables, fields, indexes, relationships, and various constraints within your database).

- **Querying Data**

  SQL statements such as SELECT with clauses such as WHERE, ORDER BY, GROUP BY, and HAVING, as well as various JOIN statements, allow you to retrieve, filter, sort, and manipulate data stored in your database.

- **Updating Data**

  The UPDATE statement allows you to modify existing data in a table. Using the SET clause within the UPDATE statement, you specify the columns to be updated and their values, and the WHERE clause can be used to specify which records should be updated.

- **Inserting Data**

  The INSERT INTO statement is used to add new data, such as new records to a table.

- **Deleting Data**

  The DELETE statement is used to remove records from a table.

Key Differences Between SQL and Access SQL

SQL and Access SQL share many core concepts and commands since they are both based on standard SQL. There are, however, some differences and unique features specific to Access SQL that provide enhanced capabilities for managing data within the Access environment. For example:

- Domain aggregate functions such as DCount, DMax, and DMin are unique to Access SQL.

- The TRANSFORM statement used in Access crosstab queries is not a part of standard SQL syntax.

- In Access SQL, dates must be enclosed in # signs (#2024-01-01#), while standard SQL uses single quotes ('2024-01-01').

- Access SQL allows for parameter queries to be used directly in the query design, while standard SQL typically uses placeholders such as the question mark (?) you saw in one of the previous chapter's procedures.

- Access SQL supports action queries such as make table, append, update, and delete.

- Access SQL is tightly integrated with Access' graphical Query Builder, which allows the user to build queries visually and see the corresponding SQL code using the SQL view.

- Access SQL can have different names and behaviors for data types. For example, Access uses `COUNTER` for auto-increment fields, while standard SQL might use `SERIAL` or `IDENTITY`.

SQL Specification and Access SQL

The SQL specification (known as *ANSI SQL-89*) was first published in 1989 by the American National Standards Institute (ANSI). The ANSI SQL standard was revised in 1992; this version is referred to as *ANSI SQL-92* or *SQL-2*. This revised specification is supported by the major database vendors, many of whom have created their own extensions of the SQL language.

In Microsoft Access, there are two different ANSI SQL query modes that you can use: ANSI-89 (often referred to as Microsoft Jet SQL) and ANSI-92. Each mode has its own syntax and features, and they are not fully compatible with each other. This means you need to choose which mode to use for your database because mixing them can lead to unexpected results or errors.

- **ANSI-89 (Microsoft Jet SQL)**

  This is the default SQL dialect for Access and it has been in use since early versions. It works well with the Jet database engine, which is used by Access for managing databases. The ANSI-89 syntax may not be compatible with other SQL databases. For example, it uses an asterisk (`*`) for any number or characters and the question mark (`?`) for a single character in queries that use the `LIKE` clause, and a pound sign (`#`) to denote dates:

  ```
  SELECT * FROM Customers WHERE State LIKE 'W*';
  SELECT * FROM Orders WHERE OrderDate = #2024-01-01#;
  ```

- **ANSI-92**

  This query mode is closer to the SQL-92 standard, therefore it is more compatible with other SQL database systems. It also provides more advanced SQL features. It uses the percent sign (`%`) for any number of characters and an underscore (`_`) for a single character in `LIKE` queries, and single quotes to denote dates:

  ```
  SELECT * FROM Customers WHERE State LIKE 'W%';
  SELECT * FROM Orders WHERE OrderDate = '2024-01-01';
  ```

Because the two ANSI SQL query modes are not compatible, you must decide which query mode you are going to use for the current database. This can easily be done in the Access user interface, as outlined in Hands-On 12.1.

> **NOTE** *All code files and figures for the hands-on projects may be found in the companion files.*

⊙ Hands-On 12.1 Setting the ANSI-92 SQL Query Mode

1. Start Access and create a new database named `Chap12.accdb` in your `C:\ VBAAccess2024_ByExample` folder.
2. Click the File tab and select Options.
3. In the left pane of the Access Options window, select Object Designers.
4. In the right pane, in the Query design section, look for the SQL Server Compatible Syntax (ANSI 92) area (see Figure 13.1). Set the query mode to ANSI92 by clicking the This database checkbox. When This database checkbox is not selected, the query mode is assumed to be ANSI-89 SQL.

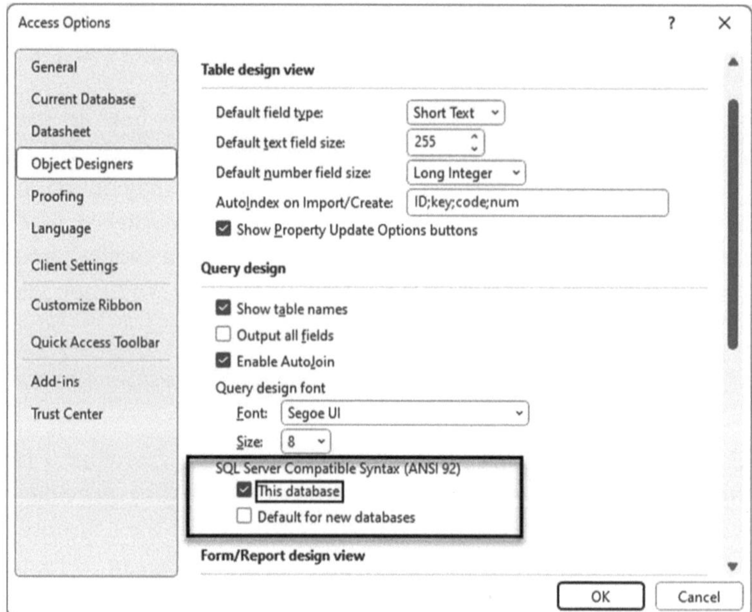

FIGURE 12.1. Use the Access Options window to set the ANSI 92 query mode for the current database or all new databases.

5. Click OK to exit the Access Options window.
   Access displays a message as shown in Figure 12.2.
6. Click OK to accept the message.
   The Access database will close and reopen with the new settings in effect.

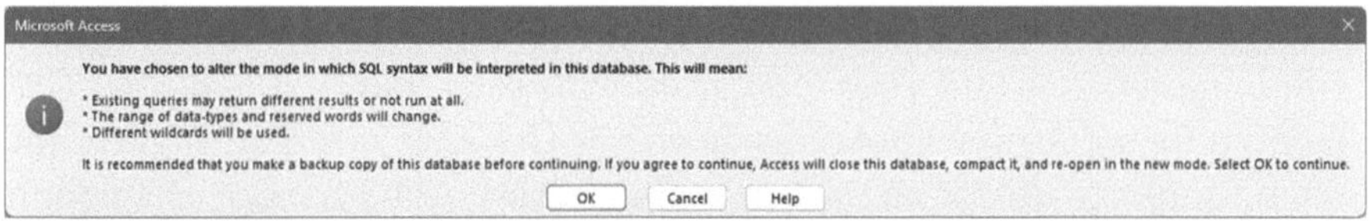

FIGURE 12.2.   When you change the query mode to ANSI 92, Microsoft Access displays an informational message alerting you to possible problems.

Understanding the differences between ANSI-89 and ANSI-92 SQL query modes in Access is crucial for maintaining compatibility and leveraging the appropriate features for your database. Use ANSI-92 if you need to ensure compatibility with other SQL Server databases or SQL-based systems. Older Access databases may use ANSI-89 syntax, and converting them to ANSI-92 could require significant code changes.

The Categories of SQL

SQL can be divided into two main categories that are crucial for managing and interacting with your database but serve different purposes.

- **Data Definition Language (DDL)**

  Offers several SQL statements to manage database security and to create and alter database components (such as tables, indexes, relationships, views, and stored procedures). These statements are `CREATE TABLE`, `DROP TABLE`, `ALTER TABLE`, `CREATE INDEX`, `DROP INDEX`, `CHECK CONSTRAINT`, `CREATE VIEW`, `DROP VIEW`, `CREATE PROCEDURE`, `DROP PROCEDURE`, `EXECUTE`, `ALTER DATABASE`, `ADD USER`, `ALTER USER`, `CREATE USER`, `CREATE GROUP`, `DROP GROUP`, `DROP USER`, `GRANT`, and `REVOKE`.

  You will learn about the statements related to handling user and group security in the next chapter.

- **Data Manipulation Language (DML)**

  Offers SQL statements that allow you to retrieve and manipulate data contained in the database tables, as well as perform transactions. These statements are `SELECT`, `UNION`, `UPDATE`, `DELETE`, `INSERT INTO`, `SELECT INTO`, `INNER JOIN`, `LEFT JOIN`, `RIGHT JOIN`, `TRANSFORM`, `PARAMETERS`, `BEGIN TRANSACTION`, `COMMIT`, and `ROLLBACK`.

You will work with many of the SQL statements mentioned in this introduction to Access SQL in this chapter's example procedures. I assume you are already familiar with using DAO and ADO, discussed in Part II of this book. You can use both ADO and DAO to execute DDL and DML statements within Access

VBA procedures. Each has its advantages, and the choice depends on your specific requirements and your familiarity with each library. Recall that DAO is tailored for working with Access databases (Jet/ACE database engine) and it's often simpler to use for operations within Access. ADO is more useful for projects that require interaction with multiple data sources or more advanced data manipulation.

USING JOINS IN ACCESS SQL

Joins are an important part of Access SQL as they allow you to construct complex queries that combine data from multiple tables, making it easier to view and analyze data. Joins also help in maintaining and enforcing relationships between tables, ensuring data consistency and accuracy.

Types of Joins

In Access, there are three types of joins: INNER JOIN, LEFT JOIN, and RIGHT JOIN. When working with SQL joins, we often use the terms "left table" and "right table" to refer to the order in which tables are specified in the join clause. This terminology is especially important when dealing with outer joins (LEFT JOIN and RIGHT JOIN)

- The left table is the table that appears to the left of the JOIN keyword in the SQL statement.
- The right table is the table that appears to the right of the JOIN keyword in the SQL statement.

INNER JOIN

This join is used for combining rows from two tables where there is a match in both tables. This join will only return rows where the join condition is met. For example, the following SQL statement uses the INNER JOIN to return only the customers who have placed orders:

```
SELECT Customers.CustomerName, Orders.OrderDate
FROM Customers
INNER JOIN Orders ON Customers.CustomerID = Orders.CustomerID;
```

LEFT JOIN (or LEFT OUTER JOIN)

This join returns all rows from the left table and the matched rows from the right table. If no match is found, NULL values are returned for columns from the right table.

For example, the following SQL statement uses the LEFT JOIN to return all customers, including those who have not placed any orders. For customers without orders, OrderDate will be NULL.

```
SELECT Customers.CustomerName, Orders.OrderDate
FROM Customers
LEFT JOIN Orders ON Customers.CustomerID = Orders.CustomerID;
```

In the above query, Customers is the left table (it appears to the left of the JOIN keyword) and Orders is the right table (it appears to the right of the JOIN keyword).

RIGHT JOIN (or RIGHT OUTER JOIN)

This join returns all rows from the right table and the matched rows from the left table. If no match is found, NULL values are returned for columns from the left table.

For example, the following SQL statement uses the RIGHT JOIN to return all orders, including those without a corresponding customer. For orders without a matching customer, CustomerName will be NULL.

```
SELECT Customers.CustomerName, Orders.OrderDate
FROM Customers
RIGHT JOIN Orders ON Customers.CustomerID = Orders.CustomerID;
```

In the above query, Customers is the left table (it appears to the left of the JOIN keyword) and Orders is the right table (it appears to the right of the JOIN keyword).

In SQL, there is also another join, FULL OUTER JOIN, which is not directly supported in Access SQL. This join returns all rows when there is a match in either table. By combining LEFT JOIN with RIGHT JOIN using the UNION operator, you can achieve the results of a FULL OUTER JOIN. For example, the following SQL statement will return all customers and all orders, and will show NULL values where there is no match.

```
SELECT Customers.CustomerName, Orders.OrderDate
FROM Customers
LEFT JOIN Orders ON Customers.CustomerID = Orders.CustomerID
UNION
SELECT Customers.CustomerName, Orders.OrderDate
FROM Customers
RIGHT JOIN Orders ON Customers.CustomerID = Orders.CustomerID;
```

When joining multiple tables, it is important to understand the structure of those tables and their relationships. Your tables should be indexed on the join fields so that your queries can run efficiently without slowing down the performance of your database.

Another thing to keep in mind is the importance of using table aliases, especially when there are many tables participating in the join. For example, the following SQL statement uses table aliases for each table:

```
SELECT c.CustomerName, o.OrderDate, p.ProductName, d.Quantity
FROM Products AS p
INNER JOIN ((Customers AS c INNER JOIN Orders AS o
ON c.CustomerID = o.CustomerID)
INNER JOIN OrderDetails AS d
ON o.OrderID = d.OrderID)
ON p.ProductID = d.ProductID;
```

The above SQL statement joins four tables to retrieve customer names, order dates, product names, and quantities for each order. You can try it out on the `SELECT` query in the `NorthwindStarter` database.

CREATING TABLES

By using the Access SQL `CREATE TABLE` statement and the `Execute` method of either the DAO `Database` object or the ADO `Connection` object, you can define a new table, its fields, and field constraints. The `CREATE TABLE` statement can only be used with Microsoft Jet and Microsoft Access engine databases. The two examples that follow illustrate how to create a table named `tblSchools` in the currently open database and in a new database using ADO.

> **Hands-On 12.2   Creating a Table in the Current Database (DDL with ADO)**

1. In the `Chap12.accdb` database that you created in Hands-On 12.1, switch to the VBE window and choose Tools | References. In the References dialog box, scroll down to locate Microsoft ActiveX Data Objects 6.1 Library. Click the checkbox to the left of this library name to set a reference to it and click OK to exit the dialog box.
2. Choose Insert | Module to add a new module to the current VBA project.
3. In the module's Code window, type the following `CreateTable` procedure:

```
Sub CreateTable()
    ' you must set up a reference to
    ' the Microsoft ActiveX Data Objects Library
    ' in the References dialog box
    Dim conn As ADODB.Connection
    Dim strTable As String
    Dim strSQL As String
```

```
On Error GoTo ErrorHandler

Set conn = CurrentProject.Connection

strTable = "tblSchools"
strSQL = "CREATE TABLE " & strTable
strSQL = strSQL & "(SchoolID AUTOINCREMENT(100, 5), "
strSQL = strSQL & "SchoolName CHAR, "
strSQL = strSQL & "City CHAR (25), "
strSQL = strSQL & "District CHAR (35), "
strSQL = strSQL & "YearEstablished DATE);"

Debug.Print strSQL

conn.Execute strSQL

    Application.RefreshDatabaseWindow
ExitHere:
  conn.Close
  Set conn = Nothing
  Exit Sub
ErrorHandler:
  MsgBox Err.Number & ":" & Err.Description
  Resume ExitHere
End Sub
```

4. Position the insertion point anywhere within the code of the `CreateTable` procedure and press F5 or choose Run | Run Sub/UserForm to execute the procedure.

   This procedure uses ADO to establish a connection to the current database (`Chap12.accdb`). The ADO `Connection` object's `Execute` method is used to execute the DDL `CREATE TABLE` statement that defines a new table and its fields. The first field is named `SchoolID` and its data type is defined as `AutoNumber`. The seed and increment values of `AutoNumber` columns are specified using the following syntax:

   ```
   Column_name AUTOINCREMENT (seed, increment)
   ```

   The table `tblSchools` has an `AutoNumber` column with a seed of `100` and an increment of `5`:

   ```
   SchoolID AUTOINCREMENT(100, 5)
   ```

   When you switch to the database window, open this table in datasheet view, and proceed to enter records, the `SchoolID` for the first record will be `100`, the second will be `105`, the third `110`, and so on.

Three fields are defined as `Text` fields and one field as a `Date/Time` field. `Text` fields are defined using the `CHAR` data type (see Table 12.1). To specify the size of the `Text` field, put the appropriate value between parentheses. If the size of the `Text` field is not specified, it is assumed to be 255 characters long. When you examine the code of the `CreateTable` procedure and compare the resultant table in Figure 12.3, you will notice that Access SQL uses different data types than those available in the Table Design window. See Table 12.1 for the comparison of data types.

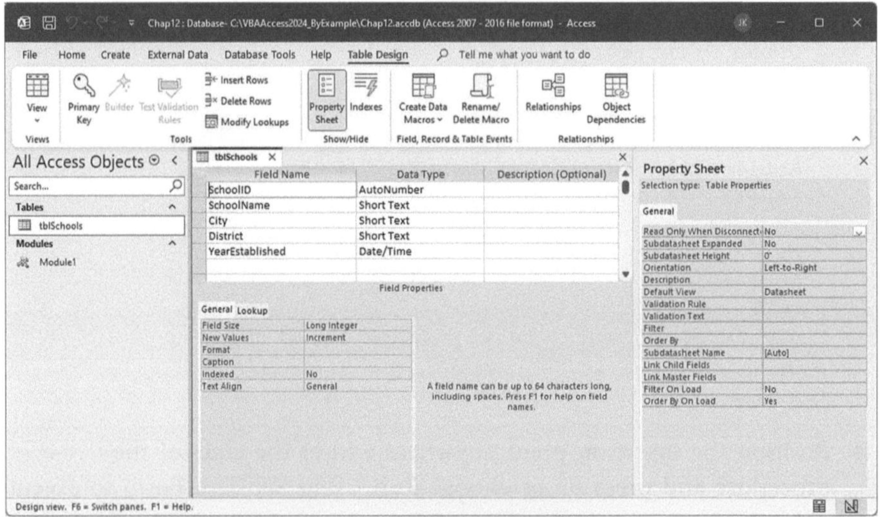

FIGURE 12.3.   The tblSchools table was generated by the CreateTable procedure in Hands-On 12.2 using the Microsoft Access SQL statement CREATE TABLE.

TABLE 12.1.   Table design data types and their Access SQL equivalents.

Table Design Data Types	Access SQL Data Types Used to Create Tables
Text	CHAR or VARCHAR
Memo	LONGTEXT
Number (Field Size = Byte)	BYTE
Number (Field Size = Integer)	SHORT
Number (Field Size = Long Integer)	LONG
Number (Field Size = Single)	SINGLE
Number (Field Size = Double)	DOUBLE
Date/Time	DATETIME

Table Design Data Types	Access SQL Data Types Used to Create Tables
Date/Time Extended (introduced in Access 2021)	No equivalent Access SQL data type
Currency	CURRENCY or MONEY
AutoNumber (Field Size = Long Integer)	AUTOINCREMENT or COUNTER
AutoNumber (Field Size = Replication Id)	GUID
Yes/No	BIT
OLE Object	LONGBINARY

The `RefreshDatabaseWindow` method of the `Application` object ensures that the database window is updated after the creation of the new table object.

Sometimes you may be required to create a new database and a new table in one procedure. Hands-On 12.3 demonstrates how to create a table in a brand-new database.

⊙ Hands-On 12.3   Creating a Table in a New Database (DDL with ADO/ADOX)

1. In the VBE window, choose Tools | References. In the References dialog box, scroll down to locate Microsoft ADO Ext. 6.0 for DDL and Security Object Library. Click the checkbox to the left of the library name to set a reference to it. Also, make sure that Microsoft ActiveX Data Objects 6.1 Library is selected. Click OK to exit the dialog box.

2. In the module's Code window, enter the following `CreateTableInNewDB` procedure:

```
Sub CreateTableInNewDB()
    ' use the References dialog box
    ' to set up a reference to
    ' Microsoft ADO Ext. 6.0 for
    ' DDL and Security Object Library
    ' and Microsoft ActiveX Data
    ' Objects 6.1 Library
    Dim cat As ADOX.Catalog
    Dim conn As ADODB.Connection
    Dim strDb As String
    Dim strTable As String
    Dim strConnect As String

    On Error GoTo ErrorHandler

    Set cat = New ADOX.Catalog
```

```vba
    strDb = CurrentProject.Path & "\Sites.accdb"

    strConnect = "Provider = Microsoft.ACE.OLEDB.12.0;" & _
     "Data Source=" & strDb & ";"


    ' create a new database file
    cat.Create strConnect
    MsgBox "The database was created (" & strDb & ")."

    ' set connection to currently open catalog
    Set conn = cat.ActiveConnection

    strTable = "tblSchools"
    conn.Execute "CREATE TABLE " & strTable & _
     "(SchoolID AUTOINCREMENT(100, 5), " & _
     "SchoolName CHAR," & _
     "City CHAR (25), District CHAR (35), " & _
     "YearEstablished DATE);"
ExitHere:
  Set cat = Nothing
  Set conn = Nothing
  Exit Sub
ErrorHandler:
  If Err.Number = -2147217897 Then
  ' delete the database file if it exists
    Kill strDb
  ' start from statement that caused this error
    Resume 0
  Else
    MsgBox Err.Number & ": " & Err.Description
    GoTo ExitHere
  End If
End Sub
```

3. Position the insertion point anywhere within the `CreateTableInNewDB` procedure and press F5 or choose Run | Run Sub/UserForm to execute the procedure.

The `CreateTableInNewDB` procedure shown here creates a new database named `Sites.accdb` in the current folder. New Access databases can be created by using the `Create` method of the ADOX `Catalog` object. Before creating a table in the new database, set the `conn` object variable to the currently open `Catalog`, like this:

```vba
Set conn = cat.ActiveConnection
```

Use the `Connection` object's `Execute` method to create a new table named `tblSchools`. Like other procedure examples in this section, this table contains an `AutoNumber` field with a sequence starting at 100 that will be incremented by 5 as new columns are added. Notice that the error-handling code demonstrated in this procedure is slightly different from previous examples. If you know the type of error that is most likely to occur, you can check for the error number in the error handler and execute the appropriate statement when the condition is met. If the database already exists, it will be deleted using the VBA `Kill` statement (don't do this in a production environment unless you are absolutely certain this is what you want to do). The statement `Resume 0` in the error-handling code will return the code execution to the line that caused the error. If other errors are encountered, error information will appear in a message box and the code execution will continue from the line following the `ExitHere` label.

DELETING TABLES

It's time to remove some of our test data. You can use the `DROP TABLE` statement to delete an existing table from a database. Note that a table must be closed before it can be deleted. The procedure in Hands-On 12.4 will delete the `tblSchools` table that was created in Hands-On 12.2.

⦿ Hands-On 12.4   Deleting a Table

This hands-on exercise requires the prior completion of Hands-On 12.2.

1. In the VBE window, choose Insert | Module.
2. In the module's Code window, enter the following `DeleteTable` procedure:

```vba
Sub DeleteTable()
  Dim conn As ADODB.Connection
  Dim strTable As String

  On Error GoTo ErrorHandler
  Set conn = CurrentProject.Connection

  strTable = "tblSchools"
  conn.Execute "DROP TABLE " & strTable
  Application.RefreshDatabaseWindow
ExitHere:
  conn.Close
  Set conn = Nothing
```

```
    Exit Sub
ErrorHandler:
  If Err.Number = -2147217900 Then
    DoCmd.Close acTable, strTable, acSavePrompt
    Resume 0
  Else
    MsgBox Err.Number & ":" & Err.Description
    Resume ExitHere
  End If
End Sub
```

3. Position the insertion point anywhere within the code of the `DeleteTable` procedure and press F5 or choose Run | Run Sub/UserForm to execute the procedure.

USING SQL STATEMENTS IN THE QUERY DESIGN

SQL DDL statements can be invoked directly in the Access user interface's Data Definition Query window by following these steps:

1. Choose Create | QueryDesign.
2. Choose Query Design | Data Definition.
3. Save the query when prompted.
4. Enter the following statement in the Data Definition Query window:

```
DROP TABLE tblSchools;
```

5. Choose Query Design | Run.
   If you ran the procedure in the previous hands-on exercise, Access will display the message that the `tblSchools` does not exist.

USING DDL STATEMENTS WITH TABLES

Using DDL statements to manage the structure of your database can be quite different depending on whether the tables are empty or contain data. Here are the key considerations and potential issues to watch for with both scenarios:

- Using DDL with Empty Tables

   DDL operations are faster on empty tables because there is no data to manipulate or index. You can freely change data types, add constraints, or drop columns without worrying about the impact on existing data.

- Using DDL with Filled Tables

  DDL operations on large tables can be time-consuming and might temporarily affect database operations. Structural changes may require indexes to be rebuilt, which can also impact the performance. Dropping columns or changing data types might result in data loss if not handled correctly. Always back up your data before performing DDL operations. Also make sure that any of the structural (schema) changes do not violate data integrity. For example, adding a NOT NULL constraint to an existing column with NULL values would cause an error.

To avoid any issues, test your DDL statements on a copy of the database to ensure they perform as expected. Making changes incrementally and verifying the results after each step is better than running the statements against the full data set. When changing data types, always ensure that the new data type can accommodate existing data. Robust error handling will help manage any issues that arise during the execution of DDL statements.

MODIFYING TABLES WITH DDL

You can modify a table definition by altering, adding, or dropping columns and constraints. *Constraints* allow you to enforce integrity by creating rules for a table. The procedures in the following sections illustrate how to use Access SQL DDL statements to perform the following database tasks:

- Add new columns to a table
- Change the column's data type
- Change the size of a Text column
- Delete a field from a table
- Add a primary key to an existing table
- Add a unique, multiple-field index to an existing table
- Delete an index
- Set a default value for a column in a table
- Change the seed and increment values of AutoNumber columns

Adding New Fields to a Table

Use the ALTER TABLE statement followed by a table name to modify the design of a table after it has been created with the CREATE TABLE statement. Prior to modifying the structure of an existing table, it's recommended that you make a backup copy of the table.

The ALTER TABLE statement can be used with the ADD COLUMN clause to add a new field to the table. For example, the procedure in Hands-On 12.5 adds a Currency field called Budget2025 to the tblSchools table using the following statement:

```
ALTER TABLE tblSchools ADD COLUMN Budget2025 MONEY
```

When you add a new field to a table, you should specify the name of the field, its data type, and, for Text and Binary fields, the size of the field.

Hands-On 12.5   Adding a New Field to an Existing Table

1. Run the procedure in Hands-On 12.2 to create the tblSchools table in the current database if you deleted the table in Hands-On 12.4.
2. In the VBE window, choose Insert | Module.
3. In the module's Code window, enter the following AddNewField procedure:

```
Sub AddNewField()
   Dim conn As ADODB.Connection
   Dim strTable As String
   Dim strCol As String

   On Error GoTo ErrorHandler
   Set conn = CurrentProject.Connection

   strTable = "tblSchools"
   strCol = "Budget2025"

   conn.Execute "ALTER TABLE " & strTable & _
     " ADD COLUMN " & strCol & " MONEY;"
ExitHere:
   conn.Close
   Set conn = Nothing
   Exit Sub
ErrorHandler:
   MsgBox Err.Number & ":" & Err.Description
   Resume ExitHere
End Sub
```

4. Position the insertion point anywhere within the code of the AddNewField procedure and press F5 or choose Run | Run Sub/UserForm to execute the procedure.
5. Open the modified table to verify that the new column was created as specified.

Changing the Data Type of a Table Column

You can use the ALTER COLUMN clause in the ALTER TABLE statement to change the data type of a table column. You must specify the name of the field, the desired data type, and the size of the field, if required. The procedure in Hands-On 12.6 changes the data type of the SchoolID field in the tblSchools table from AutoNumber to a 15-character Text field.

Hands-On 12.6   Changing the Field Data Type

This hands-on exercise uses the tblSchools table created in Hands-On 12.2 and recreated in Hands-On 12.5.

1. In the same module where you entered the procedure in Hands-On 12.5, enter the following ChangeFieldType procedure:

```
Sub ChangeFieldType()
    Dim conn As ADODB.Connection
    Dim strTable As String
    Dim strCol As String

    On Error GoTo ErrorHandler
    Set conn = CurrentProject.Connection

    strTable = "tblSchools"
    strCol = "SchoolID"

    conn.Execute "ALTER TABLE " & strTable & _
      " ALTER COLUMN " & strCol & " CHAR(15);"
ExitHere:
    conn.Close
    Set conn = Nothing
    Exit Sub
ErrorHandler:
    MsgBox Err.Number & ":" & Err.Description
    Resume ExitHere
End Sub
```

2. Position the insertion point anywhere within the code of the ChangeFieldType procedure and press F5 or choose Run | Run Sub/UserForm to execute the procedure.
3. Verify that the procedure you ran made the intended change to the SchoolID data type.

Changing the Size of a Text Column

It's easy to increase or decrease the size of a `Text` column. Simply use the `ALTER TABLE` statement followed by the name of the table, and the `ALTER COLUMN` clause followed by the name of the column whose size you want to modify. Then specify the data type of the column and the new column size. The following statement will modify the size of the `SchoolName` field from the default 255 characters to 40:

```
strTable = "tblSchools"
strCol = "SchoolName"

conn.Execute "ALTER TABLE " & strTable & _
  " ALTER COLUMN " & strCol & " CHAR(40);"
```

Write a VBA procedure that uses the above statement.

Deleting a Column from a Table

Use the `DROP COLUMN` clause in the `ALTER TABLE` statement to delete a column from a table. You only need to specify the name of the field you want to remove. The following statement will remove the specified field from the specified table:

```
strTable = "tblSchools"
strCol = "SchoolName"

conn.Execute "ALTER TABLE " & strTable & _
  " DROP COLUMN " & strCol & ";"
```

Write a VBA procedure that deletes the `Budget2025` column from the `tblSchools` table.

Setting a Default Value for a Table Column

Specifying a default value for a field automatically enters that value in the field each time a new record is added to a table unless the user provides a value for the field. Using DDL, you can add a default value for an existing column with the `SET DEFAULT` clause. The required syntax is as follows:

```
ALTER TABLE table_name ALTER [COLUMN] column_name SET DEFAULT
default-value;
```

The `[COLUMN]` in the syntax is optional. For example, the following code sets the default value for the `City` column:

```
strTable = "tblSchools"
strCol = "City"
strDefVal = "Boston"
```

```
strSQL = "ALTER TABLE " & strTable & _
  " ALTER " & strCol & " SET DEFAULT " & strDefVal
```

Hands-On 12.7   Setting a Default Value

This hands-on exercise uses the `tblSchools` table created in Hands-On 12.2.

1. In the same module where you entered previous hands-on exercises, enter the following `SetDefaultFieldValue` procedure:

```
Sub SetDefaultFieldValue()
    Dim conn As ADODB.Connection
    Dim strTable As String
    Dim strCol As String
    Dim strDefVal As String
    Dim strSQL As String

    On Error GoTo ErrorHandler
    Set conn = CurrentProject.Connection

    strTable = "tblSchools"
    strCol = "City"
    strDefVal = "Boston"
    strSQL = "ALTER TABLE " & strTable & _
      " ALTER " & strCol & " SET DEFAULT " & strDefVal

    conn.Execute strSQL

ExitHere:
    conn.Close
    Set conn = Nothing
    Exit Sub
ErrorHandler:
    MsgBox Err.Number & ":" & Err.Description
    Resume ExitHere
End Sub
```

2. Position the insertion point anywhere within the code of the `SetDefaultFieldValue` procedure and press F5 or choose Run | Run Sub/ UserForm to execute the procedure.

Changing the Seed and Increment Values of AutoNumber Columns

When a table contains a field with an `AutoNumber` data type, you can set a seed value and an increment value. The seed value is the initial value for the column, and the increment value is the number added to the seed value to obtain a new counter value for the next record. If not specified, both the seed and increment values default to 1. You can use DDL to change the seed and increment values of `AutoNumber` columns by using one of the following three statements:

```
ALTER TABLE Table_name
ALTER COLUMN Column_name AUTOINCREMENT (seed, increment)

ALTER TABLE Table_name
ALTER COLUMN Column_name COUNTER (seed, increment)

ALTER TABLE Table_name
ALTER COLUMN Column_name IDENTITY (seed, increment)
```

The example procedure in Hands-On 12.8 modifies the seed value of the existing `AutoNumber` column in the `SchoolID` column to start at 1000. Because we changed the `SchoolID` column's data type to the `Text` data type in one of the earlier hands-on exercises, you will modify the `SchoolID` column in the `Sites.accdb` file you created in Hands-On 13.3 earlier in this chapter.

Hands-On 12.8   Changing the Start (Seed) Value of the AutoNumber Field

This hands-on exercise uses the `Sites.accdb` database file and `tblSchools` table created in Hands-On 12.3.

1. In the same module where you entered previous hands-on exercises, enter the following `ChangeAutoNumber` procedure:

```
Sub ChangeAutoNumber()
  Dim conn As ADODB.Connection
  Dim strDb As String
  Dim strConnect As String
  Dim strTable As String
  Dim strCol As String
  Dim intSeed As Integer

  On Error GoTo ErrorHandler

  strDb = CurrentProject.Path & "\" & "Sites.accdb"

  strConnect = "Provider = Microsoft.ACE.OLEDB.12.0;" & _
    "Data Source=" & strDb & ";"

  strTable = "tblSchools"
  strCol = "SchoolID"
  intSeed = 1000

  Set conn = New ADODB.Connection
```

```
  conn.Open strConnect
  conn.Execute "ALTER TABLE " & strTable & _
    " ALTER COLUMN " & strCol & _
    " COUNTER (" & intSeed & ");"
ExitHere:
  conn.Close
  Set conn = Nothing
  Exit Sub
ErrorHandler:
  If Err.Number = -2147467259 Then
    MsgBox "The database file cannot be located.", _
    vbCritical, strDb
    Exit Sub
  Else
    MsgBox Err.Number & ":" & Err.Description
    Resume ExitHere
  End If
End Sub
```

2. Position the insertion point anywhere within the code of the `ChangeAuto-Number` procedure and press F5 or choose Run | Run Sub/UserForm to execute the procedure.
3. Launch Access with the `Sites.accdb` database and open the `tblSchools` table.
4. Enter a couple of new records in this table. In the `YearEstablished` field, enter the date in the format `mm/dd/yyyy`. Note that the first new record is numbered `1000`, the second `1001`, the third `1002`, and so on.
5. Close the `Sites.accdb` database file.

WORKING WITH PRIMARY KEYS AND INDEXES

Indexes speed the processes of finding and sorting records. You should create indexes for fields that are frequently used in searches and in sorting. You can create an index on a new or existing table. An index can be made of one or more fields. This section presents a number of procedures that use DDL statements to define indexes and primary keys.

Adding a Primary Key to a Table

You can use the `ADD CONSTRAINT` clause in the `ALTER TABLE` statement to define one or more columns as a primary key. The primary key is defined using the `PRIMARY KEY` keyword.

```
strTable = "tblSchools"
strCol = "SchoolID"

conn.Execute "ALTER TABLE " & strTable & _
  " ADD CONSTRAINT pKey PRIMARY KEY " & _
  "(" & strCol & ");"
```

Note that we changed the data type of the `SchoolID` to a `Text` data type in an earlier procedure. In the following procedure, we first change the `SchoolID` data type to `Long Integer` and then create a primary key on this field.

⊚ Hands-On 12.9   Adding a Primary Key to a Table

1. Add a new module to your VBA project and enter the following `Modi-fySchoolIDField_ADO` procedure:

```vba
Sub ModifySiteIDFieldADO()
    Dim conn As ADODB.Connection
    Dim strSQL As String
    Dim strTableName As String
    Dim strFieldName As String

    ' Define table and field names
    strTableName = "tblSchools"
    strFieldName = "SchoolID"

    On Error GoTo ErrorHandler

    ' Initialize the connection string
    Set conn = CurrentProject.Connection


    ' Alter the column type to Long Integer
    strSQL = "ALTER TABLE " & strTableName & _
        " ALTER COLUMN " & strFieldName & " LONG;"
    conn.Execute strSQL

    ' Add Primary Key constraint
    strSQL = "ALTER TABLE " & strTableName & _
      " ADD CONSTRAINT pKey PRIMARY KEY (" & strFieldName & ");"
    conn.Execute strSQL

    MsgBox "The SchoolID field has been modified.", vbInformation

    ' Clean up
```

```
    conn.Close
    Set conn = Nothing
    Exit Sub

ErrorHandler:
    MsgBox "An error occurred: " & Err.Description, vbCritical
    If Not conn Is Nothing Then conn.Close
    Set conn = Nothing
End Sub
```

2. Choose Run | Run Sub/UserForm to execute the procedure.

3. Open the `tblSchools` table to verify the existence of the primary key.

Recall that when we created the `tblSchools` table (see Hands-On 12.2), we defined the `SchoolID` as the `AutoNumber` field. In Access SQL, you can't directly use the `ALTER COLUMN` statement to create an `AutoNumber` field. You can, however, achieve this by creating a new field and setting its data type to `AutoNumber` (or `COUNTER`), copying the data from the original field (if necessary), and then renaming fields as needed.

Adding a Multiple-Field Index to a Table

Use the `ADD CONSTRAINT` clause and the `UNIQUE` keyword in the `ALTER TABLE` statement to add a multiple-field index. The `UNIQUE` keyword prevents duplicate values in the index.

Hands-On 12.10   Adding a Unique Index Based on Two Fields

This hands-on exercise uses the `tblSchools` table created in Hands-On 12.2.

1. In a new module, enter the following `AddMulti_UniqueIndex` procedure:

```
Sub AddMulti_UniqueIndex()
    Dim conn As ADODB.Connection
    Dim strTable As String
    Dim strCol As String

    On Error GoTo ErrorHandler
    Set conn = CurrentProject.Connection

    strTable = "tblSchools"
    strCol = "SchoolID, District"

    conn.Execute "ALTER TABLE " & strTable & _
      " ADD CONSTRAINT multiIdx UNIQUE " & _
```

```
     "(" & strCol & ");"
ExitHere:
   conn.Close
   Set conn = Nothing
   Exit Sub
ErrorHandler:
   MsgBox Err.Number & ":" & Err.Description
   Resume ExitHere
End Sub
```

2. Position the insertion point anywhere within the code of the `AddMulti_UniqueIndex` procedure and press F5 or choose Run | Run Sub/UserForm to execute the procedure. Figure 12.4 shows the result.

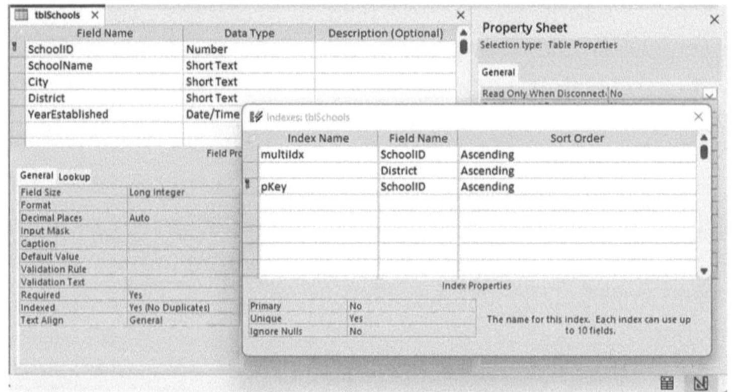

FIGURE 12.4.   The tblSchools table shown here contains a primary key and a unique index based on two fields.

Deleting an Index and an Indexed Field

Deleting an index field is a two-step process:

- Use the `DROP CONSTRAINT` clause to delete an index. You must specify the index name.
- Use the `DROP COLUMN` clause to delete the desired column. You must specify the column name.

Both clauses must be used in the `ALTER TABLE` statement.

The procedure in Hands-On 12.11 deletes the `District` column from the `tblSchools` table. Recall that the procedure in Hands-On 12.10 added a multiple-field index based on the `SchoolID` and `District` columns.

Hands-On 12.11   Deleting a Field that Is Part of an Index

This hands-on exercise uses the `tblSchools` table created in Hands-On 12.2. You must perform Hands-On 12.10 prior to running this procedure.

1. In the same module where you entered previous hands-on exercises, enter the following `DeleteIdxField` procedure:

```
Sub DeleteIdxField()
    Dim conn As ADODB.Connection
    Dim strTable As String
    Dim strCol As String
    Dim strIdx As String

    On Error GoTo ErrorHandler
    Set conn = CurrentProject.Connection

    strTable = "tblSchools"
    strCol = "District"
    strIdx = "multiIdx"

    conn.Execute "ALTER TABLE " & strTable & _
        " DROP CONSTRAINT " & strIdx & ";"

    conn.Execute "ALTER TABLE " & strTable & _
        " DROP COLUMN " & strCol & ";"

ExitHere:
    conn.Close
    Set conn = Nothing
    Exit Sub
ErrorHandler:
    MsgBox Err.Number & ":" & Err.Description
    Resume ExitHere
End Sub
```

2. Position the insertion point anywhere within the code of the `DeleteIdxField` procedure and press F5 or choose Run | Run Sub/UserForm to execute the procedure.
3. Verify that only the primary key exists in the `tblSchools` table.

CREATING INDEXES WITH RESTRICTIONS

You can use the CREATE INDEX statement to add an index to an existing table. The CREATE INDEX statement can be used with the following options:

- PRIMARY option—Creates a primary key index that does not allow duplicate values in the key
- DISALLOW NULL option—Creates an index that does not allow adding records with Null values in the indexed field
- IGNORE NULL option—Creates an index that does not include records with Null values in the key

Use the WITH keyword to declare the preceding index options. The procedure in Hands-On 12.12 designates the SupplierID field as the primary key by using the PRIMARY option (see Figure 12.3).

(⊙) Hands-On 12.12   Creating a Primary Key Index with Restrictions

1. Switch to the VBE window and insert a new module.
2. In the module's Code window, enter the following Index_WithPrimaryOption procedure:

```
Sub Index_WithPrimaryOption()
  Dim conn As ADODB.Connection
  Dim strTable As String

  strTable = "Supplier"
  On Error GoTo ErrorHandler

  Set conn = CurrentProject.Connection

  conn.Execute "CREATE TABLE " & strTable _
    & "(SupplierID INTEGER, " _
    & "SupplierName CHAR (30), " _
    & "SupplierPhone CHAR (12), " _
    & "SupplierCity CHAR (19), " _
    & "CONSTRAINT idxSupplierName UNIQUE " _
    & "(SupplierName));"
  Application.RefreshDatabaseWindow

  conn.Execute "CREATE INDEX idxPrimary ON " & strTable _
    & "(SupplierID) WITH PRIMARY;"
```

```
ExitHere:
  conn.Close
  Set conn = Nothing
  Exit Sub
ErrorHandler:
  MsgBox Err.Number & ":" & Err.Description
  Resume ExitHere
End Sub
```

3. Run the `Index_WithPrimaryOption` procedure.

The index created by this procedure has the Primary and Unique properties set to Yes in the Indexes dialog box. This means that the index is a primary key and every value in this index must be unique. You can prohibit the entry of `Null` values in the indexed fields by using the `DISALLOW NULL` option, as shown in the next example procedure.

(◉) Hands-On 12.13   Creating an Index that Disallows Null Values

1. Switch to the VBE window and insert a new module.
2. In the module's Code window, enter the following `Index_WithDisal-lowNullOption` procedure:

```
Sub Index_WithDisallowNullOption()
  Dim conn As ADODB.Connection
  Dim strTable As String

  strTable = "Supplier3"
  On Error GoTo ErrorHandler
  Set conn = CurrentProject.Connection

  conn.Execute _
   "CREATE INDEX idxSupplierCity ON " & strTable _
   & "(SupplierCity) WITH DISALLOW NULL;"
ExitHere:
  conn.Close
  Set conn = Nothing
  Exit Sub
ErrorHandler:
  MsgBox Err.Number & ":" & Err.Description
  Resume ExitHere
End Sub
```

3. Run the `Index_WithDisallowNullOption` procedure.

Figure 12.5 displays the indexes in the `Supplier` table.

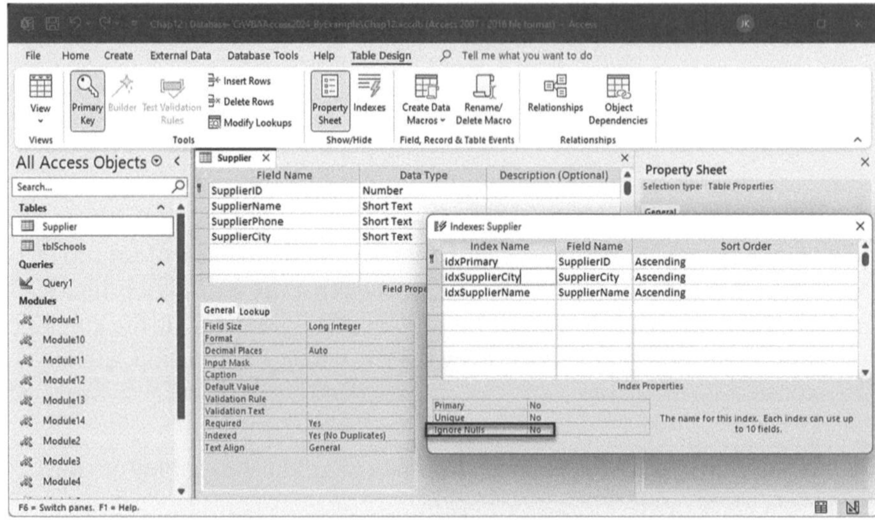

FIGURE 12.5. The index called idxSupplierCity does not allow Null values.

You can prevent records with `Null` values in the indexed fields from being included in the index by using the `IGNORE NULL` option, as illustrated in Hands-On 12.14. Figure 12.6 shows the result after running this procedure.

Hands-On 12.14 Creating an Index with the Ignore Null Option

1. Switch to the VBE window and insert a new module.
2. In the module's Code window, enter the following `Index_WithIgnoreNullOption` procedure:

```
Sub Index_WithIgnoreNullOption()
  Dim conn As ADODB.Connection
  Dim strTable As String

  strTable = "Supplier"

  On Error GoTo ErrorHandler

  Set conn = CurrentProject.Connection
  conn.Execute "CREATE INDEX idxSupplierPhone ON " _
  & strTable & "(SupplierPhone) WITH IGNORE NULL;"
```

```
ExitHere:
  conn.Close
  Set conn = Nothing
  Exit Sub
ErrorHandler:
  MsgBox Err.Number & ":" & Err.Description
  Resume ExitHere
End Sub
```

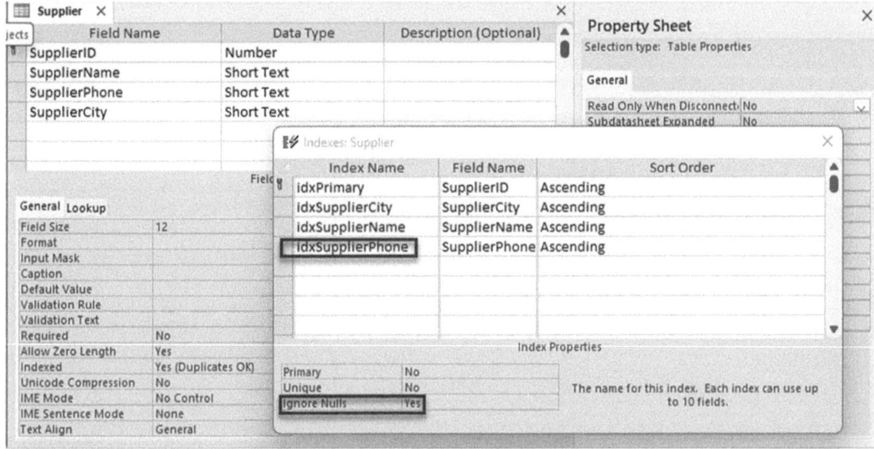

FIGURE 12.6.   The index called idxSupplierPhone allows Null values in the SupplierPhone field. Records containing Null values, however, will be excluded from any searches that use that index.

UNDERSTANDING TABLE CONSTRAINTS

When creating tables in a database, you often need to define rules regarding the values allowed in columns (fields). As mentioned earlier, constraints allow you to enforce integrity by creating rules for a table. The five types of constraints are listed in Table 12.2.

TABLE 12.2.   Table constraints.

Constraint Name	Usage
PRIMARY KEY	Identifies the column or set of columns whose values uniquely identify a row in a table.
FOREIGN KEY	Defines the relationship between tables and maintains data integrity when records are being added, changed, or deleted in a table.

(Contd.)

Constraint Name	Usage
UNIQUE	Ensures that no duplicate values are entered in a specific column or combination of columns that is not a table's primary key.
NOT NULL	Specifies that a column cannot contain a `Null` value. Primary key columns are automatically defined as `NOT NULL`. NOTE: A `Null` value is not the same as zero (0), blank, or a zero-length character string (`""`). A `Null` value indicates that no entry has been made. You can determine whether a field contains a `Null` value by using the `IsNull` function.
CHECK	Enforces integrity by limiting the values that can be placed in a column.

When constraints are added, all existing data is verified for constraint violations.

Using CHECK Constraints

Tables and columns can contain multiple CHECK constraints. A CHECK constraint can validate a column value against a logical expression or another column in the same or another table. What you can't do with the CHECK constraint is to specify the custom validation message, as is possible to do in the Access user interface.

The procedure in Hands-On 12.15 uses a PRIMARY KEY constraint explicitly named `PrimaryKey` to identify the ID column as the primary key. The CHECK constraint used in this procedure ensures that only numbers within the specified range are entered in the `YearsWorked` column. You can apply CHECK constraints to a single column or multiple columns. When a table is deleted, CHECK constraints are also dropped.

(◉) Hands-On 12.15   Using a CHECK Constraint to Specify a Condition for All Values Entered for the Column

1. Choose Insert | Module to add a new module to the current VBA project.
2. In the module's Code window, type the `CheckColumnValue` procedure shown below.

```
Sub CheckColumnValue()
    ' you must set up a reference to the
    ' Microsoft ActiveX Data Objects Library
    ' in the References dialog box
    Dim conn As ADODB.Connection
    Dim strTable As String
    Dim strSQL As String

    strTable = "tblAwards"
    strSQL = "CREATE TABLE " & strTable
```

```
    strSQL = strSQL & "(ID AUTOINCREMENT CONSTRAINT "
    strSQL = strSQL & "PrimaryKey PRIMARY KEY,"
    strSQL = strSQL & "YearsWorked INT, CONSTRAINT FromTo "
    strSQL = strSQL & "CHECK (YearsWorked BETWEEN 1 AND 30));"

    On Error GoTo ErrorHandler
    Set conn = CurrentProject.Connection

    conn.Execute strSQL
    Application.RefreshDatabaseWindow
ExitHere:
    conn.Close
    Set conn = Nothing
    Exit Sub
ErrorHandler:
    MsgBox Err.Number & ":" & Err.Description
    Resume ExitHere
End Sub
```

3. Run the `CheckColumnValue` procedure.
   The `CheckColumnValue` procedure creates the `tblAwards` table with the CHECK constraint.

4. Open the `tblAwards` table and enter a value in the `YearsWorked` column that does not fall between 1 and 30. You should receive the message shown in Figure 12.7.

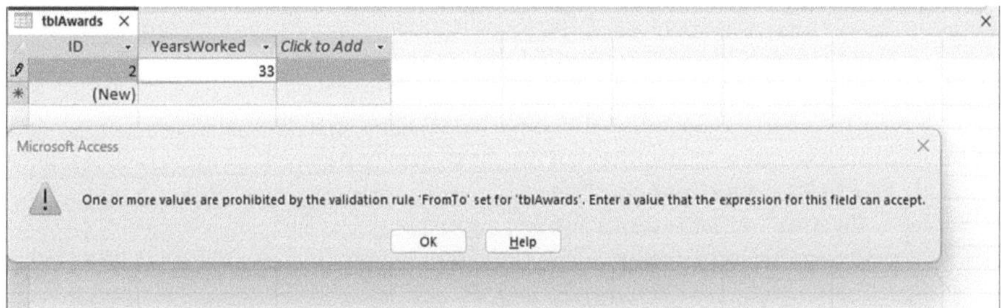

FIGURE 12.7. This message appears when you attempt to enter a value in the YearsWorked column that is not within the range of values specified by the FromTo constraint.

The next hands-on exercise demonstrates how to create a CHECK constraint to ensure that the value of the `Items` column in the `tblBookOrders` table is less than the value of the `MaxUnits` column in the `tblSupplies` table for the specified ISBN. This hands-on exercise also illustrates how to use the SQL DML statements INSERT INTO, BEGIN TRANSACTION, COMMIT TRANSACTION, and ROLLBACK TRANSACTION.

⊙ **Hands-On 12.16   Creating a Table with a Validation Rule Referencing a Column in Another Table**

1. In a new module, enter the `ValidateAgainstCol_InAnotherTbl` procedure shown here:

```
Sub ValidateAgainstCol_InAnotherTbl()
  Dim conn As ADODB.Connection
  Dim strTable1 As String
  Dim strTable2 As String
  Dim InTrans As Boolean

  strTable1 = "tblSupplies"
  strTable2 = "tblBookOrders"

  On Error GoTo ErrorHandler

  Set conn = CurrentProject.Connection

  conn.Execute "BEGIN TRANSACTION"
  InTrans = True
  conn.Execute "CREATE TABLE " & strTable1 & _
    "(ISBN CHAR CONSTRAINT " & _
    "PrimaryKey PRIMARY KEY, " & _
    "MaxUnits LONG);", adExecuteNoRecords

  conn.Execute "INSERT INTO " & strTable1 & _
    " (ISBN, MaxUnits) " & _
    " Values ('158-76609-09', 5);", _
    adExecuteNoRecords

  conn.Execute "INSERT INTO " & strTable1 & _
    " (ISBN, MaxUnits) " & _
    " Values ('167-23455-69', 7);", _
    adExecuteNoRecords

  conn.Execute "CREATE TABLE " & strTable2 & _
    "(OrderNo AUTOINCREMENT CONSTRAINT " & _
    "PrimaryKey PRIMARY KEY, " & _
    "ISBN CHAR, Items LONG, " & _
    "CONSTRAINT OnHandConstr CHECK " & _
    "(Items <(SELECT MaxUnits FROM " & strTable1 & _
    " WHERE ISBN = " & strTable2 & ".ISBN)));", _
    adExecuteNoRecords
```

```
conn.Execute "COMMIT TRANSACTION"
  InTrans = False
  Application.RefreshDatabaseWindow
ExitHere:
  conn.Close
  Set conn = Nothing
  Exit Sub
ErrorHandler:
  If InTrans Then
    conn.Execute "ROLLBACK TRANSACTION"
    Resume ExitHere
  Else
    MsgBox Err.Number & ":" & Err.Description
    Exit Sub
  End If
End Sub
```

2. Position the insertion point anywhere within the code of the `ValidateAgainstCol_InAnotherTbl` procedure and press F5 or choose Run | Run Sub/UserForm to execute the procedure.

    This procedure creates two tables: `tblSupplier` and `tblBookOrders`. Because the `Items` column in the `tblBookOrders` needs to be validated against the contents of the `MaxUnits` column in the `tblSupplies`, we wrapped the process of creating these tables and entering data in the `tblSupplies` table into a transaction. To trap errors that could occur during the procedure execution, we declared a Boolean variable named `InTrans` to help us determine whether an error occurred during the transaction; if the value of `InTrans` is `True`, we will cancel the transaction.

    Notice that in the Access SQL syntax, we use the `BEGIN TRANSACTION` statement to start the transaction, the `COMMIT TRANSACTION` statement to save the results of the transaction, and the `ROLLBACK TRANSACTION` statement to cancel any changes. These transaction statements can only be used through the OLE DB provider for Microsoft Jet and ADO. They will cause an error when used with the Access user interface or DAO.

    In this example procedure, we used the `adExecuteNoRecords` option to specify that no rows should be returned. You can use this setting with the `Connection` or `Command` object's `Execute` method to improve performance when no rows are returned or when you don't plan to access the returned rows in your procedure code. If you omit this setting, your ADO code will still execute successfully, but ADO will unnecessarily create a `Recordset` object as the return value for the `Execute` method. Using the `adExecuteNoRecords` setting is one of several techniques for optimizing data access using ADO.

3. Open the `tblBookOrders` table and enter the record shown at the top of Figure 12.8.
   When you try to save this record or move to the next data row, Access will display a message informing you that the value you are trying to enter is prohibited.

4. Click OK to dismiss the message box, then press Esc to cancel the data entry.

5. Enter the value of 4 in the Items column. This time, Access approves the entry and no error message is displayed.

6. Close the `tblBookOrders` table.

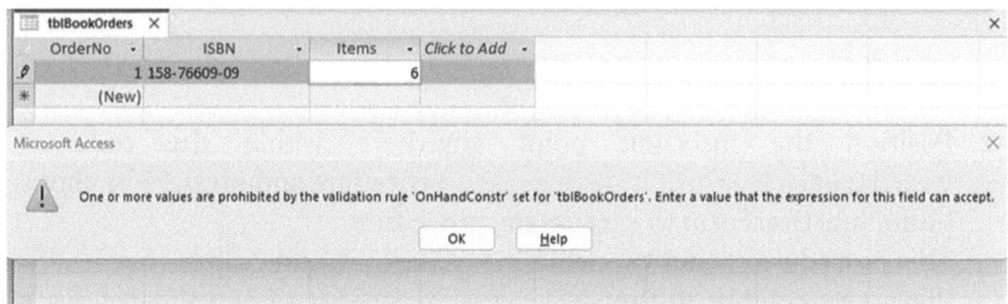

FIGURE 12.8.   When you attempt to enter a value that does not meet the validation rule, Access displays an error message.

7. In the object navigation pane on the left side of the database window, right-click the tblBookOrders table and choose Delete. Click Yes to confirm the deletion. Access will respond with the error message shown in Figure 12.9.

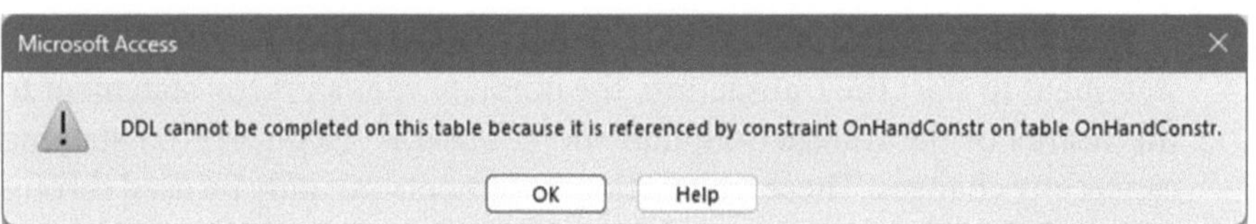

FIGURE 12.9.   If you try to manually delete a table referenced by the CHECK constraint, Access will display an error message.

ESTABLISHING RELATIONSHIPS BETWEEN TABLES

To establish a link between the data in two tables, add one or more columns that hold one table's primary key values to the other table. This column becomes a *foreign key* in the second table. Using SQL, you can use a FOREIGN KEY constraint to reference another table. Foreign keys can be single-column or multicolumn.

A `FOREIGN KEY` constraint enforces referential integrity by ensuring that changes made to data in the primary key table do not break the link to data in the foreign key table. For example, you cannot delete a record in a primary key table or change a primary key value if the deleted or changed primary key value corresponds to a value in the `FOREIGN KEY` constraint of another table. The `REFERENCES` clause identifies the parent table of the relation.

To create a brand-new table and relate it to an existing table, the following steps are required:

1. Use the `CREATE TABLE` statement followed by a table name.

```
CREATE TABLE tblOrder_Details
```

2. Follow the table name with one or more column definitions. A *column definition* consists of `ColumnName` followed by the data type and column size (if required).

```
InvoiceID CHAR, ProductId CHAR, Units LONG, Price MONEY
```

3. To designate a primary key, use the `CONSTRAINT` clause followed by the constraint name, the `PRIMARY KEY` clause, and the name of the column or columns to be designated as the primary key.

```
CONSTRAINT PrimaryKey PRIMARY KEY (InvoiceId, ProductId)
```

4. To designate a foreign key, use the `CONSTRAINT` clause followed by the constraint name, the `FOREIGN KEY` clause, and the name of the column to be designated as the foreign key.

```
CONSTRAINT fkInvoiceId FOREIGN KEY (InvoiceId)
```

5. Use the `REFERENCES` clause to specify the parent table to which a relationship is established.

```
REFERENCES tblProduct_Orders
```

6. If required, specify `ON UPDATE CASCADE` and/or `ON DELETE CASCADE` to enable referential integrity rules with cascading updates or deletes.

```
ON UPDATE CASCADE ON DELETE CASCADE
```

<table>
<tr><td>NOTE</td><td>You may choose not to enforce referential integrity rules by specifying <code>ON UPDATE NO ACTION</code> or <code>ON DELETE NO ACTION</code>, or skipping the <code>ON UPDATE</code> or <code>ON DELETE</code> keywords. If you choose this path, you will not be able to change the value of a primary key if matching records exist in the foreign table.</td></tr>
</table>

The next hands-on exercise demonstrates how to correctly combine the preceding example statements into a single SQL statement.

Hands-On 12.17   **Relating Two Tables and Setting up Cascading Referential Integrity Rules**

1. In the VBE window, choose Insert | Module.
2. In the module's Code window, enter the `RelateTables` procedure shown here:

```
Sub RelateTables()
   Dim conn As ADODB.Connection
   Dim strPrimaryTbl As String
   Dim strForeignTbl As String

   strPrimaryTbl = "tblProduct_Orders"
   strForeignTbl = "tblOrder_Details"

   On Error GoTo ErrorHandler

   Set conn = CurrentProject.Connection

   conn.Execute "CREATE TABLE " & _
     strPrimaryTbl & _
     "(InvoiceID CHAR(15), " & _
     "PaymentType CHAR(20), " & _
     " PaymentTerms CHAR(25), " & _
     "Discount LONG, " & _
     " CONSTRAINT PrimaryKey " & _
     "PRIMARY KEY (InvoiceID));", _
     adExecuteNoRecords

   conn.Execute "CREATE TABLE " & _
     strForeignTbl & _
     "(InvoiceID CHAR(15), " & _
     "ProductID CHAR(15), " & _
     " Units LONG, Price MONEY, " & _
     "CONSTRAINT PrimaryKey PRIMARY KEY " & _
     "(InvoiceID, ProductID), " & _
     "CONSTRAINT fkInvoiceID " & _
     "FOREIGN KEY (InvoiceID) " & _
     "REFERENCES " & strPrimaryTbl & _
     " ON UPDATE CASCADE ON DELETE CASCADE);", _
     adExecuteNoRecords
   Application.RefreshDatabaseWindow
ExitHere:
```

```
    conn.Close
    Set conn = Nothing
    Exit Sub
ErrorHandler:
    MsgBox Err.Number & ":" & Err.Description
    Resume ExitHere
End Sub
```

3. Position the insertion point anywhere within the code of the `RelateTables` procedure and press F5 or choose Run | Run Sub/UserForm to execute the procedure.

   The `RelateTables` procedure creates and joins two tables. A primary key table named `tblProduct_Orders` is created with a primary key on the `InvoiceID` field. The foreign key table named `tblOrder_Details` is created with a multifield primary key index based on the `ProductID` and `InvoiceID` fields. The `REFERENCES` clause specifies the `tblProduct_Orders` table as the parent table. The created relationship has the referential integrity rules enforced via the `ON UPDATE CASCADE` and `ON DELETE CASCADE` statements.

   The outcome of the `RelateTables` procedure is illustrated in the following figures. Figure 12.10 displays the one-to-many relationship between `tblProduct_Orders` and `tblOrder_Details`.

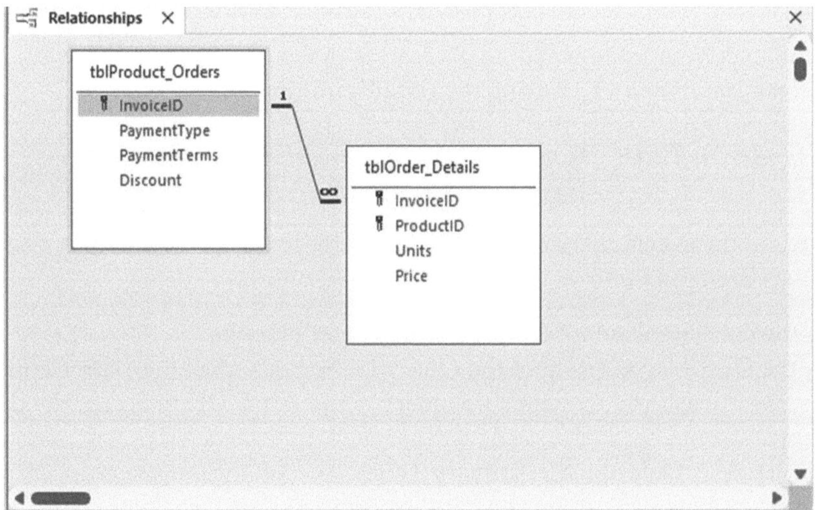

FIGURE 12.10.   To access the Relationships window, choose Database Tools | Relationships.

Figure 12.11 presents the Edit Relationships window in which both cascading updates and deletes are selected.

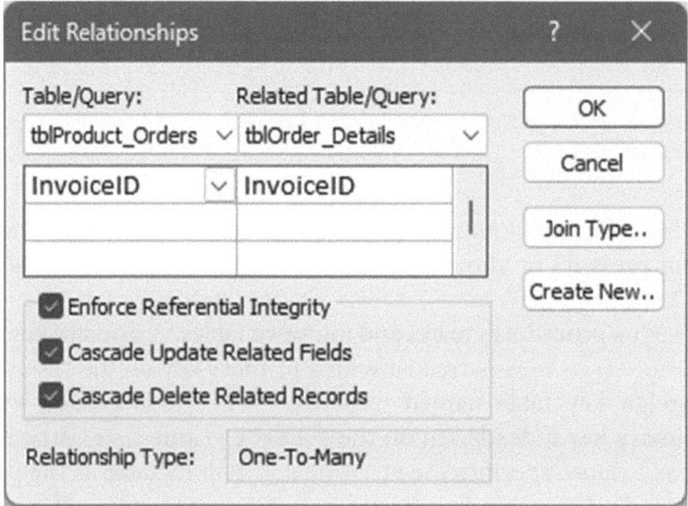

FIGURE 12.11.   To access the Edit Relationships window, choose Relationships Design | Edit Relationships.

USING THE DATA DEFINITION QUERY WINDOW

To enhance your understanding of creating tables and relationships with DDL, perform Hands-On 12.18 using the Data Definition Query window.

Hands-On 12.18   Running DDL Statements in the Access User Interface

Each of the statements in this hands-on exercise can be executed by choosing Query Design | Run.

1. In the database window, choose Create | Query Design.
2. In the Query Type group of the Query Design tab, click the Data Definition. Access will ask you to supply the query name. Click OK to accept the default name.
3. To create a table on the primary (one) side of the relationship, type the following statement on one line in the query window (see Figure 12.12):

```
CREATE TABLE myPrimaryTbl(ID COUNTER CONSTRAINT pKey
 PRIMARY KEY, COUNTRY TEXT(15));
```

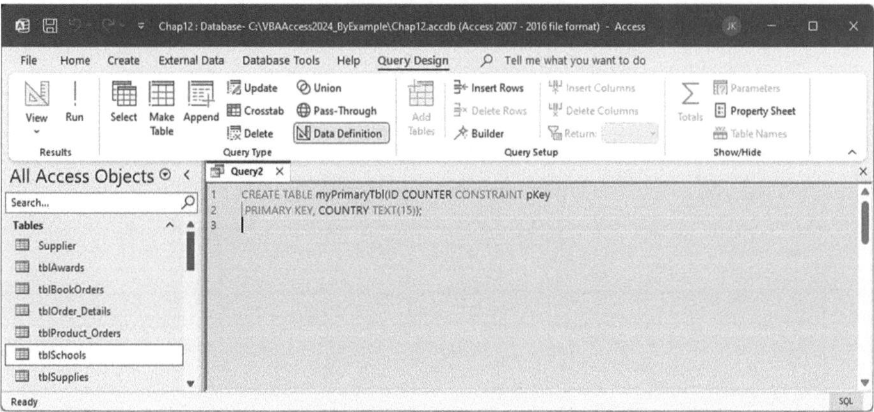

FIGURE 12.12.   Using the Data Definition Query window to enter SQL statements.

4. Click the Run button in the Query Design ribbon to execute the `Create Table` statement. You should see a new table named `myPrimaryTbl` in the database navigation pane.

5. To create a table on the foreign (many) side of the relationship, delete the preceding statement, then type the following statement and run the query:

```
CREATE TABLE myForeignTbl(ID LONG, Region TEXT (15));
```

After running the above data definition query, you should see `myForeignTbl` in the database navigation pane.

6. To create a one-to-many relationship between `myPrimaryTbl` and `myForeignTbl`, delete the preceding statement, then type the following statement on one line in the query window and run the query:

```
ALTER TABLE myForeignTbl ADD CONSTRAINT Rel FOREIGN KEY(ID)
  REFERENCES myPrimaryTbl (ID);
```

You have just related two tables.

7. In the database window, choose Database Tools | Relationships.

8. In the Relationships window, click the All Relationships button on the Ribbon.
   This will add both tables (`myPrimaryTbl` and `myForeignTbl`) to the Relationships window (see Figure 12.13).

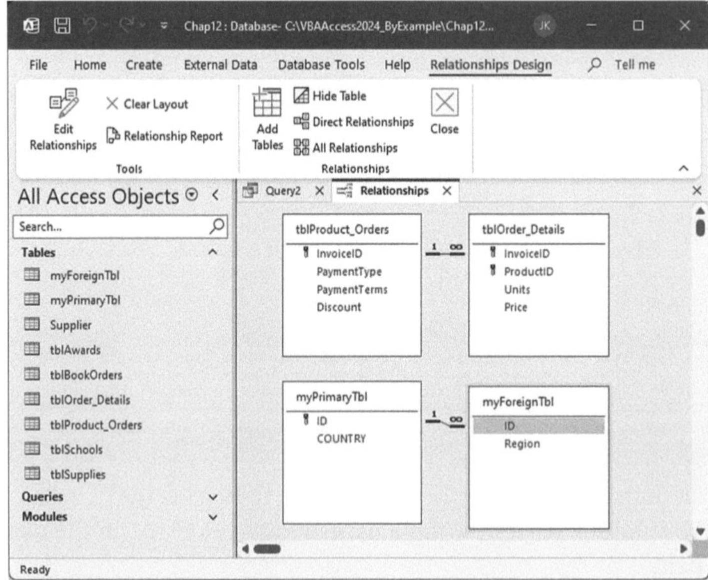

FIGURE 12.13. Notice that the tables you created by running the DDL statements in steps 3 and 5 are joined on the ID column (see step 6).

9. Right-click the line that joins the `myPrimaryTbl` and `myForeignTbl` tables and choose Edit Relationship to open the Edit Relationships dialog box, as shown in Figure 12.14. You can also double-click the line to open this dialog box.

10. Click Cancel to exit the Edit Relationships window, and click Close to close the Relationships window.

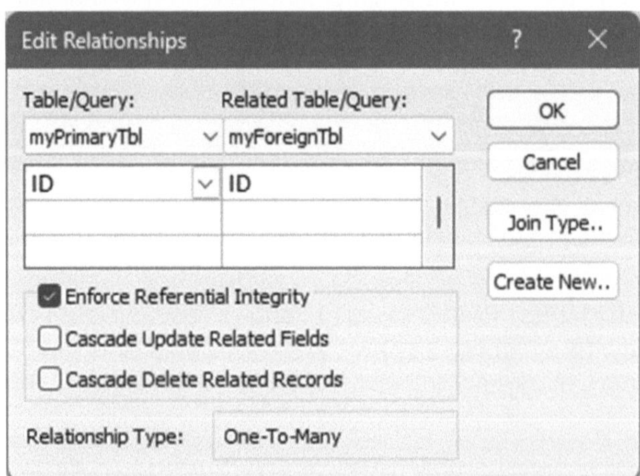

FIGURE 12.14. You can edit relationships between tables via the Edit Relationships window.

11. To delete the relationship between the tables, type the following statement in the Data Definition Query window (overwriting the previously entered statement) and run the query:

```
ALTER TABLE myForeignTbl DROP CONSTRAINT Rel;
```

12. To delete the table on the one side (`myPrimaryTbl`), type the following statement in the Data Definition Query window (overwriting the preceding statement) and run the query:

```
DROP TABLE myPrimaryTbl;
```

The table named `myPrimaryTbl` should be removed from the database.

13. To delete the table on the many side (`myForeignTbl`), type the following statement in the Data Definition Query window (overwriting the preceding statement) and run the query:

```
DROP TABLE myForeignTbl;
```

The table named `myForeignTbl` should be removed from the database.

14. Close the Data Definition Query window without saving the query.

CREATING AND USING VIEWS AND STORED PROCEDURES

Advanced DDL statements are used for creating, altering, and deleting two special database objects known as views and stored procedures. These objects are used to perform various query operations. *Views* are like select queries; however, they don't provide the ORDER BY clause to sort your data or use parameters to filter records. *Stored procedures* perform the same operations as action and parameter queries. They can also be used for creating sorted select queries. Stored procedures are saved precompiled so that at runtime, the procedure executes much faster than a standard SQL statement. Learning how to create and use views and stored procedures will give you more control over your database.

Creating a View

If you want users to view and update data in a table or set of tables, but you do not want them to open the underlying tables directly, you can create a view. An SQL *view* is like a virtual table. Similar to an Access select query, a view can display data from one or more tables. Instead of providing all the available data in your tables, you decide exactly what fields you'd like to include for viewing.

To create a view, use a SELECT statement to select the columns you want to include in the view and the FROM keyword to specify the table. Next, associate the SELECT statement with a CREATE VIEW statement. The syntax looks like this:

```
CREATE VIEW viewName [(columnNames)]
AS
SELECT (columnNames)
FROM tableName;
```

Views must have unique names in the database. The name of the view cannot be the same as the name of an existing table. Specifying the names of columns following the name of the view is optional (note the square brackets in the preceding syntax). Column names must be specified in the SELECT statement. Use the asterisk (*) to select all columns.

Let's add some context to the preceding syntax. The following example statement creates a view that lists only orders with a freight amount of less than $20.

```
CREATE VIEW cheapFreight
AS
SELECT Orders.OrderID,
Orders.[Shipping Fee],
Orders.[ShipCountry/Region]
FROM Orders
WHERE Orders.[Shipping Fee] < 20;
```

The SELECT statement that defines the view cannot contain any parameters and cannot be typed directly in the SQL pane of the Query window. It must be used through the ADO Connection object's Execute method after establishing the connection to a database, as illustrated here:

```
Sub Create_View_CheapFreight()
  Dim conn As ADODB.Connection
  Set conn = CurrentProject.Connection

  conn.Execute "CREATE VIEW CheapFreight AS " & _
    "SELECT Orders.[Order ID], Orders.[Shipping Fee], " & _
    "Orders.[Ship Country/Region] " & _
    "FROM Orders WHERE Orders.[Shipping Fee] < 20;"

  Application.RefreshDatabaseWindow
  conn.Close
  Set conn = Nothing
End Sub
```

To return data from the CheapFreight view, simply double-click its name in the Navigation Pane.

A view can be used as if it were a table. The following statement can be used to return all records from the `CheapFreight` view:

```
SELECT * FROM CheapFreight;
```

Remember that a view never stores any data; it simply returns the data as stated in the `SELECT` statement used in the view definition. Because a view is like a select query, you can use the `OpenQuery` method of the Access `DoCmd` object to open it from your VBA code:

```
Sub OpenView()
  DoCmd.OpenQuery "CheapFreight", acViewNormal
End Sub
```

The `OpenQuery` method is used to carry out the `OpenQuery` action in Visual Basic.

To get working experience with views, let's proceed to the hands-on section. We will start by creating a view called `vw_Employees`. This view is based on the `Employees` and `Orders` tables and contains four columns (`Employee ID`, `Full Name`, `Job Title`, and `Order ID`).

Hands-On 12.19   Creating a View Based on Tables

1. Copy the `Northwind 2007.accdb` database from the companion files to your `VBAAccess2024_ByExample` folder.
2. Choose External Data | New Data Source | From Database | Access.
3. In the File name box of the Get External Data dialog box, enter `C:\VBAAccess2024_ByExample\Northwind 2007.accdb` and click OK.
4. In the Import Objects dialog box, choose the Tables tab and select the Employees, Orders, and Shippers tables, then click OK.
5. Click Close to exit the Get External Data dialog box.
   The Employees, Orders, and Shippers tables are now listed in the Navigation Pane.
6. Switch to the VBE window and choose Insert | Module to add a new module to the current VBA project.
7. In the module's Code window, type the following `Create_View` procedure:

```
' Don't forget to set up a reference to the
' Microsoft ActiveX Data Objects 6.1 Library
' in the References dialog box

Sub Create_View()
  Dim conn As ADODB.Connection
```

```
    Set conn = CurrentProject.Connection

    On Error GoTo ErrorHandler

    conn.Execute _
    "CREATE VIEW vw_Employees AS " & _
     "SELECT Employees.ID AS [Employee ID], " & _
     "[First Name] & chr(32) & [Last Name] " & _
     "AS [Full Name], " & _
     "[Job Title], Orders.[Order ID] " & _
     "AS [Order ID] " & _
     "FROM Employees " & _
     "INNER JOIN Orders ON " & _
     "Orders.[Employee ID] = Employees.ID;"
     Application.RefreshDatabaseWindow
ExitHere:
   If Not conn Is Nothing Then
      If conn.State = adStateOpen Then conn.Close
   End If
   Set conn = Nothing
   Exit Sub
ErrorHandler:
   If Err.Number = -2147217900 Then
      conn.Execute "DROP VIEW vw_Employees"
      Resume
   Else
      MsgBox Err.Number & ":" & Err.Description
      Resume ExitHere
   End If
End Sub
```

8. Run the `Create_View` procedure.
This procedure creates a view named `vw_Employees`. If the view already exists, it will be deleted using the `DROP VIEW` statement. The `chr(32)` statement will insert a space between the first and last name. Another way to add a space is by using the `Space` function, like this: `Space(1)`. Notice that views don't differ much from saved queries. When you open the view created by the `Create_View` procedure in design view, you will notice that this view is simply a select query. Because the query defined by the `SELECT` statement is updatable, the `vw_Employees` view is also updatable. If the query were not updatable, the view would be read-only.

Views cannot contain the `ORDER BY` clause. To return the records in a specific order, you might want to use the view in a stored procedure, as discussed later in this chapter.

Enumerating Views

You can find out the names of the views that have been created by iterating through the `Views` collection of the ADOX `Catalog` object, as illustrated below:

```vba
' Don't forget to set up a reference to the
' Microsoft ADO Ext. 2.8 for DDL and Security

Sub List_Views()
  Dim cat As New ADOX.Catalog
  Dim myView As ADOX.View

  cat.ActiveConnection = CurrentProject.Connection

  For Each myView In cat.Views
    Debug.Print myView.Name
  Next myView
End Sub
```

Deleting a View

Use the `DROP VIEW` statement to delete a particular view from the database. You must specify the name of the view you want to delete. The following example procedure deletes a view named `vw_Employees` that was created by the procedure in Hands-On 12.19.

Note that both the `CREATE VIEW` and `DROP VIEW` statements can only be executed using the `Execute` method of the ADO `Connection` object.

◉ Hands-On 12.20   Deleting a View

1. In a new module, enter the `Delete_View` procedure shown here:

```vba
Sub Delete_View()
  Dim conn As ADODB.Connection

  Set conn = CurrentProject.Connection

  On Error GoTo ErrorHandler
  conn.Execute "DROP VIEW vw_Employees"
ExitHere:
  If Not conn Is Nothing Then
    If conn.State = adStateOpen Then conn.Close
  End If
  Set conn = Nothing
  Exit Sub
```

```
ErrorHandler:
  If Err.Number = -2147217865 Then
    MsgBox "The view was already deleted."
    Exit Sub
  Else
    MsgBox Err.Number & ":" & Err.Description
    Resume ExitHere
  End If
End Sub
```

2. Run the `Delete_View` procedure.

Creating a Stored Procedure

Stored procedures allow you to perform bulk operations that delete, update, or append records. Unlike views, stored procedures allow the use of the ORDER BY clause and parameters. Use the CREATE PROCEDURE (or CREATE PROC) statement to create a stored procedure. You must specify the name of the stored procedure and the AS keyword followed by the desired SQL statement that performs the required database operation. The syntax is as follows:

```
CREATE PROC[EDURE] procName
[(param1 datatype1 [, param2 datatype2 [, ...] ])]
AS sqlStatement;
```

The name of the stored procedure cannot be the same as the name of an existing table. To pass values to a stored procedure, include parameters after the procedure name. Parameter names are followed by a data type and are separated by commas. The parameters are listed in parentheses (see Hands-On 12.21 in the next section). Up to 255 parameters can be specified in the parameter list. If the stored procedure does not require parameters, the AS keyword immediately follows the name of the stored procedure.

The SQL statement for the stored procedure can be prepared in the Access Query Design window and then copied to the VBA procedure from the SQL view and appropriately formatted.

To return the employee records from the vw_Employees view (see Hands-On 12.19) ordered by Full Name, the following stored procedure can be written:

```
CREATE PROCEDURE usp_EmpByFullName
AS
  SELECT * FROM vw_Employees
  ORDER BY [Full Name];
```

This stored procedure selects all columns that exist in the `vw_Employees` view and orders the returned data by the Full Name field. Notice that this procedure does not require any parameters. You might want to precede the name of the stored procedure with a prefix indicating the type of stored procedure. The `usp` prefix is often used to indicate a user-defined stored procedure.

Like views, stored procedures are created via the ADO `Connection` object's `Execute` method after establishing a connection to the database. Therefore, you can use the following VBA code to create the `usp_EmpByFullName` stored procedure. If you want to try this on your own, make sure to rerun the procedure that creates `vw_Employees`, as this view was deleted in the previous hands-on exercise:

```
Sub Create_StoredProc()
  Dim conn As ADODB.Connection

  Set conn = CurrentProject.Connection
  conn.Execute "CREATE PROCEDURE usp_EmpByFullName AS " & _
    "SELECT * FROM vw_Employees " & _
    "ORDER BY [Full Name];"

  Application.RefreshDatabaseWindow

  conn.Close
  Set conn = Nothing
End Sub
```

Once created, stored procedures can be executed in the Access user interface by double-clicking the stored procedure name in the database navigation pane, or with VBA code by calling the EXECUTE statement with the ADO `Connection` object's `Execute` method.

Creating a Parameterized Stored Procedure

Most advanced stored procedures require one or more parameters. The parameters are then used as part of the SQL statement, usually the WHERE clause. When creating a parameterized stored procedure, Access allows you to specify up to 255 parameters in the parameters list. The stored procedure parameters must be separated by commas and enclosed in parentheses.

In Hands-On 12.21, a stored procedure is created that allows you to insert a new record into the `Shippers` table on the fly by supplying the required parameter values. Note that the SQL DML INSERT INTO statement is used for adding new records to a table.

Hands-On 12.21   Creating a Stored Procedure that Accepts Parameters

1. In a new module, enter the following `Create_SpWithParam` procedure:

```vba
Sub Create_SpWithParam()
  Dim conn As ADODB.Connection

  On Error GoTo ErrorHandler

  Set conn = CurrentProject.Connection

  conn.Execute _
  "CREATE PROCEDURE usp_procEnterData " & _
   "(@Company TEXT (50), " & _
   "@Tel TEXT (25)) AS " & _
   "INSERT INTO Shippers " & _
   "(Company, [Business Phone]) " & _
   "VALUES (@Company, @Tel);"
  Application.RefreshDatabaseWindow
ExitHere:
  If Not conn Is Nothing Then
    If conn.State = adStateOpen Then conn.Close
  End If
  Set conn = Nothing
  Exit Sub
ErrorHandler:
  If InStr(1, Err.Description, _
    "procEnterData") Then
      conn.Execute "DROP PROC usp_procEnterData"
    Resume
  Else
    MsgBox Err.Number & ":" & Err.Description
    Resume ExitHere
  End If
End Sub
```

2. Run the `Create_SpWithParam` procedure.
   The preceding stored procedure requires two values to be entered at runtime. The first value is passed by the `@Company` parameter and the second value by the `@Tel` parameter. In this example, the names of the parameters have been preceded with the `@` sign for easy migration of the stored procedure into the SQL Server environment. If you omit the `@` sign, the procedure will still execute

correctly in Access. If the procedure already exists, it will be dropped using the `DROP PROC` statement.

Like views, stored procedures appear in the database navigation pane in the Access application window. Because we used the SQL `INSERT INTO` statement, Access treats this stored procedure as a parameterized append query.

3. Run the stored procedure named `usp_procEnterData` by double-clicking its name in the database navigation pane of the Access application window. Figures 12.15 through 12.18 outline the process of running this stored procedure, and Figure 12.19 shows the newly inserted record in the `Shippers` table.

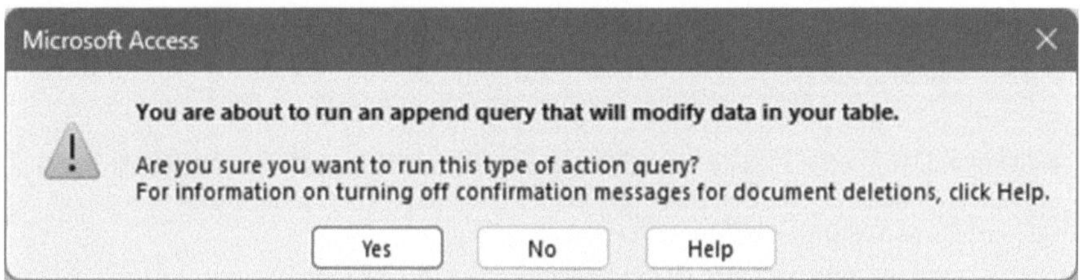

FIGURE 12.15.   When you double-click a stored procedure name in the database navigation pane of the Access database window, Access displays this message when the stored procedure expects parameters, and its SQL statement attempts to insert data into a table.

FIGURE 12.16. Because the stored procedure expects some input, you are prompted for the first parameter value

FIGURE 12.17. Here you are prompted to enter the phone number for the second stored procedure parameter.

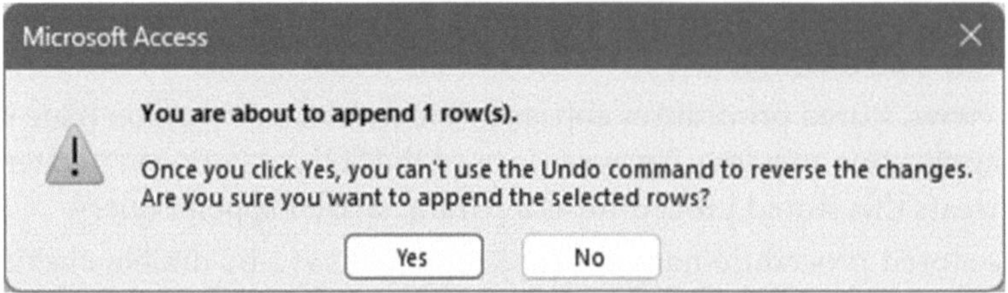

FIGURE 12.18. Once all input has been gathered via the parameters, Access informs you about the action that is to be performed. Click Yes to execute the stored procedure or No to cancel.

ID	Company	Last Name	First Name	E-mail Address	Job Title	Business Phone	Home
1	Shipping Company A						
2	Shipping Company B						
3	Shipping Company C						
4	Speedy Deliveries					800-235-0929	
(New)							

FIGURE 12.19. After clicking Yes, Access runs the append query. To view the result of this operation, double-click the Shippers table in the Navigation Pane. Notice that a new record (Speedy Deliveries) was added to the Shippers table.

Examining the Contents of a Stored Procedure

You can examine the contents of the parameterized stored procedure created in Hands-On 12.21 by right-clicking on the usp_procEnterData procedure in the database navigation pane and choosing Design View. Figure 12.20 displays the design view of an append query. Other stored procedures that you create may be presented as different action queries.

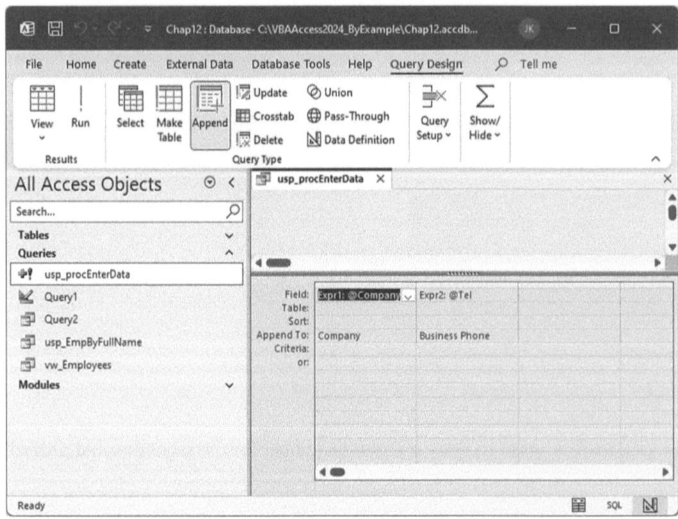

FIGURE 12.20. To view or modify the contents of a stored procedure, open it in design view.

To examine the SQL statements used by Access to execute your stored procedure, switch to the SQL view (click Query Design | View and select SQL View) or click the SQL button in the status bar. Figure 12.21 shows the SQL statement used.

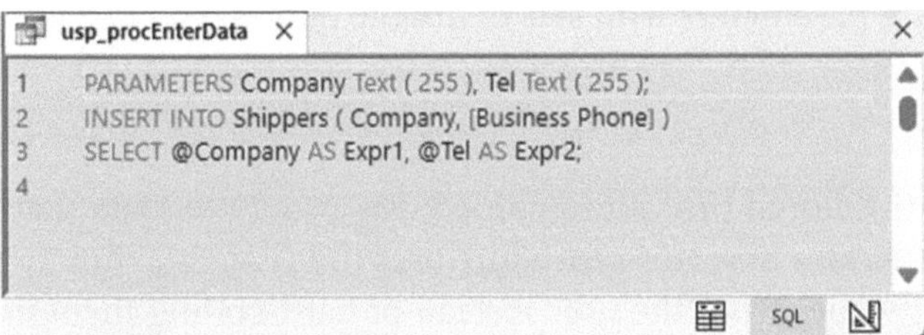

FIGURE 12.21.   The SQL view of the Query window displays the underlying SQL statement of the parameterized stored procedure.

Executing a Parameterized Stored Procedure

In the preceding section, you learned how to run a parameterized stored procedure from the Access user interface. To execute an existing stored procedure from VBA code, use the `Execute` method of the ADO `Connection` or `Command` object. Here's how:

- With the `Execute` method of the `Connection` object:

```
conn.Execute "usp_procEnterData"
```

- With the `Execute` method of the `Command` object:

```
cmd.CommandText = "usp_procEnterData"
cmd.CommandType = adCmdStoredProc

cmd.Execute
rst.Open cmd
```

If the stored procedure requires parameters, parameter values follow the procedure name as a comma-separated list. Here's an example procedure that executes the `usp_procEnterData` stored procedure and contains the values for its two parameters:

```
Sub RunProc_WithParam()
  Dim conn As ADODB.Connection

  Set conn = CurrentProject.Connection
```

```
  conn.Execute _
"usp_procEnterData ""My Company2"", ""(234) 334-3344"""
  conn.Close
  Set conn = Nothing
End Sub
```

Instead of surrounding parameters with sets of double quotes, you can use single quotes, like this:

```
conn.Execute "usp_procEnterData 'My Company2', '(234) 334-3344'"
```

In Hands-On 12.22, the stored procedure named usp_procEnterData that was created earlier is run. Notice how this procedure uses the `InputBox` function to obtain the parameter values from the user instead of hard-coding them in the `Execute` method of the `Connection` object (as shown in the preceding example). Yet another way of providing parameter values to a stored procedure would be via an Access form. This is left for you to try on your own.

⊚ Hands-On 12.22   Executing a Parameterized Stored Procedure

1. In a new module, enter the following `Execute_StoredProcWithParam` procedure:

```
Sub Execute_StoredProcWithParam()
  Dim conn As ADODB.Connection
  Dim param1 As String
  Dim param2 As String
  Dim strSQL As String

  On Error GoTo ErrorHandler

  Set conn = CurrentProject.Connection

  param1 = InputBox("Please enter " & _
            "company name:", "Company")
  param2 = InputBox("Please enter " & _
            "the phone number:", "Phone")

  strSQL = "usp_procEnterData '" & param1 & "', '" & param2 & "'"

  If param1 <> "" And param2 <> "" Then

    conn.Execute (strSQL)

  End If
```

```
ExitHere:
  If Not conn Is Nothing Then
    If conn.State = adStateOpen Then conn.Close
  End If
  Set conn = Nothing
  Exit Sub
ErrorHandler:
  MsgBox Err.Number & ":" & Err.Description
  Resume ExitHere
End Sub
```

2. Run the `Execute_StoredProcWithParam` procedure.
When you run the parameterized stored procedure in Hands-On 12.22, Access displays an input box for each parameter. After you have supplied values for both required parameters, a new record is entered into the `Shippers` table.

Deleting a Stored Procedure

Use the `DROP PROCEDURE` (or `DROP PROC`) statement to delete a stored procedure. The syntax looks like this:

```
DROP PROC[EDURE] procedureName
```

The following example procedure deletes the stored procedure named `usp_procEnterData` from the current database;

```
Sub Delete_StoredProc()
  Dim conn As ADODB.Connection

  On Error GoTo ErrorHandler

  Set conn = CurrentProject.Connection

  conn.Execute "DROP PROCEDURE usp_procEnterData; "
ExitHere:
  If Not conn Is Nothing Then
    If conn.State = adStateOpen Then conn.Close
  End If
  Set conn = Nothing
  Exit Sub
ErrorHandler:
  If InStr(1, Err.Description, "cannot find") Then
    MsgBox "The procedure you want to delete " & _
      "does not exist.", _
      vbDefaultButton1 + vbInformation, _
      "Request failed"
```

```
      Else
        MsgBox Err.Number & ":" & Err.Description
      End If
      Resume ExitHere
   End Sub
```

Changing Database Records with Stored Procedures

Stored procedures can perform various actions similar to what Access action queries and select queries with parameters can do. For example, the VBA code in Hands-On 12.23 creates a stored procedure that, when executed, deletes a record from a specific table. It is a recommended practice to always make a backup copy of your table before trying out statements that perform CRUD (Create, Read, Update, Delete) operations, as incorrectly written statements may cause all records, instead of just one, to be deleted or updated.

(◉) Hands-On 12.23   Create a Stored Procedure that Deletes a Record

1. Switch to the VBE window and insert a new module.

2. In the module's Code window, enter the `CreateProc_DeleteRecordFromTable` procedure shown here:

```
Sub CreateProc_DeleteRecordFromTable(strTable As String)
   Dim conn As ADODB.Connection

   On Error GoTo ErrorHandler

   Set conn = CurrentProject.Connection
   conn.Execute "CREATE PROCEDURE usp_DeleteRec " & _
     "(ID Integer) " & _
     "AS " & _
     "DELETE FROM " & strTable & " WHERE " & _
     strTable & ".ID = ID;"

     Application.RefreshDatabaseWindow
ExitHere:
   If Not conn Is Nothing Then
     If conn.State = adStateOpen Then conn.Close
   End If
   Set conn = Nothing
   Exit Sub
ErrorHandler:
   If InStr(1, Err.Description, "already exists") Then
     conn.Execute "DROP PROCEDURE usp_DeleteRec; "
     Resume 0
```

```
Else
   MsgBox Err.Number & ":" & Err.Description
End If
Resume ExitHere
End Sub
```

3. Enter a new record in the `Shippers` table and note the IDs of the created record.

4. In the VBE window, activate the Immediate window by pressing Ctrl+G or choose View | Immediate Window. Type the following statement and press Enter:

```
CreateProc_DeleteRecordFromTable "Shippers"
```

The above statement calls the procedure and passes to it the name of the table from which you want to delete a record.

5. In the database navigation pane, double-click the `usp_DeleteRec` query and click Yes to confirm that you want to run this action query.

6. Enter the ID for the `Shipper` record you want to delete and click OK.

7. Click Yes to confirm the deletion of one record.

8. Open the `Shippers` table to verify that the specified record was deleted.

USING ChatGPT WITH ACCESS

Retrieving data is one of the most common tasks in day-to-day database operations. The `SELECT` statement is an essential part of SQL for retrieving data. It offers a wide range of functionalities, from simple data queries to complex data manipulations. There is, however, also a `SELECT INTO` statement that you may not be familiar with. Let's find out how ChatGPT can answer the following inquiry to make clear the differences between these two statements:

User Prompt: *What is the difference between SELECT and SELECT INTO statements in Access SQL?*

Another question you may have that might require further clarification is about the `UNION` statement that works together with the `SELECT` statements. We used `UNION` in one of this chapter's examples, but there's more to it than that. Ask ChatGPT to elaborate on this topic so you can fully grasp its potential and application in complex queries, such as the following:

User Prompt: *Give me some examples of using the UNION statement in complex queries in Access. Use the NorthwindStarter database.*

ChatGPT's responses to the aforementioned user prompts can be found in the companion files. See `Chapter 12 - Using ChatGPT with Access`. Note that ChatGPT's answers will be different depending on how a question is asked. For example, you can give it the following prompt to get a better grasp on `UNION`:

User Prompt: *Elaborate on the topic of the UNION statement so that I can fully grasp its potential.*

SUMMARY

In this chapter, we explored the basic and advanced aspects of using SQL within Microsoft Access. You learned how Access SQL differs from the standard SQL. You worked with many VBA procedures that used Access SQL statements to create, update, and delete database objects and create relationships between tables, as well as retrieving data from tables and adding, modifying, or removing records. You saw examples of different types of SQL JoinS, which should help you in creating basic and more advanced queries.

You also learned how to:

- Add, modify, and delete fields and indexes in tables.
- Change the seed and increment values for `AutoNumber` fields.
- Change a field's data type.
- Assign default values to table fields.

You were introduced to the topic of constraints and learned how to:

- Create indexes with restrictions.
- Enforce data integrity by creating rules for tables with constraints.
- Validate data against another column in the same table or a column located in another table.
- Use the Access Data Definition Query window to delete tables that have constraints and remove constraints from a table.

You saw how various DDL and DML statements are used to perform database tasks.

Advanced Topics Covered

This chapter also introduced you to two powerful database objects you can use in Access: views and stored procedures. You learned about:

- Views—You saw how they are used as virtual tables to make specific rows and columns from one or more tables available to your Access users. Views are similar to SELECT statements, except they cannot contain the ORDER BY clause to sort the data and they do not allow parameters. Views can be used in queries to hide from users the complexity of joins between the tables.

- Stored Procedures—Though Access doesn't natively support stored procedures like SQL Server, we learned how to use SQL statements to create both simple and parameterized stored procedures that function similarly to Access action queries.

Finally, you learned how converting your Access queries into views and stored procedures can facilitate the migration of your Access applications to an SQL Server environment if that is something you end up doing.

This chapter concludes Part III of this book. In Part IV, we will work programmatically with Access security.

Part **IV**

IMPLEMENTING DATABASE SECURITY IN MICROSOFT ACCESS

This part of the book focuses on various methods of securing Microsoft Access databases. Whether you are creating an Access database for yourself or others, security should never be taken lightly. Before deciding on any particular security model for your Access database, familiarize yourself with various security features offered in the .mdb and .accdb file formats to ensure that your data remains protected and access to it is controlled effectively.

Chapter 13   Security Measures in Access .accdb File Format Databases
Chapter 14   Security Measures in Access .mdb File Format Databases

13 SECURITY MEASURES IN ACCESS *.ACCDB* FILE FORMAT DATABASES

Implementing security in Microsoft Access significantly depends on the file format of your database. Let's take a look at how security features differ between `.mdb` and `.accdb` databases:

1. Security in `.mdb` File Format

   The `.mdb` file format, which was used by Access versions up to 2003, supports *user-level security* that allows administrators to create user accounts and assign them to groups. Permissions can be set for different database objects (tables, queries, forms, and reports) for individual users and groups. The user and group information and their permissions are stored in a *workgroup information file* (`system.mdw`), and to enforce the security features, that file must be referenced when opening the database. The next chapter will walk you through securing a database in the `.mdb` file format.

2. Security in `.accdb` File Format

   The `.accdb` file format, which was introduced with Access 2007, does not support traditional user-level security. Instead, security is managed using alternative methods, such as database password protection, custom VBA solutions for user authentication, and integration with SharePoint, SQL Server, or cloud services such as Dataverse. We discuss each of these security measures in this chapter.

DATABASE PASSWORD PROTECTION IN ACCESS .ACCDB DATABASES

Password protection in Access `.accdb` databases involves encrypting the database with a password, ensuring that only authorized users can open it. This encryption is applied to the entire database file. You can set up a database password manually in the Access user interface, or programmatically by using DDL, DAO, or ADO.

Setting a Database Password Manually

To set up a database password, perform the following steps:

1. Open the `.accdb` database you want to secure.
2. Choose File | Info | Encrypt with Password (see Figure 13.1).

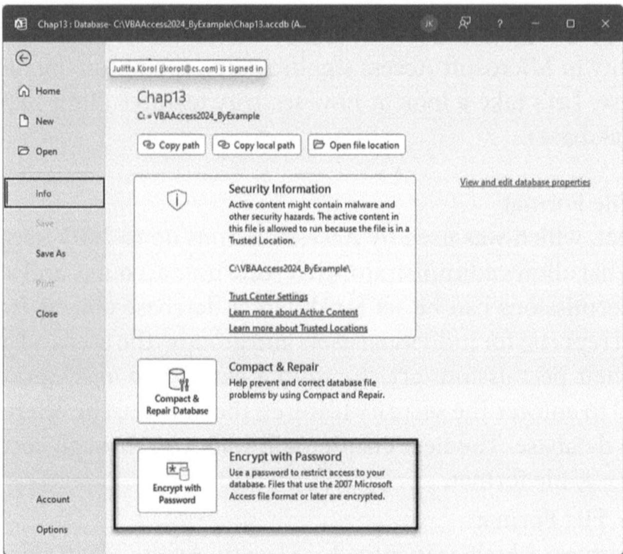

FIGURE 13.1.   Encrypting a database with a password.

When you click the Encrypt with Password button, Access will inform you that you must have the database open for exclusive use to set or remove the database password. You will be given the following instructions, which you must follow to continue:

   a.   Close the database and then reopen it by clicking the File tab.

   b. Click the Open category, and then click the Browse button.

   c. In the Open dialog box, click the arrow next to the Open button, and then select Open Exclusive (see Figure 13.2).

3. With the database reopened in exclusive mode, repeat step 2.

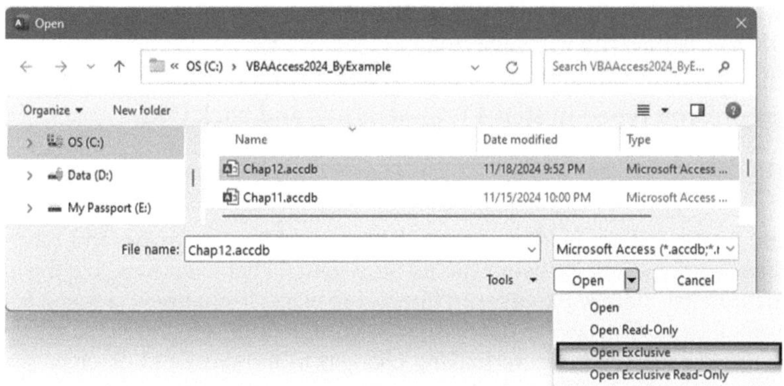

FIGURE 13.2.   Opening a database in Exclusive mode.

4. In the Set Database Password dialog box, enter and confirm the password to encrypt the database. For example, to encrypt the previous chapter's database (`Chap12.accdb`), let's enter `Chapter12` in both the Password and Verify text boxes.

5. Click OK to close the Set Database Password dialog box.

    Access displays the message shown in Figure 13.3. What does it mean?

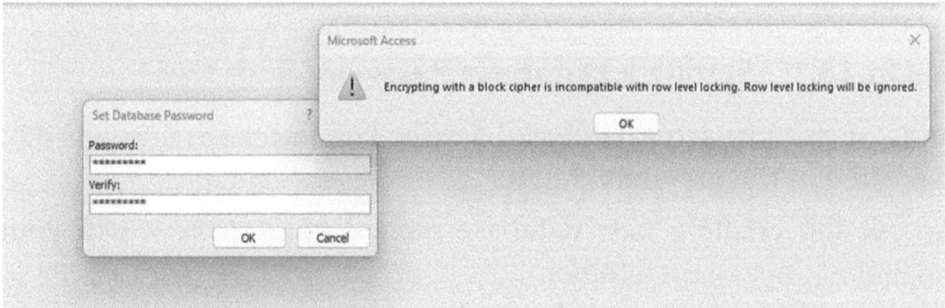

FIGURE 13.3.   When setting a database password, Access informs you that row-level locking will be ignored.

When you encrypt a database with a password, a block cipher method is used. This is a type of encryption that encrypts the whole database file, not just individual records (or rows). Row-level locking that allows you to lock only the record that you are editing, not the whole page or a table, is incompatible with block cipher encryption. Therefore, when you encrypt a database with a password, row-level locking will be ignored and page-level locking will be used. This means that when you edit a record, the whole page that contains that record will be locked, and other users will not be able to access it. This can cause conflicts or delays if multiple users are trying to access the same data.

6. Click OK to dismiss the message box.

7. Close the database file and reopen it. When prompted for a password, enter the password you typed in step 4 (`Chapter12`), and click OK.

Password Rules

It is important to use strong, unique passwords that combine uppercase and lowercase letters, numbers, and symbols. Password should be at least 8 characters long, but the longer the password the better. Store your password in a secure place; if you lose it or forget it, there is no way to retrieve it. Change the database password periodically to maintain security. Always back up your database before making changes to the password or other security settings.

Using DAO to Set or Reset a Database Password

You can use DAO to set or change the database password programmatically. Let's try it out.

NOTE	*All code files and figures for the hands-on projects may be found in the companion files.*

⊙ Hands-On 13.1   Setting a Database Password with DAO

This hands-on exercise sets a database password on the `Chap12.accdb` database file you created in the previous chapter.

1. Start Access and create a new database named `Chap13.accdb` in your `C:\VBAAccess2024_ByExample` folder.

2. Switch to the VBE window and choose Insert | Module to add a new module to the current VBA project.

3. In the module's Code window, type the following `SetDatabasePwd_DAO` procedure:

```vba
Sub SetDatabasePwd_DAO()
    Dim db As DAO.Database
    Dim strDatabasePath As String
```

```vba
    Dim strOldPassword As String
    Dim strNewPassword As String

    ' Path to your database
    strDatabasePath = "C:\VBAAccess2024_ByExample\Chap12.accdb"
    ' New password
    strNewPassword = "Secret12"
    ' Try to open the database without a password
    On Error Resume Next
   Set db = DBEngine.Workspaces(0).OpenDatabase(strDatabasePath,
                                                       True)
    ' Error 3031 indicates the database is password protected
    If Err.Number = 3031 Then
      ' Prompt for the current password
      strOldPassword = InputBox("Enter the current password:", _
          "Password Required")
      On Error GoTo 0
      ' Open the database with the current password
   Set db = DBEngine.Workspaces(0).OpenDatabase(strDatabasePath, _
          True, False, "MS Access;PWD=" & strOldPassword)
    Else
      On Error GoTo 0
    End If
    ' Check if database is opened
    If Not db Is Nothing Then
      ' Change the database password
        db.NewPassword strOldPassword, strNewPassword
      ' Close the database
        db.Close
        Set db = Nothing
        MsgBox "Password updated successfully!", vbInformation
    Else
        MsgBox "Failed to open the database.", vbExclamation
    End If
End Sub
```

4. Run the `SetDatabasePwd_DAO` procedure.

Notice that once the database is successfully opened, the password is changed using the `NewPassword` method. The new password for the `Chap12.accdb` database is now `Secret12`. The previous password was `Chapter12` (see the section on setting the database password manually).

Using ADO to Set or Reset a Database Password

You can also use ADO to set the database password. To set a new database password or change an existing password, use the DDL ALTER DATABASE PASSWORD statement in the following format:

```
ALTER DATABASE PASSWORD newPassword oldPassword
```

When setting the password for the first time, use Null for the old password. The Access database must be opened in exclusive mode to perform password operations. Therefore, when using ADO, set the ADO Connection object's Mode property to adModeShareExclusive before opening a database.

(◉) Hands-On 13.2 Setting a Database Password with ADO

1. In the VBE window, choose Tools | References. In the References dialog box, scroll down to locate Microsoft ActiveX Data Objects 6.1 Library. Click the checkbox to the left of this library name to set a reference to it and click OK to exit the dialog box.
2. Choose Insert | Module to add a new module to the current VBA project.
3. In the module's Code window, type the following SetDatabasePwd_ADO function procedure:

```
Function SetDBPwd_ADO(strFullFilePath As String, newPwd As String)
  Dim conn As ADODB.Connection
  On Error GoTo ErrorHandler
  Set conn = New ADODB.Connection
  With conn
    .Mode = adModeShareExclusive
    .Open "Provider = Microsoft.ACE.OLEDB.12.0;" & _
    "Data Source=" & strFullFilePath & ";"
    .Execute "ALTER DATABASE PASSWORD " & newPwd & " null"
  End With
ExitHere:
  If Not conn Is Nothing Then
    If conn.State = adStateOpen Then conn.Close
  End If
  Set conn = Nothing
  Exit Function
ErrorHandler:
  MsgBox Err.Number & ":" & Err.Description
  Resume ExitHere
End Function
```

4. Execute the `SetDBPwd_ADO` function from the Immediate window by typing the following statement and pressing Enter:

```
SetDBPwd_ADO "C:\VBAAccess2024_ByExample\Chap11.accdb",
                                       "Chapter11"
```

After opening a database in exclusive mode, this function procedure changes the database password from `Null` to `Chapter11`. In the function's code, the new password (`Chapter11`) is listed first, followed by the old password (`Null`). Notice how this function uses the `State` property of the ADO `Connection` object to determine whether the connection to the database is open.

`State` returns `adStateOpen` if the `Connection` object is open and `adState-Closed` if it is not.

Activate the `C:\VBAAccess2024_ByExample\Chap11.accdb` database and see whether you can open it by providing the password set in this hands-on exercise.

Removing a Database Password

To remove a database password, replace the existing password with `Null`. The password can be removed by using the `ALTER DATABASE PASSWORD` statement, as illustrated in the preceding section. When the database is secured with a password, you will need to use the `Jet OLEDB:Database Password` property to specify the password to open the database. This is an OLE DB provider for Microsoft Jet 4.0/ACE–specific property of the `Connection` object. The following procedure shows how to remove the password `Chapter11` from the `Chap11.accdb` database that was set by the `SetDBPwd_ADO` function procedure in Hands-On 13.2.

◉ Hands-On 13.3   Removing a Database Password

1. In the same module where you entered the `SetDBPwd_ADO` function (Hands-On 13.2), enter the `ResetDBPwd_ADO` function procedure shown here:

```
Function ResetDBPwd_ADO(strFullFilePath As String, _
    strNewPwd As String, strOldPwd As String)

    Dim conn As ADODB.Connection

    On Error GoTo ErrorHandler
    Set conn = New ADODB.Connection
```

```
   With conn
   .Mode = adModeShareExclusive
   .Open "Provider = Microsoft.ACE.OLEDB.12.0;" & _
     "Data Source=" & strFullFilePath & _
     "; Jet OLEDB:Database Password=" & strOldPwd & ";"
     .Execute "ALTER DATABASE PASSWORD " & _
        strNewPwd & " " & strOldPwd
   End With
 ExitHere:
   If Not conn Is Nothing Then
     If conn.State = adStateOpen Then conn.Close
   End If
   Set conn = Nothing
   Exit Function
 ErrorHandler:
   MsgBox Err.Number & ":" & Err.Description
   Resume ExitHere
 End Function
```

2. Execute the `ResetDBPwd_ADO` function from the Immediate window by typing the following statement on one line and pressing Enter:

```
ResetDBPwd_ADO "C:\VBAAccess2024_ByExample\Chap11.accdb",
"null", "Chapter11"
```

3. Execute the `ResetDBPwd_ADO` function again but this time reset the password on the `Chap12.accdb` database:

```
ResetDBPwd_ADO "C:\VBAAccess2024_ByExample\Chap12.accdb",
"null", "Secret12"
```

Recall that the old password was **Secret12**. Now, both the **Chap11** and **Chap12** databases have been decrypted.

When you set a password to encrypt the database, access is restricted to authorized users who know the password. There is, however, always a risk that users could share the database password with unauthorized individuals, which can compromise the security of your data. To avoid this, you can take additional steps to enhance the security of your database.

IMPLEMENTING CUSTOM USER AUTHENTICATION WITH VBA

You can programmatically manage security with a custom login form and VBA code that controls access to the database. At a minimum, the login form should prompt users for a username and a password and your code should validate these credentials against the Users table before granting access to the database. In Custom Project 13.1, you will perform the following tasks:

- Part I—Create the Users table.
- Part II—Create a login form.
- Part III—Add VBA code to the login form.
- Part IV—Create a main form for authenticated users.
- Part V—Add VBA code to handle various main form controls.
- Part VI—Add users to the Users table and acquire test data.
- Part VII—Test your custom user authentication process.
- Part VIII (Optional)—add enhancements to the custom user authentication process.

Custom Project 13.1   Implementing Custom User Authentication

Part I: Creating the Users Table

To restrict access to your database to only authorized users, you need a table to store user credentials. This table can be easily created in the table design view in the Access application window. With this being a programming book, however, let's use what we already know about table creation in VBA.

1. In the current Chap13.accdb database, on the VBE screen, insert a new module and save it as CustProject_Tables.
2. Enter the following VBA procedure that uses DDL SQL statements to create the Users table:

```
Sub CreateUsersTable()
    Dim db As DAO.Database
    Dim strSQL As String

    ' Get the current database
    Set db = CurrentDb()

    ' Define the SQL statement to create the Users table
    strSQL = "CREATE TABLE Users (" & _
            "UserID AUTOINCREMENT PRIMARY KEY, " & _
            "Username TEXT(50) NOT NULL UNIQUE, " & _
            "Password TEXT(50) NOT NULL);"
```

```
        ' Execute the SQL statement
        db.Execute strSQL

        ' Notify the user
        MsgBox "Users table created successfully.", vbInformation
    End Sub
```

3. Run the `CreateUsersTable` procedure.
   You may need to refresh the database navigation pane to view this table.

Part II: Creating the Login Form

The login form should contain two text box controls for Username and Password and a Login button. You can easily create this form using Form Design on the Create tab. Again, however, why not try to get a bit ahead and learn something new by creating this form entirely with VBA?

1. On the VBE screen, insert a new module and save it as `CustProject_Forms`.
2. In the module, enter the following VBA code:

```
Sub CreateLoginForm()
    Dim frm As Access.Form
    Dim txtUsername As Access.TextBox
    Dim txtPassword As Access.TextBox
    Dim btnLogin As Access.CommandButton
    Dim lblUsername As Access.Label
    Dim lblPassword As Access.Label
    Dim frmName As String

    frmName = "LoginForm"
      ' Create a new form and set form properties
    Set frm = CreateForm
    With frm
        .Caption = "Login Form"
        .Width = 6000
        .Section(0).Height = 3000
        .PopUp = True
        .AutoResize = True
        .FitToScreen = True
        .ScrollBars = False
        .RecordSelectors = False
        .NavigationButtons = False
        .BorderStyle = 3 'Dialog
    End With
    ' Save the form with the desired name
    DoCmd.Save , frmName
```

```
    ' Add controls to the form
    ' Create Username Label
    Set lblUsername = CreateControl(frmName, acLabel, _
        acDetail, , , 900, 400, 1100, 250)
    lblUsername.Caption = "Username:"

    ' Create Username Text Box
    Set txtUsername = CreateControl(frmName, acTextBox, _
        acDetail, , , 2200, 400, 2200, 250)
    txtUsername.Name = "txtUsername"
    ' Create Password Label
    Set lblPassword = CreateControl(frmName, acLabel, _
        acDetail, , , 980, 900, 1000, 250)
    lblPassword.Caption = "Password: "

    ' Create Password Text Box
    Set txtPassword = CreateControl(frmName, acTextBox, _
        acDetail, , , 2200, 900, 2200, 250)
    txtPassword.Name = "txtPassword"
    txtPassword.InputMask = "Password"

    ' Create Login Button
    Set btnLogin = CreateControl(frmName, acCommandButton, _
        acDetail, , , 2200, 1400, 1000, 500)
    With btnLogin
        .Name = "btnLogin"
        .Caption = "Login"
        .OnClick = "[Event Procedure]"
    End With
    ' Save and close the form
    DoCmd.Save acForm, frmName
    DoCmd.Close acForm, frmName
End Sub
```

The `CreateControl` function is used to programmatically add controls to a
form or report in Access. Notice that this function takes the following parameters:

- `FormName`—This is the name of the form or report to which you want to
  add the control. If you're creating the control on the active form or report,
  you can pass an empty string.

- `ControlType`—This is the type of control to create. It may be one of the
  intrinsic constants, for example, `acTextBox` (text box control), `acLabel`
  (label control), `acCommandButton` (command button control), etc.

- `Section`—This is the section of the form or report where the control will be placed. It may be one of the intrinsic constants: `acDetail` (detail section), `acHeader` (header section), `acFooter` (footer section), etc.

- `Parent`—This parameter is optional. It specifies the parent control if the new control is to be a child control. If not specified, the control is placed directly on the form or report. We can put a comma in its place.

- `ColumnName`—This parameter is optional. It specifies the name of the field in the form or report's record source that the control will be bound to. Use an empty string for unbound controls. Here, we used a comma.

- `Left`, `Top`, `Width`, and `Height`—These are optional parameters that specify the position of the control from the left and top edge of the section, and the width and height of the control. All the measurements are provided in twips.

<table>
<tr><td>NOTE</td><td>A twip is equal to 1/20 point. 1 inch is 1440 twips and 1 cm is 567 twips. Twips are used to ensure that the placement and proportion of the screen elements in your application will appear the same on all displays.</td></tr>
</table>

3. Run the `CreateLoginForm` procedure.

   This procedure creates a login form as depicted in Figure 13.4.

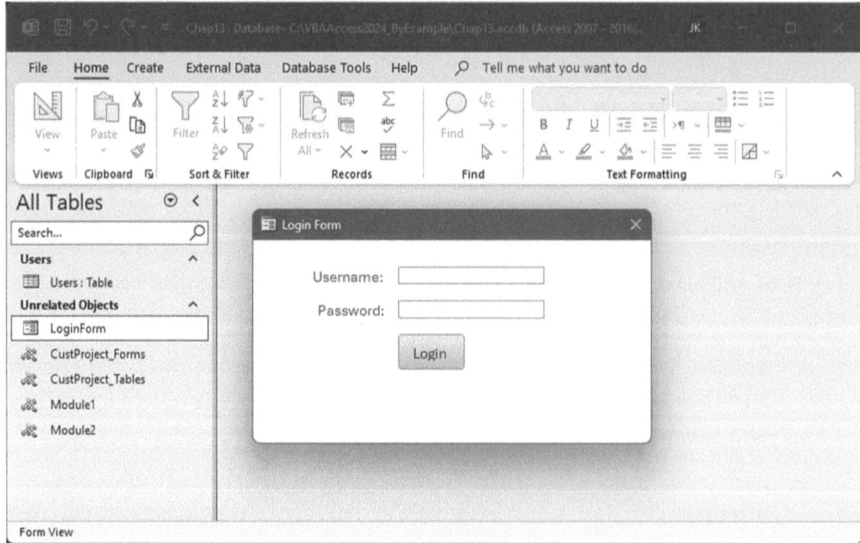

FIGURE 13.4.   An Access login form created with VBA.

Notice that the `CreateLoginForm` procedure has [Event Procedure] in the onClick event of the Login button (`btnLogin`). Right now, Access does not know what event procedure it should execute when a user clicks the Login button.

Procedures for click events must be defined in the form's module.

4. Open `LoginForm` in design view and select the Login button.
   In the Property Sheet of `btnLogin`, notice [Event Procedure] in the On Click property (the Event tab).

5. Click the ellipsis (three dots) button next to the On Click property.
   Access will create a `Form_LoginForm` class module under Microsoft Access Class Objects and enter the stub of the `btnLogin_Click` procedure for you to fill in.

6. Complete this procedure as follows:

```
Private Sub btnLogin_Click()
  Call HandleLogin
End Sub
```

`HandleLogin` is the procedure Access will call when the Login button is clicked. You will write this procedure in a standard module in the next part of this project. Note that you could also write the code you need for this button directly inside the `btnLogin_Click`, but to keep the code modular and easier to maintain, we will write all the procedures we need for the click events in a standard module.

Part III: Adding VBA Code to the Login Form

In step 6 in Part II of this project, we specified that when the user clicks the Login button, the `OnClick` event procedure should call the `HandleLogin` procedure. Let's write the VBA code for this procedure.

1. In the VBE window, insert a new standard module and save it as `CustProject_Procedures`.

2. In the `CustProject_Procedures` code module, write the following `HandleLogin` procedure:

```
' Store the logged-in user's name in a global variable
' This variable must appear at the very top of the module
' Before any procedure code

Dim CurrentUsername As String
```

```vba
Sub HandleLogin()
    Dim frm As Access.Form
    Dim strUsername As String
    Dim strPassword As String
    Dim strSQL As String
    Dim rs As DAO.Recordset
    Dim inputHash As String

    Set frm = Forms("LoginForm")
    strUsername = frm!txtUsername.Value
    strPassword = frm!txtPassword.Value
    inputHash = HashPassword(strPassword)

    strSQL = "SELECT * FROM Users WHERE Username='" & _
    strUsername & "' AND Password='" & inputHash & "';"
    Set rs = CurrentDb.OpenRecordset(strSQL)
    If Not rs.EOF Then
        CurrentUsername = strUsername
        MsgBox "Login successful", vbInformation
        ' Open the main form and close the login form
        DoCmd.OpenForm "MainForm"
        DoCmd.Close acForm, "LoginForm"
        ' Update the welcome message in the subform
        With Forms!MainForm!subFrmControl.Form. _
                                    Controls("lblWelcome")
            .Caption = "Welcome, " & CurrentUsername & "!"
        End With
    Else
        MsgBox "Invalid username or password", vbExclamation
        frm!txtPassword.SetFocus
    End If
    rs.Close
    Set rs = Nothing
End Sub
```

Note that you don't need to run the `HandleLogin` procedure. Access will execute this procedure when you start working with the Login form, after clicking the Login button. This procedure will check Username and Password against the existing entries in the `Users` table, and if the user can be successfully validated, a message box will be shown about successful login and the `MainForm` will be opened. If successful login, we will store the username in the global variable `CurrentUsername` so we can access it from the main form to welcome the user by their name (see Part IV of this project).

Notice that the `HandleLogin` procedure calls the `HashPassword` function, passing to it the user password. We will write this function in Part VI of this project.

<table>
<tr><td rowspan="1">NOTE</td><td>Password hashing is used to transform a plain-text password into a fixed-length string of characters. Using the hashing mechanism, passwords can be securely stored in a table. This security practice helps protect user credentials from being easily compromised. During the login process, the entered password is hashed and compared with the stored hash.</td></tr>
</table>

The `MainForm` is your custom form that users should be sent to after they are successfully logged in. This form should serve as the central hub for your application's functionality and include various features, such as navigation that allows users to get into different parts of the application and provides access to the primary functions of the application, such as data entry, reporting, and specific tools included in your application. It should also provide a way for your users to securely log out of the application. You can view the example of a main form when you log in to the `NorthwindStarter` database. Access will show you the Main Menu form with a navigation pane where you have access to the different parts of the application (Order, Customers, Reports, Employees, Products, etc.). By examining the structure of this form and its various controls, you can learn how to create a similar form for your own application. Note that that form uses embedded macros for most of its tasks. These macros are covered in a separate chapter of this book.

Now, let's proceed to the next part of our project, where we use VBA code to create our main form.

Part IV: Creating the Main Form with VBA

Our main form will contain an area for navigation buttons that will open different tables in our database application and an embedded subform that will welcome the user and provide the logout button. Note that this is a demo project that you can take further on your own by adding more controls to the relevant areas of the main form and its subform.

1. In the VBE, in the `CustProject_Forms` module that we created earlier when we wrote the `CreateLoginForm` procedure, enter the `CreateSubForm` and `CreateMainForm` procedures:

```vba
Sub CreateSubForm()
    Dim frm As Access.Form
    Dim lblWelcome As Access.Label
    Dim btnLogout As Access.CommandButton
    Dim lblHeader As Access.Label
    Dim lblFooter As Access.Label
    Dim frmName As String

    frmName = "MainSubForm"
    ' Create a new form
    Set frm = CreateForm
    frm.Caption = "Main Sub Form"

    'Add Form Header and Footer
    RunCommand acCmdFormHdrFtr
     ' Set background color for the Footer to Light Blue
    frm.Section(2).BackColor = 15783096
     ' Save the form with the specified name
    DoCmd.Save , frmName

     ' Add "Demo" text to the Header section
    Set lblHeader = CreateControl(frmName, acLabel, _
        acHeader, , , 100, 50, 5000, 250)
    With lblHeader
        .Caption = "Demo"
        .Name = "lblHeader"
    End With
     ' Add the current date to the Footer section
    Set lblFooter = CreateControl(frmName, acLabel, _
        acFooter, , , 100, 50, 5000, 250)
    With lblFooter
        .Caption = Format(Date, "Long Date")
        .Name = "lblFooter"
    End With
    ' Add a welcome label to the form
    Set lblWelcome = CreateControl(frmName, acLabel, _
        acDetail, , , 1000, 500, 5000, 250)
    With lblWelcome
        .Caption = "Welcome, [Username]!"
        .Name = "lblWelcome"
    End With
     ' Add a logout button to the form
    Set btnLogout = CreateControl(frmName, acCommandButton, _
        acDetail, , , 1000, 1000, 1500, 500)
    With btnLogout
        .Name = "btnLogout"
```

```vba
        .Caption = "Logout"
        .OnClick = "[Event Procedure]"
    End With
    ' Set form dimensions
    With Forms(frmName)
        .InsideWidth = 6000
        .InsideHeight = 1000
    End With

    ' Save and close the form
    DoCmd.Save , frmName
    DoCmd.Close acForm, frmName
End Sub

Sub CreateMainForm()
    Dim frm As Access.Form
    Dim btnOrders As Access.CommandButton
    Dim btnCustomers As Access.CommandButton
    Dim btnProducts As Access.CommandButton
    Dim btnEmployees As Access.CommandButton
    Dim rect As Access.Rectangle
    Dim subFrmControl As Access.SubForm
    Dim frmName As String

    frmName = "MainForm"
    ' Create a new form and set form properties
    Set frm = CreateForm
    frm.Caption = "Main Form"

    ' Save the form with the desired name
    DoCmd.Save , frmName
    ' Add a rectangle to the left-hand side
    Set rect = CreateControl(frmName, acRectangle, _
        acDetail, , , 100, 100, 2000, 6000)
    rect.BackColor = RGB(220, 220, 220)
    ' Add buttons to the rectangle for
    ' Orders, Customers, Products, and Employees
    Set btnOrders = CreateControl(frmName, acCommandButton, _
        acDetail, , , 300, 500, 1500, 500)
    With btnOrders
        .Name = "btnOrders"
        .Caption = "Orders"
        .OnClick = "[Event Procedure]"
    End With
    ' Customers Button
```

```vba
    Set btnCustomers = CreateControl(frmName, acCommandButton, _
        acDetail, , , 300, 1200, 1500, 500)
    With btnCustomers
        .Name = "btnCustomers"
        .Caption = "Customers"
        .OnClick = "[Event Procedure]"
    End With
    ' Products Button
    Set btnProducts = CreateControl(frmName, acCommandButton, _
        acDetail, , , 300, 1900, 1500, 500)
    With btnProducts
        .Name = "btnProducts"
        .Caption = "Products"
        .OnClick = "[Event Procedure]"
    End With
    ' Employees Button
    Set btnEmployees = CreateControl(frmName, acCommandButton, _
        acDetail, , , 300, 2600, 1500, 500)
    With btnEmployees
        .Name = "btnEmployees"
        .Caption = "Employees"
        .OnClick = "[Event Procedure]"
    End With
    ' Add a subform control to the right of the rectangle
    Set subFrmControl = CreateControl(frmName, acSubform, _
        acDetail, , "MainSubForm", 2300, 100, 5500, 6000)
    subFrmControl.Name = "subFrmControl"
    subFrmControl.SourceObject = "MainSubForm"
    ' Save and close the form
    DoCmd.Save , frmName
    DoCmd.Close acForm, frmName
End Sub
```

2. Run the `CreateSubForm` procedure.

3. Run the `CreateMainForm` procedure.

Figure 13.5 shows the main form with its subform in the form view.

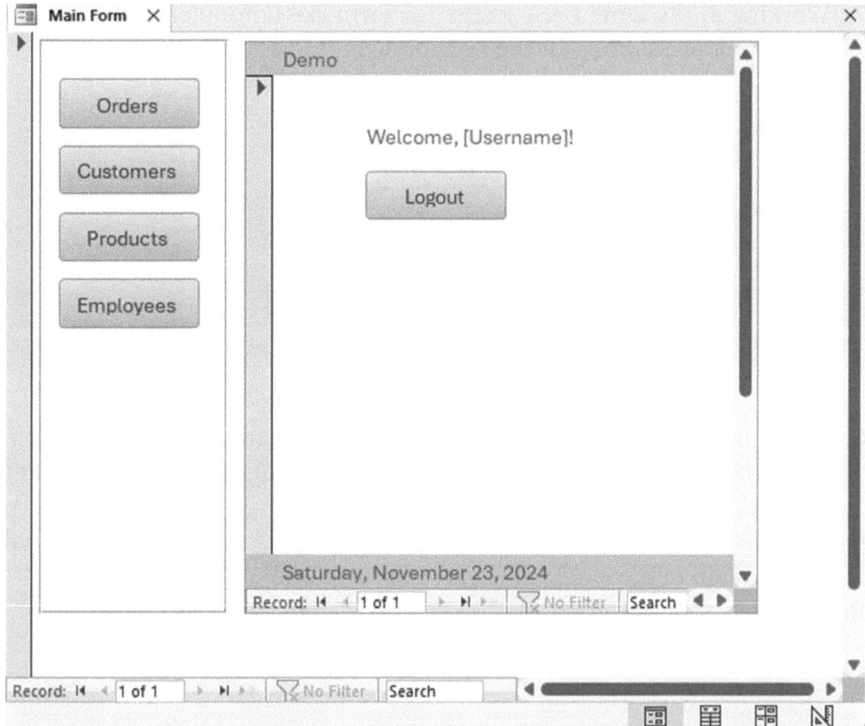

FIGURE 13.5.   The main form with its Demo subform created entirely with the VBA code.

Notice that the `CreateSubForm` and `CreateMainForm` procedures specified the [Event Procedure] in the On Click property for various buttons placed on these forms. Like with the `LoginForm`, we need to define the click event procedures in the respective form modules.

4. Open the main form in design view and select the Orders button.
   In the Property Sheet of `btnOrders`, notice [Event Procedure] in the On Click property (the Event tab).

5. Click the ellipsis (three dots) button next to the On Click property.
   Access will create a `Form_MainForm` class module under Microsoft Access Class Objects and will enter the stub of the `btnOrders_Click` procedure for you to fill in.

6. Complete this click event procedure as follows:

```
Private Sub btnOrders_Click()
    Call OpenOrders
End Sub
```

7. Working in the same `Form_MainForm` form class module, enter the following click event procedures for the remaining buttons:

```vba
Private Sub btnCustomers_Click()
    Call OpenCustomers
End Sub

Private Sub btnEmployees_Click()
    Call OpenEmployees
End Sub

Private Sub btnProducts_Click()
    Call OpenProducts
End Sub
```

8. In the main form's subform, click the Logout button to select it, and in the Properties sheet of `btnLogout`, click the ellipsis button (three dots) next to the OnClick event property.

9. Access will create a form class module named `Form_MainSubform` and give you the stub of the `btnLogout_Click` procedure.

10. Complete the code of the `btnLogout_Click` procedure as follows:

```vba
Private Sub btnLogout_Click()
    Call LogoutUser
End Sub
```

The click events are not completed, but we still need to write VBA code for all the procedures we called.

Part V: Adding VBA Code to Handle Various Control Button Events

1. On the VBE screen, in the `CustProject_Procedures` module, enter the following procedures for opening various tables and handling user logout.

```vba
' Procedure to handle opening Orders table
Sub OpenOrders()
    DoCmd.OpenTable "Orders", acViewNormal, acReadOnly
End Sub

' Procedure to handle opening Customers table
Sub OpenCustomers()
    DoCmd.OpenTable "Customers", acViewNormal, acReadOnly
End Sub

' Procedure to handle opening Products table
Sub OpenProducts()
```

```
        DoCmd.OpenTable "Products", acViewNormal, acReadOnly
End Sub

' Procedure to handle opening Employees table
Sub OpenEmployees()
        DoCmd.OpenTable "Employees", acViewNormal, acReadOnly
End Sub

' Procedure to handle user logout
Sub LogoutUser()
        MsgBox "You have been logged out.", vbInformation
        DoCmd.Close acForm, "MainForm"
        DoCmd.OpenForm "LoginForm"
End Sub
```

Part VI: Adding Users to the Users Table and Acquiring Test Data

In this part of our project, we will add four users to our `Users` table. This requires that we insert four records into the two fields in the `Users` table. We can use the `Array` function to store the names of users and their passwords and then loop through the users and insert them into the `Users` table. As mentioned earlier, to securely store user credentials, we should use password hashing. In the .NET environment, there is a special assembly called `System.Security.Cryptography` that can handle the 256-bit (SHA-256) password-hashing algorithm. Unfortunately, Microsoft Access VBA does not support directly referencing .NET assemblies. Therefore, to proceed with this project, we will create a simple `HashPassword` function that will use ASCII values of the characters in the password, and then convert the hash to a hexadecimal string.

1. On the VBE screen, in the `CustProject_Procedures` module, enter the following procedure and function:

```
Sub PopulateUsersTable()
        Dim strSQL As String
        Dim strUsername As String
        Dim strPassword As String
        Dim strHashedPassword As String
        Dim users As Variant
        Dim i As Integer

        ' Define an array of users and passwords
        users = Array( _
            Array("Yolanda", "password1"), _
            Array("Robert", "password2"), _
            Array("Arnie", "password3"), _
```

```
        Array("Donna", "password4") _
    )
    ' Loop through the users and insert them into the Users table
    For i = LBound(users) To UBound(users)
        strUsername = users(i)(0)
        strPassword = users(i)(1)
        strHashedPassword = HashPassword(strPassword)

        strSQL = "INSERT INTO Users (Username, Password) " & _
         "VALUES ('" & strUsername & "', '" & strHashedPassword  & "');"
        CurrentDb.Execute strSQL
    Next i
    MsgBox "Users table populated with 4 users.", vbInformation
End Sub

Function HashPassword(password As String) As String
    Dim i As Integer
    Dim hash As Long
    Dim result As String

    ' Initialize hash value
    hash = 0
    ' Compute a simple hash
    For i = 1 To Len(password)
        hash = (hash + Asc(Mid(password, i, 1))) Mod 65535
    Next i
    ' Convert hash value to hexadecimal string
    result = Hex$(hash)
    HashPassword = result
End Function
```

2. Execute the `PopulateUsersTable` procedure and notice that upon its execution, the `Users` table contains the entries shown in Figure 13.6.

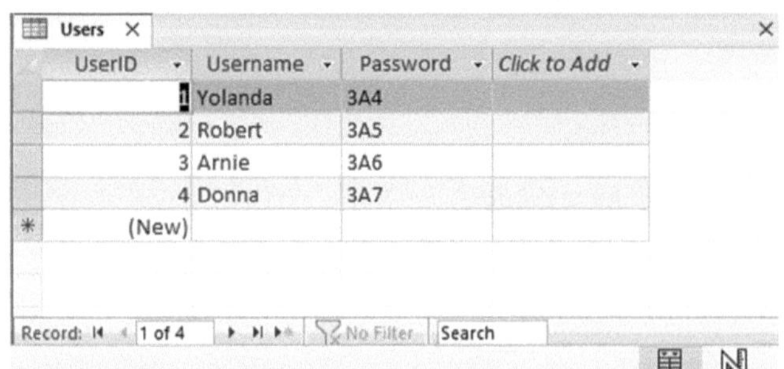

FIGURE 13.6. The Users table is populated with four user credentials.

Before we can begin testing our project, we need a few tables in our database. Let's write the VBA code that will get the needed tables from the `NorthwindStarter` database.

3. Add the following procedure to the `CustProject_Procedures` module:

```vba
Sub ImportNorthwindTables()
    Dim sourceDB As String
    Dim tableNames As Variant
    Dim i As Integer

    ' Path to the Northwind Starter database
    sourceDB = "C:\VBAAccess2024_ByExample\NorthwindStarter.accdb"

    ' Array of table names to import
    tableNames = Array("Orders", "Customers", "Products", "Employees")

    ' Loop through the table names and import each one
    For i = LBound(tableNames) To UBound(tableNames)
        DoCmd.TransferDatabase acImport, "Microsoft Access", _
        sourceDB, acTable, tableNames(i), tableNames(i), False
    Next i

    MsgBox "Tables imported successfully.", vbInformation
End Sub
```

4. Run the `ImportNorthwindTables` procedure. Make sure that the `NorthwindStarter` database is closed before running this procedure or you will get an error.

You have now completed the basic user authentication project, and you can proceed to the testing part.

Part VII: Testing Your Custom User Authentication Process

1. In the Access application Navigation Pane, double-click the LoginForm.

2. In the Login dialog box, enter `Yolanda` in the Username text box and `password1` in the Password text box, and then click Login.

3. Click OK in response to the message about the successful login.
Now Yolanda is welcomed to your custom interface and can proceed with her work via the provided controls in the main form (see Figure 13.7). She can view the data in different tables by clicking the corresponding button. She can also log out using the Logout button.

4. Click each of the buttons to test whether they all work as intended and make code corrections if necessary.
5. Click the Logout button to close the main form.

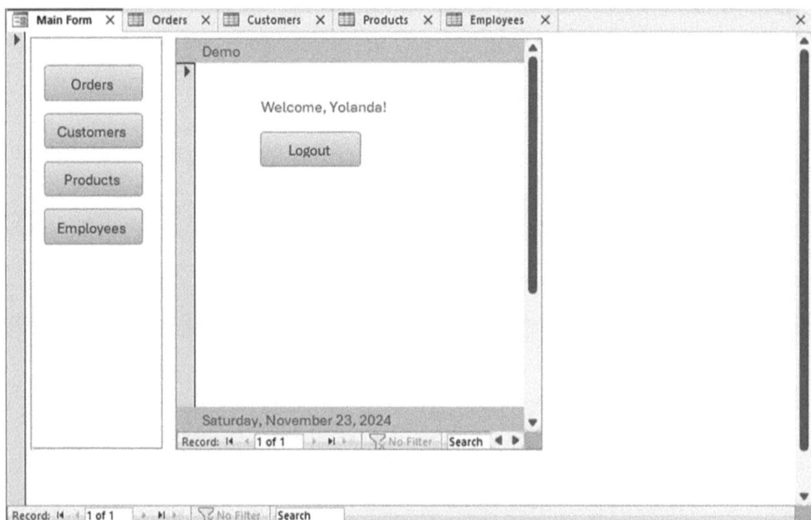

FIGURE 13.7. After the successful login, the user is welcomed by their name.

Part VIII (Optional): Adding Enhancements to the Custom User Authentication Process

Note that in a real-world scenario, the `HandleUser` and `LogoutUser` procedures should include tasks such as logging user activity in your custom `UserActivity` table and clearing any specific session data or variables to ensure that sensitive information is removed from memory. You can further enhance the Login form with additional security features that provide role-based access control based on job functions and assign permissions to these roles. For example, you can add the following tables to your project and then write your own VBA code to handle these added features.

```
CREATE TABLE Roles (
    RoleID AUTOINCREMENT PRIMARY KEY,
    RoleName TEXT(50) NOT NULL UNIQUE
);

CREATE TABLE UserRoles (
    UserID INT,
    RoleID INT,
```

```
    FOREIGN KEY (UserID) REFERENCES Users(UserID),
    FOREIGN KEY (RoleID) REFERENCES Roles(RoleID)
);

CREATE TABLE UserActivity (
    ActivityID AUTOINCREMENT PRIMARY KEY,
    UserID INT,
    Activity TEXT(255),
    ActivityDate DATETIME,
    FOREIGN KEY (UserID) REFERENCES Users(UserID)
);
```

You can get further guidance on these enhancements by following the prompts later in this chapter in the section titled Using ChatGPT with Access.

OTHER FEATURES FOR ENHANCED DATABASE SECURITY

The following features can be added to enhance the security of your Access databases:

- Activity Logging

  You should write VBA code to track user activity within the database. This will help you identify unauthorized access or suspicious behavior.

- Audit Trails

  You can write VBA procedures or Access data macros to record changes made to the data, including who made the changes and when.

- Enforced Password Policy

  You can require users to change their passwords regularly and enforce policies for strong passwords. Monitor any signs of shared credentials.

- Least Privilege Principle

  Grant users the minimum level of access necessary for performing their tasks.

- Implementation of Two-Factor Authentication (2FA)

  2FA adds an extra layer of security. This can be a code sent to the user's phone.

- Integration with Cloud Services

  Use Microsoft Dataverse to securely store and manage data in the cloud. With Dataverse, you have access to advanced security features, such as role-based security, data encryption, and auditing. Microsoft Access introduced integration with Dataverse in May 2022. This integration allows users to migrate their Access data to Dataverse, enabling cloud-based storage, enhanced security, and the ability to create mobile and Web applications using Power Platform. Microsoft Power Platform is a suite of various tools designed to analyze data, automate various processes, create applications, and interact with intelligent agents. It includes Power BI (a business analytics tool), Power Apps (a no-code application builder), Power Automate (a workflow automation tool), and Power Virtual Agents (a platform for creating powerful chatbots that can handle a range of customer and internal interactions). Power Platform offers a wide array of connectors that allow you to integrate with various data sources, services, and applications, both Microsoft and third-party.

In Access 2024, you can connect to Dataverse by choosing External Data | New Data Source | From Online Services | From Dataverse. Enter your Dataverse environment details, such as Server URL and an organization name or an additional identifier for your Dataverse environment, and select the tables to import or link. Note that working with Dataverse is beyond the scope of this book as it requires setting up advanced environments and applications that you may not have access to. If you're interested in exploring this topic further, at the time of writing, the following resources are available:

o Get started using Dataverse – Training | Microsoft Learn
  https://learn.microsoft.com/en-us/training/paths/get-started-cds/?form=MG0AV3

o Migrate Microsoft Access data to Microsoft Dataverse – Power Apps | Microsoft Learn
  https://learn.microsoft.com/en-us/power-apps/maker/data-platform/migrate-access-to-dataverse?form=MG0AV3

● SharePoint Integration

If you have access to Microsoft SharePoint, you can store data in SharePoint lists to leverage SharePoint's security and permission management features. You can also link Access to SharePoint lists to synchronize data.

USING ChatGPT WITH ACCESS

In Custom Project 13.1, I made Part VIII optional for you so you could add, on your own, enhanced security features with the help of the assistant that is always ready at your command—ChatGPT. Below are some user prompts to get you started:

User Prompt: *Give me some data for the Roles table.*

User Prompt: *Show me the Create Table SQL Statement for the Permissions table.*

User Prompt: *Give me some data for the Permissions table.*

User Prompt: *Verify this: Write procedures or Access data macros to record changes made to the data, including who made the changes and when.*

Note that these prompts are specific to the custom login authentication project I worked on with ChatGPT to deliver this material to you. Creating a brand-new project and breaking it down step by step for someone to follow along is a daunting task. While ChatGPT provided me with the initial code for the tasks I wanted to show and automate, it introduced lots of errors that had to be debugged one by one. For example, when creating forms, it set form properties that did not exist, causing the procedure to fail. Hashing passwords had to be recoded as the suggested procedure could not be run in Access. Despite these hiccups, working with ChatGPT was a pleasant experience. I hope you can learn from it as well.

The prompts and the responses obtained from ChatGPT are available in the companion files in a document titled `Chapter 13 - Using ChatGPT with Access`.

SUMMARY

You have reached the end of this chapter! If you followed along, you should have gained a wealth of new insights and skills relating to handling Access database security, as well as writing procedures that create dynamic forms and controls programmatically using VBA.

You learned how to set and reset a database password using VBA and implemented custom user authentication by creating a login form with hashed passwords. You handled user login and logout actions. You also wrote a procedure to create and populate the `Users` table and imported several tables from another database using VBA. You then added buttons to the main form to open these tables.

In summary, this chapter discussed various features that you can use to enhance the security of your Access databases, even without traditional user-level security.

The next chapter focuses on the traditional user-level security that is only available in legacy Access databases, easily recognized by the `.mdb` file format.

Chapter 14

Security Measures in Access .mdb File Format Databases

In the previous chapter, we explored various security measures to enhance the security of your Access .accdb file format databases, even without the traditional user-level security tools that are available in the older .mdb databases. The .accdb format, introduced in Access 2007, offers improved encryption and integration with SharePoint and Web services such as Dataverse, but lacks the granular user-level security model present in .mdb files.

In this chapter, we will cover tools that allow you to define user accounts, groups, and permissions so you can control access to specific database objects based on user roles. In .mdb databases, Access provides a *security wizard* to help set up and manage user-level security. This includes creating a special file known as the Workgroup Information File (WIF), which manages user accounts and permissions in .mdb databases. This file, with an .mdw extension, acts as a directory for users and groups, specifying which database objects they have permission to access.

Access .mdb databases are still in use, primarily by organizations that have legacy databases created before Access 2007. These organizations might still be using older versions of Access and have not yet migrated to the newer .accdb format due to various reasons, such as resource constraints or compatibility issues. The migration process can be quite resource-intensive, requiring thorough testing to ensure that all functions and customizations work as expected in the newer format.

If you need to use the traditional-level security features, you might consider converting your `.accdb` database into an `.mdb` file. This process involves saving your database in the older format, which can be done by choosing the Save As option in Access. Keep in mind that while doing so might provide you with the desired security features, you may lose some of the benefits of the `.accdb` file format, such as better support for newer features and integrations. Deciding whether to convert your `.accdb` database into an `.mdb` file depends on your specific needs and the trade-offs you are willing to make.

SETTING A DATABASE PASSWORD

Similar to `.accdb` databases, in `.mdb` database files, you can set a database password to help prevent unauthorized access to your database. In Hands-On 14.1, we will create a new Access database in the `.mdb` file format and secure it with a password. We will also bring data into this database and learn how to unset the database password.

NOTE	*All code files and figures for the hands-on projects may be found in the companion files.*

> ◉ **Hands-On 14.1**   **Creating an Access MDB Database and Securing it with a Password**

1. Start Microsoft Access and click the blank database button.
2. Switch to your `VBAAccess2024_ByExample` folder and enter `Chap14` in the File name text box. In the Save as type dropdown, choose Microsoft Access Databases (2002-2003 format)(*.mdb) and click OK, then click the Create button.
   You should now have a database in the selected file format.

   You may have noticed that Access provides an `.mdb` file format for Access 2000 and Access 2002–2003. The choice between these two formats depends on your specific needs and compatibility requirements.

   - Access 2000 format offers broad compatibility with older versions of Access and is recommended if you need to share the database with users who might be using very old versions of Access. This format may lack some features and improvements introduced in later versions.

- Access 2002–2003 format offers better support for newer functionality and improved performance. It includes more features and enhancements over the Access 2000 format and is recommended if you are working in an environment where users are using Access 2002 or later.

    Let's add some tables to this new database.

3. Choose External Data | New Data Source | From Database | Access.
4. In Get External Data-Access Database, in the File name box, enter `C:\ VBAAccess2024_ByExample\NorthwindStarter.accdb` and click OK.
    Access displays an informational message notifying you that field types such as attachment fields and calculated fields are not supported in the `.mdb` and `.adp` database formats. If any unsupported field types exist in the source database tables, those fields will not be imported.
5. Click OK to continue.
6. In the Import Objects dialog box in the Tables tab, select Customers, Employees, OrderDetails, Orders, OrderStatus, and Products, click OK, and then click Close.
7. Open the `Employees` table in design view.
    Notice that the Attachments field that was of the `Attachment` data type in the `.accdb` database is now of the `Long Text` data type, which stores only the name of the image file. Always keep in mind that going from the newer to the older format will remove any features that are incompatible with the older format. These features, which might have been integral to your database's functionality, design, or security, will no longer be available and could significantly impact your workflow. As a result, you may need to spend additional time and effort reworking or replacing those features with alternatives that are supported by the older format.

    Now, let's proceed to secure this database with a password.

8. Close the `Chap14.mdb` file. Do not exit Access.
9. Reopen it in exclusive mode: choose File, click Open, and then select Browse.
10. In the Open dialog box, under File name, choose Chap14.mdb and click Open, then choose Open Exclusive.
11. Click File | Info and click the Set Database Password button.
12. In the Set Database Password dialog box, enter and confirm the password. Enter `Chapter14` in the Password box, retype it in the Verify box, and then click OK.
    When setting the password for your own database, make sure to use a strong password that combines uppercase and lowercase letters, numbers, and

symbols. Make a note of your password as forgetting it will make the database inaccessible.

13. Close the database and reopen it, providing `Chapter14` when prompted for a password.
    Let's remove the database password for now.

14. Choose File | Info and click Unset Database Password.
    Access will inform you that you must open the database in exclusive mode to set or remove the password. This is the same process we just performed when setting the database password.

15. Follow the instructions in steps 8-10. Enter the password when prompted, then click OK.

16. Click File | Info | Unset Database Password.

17. In the Unset Database Password, type your current password, `Chapter14`, and click OK.

18. Close and reopen the `Chap14.mdb` database.
    You should no longer be prompted for the password.

MANAGING THE SECURITY AND PERMISSIONS OF YOUR ACCESS MDB DATABASES

To work with security in your Access `.mdb` database, Access provides several options that you can access via File | Info. On the Info screen, there's a button for managing users and permissions (see Figure 14.1). Its dropdown reveals the following options:

- User and Group Permissions—This option allows you to assign or revoke permissions for specific database objects (such as tables, queries, forms, and reports) for users and groups. You can define who can read, write, or modify each object.

- User and Group Accounts—This option lets you create, delete, and manage user accounts and groups. You can add new users, set passwords, and assign users to groups to manage permissions more efficiently.

- User-Level Security Wizard—This wizard helps you set up user-level security for your database by guiding you through the process of creating a WIF, defining user accounts, and setting permissions. It simplifies the security setup, making it easier to manage access control.

- Encode / Decode Database—This option allows you to encode (encrypt) or decode (decrypt) your database. Encoding your database enhances its security by protecting the data from unauthorized access. Decoding reverses the process, making the database readable again.

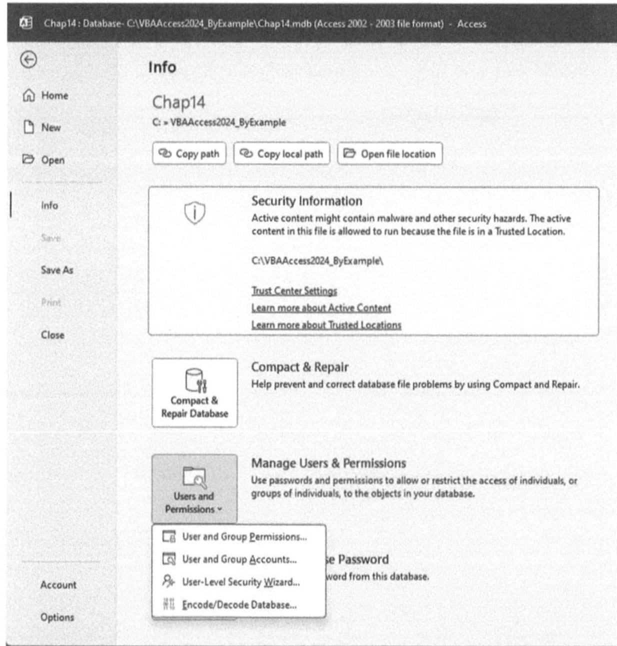

FIGURE 14.1.   Built-in tools for managing security in an .mdb database.

To implement user-level security, you create group and user accounts and assign permissions to groups and users to perform operations on various database objects. You can perform these tasks within the Access interface by using dialog boxes (see Figures 14.2 and 14.3) accessed via the options in the Users and Permissions dropdown (see Figure 14.1) or programmatically with VBA by using DAO, as demonstrated later in this chapter.

FIGURE 14.2.   The User and Group Accounts dialog box.

FIGURE 14.3.   The User and Group Permissions dialog box.

IMPLEMENTING USER-LEVEL SECURITY

User-level security is a relatively complex process that secures the code and objects in your database so that users can't accidentally modify or change them. With this type of security, you can provide the most restrictive access to the database and the objects it contains. When you use user-level security, a *WIF* is used to determine who can open a database and what objects are available to them.

The WIF holds group and user information, including passwords. The information contained in this file determines not only who can open the database but also the permissions users and groups have on the objects in the database. This file contains built-in groups (Admins and Users) and a generic user account (Admin) with unlimited privileges on the database and the objects it contains.

Understanding WIFs

To successfully run the procedures in this chapter, you need to know the location of the WIF on your computer. This file, also known as *system database* (System.mdw), is created automatically on your computer when you create an .mdb format database (see Table 14.1). This file, which can also be named System1.mdw, System2.mdw, and so on, is stored in the AppData folder on your main system drive (C:\). This is a hidden folder, so to browse it, you must first enable hidden files:

- In Windows 10—Activate File Explorer and click the View tab. Check Hidden Items in the View/Hide section of the ribbon.

- In Windows 11—Activate File Explorer and choose View | Show | Hidden Items.

Now you should be able to access the path, where <username> is the name of your user profile. Take a few minutes right now to locate the System.mdw file on your machine using Table 14.1.

TABLE 14.1.   The WIF in different versions of Access.

Access Version	Default Workgroup Information Filename	Workgroup Information File Location
2000	System.mdw	C:\Program Files\Common Files\System
2002–2003	System.mdw	C:\Documents and Settings\<username>\Application Data\ Microsoft\Access

(Contd.)

Access Version	Default Workgroup Information Filename	Workgroup Information File Location
2007–2010	System.mdw	C:\Users\<username>\AppData\Roaming\Microsoft\Access\System.mdw
2013–2024	System.mdw	C:\Users\<username>\AppData\Roaming\Microsoft\Access\System.mdw

You can also find the location and name of the WIF from the Immediate window on the VBE screen. Switch to the VBE screen, press Ctrl+G to activate the Immediate window, and type the following statement on one line (beginning with a question mark). Then, press Enter to execute:

```
? CurrentProject.Connection.Properties("Jet OLEDB:System
Database").Value
```

When you press Enter, Access displays the full path of the WIF that the currently open database uses for its security information. `Jet OLEDB:System Database` is a provider-specific property of the OLE DB provider for Microsoft Jet in the ADO Properties collection of the `Connection` object.

Access uses the WIF to store the following information:

- The name of each user and group
- The list of users who belong to each group
- The encrypted logon password for each workgroup user
- The Security Identifier (SID) of each user and group in binary format

Once you add user and group accounts to your database, the WIF will contain vital security information. *You don't want to lose this information.* Always take the time to make a backup copy of the system file and store it in a safe location. This way, if the original file gets corrupted, you'll be able to quickly restore your backup file and avoid having to recreate user and group accounts.

The WIF is like any other Access database file except that it contains hidden system tables with information regarding user and group accounts and their actual permissions. You cannot, however, change the security information by opening this file directly. All the security data stored in hidden system tables is encrypted and protected. Changes to the WIF are done automatically by the Jet engine when you use the built-in Access commands to manage security or when you execute VBA code.

You can use the same WIF for more than one database or you can create a separate file for each database you are securing. You can also give this file a name other than the default `System.mdw`. Most people find it best to use the same name as the database file. For example, if your secured database file is named `Assets.mdb`, you could create a WIF called `Assets.mdw` and put it in the same folder as the database file. This way, you'd know right away that these two files are associated with one another even after many weeks or months have passed since you created them. Keeping track of which WIF goes with which database can be quite challenging, especially if you are managing more than a couple of secured `.mdb` Access databases.

NOTE

If you try to open a secured database while another WIF is active, Access displays the following message:

You do not have the necessary permissions to use the <name> object. Have your system administrator or the person who created this object establish the appropriate permissions for you.

If you receive the preceding message while opening an Access database in the `.mdb` file format, you should look for the accompanying WIF and perform one of the following:

- *Set Up a Shortcut*

  Set up a shortcut to the database file that uses the /WRKGRP command-line switch to load the specified WIF when the database is opened (see Custom Project 14.1).

- *Use the Workgroup Administrator tool in Access 2024*

1. *Start Access and open any Access database.*
2. *Activate the VBE window.*
3. *Choose View | Immediate Window.*
4. *In the Immediate window, type the following statement and press Enter to execute:*

```
DoCmd.RunCommand acCmdWorkgroupAdministrator
```

5. *In the Workgroup Administrator dialog box, click Join, then click Browse.*
6. *Locate the WIF and then click Open. See Table 14.1 for the `.mdw` filenames used with various versions of Access.*
7. *In the Workgroup Administrator dialog box, click OK, then click Exit.*

Creating and Joining a WIF

When you open a database, Access reads the WIF to find out who is allowed to access the database. If security has been set up, you will be prompted for the user ID and password. Custom Project 14.1 walks you through the steps required to create and join a new WIF. Once you join the workgroup, you create a new Access database and set up a password for the `Admin` user. This information is saved in the WIF that you just joined. The WIF is created using the user-level security wizard. This option is available by choosing File | Info | Users and Permissions (see Figure 14.1 earlier).

Securing a database is a multiple-step process that starts with creating a new WIF, adding a new member to the `Admins` group, and removing the default `Admin` user from that group. You also need to remove permissions from the `Admin` user and the `Users` group and assign permissions to your own groups that you create. Don't be discouraged if you need to go over the security steps more than once. Access security is complex and can be approached from many different angles. Books of several hundred pages have been written to explain its inner workings. The approach presented here simply provides us with a secured Access database file we can use to perform the programming exercises in this chapter.

⊙ Custom Project 14.1   Securing an Access MDB Database

You must complete this project in order to work with the hands-on exercises in this chapter. You also need the `Chap14.mdb` database that we created in Hands-On 14.1.

1. In the `Chap14.mdb` database, choose File | Info | Users and Permissions | User-Level Security Wizard.

   Access will not allow you to run the security wizard if your database is protected by a database password. Access requires the database to be unprotected for the security wizard to function properly, as it needs full access to modify and set up security features. Additionally, if Access encounters any other constraints or issues, such as existing security features or corrupted files, it will notify you and provide guidance on how to proceed. This helps ensure that the security wizard can perform its tasks without interruptions or conflicts.

   If there are no issues, Access automatically activates the security wizard (see Figure 14.4).

2. Click Next to continue.

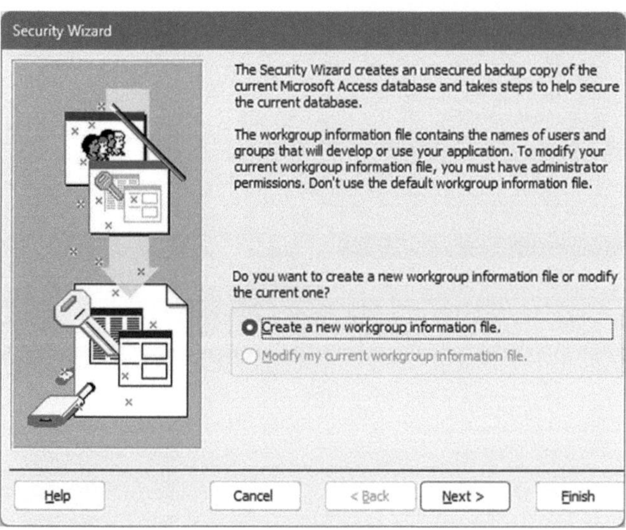

FIGURE 14.4.   Security Wizard (screen 1).

3. Another Security Wizard window appears (see Figure 14.5). Do not make any changes on this screen. Click Next to continue.

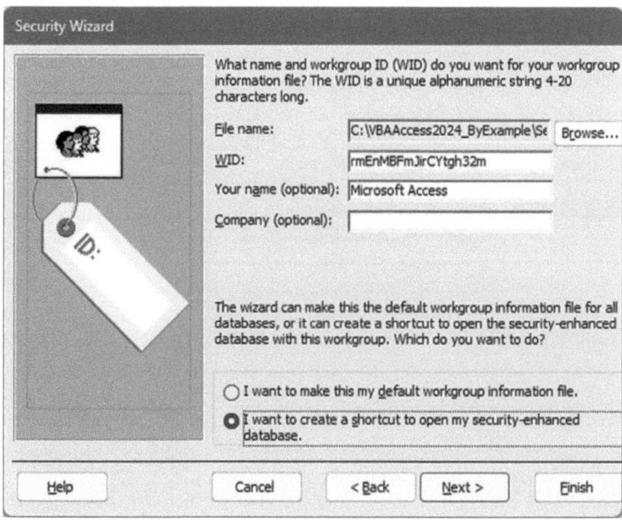

FIGURE 14.5.   Security Wizard (screen 2). The WIF named Security.mdb will store user and group account information for the current database.

4. The Security Wizard window now shows a tabbed screen that displays various database objects (Figure 14.6). Notice that the only objects we currently have are tables and they are all selected. Click Next to continue.

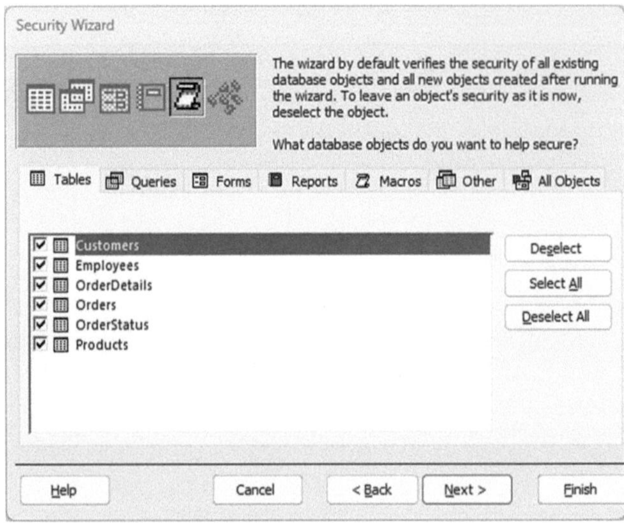

FIGURE 14.6. Security Wizard (screen 3).

5. The Security Wizard window now displays a list of optional security accounts that you could include in your new WIF (Figure 14.7). Because we will define our accounts in programming code later in this chapter, do not make any selections on this screen. Click Next to continue to the next screen.

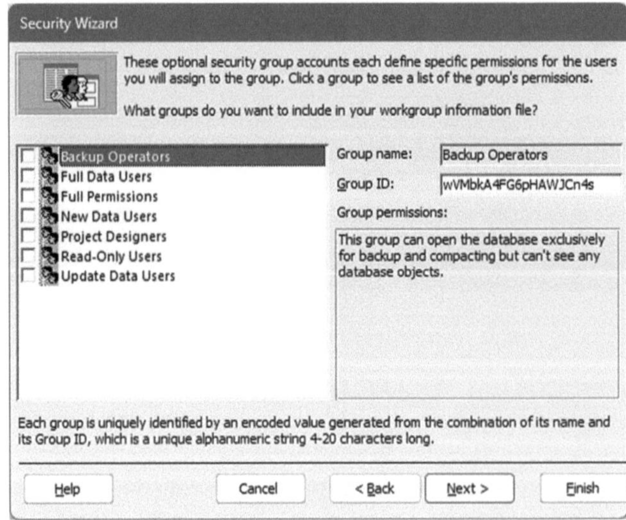

FIGURE 14.7. Security Wizard (screen 4).

6. Now the security wizard asks whether you want to grant permissions to the `Users` group (Figure 14.8). The `Users` group will have no permissions, so do

not make any changes on this screen. We will work with permissions in VBA procedures later. Click Next to continue.

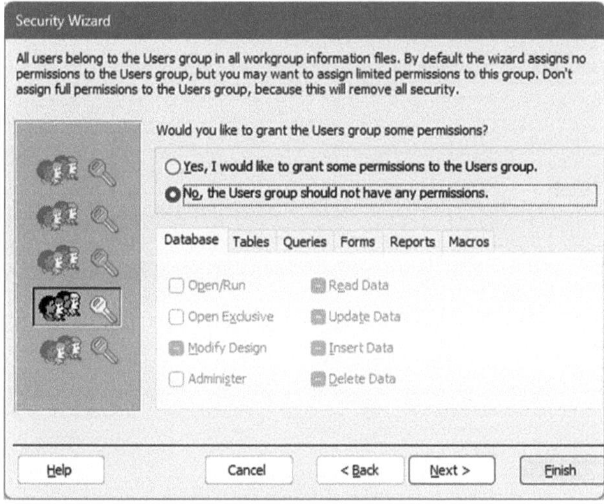

FIGURE 14.8.   Security Wizard (screen 5).

7. Now the security wizard shows a screen (Figure 14.9) where you finally can do a little bit of work. You need to define a new user in your database. This user will function as the new admin. Let's call this user `Developer` and allow them to log in to the database using `Chapter14` as the password. Fill in the User name and Password boxes as shown in Figure 14.9 and click the Add This User

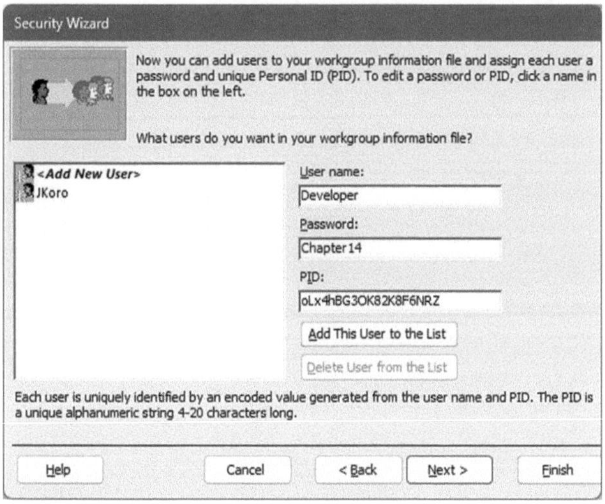

FIGURE 14.9.   Security Wizard (screen 6a).

to the List button. `Developer` should now appear in the users list (see Figure 14.10). Do not leave this screen yet.

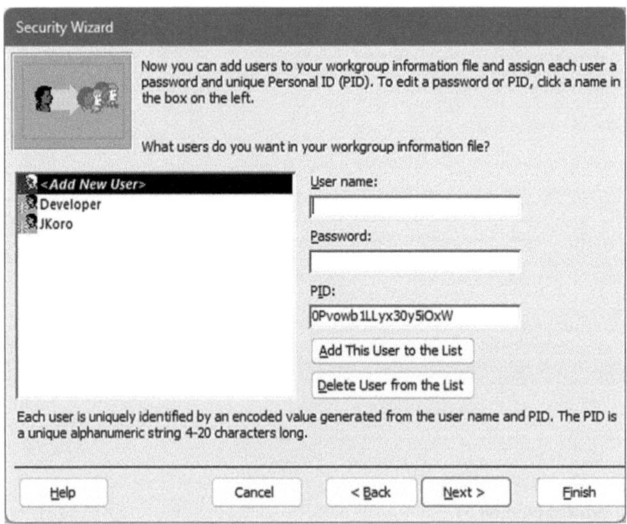

FIGURE 14.10. Security Wizard (screen 6b).

8. Now remove the user account you used to log in to Access. In the list of users, select the username you logged in with and click the Delete User from the List button. Now `Developer` is the only user in our database, as shown in Figure 14.11. Click Next to continue.

FIGURE 14.11. Security Wizard (screen 6c).

9. The security wizard shows the screen where you can assign users to groups in the WIF (Figure 14.12). Notice that the user you created in Step 8 (`Developer`) is a member of the `Admins` group. Click Next to continue.

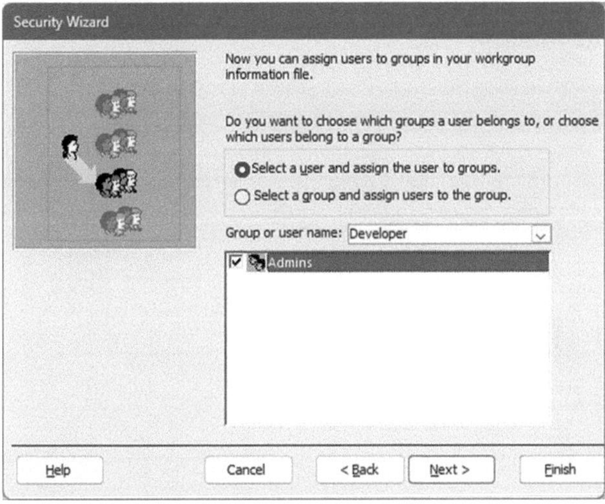

FIGURE 14.12.   Security Wizard (screen 7).

10. The security wizard has now collected all the required information, as shown in Figure 14.13. Notice that the security wizard suggests here the name of the backup copy of your unsecured database. You can change it or accept it as is. Click Finish.

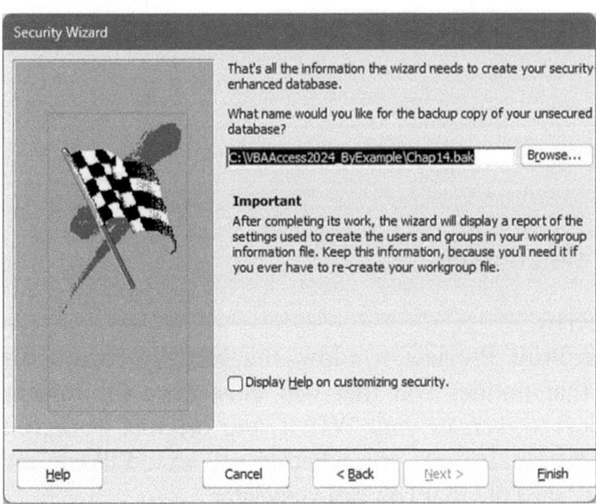

FIGURE 14.13.   Security Wizard (screen 8).

11. Access performs its final task of securing your database and displays the Security Wizard report (Figure 14.14). If you are connected to a printer, it's a good idea to take a minute now to print this report or save it to a PDF file. You can also magnify the report to read it on screen. When you are done, close the Security Wizard report window.

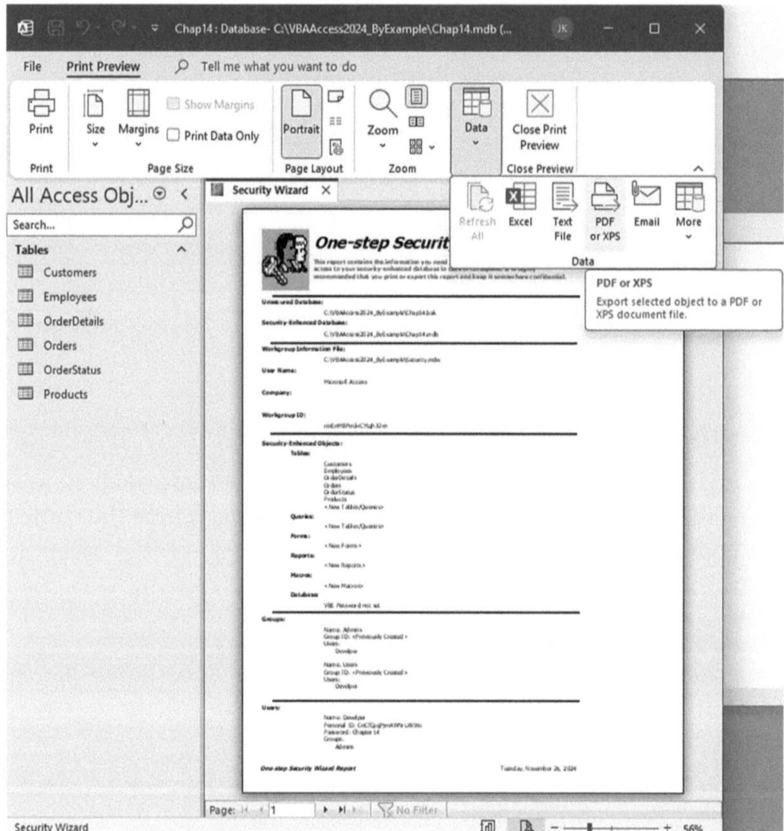

FIGURE 14.14.   Security Wizard (screen 9).

12. Click Close Print Preview.

When you close the Print Preview window, the security wizard displays a warning message that notifies you that you must have the information contained in this report to recreate your WIF if your original workgroup file is lost or corrupted. Access also asks you whether you would like to save the report as a Snapshot (`.snp`) file that you can view later.

13. Click Yes to have Access create the Snapshot file for you.
You should see the confirmation message that the security wizard has encoded your database, and to reopen your database, you must use the new workgroup file you have created by closing Access and reopening it. You'll do as suggested in the next section.

14. Click OK to this message.

15. Close the main Access window.

Opening a Secured MDB Database

The following files were added to your `C:\VBAAccess2024_ByExample` folder when you completed Custom Project 14.1:

- A WIF named `Security.mdw` that stores user and group account information for the `Chap14.mdb` database
- A snapshot file named `Chap14.snp`
- A backup copy of the `Chap14.mdb` database named `Chap14.bak`

Also, there should be a shortcut on your desktop (created by the security wizard) that allows you to quickly start the `Chap14` database using the new WIF (`Security.mdw`). If you right-click that desktop shortcut (`Chap14.mdb`) and choose Properties, you will see in the Target box the path to the WIF:

```
"C:\VBAAccess2024_ByExample\Security.mdw"
```

Note that in recent updates to Windows that are aimed at simplifying the user interface and improving usability, the Target box displays a shorter path for shortcuts and it may be harder to figure out how to create your own shortcut for a secured Access database. Previously, the target path was much longer as it included all the elements you need to correctly open the secured `.mdb` database using the specified WIF.

To create a shortcut to a secured Access `.mdb` database, so it opens with the correct security context, follow these steps:

1. Right-click on your desktop and select New | Shortcut.

2. In the Type the location of the item box, enter the target path, which includes:

- The actual path to your Access executable enclosed in double quotation marks. For example:

```
"C:\Program Files\Microsoft Office\root\Office16\MSACCESS.EXE"
```

- A space (use the spacebar).
- The full path to your secured database enclosed in double quotation marks and followed by a space and a command-line switch, `/WRKGRP`. For example:

```
"C:\VBAAccess2024_ByExample\Chap14.mdb" /WRKGRP
```

- A space (use the spacebar).
- The full path to your WIF enclosed in double quotation marks. For example:

```
"C:\VBAAccess2024_ByExample\Security.mdw"
```

The completed target path is shown here. Due to its length, it is divided into three lines:

```
"C:\Program Files\Microsoft Office\root\Office16\MSACCESS.EXE"
"C:\VBAAccess2024_ByExample\Chap14.mdb" /WRKGRP
"C:\VBAAccess2024_ByExample\Security.mdw"
```

3. Name your shortcut; for example, enter `Secured Access DB`.
4. Click Finish to create the shortcut on your desktop.

The `/WRKGRP` command-line switch tells Access that you want to start a database with a specific workgroup. If you know which user account you want to log on with, you can use the `/User` and `/Pwd` command-line switches to avoid being prompted by Access for the username and password:

```
"C:\Program Files\Microsoft Office\root\Office16\MSACCESS.EXE"
"C:\VBAAccess2024_ByExample\Chap14.mdb" /WRKGRP
"C:\VBAAccess2024_ByExample\Security.mdw"
/User "Developer" /Pwd "Chapter14"
```

The information about the username and password follows the name of the WIF and a single space.

⊙ Hands-On 14.2   Opening a Secured MDB Database

This hands-on exercise requires prior completion of Custom Project 14.1.

1. On your desktop, double-click the shortcut to `Chap14.mdb` to open the database. Because this database is secured by the WIF, a log-on box appears.
2. Enter `Developer` in the Name box and `Chapter14` in the Password box and click OK.
   If the password does not work, open the saved or printed security wizard report and check your password that is stored in the Users section. Once you open the

database, you can change the log-on password for the user by accessing User and Group Accounts (File | Info | Users and Permissions | User and Group Accounts).

Now that your secured database file is open, let's take a look at the changes the security wizard has made in User and Group Accounts.

3. Choose File | Info | Users and Permissions | User and Group Accounts. Notice that the `Admin` user is a member of the `Users` group (see Figure 14.15). If you open the Name drop-down list in the User area of this screen and select Developer, you will see that `Developer` is a member of two groups: `Admins` and `Users`.

4. Click Cancel to exit the User and Group Accounts window.

FIGURE 14.15.   In Custom Project 14.1, while running the built-in user-level security wizard, we added the Developer user to the Admins group and removed the default Admin user from the Admins group.

Having checked User and Group Accounts, you can also examine the changes made by the security wizard in the group permissions.

5. Choose File | Info | Users and Permissions | User and Group Permissions. Right now, the users `Developer` and `Admin` don't have permissions on any new objects (see Figure 14.16). To view group permissions, click the Groups option button. The `Admins` group has all the necessary permissions to administer the database while the `Users` group has no permissions at all. You will learn how to grant and revoke permissions to database objects in the example procedures in this chapter. Now, click Cancel to exit the User and Group Permissions window.

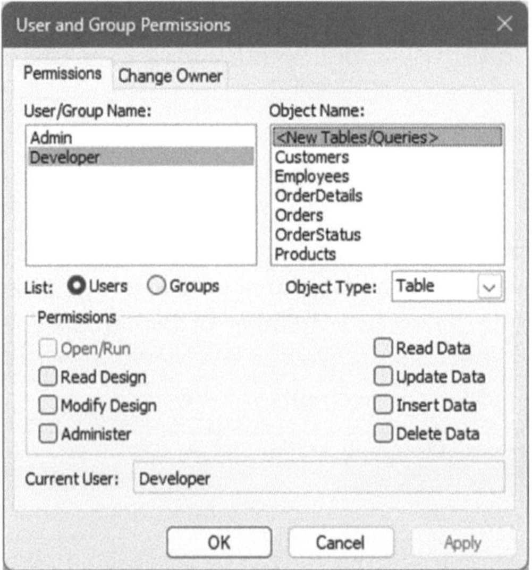

FIGURE 14.16. Use the User and Group Permissions window to check current permissions for the users Admin and Developer after running the user-level security wizard in Custom Project 14.1.

6. Close the User and Group Permissions dialog box.

Now, let's import other objects into this database. We will need them for our tests later in this chapter when we learn to handle permissions for database objects.

7. In the Access window, choose External Data | New Data Source | From Database | Access. In the Get External Data dialog box, enter `C:\VBAAccess2024_ByExample\NorthwindStarter.accdb` in the File name box and click OK.

8. Click OK to dismiss the informational message about unsupported field types.

9. In the Import Objects window, click the Queries tab, then choose Select All to select all the queries. Finally, click OK to begin importing. When the import operation is completed, click the Close button.

The queries you selected in step 7 have now been added to your database.

MANAGING USER-LEVEL SECURITY WITH VBA

To programmatically manage user-level security in Access `.mdb` databases, you can use:

- Microsoft DAO 3.6 object library

- Microsoft ADOX
- Microsoft Jet 4.0 SQL commands

In the following sections of this chapter, you will write procedures and functions that use objects from the DAO and ADO libraries, as well as SQL commands, to perform the following tasks:

- Creating a new user
- Creating a group
- Adding a user to a group
- Delete an existing user
- Removing a user from a group
- Deleting a group
- Checking and setting permissions for an object
- Changing the object owner
- List users, groups, and permissions
- Deny permissions for an object

Managing User-Level Security with DAO

In the DAO object library, the `Users` and `Groups` collections are used to manage user-level security. These collections can be accessed via the `Workspace` object of the `DBEngine`.

- The Users Collection—Contains all the user accounts in the database
- The Groups Collection—Contains all the groups in the database.

Both collections are a part of a `Workspace` object, which represents the user's environment. You can access and manipulate these collections to set and modify security settings.

Creating a New User Account with DAO

To create a new user account, you must specify the username and the user Personal Identifier (PID). The third parameter, the password, is optional but recommended.

The PID is used for additional security. It should consist of at least 4 and no more than 20 characters and digits. While it is not strictly required to set a password when creating a user account, it is highly recommended to assign a password to enhance security. A user without a password could be more vulnerable to unauthorized access.

In Microsoft Access, when you create a new user, they are automatically a member of the `Users` group. This group is a default group that includes all users of the database. The `Users` group cannot be deleted, and it includes every user account in the workgroup. The `Users` group has basic permissions that apply to all users. Note that to ensure that the new user appears in the `Users` group when you open the Users and Groups dialog box in the Access user interface, you should explicitly create a group entry for the user using the `CreateGroup` method, as shown in the next hands-on exercise.

Let's write a function to create a new user account.

(●) Hands-On 14.3   Creating a User Account

1. In the `Chap14.mdb` database, switch to the VBE window and choose Insert | Module.
2. Enter the following function procedure in the Code window:

```
Function CreateNewUser(strUserName As String, _
                        strUserPID As String, _
                        Optional strUserPwd As String) As Boolean
    Dim ws As DAO.Workspace
    Dim usr As User

    On Error GoTo ErrorHandler
     ' Initialize the workspace
     Set ws = DBEngine.Workspaces(0)

     ' Create a new user
     Set usr = ws.CreateUser(strUserName, strUserPID, strUserPwd)
     ws.Users.Append usr

     ' Explicity Add user to the Users Group
     usr.Groups.Append ws.CreateGroup("Users")

     CreateNewUser = True
     Debug.Print strUserName & " account successfully created."

     Exit Function
ErrorHandler:
     MsgBox "Error: " & Err.Description, _
         vbExclamation, "Error Creating User Account"
     CreateNewUser = False
```

```
CleanUp:
    Set usr = Nothing
    Set ws = Nothing
    Exit Function
End Function
```

3. Execute the `CreateNewUser` function from the Immediate window by entering:

```
CreateNewUser "PowerUser", "PID_Power123", "pwdPower"
```

4. Verify that the `PowerUser` appears in the `Users` group by choosing File | Info | Users and Permissions | User and Group Accounts, then select PowerUser from the User dropdown. The Member of list should indicate that `PowerUser` is a member of `Users`.

Creating a New Group Account with DAO

The `CreateGroup` method is used for creating a new group account. This method requires that you provide two arguments: the name of the new group account and the group PID. Note that there are no passwords for groups. Let's write a function that creates a new group.

◉ Hands-On 14.4   Creating a Group Account

1. In the code module, enter the following function procedure:

```
Function CreateNewGroup(strGroupName As String, _
                        strGroupPID As String) As Boolean
    Dim ws As DAO.Workspace
    Dim grp As Group

    On Error GoTo ErrorHandler
     ' Initialize the workspace
     Set ws = DBEngine.Workspaces(0)

     ' Create a new user
     Set grp = ws.CreateGroup(strGroupName, strGroupPID)
     ws.Groups.Append grp

     CreateNewGroup = True
    Debug.Print strGroupName & " group account successfully created."

    Exit Function
ErrorHandler:
    MsgBox "Error: " & Err.Description, _
        vbExclamation, "Error Creating Group Account"
```

```
    CreateNewGroup = False
CleanUp:
    Set grp = Nothing
    Set ws = Nothing
    Exit Function
End Function
```

2. Execute the `CreateNewGroup` function from the Immediate window by entering:

```
CreateNewGroup "Masters", "PID_Masters$"
```

3. Verify that the new group `Masters` appears in User and Group Accounts in the Access user interface.

Adding a User to a Group with DAO

As mentioned earlier, all newly added users in a Microsoft Access database are automatically given default membership to the `Users` group. This ensures that every user has a basic level of access as defined by the permissions of the `Users` group (we will cover that shortly). While all users are members of the `Users` group, you might need more granular control over what each user can do. Custom groups allow you to set specific permissions and manage access more effectively. Let's add our `PowerUser` to the `Masters` group.

⊚ **Hands-On 14.5   Adding a User to a Group**

1. In the code module, enter the following function procedure:

```
Function AddUserToGroup(strUserName As String, _
                strGroupName As String) As Boolean
Dim ws As DAO.Workspace
Dim grp As Group
Dim usr As User

On Error GoTo ErrorHandler
' Initialize the workspace
Set ws = DBEngine.Workspaces(0)
Set grp = ws.Groups(strGroupName)
Set usr = ws.Users(strUserName)

For Each usr In grp.Users
    If usr.Name = strUserName Then
        MsgBox "User already in this group!"
        AddUserToGroup = False
        Exit For
```

```
    Else
        grp.Users.Append ws.CreateUser(strUserName)
        AddUserToGroup = True
        Debug.Print strUserName & " was added to " & _
            strGroupName & " group."
    End If
Next
Exit Function
ErrorHandler:
    MsgBox "Error: " & Err.Description, _
        vbExclamation, "Cannot add " & strUserName & " to " & _
            strGroupName & " group."
    AddUserToGroup = False
CleanUp:
    Set grp = Nothing
    Set ws = Nothing
    Exit Function
End Function
```

2. Execute the `AddUserToGroup` function from the Immediate window by entering:

```
AddUserToGroup "PowerUser", "Masters"
```

Notice that the `AddUserToGroup` function procedure uses a `For...Each` loop to check whether the specified user is already a member of the specified group.

3. Verify that the `PowerUser` appears in the `Masters` group (check User and Group Accounts in the Access user interface).

Listing All Groups and Users with DAO

So far, you've manually verified the result of running your functions that created a new user and a new user account and added a user to a group. It's obviously not fun to constantly open a dialog box that takes many clicks to access. In the following hands-on exercise, we will write VBA code to improve this verification process.

Hands-On 14.6   Listing Users in Groups

1. Insert a new module in your VBA project and enter the following procedure:

```
Sub ListAllGroupsAndUsers()
    Dim ws As Workspace
    Dim grp As Group
    Dim usr As User
```

```vba
    ' Initialize the workspace
    Set ws = DBEngine.Workspaces(0)

    ' Loop through each group in the workspace
    For Each grp In ws.Groups
        ' Print the group name
        Debug.Print "Group: " & grp.Name

        ' Loop through each user in the group
        For Each usr In grp.Users
            Debug.Print "  User: " & usr.Name
        Next usr
    Next grp
End Sub
```

2. Run the procedure `ListAllGroupsAndUsers` and check the results in the Immediate window.

   You should see the following output:

```
Group: Admins
  User: Developer
Group: Users
  User: admin
  User: Developer
Group: Masters
  User: PowerUser
```

Notice that it's quite peculiar that the `PowerUser` doesn't appear in the `Users` group, as typically all new users should automatically be included in it. Moreover, we explicitly added the `PowerUser` to the `Users` group. To resolve this issue, you might need to add the following line of code before the `For...Each` statement:

```
ws.Groups.Refresh
```

When you rerun the updated `ListAllGroupAndUsers` procedure, not only does the Immediate window display the `PowerUser` in the `Users` group but the groups are also shown sorted alphabetically in ascending order:

```
Group: Admins
  User: Developer
Group: Masters
  User: PowerUser
Group: Users
  User: admin
```

```
User: Developer
User: PowerUser
```

Deleting a User or Group Account or Users from Groups

We all make mistakes, and working with databases and user management is no exception. When managing users and groups in Microsoft Access, errors such as creating an unintended user or group or mistakenly adding a user to the wrong group can occur. Thankfully, you can rectify these errors by writing VBA procedures designed to delete unwanted users or groups and correcting user group membership.

If you mistakenly create a user, you can delete them from the database like this:

```
Sub DeleteUser(userName As String)
    On Error Resume Next
    Dim ws As Workspace
    Set ws = DBEngine.Workspaces(0)

    ws.Users.Delete userName

    If Err.Number = 0 Then
        Debug.Print "User " & userName & " deleted successfully."
    Else
        Debug.Print "Error deleting user: " & Err.Description
    End If
    On Error GoTo 0
End Sub
```

You can also delete users based on a condition. For example, if you wanted to start from scratch, you could write a procedure that loops through the users in the `Users` group and deletes all users but the admin and `Developer`.

If you create a group account in error, you can delete it. Write your own VBA procedure that uses the following statement to delete a group account passed to the procedure (see the `DeleteUser` procedure for an example):

```
ws.Groups.Delete grpName
```

If you need to delete all custom groups and only keep the `Admins` and `Users` groups, here is the code to achieve this:

```
Sub DeleteAllGroupsExceptAdminAndUsers()
    Dim ws As Workspace
    Dim grp As Group
    Dim grpName As String
```

```vba
    ' Initialize the workspace
    Set ws = DBEngine.Workspaces(0)
    ws.Groups.Refresh

    ' Loop through each group in the workspace
    For Each grp In ws.Groups
        grpName = grp.Name
        Debug.Print grpName
        ' Check if the group name is neither Admins nor Users
        If grpName <> "Admins" And grpName <> "Users" Then
            ' Delete the group
            ws.Groups.Delete grpName
        End If
    Next grp
End Sub
```

If you need to correct user membership because a user was added to the wrong group, you can remove them from that group and add them to the correct one.

```vba
Sub CorrectUserGroupMembership(userName As String, _
    wrongGrpName As String, correctGrpName As String)
    On Error Resume Next
    Dim ws As Workspace
    Dim usr As User
    Dim wrongGrp As Group
    Dim correctGrp As Group

    Set ws = DBEngine.Workspaces(0)
    Set usr = ws.Users(userName)
    Set wrongGrp = ws.Groups(wrongGrpName)
    Set correctGrp = ws.Groups(correctGrpName)

    ' Remove user from the wrong group
    wrongGrp.Users.Delete userName
    ws.Groups.Refresh
    ' Add user to the correct group
    correctGrp.Users.Append ws.CreateUser(userName)

    If Err.Number = 0 Then
        Debug.Print "User " & userName & " moved from " & _
        wrongGrpName & " to " & correctGrpName & " successfully."
    Else
        Debug.Print "Error correcting user group membership: " & _
            Err.Description
    End If
    On Error GoTo 0
End Sub
```

For example, to remove the `PowerUser` from the `Masters` group and add it to the `Admins` group, execute the following statement from the Immediate window:

```
CorrectUserGroupMembership "PowerUser", "Masters", "Admins"
```

To verify that the changes were made correctly, rerun the `ListAllGroupsAndUsers` procedure.

Working with Object Permissions Using DAO

In Microsoft Access, the creator (owner) of a database object (such as tables, queries, forms, and reports) has rights over that object. Understanding object permissions is crucial for managing security and access within a database. As depicted in Figure 14.17, in our database, the `Developer` is the owner of the database tables. They are also the owner of queries that we imported to the database when we logged in as `Developer` in an earlier hands-on exercise.

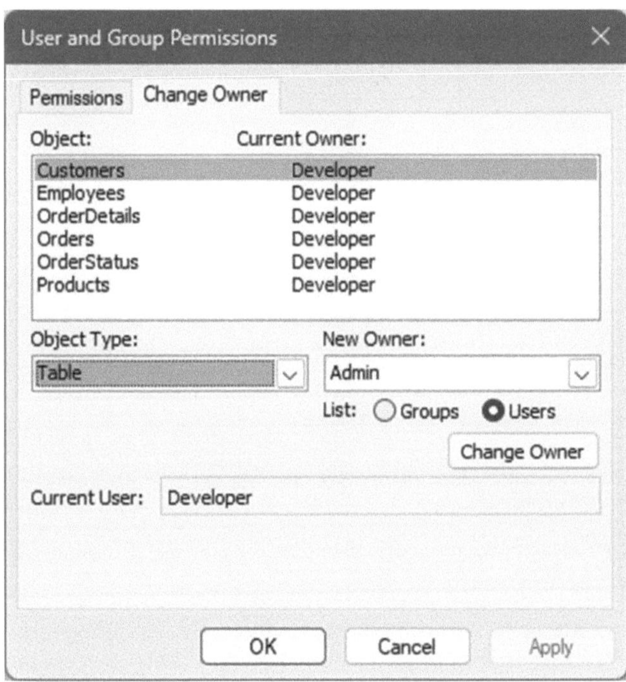

FIGURE 14.17.   The Developer user account is the object owner of the database (tables and queries that currently exist in the database).

The owner has full permissions to manage and modify the object, including the ability to grant or revoke permissions to other users or groups. This includes permissions to read, write, delete, and execute the object. Owner permissions cannot be removed by other users unless the ownership itself is transferred. To transfer ownership of an object to another user, you can use the Change Owner button (see Figure 14.17) or use appropriate SQL commands (GRANT and REVOKE), which are covered later in this chapter. It is important to regularly review object permissions to ensure they align with current security policies and access requirements. Instead of granting permissions to individual users, assign permissions to groups for more manageable and scalable security administration.

Hands-On 14.7   Changing Object Ownership

1. On the VBE screen, insert a new module and enter the following function procedure:

```
Function TransferObjectOwnership(strNewOwner As String, _
        strObjName As String, strObjType As String) As Boolean

    Dim db As Database
    Dim cont As DAO.Container
    Dim doc As DAO.Document

    On Error GoTo ErrorHandler

    ' Initialize the database
    Set db = CurrentDb

    Set cont = db.Containers(strObjType)
    Set doc = cont.Documents(strObjName)

    If (doc.AllPermissions And dbSecWriteOwner) <> 0 Then
        doc.Owner = strNewOwner
    Else
        MsgBox "You don't have permissions to change " & _
        "the ownership of " & strObjName & "."
    End If
    Exit Function
ErrorHandler:
    MsgBox Err.Number & ":" & Err.Description, vbExclamation
    Exit Function
End Function
```

2. Activate the Immediate window and execute the following statement:

```
TransferObjectOwnership "PowerUser", "Employees", "Tables"
```

In the `TransferObjectOwnership` function, we set references to the containers and document objects. In the context of Microsoft Access and DAO, containers and documents are used to manage and manipulate the various objects within a database, such as tables, queries, forms, and reports. Containers are collections that hold documents that represent individual database objects. Common containers include tables, queries, forms, reports, and modules.

You can access containers through the `Containers` collection of the `Database` object.

Documents, on the other hand, represent individual objects within a container. Each document contains properties and methods for managing the specific database object it represents. Common properties include `Name`, `Owner`, and `Permissions`. You can access documents through the `Documents` collection of a container.

In the `TransferObjectOwnership` function procedure, we use the `AllPermissions` property of the document to check whether the current user has the `dbSecWriteOwner` permission (see Table 14.2 in the next section). If the user has the necessary permissions, the `Owner` property of the document is used to set a new owner. After running the function procedure, the `PowerUser` is the owner of the `Employees` table. See the later section on how you can verify this programmatically. It is important to note that the new owner name can be a user or a group.

Setting Permissions for an Object Using DAO

When setting permissions, it's essential to understand the different types of permissions available and how to apply them. Permissions can be granted for actions such as reading, writing, and deleting data, as well as changing the ownership of objects, as you have seen demonstrated in the previous section.

In Microsoft Access, security constants are used to specify various permissions and security-related settings within a database. These constants help manage and control access to database objects, ensuring that only authorized users can perform specific actions. Table 14.2 lists common security constants used in Access. You can view them in the Object Browser by searching for `PermissionEnum` in the DAO library.

TABLE 14.2.   Security constants used in Access

Security Constant Name	Value	Description
dbSecCreate	1	Grants permission to create new objects
dbSecDBAdmin	8	Grants permission to administer the database
dbSecDBCreate	1	Grants permission to create new databases
dbSecDBExclusive	4	Grants exclusive access to the database
dbSecDBOpen	2	Grants permission to open the database
dbSecDelete	65536	Grants permission to delete objects
dbSecDeleteData	128	Grants permission to delete data
dbSecFullAccess	1048575	Grants all permissions
dbSecInsertData	32	Grants permission to insert data into tables
dbNoAccess	0	Grants no permissions
dbSecReadDef	4	Grants permission to read the definition of objects
dbSecReadSec	131072	Grants permission to read security-related information
dbSecReplaceData	64	Grants permission to replace data in tables
dbSecRetrieveData	20	Grants permission to retrieve data from tables
dbSecWriteDef	65548	Grants permission to write the definition of objects
dbSecWriteOwner	524288	Grants permission to change the ownership of objects
dbSecWriteSec	262144	Grants permission to write security-related information

Multiple conditions can be combined using the bitwise OR operator (`Or`). For example, the following can be used to grant both insert and retrieve data operations:

```
tbl.GrantPermissions "PowerUser", dbSecInsertData Or
dbSecRetrieveData
```

It is important to understand that when you set permissions for a group, every user in that group automatically inherits those permissions. Also, keep in mind that while the user and group accounts are stored in the WIF, the permissions that those users and groups have to specific objects are stored in system tables in your database.

The following example procedure demonstrates how to set permissions for the `Masters` group in the `Chap14.mdb` database. This procedure will grant the `Masters` group permissions to retrieve (`dbSecRetrieveData`) and modify (`dbSecWriteData`) data.

```
Sub SetPermissionsForMasters()
 Const dbSecRetrieveData As Long = 20
```

```vba
Const dbSecWriteData As Long = 128
Dim db As DAO.Database
Dim tbl As DAO.TableDef
Dim qry As DAO.QueryDef
Dim doc As DAO.Document
Dim strGrpName As String


 ' Initialize the database
Set db = CurrentDb

strGrpName = "Masters"

'Set permissions for all tables
For Each tbl In db.TableDefs
    If (tbl.Attributes And dbSystemObject) = 0 Then
        Set doc = db.Containers("Tables").Documents(tbl.Name)
         ' Grant permissions to Masters group
         doc.userName = strGrpName
         doc.Permissions = doc.Permissions _
            Or dbSecRetrieveData Or dbSecWriteData
         Debug.Print "Permissions set for table: " & tbl.Name
    End If
Next tbl


' Set permissions for all queries
For Each qry In db.QueryDefs
    If Left(qry.Name, 1) <> "~" And Left(qry.Name, 4) <> "MSys" Then
        On Error Resume Next
         ' Access the document representing the query
        ' you must use Tables Container to access Tables and Queries
         Set doc = db.Containers("Tables").Documents(qry.Name)
         If Not doc Is Nothing Then
             doc.userName = strGrpName
             doc.Permissions = doc.Permissions _
           Or dbSecRetrieveData Or dbSecWriteData Or dbSecWriteOwner
             Debug.Print "Permissions set for query: " & qry.Name
         Else
            Debug.Print "Error setting permissions for query: " & _
            qry.Name & " - " & Err.Description
            Err.Clear
         End If
         On Error GoTo 0
    End If
Next qry


MsgBox "Permissions have been set for Masters group.", vbInformation
End Sub
```

Checking Object Permissions Using DAO

You can programmatically check whether the specified user or group has permissions to a specific object. Notice how the `CheckPermissionsForObject` function in the companion files defines the permission constants with their appropriate values.

Additional Code in the Companion Files.

File Name: `Chap14_DAO_AdditionalCode.txt`

Description: `Checking Object Permissions using DAO (CheckPermissionsForObject)`

Denying Object Permissions Using DAO

In an earlier procedure (`SetPermissionsForMasters`), we gave the `Masters` group read and write permissions on tables and queries. Let's revoke the group's permission to read and write on the `Products` table. The permissions property is used to remove the specified permissions for the user or group by using a bitwise AND operation with the NOT operator.

Additional Code in the Companion Files.

File Name: `Chap14_DAO_AdditionalCode.txt`

Description: `Denying Object Permissions using DAO (DenyPermissionsToObject)`

Now that you've learned how to perform various security tasks using DAO, let's move on to the next topic.

Managing User-Level Security with ADO (ADOX)

To create a new group account from a VBA procedure using ADO, open the ADOX `Catalog` object by specifying the connection to the appropriate database and use the `Append` method of the `Catalog` object's `Groups` collection to add a new group account.

Creating User and Group Accounts with ADO

To create a new user account, pass the username and password to the `Append` method of the `Users` collection. Specifying a password at this time is optional. You can assign a password later with the `User` object's `ChangePassword` method.

The procedure in Hands-On 14.8 illustrates how to create two group accounts and a user account in the secured database (`Chap14.mdb`) from another Access database in the `.accdb` format.

Hands-On 14.8 Creating User and Group Accounts (ADO)

1. Close the `Chap14.mdb` database you worked with in the previous sections of this chapter.
2. Create a new Access database named `Chap14_withADO.accdb` in your `C:\VBAAccess2024_ByExample` folder.
3. Switch to VBE and choose Insert | Module.
4. Choose Tools | References and click the checkbox next to the following object libraries:
   - o Microsoft ActiveX Data Objects 6.1 Library
   - o Microsoft ADO Ext. 6.0 for DDL and Security Object Library

   After making these selections, click OK to exit the References dialog box.
5. Activate the Immediate window by choosing View | Immediate Window. Type the following statement in the Immediate window and press Enter:

```
DoCmd.RunCommand acCmdWorkgroupAdministrator
```

When you press Enter, Access loads the Workgroup Administrator tool (see Figure 14.18), which lets you check the path to the WIF that is currently being used. In Access 2024, there is no command in the user interface to display this tool. You must enter the preceding code in the Immediate window of the Access database to use the Workgroup Administrator tool.

Perform one of the following steps:

- If System.mdw appears in the Workgroup path, click OK to exit the Workgroup Administrator dialog box and proceed with step 6.

- If the Workgroup path includes the `Security.mdw` file that was created in Custom Project 14.1, click the Join button to join another workgroup (see Figure 14.18, image 1). Use the Browse button in the WIF dialog box (Figure 14.18, image 2) to select and open `System.mdw`. Refer to the beginning of this chapter for information on the default location of this file. Once you select the correct file, the dialog box should display its full path. Click OK to exit this dialog box. Access will display a message box saying you successfully joined the workgroup defined by the selected information file (Figure 14.18, image 3). Click OK to close the message and then click OK in the Workgroup Administrator dialog box to exit. Proceed to step 6.

6. In the module's Code window, enter the following `Create_UserAndGroup_ADO` procedure:

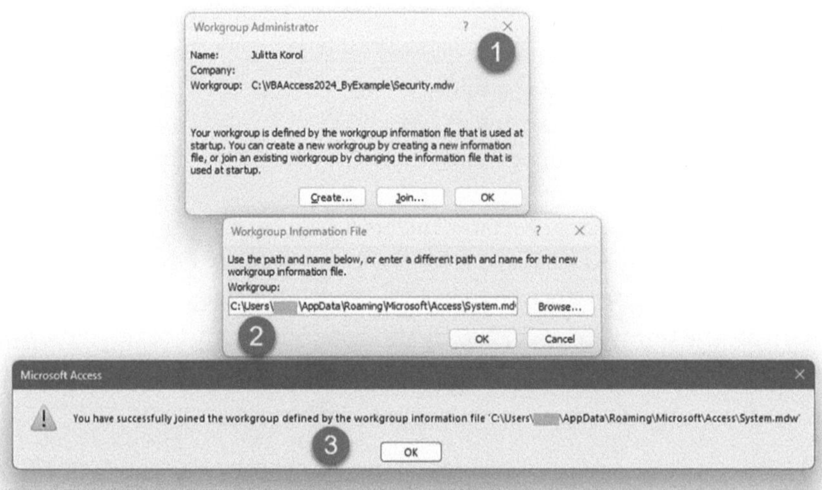

FIGURE 14.18.   Joining another WIF.

```
Sub Create_UserAndGroup_ADO()
    Dim cat As ADOX.Catalog
    Dim conn As ADODB.Connection
    Dim strPath As String
    Dim strDB As String
    Dim strSysDB As String
    Dim strGrpName1 As String
    Dim strGrpName2 As String
    Dim strUsrName As String

    On Error GoTo ErrorHandler

    strPath = "C:\VBAAccess2024_ByExample\"
    strDB = "Chap14.mdb"
    strSysDB = "Security.mdw"
    strGrpName1 = "Temps"
    strGrpName2 = "Elite"
    strUsrName = "TempUser"
    ' open connection to the database
    ' using the specified system database
    Set conn = New ADODB.Connection
    With conn
```

```
      .Provider = "Microsoft.ACE.OLEDB.12.0"
      .Properties("Jet OLEDB:System Database") = _
            strPath & strSysDB
      .Properties("User ID") = "Developer"
      .Properties("Password") = "Chapter14"
      .Open strPath & strDB
   End With

   ' Open the catalog
   Set cat = New ADOX.Catalog
   With cat
      .ActiveConnection = conn
      ' create group accounts
      .Groups.Append strGrpName1
      .Groups.Append strGrpName2
      Debug.Print "Created group accounts."
      ' create a user account
      .Users.Append strUsrName, "star"
      Debug.Print "Created user account."
      ' Add user to the group
      .Users(strUsrName).Groups.Append strGrpName1
      Debug.Print strUsrName & _
        " is a member of the " & _
      strGrpName1 & " group account."
   End With
ExitHere:
   Set cat = Nothing
   conn.Close
   Set conn = Nothing
   Exit Sub
ErrorHandler:
   MsgBox Err.Description
   Resume ExitHere
End Sub
```

7. Execute the `Create_UserAndGroup_ADO` procedure.
   Upon executing this procedure, two new group accounts, named `Temps` and `Elite`, are created in the secured `Chap14.mdb` database you created in Custom Project 14.1. A new user account named `TempUser` is added and made a member of the `Temps` group account. Notice that before opening the database, we need to set the `Jet OLEDB:System Database` property in the `Properties` collection of the ADO `Connection` object to specify the path and name of the WIF that should be active when the database is opened. We also set the user ID and password to log on to the database. After opening the database, we open the

Catalog object and use the Append method of the Catalog's Groups collection to add new group accounts. The Groups collection contains all groups in the specified WIF. The Append method of the Catalog's Users collection is used to create a new user account. This user account is then appended to the Groups collection and made a member of a group (Elite).

8. If you'd like to, take a moment now and open the Chap14.mdb database using the shortcut on your desktop. Once the database is open, choose File | Info | Manage Users and Permissions | User and Group Accounts. Notice that the database now contains the Temps and Elite groups in addition to the default Admins and Users groups (see Figure 14.19).

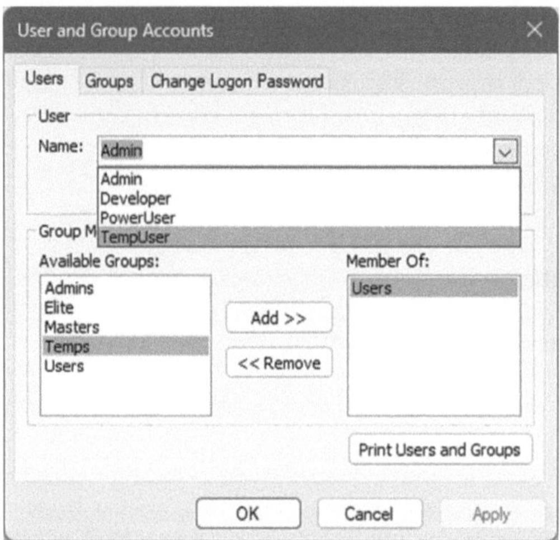

FIGURE 14.19.   The Elite and Temps group accounts are created by running the procedure in Hands-On 14.8.

9. Close the Chap14.mdb database and the Access window in which it was displayed. Be careful not to close the Chap14_withADO.accdb database you are working with.

Deleting User and Group Accounts

Use the Delete method of the Catalog object's Users collection to delete a user account. Use the Delete method of the Catalog object's Groups collection to delete a group account.

The procedure in Hands-On 14.9 deletes the user account named TempUser and the group account named Temps that were created in Hands-On 14.8.

⊙ Hands-On 14.9   Deleting User and Group Accounts (ADO)

This hands-on exercise requires the prior completion of Custom Project 14.1 and Hands-On 14.8.

1. In the VBE window of `Chap14_withADO.accdb`, choose Insert | Module.
2. In the module's Code window, enter the following `Delete_UserAndGroup` procedure:

```
Sub Delete_UserAndGroup(UserName As String, _
                        GroupName As String)
  Dim cat As ADOX.Catalog
  Dim conn As ADODB.Connection
  Dim strPath As String
  Dim strDB As String
  Dim strSysDB As String

  On Error GoTo ErrorHandler

  strPath = "C:\VBAAccess2024_ByExample\"
  strDB = "Chap14.mdb"
  strSysDB = "Security.mdw"

  ' Open connection to the database using
  ' the specified system database
  Set conn = New ADODB.Connection
  With conn
    .Provider = "Microsoft.ACE.OLEDB.12.0"
    .Properties("Jet OLEDB:System Database") = _
        strPath & strSysDB
    .Properties("User ID") = "Developer"
    .Properties("Password") = "Chapter14"
    .Open strPath & strDB
  End With

  ' Open the catalog
  Set cat = New ADOX.Catalog
  With cat
    .ActiveConnection = conn
    ' Delete user
    .Users.Delete UserName
    ' Delete group
    .Groups.Delete GroupName
  End With

ExitHere:
  Set cat = Nothing
```

```
   conn.Close
   Set conn = Nothing
   Exit Sub
ErrorHandler:
  MsgBox Err.Description
  Resume ExitHere
End Sub
```

3. To run this procedure, enter the following statement in the Immediate window and press Enter to execute it:

```
Delete_UserAndGroup "TempUser", "Temps"
```

After running the `Delete_UserAndGroup` procedure, the `Temps` group account and the `TempUser` user account are removed from the secured `Chap14.mdb` database.

Listing User and Group Accounts Using ADO

The procedure in Hands-On 14.10 demonstrates how to retrieve the names of all defined group and user accounts from the `Groups` and `Users` collections of the `Catalog` object (see Figure 14.20).

Hands-On 14.10   Listing Group and User Accounts (ADO)

1. In the VBE window of `Chap14_withADO.accdb`, choose Insert | Module.
2. In the module's Code window, enter the `List_GroupsAndUsers_ADO` procedure as shown here:

```
Sub List_GroupsAndUsers_ADO()
   Dim conn As ADODB.Connection
   Dim cat As ADOX.Catalog
   Dim grp As New ADOX.Group
   Dim usr As New ADOX.User
   Dim strPath As String
   Dim strDB As String
   Dim strSysDB As String

   strPath = "C:\VBAAccess2024_ByExample\"
   strDB = "Chap14.mdb"
   strSysDB = "Security.mdw"

   ' Open connection to the database using
   ' the specified system database
   Set conn = New ADODB.Connection
   With conn
     .Provider = "Microsoft.ACE.OLEDB.12.0"
```

```
    .Properties("Jet OLEDB:System Database") = _
        strPath & strSysDB
    .Properties("User ID") = "Developer"
    .Properties("Password") = "Chapter14"
    .Open strPath & strDB
End With

' Open the catalog
Set cat = New ADOX.Catalog
cat.ActiveConnection = conn
' list group and user accounts
For Each grp In cat.Groups
    Debug.Print "Group: " & grp.Name
Next

For Each usr In cat.Users
    Debug.Print "User: " & usr.Name
Next

Set cat = Nothing
conn.Close
Set conn = Nothing

MsgBox "Groups and users are " & _
    "listed in the Immediate window."
End Sub
```

3. Execute the `List_GroupsAndUsers_ADO` procedure.
The procedure result is shown in Figure 14.20.

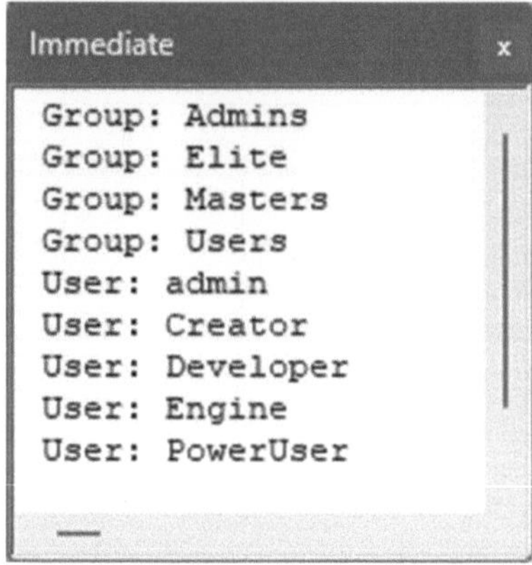

FIGURE 14.20.   The names of existing security group and user accounts are written to the
Immediate window by the procedure in Hands-On 14.10.

Notice that in addition to the user accounts you have defined, Access reveals the names of its two built-in users: `Creator` and `Engine`. To keep these built-in users from showing up in your users listing, add the following conditional statement to the `List_GroupsAndUsers_ADO` procedure:

```
If usr.Name <> "Creator" And usr.Name <> "Engine" Then
  Debug.Print "User:" & usr.Name
End If
```

Listing Users in Groups Using ADO

Sometimes you will need to know which users belong to which groups. The procedure in Hands-On 14.11 demonstrates how to obtain such a list, which is shown in Figure 14.21.

Hands-On 14.11 Listing Users in Groups (ADO)

1. In the VBE window of `Chap14.accdb`, choose Insert | Module.
2. In the module's Code window, enter the `List_UsersInGroups` procedure, as shown here:

```
Sub List_UsersInGroups()
    Dim conn As ADODB.Connection
    Dim cat As ADOX.Catalog
    Dim grp As New ADOX.Group
    Dim usr As New ADOX.User
    Dim strPath As String
    Dim strDB As String
    Dim strSysDB As String

    On Error GoTo ErrorHandler

    strPath = "C:\VBAAccess2024_ByExample\"
    strDB = "Chap14.mdb"
    strSysDB = "Security.mdw"

    ' Open connection to the database using
    ' the specified system database
    Set conn = New ADODB.Connection
    With conn
      .Provider = "Microsoft.ACE.OLEDB.12.0"
      .Properties("Jet OLEDB:System Database") = _
          strPath & strSysDB
      .Properties("User ID") = "Developer"
      .Properties("Password") = "Chapter14"
```

```vba
        .Open strPath & strDB
    End With

    ' Open the catalog
    Set cat = New ADOX.Catalog
    cat.ActiveConnection = conn
    For Each grp In cat.Groups
       Debug.Print "Group: " & grp.Name
       If cat.Groups(grp.Name).Users.Count = 0 Then
          Debug.Print vbTab & "There are no " & _
          "users in the " & grp & " group."
       End If
       For Each usr In cat.Groups(grp.Name).Users
          Debug.Print vbTab & "User: " & usr.Name
       Next usr
    Next grp
MsgBox "Groups and Users are listed " & _
    "in the Immediate window."
ExitHere:
    Set cat = Nothing
    conn.Close
    Set conn = Nothing
    Exit Sub
ErrorHandler:
    MsgBox Err.Description
    Resume ExitHere
End Sub
```

3. Execute the `List_UsersInGroups` procedure.
The procedure result is shown in Figure 14.21.

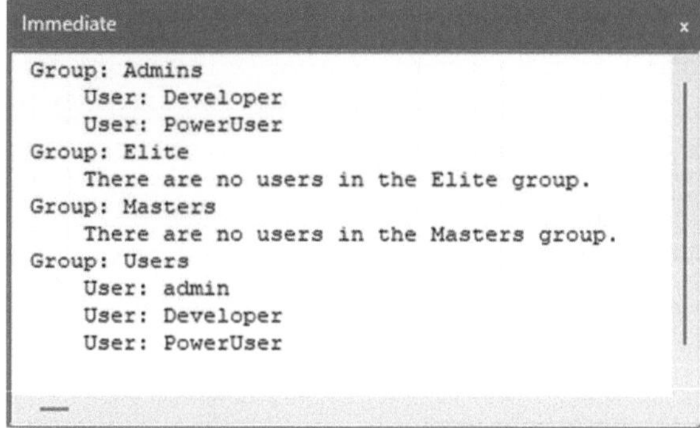

FIGURE 14.21. After running the procedure in Hands-On 14.11, security group account names and the corresponding user accounts are listed in the Immediate window.

Setting and Retrieving User and Group Permissions Using ADOX

The following sections of this chapter will get you started with using ADOX to retrieve, list, and set permissions for various database objects.

Determining the Object Owner Using ADOX

A database, and every object in the database, has an owner. The owner is the user who created that particular object. The object owner has special privileges, including the ability to assign or revoke permissions for that object. To retrieve the name of the object owner, use the `GetObjectOwner` method of a `Catalog` object. This method takes two parameters: the object's name and the object's type. For example, to determine the owner of a table, use the following syntax:

```
cat.GetObjectOwner(myObjName, adPermObjTable)
```

where `cat` is an object variable representing the ADOX `Catalog` object, `myObjName` is the name of a database table, and `adPermObjTable` is a built-in ADOX constant specifying the type of object. The constants for the `Type` parameter can be looked up in the Object Browser, as shown in Figure 14.22.

To set the ownership of an object with ADOX, use the `SetObjectOwner` method of the `Catalog` object like this:

```
cat.SetObjectOwner("Customers", adPermObjTable, "PowerUser")
```

The preceding statement says that the ownership of the `Customers` table is to be transferred to the user named `PowerUser`.

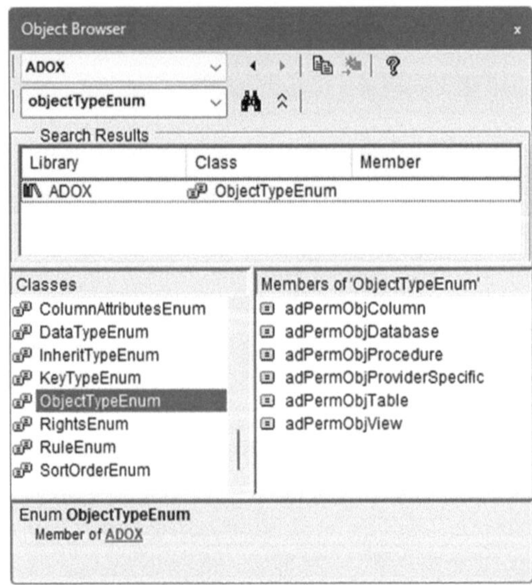

FIGURE 14.22. The Object Browser displays the available constants for the Type parameter.

Additional Code in the Companion Files.

File Name: `Chap14_ADO_AdditionalCode.txt`

Description: `Determining the Object Owner (Get_ObjectOwner)`

Setting User Permissions for an Object Using ADOX

With ADOX, you set permissions on an object by using the `SetPermissions` method. User-level security can be easier to manage if you set permissions only for groups and then assign users to the appropriate groups. Recall that permissions set for the group are automatically inherited by all users in that group. The `SetPermissions` method, which can be used for setting both user and group permissions, has the following syntax:

```
GroupOrUser.SetPermissions(Name, ObjectType, Action,
                    Rights[, Inherit] [,ObjectTypeId])
```

- `Name`—The name of the object to set permissions on.

- `ObjectType`—The type of object the permissions are set for. (See Figure 14.22 for the names of the ADOX built-in constants that can be used to specify the `Type` parameter.)

- `Action`—The type of action to perform when setting permissions. Use the `adAccessSet` constant for Access databases to specify that the group of users will have exactly the requested permissions.

- `Rights`—A `Long` value containing a bitmask indicating the permissions to set. The `Rights` argument can consist of a single permissions constant or several constants combined with the OR operator. See Figure 14.23 for the names of the ADOX built-in constants that can be used in the `Rights` argument to specify the type of permissions to set.

NOTE	*A bitmask is a numeric value intended for a bit-by-bit value comparison with other numeric values, usually to flag options in parameters or return values. In VBA, this comparison is done with bitwise logical operators, such as AND and OR. The ADOX* `GetPermissions` *and* `SetPermissions` *methods use the bitwise logical operator OR to retrieve the bitmask for the existing permissions and to add new permissions to the bitmask.*

The last two arguments (those in square brackets) are optional:

- `Inherit`—A `Long` value that specifies how objects will inherit these permissions. The default value is `adInheritNone`.

- `ObjectTypeId`—A `Variant` value that specifies the Global Unique Identifier (GUID) for a provider object type not defined by OLE DB. This parameter is required if `ObjectType` is set to `adPermObjProviderSpecific` (which is used for setting permissions for forms, reports, and macros); otherwise, it is not used. See Table 14.3 for the available GUIDs.

TABLE 14.3.   GUIDs for provider objects.

Object	GUID
Form	{c49c842e-9dcb-11d1-9f0a-00c04fc2c2e0}
Report	{c49c8430-9dcb-11d1-9f0a-00c04fc2c2e0}
Macro	{c49c842f-9dcb-11d1-9f0a-00c04fc2c2e0}

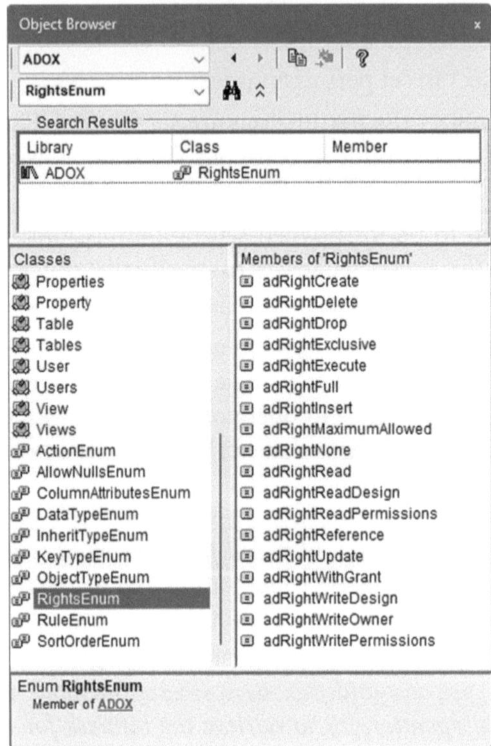

FIGURE 14.23.   In ADOX, you can use many security constants for setting permissions to database objects.

Additional Code in the Companion Files.

File Name: `Chap14_ADO_AdditionalCode.txt`

Description: `Setting User Permissions for an Object (Set_UserObjectPermissions)`

Setting User Permissions for a Database Using ADOX

To specify permissions for the database, specify an empty string (`""`) as the name of the database:

```
cat.Users("PowerUser").SetPermissions "", adPermObjDatabase, _
adAccessSet, adRightExclusive
```

This statement gives the user named `PowerUser` the right to open the database exclusively.

Additional Code in the Companion Files.

File Name: `Chap14_ADO_AdditionalCode.txt`
Description: `Setting User Permissions for a Database (Set_UserDb-Permissions_ADO)`

Setting User Permissions for a Container Using ADOX

Now that you've learned how to grant permissions to a user for a specific object such as a table or query, you may want to know how to specify permissions for an entire set of objects such as tables, queries, forms, reports, and macros.

As mentioned earlier during our work with DAO, each `Database` object has a `Containers` collection consisting of built-in `Container` objects. A `Container` object groups together similar types of `Document` objects. You can use the `Containers` collection to set security for all `Document` objects of a given type. You can set the permissions that users and groups will receive by default on all newly created objects in a database by passing in `Null` for the object name argument of the ADOX `SetPermissions` method.

⊙ Hands-On 14.12   Setting User Permissions for Containers (ADO)

1. In the VBE window, choose Insert | Module.
2. In the module's Code window, enter the `Set_UserContainerPermissions_ADO` procedure, as shown here:

```
Sub Set_UserContainerPermissions_ADO()
    Dim conn As ADODB.Connection
    Dim cat As ADOX.Catalog
    Dim strPath As String
    Dim strDB As String
    Dim strSysDB As String

    On Error GoTo ErrorHandler
```

```vba
strPath = "C:\VBAAccess2024_ByExample\"
strDB = "Chap14.mdb"
strSysDB = "Security.mdw"

' Open connection to the database using
' the specified system database
Set conn = New ADODB.Connection
With conn
   .Provider = "Microsoft.ACE.OLEDB.12.0"
   .Properties("Jet OLEDB:System Database") = _
       strPath & strSysDB
   .Properties("User ID") = "Developer"
   .Properties("Password") = "Chapter14"
   .Open strPath & strDB
End With

' Open the catalog
Set cat = New ADOX.Catalog
cat.ActiveConnection = conn

' add a user account
cat.Users.Append "PowerUser", "star"

' Set permissions for PowerUser on
' the Tables Container
cat.Users("PowerUser").SetPermissions Null, _
 adPermObjTable, _
 adAccessSet, _
 adRightRead Or _
 adRightInsert Or _
 adRightUpdate Or _
 adRightDelete, adInheritNone
 MsgBox "You have granted " & vbCrLf & _
  "permissions to PowerUser on " & _
  "the Tables Container."
ExitHere:
  Set cat = Nothing
  conn.Close
  Set conn = Nothing
  Exit Sub
ErrorHandler:
  If Err.Number = -2147467259 Then
  ' because PowerUser user already exists
  ' we ignore this statement
    Resume Next
```

```
   Else
      MsgBox Err.Description
      Resume ExitHere
   End If
End Sub
```

3. Choose Run | Run Sub/UserForm to execute the procedure.

This procedure gives the `PowerUser` account permission to design, read, update, insert, and delete data for all newly created tables and queries. Notice that `Null` is passed as the first argument of the `SetPermissions` method to indicate that permissions are to be set only on new objects of the type specified by the second argument of this method.

Checking Permissions for Objects Using ADOX

You can retrieve the permissions for a particular user or group on a particular object with the ADOX `GetPermissions` method. Because this method returns a numeric permission value for the specified object, you must write more code to decipher the returned value if you want to display the names of constants representing permissions.

Additional Code in the Companion Files.
File Name: `Chap14_ADO_AdditionalCode.txt`
Description: `Checking Permissions for a Specific Object (GetObject-Permissions_ADO)`

Changing a User Password Using ADOX

User passwords are stored in the WIF. To change a user's password in VBA code, use the ADOX `User` object's `ChangePassword` method. This method takes as parameters the user's current password and the new password. If a user does not yet have a password, use an empty string (`""`) for the user's current password.

The procedure in Hands-On 14.12 demonstrates how to change a password for the `Admin` user. Recall that `Admin` is the default user account that has a blank password. In an unsecured Access database, all users are automatically logged on using the `Admin` account. When establishing user-level security, you should start by changing the password for the `Admin` user. Changing an `Admin` password activates the Logon dialog box the next time you start Access. Only users with a valid username and password will be able to log on to the database. Although users are permitted to change their own passwords, only a user who belongs to the `Admins` group can clear a password that another user has forgotten.

◉ Hands-On 14.12 Changing a User Password (ADO)

1. Create a new Access database named `AdminPwd.mdb` in your `C:\ VBAAccess2024_ByExample` folder. Close this database before proceeding to step 2.
2. In the VBE window of the `Chap14_withADO.accdb` database, choose Insert | Module.
3. In the module's Code window, enter the `Change_UserPassword_ADO` procedure, as shown here:

```
Sub Change_UserPassword_ADO()
  Dim cat As ADOX.Catalog
  Dim strDB As String
  Dim strSysDB As String

  On Error GoTo ErrorHandler

  strDB = CurrentProject.Path & "\AdminPwd.mdb"
  ' change the path to use the default
  ' workgroup information file on your computer
  strSysDB = "C:\Users\Julitta\" & _
  "AppData\Roaming\Microsoft\Access\System1.mdw"

  ' Open the catalog, specifying the system
  ' database to use
  Set cat = New ADOX.Catalog
  With cat
    .ActiveConnection = _
    "Provider='Microsoft.ACE.OLEDB.12.0';" & _
    "Data Source='" & strDB & "';" & _
    "Jet OLEDB:System Database='" & _
        strSysDB & "';" & _
    "User Id=Admin;Password=;"

    ' Change the password for the Admin user
    .Users("Admin").ChangePassword "", "secret"
  End With

ExitHere:
  Set cat = Nothing
  Exit Sub
ErrorHandler:
  MsgBox Err.Description
  GoTo ExitHere
End Sub
```

4. Choose Run | Run Sub/UserForm to execute the procedure.

5. When you open the `AdminPwd.mdb` database after running the procedure, a Logon dialog box will appear. Enter `Admin` in the Name text box and `secret` in the Password text box, and then click OK. Remove the `Admin` password by choosing File | Info | Users and Permissions | User and Group Accounts. Click the Change Logon Password tab and type `secret` for the old password. Click the Apply button, and click OK to exit the User and Group Accounts window.

6. After removing the `Admin` password, reopen the `AdminPwd.mdb` file. The database should now open without prompting you to enter a password.

7. Close the `AdminPwd.mdb` database and exit the Access window in which the file was opened.

Managing User-Level Security with SQL Commands

Another way of managing user-level security in Access `.mdb` databases involves using SQL commands to control access to database objects. In this section, we will look at some key SQL commands that help manage who can access and modify different parts of the database, ensuring data security and integrity.

SQL Commands for Managing User-Level Security

- `CREATE USER`—Creates a new user
- `ADD USER TO GROUP`—Adds a user to a specific group
- `DROP USER`—Deletes a user
- `DROP GROUP`—Deletes a group
- `GRANT`—Grants specific permissions to a user or group
- `REVOKE`—Revokes specific permissions from a user or group.

To use the SQL commands in your VBA procedures, you need to set up a connection to the database. Use the `ADODB.Connection` object to establish a connection to your database, define and use the SQL commands to perform a specific action, and use the `Command` object to execute the SQL command against the database.

Creating a User and Granting and Revoking Permissions to Objects

The following hands-on exercise demonstrates how to create a new user, grant them permissions, and revoke permissions using SQL commands within a VBA procedure.

◉ Hands-On 14.13   Creating a User Account with Permissions

1. Create a new Access database named `Chap14_withSQL.mdb` in your `C:\VBAAccess2024_ByExample` folder. Select Microsoft Access databases (2002–2003)(*.mdb) file format.
2. Switch to the VBE window and choose Tools | References. In the References dialog box, scroll down to locate Microsoft ActiveX Data Objects 6.1 Library and Microsoft ADO Ext. 6.0 for DDL and Security. Click the checkbox to the left of each library name to set a reference and click OK to exit the dialog box.
3. Choose Insert | Module to add a new module to the current VBA project.
4. In the module's Code window, enter the `ManageUserSecurity` procedure shown here:

```vba
Sub ManageUserSecurity()
    Dim conn As ADODB.Connection
    Dim cmd As ADODB.Command
    Dim sql As String
    On Error GoTo ErrorHandler
    ' Create a new connection object
    Set conn = New ADODB.Connection
    ' Open the connection to the database secured with WIF
    conn.Open "Provider=Microsoft.ACE.OLEDB.12.0;" & _
      "Data Source=C:\VBAAccess2024_ByExample\Chap14.mdb;" & _
      "Jet OLEDB:System database=" & _
      "C:\VBAAccess2024_ByExample\Security.mdw;" & _
      "User ID=Developer;Password=Chapter14;"
    ' Create a new command object
    Set cmd = New ADODB.Command
    Set cmd.ActiveConnection = conn

    ' Define your SQL command
    sql = "CREATE USER SQLUser PWDsql"
    cmd.CommandText = sql
    cmd.Execute
    ' Grant permissions to the new user
    sql = "GRANT SELECT ON Customers TO SQLUser"
    cmd.CommandText = sql
    cmd.Execute
    ' Revoke permissions if needed
    sql = "REVOKE SELECT ON Customers FROM SQLUser"
    cmd.CommandText = sql
    cmd.Execute
ExitHere:
    ' Clean up
```

```
        conn.Close
        Set cmd = Nothing
        Set conn = Nothing
        Exit Sub
ErrorHandler:
        MsgBox Err.Number & ":" & Err.Description
        Resume ExitHere
End Sub
```

5. Run the `ManageUserSecurity` procedure.

Notice that this procedure sets up a new user account for `SQLUser` with the password `PWDsql`. A new user is created with the `SQL CREATE USER` statement that expects the username and the password. You can also provide a PID to make the account unique. The syntax of creating a user account looks like this:

```
CREATE USER userLoginName password PID
```

You can create more than one user account at a time by separating the usernames with a comma.

To grant the user `SELECT` permission on the specified table, we used the `GRANT` statement. The `SELECT` permission allows the user to read data from the table.

Next, this procedure demonstrated the `REVOKE` statement, which can be used to revoke the `SELECT` permission from the user on the specified table. When you revoke the permission, the user will no longer be able to read data from the specified table.

Adding Users to Groups

Use the `ADD  USER` statement to make a user account a member of a group. Specify the user account name followed by the `TO` keyword and a group name:

```
ADD USER userAccountName TO groupName
```

The following procedure adds the `SQLUser` created in Hands-On 14.13 to the `Elite` group.

```
Sub AddUserTOGroup()
    Dim conn As ADODB.Connection
    Dim cmd As ADODB.Command
    Dim sql As String

    On Error GoTo ErrorHandler

    ' Create a new connection object
    Set conn = New ADODB.Connection
```

```vba
    ' Open the connection to the database secured with WIF
    conn.Open "Provider=Microsoft.ACE.OLEDB.12.0;" & _
        "Data Source=C:\VBAAccess2024_ByExample\Chap14.mdb;" & _
        "Jet OLEDB:System database=" & _
        "C:\VBAAccess2024_ByExample\Security.mdw;" & _
        "User ID=Developer;Password=Chapter14;"

    ' Create a new command object
    Set cmd = New ADODB.Command
    Set cmd.ActiveConnection = conn


    ' Define SQL command to add the user to a group
    sql = "ADD USER SQLUser TO Elite"
    cmd.CommandText = sql
    cmd.Execute

ExitHere:
    ' Clean up
    conn.Close
    Set cmd = Nothing
    Set conn = Nothing
    Exit Sub
ErrorHandler:
    MsgBox Err.Number & ":" & Err.Description
    Resume ExitHere
End Sub
```

Removing a User from a Group

To delete a user from a group, use the DROP USER statement followed by the username, the FROM keyword, and the group name. For example, to delete the SQLUser account from the Elite group, use the following statement:

```
DROP USER SQLUser FROM Elite
```

Deleting a User Account

To delete a user account, use the DROP USER statement followed by the user account name:

```
DROP USER SQLUser
```

Granting Permissions for an Object

As you've seen in Hands-On 14.13, you can use the GRANT statement to assign security permissions for an object in a database to an existing user or group account.

The GRANT statement requires the following:

- A list of privileges to be granted
- The keyword ON followed by the name of a table, a non-table object, or an object container (e.g., Tables, Forms, Reports, Modules, or Scripts)

  Please note that in addition to tables, the Tables container contains queries, views, and procedures, and the Scripts container includes macros.
- The keyword TO followed by the user or group name

The syntax of the GRANT statement is shown below:

```
GRANT listOfPermissions ON tableName | objectName |
 containerName TO accountName
```

For example, the following statement can be used in your VBA procedure to grant the SELECT, DELETE, INSERT, and UPDATE permissions on all tables, queries, views, and stored procedures to the Masters group:

```
cmd.Execute "GRANT SELECT, DELETE, INSERT, " _
  & "UPDATE ON CONTAINER TABLES TO Masters"
```

Revoking Security Permissions

Use the REVOKE statement to revoke security permissions for an object from an existing user or group account. This statement has the following syntax:

```
REVOKE listOfPermissions ON tableName | objectName | container-
Name FROM accountName
```

For example, the following procedure removes the privilege of deleting objects from the Tables container from the members of the Masters group:

```
Sub RevokePermissions()
    Dim conn As ADODB.Connection
    Dim cmd As ADODB.Command
    Dim sql As String

    On Error GoTo ErrorHandler

    ' Create a new connection object
    Set conn = New ADODB.Connection

    ' Open the connection to the database secured with WIF
    conn.Open "Provider=Microsoft.ACE.OLEDB.12.0;" & _
       "Data Source=C:\VBAAccess2024_ByExample\Chap14.mdb;" & _
       "Jet OLEDB:System database=" & _
       "C:\VBAAccess2024_ByExample\Security.mdw;" & _
       "User ID=Developer;Password=Chapter14;"
```

```
' Create a new command object
Set cmd = New ADODB.Command
Set cmd.ActiveConnection = conn

' Define SQL command to revoke Delete permissions
sql = "REVOKE DELETE ON CONTAINER TABLES FROM Masters"
cmd.CommandText = sql
cmd.Execute

ExitHere:
  If Not conn Is Nothing Then
    If conn.State = adStateOpen Then conn.Close
  End If
  Set conn = Nothing
  Exit Sub
ErrorHandler:
  MsgBox Err.Number & ":" & Err.Description
  Resume ExitHere
End Sub
```

After running the above procedure, the `Masters` group does not have permission to delete data from new tables or queries (see Figure 14.24).

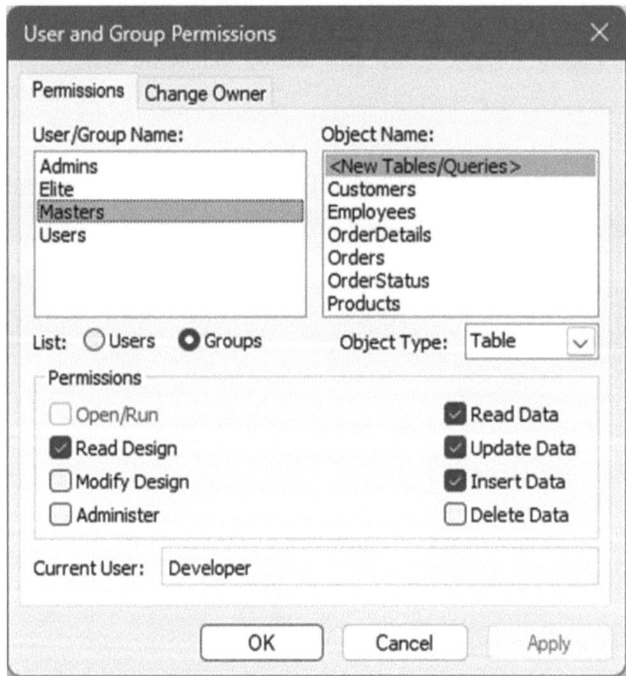

FIGURE 14.24.   Delete Data permission on new tables and queries was removed for the members of Masters.

Deleting a Group Account

Use the `DROP GROUP` statement to delete a group account. You only need to specify the name of the group account you want to delete. To delete more than one account, separate each group name with a comma. The following SQL statement used in your VBA procedure will delete the `Elite` group:

```
cmd.Execute "DROP GROUP Elite"
```

CORRECTLY OPENING A SECURED ACCESS MDB DATABASE

If you are trying to open a secured database from the recent file list in Access, Access will display the message shown in Figure 14.25. This is a scary message that most Access users and even some administrators don't know what to do with. The solution, though, is quite simple.

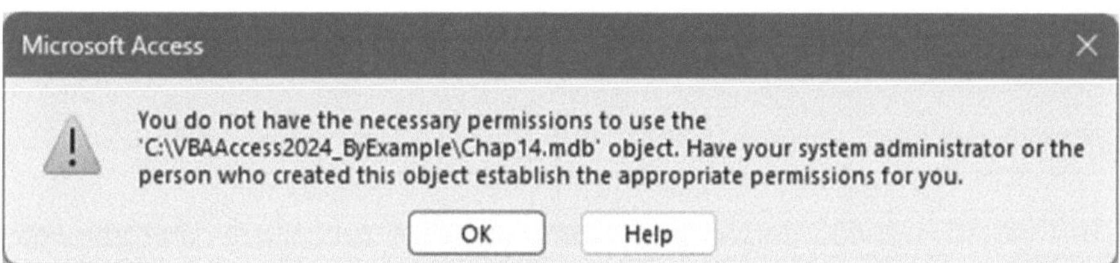

FIGURE 14.25.   This message is shown when you attempt to open a secured Access .mdb database and Access cannot find the WIF.

Recall from the beginning of this chapter that a shortcut to the `Chap14.mdb` file was placed on your desktop when you created the WIF. You must use that shortcut to open this database file. It's recommended that you keep the documentation of your shortcut handy so you can recreate it if the shortcut can no longer be found on your desktop. The shortcut ensures that Access launches with the correct workgroup file, allowing you to access your secured database without encountering permissions issues. Remember, you will need to enter the username and password to log in. In this chapter, we have been logging in to this file as `Developer` with the password `Chapter14`.

USING ChatGPT WITH ACCESS

This chapter introduced legacy topics that you may or may not use, depending on your specific needs and circumstances. Understanding these foundational concepts is, however, crucial for comprehensively managing database security in Access `.mdb` databases. The skills and knowledge gained from these legacy systems can be transferable to more contemporary technologies, enhancing your overall proficiency in database management. Some topics introduced here may require further research on your part to deepen your understanding. Again, we are lucky to have access to the newest technological inventions, and we can quickly get the answers we need. So, what should we outsource to ChatGPT in this chapter? I bet you have lots of questions. To begin with, here are two prompts that you might like to explore more:

User Prompt: *What are the numbers that the AllPermissions and adbSecWrite-Owner return?*

User Prompt: *Create a Quiz with 10 questions and answers on the topic of securing MDB databases.*

The prompts and the responses obtained from ChatGPT are available in the companion files in a document titled `Chapter 14 – Using ChatGPT with Access`.

SUMMARY

In this chapter, you delved into numerous VBA procedures that allowed you to implement user-level security in an Access `.mdb` database. Your learning included the WIF, a crucial component used to store group and user accounts, along with their permissions on various database objects. You worked with DAO to create users, assign them to groups, and set their permissions programmatically. You also learned how to use ADO to connect to the database, execute SQL commands, and manage user-level security. This included setting up connections with a secured database using the WIF. Finally, you practiced using SQL commands to manage security settings, including creating users, adding users to groups, and altering permissions. You should now be well equipped to manage user-level security in Access `.mdb` databases, using various tools and techniques to maintain control over database access and permissions.

This chapter concludes Part IV of this book, in which we focused on writing VBA procedures that deal with security aspects of Access databases in the `.accdb` and `.mdb` file formats.

Part **V**

VBA Programming in Access Forms and Reports

The behavior of Access objects such as forms, reports, and controls can be modified by writing programming code known as an event procedure or an event handler. In this part of the book, you will learn how you make your forms, reports, and controls perform useful tasks by writing event procedures in class modules.

Chapter 15   Using VBA to Interact with Forms and Form Controls
Chapter 16   Using VBA to Interact with Reports and Report Controls

15

USING VBA TO INTERACT WITH FORMS AND FORM CONTROLS

Microsoft Access has always offered users a great number of features in the form design area. Its form features include various methods of creating forms and using different types of controls and styles. This chapter assumes that you know how to create forms by using the form design tools in Access to layout fields, labels, buttons, and their controls, and are now ready to learn how to enhance your forms using VBA programming.

Designing user-friendly forms in Access is a vital skill for creating intuitive and efficient database applications that cater to specific business needs. Your forms allow you to control how data is presented and interacted with. Controls that you place on your forms can be bound to data sources such as tables or queries, enabling real-time interaction with your database. The custom forms you create can range from simple data entry forms to complex interfaces with embedded subforms, tab controls, and VBA code for advanced functionality.

When designing a custom form, consider the end user's experience. Use tab controls to organize information into logical sections, ensuring that users can easily navigate the form. Include command buttons for common actions such as saving records, navigating between controls, and running specific queries. Use VBA to implement validation rules and error handling to prevent data entry mistakes and provide helpful feedback to your users.

CONTROLLING FORMS WITH FORM PROPERTIES

As you know, each form you create in Access comes with a variety of properties that can significantly enhance both its appearance and functionality. You can view these properties by opening the form in design view and selecting Property Sheet on the Form Design tab in the Ribbon. To select the form itself, click the form selector in the top corner of the form (where the rules meet). This ensures that you're viewing properties for the entire form, not just a specific control.

In the Property Sheet (see Figure 15.1), you'll see various tabs, such as Format, Data, Event, Other, and All. These tabs organize different properties that you can set or modify. To change or make your adjustments to a property, click on the property name you want to change. For example, you might set the Record Source property to a specific table or query, or change the Back Color property to update the form's background. If you're unsure about a specific property, pressing F1 for help will often give you a detailed explanation.

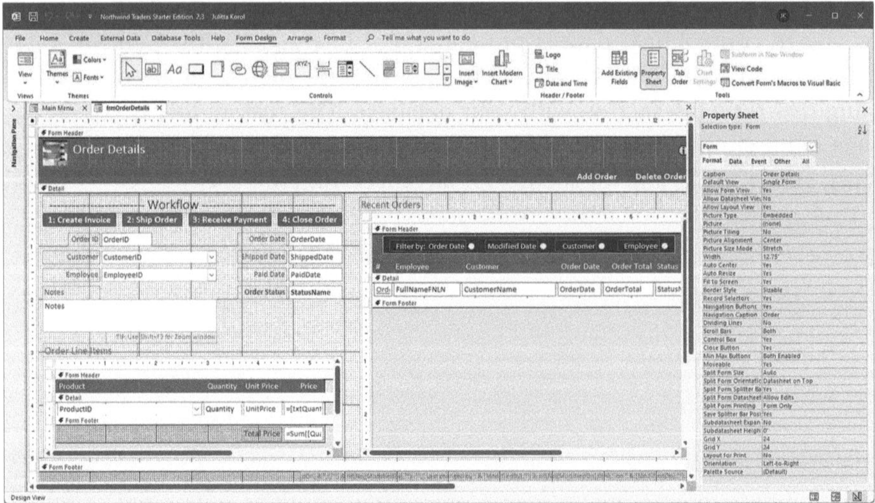

FIGURE 15.1. The Order Details form in design view and its Property Sheet.

There is one form property, called `Has Module`, that you may not be familiar with. This property, which you can find on the Properties Sheet's Other tab, determines whether the form has an associated class module. Note that any VBA code written for a form or its controls resides in the form class module. When you create a new form, the `Has Module` property is set to `No`, making it a lightweight object. Forms without class modules load and display faster, and this also helps with reducing the size of the database.

Reviewing and understanding the form properties, especially those designed by others, can be time-consuming. What if we designed a custom form that streamlines the process of reviewing form properties? This project will involve creating a form that allows you to quickly view all forms in a database and display properties that differ from the default settings. This is a multistep project that will introduce you to working with the form and its controls by writing the required event procedures in form modules.

NOTE	*All code files and figures for the hands-on projects may be found in the companion files.*

Custom Project 15.1   Designing and Programming a Custom Form

Part 1: Create a New Database and Populate It with Data

1. Create a new database named `Chap15.accdb` in your `VBAAccess2024_ByExample` folder.
2. Use External Data | New Data Source | From Database | Access to import all the tables, queries, forms, and reports from the `Northwind 2007.accdb` database that is included in the companion files.

Part 2: Create a Custom Form Using Access' Built-In Form Tools

1. Choose Create | Form Design and save `Form1` as `FormInspector`.
2. Position and size the controls as shown in Figure 15.2.

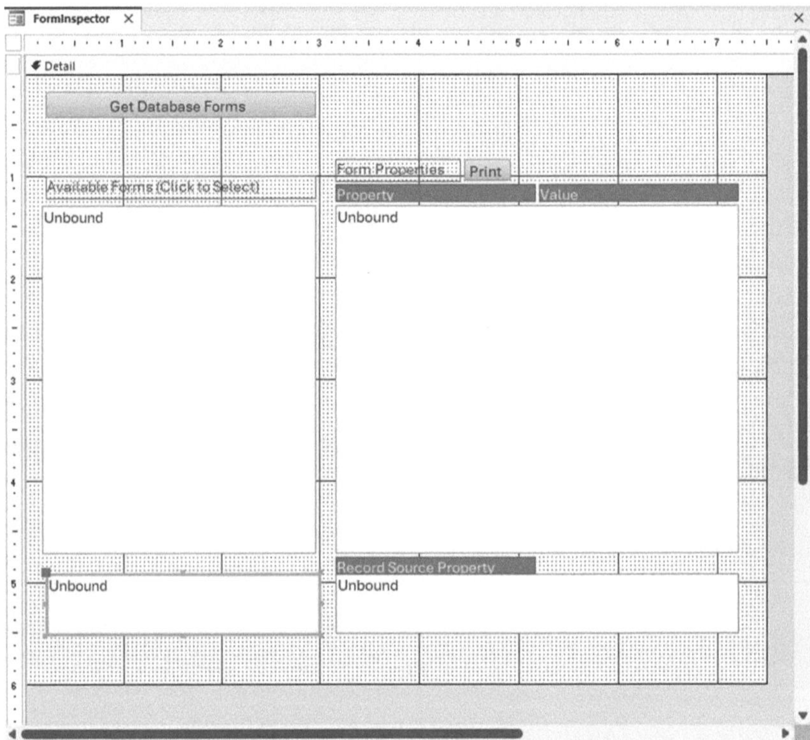

FIGURE 15.2.   Custom form in design view as used in Custom Project 15.1.

Table 15.1 lists the control types used and their initial properties that must be set prior to writing any programming code.

TABLE 15.1.   Controls used in the FormInspector form.

Control Type	Property Name	Property Value
Command Button	Name Caption Back Color	cmdGetForms Get Database Forms Accent 1, Lighter 40% (choose blue)
List Box Control	Name Column Heads Column Count Width Height	lstForms No 1 2.7917" 3.4167"
List Box Control Label	Caption	Available Forms (Click to Select)

Control Type	Property Name	Property Value
List Box Control	Name Column Count Column Widths Column Heads Width Height	lstProperties 2 2";2" No 4.0417" 3.4167"
NOTE: The two label controls over the lstProperties list box will serve as its column heads, so you can format their appearance according to your needs.		
Label (above the first column)	Caption Back Color For Color	Property Accent 6 (choose green) Text Light (choose white)
Label (above the second column)	Caption Back Color For Color	Value Accent 6 (choose green) Text Light (choose white)
Label	Caption	Form Properties
Command Button	Name Caption Visible Back Color	cmdPrint Print No Accent 1, Lighter 40% (choose blue)
There is a text box under each list box control.		
Text Box (on the left)	Name Visible	txtHiddenProperties No
Text Box (on the right)	Name Visible Can Grow Can Shrink ScrollBars	txtRecordSource No Yes Yes Vertical
Label (over the txtRecordSource)	Name Caption Visible Back Color Fore Color	lblRecordSource Record Source Property No Accent 6 (choose green) Text Light (choose white)

This is the basic form design; you can polish it up later if needed.

Note that to make a text box multiline, you should set the Can Grow and Can Shrink properties to Yes. This allows the text box to expand or contract based on its content. ScrollBars set to Vertical will allow users to scroll through longer text.

3. Save your form and display it in form view. The form should appear as shown in Figure 15.3.

   Next, we will make this form perform the desired tasks using VBA code. Writing code for a form in Microsoft Access involves creating event procedures that respond to user actions, such as clicking buttons or selecting items from a list. Events are explained in detail in a separate section of this chapter. In our `FormInspector` form, we will perform the following tasks in various event procedures:

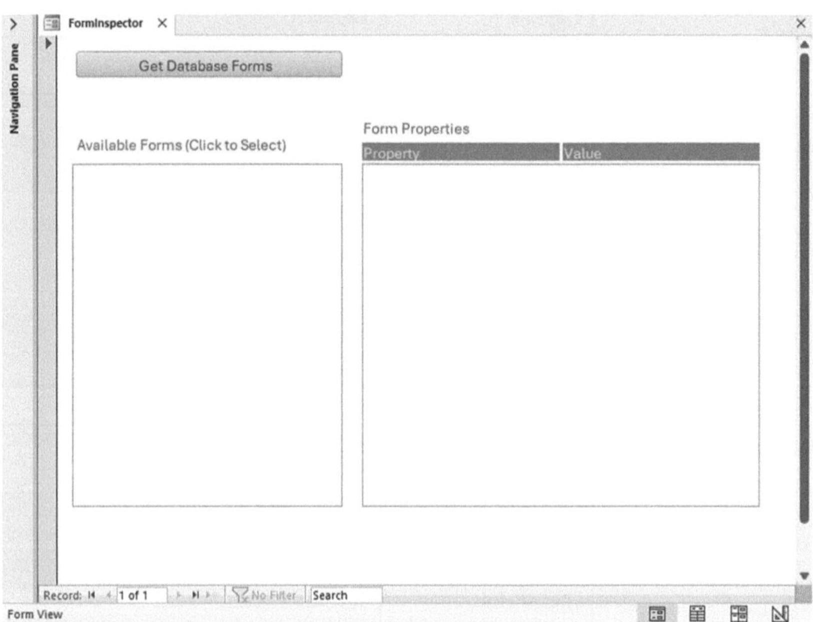

FIGURE 15.3. Custom form in form view as used in Custom Project 15.1.

1. Set the initial form properties (Form Load).
2. Populate the forms list box when a button is clicked (Button Click).
3. Update the properties list box when a form is selected (List Box Update).
4. Update the hidden text box and Record Source text box (Text Box Update).
5. Print to a text file the selected form properties (Button Click).

In addition, we will implement special handling for the `RecordSource` property. `RecordSource` can be a complex SQL query, which might be lengthy. It can span multiple lines, unlike other properties, which typically have single-line values. This requires a dedicated text box with scroll capabilities to display the full content. The `RecordSource` defines the data source for the form, essentially determining what data is available for display and interactions. This makes it a critical property for understanding and debugging forms. In the Access User Interface (UI), list boxes and text boxes have size limitations. The `RecordSource` often exceeds these limits, requiring a special approach to ensure the entire query is visible. In our `FormInspector` form, we use a separate text box (`txtRecordSource`) to display the full `RecordSource` content, along with a label (`lblRecordSource`) for identification. The text box and label will be shown only if the `RecordSource` property exists and contains a value, ensuring that the UI remains clean and uncluttered. When the `RecordSource` property is selected from the list of properties, the text box will be automatically populated with the full content and made visible.

This custom project uses a hidden text box (`txtHidenProperties`) to store a concatenated string of properties and their values. This intermediate data storage simplifies transferring this information between different parts of the form and facilitates further processing. When the Print button is clicked, the hidden text box acts as a buffer, holding the complete data string ready for output to the text file that we will create.

Using Hidden Text Boxes in Access Custom Forms

In Access, a hidden text box can serve several important purposes:

1. Storing Intermediate Data
   This is demonstrated in this custom project.

2. User Interface Management
   By keeping intermediate data hidden, you can maintain a clean and user-friendly interface. This ensures that users see only relevant and essential information without unnecessary details cluttering the form. Also, the hidden text box allows the form to manage data in the background, performing necessary tasks without exposing these operations to the user.

3. Data Integrity
   Storing data in the hidden text box ensures that the data is consistently accessible throughout the form's lifecycle. By using a hidden text box, you can safely handle and manipulate data within the form without risking accidental user modifications.

4. Synchronization
   The hidden text box ensures that when properties are updated or a new form is selected, all relevant data is updated efficiently and consistently across the form.

Part 3: Writing Your First Event Procedure to Handle the Form_Load Event

The `Form_Load` event in Microsoft Access is a very important event that occurs when a form is opened and loaded into memory but before it becomes visible

to the user. This event is frequently used to initialize form controls and set up
any necessary data or parameters the form might need for user interaction.

> ## Use Cases for the Form_Load Event
>
> - **Initializing Controls**
>
>   This includes setting default values for controls on the form and adjusting properties such as
>   visibility, enabled state, or formatting based on specific conditions.
>
> - **Populating Controls with Data**
>
>   This includes filling list boxes and combo boxes with data from tables or queries, as well as
>   setting the `RowSource` property for controls dynamically based on certain criteria.
>
> - **Setting Initial Conditions**
>
>   This includes adjusting the form's appearance, such as setting the form's caption or making
>   certain sections visible or hidden. Use this event to apply user-specific settings or preferences
>   (e.g., theme, layout) when the form loads.
>
> - **Running Setup Code**
>
>   This includes any initialization routines or setup code that must run before the user interacts
>   with the form. You can also log and track here the form-loading event and usage statistics.

1. In the form design view, activate the Property Sheet and choose Form from the
   Property Sheet dropdown.
2. Click the Event tab in the Property Sheet for the form and then click the ellipsis
   button (three dots) next to the On Load event property.
3. In the Choose Builder dialog box, select Code Builder and click OK.
   On the VBE screen, Access creates the form class module for that specific
   form. This module is where you write and store the VBA code that controls
   the behavior of your form and its controls. When you choose Code Builder
   for a form control's event, Access automatically creates a corresponding event
   procedure in the form's class module. You should see the following event
   procedure stub, which you must complete with your desired code:

```
Private Sub Form_Load()

End Sub
```

This stub is created by Access, and you then need to fill it with the code that
performs the actions you want when the event occurs. For instance, you might
need to initialize controls, set default values, or load data when the form loads.

> | **NOTE** | *If you select the wrong event property by mistake, simply delete the automatically generated lines from the class module, and then go back to the Property Sheet to select the correct property you want to work with.* |

What Is a Form Class Module?

A form class module is a container for event procedures and other VBA code specific to a particular form. Each form in Access can have its own class module, which is used to handle events, manipulate controls, and perform various tasks related to that form.

4. Complete the `Form_Load` event procedure, as shown below:

```
Private Sub Form_Load()
    ' Ensure RowSourceType is set correctly during form load
    Me.lstProperties.RowSourceType = "Value List"
    Me.lstForms.RowSource = ""
    Me.txtRecordSource.Visible = False
    Me.lstProperties.RowSource = ""
    Me.cmdPrint.Visible = False
End Sub
```

Note that in VBA, particularly within the context of Access form modules, the `Me` keyword is used to refer to the current instance of the form. It provides a convenient way to access the properties and methods of the form and its controls without having to explicitly name the form. By using `Me`, you avoid hard-coding the form's name in your code, which makes your code more flexible and easier to reuse in other forms.

You have not written the `Form_Load` event procedure that Access will execute when you open the form. You can verify that the `Form_Load` event procedure executes when the form opens by setting a breakpoint in the VBA editor. Do this by clicking in the margin to the left of the Private Sub Form_Load() line. A red dot will appear, and the line will be highlighted in red, indicating that a breakpoint is set. When you switch back to Access and open the form in form view, the VBA editor will automatically open, and execution will pause at the breakpoint, allowing you to step through the code line by line (see the earlier chapter in this book on using various debugging techniques). By using breakpoints and stepping through your code, you can verify that the `Form_Load` event procedure executes as expected and performs the necessary initialization tasks.

Part 4: Writing an Event Procedure to Fill the Forms List Box (cmdGetForm)

To write event procedures for other controls on your form, you can use the Code Builder, as we did in the previous step, or you can work directly in the form class module using the following guidelines:

- Find the form you are working on under Forms in the Project Explorer.
- Double-click the form to open its class module.
- Choose Control and Event.

  At the top of the code window, you will see two drop-down lists. The left list is the Control box, and the right list is the Event box.

  o Select the control name from the Control box.
  o Choose the event you want to write code for from the Event box. This will automatically create an event procedure stub for you to complete.

1. In the `Forms_FormInspector` code module, select `cmdGetForms` from the Control box and the Click property from the Event box.
2. Complete the `cmdGetForms_Click` event procedure, as shown below:

```
Private Sub cmdGetForms_Click()
    Dim db As DAO.Database
    Dim doc As DAO.Document
    Dim frm As Access.Form

    ' Set the form variable to the current form
    Set frm = Me

    ' Access the current database
    Set db = CurrentDb

    ' Set the row source type of the list box
    Me.lstForms.RowSourceType = "Value List"

    ' Loop through each document in the Forms container
    ' and add to the list box
    For Each doc In db.Containers("Forms").Documents
        ' Exclude the current form
        If doc.Name <> Me.Name Then
            frm!lstForms.AddItem doc.Name
        End If
    Next doc

    ' Prevent users from adding more items to the list box
    Me.lstForms.AllowValueListEdits = False
```

```
    ' Select the first item in the list box
    If Me.lstForms.ListCount > 0 Then
        Me.lstForms = Me.lstForms.ItemData(0)
    End If

    ' Trigger the After Update event to refresh the properties
    Call lstForms_AfterUpdate

    ' Clean up
    Set db = Nothing
End Sub
```

In this click event procedure, which will execute when the user clicks the cmdGetForm button, we tell Access to retrieve the names of the current database's forms, excluding the current form, from the DAO Documents collection of the DBEngine Containers Forms collection. Before loading the form names into the lstForms list box, it is important to ensure that the RowSourceType is set to Value List. To prevent users from adding more items to the list box, the procedure sets the AllowValueListEdit property of the lstForms list box to False. Then, the procedure checks whether the list box contains items (ListCount >0). If so, it selects the first item using ItemData(0). Finally, the lstProperties list box must be refreshed so the properties of the selected form can be loaded. This is done by calling the lstForms_AfterUpdate event procedure, which we will write next.

Part 5: Writing an Event Procedure to Update the Properties List Box (lstForms_AfterUpdate)

Now you need to ensure that after the list box with the form names is populated, and a form is selected, the properties list box is refreshed. This procedure involves the following tasks:

1. Retrieve the selected form name from the list box and open it in design view.
2. Loop through the form's properties, excluding binary data properties and other properties you don't need, and concatenate them into a string.
3. Populate the lstProperties list box with the property names and values. We want the properties to appear alphabetically in the list box, so we will need to include a sorting routine.
4. Handle the RecordSource special case, as explained earlier. Check that the RecordSource property exists and is not empty. If so, retrieve its full value and display it in a text box.
5. Make the Print button visible so the property list can be printed to a text file.

6. Ensure that the RecordSource text box and its label are visible only when the RecordSource is selected. Note that as we are only displaying the properties that may have changed, if the RecordSource property of any selected form is empty, we will not display it in the lstProperties list box.

As you can see, there are numerous conditions you must handle in this event procedure.

1. In the `Forms_FormInspector` code module, select lstForms from the Control box and the AfterUpdate property from the Event box.

2. Complete the `lstForms_AfterUpdate` event procedure, as shown below:

```
Private Sub lstForms_AfterUpdate()
    Dim frmName As String
    Dim frm As Access.Form
    Dim prop As Property
    Dim propValue As Variant
    Dim strProperties As String
    Dim excludeProps As Variant
    Dim propNames() As String
    Dim propValues() As String
    Dim propCount As Integer
    Dim i As Integer
    Dim hasRecordSource As Boolean

    ' Properties to exclude
    excludeProps = Array("PictureData", "ImageData", _
        "PrtDevMode", "PrtDevModeW", "PrtDevNames", _
        "PrtMip", "PrtDevNamesW")

    ' Get the selected form name from the list box
    frmName = Me.lstForms.Value

    ' Open the selected form in Design View
    DoCmd.OpenForm frmName, acDesign
    Set frm = Forms(frmName)

    ' Retrieve the full RecordSource directly
    Dim fullRecordSource As String
    fullRecordSource = frm.RecordSource

    ' Initialize the properties arrays
    propCount = 0
    ReDim propNames(1 To 1)
    ReDim propValues(1 To 1)
```

```vba
' Initialize flag for RecordSource property
hasRecordSource = False

' Loop through the form's properties
' and collect names and values
On Error Resume Next
For Each prop In frm.Properties
    propValue = prop.Value
    ' Check if the property should be excluded
    If Not IsNull(propValue) And _
        propValue <> "" And Not IsObject(propValue) Then
        For i = LBound(excludeProps) To UBound(excludeProps)
            If prop.Name = excludeProps(i) Then
                propValue = Null
                Exit For
            End If
        Next i
    End If
    ' Only collect properties that are not excluded
    ' and have non-default value
    If Not IsNull(propValue) And propValue <> "" Then
        propCount = propCount + 1
        ReDim Preserve propNames(1 To propCount)
        ReDim Preserve propValues(1 To propCount)
        propNames(propCount) = prop.Name
        propValues(propCount) = propValue

        ' Check if the property is RecordSource
        If prop.Name = "RecordSource" Then
            hasRecordSource = True
        End If
    End If
Next prop
On Error GoTo 0

' Sort the properties alphabetically by name
Dim j As Integer, k As Integer
Dim tempName As String
Dim tempValue As Variant
For j = 1 To propCount - 1
    For k = j + 1 To propCount
        If propNames(j) > propNames(k) Then
            ' Swap property names
            tempName = propNames(j)
```

```vba
                propNames(j) = propNames(k)
                propNames(k) = tempName

                ' Swap property values
                tempValue = propValues(j)
                propValues(j) = propValues(k)
                propValues(k) = tempValue
            End If
        Next k
    Next j

    ' Configure the list box
    Me.lstProperties.ColumnCount = 2
' Me.lstProperties.ColumnHeads = True
    Me.lstProperties.RowSourceType = "Value List"
    Me.lstProperties.RowSource = ""   ' Clear existing items
' Me.lstProperties.AddItem "Property;Value"

    ' Initialize properties string
    strProperties = "Form Properties for " & frmName & vbCrLf
                                            & vbCrLf
    strProperties = strProperties & "Property" & vbTab & "Value"
                                            & vbCrLf
    strProperties = strProperties & "--------" & vbTab &
                                    "-----" & vbCrLf

    ' Add sorted properties to list box and string
    For i = 1 To propCount
      Me.lstProperties.AddItem propNames(i) & ";" & propValues(i)
        ' Add property name and value to the string variable
        strProperties = strProperties & propNames(i) & _
            vbTab & propValues(i) & vbCrLf
    Next i

    ' Store the properties string in the hidden text box
    Me.txtHiddenProperties.Value = strProperties

    ' Always hide the RecordSource text box initially
    Me.txtRecordSource.Value = ""
    Me.txtRecordSource.Visible = False
    Me.lblRecordSource.Visible = False

    ' Check if the RecordSource exists and is not empty
    If hasRecordSource And frm.RecordSource <> "" Then
```

```
    ' Retrieve the full RecordSource directly
    fullRecordSource = frm.RecordSource

    ' Display the full RecordSource in the text box
    Me.txtRecordSource.Value = fullRecordSource
    Me.txtRecordSource.Visible = True
    Me.lblRecordSource.Visible = True

    ' Select the RecordSource property in the list box
    For i = 0 To Me.lstProperties.ListCount - 1
      If Me.lstProperties.Column(0, i) = "RecordSource" Then
          Me.lstProperties.Selected(i) = True
          Exit For
        End If
    Next i
  End If

  ' Display the Print button
  Me.cmdPrint.Visible = "True"


  ' Close the form and return to Form View
   DoCmd.Close acForm, frmName, acSaveNo

  ' Clean up
  Set frm = Nothing
End Sub
```

Using the AfterUpdate Event

The `AfterUpdate` event for a list box in Access is triggered after the user makes a selection from the list box and the selection is changed. This event is commonly used to perform actions based on the user's selection, such as updating other controls on the form or processing the selected data. Use this event to populate or update other controls on the form based on the selected item, or to show additional information related to the selected item. The `AfterUpdate` event is also used to enable or disable other controls depending on the selection.

By effectively using the `AfterUpdate` event, you can create dynamic and responsive Access forms that react to user actions in real time.

After declaring a number of variables for the `lstForms_AfterUpdate` event procedure, we define an array that contains the names of properties we want to exclude. In Access, some form properties contain binary data or special characters (`PictureData`, `ImageData`, `PrtDevMode`, etc.) that are not readable as plain text. Excluding these properties will result in a cleaner output when we write the properties to a text file.

To retrieve the selected form properties, the form is opened in design view and the properties are read by looping through the form `Properties` collection. We exclude properties that have no value (`IsNull`), are blank (`""`), or are binary (`Not IsObject`). All other properties that have non-default values (are non-null and non-empty) are collected. The `propCount` variable keeps track of the number of properties that meet the criteria (non-excluded and non-default value). The `ReDim Preserve` statement, discussed in the chapter on arrays, dynamically resizes the arrays (`propName` and `propValues`) to accommodate the new property. Recall that the `ReDim Preserve` statement resizes the array while preserving its existing contents. The following lines store the current property's name and value in the newly resized arrays:

```
propNames(propCount) = prop.Name
propValues(propCount) = propValue
```

The first line adds the property name to the `propNames` array at the index `propCount`. The second line adds the property value to the `propValues` array at the index `propCount`.

If the current property's name is `RecordSource`, we set the Boolean variable `hasRecordSource` to `True`. We need this later to handle special processing for the `RecordSource` property to ensure its value is fully retrieved and displayed.

The next code segment performs the sorting routine to ensure that property names are displayed alphabetically by name.

When you retrieve the names of the properties from a form or control in Microsoft Access using VBA, the properties are generally returned in the order they are stored within the internal structure of the form or control object. This order is not explicitly defined and can seem arbitrary. The order of properties as retrieved from the form or control cannot be changed within the object's native internal structure. You can, however, change the way you process or display these properties in your VBA code.

Sorting and Customizing the Order of Properties

You can sort and customize the order of properties after retrieving them by using an array. Arrays are easier to manage for sorting purposes.

The sorting code fragment in the `lstForms_AfterUpdate` event procedure uses a simple bubble sort algorithm to sort the property names and their corresponding values alphabetically. The code initializes the `j` and `k` variables as loop counters and the `tempName` and `tempValue` variables as temporary variables used for swapping. The sorting task is performed via two loops:

1. The outer loop (`For j = 1 to propCount - 1`) runs from the first element to the second-to-last element in the `propName` array. This ensures each element is compared with all subsequent elements.
2. The inner loop (`For k = j + 1 to propCount`) runs from the element immediately following the current element in the outer loop (`j`) to the last element in the `propNames` array. This ensures each element is compared with all subsequent elements.

Next, comparison and swapping are performed.

1. If `propNames(j) > propNames(k)`, then it compares the current element (`propNames(j)`) with the next element (`propNames(k)`).
2. If `propNames(j)` is greater than `propNames(k)`, the elements are swapped:

   a. `tempName` stores the current element (`propNames(j)`).

   b. `propNames(j)` is assigned the value of the next element (`propNames(k)`).

   c. `propNames(k)` is then assigned the value of `tempName`.

3. The corresponding property values in `propValues` are also swapped using `tempValue`.

   The bubble sort algorithm repeatedly steps through the list, compares adjacent elements, and swaps them if they are in the wrong order. This process is repeated until the list is sorted. In this case, the sorting is done alphabetically by property name.

After we have our list of properties all sorted, we set various properties for the list box control and initialize the properties for the string that will be written to the txtHiddenProperties text box. We also add the properties to the list box. The remaining code ensures that the RecordSource text box and its label are only displayed when the form contains the RecordSource (recall that in this project, we are not displaying a RecordSource property if it is blank). If the user clicks on another property in the Properties list, the RecordSource text box and its label should not be visible. We end the procedure by making the Print button (`btnPrint`) visible and closing the form that was open in design view for the purpose of accessing its properties.

Part 6:   Writing an Event Procedure for the Properties List Box (lstProperties_AfterUpdate)

When a selection is made in the lstProperties list box and the selected property is RecordSource, the full value of the RecordSource must be retrieved from the selected form design view. If another property is selected, the text box is cleared and hidden and so is its label. To handle these conditions, VBA code must be written in the `lstProperties_AfterUpdate` event procedure.

1. In the `Forms_FormInspector` code module, select lstProperties from the Control box and the AfterUpdate property from the Event box.
2. Complete the `lstProperties_AfterUpdate` event procedure as shown below:

```
Private Sub lstProperties_AfterUpdate()
    ' Check if the selected property is "RecordSource"
    If Me.lstProperties.Column(0) = "RecordSource" Then
        ' Retrieve the full RecordSource directly
        Dim frmName As String
        Dim fullRecordSource As String
        frmName = Me.lstForms.Value

        ' Open the form in Design View to access its properties
        DoCmd.OpenForm frmName, acDesign
        fullRecordSource = Forms(frmName).RecordSource

        ' Set the value in the text box and make it visible
        Me.txtRecordSource.Value = fullRecordSource
        Me.txtRecordSource.Visible = True
        Me.lblRecordSource.Visible = True

        ' Close the form and return to Form View
        DoCmd.Close acForm, frmName, acSaveNo

    Else
        ' Clear and hide the text box if another property is
          selected
        Me.txtRecordSource.Value = ""
        Me.txtRecordSource.Visible = False
        Me.lblRecordSource.Visible = False
    End If
End Sub
```

Part 7: Writing an Event Procedure to Handle the Print Button (cmdPrint_Click)

When you design your custom forms, you may want to print some data. You could create a simple form that has a combo box and a Print button and uses VBA to retrieve the list of printers, and then call this form from your project. This is something you can try on your own. In this project, we use the Print button to save the form properties to a text file on your computer.

NOTE	*We will not retrieve or use printers in this project. You can find an example of loading printer names into a combo box in the* `frmPrinterSelection` *form in the* `Chap15.accdb` *database in the companion files. Another approach to offer printing from your custom forms is by creating and using a report for printing. This approach ensures the content is printed correctly using Access' native printing functionality.*

1. In the `Forms_FormInspector` code module, select cmdPrint from the Control box and the Click property from the Event box.
2. Complete the `cmdPrint_Click` event procedure, as shown below:

```
Private Sub cmdPrint_Click()
    Dim strPrintContent As String
    Dim filePath As String
    Dim fileNumber As Integer

    ' Retrieve the properties string from the hidden text box
    strPrintContent = Nz(Me.txtHiddenProperties.Value, "")

    ' Check if the content is not empty
    If strPrintContent = "" Then
        MsgBox "No properties to save.", vbExclamation
        Exit Sub
    End If

    ' Define the file path and name
    filePath = "C:\VBAAccess2024_ByExample\FormProperties.txt"

    ' Get a free file number
    fileNumber = FreeFile

    ' Open the file for output
    Open filePath For Output As #fileNumber

    ' Write the content to the file
    Print #fileNumber, strPrintContent
```

```
    ' Close the file
    Close #fileNumber

    ' Confirm to the user
    MsgBox "Form properties saved to " & filePath, vbInformation
End Sub
```

The first line of code retrieves the value from a hidden text box control named `txtHiddenProperties` and assigns it to the variable `strPrintContent`.

Handling Null Values

The `Nz` function is used to handle any potential `Null` values. Its syntax is:

```
Nz(expression, [valueifnull]
```

The expression is the field or control that might contain a null value, in this case, `Me.txtHiddenProperties.Value`. An optional argument, `[valueifnull]`, specifies what to return if the expression is null. If not provided, `Nz` returns `0` (zero) for numeric fields or an empty string (`""`) for text fields. Using the `Nz` function prevents potential run-time errors when the variable is used later in the code for printing or processing.

Next, the code demonstrates how to write to a file using low-level file Input/Output (I/O) functions in VBA. These functions provide a straightforward way to handle file operations.

Understanding Low-Level File I/O

The `Open`, `Print`, and `Close` statements are considered low-level file I/O functions. These functions operate directly on files, giving you fine-grained control over file operations.

The `FreeFile` function is used to obtain the next available file number. This is crucial to avoid conflicts with other files that might be open simultaneously. Each file you open in VBA is assigned a unique file number.

❏ The `Open` statement is used to open a file in a specified mode (for output, in this case, which means the file is opened for writing). If the file already exists, it will be overwritten.

❏ The `Print` statement is used to write data to the file. In this case, it writes the contents of the `strPrintContent` variable to the file.

❏ The `Close` statement closes the file associated with the specified file number, ensuring that all data is properly written to the file and resources are freed.

These low-level file I/O functions are especially useful for dealing with text files when basic file operations are needed. For more complex file operations, you might consider using high-level file-handling approaches such as the `FileSystemObject` (FSO) provided by the Microsoft Scripting Runtime library.

We have now written all the procedures for our `FormInspector` form; it's time to put it to the test.

Part 8: Testing and Using the FormInspector Form

1. Save the code you have written in VBE.
2. Switch to the Access main window and open the `FormInspector` form.
3. When the form loads, click the Get Database Forms button.
   Access populates both list boxes, enables the Print button, and displays the RecordSource property box for the first form in the Available Forms list box (see Figure 15.4).

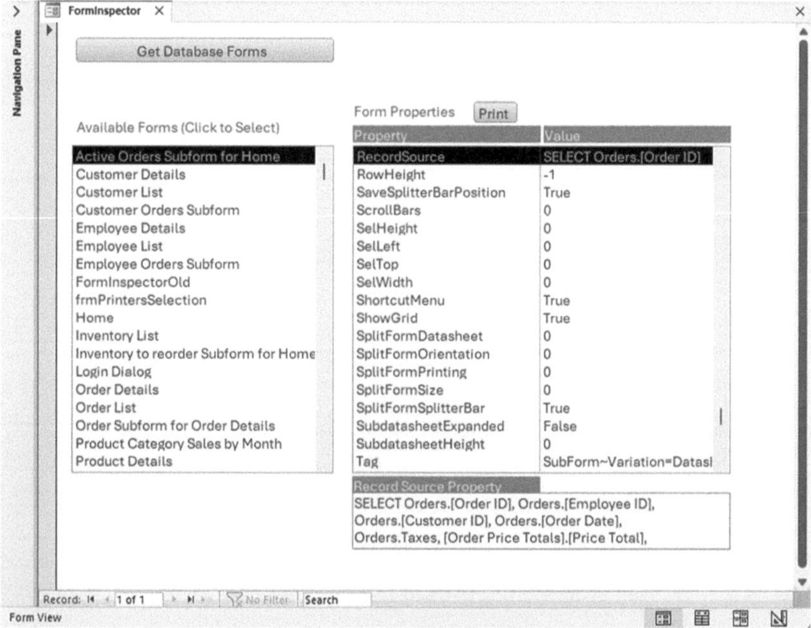

FIGURE 15.4.   The completed FormInspector form provides easy access to the selected form properties and a mechanism to print the properties to a text file.

4. Select another property in the Properties list box and notice that the RecordSource property and the label are not shown. Click on the RecordSource property and notice that the RecordSource text box and its label are again visible. Now, select another form and notice the changes in the form. All the properties are always displayed alphabetically. Some properties display 0, and you may need to write additional code to replace them with the meaningful names displayed in the form's Property Sheet.

5. Click the Print button to check out the properties list saved in a text file (see Figure 15.5).

6. Close the `FormInspector` form when finished.

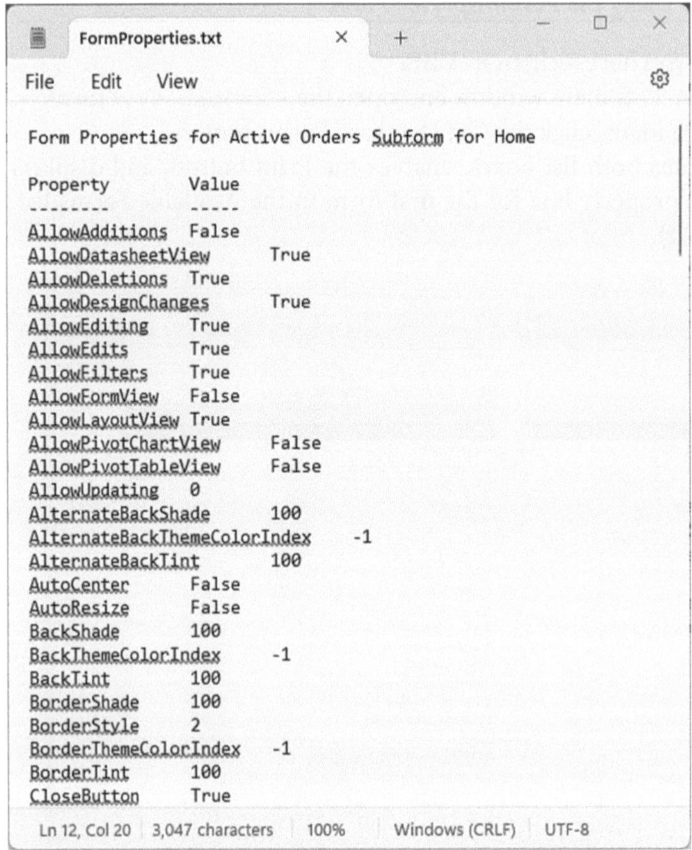

FIGURE 15.5.   The selected form properties were saved to a text file.

REFERRING TO FORMS AND THEIR CONTROLS

To successfully manipulate forms and their controls within your VBA procedures, you must follow specific rules that Access has for referring to objects:

1. Referring to Forms and Subforms
   - Current Form

   To refer to the form that is currently open or active, use the **Forms** collection of the application, followed by an exclamation mark (**!**) and the name of the form. For example, if the **Customer Details** form is open, use the following code to get the number of controls that are present on this form:

```
Dim ctrCount As Integer
ctrCount = Forms![Customer Details].Controls.Count
Debug.Print "There are " & ctrCount & " controls in this form."
```

The **Forms** collection holds all open forms in the application. You can reference any open form by its name using this collection.

Forms![Customer Details] references the form named **Customer Details** that is currently open. The exclamation mark (**!**) is used to refer to objects within collections in VBA.

.Controls.Count accesses the **Controls** collection of the specified form and counts the number of controls on that form.

The count of controls is assigned to the variable **ctrCount**. The **Debug.Print** is used to output the count of controls to the Immediate window so you can verify it.

- Specific Form

  To refer to a specific form, for example, when you want to open a form in design view, use the following statement:

```
DoCmd.OpenForm "Customer List", acDesign
```

- Subform

  In Access, when a form includes another form, the containing form is called a *main* form, and the included form is called a *subform*. The subform is typically used to display related data within the context of the main form. For example, to print the **SourceObject** of a subform placed in the **Order Details** form, you can use the following statement:

```
Print Forms![Order Details]![sbfOrderDetails].SourceObject
```

Forms![Order Details] references the main form named **Order Details** that is currently open.

![sbfOrderDetails] references the subform control named **sbOrderDetails** on the main form. This is the control on the main form that holds the subform, not the name of the subform itself.

.SourceObject is the **SourceObject** property. This property specifies the form, report, or other object that the subform control displays. Printing this property shows the name of the object currently displayed in the subform control.

Below is the VBA code that prints the **SourceObject** of the subform control in the Immediate window:

```
Sub PrintSubformSourceObject()
' Print the SourceObject of the subform control
Debug.Print Forms![Order Details]![sbfOrderDetails]. SourceObject
End Sub
```

2. Referring to Form Controls

- Control on Current Form

  You can use the Me keyword to refer to controls on the form where the code is running:

  ```
  Me.lstForms.RowSourceType = "Value List"
  ```

- Control on Another Form

  When the form is open in form view, you can display the value of the specified control in the currently selected record like this:

  ```
  MsgBox Forms![Inventory List].[Qty On Hand].value
  ```

- Control on a Subform

  The general syntax to reference a control on a subform is:

  ```
  Forms![MainFormName]![SubformControlName].Form![ControlName]
  ```

  For example:

  ```
  MsgBox Forms![Supplier Details]![Products subform].
                                 Form![Product Name].value
  ```

  Ensure you use the correct names for the main form (the primary form that contains the subform), the subform control (the control on the main form that displays the subform), and the form within the the subform control (the actual form being displayed within the subform control).

  a. `Forms![Supplier Details]` references the main form named **Supplier Details**.

  b. `![Products subform]` references the subform control named **Products subform** on the main form. This is the control that contains the subform, not the name of the subform itself. In this example, the subform name as displayed in the database navigation pane is **Supplier Products Subform**.

   c. `.Form!` accesses the form contained within the subform control. The subform control name is the name of the control on the main form that contains the subform, not necessarily the name of the subform object itself.

   d. `[Product Name]` is the specific control on the subform.

Note that when the subform is on a tab control, the syntax remains the same because the tab control does not change the structure of the form.

By following the above examples, you can easily reference forms and interact with their controls even if they are placed on subforms or tab controls within another form.

FORM MODULES AND EVENT PROGRAMMING IN ACCESS

Each form in Access can have its own module, which acts as a container for procedures and functions related to that form. Form modules enable event-driven programming, which means your code can react to events such as opening the form, changing a record, clicking a button, or even custom events you define. Events provide a way to inject custom functionality into your forms, enabling you to automate tasks, validate data, and enhance the user experience. Understanding the following terminology is crucial for extending the capabilities of Access beyond the default functionalities:

- Event—Events are things that happen to an object. Events occur when you move the mouse; press a key; make changes to data; open a form; add, modify, or delete a record; etc. An event can be triggered by the user or by the operating system.

- Event Property—Forms, reports, and controls have various event properties you can use to trigger desired actions. When an event occurs, Microsoft Access runs a procedure assigned to an event property. Event properties are listed in the Event tab of the object's Property Sheet. The name of an event property begins with `On` and is followed by the event's name. Therefore, the `On Click` event property corresponds to the `Click` event, and the `On Got Focus` event property is used for responding to the `GotFocus` event.

- Event Procedure—This is programming code you write to specify how a form, report, or control should respond to a particular event. By writing event procedures, you can modify the application's built-in response to an event.

- Event Trapping—When you assign programming code to an event property, you set an event trap. When you trap an event, you interrupt the default processing that Access would normally carry out in response to the user's keypress or mouse click.

- Sequence of Events—Events occur in a predefined order. For example, the `Click` event occurs before the `DoubleClick` event. When you perform an action, several events occur, one after the other. For instance, the following form and control events occur when you open a form:

```
Open → Load → Resize → Activate → Current → Enter (control) →
                                              GotFocus (control)
```

Closing the form triggers the following control and form events:

```
Exit (control) → LostFocus (control) → Unload → Deactivate → Close
```

To find out whether a particular event is triggered in response to a user action, you may want to place the `MsgBox` statement inside the event procedure for the event you want to test.

Events can be organized by object (form, report, or control) or by cause (what caused the event to happen). This chapter contains numerous examples of event procedures you can write to make your forms dynamic.

Access forms come with a wide range of built-in events, each corresponding to different user actions or changes in the form's state. You've already seen an example of the `Form_Load` event, which triggers when a form is opened, allowing you to initialize settings or populate controls with data. The `Click` event for a button that executes when the button is clicked is the perfect place to handle user commands such as saving data or opening another form. Similarly, events such as `AfterUpdate` for a text box can be used to validate data or perform calculations immediately after a user makes a change.

To handle various events, you write VBA code in the form's module. This code can range from simple procedures that display messages to complex logic that interacts with multiple database objects. Using VBA programming, you can automate data entry, enforce business rules, or create a great-looking UI. After completing Custom Project 15.1 in this chapter, you should know how to access the form module via the Code Builder and from VBE.

NOTE	*Form modules are only available if there are forms in your database. If your database has no forms, there won't be any form modules to access or modify.*

As you design your custom forms, you will find that some form events are used more frequently than others. The following sections provide hands-on examples of event procedures you can write for Access forms.

DATA EVENTS

Data events occur when you change the data in a control or record placed on a form, or when you move the focus from one record to another.

The Current Event

The `Current` event occurs when the form is opened or requeried and when the focus moves to a different record. Use the `Current` event to synchronize data among forms or move focus to a specific control. In the event procedure in Hands-On 15.1, we display a message box showing the product ID and product code whenever the user navigates to a different product in the `Product Details` form.

> ### (●) Hands-On 15.1   Writing the Form_Current Event Procedure

1. In the Access window of the `Chap15.accdb` database, right-click on the Product Details form and choose Design View. Make sure the form's Property Sheet is visible and the Selection Type is set to Form. To activate the Property Sheet, choose Property Sheet in the Tools section of the Form Design tab.

2. In the form's Property Sheet, click the Event tab. Click next to the On Current event property and choose [Event Procedure] from the drop-down box. Click the Build button (…).

    Access opens the VBE window and writes the stub of the `Form_Current` event procedure. Note that if there are any other events written for the form or its controls, their VBA code will be displayed in the code window.

3. Complete the code of the `Form_Current` event procedure, as shown here:

```
Private Sub Form_Current()
    ' Check the current record
    If Not Me.NewRecord And Me.CurrentRecord <> 1 Then
      ' Display a message box showing the Order ID and Order Date
        MsgBox "You are now viewing Product ID: " _
        & Me.[ID] & ", Product Code: " & Me.[Product Code]
    End If
End Sub
```

In this procedure, the `Not Me.NewRecord` statement ensures that the code only runs if the current record is not a new, unsaved record. The `Me.CurrentRecord <> 1` checks that the current record number is not 1.

4. To test this event procedure, activate the Products form that is currently open in design view. You can quickly switch to the selected form from Visual Basic by clicking the View Object button in the Project Explorer window. Next, in the Access window, click the View button on the Ribbon to display the form in form view. After the form loads, select another record. You should see the message you programmed in the `Form_Current` event procedure.

5. Close the Product Details form and save all the changes when prompted.

Ensuring that Events Work Together

Each event procedure you create can be improved further by adding necessary conditions that handle various scenarios. Ensure that the added conditions do not conflict with existing logic. Determine which events interact with each other. If necessary, modify other events to accommodate changes in the logic. Create new events if existing ones cannot handle new requirements. Keep in mind that existing events may already contain embedded macros or logic that may be affected by new conditions. If an embedded macro needs to work with programmed events, integrate the macro logic into the VBA code. This will require that you convert macros to VBA procedures for better control and customization. See the chapter on macros to find out how to perform such conversions and improve the event procedure in Hands-On 15.1, by adding more conditions and interaction with the `Form_OnLoad` event that is currently set to an embedded macro.

The BeforeInsert Event

The `BeforeInsert` event occurs when the first character is typed in a new record but before the new record is created. Use the `BeforeInsert` event to verify that the data is valid or to display information about data being added. This event is quite useful for placing default values in the fields at runtime. The `BeforeInsert` event can be canceled if the data being added does not meet specific criteria. The event procedure in Hands-On 15.2 demonstrates how to enter a default value in the Country/Region field when a user begins to enter data in the form.

⊙ Hands-On 15.2   Writing the Form_BeforeInsert Event Procedure

For this hands-on exercise, we will create a new form based on the `Customers` table.

1. Highlight the Customers table in the left pane of the Access window. Choose Create | Form Wizard.

2. Select the following fields: ID, Company, Address, City, State/Province, Zip/ Postal Code, and Country/Region. Step through the Form Wizard screens, pressing the Next button until you get to the screen where you are asked for the form's title. Type `New Customers` for the form's title, select the Modify the form's design option button, and click Finish.
   Access opens the New Customers form in design view.

3. In the Property Sheet, select Form from the drop-down box and click the Data tab. Set the Data Entry property to Yes.

4. In the form's Property Sheet, click the Event tab. Click next to the Before Insert event property and choose [Event Procedure] from the drop-down box. Click the Build button (…).
   Access opens the VBE window and writes the stub of the `Form_BeforeInsert` event procedure.

5. Complete the code of the `Form_BeforeInsert` event procedure, as shown here:

```
Private Sub Form_BeforeInsert(Cancel As Integer)
   Me.[Country/Region] = "USA"
End Sub
```

6. To test this event procedure, activate the New Customers form in form view.

7. Type `Erin Properties, Ltd.` in the Company field. Notice that as soon as you start typing, the text USA appears in the Country field.

8. Press the Esc key twice to undo the changes to the form.

9. Close the `New Customers` form and save all the changes when prompted.

The AfterInsert Event

The `AfterInsert` event occurs when a new record has been inserted. Use this event to requery the recordset when a new record is added or to display other information. The following event procedure retrieves the total number of records in the `Customers` table after a new record has been inserted in the `Customer Details` form:

```
Private Sub Form_AfterInsert()
   Dim db As DAO.Database
   Dim rst As DAO.Recordset

   Set db = CurrentDb()
   Set rst = db.OpenRecordset("Customers")

   MsgBox "Total Number of Records: " & _
    rst.RecordCount & "."
```

```
    rst.Close
    Set rst = Nothing
    Set db = Nothing
End Sub
```

The BeforeUpdate Event

The BeforeUpdate event occurs after a record has been edited but before it is written to the table. This event is triggered by moving to another record or attempting to save the current record. The BeforeUpdate event takes place after the BeforeInsert event. Use this event to validate the entire record and display a message to confirm the change. The BeforeUpdate event can be canceled if the record cannot be accepted. The following event procedure validates that certain fields are not left blank before updating a record in the Employees table, ensuring that First Name, Last Name, and Job Title are filled in before allowing the update to proceed.

```
Private Sub Form_BeforeUpdate(Cancel As Integer)
    ' Check if the required fields are filled
    If IsNull(Me.[First Name]) Or Me.[First Name] = "" Then
        MsgBox "First Name is required.", _
               vbExclamation, "Validation Error"
        Cancel = True ' Cancel the update
        Me.[First Name].SetFocus '
        Exit Sub
    End If

    If IsNull(Me.[Last Name]) Or Me.[Last Name] = "" Then
        MsgBox "Last Name is required.", _
               vbExclamation, "Validation Error"
        Cancel = True ' Cancel the update
        Me.[Last Name].SetFocus '
        Exit Sub
    End If

    If IsNull(Me.[Job Title]) Or Me.[Job Title] = "" Then
        MsgBox "Title is required.", _
               vbExclamation, "Validation Error"
        Cancel = True ' Cancel the update
        Me.[Job Title].SetFocus ' Set focus to the Title field
        Exit Sub
    End If

    ' Additional validation can be added here if needed
    ' If all validations pass, allow the update to proceed
End Sub
```

The AfterUpdate Event

The `AfterUpdate` event occurs after the record changes have been saved in the database. It is also invoked when a control loses focus and after the data in the control has changed. Use the `AfterUpdate` event to update data in other controls on the form or to move the focus to a different record or control. The event procedure in Hands-On 15.3 creates an audit trail for all newly added records, as illustrated in Figure 15.6.

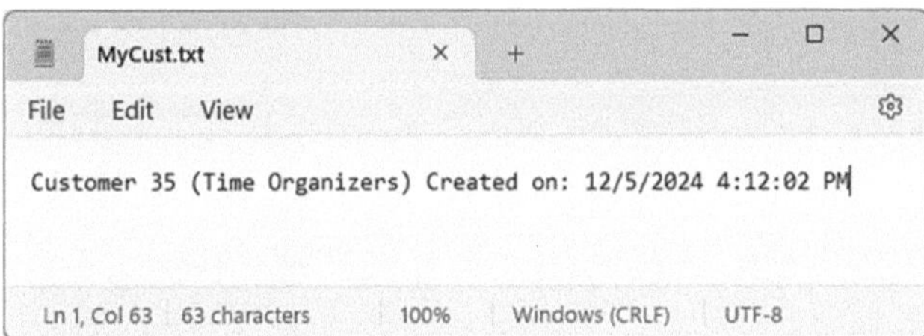

FIGURE 15.6.   The Form_AfterUpdate event procedure is used here to store information about newly added records in a text file.

Hands-On 15.3   Writing the Form_AfterUpdate Event Procedure

This hands-on exercise requires the `New Customers` form that was created in Hands-On 15.2.

1. In the VBE window, choose Tools | References. Locate and select Microsoft Scripting Runtime in the Available References list and click OK.
2. In the VBE Project Explorer window, double-click Form_New Customers.
3. Other procedures that were prepared so far in this chapter will be listed in the Code window. Enter the following `Form_AfterUpdate` event procedure below the code of the last procedure:

```
Private Sub Form_AfterUpdate()
    Dim fso As FileSystemObject
    Dim objFile As Object
    Dim strFileName As String
    Dim strPath As String
    Dim strFullPath As String

    On Error Resume Next

    strPath = "C:\VBAAccess2024_ByExample\"
    strFileName = "MyCust.txt"
    strFullPath = strPath & strFileName
```

```
Set fso = New FileSystemObject
Set objFile = fso.GetFile(strFullPath)

If Err.Number = 0 Then
  ' open text file
  Set objFile = fso.OpenTextFile(strFullPath, 8)
Else
  ' create a text file
  Set objFile = fso.CreateTextFile(strFullPath)
End If

objFile.WriteLine "Customer " & UCase(Me.ID) & _
  " (" & Me.Company & ") Created on: " & Date & " " & Time
objFile.Close
Set fso = Nothing
MsgBox "This record was logged in: " & strFullPath
End Sub
```

This event procedure first checks whether the specified text file exists on your computer. If the file is found, then the `Err.Number` statement returns 0. At this point, you want to open the file. The 8 represents the open mode for appending. Use 2 if you want to replace the contents of a file with the new data.

4. To test the event procedure, open the `New Customers` form in form view. Type `Time Organizers` in the Company box. Click the record selector to move to the next record. The message box notifies you about the location of the audit trail (the result of the `AfterUpdate` event procedure prepared in this exercise). Click OK to the message.

5. Close the `New Customers` form and save the changes to the form if prompted.

6. Open the log file you created in this hands-on exercise and check its output with Figure 15.6.

The Dirty Event

The `Dirty` event occurs when the contents of a form or the text portion of a combo box change. This event will be triggered by an attempt to enter a character directly in the form's text box or combo box. Use this event to determine whether the record can be changed. The following event procedure disallows changes to `Supplier List` form data when the job title begins with the string `Marketing`:

```
Private Sub Form_Dirty(Cancel As Integer)
  If Me.Job_Title Like "Marketing*" Then
```

```
      MsgBox "You cannot make changes in this record."
      Cancel = True
   End If
End Sub
```

The OnUndo Event

The OnUndo event occurs when the user undoes a change to a combo box control, form, or text box control. By setting the Cancel argument to True, you can cancel the undo operation and leave the control or form in its edited state. The Undo event for forms is triggered when the user clicks the Undo button, presses the Esc key, or calls the Undo method.

The Delete Event

The Delete event occurs when you select one or more records for deletion and before the records are actually removed from the table. Use this event to place restrictions on the data that can be deleted. When deleting multiple records, the Delete event occurs for each record. This enables you to confirm or cancel each deletion in your event procedure code. You can cancel the deletion in the Delete or BeforeDelConfirm event by setting the Cancel argument to True. For example, the following procedure handles the Delete event for the Customer List form:

```
Private Sub Form_Delete(Cancel As Integer)
  If ID <= 29 Then
    MsgBox "You can't delete the original records."
    Cancel = True
  Else
    If MsgBox("Do you really want to delete " & _
     "this record?", vbOKCancel, _
     "Delete Verification") = vbCancel Then
     Cancel = True
    End If
  End If
End Sub
```

If you entered any records in the previous hands-on exercises into the Customers table, you can delete them using the Customer List form. The procedure in the Delete event for this form will ensure that you don't delete any customers that you have not inserted. Note that you will be prompted twice to confirm the deletion of your own records. The first prompt is the one that you coded in the Form_Delete event procedure. The second prompt will be the default prompt that Access normally displays to confirm record(s) deletion. See the next event to find out how you can prevent this default prompt.

The BeforeDelConfirm Event

The `BeforeDelConfirm` event occurs after the `Delete` event but before the Delete Confirm message box is displayed. If you don't write your own `Before-DelConfirm` event, Access will display a standard delete confirmation message. You can use this event to write a custom deletion confirmation message. The following event procedure for the `Customer List` form demonstrates how to suppress the Access default message.

```
Private Sub Form_BeforeDelConfirm(Cancel _
 As Integer, Response As Integer)
  Response = acDataErrContinue
End Sub
```

If needed, enter a new record into the `Customers` table and use the `Customer List` form to delete this record. You should only be prompted once with your custom confirmation message that you included in the `Form_Delete` event procedure.

<table>
<tr>
<td>NOTE</td>
<td>

Instead of writing your custom confirmation message in the `Form_Delete` *event procedure, you can place it in the* `Form_BeforeDel-Confirm` *event procedure, as shown here:*

```
Private Sub Form_BeforeDelConfirm(Cancel As Integer, _
  Response As Integer)
  ' remove the default Access message box
  ' that prompts to confirm deletion
  Response = acDataErrContinue
  If MsgBox("Do you really want to delete
                this record?", _
   vbOKCancel) = vbCancel Then
    Cancel = True
  End If
End Sub
```

</td>
</tr>
</table>

The AfterDelConfirm Event

The `AfterDelConfirm` event occurs after the record is deleted or after deletion is canceled in the `BeforeDelConfirm` event procedure. Use the `AfterDelCon-firm` event to move to another record or to display a message indicating whether the deletion was successful. The `Status` argument allows you to check whether the deletion progressed normally or was canceled by the user or system. The following constants can be used for the `Status` argument in the `AfterDelConfirm` event procedure: `acDelete` (6), `acDeleteCancel` (1), `acDeleteOK` (0), or `acDeleteUserCancel` (2).

The following event procedure for the `Customer List` form displays a message when a record is successfully deleted.

```
Private Sub Form_AfterDelConfirm(Status As Integer)
  MsgBox "The selected record was deleted."
  Debug.Print "Status = " & Status
End Sub
```

If you add a new customer record and then decide to delete it, Access will execute the code in the `Form_Delete` event procedure that displays a message box asking you whether you want to delete the record. When you click Yes, Access will then check the code in the `Form_BeforeDelConfirm` procedure. The statement `Response = acDataErrContinue` will cause Access to suppress its default Delete Confirm message box and you will not be prompted again to reconfirm the deletion. Finally, `Form_AfterDelConfirm` will run and you will see a message about the successful deletion.

FOCUS EVENTS

Focus events occur when a form becomes active or inactive and when a form or form control loses or gains the focus.

The Activate Event

The Activate event occurs whenever the form receives the focus and becomes the active window. This situation occurs when the form is first opened and when the user activates the form again by clicking on the form or one of its controls. The following event procedure refreshes the form's data and displays a message indicating that the form is now active. In addition, the form's status bar is updated and the Home button is enabled if present on the form.

```
Private Sub Form_Activate()
    ' Debug print to verify the event is firing
    Debug.Print "Form_Activate event fired"

    ' Refresh the form's data
    Me.Requery
    Debug.Print "Form data re-queried"
```

```
    ' Display a message indicating that the form is now active
    MsgBox "The form is now active.", vbInformation, "Form Activated"


    ' Update the status bar
    SysCmd acSysCmdSetStatus, "The form is now active."
    Debug.Print "Status bar updated"

    ' Enable a specific button (assuming cmdSave exists on the form)
    If Not IsNull(Me.cmdHome) Then
        Me.cmdHome.Enabled = True
        Debug.Print "cmdHome button enabled"
    Else
        Debug.Print "cmdHome button not found"
    End If
End Sub
```

The Deactivate Event

The `Deactivate` event occurs when the user switches to another form or closes the form. The following event procedure clears the status bar message when the form is deactivated.

```
Private Sub Form_Deactivate()
    ' Clear the status bar message when the form is deactivated
    SysCmd acSysCmdClearStatus
End Sub
```

The GotFocus Event

The `GotFocus` event happens when a form receives the focus, if there are no visible or enabled controls on the form. The `GotFocus` event is frequently used for controls placed on the form and rarely used for the form itself.

The LostFocus Event

The `LostFocus` event happens when a form loses focus, provided there are no visible or enabled controls on the form. This event is frequently used for controls placed on the form and rarely used for the form itself.

MOUSE EVENTS

`Mouse` events occur when you move a mouse or click any of the available mouse buttons.

The Click Event

The `Click` event occurs when you click a mouse button on a blank area of a form, a form's record selector, or a control placed on the form. You have seen how this event works in the `Click` event procedures that we wrote in Custom Project 15.1.

The DblClick Event

The `DblClick` event occurs when you double-click on a blank area of the form, the form's record selector, or a control placed on the form.

The MouseDown Event

The `MouseDown` event occurs when you click and hold on a blank area of the form, the form's record selector, or a control placed on the form. This event occurs before the `Click` event. The `MouseDown` event has four arguments:

- `Button`—Identifies the state of the mouse buttons. Use `acLeftButton` to check for the left mouse button, `acRightButton` to check for the right mouse button, and `acMiddleButton` to check for the middle mouse button.
- `Shift`—Specifies the state of the Shift, Ctrl, and Alt keys when the button specified by the `Button` argument was pressed or released. Use `acShift-Mask` (1) to test for the Shift key, `acCtrlMask` (2) to test for the Ctrl key, and `acAltMask` (4) to test for the Alt key. You can test for any combination of buttons. For example, to specify that Ctrl and Alt were pressed, use the value of 6 (2 + 4) as the Shift argument.
- `x`—Specifies the horizontal (x) position from the left edge of the form or control.
- `Y`—Specifies the vertical (y) position from the top edge of the form or control.

The following event procedure displays two messages when the form's `Mouse-Down` event is fired. The first message tells whether you pressed the Alt, Ctrl, or Shift key, and the second one announces which mouse button was used.

```
Private Sub Form_MouseDown(Button As Integer, _
  Shift As Integer, _
  X As Single, _
  Y As Single)
  Debug.Print "Mouse Down"

  Select Case Shift
```

```
    Case 0
      MsgBox "You did not press a key."
    Case 1 ' or acShiftMask
      MsgBox "You pressed SHIFT."
    Case 2 ' or acCtrlMask
      MsgBox "You pressed CTRL."
    Case 3
      MsgBox "You pressed CTRL and SHIFT."
    Case 4 ' or acAltMask
      MsgBox "You pressed ALT."
    Case 5
      MsgBox "You pressed ALT and SHIFT."
    Case 6
      MsgBox "You pressed CTRL and ALT."
    Case 7
      MsgBox "You pressed CTRL, ALT, and SHIFT."
  End Select

  If Button = 1 Then ' acLeftButton
    MsgBox "You pressed the left button."
  ElseIf Button = 2 Then ' acRightButton
    MsgBox "You pressed the right button."
  ElseIf Button = 4 Then ' acMiddleButton
    MsgBox "You pressed the middle button."
  End If
End Sub
```

The MouseMove Event

The `MouseMove` event occurs when you move the mouse over a blank area of the form, the form's record selector, or a control placed on the form. The `MouseMove` event occurs before the `Click` event and has the same arguments as the `MouseDown` event.

The MouseUp Event

The `MouseUp` event occurs when you release the mouse button. It occurs before the `Click` event and uses the same arguments as the `MouseDown` and `MouseMove` events.

The MouseWheel Event

The `MouseWheel` event occurs in form view or datasheet view when the user rotates the mouse wheel on a mouse device that has a wheel. This event takes the following two arguments:

- `Page`—Returns `True` if the page was changed.

- Count—Specifies the number of lines that were scrolled with the mouse wheel.

NOTE	*Because there is no* Cancel *argument, you cannot use the* MouseWheel *event to prevent users from using the mouse wheel to scroll through records on a form.*

KEYBOARD EVENTS

Keyboard events occur when you hold down, press, or release a key on the keyboard or send a keystroke by using the SendKeys statement in Visual Basic or the SendKeys action in a macro.

The keyboard events occur in the following sequence:

KeyDown → KeyPress → KeyUp

If the form's KeyPreview property is set to Yes, all keyboard events occur first for the form, and then for the control that has the focus. When you press and hold down the key, the KeyDown and KeyPress events occur repeatedly. When you release the key, the KeyUp event occurs.

The KeyDown Event

The KeyDown event occurs when you press a key while a form or control has the focus. This event is also triggered by using the SendKeys statement in Visual Basic or the SendKeys action in a macro. If the form's KeyPreview property is set to Yes, all keyboard events occur first for the form, and then for the control that has the focus.

The KeyDown event takes the following two arguments:

- KeyCode—Determines which key was pressed. To specify keycodes, use members of the KeyCodeConstants class in the VBA object library in the Object Browser. To prevent an object from receiving the keystroke, set KeyCode to zero (0).

- Shift—Determines whether the Shift, Ctrl, or Alt key was pressed. Use acShiftMask (1) to test for the Shift key, acCtrlMask (2) to test for the Ctrl key, and acAltMask (4) to test for the Alt key. You can test for any combination of buttons. For example, to specify that Ctrl and Alt were pressed, use the value of 6 (2 + 4) as the Shift argument.

The event procedure in Hands-On 15.4 displays a message when you press one of the following keys: F1, Home, Tab, Shift, Ctrl, Alt, or Delete.

⊙ Hands-On 15.4   Writing the Form_KeyDown Event Procedure

1. Open the `Order List` form in design view. In the form's Property Sheet, make sure Form is selected and click the Event tab. Set the Key Preview property to Yes.
2. Save the `Products` form.
3. Click next to the On Key Down event property and choose [Event Procedure] from the drop-down box. Click the Build button (…).
   In the Code window, there are a couple of event procedures already written for this form. Access adds the stub of the `Form_KeyDown` event procedure for you.
4. Enter the following `Form_KeyDown` event procedure code.

```
Private Sub Form_KeyDown(KeyCode As Integer, Shift As Integer)
  Select Case KeyCode
    Case vbKeyF1
      MsgBox "You pressed the F1 key."
    Case vbKeyHome
      MsgBox "You pressed the Home key."
    Case vbKeyTab
      MsgBox "You pressed the Tab key."
  End Select

  Select Case Shift
    Case acShiftMask
      MsgBox "You pressed the SHIFT key."
    Case acCtrlMask
      MsgBox "You pressed the CTRL key."
    Case acAltMask
      MsgBox "You pressed the ALT key."
  End Select
  If KeyCode = vbKeyDelete Then
    MsgBox "Delete Key is not allowed."
    KeyCode = 0
  End If
End Sub
```

5. To test this event procedure, open the `Order List` form in form view. Press one of the following keys: F1, Home, Tab, Shift, Ctrl, Alt, or Delete. Click OK to the message.
6. Close the `Order List` form and save changes to the form when prompted.

The KeyPress Event

The `KeyPress` event occurs when you press and release a key or a key combination. This event is also triggered by using the `SendKeys` statement in Visual Basic or the `SendKeys` action in a macro. If the form's `KeyPreview` property is set to `Yes`, all keyboard events occur first for the form, and then for the control that has the focus.

The `KeyPress` event responds only to the ANSI characters generated by the keyboard, the Ctrl key combined with a character from the standard alphabet or a special character, and the Enter or Backspace key. Other keystrokes are handled by the `KeyDown` and `KeyUp` event procedures. `KeyAscii` is a read/write argument that specifies which ANSI key was pressed. To cancel the keystroke in the `KeyPress` event, set the `KeyAscii` argument to 0. The `KeyPress` event treats uppercase and lowercase letters as different characters.

The KeyUp Event

The `KeyUp` event occurs when you release a key while a form or control has the focus. This event is also triggered by using the `SendKeys` statement in Visual Basic or the `SendKeys` action in a macro. If the form's `KeyPreview` property is set to `Yes`, all keyboard events occur first for the form and then for the control that has the focus.

The `KeyUp` event takes the following two arguments:

- `KeyCode`—Determines which key was pressed. To specify keycodes, use members of the `KeyCodeConstants` class in the VBA object library in the Object Browser. To prevent an object from receiving the keystroke, set `KeyCode` to zero (0).

- `Shift`—Determines whether the Shift, Ctrl, or Alt key was pressed. Use `acShiftMask` (1) to test for the Shift key, `acCtrlMask` (2) to test for the Ctrl key, and `acAltMask` (4) to test for the Alt key. You can test for any combination of buttons. For example, to specify that Ctrl and Alt were pressed, use the value of 6 (2 + 4) as the `Shift` argument.

ERROR EVENTS

Error events are triggered by run-time errors generated either in the Access interface or by the Microsoft Jet/ACE database engine. Note that the `Error` event does not trap VBA errors.

The Error Event

The `Error` event occurs when there is a problem accessing data for the form. Use this event to suppress the standard error messages and display a custom error message instead.

The `Error` event takes the following two arguments:

- `DataErr`—Contains the number of the Microsoft Access error that occurred.
- `Response`—Determines whether error messages should be displayed. It may be one of the following constants:
  a. `acDataErrContinue`—Ignore the error and continue without displaying the default Microsoft Access error message.
  b. `acDataErrDisplay`—Display the default Microsoft Access error message. This is the default.

The event procedure shown below, written for the `Product Details` form, displays an error message when the `Unit Price` field is left blank. The `Unit Price` field is a required field in the `Products` table. This procedure defines custom error messages for different errors and logs the error details to a text file. Notice how the `Response = acDataErrContinue` suppresses the default error message from Access. You can add more code to the `Select Case` statement to handle more specific errors with custom messages.

```
Private Sub Form_Error(DataErr As Integer, _
   Response As Integer)

   Dim strErrorMsg As String
   Dim strLogMessage As String
   Dim logFilePath As String
   Dim fileNum As Integer

   ' Define the path for the error log file
   logFilePath = "C:\VBAAccess2024_ByExample\ListErrors.txt"

   ' Define custom error messages for specific DataErr values
   Select Case DataErr
       Case 2101
           strErrorMsg = "You can't save this record at this time."
       Case 3314
           strErrorMsg = "Required field not filled in."
       Case Else
           strErrorMsg = "An error occurred. Error Number: " & _
```

```
                    DataErr & vbCrLf & _
                    "Error Description: " & AccessError(DataErr)
    End Select

    ' Display the custom error message
    MsgBox strErrorMsg, vbExclamation, "Error"

    ' Log the error details
    strLogMessage = "Error Number: " & DataErr & vbCrLf & _
            "Error Description: " & Error(DataErr) & vbCrLf & _
            strErrorMsg & vbCrLf & _
            "Form Name: " & Me.Name & vbCrLf & _
            "Date and Time: " & Now & vbCrLf & _
            "----------------------------------" & vbCrLf

    ' Append the error details to the log file
    fileNum = FreeFile
    Open logFilePath For Append As #fileNum
    Print #fileNum, strLogMessage
    Close #fileNum

    ' Suppress the default error message
    Response = acDataErrContinue
End Sub
```

FILTER EVENTS

Filter events are triggered by opening or closing a filter window or when you are applying or removing a filter.

The Filter Event

The `Filter` event occurs when you design a filter to limit the form's records to those matching specified criteria. This event takes place when you select the Filter by Form or Advanced Filter/Sort option. Use this event to remove the filter that was previously set, to enter initial settings for the filter, or to call your own custom filter dialog box. To cancel the filtering command, set the `Cancel` argument for the event procedure to `True`.

The `Form_Filter` event procedure for the `Employee List` form shown below allows the use of the Ribbon's Filter by Form option but disallows the use of the Advanced Filter/Sort option.

```
Private Sub Form_Filter(Cancel As Integer, _
  FilterType As Integer)
    Select Case FilterType
      Case acFilterByForm
        MsgBox "You selected to filter records " & _
          "by form.", vbOKOnly + vbInformation, _
          "Filter By Form"
        Me.[First Name].SetFocus
        Me.[ID].Enabled = False
      Case acFilterAdvanced
        MsgBox "You are not authorized to use " & _
          " Advanced Filter/Sort.", _
          vbOKOnly + vbInformation, _
          "Advanced Filter By Form"
        Cancel = True
    End Select
End Sub
```

The ApplyFilter Event

The `ApplyFilter` event occurs when you apply the filter to restrict the records. This event takes place when you select the Apply Filter/Sort, Filter by Selection, or Remove Filter/Sort option. Use this event to change the form display before the filter is applied or undo any changes made when the `Filter` event occurred.

The `ApplyType` argument can have one of the predefined constants shown in Table 15.2.

TABLE 15.2.   ApplyType argument constants.

Constant Name	Constant Value
acShowAllRecords	0
acApplyFilter	1
acCloseFilterWindow	2
acApplyServerFilter	3
acCloseServerFilterWindow	4

The `Form_ApplyFilter` event procedure in the `Employee List` form displays a different message depending on whether the user has made a selection in the Filter by Form dialog box.

```
Private Sub Form_ApplyFilter(Cancel As Integer, _
  ApplyType As Integer)

  Dim Response As Integer
```

```vba
If ApplyType = acApplyFilter Then
  If Me.Filter = "" Then
    MsgBox "You did not select any criteria.", _
      vbOKOnly + vbCritical, "No Selection"
    GoTo ExitHere
  End If
  Response = MsgBox("The selected criteria " & _
    "is as follows:" & vbCrLf & _
    Me.Filter, vbOKCancel + vbQuestion, _
    "Filter Criteria")
End If

If Response = vbCancel Then
  Cancel = True
End If
If ApplyType = acShowAllRecords Then
  Me.Filter = ""
  MsgBox "Filter was removed."
End If
If ApplyType = acCloseFilterWindow Then
  Response = MsgBox("Are you sure you " & _
    "want to close the Filter window?", vbYesNo)
  If Response = vbNo Then
    Cancel = True
  End If
End If
ExitHere:
  With Me.ID
    .Enabled = True
    .SetFocus
  End With
End Sub
```

TIMING EVENTS

Timing events occur in response to a specified amount of time passing.

The Timer Event

The `Timer` event occurs when the form is opened. The duration of this event is determined by the value (in milliseconds) entered in the `TimerInterval` property located on the Event tab of the form's Property Sheet. Use this event to display a splash screen when the database is opened. The `Timer` event is helpful in limiting the time the record remains locked in multiuser applications.

The `Form_Timer` event procedure in the `Employee List` form will flash the Home button displaying continuously either Home or Click Me! (or the entire button if you use the commented code instead). For the code to work, you must start the timer by changing the `TimerInterval` property from `0` (stopped) to the desired interval. A timer interval of 1,000 will invoke a timer event every second. The form's `Load` event procedure sets the form's `TimerInterval` property to `250`, so the button text (or the entire button) is toggled once every quarter second. You may change the timer interval manually by typing the value next to the form's `TimerInterval` property in the Property Sheet or by placing the following statement in the `Form_Load` event:

```
Private Sub Form_Load()
    Me.TimerInterval = 250

End Sub

Private Sub Form_Timer()
  Static OnOff As Integer

  If OnOff Then
     Me.cmdHome.Caption = "Click Me!"
  Else
    Me.cmdHome.Caption = "&Home"
  End If
  OnOff = Not OnOff
End Sub
```

EVENTS RECOGNIZED BY FORM SECTIONS

In addition to trapping events for the entire form, you can write event procedures for the following form sections: `Detail`, `FormHeader`, `FormFooter`, `PageHeader`, and `PageFooter`.

Form sections respond to the following events: `Click`, `DblClick`, `MouseDown`, `MouseUp`, and `MouseMove`.

The DblClick (Form Section) Event

The `DblClick` event occurs when you double-click inside the form's header or footer section.

The `Detail_DblClick` event procedure in the `New Customers` form demonstrates how to randomly change the background color for each of the form's sections every time you double-click anywhere within the form's Detail section.

To test this event procedure, add a Footer section to the `New Customers` form you created earlier, then open the form in form view and double-click anywhere in the Detail section of the form; you will see the colors of the Detail, Header, and Footer sections change.

```
Private Sub Detail_DblClick(Cancel As Integer)
  With Me
    .Section(acHeader).BackColor = _
    RGB(Rnd * 128, _
    Rnd * 256, _
    Rnd * 255)
    .Section(acDetail).BackColor = _
    RGB(Rnd * 128, _
    Rnd * 256, _
    Rnd * 255)
    .Section(acFooter).BackColor = _
    RGB(Rnd * 128, _
    Rnd * 256, _
    Rnd * 255)
  End With
End Sub
```

UNDERSTANDING AND USING THE OPENARGS PROPERTY

It's been over a decade since Microsoft introduced in Access an extremely useful property of the `Form` and `Report` objects called `OpenArgs`. Using the `OpenArgs` property, you can pass parameters to the form or report when you open it with the `DoCmd` command. The `OpenArgs` property also comes in handy when:

1. You want to pass values from one form to another.
2. You want to move the focus to a specific record when the form opens.
3. You want to automatically populate a control on the form.
4. You want to restrict access to certain forms.

The `OpenArgs` property is a string expression. It can be used in both macros and VBA code. Only one `OpenArgs` string can be used in the `OpenForm` or `OpenReport` command; however, by combining values into one string separated by a unique character and using the built-in VBA `Split` function, you can overcome this limitation. Before we delve into a practical example, let's look at the complete syntax of the `OpenForm` method:

```
DoCmd.OpenForm FormName, View, FilterName, WhereCondition,
DataMode, WindowMode, OpenArgs
```

The parameter definitions are listed in Table 15.3.

TABLE 15.3.   Parameters used with the OpenForm method of the DoCmd object.

Parameter Name	Data Type	Description
FormName (This parameter is required.)	Variant	A string expression containing the name of a form in the current database.
View	acFormView	The acFormView constant specifies the view in which the form should open. The default is acNormal.
FilterName	Variant	A string expression containing the name of a query in the current database.
WhereCondition	Variant	A string expression containing the SQL WHERE clause without the word WHERE.
DataMode	acFormOpenDataMode	An acFormOpenDataMode constant specifies the data entry mode for the form and applies only to forms open in form view or datasheet view. The default is acFormPropertySettings.
WindowMode	acWindowMode	An acWindowMode constant specifies the window mode in which the form opens. The default is acWindowNormal.
OpenArgs	Variant	A string expression used to set the form's OpenArgs property in VBA code or in a macro.

Hands-On 15.5 demonstrates the use of the `OpenArgs` property for passing values from a custom form (`frmOpenArgs`) to a `Northwind 2007` database built-in form (`Employee List`).

◉ Hands-On 15.5   Passing Values to a Form Using the OpenArgs Property

1. Import the `frmOpenArgs` form and the `openArgsUtil` module from the `OpenArgs_Demo.accdb` database in the companion files to your `Chap15.accdb` database.
2. In the Navigation Pane on the left, double-click the frmOpenArgs to open it in form view (see Figure 15.7). You will work with this form after completing the VBA code as instructed below.

3. On the VBE screen, in the Project Explorer window, double-click the Form_Employee List, and in the selected form's code module, enter the following `Form_Event` procedure. If there is an existing `Form_Load` event for this form, just add the provided code as shown:

```
Private Sub Form_Load()
    Dim aArgs() As String
    Dim counter As Integer

    If Not IsNull(Me.OpenArgs) Then
        If Me.OpenArgs = "Customer Address Book" Then
            Me.cboReports = Me.OpenArgs
            Me.cboReports.Width = 2800
            Exit Sub
        End If

        If DelimFound(Me.OpenArgs, "|") Then
            MsgBox "Passing multiple values."
            aArgs() = Split(Me.OpenArgs, "|")
            For counter = 0 To UBound(aArgs)
                If aArgs(counter) = "frmOpenArgs" Then
                    Me.Auto_Title0.Caption = _
                        Me.Auto_Title0.Caption & _
                            " called from " & aArgs(counter)
                End If
                If aArgs(counter) = "Customer Phone Book" Then
                    Me.cboReports = aArgs(counter)
                    Me.cboReports.Width = 2800
                End If
                Debug.Print counter & ":" & aArgs(counter)
            Next counter
        Else
            Me.Auto_Title0.Caption = "Employee List"
        End If

    End If

    ' Me.TimerInterval = 250
End Sub
```

The `Form_Load` event procedure of the `Employee List` form reads the values placed in the `OpenArgs` property and makes changes to the specified form controls.

This procedure begins by checking whether the `OpenArgs` property contains any values. If the property is not Null, Access will run the remaining code prior to loading the form. Notice that to determine whether the `OpenArgs` property is passing more than one value, we make a call to the custom `DelimFound` function (see the second code excerpt below). We pass two values to the `DelimFound` function. The first value is the contents of the `OpenArgs` property; the second value is the delimiter. In this example, we are using the pipe character (|) as the delimiter. If the delimiter is found, we need to extract the values from the `OpenArgs` property by using the `Split` function:

```
aArgs() = Split(Me.OpenArgs, "|")
```

The extracted values are stored in the `aArgs` array variable (refer to Chapter 7 if you are new to arrays). The `For…Next` loop is then used to iterate through the array and assign the values to the form controls. In this process, we assign corresponding values to the `Auto_Title0` and `cboReports` controls.

4. In the same code module, enter the following `Form_Unload` event procedure:

```
Private Sub Form_Unload(Cancel As Integer)
    Me.Auto_Title0.Caption = "Employee List"
End Sub
```

In the **Form_Unload** event procedure, we make sure that the form's caption is reset to **"Employee List"**.

5. In the `frmOpenArgs` form, select the last value from the drop-down box and click the Execute button. Access displays the `Employee List` form, as shown in Figure 15.7.

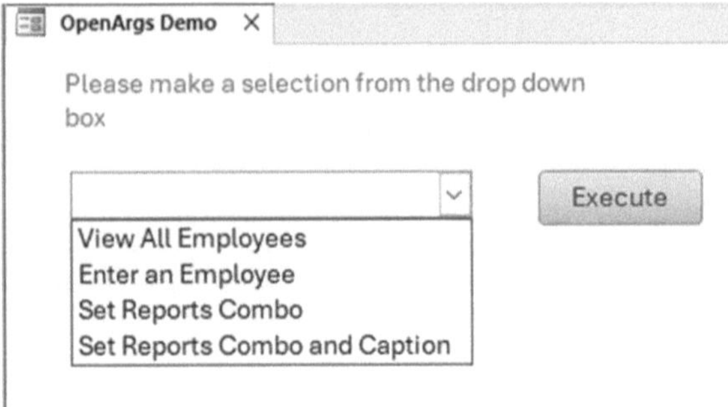

FIGURE 15.7.   Working with the OpenArgs demo (frmOpenArgs form).

In this form, we have a combo box control with four items. Every time you select an item and click the Execute button, an `Employee List` form is loaded with a slightly different effect. The code attached to the click event of the Execute button is shown below:

```
Private Sub cmdOpenEmpList_Click()
On Error GoTo Err_cmdOpenEmpList_Click
```

```
Dim strFormToOpen As String
Dim strUserSelection As String
strFormToOpen = "Employee List"

If IsOpenForm(strFormToOpen) Then
    DoCmd.Close acForm, strFormToOpen
    DoEvents
End If

If Not IsNull(cboSelection) Then
    strUserSelection = cboSelection.Value

    Select Case cboSelection
       Case "View All Employees"
         DoCmd.OpenForm FormName:=strFormToOpen, _
             View:=acNormal, WindowMode:=acWindowNormal, _
             OpenArgs:=strUserSelection
       Case "Enter an Employee"
         DoCmd.OpenForm FormName:=strFormToOpen, _
             View:=acNormal, DataMode:=acFormAdd, _
             OpenArgs:=strUserSelection
       Case "Set Reports Combo"
         DoCmd.OpenForm strFormToOpen, acNormal, _
          , , , acWindowNormal, "Customer Address Book"
       Case "Set Reports Combo and Caption"
         DoCmd.OpenForm strFormToOpen, acNormal, _
          , , , acWindowNormal, _
         Me.Name & "|" & "Customer Phone Book"

    End Select
Else
    MsgBox "Please make a selection from the combo box."
End If
Exit_cmdOpenEmpList_Click:
    Exit Sub
Err_cmdOpenEmpList_Click:
    MsgBox Err.Description
    Resume Exit_cmdOpenEmpList_Click
End Sub
```

Notice how this `Click` event procedure uses the `OpenArgs` property of the form to send different values to the `Employee List` form. To open a form, we simply use the `OpenForm` method of the `DoCmd` object and pass the name of the form as well as other parameters that define the type of view, data mode, window mode, and `OpenArgs`. The parameters can be passed by name (as shown in the first two `Select Case` statements, or inline (as shown in the last two `Select Case` statements).

The supplemental function procedures that the `Click` event procedure and the `Load` event procedures call are placed in a standard module called `openArgsUtil`.

The `IsOpenForm` function procedure returns `true` if the `Employee List` form is open and `false` if it is closed. If the form is open, the `cmdOpenEmpList_Click` event procedure will close it prior to executing the remaining code.

```
Function IsOpenForm(strFormName As String) _
    As Boolean

    IsOpenForm = Application.CurrentProject. _
        AllForms(strFormName).IsLoaded

End Function
```

The `DelimFound` function checks whether the specified delimiter can be found in the string passed in the `OpenArgs` property. This is done by using the built-in `InStr` function.

```
Function DelimFound(strOpenArgs As String, _
    strDelim As String) As Boolean

    If InStr(1, strOpenArgs, strDelim) Then
        DelimFound = True
    Else
        DelimFound = False
    End If

End Function
```

OpenArgs Demo ✕ Employee List ✕

Employee List called from frmOpenArgs

New Employee   Collect Data via E-mail   Add From Outlook   E-mail List   Reports   Customer Phone Book ⌄

ID	First Name	Last Name	E-mail Address	Business Phone	Company	Job Title
2	Andrew	Cencini	andrew@northwindtraders.cor	(123)555-0100	Northwind Trade	Vice President, Sal
1	Nancy	Freehafer	nancy@northwindtraders.com	(123)555-0100	Northwind Trade	Sales Representati
8	Laura	Giussani	laura@northwindtraders.com	(123)555-0100	Northwind Trade	Sales Coordinator
9	Anne	Hellung-Larsen	anne@northwindtraders.com	(123)555-0100	Northwind Trade	Sales Representati
3	Jan	Kotas	jan@northwindtraders.com	(123)555-0100	Northwind Trade	Sales Representati
6	Michael	Neipper	michael@northwindtraders.cor	(123)555-0100	Northwind Trade	Sales Representati
4	Mariya	Sergienko	mariya@northwindtraders.com	(123)555-0100	Northwind Trade	Sales Representati
5	Steven	Thorpe	steven@northwindtraders.com	(123)555-0100	Northwind Trade	Sales Manager
7	Robert	Zare	robert@northwindtraders.com	(123)555-0100	Northwind Trade	Sales Representati
(New)						
	9					

FIGURE 15.8. After selecting the last value from the OpenArgs Demo drop-down list (see Figure 15.7), Access displays the Employee List form with changes made to the form caption (Employee List called from frmOpenArgs) and the Reports drop-down list.

USING IMAGES IN ACCESS FORMS

Access 2007 came with better image support. Earlier versions of Access converted images from their native format and stored them as bitmaps (`.bmp`). This format caused a significant increase in the size of the database because bitmap files are not compressed. Also, any image transparency features were lost during the conversion process. If you use the Image control in Access 2007–2024 and specify the image in the Picture property, Access will store the image in its native format with no conversion. Images with transparency work just fine. You can see examples of transparent buttons and pictures in the forms that we imported from the `Northwind 2007` database.

Older `.mdb` databases do not support saving images in the native format, so there is a special database property that lets you choose whether the images should be converted to DIB (device-independent bitmap) or stored in their native format. The default setting is to store images in their native format and convert them to bitmaps for `.mdb` databases. If you want your images to be displayed in previous versions of Access, choose the second option button under the Picture Property Storage Format setting (see Figure 15.9).

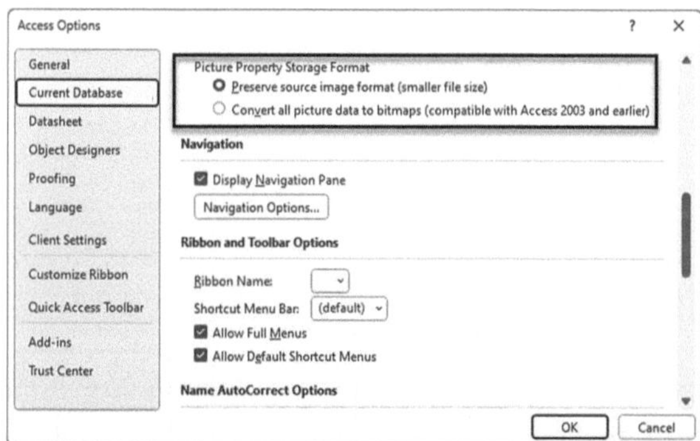

FIGURE 15.9.   You can tell Access how to store images in older versions of Access (2003 and earlier) by using the options under Picture Property Storage Format. The Access Options window can be accessed by clicking File | Options.

Access 2007 introduced a bound Image control. Access 2003 and earlier needed lots of VBA code to display images on forms and reports when the images were stored in the directories on disk. The Image control can be bound to the image path. To add an image to your form, place the form in design view and click the Image button in the Controls group of the Ribbon's Form Design tab. Click Browse and choose the image file. When you click OK, you are returned to the form design and your cursor displays a small image next to it. Click and drag on the form to define the area where you'd like the image to be placed. When you release the mouse button, the selected picture is placed in the selected area on the form. If you activate the Property Sheet for the Image control, you will see that Access has placed the filename in the Picture property (see Figure 15.10). If you don't like the picture you've chosen, you can simply click the ellipsis button (…) next to the Picture property and choose another image, or choose another image (if available) from the Image Gallery accessed via the Insert Image button.

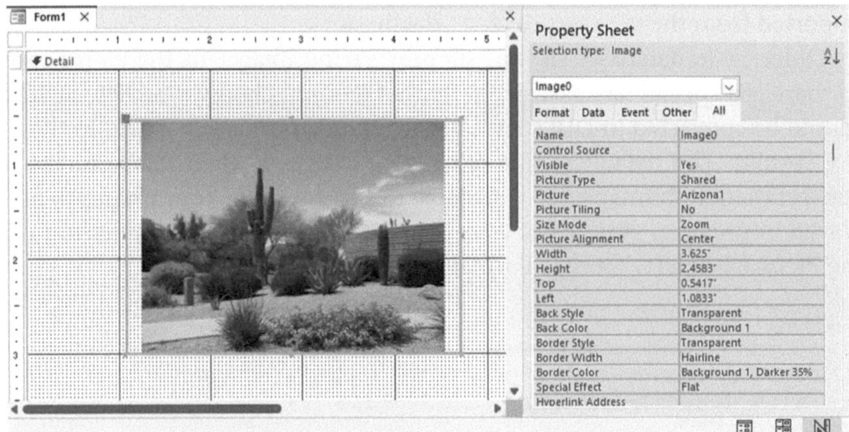

FIGURE 15.10. The picture is shown here using the Image control placed on an Access form.

USING THE ATTACHMENTS CONTROL

In the Controls group of the Form Design tab, you will find an Attachments control (📎), which enables you to attach a file or a collection of files to any database record. When you click on the Attachments field on the form, Access displays a small toolbar with three buttons (see Figure 19.15). The Forward and Backward buttons allow you to move through the attached files, and the third button opens the Attachments dialog box. You can also right-click the Attachments field and choose the same options from the shortcut menu.

Recall that earlier in this book, you wrote a VBA procedure that added an attachment field to an existing table. Let's see how you can work with attachments in an Access form.

⊙ Custom Project 15.2   Working with Attachments Control

1. In the `Chap15.accdb` database, double-click the Customers table.
2. Double-click on the paper clip icon for the third record. You should see an empty Attachments dialog box. Click the Add button, then select the California1.jpg, California2.jpg, and California3.jpg images. These files can be found in the companion files in the `External Docs` folder. When you select the files and click Open, the image names should appear in the Attachments dialog box.
3. Click OK to close the dialog box and press Ctrl+S to save the record. Notice that the paper clip column now displays the number of attached files in parentheses next to the paper clip icon for the record.
4. Close the `Customers` table.
5. Open the `Customer Details` form and activate the record for the third customer that has the California images in the Attachments control.
6. Click the image control and notice a small toolbar with three buttons (see Figure 15.11). Scroll through the attached files by clicking the Forward and Backward buttons.

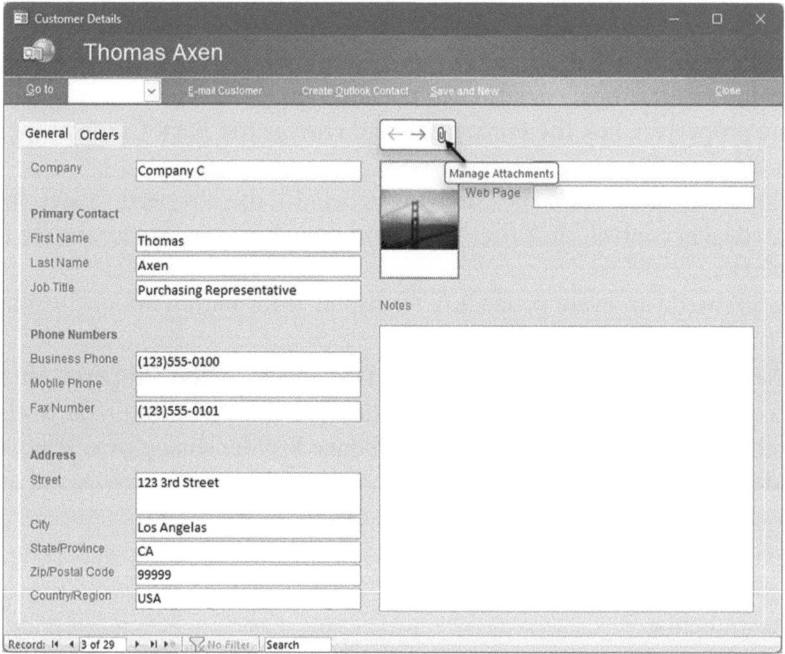

FIGURE 15.11.   The Access form uses the Attachments control to show images attached to a record.

Let's modify the form to display additional information about the attachments.

7. Switch to the form design view of the `Customer Details` form and use the Text Box control in the Controls group of the Form Design tab to add a text box to the form, as shown in Figure 15.12. Change the text box label caption to `Showing:`, as illustrated below.

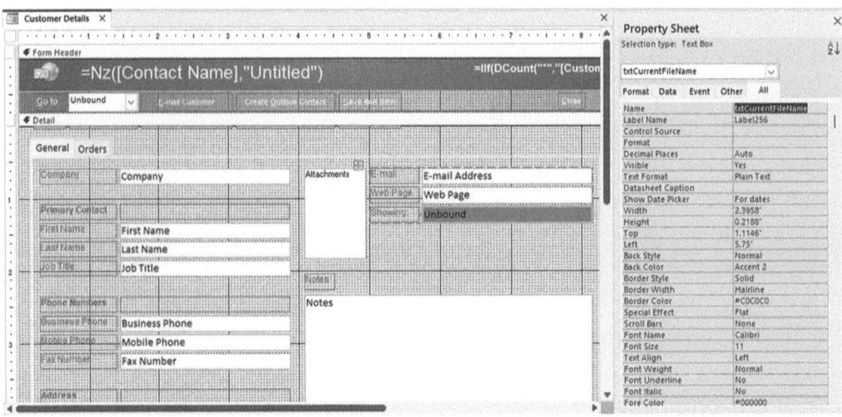

FIGURE 15.12. Placing an unbound text box control on the form.

8. In the form grid, click the unbound text box next to Current File. In the Property Sheet for this text box, click the All tab and type `txtCurrentFileName` in the Name property. Click the Format tab and change the Back Color property to any color you like.

9. In the form grid, click the Showing label. In the Property Sheet for the selected label control, click the All tab and type `lblCurrentFile` in the Name property.

   Now let's write an event procedure to display information about the attached file.

10. In the form grid, click the Attachments control. In the Property Sheet for this control, click the Event tab, then click the ellipsis button next to the On Attachment Current property. In the Choose Builder dialog box, select Code Builder and click OK.

    Access will write the stub of the `Attachments_AttachmentCurrent` event procedure.

11. Complete the code of the `Attachments_AttachmentCurrent` procedure, as shown below:

```
Private Sub Attachments_AttachmentCurrent()
```

```
      If Me.DefaultView = 0 Then
         If Me.Attachments.AttachmentCount = 0 Then
            Me.txtCurrentFileName.Visible = False
            Me.lblCurrentFile.Visible = False
         Else
            Me.txtCurrentFileName.Visible = True
            Me.lblCurrentFile.Visible = True
            Me.txtCurrentFileName = Me.Attachments.FileName
         End If
      End If
End Sub
```

Add the following `Attachments_Click` event procedure:

```
Private Sub Attachments_Click()
     If Me.DefaultView = 0 Then
       If Me.Attachments.AttachmentCount > 0 Then
         MsgBox " There are " & Me.Attachments.AttachmentCount & _
               " files attached to this record."
       End If
     End If
End Sub
```

The Attachments control comes with special properties that apply to working with the `Attachment` data type. The `FileName` property returns the name of the attached file. If you need to display the file extension, use the `FileType` property. The `AttachmentCount` property returns the number of attachments stored for the record.

The Attachments control has a special event called `AttachmentCurrent`. This event is similar to the form's `OnCurrent` event. It is triggered when you move the focus from one attachment to another. The code shown in the `Attachments_AttachmentCurrent` event procedure begins by checking whether the form's default view is set to Single Form (0). If `DefaultView` is set to display other types of Access forms, the code in the event procedure will not run. The procedure hides the txtCurrentFileName text box and its label for all records that do not have any attachments. This is done by setting the Visible property of the text box and label control to False. The `Attachments_Click` event procedure displays the number of attached files when the Attachments control is clicked and contains attached files.

12. Activate the `Customer Details` form in form view and scroll to the third customer record (see Figure 15.13).

Notice that the Showing text box displays the current attachment filename. To scroll through the available files, click the Attachments field. Access will display a message with the number of attached files. Click the Forward button in the tiny pop-up toolbar and notice the image changes and the text box with the image filename gets updated.

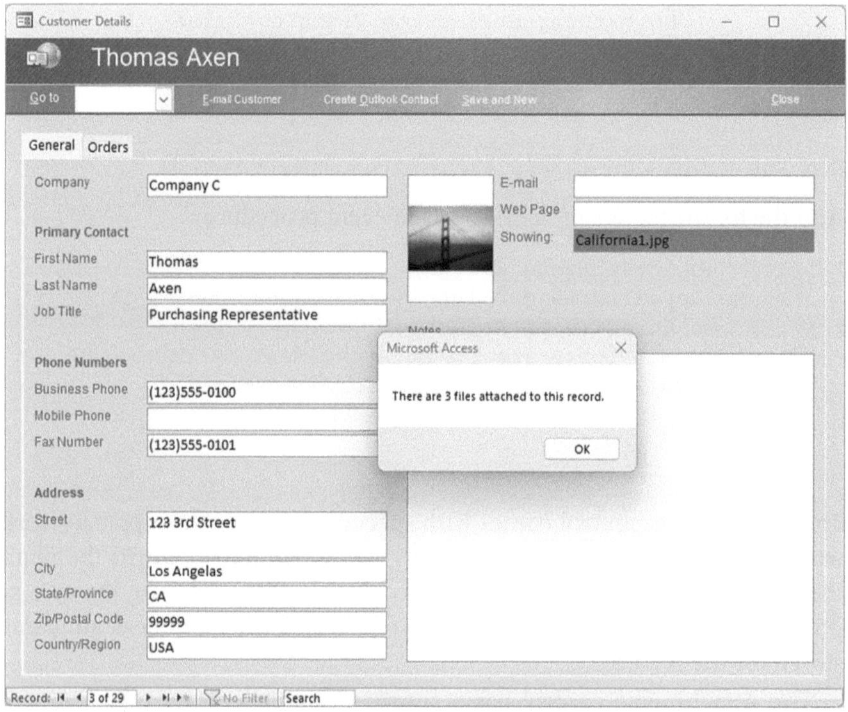

FIGURE 15.13.   The Current File text box control added to the form provides information about the attachment filename currently displayed in the Attachments control.

13. Press Ctrl+S to save changes to the `Customer Details` form, and then close this form.

USING THE DoCmd OBJECT WITH ACCESS FORMS

`DoCmd` is a powerful object in Access VBA that allows you to perform various actions in your Access database, such as opening forms, running queries, and printing reports. Here's an overview of how you can use `DoCmd` with forms.

Opening Forms

You've already seen many examples of using the `DoCmd` to open Access forms. The syntax of this command is:

```
DoCmd.OpenForm "FormName", View, FilterName, WhereCondition, DataMode, WindowMode, OpenArgs
```

TABLE 15.4.   Arguments of the OpenForm method of the DoCmd object.

Argument Name	Description
FormName	The name of the form you want to open
View	The view in which to open the form (e.g., acNormal, acDesign, acFormDS for datasheet view)
FilterName	The name of a filter to apply when the form opens
WhereCondition	A string expression that acts as a WHERE clause without the WHERE keyword
DataMode	The data entry mode (e.g., acFormAdd, acFormEdit, acFormReadOnly)
WindowMode	The window mode (e.g., acWindowNormal, acDialog, acHidden)
OpenArgs	A variant that provides an open argument

For example, to open the `Employee List` form and show only the first employee record ready for editing, try the following statement from the Immediate window:

```
DoCmd.OpenForm "Employee List", acNormal, , "ID=1", acFormEdit, acWindowNormal
```

Closing Forms

Use the following syntax to close an Access form:

```
DoCmd.Close acForm, "FormName", Save
```

- `acForm`—Indicates that the object being closed is a form
- `FormName`—The name of the form to close
- `Save`—Whether to save changes (`acSaveYes`, `acSaveNo`, `acSavePrompt`)

For example, to close the Employee List form and save the changes, use this statement:

```
DoCmd.Close acForm, "EmployeeForm", acSaveYes
```

Moving Between Records

After you open the form, use the `DoCmd` object's `GoToRecord` method to move to another record. The syntax for moving between records is shown here:

```
DoCmd.GoToRecord ObjectType, ObjectName, Record, Offset
```

- `ObjectType`—The type of object (e.g., `acDataForm` for forms)
- `ObjectName`—The name of the object
- `Record`—The record to go to (e.g., `acNext`, `acPrevious`, `acFirst`, `acLast`, `acGoTo`)
- `Offset`—A numeric expression that's the number of records to move forward or backward

For example, to move to the next record on the `Customer List` form, enter the following in the Immediate window (assuming the form is currently open in form view):

```
DoCmd.GoToRecord acDataForm, "Customer List", acNext
```

Saving Forms

When saving forms, use the following syntax:

```
DoCmd.Save ObjectType, ObjectName
```

- `ObjectType`: The type of the object (e.g., `acForm`)
- `ObjectName`: The name of the object

For example, the following statement run from the Immediate window will save the `Customer List` form (assuming the form is open):

```
DoCmd.Save acForm, "Customer List"
```

The following `Click` event procedure will save the current form, when the `btnSaveForm` is clicked:

```
Private Sub btnSaveForm_Click()
    DoCmd.Save acForm, Me.Name
End Sub
```

Using Requery with Forms and Controls

To ensure that the data displayed on the form is current and reflects any recent changes in the database, you should use the `DoCmd` object's `Requery` method. This method has the following syntax:

```
DoCmd.Requery ControlName
```

`ControlName` is the name of the control to requery. If omitted, the form or report is requeried.

The `Requery` method for forms refreshes the data for the entire form, including all its controls and subforms. The `Requery` method for controls refreshes the data for the specific control, such as a combo box or list box, without affecting the entire form.

You should use `Requery` after you've added, deleted, or modified records and need to refresh the displayed data. When navigating between records, use `Requery` to show the latest data from the database.

The following statement will refresh the data on the `Employee List` form:

```
DoCmd.Requery "Employee List"
```

To refresh the entire form after clicking the `cmdRefesh` button on the form:

```
Private Sub cmdRefresh_Click()
    Me.Requery
End Sub
```

To requery a subform, you must refer to the subform control on the main form, like this:

```
Private Sub cmdRequerySubform_Click()
    Me.[Custormer Orders subform].Form.Requery
End Sub
```

Keep in mind that requerying can slow down your application if the underlying data source is large and complex.

FORCING THE COMBO BOX DROPDOWN ON FORM_LOAD

Microsoft Access box controls have numerous properties you can manipulate with VBA to customize their behavior and appearance. For example, the following procedure demonstrates how to set various properties of the `cboEmployees` combo box:

```
Private Sub cboEmployees_GotFocus()
' set up a Combo Box control
With Me.cboEmployees
.RowSource = "SELECT ID, [First Name], [Last Name] FROM Employees"
.ColumnCount = 3
.ColumnWidths = "0;1in;1in"
.BoundColumn = 1
```

```
.LimitToList = True
.AutoExpand = True
.ListRows = 10
.ListWidth = "2.5"
End With
End Sub
```

In this example, the setup code is placed in the control's `GotFocus` event. You can also put the code in the `Form_Load` event. Notice that the `RowSource` property sets the data source to a query that selects three fields from the `Employees` table, `ID`, `[First Name]`, and `[Last Name]`, and basic properties are set to specify the control's appearance.

To have the combo box dropdown open automatically when the form loads, use the combo box `Dropdown` method:

```
Private Sub Form_Load()
    Me.cboEmployees.SetFocus
    Me.cboEmployees.Dropdown
End Sub
```

Sometimes, the `Dropdown` method might fail to open the combo box when the form is loaded. This can be caused by different reasons, which include:

- Form loading timing (the `Dropdown` method is invoked before the form is fully loaded or rendered)
- Focus issues (the combo box might not have the focus when the `Dropdown` method is called),
- Control initialization (the combo box might not be fully initialized with its data source when the `Dropdown` method is called)
- Hidden/invisible form (if the form or the combo box control is hidden or not visible when the `Dropdown` method is called)
- Event conflicts (other events or code that runs during the form loading might interfere with the `Dropdown` method)

In my experience, `Dropdown` issues are always resolved by using the `Timer` event. By introducing a slight delay before calling the `Dropdown` method, you can ensure that the form is fully loaded and rendered. The following code demonstrates this method using the event procedures for the `frmPrintersSelection` form, which is included in the `Chap15` database in the companion files.

```
Private Sub Form_Load()
    Dim prt As Printer
```

```
    Me.cmbPrinters.RowSourceType = "Value List"
    ' Populate printers combo box
    For Each prt In Application.Printers
        Me.cmbPrinters.AddItem prt.DeviceName
    Next prt
    Me.cmbPrinters.AllowValueListEdits = False
    Me.cmbPrinters.SetFocus
    ' Set the timer interval to trigger the Timer event
    Me.TimerInterval = 100
End Sub

Private Sub Form_Unload(Cancel As Integer)
    ' Clear the combo box
    Me.cmbPrinters.RowSource = ""
End Sub

Private Sub Form_Timer()
    ' Drop down the combo box
    Me.cmbPrinters.Dropdown
    ' Reset the timer interval to 0 to stop the timer
    Me.TimerInterval = 0
End Sub
```

The last statement in the `Form_Load` event sets the `TimerInterval` property to 100 milliseconds to trigger the `Form_Timer` event. In the `Form_Timer` event, we drop down the combo box and reset the `Timer` interval to stop it after the dropdown action is performed. This approach delays the dropdown action slightly, allowing the form to fully load and render, and ensures that the `Dropdown` method works correctly.

USING ChatGPT WITH ACCESS

You can gain more experience in programming Access forms by examining the code already written by the Microsoft team in the provided sample databases. These sample databases (such as `Northwind 2007` or `NorthwindStarter`) are excellent resources for learning and understanding best practices, coding techniques, and complex functions implemented by experienced developers. You can also improve your own Access forms by formulating prompts for AI companions such as ChatGPT. Be specific and detailed. The AI needs a clearly described problem with relevant details, such as form names, control names, and specific actions or outcomes. In summary, the AI needs to know what you want to achieve. If you have a complex task, break it down into smaller, more manageable parts and ask for help with each part sequentially. For example:

User Prompt:

Step1: How do I write a query for an Order Details subform?

Step2: How do I write VBA code that connects the subform with the main form that shows the customers datasheet?

Step 3: How do I make sure that when I select a customer record in the main form the corresponding records appear in the subform?

One procedure in this chapter used the `DoEvents` statement, which was purposely omitted from the code analysis. Let's put out a prompt to ChatGPT to get the needed explanation:

User Prompt: *Explain DoEvents in Access VBA programming.*

These prompts and the ChatGPT responses are provided in the `Chapter 15 - Using ChatGPT with Access` document included in the companion files.

When you get an answer, don't assume it will work perfectly right away. It is crucial to use the debugging tools and techniques you have learned to step through the code line by line. I can't stress this enough. This process will elevate your skills in VBA, and really, in any kind of programming. If a provided solution doesn't work as expected, don't hesitate to seek further assistance. Explain what went wrong, include any error messages or unexpected behaviors, and ask for troubleshooting advice. AI companions such as ChatGPT can offer refined solutions based on the detailed feedback you provide.

Access forms may seem straightforward at first glance, but the deeper you dive, the more intricate they become. You must learn how to handle various user inputs and scenarios. You must learn how to interact with multiple data sources, or you will get unexpected issues. Managing form events can be complex, especially when dealing with multiple controls and dependencies. Each problem you solve on your own or with the help of others, including AI, will build your expertise and confidence, making you a more skilled and resourceful Access developer.

SUMMARY

In this chapter, you were introduced to programming Access forms with VBA. You learned about form class modules and event procedures you can write for forms and their controls. You saw examples of various types of events that can occur on an Access form and learned how you can react to a specific form event by writing an event procedure. Be aware that if you don't write your own code to handle a particular form event, Access will use its default handler for the event.

You have also learned how to use the form's `OpenArgs` property to pass values from one form to another and explored various uses of the `DoCmd` object in programming Access forms.

This chapter's main project focused on designing a custom form that streamlines the process of reviewing form properties. This project involved creating a form that allows you to quickly view all forms in a database and display properties that differ from the default settings. This was a multistep project that introduced you to working with a form and its controls (command buttons, list boxes, and text boxes) by writing the required event procedures in form modules.

In another project, you learned about using the Attachments control in an Access form. You wrote an event procedure to display additional information about the attachments.

After trying out the numerous examples and exercises presented in this chapter, you should have a good understanding of how to write event procedures for an Access form. You should also be able to recognize the importance of form and control events in an Access database application.

The next chapter will introduce you to VBA programming in Access reports.

16
Using VBA to Interact with Reports and Report Controls

Reports have always been a very popular and widely used feature in Access. Access reporting is very interactive thanks to the report view, which allows you to easily perform sorting, copying, and filtering of data. Many of the Access form features are also available for reports. For example, to make long tabular reports easier to read, you can apply alternating row shading just by changing the Alternate Back Color property in the report's Detail section. Like forms, reports can utilize bound image controls and rich text formatting. The layout view makes it easier to design reports; because you are working with live data in layout view, you do not need to switch between the design and report views to see how the final report will look. The layout view allows formatting report sections and controls, adding new fields, applying auto-formats, grouping and sorting data, and changing many of the report's properties. Layouts can be used in reports to resize and move groups of controls together or add grid lines that grow or shrink with the data. It is very easy to design objects in layout view. You can drop any control anywhere within the layout. Your controls can span multiple rows and columns. Like forms, reports can be enhanced by applying a consistent style using themes. Report distribution is easy with the portable document format (`.pdf`) and XML Paper Specification (`.xps`) format. The feature most appreciated by all Access users is the ability to view a report as a subform on a form. Additionally, you can specify the name of a report by using the `SourceObject` property of a subform control on a form.

CREATING ACCESS REPORTS

There are many types of reports you can create in Access by working with the Report, Report Design, Report Wizard, or Labels tools included in the Reports group of the Create tab on the Ribbon. For example:

- The Report tool (see Figure 16.1) allows you to create a basic report based on the currently selected table or query. You can then add additional features, such as groups and totals.

- The Report Design tool gives you more control over creating a report by allowing you to add custom controls and add VBA code behind a report, as demonstrated later in this chapter. When using Report Design, you will not be able to see the actual data from tables and views at design time. You need to switch to Print Preview to view the entire report. To overcome this limitation, try working with the layout view. In layout view, you can add different types of controls, as well as functionality for sorting, grouping, and calculating totals. You can also apply different formatting to the layout view while viewing the actual data from your tables and queries.

- The Blank Report tool gives you a blank report where you can insert fields and place the controls the way you like to design your custom report.

- The Access Report Wizard will walk you through the report creation process by presenting various options to choose from, such as selecting a data source for your report, determining criteria such as grouping and sorting, and offering formatting options (layout, orientation, and style). The Report Wizard makes it easy to create a report based on multiple tables.

- The Labels tool is a label wizard that allows you to quickly create mailing labels using a standard or custom size for each label.

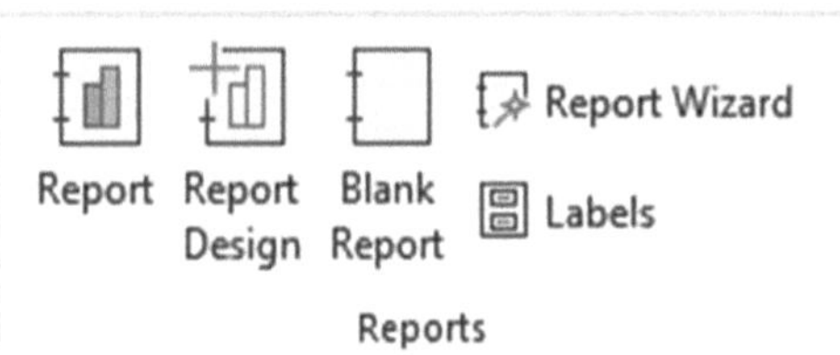

FIGURE 16.1. The Reports group on the Create tab provides several tools for creating basic and advanced reports.

Using the tools described above, you can create the following types of reports in Access:

- Detail Reports (Figures 16.2 and 16.3)

  In a detail report, there is one entry for each record included in the report. Take, for example, a sales report with a data source based on multiple tables: `Orders`, `Order Details`, `Products`, and `Customer`. In the Detail section, the records are grouped by customer and contain fields such as `Order ID`, `Order Date`, `Product ID`, `Quantity`, and `Unit Price`. The bottom of the report contains calculated fields such as total for each order: `=[Quntity] * [Unit Price]`. This type of report uses a tabular layout and can be based on a parameter query to limit the data displayed on the report based on criteria supplied by the user at runtime.

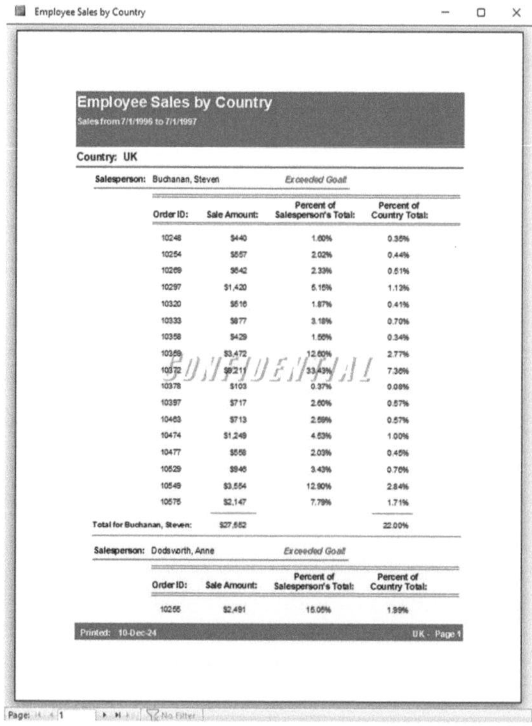

FIGURE 16.2. Detail report (source: Northwind.mdb).

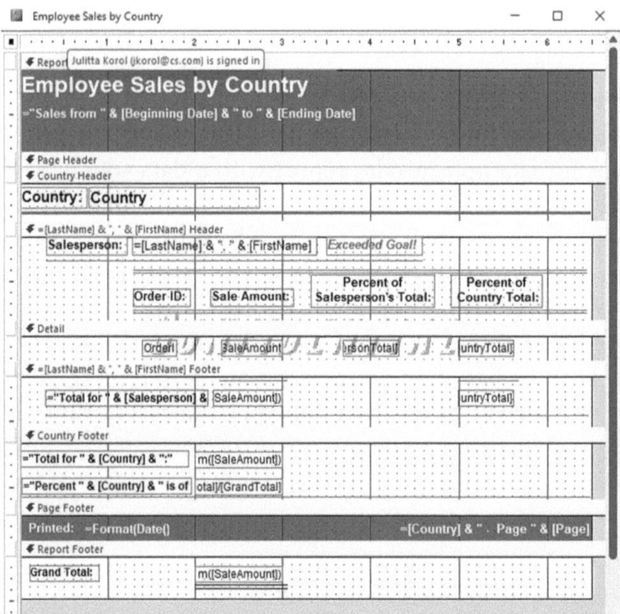

FIGURE 16.3. Detail report design view (source: Northwind.mdb).

- Summary Reports (Figures 16.4 and 16.5)

  In a summary report, you show summary data for all the records included in the report. This report focuses on aggregated data, such as totals, averages, counts, and other summary statistics. The data is often grouped by specific categories, such as departments, regions, or time period, to provide insight at a higher level. The data is usually sorted into groups to make it easier to analyze and compare. Summary reports often use filters to include only relevant data, such as data from a specific range or category.

  In a summary report, group headers introduce each section of grouped data, displaying the category or grouping field. The group footers often contain summary calculations for each group, such as subtotals, averages, or counts. There is also a report header with the report title, company logo, and report date. The report footer may contain overall summary calculations, page numbers, and other concluding information. Sometimes, charts or graphs are included to visually represent aggregated data, making trends and comparisons more apparent. Create summary reports for high-level data analysis to enable informed decision-making.

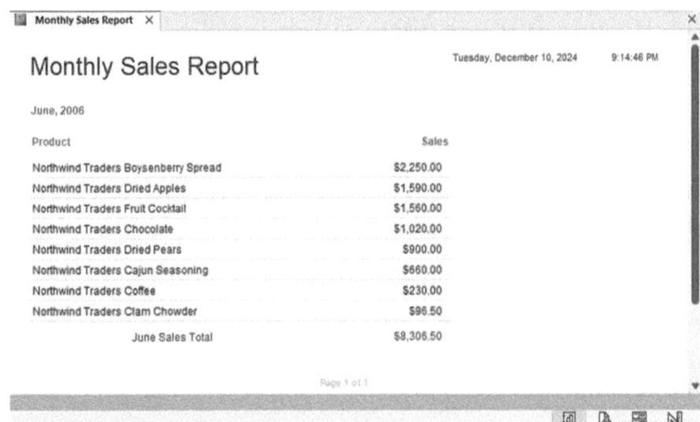

FIGURE 16.4.   Summary Report (source: Northwind 2007.accdb).

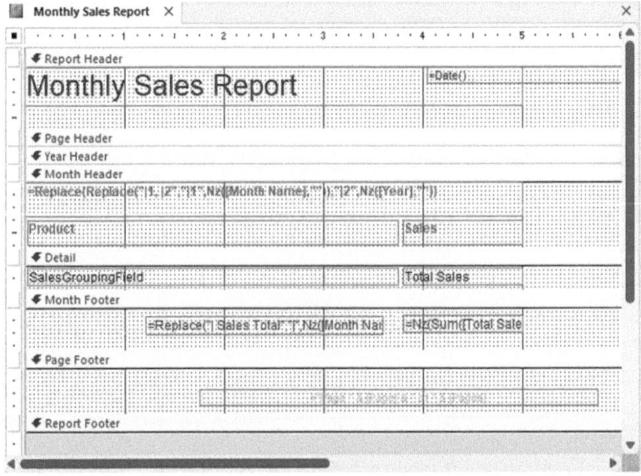

FIGURE 16.5.   Summary report in design view (source: Northwind 2007.accdb).

- Crosstabulation Reports (Figures 16.6 and 16.7)

  This report is often called a crosstab or pivot table report and is designed to summarize and analyze data by displaying it in a compact, matrix-like format. It allows you to compare different categories of data at a glance by showing the relationships between two or more sets of data. The crosstab report is organized in a grid format with rows and columns. Each row represents a unique value from a specific field, such as `Product Category`. Each column represents another unique value from a different field, such as `Year` or `Month`.

  The cells within the grid display aggregated data, such as sums, averages, counts, or other statistics. Aggregation is typically done using numerical fields. Crosstab reports have row and column headings. The row headings usually represent one dimension of your data, such as product categories, products, or regions. The column headings represent another dimension, such as time periods—months, quarters, years, or other categories. The intersection of each row and column contains the summary value, showing the aggregated data for the corresponding categories. Crosstab reports can become complex with multiple dimensions and large data sets. If you need a more flexible report, try pivot tables in Excel.

Quarterly Sales Report

Tuesday, December 10, 2024 9:52:29 PM

Q2 2006

Product	Apr	May	Jun	Total
Northwind Traders Syrup	$500.00	$0.00	$0.00	$500.00
Northwind Traders Cajun Seasoning	$0.00	$0.00	$0.00	$0.00
Northwind Traders Olive Oil	$533.75	$0.00	$0.00	$533.75
Northwind Traders Boysenberry Spre	$0.00	$0.00	$0.00	$0.00
Northwind Traders Dried Pears	$0.00	$0.00	$0.00	$0.00
Northwind Traders Curry Sauce	$1,120.00	$800.00	$0.00	$1,920.00
Northwind Traders Fruit Cocktail	$0.00	$0.00	$0.00	$0.00
Northwind Traders Chocolate Biscui	$230.00	$0.00	$0.00	$230.00
Northwind Traders Marmalade	$3,240.00	$0.00	$0.00	$3,240.00
Northwind Traders Scones	$200.00	$0.00	$0.00	$200.00
Northwind Traders Beer	$5,418.00	$0.00	$0.00	$5,418.00
Northwind Traders Crab Meat	$1,472.00	$736.00	$0.00	$2,208.00
Northwind Traders Clam Chowder	$772.00	$0.00	$0.00	$772.00
Northwind Traders Coffee	$0.00	$0.00	$0.00	$0.00
Northwind Traders Chocolate	$127.50	$0.00	$0.00	$127.50
Northwind Traders Dried Apples	$0.00	$0.00	$0.00	$0.00
Northwind Traders Long Grain Rice	$280.00	$0.00	$0.00	$280.00
Northwind Traders Ravioli	$1,950.00	$0.00	$0.00	$1,950.00
Northwind Traders Mozzarella	$3,132.00	$0.00	$0.00	$3,132.00
Northwind Traders Almonds	$0.00	$200.00	$0.00	$200.00
Northwind Traders Dried Plums	$0.00	$52.50	$0.00	$52.50
	$18,975.25	$1,788.50	$0.00	$20,763.75

Page 1 of 1

FIGURE 16.6. Crosstab report (source: Northwind 2007.accdb).

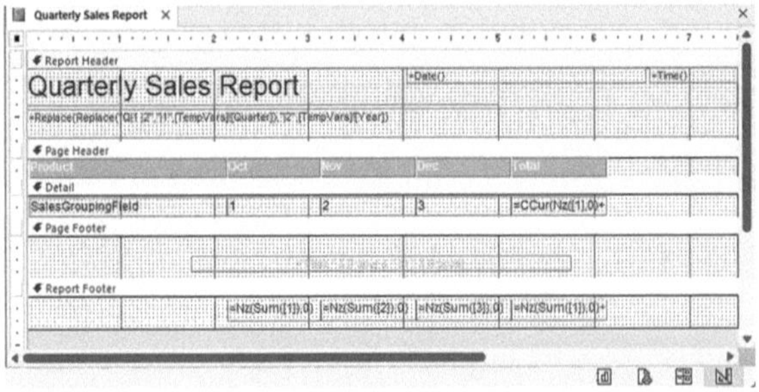

FIGURE 16.7. Crosstab report in design view (source: Northwind 2007.accdb).

• Reports with Forms (Figures 16.8 and 16.9)

In Microsoft Access, integrating reports with forms is a powerful way to enhance data visualization and user interaction. Users can generate, view, and interact with reports directly from forms, creating a more efficient workflow. You can embed reports directly into forms using subforms/ subreports. This allows users to view reports without leaving the form. Forms are often used to input parameters that dynamically generate and filter reports, providing a tailored view of the data. You can add buttons to forms to open and print reports. Combo boxes and text boxes can collect user input for filtering reports. The form can pass user-entered parameters to the report, ensuring the report displays only the relevant data.

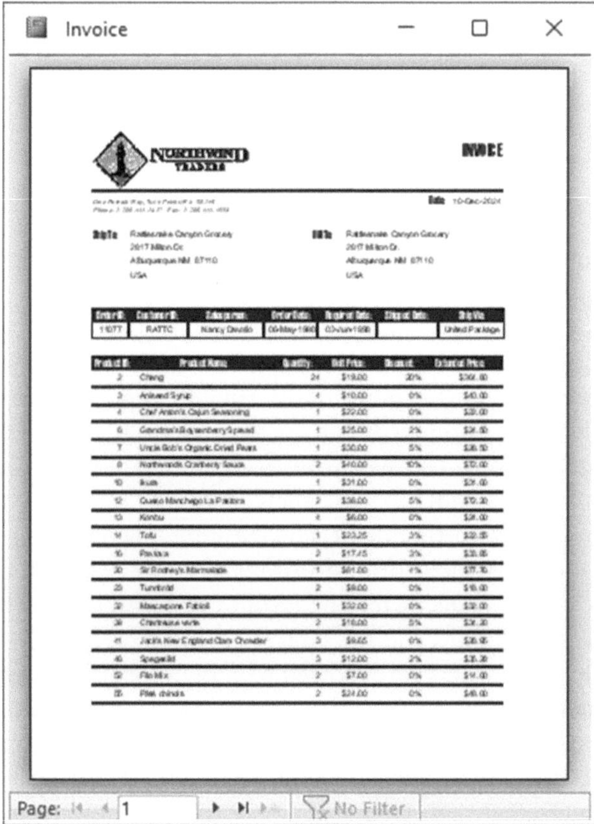

FIGURE 16.8.   Report with a Form (source: Northwind 2007.accdb).

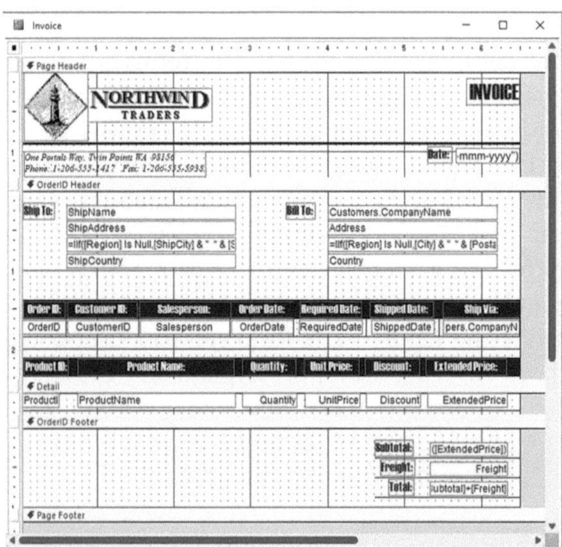

FIGURE 16.9.   Report with a form in design view (source: Northwind 2007.accdb).

- Reports with Labels (Figures 16.10 and 16.11)

  A label report is designed to print labels, such as mailing labels, product labels, or any other type of label that needs to be printed in a predefined format. Access provides predefined label layouts that match commonly used label sizes and formats, such as Avery and DYMO. Users can select the appropriate label type and layout during the report creation process. Each label can be customized with various controls, such as text boxes, images, and barcodes. The size, font, and placement of controls can be adjusted to fit your requirements. Labels are bound to a data source, such as a table or query, ensuring that each label contains specific information from a database. Label reports can use a multiple-column layout to fit several labels on a single page. The layout can be adjusted to fit the desired number of columns and rows per page. Label reports can be printed directly onto label sheets or exported to a PDF format for easy sharing and printing later.

  You can create labels for products that include details such as product name, SKU, price, and barcode. Labels can be used for many different purposes, such as inventory management; retail requirements, such as price tags; or identification purposes, such as employee badges, event passes, or equipment tags.

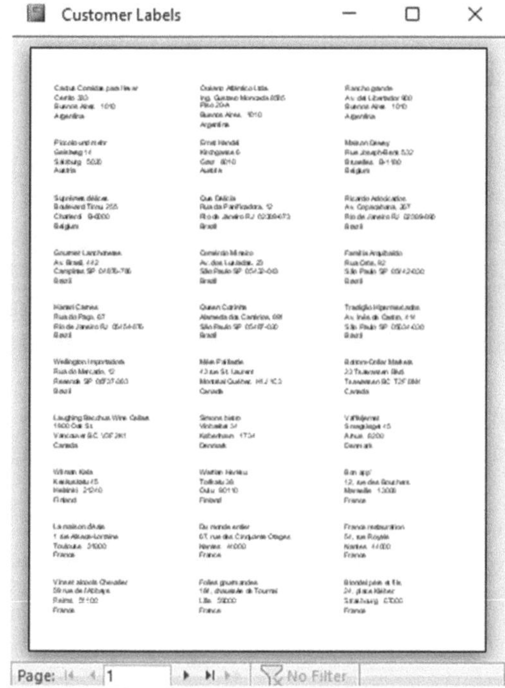

FIGURE 16.10.   Report with labels (source: Northwind.mdb).

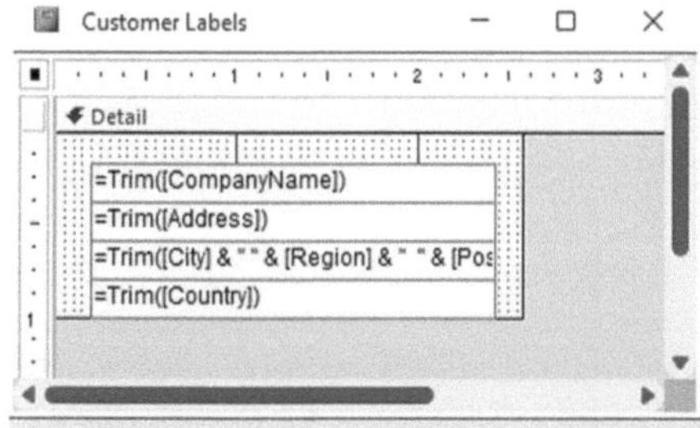

FIGURE 16.11.   Report with labels in design view (source: Northwind.mdb).

- Reports with Charts (Figures 16.12 and 16.13)

  These types of reports allow you to present data visually, making it easier to understand and analyze trends, patterns, and relationships. Charts provide a graphical representation of data, which can often reveal insights that are not immediately apparent in tabular data. You can include bar charts, line charts, pie charts, and more, serving a different purpose and different types of data comparison. These reports are bound to data sources such as tables or queries to reflect the latest data from your database. The visualizations automatically update when the underlying data changes. You can customize your graphs and charts to your liking with titles, axes, labels, legends, and colors. Use the correct chart type for your purpose:

- Bar Chart—This is suitable for comparing quantities across categories. It is often used to compare sales figures across different regions or products.
- Line Chart—This is ideal for showing trends over time. It is used to track financial metrics over time and show sales trends over months or years.
- Pie Chart—This is useful for illustrating proportions and percentages. It is often used in financial reports to show the distribution of expenses or revenue sources.
- Column Chart—This is similar to a bar chart but oriented vertically. It is used to compare operational metrics such as production output across different facilities.
- Scatter Plot—This is effective for displaying relationships between two variables. It is used to analyze the correlation between variables such as production time and defect rates.

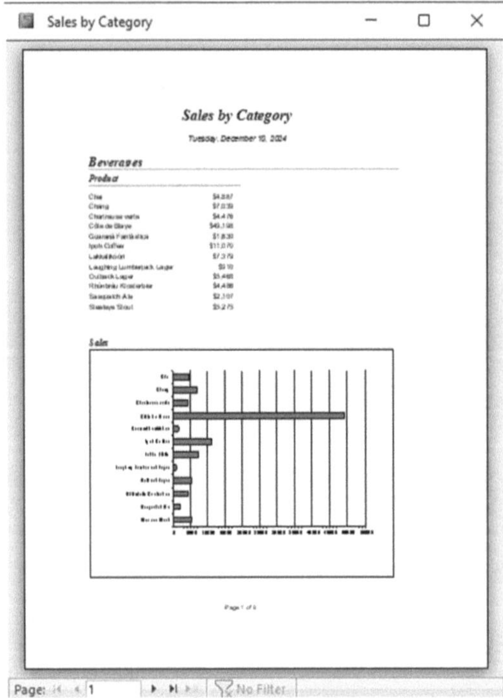

FIGURE 16.12.   Report with a chart (source: Northwind.mdb).

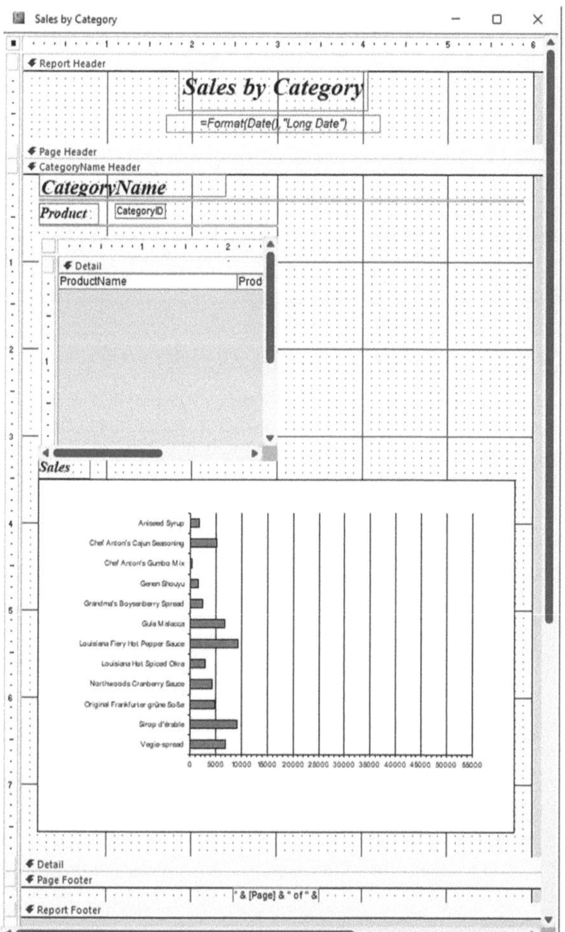

FIGURE 16.13.   Report with a chart in design view (source: Northwind.mdb).

In addition to creating Access reports via the built-in tools in Access, you can create a report with VBA by using the `CreateReport` method of the `Application` object. This process is discussed further in this chapter.

REPORT MODULES, PROPERTIES, AND EVENT PROGRAMMING IN ACCESS REPORTS

In Microsoft Access, report modules are VBA code class modules used to add custom functionality, automate tasks, and enhance the interactivity of your reports. They are similar to form modules, which we discussed in the previous chapter, but are tailored to the unique needs of reporting.

Report Properties

Like forms, reports in Microsoft Access have numerous properties that you can set to specify and enhance the appearance of your report. These properties allow you to customize everything from the layout and formatting to the behavior and data presentation of the report. The key properties of reports are listed below:

- Format Properties
  - Caption—The title or label displayed for the report
  - Font—Used for setting the font style, size, color, and other formatting options
  - Background Color—Used for defining the background color for the report or its specific sections
  - Border Style—Used for setting the style of the borders around the report or individual controls

- Layout Properties
  - Width and Height—Used to specify the dimension of the report and its section
  - Orientation—Determines whether the report is printed in portrait or landscape mode
  - Margins—Sets the margins for the report, to control how the content is spaced from the edges of the page

- Data Properties
  - Record Source—A table or query that provides data for the report
  - Filter—Used to apply a filter to restrict the data displayed in the report
  - Sort Order—Defines the order in which data is sorted in the report
  - Group By—Groups data by a specific field or expression

- Event Properties
  - On Open—VBA code to be executed when the report is opened
  - On Close—VBA code to be executed when the report is closed
  - On No Data—VBA code to be executed when there are no records to display in the report
  - On Page—VBA code to be executed when a page is formatted during printing

- Section Properties
  - o Page Header/Footer—Displays content at the top or bottom of every page
  - o Report Header/Footer—Displays content at the beginning or end of the entire report
  - o Group Header/Footer—Displays content at the beginning or end of each group of records
  - o Detail Section—Contains the main body of the report, where the detailed data is displayed

Using Report Events

When an Access report is run, a number of events can occur. The following examples demonstrate how to control what happens not only when the report is opened, activated, deactivated, or closed, but also when there are no records for the report to display or the report record source simply does not exist.

Open

The `Open` event for a report occurs when the report is opened. Use this event to display support forms or custom buttons, or to change the record source for the report. The event procedure in Hands-On 16.1 demonstrates how to change a report's record source on the fly.

NOTE	*All code files and figures for the hands-on projects may be found in the companion files.*

⊙ Hands-On 16.1   Writing the Report_Open Event Procedure

1. Start Access and create a new database named `Chap16.accdb` in your `C:\VBAAccess2024_ByExample` folder.
2. Import all the tables, queries, forms, reports, macros, and modules from the `Northwind.mdb` sample database to your `Chap16.accdb` database.
3. In the Access window's Navigation Pane, select the Customers table and choose Create | Report Wizard. Select all the fields for the report and click Next. Continue clicking Next until you get to the Report Wizard screen, where you can specify the title for your report. Type `rptCustomers` for the title and click Finish. Access opens the report in Print Preview.
4. Right-click the report tab and choose Design view from the context menu.

5. In the Report Header area, click the report title (label control) to select it. Resize the control to allow for longer text that will be entered dynamically by the event procedure in step 7.
6. Make sure the Property Sheet is displayed. You can toggle it on and off using the Property Sheet button on the Ribbon. In the Property Sheet for the selected label control, click the All tab and enter `lblCustomers` as the Name property and `Customers` as the Caption property, overwriting the previous values.
7. In the Property Sheet, select Report from the drop-down box and click the Event tab. Click next to the On Open event property and choose [Event Procedure] from the drop-down box, then click the ellipsis button (…).
8. Access opens the VBE window and writes the stub of the `Report_Open` event procedure. Complete the code of the following `Report_Open` event procedure:

```vba
Private Sub Report_Open(Cancel As Integer)
  Dim strCustName As String
  Dim strSQL As String
  Dim strWHERE As String

  On Error GoTo ErrHandler
  strSQL = "SELECT * FROM Customers"

  strCustName = InputBox("Type the first letter " & _
    " of the Company Name or type an asterisk (*) " & _
    " to view all companies.", "Show All /Or Filter")

  If strCustName = "" Then
    Cancel = True
  ElseIf strCustName = "*" Then
    Me.RecordSource = strSQL
    Me.lblCustomers.Caption = "All Customers"
  Else
    strCustName = "'" & Trim(strCustName) & "*'"
    strWHERE = " WHERE CompanyName Like " _
     & strCustName & ""
    Debug.Print strSQL
    Debug.Print strWHERE
    Me.RecordSource = strSQL & strWHERE
    Me.lblCustomers.Caption = "Selected Customers" & _
      " (" & UCase(strCustName) & ")"
  End If
```

```
  Exit Sub
ErrHandler:
  MsgBox Err.Description
End Sub
```

9. Use the Project Explorer's middle button to switch to the report's design view.
10. Choose Home | View | Print Preview. A message box will appear where you can enter an asterisk (*) to view all customers, or the first letter of a company name if you'd like to limit your records. To cancel the report, click Cancel or press the Esc key.
11. Close the report and try to preview it with another filter.

Close

The `Close` event occurs when you close the report. Use this event to close supporting forms or to perform other cleanup operations. You cannot cancel the `Close` event. Figure 16.14 shows the `Report_Close` event procedure for the `Sales by Year` report. To run this report, double-click the Sales by Year report name in the Navigation Pane. In the Sales by Year dialog form that opens, specify the report beginning and ending dates and click OK. Access will run the report and hide the form. The Sales by Year dialog form remains open while the report is open and is closed during the `Report_Close` event.

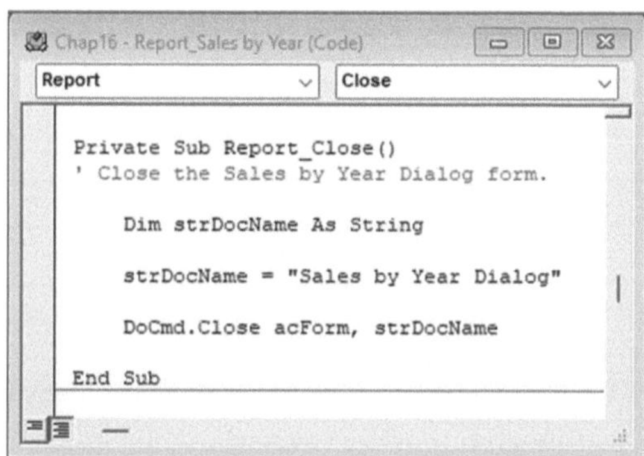

FIGURE 16.14.   The Report_Close event procedure is often used to close supporting forms.

Activate

The `Activate` event occurs when the report is opened right after the `Open` event but before the event for the first section of the report. The procedure in Hands-On 16.2 displays a message when the report is open in Print Preview and returns the name of the default printer to the Immediate window.

(◉) Hands-On 16.2   Writing the Report_Activate Event Procedure

This hands-on exercise uses the `rptCustomers` report created in Hands-On 16.1.

1. In VBE's Project Explorer window, double-click the rptCustomers report. In the Code window, below the previous procedure code, enter the following `Report_Activate` event procedure:

```
Private Sub Report_Activate()
  If Me.CurrentView = acCurViewPreview Then
    MsgBox "Activating Print Preview of " _
     & Me.Name & " report."
    Debug.Print "Default Printer: " & _
     Application.Printer.DeviceName
  End If
End Sub
```

Notice how the `CurrentView` property is used to determine the current view of an object. Table 16.1 lists the `CurrentView` property constants.

TABLE 16.1.   CurrentView property constants.

CurrentView Property Name	Value	Description
acCurViewDesign	0	The object is in design view.
acCurViewFormBrowse	1	The object is in form view.
acCurViewDatasheet	2	The object is in datasheet view.
acCurViewPivotTable	3	The object is in PivotTable view.
acCurViewPivotChart	4	The object is in PivotChart view.
acCurViewPreview	5	The object is in Print Preview.
acCurViewReportBrowse	6	The object is in report view.
acCurViewLayout	7	The object is in layout view.

2. In the Navigation Pane of the Access window, right-click the rptCustomers report and choose Print Preview. Enter your report criteria when prompted. Upon activation of the report, the `Report_Activate` event will fire with a message. Click OK to the message, and then switch to the Immediate window to check out the name of your default printer.

3. Close the `rptCustomers` report and save the changes to the report when prompted.

Deactivate

The `Deactivate` event occurs when a report loses focus to a table, query, form, report, macro, module, or database window. This event occurs before the `Close` event for the report.

NoData

The `NoData` event occurs when the record source for the report contains no records. This event allows you to cancel the report when no records are available. The event procedure in Hands-On 16.3 displays a message when the user enters criteria that are not met.

Hands-On 16.3   Writing the Report_NoData Event Procedure

This hands-on exercise uses the `rptCustomers` report created in Hands-On 16.1.

1. In VBE's Project Explorer window, double-click the Report_rptCustomers report. In the Code window, enter the following `Report_NoData` event procedure:

```
Private Sub Report_NoData(Cancel As Integer)
  MsgBox "There is no data for the criteria " & _
    "you entered."
  Cancel = True
End Sub
```

2. Switch to the Access window and open the `rptCustomers` report. Request to see customers with a company name starting with the letter x. Because there aren't any company names beginning with x, a message box will be displayed, saying that there is no data for the criteria entered, and the report will be canceled.

Page

The `Page` event occurs after a page is formatted but before it is printed. Use the `Page` event to customize the appearance of your printed reports by adding lines, circles, and graphics. The event procedure in Hands-On 16.4 will draw a red border around the report pages.

◉ Hands-On 16.4 Drawing a Page Border Using the Report_Page Event Procedure

This hands-on exercise uses the `rptCustomers` report created in Hands-On 16.1.

1. In VBE's Project Explorer window, double-click the rptCustomers report. In the Code window, enter the following `Report_Page` event procedure:

```
Private Sub Report_Page()
  Me.DrawWidth = 15 ' pixels
  Me.Line (0, 0)-(Me.ScaleWidth, Me.ScaleHeight), vbRed, B
End Sub
```

Notice that the `DrawWidth` method specifies the thickness of the line and the `Line` method draws a line with the upper-left corner at `(0, 0)` and the lower-right corner at `(Me.ScaleWidth, Me.ScaleHeight)`. The `ScaleWidth` and `ScaleHeight` properties specify the width and height of the report.

2. Switch to the Access window and open the `rptCustomers` report in Print Preview with valid filter criteria. Notice that when the report appears on the screen, a red border surrounds the pages (see Figure 16.15).

3. Close the `rptCustomers` report and save changes when prompted.

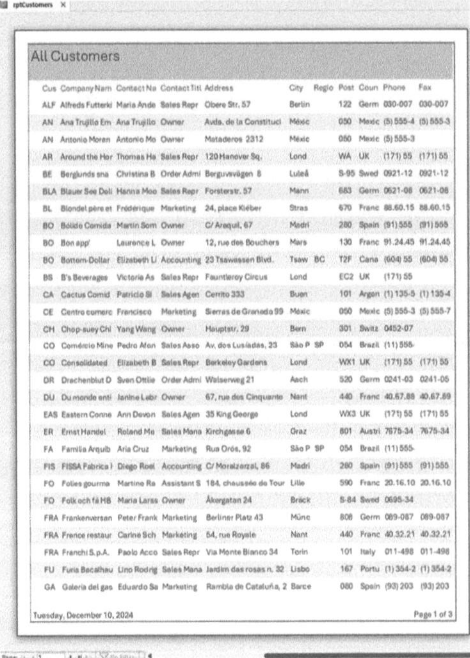

FIGURE 16.15. You can frame your Access report pages with a red line by implementing the Report_Page event procedure shown in Hands-On 16.4.

Error

The `Error` event is triggered by errors in accessing the data for the report. Use this event to replace the default error message with your custom message. The `Error` event takes the following two arguments:

- `DataErr`—Contains the number of the Microsoft Access error that occurred.

- `Response`—Determines whether error messages should be displayed. It may be one of the following constants:

  - `acDataErrContinue`—Ignore the error and continue without displaying the default Microsoft Access error message.
  - `acDataErrDisplay`—Display the default Microsoft Access error message. This is the default.

The `Report_Error` event procedure in Hands-On 16.5 illustrates how to use the value of the `DataErr` argument together with the `AccessError` method to determine the error number and its descriptive string.

The statement:

```
Response = acDataErrContinue
```

will prevent the standard Microsoft Access error message from appearing. The `Error` event for reports works the same as the `Error` event for forms—but only Microsoft Access ACE or Jet engine errors can be trapped here.

To trap errors in your VBA code, use the `On Error GoTo` statement to direct the procedure flow to the location of the error-handling statements in your procedure.

(◉) Hands-On 16.5   Writing the Report_Error Event Procedure

This hands-on exercise uses the `rptCustomers` report created in Hands-On 16.1.

1. In the Navigation Pane, rename the `Customers` table to `Customers2`.
2. In VBE's Project Explorer window, double-click the rptCustomers report. In the Code window, enter the following `Report_Error` event procedure:

```
Private Sub Report_Error(DataErr As Integer, _
  Response As Integer)
   ' obtain information about the error
  MsgBox Application.AccessError(DataErr), _
    vbOKOnly, "Error Number: " & DataErr
  If DataErr = 3070 Then
```

```
      Response = acDataErrContinue
      MsgBox "Your custom error message goes here."
   End If
End Sub
```

3. Switch to the Access window and open the `rptCustomers` report. When the input box appears prompting you for the criteria, type any letter and press OK. At this point, the `Report_Error` event will fire because the underlying data for the `rptCustomers` report does not exist. Because you renamed the `Customers` table that this report uses for its data source, Microsoft Access cannot locate the data and generates the error.

4. In the Navigation Pane, change the `Customers2` table's name back to `Customers` and open the `rptCustomers` report to ensure that it does not produce unexpected errors.

5. Close the report when finished and save the changes when prompted.

Events Recognized by Report Sections

An Access report can contain various sections, such as the report header/footer, the page header/footer, the Detail section, and group headers/footers. All report sections can respond to the `Format` and `Print` events. These events occur when you print or preview a report. In addition, the report header/footer and the Detail section recognize the `Retreat` event that occurs when Access returns to a previous section during report formatting.

Format (Report Section Event)

A `Format` event occurs for each section in a report before Access formats the section for previewing or printing. This event takes the following two arguments:

- `Cancel`—Determines whether the formatting of the section occurs. To cancel the section formatting, set this argument to `True`.

- `FormatCount`—Is an integer that specifies whether the `Format` event has occurred more than once for a section. If a section does not fit on one page and the rest of the section needs to be moved to the next page of the report, the `FormatCount` argument is set to `2`.

Use the `Format` event in the appropriate report section for changes that affect the page layout, as described in Table 16.2. For changes that don't affect page layout, use the `Print` event for the report section.

TABLE 16.2.   Effect of the Format event on report sections.

Report Sections	Description of Event
Detail	The Format event occurs for each record in the section just before Access formats the data in the record. You can access the data in the current record using the event procedure.
Group Headers	The Format event occurs for each new group. You can access the data in the group header and the data in the first record in the Detail section using the event procedure.
Group Footers	The Format event occurs for each new group. You can access the data in the group footer and the data in the last record in the Detail section via an event procedure.

The event procedure in Hands-On 16.6 demonstrates how to make reports easier to read by shading alternate rows.

Hands-On 16.6   Shading Alternate Rows Using the Detail_Format Event Procedure

This hands-on exercise uses the `rptCustomers` report created in Hands-On 16.1.

1. In VBE's Project Explorer window, double-click the rptCustomers report. In the Code window, enter the following `Detail_Format` event procedure. Do not type the `Option Compare Database` and `Option Explicit` statements if they are already present at the top of the Code window.

```
Option Compare Database
Option Explicit


Dim shaded As Boolean

Private Sub Detail_Format(Cancel As Integer, _
  FormatCount As Integer)
    If shaded Then
      Me.Detail.BackColor = vbYellow
    Else
      Me.Detail.BackColor = vbWhite
    End If
    shaded = Not shaded
End Sub
```

Notice that at the top of the module sheet (in the module's Declarations area), we have placed the following declaration statement:

```
Dim shaded As Boolean
```

This statement declares a global variable of the `Boolean` type to keep track of the alternate rows. When you run the report, upon printing the Detail section, Access will check the value of the `shaded` variable. If the value is `True`, it will change the background of the formatted row to yellow (which produces a light gray background when printed on a noncolor printer). The `shaded` value will then be set to `False` for the next row by using the following statement:

```
shaded = Not shaded
```

This statement works as a toggle. If `shaded` was `True`, it will be `False` now, and vice versa.

2. Modify the `Report_Open` event procedure as follows:
   a. Add the following statement just below the other variable declarations that are already present inside this procedure:

   ```
   Dim ctrl As TextBox
   ```

   b. Enter the following code before the `Exit Sub` statement:

   ```
   For Each ctrl In Me.Detail.Controls
       If ctrl.BackStyle = 1 Then ctrl.BackStyle = 0
   Next
   ```

   The `For Each` loop will iterate through the controls in the Detail section of the `rptCustomers` report and set the Back Style property of each text box control to 0 (Transparent).

3. Switch to the Access window and open the `rptCustomers` report in Print Preview. When the input box prompts you for the criteria, type an asterisk (*) and press OK. Click OK to the message. You should see the same data as shown in Figure 16.15 with alternate shading now in yellow.

<table>
<tr><td>
NOTE</td><td>In Access 2007–2024, you can shade alternate rows by setting the `AlternateBackColor` property for the Detail section instead of writing VBA code for the `Format` event of the Detail section.</td></tr>
</table>

4. Close the `rptCustomers` report, saving the changes when prompted.

The next hands-on exercise demonstrates how to suppress the page footer on the first page of your report by placing code in the `PageFooterSection_Format` event procedure.

⊚ Hands-On 16.7 Suppressing the Page Footer Using the PageFooterSection_Format Event Procedure

1. Using the Report Wizard, create a report called `rptProducts` based on the `Products` table. Choose the following fields for this report: `ProductID`, `ProductName`, `UnitPrice`, and `UnitsInStock`. Continue to click Next until you get the last page of the wizard asking you for the report title. Enter `rptProducts` for the new title name and select the Modify the report's design option button, then click Finish.

2. In the design view of the `rptProducts` report, select PageFooterSection from the drop-down list in the Property Sheet. Click the Event tab. Click next to the On Format property and select [Event Procedure] from the drop-down list. Click the ellipsis button (…) to activate the Code window.

3. In the Code window for `rptProducts`, enter the following `PageFooter-Section_Format` event procedure:

```
Private Sub PageFooterSection_Format(Cancel As Integer, _
  FormatCount As Integer)
    Dim ctrl As Control

    For Each ctrl In Me.PageFooterSection.Controls
      If Me.Page = 1 Then
        ctrl.Visible = False
      Else
        ctrl.Visible = True
      End If
    Next ctrl
End Sub
```

4. Switch to the Access window and open the `rptProducts` report in Print Preview. Notice that the footer section does not appear on the first page of the report. Use the page selector at the bottom of the Print Preview window to move between the pages of the report.

5. Close the `rptProducts` report and save the changes to the report when prompted.

Print (Report Section Event)

The `Print` event occurs after the data in a report section has been formatted but before the data is printed. The `Print` event occurs only for sections that are actually printed, as described in Table 16.3. To access data from sections that are not printed, use the `Format` event.

You can use the `PrintCount` argument to check whether the `Print` event has occurred more than once for a record. If part of a record is printed on one page and the rest is printed on the next page, the `Print` event will occur twice, and the `PrintCount` argument will be set to `2`. You can use the `Cancel` argument to cancel the printing of a section.

TABLE 16.3. Effect of the Print event on report sections.

Report Section	Description of Event
Detail	The Print event occurs for each record in the Detail section just before Access prints the data in the record.
Group Headers	The Print event occurs for each new group.
Group Footers	The Print event occurs for each new group.

The event procedure in Hands-On 16.8 demonstrates how to print a record range indicator in the report's footer. This indicator will display the range of records printed on each page. You can easily modify this example procedure to print the first and last customer IDs on the page (see the discussion that follows this hands-on exercise).

(◉) Hands-On 16.8   Displaying a Record Range in the Report's Footer Using the Detail_Print Event Procedure

This hands-on exercise uses the `rptCustomers` report you created in Hands-On 16.1.

1. Open the `rptCustomers` report in design view and place two unbound text boxes in the report's page footer section. You may need to make other controls in the footer area smaller to make more room.
2. Change the Name property of the first box to `txtPage` and set its Visible property to No. Delete the label control in front of this text box.
3. Name the second text box `txtRange` and set the Caption property of its label control to `Records:`.
4. In the Property Sheet for the `txtRange` text box and `Records` label, set the Display When property to Print Only (see the note at the end of this exercise).
5. In the Property Sheet, select Detail from the drop-down box and click the Event tab. Set the On Print property of the Detail section to [Event Procedure] and click the ellipsis (…) to activate the code window with the event stub.
6. Write the code for the `Detail_Print` event, as shown here:

```
Private Sub Detail_Print(Cancel As Integer, _
  PrintCount As Integer)
    Static rCount As Integer
```

```
Static start As Integer
Static firstID As String
Static lastID As String

If Me.Page <> Me.txtPage Then
   start = Me.CurrentRecord
   firstID = CustomerID
   Me.txtPage = Me.Page
   rCount = 0
End If
   rCount = rCount + 1
   lastID = CustomerID
If start <= rCount Then
   Me.txtRange = start & "-" & rCount
   ' Me.txtRange = UCase(firstID) & _
      "-" & UCase(lastID)
Else
   rCount = Me.CurrentRecord
   lastID = CustomerID
End If
End Sub
```

The `Detail_Print` event procedure is triggered for each record. It uses the `start` and `rCount` variables to keep track of the first and last items on the page.

7. In the Code window, enter the `PageHeaderSection_Print` event procedure, as shown here:

```
Private Sub PageHeaderSection_Print(Cancel As Integer, _
 PrintCount As Integer)
  Me.txtPage = 0
End Sub
```

8. To test the event procedures, switch to the Access window and open the `rptCustomers` report in Print Preview, displaying all customers.
   Notice the record range indicator at the bottom of the report page (Figure 16.16).

9. Close the `rptCustomers` report and save the changes when prompted.
   The `PageHeaderSection_Print` event procedure will set the value of the unbound `txtPage` text box to zero (0) whenever the `Print` event occurs for a new page.

rptCustomers ×

FA	Família Arquib	Aria Cruz	Marketing	Rua Orós, 92	São P	SP	054	Brazil	(11) 555-
FIS	FISSA Fabrica I	Diego Roel	Accounting	C/ Moralzarzal, 86	Madri		280	Spain	(91) 555 (91) 555
FO	Folies gourma	Martine Ra	Assistant S	184, chaussée de Tour	Lille		590	Franc	20.16.10 20.16.10
FO	Folk och fä HB	Maria Larss	Owner	Åkergatan 24	Bräck		S-84	Swed	0695-34
FRA	Frankenversan	Peter Frank	Marketing	Berliner Platz 43	Münc		808	Germ	089-087 089-087
FRA	France restaur	Carine Sch	Marketing	54, rue Royale	Nant		440	Franc	40.32.21 40.32.21
FRA	Franchi S.p.A.	Paolo Acco	Sales Repr	Via Monte Bianco 34	Torin		101	Italy	011-498 011-498
FU	Furia Bacalhau	Lino Rodrig	Sales Mana	Jardim das rosas n. 32	Lisbo		167	Portu	(1) 354-2 (1) 354-2
GA	Galeria del gas	Eduardo Sa	Marketing	Rambla de Cataluña, 2	Barce		080	Spain	(93) 203 (93) 203

Wednesday, December 11, 2024   Records: 1-29   Page 1 of 3

FIGURE 16.16.   This report displays the record range indicator at the bottom of the page (see Hands-On 16.8).

You can modify the event procedure in Hands-On 16.8 to print the first and last customer IDs on the page, as shown in Figure 16.17. Simply replace the following statement in the `Detail_Print` event procedure:

```
Me.txtRange = start & "-" & rCount
```

with the following line of code:

```
Me.txtRange = UCase(firstID) & "-" & UCase(lastID)
```

rptCustomers ×

FA	Família Arquib	Aria Cruz	Marketing	Rua Orós, 92	São P	SP	054	Brazil	(11) 555-
FIS	FISSA Fabrica I	Diego Roel	Accounting	C/ Moralzarzal, 86	Madri		280	Spain	(91) 555 (91) 555
FO	Folies gourma	Martine Ra	Assistant S	184, chaussée de Tour	Lille		590	Franc	20.16.10 20.16.10
FO	Folk och fä HB	Maria Larss	Owner	Åkergatan 24	Bräck		S-84	Swed	0695-34
FRA	Frankenversan	Peter Frank	Marketing	Berliner Platz 43	Münc		808	Germ	089-087 089-087
FRA	France restaur	Carine Sch	Marketing	54, rue Royale	Nant		440	Franc	40.32.21 40.32.21
FRA	Franchi S.p.A.	Paolo Acco	Sales Repr	Via Monte Bianco 34	Torin		101	Italy	011-498 011-498
FU	Furia Bacalhau	Lino Rodrig	Sales Mana	Jardim das rosas n. 32	Lisbo		167	Portu	(1) 354-2 (1) 354-2
GA	Galería del gas	Eduardo Sa	Marketing	Rambla de Cataluña, 2	Barce		080	Spain	(93) 203 (93) 203

Wednesday, December 11, 2024   Records: ALFKI-GA   Page 1 of 3

FIGURE 16.17.   This report displays the first and last customer IDs for a specific page at the bottom of each printed page.

NOTE	*When you open the* `rptCustomers` *report in report view instead of in Print Preview, you will notice that there is no calculated value in the Records text box at the bottom of the page. The reason for this is that in report view, there aren't any pages. The entire report is one big continuous page. Since there aren't any pages, Access cannot calculate any values that depend on the* `Page` *or* `Pages` *property. Also, it's important to remember that the* `Print` *event for report sections does not fire in report view. You can tell Access to display certain controls only in Print Preview by changing the Display When property of the control to Print Only in the Property Sheet.*

Retreat (Report Section Event)

The `Retreat` event occurs when Access returns to previous sections of the report during report formatting. For example, after formatting a report section, if Access discovers that the data will not fit on the page, it will go back to the necessary location in the report to ensure that the section can properly begin on the next page.

The `Retreat` event occurs after the `Format` event but before the `Print` event. This event applies to all report sections except page headers and footers. The `Retreat` event occurs for group headers and footers whose `KeepTogether` property has been set to `Whole Group` or `With First Detail`. This event is also triggered in subreports whose `CanGrow` or `CanShrink` property has been set to `True`.

The `Retreat` event makes it possible to undo any changes made during the `Format` event for the section. The `Retreat` event is demonstrated in the sample `Northwind.mdb` database's `Sales by Year` report that you imported earlier to the `Chap16.accdb` database. Figure 16.18 shows the `GroupFooter1_Retreat` event procedure.

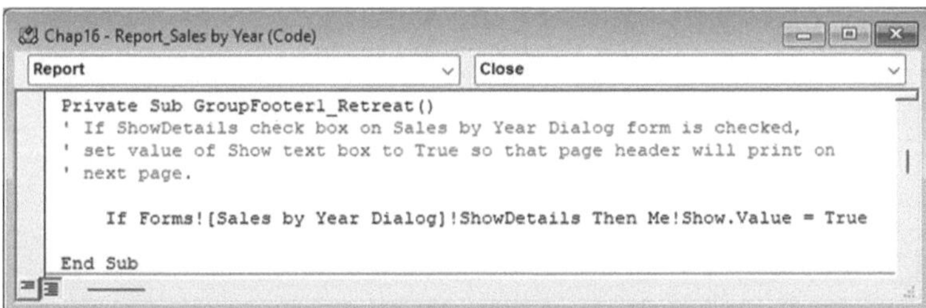

FIGURE 16.18.   The Sales by Year report in the Northwind.mdb database uses the GroupFooter1_ Retreat event procedure to control the printing of a page header.

USING THE REPORT VIEW

Reports have an interactive view called report view, as shown in Figure 16.19. This is the default view for all new reports created in Access 2007–2024. In this view, you can easily copy data by selecting it and then clicking the Copy button in the Clipboard group of the Home tab or pressing Ctrl+C.

If you need to find particular data in the report, use the Find button in the Find group of the Home tab or press Ctrl+F. Access will pop up the standard Find dialog box in which you can enter your search criteria.

Filtering and sorting are also enabled for report view via the buttons located in the Sort & Filter section of the Home tab.

A report open in report view isn't divided into pages; it is a single big page. If you have any calculations that depend on the `Page` or `Pages` property of the report, they may not return the correct results.

Certain report events, such as `Print` and `Format`, will not be triggered when the report is displayed in report view. The report view has its own event called `Paint` that is used with sections in report view. This event fires whenever a section needs to be drawn on the screen. Use this event to conditionally format controls in that view, as shown in Hands-On 16.9.

<table>
<tr><td>______

NOTE</td><td>*The* `Paint` *event fires multiple times for each section of the report because Access paints various elements of the given section separately at different times. The calculated controls and the items that require a change in background or foreground colors are each painted separately.*</td></tr>
</table>

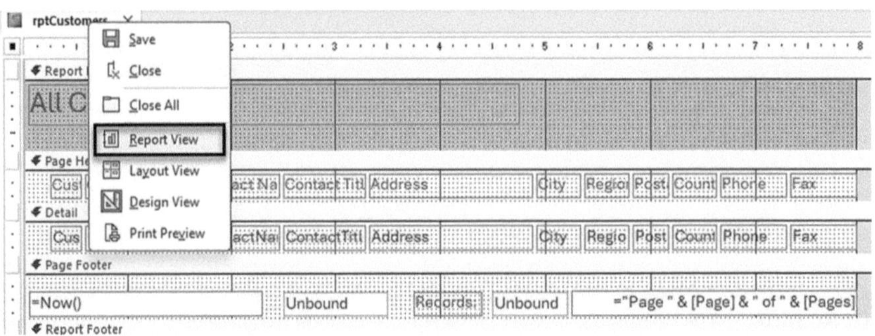

FIGURE 16.19. Access reports can be displayed using four different views: Report View, Layout View, Design View, and Print Preview. The layout view may not be available for some reports.

Hands-On 16.9   Conditionally Formatting a Control in Report View

1. In the Navigation Pane, right-click the `rptCustomers` report created earlier and choose Design View.
2. Click the Detail section and activate the Property Sheet.
3. In the Property Sheet of the Detail section, click the Event tab, select Event Procedure from the drop-down box next to the On Paint property, then click the ellipsis button (…).

Access activates the Code window and writes the stub of the `Detail_Paint` event procedure.

4. Complete the code of the `Detail_Paint` procedure, as shown here:

```
Private Sub Detail_Paint()
  If Me.City.Value = "London" Then
    Me.City.ForeColor = vbBlue
  Else
    Me.City.ForeColor = vbBlack
  End If
End Sub
```

This event procedure will set the `ForeColor` property for a control called `City` to blue when the city name is `London` and display the names of all other cities in black. This procedure will be triggered when you open the report in report or layout view.

5. Press Ctrl+S to save the changes in the Code window.
6. Press Ctrl+F11 to return to the main Access window.
7. Click the View button in the Views group of the Report Design tab.
8. Enter * (asterisk) to view all customers. Press Ctrl+F to activate the Find dialog box. Enter `London` (change the Look In field to Current document) and click Find Next. Access locates the first customer who lives in London. Click Find Next again to locate the next customer. Notice that all the occurrences of London are shown in blue.
9. Close the `rptCustomers` report and save the changes if prompted.

SORTING AND GROUPING DATA

Access offers users a convenient interface for grouping data, adding totals, and filtering. These features are available from a separate Group, Sort, and Total pane, as shown in Figure 16.20. To work with this pane, open the report in layout view, click the Report Layout Design tab, and select the Group & Sort button in the Grouping & Totals section. When you click on the Add a Group or Add a Sort button in the pane at the bottom of the report, Access will walk you through the steps required to create new report groups, add totals, or sort (Figure 16.21).

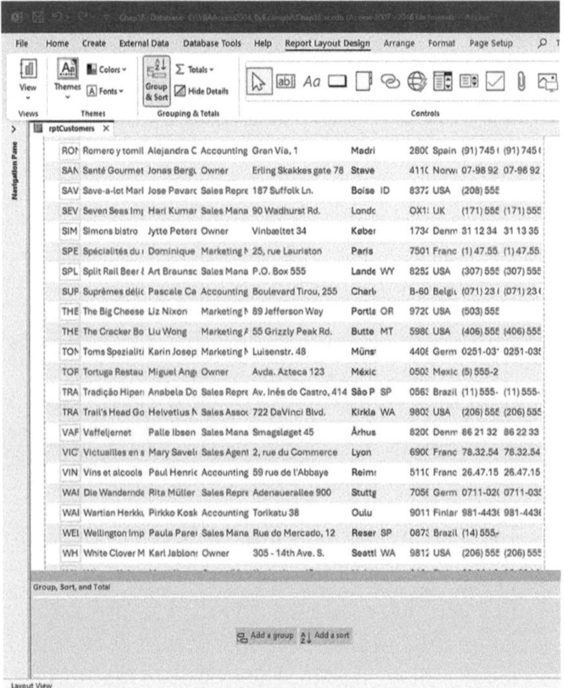

FIGURE 16.20. The Group, Sort, and Total pane provides a quick way to group and sort data and add calculations in Access reports.

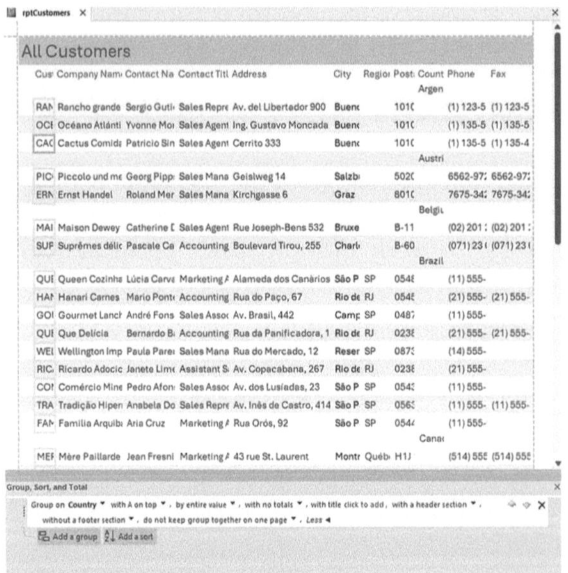

FIGURE 16.21. The Group, Sort, and Total pane indicates that the report is grouped on Country.

SAVING REPORTS IN .PDF OR .XPS FILE FORMAT

Access reports can be saved to the `.pdf` or `.xps` format, as shown in Figure 16.22. The `.pdf` format preserves document formatting and makes files easy to distribute and print. Reports distributed as `.pdf` files retain their format and are protected so that the data may not be copied or changed. Another format that you can use for your report distribution is the `.xps` format, which also retains the format of the original document.

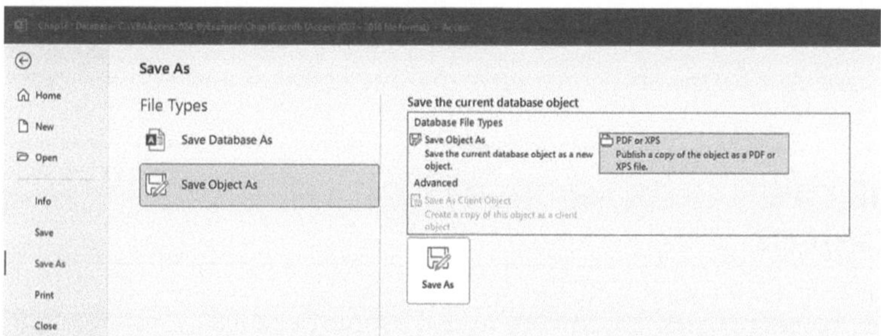

FIGURE 16.22.   To save your report to .pdf or .xps file format, open it in design view and activate report view. With the report displayed on your screen, click File | Save As. Select Save Object As, select PDF or XPS, and click the Save As button. Access will display the Publish As PDF or XPS dialog box, where you can specify the required file format, as well as the filename and destination folder.

REPORT TROUBLESHOOTING

While working with reports and event procedures, an error may suddenly prevent you from opening a report in report view. For example, Microsoft Access could display an error like this:

The Expression OnOpen you entered as the event property setting produced the following error. A problem occurred while Microsoft Access was communicating with the OLE server or ActiveX control.

This error often occurs when there's an issue with the code assigned to the `OnOpen` event of a report or form. While there are many recommendations for how to fix this error, the problem may not be at all related to what Access tells you in the error message. Access does not even allow you to debug your code by stepping through the code. Besides, before you got this error, the report and all the events you wrote for it were triggered without any issues, producing the expected results. You compiled your code multiple times, and no problems were found. If you are not able to proceed and fix the issue causing the error, there may be a deeper issue that prevents the code from executing or even reaching the debug phase. Sometimes, the report or form you created suddenly becomes corrupt. You can try creating a new report and copying the elements and code from the old report to the new one. It, however, is very time-consuming and frustrating to attempt to recreate a custom report that may contain many controls, expressions, and report sections as well as formatting properties. You could try to compact and repair the database and see whether the problem is fixed, but if this does not work for you, your best solution would be to import your report from the backup file. This is an example of why it is so important to keep regular backups of your database, especially when you are working on complex reports or forms and constantly making changes and adjustments.

USING THE OPENARGS PROPERTY OF THE REPORT OBJECT

Like forms, Access reports have a very useful property called `OpenArgs` that you can use from VBA code or a macro to pass a value to a report as the report is opened. Use the `OpenReport` method of the `DoCmd` object in the following form:

```
DoCmd.OpenReport (reportname, view, filtername,
wherecondition, windowmode, OpenArgs)
```

The `OpenArgs` argument is a string expression of the `Variant` data type. You can pass multiple values in the `OpenArgs` argument by concatenating your values.

The `OpenArgs` property can be used to set a report format or to determine what data the report should display. With the `OpenArgs` property, you can reuse the same report, instead of creating a new report for a similar requirement.

Hands-On 16.10 demonstrates how to filter a report with the help of the `OpenArgs` property.

Hands-On 16.10   **Using the OpenArgs Property to Filter an Access Report**

1. Copy the `Northwind 2007_Revised.accdb` database from the companion files to your `C:\VBAAccess 2024_ByExample` folder.
2. Open the database and cancel out of the Login dialog box.
3. In the Navigation Pane on the left, locate and double-click frmEmployeeAddress. You should see the form as shown in Figure 16.23.

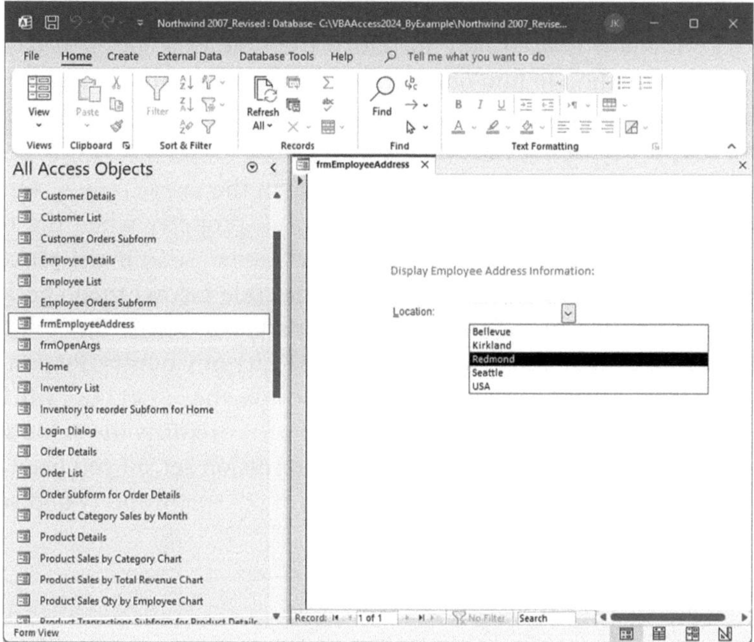

FIGURE 16.23.   The form used to filter the Employee Address Book report by City or Country/Region.

4. Choose Redmond from the combo box.

Access executes the following code in the `cboReports_AfterUpdate` event procedure:

```
Private Sub cboReports_AfterUpdate()
    Dim strFilterBy As Variant
    Dim strRpt As String

    strRpt = "Employee Address Book"

    If SysCmd(acSysCmdGetObjectState, acReport, _
        strRpt) <> 0 Then
        DoCmd.Close acReport, strRpt
    End If

    strFilterBy = Me.cboReports.Value
    DoCmd.OpenReport ReportName:=strRpt, _
        View:=acViewReport, _
        OpenArgs:=strFilterBy

End Sub
```

This event procedure closes the `Employee Address Book` report if it is open. The `SysCmd` method is used here to return the state of a specified database object. Use this method to find out whether the object is open, is a new object, or has been changed but not saved. For more information on using this method in your VBA procedures, see the online help.

Next, the procedure stores the selected value in the `strFilterBy` variable. This variable is then referenced in the `OpenArgs` property when the report is opened with the `OpenReport` method. The `Report_Load` event procedure of the `Report_Employee` address book (see the code below) then checks the `OpenArgs` property for the `Null` value. If the property is not `Null`, the `strFilter` variable is set to contain filtering criteria for the City or Country/Region field. If you selected Redmond from the form's combo box, the `strFilter` will be set to `City = 'Redmond'`. The statement `Me.OpenArgs` returns the value stored in the `OpenArgs` property. With the filtering expression set, all you need to do is tell Access to turn the filter on by using the `FilterOn` property and set the `Filter` property to the `strFilter` variable.

```vba
Private Sub Report_Load()
  Dim strFilter As String

  If IsNull(Me.OpenArgs) Then
     Exit Sub
  Else
     If Me.OpenArgs = "USA" Then
        strFilter = "[Country/Region] = '" & _
                    Me.OpenArgs & "'"
     Else
        strFilter = "City = '" & Me.OpenArgs & "'"
     End If
     Me.FilterOn = True
     Me.Filter = strFilter

  End If
End Sub
```

After the procedure finishes executing its code, you should see the `Employee Address Book` filtered by Redmond or whatever item you specified in the form's combo box (Figure 16.24).

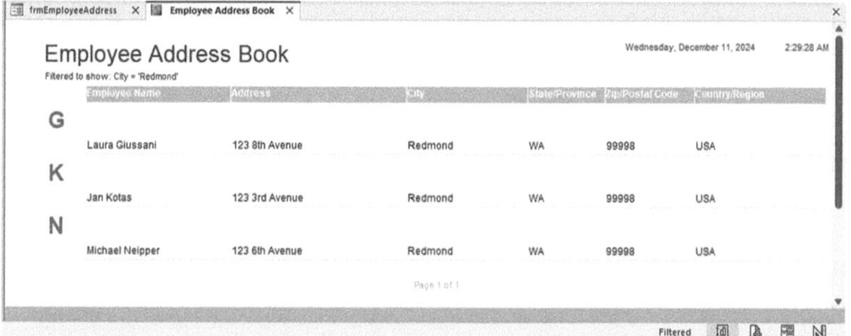

FIGURE 16.24.   This report was filtered by using the value passed in the OpenArgs property.

5. To filter the report again, make another selection from the form's combo box.

RUNNING BUILT-IN MENU COMMANDS FROM VBA

Access has a special `RunCommand` method that allows you to run various built-in menu commands from VBA. This method requires that you pass to it an `acCommand` constant. Let's look at some of the commands related to reports that you can try out right from the Immediate window.

Enter in the Immediate Window	Description
RunCommand acCmdNewObjectReport	Access displays the Report Wizard dialog box and shows the fields in the Products table that are available for your report. Notice that this command is equivalent to clicking the Report Wizard button in the Reports group of the Ribbon's Create tab.
RunCommand acCmdNewObjectDesignReport	Access displays a blank report design view. This is the same as clicking the Report Design button in the Reports group of the Ribbon's Create tab.
RunCommand acCmdNewObjectBlankReport	Access displays a blank report in layout view. This is the same as clicking the Blank Report button in the Reports group of the Ribbon's Create tab.
RunCommand acCmdNewObjectAutoReport (Make sure that some table or select query is highlighted in the Navigation Pane of the Access Application window before trying out this command.)	Access creates a report based on the fields in the selected table or query. This is the same as clicking the Report button in the Reports group of the Ribbon's Create tab.
RunCommand acCmdNewObjectLabelsReport	Access invokes the Labels report.

Below is an example VBA procedure that creates a new report based on the table passed to it.

```vba
Sub Create_NewReport(strTable As String)
  With DoCmd
    .SelectObject acTable, strTable, True
    .RunCommand acCmdNewObjectAutoReport
  End With
End Sub
```

We start this procedure by using the `SelectObject` method of the `DoCmd` object to select the specified table in the Database window. After that, we execute the `RunCommand` method, which creates a report. All table fields are used in the report layout. To call this procedure, create another report like this:

```vba
Sub ExecuteCmd()
    Create_NewReport "Shippers"
End Sub
```

> ### Looking Up Access Objects' Constants Using the Object Browser
>
> Now that you know how to execute Access' built-in Ribbon commands for reports, you can try running similar commands for forms and other Access objects. To find out the list of constants that need to be passed to the `RunCommand` method, use the Object Browser on the VBE screen (press F2, or choose View | Object Browser). In the Object Browser's Find box, enter `acCommand` and click Search. You should now see the list of members in the `acCommand` class, that is, the constants that can be used with the `RunCommand` method. Selecting any of the constants and pressing the F1 key will open the Microsoft online documentation.

CREATING A REPORT WITH VBA

As mentioned at the beginning of this chapter, you can create an Access report programmatically by using the `CreateReport` method of the `Application` object. This method creates an empty report with a page header, page footer, and a Detail section. The report is assigned a default name, `Report1`. To add controls to the report, use the `CreateControlReport` method of the `Application` object. Because an empty report is not attached to any database table or query, when creating a report programmatically, you need to specify an existing data source for the report records or create a new data source. In the following project, you will create a custom report that displays data based on the parameter crosstab query. Crosstab queries are a powerful tool for data analysis. In this project, you will create a crosstab query first in the query design view and then by writing a VBA function. Next, you will write another VBA function that creates a report and populates it with the controls to display relevant data. In this function, you will also write VBA code to create the report's event procedures. The report function will call the query function. Let's get started.

Custom Project 16.1   Programming a Query and a Report from Scratch

Part I: Creating a Crosstab Query in Query Design View

Crosstab queries calculate sums, averages, counts, and other types of aggregate totals on records and are often used for reporting purposes. A crosstab query groups the data down the left side of the datasheet and across the top. This format makes the data easier to read, analyze, and compare.

When creating a crosstab query, you can only have one column heading and one value heading to perform calculations on. You can have multiple row headings. Access' built-in Crosstab Query Wizard can be helpful in creating simple crosstab queries. If, however, you need to use more than one table or query in the crosstab query, you will first need to create a separate query with the table you want to use.

In this part, you will create a crosstab query based on three tables: `Products`, `Orders`, and `Order Details`. The data will be grouped by `Product Name` (row heading) and will display sales for each quarter of the year passed as a parameter to this query. Figure 16.25 shows the design view of the query. Figure 16.26 displays the result after running this query.

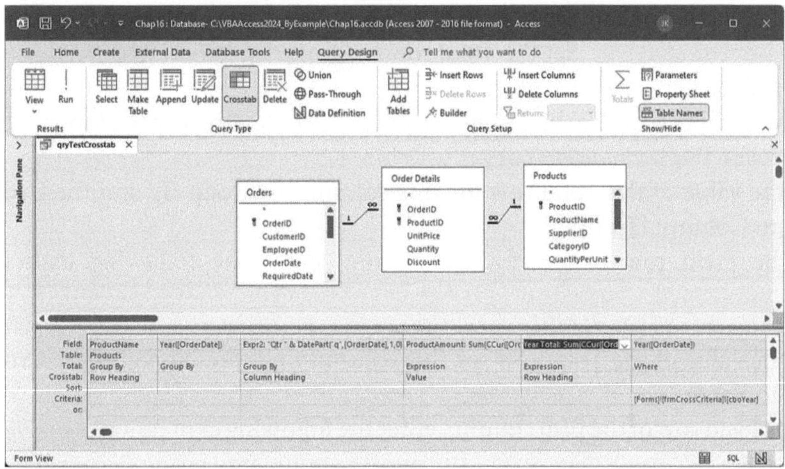

FIGURE 16.25.   Crosstab query design view.

Product Name	Year Total	Qtr 1	Qtr 2	Qtr 3	Qtr 4
Alice Mutton	$17,604.60	$2,667.60	$4,013.10	$4,836.00	$6,087.90
Aniseed Syrup	$1,724.00	$544.00	$600.00	$140.00	$440.00
Boston Crab Meat	$9,814.73	$1,768.41	$1,978.00	$4,412.32	$1,656.00
Camembert Pierrot	$20,505.40	$3,182.40	$4,683.50	$9,579.50	$3,060.00
Carnarvon Tigers	$15,950.00	$1,500.00	$2,362.50	$7,100.00	$4,987.50
Chai	$4,887.00	$705.60	$878.40	$1,174.50	$2,128.50
Chang	$7,038.55	$2,435.80	$228.00	$2,061.50	$2,313.25
Chartreuse verte	$4,475.70	$590.40	$360.00	$1,100.70	$2,424.60
Chef Anton's Cajun Seasoning	$5,214.88	$225.28	$2,970.00	$1,337.60	$682.00
Chef Anton's Gumbo Mix	$373.62			$288.22	$85.40
Chocolade	$1,282.01	$744.60	$162.56	$68.85	$306.00
Côte de Blaye	$49,198.08	$25,127.36	$12,806.10	$7,312.12	$3,952.50
Escargots de Bourgogne	$2,076.28		$265.00	$1,393.90	$417.38
Filo Mix	$2,124.15	$187.60	$742.00	$289.80	$904.75
Fløtemysost	$8,438.74	$2,906.80	$174.15	$2,541.29	$2,816.50

Record: 1 of 77   No Filter   Search

FIGURE 16.26.   Crosstab query in datasheet view.

1. In the main Access database window, choose Create | Query Design.
   At this point, you are in the empty window of the select query (notice the Select button is highlighted on the Query Design tab on the Ribbon).

2. From the list of tables in the Add Tables pane, select Products, Orders, and Order Details, and then click Add Selected Tables.

3. Close the Add Tables side pane.

4. Click the Crosstab button on the Ribbon to switch the Query type to Crosstab query.

5. Drag the ProductName from the Products table to the first column in the Query Design grid.

6. In the Crosstab row, click and select Row Heading from the dropdown.

7. In the Field row of the second column, enter the following expression: `Year([OrderDate])`. Set the Total row to Group by. When Access adds `Expr1` to the field name, leave it as is.

8. In the Field row of the third column, enter the following expression: `"Qtr " & DatePart("q",[OrderDate],1,0)`.

9. Set the value of the Total row for this column to Group By and the Crosstab row to Column Heading.

10. In the Field row of the fourth column, enter the following expression: `ProductAmount: Sum(CCur([Order Details].UnitPrice*[Quantity]*(1-[Discount])/100)*100)`.

11. Set the value of the Total row for this column to Expression and the Crosstab row to Value.

12. In the Field row of the fifth column, enter the following expression: `Year Total: Sum(CCur([Order  Details].[UnitPrice]*[Quantity]*(1-[Discount])/100)*100)`.

13. Set the value of the Total row for this column to Expression and the Crosstab row to Row Heading.

14. In the Field row of the sixth column, enter the following expression: `Year([OrderDate])`.

15. Set the value of the Total row for this column to Where, and in the Criteria row, enter the following expression:

```
[Forms]![frmCrossCriteria]![cboYear]
```

This expression will filter the data by year passed from the combo box control on a form that will be created further in this project.

To prompt the user for the year when the query is running, we will add a parameter to the query. To use parameters in a crosstab query, you must define them in the Query Parameters dialog box. When your query has parameters, you can easily get different sets of data without having to change the structure of your query for different criteria.

16. In the Show/Hide group of the Ribbon's Query Design tab, click the Parameters button.

17. Enter the parameter as shown in Figure 16.27. Notice that the parameter value is the same as the expression in the Where clause of the last column in the Query Design grid.

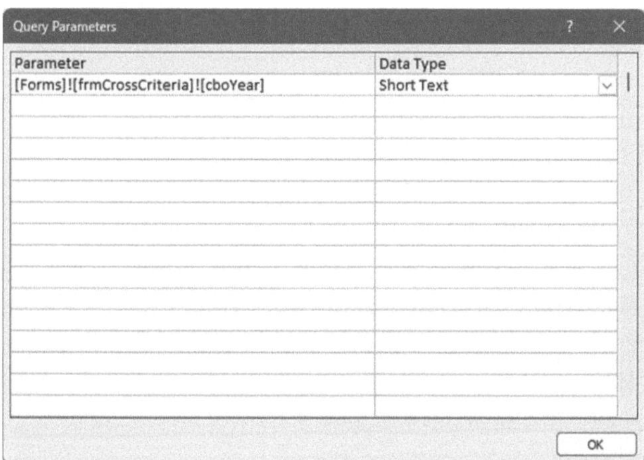

FIGURE 16.27.   Use the Query Parameter dialog box to define parameters for the crosstab query.

18. Click OK to close the Parameters dialog box.

19. Save the completed query as `qryTestCrosstab`. Enter `1996` when prompted for the parameter.

20. Double-click the qryTestCrosstab in the Navigation Pane to run it. Enter 1997 when prompted. The output of this query should match that shown in Figure 16.26.

21. Right-click the qryTestCrosstab tab and choose SQL View.
Access displays the SQL statement for the crosstab query you configured in query design view, as shown in Figure 16.28.

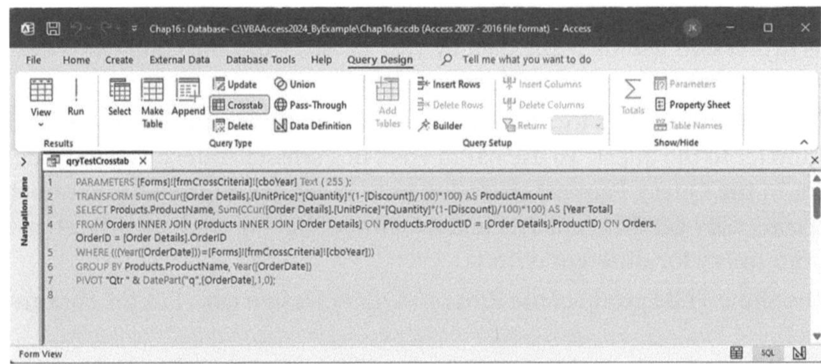

FIGURE 16.28. SQL statement for the completed crosstab query.

22. With a cursor placed anywhere in this statement, press Ctrl+A to select the entire statement. Press Ctrl+C to copy the selection to the clipboard.
You will need this statement when we write the VBA function to create the crosstab query.

23. Close the query window and choose Yes if asked to save the changes. Click Cancel if prompted for a parameter.

Part II: Creating a Query with VBA

When you must create a query programmatically, it helps to first create it manually in query design view so that you can use the ready-made SQL statement for your programming code.

Let's use the SQL statement that is on your clipboard to write the VBA function that creates the same query.

1. Switch to the VBE window and choose Insert | Module.

2. In the Module code window, enter the following function procedure:

```
Function CreateCrossTab_Qry(strQryName As String) As Boolean
Dim db As DAO.Database
Dim qryDef As QueryDef
Dim strSQL As String
```

```vba
On Error Resume Next
Set db = CurrentDb()
' test if the query with the specified name already exists
' in the QueryDefs collection of the current database
Set qryDef = db.QueryDefs(strQryName)

If Err.Number <> 0 Then
    Debug.Print Err.Number & " " & Err.Description
    Set qryDef = db.CreateQueryDef(strQryName)
    Err.Clear
End If

' prepare the SQL statement for the query
strSQL = "PARAMETERS [Forms]![frmCrossCriteria]!Text (255);"
strSQL = strSQL & "TRANSFORM Sum(CCur(" & _
    "[Order Details].UnitPrice*[Quantity]* "
strSQL = strSQL & "(1-[Discount])/100)*100) AS ProductAmount "
strSQL = strSQL & "SELECT Products.ProductName, "
strSQL = strSQL & "Sum(CCur("& _
    "[Order Details].[UnitPrice]*[Quantity]*(1-[Discount])/100)*100) "
strSQL = strSQL & "AS [Year Total] FROM Orders INNER JOIN  "
strSQL = strSQL & "(Products INNER JOIN [Order Details] "
strSQL = strSQL & "ON Products.ProductID = "
strSQL = strSQL & "[Order Details].ProductID) "
strSQL = strSQL & "ON Orders.OrderID = [Order Details].OrderID "
strSQL = strSQL & "WHERE (((Year([OrderDate])) = "
strSQL = strSQL & "[Forms]![frmCrossCriteria]![cboYear]))"
strSQL = strSQL & "GROUP BY Products.ProductName, Year([OrderDate])"
strSQL = strSQL & "PIVOT ""Qtr "" & DatePart(""q"",[OrderDate],1,0) "
strSQL = strSQL & "In (""Qtr 1"",""Qtr 2"",""Qtr 3"",""Qtr 4"");"

Debug.Print strSQL
qryDef.SQL = strSQL

' check for error
If Err.Number <> 0 Then
    Debug.Print Err.Number & " " & Err.Description
    Exit Function
End If
' make the query persistant by appending it
' to the QueryDefs collection
db.QueryDefs.Append qryDef

' Close and refresh the Query object
qryDef.Close
End Function
```

The `CreateCrossTab_Qry` function takes one argument, which is the name of the query we are going to create. This name will be passed by the function procedure that you will write in the next section. The function will return a Boolean value of `True` or `False`, so we know whether the query was created successfully. We start by pointing the object variable `db` to the current database. In the current database, we will then set the object variable `qryDef` to point to the query. Recall from earlier chapters that we use the `QueryDef` object to define a query. Next, we must check whether the query with the specified name already exists in the database. If we receive an error when trying to pass the query name to the `QueryDefs` collection, we know that the query does not exist, so we print the error number to the Immediate window and call the DAO `CreateQueryDef` method to create the query and we clear the error. If the query exists, we continue.

Next, we prepare the SQL statement for the query. Notice how you may format the statement so it is easier to understand. The statement you copied from the query that you created manually in the previous section should be used here, but it should be formatted as shown. Notice that your statement differs a bit in the `PIVOT` clause from the one displayed in the above code. This change will allow us to display all four quarters regardless of whether the data is available and will make your report based on this query look more consistent. When preparing the SQL statement, pay attention to the extra spaces and double quotes. It helps to print the contents of the prepared SQL string variable to the Immediate window so you can spot any syntax errors and spacing issues. Once you have the correct SQL string, you must use it to set the `QueryDef.SQL` property.

The `SQL` property contains the SQL statement that determines how records are selected, grouped, and ordered when a query is executed. The next error checkpoint will let you know if there was a problem with the SQL statement. We will exit the function when the error occurs. You will need to fix the problem before attempting to run the query again. If all is fine, and no error was received, you must add the query to the `QueryDefs` collection to make it permanent in your database. After that, you can close the `QueryDef` object. You are now done creating this query. If you need to create another query programmatically, all you need to do is change the SQL statement and pass a different name for the query.

3. In the VBE window, choose Debug | Compile to have it checked for any mistakes that could cause errors during the code execution. If errors are found,

Access will highlight them, and you should take time to correct them. Then, reissue the Debug Compile command to ensure that there are no more errors.

4. Now test the function by entering the following statement in the Immediate window:

```
CreateCrossTab_Qry("Quarterly Orders by Product Crosstab")
```

5. In the Navigation Pane of the Access database window, locate and run the newly created query. Enter `1996` when prompted.
6. Close the query.

Now, let's move on to creating our report.

Part III: Creating a Report with VBA

<table>
<tr><td>NOTE</td><td>The report will use an image in the report header section and a text file with some event procedure code for the report.</td></tr>
</table>

1. Copy the `Images` folder from the companion files to your `VBAAccess2024_ByExample` folder.
2. Copy the `ReportEvents.txt` file from the companion files to your `VBAAccess2024_ByExample` folder.
3. Return to the VBE screen and choose Insert | Module. In the Module code window, enter the function procedure located in the companion files named `functionCreateReport_Crosstab.txt`.

<table>
<tr><td>NOTE</td><td>You can also choose File | Import File in the VBE window and select functionCreateReport_Crosstab.bas from the companion files.</td></tr>
</table>

4. Set several breakpoints in various parts of the function procedure and run the function from the Immediate window using this statement:

```
CreateReport_Crosstab 1996
```

5. Walk through the procedure by pressing the F8 key or clicking the Step Into button on the Debug toolbar. Refer to Chapter 8 if you need a refresher on the process of debugging VBA code.
   Notice that the function begins by calling the procedure that creates a crosstab query. Next, a reference is created to the crosstab query and a parameter is set.

We also open a recordset based on the query. These tasks are performed in the following code snippet:

```
' call function to create query
CreateCrossTab_Qry (strQryName)

' get the parameter query
Set qdf = db.QueryDefs(strQryName)

' provide the parameter value
qdf.Parameters(0) = yr

' Open a Recordset based on the parameter query
Set rst = qdf.OpenRecordset()
```

Now we are ready to create a blank report and set some of its properties. Here is the code snippet:

```
'Create the Report object
Set rpt = CreateReport

'Add ReportHeader/Footer to the empty report
RunCommand acCmdReportHdrFtr
rpt.Caption = strQryName
```

Now it's time to create report controls. Each control is created using the `CreateReportControl` method, which requires the following parameters: `ReportName` and `ControlType`. There are also a few optional parameters that specify the section that will contain the new control, the name of the parent control, the name of the field to which the control will be bound if it is a data-bound control, the coordinates for the right and left corners of the control in twips, and finally the width and height of the control in twips. The following code snippet demonstrates how we can add an image control to the `ReportHeader` section:

```
'Create report controls
Set rptCtl = CreateReportControl(rpt.Name, acImage, acHeader)
With rptCtl
    .Height = 400
    .Width = 400
    .Top = 0
    .Name = "Auto_Logo0"
    .Picture = CurrentProject.path & "\Images\redstar.gif"
End With
```

<table>
<tr><td>**NOTE**</td><td>*If you get stuck here while debugging this function, click Debug in the message box and ensure that you have the* Images *folder in your working directory. See the note at the beginning of this section.*</td></tr>
</table>

Our report has text boxes and labels, and here is how we can add them:

```
Set rptCtl = CreateReportControl(rpt.Name, acLabel, acPageHeader)
With rptCtl
    .Height = 280
    .Width = 1200
    .Top = 0
    .Caption = "Order Year:"
End With
Set rptCtl = CreateReportControl(rpt.Name, acTextBox, acPageHeader)
With rptCtl
    .Height = 280
    .Width = 1080
    .Top = 0
    .Left = 1250
    .ControlSource = "=[Forms]![frmCrossCriteria]![cboYear]"
End With
```

Note that that all screen measurements are given in twips. A twip is equal to 1/20 point. 1 inch is 1440 twips and 1 cm is 567 twips. Twips are used to ensure that the placement and proportion of screen elements in your application will appear the same on all displays.

Next, we need to lay out the label text box controls for each field returned by the query. We do this with the help of the `For ...Next` loop and the `Recordset` object. See the code snippet below:

```
' Create corresponding label and text box controls for each field
For i = 0 To rst.Fields.Count - 1
    ' Create new text box control and size to fit data.
    Set txtNew = CreateReportControl(rpt.Name, acTextBox, _
    acDetail, , rst.Fields(i).Name, lngLeft, 0)
    If i = 0 Then
        txtNew.Width = 3500
    Else
        'txtNew.SizeToFit
    End If

    ' Create new label control and size to fit data.
```

```
        Set lblNew = CreateReportControl(rpt.Name, acLabel, _
          acPageHeader, , rst.Fields(i).Name, _
          lngLeft, 400, 1400, txtNew.Height)

      With lblNew
          .FontSize = 12
          .FontName = "Haettenschweiler"
          .TextAlign = 2
      End With

       ' Increment top value for next control
       If i = 0 Then
          lngLeft = lngLeft + txtNew.Width '+ 25
          Debug.Print lngLeft
       Else
          lngLeft = lngLeft + txtNew.Width '+ 25
           Debug.Print lngLeft
       End If
Next
```

In the following code, we make some visual adjustments to the report and put
a timestamp in the footer section. We also specify the query as the report's
`RecordSource` property.

```
With rpt
' Create timestamp on footer
    With CreateReportControl(.Name, acLabel, _
        acPageFooter, , Now(), 0, 0)
    End With

    .Section(acDetail).Height = 420
    .Section("detail").Height = 0
    .RecordSource = strQryName
    'make PageHeaderSection visible
    .Section(3).Visible = True
    .DefaultView = 0 'show report in Print Preview
End With
```

Before finishing our report creation tasks, we need to add some event
procedures. We start by setting a reference to the report module. Next, we
use the `CreateEventProc` method to create the first event procedure that will
run when the report is opened. We also prepare the variable that will hold the
procedure code.

```
' return reference to report module
Set mdl = rpt.Module
```

```
' add event procedure
lngReturn = mdl.CreateEventProc("Open", "Report")
strCode = strCode & vbCrLf & "Dim strDocName As String"
strCode = strCode & vbCrLf & "strDocName = ""frmCrossCriteria"""
strCode = strCode & vbCrLf & "' Open form."
strCode = strCode & vbCrLf & "DoCmd.OpenForm strDocName"
strCode = strCode & ", , , , , acDialog"
strCode = strCode & vbCrLf & "If IsLoaded(strDocName) "
strCode = strCode & "= False Then Cancel = True"
```

NOTE	*This is another place where you will get stuck while running this function because the above code references a nonexisting form. Click Continue in the error message when you are advised that you can't enter break mode at this time. In the next message, Run-time error '2102', where Access tells you that the form name is misspelled or refers to a form that does not exist, click End. The report will be generated without any issues; we will take care of the form issue in the next section.*

Notice that formatting the code of the event procedure as shown above can be very tedious and frustrating. To avoid errors, you must pay close attention to the single and double quotation marks, spaces, and commas. The good news is that there is a better way. Simply write your event procedures in a text file and add the text file to the module like this:

```
' Insert other event procedures from a text file
mdl.AddFromFile "C:\VBAAccess2024_ByExample\ReportEvents.txt"
```

Before we are done with the report creation, we need to save the report and perhaps display it in Print Preview. The final statements in the function are as follows:

```
'save the report with specified name
DoCmd.Save , strRptName

'open the report in Print Preview
DoCmd.OpenReport strRptName, acViewPreview

Set rpt = Nothing
rst.Close
set db = Nothing
```

Finally, Figure 16.29 displays our programmatically generated report. It is shown in design view because we encountered an error with the form that provides the parameter to the report.

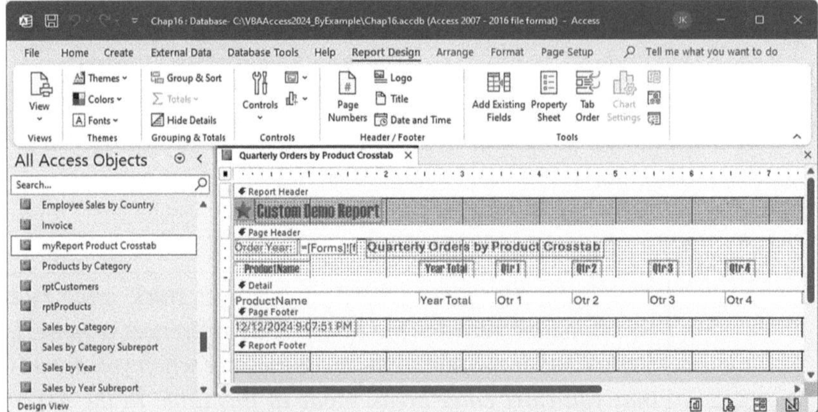

FIGURE 16.29. The Custom Demo Report in design view generated using VBA code.

Now that we have the report ready, let's see how we can provide a user-friendly interface for running it. This will allow us to display the report output.

Part IV: Creating a Custom Form for the Query's Parameters

Prompting the user for parameters should be a pleasant experience. The user may not know what type of parameter is expected or what range of data is available for a specific report. When a report is based on a parameter query, creating a customized form for the query's criteria will make it less cumbersome for the user to use your custom report. In this section, you will create the form shown in Figure 16.30. This form will include a combo box listing the years for which the report can be requested. The command button will run the report only when a selection is made from the combo box. Let's set this up.

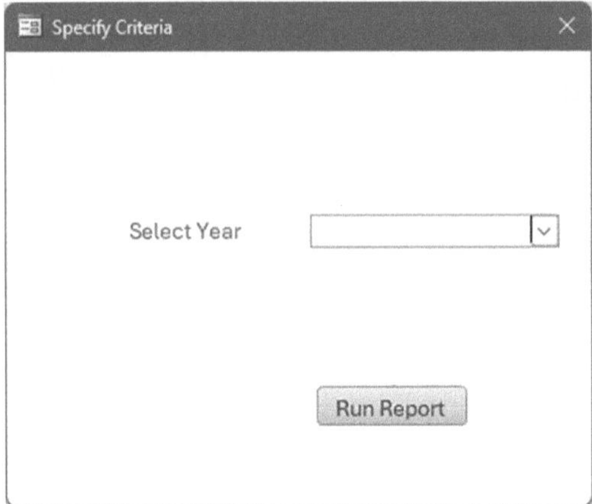

FIGURE 16.30. This custom form is used to provide the Year parameter for the report.

1. In the Access database window, choose Create | Form Design to create a blank form.
2. In the Form Design Tools group, click the Property Sheet button.
3. Click a combo box control in the Controls section of the Ribbon and click in the Form Detail section. If the Combo Box Wizard appears, click Cancel. The control should appear in its default size. Drag the combo control to position it as shown in Figure 16.30 and drag its side handles a bit to expand it.
4. Click on the combo control's label to select it, and in the Property Sheet, click the All tab, and change the Caption property to `Select Year`.
5. Click the Unbound combo box control, and in the Property Sheet, change its Name property to `cboYear`.
6. In the Property Sheet for `cboYear`, click the Data tab. In the Row Source property, enter the following statement:

```
SELECT DISTINCT Year([OrderDate]) FROM Orders GROUP BY [OrderDate];
```

This will provide the combo box with the list of available years for the report. To get more room for data entry, you can press Shift+F2 when the cursor is in the Row Source property field.

On the Data tab, set other property values for the `cboYear` control, as follows:

Limit To List	Yes
Allow Value List Edits	No
Show Only Row Source Values	Yes

7. Click the command button control in the Controls section of the Ribbon and click in the Form Detail section. Cancel the Command Button Wizard if it appears. The control should appear in its default size. Drag the command button to the position shown in Figure 16.30. While the command button is selected, use the Property Sheet to change the Name property to `cmdRunProductsRpt` and the Caption property to `Run Report`.
8. In the Property Sheet for the `cmdRunProductsRpt` command button, click the Event tab and set the On Click event to [Event Procedure], then click the ellipsis button (…). Access will open the report module with the stub of the `cmdRunProductsRpt_Click` procedure. Complete this procedure as follows.

```
Private Sub cmdRunProductsRpt_Click()
    Dim strRptName As String
    Dim strMsg As String
    Dim strTitle As String
```

```
    strRptName = "myReport Product Crosstab"
    strMsg = "Please Open the report: " & strRptName
    strTitle = "Open the Report"

    'check if report is open
    If Application.CurrentProject.AllReports(strRptName).
                               IsLoaded = True Then
        If IsNull(Me.cboYear) Or Me.cboYear = "" Then
            MsgBox "Please select value for the year.", _
                    vbInformation, "Year selection?"
            With Me.cboYear
                .SetFocus
                .Dropdown
            End With
        Else
            ' Hide form.
            Me.Visible = False
        End If
    Else
        MsgBox strMsg, vbInformation, strTitle
        'close the form
        DoCmd.Close
    End If
End Sub
```

This procedure will ensure that criteria were selected from the dropdown and the user runs the report not by launching the form but by clicking the report name in the Navigation Pane.

9. Press the Save button on the toolbar to make sure your changes are saved. When prompted for the form name, enter `frmCrossCriteria`.
Let's continue by setting the form properties.

10. Back in the form design view, use the Property Sheet's drop-down list to select Form. Click the Format tab and set the form's Caption property to Specify Criteria. Set other property values for the form, as follows:

Pop Up	Yes
Border Style	Dialog
Record Selectors	No
Navigation Buttons	No
Scroll Bars	Neither
Width	3.9583"

Set the form's height to 3" by dragging the sizing handle of the form (Figure 16.31).

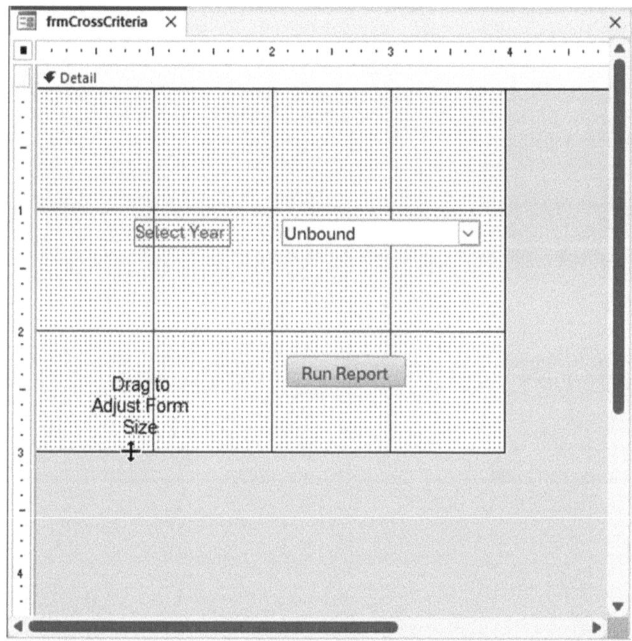

FIGURE 16.31.   Resizing the form.

The criteria form is now set up.

11. Close the form and save your changes before proceeding to the next section.

Part V: Running the Form and Report

1. In the Navigation Pane, double-click the `frmCrossCriteria` form you created in the previous section.
2. When Access opens the form, click the Run Report button.
The click event attached to this button checks whether the specified report is open. The `Else` clause of the event procedure will run now because you have not clicked the report name in the Navigation Pane. Click OK to the message that tells you that you should open the report. Access will close the form.
3. In the Navigation Pane of the Access database window, in the Reports section, locate and double-click the myReport Product Crosstab.
Access opens the `frmCrossCriteria`, where you are prompted to select a year. Note that if you are working with multiple monitors, the form may pop up on a different screen.

4. Select any year from the drop-down box and click Run Report.
   Access opens the report in Print Preview, as shown in Figure 16.32. Here, you have options to format, print, email, or save your report in other file formats.

5. Close the report Print Preview.

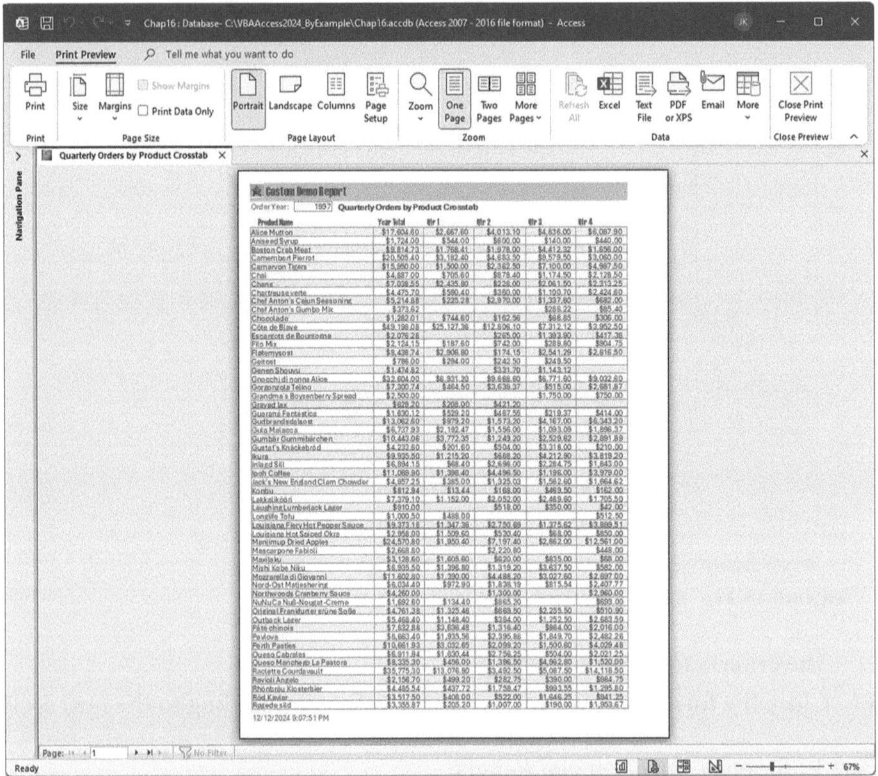

FIGURE 16.32. The Custom Demo Report shown in Print Preview.

Action Item 16.1
On your own, add another command button to the s form. Set its Name property to `cmdCancel` and its Caption property to `Cancel`. Write an event procedure for the `cmdCancel` button's `Click` event. The code of this procedure should close the form when the Cancel button is clicked.

USING ChatGPT WITH ACCESS

What else can you find out or do with Access reports? Let's chat a bit with our AI assistant on this topic.

User Prompt: What problems should I watch for when creating reports with Access VBA? Also, please provide a summary of key VBA methods in programming Access reports.

User Prompt: Can you give me guidance on programming Access report sections with VBA? Where do I begin?

User Prompt: How do I create an interactive report in Access?

These prompts and ChatGPT's responses are provided in the `Chapter 16 – Using ChatGPT with Access` document included in the companion files. As you read through the responses, bear in mind all the notes and precautions that were already discussed in our previous ChatGPT sessions.

SUMMARY

In this chapter, you were introduced to programming Access reports with VBA. You worked with several events that fire when the report is run. By writing your own event procedures, you can specify what happens when the report is opened, activated, deactivated, or closed. You can also display a custom message when an error occurs or the report does not contain any data, or you can make last-minute changes to the report format before it is printed or previewed. After that, you learned that, like forms, Access reports have a very useful property called `OpenArgs` that is handy when you need to pass a value to a report to filter its data. This allows you to reuse the same report to provide different displays of your data.

In the main project of this chapter, you created a report entirely with VBA. This was a multistep project where you created a crosstab query for the report's data source and designed a form that provided a parameter to your report. During this project, you learned how to use various VBA methods to create your report, add controls to the report, and set up their properties. In addition, you saw how you can create event procedures inline, within your function code, or by inserting the code straight from the earlier-prepared text files.

This chapter barely scratched the surface of what is possible and doable with reports. There are numerous templates Microsoft provides that you can study on your own to gain more insight into designing very appealing, informative, and interactive reports. You can also try out several examples of creating and customizing reports, including their various sections, which I go through step by step in my recent book titled *Access 365 Project Book – Hands-On Database*

Creation, ISBN 9781683920946, published by Mercury Learning and Information, an Imprint of DeGruyter Inc.

This chapter concludes Part V of this book. In the next chapter, you will be working with the menu interface in Access, commonly referred to as RibbonX.

VI

Enhancing the User Experience

Since its 2007 release, Access, like other Microsoft 365 applications, has used the Ribbon interface for its main menu system. Knowing how the Ribbon works and how you can modify it to customize your Access databases will enhance the experience of your database users. We will cover this topic in one big chapter with numerous illustrated hands-on examples and programming code written in VBA and XML.

Chapter 17   Programming the Ribbon Interface in Access

17 PROGRAMMING THE RIBBON INTERFACE IN ACCESS

Beginning with its 2007 version, Access, like other Microsoft 365 applications, has used the RibbonX interface for its menu system. The latest update to the Ribbon UI in Access was part of the Office visual refresh that was introduced to align with the design of Windows 11. This refresh includes a more rounded look to the Office Ribbon bar and small changes in the design of various buttons. These updates ensure a consistent look and feel across different Office applications, making it easier for users to switch between them. To get a bit more screen space, users can now quickly toggle the visibility of the Ribbon by pressing Ctrl+F1.

This chapter provides an overview of the programing elements available in the Ribbon and shows how you can customize the menu system in your Access database applications. In the following sections, we will examine many examples that demonstrate the use of different Ribbon features. Because RibbonX is based on Extensible Markup Language (XML), if you are new to XML, I recommend you start with Chapter 20 (Using XML in Access) before working through the examples in this chapter.

UNDERSTANDING AND EXPLORING THE RIBBON INTERFACE

Upon opening an existing Access database or creating a new one, you see a rounded Ribbon bar with various options. The current version changed the position and the way you activate the Quick Access Toolbar (QAT) customization options. This toolbar is now positioned directly above the Ribbon, providing a more streamlined and accessible interface. You can still customize the QAT by adding your frequently used commands, making it easier to access essential tools without navigating through the Ribbon. Figure 17.1 shows the QAT with its many available customization options.

The QAT allows you to add as many commands as you wish. You can add built-in commands to the QAT by using any of the following methods:

- Click the drop-down arrow in the QAT and select one of the listed commands or click More Commands. Access will add the chosen commands along the QAT itself in the order they were added, starting from the left side of the toolbar. Each command is represented by its icon, and if space allows, a text label may appear. Removing a command from the QAT is just as easy. Right-click on its icon on the QAT and select Remove from QAT.

- Click File | Options and choose QAT. In the Access Options dialog, choose the command from the list on the left and click Add to move it to the QAT on the right, then click OK to apply the changes.

Note that by default, the QAT is positioned above the Ribbon, but you can reposition it below the Ribbon by clicking Show Below the Ribbon in the Customize QAT dropdown. The QAT remains visible regardless of which tab you have selected in the Ribbon, ensuring your essential commands are always accessible.

Together with the title bar and the tabs, the QAT belongs to a large rectangular area called the Ribbon. This area is positioned at the top of the UI window. The QAT was designed for the convenience of end users. Developers should not alter this toolbar. If, however, you have a valid reason to hide the contents of this toolbar or add other buttons to it, you can apply your own customizations.

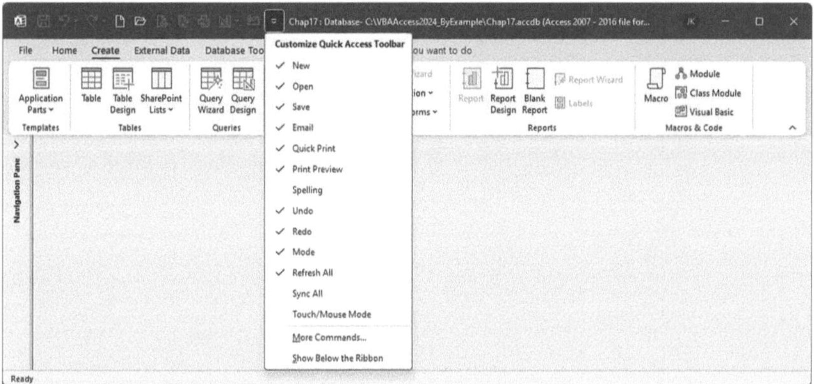

FIGURE 17.1.   Accessing the QAT in Access 2024.

The Ribbon has tabs and groups with various commands. All this can be customized to your specific needs. You can access the Ribbon customization options in one of these ways:

- Right-click in the empty space at the end of the Ribbon bar and choose Customize the Ribbon… (see Figure 17.2). Notice that another option allows you to collapse the Ribbon.

- Click File | Options and choose Customize Ribbon in the Access Options dialog (Figure 17.3). Choose the command from the list on the left and click Add to move it to the specific tab on the right, then click OK to apply the changes. The customized Ribbon immediately updates to include your changes. If you make a mistake by adding commands to the wrong tab, click the Reset button in the Access Options (Customize the Ribbon) dialog. This will revert it to the default Ribbon settings.

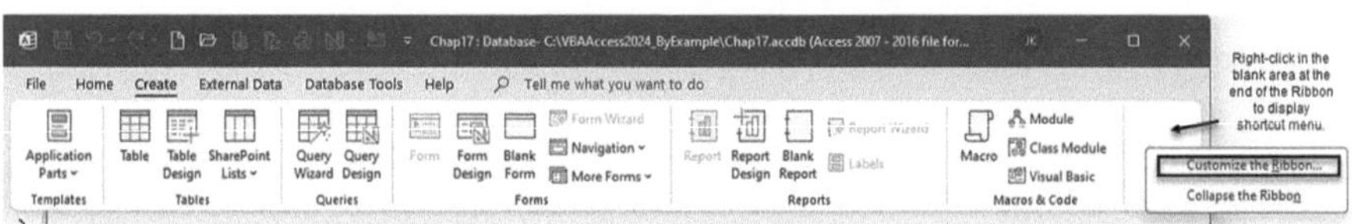

FIGURE 17.2.   Accessing the Ribbon customization interface via a right-click menu.

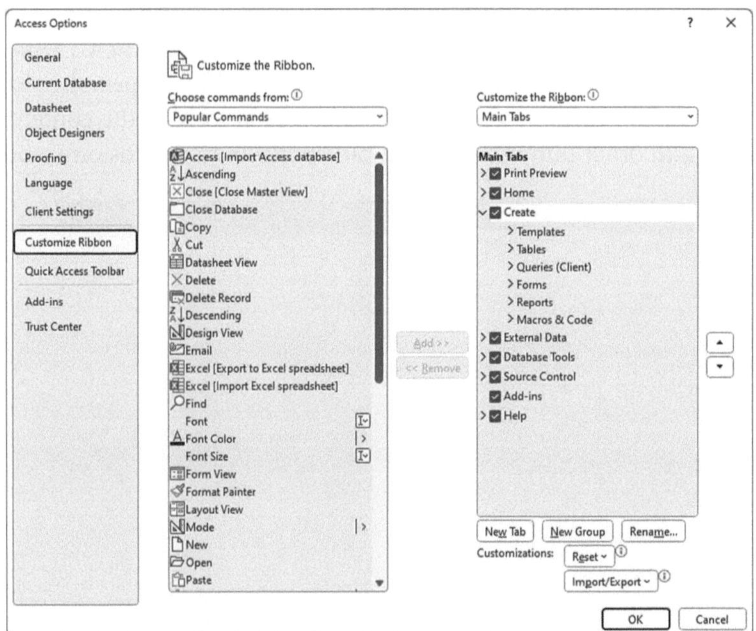

FIGURE 17.3.   Accessing the Ribbon customization interface via the Access Options dialog.

WORKING WITH THE NAVIGATION PANE

When an Access database is open, you can easily access all of your database objects via the Navigation Pane on the left side of the window (see Figure 17.4). If you need more screen real estate, you can hide the Navigation Pane by clicking on the Shutter Bar Open/Close button (the double arrow at the top of the pane) or by pressing F11.

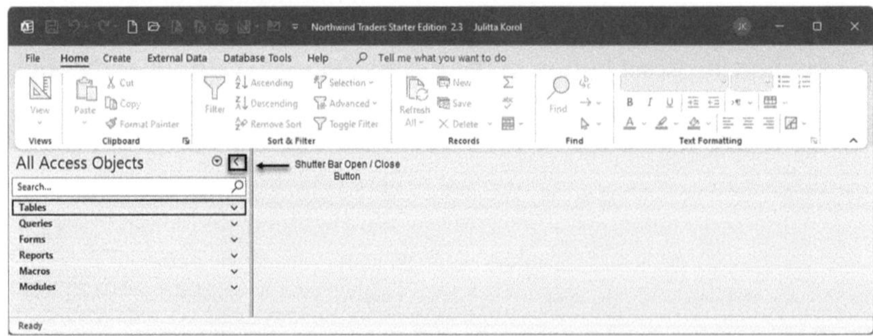

FIGURE 17.4.   The database navigation pane in Access 2024 shows all available database objects organized into different categories. It can be hidden by clicking the Shutter Bar Open/Close button.

Use the Navigation Pane to organize your objects by type, date created or modified, or related table, or create your own custom groups of objects. By clicking on the down arrow button at the top of the Navigation Pane, you can define how you view and manage the database (see Figure 17.5).

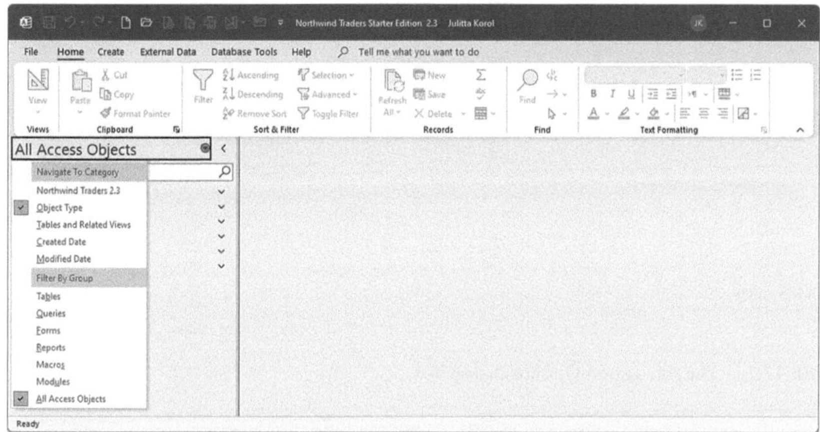

FIGURE 17.5.   Grouping options in the database navigation pane.

To sort and filter your database objects, click the search bar, or access the navigation options by right-clicking the Shutter Bar Open/Close Button anywhere at the top bar of the Navigation Pane above the search bar (see Figure 17.6).

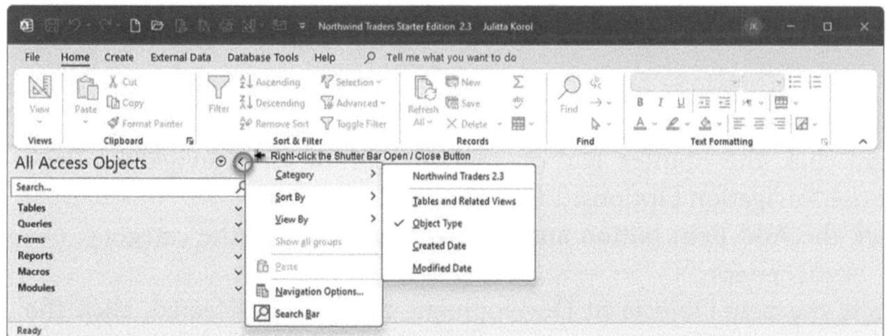

FIGURE 17.6.   Objects in the database navigation pane can be easily categorized, sorted, and filtered. Use the search bar to locate hard-to-find objects. Use the Navigation Options tool to create custom groups of objects.

The Navigation Options dialog box (see Figure 17.7) allows you to create any number of custom groups for organizing your objects according to specific database needs.

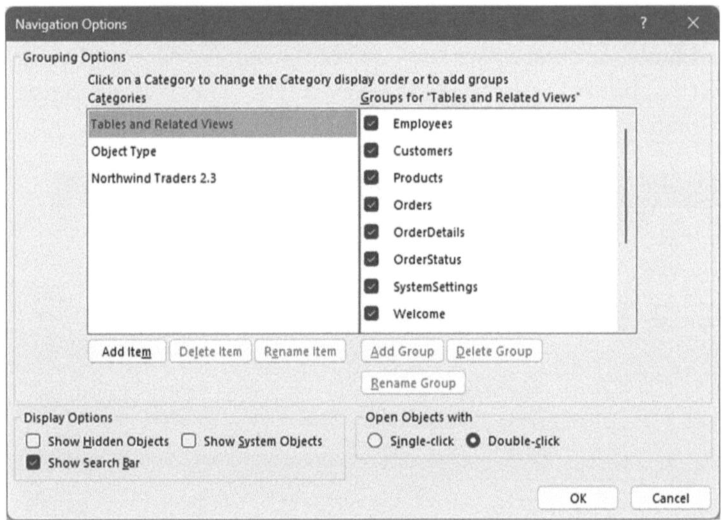

FIGURE 17.7.   The Navigation Options dialog box.

The exercise in Hands-On 17.1 will walk you through the process of creating a custom group in the Navigation Pane to help track your development efforts.

> **NOTE**   *All code files and figures for the hands-on projects may be found in the companion files.*

Hands-On 17.1   Adding a Custom Group to the Navigation Pane

1. Open the `C:\VBAAccess2024_ByExample\Northwind 2007.accdb` database. Cancel the login box.
2. Right-click the Shutter bar or the top bar of the Navigation Pane and choose Navigation Options… (see Figure 17.6 earlier).
3. Click the Add Item button and type a new name for the category: `Objects in Development`.
4. While the new Objects in Development category is selected, click the Add Group button and enter `Dev Tables` for the new group name.
5. Click the Add Group button again to add another group named `Dev Queries`.
6. Add two more groups under Objects in Development named `Dev Forms` and `Dev Reports`. See Figure 17.8 for the final output.

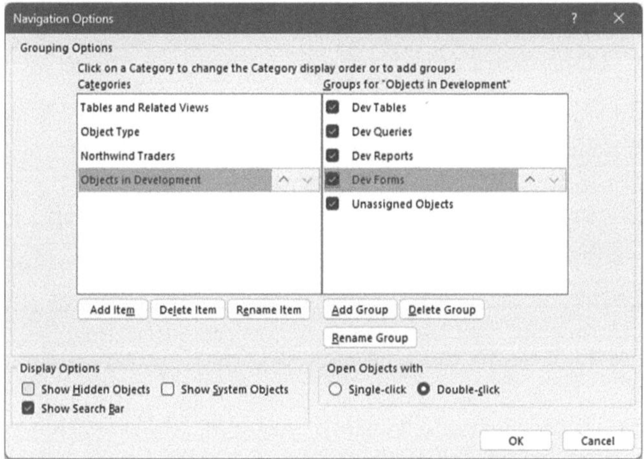

FIGURE 17.8.   Creating custom groups in Navigation Options.

7. Click OK to close the Navigation Options dialog box.
8. Click on the down arrow button at the top of the Navigation Pane and choose Objects in Development (Figure 17.9).

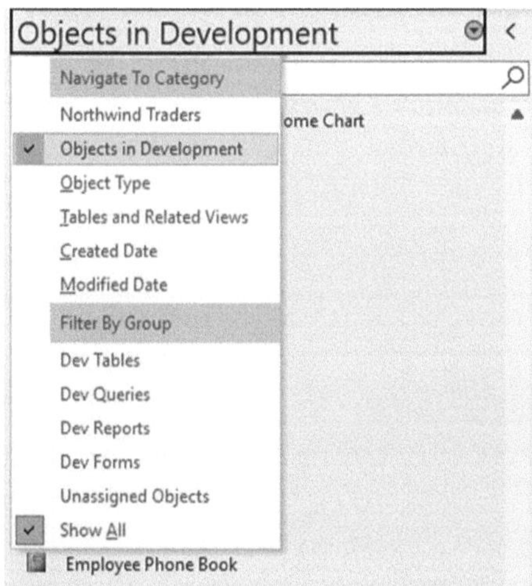

FIGURE 17.9.   Displaying a custom group in the Navigation Pane.

The next logical step is placing some database objects into your custom groups. Hands-On 17.2 requires prior completion of Hands-On 17.1.

> ### Hands-On 17.2   Assigning Objects to Custom Groups in the Navigation Pane

1. In the `Northwind 2007.accdb` database you opened in Hands-On 17.1, right-click the Customers table and choose Copy.
2. Right-click anywhere in the Navigation Pane and choose Paste. In the Paste Table As dialog box, enter `Companies` for the new name of the table and select the Structure Only option button. Click OK to exit the dialog box.
3. Choose Objects in Development from the drop-down list at the top of the Navigation Pane.
4. Drag the Companies table from the Unassigned Objects group to the Dev Tables group.

   When you place a database object into a custom group in the Navigation Pane, Access creates a shortcut to this object (see Figure 17.10). You can rename your shortcut by right-clicking its name and choosing Rename Shortcut. You can also hide the shortcut in the group or remove it from the group, provided the Navigation Pane has not been locked (this is discussed in the next section). In addition to the Hidden attribute, each shortcut has a Disable Design View shortcuts attribute you can set to prevent users from switching to design view when using the shortcut. You must restart your Access database for this property change to take effect. To display the shortcut properties as shown in Figure 17.10, right-click on the Companies shortcut under the Dev Tables group and choose Table Properties. Remember, you can drag any object listed in the Unassigned Objects group into your custom groups.

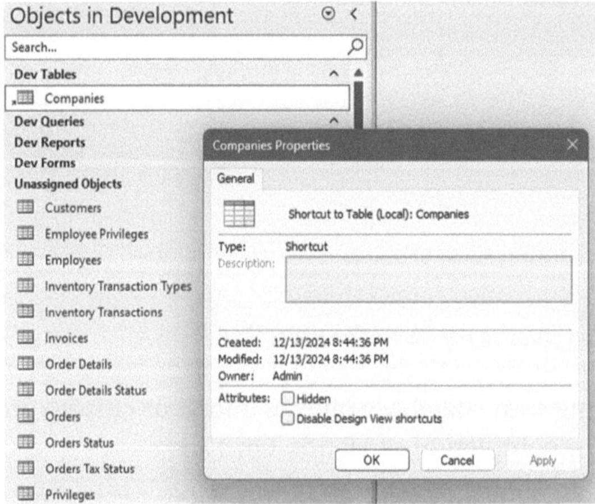

FIGURE 17.10.   The Navigation Pane with custom groupings.

USING VBA TO CUSTOMIZE THE NAVIGATION PANE

You can lock down and customize the Navigation Pane programmatically by using the following methods of the `DoCmd` object: `LockNavigationPane`, `NavigateTo`, and `SetDisplayedCategories`. There are also two methods of the `Application` object (`ExportNavigationPane` and `ImportNavigationPane`) that enable you to quickly apply the same Navigation Pane customizations to any Access database.

Locking the Navigation Pane

To prevent users from deleting database objects that are displayed in the Navigation Pane, use the following statement:

```
DoCmd.LockNavigationPane True
```

The `LockNavigationPane` method of the `DoCmd` object requires a `Lock` argument. Use the Boolean value of `True` to lock the Navigation Pane and `False` to unlock it.

Controlling the Display of Database Objects

To automatically navigate to a specific category in the Navigation Pane upon the startup of your Access database or to display only certain objects in the category, use the `NavigateTo` method of the `DoCmd` object. This method takes two arguments: `Category` (required) and `Group` (optional). The `Category` argument specifies the category you want to navigate to. This argument can be the name of your custom category, such as the Objects in Development category you created in Hands-On 17.1, or a constant representation of the Object Type, Tables and Views, Created Date, and Modified Date categories. The `Group` argument is optional. If you omit it, the Navigation Pane will display all database objects arranged by the criteria specified in the `Category` argument. See Table 17.1 for valid `Group` arguments for the various `Category` arguments.

TABLE 17.1.   Category and Group arguments used in the NavigateTo method.

Category Argument	Category Argument Constant	Group Argument	Group Argument Constant
Object Type	acNavigationCategoryObjectType	Tables	acNavigationGroupTables
		Forms	acNavigationGroupForms
		Reports	acNavigationGroupReports
		Queries	acNavigationGroupQueries
		Pages	acNavigationGroupPages
		Macros	acNavigationGroupMacros
		Modules	acNavigationGroupModules

(Contd.)

Category Argument	Category Argument Constant	Group Argument	Group Argument Constant
Tables and Views	acNavigationCategoryTablesAnd-Views	Name of a specific table or view in your database	
Modified Date	acNavigationCategoryModified-Date	Today Yesterday Last Month Older	acNavigationGroupToday acNavigationGroupYesterday acNavigationGroupLastMonth acNavigationGroupOlder
Created Date	acNavigationCategoryCreatedDate	Today Yesterday Last Month Older	acNavigationGroupToday acNavigationGroupYesterday acNavigationGroupLastMonth acNavigationGroupOlder
Custom	Name of your custom category	Name of one of the custom groups you have created for the specified custom category	

Let's get some practice with the `NavigateTo` method.

Hands-On 17.3   Using the NavigateTo Method to Control the Display of Database Objects in the Navigation Pane

1. In the `Northwind 2007.accdb` database, press Alt+F11 to switch to the VBE window. Press Ctrl+G (or choose View | Immediate Window) to open the Immediate window.
2. In the Immediate window, type each of the following `DoCmd.NavigateTo` statement examples on one line, pressing Enter to execute each statement. After the execution of each statement, check the resulting display in the Navigation Pane of the Access main window. Two monitors create the perfect environment for this exercise.

Enter on One Line in the Immediate Window	Description
DoCmd.NavigateTo "acNavigationCategory-CreatedDate"	This statement will navigate to the Created Date category and display all database objects.
DoCmd.NavigateTo "acNavigationCategoryOb-jectType", "acNavigationGroupForms"	This statement will navigate to the Object Type category and select the Forms group.
DoCmd.NavigateTo "acNavigationCategory-TablesAndViews", "Invoices"	This statement will navigate to the Invoices table in the Tables and Views category.

Enter on One Line in the Immediate Window	Description
DoCmd.NavigateTo "Objects in Development", "Dev Tables"	This statement will navigate to the Dev Forms group objects in the Objects in Development category created in Hands-On 17.1.
DoCmd.NavigateTo "acNavigationCategory-ModifiedDate", "acNavigationGroupOlder"	This statement will navigate to the Modified Date category and display all the database objects beginning with a date earlier than the previous month.

Figure 17.11 displays all the statements entered in the Immediate window.

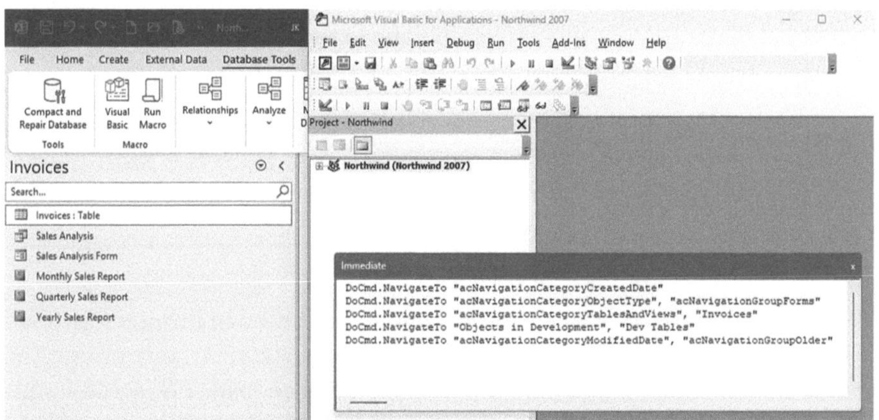

FIGURE 17.11.   Testing navigation statements in the Immediate window.

3. When finished, press Ctrl+G, Ctrl+A, and then the Delete key to remove the contents of the Immediate window.

Setting Displayed Categories

The `SetDisplayedCategories` method of the `DoCmd` object is used to specify which categories should be displayed under Navigate To Category in the title bar of the Navigation Pane. Use this method to show and hide groups from the top bar of the Navigation Pane. For example, the following statement will remove the custom category Objects in Development from the Navigation Pane title bar's drop-down list:

```
DoCmd.SetDisplayedCategories False, "Objects in Development"
```

Notice that the `SetDisplayedCategories` method uses two arguments. The first argument specifies whether to show or hide the category. Use the Boolean value of `False` to hide the category specified in the second argument of this method or `True` to show the category. The second argument denotes the name of the category you want to show or hide. Do not specify this argument if you want to show or hide all categories.

Saving and Loading the Configuration of the Navigation Pane

The configuration of the Navigation Pane can be saved at any time with the `ExportNavigationPane` method of the `Application` object. This method requires one argument—the path and the name of the XML file where you want to save the configuration of the Navigation Pane. For example, the following statement entered on a single line in the Immediate window will save the current configuration of the Navigation Pane to the specified folder:

```
Application.ExportNavigationPane "C:\VBAAccess2024_ByExample\
North2007NavConfig.xml"
```

To load a saved Navigation Pane configuration from the XML file, use the `ImportNavigationPane` method of the `Application` object:

```
Application.ImportNavigationPane "C:\VBAAccess2024_ByExample\
North2007NavConfig.xml", False
```

Notice that the `ImportNavigationPane` method used in the previous statement has two arguments. The first one specifies the path and name of the XML file that contains the Navigation Pane configuration to load. The second argument is optional. When set to `True`, the imported categories will be appended to the existing categories. The default value is `False`.

Hands-On 17.4 demonstrates how to save the current configuration of the Navigation Pane and then load it into another Access database.

> **Hands-On 17.4   Saving and Loading the Configuration of the Navigation Pane**

1. In the VBE window of the `Northwind 2007.accdb` database, type the following statement on one line in the Immediate window and press Enter to execute:

```
Application.ExportNavigationPane "C:\VBAAccess2024_ByExample\
North2007NavConfig.xml"
```

2. Switch to Windows File Explorer and check that the `North2007NavConfig.xml` file is indeed in the `VBAAccess2024_ByExample` folder.
3. Double-click the filename and open it in your browser. Figure 17.12 displays the partial content of the configuration file.
The XML file contains the objects and structure of the Access Navigation Pane. This file includes information about the contents of the Navigation

Pane system tables: `MSysNavPaneGroupCategories`, `MSysNavPaneGroups`, `MSysNavPaneGroupToObjects`, and `MSysNavPaneObjectIDs`.

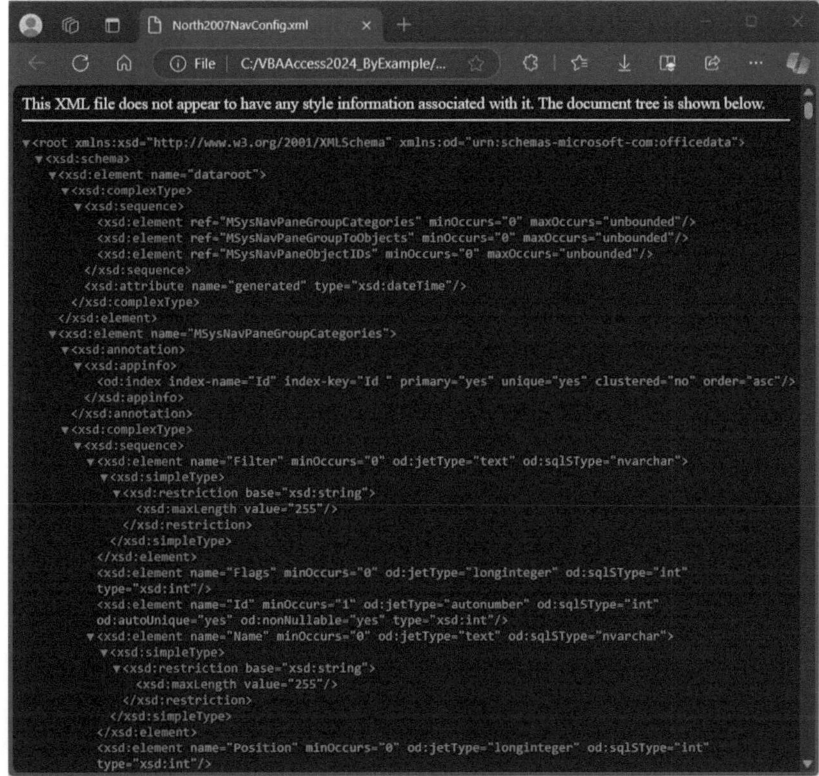

FIGURE 17.12.   The current configuration of the Navigation Pane is saved in this XML file.

4. Close the Browser window and then close the `Northwind 2007.accdb` database.

5. Create a new Access database named `Load_North2007NavConfig.accdb` in your `C:\VBAAccess2024_ByExample` folder.

6. Click the top bar of the Navigation Pane and view the Navigation Pane title bar's drop-down list before proceeding to import the saved configuration file.

7. Press Alt+F11, then press Ctrl+G to activate the Immediate window. Type the following statement on one line and press Enter to execute:

```
Application.ImportNavigationPane "C:\VBAAccess2024_ByExample\
North2007NavConfig.xml", False
```

8. Press Alt+F11 to switch back to the Access application window.
9. Click the top bar of the Navigation Pane and display the Navigation Pane title bar's drop-down list again (see Figure 17.13).

Notice the additional entries in the drop-down list: Northwind Traders and Objects in Development.

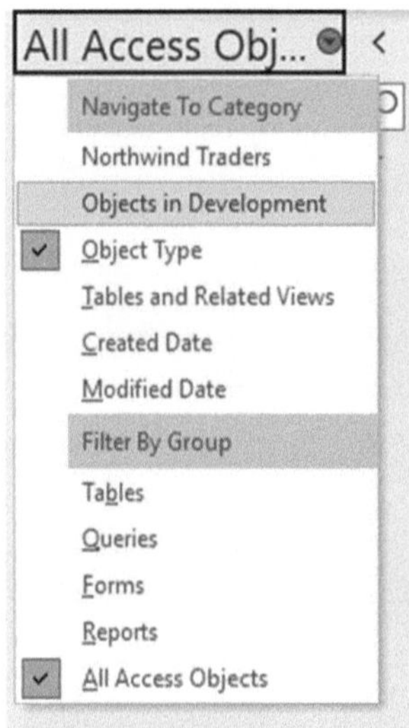

FIGURE 17.13.   The Navigation Pane can be easily modified using the external XML file containing the custom configuration settings.

Now that you know how to manually and programmatically control the Navigation Pane, you should find it easy to provide users with the needed customization of the Access database navigation system. The next section will expand your knowledge of the Access UI by giving you a quick overview of the Ribbon. You need to understand the types of the elements that are available on the Ribbon so you can program them later in this chapter.

A QUICK OVERVIEW OF THE ACCESS 2024 RIBBON INTERFACE

All Access program commands can be accessed from the Ribbon. Each tab on the Ribbon provides access to features and commands related to a particular database task. For example, you can use the Create tab to quickly create new tables, forms, reports, queries, macros, modules, and Microsoft Windows SharePoint services lists (see Figure 17.14). Related commands within a tab are organized into groups. For example, the Create tab divides its commands into six groups: Templates, Tables, Queries, Forms, Reports, and Macros & Code. This type of organization makes it easy to locate a particular command.

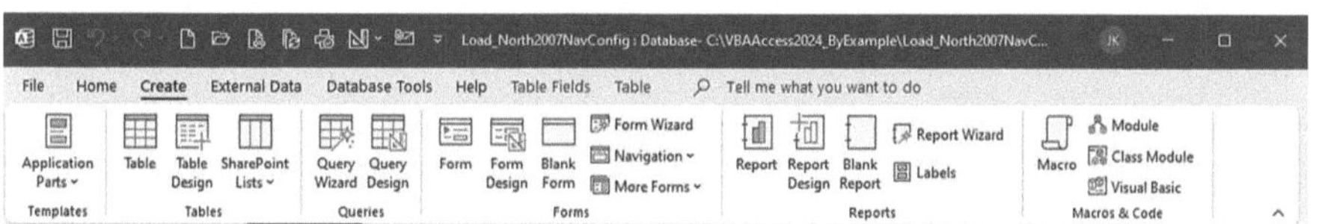

FIGURE 17.14.   All Access commands related to creating various database objects are grouped on the Create tab.

Various program commands are displayed as large or small buttons. Large buttons denote frequently used commands, while small buttons show specific features of the main commands. For example, in the Forms group, there is a large Form button and a small Form Wizard button. Some large and small command buttons include drop-down lists of other specialized commands. For example, the small More Forms drop-down button contains additional methods for creating a form: Multiple Items, Datasheet, Split Form, and Modal Dialog (Figure 17.15).

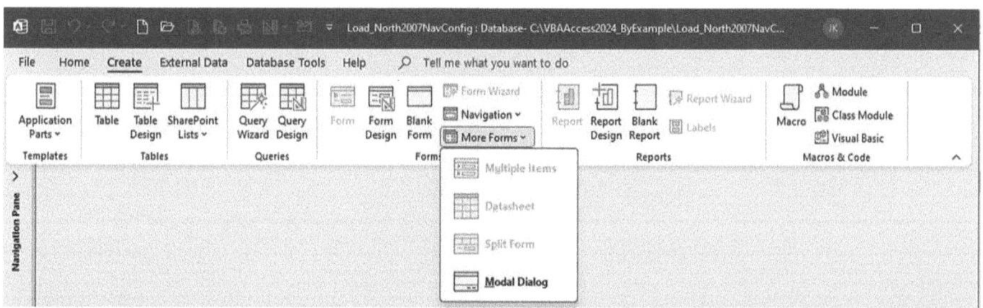

FIGURE 17.15.   Additional commands can be accessed by clicking on the down arrow to the right of the button control.

Some controls that you find on the Ribbon may be disabled until certain other options are chosen because these selected options do not display commands. Instead, they provide a visual clue of the output you might expect when a specific option is selected. These types of controls are known as *galleries*. Gallery controls are often used to present various formatting options, as shown in Figure 17.16.

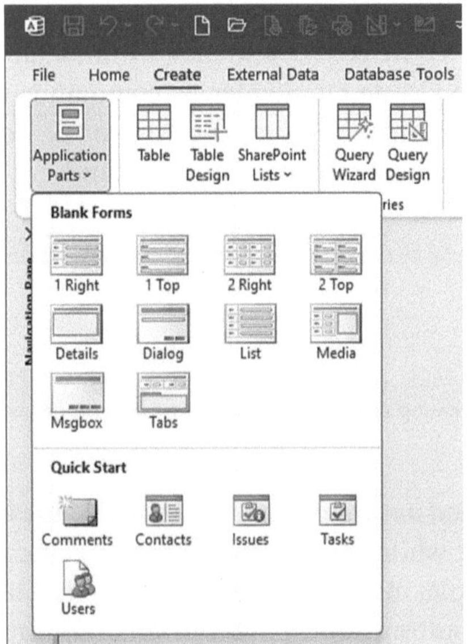

FIGURE 17.16.   Clicking on the Application Parts button in the Template group of the Create tab displays a gallery of different types of blank form layouts.

Some tab groups have dialog box launchers in the bottom-right corner (see Figure 17.17) that display a dialog box in which you can set several advanced options at once.

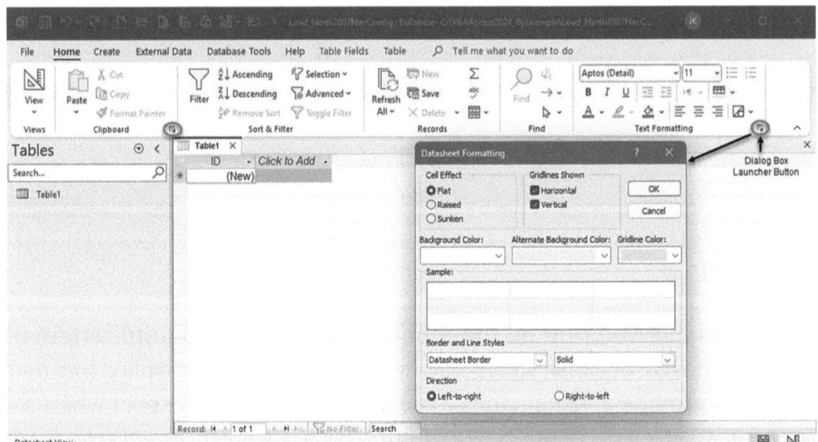

FIGURE 17.17   Notice two launcher buttons circled in this figure. The clipboard launcher button in the Clipboard group of the Ribbon when clicked provides quick access to the contents of your Windows clipboard. The dialog box launcher button in the bottom-right corner of the Text Formatting group on the Ribbon's Home tab displays the Datasheet Formatting dialog box.

In addition to the main Ribbon tabs, there are also contextual tabs that contain commands that apply to what you are doing at a given moment. When a particular object is selected, the Ribbon displays a contextual tab that provides commands for working with that object. For example, when a table is open in datasheet view, the Ribbon displays a contextual tab called Table Fields. Clicking on the Table Fields tab shows Ribbon options pertaining to this choice (see Figure 17.18). The contextual tab disappears when you cancel the selection of the object. In other words, close the datasheet and the Table Fields tab will be gone.

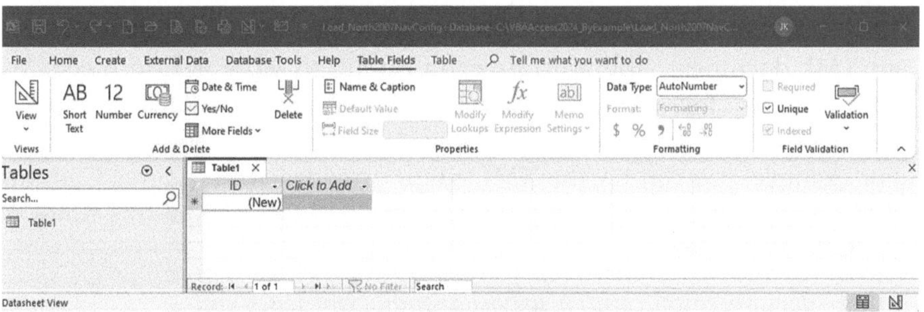

FIGURE 17.18.   A contextual tab (Table Fields) in the Ribbon.

Now that you've reviewed the main features of the Ribbon interface, let's look at how you can extend it with your own tabs and controls. The next section introduces you to Ribbon programming.

RIBBON PROGRAMMING WITH XML, VBA, AND MACROS

The components of the Ribbon UI can be manipulated programmatically using XML or other programming languages. Refer to Chapter 20 (Using XML in Access) for an introduction to using XML with Access.

All Microsoft 365 applications use the Ribbon and rely on the programming model known as Ribbon extensibility, or *RibbonX.*

This section introduces you to customizing Access 2024 Ribbons by using the XML markup language. No special tools are required to perform these customizations. XML is a plain-text format; therefore, you can use any text editor to create your customization files. In the examples that follow, we'll be using the simple Windows Notepad.

Your customizations can be stored in a special Access table, in a VBA procedure, or in another Access database, or they can be linked to an Excel spreadsheet. When storing your customizations in a location other than the Access table, you must call the `LoadCustomUI` method of the `Application` object to load your XML markup manually and then set the Ribbon name in your program at runtime. Ribbon customizations can be applied to the entire application or to specific forms and reports.

Tools for Ribbon Programming

Simple text editors such as Notepad do not provide tools for validating your XML markup, and validation is a big requirement when you are working with an XML document. You must be extra careful to write well-formed XML or your code will fail. If you are planning on performing extensive Ribbon customizations, I recommend that you consider acquiring a dedicated XML editor. For example, you can try the XML editor provided with the free Community Edition of Microsoft Visual Studio. You can read more about this editor using the following link:

https://docs.microsoft.com/en-us/visualstudio/xml-tools/xml-editor?view=vs-2022

Another text editor that can come in handy is the free Notepad++ . You can download it from this link:

https://notepad-plus-plus.org

Once installed, use the Plugins menu to access the Plugin Admin, where you can search for and install XML Tools. The XML Tools plugin will provide you with extensive menu options for working with and validating XML documents.

None of these special tools are necessary for the completion of this chapter's Ribbon customizations. Each new tool, especially an advanced one, requires that you first familiarize yourself with its interface, which can delay your progress if you need to learn something in a hurry. So, to get started with XML programming without further delays, the built-in Windows Notepad will do.

Creating the Ribbon Customization XML Markup

To make custom changes to the Ribbon UI, you must prepare an XML markup file that specifies all your customizations. The XML markup file that we are going to prepare and use in Hands-On 17.5 is shown in Figure 17.19. After implementation, this customization will appear in your Access database, as shown in Figure 17.20.

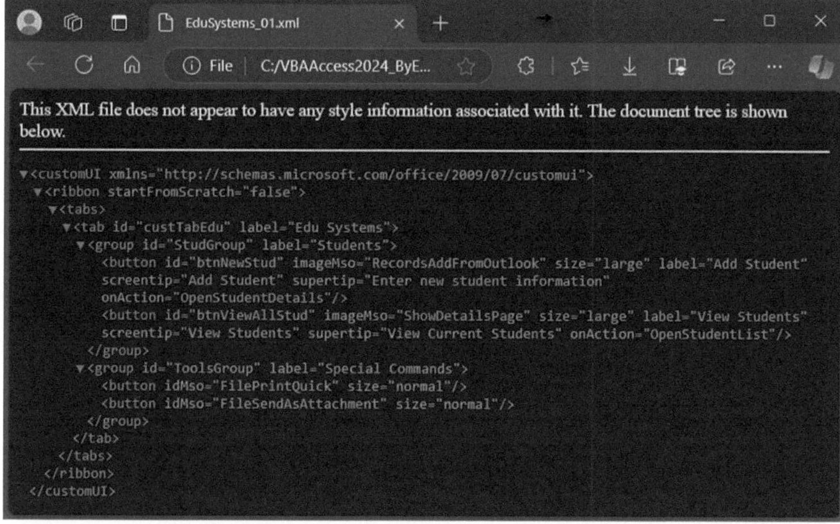

FIGURE 17.19.   This XML file defines a new tab with two groups for the existing Access 2024 Ribbon. See the output this file produces in Figure 17.20.

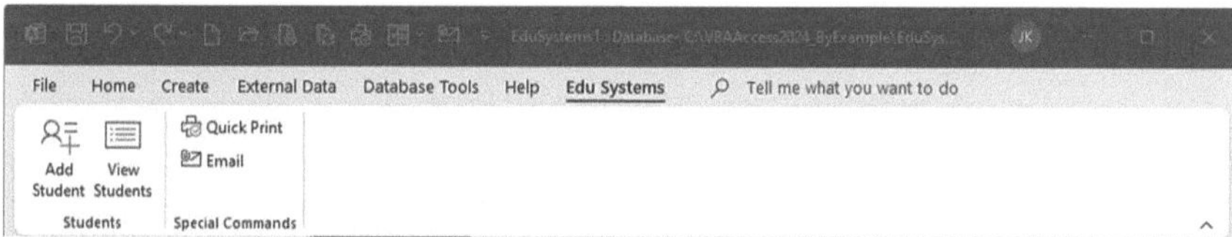

FIGURE 17.20.   The custom Edu Systems tab is based on the XML markup file shown in Figure 17.19.

◉ Hands-On 17.5   Creating an XML Document with Ribbon Customizations

1. Close the `Load_North2007NavConfig.accdb` database that you prepared and worked with earlier.

2. Open Windows Notepad and type the following XML markup, or copy the code from the `EduSystems_01.txt` in the companion files.

```
<customUI xmlns="http://schemas.microsoft.com/office/2009/07/
                   customui">
  <ribbon startFromScratch="false">
  <tabs>
  <tab id="custTabEdu" label="Edu Systems">
  <group id="StudGroup" label="Students">
  <button id="btnNewStud" imageMso="RecordsAddFromOutlook"
  size="large" label="Add Student" screentip="Add Student"
  supertip="Enter new student information"
```

```
 onAction="OpenStudentDetails" />
<button id="btnViewAllStud" imageMso="ShowDetailsPage"
size="large" label="View Students" screentip="View Students"
supertip="View Current Students" onAction="OpenStudentList" />
</group>
<group id="ToolsGroup" label="Special Commands">
<button idMso="FilePrintQuick" size="normal" />
<button idMso="FileSendAsAttachment" size="normal" />
</group>
</tab>
</tabs>
</ribbon>
</customUI>
```

Let's go over the contents of this file.

Every XML document consists of several elements, called *nodes*. In any XML document, there must be a root node, also known as a top-level element. In the Ribbon customization file shown above, the root note is `<customUI>`. The root's purpose is to specify the current Office RibbonX XML *namespace* (`xmlns`):

```
<customUI xmlns="http://schemas.microsoft.com/office/2009/07/
customui">
```

Namespaces are used to uniquely identify elements in the XML documents and avoid name collisions when elements with the same name are combined in the same document.

The `xmlns` attribute of the `<customUI>` XML tag holds the name of the default namespace to be used in the Ribbon customization. Notice that the root element encloses all other elements of this XML document: ribbon, tabs, tab, group, and button. Each element consists of a beginning and ending tag. For example, `<customUI>` is the name of the beginning tag and `</customUI>` is the ending tag.

The actual Ribbon definition is contained within the `<ribbon>` tag:

```
<ribbon startFromScratch="false">
[Include xml tags to specify the required ribbon customization]
</ribbon>
```

The `startFromScratch` attribute of the `<ribbon>` tag defines whether you want to replace the built-in Ribbon with your own (`true`) or add a new tab to the existing Ribbon (`false`).

> **Hiding the Elements of the Access UI**
>
> Setting `startFromScratch="true"` in the `<ribbon>` tag will hide the default Ribbon as well as the contents of the QAT. The File tab will be left with only four commands: New, Open, Save As, and Close Database.

To create a new tabset in the Ribbon, use the `<tabs>` tag. Each tab element is defined with the `<tab>` tag. The `label` attribute of the tab element specifies the name of your custom tab. The name in the `id` attribute is used to identify your custom tab:

```
<tabs>
<tab id="custTabEdu" label="Edu Systems">
```

Ribbon tabs contain controls organized in groups. You can define a group for the controls on your tab with the `<group>` tag. The example XML markup file defines the following two groups for the Edu Systems tab:

```
<group id="StudGroup" label="Students">
<group id="ToolsGroup" label="Special Commands">
```

Like the tab node, the group nodes of the XML document contain the `id` and `label` attributes. Placing controls in groups is easy. Notice that the group labeled `Students` has two custom button controls, identified by the `<button>` elements. The group labeled `Special Commands` also contains two buttons; however, unlike the `Students` group, the buttons placed here are built-in Office system controls rather than custom controls. You can quickly determine this by looking at the `id` attribute for the control. Any attribute that ends with `Mso` refers to a built-in Office item:

```
<button idMso="FilePrintQuick" size="normal" />
```

You can download control IDs for built-in controls in all applications that use the Office Fluent UI (another name for the Ribbon) from the GitHub repository:

https://github.com/OfficeDev/office-control-ids

As mentioned earlier in this chapter, buttons placed on the Ribbon can be large or small. You can define the size of the button with the `size` attribute set to `"large"` or `"normal"`. Buttons can have additional attributes, as shown here:

```
<button id="btnNewStud" imageMso="RecordsAddFromOutlook"
size="large" label="Add Student"
screenTip="Add Student" supertip="Enter new student information"
onAction="OpenStudentDetails" />
```

The `imageMso` attribute denotes the name of the existing Office icon. You can use images provided by any Microsoft 365 application. To provide your own image, you must use the `getImage` attribute in your XML markup (see more information in the section Using Images in Ribbon Customizations later in this chapter).

The `screentip` and `supertip` attributes allow you to specify the short and longer text that should appear when the mouse pointer is positioned over the button.

Callback Procedures in Ribbon Programming

The controls that you specify in XML markup perform their designated actions via *callback procedures*. For example, the `onAction` attribute of a button control contains the name of the callback procedure that is executed when the button is clicked. When that procedure completes, it calls back the Ribbon to provide the status or modifies the Ribbon. You will write the callback procedures for the `onAction` attribute in the next section of this chapter (see Custom Project 17.1).

Note that buttons borrowed from the Office system do not require the `onAction` attribute. When clicked, these buttons will perform their default built-in action.

Before finishing off the XML Ribbon customization document, always make sure that you have included all the required ending tags:

```
</tab>
</tabs>
</ribbon>
</customUI>
```

 (◉) **Hands-On 17.5   Continued...**

3. Save the text file you created in step 1 as `C:\VBAAccess2024_ByExample\EduSystems_01.xml`.

   By entering the XML extension, the text file is saved as an XML document.

4. To ensure that this XML document is well formed (it follows the formatting rules for XML), open the created `.xml` file in a browser.

   If the browser can read the document, then its output should match Figure 17.19. If the browser finds problems with the document, it will show you the incorrect statement. It is up to you to figure out what correction is required. Open the file in Notepad, correct the erroneous code, save the file, and test it again by loading it in the browser. This is one of the situations where dedicated XML tools would help you a lot with your debugging and any validation issues.

5. Close the browser.

At this point, you should have a well-formed XML document with your first Ribbon customization.

Now that you know how to structure an XML document for Ribbon customizations, you should find it straightforward to add other features to the Access Ribbon as they are discussed in this chapter.

Loading Ribbon Customizations from an External XML Document

Since your first Ribbon customization is already in an external XML document, we will go ahead and load it into Access using the combination of VBA and macros. In a later section of this chapter, you will learn how to load the same XML markup into a local Access table and have Access take care of the Ribbon modifications at startup.

Custom Project 17.1 walks you through the steps required to integrate Ribbon customizations into your database application.

 **Custom Project 17.1   Applying Ribbon Customizations from an External XML File**

This custom project depends on the XML document prepared in Hands-On 17.5.

Part 1: Setting Access Options

1. Copy the `EduSystems1.accdb` database from the companion files to your `C:\VBAAccess2024_ByExample` folder. This database is a copy of a database generated from the Students template provided by Microsoft Corporation. We will use this database to build Ribbon customizations in this chapter.

2. Open the `EduSystems1` database and click File | Options, then Client Settings.

3. In the General section, make sure that the Show add-in user interface errors option is selected (Figure 17.21).

When you enable this option, you will be able to see error messages if errors are encountered when you load your Ribbon customizations.

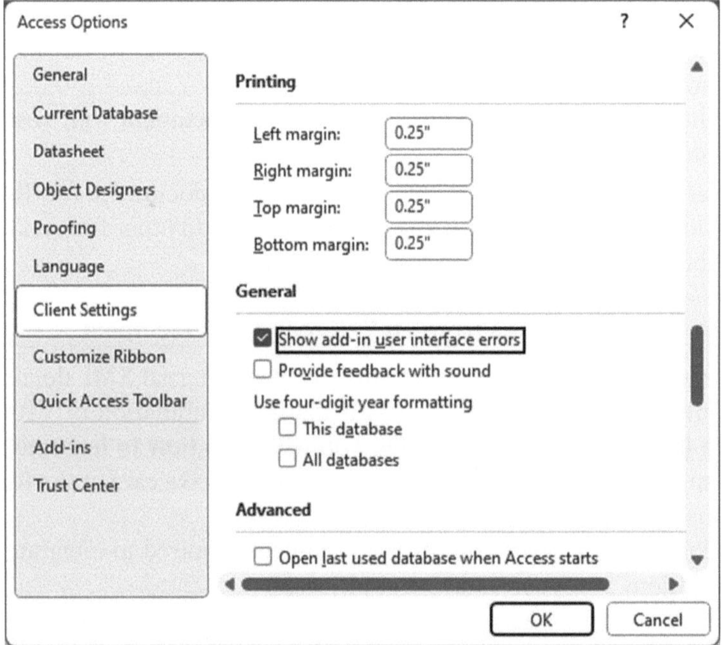

FIGURE 17.21.   When you check Show add-in user interface errors, Access will notify you about any problems in the Ribbon XML.

4. Click OK to close the Access Options dialog box.
5. Click OK to the message that you must close the current database for the specified option to take effect.
6. Close the `EduSystem1.accdb` database and reopen it.

Part 2: Setting Up the Programming Environment

1. Choose Database Tools | Visual Basic to switch to the VBE window.
2. Choose Tools | References. In the References dialog box, add references to the following two libraries: Microsoft Office 16.0 Object Library and Microsoft Scripting Runtime (Figure 17.22). Scroll down the list until you find these libraries and select them, then click OK to exit the References dialog.

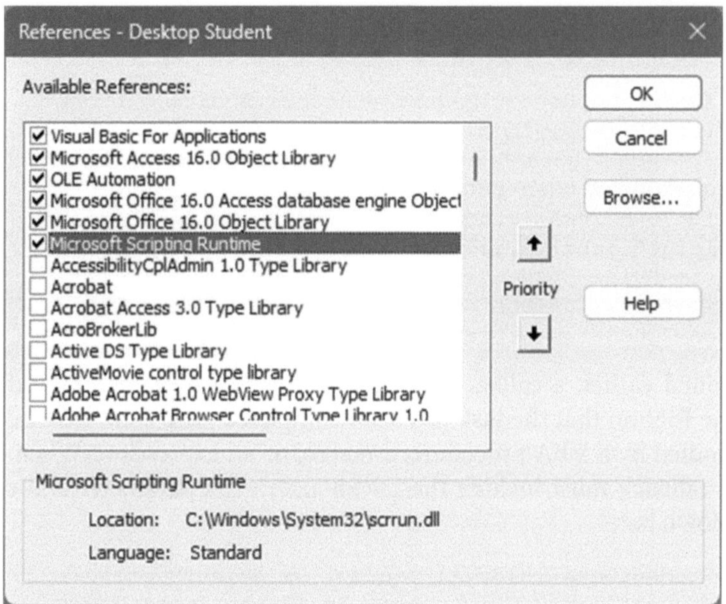

FIGURE 17.22.   To avoid compile errors, you must set library references as shown here.

3. Choose Insert | Module.
In the Properties window, change the Name property of the module to `RibbonModification`.

Part 3: Writing VBA Code

1. In the `RibbonModification` Code window, enter the following VBA procedures, or copy and paste the VBA code from `RibbonVBA.txt` in the companion files:

```
Sub OpenStudentDetails(ByVal control As IRibbonControl)
  DoCmd.OpenForm "Student Details", acNormal, , , acFormAdd
End Sub

Sub OpenStudentList(ByVal control As IRibbonControl)
  DoCmd.OpenForm "Student List", acNormal
End Sub
```

Notice that both preceding procedures open the specified Access forms. In addition, the `OpenStudentDetails` procedure opens the `Student Details` form in Add mode (`acFormAdd`). You may recall that these procedures

(`OpenStudentDetails` and `OpenStudentList`) are the names of the callback procedures that were specified in the `onAction` attribute of the button XML:

```
<button id="btnNewStud" imageMso="RecordsAddFromOutlook"
  size="large" label="Add Student"
 screentip="Add Student" supertip="Enter new student information"
  onAction="OpenStudentDetails" />
<button id="btnViewAllStud" imageMso="ShowDetailsPage"
  size="large" label="View Students"
  screentip="View Students"
  supertip="View Current Students"
  onAction="OpenStudentList" />
```

As mentioned earlier, a callback procedure executes some action and then notifies the Ribbon that the task has been completed. The `onAction` callback can be handled by a VBA procedure, a macro, or an expression. When using VBA, the callback must include the `IRibbonControl` parameter and return type, as shown here:

```
Sub OpenStudentDetails(ByVal control As IRibbonControl)
Sub OpenStudentList(ByVal control As IRibbonControl)
```

The `IRibbonControl` parameter is the control that was clicked. This control is passed to your VBA code by the Ribbon. For VBA to recognize this parameter, we added a reference to the Microsoft Office 16.0 object library in Part 2 of this project.

The IRibbonControl Properties

You can view the properties (`Context`, `Id`, and `Tag`) of the `IRibbonControl` object in the Object Browser. The `Context` property returns the active window that contains the Ribbon interface. The `Id` property contains the ID of the control that was clicked. The `Tag` property can be used to store additional information with the control. To use this property, you need to add the tag attribute to the XML markup. You can write a more generic procedure to handle the callbacks by using the `Tag` property. For example, instead of writing a separate procedure to open the `Student Details` and `Student List` forms as we did in this example, you could write a single procedure like this:

```
Sub OpenFrm(ByVal control AS IRibbonControl)
  Select Case control.Id
    Case "btnNewStud"
      DoCmd.OpenForm "Student Details", acNormal, , , acFormAdd
    Case "btnViewAllStud"
      DoCmd.OpenForm "Student List", acNormal
  End Select
End Sub
```

Next, you would need to add the `Tag` attribute to the XML markup and change the `onAction` callback to the `OpenFrm` procedure name:

```
<button id="btnNewStud" imageMso="RecordsAddFromOutlook"
  size="large" label="Add Student"
  screentip="Add Student" supertip="Enter new student information"
  onAction="OpenFrm" tag="Student Details" />
<button id="btnViewAllStud" imageMso="ShowDetailsPage"
  size="large" label="View Students"
  screentip="View Students"
  supertip="View Current Students"
  onAction="OpenFrm" tag="Student List" />
```

You can see the implementation of the preceding technique in the `EduSystems2.accdb` database and the `EduSystems_02.xml` document located in the companion files.

2. In the `RibbonModification` code module, enter the following `LoadRibbon` function procedure, or copy and paste the procedure code from the `RibbonVBA. txt`:

```
Public Function LoadRibbon()
  Dim strXML As String
  Dim oFso As New FileSystemObject
  Dim oTStream As TextStream

  ' Open the file containing the Ribbon customizations
  ' and return a TextStream object that will be used
  ' for reading from the file
  Set oTStream = oFso.OpenTextFile( _
      "C:\VBAAccess2024_ByExample" & _
      "\EduSystems_01.XML", ForReading)

  ' Read the entire stream into a string variable
  strXML = oTStream.ReadAll

  ' Close the TextStream object
  oTStream.Close

  ' Free up resources
  Set oTStream = Nothing
  Set oFso = Nothing

  ' load XML markup that represents a customized Ribbon
  Application.LoadCustomUI "EduTabR", strXML
End Function
```

This procedure uses the `LoadCustomUI` method of the `Application` object to load into Access the XML markup that contains your Ribbon customizations. To use this method, you must pass the name of the Ribbon and the XML code that defines the customized Ribbon. In this example, `EduTabR` is the name of our customized Ribbon. You can name your Ribbon anything you want. The `strXML` variable contains the XML markup. Because the XML markup must be passed as a text string, the procedure begins by accessing the `FileSystemObject` from Microsoft Scripting Runtime (see Part 2 where you added a reference to this library) and reading the contents of the XML file using the `ReadAll` method of the `TextStream` object.

In Part 4 of this custom project, you will call the `LoadRibbon` function from the `AutoExec` macro to make the custom Ribbon available to your database application on startup.

3. Click the Save button to save changes in the `RibbonModification` module.
4. Choose Debug | Compile Desktop Student to ensure that the VBA code does not contain spelling or other errors. If errors are found, correct them before proceeding to the next step.
5. Press Alt+Q to close the VBE window and return to Microsoft Access.

Part 4: Calling the LoadRibbon function from an Autoexec Macro

1. In the Access window's Navigation Pane, right-click the AutoExec macro name and select Design View.
2. In the macro design window (see Figure 17.23), select RunCode from the Add New Action drop-down list. Enter `LoadRibbon()` in the Function Name text box. The function name should automatically appear when you start typing its name.
3. Press Ctrl+S or click the Save icon in the title bar to save the changes to the `AutoExec` macro.

   Notice that the `AutoExec` macro already contains other actions defined by the Microsoft developers team. An Access macro named `AutoExec` runs automatically each time you open the database. If you need to open a database without running this macro, or to bypass other startup options, you must hold down the Shift key when double-clicking the database. For more information about using macros in Access 2024, refer to Chapter 19 (Getting Comfortable with Access Macros and Templates).
4. To run the `AutoExec` macro right now, click the Run button on the Macro Design tab.

If you click the Run button and receive no error, the macro has run successfully, and your Ribbon customization (`EduTabR`) has been loaded. Access will automatically close the Macro Designer dialog but will leave the AutoExec tab open.

For the changes in the Ribbon to become visible, you must complete the steps in Part 5 of this custom project.

5. Close the AutoExec tab.

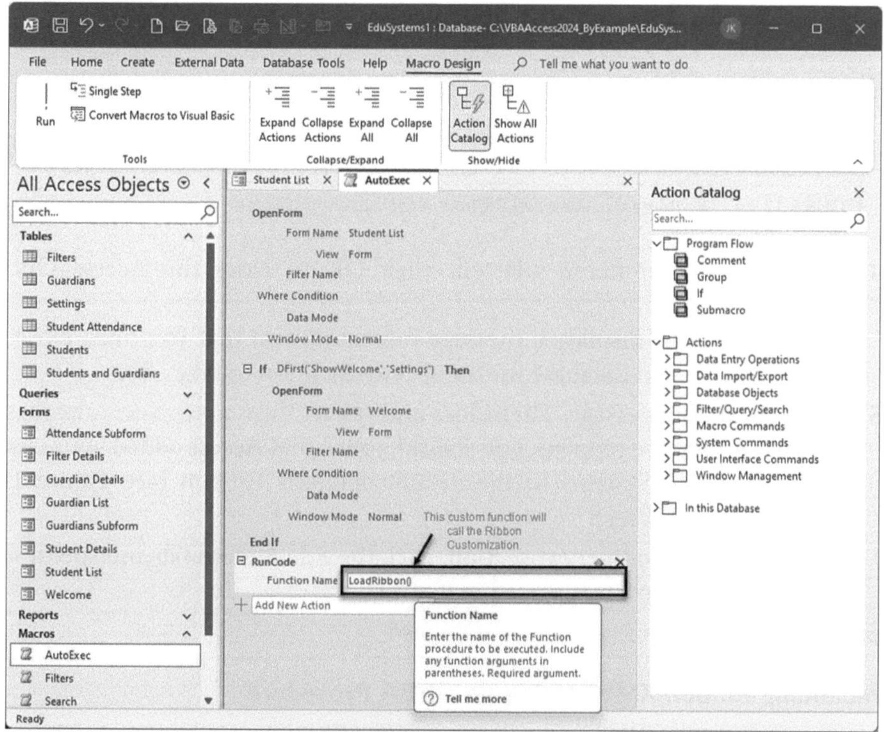

FIGURE 17.23.   To load a Ribbon customization in your Access database when the database is loaded, enter the custom LoadRibbon() function in the AutoExec macro.

Part 5: Applying the Customized Ribbon

1. Click the File tab, and then click Options.
2. In the left pane of the Access Options dialog, click the Current Database option.
3. In the Ribbon and Toolbar Options section, choose EduTabR from the Ribbon Name list (Figure 17.24).

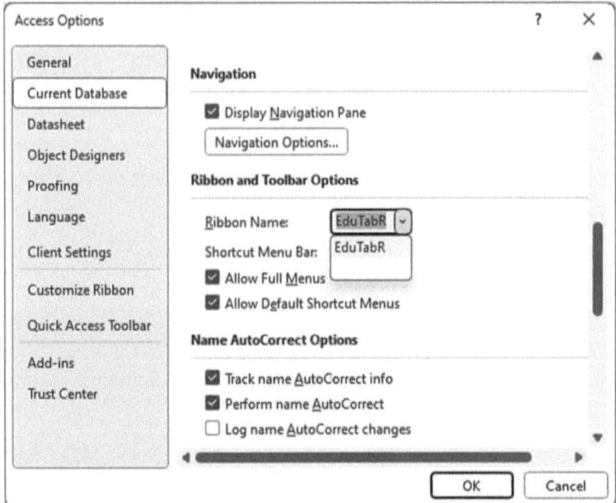

FIGURE 17.24.   Enabling a customized Ribbon in the current database.

4. With the Ribbon name selected, click OK to close the Access Options dialog.
   Microsoft Access displays a message informing you that you must close and reopen the current database for the specified option to take effect.

5. Click OK to the message. Then close and restart the `EduSystems1` database. When the database reopens, you should notice that Access added your custom tab named Edu Systems to the default database Ribbon (see Figure 17.20 earlier in this chapter).

   Before going on to the next section, click the Edu System tab and spend some time testing the controls placed in it.

6. Close the `EduSystems1.accdb` database.

Embedding Ribbon XML Markup in a VBA Procedure

In Custom Project 17.1, you learned how to load a Ribbon customization from an external XML document. Because the name and path of this document are hard-coded in the `LoadRibbon` function, prior to loading the database, you must make sure that the XML markup file exists in the specified folder or Access will greet you with one or more error messages.

   If you don't want to worry about the location of the XML markup file, you can place the XML markup directly inside the VBA function procedure that loads the Ribbon, as shown in Figure 17.25. While the formatting of the XML string is more time-consuming than referencing the file directly, it will ensure that your Ribbon markup travels with the database. Placing Ribbon XML markup inside a VBA procedure is not recommended if you plan on using the same Ribbon customizations in more than one database. If the Ribbon needs to be modified, you would need to make changes in several places, which can become very confusing.

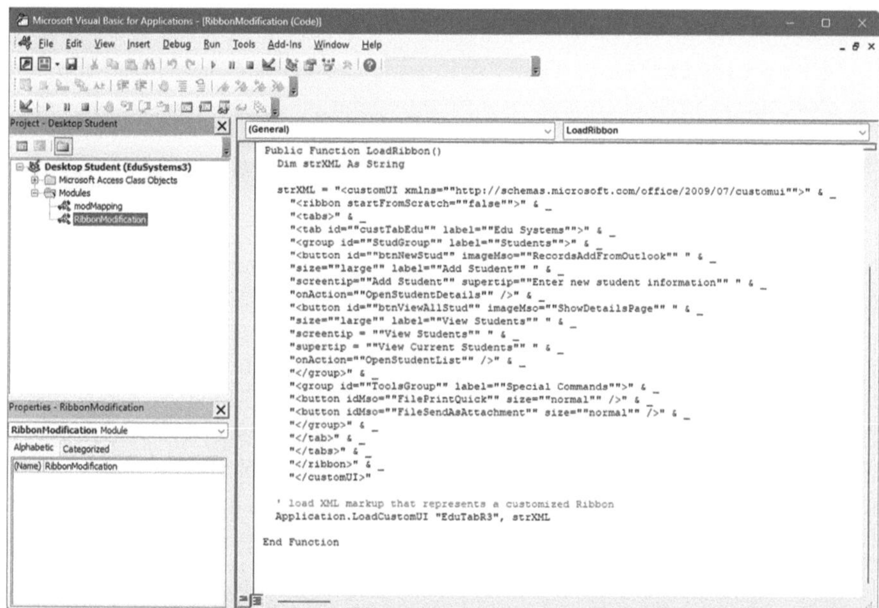

FIGURE 17.25. Ribbon XML markup can be embedded inside the VBA procedure. To try this out, copy the EduSystems3.accdb database from the companion files to your VBAAccess2024_ByExample folder and then open the database. Opening the database directly from the companion files or another folder will generate an error.

Storing Ribbon Customization XML Markup in a System Table

If you store your Ribbon customization XML markup in a local database table, your XML code will be loaded automatically at startup and you won't need to write a special VBA function to load your markup as you did in Custom Project 17.1.

To store your XML in a table, you must create a system table named USys-Ribbons. This table must include two fields: a text field named RibbonName and a memo field named RibbonXML. Access expects these specific column names and data types to read your Ribbon customizations. Any additional fields in this table will be ignored.

In the `RibbonName` field, you must enter a unique name that identifies your custom Ribbon. The `RibbonXML` field must contain the XML customization markup to be applied to the Ribbon.

The `USysRibbons` table is a hidden system table. To show this table in the Navigation Pane, you must tell Access to show system objects (see the next sidebar). You can define multiple Ribbons in your database application by adding a new record to the `USysRibbons` table.

Let's proceed to Hands-On 17.6, in which you create the `USysRibbons` table to store the Ribbon customization prepared earlier in this chapter.

Hands-On 17.6   Creating a Local System Table to Store Ribbon Customization

This hands-on exercise requires the XML document prepared in Hands-On 17.5.

1. Copy the Access database named `EduSystems_Local.accdb` from the companion files to your `C:\VBAAccess2024_ByExample` folder.
2. Open the `EduSystems_Local.accdb` database and click Create | Table Design.
3. In table design view, enter the table structure shown in Figure 17.26.
4. To make the `RibbonName` field the primary key, select this field and click the Primary Key button in the Tools group of the Table Design tab.
5. Save the table as `USysRibbons`. (Press Ctrl+S or click the Save button to open the Save As dialog box.)

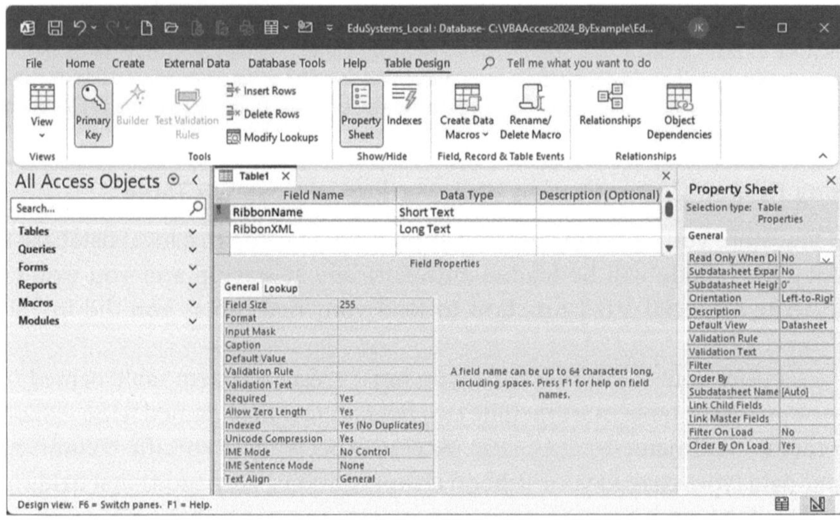

FIGURE 17.26.   USysRibbons is a special system table used for storing Ribbon customizations.

6. Open the `C:\VBAAccess2024_ByExample\EduSystems_01.xml` in Windows Notepad. Press Ctrl+A to select all text and Ctrl+C to copy it to the clipboard, then close Notepad.

7. Back in the main Access window, in the Table Design tab, click the View button and open the `USysRibbons` table in the datasheet view. If you closed this table after you saved it, read the sidebar at the end of this hands-on exercise on how to enable system objects in the database navigation pane.

8. In the USysRibbon datasheet, in the RibbonName field, enter `TestRibbonTab`.

9. When the cursor moves to the RibbonXML field, press Ctrl+V to paste the entire contents of the `EduSystems_01.xml` document that you earlier copied to the clipboard. Expand the row and column widths so that the entire XML markup is visible. Make changes in the `onAction` attribute of the buttons, as shown in Figure 17.27. In the `onAction` attribute for `btnNewStud`, enter `RibbonLib.OpenStudentDetails`. In the `onAction` attribute for `btnViewAllStud`, enter `RibbonLib.OpenStudentList`.

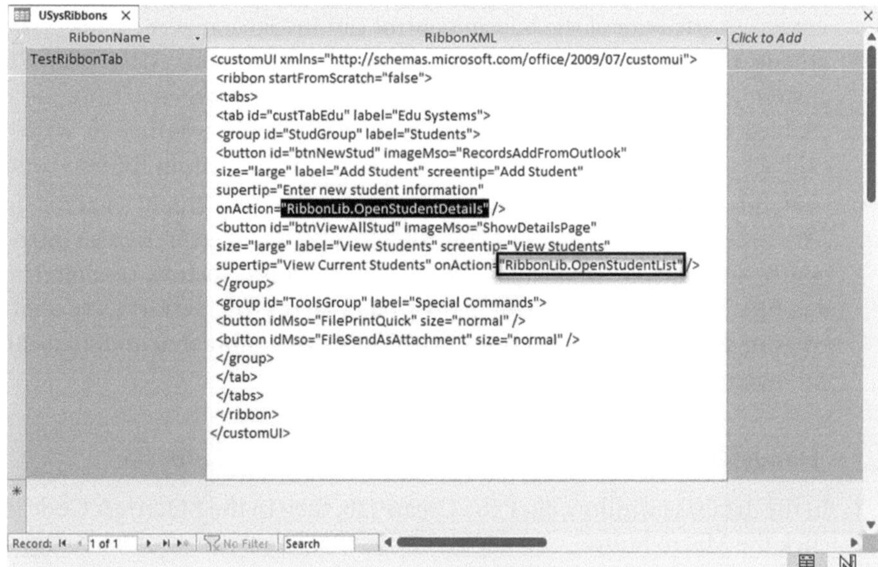

FIGURE 17.27.   The USysRibbons table with a record defining Ribbon customization. To define multiple Ribbons in your application, simply add a new record to this table.

10. Save and close the `USysRibbons` table.

> ### Showing System Objects in the Navigation Pane
>
> By default, system tables do not show in the Navigation Pane. If you need to open the `USysRibbons` table to correct any errors or add a new record, you must enable the system objects in the Navigation Options dialog box, as follows:
>
> 1. Click the File tab, then click Options.
> 2. Click Current Database, then in the Navigation section, click the Navigation Options button.
> 3. Select Show System Objects and click OK to close the Navigation Options dialog box.
> 4. Click OK to exit the Access Options dialog box. You may be asked to restart the database.
> 5. Close and reopen the `EduSystems_Local` database.
>
> The USysRibbons table should now be listed under the Tables category in the database navigation view.

The next step is to enter callbacks that are needed for the button actions.

In Custom Project 17.1, you wrote VBA callback procedures for the `btnNewStud` and `btnViewAllStud` buttons. Instead of a VBA callback, the `onAction` attribute of the button control can invoke a macro. Macro callbacks do not require that you return a value to the Ribbon. Also, your Ribbon customization can be functional even in safe mode (when VBA code is not enabled for the database). It is up to you to decide whether to write VBA callbacks or to create simple macro actions for your custom Ribbon controls.

Hands-On 17.7 demonstrates how you can implement macros in the `onAction` attribute for various controls. This hands-on exercise also introduces you to submacros. *Submacros* are like subroutines. Instead of cluttering the database navigation pane with many small macros that perform a specific task, you can define a series of actions in one place as a submacro and then call that submacro whenever it's needed.

⦿ Hands-On 17.7   Using Macros Instead of VBA Callbacks

1. In the database window, click the Create tab, then in the Macros & Code group, click the Macro button.
2. In the Macro Design window, select Submacro from the Add New Action drop-down list. This option appears toward the top of the drop-down list.
3. In the Submacro name text box, enter `OpenStudentDetails`.
4. Specify the form settings as shown in Figure 17.28:
    a. Select OpenForm from the Add New Action drop-down list.
    b. Select StudentDetails from the Form Name drop-down list.
    c. Select Add from the Data Mode drop-down list.

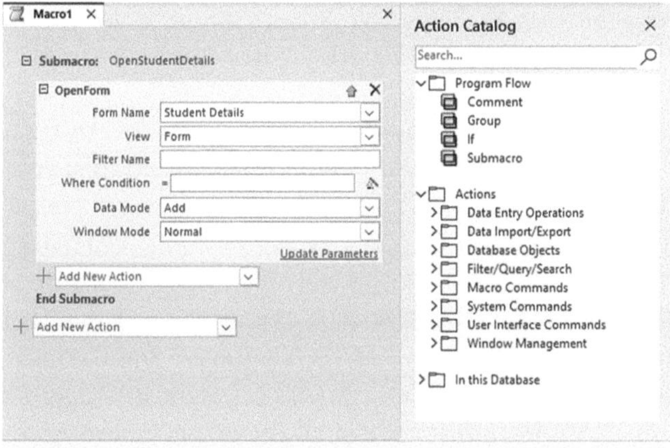

FIGURE 17.28.   Creating the OpenStudentDetails submacro.

You have now completed the first submacro. Let's create the next one.

5. Select Submacro from the Add New Action drop-down list located below End Submacro.
6. In the Submacro name text box, enter `OpenStudentList.`
7. Specify the form settings as shown in Figure 17.29:
   a. Select OpenForm from the Add New Action drop-down list.
   b. Select Student List from the Form Name drop-down list.

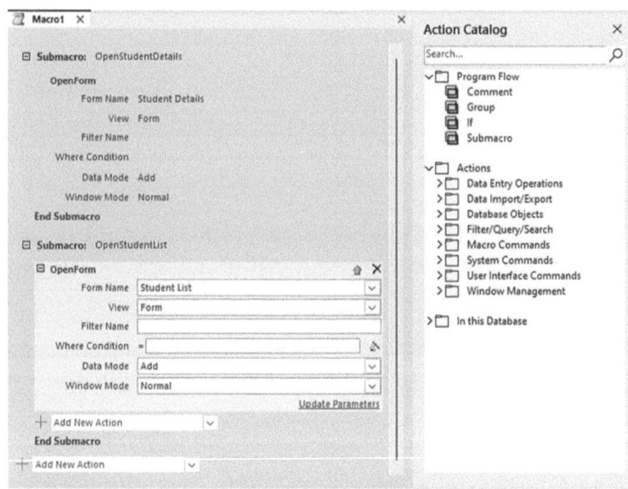

FIGURE 17.29.   Creating the OpenStudentList submacro.

8. Press Ctrl+S to invoke the Save As dialog box. Enter `RibbonLib` for your macro name. This macro contains the two submacros created in earlier steps.

9. Close the `RibbonLib` macro.

   Now that your macro callbacks are ready, you must tell Access to read your Ribbon definition from the `USysRibbons` system table. To do this, you must close and restart the database.

10. Restart Access and then reload the `EduSystems_Local.accdb` database.

    When the application starts, Access looks for the `USysRibbons` system table. If the table exists, Access proceeds to read the data. If any errors are encountered in the Ribbon definition and you have set the option to Show add-in user interface errors (see Figure 17.21 earlier), you will see error messages like the one shown in Figure 17.30. You must correct all the errors before Access can display your customization in the Ribbon.

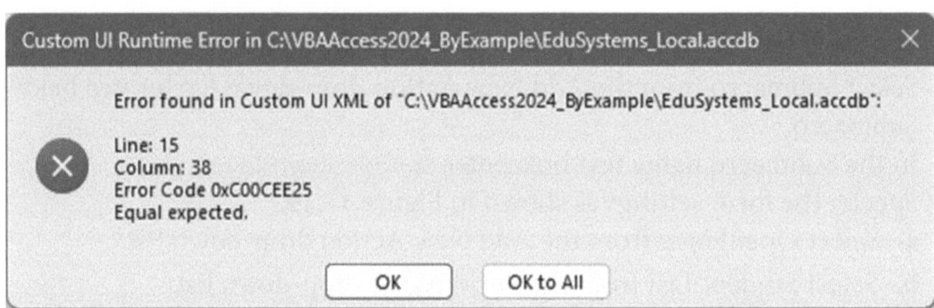

FIGURE 17.30. Upon loading the database, Access displays an error message if errors are found in the Ribbon customization markup.

If there are no errors, Access loads your customization; however, before you can see the Ribbon, you need to tell Access to apply your Ribbon customization when the application is started.

11. Click the File tab, then click Options.

12. Click Current Database. In the Ribbon and Toolbar Options section, choose the name of your customized Ribbon from the Ribbon Name list: TestRibbonTab.

13. Click OK to close the Access Options window.

    Access will advise you that you must close and restart the application before the changes take effect.

14. Click OK to the message, then close and restart the database.

    When the `EduSystems_Local` database is reloaded, you should see your custom Ribbon tab named Edu Systems. Take the time to test the controls placed on this tab to make sure that the macro actions are invoked correctly.

15. Close the `EduSystems_Local.accdb` database.

> | **NOTE** | *If you don't want Access to automatically load Ribbon customizations from the* `USysRibbons` *table, simply rename this table.* |

Assigning Ribbon Customizations to Forms and Reports

In addition to customizing the main database Ribbon, Access allows you to create Ribbons that are associated with a particular form or report. To display Ribbon content for forms and reports, you can use a contextual tabset called `AccessFormReportExtensibility`. This tabset is hidden by default; however, it will become visible when it has controls to display. You will insert some commands into this contextual tabset in Custom Project 17.2.

Because the contextual tabset takes focus when the form or report is first opened, your users will be able to see right away the special controls you've made available for them. These controls can include built-in icons from other Access tabs or your own custom buttons and other types of controls, as discussed later in this chapter.

Keep in mind that Ribbon customizations for forms and reports are only displayed when a form or report is loaded or activated, and they are removed when the object is closed or deactivated. While a specific form or report is in use, you may also hide other built-in Ribbon items. You can do this by setting the `Visible` attribute of a Ribbon item to `False`. This will prevent users from using features of the program that you don't want to be available.

To assign a custom Ribbon to a form or report, you must open a form or report in design or layout view. On the Other tab of the Property Sheet, choose the Ribbon you want to apply from the Ribbon Name list.

◎ Custom Project 17.2   Creating and Assigning Ribbon Customization to a Report

This custom project requires access to the `EduSystems_Local.accdb` database and the `USysRibbons` table that was created in Hands-On 17.6.

Part 1: Creating Ribbon Customization for a Report Using a Local System Table

1. Open the `C:\VBAAccess2024_ByExample\EduSystems_Local.accdb` database.

This database will display a custom tab named Edu Systems. Recall that the XML markup for this customization is stored in the local system table named

`USysRibbons`. In this exercise, you will add another record to this table to specify a Ribbon customization for an Access report. Before you proceed to the next step, make sure that the `USysRibbons` table is displayed in the Navigation Pane. To unhide the table, follow the steps outlined in the previous sidebar, Showing System Objects in the Navigation Pane.

2. Open the `USysRibbons` table and enter a new record for the Ribbon named `AlergMedRpt`, as shown in Figure 17.31. Copy the XML markup file from `EduSystems_04.xml` in the companion files.

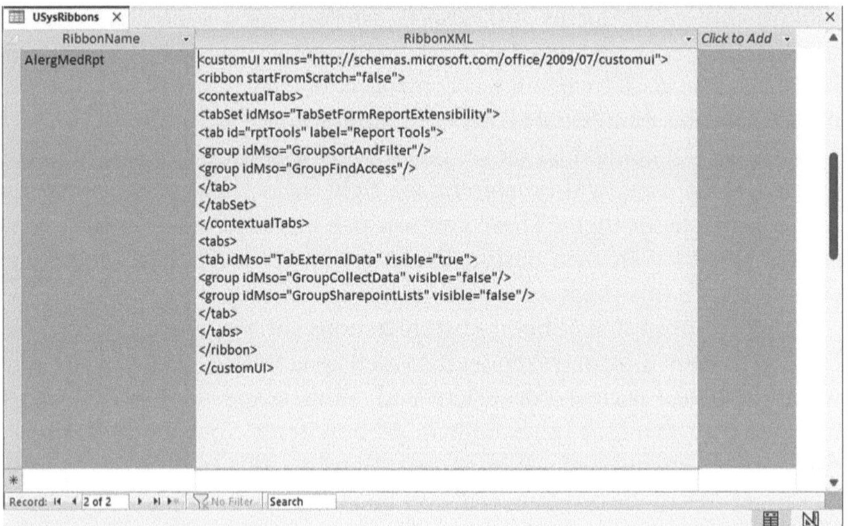

FIGURE 17.31.   Entering Ribbon customization for a report into the new record of the USysRibbons table.

As mentioned earlier, the `RibbonXML` field contains the XML markup you want to apply to a report. The `RibbonName` can be any name you want to use to identify this customization. To have Access use the special contextual tabset available for forms and reports, you must use the `<contextualTabs>` XML tag. Within this tag, use the `<tabSet>` tag. Because this tabset is defined by Access, you must specify `TabSetFormReportExtensibility` in the `idMso` attribute:

```
<contextualTabs>
<tabSet idMso="TabSetFormReportExtensibility">
```

In the next statement, assign a custom ID and a name to the tab that will contain your customization:

```
<tab id="rptTools" label="Report Tools">
```

The preceding XML statement tells Access to place the focus on the Report Tools tab when the report is opened. The next two XML statements define the controls you want to display:

```
<group idMso="GroupSortAndFilter" />
<group idMso="GroupFindAccess" />
```

In this example, you are telling Access to simply add the Sort and Filter and Find groups from its library of built-in controls. As mentioned earlier, you can download the list of control IDs from the GitHub repository. Because you are not defining other customizations to appear on this tab, you need to close this XML group by including the closing tags:

```
</tabSet>
</contextualTabs>
```

When the report is loaded, you also want to disable certain built-in features, such as controls that collect data and use SharePoint lists. This can be done by setting the `visible` attribute of the named built-in control groups to `false`:

```
<tabs>
<tab idMso="TabExternalData" visible="true">
<group idMso="GroupCollectData" visible="false" />
<group idMso="GroupSharepointLists" visible="false" />
</tab>
</tabs>
```

To finish off the customization markup, you must include the ending tags:

```
</ribbon>
</customUI>
```

3. Press Ctrl+S to save changes to the `USysRibbons` table.
4. Close the `USysRibbons` table.

Part 2: Making Access Aware of the New Customization

Remember that the Ribbon customization cannot be displayed until you close and reopen the database:

1. Exit Access and reopen the `EduSystems_Local.accdb` database.
   When Access loads, it will read the Ribbon customizations from the `USysRibbons` table. Now is the time to tell Access to load the customized Ribbon for a specific report.

<table>
<tr><td>NOTE</td><td>You should follow the same steps for creating and assigning Ribbon customizations for a form. Of course, your XML markup for a form ought to include the features related to forms and not reports.</td></tr>
</table>

Part 3: Assigning a Ribbon Customization to a Report

1. In the Navigation Pane, right-click the Allergies and Medications report and choose Design View.
2. If the Property Sheet is not displayed, press Alt+Enter to display it or click the Property Sheet button in the Ribbon. Make sure Report is selected in the selection list at the top of the Property Sheet.
3. In the Property Sheet, click the Other tab, click the down arrow next to the Ribbon Name property, and choose AlergMedRpt from the drop-down list (see Figure 17.32).
4. Press Ctrl+S to save the changes.
5. Close the Allergies and Medications report, then reopen it.
   Notice that when the report opens, the focus is on your custom Ribbon tab named Report Tools (Figure 17.33).
6. Click the External Data tab and notice that only two control groups are shown: Import & Link and Export. The Collect Data tab that normally appears for reports is removed from the Ribbon. This report group is made invisible when the Allergies and Medications report is active, and appears on the External Data tab when any other report is open. Open another report to check this out.
7. Close the Allergies and Medications report when you are finished viewing Ribbon customizations.
8. Close the `EduSystems_Local.accdb` database.

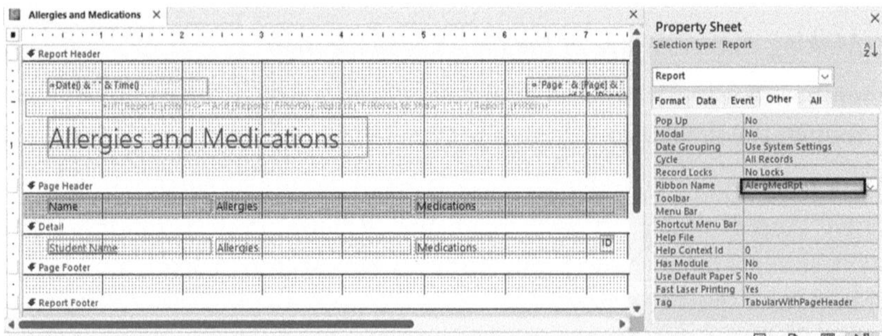

FIGURE 17.32.   Use the Ribbon Name property of the report to assign your Ribbon customization to the active report.

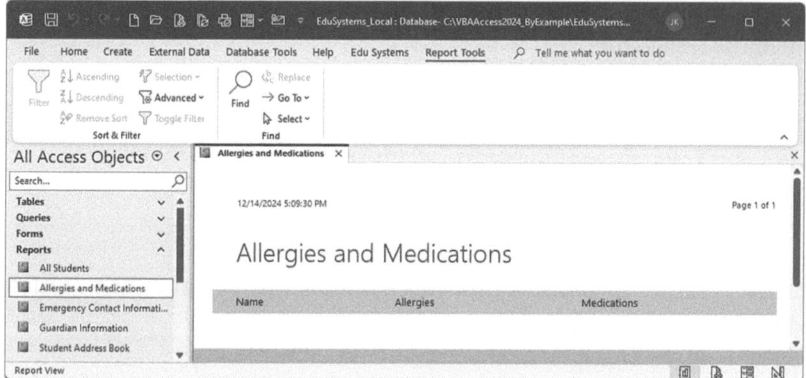

FIGURE 17.33.   The custom Report Tools tab appears in the Access Ribbon when the Allergies and Medications report is opened.

USING IMAGES IN RIBBON CUSTOMIZATIONS

The images you have used so far in your Ribbon customizations are images provided by any Microsoft 365 application that implements the Ribbon. You already know that to reuse an icon from the Office application, you must use the `imageMso` attribute of a control. Instead of using built-in Office images, however, you can also use your own BMP, GIF, and JPEG image files. These images can be stored in a directory on your computer or a network drive, or in an Access table, then passed to your Ribbon controls via the `loadImage` callback for the Ribbon or the `getImage` callback for a control.

Requesting Images via the loadImage Callback

You can specify the name of a custom image file to be loaded for a specific control on the Ribbon by using the image attribute. When you request an image via the image attribute, the `loadImage` callback is called. To load images dynamically with one procedure call, define the callback procedure name in the `loadImage` attribute of the `customUI` node. Here's a fragment of the XML markup file that we'll use in Custom Project 17.3 to implement this method of loading images:

1. In the first line of your Ribbon customization markup (inside the `<customUI>` tag), use the `loadImage` attribute and specify the name of the callback procedure:

```
<customUI xmlns="http://schemas.microsoft.com/office/2009/07/
                 customui"
loadImage="OnLoadImage">
```

2. When defining your Ribbon controls, use the image attribute and specify the name of the image file:

```
<group id="ImagesGroup" label ="Special Features">
<button id="btnNotes" label="Open Notepad"
image="Note.gif" size="large" onAction="OpenNotepad" />
<button id="btnComputer" label="Computer folder"
image="MyFolder.gif" size="normal" />
</group>
```

3. Write the `loadImage` callback procedure (`OnLoadImage`) in a VBA module:

```
Public Sub OnLoadImage(imgName As String, ByRef image)
  Dim strImgFileName As String
  strImgFileName = "C:\VBAAccess2024_ByExample\images\" & imgName

  Set image = LoadPicture(strImgFileName)
End Sub
```

To load a picture from a file, you must use the `LoadPicture` function. This function is a member of the `stdole.StdFunctions` library. The library file, which is called `stdole2.tlb`, is installed in the `System` or `System32` folder on your computer and is available to your VBA procedures without setting additional references. The `LoadPicture` function returns an object of type `IPictureDisp` that represents the image. You can view objects, methods, and properties available in the `stdole` library by activating the Object Browser in the VBE window.

4. Write the callback procedure for the button labeled `OpenNotepad`:

```
Public Sub OpenNotepad(ctl As IRibbonControl)
  Shell "Notepad.exe", vbNormalFocus
End Sub
```

The `OpenNotepad` procedure tells Access to use the `Shell` function to open Windows Notepad. Notice that the name of the program's executable file is in double quotation marks. The second argument of the `Shell` function is optional. This argument specifies the window style, that is, how the program will appear once it is launched. The `vbNormalFocus` constant will open Notepad in a normal-size window with focus. If the window style is not specified, the program will be minimized with focus (`vbMinimizedFocus`).

Let's proceed to Custom Project 17.3, which adds two new buttons with custom images to the Ribbon.

⊚ Custom Project 17.3   Loading Custom Images Using the loadImage Callback

This project requires access to the `EduSystems_Local.accdb` database and the `USysRibbons` table that was created in Hands-On 17.6. To use custom images, copy the `Images` folder from the companion files to your `C:\VBAAccess2024_ByExample` folder.

Part 1: Creating Ribbon Customization for Loading Custom Images

1. Open the `C:\VBAAccess2024_ByExample\EduSystems_Local.accdb` database.
2. In the Navigation Pane, double-click the USysRibbons table to open it. If you cannot find this table, refer to Part 1 in Custom Project 17.2.
3. Enter a new record for the Ribbon named `CustomImage1`, as shown in Figure 17.34. You can copy the XML markup from the `EduSystems_05.txt` file in the companion files.

   In the first line of the Ribbon customization markup (inside the `<customUI>` tag), notice that we've added the `loadImage` attribute. This attribute specifies the name of the callback procedure, `OnLoadImage`, that will handle loading the custom images included in the Special Features group. The Special Features group contains two images to be loaded from the `C:\VBAAccess2024_ByExample\Images` folder. Notice that the names of these images are specified in the image attribute of each button control in this group. You do not need to specify the file path; the `OnLoadImage` procedure will contain this information. For the button to perform some action, you need to include the `onAction` attribute with the name of the macro, VBA procedure, or expression to be executed. This example does not define the `onAction` callback for the button named Computer Folder. To test your skills, you can add your own action for this button when you have completed this project.

4. Press Ctrl+S to save changes to the `USysRibbons` table.
5. Close the `USysRibbons` table.

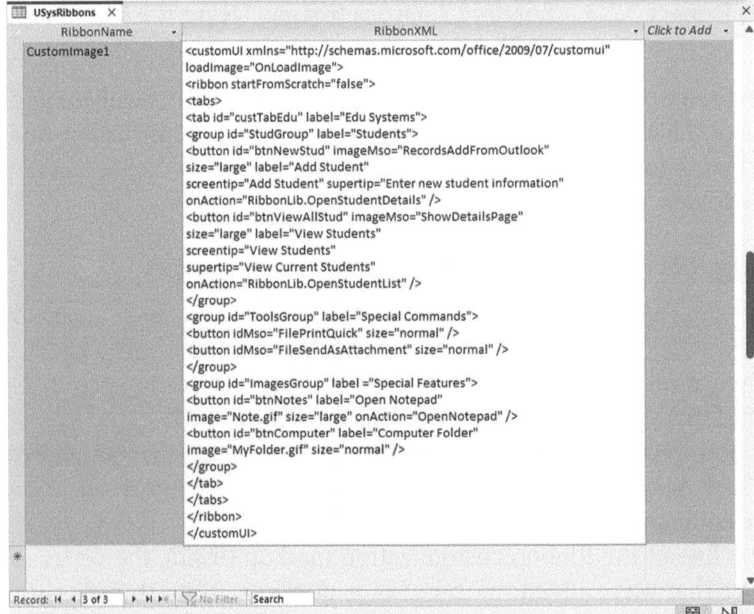

FIGURE 17.34. Entering Ribbon customization for loading custom images. Notice that this is the third record in the USysRibbons table.

Part 2: Setting Up the Programming Environment

1. Press Alt+F11 to switch to the VBE window.
2. Choose Tools | References. In the References dialog box, add a reference to the following library: Microsoft Office 16.0 Object Library.
3. Click OK to close the References dialog box.

Part 3: Writing the VBA Callback Procedures

1. Choose Insert | Module.
2. In the module Code window, enter the following VBA procedures:

```vba
Public Sub OnLoadImage(imgName As String, ByRef image)
  Dim strImgFileName As String
  strImgFileName = "C:\VBAAccess2024_ByExample\images\" & imgName

  Set image = LoadPicture(strImgFileName)
End Sub


Public Sub OpenNotepad(ctl As IRibbonControl)
  Shell "Notepad.exe", vbNormalFocus
End Sub
```

> **NOTE**   *For explanations of these procedures, please refer to the beginning of this section.*

3. Press Ctrl+S to save the changes in the Code window. When asked to name your module, enter any name you want.
4. Choose File | Close and Return to Microsoft Access.

Part 4: Making Access Aware of the New Customization

Recall that the Ribbon customization cannot be displayed until you close and reopen the database.

1. Close and reopen the `EduSystems_Local.accdb` database.
   When Access loads, it will read the Ribbon customizations from the `USysRibbons` table.
2. Click the File tab, then click Options.
3. Click the Current Database option. In the Ribbon and Toolbar Options section, choose CustomImage1 from the Ribbon Name list.
4. Click OK to close the Access Options window.
   Access displays a message informing you that you must close and reopen the current database for the specified option to take effect.
5. Click OK to the message. Then, close and restart the `EduSystems_Local` database.
   When the database reopens, you should see the default database Ribbon with your custom tab named Edu Systems (Figure 17.35).

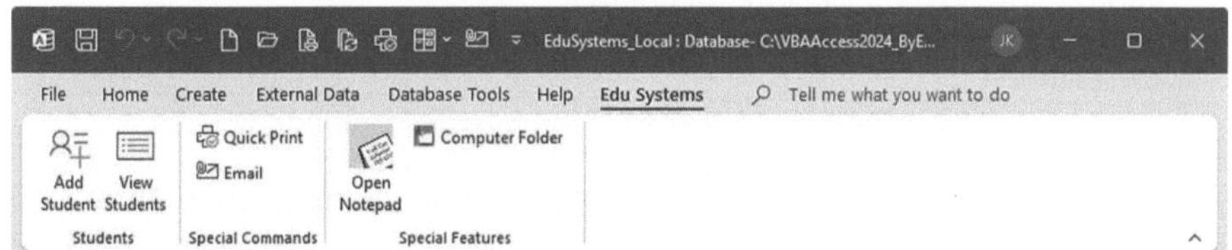

FIGURE 17.35.   The Ribbon customization as defined in Custom Project 17.3 with two image buttons in the Special Features group of the Edu Systems tab.

6. Click the Open Notepad button to open Windows Notepad. Then, close Notepad.

Before moving on to the next section, take some time to modify the Ribbon XML to include the `onAction` callback for the button labeled Computer Folder and write your own custom VBA procedure to execute when this button is clicked. For example, you can make this button display a dialog box asking the user for the name of the folder to create, then use the VBA built-in function `MkDir` to create it. Use the Object Browser to locate this function. Remember that you will have to close and reopen the database for Access to recognize your Ribbon modifications.

Requesting Images via the getImage Callback

Custom images can also be loaded to the Ribbon using the `getImage` attribute of a control. The procedure you specify in this attribute will retrieve the correct image from the specified location using the same `LoadPicture` function you worked with in the previous section. The following XML markup adds two new controls with custom images to the Special Features group that was defined in Custom Project 17.3:

```
<customUI xmlns="http://schemas.microsoft.com/office/2009/07/
loadImage="OnLoadImage">
  <ribbon startFromScratch="false">
  <tabs>
  <tab id="custTabEdu" label="Edu Systems">
  <group id="StudGroup" label="Students">
  <button id="btnNewStud" imageMso="RecordsAddFromOutlook"
  size="large" label="Add Student"
  screentip="Add Student" supertip="Enter new student
information"
  onAction="RibbonLib.OpenStudentDetails" />
  <button id="btnViewAllStud" imageMso="ShowDetailsPage"
  size="large" label="View Students"
  screentip="View Students"
  supertip="View Current Students"
  onAction="RibbonLib.OpenStudentList" />
  </group>
  <group id="ToolsGroup" label="Special Commands">
  <button idMso="FilePrintQuick" size="normal" />
  <button idMso="FileSendAsAttachment" size="normal" />
  </group>
  <group id="ImagesGroup" label="Special Features">
  <button id="btnNotes" label="Open Notepad"
  image="Note.gif" size="large"
  onAction="OpenNotepad" />
  <button id="btnComputer" label="Computer Folder"
  image="MyFolder.gif" size="normal" />
  <button id="btnRedStar" label="Honor Student"
  getImage="OnGetImage" size="large" />
  <gallery id="glHolidays" label="Holidays" columns="3" rows="4"
```

```
getImage="OnGetImage" getItemCount="OnGetItemCount"
getItemLabel="OnGetItemLabel" getItemImage="OnGetItemImage"
getItemID="onGetItemID" onAction="onSelectedItem" />
</group>
</tab>
</tabs>
</ribbon>
</customUI>
```

In the preceding Ribbon customization markup, we are using all the controls that have been added thus far in this chapter's hands-on exercises and projects. In addition, the Special Features group now includes a new button labeled Honor Student and a gallery control labeled Holidays.

```
<button id="btnRedStar" label="Honor Student"
  getImage="OnGetImage" size="large" />
<gallery id="glHolidays" label="Holidays" columns="3" rows="4"
  getImage="OnGetImage" getItemCount="OnGetItemCount"
  getItemLabel="OnGetItemLabel" getItemImage="OnGetItemImage"
  getItemID="onGetItemID" onAction="onSelectedItem" />
```

In this XML markup, the gallery control will perform the action specified in the `onSelectedItem` callback procedure. To specify your own callback procedure for the Honor Student button, you must add the `onAction` attribute to this button, then write the appropriate VBA code. Notice that the gallery control has many attributes that contain static text or define callbacks. We will discuss them later. Right now, let's focus on the image-loading process. Both the button and gallery controls use the `getImage` attribute with the `OnGetImage` callback procedure. This procedure will tell Access to load the appropriate image to the Ribbon for each of these controls:

```
Public Sub OnGetImage(ctl As IRibbonControl, ByRef image)
Select Case ctl.id
    Case "btnRedStar"
      Set image = _
      LoadPicture("C:\VBAAccess2024_ByExample\images\redstar.gif")
    Case "glHolidays"
      Set image = _
      LoadPicture("C:\VBAAccess2024_ByExample\images\Square0.gif")
End Select
End Sub
```

The decision as to which image should be loaded is based on the ID of the control in the `Select Case` statement. The gallery control also uses the `OnGet-`

`ItemImage` callback procedure (defined in the `getItemImage` attribute) to load custom images for its drop-down selection list (see Figure 17.36).

Use the columns and rows attributes to specify the number of columns and rows in the gallery when it is opened. If you need to define the height and width of images in the gallery, use the `itemHeight` and `itemWidth` attributes (these are not used in this example due to the simplicity of the utilized images). The `getItemCount` and `getItemLabel` attributes contain callback procedures that provide information to the Ribbon on how many items should appear in the drop-down list and the names of those items. The `getItemImage` attribute contains a callback procedure specifying the images to be displayed next to each gallery item. The `getItemID` attribute specifies the `onGetItemID` callback procedure that will provide a unique ID for each of the gallery items.

Now that we've discussed the Ribbon customization markup, let's go over the VBA callbacks that are referenced in it. The following procedures must be added to the VBA module for the preceding XML markup to work:

```
Public Sub OnGetItemCount(ctl As IRibbonControl, ByRef count)
   count = 12
End Sub
```

In this procedure, we use the `count` parameter to return to the Ribbon the number of items we want to place in the gallery control.

```
Public Sub OnGetItemLabel(ctl As IRibbonControl, _
   index As Integer, ByRef label)
   label = MonthName(index + 1)
End Sub
```

This procedure will label each of the gallery items. The VBA `MonthName` function is used to retrieve the name of the month based on the value of the index. The initial value of the index is zero (`0`). Therefore, `index + 1` will return February. To display the month's name abbreviated (Jan, Feb, etc.), specify `True` as the second parameter to this function:

```
label = MonthName(index + 1, True)
```

If you are using a localized version of Microsoft 365 or standalone Access (French, Spanish, etc.), the `MonthName` function will return the name of the month in the specified interface language.

The next callback procedure shows how to load images for each gallery item:

```
Public Sub OnGetItemImage(ctl As IRibbonControl, _
   index As Integer, ByRef image)
```

```
   Dim imgPath As String

    imgPath = "C:\VBAAccess2024_ByExample\images\square"
    Set image = LoadPicture(imgPath & index + 1 & ".gif")
  End Sub
```

Each item in the gallery must have a unique ID, so the `onGetItemID` callback uses the `MonthName` function to specify the ID:

```
Public Sub onGetItemID(ctl As IRibbonControl, _
  index As Integer, ByRef id)

    id = MonthName(index + 1)

End Sub
```

The last procedure you need to write for the gallery control should define the actions to be performed when an item in the gallery is clicked. This is done via the following `onSelectedItem` callback that was specified in the `onAction` attribute of the XML markup:

```
Public Sub onSelectedItem(ctl As IRibbonControl, _
  selectedId As String, _
  selectedIndex As Integer)

  Select Case selectedIndex
    Case 6
      MsgBox "Holiday 1: Independence Day, July 4th", _
        vbInformation + vbOKOnly, _
        selectedId & " Holidays"
    Case 11
      MsgBox "Holiday 2: Christmas Day, December 25th", _
        vbInformation + vbOKOnly, _
        selectedId & " Holidays"
    Case Else
      MsgBox "Please program holidays for " & selectedId & ".", _
        vbInformation + vbOKOnly, _
        " Under Construction"
  End Select
End Sub
```

In the preceding callback procedure, the `selectedId` parameter returns the name that was assigned to the label, while the `selectedIndex` parameter is the position of the item in the list. The first item in the list (`January`) is indexed with zero (`0`), the second with `1`, and so forth. In this procedure, we have just coded two holidays: one for the month of July (`selectedIndex-6`) and one for

December (`selectedIndex=11`). The `Case  Else` clause in the `Select  Case` statement provides a message when other months are selected.

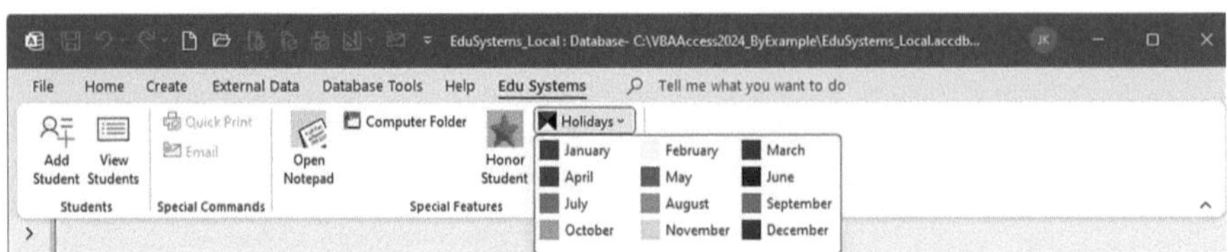

FIGURE 17.36. Customized Ribbon with the gallery control.

To implement the Ribbon customization shown in Figure 17.32, follow the steps outlined in Hands-On 17.8.

Hands-On 17.8 Loading Custom Images Using the getImage Callback

This hands-on exercise requires access to the `EduSystems_Local.accdb` database and the `USysRibbons` table that was created in Hands-On 17.6. This exercise assumes that you have also completed Custom Project 17.3, which presented a method of loading images via the `loadImage` callback. By now, you should be very familiar with the Ribbon customization process, and thus this exercise outlines only the main steps you need to take to complete it.

For a detailed explanation of the process, refer to the previous exercises and projects. The images used in this example are located in the `C:\VBAAccess2024_ByExample\Images` folder.

1. In the `USysRibbons` table of the `EduSystems_Local` database, add a new record. In the RibbonName field, enter `CustomImage2` for the name of the new Ribbon customization. In the RibbonXML field, paste the XML markup from the `EduSystems_06.txt` file in the companion files. Press Ctrl+S to save the changes, then close the `USysRibbons` table.
2. Press Alt+F11 to switch to the VBE window. You should see one module with the VBA procedures that were added in Custom Project 17.3. You do not need to create a new module for this customization. In the same module, enter the VBA procedures discussed earlier in this section (`OnGetImage`, `OnGetItemCount`, `OnGetItemLabel`, `OnGetItemImage`, `onGetItemID`, and `onSelectedItem`). Press Ctrl+S to save the changes in your module and exit VBE. All these VBA callback procedures can be also copied from the `EduSystems_HandsOn_17.8.txt` file located in the companion files.
3. Close Access and restart the `EduSystems_Local` database. When the database is reloaded, click the File tab and select Options. In the Access Options

window, click Current Database and select your new Ribbon (CustomImage2) from the Ribbon Name list in the Ribbon and Toolbar Options section. Click OK to close the Access Options window. Access will display a message informing you that you must close and reopen the current database for the specified option to take effect. Click OK to the message. Then, close and restart the `EduSystems_Local` database.

The customized Ribbon should appear as shown earlier in Figure 17.36. Test the gallery control by clicking on some of the month items.

More About Loading Custom Images

Instead of loading custom images from a computer folder, you can create an Access table to store your images and then use the `Recordset` object in the `getImage` callback to read the images from the table. This table should contain at least two fields: the `ControlID` field with the name of the control and the `ImageFileName` field specifying the name of the image file for the control. Custom images can also be stored and loaded from an `Attachment` field, which is available in Access databases created in the `.accdb` file format.

Understanding Attributes and Callbacks

Ribbon controls have properties defined by attributes, such as `id`, `label`, `enabled`, and `screentip`. By using a specific attribute, you can modify the appearance of a control at either design time or runtime. To define a control attribute at runtime, simply set it to an allowable value right in the Ribbon customization XML markup. For example, you can provide the name for your control in the `label` attribute. The control `label` can contain up to 1,024 characters.

If the attribute value is unknown at design time, add the prefix `get` to the design-time attribute name and specify the name of the callback procedure or macro as the attribute value. For example, if the control's label needs to be defined at runtime, use the `getLabel` attribute and specify the name of the callback procedure:

```
<group id="Today's Events" getLabel="getEventDate">
```

When the Ribbon is loaded, the procedure in the `getLabel` attribute will run and provide the actual value of the attribute:

```
Public Sub getEventDate(ctl As IRibbonControl, _
  ByRef ReturnValue As Variant)

  ReturnValue = "Events for " & Format(Now(), "mm/dd/yyyy")
End Sub
```

This procedure will display the current date in the name of the group label. Although many times you will see the callback procedure name prefixed with `get` or `onGet`, keep in mind that you do not have to give the callback procedure the same name as the attribute it is used with. Use any name that makes sense to you. The only requirement is that the callback procedure matches a particular *signature*, which is the declaration of the procedure, the parameters, and return types. For example, the callback for the `onAction` attribute of a button control has the following signature:

```
Public Sub NameOfCallback(control As IRibbonControl)
```

`IRibbonControl` is the control that was clicked. This control is passed to your procedure by the Ribbon. You can specify your own name for the control parameter. For example:

```
Public Sub NameOfCallback(ctl As IRibbonControl)
```

Before using the `IRibbonControl`, you need to add a reference to the Microsoft Office 16.0 object library in your VBA project. The `onAction` attribute is a special type of attribute that does not need to be prefixed by the word `get` to point to a callback procedure.

USING VARIOUS CONTROLS IN RIBBON CUSTOMIZATIONS

Now that you know how to go about creating the XML markup for your Ribbon customizations, as well as loading and applying the custom Ribbon to a database, form, or report, let's look at other types of controls you can show in the Ribbon to give your database application a more polished and professional look. You can reuse the `EduSystems_Local` database used in the earlier examples to create additional Ribbon customizations that utilize the controls discussed in this section.

Creating Toggle Buttons

A *toggle button* is a button that alternates between two states. Many formatting features, such as Bold, Italic, and Format Painter, are implemented as toggle buttons. When you click a toggle button, the button stays down until you click it again. To create a toggle button, use the `<toggleButton>` XML tag, as shown here:

```
<toggleButton id="tglNewStudent" label="New Student
                                        Questionnaire"
size="normal" getPressed="OnGetPressed" onAction="ShowHideQ" />
```

You can add a built-in image to the toggle button with the `imageMso` attribute, or use a custom image, as discussed earlier in this chapter. To find out whether the toggle button is pressed, include the `getPressed` attribute in your XML markup. The `getPressed` callback procedure provides two arguments—the control that was clicked and the pressed state of the toggle button:

```
Sub OnGetPressed(control As IRibbonControl, _
 ByRef pressed)

  If control.id="tglNewStudent" then
    pressed = False
  End If
End Sub
```

The preceding callback routine will ensure that the specified toggle button is not pressed when the Ribbon is loaded.

To perform an action when the toggle button is clicked, set the `onAction` attribute to the name of your custom callback procedure. This callback also provides two arguments—the control that was clicked and the state of the toggle button:

```
Sub ShowHideQ(control As IRibbonControl, pressed As Boolean)
  If pressed Then
    MsgBox "The toggle button is pressed."
  Else
    MsgBox "The toggle button is not pressed."
  End If
End Sub
```

If the toggle button is pressed, the value of the pressed argument will be `True`; otherwise, it will be `False`. The toggle button named New Student Questionnaire is shown in Figure 17.37.

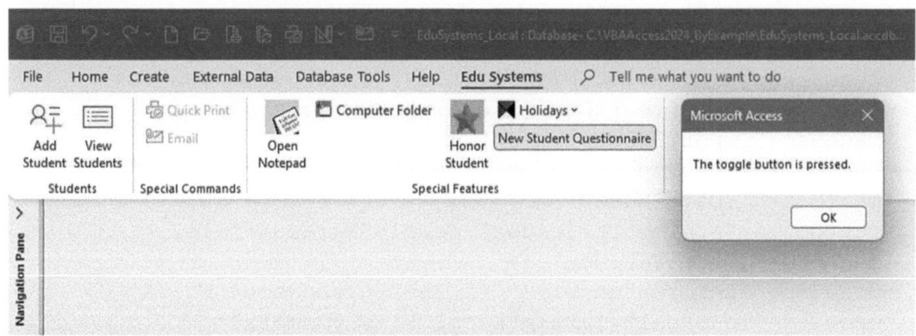

FIGURE 17.37.   The custom toggle button Student Questionnaire will become highlighted when pressed and will return to its normal state when clicked again.

<table>
<tr><td>NOTE</td><td>The XML markup for adding the Toggle button to the current Edu Systems tab can be found in the EduSystems_07.txt file in the companion files. The VBA callback code is located in the EduSystems_07_withToggle_VBA.txt file.</td></tr>
</table>

<table>
<tr><td>NOTE</td><td>For each of the discussed controls, continue to make new records in the USysRibbons table and copy the XML customization code from the provided text file. See Figure 17.45 later in this chapter for the names of the created Ribbon tabs. If preferred, use your own names. If you find it difficult to do data entry in the RibbonXML field due to the length of the XML markup, press Shift+F2 for the Zoom dialog. Test each button before moving on to create a new button. This way, if any errors occur upon loading your modified Ribbon customization, it will be easier to troubleshoot them.</td></tr>
</table>

Creating Split Buttons, Menus, and Submenus

A *split button* is a combination of a button or toggle button and a menu. Clicking the button performs one default action, and clicking the drop-down arrow opens a menu with a list of related options to select from. To create the split button, use the `<splitButton>` tag. Within this tag, you need to define a `<button>` or `<toggleButton>` control and the `<menu>` control, as shown in the following XML markup:

```
<group id="OtherControlsGroup" label="Other Controls" >
<splitButton id="btnSplit1" size="large" >
<button id="btnImport" label="Import More"
imageMso="ImportAccess" />
<menu id="mnuImport" label="More Import Formats"
itemSize="normal" >
<menuSeparator id="mnuDiv1" title="Other Databases" />
<button id="btnImportODBC" label="ODBC database"
imageMso="ImportOdbcDatabase" />
<button id="btnImportDbase" label="Dbase file"
imageMso="ImportDBase" />
<button id="btnImportParadox" label="Paradox file"
imageMso="ImportParadox" />
<menuSeparator id="mnuDiv2" title="Spreadsheet Files" />
<menu id="mnuExcel" label="Excel File Formats"
imageMso="ImportExcel" itemSize="normal" >
```

```
<checkBox id="xlsFormat" label="xls file" />
<checkBox id="xlsxFormat" label="xlsx file" />
</menu>
<button id="btnImportLotus" label="Lotus 1-2-3 file"
imageMso="ImportLotus" />
<menuSeparator id="mnuDiv3" title="Other Files" />
<button id="btnText" label="Text file"
imageMso="ImportTextFile" />
<button id="btnXML" label="XML file" imageMso="ImportXmlFile" />
<button id="btnHTML" label="HTML file"
imageMso="ImportHtmlDocument" />
<button id="btnOutlook" label="Outlook folder"
imageMso="ImportOutlook" />
<button id="btnSharepoint" label="SharePoint List"
imageMso="ImportSharePointList" />
</menu>
</splitButton>
</group>
```

> **NOTE** *The* `<checkBox>` *tag used in the preceding example XML is discussed in detail in the next section.*

You can specify the size of the items in the menu using the `itemSize` attribute. To display a description for each menu item below the item label, set the `itemSize` attribute to `large` (`itemSize="large"`) and use the `description` attribute to specify the text. The `<menuSeparator>` tag can be used inside the menu node to break the menu into sections. Each menu segment can then be titled using the title attribute, as shown in the preceding example. You can add the `onAction` attribute to each menu button to specify the callback procedure or macro to execute when the menu item is clicked. In addition to button controls, menus can contain toggle buttons, checkboxes, gallery controls, split buttons, nested menus, and dynamic menus.

See `EduSystems_08_withSplitPlusMenus.txt` in the companion files for the XML code used to produce the custom split button shown in Figure 17.38.

Figure 17.38 displays the Ribbon with split buttons, menus, and submenus created in this section.

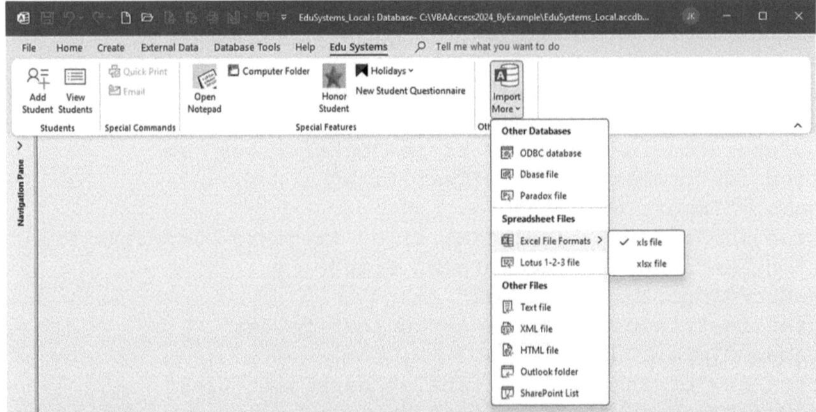

FIGURE 17.38.   Custom split button controls can use the built-in Office images. They can also contain menus and submenus consisting of checkboxes.

Creating Checkboxes

The checkbox control is used to provide an option, such as true/false or on/off. It can be included inside a menu control, as was demonstrated in the previous section, or used as a separate control on the Ribbon. To create a checkbox, use the <checkBox> tag, as shown in the following XML:

```
<separator id="OtherControlsDiv1" />
<labelControl id="TitleForBox1" label="Areas of Interest (please
  check below)" />
<box id="boxLayout1">
<checkBox id="chkSafety" label="School Safety"
  enabled="true" visible="true"
  onAction="DoSomething" />
<checkBox id="chkHealth" label="Health" enabled="false" />
<checkBox id="chkSportsMusic" getLabel="onGetLabel" />
</box>
```

In the preceding XML markup, the <separator> tag will produce the vertical bar that visually separates controls within the same Ribbon group (see Figure 17.39).

The <labelControl> tag can be used to display static text anywhere in the Ribbon. In this example, we use it to place a header over a set of controls. To control the layout of various controls (to display them horizontally instead of vertically), use the <box> tag. You can define whether a checkbox should be visible or hidden by setting the visible attribute to true or false. To disable a checkbox, set the enabled attribute to false; this will cause the checkbox to appear grayed out. Notice that the checkbox labeled Health is not active (it is grayed out).

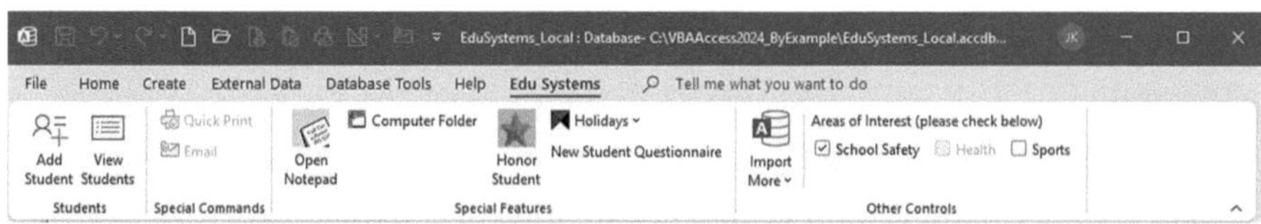

FIGURE 17.39.   These checkbox controls are laid out horizontally.

See `EduSystems_09_withCheckBoxes.txt` in the companion files for the XML code used to produce the checkbox controls shown in Figure 17.39. The required VBA code can be found in `EduSystems_09_withCheckBoxes_VBA.txt`.

Similar to other controls, labels for checkboxes can contain static text in the `label` attribute, or they can be assigned dynamically using the callback procedure in the `getLabel` attribute:

```
<checkBox id="chkSportsMusic" getLabel="onGetLabel" />
```

The `getLabel` attribute points to the `onGetLabel` callback procedure, which needs to be added to your VBA module:

```
Public Sub onGetLabel(ctl As IRibbonControl, ByRef label)
  If ctl.id = "chkSportsMusic" And _
    Weekday(Now(), vbWednesday) Then
      label = "Sports"
  Else
      label = "Music"
  End If
End Sub
```

This procedure will run automatically when the Ribbon loads. If today is Wednesday, you will see a checkbox for Sports; otherwise, it will be Music.

The action of the checkbox control is handled by the callback procedure in the `onAction` attribute:

```
<checkBox id="chkSafety" label="School Safety"
    enabled="true" visible="true"
    onAction="DoSomething" />
```

The `DoSomething` procedure must be added to the VBA module for the School Safety checkbox to respond to a user's click:

```
Public Sub DoSomething(ctl As IRibbonControl, _
 pressed As Boolean)
```

```
   If ctl.id = "chkSafety" And pressed Then
     MsgBox "Safety is our number one concern."
   Else
     MsgBox "Sorry to hear that safety is not your concern."
   End If
End Sub
```

To get the checked state for a checkbox, point to your callback procedure in the `getPressed` attribute, similar to what we did earlier with the toggle button. The default VBA syntax for this callback is as follows:

```
Sub GetPressed(control As IRibbonControl, ByRef return)
```

<table>
<tr><td>

NOTE

</td><td>

As mentioned earlier, callback procedures don't need to be named the same as the attribute they are used with. Also, you may change the callback's argument names as desired.

</td></tr>
</table>

Creating Edit Boxes

Use the `<editBox>` tag to provide an area on the Ribbon where users can type text or numbers:

```
<editBox id="txtFullName" label="First and Last Name:"
sizeString="AAAAAAAAAAAAAAA" maxLength="25"
onChange="onFullNameChange" />
```

Figure 17.40 shows the result of the preceding XML markup.

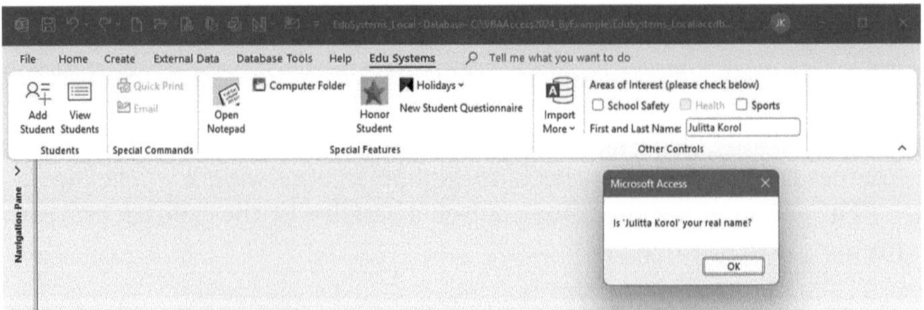

FIGURE 17.40.   An edit box control allows data entry directly on the Ribbon.

See the `EduSystems_10_withEditBoxes.txt` file in the companion files for the XML code used to produce the edit box control shown in Figure 17.40. The required VBA code can be found in `EduSystems_10_withEditBoxes_VBA.txt`.

The `sizeString` attribute specifies the width of the edit box. Set it to a string that will give you the width you want. The `maxLength` attribute allows you to limit the number of characters and/or digits that can be typed in the edit box. If the text entered exceeds the specified number of characters (25 in this case), Access automatically displays a balloon message on the Ribbon: The entry may contain no more than 25 characters.

When the entry is updated in an edit box control, the callback procedure specified in the `onChange` attribute is called:

```
Public Sub onFullNameChange(ctl As IRibbonControl, _
  text As String)
   If text <> "" Then
     MsgBox "Is '" & text & _
       "' your real name?"
   End If
End Sub
```

When the user enters text in the edit box, the procedure displays a message box.

Creating Combo Boxes and Dropdowns

There are three types of drop-down controls that can be placed on the Ribbon: combo box, drop-down, and gallery.

These controls can be dynamically populated at runtime by writing callbacks for their `getItemCount`, `getItemID`, `getItemLabel`, `getItemImage`, `getItem-Screentip`, or `getItemSupertip` attributes.

The combo box and drop-down controls can also be made static by defining their drop-down content using the `<item>` tag, as shown here:

```
<separator id="OtherControlsDiv2" />
<comboBox id="cmbLang" label="Languages"
supertip="Select Language Guide"
  onChange="OnChangeLang" >
  <item id="English" label="English" />
  <item id="Spanish" label="Spanish" />
  <item id="French" label="French" />
  <item id="German" label="German" />
  <item id="Russian" label="Russian" />
</comboBox>
```

To separate the combo box control from other controls in the same Ribbon group, this example uses the `<separator>` tag. Each `<item>` tag specifies a new drop-down row.

A combo box is a combination of a drop-down list and a single-line edit box, allowing the user to either type a value directly into the control or choose from the list of predefined options. Use the `sizeString` attribute to define the width of the edit box.

The combo box control does not have the `onAction` attribute. It uses the `onChange` attribute, which specifies the callback to execute when the item selection changes:

```
Public Sub OnChangeLang(ctl As IRibbonControl, _
 text As String)

  MsgBox "You selected the " & text & " language guide."
End Sub
```

The `onChange` callback provides only the text of the selected item; it does not give you access to the selected index. If you need the index of the selection, use the drop-down control instead, as shown here:

```
<dropDown id="drpBoro" label="City Borough"
  supertip="Select School Borough"
  onAction="OnActionBoro" >
  <item id="M" label="Manhattan" />
  <item id="B" label="Brooklyn" />
  <item id="Q" label="Queens" />
  <item id="I" label="Staten Island" />
  <item id="X" label="Bronx" />
</dropDown>
```

The `onAction` callback of the drop-down control will give you both the selected item's ID and its index:

```
Public Sub OnActionBoro(ctl As IRibbonControl, _
 ByRef SelectedID As String, _
 ByRef SelectedIndex As Integer)

  MsgBox "Index=" & SelectedIndex & " ID=" & SelectedID
End Sub
```

Figure 17.41 shows the combo box and drop-down controls created in this section.

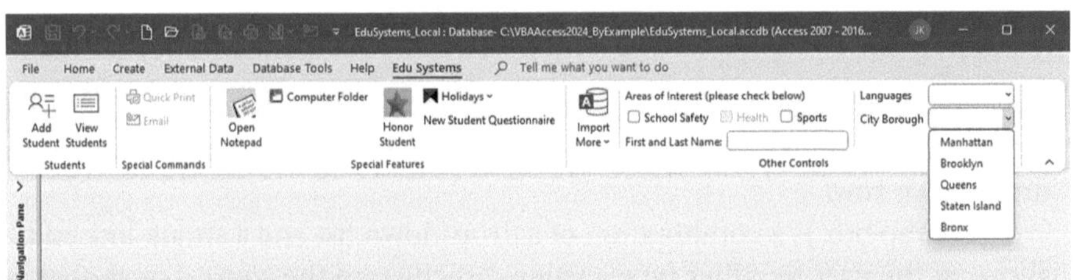

FIGURE 17.41.   The Languages combo box and City Borough drop-down controls look the same on the Ribbon.

See the `EduSystems_11_withComboAndDropDowns.txt` file in the companion files for the XML code used to produce the combo and drop-down controls shown in Figure 17.41. The required VBA code can be found in `EduSystems_11_withComboAndDropDowns _VBA.txt`.

Creating a Gallery Control

The gallery control in the Access Ribbon is designed to help users quickly choose from a set of options. Instead of just displaying commands, the gallery control shows the results of those commands, making it easier for users to select the desired outcome. The gallery control displays a collection of items, such as icons, images, or other visual elements, allowing users to visually select an option. The gallery control was introduced earlier in this chapter in the section titled Requesting Images via the getImage Callback. This control cannot be static; it must be dynamically populated at runtime.

Creating a Dialog Box Launcher

Some Ribbon tabs have a small dialog launcher button at the bottom-right corner of a group (see Figure 17.17 earlier). You can use this button to open a dialog box that allows the setup of multiple options at once, or you can display a form that contains specific information. To add a custom dialog launcher button to the Ribbon, use the `<dialogBoxLauncher>` tag, as shown here:

```
<dialogBoxLauncher>
  <button id="Launch1"
  screentip="Show Product Key"
  onAction="OnActionLaunch" />
</dialogBoxLauncher>
```

The dialog box launcher control must contain a button. The `OnAction` attribute for the button contains the callback procedure that will execute when the button is clicked:

```
Public Sub OnActionLaunch(ctl As IRibbonControl)
  ' open the About Microsoft Office Access box
  DoCmd.RunCommand acCmdAboutMicrosoftAccess
End Sub
```

The dialog box launcher control must appear as the last element within the containing group element in the XML markup.

The entire definition of the custom Edu Systems Ribbon tab created in this chapter and depicted in Figure 17.42 is available in the `EduSystems_12_withDialogLauncher.txt` file in the companion files.

The required VBA procedure can be found in `EduSystems_12_withDialo-gLauncher_VBA.txt`.

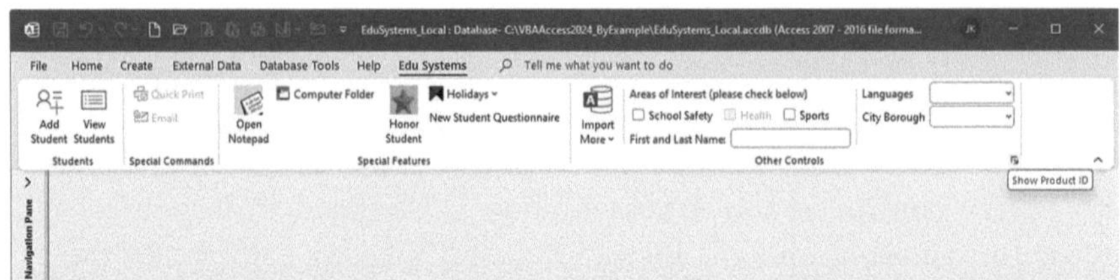

FIGURE 17.42.   A dialog box launcher control on the Ribbon will display the Product License, Session ID, Third Party Notices, and Microsoft Software License Terms (not depicted in this image).

Disabling a Control

You can disable a built-in or custom Ribbon control by using the `enabled` or `getEnabled` attribute. Here's how we disabled our custom checkbox control earlier by using the `enabled` attribute:

```
<checkBox id="chkHealth" label="Health" enabled="false" />
```

Use the `getEnabled` attribute to disable a control based on some conditions or simply display a "not authorized" message.

The following XML code shows how to disable the built-in Relationships button on the Ribbon's Database Tools tab:

```
<!-- Built-in commands section -->
<commands>
  <command idMso="DatabaseRelationships"
onAction="DisableRelations" />
</commands>
```

To make your XML code more readable, you can include comments between the `<!--` and `-->` characters. The `<command>` tag can be used to refer to any built-in command. This tag must appear in the `<commands>` section of the XML code.

To see the exact position of the above XML markup in the Ribbon customization, open the `EduSystems_13_DisableAndRepurpose.txt` file in the companion files. Notice the built-in command section just before the line:

```
<ribbon startFromScratch="false">
```

The `onAction` attribute contains the following callback procedure that will display a message when the Relationships button is clicked:

```
Sub DisableRelations(ctl As IRibbonControl, _
 ByRef cancelDefault)

  MsgBox "You are not authorized to use this function."
```

```
      cancelDefault = True
End Sub
```

You can add more code to this procedure if you need to cancel the control's default behavior only when certain conditions have been satisfied.

Repurposing a Built-In Control

It is possible to change the purpose of a built-in Ribbon button. For example, when the user clicks the Database Documentor button (Database Tools | Analyze group) while the Student List form is open, you could display a Database Properties dialog box instead of the default Documentor dialog box:

```
<command idMso="DatabaseDocumentor" onAction="ShowDbProperties" />

Public Sub ShowDbProperties(ctl As IRibbonControl, _
  ByRef cancelDefault)

  If CurrentProject.AllForms("Student List").IsLoaded Then
    ' display Database Properties dialog box instead
    DoCmd.RunCommand acCmdDatabaseProperties
  Else
    cancelDefault = False
  End If
End Sub
```

Only simple buttons that perform an action when clicked can be repurposed. You cannot repurpose advanced controls such as combo boxes, dropdowns, or galleries.

See `EduSystems_13_DisableAndRepurpose.txt` for the XML code.

The matching VBA file can be found in `EduSystems_13_DisableAndRepurpose_VBA.txt`. The output is displayed in Figure 17.43.

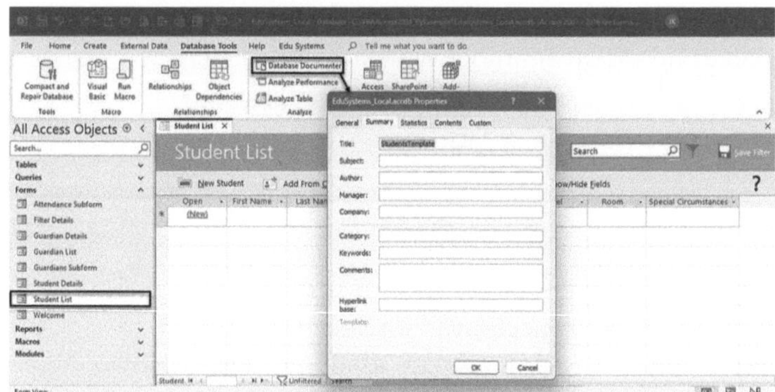

FIGURE 17.43. The built-in Database Documenter button has been repurposed and displays a different dialog box when the Student List form is open.

Refreshing the Ribbon

So far in this chapter, you've seen how to use callback procedures to specify the values of control attributes at runtime. What if you need to update your custom Ribbon or the controls placed in the Ribbon based on what the user is doing in your application? The good news is that you can change the attribute values at any time by using the `InvalidateControl` method of the `IRibbonUI` object. To use this object, start by adding the `onLoad` attribute to the `customUI` element in your Ribbon customization XML:

```
<customUI xmlns="http://schemas.microsoft.com/office/2009/07/
customui"
loadImage="OnLoadImage" onLoad="RefreshMe" >
```

The `onLoad` attribute points to the callback procedure that will give you a copy of the Ribbon that you can use to refresh anytime you want. In this example, the `onLoad` callback procedure name is `RefreshMe`.

Let's say you have a checkbox that is disabled when the Ribbon is first loaded and you would like to enable it when the user enters text in an edit box. Also, upon entry you want the text of the edit box to appear in uppercase. To implement the `onLoad` callback, start by declaring a `Public` module-level variable of type `IribbonUI` in your VBA code module:

```
Public objRibbon As IribbonUI
```

The preceding statement should appear in the declaration section at the top of the VBA module. To keep track of the state of the two Ribbon controls we are interested in, declare two `Private` module-level variables:

```
Private strUserTxt As String
Private isCtlEnabled As Boolean
```

Next, enter the callback procedure that will store a copy of the Ribbon in the `objRibbon` variable and assign an initial value to the `isCtlEnable` variable:

```
' callback for the onLoad attribute of customUI
Public Sub RefreshMe(ribbon As IRibbonUI)
  Set objRibbon = ribbon
  isCtlEnabled = False
End Sub
```

When the Ribbon loads, the checkbox control will be disabled. You will also have a copy of the `IRibbonUI` object saved for later use.

Now, let's take a look at the XML markup used in this scenario:

```
<checkBox id="chkHealth" label="Health"
getEnabled="onGetEnabled_Health" />
```

```
<editBox id="txtFullName" label="First and Last Name:"
  sizeString="AAAAAAAAAAAAAAAAA" maxLength="25"
  getText="getEditBoxText" onChange="onFullNameChangeToUcase" />
```

These checkbox and edit box controls were introduced earlier in this chapter. In order to change the enabled state of the checkbox control based on the user action, the `getEnabled` attribute must be used. The callback procedure for this attribute is shown below:

```
Public Sub onGetEnabled_Health(control As IRibbonControl, _
  ByRef enabled)
    enabled = isCtlEnabled
End Sub
```

When the Ribbon is loaded, the `onGetEnabled_Health` procedure will provide the value for the `getEnabled` attribute. The Health checkbox will be displayed in the Ribbon in its disabled mode because we have set the value of the `isCtlEnabled` variable to `False` in the `RefreshMe` procedure.

The edit box control contains two attributes that require callback procedures. The `getText` attribute points to the following callback:

```
Public Sub getEditBoxText(control As IRibbonControl, _
  ByRef text)
    text = UCase(strUserTxt)
End Sub
```

The preceding callback uses the VBA built-in `UCase` function to change the text that the user entered in the edit box to uppercase letters. When text is updated in the edit box, the procedure in the `onChange` attribute is called:

```
Public Sub onFullNameChangeToUcase(ByVal control As
IRibbonControl, _
 text As String)

  If text <> "" Then
    strUserTxt = text
    objRibbon.InvalidateControl "txtFullName"
    isCtlEnabled = True
  Else
    isCtlEnabled = False
  End If
  objRibbon.InvalidateControl "chkHealth"
End Sub
```

The preceding callback begins by checking the value of the `text` parameter provided by the Ribbon. If this parameter contains a value other than an empty string (" "), the text the user entered is stored in the `strUserTxt` variable.

Before a change can occur in the Ribbon control, you need to mark the control as invalid. This is done by calling the `InvalidateControl` method of the `IRibbonUI` object that we have stored in the `objRibbon` variable:

```
objRibbon.InvalidateControl "txtFullName"
```

This statement will tell the `txtFullName` control to refresh itself the next time it is displayed. When the control is invalidated, it will automatically call its callback functions.

The `getEditBoxText` callback procedure in the `onChange` attribute will execute, causing the text entered in the `txtFullName` edit box control to appear in uppercase letters.

The second action that we want to perform is to enable the `chkHealth` checkbox control when the user enters text in the edit box control and keep this button disabled when the edit box control is empty. This is done by setting the `isCtlEnabled` Boolean variable to `True` or `False` and invalidating the `chkHealth` checkbox control. When the `chkHealth` control is marked as invalid, it will call its callback functions. The `onGetEnabled_Health` callback procedure in the `getEnabled` attribute will execute, causing the control to appear in the enabled state if the `txtFullName` edit box control contains any text.

<table>
<tr><td>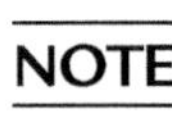
NOTE</td><td>The `IRibbonUI` object has only two methods: `InvalidateControl` and `Invalidate`. Use the `InvalidateControl` method to refresh an individual control. Use the `Invalidate` method to refresh all controls in the Ribbon.</td></tr>
</table>

Figure 17.44 shows the Ribbon after it has been refreshed.

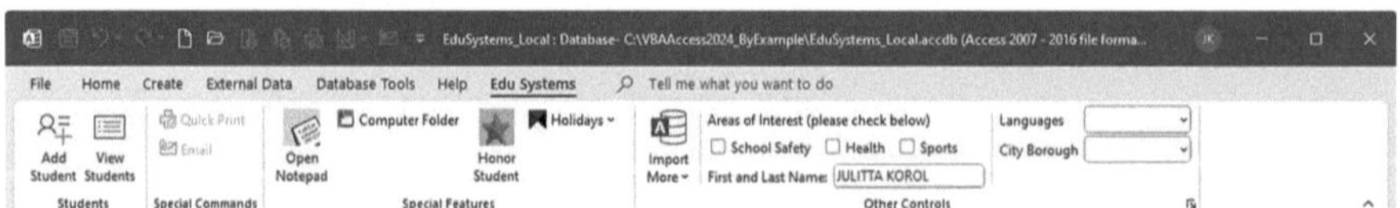

FIGURE 17.44. The Ribbon controls are shown here after the Ribbon refresh. The Health checkbox is enabled upon entry of text in the First and Last Name edit box and disabled when the entry is deleted. The first and last names now appear in uppercase letters.

The XML markup for the final Ribbon customization is contained in the `EduSystems_14_WithRefresh.txt` file in the companion files and the VBA code is found in `EduSystems_14_WithRefresh_VBA.txt`.

You can find the completed customizations demonstrated in the preceding sections of this chapter in the `EduSystems_Local.accdb` file in the `VBAAccess2024_ByExample` folder in the companion files.

Figure 17.45 displays the names of all custom Ribbons we created in this database. If you followed along and completed all the exercises, your `USysRibbons` table should contain 12 records, each one representing a different Ribbon.

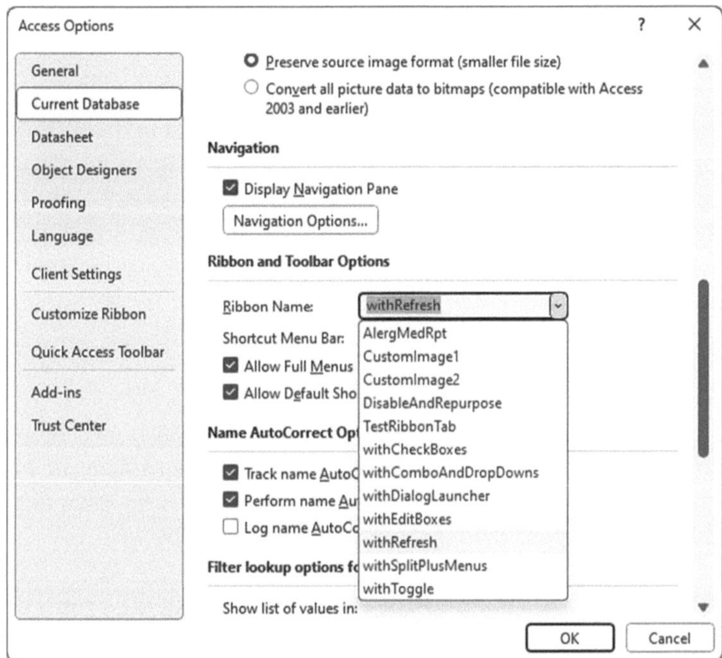

FIGURE 17.45.   Each time you apply a different Ribbon customization, you need to close and reopen the Access database. When the Ribbon customization requires VBA callbacks, you must exit Access and then reopen the database.

`withRefresh` is the last Ribbon customization for this chapter. It has demonstrated all the Ribbon features that were discussed and introduced in the previous sections.

THE COMMANDBARS OBJECT AND THE RIBBON

You can make your custom Ribbon button match any built-in button by using the `CommandBars` object. This object has been extended with several `Get` methods that expose the state information for the built-in controls: `GetEnabledMso`, `GetImageMso`, `GetLabelMso`, `GetPressedMso`, `GetScreentipMso`, `GetSupertipMso`, and `GetVisibleMso`.

Use these methods in your callbacks to check the built-in control's properties. For example, the following statement will return `False` if the Ribbon's built-in Cut button is currently disabled (grayed out), and `True` if it is enabled (ready to use):

```
MsgBox Application.CommandBars.GetEnabledMso("Cut")
```

Notice that the `GetEnabledMso` method requires the name of the built-in control. To see the result of the preceding statement, simply type it in the Immediate window and press Enter.

The `GetImageMso` method is very useful if you'd like to reuse any of the built-in button images in your own controls. This method allows you to get the bitmap for any `imageMso` tag. For example, to retrieve the bitmap associated with the Cut button on the Ribbon, enter the following statement in the Immediate window:

```
MsgBox Application.CommandBars.GetImageMso("Cut", 16, 16)
```

The preceding `GetImageMso` method uses three arguments: the name of the built-in control and the width and height of the bitmap image in pixels. Because this method returns the `IPictureDisp` object, it is very easy to place the retrieved bitmap onto your own custom Ribbon control by writing a simple VBA callback for your control's `getImage` attribute.

In addition to the methods that provide information about the properties of the built-in controls, the `CommandBars` object also includes a handy `ExecuteMso` method that can be used to trigger the built-in control's default action. This method is quite useful when you want to perform a click operation for the user from within a VBA procedure or want to conditionally run a built-in feature.

Let's take a look at the example implementation of the `GetImageMso` and `ExecuteMso` methods. Here's the XML definition for a custom Ribbon button (see Figure 17.46):

```
<button id="btnRptWizard" label="Use Report Wizard"
                            size="normal"
  getImage="onGetBitmap" onAction="DoDefaultPlus" />
```

The preceding XML code can be added to any of the custom Ribbon definitions you've already defined in the `USysRibbons` table. Now, let's look at the VBA part.

Suppose you want the button to use the same image as the built-in button labeled Report Wizard. When the button is clicked, you'd like to display the built-in Report Wizard dialog box only when a certain condition is true. Here is the code you need to add to your VBA module:

```
Sub onGetBitmap(ctl As IRibbonControl, ByRef image)
  Set image = Application.CommandBars. _
  GetImageMso("CreateReportFromWizard", 16, 16)
End Sub
```

When the Ribbon is loaded, the `onGetBitmap` callback automatically retrieves the image bitmap from the Report Wizard button's `imageMso` attribute and assigns it to the `getImage` attribute of your button. When your button is clicked and the Student List form is selected in the Navigation Pane, the Report Wizard dialog box will pop up; if the specified object is not selected, the user will see a message box:

```
Sub DoDefaultPlus(ctl As IRibbonControl)
  If Application.CurrentObjectName = "Student List" Then
    Application.CommandBars.ExecuteMso "CreateReportFromWizard"
  Else
    MsgBox "To run this Wizard you need to select " & _
      " the Student List Form", _
    vbOKOnly + vbInformation, "Action Required"
  End If
End Sub
```

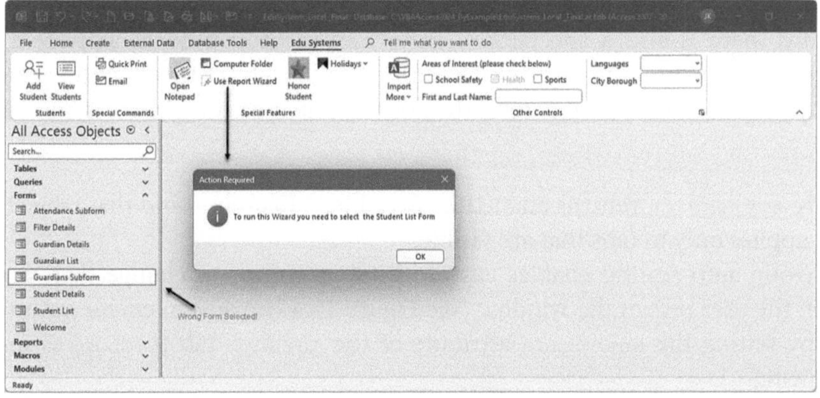

FIGURE 17.46. The custom button (Use Report Wizard) in the Special Features group of the Edu Systems tab uses a built-in image and runs a built-in Access feature based on the condition specified in the callback assigned to its onAction attribute. Notice the new database name is EduSystems_Local_ Final, which is a copy of the EduSystems_Local database and contains all the controls created so far in this chapter.

To continue with the Ribbon customizations described in this section, make a copy of the `EduSystem_Local` database and save it as `EduSystems_Local_ Final.accdb`.

You can find the XML markup discussed in this section in the `EduSystems_15_withCommandBars.txt` file in the companion files.

The sample VBA code is included in `EduSystems_15_withCommandBars_VBA.txt`.

TAB ACTIVATION AND GROUP AUTO-SCALING

Tab activation makes it possible to activate a specific tab in response to some event. To activate a custom tab on the Access 2024 Ribbon, use the `ActivateTab` method of the `IRibbonUI` object by passing to it the ID of the custom string. For example, to activate the Edu Systems tab you created in this chapter, try the following statement in the Immediate window while any of the default Access tabs is active:

```
objRibbon.ActivateTab "custTabEdu"
```

Recall that `objRibbon` is the module-level `Public` variable we declared earlier for accessing the `IRibbonUI` object. To activate a built-in tab, use the `ActivateTabMso` method. For example, the following statement activates the Create tab:

```
objRibbon.ActivateTabMso "TabCreate"
```

Finally, there is also a special `ActivateTabQ` method used to activate a tab shared between multiple add-ins. In addition to the tab ID, this method requires that you specify the namespace of the add-in. The syntax is shown here:

```
expression.ActivateTabQ(tabID As String, namespace as String)
```

where `expression` returns an `IRibbonUI` object. Keep in mind that tab activation applies only to tabs that are visible.

Group auto-scaling enables custom Ribbon groups to change their layout when the user resizes the window (see Figure 17.47). You can enable auto-scaling by setting the `autoScale` attribute of the `<group>` tab to `true`, as in the following:

```
<group id="ImagesGroup" label="Special Features" autoScale="true">
```

Notice that the value of the `autoScale` attribute is entered in lowercase. Auto-scaling is set on a per-group basis.

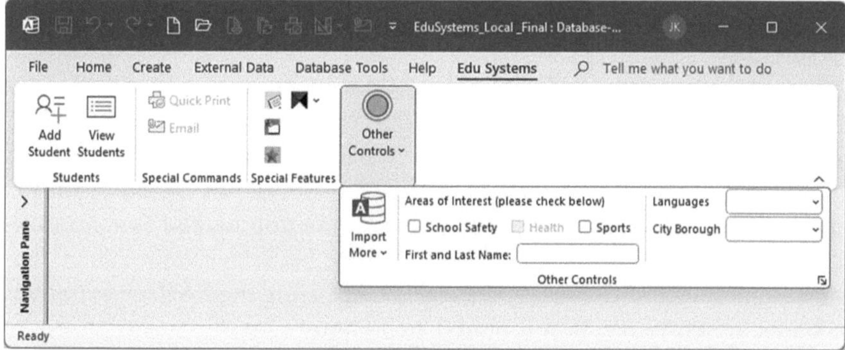

FIGURE 17.47.   The commands in the Other Controls group of the Ribbon are automatically compressed to a single button when the Access application window is made smaller. To change the icon that appears when the group is compressed, assign an image to the group itself. When you set the autoScale attribute to true, the group of controls in Special Features will change its layout to best fit the resized window.

You can find the Ribbon customizations discussed in this section in the `EduSy-stems_16_WithAutoScale.txt` file in the companion files.

CUSTOMIZING THE BACKSTAGE VIEW

The Access File tab provides an entry point to a part of the Office UI known as the backstage view. This view is specifically designed for working with a database as a whole. It contains commands known as *fast commands* that provide quick access to common functionality, such as saving, opening, or closing a database. Here, you will also find the Exit command for exiting Access and the Options command for customizing numerous Access features.

In addition to fast commands, the navigation bar on the left-hand side of the backstage view includes several tabs that group related tasks. For example, clicking the Print tab in the navigation bar displays all the information related to the installed printers and allows you to easily access and change many of the print settings.

The Info tab organizes tasks related to compacting and repairing a database and encrypting it with a password. As an Access developer already familiar with Ribbon UI customization, you should feel very comfortable with customizing the backstage view. Like the Ribbon, the backstage view uses XML markup. The backstage view is a perfect place to include custom solutions that present summaries of business processes or workflows. In this section, you'll perform some simple operations in the backstage view to get started with the customization of this interface.

The backstage view XML markup should be entered between the `<backstage>` and `</backstage>` elements within the `<customui>` and `</customui>` tags and below any Ribbon customization markup.

The `EduSystems_17_WithBackstageView.txt` file in the companion files contains the XML markup that adds a custom button named Synchronize and a custom tab named Endless Possibilities to the backstage view. When you add a new Ribbon record to the `USysRibbons` table using the XML code in that file, the backstage customization should match Figure 17.48.

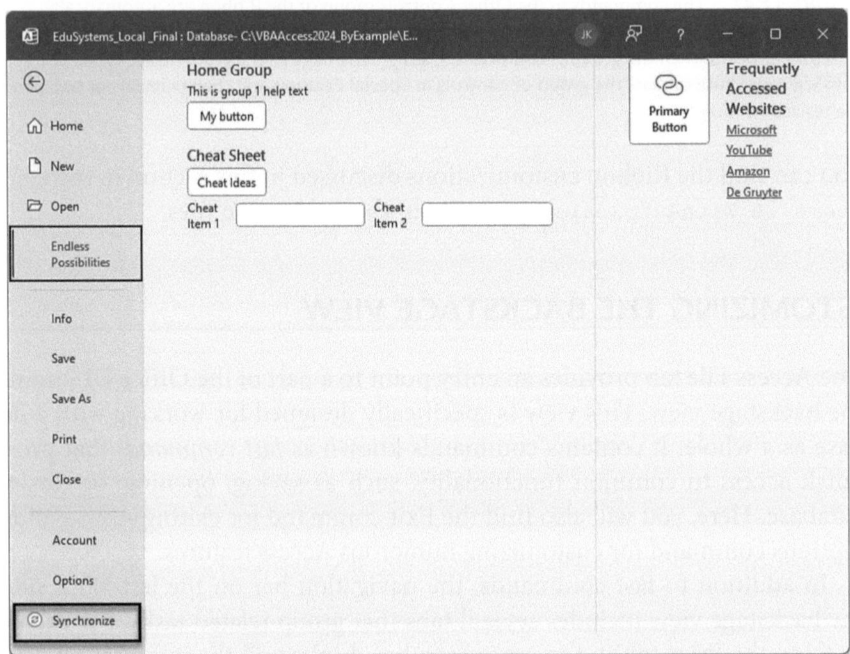

FIGURE 17.48. The backstage view is highly customizable. The Synchronize button and the Endless Possibilities tab were created by adding custom XML markup to the USysRibbons system table and the required VBA callbacks in a VBA module.

Open the `EduSystems_17_WithBackstageView.txt` file to analyze its XML markup. Note that the `<button>` element is used to incorporate into the navigation bar of the backstage view a custom command labeled Synchronize:

```
<button id="btnSync" label="Synchronize" imageMso="SyncNow"
isDefinitive="true" insertBeforeMso="FileClose" onAction="onActi
onCopyToArchive" />
```

The <button> element contains the `isDefinitive` attribute. When this attribute is set to `true`, clicking the button will trigger the callback procedure defined in the `onAction` attribute and then automatically close the backstage view. The `onAction` callback for the custom Synchronize button is shown here. The callback calls the `CreateDbCopy` procedure, which allows you to make a copy of the specified database.

```vba
Sub onActionCopyToArchive(ctl As IRibbonControl)
  CreateDbCopy
End Sub

Sub CreateDbCopy()
  Dim fso As Object
  Dim dbName As String
  Dim dbNewName As String

  On Error GoTo ErrorHandler

  Set fso = CreateObject("Scripting.FileSystemObject")

  dbName = InputBox("Enter the name of the database " & _
    "you want to copy: " & _
    "(C:\VBAAccess2024_ByExample\Chap16.accdb)", _
    "Create a copy of")

  If dbName = "" Then Exit Sub
  If Dir(dbName) = "" Then
    MsgBox dbName & " was not found. " & Chr(13) _
    & "Check the database name or path."
    Exit Sub
  End If

  dbNewName = InputBox("Enter the name for the " & _
    "copied database:" & Chr(13) & _
    "(C:\VBAAccess2024_ByExample\Chap16Ver2.accdb)", _
    "Save As")
  If dbNewName = "" Then Exit Sub

  If Dir(dbNewName) <> "" Then
    Kill dbNewName
  End If

  fso.CopyFile dbName, dbNewName
  Set fso = Nothing
```

```
   Exit Sub
ErrorHandler:
   MsgBox Err.Number & ":" & Err.Description
End Sub
```

The backstage view XML markup also adds to the navigation bar of the back-stage view a custom tab labeled Endless Possibilities. Each `<tab>` element can have one or more columns. Our example contains two columns. Each tab can contain multiple `<group>` elements. Here, we have two groups in the first column and one group in the second column. The Backstage group can contain different types of controls.

You can group the controls into the following three types of sections:

<primary item>	This element is used to specify the most important item in the group. The primary item control can be a button or a menu with buttons, toggle buttons, checkboxes, or another menu.
<topItems>	This element defines controls that will appear at the top of the group.
<bottomItems>	This element defines the controls that will appear at the bottom of the group.

The layout of controls in the backstage view is defined using the `<layoutContainer>` element. This element's `layoutChildren` attribute can define the layout of controls as horizontal or vertical. The second column of our example XML markup uses the `onActionExecHyperlink` callback procedure for the hyperlinks shown in Figure 17.48.

```
Sub onActionExecHyperlink(ctl As IRibbonControl, _
   ByRef target)
   Select Case ctl.ID
   Case "YouTube"
     target = "http://www.YouTube.com"
   Case "amazon"
     target = "http://www.amazon.com"
   Case "deg"
     target = "https://www.degruyter.com"
   Case "msft"
     target = "http://www.Microsoft.com"
   Case Else
     MsgBox "You clicked control id " & ctl.ID & _
     " that has not been programmed!"
   End Select
End Sub
```

Hiding Backstage Buttons and Tabs

The following XML will hide the Options button in the backstage view navigation bar:

```
<button idMso="ApplicationOptionsDialog" visible="false" />
```

The backstage view uses the following button IDs: `FileSave`, `FileSaveAs`, `FileOpen`, `FileClose`, `ApplicationOptionsDialog`, and `FileExit`.

To hide the Info tab in the backstage view, use this markup:

```
<tab idMso="TabInfo" visible="false" />
```

The backstage view has the following tab IDs: `TabInfo`, `TabRecent`, `TabNew`, `TabPrint`, `TabShare`, and `TabHelp`.

Things to Remember when Customizing the Backstage View

❑ The maximum number of allowed tabs is 255.

❑ You cannot reorder built-in tabs.

❑ You can add your custom tab before or after the built-in tab.

❑ You cannot modify the column layout of any built-in tab.

❑ You cannot reorder built-in groups; however, you can specify the order of groups you create.

CUSTOMIZING THE QUICK ACCESS TOOLBAR (QAT)

As mentioned at the beginning of this chapter, the QAT has changed its location and look in the current version of Access. The QAT can only be customized at the start by setting the `startFromScratch` attribute to `true` in the Ribbon XML customization file:

```
<ribbon startFromScratch="true">
```

The preceding XML markup will hide all built-in tabs. You must add your own custom tabs, as demonstrated earlier in this chapter.

The QAT modifications are specified using the `<qat>` element. Within this element, you should use the `<documentControls>` element to specify the controls that you want to appear in the QAT. The following XML markup creates the custom QAT shown in Figure 17.49. You can find this code in the `Custom-UI_withQAT.txt` file located in the companion files.

The example VBA procedure that opens the Calculator is included in the `CustomUI_withQUAT_VBA.txt` file.

```
<customUI
xmlns="http://schemas.microsoft.com/office/2009/07/customui" >
<ribbon startFromScratch="true">
  <qat>
    <documentControls>
      <button id="btnCalc2" label="Calculator"
      imageMso="SadFace" onAction="OpenCalculator" />
      <button idMso="FilePrintQuick" />
    </documentControls>
  </qat>
</ribbon>
</customUI>
```

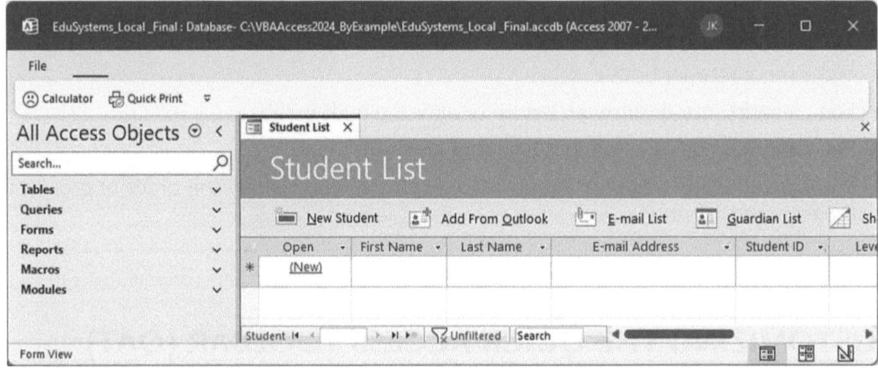

FIGURE 17.49.   Customized QAT shown below the Ribbon displays two buttons: Calculator and Quick Print.

The button labeled Calculator that is represented by the `SadFace` image calls the `OpenCalculator` procedure, shown here:

```
Public Sub OpenCalculator(ctl As IRibbonControl)
Shell "Calc.exe", vbNormalFocus
End Sub
```

The `EduSystems_Local_Final.accdb` database in the `VBAAccess2024_ByExample` folder in the companion files contains all the Ribbon customizations introduced in this chapter.

USING ChatGPT WITH ACCESS

Ribbon programming is not something that every developer might dive into regularly, but it's an invaluable skill that can significantly enhance the user experience in your Access applications. Ribbon programming involves understanding and writing XML, which may be unfamiliar to some developers. Integrating VBA with XML to define and control ribbon behavior adds another layer of complexity. I'm sure you've experienced it yourself while working on this chapter's projects and hands-on exercises. Learning how to create and manage custom ribbons requires time and effort, and the debugging process can be challenging, especially if errors are difficult to identify.

Let's review some Ribbon customization topics that were introduced in this chapter by engaging a bit with ChatGPT.

User Prompt: *How can I create my own Ribbon in an Access database?*

User Prompt: *Can you suggest practical applications of custom Ribbons?*

User Prompt: *Can you provide me with an example of a fully customized backstage view in Access?*

User Prompt: *I need more guidance in writing VBA callbacks for the Ribbon customizations.*

User Prompt: *How much XML do I need to know to program the Access Ribbon?*

User Prompt: *Did Access 2024 introduce any new features to the Ribbon interface?*

These prompts and the ChatGPT responses are provided in the `Chapter 17 - Using ChatGPT with Access` document included in the companion files.

SUMMARY

This chapter introduced you to using and customizing the Access 2024 UI. After a short overview of the Access Ribbon and the QAT, we looked at numerous features of the Access Navigation Pane. You learned how to use the Navigation Pane to access and organize your database objects by using both manual techniques and VBA code.

You learned how to create XML Ribbon customization markup and load it in your database by using the `LoadCustomUI` method of the `Application` object and via a special Access system table called `USysRibbons`. You also learned how

Ribbon customizations can be assigned to forms or reports. You spent quite a bit of time in this chapter familiarizing yourself with various controls that can be added to the Ribbon and wrote callback procedures in order to set your controls' attributes at runtime. In addition to Ribbon customizations, you learned how to modify the backstage view and the QAT.

While this chapter introduced many controls and features of the Ribbon, it did not attempt to cover all there is to know about this interface. After all, this book is about VBA programming in Access in general, not just the Ribbon. The knowledge and experience you gained in this chapter can be applied to customizing the Ribbon in all of the Microsoft 365 applications.

In the next chapter, you'll be introduced to more advanced concepts in Access VBA programming.

Part **VII**

ADVANCED VBA PROGRAMMING CONCEPTS

Microsoft Access offers numerous built-in objects that you can access from your VBA procedures to automate many aspects of your databases. You are not, however, limited to using these built-in objects. VBA allows you to create your own objects and collections of objects, complete with their own methods and properties.

In this part of the book, you will learn how Object-Oriented Programming (OOP) in VBA can help you create robust, efficient, and user-friendly database applications in Access. In the next chapter, you'll be working on a new type of module, known as a class module. You will learn how to create and use classes and objects to encapsulate data and behavior, so you can protect your data by keeping it hidden within the object and only allowing it to be accessed or modified through specified methods. This will help you maintain clean and organized code by grouping related properties and behaviors together. While building a simple movie tracker system, you will define properties to store data, methods to perform actions, and events to handle specific conditions or triggers.

Chapter 18   Creating Classes, Objects, Properties, Methods, and Events

18 CREATING CLASSES, OBJECTS, PROPERTIES, METHODS, AND EVENTS

So far in this book, you have learned that there are many ways to perform the same tasks in Access. You've written many procedures and functions that contained programming code that you might want to reuse in other Access projects. As your Access applications become more complex, you may find that your code is scattered all over the place and is difficult to maintain. Copying code from place to place and modifying procedures to include more arguments and enhancements because of the ever-changing requirements will lead to creating code that is difficult to manage. Access, however, has a special feature known as a *class module* that allows you to create code that is self-contained and reusable. The class helps you organize your code into manageable objects that you can easily reuse and adjust when necessary. Classes also make it easier to share your programming code with others. The class hides its inner workings from the rest of the program. Any programmer can use the class without knowing how that class was put together. It's like driving a car; a driver does not need to know the intricate details of how a car is manufactured to be able to drive it.

By getting acquainted with classes, you'll be able to move from the procedural programming that you're already familiar with into OOP, where you program by creating objects that may contain data defined as attributes or properties and code defined as procedures or methods. Objects are the basic units of OOP and are created by adding class modules to your Access applications. A class is like a cookie cutter. Once you create it, you can make any number of cookies. In Access, your cookies will be the custom objects you create from a class defined in a class module.

IMPORTANT TERMINOLOGY

In this chapter, you will work with advanced VBA concepts: VBA classes, class objects, collection classes, and events. Let's start by reviewing the following terms:

- Classes, Objects, and Object Instances

  Object—An object is a logical representation of a thing. This thing can be a physical entity, such as a person, a car, a customer or an employee, or a logical entity, such as an order, a transaction, or a report. It can also be something related to your specific Access application, such as a process that simplifies data validation or the manipulation of data. In other words, an object is anything you need to define. When you create an instance of a class, you get an object. The object is anything you need to define based on the class blueprint. Creating an instance of a class results in an object that embodies the attributes and methods defined by that class. Each object will have unique values for the attributes specified by the class. For example, if you have a class called `clsMovie`, each object created from this class would have its specific attributes, such as title, director, genre, and release year. This object can perform actions (methods) such as getting, adding, and removing, which are defined by the class but executed based on its unique attributes. Objects allow for creating multiple instances with similar functionality yet distinct identities.

  Class—This is a definition of an object that includes its name, properties, methods, and events. The class acts as a sort of object template (blueprint) from which an instance of an object is created at runtime.

  Instance—A specific object that belongs to a class is referred to as an *instance of the class*. When you create an instance, you create a new object that has the properties and methods defined by the class.

- Properties and Methods

  Properties—Attributes or data stored in an object (e.g., `Title`, `Directory`, `Genre`, and `ReleaseYear` in the `clsMovie` class that you will create in this chapter).

Methods—Functions or procedures that operate on the object (e.g., getting, adding, and removing movies in a `clsMovieCollection` class).

- Module and Class Modules

  Module—A module that contains procedures and functions that can be used throughout the database.

  Class Module—A module that contains the definition of a class, including its property and method definitions.

  Form Module—A module that contains the VBA code for all event procedures triggered by events occurring in a user form or its controls. A form module is a type of class module.

  Report Module—A module that contains the VBA code for all event procedures triggered by events occurring in a report or its controls. A report module is a type of class module.

- Collections

  Collection Class—A built-in class in VBA used to manage groups of related objects (e.g., `Collection` to manage multiple `clsMovie` objects). Use methods to add (`add`) and remove (`Remove`) items from the collection. Use loops to iterate through items in the collection for operations such as displaying data or applying actions to each item.

- Encapsulating Data and Behavior

  Encapsulation—The principle of bundling the data (attributes) and methods (functions) that operate on the data into a single unit or class. Encapsulation can:
  - Protect Your Data—By keeping the object's data hidden and only allowing it to be modified through defined methods, you can ensure that the data can't be accidentally changed in unexpected ways.
  - Increase Flexibility—Your application can be changed easily without affecting other parts of your code.
  - Maintain Clean Code—Encapsulation helps keep your code organized by bundling related properties and methods together in one place, making it easier to understand and maintain.
  - Increase Security—Encapsulation adds a layer of security to your code by controlling how data is accessed and modified, ensuring that it is used in safe and predictable ways.
  - Data Reusability—When you encapsulate functionality into a class, you can easily reuse it in different parts of your program or even in different projects, reducing redundancy and saving development time.

- Events and Event Procedures

Event—An action recognized by an object, such as a mouse click or a keypress, for which you can define a response. Events can be triggered by a user action, a VBA statement, or the system. In addition to form and report events and events for their controls, class modules also have `Class_Initialize` and `Class_Terminate` events, which provide control over how various variables and resources used by the class module are initialized and cleaned up.

`Event` is also a statement used to declare a user-defined event. The `Event` declaration must appear in a class module.

Event Procedure—A procedure that is automatically executed in response to an event triggered by the user, program code, or the system.

Event Sink—A class that implements an event. Only classes can sink events.

Event Source—An object that raises events. An event source can have multiple event sinks. Note that the source and sink terminology is derived from electronics. A device that outputs current when active is said to be sourcing current. A device that draws current into it when active is said to be sinking current.

`WithEvents`—A keyword that allows you to handle an object's events inside classes other than form or report classes. The variable that you declare for the `WithEvents` keyword is used to handle an object's events.

`RaiseEvent`—A statement used to call a custom event. The custom event must first be declared using the `Event` statement.

CREATING CUSTOM OBJECTS IN CLASS MODULES

There are two module commands available in VBE's Insert menu: Module and Class Module. So far, you've used a module to create subprocedures and function procedures. You have also used special forms of class modules (form and report class modules) while working with forms and reports. You'll use a stand-alone class module for the first time in this chapter to create a custom movie object and define its properties and methods.

To create a new VBA object, you must insert a class module into your VBA project and add the required code to that module. Before you do so, however, you need a basic understanding of what a class is. If you refer to the list of terms in an earlier section of this chapter, you will notice that we said that a *class* is a sort of object template. A frequently used analogy is comparing an object class to a cookie cutter. Just like a cookie cutter defines what a cookie will look like, the definition of the class determines how a particular object should look and how it should behave. Before you can use an object class, you must first create a new *instance* of that class. Object instances are the cookies. Each object instance has the characteristics (properties and methods) defined by its class. Just as you can cut out many cookies using the same cookie cutter, you can create multiple instances of a class. You can change the properties of each instance of a class independently of any other instance of the same class.

A *class module* lets you define your own custom classes, complete with custom properties and methods. You can create the properties for your custom objects by writing property procedures in a class module. The object methods are created in a class module by writing subprocedures or function procedures.

After building your object in the class module, you can use it in the same way you use other Access built-in objects. You can also export the object class outside the VBA project to other VBA-capable applications.

Creating a Class

Working with classes can seem a daunting task when you've already gotten used to procedural programming. Again, working by example can make it much easier for you to understand how classes can help you break your bigger programming problems into reusable and organized components.

The following sections of this chapter walk you through the process of creating and working with a custom object called `clsMovie`. This object will represent a movie. It will have properties such as `Title`, `Director`, `Genre`, and `ReleaseYear`. It will also have methods to get, add, and remove a movie.

<table>
<tr><td>**NOTE**</td><td>*All figures and files for the hands-on projects can be found in the companion files.*</td></tr>
</table>

⦿ Custom Project 18.1 (Part 1)   Creating a Class Module

1. Start Access and create a new database named `Chap18.accdb` in your `C:\VBAAccess2024_ByExample` folder.
2. Press Alt+F11 to switch to the VBE window and choose Insert | Class Module.
3. In the Project Explorer window, highlight the Class1 module and use the Properties window to rename the class module `clsMovie` (see Figure 18.1).

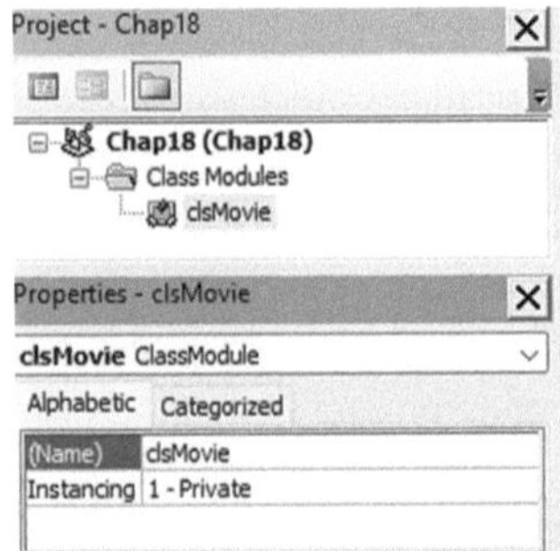

FIGURE 18.1. Use the Name property in the Properties window to rename the Class module.

Naming a Class Module

Every time you create a new class module, Access gives the class a default name of `Class1`, `Class2`, and so forth. Before working with the class, give it your own meaningful name. Set the name of the class module to the name you want to use in your VBA procedures using the class. The name you choose for your class should be easily understood and should identify the "thing" the object class represents.

Class Variables

After adding and renaming the class module, the next step is to declare the variables that will hold the data you want to store in your custom `clsMovie` object. As mentioned earlier, this object will have the `Title`, `Director`, `Genre`, and `ReleaseYear` properties. Each item of data you want to store in an object should be assigned a variable.

Class variables are called *data members* and are declared with the `Private` keyword. Using the `Private` keyword in a class module hides the data members and prevents other parts of the application from referencing them. Only the procedures within the class module in which the private variables were defined can modify the value of these variables.

Because the name of a variable also serves as a property name, use meaningful names for your object's data members. In this example, we will preface the class variable names with `p` to indicate that they are private variables.

◉ Custom Project 18.1 (Part 2)   DeclaringClass Members

1. Type the following declaration lines at the top of the `clsMovie` class module's code window:

```
Option Compare Database
```

```
Option Explicit

' Variable declarations
Private pTitle As String
Private pDirector As String
Private pGenre As String
Private pReleaseYear As Integer
```

When you declare the class member variables using the `Private` keyword, these variables can only be accessed through the property code, as detailed in the next part of this custom project. By using the property code, you can ensure that the values stored in these variables are valid and adhere to the specific rules of your application.

Creating and Using Property Procedures

Declaring variables with the `Private` keyword ensures that they cannot be directly accessed from outside the object. This means that VBA procedures outside the class module will not be able to set or read data stored in those variables. To enable other parts of your VBA application to set or retrieve the movie data, you must add special property procedures to the `clsMovie` class module. There are three types of property procedures:

- Property Get—This type of procedure allows other parts of the application to get or read the value of a property. This property procedure works like a VBA function that returns some value.

- Property Let—This type of procedure allows other parts of the application to set the value of a property. This property procedure is used with simple data types, such as numeric, string, and date properties.

- Property Set—This type of procedure is used instead of Property Let when setting the reference to an object. For example, it can be used when setting a property for a `Recordset` object or another object data type.

Property procedures are executed when an object property needs to be set or retrieved. The Property Get procedure can have the same name as the Property Let procedure. You should create property procedures for each property of the object that can be accessed by another part of your VBA application.

If you only create a Property Get procedure, the property becomes read-only and its value can't be changed by the program using the object. If you create only the Let or Set property procedure, the property becomes write-only, and its value can't be viewed by the calling program. Write-only properties are often used for sensitive information, such as passwords and login credentials.

The easiest of the three types of property statements to understand is the Property Get procedure. Let's examine the syntax of the property procedures by taking a close look at the Property Get `LastName` procedure.

Property procedures contain the following parts:

- A procedure declaration line that includes the `Property` keyword
- An assignment statement
- The `End Property` keywords

A procedure declaration line specifies the name of the property and the data type:

```
Property Get Title() As String
```

`Title` is the name of the property and `As String` determines the data type of the property's return value. The procedure declaration line must include the `Property` keyword.

Property Get procedures are always public by default, so they can be exposed to the other parts of your application. You can use the `Public` keyword in front of the `Property` keyword to explicitly specify the property procedure's scope:

```
Public Property Get Title() As String
```

An assignment statement is similar to the one used in a function procedure:

```
Title = pTitle
```

`Title` is the name of the property and `pTitle` is the data member variable that holds the value of the property you want to retrieve or set. The `pTitle` variable should be defined with the `Private` keyword at the top of the class module. Here's the complete Property Get procedure:

```
Property Get Title() As String
   Title = pTitle
End Property
```

The above property procedure retrieves the movie title.

Property Get procedures can also return a result from a calculation, like this:

```
Property Get Royalty()
   Royalty = (Sales * Percent) - Advance
End Property
```

The `End Property` keywords specify the end of the property procedure.

Immediate Exit from Property Procedures

Just as the `Exit Sub` and `Exit Function` keywords allow you to exit early from a subroutine or a function procedure, the `Exit Property` keywords give you a way to immediately exit from a property procedure. Program execution will continue with the statements following the statement that called the Property Get, Property Let, or Property Set procedure.

Creating the Property Get and Property Let Procedures

The `clsMovie` class object has four properties that need to be exposed to the VBA procedures that we will write later. When working with the `clsMovie` object, you will need to get information about the movie title, director, genre, and release year. For each of these properties, you will need to write a Property Get procedure. In addition to retrieving values stored in data members (private variables) with Property Get procedures, you must prepare corresponding Property Let procedures to allow other procedures to change the values of these variables as needed. The only time you don't define a Property Let procedure is when the value stored in a private variable is meant to be *read-only*.

⊙ **Custom Project 18.1 (Part 3)   Writing Property Get and Property Let Procedures**

1. Type the following Property Get and Property Let procedures in the `clsMovie` class module, just below the declaration section that you entered in Part 2 of this custom project:

```
' Property procedures
Public Property Get Title() As String
    Title = pTitle
End Property

Public Property Let Title(Value As String)
    pTitle = Value
End Property

Public Property Get Director() As String
    Director = pDirector
End Property

Public Property Let Director(Value As String)
    pDirector = Value
End Property
```

```
Public Property Get Genre() As String
    Genre = pGenre
End Property

Public Property Let Genre(Value As String)
    pGenre = Value
End Property

Public Property Get ReleaseYear() As Integer
    ReleaseYear = pReleaseYear
End Property

Public Property Let ReleaseYear(Value As Integer)
    pReleaseYear = Value
End Property
```

Notice that each movie property requires a separate Property Get procedure. Each of the preceding Property Get procedures returns the current value of the property. Notice also how a Property Get procedure is like a function procedure. Like function procedures, the Property Get procedures contain an assignment statement.

The Property Let procedures require at least one parameter that specifies the value you want to assign to the property. The data type of the parameter passed to the Property Let procedure must be the same data type as the value returned from the Property Get or Property Set procedure with the same name. Notice that the Property Let procedures have the same names as the Property Get procedures.

Defining the Scope of Property Procedures

You can place the `Public`, `Private`, or `Static` keyword before the name of a property procedure to define its scope. To indicate that the Property Get procedure is accessible to procedures in all modules, use the following statement format:

```
Public Property Get Director() As String
```

To make the Property Get procedure accessible only to other procedures in the module where it is declared, use the following statement format:

```
Private Property Get Director() As String
```

To preserve the Property Get procedure's local variables between procedure calls, use the following statement format:

```
Static Property Get Director() As String
```

If not explicitly specified using either `Public` or `Private`, property procedures are public by default. Also, if the `Static` keyword is not used, the values of local variables are not preserved between procedure calls.

Creating the Class Methods

Apart from properties, objects may have one or more methods. A *method* is an action that the object can perform. Methods allow you to manipulate the data stored in a class object. Methods are created with subroutines or function procedures. To make a method available outside the class module, use the `Public` keyword in front of the subprocedure or function definition. As we will be managing a collection of movies, we will create a new class named `clsMovieCollection` and we will use it to write methods that will allow us to add, remove, and get a movie.

⊚ Custom Project 18.1 (Part 4)   Creating the clsMovieCollection Class and Writing VBA Code

1. Insert another class module and name it `clsMovieCollection`.
2. In this class, we will manage a collection of `clsMovie` objects.
3. Type the following subprocedures and functions in the `clsMovieCollection` class module:

```
Private colMovies As Collection

' Initialize the collection
Private Sub Class_Initialize()
    Set colMovies = New Collection
End Sub

' Add a movie
Public Sub AddMovie(ByVal movie As clsMovie)
    colMovies.Add movie, movie.Title
End Sub

' Remove a movie
Public Sub RemoveMovie(ByVal Title As String)
    colMovies.Remove Title
End Sub

' Get a movie by title
Public Function GetMovie(ByVal Title As String) As clsMovie
    On Error Resume Next
    Set GetMovie = colMovies(Title)
```

```vba
    On Error GoTo 0
End Function

' Get the number of movies
Public Property Get Count() As Long
    Count = colMovies.Count
End Property

Public Property Get Movies() As Collection
    Set Movies = colMovies
End Property

Public Function MovieExists(ByVal Title As String) As Boolean
    Dim movie As clsMovie
    On Error Resume Next
    Set movie = colMovies(Title)
    If Not movie Is Nothing Then
        MovieExists = True
    Else
        MovieExists = False
    End If
    On Error GoTo 0
End Function
```

Notice that the first line in the code above declares a private collection named `colMovies`. A collection is a type of object that can hold multiple items, in this case, movie objects.

The first procedure, `Private Sub Class_Initialize()`, is a special class method that initializes the collection when an instance of the class is created. We use the `New` keyword to create a new collection object and assign it to `colMovies`.

Custom classes recognize only two events: `Class_Initialize` and `Class_Terminate`. These events are triggered when an instance of the class is created and destroyed, respectively. The `Initialize` event is a good place to perform initialization of the objects created from the class.

The `Terminate` event occurs when all references to an object have been released. This is a good place to perform any necessary cleanup tasks. For example, if your class interacts with a database, you should close any open database connections and set the connection object to `Nothing`. You should also release any other objects or resources that the class is holding. For example, the `clsMovies` should be set to `Nothing` to free up memory. Optionally, you can include a debug statement to log a message when the class instance is terminated. This can help you during the debugging process to ensure that the `Terminate` event is being triggered:

```
Private Sub Class_Terminate()
    ' Release objects or resources
    Set colMovies = Nothing

    ' Debugging purposes
    Debug.Print "clsMovieCollection instance is being terminated."
End Sub
```

The next procedure allows you to add a movie object to the collection using the `Add` method. The movie title is used as the key for easy retrieval.

Next, we have a procedure that removes a movie from the collection by its title. We use the `Remove` method to remove the specified movie from the collection.

To retrieve a movie object from the collection, we wrote a function procedure named `GetMovie` and passed to it the movie title. We included the `On Error Resume Next` statement, which tells the program to continue executing the next line of code if an error occurs. The `On Error GoTo 0` line will reset the error handling, so subsequent errors will stop the code execution.

The following are the property `Get Count` and `Get Movies` procedures, where we use the `Count` function to retrieve the number of movie objects in the collection and return the entire `colMovies` collection, allowing external code to interact with the collection of movies. The `MovieExists` function checks whether a movie with a given title exists in the collection and returns `True` or `False`.

The line `If Not movie is Nothing Then` checks that the movie object is not `Nothing` (i.e., it was found in the collection).

About Class Methods

- Only those methods that will be accessed from outside of the class should be declared as `Public`. All others should be declared as `Private`.
- Methods perform some operation on the data contained within the class.
- If a method needs to return a value, write a function procedure. Otherwise, create a subprocedure.

Before we create the form to test our `clsMovie` and `clsMovieCollection`, let's define the table that will store our movie collection.

◉ Custom Project 18.1 (Part 5)   Creating a Movie Table

1. Create a new table named `Movies` with the field names and data types as depicted in Figure 18.2.
2. Make the `ID` field the primary key.

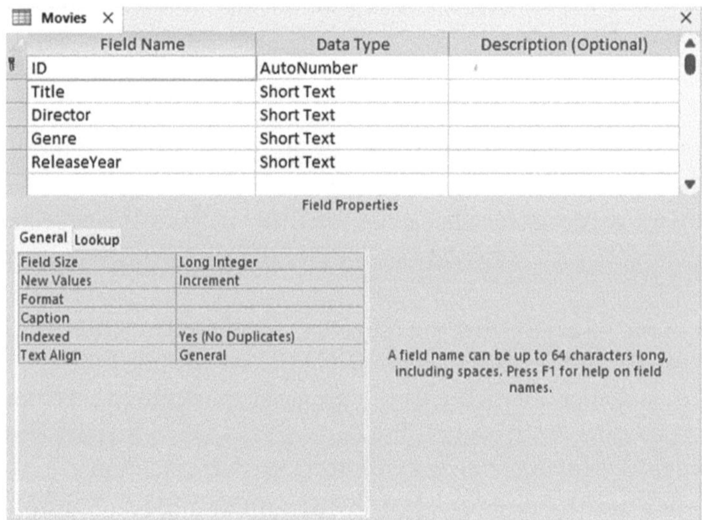

FIGURE 18.2.   The Movies table design view.

◉ Custom Project 18.1 (Part 6)   Populating the Movies table with Movie Data

1. Open the `Movies` table in the datasheet view and enter a couple of your favorite movies, or import the movies from the `Movies.txt` file included in the companion files. When importing the movie list, make sure to skip the `ID` field. You can get to this option by clicking the Advanced button on the first screen of the Import Text Wizard.
   With the table ready, let's move on to creating a custom form that will allow us to display, add, and remove movies from the movie collection.

◉ Custom Project 18.1 (Part 7)   Creating the Movies Form

1. Create a new form in Access and name it `frmMovies`.
   This form should have three sections: form header, Details, and form footer. To activate the form header/footer, right-click the blank form in design view and select Form Header/Footer from the shortcut menu.

2. Include the following controls (see Figure 18.3):
The form header section:

- An image control (retrieve the image named `IMG_MovieReel1` from the `Images` folder in the companion files) and use the image name to set the Picture property of this image control
- A label with the `MovieTracker` caption
- A command button captioned Close and named `btnClose`
- A rectangle control with the Height property set to `0.0833"` and the Background property set to Blue (Accent 4) or any other color you like

The Detail Section:

- A list box control named `lstMovies` and a label captioned Movies:. Set the Font Size property of lstMovies to `10`.
- A command button named `btnAdd` and captioned Add New.
- Text boxes named `txtTitle`, `txtDirector`, `txtGenre`, and `txtRelease-Year` with the corresponding labels.
- A command button named `btnUpdate` and captioned Update.
- A command button named `btnRemove` and captioned Remove.
- A command button named `btnSave` and captioned Save. Note this button is not visible in Figure 18.3 as it is positioned right behind the Update button.

The Footer Section:

- A label control named `lblItemCount` and captioned List Box Count

3. Using the Property Sheet, select the form from the drop-down list in the Property Sheet and set the following Form properties:

PopUp	Yes
Default View	Single Form
Allow Form View	Yes
Allow Datasheet View	No
Allow Layout View	No
Record Selectors	No
Navigation Buttons	No
Scroll Bars	Neither
Min Max Buttons	None

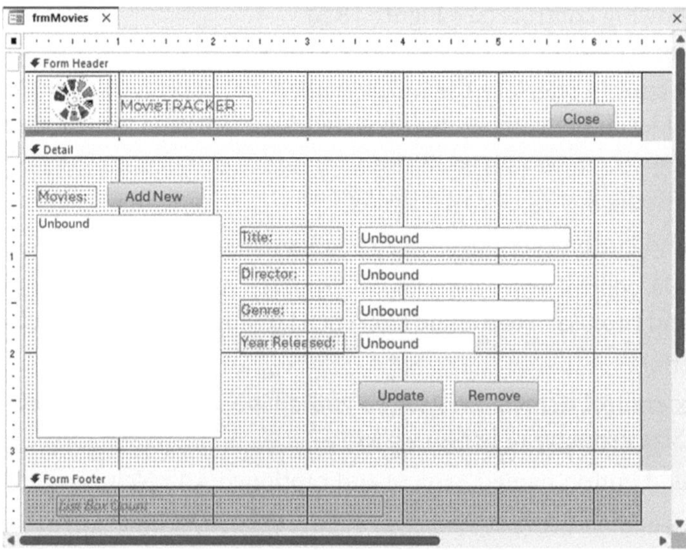

FIGURE 18.3.   The frmMovies Form in the form design view.

Writing Event Procedures

The `frmMovies` form provides the user interface. Users will be able to add, view, and remove movies through the form. For users to interact with the form and its various controls, you need to write VBA code in the form class module. The form uses button click events to interact with the `MovieCollection` class, adding, removing, updating, and saving movies. The form also needs VBA code in the `Form_Load` event procedure to retrieve the movies from the `Movies` table (if available) into the `lstMovies` list box. Upon loading, the `lstMovies After_Update` event procedure should display the selected movie details in the corresponding text boxes. The Add New button should clear the text boxes, hide the Update and Remove buttons, and make the hidden Save button visible so that new movies can be added to the collection of movies in the list box and saved into the `Movies` table. Other form interaction details will be revealed as we proceed with this project.

⊙ **Custom Project 18.1 (Part 8)   Writing VBA Code for the frmMovies Form**

Writing the Form_Load Event Procedure

1. Open the `frmMovies` form in design view, and in the Property Sheet, select Form from the drop-down list. Click the Event tab, click in the On Load

property, select [Event Procedure], and then click the ellipsis (…) button. Access will open the VBE screen with the Code window for the `Form_frmMovies` form with the stub of the `Form_Load` event procedure that you will need to complete. This procedure will initialize a form that displays a collection of movies in a list box when the form is loaded. To access the movie collection, you will need to declare two `Private` variables: `movieCollection` is an instance of the `clsMovieCollection` class, and `currentMovie` is an instance of the `clsMovieClass`.

2. Enter the following variable declaration at the top of the `Form_frmMovies` code window, just below the `Option Explicit` statement:

```
Option Compare Database
Option Explicit

' Variable declarations
Private movieCollection As clsMovieCollection
Private currentMovie As clsMovie
```

3. Complete the code of the `Form_Load` event procedure, as shown below:

```
Private Sub Form_Load()
    Dim db As DAO.Database
    Dim rst As DAO.Recordset

    Me.btnUpdate.Visible = True
    Me.btnAdd.Visible = True
    Me.btnSave.Visible = False

    'Initialize the movieCollection object
    Set movieCollection = New clsMovieCollection

    'Open the Movies Table
    Set db = CurrentDb
    Set rst = db.OpenRecordset("Movies", dbOpenDynaset)

    'Clear the list box before loading movies
    Me.lstMovies.RowSourceType = "Value List"
    Me.lstMovies.RowSource = ""

    Do While Not rst.EOF
        Dim movie As clsMovie
        Set movie = New clsMovie
        movie.Title = rst!Title
        movie.Director = rst!Director
        movie.Genre = rst!Genre
```

```
        movie.ReleaseYear = rst!ReleaseYear

        movieCollection.AddMovie movie
        Me.lstMovies.AddItem movie.Title
        rst.MoveNext
    Loop

    If Me.lstMovies.ListCount > 0 Then
        'Select the first item in the list box
        Me.lstMovies.Selected(0) = True
    End If

    rst.Close
    Set rst = Nothing
    Set db = Nothing
End Sub
```

Notice that the first code lines in this procedure set the visibility of three buttons (`btnUpdate`, `btnAdd`, and `btnSave`) on the form; `btnSave` is initially hidden. The next line creates a new instance of the `clsMovieCollection` class and assigns it to the `movieCollection` variable. The following code block opens the `Movies` tables from the current database (`db`) and sets the recordset (`rst`) to contain the data from the `Movies` table. Before loading movies into the list box, we clear the list box (`lstMovies`) by setting its `RowSourceType` to `"Value List"` and its `RowSource` to an empty string. Next, we iterate through each record in the `rst` recordset, creating a new `clsMovie` object and setting the properties of the `clsMovie` object to the corresponding fields in the current record (`Title`, `Director`, `Genre`, and `ReleaseYear`). Once the properties are set, the `clsMovie` object is added to the `movieCollection` and the title of the movie is added to the list box (`lstMovies`). The recordset then moves to the next record and the process repeats for the next movie in the `Movies` table until there are no more records to read. Finally, we check whether there are any items in the `lstMovies` list box, and if there are, we select the first item. Before ending this procedure, we must close the recordset (`rst`) and set the recordset and database objects to `Nothing` to release resources.

When you open the form in form view, Access will execute the code in the `Form_Load` event procedure, and you should see the first movie title selected in a list box.

To view the details of the selected movie title, you must write the `lstMovies_Update` event procedure.

Writing the lstMovies_AfterUpdate Event Procedure

The `lstMovies_AfterUpdate` event procedure code should address the visibility of buttons on the form and display the movie details in text boxes each time the selection in the list box changes. The current movie details should also be preserved so we know if any of the values were changed when the user clicks the `btnUpdate` button.

1. Write the following procedures in the `Form_frmMovies` Code window:

```vba
Private Sub lstMovies_AfterUpdate()
    Dim selectedTitle As String
    Dim movie As clsMovie

    Me.btnSave.Visible = False
    Me.btnUpdate.Visible = True
    Me.btnRemove.Visible = True

    If Me.lstMovies.ListIndex >= 0 Then
        selectedTitle = Me.lstMovies.Value

        On Error GoTo Error_Handler

        ' Find the selected movie in the collection
        For Each movie In movieCollection.Movies
            If movie.Title = selectedTitle Then
                Set currentMovie = movie
                Exit For
            End If
        Next movie

        ' Display the movie details in the text fields
        If Not currentMovie Is Nothing Then
            Me.txtTitle.Value = currentMovie.Title
            ' Ensure that the user can't update the Title
            Me.txtTitle.Enabled = False
            Me.txtDirector.Value = currentMovie.Director
            Me.txtGenre.Value = currentMovie.Genre
            Me.txtReleaseYear.Value = currentMovie.ReleaseYear
        Else
            MsgBox "Selected movie not found in the collection.", _
                vbExclamation, "View Error"
        End If
        Call StoreValuesInTag
        Exit Sub
    End If
```

```
Error_Handler:
 MsgBox "An error occurred: " & Err.Description, _
vbCritical, "Error"
End Sub

Private Sub StoreValuesInTag()
    Dim ctl As Control

    ' Loop through all controls on the form
    For Each ctl In Me.Controls
        ' Check if the control is a text box
        If TypeName(ctl) = "TextBox" Then
            ' Store the current value in the Tag property
            ctl.Tag = ctl.Value
        End If
    Next ctl
End Sub
```

The `AfterUpdate` event contains the logic you want to run when a movie title is selected in a list box. To keep track of the currently displayed movie details, we call the `StoreValuesInTag` procedure, which loops through the form's text box controls and stores the current value of each text box in its `Tag` property. You can call this procedure when the form loads or when a record changes to ensure the `Tag` property is always up to date. To check the `Tag` property of any control on your form, use the Immediate window in the VBA editor by pressing Ctrl+G. For example, to retrieve the `Tag` property value from the `txtTitle` text box in the `frmMovies` form, use the following syntax:

```
? Forms!frmMovies.txtTitle.Tag
```

Using the Tag Property

The `Tag` property is an extra property that you can use to store any value you want. This property can be read and modified at runtime. The `Tag` property is available for forms, form sections, reports, report sections, and controls. You can set this property in the Property Sheet or in a VBA procedure.

Writing the Form_Current Event Procedure

After the form loads, it would be nice to display the total number of movies that were loaded into the list box. Recall that the form footer contains the `lblItem-Count` label control. Using the `ListCount` property of the `lstMovies` list box control, we can easily update the label's caption to display the total movie count.

1. Include the following VBA code in the `Form_Current` event procedure, as shown below:

```
Private Sub Form_Current()
    ' Update the item count in the form footer
    Me.lblItemCount.Caption = "Total Movies: " & Me.lstMovies.
ListCount
End Sub
```

Recall that the `Form_Current` event occurs when the form is opened or requeried and when the focus moves to a different record. This event will happen right after the `Form_Load` event.

Testing the Project Progress (Test 1)

It's time to find out how far we've progressed. Figure 18.4 displays the `frmMovies` form with the selected movie details. Notice that the list box contains 12 movie titles, and upon the form loading, the first item in the list is selected. As you move through the items in the list, the values of the text boxes are automatically updated for the selected movie item. The next part of this project is writing VBA code that handles each of the displayed buttons. We'll start with the simplest one, the Close button.

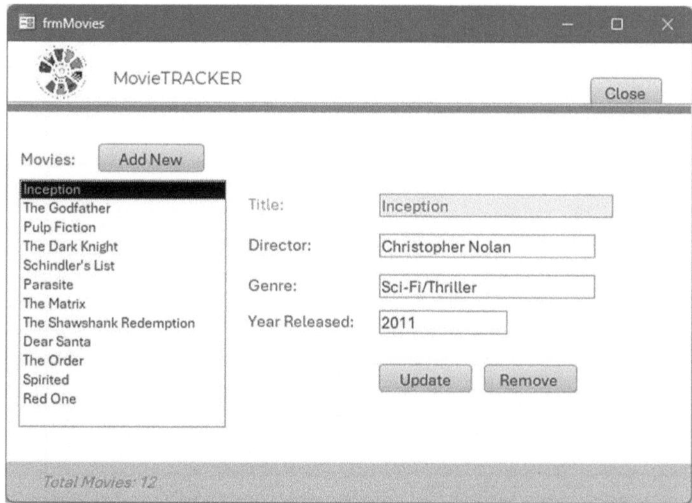

FIGURE 18.4.   The frmMovies form displays the selected movie title details.

Writing the btnClose_Click Event Procedure

When clicked, the Close button should close the form. This is easily done using the `Close` method of the `DoCmd` object.

1. In the `Form_frmMovies` Code window, enter the following event procedure:

```
Private Sub btnClose_Click()
    DoCmd.Close
End Sub
```

Writing the btnUpdate_Click Event Procedure

When the user updates any text box value (`Director`, `Genre`, or `ReleaseYear`) and clicks the Update button, the `btnUpdate_Click` procedure should:

- Verify that the record has indeed changed.
- If the record has changed, update the movie properties in the `movieCollection`.
- Save the updated changes back to the `Movies` table.

After the successful update, the form should:

- Reload to reflect the changes.
- Highlight the previously selected title in the `lstMovies` list box.

1. Write the following procedures that will handle movie updates:

```
Private Sub btnUpdate_Click()
    Set currentMovie = New clsMovie

    On Error GoTo Error_Handler

    If HasRecordChanged() And Not currentMovie Is Nothing Then
        ' Update the movie properties with new values
        currentMovie.Director = Me.txtDirector.Value
        currentMovie.Genre = Me.txtGenre.Value
        currentMovie.ReleaseYear = Me.txtReleaseYear.Value

        ' Escape apostrophes in the title
        Dim escapedTitle As String
        escapedTitle = Replace(Me.txtTitle, "'", "''")

        ' Update the Movies table
        Dim db As DAO.Database
        Dim rst As DAO.Recordset


        Set db = CurrentDb
        Set rst = db.OpenRecordset("Movies", dbOpenDynaset)
```

```
        rst.FindFirst "Title='" & escapedTitle & "'"
        If Not rst.NoMatch Then
            rst.Edit
            rst!Director = currentMovie.Director
            rst!Genre = currentMovie.Genre
            rst!ReleaseYear = currentMovie.ReleaseYear
            rst.Update
            MsgBox "Movie details updated successfully!", _
                vbInformation, "Success"

            Dim selectedTitle As String
            selectedTitle = Me.lstMovies.Value

            ' Refresh the list box
            Call Form_Load

            'Select the first item in the list box
            Me.lstMovies.Selected(0) = True

            ' Cleanup
            rst.Close
            Set rst = Nothing
            Set db = Nothing
        Else
           MsgBox "The Movie " & escapedTitle & " was not found."
        End If

    Else
        MsgBox "There is nothing to update.", vbInformation
    End If

    Exit Sub
Error_Handler:
    MsgBox "An error occurred: " & Err.Description, _
        vbCritical, "Error"
End Sub
```

The `btnUpdate_Click` event procedure is triggered when the user clicks the Update button. The `HasRecordChanged` function checks whether there have been any changes in the form's enabled text boxes (e.g., `Director`, `Genre`, or `ReleaseYear`). If changes are detected (`HasRecordChanged` returns `True`), the movie properties are updated with the new values. A DAO recordset is opened to locate and update the changed record in the `Movies` table with the new values. The `Form_Load` event procedure is called to reload the form. This ensures that the updated values are reflected in the `lstMovies` list box. The first movie title in the `lstMovies` list box is then selected. This sequence of events ensures that any changes made by the user are correctly reflected in both the movie properties and the database table, and that the user interface is updated to show these changes.

```
Function HasRecordChanged() As Boolean
    Dim ctl As Control

    ' Assume no changes initially
    HasRecordChanged = False

    ' Loop through all controls on the form
    For Each ctl In Me.Controls
        ' Check if the control is a text box
        If TypeName(ctl) = "TextBox" Then
        ' Check if the value has actually changed,
        ' considering data types
            If Not IsNull(ctl.Value) And Not IsNull(ctl.Tag) Then
                ' Handle numeric values (e.g., year)
                If IsNumeric(ctl.Value) And IsNumeric(ctl.Tag) Then
                    If CDbl(ctl.Value) <> CDbl(ctl.Tag) Then
                    ' Exit the function if a change is detected
                        HasRecordChanged = True
                        Exit Function
                    End If
                ' Handle string values
                ElseIf CStr(ctl.Value) <> CStr(ctl.Tag) Then
                    HasRecordChanged = True
                    Exit Function
                End If
            ElseIf IsNull(ctl.Value) And Not IsNull(ctl.Tag) Or _
                Not IsNull(ctl.Value) And IsNull(ctl.Tag) Then
                    HasRecordChanged = True
                    Exit Function
            End If
        End If
    Next ctl
End Function
```

The `HasRecordChanged` function initially assumes no changes have been made to the record by setting the function's result `HasRecordChanged` to `False`. The function then loops through each control on the form, checking whether the current control is a text box. To ensure that the `HasRecordChanged` function accurately detects changes, we have added additional checks.

The first `If` statement checks that both the control's value and tag are `Not Null`. Recall that we have stored the original value of each text box control in the control's `Tag` property in the `lstMovies_AfterUpdate` event procedure. Next, we use various `If` statements for different comparisons, considering data types (`Numeric` value, `String` value, and `Null` value).

The `IsNumeric` function checks that both the current value and the tag value are numeric. The `CDbl` function converts both values to `Double` and compares them. If they are not equal, it means the value has changed, so the `HasRecordChanged` is set to `True` and the function exits immediately, as a change has been detected. The `CDbl` function converts a value to a double-precision floating-point number. When comparing a year entry from a text box to the `Tag` property, you may use the `CDbl` function to ensure that both values are treated as numbers.

If the values are not numeric, the values are converted to strings for proper comparison using the `CStr` function. If they are not equal, it means the value has changed, so the `HasRecordChanged` is set to `True` and the function terminates, as a change has been detected.

Finally, the `IsNull` value comparison handles cases where one value is `Null` and the other is not. If they are different, it means the value has changed.

Writing the btnRemove_Click Event Procedure

Let's assume that any movie selected in the `lstMovies` list box can be removed from the `movieCollection` and the `lstMovies` list box upon clicking the Remove button (`btnRemove`).

The movie title and its details will not, however, be removed from the `Movies` table.

1. Enter the following `btnRemove_Click` event procedure in the `Form_frmMovies` code window:

```vba
Private Sub btnRemove_Click()
    Dim selectedTitle As String

    If Me.lstMovies.ListIndex >= 0 Then
        selectedTitle = Me.lstMovies.Value
        movieCollection.RemoveMovie selectedTitle
        Me.lstMovies.RemoveItem Me.lstMovies.ListIndex
        MsgBox selectedTitle & _
        " was removed from the collection only!", vbInformation
        Me.lstMovies.Selected(0) = True
```

```
        ' Enter the add mode
        Call btnAdd_Click

        ' Update the item count in the form footer
        Me.lblItemCount.Caption = "List Items: " & _
            Me.lstMovies.ListCount & _
            " | Total Movies: " & DCount("*", "Movies")
    End If
End Sub
```

The `btnRemove_Click` event procedure handles the removal of a selected movie from the list and the collection and informs the user about the removal, then sets the form to "add mode" and updates the item count on the form. The `RemoveMovie` method from the `movieCollection` object is called to remove the selected movie from the collection. The `ListIndex` property of `lstMovies` is used to remove the selected item from the list box. The `btnAdd_Click` procedure (we'll write it next) switches the form to an "add mode" for adding new movies. This prepares the form for adding a new movie after removing one. The last statement in the procedure updates the Caption property of the `lblItemCount` label to reflect the current number in the `lstMovies` list and the total number of movies in the database.

The `DCount` function allows us to count records in a table without having to bind the form to the data source: `DCount("*", "Movies")` returns the total number of records in the specified table.

Writing the btnAdd_Click and btnSave_Click Event Procedures

To add a new movie to the `movieCollection` and the `Movies` table, the user can click the Add Movie button (`btnAdd`) located above the `lstMovies` list box. A movie can also be added after clicking the Remove button, as shown in the `btnRemove_Click` event procedure earlier.

Clicking the Add New button on the form should:

- Disable any movie selection in the list box.
- Remove all the values from the text boxes.
- Enable the Title text box and move focus to this box so the user can start entering a new movie title.
- Hide the Update and Remove buttons.
- Make the hidden Save Movie button visible, so the user can save the newly entered movie.

1. Enter the following procedures in the `Form_frmMovies` code window:

```
Private Sub btnAdd_Click()
    Dim i As Integer

    ' Deselect all items in the list box
    For i = 0 To Me.lstMovies.ListCount - 1
        Me.lstMovies.Selected(i) = False
    Next i

    ' Clear the text boxes
    ClearControls

    ' handle buttons
    Me.btnSave.Visible = True
    Me.btnUpdate.Visible = False
    Me.btnRemove.Visible = False
End Sub
```

The `btnAdd_Click` event procedure calls the following `ClearControls` procedure:

```
Private Sub ClearControls()
    ' Clear form controls
    With Me
        .txtDirector = ""
        .txtGenre = ""
        .txtTitle = ""
        .txtReleaseYear = ""
        .txtTitle.Enabled = True
        .txtTitle.SetFocus
    End With
End Sub
```

In the `btnSave_Click` event procedure shown below, we don't allow saving the record, unless there is a value in the Title text box. If other text boxes are left empty, we set a default `"Unknown"` value. Notice how this procedure calls the `MovieExists` method from the `clsMovieCollection` to check whether the movie already exists in the collection.

```
Private Sub btnSave_Click()
    Dim newMovie As clsMovie
    Set newMovie = New clsMovie

    On Error GoTo Error_Handler
    ' check if movieCollection is initialized
```

```vba
If movieCollection Is Nothing Then
    Set movieCollection = New clsMovieCollection
End If


' Validate and set movie properties from form controls
If IsNull(Me.txtTitle.Value) Or Me.txtTitle.Value = "" Then
    MsgBox "Title is required.", vbExclamation, "Input Error"
    Me.txtTitle.SetFocus
    Exit Sub
Else
    newMovie.Title = Me.txtTitle.Value
End If


If Not IsNull(Me.txtDirector.Value) And _
   Me.txtDirector.Value <> "" Then
    newMovie.Director = Me.txtDirector.Value
Else
    ' Default value if Director is empty
    newMovie.Director = "Unknown"
End If


If Not IsNull(Me.txtGenre.Value) And _
   Me.txtGenre.Value <> "" Then
      newMovie.Genre = Me.txtGenre.Value
Else
    ' Default value if Genre is empty
    newMovie.Genre = "Unknown"
End If


If IsNumeric(Me.txtReleaseYear.Value) And _
   Me.txtReleaseYear.Value <> "" Then
      newMovie.ReleaseYear = Me.txtReleaseYear.Value
Else
    ' Default value if ReleaseYear is empty or not numeric
    newMovie.ReleaseYear = 0
End If


' Check if the movie already exists
If movieCollection.MovieExists(newMovie.Title) Then
    MsgBox "The movie already exists in the collection.", _
        vbExclamation, "Duplicate Entry"
    Exit Sub
End If


'Check if the title already exists in the table
Dim ID As Variant
```

```vba
ID = DLookup("ID", "Movies", "Title = '" & newMovie.Title & "'")

If Not IsNull(ID) Then
 MsgBox "The movie with this title exists in the table." & _
        vbCrLf & "Reload the form to view it."
        Exit Sub
End If

' Add new movie to the collection
movieCollection.AddMovie newMovie

'Insert new movie into the Movies table
Dim db As DAO.Database
Dim rst As DAO.Recordset
Set db = CurrentDb
Set rst = db.OpenRecordset("Movies", dbOpenDynaset)

With rst
    .AddNew
    !Title = newMovie.Title
    !Director = newMovie.Director
    !Genre = newMovie.Genre
    !ReleaseYear = newMovie.ReleaseYear
    .Update
End With

rst.Close
Set rst = Nothing
Set db = Nothing

'Update the list box
Me.lstMovies.RowSourceType = "Value List"
Me.lstMovies.AddItem newMovie.Title

' Clear text boxes after saving
ClearControls

MsgBox "Record saved successfully!", vbExclamation
' prepare the form for the new record entry
Call btnAdd_Click

' Update the item count in the form footer
Me.lblItemCount.Caption = "List Items: " & _
    Me.lstMovies.ListCount & _
    " | Total Movies: " & DCount("*", "Movies")
Exit Sub
```

```
Error_Handler:
    MsgBox "An error occurred: " & Err.Description, vbCritical,
"Error"
End Sub
```

The `currentMovie` variable stores the currently viewed movie, allowing updates to be applied to the correct record in the table.

Testing the Project Progress (Test 2)

All the procedures are not completed, and we can test the Remove and Add New buttons.

1. Open the `frmMovies` form in form view, select any movie in the list box, click the remove button, and click OK to confirm the message box. The movie should no longer appear in the list box and the `lstCountItems` label in the form's footer should indicate a different count for the movie and item totals. Also, upon the movie's removal from the collection, the form should be ready for a new data entry.

2. Click the Save button with nothing filled in the text boxes and notice the error message appears, as shown in Figure 18.5.

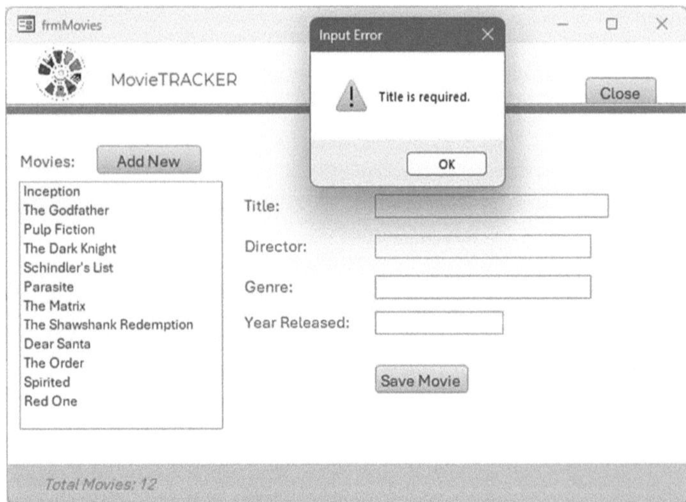

FIGURE 18.5.   The frmMovies form prepared for data entry.

3. In the Title text box, type the movie name that already exists in the list box, and click the Save Movie button. You should see a message that the movie already exists in the collection.

4. Click the Add New button to clear any entries in text boxes and type your favorite movie title that's not already in the list box, then click the Save Movie button.
   You should see the Record saved successfully! message.
5. Click OK to the message and notice the newly added movie title now appears in the list box.
6. Select the newly added title in the list box and notice the text boxes populate with the name of the movie and default values for all other movie details.
7. Perform other tests of your own to ensure that all the code is working as desired. You may need to add additional code to the `Form_frmMovies` form module to handle conditions that were not addressed in prior code.

Effective Code Analysis

To effectively analyze the code as the form loads and is being worked with, adding breakpoints can help you understand the flow of execution and identify any issues. Locate important subroutines and functions within the `Form_frmMovies` form module. The key locations include:

- `Form_Load` (the event that runs when the form is first loaded)
- `Form_Current` (the event that runs when the form's current record changes)
- Button click events (e.g., `btnAdd_Click`, `btnRemove_Click`) that handle user interactions
- Any custom subroutines or functions that perform significant actions.

To add a breakpoint, click on the left margin next to the line of code where you want to add a breakpoint, or press F9. The line should be highlighted to indicate a breakpoint. When you open the form, the code execution will stop at the breakpoints you've added. Step through the code line by line using F8 and observe the sequence of execution and the values of variables. You can press F5 to continue execution until the next breakpoint is encountered.

Creating an Instance of a Class

Creating an object is often called *creating an instance of a class* or *instantiating an object*. It is important to understand the difference between a class and an object. A class is like a data type; it defines a type of object. It is not itself an object, but a template that you can use to create as many objects as you want. In other words, multiple objects can be created from a single class. Each object is considered a completely different entity with distinct properties. Before the object can be created, an object variable must be declared to store the reference to the object. If the name of the class module is `clsMovie`, then a new instance of this class can be created with the following statement:

```
Dim currentMovie As New clsMovie
```

The `currentMovie` variable represents a reference to an object of the `clsMovie` class. When you declare the object variable with the `New` keyword, VBA creates the objects and allocates the memory for it. The object isn't instantiated, however, until you refer to it in your procedure by assigning a value to its property or by running one of its methods.

You can also create an instance of the object by declaring an object variable with the data type defined by the class of the object, as in the following examples used in our `MovieTracker` project:

```
'  Declarations at the top of the form class module
Private movieCollection As clsMovieCollection
Private currentMovie As clsMovie

' initializing the object within the Form_Load procedures
Set movieCollection = New clsMovieCollection

' initializing the object within btnUpdate_Click event procedure
Set currentMovie = New clsMovie
```

If you don't use the `New` keyword with the `Dim` statement, VBA does not allocate memory for your custom object until your procedure needs it.

CREATING AND WORKING WITH COLLECTION CLASSES

In Chapter 7 of this book, you used collections to track and manipulate data in your VBA program. At that time, you learned that collections complement the capabilities of arrays, allowing you to store and process large amounts of data without the need to create multiple variables. To track data, you declared the collection at the top of the standard module using the `Dim` keyword:

```
Dim myCollection as New Collection
```

Then, you used the `Add` method to add specific items to your collection:

```
myCollection.Add "item1"
myCollection.Add "item2"
myCollection.Add "item3"
```

You also learned how to add elements in any position by using the optional `Before` and `After` arguments. You counted your collection items using the `Count` property and removed your items using the `Remove` method. Now that you are familiar with the concept of a collection, let's take it a bit further.

The Collection Object

Collections are often created to hold objects, and they play an important role in the object models of Microsoft 365 applications (e.g., Access, Excel, Word, PowerPoint, Outlook, OneNote, and Visio), as well as other applications that support VBA. You've already used many of the built-in collections in Access. For example, recall the `TableDefs` or `QueryDefs` collections that you worked with in earlier chapters of this book. In Word, the `Documents` collection stores all open documents, and the `Paragraphs` collection stores each paragraph in the current document; in Excel, there is a collection of `Workbooks`, `Worksheets`, and so on. One can manipulate these collections using the familiar `For Each… Next` loop. Each collection is a class that can contain instances of other classes or entire groups (collections) of related classes.

The VBA collection objects have the familiar `Add`, `Remove`, and `Items` methods, and the `Count` property. The `Add` method adds a member to the collection and has the following syntax:

```
CollectionObjectName.Add(Item, [Key], [Before]. [After])
```

Notice that the parameters in brackets are optional. The `Key` is a unique string that specifies a key that can be used to identify the collection member instead of its ordinal position in the collection. The `Before` and `After` arguments specify that the new member is to be added at the position immediately preceding an existing member in the collection or immediately following the existing member in the collection. You can only specify a `Before` or `After` position, but not both.

The only required parameter of the `Add` method is `Item`, which is a pointer to the object instance. Do not confuse the `Item` parameter with the `Item` method that is used to specify an object by its ordinal position in the collection:

```
CollectionObjectName.Item(Index)
```

The `Index` argument specifies the position of an existing collection member. The index must be between `1` and the collection's `Count` property. Unlike the built-in Access collections, which are zero-based, the first item in the custom collection object is at position 1. The `Index` argument is also used to provide the position of the existing collection member when removing it from a collection:

```
CollectionObjectName.Remove(Index)
```

The read-only `Count` property returns a `Long Integer` containing the number of objects in a collection:

```
Debug.Print CollectionObjectName.Count
```

The Collection Class

So far, we have used untyped collections. These collections allowed you to put anything in them and were easy to create. What if you're writing an application that must restrict the type of item that can be added to the collection? In this case, a strongly typed collection class is what you need. Strongly typed collections are custom collection classes that will only accept objects of the same type. While they are not as easy to create as untyped collections that are built into VBA, custom collection classes give you more control over what is added to the collection and allow you to catch errors early in the development process instead of at runtime. You create a collection class in a class module.

To get started with creating and using collection classes in Access, assume that you are writing an application that keeps track of a computer inventory in your company. On the VBE editor screen, you've added two class modules and a standard module. The first class module, named `clsAsset`, contains several public variable declarations for your asset object and one `Property Get AssetInfo` procedure that is used to retrieve asset information:

```
' class module: clsAsset
Option Compare Database
Option Explicit

' Declare asset variables
Public assetType As String
Public Manufacturer As String
Public Model As String
Public SerialNo As String

Property Get AssetInfo() As String
    AssetInfo = assetType & _
        " | " & Manufacturer & _
        " | " & Model & _
        " | " & SerialNo & vbCrLf
End Property
```

The second class module is named `clsAssetCollection` and contains the code shown in Figure 18.6.

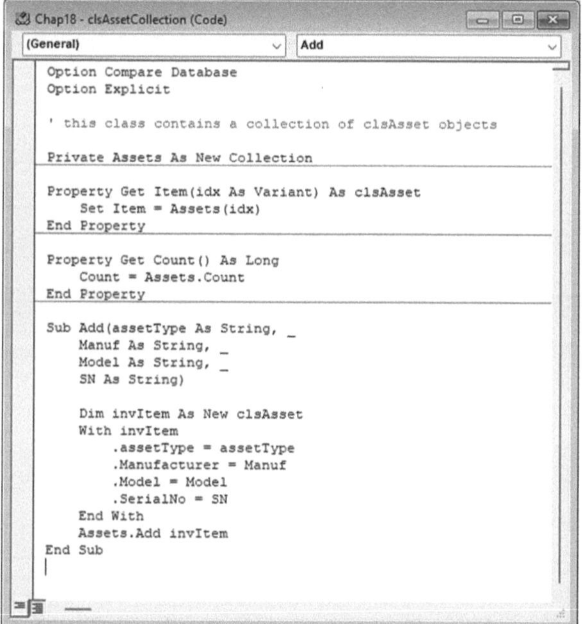

FIGURE 18.6.   Class collection module named clsAssetCollection.

Notice that the collection object variable is named `Assets` and is declared at the top of the `clsAssetCollection` module. The first `Property Get Item` allows you to retrieve asset information for a specific asset object, while the second `Property Get Count` returns the total number of items placed in the collection. The custom `Add` method is used to create an inventory item and add it to the collection. The `invItem` object variable represents an asset object created from the `clsAsset` class.

To work with asset objects and the `Assets` collection, we need a procedure in a standard module. This procedure should call the `Add` method from the `clsAssetCollection` class module to create an asset and add it to the `Assets` collection. The following code is to be entered in a standard module:

```
Option Compare Database
Option Explicit


Sub AddItemsToInventory()
    ' create a new collection based on clsAssetCollection class
    ' to store computer assets
    Dim Assets As New clsAssetCollection

    'add assets to the collection
```

```vba
Assets.Add "Laptop", "Dell", "XPS-13", "XYZ89JWZ28"
Assets.Add "Desktop", "Lenovo", "ThinkCentre M90q Gen 2 _
    Tiny", "YGU23HY7899"

'list all inventory items
Dim invAsset As clsAsset
Dim invItemNo As Integer

For invItemNo = 1 To Assets.Count
    Debug.Print Assets.Item(invItemNo).AssetInfo
Next invItemNo
End Sub
```

For this demo procedure, we've hard-coded the asset data. You can create a custom Access form to collect asset information from the user or read it directly from a text file. The `AddItemsToInventory` procedure declares the `Assets` collection class and calls the `Add` method from the `clsAssetCollection` class module to create a new asset and add it to the inventory. Next, the `For...` loop is used to iterate through the collection and retrieve `AssetInfo` for each stored asset. To better understand how an asset is created, added, and retrieved from the collection, run the `AddItemsToInventory` procedure by stepping through its code.

After running the procedure, the collection content is shown in the Immediate window:

Laptop | Dell | XPS-13 | XYZ89JWZ28
Desktop | Lenovo | ThinkCentre M90q Gen 2 Tiny | YGU23HY7899

The same output can be obtained using another procedure that utilizes the built-in VBA collection instead of the custom collection class:

```vba
Sub CreateNewAssets_BuitInCollection()
    ' declare an untyped built-in VBA collection object
    Dim colAssets As New Collection

    'create two assets
    Dim oAsset1 As New clsAsset
    Dim oAsset2 As New clsAsset

    ' assign values to asset properties
    With oAsset1
        .assetType = "Laptop"
        .Manufacturer = "Dell"
        .Model = "XPS-13"
        .SerialNo = "XYZ89JWZ28"
```

```vba
End With

With oAsset2
    .assetType = "Desktop"
    .Manufacturer = "Lenovo"
    .Model = "ThinkCentre M90q Gen 2 Tiny"
    .SerialNo = "YGU23HY7899"
End With


' Print asset information to the Immediate Window
Debug.Print oAsset1.AssetInfo & vbCrLf & oAsset2.AssetInfo

' add both assets into a untyped (built-in VBA) collection
colAssets.Add oAsset1
colAssets.Add oAsset2

' use the for each loop to loop over the collection
Dim myAsset As clsAsset
For Each myAsset In colAssets
    Debug.Print myAsset.AssetInfo
Next
End Sub
```

In the code above, all seems to work fine until you add something else to the collection that is not an object:

```vba
' add both assets into a untyped (built-in VBA) collection
colAssets.Add oAsset1
colAssets.Add oAsset2
colAssets.Add CurrentDb.Name
```

The third code line in the snippet above will generate an error at runtime but not at compile time. What does this mean? When you write your code and choose Debug | Compile, Access checks for syntax errors. If no errors are found, you assume that you've written perfect code and things will go smoothly, but then you are faced with Run-time error: "424 Object Required". Don't you just hate this error? The program fails while looping through the collection, expecting an object and not a string. By using a custom collection class as we did in the previous example, you can expose errors at compile time so you can handle your errors while you're still in the development phase.

ADVANCED EVENT PROGRAMMING

So far in this book, you've worked with event procedures that executed from the form or report class module when a certain event occurred for a form, report, or control. You have probably noticed that event programming, as you've seen it implemented in the form and report class modules, requires that you copy and paste your existing event code into new form or report events in order to obtain exactly the same functionality.

For instance, say you added certain features to a text box on one form and now you'd like to have a text box on other forms behave in the same way. You could react to the text box's events in the same way on all your forms by entering the same event procedure code in a form class module for each form, or you could save keystrokes by learning how to centralize and reuse your event code.

Action Item. 18.1

Earlier in this chapter, we created and worked with the `clsMovie` class. `Chap18.accdb` in the companion files (see the `Completed Files` folder) includes the `frmMovies2` form, which is an enhanced version of the `frmMovies` form you worked with in this chapter. The `frmMovies2` form includes additional controls to allow users to include a movie poster when adding or updating a movie (see Figure 18.7). The form's data is loaded from the `Movies2` table, which includes an additional field named `ImagePath` to store the path to the image file. Sample images are included in the `Images` folder in the companion files, or you can

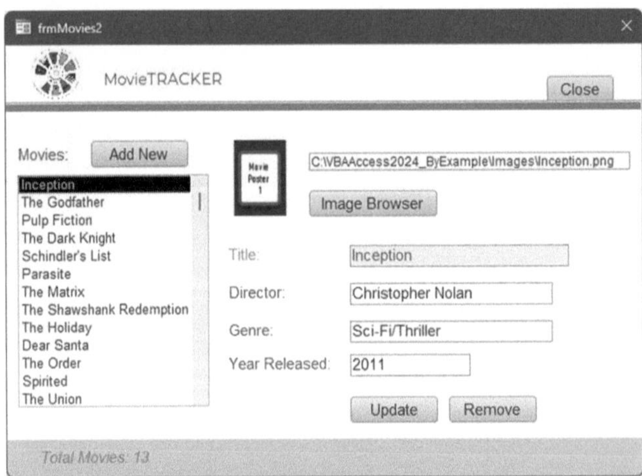

FIGURE 18.7.   The Enhanced frmMovies2 form contains additional controls and demonstrates the use of advanced event programming.

add your own. The additional VBA code in the `Form_frmMovies2` class module demonstrates how to raise custom events when a movie is added or removed. Look for the following declarations and event-handler code at the top of the `Form_frmMovies2` form module:

```
Private currentMovie As clsMovie
Private WithEvents movieCollection As clsMovieCollection

' Event handler for MovieAdded event
Private Sub movieCollection_MovieAdded(ByVal Title As String)
    Debug.Print "Movie added: " & Title
End Sub

' Event handler for MovieRemoved event
Private Sub movieCollection_MovieRemoved(ByVal Title As String)
    Debug.Print "Movie removed from the collection: " & Title
End Sub
```

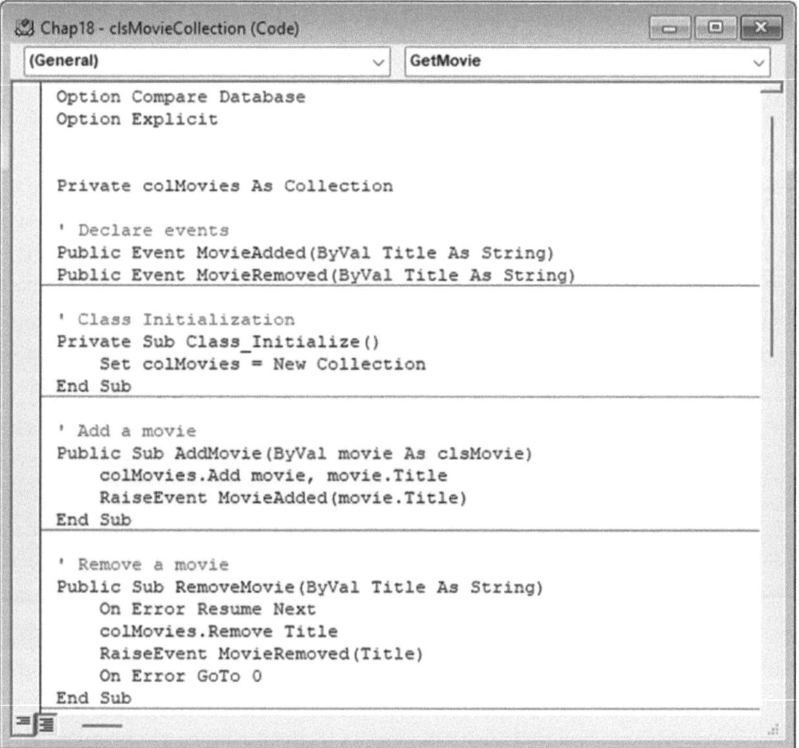

FIGURE 18.8. The enhanced clsMovieCollection class module contains additional code and declarations for handling MovieAdded and MovieRemoved events.

In the variable declaration, notice the use of the `WithEvents` keyword. This keyword allows the form to sink events from the `movieCollection` object.

The `clsMovieCollection` class module also includes additional code to handle the `MovieAdded` and `MovieRemoved` events (see Figure 18.8). These handlers print a message to the Immediate window when the events are raised.

Use the `Public Event` keywords to declare events in your class.

Use the `WithEvents` keyword to declare an object variable that can sink events. You must write event handler procedures to respond to the events.

Use the `RaiseEvent` statement to trigger events within your class. Raising events in VBA allows your objects to notify other parts of your application when certain actions or changes occur. This is useful for creating interactive and responsive applications. The `RaiseEvent` statement is used within the `AddMovie` and `RemoveMovie` methods to trigger these events when a movie is added or removed.

When you interact with the controls on the `frmMovies2` form, be sure to examine the Immediate window to see which events were triggered and what output was generated.

Sinking Events in Standalone Class Modules

Instead of writing your event procedures in the form and report class modules, you can make the maintenance of your Microsoft Access applications much simpler by writing the event code in class modules. In addition to creating custom objects, as we have seen earlier in this chapter while working with the `MovieTracker` project, standalone class modules can implement object events.

The process of listening to an object's events is called *sinking the event*. To sink (handle) events in a standalone class module, you must use the `WithEvents` keyword. This keyword will tell the class that you want to sink some or all of the object's events in the class module. You determine which events you want to sink by writing the appropriate event code. Remember that only classes can sink events. Therefore, the `WithEvents` keyword can only be used in class modules. You can use the `WithEvents` keyword to declare as many individual variables as you need; however, you cannot create arrays using `WithEvents`.

As mentioned in the Important Terminology section at the beginning of this chapter, an object that generates events is called an *event source*. The process of broadcasting an event is called *sourcing the event*. To handle events raised by an event source, you must declare an object variable using the `WithEvents` keyword. For example, to react to form events in a standalone class module, you would need to enter the following module-level variable declaration:

```
Private WithEvents m_frm As Access.Form
```

In this statement, `m_frm` is the name of the object variable that references the `Form` object. While you can use any variable name you want, this variable cannot be a generic object type. That means you cannot declare it as `Object`. If the variable were declared as `Object`, Visual Basic wouldn't know what type library should be used. Therefore, it would not be able to provide you with the names of events for which you can write code.

Now, let's walk through these new concepts step by step. Custom Project 18.2 demonstrates how to create a record logger class that handles a form's `AfterUpdate` event. Each time the `AfterUpdate` event occurs, this class will enter information about the newly created record into a text file.

(◉) Custom Project 18.2   Sinking Events in a Standalone Class Module

Part 1: Database File Preparation

1. In the `Chap18.accdb` database, choose Create | Form Wizard. Select the `Movies` table from the Tables/Queries drop-down list, select all the fields from this table, and choose Next. Choose Columnar layout for your form and click Next. Enter `frmMovies3` as the form's title and click Finish.
2. Switch to the form design view and use the Property Sheet to set the form's Pop Up property to Yes, and the form's Data Entry property to Yes.
3. Select the ID text box on the form, and in the Property Sheet, set the Enabled property to No.
4. Save and close the `frmMovies3` form.

Part 2: Creating the clsRecordLogger Class

1. Choose Database Tools | Visual Basic to activate the VBE window.
2. In the Project Explorer window, select Chap18 (Chap18) and choose Insert | Class Module. A new class will appear in the Project Explorer window. Use the Name property in the Properties window to change the name of the class to `clsRecordLogger`.
3. In the `clsRecordLogger` class module's code window, enter the following module-level variable declaration just below the `Option Compare Database` and `Option Explicit` statements:

```
Private WithEvents m_frm As Access.Form
```

After declaring the object variable using `WithEvents`, the variable name `m_frm` appears in the Object box in your class module (see Figure 18.9). When you select this variable from the drop-down list, the valid events for that object will appear in the Procedure drop-down box on the right-hand side.

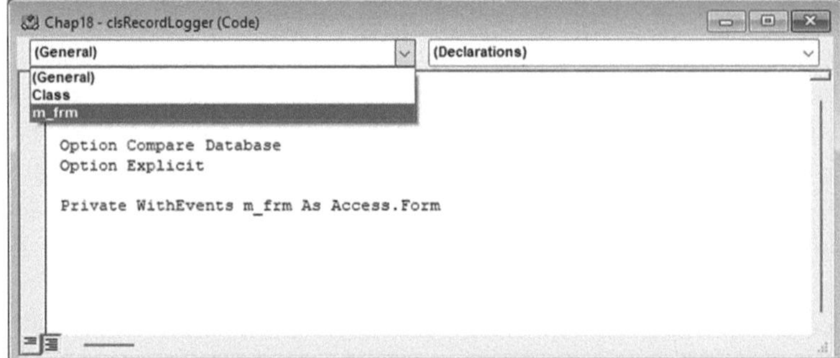

FIGURE 18.9.   The Object drop-down list in the clsRecordLogger's Code window lists the m_frm object variable that was declared using the WithEvents keyword.

4. In the `clsRecordLogger` class module's code window, enter the following property procedure just below the variable declaration line:

```
Public Property Set Form(cur_frm As Form)
  Set m_frm = cur_frm
  m_frm.AfterUpdate = "[Event Procedure]"
End Property
```

To sink events in a standalone class module, you must tell the class which specific form's events the class should be responding to. You do this by writing the Property Set procedure. Recall from an earlier discussion that Property Set procedures are used to assign a reference to an object. Therefore, the statement:

```
Set m_frm = cur_frm
```

will assign the current form (passed in the `cur_frm` variable) to the `m_frm` object variable declared in step 3. Pointing the object variable (`m_frm`) at the object (`cur_frm`) isn't enough. Access will not raise the event unless the object's Event property is set to [Event Procedure]. Therefore, the second statement in the preceding procedure will ensure that Access knows that it must raise the form's `AfterUpdate` event.

5. Choose Tools | References and add the reference to Microsoft Scripting Runtime Library. You will need this library to gain access to the `FileSystemObject` in the next step. Close the References dialog box after setting the specified reference.

6. In the `clsRecordLogger` class module's code window, enter the following `m_frm_AfterUpdate` event procedure:

```
Private Sub m_frm_AfterUpdate()
  Dim fso As FileSystemObject
```

```
    Dim myFile As Object
    Dim strFileN As String
    Dim ctrl As Control

    On Error Resume Next

    Set fso = New FileSystemObject
    strFileN = "C:\VBAAccess2024_ByExample\MyMovies.txt"
    Set myFile = fso.GetFile(strFileN)

    If Err.Number = 0 Then
      ' open text file
      Set myFile = fso.OpenTextFile(strFileN, 8)
    Else
      ' create a text file
      Set myFile = fso.CreateTextFile(strFileN)
    End If
    If IsNull(m_frm.Title) Or m_frm.Title = "" Then
      MsgBox "You must enter the movie title."
      m_frm.Title.SetFocus
      Exit Sub
    End If

    For Each ctrl In m_frm.Controls
      If ctrl.ControlType = acTextBox And _
        InStr(1, ctrl.Name, "Title") Then
        myFile.WriteLine "Title:" & ctrl.Value & _
        " Added on: " & Date & " " & Time & _
        " (Form: " & m_frm.Name & ")"
        MsgBox "See the audit trail in " & strFileN & "."
        Exit For
      End If
    Next

    myFile.Close
    Set fso = Nothing

    ' Requery the form to display a new data entry screen
    m_frm.Requery
    Call m_frm.Form_Click
End Sub
```

The code inside the `m_frm_AfterUpdate` event procedure will be executed after Access finds that the form's `AfterUpdate` property is set to [Event Procedure]. This code tells Access to open or create a text file named `MyMovies.txt` and write a line consisting of the value of the Title text box control on the form, the date and time the record was inserted or modified, and the name of the form. Notice how the `InStr` function is used to locate the control whose name contains the `Title` string. The first argument of the `InStr` function determines the character position where the search should begin, the second argument is the string being searched, and the third argument is the string expression being sought within the string specified in the second argument.

7. Save the code that you wrote in the class module by clicking the Save button on the toolbar or choosing File | Save. When the Save As dialog box appears with clsRecordLogger in the text box, click OK.

   For the events to actually fire, you must instantiate the class and pass it the object whose events you want to track. This requires a couple of lines of code in your form's class module.

Part 3: Creating an Instance of the Custom Class in the Form's Class Module

1. Switch to the Access window by pressing Alt+F11. In the database navigation pane, right-click the frmMovies3 form you created earlier and select Design View.

2. Click the Property Sheet button on the Ribbon and select Form in the drop-down list; then, activate the Event tab. Click next to the On Open property and select [Event Procedure], then click the ellipsis (…) button.

   Access activates the Code window and writes the procedure stub for the `Form_Open` event.

3. Complete the code of the `Form_Open` event procedure, as shown below (note that you must also declare the `RecordLogger` `Private` variable at the top of the form's class module):

```
Private RecordLogger As clsRecordLogger

Private Sub Form_Open(Cancel As Integer)
   Set RecordLogger = New clsRecordLogger
   Set RecordLogger.Form = Me
End Sub
```

To instantiate a custom class module, we begin by declaring a module-level object variable, `RecordLogger`, as the name of our custom class, `clsRecordLogger`. You can choose any name you wish for your variable name. Next, we instantiate the class in the `Form_Open` event procedure by using the `Set` statement. Notice that you must use the `New` keyword to create a new object of a particular class. By setting the reference to an actual instance of the object when the form first opens, we ensure that the object refers to an actual object by the time the event is first fired. The second statement in the `Form_Open` event procedure sets the `Form` property (which was defined by the property procedure in the class module) to the `Form` object whose events we want to sink. The `Me` keyword represents the current instance of the form class.

When we are done pointing the object variable to the instance of the custom class, it is a good idea to release the variable reference. We can do this by setting the object variable `RecordLogger` to `Nothing` in the `Form_Close` event procedure.

4. Enter the following `Form_Close` event procedure in the form's class module code window:

```
Private Sub Form_Close()
   Set RecordLogger = Nothing
End Sub
```

Notice that the last statement in the `clsRecordLogger` class module (see the `m_frm_AfterUpdate` event procedure in Part 2, step 6) calls the `Form_Click` event procedure. We must write the code for this procedure in the form class module.

5. Enter the following `Form_Click` procedure in the form's class module:

```
Private Sub Form_Click()
    DoCmd.GoToControl "Title"
End Sub
```

This procedure instructs Access to select the Title text on the form so the user can start entering the movie information.

The complete code for the `Form_frmMovies3` form class module is shown in Figure 18.10.

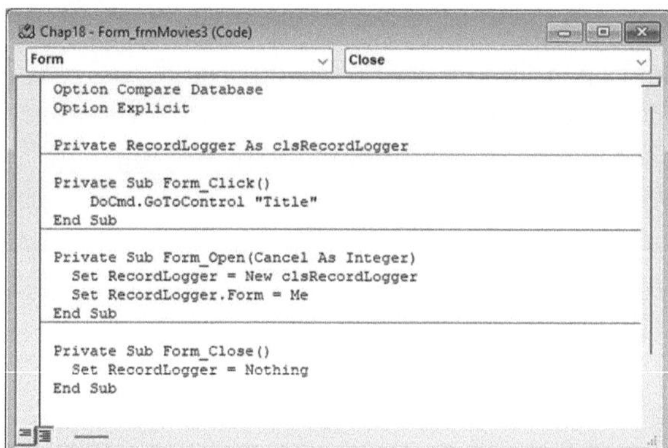

FIGURE 18.10. To sink form events in a custom class module, clsRecordLogger, you must enter VBA event procedures in the Form_frmMovies3 class module.

6. Press Ctrl+S to save the module code, or click the Save button on the toolbar.
7. In the Access main window, close the `frmMovies3` form.

Now all the required code has been written in both the standalone class module and in the form class module. Let's test our project.

Part 4: Testing the clsRecordLogger Custom Class

1. Open the `frmMovies3` form in form view.
2. Enter a movie title of your choice in the Title text box and click the record selector on the left side of the form to save the record (see Figure 18.11).

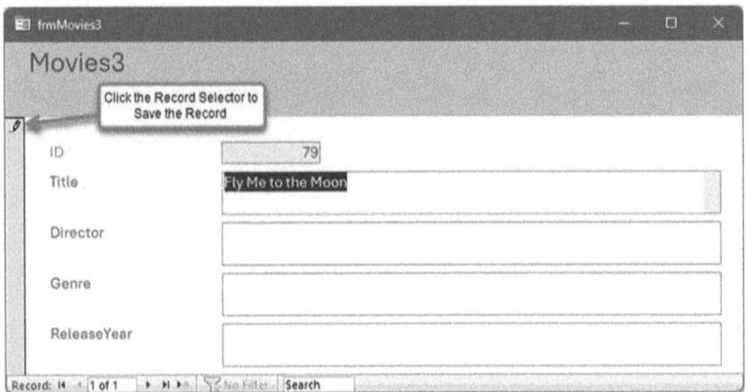

FIGURE 18.11. The frmMovies3 form in data entry mode is used for testing out the custom clsRecordLogger class.

When you save the newly entered record, a message box appears with the text See the audit trail in C:\VBAAccess2024_ByExample\MyMovies.txt. Recall that this message was programmed inside the `m_frm_AfterUpdate()` event procedure in the `clsRecordLogger` class module. It looks like our custom class has successfully sunk the `AfterUpdate` event. The form's `AfterUpdate` event was propagated to the custom class module.

3. Click OK to close the message box.
4. Activate File Explorer and open the `C:\VBAAccess2024_ByExample\MyMovies.txt` file.

The `MyMovies.txt` file (see Figure 18.12) displays the record log.

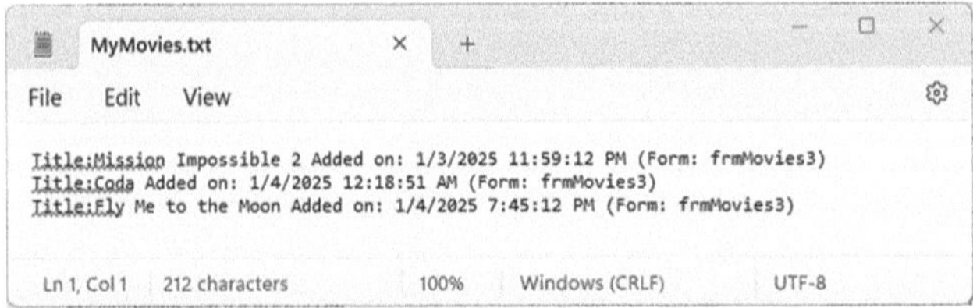

FIGURE 18.12. The MyMovies.txt file is used by the clsRecordLogger custom class for tracking record additions.

5. Close the `MyMovies.txt` file.
6. Add a few more records to the `frmMovies3` form and check out the `C:\VBAAccess2024_ByExample\MyCust.txt` file.
7. Close the `frmMovies3` form.

   Now that you know how to sink the form's `AfterUpdate` event outside the form class module, you can use the same idea to sink other form events in a class module and make your code easier to implement and maintain. Just remember that if you want to sink events in a standalone class module, you must write code in two places: in your class module and in your form or report class module. The standalone class module must contain a module-level `WithEvents` variable declaration, and you must set the reference to an actual instance of the object in the form or report module.

<table>
<tr><td rowspan="2">**NOTE**</td><td>*The code you've written in this project can be reused in another Access form. If your record log text file will be used to track various types of information in different forms, consider giving it a more generic name.*</td></tr>
</table>

Writing Event Procedure Code in Two Places

If you write event procedure code for the same event both in the form module and in the class module, the code defined in the form class module will run first, followed by the code in the custom class module. You can easily test this by entering the following `Form_AfterUpdate` event procedure code in the `Form_frmMovies3` class module prepared in Custom Project 18.2:

```
Private Sub Form_AfterUpdate()
  MsgBox "Transferring control to the custom class."
  ' when you click OK to this message, the code
  ' inside the AfterUpdate procedure in the custom
  ' class module will run
End Sub
```

When you open the form and add and save a new record, the `Form_AfterUpdate` event will fire and you will see the message about transferring control to the custom class. Next, the `AfterUpdate` event procedure will run in the custom class, and you will see a message informing you that you can view the audit trail in the specified text file.

Responding to Control Events in a Class Module

Everyone designing Microsoft Access forms sooner or later realizes that it takes a long time to customize some of the controls placed on the form. It's no wonder, then, that once the control is working correctly, there is a tendency toward copying the control and its event procedures to a new form that requires a control with the same functionality. If you followed this chapter carefully, you will already know a better (and a neater) solution. By using the `WithEvents` keyword, you can create an object variable that points to the control raising the events. Instead of responding to control events in the form module, you will react to these events in a different location: a standalone class module. This lets you write centralized code that is easy to implement in other form controls of the same type.

Suppose you need a text box that converts lowercase letters to uppercase and disallows numbers. Hands-On 18.1 demonstrates how to create a text box with these features and hook it up to any Microsoft Access form.

Hands-On 18.1   Responding to Control Events in a Class Module

This hands-on exercise requires prior completion of Custom Project 18.1.

1. Activate the VBE window and choose Insert | Class Module.
   A new class will appear in the Project Explorer window.
2. In the Properties window, click the (Name) property and type `clsUCaseBox`.
   You should see the clsUCaseBox entry under the Class Modules folder in the Project Explorer.
3. In the `clsUCaseBox` class module's Code window, enter the following code:

```
Private WithEvents txtBox As Access.TextBox

Public Function InitializeMe(myTxt As TextBox)
   Set txtBox = myTxt
   txtBox.OnKeyPress = "[Event Procedure]"
End Function

Private Sub txtBox_KeyPress(KeyAscii As Integer)
   Select Case KeyAscii
     Case 48 To 57
       MsgBox "Numbers are not allowed!"
       KeyAscii = 0
     Case Else
        ' convert to uppercase
       KeyAscii = Asc(UCase(Chr(KeyAscii)))
   End Select

   With txtBox
```

```
      .FontBold = True
      .FontItalic = True
      .BackColor = vbYellow
   End With
End Sub
```

Notice that to respond to a control's events in a standalone class module you start by declaring a module-level object variable using the `WithEvents` keyword.

Because the form can contain more than one text box control, we should tell the class which text box it needs to respond to. We do this by creating a Property Set procedure (like the one created in Custom Project 18.1) or a function procedure like the one shown above. We called this function `InitializeMe`, but you can use any name you wish. A function entered in a class module serves as an object's method. We will call the `InitializeMe` method later from a form class module and pass it the actual control we want it to respond to. The `InitializeMe` method will assign the passed-in control to the `WithEvents` object variable like this:

```
Set txtBox = myTxt
```

Next, we set the text box `KeyPress` property to [Event Procedure] to tell the class that we are interested in tracking this event.

Finally, we write the event procedure code for the text box control's `KeyPress` event. This code begins by checking the value of the key that was pressed by the user. If a number was entered, the user is advised that numbers aren't allowed, and the digit is removed from the text box by setting the value of `KeyAscii` to zero (0). Otherwise, if the user typed a lowercase letter, the character is converted to uppercase. `KeyAscii` is an integer that returns a numerical ANSI keycode. To convert the `KeyAscii` argument into a character, we use the `Chr` function. Once we've converted a key into a character, we use the `UCase` function to convert it to the uppercase. Finally, we translate the character back to an ANSI number by using the `Asc` function. The `txtBox_KeyPress` event procedure ends by adding some visual enhancements to the text box. The text entered in it will appear in bold italic type on a yellow background.

4. Save the code you entered in the `clsUCaseBox` class module's Code window by pressing the Save button on the toolbar.

5. In the Project Explorer window, double-click Form_frmMovies3. The `Form_frmMovies3` class module's code window should already contain the code you entered while working with Custom Project 18.1 earlier in this chapter. To

connect the `clsUCaseBox` class module with the actual text box, you must enter the following code in a form's class module (do not enter it yet):

```
' module-level variable declaration
Private mTextBox1 As clsUCaseBox

Private Sub Form_Open(Cancel As Integer)
  Set mTextBox1 = New clsUCaseBox
  mTextBox1.InitializeMe Me.Controls("Genre")
End Sub

Private Sub Form_Close()
  Set mTextBox1 = Nothing
End Sub
```

Because the `frmMovies3` form already contains a call to the `clsRecordLogger` class created earlier, all the procedures we need are already in place; therefore, we will simply add the appropriate lines of code to the existing procedures.

6. In the `Form_frmMovies3` code window, enter the following module-level variable declaration just above the `Form_Open` event procedure (see Figure 18.13):

```
Private mTextBox1 As clsUCaseBox
```

This statement declares the `mTextBox1` class variable. This variable is used in instantiating the `clsUCaseBox` object and connecting it with the actual text box control on the form (see the next step).

7. Enter the following lines of code before the `End Sub` statement of the `Form_Open` event procedure:

```
Set mTextBox1 = New clsUCaseBox
mTextBox1.InitializeMe Me.Controls("Genre")
```

Before our `clsUCaseBox` class can respond to a text box's events, you need these two lines of code; the first one sets the class variable `mTxtBox1` to a new instance of the `clsUCaseBox` class, and the second one calls the class `InitializeMe` method and supplies it with the name of the text box control.

8. Enter the following line of code before the `End Sub` statement of the `Form_Close` event procedure:

```
Set mTextBox1 = Nothing
```

When we are done with the object variable, we set it to `Nothing` to release the resources that have been assigned to it.

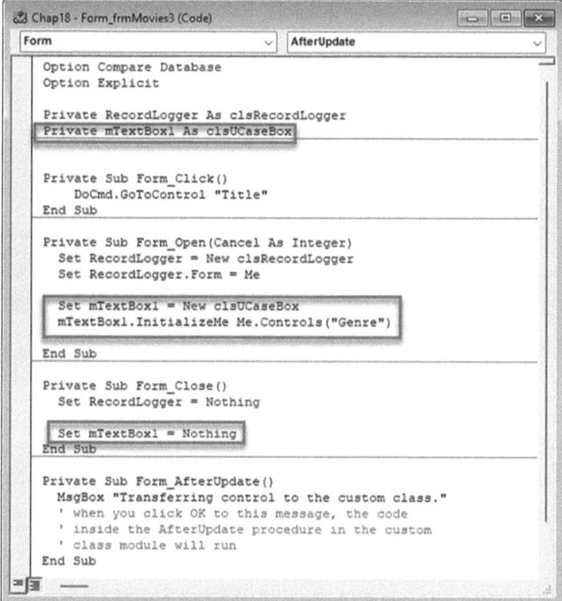

```
Chap18 - Form_frmMovies3 (Code)

Form                                    AfterUpdate

    Option Compare Database
    Option Explicit

    Private RecordLogger As clsRecordLogger
    Private mTextBox1 As clsUCaseBox


    Private Sub Form_Click()
        DoCmd.GoToControl "Title"
    End Sub

    Private Sub Form_Open(Cancel As Integer)
        Set RecordLogger = New clsRecordLogger
        Set RecordLogger.Form = Me

        Set mTextBox1 = New clsUCaseBox
        mTextBox1.InitializeMe Me.Controls("Genre")

    End Sub

    Private Sub Form_Close()
        Set RecordLogger = Nothing

        Set mTextBox1 = Nothing
    End Sub

    Private Sub Form_AfterUpdate()
        MsgBox "Transferring control to the custom class."
        ' when you click OK to this message, the code
        ' inside the AfterUpdate procedure in the custom
        ' class module will run
    End Sub
```

FIGURE 18.13.   The form class module shows code that instantiates and hooks up objects created in the clsRecordLogger and clsUCaseBox class modules with the form and a text box control.

9. Save the changes made in the code window by clicking the Save button on the toolbar.

10. Open the `frmMovies3` form in the form view and enter the movie title of your choice, then click the Genre text box and enter the movie genre.
Notice that as you type, the characters you enter are converted to uppercase (see Figure 18.14). They are also made bold and italic and appear on a yellow background. If you happen to press a number key, which is disallowed by your custom `KeyPress` event, you receive an error message.

FIGURE 18.14.   The Genre text box control is driven by the events defined in the clsUCaseBox class module.

11. Click on the record selector to save the record.

Because the `Movies3` form also responds to the `AfterUpdate` event that we programmed earlier, you should see an additional message when you save the form.

12. Close the `frmMovies3` form.

Declaring and Raising Events

As mentioned earlier, standalone class modules automatically support two events: `Initialize` and `Terminate`. Use the `Initialize` event to give the variables in your classes initial values. The `Initialize` event is called when you make a new instance of a class. The `Terminate` event is called when you set the instance to `Nothing`. In addition to these default events, you can define custom events for your class module.

To create a custom event, use the `Event` statement in the declaration section of a class module. For example, the following statements declare two events, named `MovieAdded` and `MovieRemoved`, which require one argument (see Figure 18.15):

```
Public Event MovieAdded(ByVal Title As String)
Public Event MovieRemoved(ByVal Title As String)
```

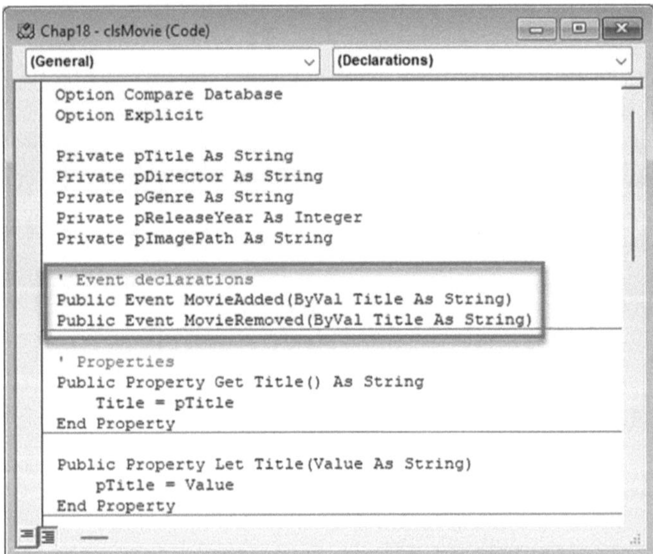

FIGURE 18.15. Creating user-defined, custom events in a class module requires the use of the Event statement.

The `Event` statement declares a user-defined event. This statement is followed by the name of the event and any arguments that will be passed to the event procedure. Arguments are separated by commas. An event can have `ByVal` and `ByRef` arguments. Recall that when passing the variable `ByRef`, you are actually passing the memory location of the variable. If you pass a variable `ByVal`, you are sending a copy of the variable.

When declaring events with arguments, bear in mind that events cannot have named arguments, optional arguments, or `ParamArray` arguments. The `Public` keyword is optional as events are public by default.

Use the `RaiseEvent` statement to fire the event. This is usually done by creating a method in a class module. For example, here's how you could trigger the `MovieAdded` and `MovieRemoved` events (see Figure 18.16):

```
' Add a movie
Public Sub AddMovie(ByVal movie As clsMovie)
    colMovies.Add movie, movie.Title
    RaiseEvent MovieAdded(movie.Title)
End Sub


' Remove a movie
Public Sub RemoveMovie(ByVal Title As String)
    On Error Resume Next
    colMovies.Remove Title
    RaiseEvent MovieRemoved(Title)
    On Error GoTo 0
End Sub
```

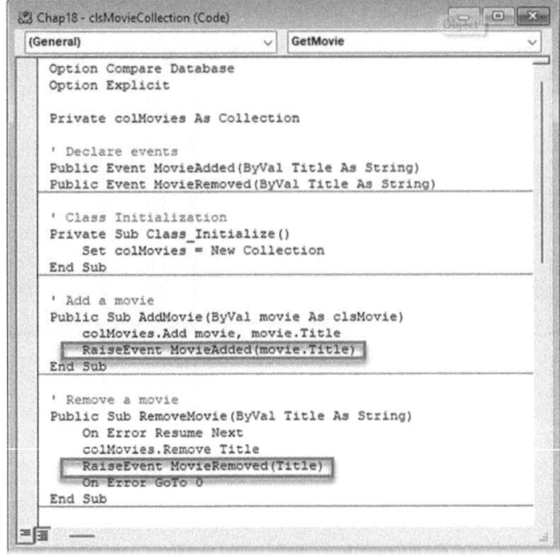

FIGURE 18.16.   To fire custom events, use write methods that use the RaiseEvent statement.

Notice that the `RaiseEvent` statement must be followed by the name of the event you want to fire and optionally one or more arguments you want to pass to the event. Arguments must be enclosed in parentheses.

Events can only be raised in the module in which they are declared using the `Event` statement. After declaring the event and writing the method that will be used for raising the event, you need to switch to the form class module and perform the following tasks:

- Declare a module-level variable of the class type using the `WithEvents` keyword.
- Assign an instance of the class containing the event to the object defined using the `WithEvents` statement.
- Write a procedure that calls the class method.
- Write the event-handler code.

Figure 18.17 shows the declaration of a module-level variable of the class type using the `WithEvents` keyword in the `Form_frmMovies2` form in the `Chap18.accdb` database (see the `Completed Files` folder in the companion files) and two event procedures that handle the `MovieAdded` and `MovieRemoved` events. The `Form_Load` event procedure has the required assignment statement. To understand when and how these events fire, set up a few breakpoints in `clsMovie`, `clsMovieCollection`, and `Form_frmMovies2`, then open and interact with the `Movies2` form. Modify the code as needed to get more experience in event programming.

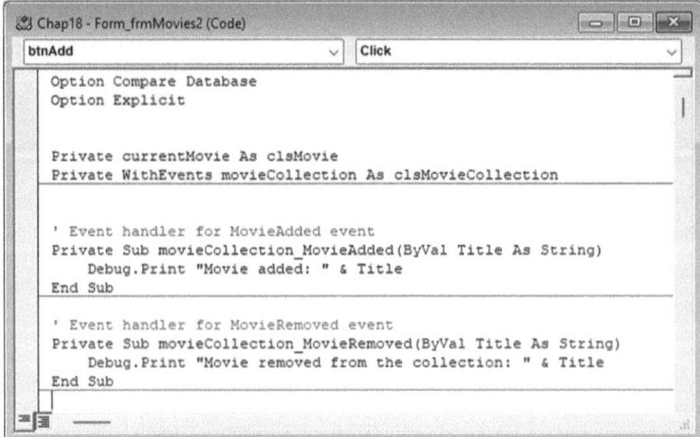

FIGURE 18.17.   The form class module shows code that uses a custom object with its events.

USING ChatGPT WITH ACCESS

If you're looking for an extra hands-on project to enhance your understanding of the topics covered in this chapter, ChatGPT can give you some suggestions and write VBA code for you so you can quickly get started. Just give it a detailed prompt and you'll soon have something new to work on. While the AI-generated code may need a few corrections here and there, having some code already written for you is far superior to starting from scratch. This can save you valuable time and effort, allowing you to focus on refining and enhancing the code, rather than building it from the ground up. Furthermore, the AI can help bridge any knowledge gaps you might have, providing a solid foundation to work from. You can also expand on the initial suggestions by forming requests for improvements.

User Prompt: *Demonstrate the use of classes in Access VBA. This project should include a form that requires the use of a class and its members and perform some event programming. Including collection classes is also desirable.*

ChatGPT/Microsoft Copilot's Response:
Let's create an Access project that uses classes and collection classes, with a form that interacts with these classes through event programming. We'll build a simple Contact Management System where users can add, view, and delete contacts.

Another prompt that will get more Access VBA programming skills under your belt is shown below:

User Prompt: *Can you walk me through creating a form with a Web browser control?*

ChatGPT/Microsoft Copilot's Response:
Absolutely! Adding a Web Browser Control to a form in Access allows you to display web content directly within your database application. This can be useful for displaying web pages, embedding web-based resources, or integrating online tools. Here's a step-by-step guide to help you create a form with a Web Browser Control:

I personally followed the AI instructions and included the completed Web browser control project in the completed `Chap18.accdb` database in the companion files. Please note that Access provides two Web browser controls, and selecting the correct one is essential for the successful completion of this project.

Due to space constraints, I wasn't able to introduce you to the digital signature and code-signing features available in Access 2024. It is important that you familiarize yourself with these topics when you get a chance. ChatGPT will give you details on both.

User Prompt: *Give me the details of the digital signature feature in Access 2024.*

User Prompt: *Tell me about the code-signing feature in Access. Is it different from the digital signature you just explained?*

ChatGPT/Microsoft Copilot's Response:
Yes, the code signing feature in Access is related to, but distinct from, the digital signature feature I explained earlier.

All user prompts shown above and the AI-generated responses are included in the companion files. Refer to the `Chapter 18 - Using ChatGPT with Access` document.

SUMMARY

In this chapter, you learned how to create and use your own custom objects and collections in VBA procedures. Although you can easily build Access database applications without using your own classes, understanding the essentials of OOP can help you manage and understand more advanced Microsoft Access database projects. You learned that a class is a template that can be used to create one or more objects.

A class consists of the following:

- Properties that contain information about it
- Methods that are used to take some actions and process some information
- Events that notify the program of some changes

You used a class module to create a user-defined (custom) object. You saw how to define your custom object's properties using the Property Get and Property Let procedures. You also learned how to write methods for your custom object and saw how to make the class module available to the user with a custom form. Finally, you learned how to analyze the class code by stepping through it, as well as learning about creating and using collection classes in Access.

Next, you were introduced to many advanced concepts in event-driven programming. You learned how you can make your code more manageable and portable by responding to events in standalone class modules. This chapter has also shown you the process of creating your own events for a class and raising them from a public method by calling the `RaiseEvent` statement.

The important thing to understand is that while events happen in Access all the time (whether or not you respond to them), you are the one to decide where to respond to the built-in events. Also, if you ever find yourself short of an event, you can always create one that does exactly what you need by using the event programming skills acquired in this chapter.

This chapter barely scratched the surface of what's possible to do with custom classes, collections, and events. Understanding and utilizing these new concepts in your Access VBA programming journey will require more effort and experimentation on your part.

In the next chapter, we will move on to another topic in Access development. You will learn about creating and using different types of macros and converting embedded macros to VBA. You will also learn about the inner workings of Access database templates.

Part **VIII**

VBA AND *MACROS*

Writing VBA code is not the only way to provide rich functionality to your Access database users. Macros have long been used to enhance the user experience without writing a single line of VBA code. The Macro Builder allows you to include complex logic, business rules, and error handling in your macros.

In this part of the book, you are introduced to three types of macros that you can create in Access 2024. In addition, you will learn how to convert macros to VBA and get started with built-in templates that extensively use macros.

Chapter 19   Getting Comfortable with Access Macros and Templates

19 GETTING COMFORTABLE WITH ACCESS MACROS AND TEMPLATES

While programming Access applications, there are two other areas of Access that you need to become acquainted with: macros and templates. Macros in Access have been around longer than the VBA language. When Access 2 came out in 1992, it included a macro language called Access Basic that contained a subset of Visual Basic 2.0's core syntax. Access 95 replaced Access Basic with VBA, but until Access 97, macros were the most common means of automating database tasks. When Access 2000 came out, many successful macro users had already moved to the new programming platform to take advantage of the language model that offered more control over Access. In fact, in versions 2000 through 2003, Microsoft recommended VBA to automate Access applications, and macros were supported mainly for backward compatibility.

The outlook on macros changed with the release of Access 2007. After performing some extensive research, Microsoft found out that many users were intimidated by the programming environment that Access provided but were quite successful at creating macros. It seems that it is much simpler to pick a macro action and set a couple of parameters than it is to write VBA code. Because most Access applications created by end users are loaded with macros, Microsoft decided to improve the "macro experience" in Access 2007 by adding event handling, temporary variables (`TempVars`), better error handling, and a new type of macro called an embedded macro. In Access 2010, Microsoft added a macro sandbox, a security feature designed to prevent potentially unsafe expressions from running in your database. Access 2010 also brought a powerful enhancement known as data macros.

In 2024, Microsoft Access introduced several updates and improvements to its macro functionality, enhancing both performance and security. Additional security measures were added to protect users from potentially harmful macros. Many updates have been made to better handle errors when running macros, providing more detailed error messages and ensuring that macros run more efficiently, especially when dealing with large data sets and complex operations.

In this chapter, you will work with the Macro Builder and learn how to create standalone and embedded macros in Access 2024. We will also take a look at the `.accdt` file format used with Access desktop database templates.

MACROS OR VBA?

You can use both VBA and macros to automate your Access applications. While macros have become very powerful, whether you use macros or VBA will depend on what you want to do. Macros can perform just about any task you can do with the Access user interface by using the keyboard or the mouse. They provide an easy way of opening and closing various Access objects (tables, queries, forms, and reports). You can also use them to automate repetitive tasks, execute commands on the Access Ribbon, set values for form and report controls, import and export spreadsheets and text files, display informative messages, or even sound a beep. With data macros, you can also enforce business rules at a table level. These are just a few examples of what macros can do.

Macros cannot create and manipulate database objects the way we did with VBA using DAO or ADO. They also cannot step through records in a recordset and perform operations on each record. For these types of operations, you need to write VBA code. You must also use VBA when you need to pass parameters to your procedures, call DLLs, create custom functions, or determine whether a file exists on the system.

Even if you don't want to get started with macros now that you know how to write code in VBA, you still need to understand how macros are used in Access, as Microsoft makes extensive use of macros in their templates and the Access built-in Command Button Wizard creates embedded macros.

ACCESS 2024 MACRO SECURITY

In Microsoft's documentation, the term "macro security" applies to macros and VBA, as well as other executable content that could be harmful when allowed to run.

In Chapter 1, we specified that Access should trust any database file opened from a designated trusted folder (see Hands-On 1.4). This enabled you to work with this book's examples without having to constantly deal with the Access security warning. When a database is not in a trusted location, Access 2024 will display a security prompt asking whether you want to enable macros. This gives you control over running macros in potentially untrusted environments. Access 2024 includes settings in the Trust Center that allow you to manage macro security, such as enabling and disabling macros with notifications (see Figure 19.1).

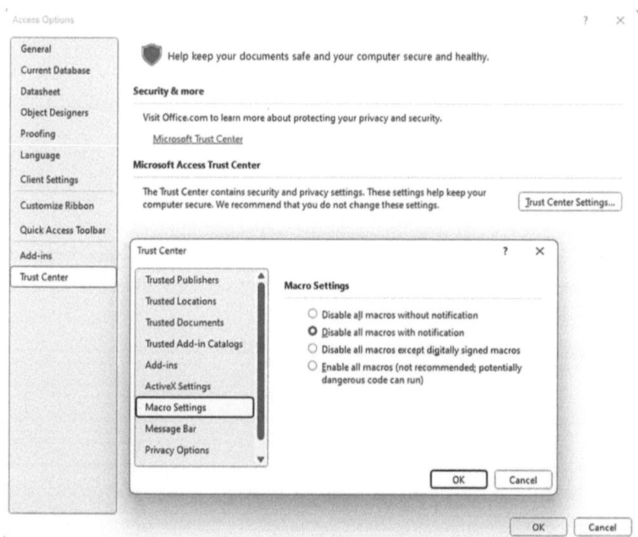

FIGURE 19.1.   The Macro Settings options allow you to specify whether the macros should be disabled or allowed to run and whether you should see a notification when macros are disabled.

You can change your macro settings at any time by following these steps:

1. Click the File tab, then click Options.
2. In the Access Options dialog box, click the Trust Center tab, then click Trust Center Settings.
3. In the Trust Center dialog box, select Macro Settings.

If the Disable all macros with notification option is selected, you may want to leave that setting as is. This option allows you to enable the disabled content only for this session by clicking the Enable Content button in the SECURITY WARNING message bar when a database file is opened.

You can access advanced security options by clicking the message text to the left of the Enable Content button in the SECURITY WARNING message bar (Figure 19.2). This will activate the Backstage View Info tab, where you can click the Enable Content button to bring up a menu of additional options, as shown in Figure 19.3. When you click Advanced Options, Access displays the dialog box shown in Figure 19.4.

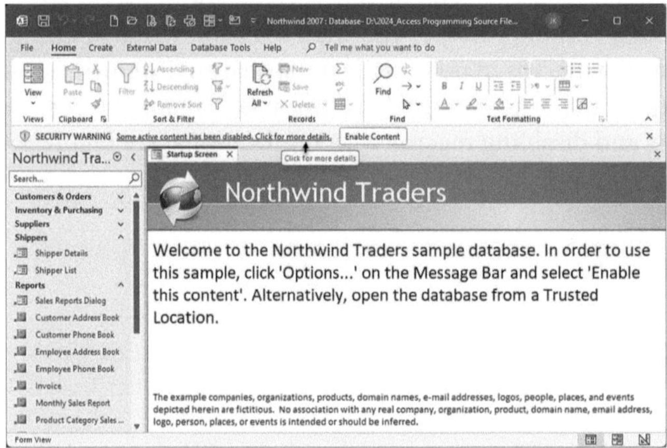

FIGURE 19.2. A security warning message appears on an attempt to load a database file containing content that could possibly harm your computer.

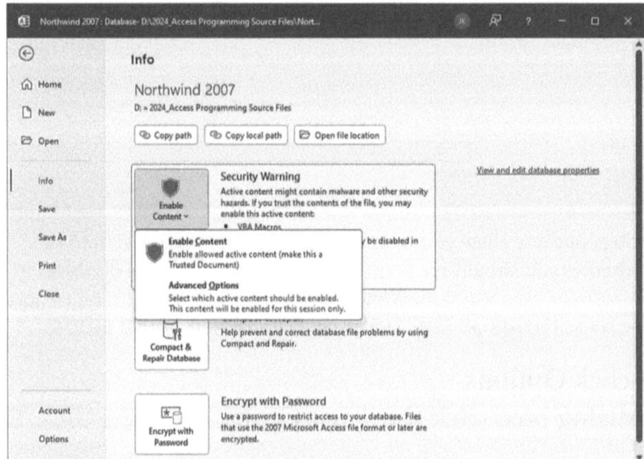

FIGURE 19.3. The Info tab in the backstage view displays information related to the security warning message and a brief description of the active content. By clicking on the Enable Content button, you can either enable all content in the current database or choose Advanced Options, which allows you to specify which active content should be enabled.

FIGURE 19.4.   The Microsoft Office Security Options dialog box allows you to temporarily enable disabled programming content by selecting the Enable content for this session radio button.

If you select the first radio button in Figure 19.4, Access will open the database in sandbox mode, which means that it will turn off all executable content, such as:

- VBA Code and Any References to It
- Unsafe Expressions

  An unsafe expression contains functions that could allow a user to modify the database or gain access to resources outside the database.
- Unsafe Macro Actions

  These are actions that could allow a user to modify the database or gain access to resources outside the database.
- Certain Types of Queries, such as:
  - Action Queries
    These are queries that could allow a user to make unauthorized additions, changes, or deletions of database data.
  - DDL Queries
    These are queries that are used to create or alter objects in a database, such as tables or procedures.

- o SQL Pass-Through Queries
  These queries allow a user to send commands directly to a database server that supports the ODBC standard.
- ActiveX Controls

  These are small programs that have unrestricted access to your computer's file system that could be used to take control of your computer.

If you plan on distributing your Access database in the `.accdb` file format, you can use the `IsTrusted` property of the `CurrentProject` object to test whether your application has its executable content disabled. Use this property in an AutoExec macro to check whether your application can load (see the next section).

USING THE AUTOEXEC MACRO

The most important macro that every Access programmer needs to be familiar with is the AutoExec macro. This macro has been with Access since the very beginning. An AutoExec macro runs automatically when the database is opened. This is very convenient, especially when you need to check whether the rest of your application will load. Let's see how Microsoft does this in the `NorthwindStarter` database.

NOTE	*All files and images for the hands-on projects may be found in the companion files.*

(•) Hands-On 19.1   Understanding and Using the AutoExec Macro

1. Open the `NorthwindStarter` database from your trusted folder.
   When Access starts, notice the appearance of the SECURITY WARNING message bar with the Enable Content button, as was shown earlier in Figure 19.2.
2. Click Continue if you are presented with a Welcome screen.
3. In the Login dialog, select any employee and click Login.
4. In the Navigation Pane, select All Access Objects and activate the Macros group. Right-click the AutoExec macro name and choose Design View.
   Access displays the contents of the AutoExec macro, as shown in Figure 19.5. Notice that the Macro Design tab displays the Ribbon with various tools related to running macros and working within the Macro Builder window.

Read through the next section where we discuss various elements of this window and look at the contents of the AutoExec macro.

5. Close the AutoExec macro by right-clicking the AutoExec tab and choosing Close.

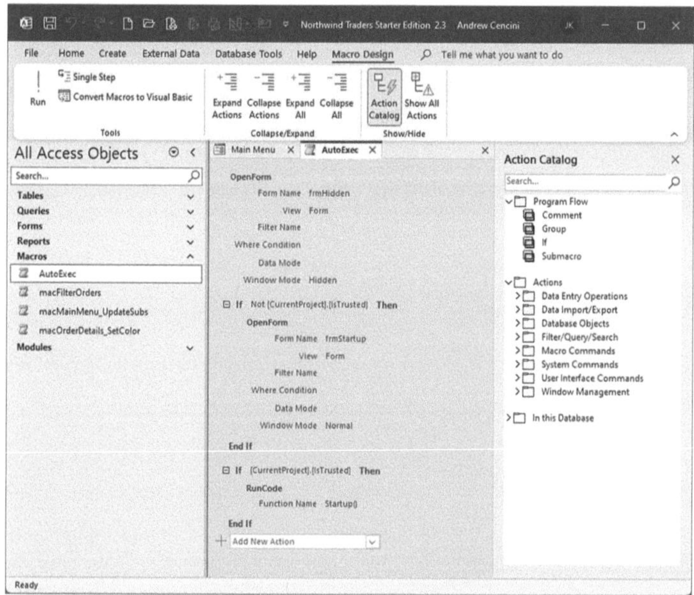

FIGURE 19.5. The contents of the AutoExec macro in the NorthwindStarter 2 sample database.

UNDERSTANDING MACRO ACTIONS, ARGUMENTS, AND PROGRAM FLOW

A macro can have more than one action, but you must specify at least one action when you create a macro. When you open the Macro Builder with an existing macro, you will see macro actions with various conditions filled in. At the bottom of the macro, there is an Add New Action drop-down list preceded by a plus sign icon. This is where you select the next action you want to add to the macro. When you select an action from the drop-down list, the macro design area will expand to show more options. For example, if the selected action requires additional data, a list of arguments is displayed. Access has a long list of macro actions to pick from.

If you are not sure which action to select to perform a particular task, you can browse the Action Catalog that appears to the right of the macro content window (see Figure 19.5 earlier). All available macro actions are grouped by subject in the Action Catalog. When you expand the list of actions and select a specific action, you will see the description of the selected macro action at the bottom of the Action Catalog (see Figure 19.6).

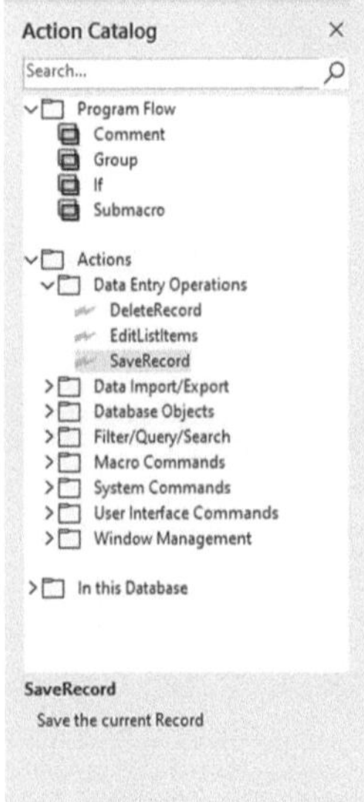

FIGURE 19.6. The Action Catalog. A description of the selected macro action appears at the bottom of the window.

In addition to a hierarchical listing of macro actions, the Action Catalog contains several program flow constructs that you can apply to your macros. These are shown at the top of the Action Catalog.

- Use Comment to document your macros.
- Use Group to organize your macro actions in a named block that can be easily collapsed, moved, or copied.
- Use the If construct to create macros based on a condition. Your condition could test a value in a field or evaluate the result of a function. You can use any expression that evaluates to true/false (yes/no). To add conditional logic to your macro, double-click or drag the If to the macro design area. The macro actions will execute when the condition defined at the top of the `If` block is true. If the condition is not true, the action will be skipped, and the macro control will move to the next row. Actions that

should not be executed when the condition is true are preceded with `Not`, as shown in Figure 19.5 earlier.

- Use Submacro to create a named collection of macro actions, as discussed later in this chapter.

To see all the available actions in the catalog, click the Show All Actions button on the Ribbon. Macro actions that are considered unsafe are denoted by a yellow warning sign that appears to the left of the macro action name. Examples of unsafe macro actions are `CopyObject`, `DeleteObject`, and `RenameObject`; a few others are also listed under the Database Objects category in the Action Catalog.

The AutoExec macro included in the `NorthwindStarter` database and shown in Figure 19.7 uses the `OpenForm` macro action.

This action (found in the Database Objects section of the Action Catalog) is used to open a specified form. The form name can be selected from a drop-down list when you click the Form Name box. All forms in the current database will be shown. You can also specify the view in which the form will open. The default view is Form; you can select the view from the View drop-down box. Note that

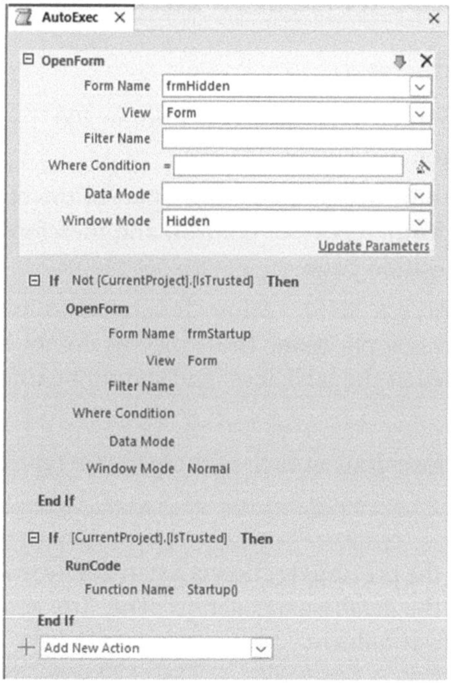

FIGURE 19.7.   The AutoExec macro is shown here in edit mode.

not all arguments need to be filled in. You can easily look up the meaning of an action's arguments by moving your mouse over the argument name.

In this example, upon startup, Access will open the `frmHidden` form in hidden window mode, meaning the user will not be able to see it. You can view the contents of the `frmHidden` form by opening it from the database navigation pane.

Next, the macro checks whether the database is in a trusted location. The `IsTrusted` property of the `CurrentProject` object is used to test whether the application has its executable content disabled. If the `CurrentProject` (database) is *not trusted*, Access opens the `frmStartup` form, which prompts the user to enable macros. If the database is *trusted*, Access will run the `Startup` function, which checks various settings to determine which forms need to be opened. You can examine the VBA code included in this function by choosing the `modStartup` module in the database navigation pane.

NOTE	*To open an Access database without running the AutoExec macro, hold down the Shift key while opening the database.*

CREATING AND USING MACROS IN ACCESS 2024

Access 2024 supports three types of macros:

- Standalone Macros (Also Used in Versions of Access Prior to 2007)—Are visible in the database navigation pane under Macros.
- Embedded Macros (Introduced in Access 2007)—Are part of the object in which they are embedded (form, report, or control) and therefore are not visible in the database navigation pane.
- Data Macros (introduced in Access 2010)—Allow developers to implement business rules in an Access application. These macros do not have a user interface; they are applied at the table level and cannot be used to open a form or a report.

In the following sections, we take a closer look at each of these macro types.

Creating Standalone Macros

The AutoExec macro we looked at in the previous section is a standalone macro. Once created, this macro appears in the database navigation pane. The general steps to create a standalone macro are as follows:

1. Click Macro in the Macros & Code group of the Create tab (Figure 19.8).

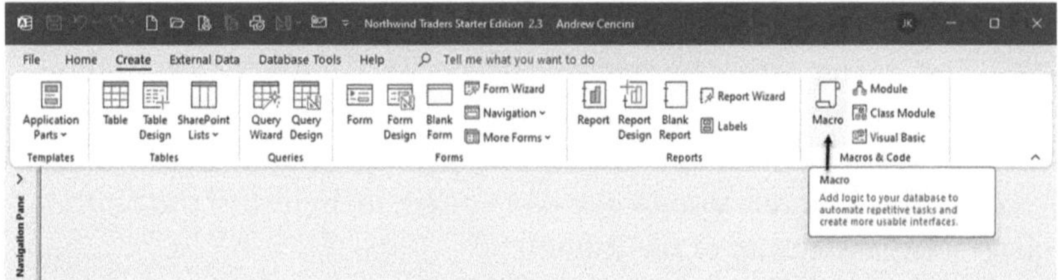

FIGURE 19.8. Creating a standalone macro.

Access displays the Macro Builder window with one drop-down box, as shown in Figure 19.9. As you can see, the layout has a collapsible drop-down interface.

2. Choose the action from the drop-down list to the right of the plus sign.
When the Ribbon's Show All Actions button is selected, this list displays all the available macro actions. When this button is not selected, you will see a shorter list of actions that are allowed to run even if the database is not trusted.

You can also add a macro action to the macro design surface by double-clicking an action in the Action Catalog or dragging an action onto the macro design surface. To activate the Action Catalog, click the Action Catalog button in the Macro Design tab of the Ribbon.

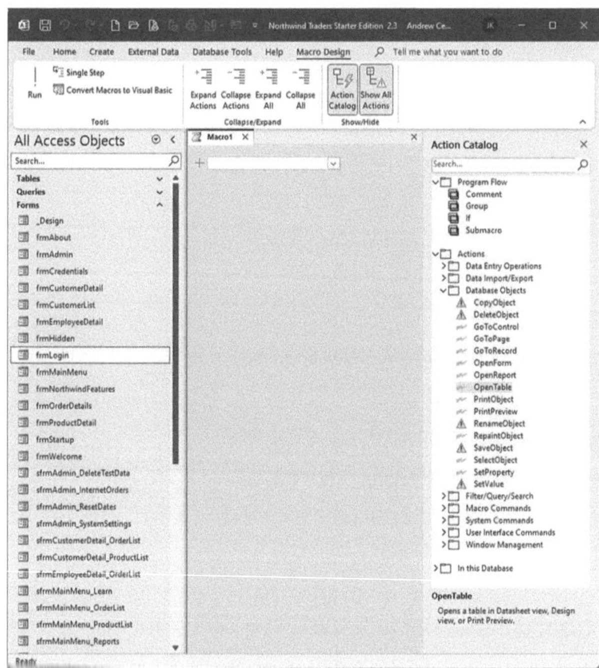

FIGURE 19.9. The initial Macro Design window.

3. If the macro action you select requires arguments, Access displays an inline dialog box where you can specify the required values (see Figure 19.10). Default argument values are prefilled for you. Notice that the code blocks are collapsible. You can expand or collapse the code areas by clicking the +/- controls to the left side of the code block or by using the buttons in the Collapse/Expand group of the Ribbon.

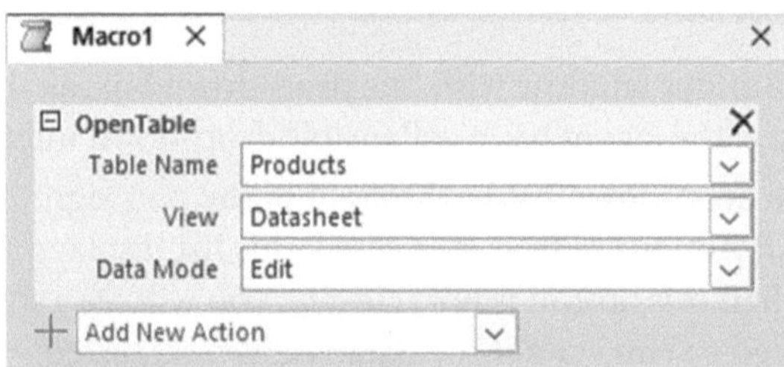

FIGURE 19.10. The OpenTable macro action opens a table. You need to specify the required arguments: the name of the table to open, the type of view for the presentation of the data, and the data mode.

4. If desired, add another macro action, as shown in Figure 19.11.

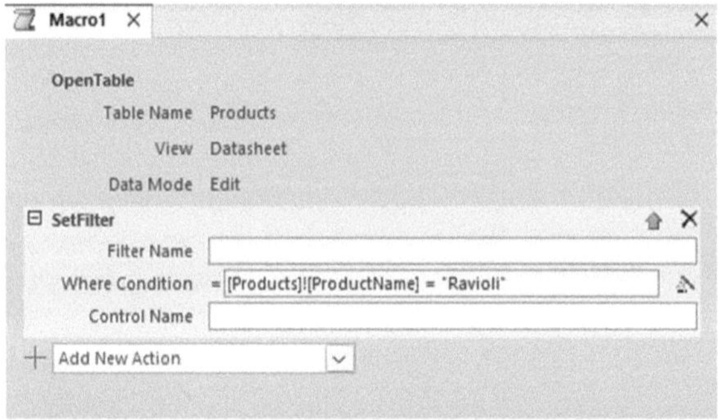

FIGURE 19.11. You can restrict the number of records in a table by using the SetFilter macro action.

To build the macro filter condition, click the builder button to the right of the Where Condition box. Access will display the Expression Builder dialog (see Figure 19.12), where you can create and edit expressions for various actions and conditions within your macros.

Navigate through the Expression Elements pane to find and select the required type of function, database object (tables, queries, forms, or reports), operator, constant, or a common expression you want to use; then, in the

Expression Categories pane, double-click the function, field, operator, constant or common expression to add them to the expression pane. Complete the expression by typing in any additional values you need, then click OK to return to the Macro Design area. The Expression Builder offers the IntelliSense feature, which provides guidance as you type an expression. If any errors are found in the expression when you try to save your macro, you will be prompted to return to the Expression Builder to correct the errors.

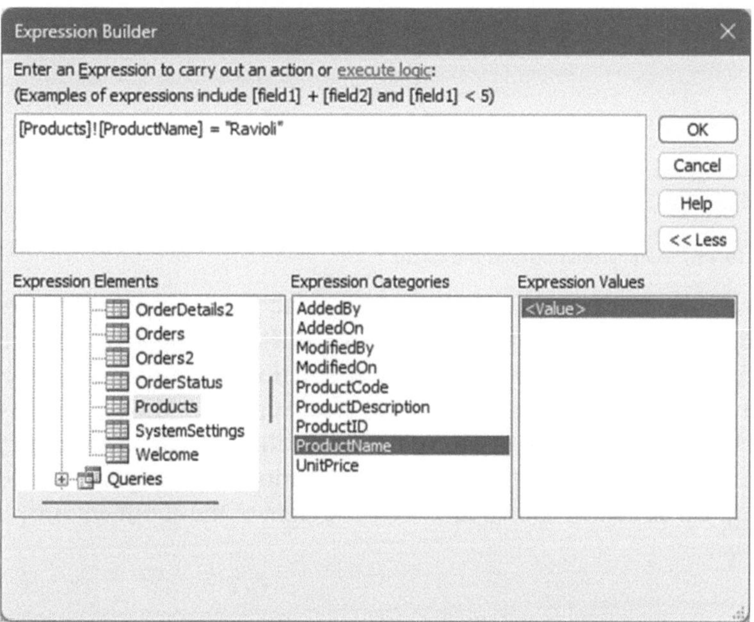

FIGURE 19.12. Creating a macro expression using the Expression Builder.

5. If the macro action should be conditionally executed (see Figure 19.13), choose the `If` block from the Actions drop-down box. Type your conditional expression in the text box or click the Builder button next to the expression box to invoke the Expression Builder. Because macro actions within the `If` block only run when the conditional expression resolves to `True`, the expression you enter must be of the Boolean type (`True`/`False`). If the condition evaluates to `False`, the action specified within the `If` block will be skipped.

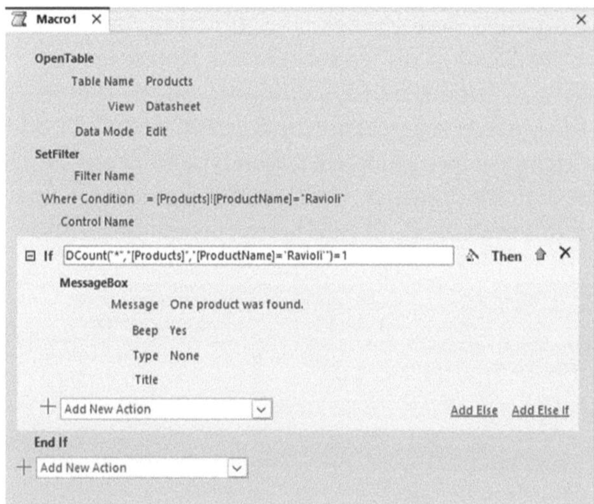

FIGURE 19.13. Adding conditions to the macro.

6. To make your macro actions easy to understand for yourself and others, you can add comments to the macro (see Figure 19.14). Comments are optional. To add a comment, choose Comment from the Actions drop-down box and type the text in the provided box. You can also type // in an Add New Action drop-down box. Comments are easy to spot because they appear as green text. You can move the comment to the appropriate location in your macro by clicking the Move Up and Move Down arrows to the right of the comment box.

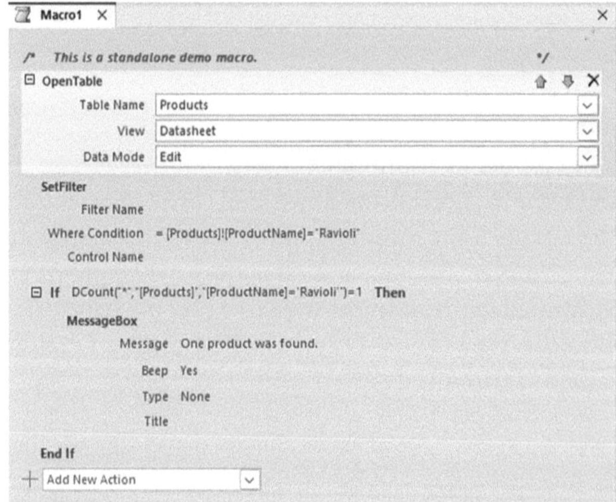

FIGURE 19.14. Comments can be added anywhere within your macro code block.

7. To add another action to your macro, select an action from the Actions dropdown.

   To add an action between the actions you've already entered, first select the desired action from the Actions dropdown, and then move it to the appropriate location within your macro using the Move Up and Move Down arrows.

   To delete an action, select it and click the X button. You can also right-click the action and choose Delete from the menu.

> **NOTE**   *If you add an action that is considered "unsafe," Access displays a yellow warning sign to the left of the macro action name. An unsafe action will not execute if the database is not trusted.*

For more complex macros, you may want to use a program flow construct known as a *group*. With this construct, you can put multiple actions and program flows into a group block so you can expand or collapse an entire group for better readability.

8. When you are done entering all actions for your macro, press Ctrl+S to save your macro, or right-click the Macro tab and choose Save. Enter the macro name `mcrOpenProducts_Ravioli` in the Save As dialog box and click OK.
9. Close the Macro Design window.

   The saved macro appears in the database navigation pane.

Running Standalone Macros

You can run standalone macros from the design view, the database navigation pane, another macro, or a VBA procedure, or in response to an event on a form, report, or control.

- Running a Macro from Design View—If the standalone macro is open in design view, you can click the Run button (with the exclamation point) in the Tools group of the Macro Design tab to run the macro.

  In design view, you can also run your macro one action at a time by selecting the Single Step button and then clicking the Run button (see Error Handling in Macros later in this chapter).

- Running a Macro from the Database Navigation Pane—In the database navigation pane, right-click the macro name and choose Run from the shortcut menu, but make sure you know what the macro will do before you run it. A badly designed macro could wipe out all the data in your database without asking you if you want to proceed.

When you right-click a macro in the database navigation pane and that macro contains submacros, the Run command will only execute the first submacro (see Creating and Using Submacros in the next section).

- Running a Macro from Another Macro—To run a macro from another macro, you must create at least two macros. The main macro should include the `RunMacro` action. Set the `Macro Name` argument of this action to the name of the macro you want to run. When you run the main macro, both macros will execute.

- Running a Macro from a VBA Procedure—The `RunMacro` method of the `DoCmd` object carries out the `RunMacro` action in VBA.

   To run a standalone macro, use the following statement:

   ```
   DoCmd.RunMacro "YourMacroName"
   ```

   Optionally, you may specify how many times the macro should be run:

   ```
   DoCmd.RunMacro "YourMacroName", 2
   ```

   To run a macro with submacros, use the name of the main macro followed by a period and the name of the submacro:

   ```
   DoCmd.RunMacro "Sales.AddProducts"
   ```

- Running a Macro in Response to an Event on a Form, Report, or Control—A standalone macro can be bound to events for forms, reports, or controls. For example, if your form contains a button that needs to open another form and you have previously created a macro that performs this action, you can specify the macro name in the `OnClick` property of the button.

Creating and Using Submacros

Instead of having a large number of standalone macros listed in the database navigation pane, consider storing related macros together using submacros. Submacros are similar to VBA subroutines in VBE modules. Figure 19.15 shows submacros that can be attached to the `Suppliers` form in the `Northwind.mdb` database. Notice how this single macro object named `Suppliers` stores a number of submacros, each of which performs a different action. To create submacros within a particular macro, you must give each submacro a unique name.

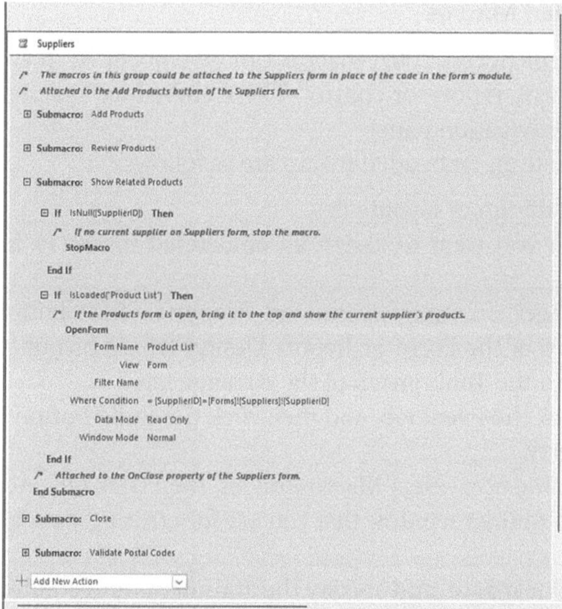

FIGURE 19.15.   The Suppliers macro in the sample Northwind.mdb database contains submacros that can be used in the Suppliers form.

The general steps to create submacros are as follows:

1. Click the Macro button in the Macros & Code group of the Create tab.
2. Select Submacro from the Add New Action drop-down list. Access enters the default name for your submacro. Replace the suggested name with the desired name.
3. Specify the macro actions for your submacro.
4. Add another submacro if desired and specify the actions to perform.
5. Save the macro by pressing Ctrl+S and typing the name for the macro. The name you specify is the name of the main macro that contains the submacros. This name will appear in the Navigation Pane under Macros.
6. Close the Macro Builder window.

As mentioned earlier, when a macro contains submacros, right-clicking the macro in the database navigation pane and choosing Run will execute only the first submacro.

Submacros are frequently implemented in forms and reports. To gain a better understanding of submacros, study the Suppliers macro and the `Suppliers` form in the `Northwind.mdb` database. Another excellent example of using submacros is the Customer Labels Dialog macro attached to the `Customer Labels Dialog` form in the `Northwind.mdb` database.

Creating and Using Embedded Macros

Beginning with the release of Access 2007, macros can be embedded in any of the events provided by a form, report, or control. These embedded macros are not visible in the database navigation pane.

The general steps to create an embedded macro are as follows:

1. Open a form or report in design or layout view.
2. Select an object to which you want to assign an embedded macro (a form, report, or control).
3. Activate the Property Sheet. In design view, the Property Sheet button is located in the Tools group of the Form or Report Design tab. In layout view, you will find this button in the Tools group of the Arrange tab.
4. In the Property Sheet, click the Event tab, and then click the Build button (…) next to the desired property.
5. In the Choose Builder dialog box, select Macro Builder, then click OK. Access will open the same Macro Builder window that you use for creating standalone macros.
6. Choose the actions for your macro, and specify the arguments and conditions if required.
7. Press Ctrl+S to save your macro, then click the Close button in the Close group of the Macro Design tab. Access closes the Macro Design view and enters [Embedded Macro] in the event property (see Figure 19.16).

To modify the embedded macro, click on the Build button (…) next to the property with [Embedded Macro]. Access will open the Macro Builder (design view), where you can make the required modifications.

You cannot reference an embedded macro from other macros. To reference a macro from another macro, you must create a standalone macro.

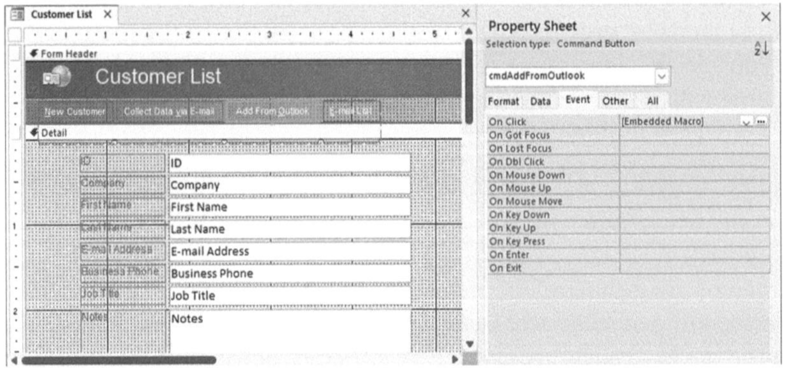

FIGURE 19.16.   Assigning an embedded macro to the event property of a form's command button in the Northwind 2007.accdb database.

Copying Embedded Macros

Because embedded macros are part of the object in which they are created, the macro behind the control is automatically copied when you copy the form, report, or control.

You can also copy an embedded macro from one event property to another. This is possible thanks to so-called "shadow properties." What this means is that for each event property of a control, form, or report, there is a "shadow" event property that contains the embedded macro for that property. For example, if your form's On Load event property is set to [Embedded Macro], then the shadow property called On Load Macro contains its embedded macro. The On Click event property has the On Click Macro property if you are using the embedded macro to trigger the On Click event. If the event property is empty, then there is no shadow property.

Hands-On 19.2 demonstrates how to use VBA to copy an embedded macro from the `Shipper Details` form to the `Supplier List` form in the `Northwind 2007.accdb` database.

⊙ Hands-On 19.2   Copying Embedded Macros

1. In the `Northwind 2007.accdb` database, open the `Supplier List` form in design view.
2. In the Form Header section, right-click the Home button and choose Copy.
3. Right-click anywhere in the empty area of the Form Header section and choose Paste. The copied button appears in the upper-left corner of the Form Header section. Leave the button in this location for now until we change some of its properties. The button has the same label as the original button and a default name beginning with Command and followed by some numbers, such as Command273. You will need to change the button's Name and Caption properties.
4. While the button is selected, click the Property Sheet button in the Tools group of the Form Design tab. Click the All tab and change the button's Name property to `cmdClose` and the Caption property to `&Close`. The ampersand in front of the letter `c` assigns a keyboard shortcut to the button.
5. Position the Close button to the left of the Home button, as shown in Figure 19.17.

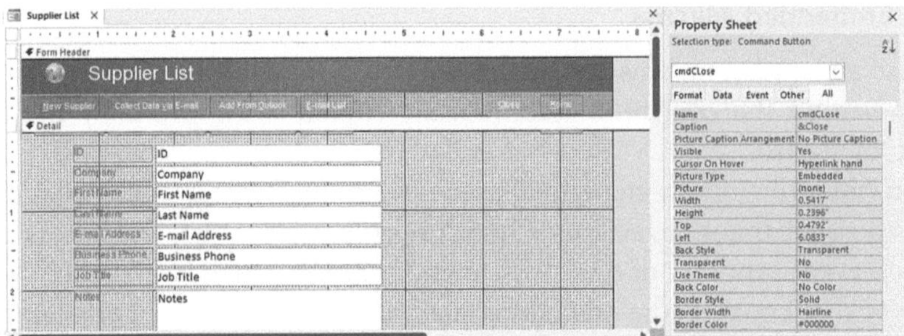

FIGURE 19.17. Use the Property Sheet to change the Name and Caption properties of the Close command button.

6. Press Ctrl+S to save the changes to the form.
7. While the Close button is selected, click the Event tab in the Property Sheet. Notice that when you copied the Home button, Access also copied the embedded macro attached to the On Click event property (see Figure 19.18). At this point, you could simply click the Build button (…) to modify this macro to have it close the `Supplier List` form instead of opening the `Home` form. The purpose of this exercise, however, is to show you how to use VBA to copy an embedded macro from one property to another. We will overwrite this embedded macro with a different one by writing a VBA procedure in the next steps.

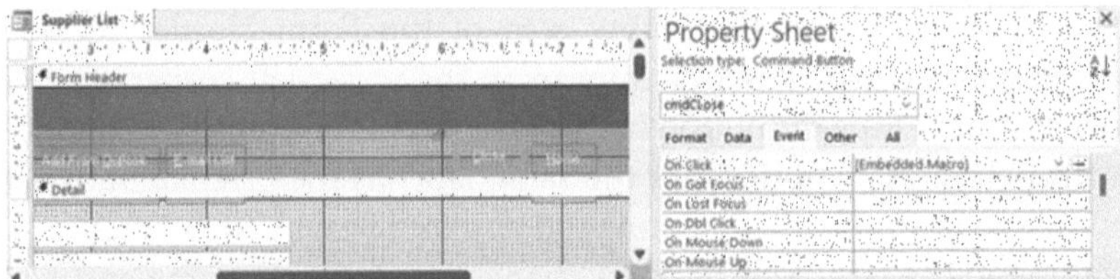

FIGURE 19.18. When you copied the Home button, the new button inherited the embedded macro assigned to the On Click event property.

8. Press Alt+F11 to activate the VBE window, and choose Insert | Module.
9. In the module's Code window, enter the following `Copy_OnClickMacro` procedure:

```
Sub Copy_OnClickMacro()
  Dim ctl As Control

    ' open in the Design view the Supplier List form
    DoCmd.OpenForm "Supplier List", acDesign

    ' only run the code if the specified control
```

```
' exists on the form
For Each ctl In Forms("Supplier List").Controls
   If TypeOf ctl Is CommandButton Then
      If StrComp(ctl.Name, "cmdClose", vbTextCompare) = 0 Then

         ' open in the Design view the Shipper Details form
         ' this form contains an embedded macro in the OnClick
         ' event of cmdClose button

         DoCmd.OpenForm "Shipper Details", acDesign

         ' copy macro from the OnClick event property of the
         ' cmdClose button on the Shipper Details form
         ' to the OnClick event property of the cmdClose button
         ' on the Supplier List form

      Forms("Supplier List").Controls("cmdClose").OnClickMacro = _
         Forms("Shipper Details").Controls("cmdClose").OnClickMacro
      DoCmd.Save acForm, "Supplier List"
      DoCmd.Close acForm, "Shipper Details"
      MsgBox "The embedded macro was successfully copied."
      Exit Sub
    End If
   End If
  Next

  MsgBox "Operation could not be performed. " & vbCrLf & _
  "Ensure that the specified control exists."
End Sub
```

In this procedure, we begin by opening the `Supplier List` form in design view
and iterating through the form's controls to find out whether the form contains
the control named `cmdClose`. We use the `TypeOf…Is` expression to specifically
look for the `CommandButton` control. Because the `Supplier List` form contains
several buttons, we can use the `StrComp` function to determine whether we
found the correct button. This function will tell us if the string specified in the
second argument is found in the string specified in the first argument. The third
argument of the `StrComp` function tells Access to perform the comparison of
the two text strings. If the `StrComp` function returns zero (0), then we found the
control we were looking for and we can proceed to open the `Shipper Details`
form and copy the embedded macro assigned to the On Click event property
of this form's `cmdClose` button to the On Click event property of the `Supplier
List`'s equivalent button. Once we are finished copying, we can simply exit the
procedure using the early exit expression `Exit Sub`.

If the `Supplier List` form does not contain the button with the specified name, we display a message.

10. Run the `Copy_OnClickMacro` procedure.
    If you followed all the steps of this hands-on exercise, you should see a message stating that the embedded macro was successfully copied. Click OK to close the message box. If you got a different message, check the code for any errors and ensure that the `Supplier List` form has the `cmdClose` button. Then, rerun the procedure.
11. Press Ctrl+S to save changes in the module. Access will ask you to assign a new name to the module. Click OK to accept the default name.
12. Close the VBE window and return to the main Access window.
13. In the Property Sheet for the `cmdClose` button, click the Build (…) button next to the On Click event property on the Event tab. Access opens the Macro Design view, as shown in Figure 19.19. This macro will close the form when the user clicks the Close button on the `Supplier List` form.

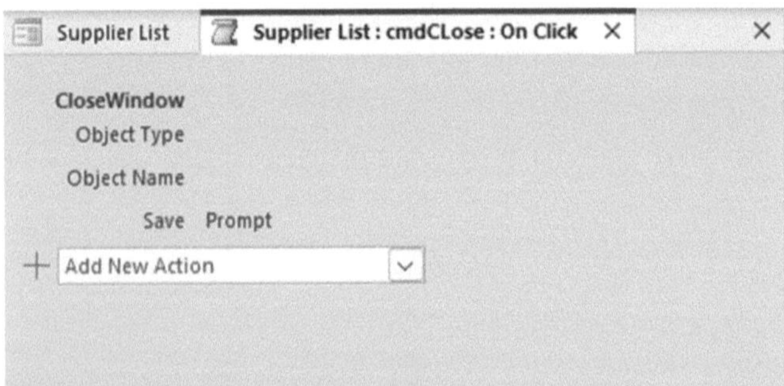

FIGURE 19.19.   Examining an embedded macro after it's been copied from another event property.

14. Exit the Macro Design view by clicking the Close button in the Ribbon.
15. Right-click the Supplier List tab, and choose Form View.
16. Click the Close button in the Header section of the `Supplier List` form to close this form. This will execute the embedded macro you copied in this hands-on.

Examining Shadow Properties

You can see the contents of the `OnClickMacro` shadow property by typing the following statement in the Immediate window and pressing Enter (the form must be open for this to work):

```
?Forms("Supplier List").Controls("cmdClose").OnClickMacro
```

You should see the output shown in Figure 19.20.

```
Immediate                                                                    [X]
 ?Forms("Supplier List").Controls("cmdClose").OnClickMacro
 Version =196611
 ColumnsShown =8
 Begin
     Action ="Close"
     Argument ="-1"
     Argument =""
     Argument ="0"
 End
 Begin
     Comment ="_AXL:<?xml version=\"1.0\" encoding=\"UTF-16\" standalone=\"no\"?>\015\012<UserI"
         "nterfaceMacro For=\"cmdCLose\" xmlns=\"http://schemas.microsoft.com/office/acces"
         "sservices/2009/11/application\"><Statements><Action Name=\"CloseWindow\"/></Stat"
         "ements></UserInterfaceMacro>"
 End
```

FIGURE 19.20. Examining the Shadow property – OnClickMacro.

Access has a large number of hidden properties that make it possible to get and set embedded macros. The property name begins with the name of the event property and ends with `EmMacro`, such as `OnClickEmMacro` and `AfterUpdateEmMacro`. Try the following statement in the Immediate window (the form must be open for this to work), and notice that it produces the same output as the previous statement:

```
?Forms("Supplier List").Controls("cmdClose").
                           Properties("OnClickEmMacro").Value
```

With this knowledge, it is easy to create a standalone macro from an embedded macro. Here's an example VBA procedure that does just that:

```
Sub SaveEmToStandalone()
Dim strMacro As String
Dim objFileSys As Object
Dim objFile As Object
Dim strFileName As String

' open in the Design view the form that contains
' the embedded macro
DoCmd.OpenForm "Login Dialog", acDesign

' to write an embedded macro to a file use the
' Value property
strMacro = Forms("Login Dialog"). _
Controls("cboCurrentEmployee"). _
Properties("AfterUpdateEmMacro").Value

' close the form
```

```
DoCmd.Close acForm, "Login Dialog"

' Create a text file
strFileName = "C:\VBAAccess2024_ByExample\cboAfterUpdate.txt"

Set objFileSys = CreateObject("Scripting.FileSystemObject")
Set objFile = objFileSys.CreateTextFile(strFileName, True)

' Write strMacro to the text file
objFile.Write strMacro
' Close the file
objFile.Close

' Use the undocumented LoadFromText method of
' the Application object to create a standalone macro
' from the text file
Application.LoadFromText acMacro, _
 "cboEmployeeAfterUpdate", strFileName

End Sub
```

The `LoadFromText` method of the `Application` object makes it possible to create various Access database objects (including macros) from information that was previously saved to a text file. The `LoadFromText` method requires that you specify the object type, the object name, and the name of the text file.

After running this procedure, you should see the `cboEmployeeAfterUpdate` macro listed in the Navigation Pane under Macros.

Working in Sandbox Mode

By default, Access runs in sandbox mode, which means that the program blocks all the expressions in field properties and controls that are considered unsafe. A *safe expression* is one that does not use functions that could be used to access drives or other resources on a user's computer to damage data or files. When Access is running in sandbox mode, any expressions that use unsafe macro actions are marked with a yellow warning sign.

Access allows you to disable sandbox mode by setting the macro security level to low; however, for security reasons, this setting is not recommended. If you trust the database and want to run unsafe expressions that the sandbox mode blocks without having to change your current macro security, you can disable sandbox mode by changing the registry key. Modifying the Windows Registry, however, is beyond the scope of this chapter.

Generating Macros Using the Command Button Wizard

You do not have to write all your macros from scratch. Access provides a built-in tool known as the Command Button Wizard. If you are working with the database in .accdb format, the wizard will generate embedded macros to open forms, run queries, find records, apply filters, or print reports. For older databases in the .mdb file format, the Command Button Wizard creates VBA code.

Understanding Data Macros

Prior to Access 2010, macros could only be attached or embedded in forms and reports. Access programmers had long asked for a feature similar to SQL triggers that would enable them to automatically update data in a table or track when a record was last modified or deleted. Microsoft answered this programming request in Access 2010 by introducing *data macros*. A data macro contains one or more actions that execute in response to a table event.

With data macros, programmers can enforce complex business rules at the table level. For example, by attaching a data macro to a table, you can control what happens to a table's data when the user interacts with the data via an Access form. You can specify what occurs after data is inserted, updated, or deleted. For instance, you may want to verify the accuracy of table data, send an email notification to the database manager about the changes that occurred to the data, or automatically update fields in another table.

By using data macros attached to the After Insert, After Update, and After Delete events, you can check and modify records in the current table or other tables. You can use the `For Each Record` construct to iterate through a set of records in a table to update records that meet certain criteria or accumulate the totals. You can also perform specific actions before data is inserted, changed, or deleted.

The Before Change data macro event will allow you to check a value in another table and, if necessary, prevent a change or insert from happening. You can use an `IsInsert` property to detect whether it's an insert or an update operation. You can find out whether the value of a specific field has changed by using the `Updated` function, and, if the value of a field has changed, you can use the `Old` property to find out the previous value of the field.

Before deleting records, you can use the Before Delete data macro event to determine whether the record can be deleted. You can also update an audit file to indicate that the record was deleted.

By using data macros, you can guarantee that your business logic is executed even if the user modifies a record outside the forms you provide such as in datasheet view or by running another macro or a VBA procedure. Your data macros will run silently in the background regardless of how the data is accessed. With data macros, you no longer need to attach the same macro to a number of forms. All you need to do is add the logic to the table. Any form based on that table will inherit that logic.

In addition to *event data macros* that are triggered by table events, you can create standalone *named data macros*. Named data macros allow you to save time by incorporating the common tasks into one macro. Instead of repeating the same actions in multiple data macros, simply create a named data macro and call it from a data event. Named macros can be called using the `RunDataMacro` action.

Keep in mind that data macros do not have any user interface; they are stored within a table itself and therefore do not show up in the database navigation pane. Do not attempt to use data macros to handle multivalue and attachment data types as they are not supported. Also, keep in mind that data macros can only be attached to events in local tables, not linked tables.

Creating a Data Macro

In the following hands-on exercise, you will work with the `Purchase Order Details` table in the `Northwind 2007` database. You'll write a data macro to ensure that the order quantity cannot be modified if the order was already posted to inventory or the Date Received field contains a date value. The following VBA procedure has already been written by the Microsoft team to validate the Quantity field in the `Purchases Subform for Purchase Order Details` form:

```
Private Sub Quantity_BeforeUpdate(Cancel As Integer)
   If Me![Posted To Inventory] Or _
     Not IsNull(Me![Date Received]) Then
         MsgBoxOKOnly CannotModifyPurchaseQuantity
     Cancel = True
   End If
End Sub
```

While this procedure works just fine for controlling data entry operations on the form, it has no effect on data manipulations performed directly at the table level. By creating a Before Change data macro, you can ensure that this test scenario is addressed no matter how data is being accessed.

⊚ Hands-On 19.3   Creating and Testing a Data Macro

1. Open the `Purchase Order Details` table in the `Northwind 2007.accdb` database.
2. Select the Table tab on the Ribbon and click the Before Change button (Figure 19.21).

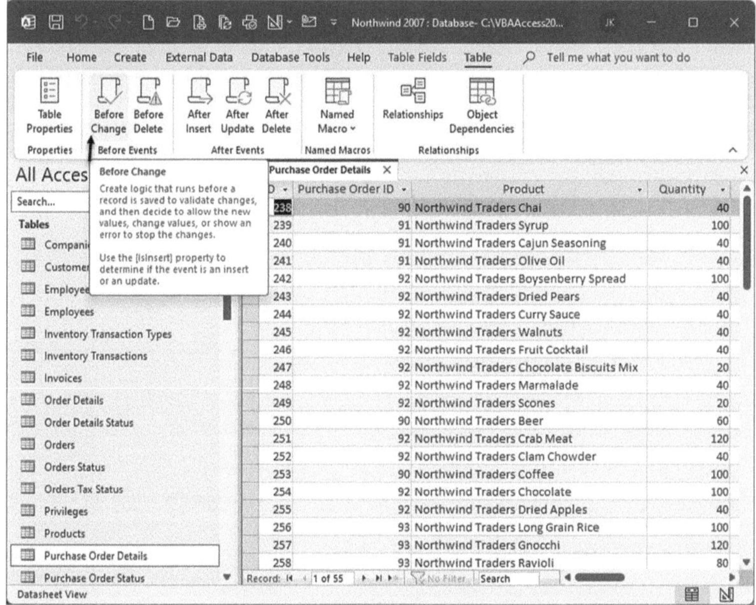

FIGURE 19.21.   Creating a data macro from the table's datasheet view.

Table 19.1 lists five events that can trigger a data macro.

TABLE 19.1.   Data macro events.

Event Name	Event Description
Before Change	Runs before a record is about to be updated. Use it to validate changes before saving them to the table. You can include logic to allow new values or show an error to reject the changes. Use the IsInsert property to determine whether the change is an insert or an update.
Before Delete	Runs before a record is about to be deleted. You can include logic that validates the deletion and allows it, or cancels the deletion and raises an error.
After Insert	Runs after a new record has been added to the table.

(Contd.)

Event Name	Event Description
After Update	Runs after a record has been edited in the table. Use the Updated("Field Name") function to determine whether a specific field has changed. Use Old.[Field Name] to find out the value the field had before the record was changed.
After Delete	Runs after a record has been deleted from the table. Use Old.[Field Name] to find out the value the field had before the record was deleted.

3. When you click the event name, Access opens the Macro Builder (Figure 19.22).

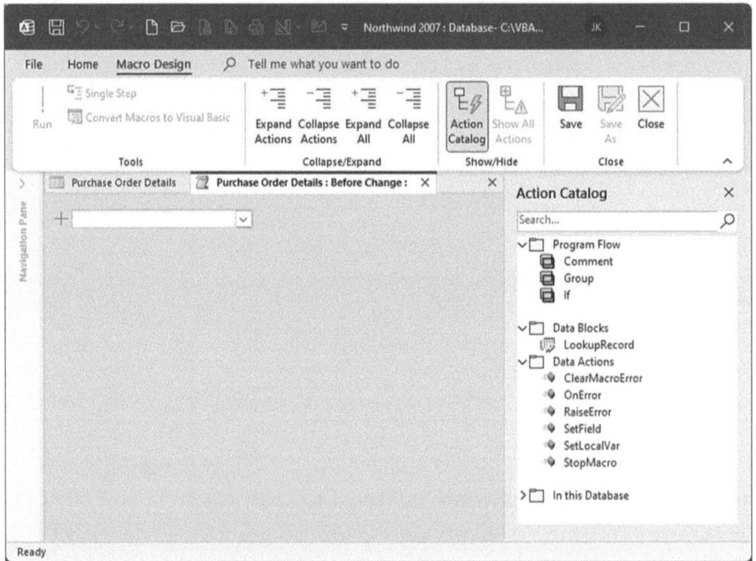

FIGURE 19.22. Macro Builder for writing data macros.

The Action Catalog shows three categories of actions that can be specified for a data macro: Program Flow, Data Blocks, and Data Actions. The actions listed in each category depend on the type of table event you have selected.

When you are working with data macros, the only Program Flow constructs are comments (used for documenting your data macro), groups (used for organizing your macro), and `If` blocks (for applying conditional logic).

Data Blocks contain constructs that are used to perform specific operations on database records such as looking up a record in a table (`LookupRecord`), adding a record to a table (`CreateRecord`), modifying an existing record in a table (`EditRecord`), and looping through every record in a table

(`ForEachRecord`). Notice that only the `LookupRecord` data block is available for the Before Change event. When you select a construct from the Data Blocks category, you can add one or more actions and these actions will be performed as part of the data block. You can even nest data blocks. For example, you can set up a `ForEachRecord` data block to iterate through every record in a table and, depending on your conditional logic, create the `CreateRecord` data block to add a record to another table based on the found record.

The Data Actions category in the Action Catalog lists the available data actions. Some table events have more actions than others. You can find the description of an event by selecting it and then checking the bottom of the Action Catalog (see Figure 19.23).

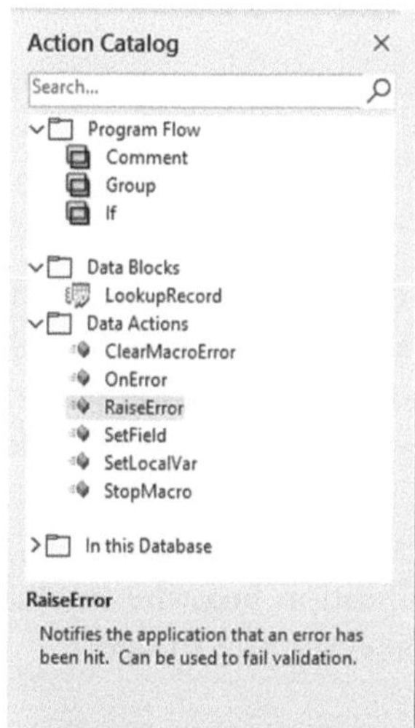

FIGURE 19.23. Adding an If block to the data macro.

4. Double-click the `If` construct in the Program Flow section. Access adds a conditional block, as shown in Figure 19.24.

5. In the `If` box, enter the following conditional expression on one line:

```
Updated("Quantity") And ([Posted To Inventory] Or Not
    IsNull([Date Received]))
```

6. Select SetLocalVar from the Add New Action dropdown located within the `If...Then...End If` block.

7. Enter `strMsg` in the Name box and `""` (an empty string) in the Expression box, as shown in Figure 19.23.

The `SetLocalVar` action allows you to create a local variable. In this macro, you'll use a local variable named `strMsg` to store the error message text that you'll retrieve from the `Strings` table that is a part of the `Northwind 2007.accdb` database. Notice that the initial value of the `strMsg` variable is set to an empty string.

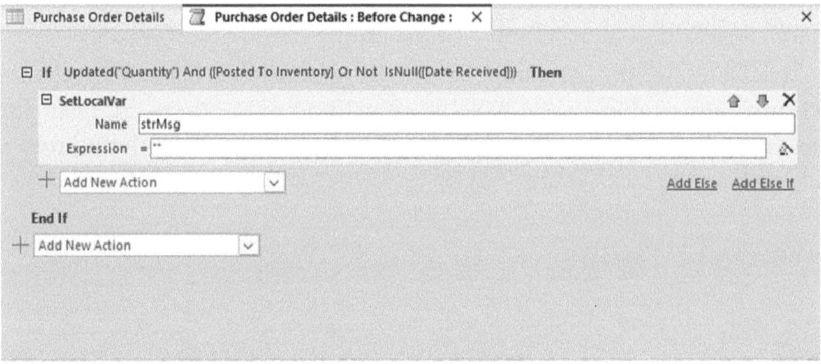

FIGURE 19.24.   Adding a local variable to your data macro.

8. Select `LookupRecord` from the Add New Action dropdown located within the `If...Then...End If` block. The Macro Design tool adds a `LookupRecord` block.
9. Fill in the block as depicted in Figure 19.25. Choose Strings from the Look Up A Record In drop-down box, and enter `[Strings].[String ID] = 31` for the Where Condition.

   This condition tells the macro to find the thirty-first record in the `Strings` table. Notice that as you start typing in the Where Condition box, the IntelliSense technology is at work displaying appropriate choices for you to select.

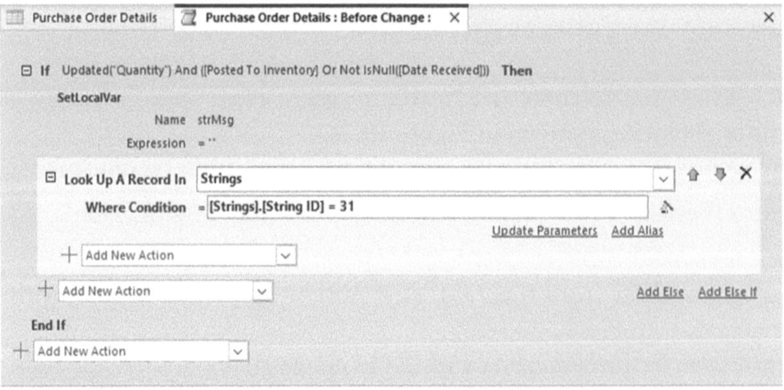

FIGURE 19.25.   Adding an action to look up a record in a table.

10. Within the `LookupRecord` block, add a new `SetLocalVar` action. In the Name box, enter the name of the local variable `strMsg` that you declared at the beginning of the macro. In the Expression box, enter `[Strings].[String Data]`, as shown in Figure 19.26.

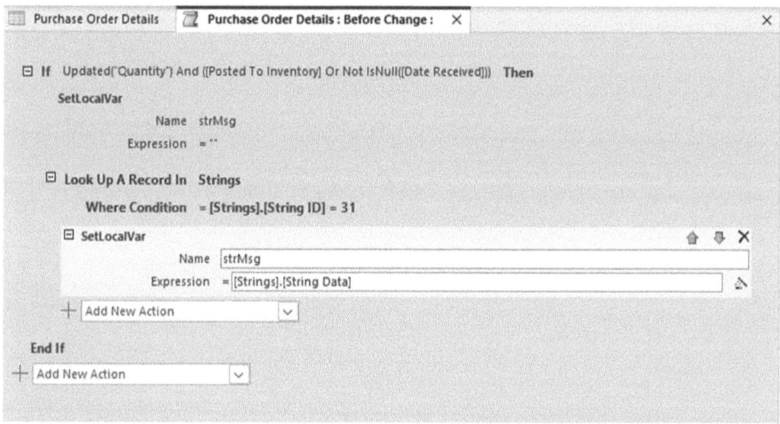

FIGURE 19.26.   Storing data retrieved by the LookupRecord action in a local variable.

11. In the Add New Action drop-down box within the `LookupRecord` block, choose Comment. When a text box appears, enter the following text: `Record Lookup Completed`. Figure 19.27 shows the result of adding a comment. The comments appear in green italics between the `/*` and `*/` delimiters.

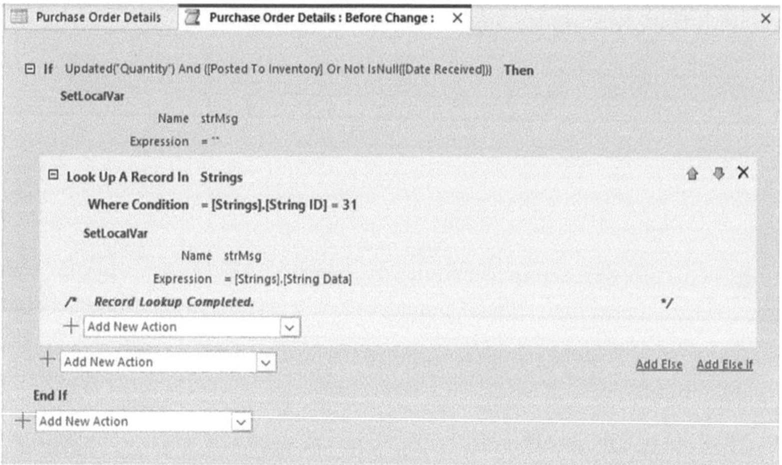

FIGURE 19.27.   Adding a comment to a macro.

12. In the Add New Action drop-down box located outside the LookupRecord block, choose RaiseError. Enter `100` in the Error Number box and `=[strMsg]` in the Error Description box. This will tell the macro to display the text stored in the local variable `strMsg` when an error occurs. Be sure to enter the equal sign before the variable name. Figure 19.28 displays the completed macro.

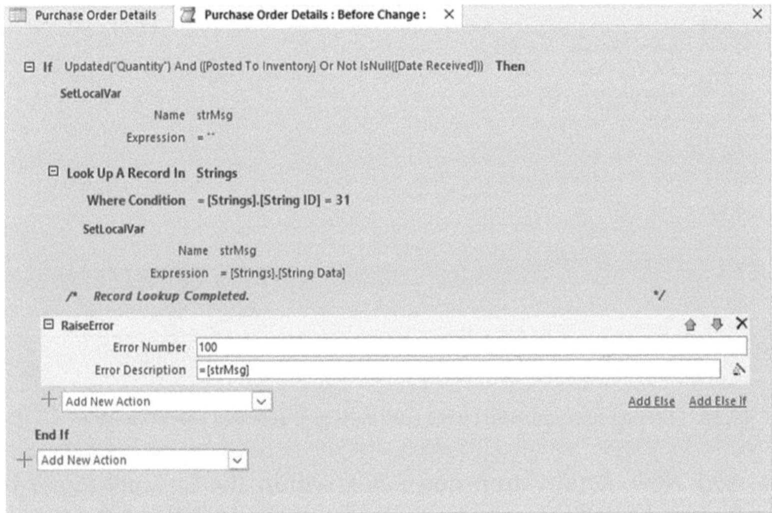

FIGURE 19.28. Adding a macro action to raise an error.

13. Click the Save button to save your macro, then click the Close button to close the Macro Builder. Notice that when a macro is defined for a table event, the button with the event name has a shaded background (see Figure 19.29).

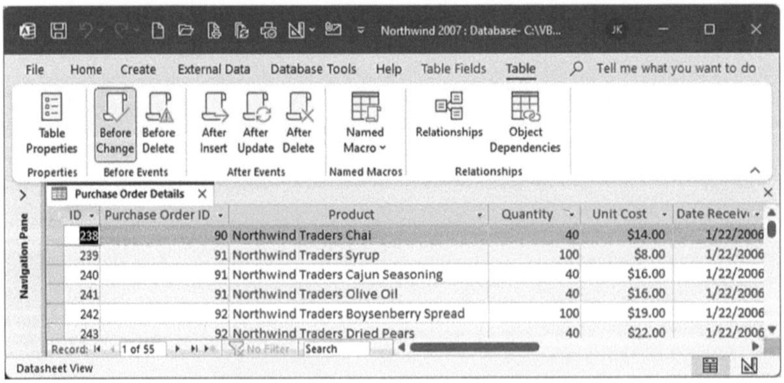

FIGURE 19.29. The highlighted Before Change button on the Ribbon indicates that there is a data macro attached to this event.

To test your macro, you need to perform the action that will trigger the event for which you defined the macro.

14. In the `Purchase Order Details` table, enter a different value in the Quantity field for any record that has both a checkmark in the Posted To Inventory field and a value in the Date Received field. When you attempt to save the record after making a change to the Quantity field, Access displays the error message shown in Figure 19.30. The error message is retrieved from the `Strings` table. Click OK to the message and then press the Esc key to exit the edit mode.

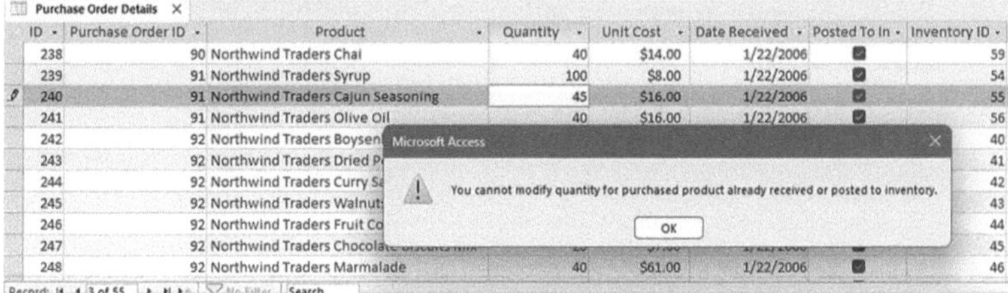

FIGURE 19.30.   The error raised by the data macro assigned to the Before Change event.

NOTE	*A form based on a table that contains a data macro will inherit the logic defined in the table. This means that you no longer need to write separate VBA code in the form class modules to respond to events that are already handled at a table level.*

Creating a Named Data Macro

As mentioned earlier, in addition to writing data macros that are triggered by a table event, you can create named data macros. You can pass arguments to these macros and call them from anywhere within your application. To create a named data macro, follow these general guidelines:

1. In the database navigation pane, double-click the desired table to open it.
2. Select the Table tab on the Ribbon.
3. In the Named Macros group, choose Named Macro | Create Named Macro (Figure 19.31).

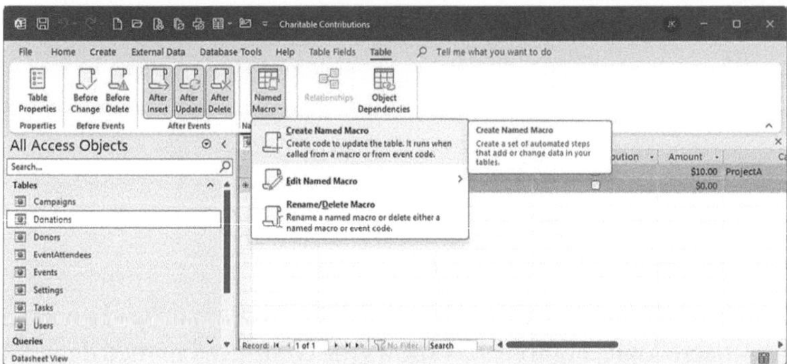

FIGURE 19.31.   Creating a named data macro.

Access opens the Macro Builder, as shown in Figure 19.32. Notice that the Action Catalog lists a number of data actions that you can use in your named data macro logic.

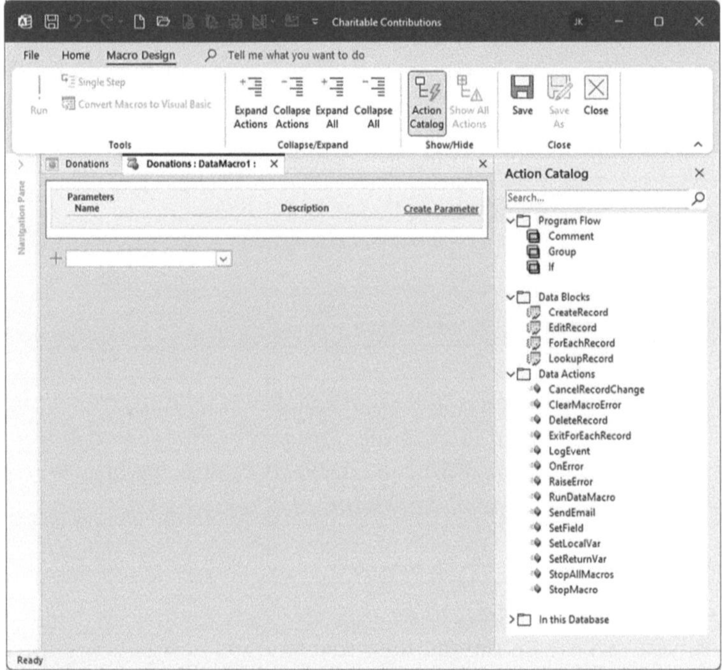

FIGURE 19.32. The Macro Builder window for creating a named data macro.

4. If you need to pass parameters to your macro, click the Create Parameter hyperlink at the top of the Macro Builder screen. Enter the name of the parameter in the Name box. You may also enter a description in the Description box (Figure 19.33).

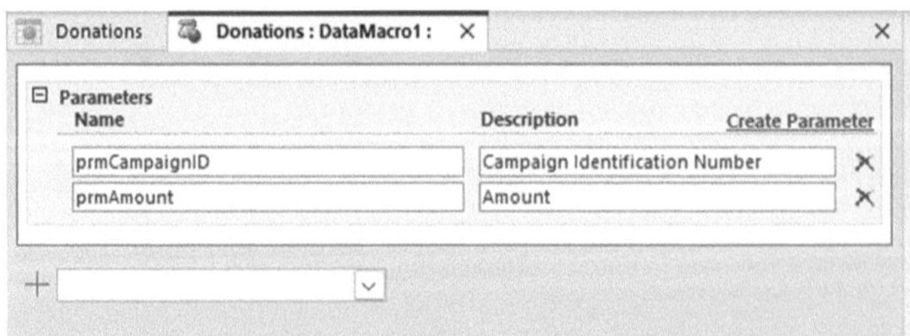

FIGURE 19.33. Specifying parameters in the named data macro.

5. Select an appropriate action from the Add New Action drop-down box to specify your macro logic. Figure 19.34 shows the completed named data macro.

6. When you are done with the macro logic, save the macro by clicking the Save As button on the Ribbon.

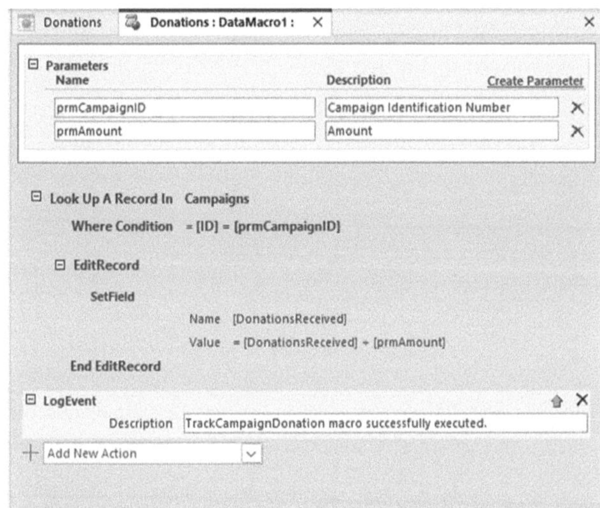

FIGURE 19.34. The completed named data macro.

<table>
<tr><td>NOTE</td><td>The named data macro depicted in Figure 19.34 is available in the Charitable Contributions Web Database created from a template supplied with an earlier version of Access and, for your convenience, included in the companion files. Follow these steps to open the database:

1. Copy the Charitable Contributions Web Database.accdb file from the companion files to your C:\VBAAccess2024_ByExample folder.
2. Double-click the copied file to open it in Access.
3. In the Login window, click the New User hyperlink.
4. In the User Details window, enter your name in the Full Name text box, and click Save & Close.
5. Select your name in the Login window and click Login.
6. When prompted, click the Enable Content button in the message bar. This will activate the Login window. Select your name and click Login.
7. Open the Navigation Pane and double-click the Donations table.
8. Click the Table tab and select Named Macros | Edit Named Macro | TrackCampaignDonation to view the data macro and access the named macros in this table.</td></tr>
</table>

Editing an Existing Named Data Macro

You can edit an existing named data macro by clicking the Named Macro button on the Ribbon and selecting Edit Named Macro. Access will display the list of available macros to edit, as shown in Figure 19.35.

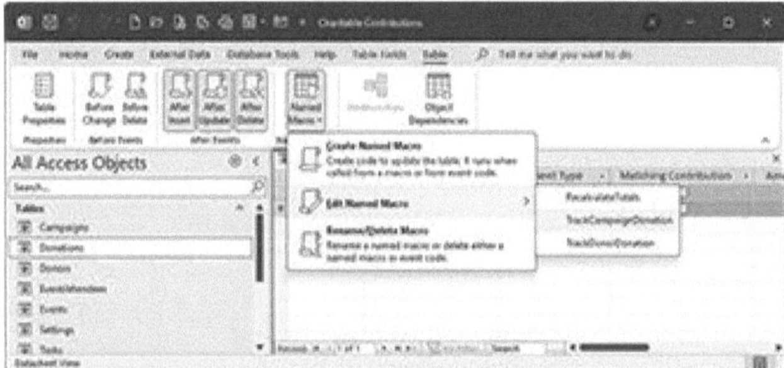

FIGURE 19.35.   If the table contains named data macros, the macro names are listed under the Edit Named Macro option.

Calling a Named Data Macro from Another Macro

You can run a named macro from another macro using the `RunDataMacro` action. Figure 19.36 shows two named data macros that are run from within the After Insert data macro in the `Donations` table. Notice that to run a named macro, you need to:

- Specify the `RunDataMacro` action.
- Specify the named macro name (`Donations.TrackDonorDonation`, `Donations.TrackCampaignDonation`).
- Specify the values for the parameters that the named data macro expects.

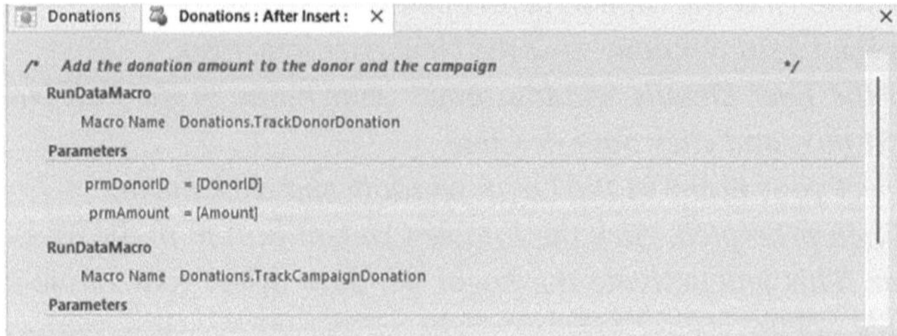

FIGURE 19.36.   Running named macros from the After Insert data macro in the Donations table.

Using ReturnVars in Data Macros

A powerful feature in data macros is their ability to return values to other macros by using `ReturnVars`.

`ReturnVars` can be compared to values returned by functions in VBA procedures. You can specify the `ReturnVars` by using the `SetReturnVar` action in a named data macro, as depicted in Figure 19.37. After selecting the `SetReturnVar` macro action from the Add New Action drop-down box, enter the name of the `ReturnVar` in the Name box and specify the value or expression in the Expression box. For example, to return the number of backordered inventory items, the example macro in Figure 19.40 sets up a `ReturnVar` named `retBackOrdered` and sets its value in the Expression box to `[BackOrdered]`, which is the name of the field in the `Inventory` table. The number of backordered items will be returned by the `LookupRecord` macro action for the specified `ProductID`. Notice that all return variables are initialized at the top of the macro.

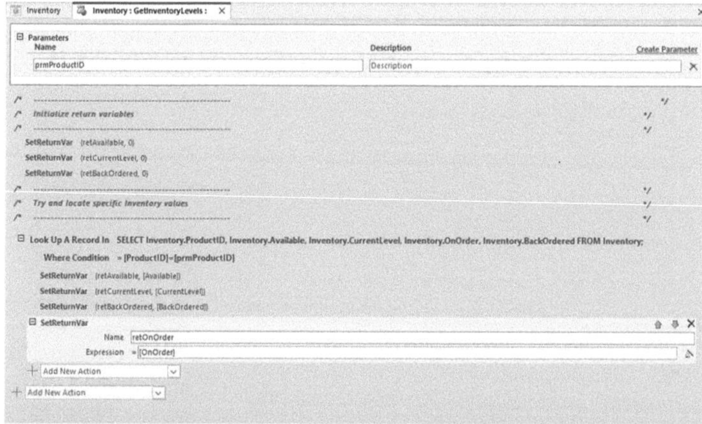

FIGURE 19.37.   The named data macro GetInventoryLevels located in the Inventory table of the Northwind Web database created from a template generated by an earlier version of Access demonstrates the use of return variables. You can open this database from the companion files.

NOTE	*Access 2010 introduced a new type of database file known as Access Web Database. You could use Access Web Databases to publish your Access data to a Microsoft SharePoint server running Access services. Once published, your database could be used in an Internet browser. Because Access Web Database is not compatible with VBA, all programming had to be done using macros. In Access 2010, to design an Access Web application, you had to choose File	New and click Blank Web Database. Well, this option is not available in Access 2016–2024. Simply put, Microsoft has retired the Web apps. While you can open, design, and publish existing Access 2010 Web databases in Access 2016–2024, it is no longer possible to create new Access Web databases.*

To get the return value, you must first call the macro. The GetInventoryLevels macro (shown in Figure 19.37) is called from the embedded macro (see Figure 19.38) that is attached to the After Update event of the `chkPostedToInventory` checkbox control. This control is located on the `PurchaseOrderLineItemsReceiving` form in the `Northwind Web` database.

Notice that to reference the return variable in a macro, you must use the `ReturnVars` command like this:

```
= [ReturnVars]![retBackOrdered]
```

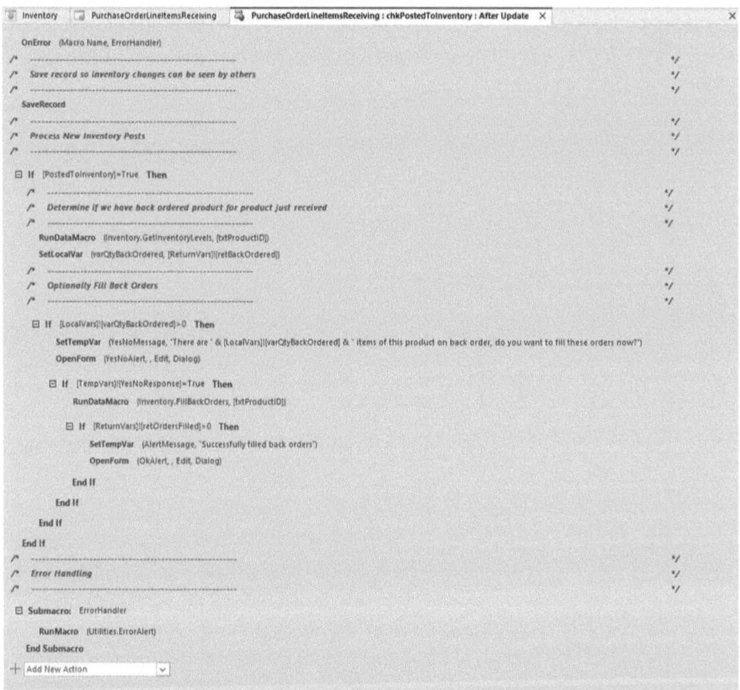

FIGURE 19.38. Referencing return variables (ReturnVars) inside a macro attached to the After Update event of a control placed on a form. Notice that the value of the return variable is being retrieved into a local variable named varQtyBackOrdered.

Tracing Data Macro Execution Errors

Access automatically writes all errors encountered during the execution of your data macros in a system table called `USysApplicationLog`. Any failure that occurs while executing a named data macro or a data macro attached to an event will be reported in this table. By default, the `UsysApplicationLog` table is created the first time Access encounters a data macro error. There are a couple of ways to access this table:

- Using the Backstage View (see Figure 19.39)

  If the `UsysApplicationLog` table is present in your database, select the File tab, and click the View Application Log Table button to open the table.

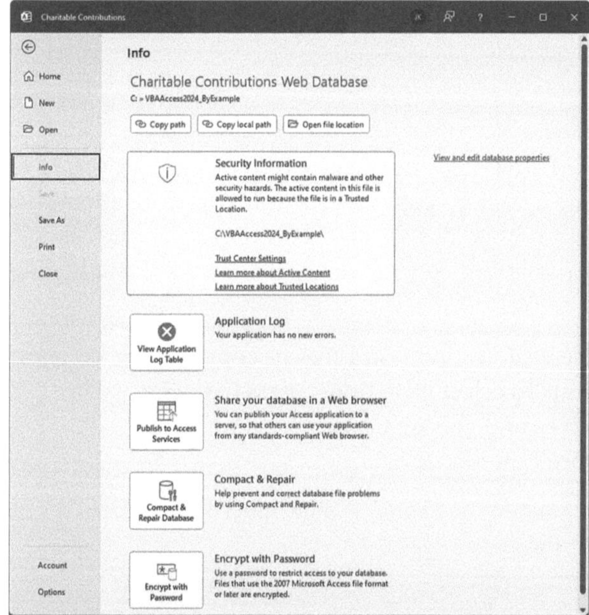

FIGURE 19.39.   Accessing the UsysApplicationLog table in the Backstage View.

- Using the Navigation Pane (see Figure 19.40)

  Before you can access the `UsysApplicationLog` table from the Navigation Pane, you must tell Access to display system objects. To do this, select File | Options and click Current Database. Scroll down to the Navigation section and click the Navigation Options button. Select the Show System Objects box at the bottom of the Navigation Options dialog box and click OK.

You can use `UsysApplicationLog` to view the details of errors that occurred during data macro execution. Access provides a special action called `LogEvent` that allows you to write your own messages to the log table. You can keep track of the data macros that ran by adding the `LogEvent` action to the end of your named macro and setting its Description field to whatever message you want to write. Figure 19.40 displays the contents of the `UsysApplicationLog` table after adding data to the `Donations` table.

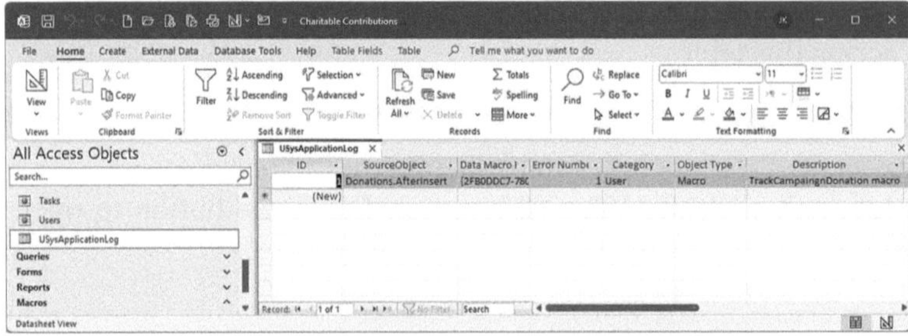

FIGURE 19.40. Viewing the contents of the UsysApplicationLog table.

Copying Macros

Access stores macros as XML. Saving your macro as XML enables you to email it to someone else or create a backup copy of your macro before attempting to edit its logic.

You can copy the XML markup of your data macro to a text editor using these steps:

1. Open the macro and select the action you'd like to copy. A gray box appears around the selected action. To select all actions, press Ctrl+A.
2. Right-click the selected area and choose Copy.
3. Open Notepad and choose Edit | Paste.

Figure 19.41 shows the `RecalculateTotals` data macro copied to Windows Notepad.

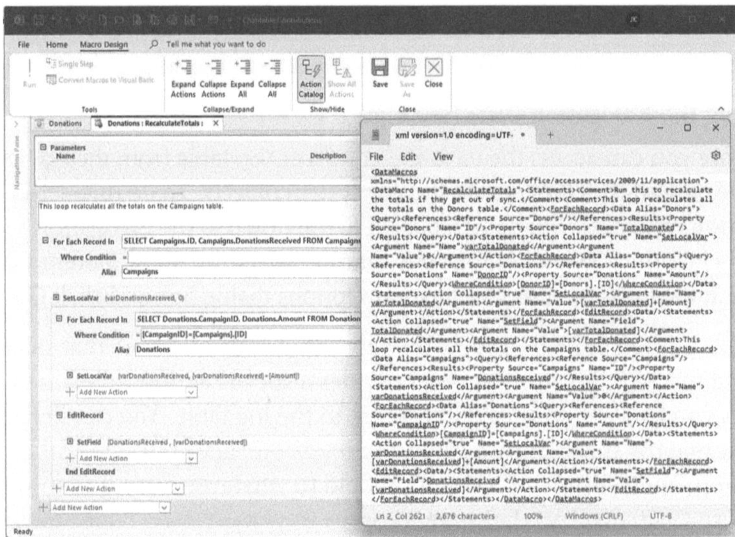

FIGURE 19.41. Copying the macro content to a text file.

Error Handling in Macros

Access provides special macro actions that give macros the capability to handle errors: `OnError`, `ClearMacroError`, and `SingleStep`. A `MacroError` object provides you with information about the error received and allows you to create user-friendly error messages. The `OnError` action is similar to the `On Error` statement in VBA. This action specifies how errors should be handled when a run-time error occurs. The `OnError` action has two arguments, as shown in Table 19.2.

TABLE 19.2.   OnError action arguments.

Arguments	Description
Go To (This argument is required.)	Specifies how macros should handle errors. The Go To argument can be set to Next, Macro Name, or Fail. • Next—The error is recorded in the MacroError object, and the execution of the macro moves to the next macro action. This is similar to the On Error Resume Next statement in VBA. • Macro Name—Macro execution is passed to the macro that is named in the Macro Name argument. This is similar to the On Error GoTo statement in VBA. • Fail—Access will stop the execution of the macro and display an error. This is similar to On Error GoTo 0 in VBA.
Macro Name (This argument is optional.)	If the Go To argument is set to Macro Name, the name of the macro in the current macro group will handle the error.

The `OnError` action suppresses standard error messages displayed by Access when an error occurs. When you use this action in your macro, you should use the error information saved in the `MacroError` object to display a user-friendly message about the error.

The `MacroError` object has the following properties: `ActionName`, `Arguments`, `Condition`, `Description`, `MacroName`, and `Number`. You can check the `MacroError` object's `Number` property to find out whether an error occurred. If there was no error, the `Number` property will return zero (0). If, however, `[MacroError].[Number] <> 0`, then you should handle the error right away.

By default, the `MacroError` object is cleared at the end of the macro execution; however, you can clear it right after the error has been handled by using the `ClearMacroError` action. This action will reset the error number in the `MacroError` object back to 0 and clear other information stored in the object, such as macro name, action name, condition, arguments, and description. The `MacroError` object contains information about only one error at a time; if more than one error occurred, only the error information about the last error can be retrieved. Therefore, when writing longer macros, use the `ClearMacroError` action right after handling the first error so the `ErrorObject` will be able to capture information about the next error that might occur.

Use the `StopMacro` action to stop the currently running macro. In Figure 19.42, the `StopMacro` action is run right after the user receives the message about the macro error.

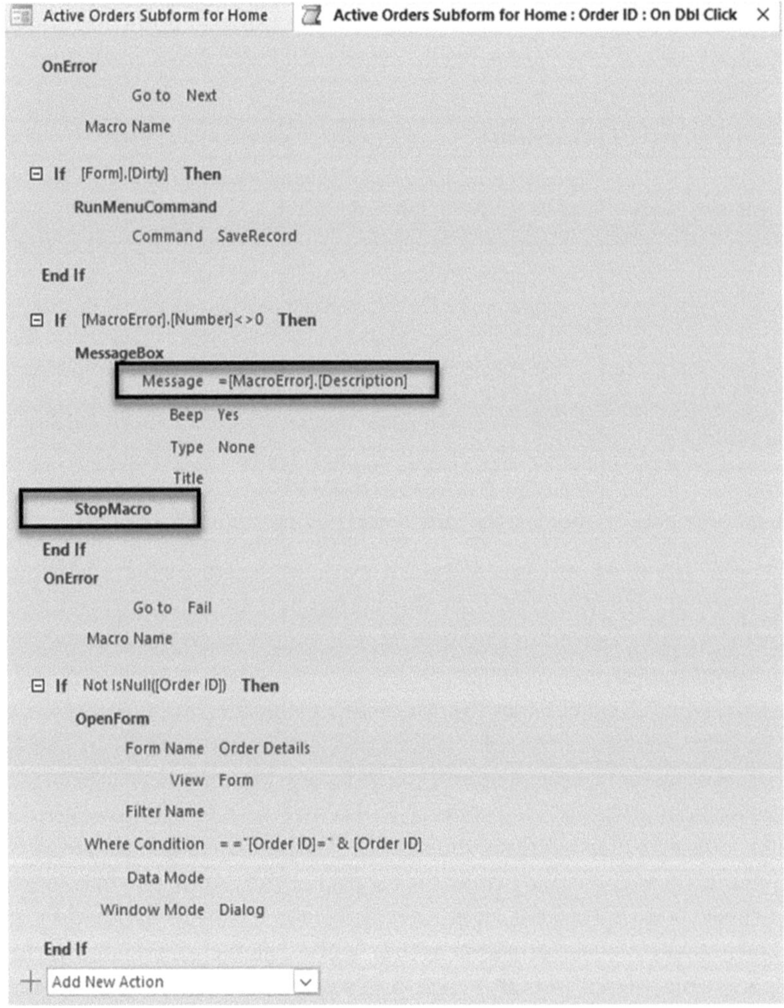

FIGURE 19.42.   Error handling in an Access macro located in the Northwind 2007.accdb database (see the On Dbl Click event for the Order ID field in the Active Orders Subform for Home).

To debug a macro that is not working properly, click the Single Step button in the Tools group of the Macro Design tab and then click the Run button, or use the `SingleStep` macro action just before an action that you suspect is causing a problem. This action pauses the macro and opens the Macro Single Step dialog box (see Figure 19.43), which displays information about the current macro action (macro name, condition, action name, arguments, and error number). The Macro Single Step dialog box contains the three buttons described in Table 19.3.

TABLE 19.3. Buttons available in the Macro Single Step dialog box.

Button Name	Description
Step	Move to the next macro action.
Stop All Macros	Stop the current macro and any other macros that may be running.
Continue	Use this button to exit Single Step mode and continue the normal execution of the macro.

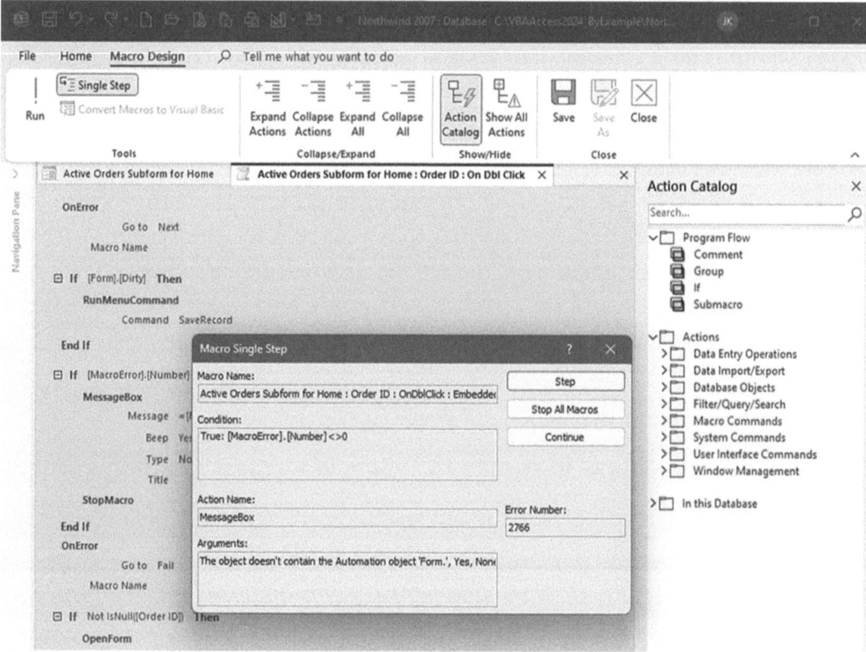

FIGURE 19.43. Debug your macros by selecting the Single Step option on the Ribbon and clicking the Run button.

If you open the Macro Single Step dialog box using the Single Step button on the Ribbon, you must click this button again when you are done debugging your macro or the next macros that you run will also be run using Single Step mode.

Using Temporary Variables in Macros

The functionality to add temporary variables (`TempVars`) has been in Access since its 2007 release. This functionality applies to both VBA and macros. Recall that the `TempVar` object of the `TempVars` collection allows you to get or set a value for a variable. Each `TempVar` object has a name and value property. In macros, there are three macro actions that relate to `TempVars`:

- `SetTempVar` (name, expression)—This macro action is used to create a new temporary variable that can be used as a condition or argument in subsequent macro actions. Temporary variables are global; therefore, you can use them in another macro, in an event procedure, or on a form or report.

- The first argument of the `SetTempVar` macro action assigns a name to the temporary variable. The second argument is the expression that Access should use to set the value for this temporary variable. You can define up to 255 temporary variables at one time.

- `RemoveTempVar` (name)—This macro action is used to remove the temporary variable. Use the `name` argument to provide the name of the variable to remove. It is recommended that you remove the temporary variable once you've finished working with it. If you don't remove your temporary variables, they will be removed automatically when you close the database.

- `RemoveAllTempVar`—This macro action is used to remove all temporary variables from the `TempVars` collection.

Figure 19.44 shows how to specify the name of a report by using a temporary variable.

NOTE	*Because both macros and VBA use the same `TempVars` collection, it is easy to share data between your macros and VBA procedures.*

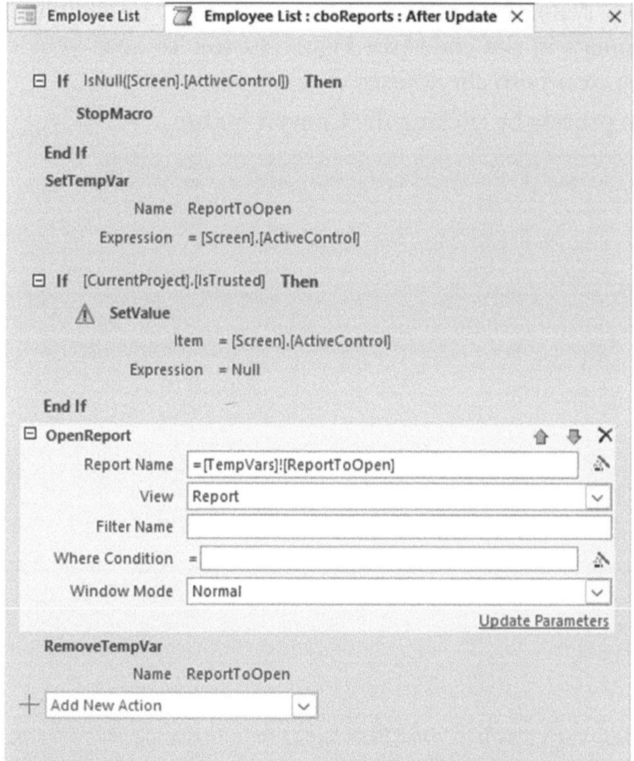

FIGURE 19.44.   Using temporary variables in an Access macro.

CONVERTING MACROS TO VBA CODE

The ability to convert standalone macros to VBA code has been available since Access 97. With the introduction of embedded macros, Access also provides a button to convert to VBA macros that are stored in an event property of a form, report, or control (see Figure 19.45).

Converting a Standalone Macro to VBA

To convert a standalone macro to VBA, follow these steps:

1. In the Navigation Pane, under Macros, right-click the macro you want to convert, then click Design View.
2. In the Tools group of the Design tab, click Convert Macros to Visual Basic (see Figure 19.45).

Access will display a dialog box asking whether you want to include error handling and comments in the code (see Figure 19.46). To keep your code very simple, you can clear both checkboxes.

3. Start the conversion process by clicking the Convert button.

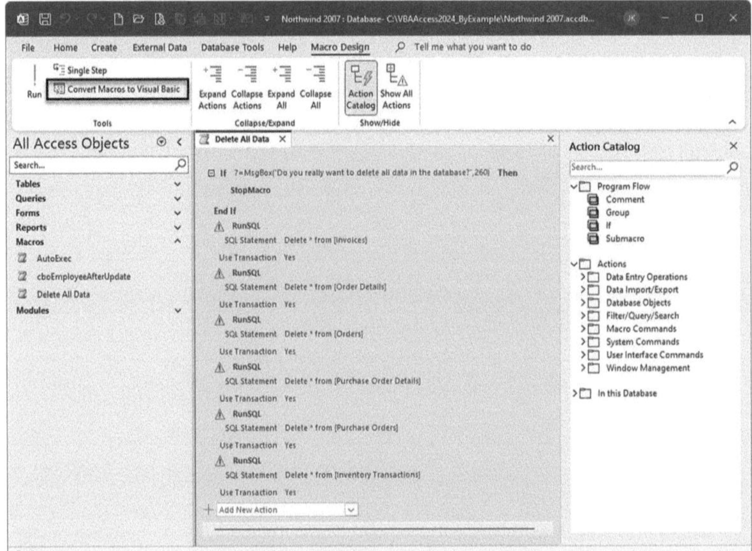

FIGURE 19.45.   Click the Convert Macro to Visual Basic button to convert a standalone macro to VBA code.

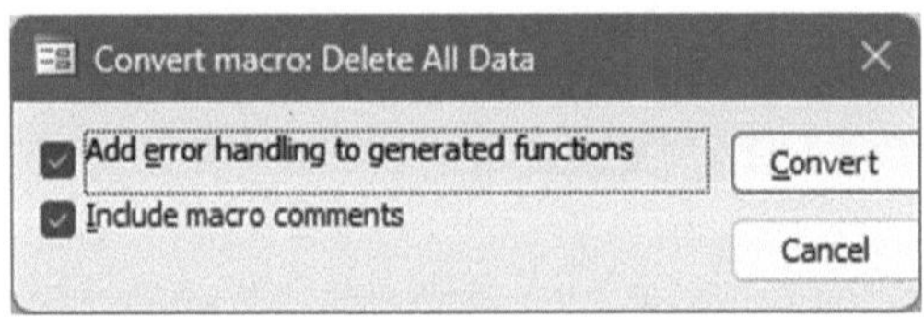

FIGURE 19.46.   Access displays this dialog box when you click the Convert Macros to Visual Basic button (see Figure 19.45).

Upon completion of the macro conversion process, Access displays a message stating that the conversion is finished. Click OK to the message and review the Modules group in the database navigation pane. You should see a separate module for the converted macro. The name of the module is Converted Macro followed by a dash and the name of the macro you converted. For example, after converting the Delete All Data macro, the name of the VBA module is Converted Macro – Delete All Data. To view the converted macro, double-click the converted module's name. This will open the VBE window, as shown in Figure 19.47.

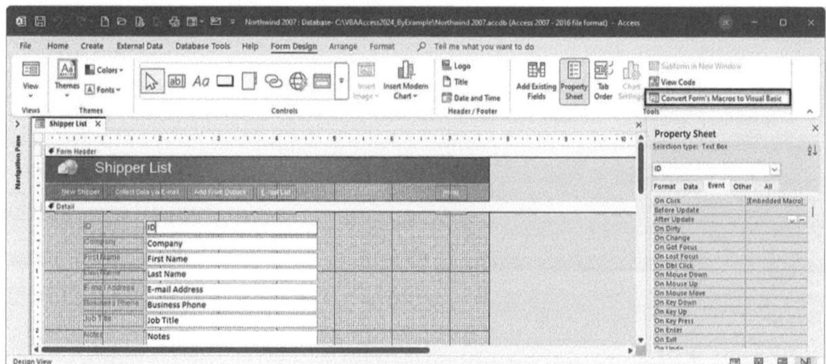

```
Northwind 2007 - Converted Macro- Delete All Data (Code)

(General)                                                    Delete_All_Data

Option Compare Database
Option Explicit


'----------------------------------------------------------
' Delete_All_Data
'
'----------------------------------------------------------
Function Delete_All_Data()
On Error GoTo Delete_All_Data_Err

    If (Eval("7=MsgBox(""Do you really want to delete all data in the database?"",260)")) Then
        Exit Function
    End If
    DoCmd.RunSQL "Delete * from [Invoices]", -1
    DoCmd.RunSQL "Delete * from [Order Details]", -1
    DoCmd.RunSQL "Delete * from [Orders]", -1
    DoCmd.RunSQL "Delete * from [Purchase Order Details]", -1
    DoCmd.RunSQL "Delete * from [Purchase Orders]", -1
    DoCmd.RunSQL "Delete * from [Inventory Transactions]", -1


Delete_All_Data_Exit:
    Exit Function

Delete_All_Data_Err:
    MsgBox Error$
    Resume Delete_All_Data_Exit

End Function
```

FIGURE 19.47.   This VBA code was generated by Access from a standalone macro.

You can modify the code generated by the macro conversion process to suit your needs.

Converting Embedded Macros to VBA

To convert embedded macros, open the form or report in design view. You should see the button named Convert Form's Macros to Visual Basic in the Macro group, as shown in Figure 19.48.

FIGURE 19.48.   Converting embedded macros to VBA using the Convert Form's Macros to Visual Basic button.

After clicking the Convert Form's Macros to Visual Basic button, Access displays the same dialog box shown earlier in the conversion process for standalone macros (see Figure 19.45). When you click the Convert button, Access begins the conversion process, and when this process completes, you will see a message about the successful completion of the conversion. Click OK to the message. Next, activate the Property Sheet, and notice that form and control event properties that were previously been set to [Embedded Macro] now display [Event Procedure]. You can click the Build button (…) to view the VBA code.

Figure 19.49 shows the VBA procedure that was generated for the embedded macro attached to the Click event of the ID text box control placed on a form. Notice that for each converted macro, Access writes its equivalent XML macro code as a comment at the top of the VBA procedure.

If after the conversion process you still want to keep the [Embedded Macro] setting in the event properties of a form, report, or control, perform these steps:

1. Save the VBA code generated by the macro conversion to a file by choosing File | Export File in the VBE window. Access will create a file with the `.cls` extension.
2. To view the contents of this file, right-click its name in Windows Explorer and choose Open With | Choose Program. Select Notepad and click OK.
3. In Access, close the form and answer No when prompted for changes. Access will revert the [Event Procedure] setting in the event properties to [Embedded Macro].

```
ID                                              ∨   Click                                              ∨
'-----------------------------------------------------------------------
' ID_Click
'
'-----------------------------------------------------------------------
Private Sub ID_Click()
On Error GoTo ID_Click_Err

    ' _AXL:<?xml version="1.0" encoding="UTF-16" standalone="no"?>
    ' <UserInterfaceMacro For="E-mail Address" xmlns="http://schemas.microsoft.com/offic
    ' _AXL:t IsNull([Screen].[ActiveControl])</Condition><Statements><Action Name="EMail
    On Error Resume Next
    If (Form.Dirty) Then
        DoCmd.RunCommand acCmdSaveRecord
    End If
    If (MacroError.Number <> 0) Then
        Beep
        MsgBox MacroError.Description, vbOKOnly, ""
        Exit Sub
    End If
    On Error GoTo 0
    DoCmd.OpenForm "Shipper Details", acNormal, "", "[ID]=" & Nz(ID, 0), , acDialog
    If (Not IsNull(ID)) Then
        TempVars.Add "CurrentID", ID
    End If
    If (IsNull(ID)) Then
        TempVars.Add "CurrentID", Nz(DMax("[ID]", Form.RecordSource), 0)
    End If
    DoCmd.Requery ""
    DoCmd.SearchForRecord , "", acFirst, "[ID]=" & TempVars!CurrentID
    TempVars.Remove "CurrentID"


ID_Click_Exit:
    Exit Sub

ID_Click_Err:
    MsgBox Error$
    Resume ID_Click_Exit

End Sub
```

FIGURE 19.49. VBA code from a converted embedded macro.

ACCESS TEMPLATES

Access comes with several prebuilt templates that give users a head start with various types of projects. In Access 2024, the templates are listed when you click the New button, as shown in Figure 19.50. You can also search online for more templates.

Access template files are recognized by the `.accdt` file extension. By default, Access stores its template files in the `C:\Users\username\AppData\Roaming\Microsoft\Templates` folder. Please note that `AppData` is a hidden Windows folder, and you will need to unhide it in the File Explorer in order to access its content.

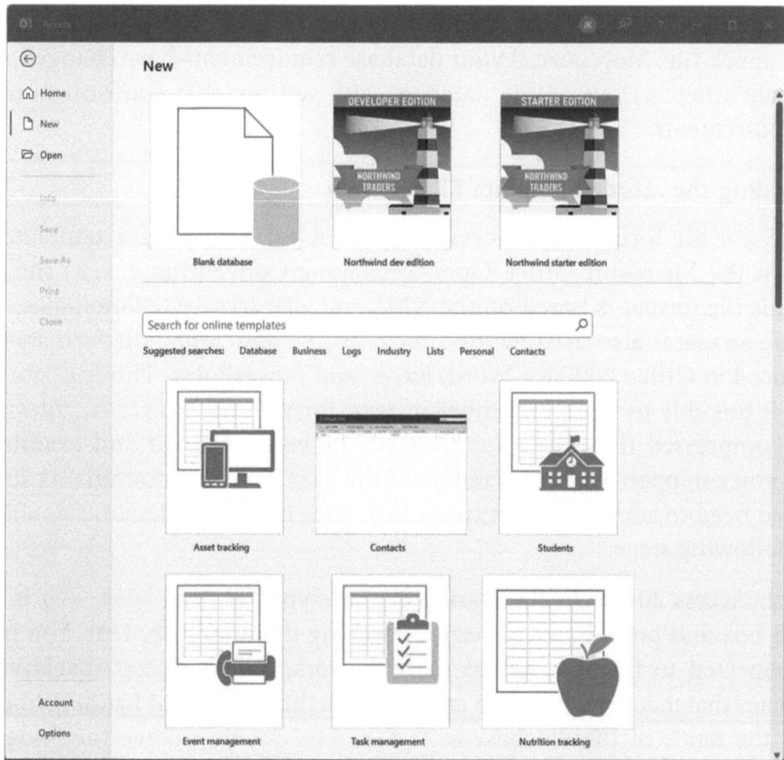

FIGURE 19.50.   Creating an Access database based on a specific template.

Creating a Custom Blank Database Template

When you select the Blank database button and click the Create button, Access provides you with an empty database that you can customize to suit your specific needs. If you are like many users, you might start your next database project by again clicking the Blank database button and proceeding to implement many of the same customizations that you applied to the previous database project. If you have been working like this, however, you are not taking advantage of the startup template—`Blank.accdb`. Instead of customizing each new blank database, simply create a new database called `Blank.accdb` in the template folder and customize it to include specific database properties, VBA references, custom functions, Ribbon customizations, default forms and reports, and customized controls, as well as any other special configuration settings that you normally use in your database applications. The next time you click the Blank database button in the backstage view, Access will make a copy of your `Blank.accdb` database so you won't need to start from scratch. Your new database will already contain the common settings that you saved in the `Blank.accdb` file. Moreover, if your database requirements have changed, you can create a new `Blank.accdb` database with settings that conform to these new requirements.

Understanding the .accdt Template File Format

The `.accdt` file format that Access 2024 uses for its database templates is based on the Microsoft Office Open Packaging Convention (`.opc`) file format. This file format is based on the XML and ZIP archive technologies. The `.opc` file format is also used by the `.docx`, `.xlsx`, and `.pptx` file formats first introduced in Office 2007 for Word, Excel, and PowerPoint. The `.opc` format makes it possible to store a number of text, image, and `.xml`/`.xsd` files in a single compressed file. The `.opc` files can be easily opened and examined. Before you can open an Access template file (`.accdt`) and examine its structure, you need to add the `.zip` extension at the end of the filename, as shown in the following steps:

1. Launch Access 2024. On the startup screen, type `lending library` in the search box and press Enter to begin searching the online content. You must be connected to the Internet to make it work. When Access displays the templates that match your search criteria, click the one named Lending library. Enter the name of the database as `MyLibrary.accdb`, change the folder to `C:\VBAAccess2024_ByExample`, and then click the Create button. Access downloads the template file and creates the specified desktop database. The resulting database is shown in Figure 19.51.

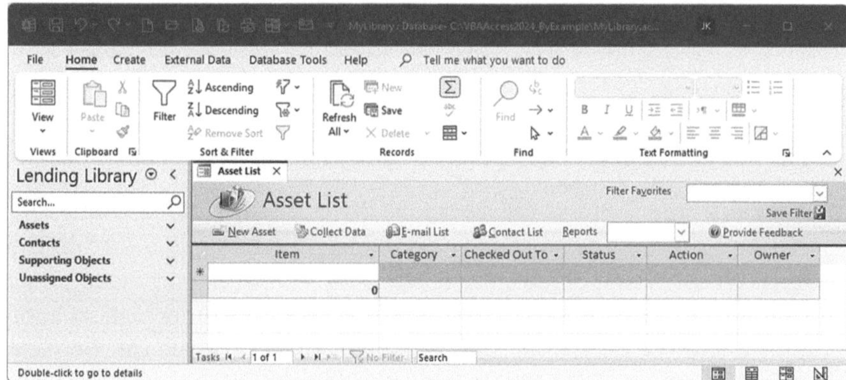

FIGURE 19.51.   The MyLibrary database is based on the Lending Library template downloaded from the Microsoft Access online templates.

2. Close the `MyLibrary.accdb` database file and exit Access.
3. Locate the downloaded `Lending library.accdt` template file. By default, templates are stored in your `\Users\username\AppData\Roaming\Microsoft\Templates` folder.
4. Rename the file `Lending library.accdt.zip`, as shown in Figure 19.52.
5. When the Rename dialog box appears, click Yes to confirm that you want to change the filename extension. Click Continue, if prompted to provide administrator permission to rename this file. The file format should now change to the ZIP archive.

Name	Date modified	Type	Size
LiveContent	10/17/2023 2:20 AM	File folder	
SmartArt Graphics	3/24/2024 11:12 PM	File folder	
Lending library.accdt.zip	12/27/2024 2:25 PM	Compressed (zipped) Folder	879 KB
Normal.dotm	3/25/2024 4:15 PM	Microsoft Word Macro-Enabled Template	20 KB

FIGURE 19.52.   By adding the .zip file extension to the .accdt file format, you can turn it into a ZIP archive that you can examine and modify depending on your needs.

6. To open the `Lending library.accdt.zip` file, right-click the filename and choose Open With | Compressed (zipped) Folders or File Explorer, or simply Open, if you're using Windows 11. The folders that make up the document are shown in Windows File Explorer (see Figure 19.53).

Name	Type	Compressed size	Password ...	Size	Ratio	Date modified
_rels	File folder					
docProps	File folder					
template	File folder					
[Content_Types].xml	Microsoft Edge HTML Document	1 KB	No	1 KB	53%	12/29/1899 7:00 PM

FIGURE 19.53. The directory structure of an Access template file.

Notice that the archive file contains the following three folders: `_rels`, `docProps`, and `template`. The `_rels` folder contains one `.xml` file with the extension `.rels` that defines the relationships between various files included in the file package. Access uses this file to find out information about the template and the database. The contents of the `.rels` file can be viewed in Notepad, as shown in Figure 19.54.

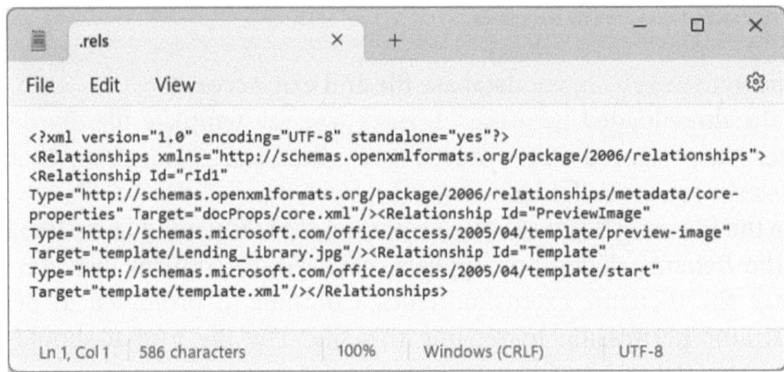

FIGURE 19.54. The contents of the .rels .xml file in the _rels folder.

The `docProps` folder contains the `core.xml` file that describes the core document properties, such as `creator name`, `identifier`, `title`, `description`, `keywords`, `category`, `version`, and `lastModifiedBy` (see Figure 19.55).

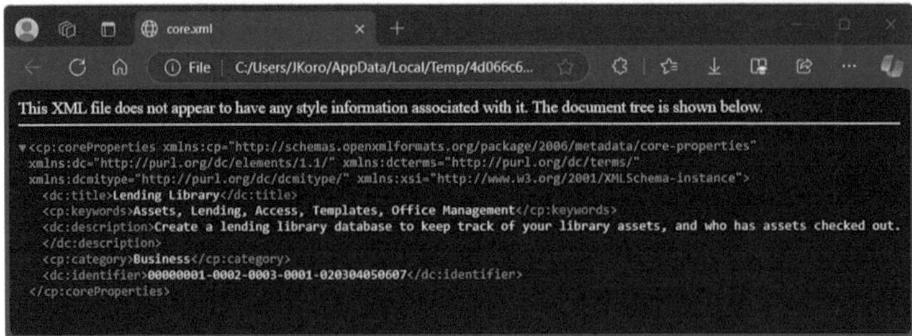

FIGURE 19.55. The contents of the core.xml file in the docProps folder.

When you double-click the `template` folder, you will see two subfolders named `_rels` and `database`, as well as a `template.xml` file and a `.jpg` image. The `template.xml` file contains information about the format of the template file (Figure 19.56).

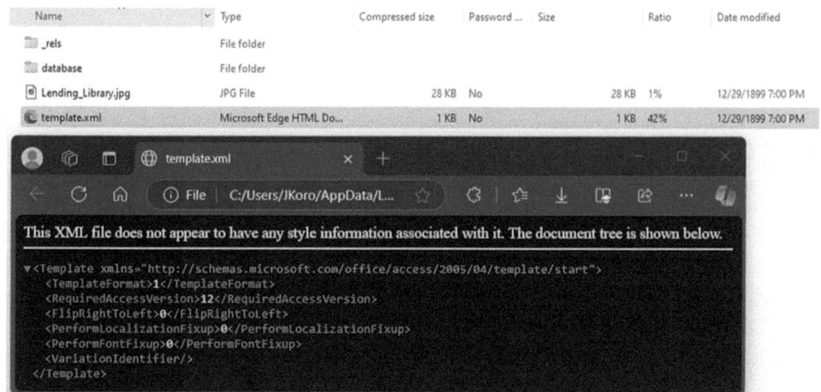

FIGURE 19.56.   The contents of the template folder and the Template.xml file.

You can find out a lot of information about the contents and structure of the `.accdt` file by opening the `database` folder (Figure 19.57).

Name	Type	Compressed size	Password protected	Size	Ratio	Date modified
objects	File folder					
databaseProperties.xml	Microsoft Edge HTML Document	1 KB	No	1 KB	59%	12/29/1899 7:00 PM
navpane.xml	Microsoft Edge HTML Document	5 KB	No	50 KB	92%	12/29/1899 7:00 PM
relationships.xml	Microsoft Edge HTML Document	1 KB	No	2 KB	73%	12/29/1899 7:00 PM
vbaReferences.xml	Microsoft Edge HTML Document	1 KB	No	1 KB	48%	12/29/1899 7:00 PM

FIGURE 19.57.   The contents of the database folder.

The `databaseProperties.xml` file in the `database` folder stores various database settings and properties. You can modify this file to include additional properties that need to be set by adding new nodes to the file.

The `navpane.xml` file contains information about the structure of the database navigation pane. It also contains the data for the database navigation pane system tables: `MSysNavPaneGroupCategories`, `MSysNavPaneGroups`, `MSysNavPaneGroupToObjects`, and `MSysNavPaneObjectIDs`.

The `relationships.xml` file contains the contents of the `MSysRelationships` system table.

The `vbaReferences.xml` file contains all VBA project references that Access needs to set.

In the `objects` folder, you will find many other files that describe different database objects (Figure 19.58).

Name	Type	Compressed size
_rels	File folder	
properties	File folder	
sampleData	File folder	
formAssetDetails.txt	Text Document	65 KB
formAssetList.txt	Text Document	44 KB
formCheckIn.txt	Text Document	32 KB
formCheckOut.txt	Text Document	30 KB
formContactCurrentLendingSubfo...	Text Document	6 KB
formContactDetails.txt	Text Document	64 KB
formContactDetails0x7EAddFuriga...	Text Document	66 KB
formContactDetails0x7EFlipAddres...	Text Document	65 KB
formContactDetails0x7EFlipName.t...	Text Document	65 KB
formContactList.txt	Text Document	40 KB
formContactList0x7EAddFurigana.t...	Text Document	41 KB
formContactList0x7EFlipAddress.txt	Text Document	40 KB
formContactList0x7EFlipName.txt	Text Document	40 KB
formFilterDetails.txt	Text Document	39 KB
formLendingHistory.txt	Text Document	7 KB
macroFilters.txt	Text Document	2 KB
macroTransactions.txt	Text Document	1 KB
queryAssetsWithTransactions.txt	Text Document	2 KB
queryContactsExtended.txt	Text Document	2 KB
queryContactsExtended0x7EAddFu...	Text Document	2 KB
queryContactsExtended0x7EFlipAd...	Text Document	2 KB
queryContactsExtended0x7EFlipNa...	Text Document	2 KB
queryCurrentTransactions.txt	Text Document	2 KB
reportAllAssets.txt	Text Document	9 KB

FIGURE 19.58.   Files in the objects folder contain information about different database objects in the template file as well as information about sample data and properties for each object included in the template.

You can open any of the files listed in Figure 19.58 and examine the type of information being stored. Because this chapter covered macros, look inside the `macroFilters.txt` file to find out how Access stores the embedded macros.

<table>
<tr><td>____
NOTE</td><td>When you are done reviewing the template files, change the name of the <code>Lending library.accdt.zip</code> file back to its original name—<code>Lending Library.accdt</code>.</td></tr>
</table>

USING ChatGPT WITH ACCESS

The more time you spend with Access macros, the more you'll realize their potential in streamlining your work and enhancing your productivity. Access macros offer a visual way to define your logic without needing to write extensive VBA code; however, combining macros with VBA will provide you with more flexibility and control.

With macros, you can quickly open forms and reports, validate user input, and execute many complex actions with a single click. If you need more guidance on specific macro actions or tips on optimizing your macros, ChatGPT is at your command. Let's compose a few prompts to take our macros skillset to a higher level:

User Prompt: Please provide the top 5 macro actions in Access with examples.

According to ChatGPT, the top 5 macro actions are `OpenForm`, `SetValue`, `MessageBox`, `OpenReport`, and `RunMacro`.

User Prompt: Is there a way to quickly discover all the embedded macros in a particular database?

Absolutely. You can use the Database Documenter or write a VBA procedure to quickly discover all the embedded macros in a particular database.

User Prompt: Provide a few examples of using an AutoExec macro in Microsoft Access.

The provided examples for the AutoExec macro include opening a main navigation form, displaying a welcome message, maximizing the Application window, checking for updates and the notifying user, and setting user-specific environment settings.

User Prompt: Explain the purpose of data macros in the NorthwindStarter database.

The complete chat is included in the companion files. Refer to the `Chapter 19 - Using ChatGPT with Access` document. Also, make sure to check out the `Northwind 2007.accdb` database in the completed files for the VBA procedure that prints to a text file all embedded macros in forms and reports, along with their associated controls and events.

SUMMARY

This chapter introduced you to working with macros in Access 2024. You learned about macro security, created standalone and embedded macros, and worked with data macros. You also saw examples of return variables (`Return-Vars`), local variables, and temporary variables (`TempVars`), and examined the error-handling actions in macros. You learned how standalone and embedded macros can be easily converted to Visual Basic code. Because Access uses embedded macros extensively in its templates, we examined the structure and contents of the `.accdt` file format.

This chapter concludes Part VIII of the book, which focused on getting familiar with the macro interface and template file structure in Access 2024.

In Part IX, you will learn how to use your Access VBA skills with XML and Web services.

# Part IX — WORKING TOGETHER: VBA, XML, AND REST API

Extensible Markup Language (XML) has long been the standard format for sharing data regardless of the originating application or the operating system. In this part of the book, you will learn how XML is used in Access to bring external data to your database, as well as providing your data to other applications. You will also learn about REST APIs, the newest and most flexible method of integrating applications.

Chapter 20   Using XML in Access
Chapter 21   Access and REST API

USING XML IN ACCESS

In Chapter 17, we used XML to customize the application's interface and behavior, particularly when it comes to the Ribbon and backstage view. This chapter provides an overview of how XML can be utilized in Access beyond Ribbon customization. With XML, you can import structured data into your Access database. This is quite useful when you need to integrate data from different systems or applications that provide data in XML format. You can also export data from your Access tables or queries into XML files, which can then be used for data exchange with other systems, for backup, or for data analysis in other applications.

XML AND ACCESS

XML has been supported in Access since its 2002 version. This support has allowed users to take full advantage of XML's structured format for seamless data exchange.

XML is a powerful platform-independent markup language designed for the creation of structured documents. Unlike other data formats, XML is both human-readable and machine-readable, making it an ideal choice for data storage and exchange across different platforms and applications.

XML documents are simple text files that can be read and processed by any XML parser, regardless of the operating system or hardware. XML uses tags (such as `<order></order>`, `<item></item>`, and `<unitPrice></unitPrice>`) to define elements and structure the data. A *parser* is a software engine, usually a DLL, that can read and extract data from XML.

While Hypertext Markup Language (HTML) uses fixed, non-customizable tags to provide formatting instructions that should be applied to the data, XML is *extensible*, which means that it is not restricted to a set of predefined tags. XML allows you to define your own tags. The XML parser does not care what tags you use; it only needs to be able to find the tags and confirm that the XML document is well formed. A document that follows the formatting rules for XML is considered a well-formed document.

In addition to being well formed, an XML document must also be valid. When a document is *valid*, it follows the predefined rules for valid data. These rules are defined in a Document Type Definition (DTD) or schema file, which is written in XML. DTD is an older method of data validation. XML Schema Definition (XSD) files are easily recognized by the `.xsd` file extension. These files contain information about the structure of the XML tags, data types, and constraints. You can have Access generate these files automatically for you when you export your database data into XML documents.

Later in this chapter, you will see how Access uses a schema to determine the types of elements and attributes an XML document should contain, how these elements and attributes should be named, whether they're optional or required, their data types and default values, and the relationships between the elements. Another file type you will be working with is Extensible Stylesheet Language (XSL), which has an `.xsl` extension (don't confuse it with the older Excel XLS file format). It defines how the XML data is supposed to look. You will have a chance to apply a stylesheet to a raw XML document to make it look attractive to an end user. A part of XSL is transformations (XSLT). You will use XSLT later in this chapter to define the structure of your XML data.

Because of its extensibility, XML makes it easy to describe any data structure and send it anywhere across the Web using common protocols such as Hypertext Transfer Protocol (HTTP) or File Transfer Protocol (FTP).

Although XML was designed specifically for delivering information over the World Wide Web, it is also utilized in other areas, such as storing, sharing, and exchanging data.

STRUCTURE OF XML DOCUMENTS

XML documents consist of elements, attributes, and text content, all enclosed within tags, as shown in the example below, which describes a list of books.

```
<books>
  <book>
    <title>Access 2024 / Microsoft 365 Programming by Example</title>
    <author>Julitta Korol</author>
    <publisher>DeGruyter, Inc.</publisher>
    <yearPublished>2025</yearPublished>
  </book>
  <book>
<title>Excel 2024 / Microsoft 365 Programming by Example</title>
    <author>Julitta Korol</author>
    <publisher> DeGruyter, Inc. </publisher>
    <yearPublished>2025</yearPublished>
    </book>
</books>
```

Notice how the `<books>` tag describes the entire document. The `<books>` tag is a root element. It tells people that this document contains information about books. An XML document must have one root element. While in an HTML document the root element is always `<html>`, in an XML document, you can name your root element anything you want.

Element names must begin with a letter or underscore character. The root element must enclose all other elements, and elements must be properly nested. The XML data must be hierarchical; the beginning and ending tags cannot overlap. At the end of the document, you will find an ending tag `</books>`. Make sure that all element tags are closed (a beginning tag must be followed by an ending tag). Let's look at another example below:

```
<Sessions>5</Sessions>
```

You can use shortcuts, such as a single slash (/), to end the tag so you don't have to type the full tag name. For example, if the current `<Sessions>` element is empty (does not have a value), you could use the following tag:

```
<Sessions />
```

Tag names are case-sensitive: The tags `<Title>` and `</Title>` aren't equivalent to `<TITLE>` and `</TITLE>`.

XML documents can be element- or attribute-based. If you use attributes, the books information can be presented as follows:

```
<books>
<book title="Access 2024 / Microsoft 365 Programming by
Example" author="Julitta Korol" publisher = "DeGruyter, Inc."
yearPublished=2025 />

<book title="Excel 2024 / Microsoft 365 Programming by
Example author="Julitta Korol" publisher = "DeGruyter, Inc."
yearPublished=2025 />
</books>
```

Notice that all text attributes are inside quotation marks. You cannot have more than one attribute with the same name within the same element.

EXPORTING XML DATA FROM ACCESS

In Access, you can export tables, queries, forms, and/or reports to XML files. There is no XML support for macros or modules. When you export a form or report, you actually export the data from the form or report's underlying table or query.

Access uses a special XML vocabulary known as *ReportML* for representing its objects as XML data. ReportML is an XML file that contains tags describing properties, methods, events, and attributes of the Access object being exported. This file is generated automatically by Access when you begin the export process and is used by Access to generate the final output files.

To allow XML data to be viewed in browsers in a user-friendly format, ReportML relies on a rather complicated stylesheet that contains formatting instructions. We examine stylesheets later in this chapter.

After the formatting instructions contained in the stylesheet have been applied to the XML file, the ReportML file is automatically deleted.

No matter what Access object you need to export to XML, you always follow the same procedure:

- Export all data:
- Select the appropriate object (table, query, report, or form) in the database window.
- Choose External Data | More | XML File or right-click the object name in the Navigation Pane and select Export | XML File from the shortcut menu.

- Export a single record or a set of filtered or sorted records:
- Open the appropriate object and follow these steps:

You want to...	Step 1	Step 2
Export a single record	Select that record	Choose External Data | More | XML File, specify the name of the export file you want to create, and click OK. Click the More Options… button, and in the Records to Export area, select Current Record.
Export filtered records	Apply a filter to the records	Choose External Data | More | XML File and select the appropriate options.
Export records in a predefined order	Arrange records in the order you want	Choose External Data | More | XML File and select the appropriate options.

The following hands-on exercise demonstrates how to use the Export command to save the `Products` table in XML format.

> **NOTE** *All code files and figures for the hands-on projects may be found in the companion files.*

⊙ Hands-On 20.1   Exporting an Access Table to an XML File

1. Use File Explorer to create a new folder named `C:\VBAAccess2024_XML` for this chapter's practice files.
2. Copy the sample `Northwind 2007.accdb` database from the companion files to the `VBAAccess2024_XML` folder and open it. If you get a security warning message that some active content has been disabled, click OK and then click Enable Content button below the Ribbon.
3. Log in as Andrew Cencini.
4. Use the Access Options dialog to add the `C:\VBAAccess2024_XML` folder to your trusted locations. Refer to the section titled Placing a Database in a Trusted Location in Chapter 1 for more details.
5. In the Access window's Navigation Pane, choose Tables and Related Views from the Northwind Traders dropdown, and open the `Products` table.
6. Click the External Data tab, and, in the Export group of the Ribbon, click the More dropdown and choose XML File.
7. In the File name box, enter `C:\VBAAccess2024_XML\Products.xml` and click OK.
   In the Export XML dialog box that appears, there are three checkboxes (see Figure 20.1). The first one will tell Access to generate an XML file containing

the data from the `Products` table. The second one specifies that Access should create an XSD file with the data definition. The third checkbox tells Access to generate the stylesheet (XSL) file that will contain formatting specifications.

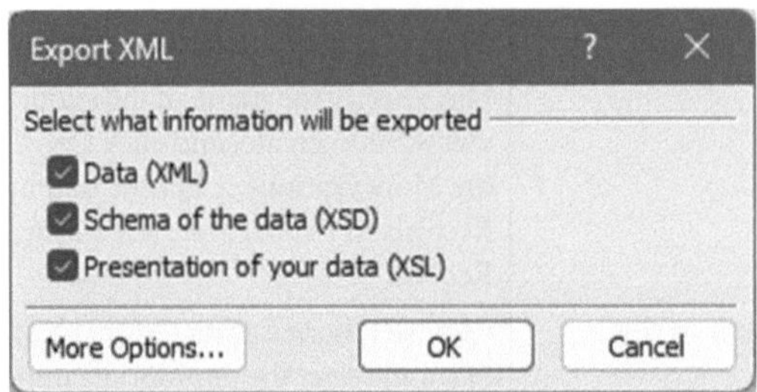

FIGURE 20.1.   The Export XML dialog box displays three checkboxes; the first one is selected by default. The More Options button allows for more customizations.

8. Select all the checkboxes and click OK to proceed with the export.
   When the export operation completes, Access displays the Export - XML File window, where you are given a chance to save the export steps so that you can repeat them in the future without using the wizard.

9. Click Close to exit the Export - XML File window without saving the export steps.

Understanding the XML Data File

In Hands-On 20.1, you prepared the `Products.xml` file. Let's switch to Windows File Explorer and examine the contents of your `Access2024_XML` folder.

Hands-On 20.2   Examining the Contents of an XML Data File

1. Open the `C:\VBAAccess2024_XML` folder.
   Figure 20.2 displays the contents of the `Access2024_XML` folder after exporting the `Products` table to an XML file.

Name	Date modified	Type	Size
Northwind 2007.accdb	12/17/2024 8:05 PM	Microsoft Access Database	3,928 KB
Northwind 2007.laccdb	12/17/2024 8:01 PM	Microsoft Access Record-Locking Information	1 KB
Products.htm	12/17/2024 8:10 PM	Microsoft Edge HTML Document	2 KB
Products.xml	12/17/2024 8:10 PM	Microsoft Edge HTML Document	27 KB
Products.xsd	12/17/2024 8:10 PM	XML Schema File	25 KB
Products.xsl	12/17/2024 8:10 PM	XSLT Stylesheet	19 KB

FIGURE 20.2.   After exporting the Products table to XML with all three checkboxes selected in the Export XML dialog box, Access creates four files.

2. Highlight the `Products.xml` and choose Open With. Select Microsoft Edge or another browser of your choice. Access displays the `Products` data in XML format, as shown in Figure 20.3.


```
<dataroot xmlns:od="urn:schemas-microsoft-com:officedata" xmlns:xsi="http://www.w3.org/2001/XMLSchema-instance"
  xsi:noNamespaceSchemaLocation="Products.xsd" generated="2024-12-17T20:10:49">
  <Products>
    <Supplier_x0020_IDs>
      <Value>4</Value>
    </Supplier_x0020_IDs>
    <ID>1</ID>
    <Product_x0020_Code>NWTB-1</Product_x0020_Code>
    <Product_x0020_Name>Northwind Traders Chai</Product_x0020_Name>
    <Standard_x0020_Cost>13.5</Standard_x0020_Cost>
    <List_x0020_Price>18</List_x0020_Price>
    <Reorder_x0020_Level>10</Reorder_x0020_Level>
    <Target_x0020_Level>40</Target_x0020_Level>
    <Quantity_x0020_Per_x0020_Unit>10 boxes x 20 bags</Quantity_x0020_Per_x0020_Unit>
    <Discontinued>0</Discontinued>
    <Minimum_x0020_Reorder_x0020_Quantity>10</Minimum_x0020_Reorder_x0020_Quantity>
    <Category>Beverages</Category>
  </Products>
  <Products>
    <Supplier_x0020_IDs>
      <Value>10</Value>
    </Supplier_x0020_IDs>
    <ID>3</ID>
    <Product_x0020_Code>NWTCO-3</Product_x0020_Code>
    <Product_x0020_Name>Northwind Traders Syrup</Product_x0020_Name>
    <Standard_x0020_Cost>7.5</Standard_x0020_Cost>
    <List_x0020_Price>10</List_x0020_Price>
    <Reorder_x0020_Level>25</Reorder_x0020_Level>
    <Target_x0020_Level>100</Target_x0020_Level>
    <Quantity_x0020_Per_x0020_Unit>12 - 550 ml bottles</Quantity_x0020_Per_x0020_Unit>
    <Discontinued>0</Discontinued>
    <Minimum_x0020_Reorder_x0020_Quantity>25</Minimum_x0020_Reorder_x0020_Quantity>
    <Category>Condiments</Category>
  </Products>
```

FIGURE 20.3.   The tree-like structure of the XML document.

With the XML file open in the browser, you can see the hierarchical layout of an XML document very clearly. The down arrows (or plus/minus signs in Windows 10 and earlier) make it possible to display the document as a collapsible tree. Scroll down to see the data for all the products.

The first line in the generated XML document is a dataroot element that defines two namespaces:

```
xmlns:od="urn:schemas-microsoft-com:officedata"
xmlns:xsi="http://www.w3.org/2001/XMLSchema-instance"
```

A *namespace* is a collection of names in which each name is unique. XML namespaces are used in XML documents to ensure that the tags used for element names do not conflict with one another and are unique within a set of names (a namespace).

For example, the `<TITLE>` tag will certainly have a different meaning and content in an XML document generated from the `Books` table than the `<TITLE>` element used to describe the courtesy titles of your customers. If the two XML documents containing the `<TITLE>` tag were to be merged, there would be an element name conflict. Therefore, to distinguish between tags that have the same names but need to be processed differently, namespaces are used.

The attribute `xmlns` is an XML keyword used for declaring a namespace. The namespace is identified by a Uniform Resource Identifier (URI)—either a Uniform Resource Locator (URL) or a Uniform Resource Name (URN). The URI used as an XML namespace name is simply an identifier; it is not guaranteed to point to anything. Most namespaces use URIs for the namespace names because URIs are guaranteed to be unique. The use of a namespace is identified via a name prefix, which is mapped to a URI to select a namespace.

For example, in the context of the `Products.xml` document, the `od` prefix is associated with the `urn:schemas-microsoft-com:officedata` namespace and the `xsi` prefix identifies the `http://www.w3.org/2001/XMLSchema-instance` namespace. These prefixes may be associated with other namespaces outside of this XML document. Notice that the prefix is separated from the `xmlns` attribute with a colon and the URI is used as the value of the attribute.

In addition to namespaces, the dataroot element specifies where to find the schema file. This is done by using two attributes: the location of a schema file that defines the rules of an XML document and the date the file was generated.

If you expand the dataroot element, you will notice that it encloses all the elements in the Access XML file. Each element in a tree structure is called a *node*.

The dataroot node contains child nodes for each row of the `Products` table. Notice that the table name is used for each element representing a row. Within row elements, there is a separate element for each table column, such as ID, Supplier IDS, and Product Code. Notice that each XML element contains a start tag, the element data, and the end tag. The elements listed under `Products` are children of the `Products` element. In turn, each `Products` element is a child of the dataroot element. XML documents can be nested to any depth provided that each inner node is entirely contained within the outer node.

At the end of the XML document, you should see the ending dataroot element: `</dataroot>`.

3. Close the browser containing the `Products.xml` file.

Understanding the XML Schema File

Now, let's review another type of XML file that was created by Access during the export to XML process—the XML schema file (XSD).

Schema files describe XML data using the XSD language and allow the XML parser to validate the XML document. An XML document that conforms to the structure of the schema is said to be *valid*.

Here are some examples of the types of information that can be found in an XML schema file:

- Elements that are allowed in each XML document
- Data types of allowed elements
- Number of allowed occurrences of a given element
- Attributes that can be associated with a given element
- Default values for attributes
- Child elements of other elements
- The sequence and number of child elements

(●) Hands-On 20.3   Examining the Contents of an XML Schema File

1. Use Notepad to open the `Products.xsd` file located in the `VBAAccess2024_XML` folder. Access displays the contents of the `Products.xsd` file, as shown in Figure 20.4.

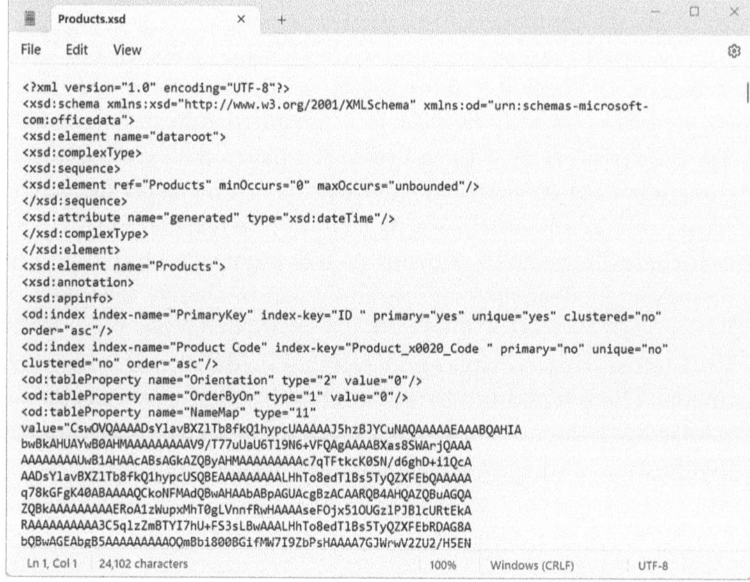

```
Products.xsd                    ×    +

File   Edit   View

<?xml version="1.0" encoding="UTF-8"?>
<xsd:schema xmlns:xsd="http://www.w3.org/2001/XMLSchema" xmlns:od="urn:schemas-microsoft-
com:officedata">
<xsd:element name="dataroot">
<xsd:complexType>
<xsd:sequence>
<xsd:element ref="Products" minOccurs="0" maxOccurs="unbounded"/>
</xsd:sequence>
<xsd:attribute name="generated" type="xsd:dateTime"/>
</xsd:complexType>
</xsd:element>
<xsd:element name="Products">
<xsd:annotation>
<xsd:appinfo>
<od:index index-name="PrimaryKey" index-key="ID " primary="yes" unique="yes" clustered="no"
order="asc"/>
<od:index index-name="Product Code" index-key="Product_x0020_Code " primary="no" unique="no"
clustered="no" order="asc"/>
<od:tableProperty name="Orientation" type="2" value="0"/>
<od:tableProperty name="OrderByOn" type="1" value="0"/>
<od:tableProperty name="NameMap" type="11"
value="CswOVQAAAADsYlavBXZ1Tb8fkQ1hypcUAAAAAJ5hzBJYCuNAQAAAAAEAAABQAHIA
bwBkAHUAYwB0AHMAAAAAAAAAV9/T77uUaU6T19N6+VFQAgAAAABXas8SWArjQAAA
AAAAAAAAUwB1AHAAcABsAGkAZQByAHMAAAAAAAAAc7qTFtkcK0SN/d6ghD+i1QcA
AADsYlavBXZ1Tb8fkQ1hypcUSQBEAAAAAAAAALHhTo8edT1Bs5TyQZXFEbQAAAAA
q78kGFgK40ABAAAAQCkoNFMAdQBwAHAAbABpAGUAcgBzACAARQB4AHQAZQBuAGQA
ZQBkAAAAAAAAAERoA1zWupxMhT0gLVnnfRwHAAAAseFOjx51OUGz1PJB1cURtEkA
RAAAAAAAAAA3C5q1zZmBTYI7hU+FS3sLBwAAALHhTo8edT1Bs5TyQZXFEbRDAG8A
bQBwAGEAbgB5AAAAAAAAAAOQmBbi800BGifMW7I9ZbPsHAAAA7GJWrwV2ZU2/H5EN

Ln 1, Col 1    24,102 characters                          100%    Windows (CRLF)    UTF-8
```

FIGURE 20.4.   The partial view of the schema file shown here defines the data in the Products.xml document.

In the `Products.xsd` file currently open in Notepad, you will notice several `xsd` declarations and commands that begin with the `<xsd>` tag followed by a colon and the name of the command. You will also notice the names of the elements and attributes that are allowed in the `Products.xml` file as well as the data types for each element. The names of the data types begin with the `od` prefix followed by a colon. The schema file also specifies the number of times an element can be used in a document based on the schema. This is done via the `minOccurs` and `maxOccurs` attributes.

2. Close Notepad and the `Products.xsd` file.

<table>
<tr><td rowspan="2">NOTE</td><td>To learn more about XML schemas, check out the following links:</td></tr>
<tr><td>http://www.w3.org/TR/xmlschema-0/
http://www.w3.org/TR/xmlschema-1/
http://www.w3.org/TR/xmlschema-2/</td></tr>
</table>

Understanding the XSL Transformation Files

When you examined the contents of the `Products.xml` document earlier in this chapter, you may have noticed that the file did not contain any formatting instructions. Although it is easy to display the XML file in any browser, end users expect to see documents that are nicely formatted. To meet their expectations, the raw XML data is usually formatted with XSL.

When you exported the `Products` table to XML and selected the Presentation of your data (XSL) checkbox in the Export XML dialog box (see Hands-On 20.1), Access generated an XSL file. XSL is a transformation style language that uses XSL Transformations (XSLT) to create templates that are applied to the source document data to create the target document. The target document can be another XML document, an HTML page, or even a text-based file.

XSL files include all the XSLT transforms that are needed to define how the data is to be presented. Transformations allow you to change the order of elements and selectively process elements. Later in this chapter, you create XSL files with XSLT transforms to display only selected fields from Access-generated XML documents. There is no limit to the number of stylesheets that can be used with a particular XML document. By creating more than one XSL file, you can present different styles of the same XML document to various users.

⦿ Hands-On 20.4   Examining the Contents of an XSL File

1. Use Notepad to open the `Products.xsl` file located in the `C:\VBAAccess2024_XML` folder. Access displays the contents of the `Products.xsl` file, as shown in Figure 20.5.

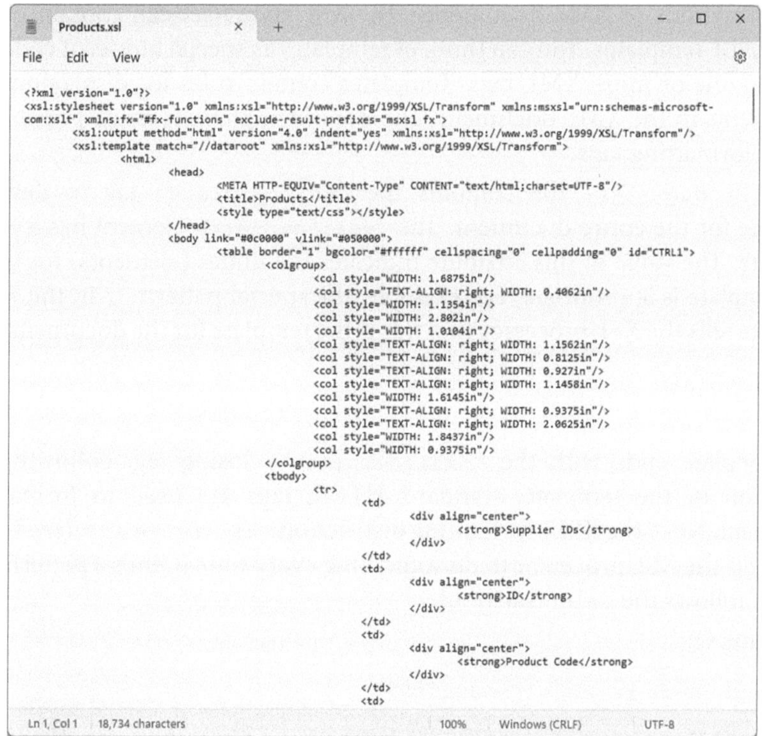

FIGURE 20.5.   The XSL stylesheet document is just another XML document that contains HTML formatting instructions and XSLT formatting elements for transforming raw XML data into HTML.

When you expand all the nodes and scroll through the contents of the `Products.xsl` file, you will notice a number of XSLT formatting elements, such as `<xsl:template>`, `<xsl:for-each>`, and `<xsl:value-of>`. You will also find many HTML formatting instructions, such as `<head>`, `<title>`, `<style>`, `<body>`, `<tbody>`, `<table>`, `<colgroup>`, `<col>`, `<tr>`, `<td>`, `<div>`, and `<strong>`.

The first line of the stylesheet code declares that this is an XML document that follows the XML 1.0 standard (version). An XSL document is a type of XML document. While XML documents store data, XSL documents specify how the data should be displayed.

The second line declares the namespace that will be used to identify the tags in the XSL document. The third line specifies that HTML should be used to display the data.

The next line is the beginning of the formatting section. Before we look at the XSLT tags, you need to know that XSL documents use templates to perform transformations of XML documents. The XSL stylesheet can contain one or more XSLT templates. You can think of templates as special blocks of code that apply to one or more XML tags. Templates contain rules for displaying a set of elements in the XML document. The use of templates is made possible via special formatting tags.

The `Products.xsl` file contains the `<xsl:template>` tag to define a template for the entire document. The `<xsl:template>` element has a `match` attribute. The value of this attribute indicates the nodes (elements) for which this template is appropriate. For example, the special pattern `//` in the `match` attribute tells the XSL processor that this is the template for the document root:

```
<xsl:template match="//dataroot"
xmlns:xsl="http://www.w3.org/1999/XSL/Transform">
```

The template ends with the `</xsl:template>` closing tag. Following the definition of the template, standard HTML tags are used to format the document. Next, the XSLT formatting instruction `<xsl:for-each>` (see Figure 20.6) tells the XSL processor to do something every time it finds a pattern. The pattern follows the `select` attribute.

For example:

```
<xsl:for-each select="Products">
```

tells the XML processor to loop through the `<Products>` elements. The loop is closed with a closing loop tag:

```
</xsl:for-each>
```

The XSLT formatting instruction `<xsl:value-of>` tells the XSL processor to retrieve the value of the tag specified in the `select` attribute.

For example, here we tell the XML processor to select the `ID` column:

```
<xsl:value-of select="ID">
```

Because this formatting instruction is located below the `<xsl:for-each>` tag, the XSL processor will retrieve the value of the `ID` column for each `Products` element. The `select` attribute uses the XML Path (XPath) language expression to locate the child elements to be processed.

If you scroll down the `Products.xsl` file, you will also notice that Access has generated several VBScript functions to evaluate expressions and running sums. To prevent the XSL processor from parsing these functions, the `function` section is placed within the `CDATA` directive (`<![CDATA[...`), as shown in Figure 20.7.

2. Close the browser containing the `Products.xsl` file.

```
<tbody id="CTRL2">
    <xsl:for-each select="Products">
            <!-- Cache the current node incase the a field is formatted -->
            <xsl:value-of select="fx:CacheCurrentNode(.)"/>
            <tr>
                <td>
                    <xsl:value-of select="Supplier_x0020_IDs"/>
                </td>
                <td>
                    <xsl:value-of select="ID"/>
                </td>
                <td>
                    <xsl:value-of select="Product_x0020_Code"/>
                </td>
                <td>
                    <xsl:value-of select="Product_x0020_Name"/>
                </td>
                <td>
                    <xsl:value-of select="Description" disable-output-escaping="yes"/>
                </td>
                <td>
                    <xsl:value-of select="fx:FormatFromXSL('Standard_x0020_Cost', 'Currency', 'auto', '1033', 6)"/>
                </td>
```

FIGURE 20.6.   The XSLT formatting instructions in the Products.xsl file.

```
</xsl:template>
<msxsl:script language="VBScript" implements-prefix="fx" xmlns:msxsl="urn:schemas-microsoft-com:xslt"><![CDATA[
Option Explicit

' *****************************************************************************
' **   Functions dynamically generated to evaluate expressions used as a Control Source
' *****************************************************************************


' *****************************************************************************
' **   Functions dynamically generated to evaluate running sums
' *****************************************************************************


' This function will calculate the running sums and expressions for the Detail section
Function CalculateExpressions_Detail(CurrentNode, GroupNodes)
        PrepExpressions CurrentNode, GroupNodes


        On Error Resume Next


        CalculateExpressions_Detail = ""
End Function


' This function will calculate the running sums and expressions for the Global section
Function CalculateExpressions_Global(CurrentNode, GroupNodes)
        PrepExpressions CurrentNode, GroupNodes


        On Error Resume Next


        CalculateExpressions_Global = ""
End Function
```

FIGURE 20.7.   The VBScript functions were automatically added to the Products.xsl file.

What Exactly Is XPath?

XPath is a query language used to create expressions for finding data in an XML data file. These expressions can manipulate strings, numbers, and Boolean values. They can also be used to navigate an XML tree structure and process its elements with XSLT instructions. XPath is designed to be used by XSLT. With XPath expressions, you can easily identify and extract from the XML document specific elements (nodes) based on their type, name, values, or the relationship of a node to other nodes. When preparing stylesheets for transforming your XML documents into HTML, you will often use various XPath expressions in the `select` attribute.

<table>
<tr><td>NOTE</td><td>For more information about XSL, visit http://www.w3.org/TR/xsl/</td></tr>
</table>

VIEWING XML DOCUMENTS FORMATTED WITH STYLESHEETS

When you exported the `Products` table to XML format, Access applied XSLT transforms to turn the XML data into an HTML file called `Products.htm`. Figure 20.8 displays the contents of this file. Let's spend a few minutes reviewing the code statements in this file.

Notice that when the HTML page loads, it executes the VBScript `Apply-Transform` function, which appears in the `<SCRIPT>` block just below the ending `</BODY>` tag.

VBScript is a scripting language introduced by Microsoft in 1996. It uses a software component called the XML Document Object Model (DOM) that provides methods and properties for working with XML programmatically, allowing you to output and transform the XML data.

The `DOMDocument` object is the top level of the XML DOM hierarchy and represents a tree structure composed of nodes. You can navigate through this tree structure and manipulate the data contained in the nodes by using various methods and properties. Because every XML object is created and accessed from `DOMDocument`, you must first create the `DOMDocument` object to work with an XML document.

The `ApplyTransform` function begins by setting an object variable (`objData`) to an instance of `DOMDocument` that's returned by a custom `CreateDOM` function. This function creates a reference to the `DOMDocument` via the `CreateObject` method of the `Server` object. Because different versions of the MSXML parser may be installed on a client machine (`DOMDocument6`, `DOMDocument5`, `DOMDocument4`, etc.), the function attempts to instantiate the `DOMDocument` object using the most recent version. If such a version is not found, it looks for older versions of the MSXML parser that may exist. It is extremely important that only one version of the `DOMDocument` is used, since mixing `DOMDocument` objects from different versions of the MSXML parser can cause ugly errors.

Once the `DOMDocument` object has been instantiated, the `LoadDOM` function listed at the bottom of the page is called. This function expects two parameters: `objDOM`, which is the `objData` variable referencing the `DOMDocument`, and `strX-MLFile`, which is the name of the file to load into the `DOMDocument` object. To

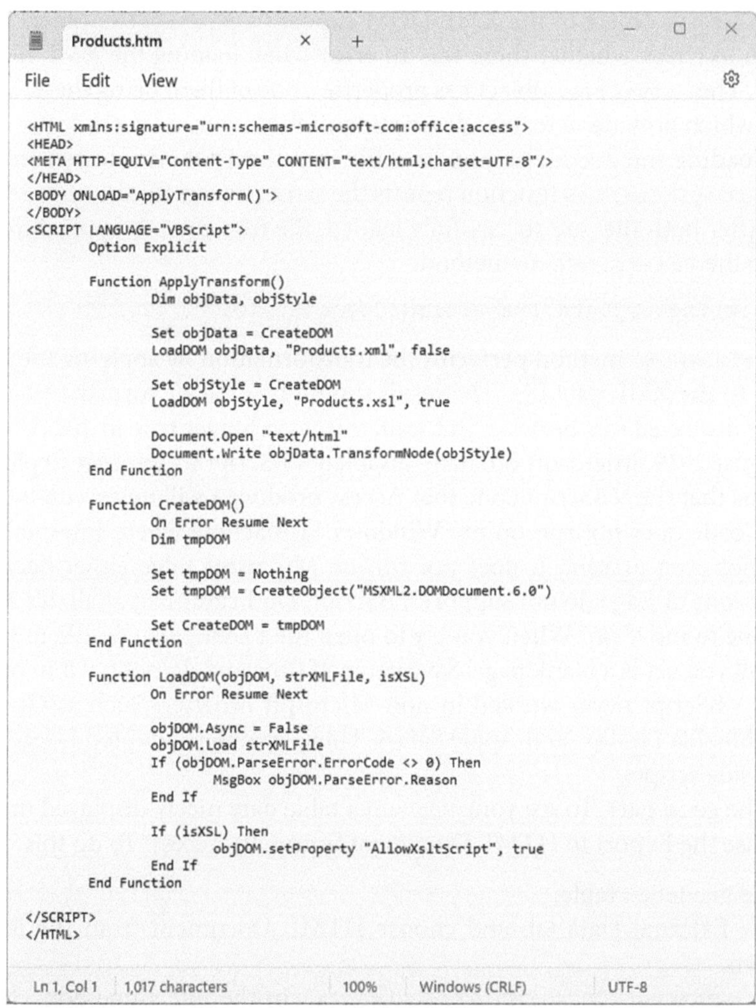

```
<HTML xmlns:signature="urn:schemas-microsoft-com:office:access">
<HEAD>
<META HTTP-EQUIV="Content-Type" CONTENT="text/html;charset=UTF-8"/>
</HEAD>
<BODY ONLOAD="ApplyTransform()">
</BODY>
<SCRIPT LANGUAGE="VBScript">
        Option Explicit

        Function ApplyTransform()
                Dim objData, objStyle

                Set objData = CreateDOM
                LoadDOM objData, "Products.xml", false

                Set objStyle = CreateDOM
                LoadDOM objStyle, "Products.xsl", true

                Document.Open "text/html"
                Document.Write objData.TransformNode(objStyle)
        End Function

        Function CreateDOM()
                On Error Resume Next
                Dim tmpDOM

                Set tmpDOM = Nothing
                Set tmpDOM = CreateObject("MSXML2.DOMDocument.6.0")

                Set CreateDOM = tmpDOM
        End Function

        Function LoadDOM(objDOM, strXMLFile, isXSL)
                On Error Resume Next

                objDOM.Async = False
                objDOM.Load strXMLFile
                If (objDOM.ParseError.ErrorCode <> 0) Then
                        MsgBox objDOM.ParseError.Reason
                End If

                If (isXSL) Then
                        objDOM.setProperty "AllowXsltScript", true
                End If
        End Function

</SCRIPT>
</HTML>
```


FIGURE 20.8.   Access-generated Products.htm file opened in Windows Notepad.

ensure that the browser waits until all the data is loaded before rendering the
rest of the page, the `Async` property of the `DOMDocument` is set to `False`:

```
objDOM.Async = False
objDOM.Load strXMLFile
```

The `Load` method is used to load the supplied file into the `objData` object variable. This method returns `True` if it successfully loaded the data and `False` otherwise. If there is a problem with loading, a description of the error is returned
in a message box.

The `Document` object of the XML DOM exposes a `parseError` object that allows you to check whether there was an error when loading the XML file or stylesheet. The `ParseError` object has properties, one of them being the `Reason` property, which provides a textual description of the error.

After loading the `Products.xml` data file into the DOM software component, the `ApplyTransform` function repeats the same process for the `Products.xsl` file. After both files are successfully loaded, the transform is applied to the data using the `TransformNode` method:

```
document.Write objData.TransformNode(objStyle)
```

The `TransformNode` method performs the transformation by applying the XSL stylesheet to the XML data file. The result should be a nicely formatted `Products` table displayed in a browser. But wait, this is no longer true in 2024!

In August 2019, Microsoft officially disabled VBScript in Internet Explorer. This means that the VBScript code that Access produced will never run by default. The code does not run on my Windows 11 machine where Internet Explorer is not even present. It does not run on Microsoft Edge either because recent versions of Edge do not support VBScript. Do I care? Not at all. It's 2025 and it's time to move on. When you try to open the `Products.htm` file in your browser, all you get is a blank page. Save yourself time and do not try it in other browsers. VBScript never worked in non-Microsoft browsers such as Google Chrome, Mozilla Firefox, and Apple Safari. Those browsers adopted JavaScript for client-side scripts.

Now, the good part. To see your `Products` table data nicely displayed in any browser, use the Export to HTML Document feature in Access. To do this:

1. Open the `Products` table.
2. Click the External Data tab and choose HTML Document from the More dropdown.
3. Enter `C:\VBAAccess2024_XML\Products.html` in the File name box, check the box next to Export data with formatting and layout, and click OK.
4. In the HTML Output Options dialog box, click OK while the Default encoding is selected.
5. Click Close to exit the Save Export Step dialog.
6. Double-click the `Products.html` file in the `C:/VBAAccess2024_XML` folder. Note that there are two HTML files in this folder. The one with `.htm` was generated by Access when we exported the table to XML format, and the other one, with the `.html` extension, is the file you generated just now with these instructions.

The result of exporting to an HTML document is shown in Figure 20.9.

Products

Supplier IDs	ID	Product Code	Product Name	Description	Standard Cost	List Price	Reorder Level	Target Level	Quantity Per Unit	Discontinued	Minimum Reorder Quantity	Category	Attachments
Supplier D	1	NWTB-1	Northwind Traders Chai		$13.50	$18.00	10	40	10 boxes x 20 bags	No	10	Beverages	0
Supplier J	3	NWTCO-3	Northwind Traders Syrup		$7.50	$10.00	25	100	12 - 550 ml bottles	No	25	Condiments	0
Supplier J	4	NWTCO-4	Northwind Traders Cajun Seasoning		$16.50	$22.00	10	40	48 - 6 oz jars	No	10	Condiments	0
Supplier J	5	NWTO-5	Northwind Traders Olive Oil		$16.01	$21.35	10	40	36 boxes	No	10	Oil	0
Supplier B, Supplier F	6	NWTJP-6	Northwind Traders Boysenberry Spread		$18.75	$25.00	25	100	12 - 8 oz jars	No	25	Jams, Preserves	0
Supplier B	7	NWTDFN-7	Northwind Traders Dried Pears		$22.50	$30.00	10	40	12 - 1 lb pkgs.	No	10	Dried Fruit & Nuts	0
Supplier H	8	NWTS-8	Northwind Traders Curry Sauce		$30.00	$40.00	10	40	12 - 12 oz jars	No	10	Sauces	0
Supplier B, Supplier F	14	NWTDFN-14	Northwind Traders Walnuts		$17.44	$23.25	10	40	40 - 100 g pkgs.	No	10	Dried Fruit & Nuts	0
Supplier F	17	NWTCFV-17	Northwind Traders Fruit Cocktail		$29.25	$39.00	10	40	15.25 OZ	No	10	Canned Fruit & Vegetables	0
Supplier A	19	NWTBGM-19	Northwind Traders Chocolate Biscuits Mix		$6.90	$9.20	5	20	10 boxes x 12 pieces	No	5	Baked Goods & Mixes	0

FIGURE 20.9.   Access-generated Products.html file opened in the Microsoft Edge browser.

ADVANCED XML EXPORT OPTIONS

When you exported the `Products` table to XML format, you may have noticed the More Options… button in the Export XML dialog box. Pressing this button opens a window with three tabs, as shown in Figure 20.10. Each tab organizes options for the types of XML objects that you can export. The Data tab contains options for the XML document, the Schema tab lists options for the XSD document, and the Presentation tab provides options for generating the XSL document.

Data Export Options

The options shown on the Data tab (see Figure 20.10) control the data that is exported to the XML documents. These options are grouped into three main areas.

The Data to Export section displays data that you may want to export. In this particular scenario, the `Customers` table has been chosen for export. Because this table is directly related to the `Orders` table in the `Northwind 2007` database, the `Orders` table is displayed as a child node of `Customers`. The `Orders` table is related to the `Order Details` table and so on. Clicking on the plus sign in front of the [Lookup Data] node will display the names of tables that provide lookup information for the main tables. By clicking on the checkbox, you may export just the table that you originally requested, or you can export the customers' data along with all the orders, and perhaps include lookup information.

Below the Data to Export section is the Export Location area, which shows the filename for the XML document that will be created when you click the OK button. You can change the location of this document by using the Browse button. Simply navigate to the folder where you want to save the XML file. You can also change the name of the document by replacing the name shown in the text box with another name.

The area to the right of the Data to Export section allows you to specify which records you want to export. This area contains three option buttons that allow you to export all records, filtered records, or the current record. Notice that only one option is enabled in Figure 20.10.

When you highlight the table to export in the database window and then choose the Export command from the File menu, only the All Records option button will be enabled in the Records To Export section. Opening the table prior to choosing the Export command tells Access to enable the All Records and Current record option buttons. Also, if you open the table and apply a filter to the data, then select the Export command, Access will enable the Apply existing filter option button in addition to the other two options.

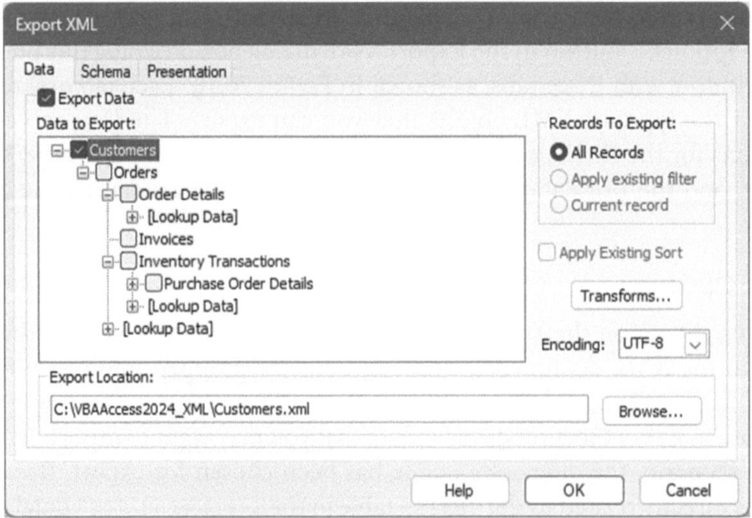

FIGURE 20.10.   Use the Data tab in the Export XML window to set advanced data options.

The other options on the Data tab are Apply Existing Sort, Transforms…, and Encoding. The Apply Existing Sort checkbox is enabled if the exported object is open and a sort is applied. Access will export the data in the specified sort order. Clicking the Transforms… button allows you to select a custom XSL transform file to apply to the data during export. You can choose from the transforms you have written yourself or received with the XML data.

Use the Encoding drop-down list to select UTF-8 or UTF-16 encoding for the exported XML. The default is UTF-8.

When you export an object from an Access database file, Access exports static data. This means that the exported object is not automatically updated when the data changes. If the data in the Access database has changed since you exported an Access object to an XML data file, you will need to re-export the object so the new data is available to the client application.

NOTE	*Exporting live data is supported by Access data projects (.adp file format) in Access 2010. Support for ADP was removed in Access 2013, therefore additional options related to Access data projects are not discussed here.*

Schema Export Options

The options shown on the Schema tab (see Figure 20.11) control the way the schema file for the object is exported. Advanced schema options are presented in two sections: Export Schema and Export Location.

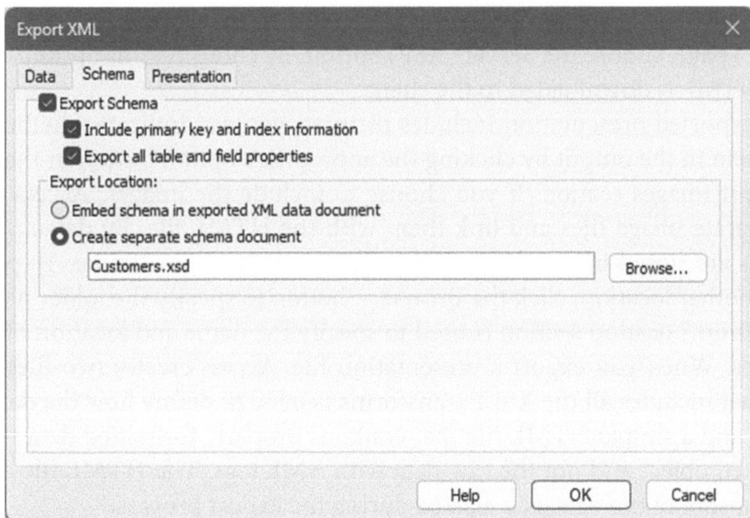

FIGURE 20.11. Use the Schema tab in the Export XML dialog box to set advanced schema options.

The Export Schema section has two checkboxes. By selecting the Export Schema checkbox, you indicate that you want to export the object's schema as an XSD file. This selection is the same as choosing the Schema of the data (XSD) option in the first Export XML dialog box (see Figure 20.1). The checkboxes under Export Schema allow you to specify whether you want to include primary key and index information in the XSD schema file, and whether to export all table and field properties.

The Export Location section has two option buttons used to specify whether the schema information must be embedded in the exported XML data document or stored in a separate schema file. You can enter the filename in the provided text box and specify the location of the schema file by clicking the Browse… button.

Presentation Export Options

The selections on the Presentation tab (see Figure 20.12) specify available options for the XSL files. The Export Presentation (HTML 4.0 Sample XSL) checkbox allows you to indicate whether you want to export the object's presentation. Choose the Client (HTML) option in the Run from section if you want the presentation to run on the client. Access will create an HTML file with the script necessary to perform the transform. The script will be executed on the client (user) machine. While this selection reduces the load on the server, a client application will need to download a few files (HTML document, XML data file, and XSD schema file) to present the data in the browser. If the XSL file is going to be placed on the Web server and called from a classic Active Server Page (ASP) page, choose the Server (ASP) option. By choosing this option, only the final HTML is downloaded to the client.

If the exported presentation includes pictures, you can indicate whether to include them in the output by clicking the appropriate option button in the Include report images section. If you choose to include the images, Access will create separate image files and link them with the HTML file. By default, the image files are stored in the `Images` folder of the main export folder. To place them in another location, click the Browse… button to specify the folder name.

The Export Location section is used to specify the name and location of the export files. When you export a presentation file, Access creates two files: an XSL file that includes all the XSLT transforms needed to define how the data is presented and a simple HTML file that contains properly formatted data from the exported object and not the raw data with XML tags. The HTML file contains a snapshot of the data as it existed during the export process.

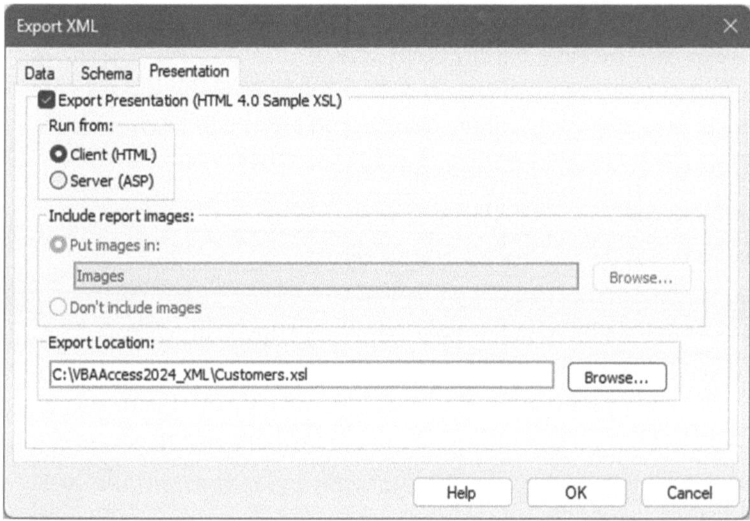

FIGURE 20.12.   Use the Presentation tab in the Export XML dialog box to set advanced presentation options.

(⊙) **Hands-On 20.5   Advanced Export of the Customers table to XML and ASP**

1. Open the `Customers` table in the `VBAAccess2024_XML\Northwind 2007.accdb` database.
2. Choose External Data | More | XML File.
3. Enter `C:\VBAAccess2024_XML\Customers_Server.xml` in the File name box and click OK.
4. In the Export XML dialog box, make sure the first two checkboxes are selected and then click the More Options… button.
5. In the Data tab of the Export XML dialog box, ensure that the Customers table is selected for Export of All Records and the export location is pointed to `C:\VBAAccess2024_XML\Customers_Server.xml`.
6. Click the Schema tab in the same Export XML dialog box.
7. In the Schema tab, make sure that a separate schema document option button is selected and both checkboxes are checked under the Export Schema section. Enter the full path and name of the schema file as `C:\VBAAccess2024_XML\Customers_Server.xsd`. Do not click OK.
8. Click the Presentation tab in the same Export XML dialog box.
9. Select Export Presentation (HTML 4.0 Sample XSL) and run it from Server (ASP). Enter `C:\VBAAccess2024_XML\Customers_Server.xsl`.

10. Click OK to finish setting up the Export XML.

11. Click Close to exit the Save Export Steps screen.

12. Open the File Explorer and ensure that Access has generated four new files in the `C:\VBAAccess2024_XML` folder. You should see the following files:

Customers_Server.asp	Active Server Page
Customers_Server.xml	XML Document
Customers_Server.xsd	XML Schema File
Customers_Server.xsl	XSLT Stylesheet

Now that the `Customers` data has been generated, how can you view this data? ASP is a text file with an `.asp` extension. Because this file is located on your computer, you can open it with Windows Notepad. Once this file is placed on a Web server, however, only authorized people will be able to access it.

13. Use Windows Notepad to open the `Customers_Server.asp` file to view its source code (see Figure 20.13).

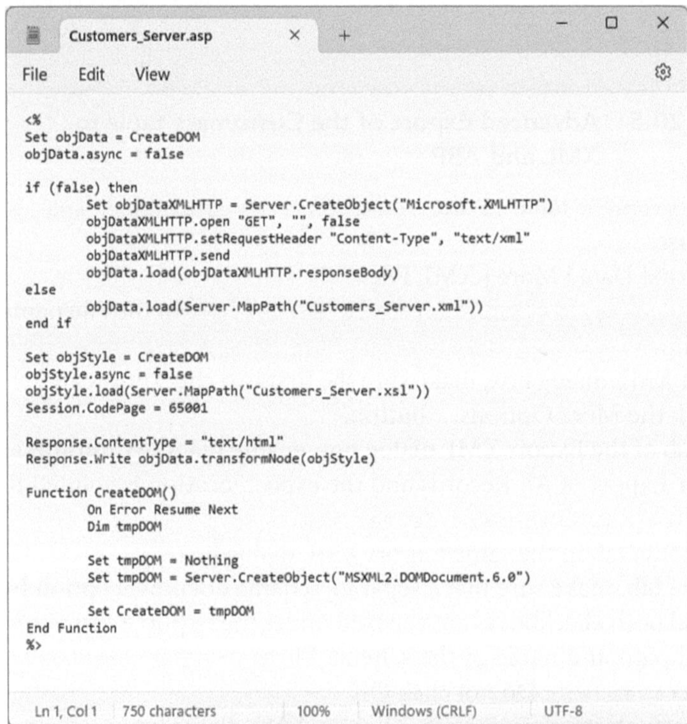

```
<%
Set objData = CreateDOM
objData.async = false

if (false) then
        Set objDataXMLHTTP = Server.CreateObject("Microsoft.XMLHTTP")
        objDataXMLHTTP.open "GET", "", false
        objDataXMLHTTP.setRequestHeader "Content-Type", "text/xml"
        objDataXMLHTTP.send
        objData.load(objDataXMLHTTP.responseBody)
else
        objData.load(Server.MapPath("Customers_Server.xml"))
end if

Set objStyle = CreateDOM
objStyle.async = false
objStyle.load(Server.MapPath("Customers_Server.xsl"))
Session.CodePage = 65001

Response.ContentType = "text/html"
Response.Write objData.transformNode(objStyle)

Function CreateDOM()
        On Error Resume Next
        Dim tmpDOM

        Set tmpDOM = Nothing
        Set tmpDOM = Server.CreateObject("MSXML2.DOMDocument.6.0")

        Set CreateDOM = tmpDOM
End Function
%>
```

FIGURE 20.13.   The source code of the Customers_Server.asp file generated by Access.

ASP files allow you to create dynamic Web pages where information is updated dynamically from the connected data source. In this case, the data source is the Access-generated XML file. ASP files can include standard HTML formatting tags, embedded scripting statements, and references to other files. VBScript, which is a subset of VBA, is the scripting language for ASP. As you review the file, you will notice that it begins with `<%` and ends with the `%>` delimiter. The statements that appear between these delimiters constitute the VBScript code that will be executed on the Web server once the connection with it is established.

The VBScript code uses a software component called the XML DOM. The DOM offers methods and properties for working with XML programmatically, allowing you to output and transform the XML data.

The `DOMDocument` object is the top level of the XML DOM hierarchy and represents a tree structure composed of nodes. You can navigate through this tree structure and manipulate the data contained in the nodes by using various methods and properties. Because every XML object is created and accessed from `DOMDocument`, you must first create the `DOMDocument` object to work with an XML document. Therefore, the first statement in the `Customers_Server.asp` file sets an object variable (`objData`) to an instance of `DOMDocument` that's returned by a custom `CreateDOM` function:

```
Set objData = CreateDOM
```

The `CreateDOM` function sets a reference to the `DOMDocument` via the `CreateObject` method of the `Server` object. Once the `DOMDocument` object has been instantiated, the second statement in the file ensures that the browser waits until all the data is loaded before rendering the rest of the page. This is done by setting the `Async` property of the `DOMDocument` to `false`.

The next step is to make sure that we can send and receive information to and from a Web server. This is done by creating an instance of the `Microsoft.XMLHTTP` object. We store the reference to this object in the object variable `objDataXMLHTTP`. The `open` method is then used to open the connection to a Web server. The `open` method takes several arguments:

- The first argument specifies the type of HTTP protocol being called. In this case, we use the simple `GET` protocol.
- The second argument contains the `URL` that is being targeted. In this case, we use an empty string (`""`) to indicate that we are calling the current ASP page.

- The third argument, which is set to `false`, tells the browser to send the request and wait for the reply.
- The next statement sends some extra information to the server to inform it about the type of data being sent to it. This is done via the `setRequestHeader` property of the `XMLHTTP` object.
- The `Content-Type` header informs the server that the document being sent is the XML document. Notice that `Content-Type` is set to `text/xml`.

The code then uses the `send` method to send the request via the `HTTP GET` protocol specified in the `open` method. `send` opens a connection to the Web server and sends the header information that was specified earlier. At this point, the Web server will send back a set of headers with the status information so the browser can display error messages, if necessary. If the connection succeeds, the statement in the `Else` clause will load the specified XML file for processing by the Web server.

The `Load` method is used to load the supplied file into the `objData` object variable. This method returns `True` if it successfully loaded the data and `False` otherwise. After loading the `Customer_Server.xml` data file into the DOM, the transform is applied to the data using the `transformNode` method. The `transformNode` method performs the transformation by applying the XSL stylesheet to the XML data file.

After both XML and XSL files have been processed, the following statement is executed:

```
objData.load(objDataXMLHTTP.responseBody)
```

The `responseBody` property of the `XMLHTTP` object returns the data from the server as an HTML document, as depicted in Figure 20.14.

14. Close the `Customers_Server.asp` file.

    Now that you know what the VBScript code looks like, let's prepare your environment for running this code. In the next step, you are referred to Appendix C, where you will find step-by-step instructions on how to set up Internet Information Services (IIS) on your computer. IIS is a built-in Web server provided by the Microsoft Windows operating system. Because this server is turned off by default, you will need to enable and configure it before it can be accessed.

15. Go to Appendix C and follow the steps of setting up and configuring IIS. Once completed, return here and continue with step 16.

16. Open your favorite browser and, in the address bar, type the following URL and press Enter: `http://localhost/acc_xml/Customers_Server.asp`. `localhost` is the name of the Web server that you enabled on your computer. `acc_xml` is the name of the virtual folder where the ASP script and other supporting files are located. Your browser sends the request to the Web server to process the `Customers_Server.asp` file, and once the request is processed, your browser receives the response, and the resulting data is shown in Figure 20.14. If you encountered an error, read on to find out how to correct it.

ID	Company	Last Name	First Name	E-mail Address	Job Title	Business Phone	Home Phone	Mobile Phone	Fax Number	Address	City	State/Province	ZIP/Postal Code	Country/Region	Web Page	Notes	Attachments
1	Company A	Bedecs	Anna		Owner	(123)555-0100			(123)555-0101	123 1st Street	Seattle	WA	99999	USA			
2	Company B	Gratacos Solsona	Antonio		Owner	(123)555-0100			(123)555-0101	123 2nd Street	Boston	MA	99999	USA			
3	Company C	Axen	Thomas		Purchasing Representative	(123)555-0100			(123)555-0101	123 3rd Street	Los Angelas	CA	99999	USA			
4	Company D	Lee	Christina		Purchasing Manager	(123)555-0100			(123)555-0101	123 4th Street	New York	NY	99999	USA			
5	Company E	O'Donnell	Martin		Owner	(123)555-0100			(123)555-0101	123 5th Street	Minneapolis	MN	99999	USA			
6	Company F	Pérez-Olaeta	Francisco		Purchasing Manager	(123)555-0100			(123)555-0101	123 6th Street	Milwaukee	WI	99999	USA			
7	Company G	Xie	Ming-Yang		Owner	(123)555-0100			(123)555-0101	123 7th Street	Boise	ID	99999	USA			
8	Company H	Andersen	Elizabeth		Purchasing Representative	(123)555-0100			(123)555-0101	123 8th Street	Portland	OR	99999	USA			
9	Company I	Mortensen	Sven		Purchasing Manager	(123)555-0100			(123)555-0101	123 9th Street	Salt Lake City	UT	99999	USA			

FIGURE 20.14.   Customers data is generated from Access by running an ASP that queries the data contained in an XML file and formats it with the stylesheet.

NOTE

Errors happen everywhere. There are no perfect programs, thus programmers need to acquire skills to troubleshoot various types of errors, whether they are their own or created by others. Here, is a file created entirely by Access, without us messing with its code, which may produce the following error:

```
msxml6.dll error '80004005'
Security settings do not allow the execution of
script code within this stylesheet.
/acc_xml/Customers_Server.asp, line 21
```

What seems to be the problem? How do you fix this security issue? The error references a specific line. Open the file in Notepad and see which line it is. If you turn on the Status bar from the View menu, you will be able to easily identify the line number as you click around. It looks like the problem is on the line with the following code:

```
Response.Write objData.transformNode(objStyle)
```

> *Here, the server is trying to work with the stylesheet, and it needs some permissions. In programming, the rights are often given by setting properties of objects. The following statement placed above the problem line should provide the needed correction:*
>
> ```
> objStyle.setProperty "AllowXsltScript", true
>
> Response.Write objData.transformNode(objStyle)
> ```
>
> *To find out the solution to an issue you encounter while executing code written by yourself or others, Google the error code and error message to see whether a solution was already posted somewhere. If not, try to look at other code that Access has generated to see whether you can spot any differences. In this case, I compared the* `Products.htm` *file generated by Access that contains the client-side VBScript code and found that it contained the following line, which was not included in the server-side VBScript code:*
>
> ```
> objDOM.setProperty "AllowXsltScript", true
> ```
>
> *The problem was fixed by adding the same statement to the problem file, just making sure that it references the correct object.*
>
> *If you encounter other types of errors, for example, A provider cannot be found, you may need to download the 2007 Office System Driver Data Connectivity Components. It's hard to foresee what kinds of errors you may be faced with while working with this book, as your machine will be configured differently than mine and may be missing some older components that are still required to run on newer systems and that are never installed until they are needed. Each system is unique and the recommended troubleshooting steps may or may not work. Solving your own problems is a skill that takes time to build; the more troubleshooting you perform by yourself, the more skillful you become.*

17. When you fix the error, go back to step 16 to test the file again.

18. Close the browser and proceed to the next section.

APPLYING XSLT TRANSFORMS TO EXPORTED DATA

When exporting Access data to XML format, you can use custom transformation files (XSL) to modify the data after you export it. Hands-On 20.6 demonstrates how to create a custom stylesheet for use after export. This stylesheet assumes that for each customer in the Customers table, we want to display only selected columns from the Orders table. You will learn how to apply this custom stylesheet in Hands-On 20.7.

⦿ Hands-On 20.6   Creating a Custom Transformation File

1. Open Notepad and enter the following statements:

```
<?xml version="1.0" encoding="UTF-8"?>
<xsl:stylesheet version="1.0" xmlns:xsl=
                          "http://www.w3.org/1999/XSL/Transform">
<xsl:output method="html" version="4.0" indent="yes"/>

<xsl:template match="dataroot">
  <html>
  <body>
  <h2 style="font-family:Verdana">Customer Orders</h2>
  <p/>
  <xsl:apply-templates select="Customers"/>
  </body>
  </html>
</xsl:template>

<xsl:template match="Customers">
<table>
  <tr>
  <td style="background-color:#FFCC33; color:#000000;">
  <xsl:value-of select="ID"/>
  </td>
  <td><b>
  <xsl:value-of select="Company"/>
  </b></td>
  </tr>
</table>
<table cellpadding="5" cellspacing="5">
  <tr style="background-color:black; color:white;">
  <td style="background-color:black; width:10px;"/>
  <td>Order ID</td>
  <td>Order Date</td>
  <td>Shipped Date</td>
  <td>Shipping Fee</td>
  </tr>
  <xsl:apply-templates select="Orders"/>
</table>
</xsl:template>
```

```
<xsl:template match="Orders">
<tr>
<td style="background-color:black; width:10px;"/>
<td><xsl:value-of select="Order_x0020_ID"/></td>
<td><xsl:value-of select="substring(Order_x0020_Date,
                                    1, 10)"/></td>
<td><xsl:value-of select="substring(Shipped_x0020_Date,
                                    1, 10)"/></td>
<td>$<xsl:value-of select="format-number(Shipping_x0020_
                                    Fee,'####0.00')"/>
</td>
</tr>
</xsl:template>

</xsl:stylesheet>
```

2. Save the file as `C:\VBAAccess2024_XML\ListCustOrders.xsl`. You must include the file extension to ensure that the file is not saved as text.
3. Close Notepad.

   The `ListCustOrders.xsl` file will be used to transform XML to HTML in the next hands-on exercise. Because the XSLT stylesheet is an XML document, we need to start out with a standard XML declaration like this:

```
<?xml version="1.0" encoding="UTF-8"?>
```

Next, we define the namespace for the stylesheet and declare its prefix like this:

```
<xsl:stylesheet version="1.0"
xmlns:xsl="http://www.w3.org/1999/XSL/Transform">
```

On the third line, we use the `<xsl:output>` tag to indicate that XSLT should transform the XML into HTML:

```
<xsl:output method="html" version="4.0" indent="yes"/>
```

The `<xsl:output>` tag has three attributes: `method`, `version`, and `indent`. The `method` attribute specifies the format of the output. This can be XML, HTML, or text. The `version` attribute sets the version number for the output format. The `indent` attribute, which is set to `"yes"` in this example, indicates that the XML should be indented. This will make the final XML document more readable when viewed in the browser.

   The remaining part of the XSL file contains transformation instructions for the XML document element nodes. We begin by creating the root template. The `<xsl:template>` tag initiates a template within a stylesheet. Because a template must indicate which nodes we want to use, we use the tag's `match` attribute to supply the node information:

```
<xsl:template match="dataroot">
```

This tells the XSLT processor to extract the XML document's root node. The root node provides a base node upon which we will build the HTML Web page. Notice that in the root template, we need to include the `<html>` and `<body>` tags to create the structure of the final document. HTML tags such as `<h2>`, `<font>`, and `<p>` are used to add the required formatting. In the root template, we are also telling the XSLT processor that it should apply the template rules found in the `Customers` template (defined further down in the file):

```
<xsl:apply-templates select="Customers"/>
```

When the XSLT processor encounters the `<xsl:apply-templates>` instruction, it will proceed to the following line:

```
<xsl:template match="Customers">
```

This line marks the beginning of the `Customers` template rule. Within it, there are HTML tags as well as other XSLT processing instructions. For example, to output the ID, we use the `<xsl:value-of>` tag with the select attribute like this:

```
<xsl:value-of select="ID"/>
```

Because the `<xsl:value-of>` tag does not have any content, you must end it with the forward slash (/). Notice that we placed the value of the `ID` field in a table cell. Using the same approach, we can output the `Company` column, like this:

```
<xsl:value-of select="Company"/>
```

Next, we define the column headings for the `Orders` table. For a special effect, we add to the output a 10-pixel-wide dummy column with a black background:

```
<td style="background-color:black; width:10px;"/>
```

We also tell the XSLT processor to apply the `Orders` template:

```
<xsl:apply-templates select="Orders"/>
```

The `Orders` template rules indicate how to extract values for each of the defined column headings. This is done by using the `<xsl:value-of>` tag with the `select` attribute, like this:

```
<td><xsl:value-of select="Order_x0020_ID"/></td>
```

```
<td><xsl:value-of select="substring(Order_x0020_Date,
                                    1, 10)"/></td>
<td><xsl:value-of select="substring(Shipped_x0020_Date,
                                    1, 10)"/></td>
<td>
$<xsl:value-of select="format-number(Shipping_x0020_
                                    Fee,'####0.00')"/>
</td>
```

Notice that the space found in the column name must be replaced with _x0020_.

To obtain only the date portion from the Order Date and Shipped Date columns, we use the XPath `substring` function in the `select` attribute. This function has the same syntax as the VBA `Mid` function, allowing you to extract a specified number of characters from a string starting at a specific position. The following expression tells the XSLT processor to retrieve only the first 10 characters from the value found in the Order Date column:

```
<xsl:value-of select="substring(Order_x0020_Date, 1, 10)"/>
```

To correctly format the Shipping Fee column, the `format-number` XPath expression is used like this:

```
$<xsl:value-of select="format-number(Shipping_x0020_
                                    Fee,'####0.00')"/>
```

This tells the XSLT processor to format the value found in the Shipping Fee column as a number using two decimal places.

Each of the defined template rules ends with the `</xsl:template>` ending tag and the stylesheet itself ends with the `</xsl:stylesheet>` tag.

This concludes your first custom stylesheet. While this is a basic stylesheet to get you started, in real life, you will probably want to create stylesheets that can use the following:

- Batch-processing nodes (`<xsl:for-each>` tag with the `select` attribute)
- Conditional processing of nodes (`<xsl:if>` tag with the `test` attribute)
- Decisions based on conditions (`<xsl:choose>` tag and `<xsl:when>` tag with the `test` attribute)
- Sorting nodes before processing (`<xsl:sort>` tag with the `select` attribute)

NOTE	*For more information about XSLT, visit the following link: http://www.w3.org/TR/xslt#section-Applying-Template-Rules*

Now that you have a custom stylesheet, let's see what you can do with it. Hands-On 20.7 demonstrates how to export data from an Access table directly to an HTML file and apply a custom transform so that only the specified columns are displayed.

(◉) Hands-On 20.7   Exporting Data and Applying a Custom XSL File

1. Make sure that you open the `C:\VBAAccess2024_XML\Northwind 2007.accdb` database.
2. In the Navigation Pane, right-click the Customers table and choose Export | XML File.
3. In the File name box, enter `C:\VBAAccess2024_XML\ListCustOrders.xml` and click OK.
4. In the Export XML dialog box, make sure that the first two checkboxes are selected. Click the More Options… button.
5. In the Data to Export area, the Customers table is automatically selected. Click the checkbox next to the Orders table to include it in the export.
6. Click the Transforms button.
7. In the Export Transforms window that appears, click the Add button, switch to the `C:\VBAAccess2024_XML` folder, and select the ListCustOrders.xsl file that you created in the previous hands-on exercise. Click the Add button to add this file to the list of transforms. The transformation file appears in the list, as shown in Figure 20.15.
8. In the Export Transforms window, click OK.

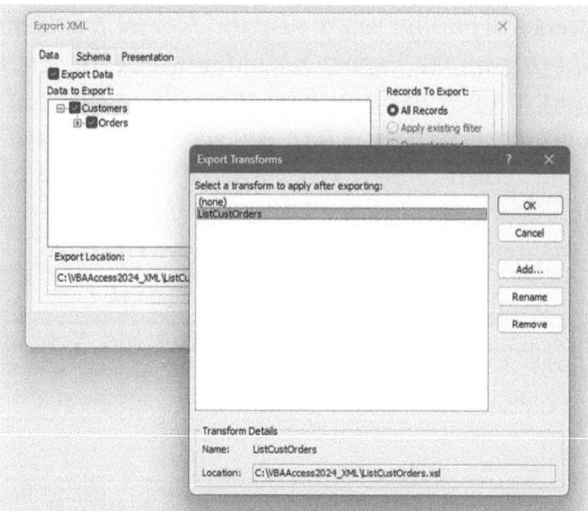

FIGURE 20.15.   Use this window to indicate a transformation file (stylesheet) to be used after export.

9. Back in the Export XML dialog box, change the file extension from `.xml` to `.html`, as shown in Figure 20.16.

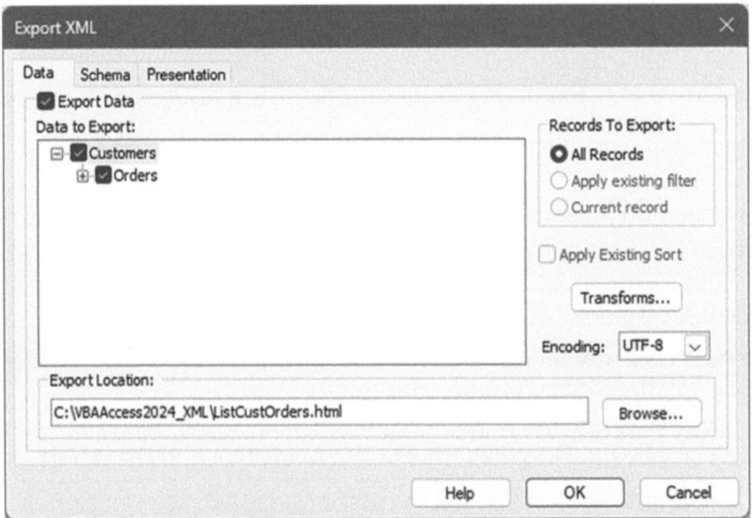

FIGURE 20.16.   To export XML data directly to the HTML file, you must choose the transformation file using the Transforms button and change the file extension from .xml to .html.

10. Click the OK button to begin the export.

11. Upon the successful export operation, click Close.

NOTE	*If the selected transformation file is invalid, you will see an error message. Access will prompt you to save the data for troubleshooting and will bring up the Export XML dialog box. At this time, you may want to open the transformation file in Notepad and make appropriate corrections. Once you save the corrected XSL file, you should return to the Export XML dialog box to try the export again. Before you click the OK button in the Export XML dialog box, ensure that the appropriate tables are selected.*

12. Close the `Northwind 2007` database and exit Access.

13. In the File Explorer, double-click the ListCustOrders.html file. Your output should match Figure 20.17.

14. Close the browser window.

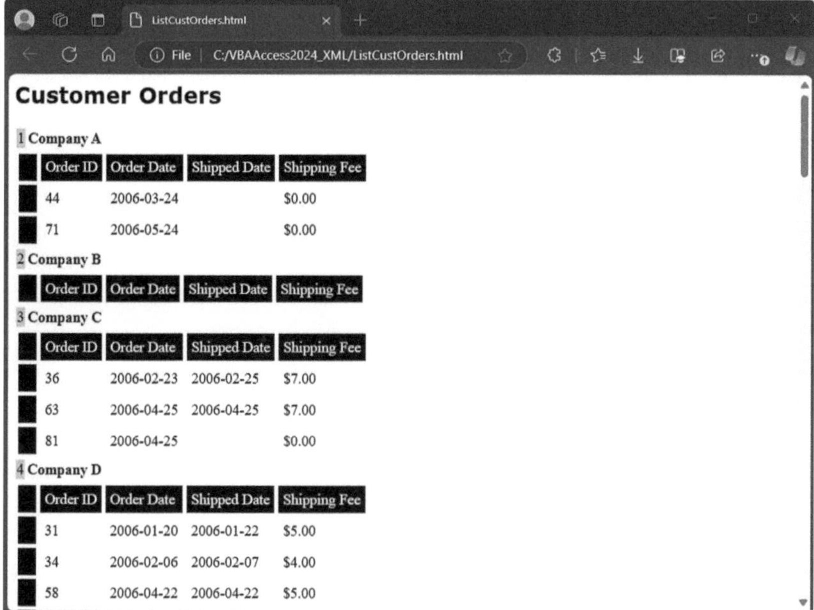

FIGURE 20.17.   XML data can be formatted any way you like by applying a custom transformation.

IMPORTING XML DATA TO ACCESS

The Access built-in Import command allows you to import an XML data or schema document to a database. When you import a structure or data from an XML file, Access assigns the `Text` data type to all the fields in a table. When you import a structure from an XSD schema file, however, each field is assigned a data type that closely matches the data type specified in the schema. You can change the data types after importing data or a table structure as long as the fields' data allows such a change.

Importing a Schema File

When you import a schema, Access creates a new empty table with the structure of the imported schema. Earlier in this chapter, when you exported the `Prod-ucts` table to XML format, Access also created the schema of that table. Hands-On 20.8 shows how to import this schema document to a new Access database.

⊚ Hands-On 20.8   Importing a Schema File (XSD) to an Access Database

1. Create a new Access database named `C:\VBAAccess2024_XML\Chap20.accdb`.
2. In the Access window, choose External Data, and then select New Data Source | From File | XML File.
3. In the Get External Data - XML File window, type `C:\VBAAccess2024_XML\Products.xsd` in the File name box and click OK.
   Access displays the Import XML dialog box, as shown in Figure 20.18.

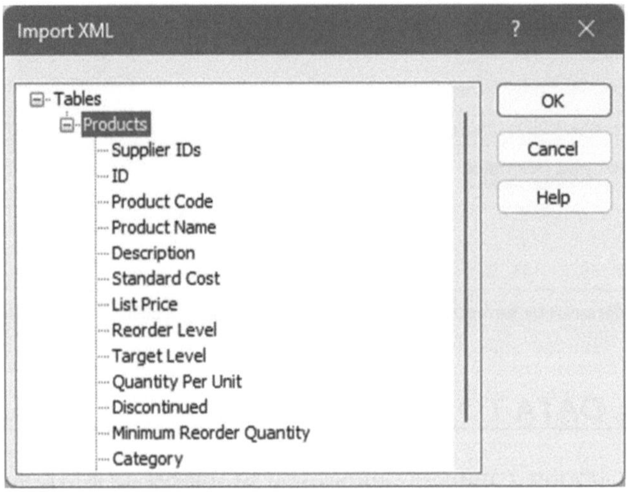

FIGURE 20.18.   When importing a schema file to an Access database, the Import XML dialog box displays the table name, and its columns as defined in the schema.

Notice that you cannot indicate which columns you would like to import. Access always imports the entire XSD file.

4. Click OK to perform the import. When the import operation is completed, click Close.
   The `Products` table appears in the Navigation Pane of the Access window. Figure 20.19 shows this table opened in design view.
5. Close the `Chap20.accdb` database.

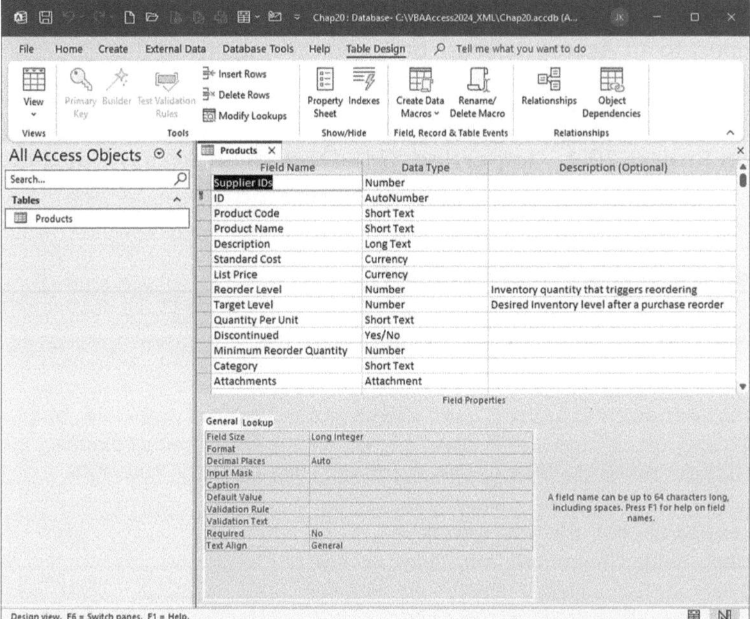

FIGURE 20.19.   The Products table was created by importing the Products.xsd schema file.

Importing an XML File

When importing an XML data file to an Access database, you can use the Import Options section to specify whether you want to import structure only, import structure and data, or append data to an existing table. When you append data to an existing table, Access compares the structure of the imported table with the table structures that are already in the database. If Access cannot find a table structure matching the imported table, the data is placed in a new table; otherwise, it is appended to the existing table. You can also click the Transform button in the Import XML dialog box to specify a transformation file that you want to apply when the XML data is imported. It is important to point out that when XML data is imported to an Access database, it is not linked with the original XML file. This means that to refresh the data in the table, you need to repeat the import process.

The following project demonstrates how to import XML data to an Access database and modify the data before import using a transformation file. We will perform the tasks outlined here:

- Create a custom transformation file to be used after the XML data import

- Export the `Customers` table and the related `Orders` table to an XML file.
- Import to an Access database only two columns from the `Customers` table and five columns from the `Orders` table.

> **Custom Project 20.1   Importing XML Data to an Access Database and Applying a Transform**

Part 1: Creating a Custom Transformation File

1. Open Notepad and enter the following statements:

```
<?xml version="1.0" encoding="UTF-8"?>
<xsl:stylesheet version="1.0" xmlns:xsl="http://www.w3.org/1999/
                                        XSL/Transform">
<xsl:output method="html" version="4.0" indent="yes"/>

<xsl:template match="dataroot">
  <html>
  <body>
  <table>
  <xsl:apply-templates select="Customers"/>
  </table>
  <table>
  <xsl:apply-templates select="Customers/Orders"/>
  </table>
  </body>
  </html>
</xsl:template>

<xsl:template match="Customers">
  <Customer>
  <ID>
  <xsl:value-of select="ID"/>
  </ID>
  <Company>
  <xsl:value-of select="Company"/>
  </Company>
  </Customer>
</xsl:template>

<xsl:template match="Customers/Orders">
  <Order>
```

```
<OrderID>
<xsl:value-of select="Order_x0020_ID"/>
</OrderID>
<CustomerID>
<xsl:value-of select="Customer_x0020_ID"/>
</CustomerID>
<OrderDate>
<xsl:value-of select="substring(Order_x0020_Date, 1, 10)"/>
</OrderDate>
<ShippedDate>
<xsl:value-of select="substring(Shipped_x0020_Date, 1, 10)"/>
</ShippedDate>
<ShippingFee>
<xsl:value-of select="format-number(Shipping_x0020_
                                   Fee,'####0.00')"/>
</ShippingFee>
</Order>
</xsl:template>

</xsl:stylesheet>
```

2. Save the file as `C:\VBAAccess2024_XML\CustomerOrders.xsl`. You must include the file extension to ensure that the file is not saved as text.

3. Close Notepad.

    After creating a similar stylesheet in Hands-On 20.6, you should be familiar with the contents of the `CustomerOrders.xsl` file. All that's different here are the `<Customer>` and `<Order>` tags that specify the names of Access tables where we want to place our XML data. When importing data, tables are named according to the name of the XML element being imported. If the Access database already has a table with the specified name, a number is appended to the name.

Part 2: Exporting the Customers and Related Orders Tables to an XML File

1. Open the `C:\VBAAccess2024_XML\Northwind 2007.accdb` database and log in as Andrew Cencini.

2. In the Navigation Pane, right-click the Customers table and choose Export | XML File.

3. In the Export - XML File window, type `C:\VBAAccess2024_XML\CustomerOrders.xml` in the File name box and click OK.

4. Access displays the Export XML dialog box with three checkboxes; the first two checkboxes should be selected. Click the More Options… button.

5. In the Data to Export area of the Export XML dialog box, select the checkbox next to the Orders table. The Customers and Orders tables should both be selected.
6. Click OK to perform the export of all the records in the selected tables. When the export operation is completed, click Close.
7. Close the `Northwind 2007.accdb` database.

Part 3: Importing Selected Columns to an Access Database

1. Open the `C:\VBAAccess2024_XML\Chap20.accdb` database file that you created in Hands-On 20.8.
2. In the Access window, choose External Data, and then select New Data Source | From File | XML File.
3. In the Get External Data - XML File window, type `C:\VBAAccess2024_XML\CustomerOrders.xml` in the File name box and click OK.
   Access displays the Import XML window with the file's `Customers` and `Orders` tables listed. By expanding nodes in the tree structure, you can see the columns in each table, but you cannot indicate which columns to import, as Access always imports the entire file by default. You can, however, tell Access to perform a custom XSLT transform to import only the columns needed.
4. In the Import XML window, click the Transform button.
5. In the Import Transforms window that appears, click the Add button to apply a transform before importing.
   Access displays the Add New Transform window. Switch to the `VBAAccess2024_XML` folder and select the CustomerOrders.xsl stylesheet file that you created in Part 1 of this project. Click the Add button to add this file to the list of transforms.
6. In the Import Transforms window, click OK.
7. Back in the Import XML window, make sure that the Structure and Data option button is selected under Import Options and click OK. When Access finishes importing the `C:\VBAAccess2024_XML\CustomerOrders.xml` document, click Close.
   In the Navigation Pane of the Access window, notice the appearance of two new tables: `Customer` and `Order`. Open both tables and check their contents. As you can see, Access applied the custom stylesheet before importing the data and only the columns specified in the stylesheet were imported (see Figure 20.20).

8. Open the `Orders` table in design view. Notice that all the fields in this table have been assigned the `Text` data type.
   After importing data or table structure you can change the fields' data types.

9. Change the data type of `OrderID` and `CustomerID` to `Number`, `OrderDate` and `ShippedDate` to `Date/Time`, and `ShippingFee` to `Currency` to match the original `Orders` table.

10. Save the modified `Orders` table and click Yes when Access notifies you that some data may be lost.

11. Close the `Chap20.accdb` database.

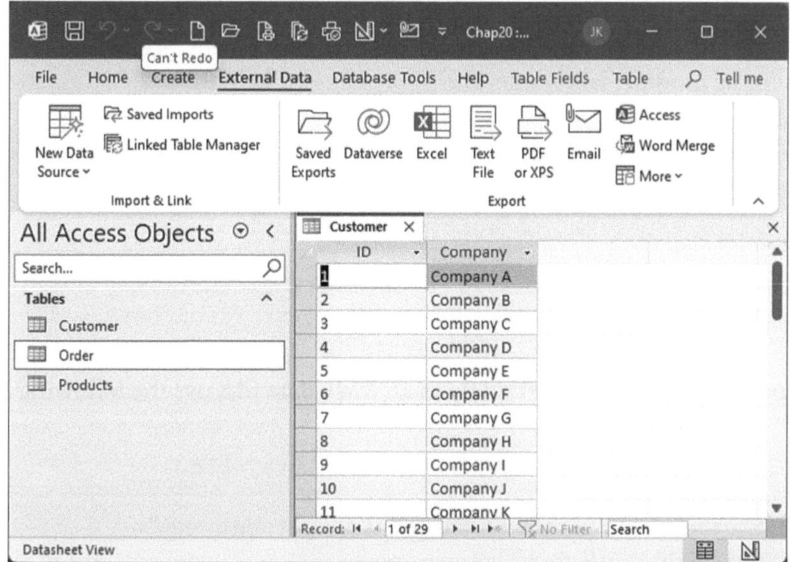

FIGURE 20.20.   Applying a custom transform prior to XML data import will allow you to limit the number of imported columns.

USING VBA TO EXPORT AND IMPORT XML DOCUMENTS

You've now mastered the use of Access 2024 built-in commands for exporting and importing XML data. Let's look at the tools that are available for programmers who want to perform these XML operations programmatically. In the following sections of this chapter, you will learn how to work with XML using:

- The `ExportXML` and `ImportXML` methods from the Microsoft Access 16.0 object library

- The `TransformXML` method

Exporting to XML Using the ExportXML Method

Use the Microsoft Access 16.0 object library's `ExportXML` method of the `Application` object to export XML data, schemas (XSD), and presentation information (XSL) from a Microsoft Access database.

The `ExportXML` method takes a number of arguments. In its simplest form, the `ExportXML` method looks like this:

```
Application.ExportXML ObjectType:=acExportTable, _
DataSource:="Customers", _
DataTarget:= "C:\VBAAccess2024_XML\North_Customers.xml"
```

The preceding statement, when typed on a single line (without the underscore characters) in VBE's Immediate window or inside a VBA procedure stub in a Visual Basic module, will render the `Customers` table in the `North_Customers.xml` file.

To export the XML `Products` table with its schema and presentation information placed in separate files, use the following statement:

```
Application.ExportXML ObjectType:=acExportTable, _
DataSource:="Products", _
DataTarget:= "C:\VBAAccess2024_XML\North_Products.xml", _
SchemaTarget:= "C:\VBAAccess2024_XML\North_ProdSchema.xsd", _
PresentationTarget:= "C:\VBAAccess2024_XML\North_ProdReport.xsl"
```

To export a specific customer's data to an XML data file, use the following statement:

```
Application.ExportXML ObjectType:=acExportTable, _
DataSource:="Customers", _
DataTarget:="C:\VBAAccess2024_XML\OneCustomer.xml", _
WhereCondition:="ID = 4"
```

<table>
<tr><td>NOTE</td><td>

Follow these steps to try out the preceding statements:
1. *Open the* `Northwind 2007.accdb` *database as Andrew Cencini.*
2. *Switch to the VBE window (Choose Database Tools | Visual Basic).*
3. *Insert a new standard module (Insert | Module),*
4. *Create a subprocedure named* `Test_ExportToXML` *(choose Insert | Procedure, enter the procedure name, and click OK).*
5. *Type each of the preceding statements inside the procedure stub.*
6. *Execute the procedure (Run | Run Sub/UserForm).*
7. *Locate and check out the newly created XML files in your* `C:\VBAAccess2024_XML` *folder.*

</td></tr>
</table>

Hands-On 20.9 demonstrates how to export to XML three tables: Customers, Orders, and Order Details.

⊙ Hands-On 20.9   Exporting Multiple Tables to an XML Data File

1. In the C:\VBAAccess2024_XML\Chap20.accdb database, switch to the VBE window.
2. Choose Insert | Module to add a standard module to the current VBA project.
3. In the module's Code window, enter the following Export_CustomerOrderDetails procedure:

```
Sub Export_CustomerOrderDetails()
    Dim objAppl As New Access.Application
    Dim objOtherTbls As AdditionalData
    Dim strPath As String
    Dim strDBName As String

    strPath = "C:\VBAAccess2024_XML\"
    strDBName = "Northwind 2007.accdb"

    On Error GoTo ErrorHandler
    objAppl.OpenCurrentDatabase (strPath & strDBName)
    objAppl.Visible = False

    Set objOtherTbls = objAppl.CreateAdditionalData

    ' include the Orders and OrderDetails tables
    ' in export
    objOtherTbls.Add "Orders"
    objOtherTbls.Add "Order Details"

    ' export Customers, Orders, and Order
    ' Details table into one XML data file

    objAppl.ExportXML ObjectType:=acExportTable, _
    DataSource:="Customers", _
    DataTarget:=strPath & "CustomerOrdersDetails.xml", _
    AdditionalData:=objOtherTbls

    MsgBox "Export operation completed."

Exit_Here:
    On Error Resume Next
    objAppl.CloseCurrentDatabase
```

```
    Set objAppl = Nothing
    Exit Sub
ErrorHandler:
    MsgBox Err.Number & ": " & Err.Description
    Resume Exit_Here
End Sub
```

4. Place the insertion point anywhere within the `Export_CustomerOrderDetails` procedure code and choose Run | Run Sub/UserForm.
   Access executes the procedure code and displays a message.

5. Click OK to clear the informational message.

6. Switch to File Explorer and locate and open the `C:\VBAAccess2024_XML\` `CustomerOrdersDetails.xml` file.
   Notice that all the requested data was placed into one file. If the expected `.xml` file was not created, double-check the spelling of variables in your procedure. Make sure that the `Option Explicit` statement appears at the top of the module, above your procedure code.

7. Exit the File Explorer.

   In the above procedure code, the `Application` object refers to the active Access application, which in this case is the `Chap20.accdb` database where you wrote the procedure code shown here. Because this database does not contain the tables you want to export, you used the `New` keyword to create a new instance of the Access `Application` object and then opened another Access database (`Northwind 2007.accdb`) using the `OpenCurrentDatabase` method. You can use the `OpenCurrentDatabase` method to open an existing Access database as the current database.

   Using the `AdditionalData` object, you can export any set of Access tables to an XML data file. To use this object, follow these steps:

1. Declare an object variable as `AdditionalData`:

   ```
   Dim objOtherTbls As AdditionalData
   ```

2. Create the `AdditionalData` object using the `CreateAdditionalData` method of the `Application` object and set the object variable to the newly created object:

   ```
   Set objOtherTbls = objAppl.CreateAdditionalData
   ```

3. Use the `AdditionalData` object's `Add` method to add table names to the object:

   ```
   objOtherTbls.Add "Orders"
   objOtherTbls.Add "Order Details"
   ```

4. Pass the `AdditionalData` object to the `ExportXML` method:

```
objAppl.ExportXML ObjectType:=acExportTable, _
DataSource:="Customers", _
DataTarget:=strPath & "CustomerOrdersDetails.xml", _
AdditionalData:=objOtherTbls
```

Transforming XML Data with the TransformXML Method

While stylesheets are often used to render XML files into HTML for display in a Web browser, they can also be used to transform XML files into other XML files.

In this section, you will learn how the `TransformXML` method is used to apply an XSL stylesheet to an XML data file to transform it into another XML file.

The `TransformXML` method takes a number of arguments. In its simplest form, the `TransformXML` method looks like this:

```
Application.TransformXML _ DataSource:="C:\VBAAccess2024_XML\
InternalContacts.xml", _
 TransformSource:="C:\VBAAccess2024_XML\Extensions.xsl", _
 OutputTarget:="C:\VBAAccess2024_XML\EmpExtensions.xml"
```

The preceding statement can be used inside a VBA procedure stub to programmatically apply the specified stylesheet.

Custom Project 20.2 demonstrates how to transform an XML data file into another XML file. We will start by creating a custom stylesheet named `Extensions.xsl` that will transform the `InternalContacts.xml` file (generated from the `Northwind.mdb` database `Employees` table) into an XML file named `EmpExtensions.xml`. Next, we will write a VBA procedure to export the XML source file and perform the transformation. Finally, we will import the resulting XML data file into Access.

⊙ Custom Project 20.2   Applying a Stylesheet to an XML Data File with the TransformXML Method

Part 1: Creating a Custom Stylesheet for Transforming an XML Source File into Another XML Data File

1. Open Notepad and enter the following statements:

```
<?xml version="1.0"?>
<xsl:stylesheet version="1.0" xmlns:xsl="http://www.w3.org/1999/
XSL/Transform">
<xsl:output method="xml" indent="yes"/>
<xsl:template match="/">
```

```
<dataroot>
<xsl:for-each select="//Employees">
<Extensions>
  <LastName>
  <xsl:value-of select="LastName" />
  </LastName>
  <FirstName>
  <xsl:value-of select="FirstName" />
  </FirstName>
  <Extension>
  <xsl:value-of select="Extension" />
  </Extension>
</Extensions>
</xsl:for-each>
</dataroot>
</xsl:template>
</xsl:stylesheet>
```

Look at the preceding stylesheet and notice that we have asked the XSL processor to produce the output in XML format:

```
<xsl:output method="xml" indent="yes"/>
```

Next, we used the following instruction:

```
<xsl:template match="/">
```

This instruction defines a template for the entire document. The special pattern "/" in the `match` attribute tells the XSL processor that this is a template for the document root. Because each XML document must have a root node, we proceeded to define `<dataroot>` as the document root. You can use any name you want for this purpose. Next, we told the XSL processor to get all the `Employees` nodes from the source XML data file:

```
<xsl:for-each select="//Employees">
```

The first forward slash in the preceding instruction represents the XML document root. This is the same as:

```
<xsl:for-each select="dataroot/Employees">
```

Next, we proceed to extract data from the required nodes. We are only interested in three columns from the source XML data file: `FirstName`, `LastName`, and `Extension`. We can create the necessary elements using the `<xsl:value-of>` tag with the `select` attribute specifying the element name:

```
<LastName>
```

```
  <xsl:value-of select="LastName" />
</LastName>
<FirstName>
  <xsl:value-of select="FirstName" />
</FirstName>
<Extension>
  <xsl:value-of select="Extension" />
</Extension>
```

Next, we tell the XSL processor to place the defined elements under the `<Extensions>` node. When importing the resulting XML file to Access, Access will create an `Extensions` table with three columns: LastName, FirstName, and Extension. You can use any name you want when specifying the container node for your elements. To finish the stylesheet, we must write the necessary closing tags:

```
</xsl:for-each>
</dataroot>
</xsl:template>
</xsl:stylesheet>
```

2. Save the file as `C:\VBAAccess2024_XML\Extensions.xsl`. You must include the `.xsl` file extension to ensure that the file is not saved as text.
3. Close Notepad.

   With the stylesheet ready, let's write a VBA procedure to actually export the source data and perform the transformation.

Part 2: Writing a VBA Procedure to Export and Transform Data

1. Copy the `Northwind.mdb` database from the companion files to your `C:\VBAAccess2024_XML` folder.
2. In the `Chap20.accdb` database, choose External Data and click New Data Source | From Database | Access.
3. In the File name box, enter `C:\VBAAccess2024_XML\Northwind.mdb` and click OK.
4. In the Import Object dialog box, click the Tables tab, select Employees, and click OK.
5. Click Close to exit the Get External Data – Access Database dialog box. You should see the `Employees` table in the Navigation Pane.
6. Choose Database Tools | Visual Basic.
7. In the VBE window, choose Insert | Module to add a standard module to the current VBA project.

8. In the module's Code window, enter the following `Transform_Employees` procedure:

```vba
Sub Transform_Employees()
Dim strPath As String
   ' use the ExportXML method to
   ' create a source XML data file

strPath = "C:\VBAAccess2024_XML\"
  Application.ExportXML _
    ObjectType:=acExportTable, _
    DataSource:="Employees", _
    DataTarget:=strPath & "InternalContacts.XML"

  MsgBox "The export operation completed."

  ' use the TransformXML method
  ' to apply the stylesheet
  ' that transforms the source
  ' XML data file into
  ' another XML data file
  Application.TransformXML _
   DataSource:=strPath & "InternalContacts.xml", _
   TransformSource:=strPath & "Extensions.xsl", _
   OutputTarget:=strPath & "EmpExtensions.xml", _
   WellFormedXMLOutput:=False

  MsgBox "The transform operation completed."
End Sub
```

The first part of this procedure exports the `Employees` table to an XML file named `InternalContacts.xml`. The second part of this procedure applies the `Extensions.xsl` stylesheet prepared in Part 1 of this custom project to the `InternalContacts.xml` data file. The resulting XML document after the transformation is named `EmpExtensions.xml`. A portion of this file is shown in Figure 20.21.

9. Choose Run | Run Sub/UserForm or press F5 to run the `Transform_Employees` procedure.
10. Save the changes in the module and exit the VBE window.

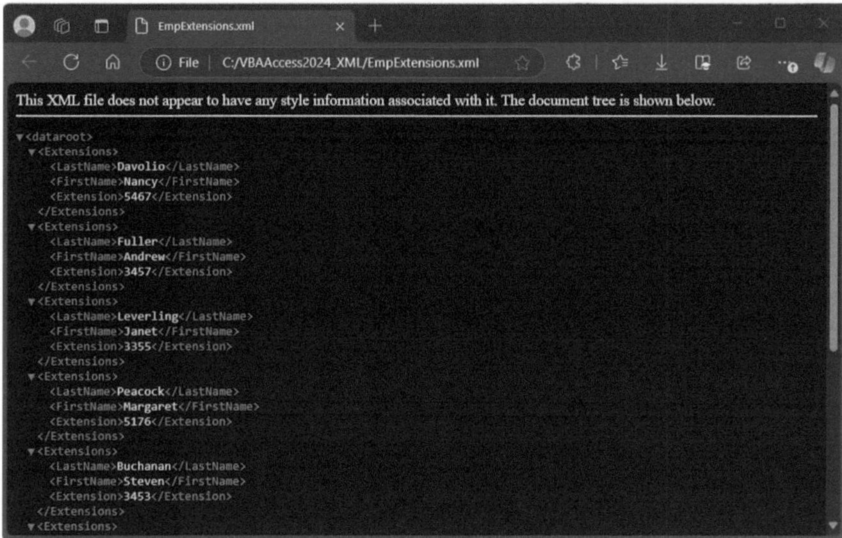

FIGURE 20.21.   Partial contents of the EmpExtensions.xml file.

After transforming the source XML data file into another XML document, it's time to bring it into Access.

Part 3: Importing the Transformed XML Data File to Access

1. In `Chap20.accdb`, choose External Data | New Data Source | From File | XML File.
2. In the File name box, type `C:\VBAAccess2024_XML\EmpExtensions.xml` and click OK. Access displays the Import XML dialog box listing the Extensions table with three columns: LastName, FirstName, and Extension.
3. In the Import XML dialog box, click OK to perform the import.
4. Click Close to exit the Import XML window.
   In the Navigation Pane of the Access window, notice the appearance of the `Extensions` table.
5. Open the `Extensions` table to examine its contents, then close it.
   A nice thing about XSLT transformations is that you can apply different stylesheets to the same XML data file to create and view the resulting document in different formats.

   For example, let's assume that in the `Extensions` table, you'd like to combine the LastName and FirstName columns into one column and sort the data by LastName. To do this, you could create the `Extensions SortByEmp.xsl` stylesheet and apply it to `InternalContacts.xml`.

Part 4: Creating Another Transformation

1. Open Notepad and prepare the following stylesheet.

```
<?xml version="1.0"?>
    <xsl:stylesheet version="1.0"
    xmlns:xsl="http://www.w3.org/1999/XSL/Transform">
    <xsl:output method="xml" indent="yes"/>
      <xsl:template match="/">
      <dataroot>
      <xsl:apply-templates select="dataroot/Employees">
      <xsl:sort select="LastName" order="ascending" />
      </xsl:apply-templates>
      </dataroot>
      </xsl:template>

      <xsl:template match="//Employees">
      <Extensions>
      <FullName>
      <xsl:value-of select="LastName" />
      <xsl:text>, </xsl:text>
      <xsl:value-of select="FirstName" />
      </FullName>
      <Extension>
      <xsl:value-of select="Extension" />
      </Extension>
      </Extensions>
      </xsl:template>
    </xsl:stylesheet>
```

2. Save the stylesheet as `C:\VBAAccess2024_XML\Extensions_SortByEmp.xsl`.
The preceding stylesheet uses the `<xsl:apply-templates>` tag to tell the XSL
processor to select the child elements of the `dataroot/Employees` node. For
each child element, it will find in the stylesheet the matching template rule and
process it:

```
<xsl:apply-templates select="dataroot/Employees">
 <xsl:sort select="LastName" order="ascending" />
</xsl:apply-templates>
```

The `<xsl:sort>` tag specifies how the resulting XML document should be
sorted. The `select` attribute of this tag is set to `LastName`, indicating that the
file should be sorted by the `LastName` element. The `order` attribute defines the
sort order as ascending.

Next, the stylesheet uses the template rule that begins with the `<xsl:template>` tag. Its `match` attribute specifies which nodes in the document tree the template rule should process:

```
<xsl:template match="//Employees">
```

The `//Employees` expression in the `match` attribute is equivalent to `dataroot/Employees`.

Next, you need to define the document node in the output file as `Extensions` and proceed to define its child elements as `FullName` and `Extension`:

```
<Extensions>
 <FullName>
 <xsl:value-of select="LastName" />
 <xsl:text>, </xsl:text>
 <xsl:value-of select="FirstName" />
 </FullName>
 <Extension>
 <xsl:value-of select="Extension" />
 </Extension>
</Extensions>
```

The element `FullName` should contain the last name of the employee followed by a space and the first name. You can obtain the values of these fields with the `<xsl:value-of>` tag and use the `<xsl:text> </xsl:text>` tag pair to output a comma followed by a space between the last name and first name. Since there is nothing special about the `Extension` element, you can simply use the `<xsl:value-of>` tag to obtain this element's value.

Finally, you must complete the template and the stylesheet with the required closing tags:

```
</xsl:template>
</xsl:stylesheet>
```

3. To apply the preceding stylesheet to the source XML file, switch to the VBE window and enter the following VBA procedure.

```
Sub Transform_ContactsSort()
 Dim strPath As String

 strPath = "C:\VBAAccess2024_XML\"

 ' use the ExportXML method to create
 ' a source XML data file
```

```
'objAppl.ExportXML ObjectType:=acExportTable, _

 Application.ExportXML ObjectType:=acExportTable, _
 DataSource:="Employees", _
 DataTarget:=strPath & "InternalContacts.xml"

' use the TransformXML method
' to apply the stylesheet that
' transforms the source XML data
' file into another XML data file

Application.TransformXML _
   DataSource:=strPath & "InternalContacts.xml", _
   TransformSource:=strPath & "Extensions_SortByEmp.xsl", _
   OutputTarget:=strPath & "EmpExtensions.xml", _
   WellFormedXMLOutput:=False

End Sub
```

4. Choose Run | Run Sub/UserForm or press F5 to run the `Transform_ ContactsSort` procedure.
5. Save the module changes and exit the VBE window.
6. Follow the steps from Part 3 above to import the `EmpExtensions.xml` file to Access.

   You should see the `Extensions1` table in the database window. When opened, this table displays a sorted list of employees with their extensions (see Figure 20.22).

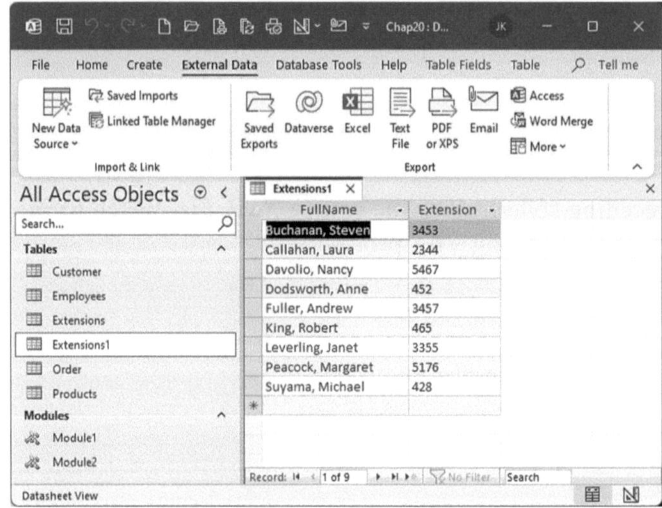

FIGURE 20.22.   The Extensions table after it was reformatted with another stylesheet.

Importing to XML Using the ImportXML Method

Use the `ImportXML` method to programmatically import an XML data file and/ or schema file. The `ImportXML` method requires that you specify the full path of the XML file to import. The second argument, `ImportOptions`, is optional (see Table 20.1).

TABLE 20.1.   Arguments of the ImportXML method (in order of appearance).

Argument Type	Data Type	Description
`DataSource` (required)	String	Specifies the full path of the XML file to import.
`ImportOptions` (optional)	`acImportXMLOption` Use one of the following constants: | Constant	Value
---	---
acAppendData	2
acStructureAndData	1
acStructureOnly	0		Specifies whether to import structure only (0), import structure and data (1) (default), or append data (2).

The following procedure will import the structure of the `Extensions` table from the `EmpExtensions.xml` file:

```
Sub Import_XMLFile()
Application.ImportXML _
  DataSource:="C:\VBAAccess2024_XML\EmpExtensions.xml", _
  ImportOptions:=acStructureOnly
End Sub
```

The result should be an empty `Extensions2` table in your `Chap20.accdb` database.

MANIPULATING XML DOCUMENTS PROGRAMMATICALLY

You can create, access, and manipulate XML documents programmatically using the XML DOM. The DOM has objects, properties, and methods for interacting with XML documents. To use the XML DOM from your VBA procedures, take a few minutes now to set up a reference to the MSXML object library:

1. Switch to the VBE window in `Chap20.accdb` and choose Tools | References.
2. In the References window, select Microsoft XML, v6.0 (see Figure 20.23) and click OK.
   If you don't have version 6.0 installed, select the lower version of this object type library, or upgrade your browser to the higher version so that the most recent library is available.

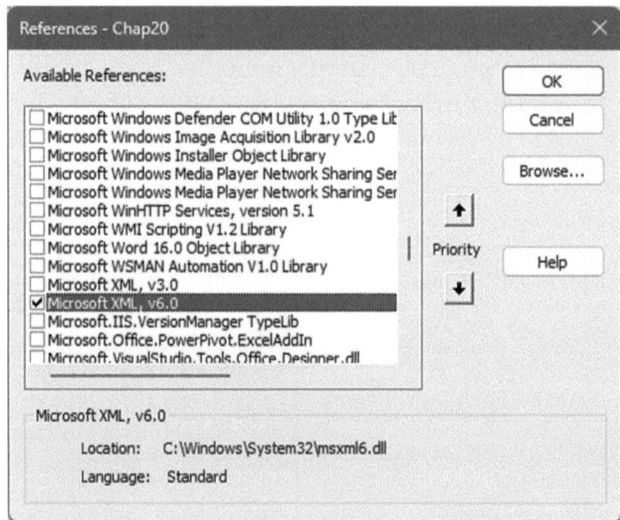

FIGURE 20.23. To work with XML documents programmatically, you need to reference the Microsoft XML object type library.

3. With the reference set, open the Object Browser (press F2) and examine the XML DOM's objects, methods, and properties (see Figure 20.24).

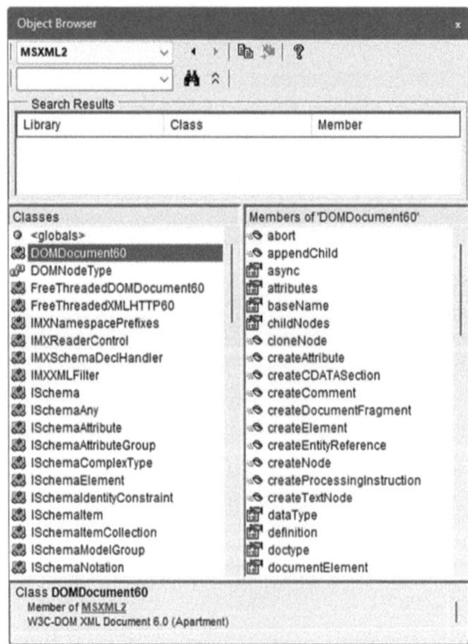

FIGURE 20.24. To view objects, properties, and methods exposed by the XML DOM, open the Object Browser after setting up a reference to the Microsoft XML object type library (see Figure 20.22).

4. Close the Object Browser window.

The `DOMDocument` object is the top level of the XML DOM object hierarchy. This object represents a tree structure composed of nodes. You can navigate through this tree structure and manipulate the data contained in the nodes by using various methods and properties. The following sections demonstrate how to read and manipulate XML documents by using VBA procedures.

Loading and Retrieving the Contents of an XML File

Hands-On 20.10 shows how to open an XML data file and retrieve both the raw data and the actual text stored in XML nodes.

(◉) Hands-On 20.10   Loading and Retrieving the Contents of an XML File

1. In the VBE window of the `Chap20.accdb` database, choose Insert | Module to add a new standard module to the current VBA project.
2. In the module's Code window, enter the following `ReadXMLDoc` procedure:

NOTE	*For this procedure to work correctly, you must set up the reference to the Microsoft XML object type library as instructed at the beginning of this section.*

```
Sub ReadXMLDoc()
  Dim xmldoc As MSXML2.DOMDocument60
  Dim strPath As String

  strPath = "C:\VBAAccess2024_XML\"
  Set xmldoc = New MSXML2.DOMDocument60

  xmldoc.Async = False
  If xmldoc.Load(strPath & "InternalContacts.xml") Then
    Debug.Print xmldoc.XML
    ' Debug.Print xmldoc.Text
  End If
End Sub
```

To work with an XML document, we begin by creating an instance of the `DOMDocument` object as follows:

```
Dim xmldoc As MSXML2.DOMDocument60
Set xmldoc = New MSXML2.DOMDocument60
```

MSXML uses an asynchronous loading mechanism by default for working with documents. *Asynchronous* loading allows you to perform other tasks during long database operations, such as providing feedback to the user as MSXML parses the XML file or giving the user the chance to cancel the operation. Before calling the `Load` method, however, it's a good idea to set the `Async` property of the `DOMDocument` object to `False` to ensure that the XML file is fully loaded before other statements are executed. The `Load` method returns `True` if it successfully loaded the data and `False` otherwise. Having loaded the XML data into a `DOMDocument` object, you can use the `XML` property to retrieve the raw data or use the `Text` property to obtain the text stored in document nodes.

3. Position the insertion point anywhere within the code of the `ReadXMLDoc` procedure and choose Run | Run Sub/UserForm. The procedure executes and writes the contents of the XML file into the Immediate window, as shown in Figure 20.25.

4. In the code of the `ReadXMLDoc` procedure, comment the first `Debug.Print` statement and uncomment the second statement that reads `Debug.Print xmldoc.Text`.

5. Run the `ReadXMLDoc` procedure again, then check out the Immediate window.

   This time, the Immediate window should show the entry as one long line of text.

```
Immediate                                                                                    x

<?xml version="1.0"?>
<dataroot xmlns:od="urn:schemas-microsoft-com:officedata" generated="2024-12-19T17:38:43">
    <Employees>
        <EmployeeID>1</EmployeeID>
        <LastName>Davolio</LastName>
        <FirstName>Nancy</FirstName>
        <Title>Sales Representative</Title>
        <TitleOfCourtesy>Ms.</TitleOfCourtesy>
        <BirthDate>1968-12-08T00:00:00</BirthDate>
        <HireDate>1992-05-01T00:00:00</HireDate>
        <Address>507 - 20th Ave. E.
Apt. 2A</Address>
        <City>Seattle</City>
        <Region>WA</Region>
        <PostalCode>98122</PostalCode>
        <Country>USA</Country>
        <HomePhone>(206) 555-9857</HomePhone>
        <Extension>5467</Extension>
        <Photo>EmpID1.bmp</Photo>
        <Notes>Education includes a BA in psychology from Colorado State University.  She also
        <ReportsTo>2</ReportsTo>
    </Employees>
    <Employees>
```

FIGURE 20.25. By using the XML property of the DOMDocument object, you can retrieve the raw data from an XML file.

Working with XML Document Nodes

An XML document can contain nodes of different types. It can have a node that provides access to the entire XML document or one or more element nodes representing individual elements. Some nodes represent comments and processing instructions and others hold the text content of a tag. To determine the type of node, use the `nodeType` property of the `IXMLDOMNode` object. Node types are identified by either a text string or a constant.

For example, the node representing an element can be referred to as `NODE_ELEMENT` or `1`, while the node representing the comment is named `NODE_COMMENT` or `8`. See the MSXML2 library in the Object Browser for the names of other node types.

In addition to node types, nodes can have parent, child, and sibling nodes. The `hasChildNodes` method lets you determine whether a `DOMDocument` object has child nodes. There's also a `childNodes` property, which simplifies retrieving a collection of child nodes. Before you start looping through the collection of child nodes, it's a good idea to use the length property of the `IXMLDOMNode` object to determine how many elements the collection contains.

The following hands-on exercise uses the `InternalContacts.xml` file to demonstrate how to work with XML document nodes.

◉ Hands-On 20.11   Working with XML Document Nodes

1. In the same module where you entered the `ReadXMLDoc` procedure in the previous hands-on exercise, enter the following `LearnAboutNodes` procedure:

```vba
Sub LearnAboutNodes()
    Dim xmldoc As MSXML2.DOMDocument60
    Dim xmlNode As MSXML2.IXMLDOMNode
    Dim strPath As String

    strPath = "C:\VBAAccess2024_XML\"
    Set xmldoc = New MSXML2.DOMDocument60
    xmldoc.Async = False

    xmldoc.Load (strPath & "InternalContacts.xml")
    If xmldoc.hasChildNodes Then
      Debug.Print "Number of child Nodes: " & _
        xmldoc.childNodes.length
      For Each xmlNode In xmldoc.childNodes
        Debug.Print "Node name:" & xmlNode.nodeName
        Debug.Print vbTab & "Type:" & _
          xmlNode.nodeTypeString _
```

```
        & "(" & xmlNode.nodeType & ")"
      Debug.Print vbTab & "Text: " & xmlNode.Text
    Next xmlNode
  End If
  Set xmldoc = Nothing
End Sub
```

Notice that this procedure uses the `hasChildNodes` property of the `DOMDocument` object to check whether there are any child nodes in the loaded XML file. If child nodes are found, the `length` property of the `childNodes` collection returns the total number of child nodes found. Next, the procedure loops through the `childNodes` collection and retrieves the node name using the `nodeName` property of the `IXMLDOMNode` object.

The `nodeTypeString` property returns the string version of the node type (for example, processing instruction, element, text, etc.) and the `nodeType` property is used to return the enumeration value. Finally, the `Text` property of the `IXMLDOMNode` object retrieves the node text.

2. Position the insertion point anywhere within the code of the `LearnAboutNodes` procedure and choose Run | Run Sub/UserForm.

3. Running the `LearnAboutNodes` procedure produces output like this in the Immediate window:

```
Number of child Nodes: 2
Node name:xml
    Type:processinginstruction(7)
    Text: version="1.0" encoding="UTF-8"
Node name:dataroot
    Type:element(1)
    Text: 1 Davolio Nancy Sales Representative Ms. 1968-12-
          08T00:00:00 1992-05-01T00:00:00 507 - 20th Ave. E.
… (and so on)
```

Retrieving Information from Element Nodes

Let's assume that you want to read information from only text element nodes. Use the `getElementsByTagName` method of the `DOMDocument` object to retrieve an `IXMLDOMNodeList` object containing all the element nodes. This method takes an argument specifying the tag name to search for. To search for all the element nodes, use "*" as the tag to search for.

The following hands-on exercise demonstrates how to obtain data from XML document element nodes.

◉ Hands-On 20.12   Retrieving Information from Element Nodes

1. In the VBE window, enter the following `IterateThruElements` procedure below the last procedure code you entered in Hands-On 20.11:

```
Sub IterateThruElements()
Dim xmldoc As MSXML2.DOMDocument60
Dim xmlNode As MSXML2.IXMLDOMNode
Dim xmlNodeList As MSXML2.IXMLDOMNodeList
Dim myNode As MSXML2.IXMLDOMNode
Dim strPath As String

strPath = "C:\VBAAccess2024_XML\"

Set xmldoc = New MSXML2.DOMDocument60
xmldoc.Async = False
xmldoc.Load (strPath & "InternalContacts.xml")
Set xmlNodeList = xmldoc.getElementsByTagName("*")
For Each xmlNode In xmlNodeList
  For Each myNode In xmlNode.childNodes
    If myNode.nodeType = NODE_TEXT Then
      Debug.Print xmlNode.nodeName & _
        "=" & xmlNode.Text
    End If
  Next myNode
Next xmlNode
Set xmldoc = Nothing
End Sub
```

The `IterateThruElements` procedure retrieves the XML document name and the corresponding text for all the text elements in the `InternalContacts.xml` file. Notice that this procedure uses two `For Each...Next` loops. The first one (the outer loop) iterates through the entire collection of element nodes. The second one (the inner loop) uses the `nodeType` property to find only those element nodes that contain a single text node.

2. Position the insertion point anywhere within the code of the `IterateThruElements` procedure and choose Run | Run Sub/UserForm. Running the `IterateThruElements` procedure produces the following results:

```
EmployeeID=1
LastName=Davolio
FirstName=Nancy
Title=Sales Representative
TitleOfCourtesy=Ms.
```

```
BirthDate=1968-12-08T00:00:00
HireDate=1992-05-01T00:00:00
Address=507 - 20th Ave. E.
Apt. 2A
City=Seattle
Region=WA
PostalCode=98122
Country=USA
HomePhone=(206) 555-9857
Extension=5467
Photo=EmpID1.bmp
Notes=Education includes a BA in psychology from Colorado State
University.   She also completed "The Art of the Cold Call."
Nancy is a member of Toastmasters International.
ReportsTo=2
EmployeeID=2
LastName=Fuller
FirstName=Andrew
...(and so on)
```

Retrieving Specific Information from Element Nodes

You can list all the nodes that match a specified criterion by using the `select-Nodes` method. The following hands-on exercise prints to the Immediate window the text for all `Title` nodes that exist in the `InternalContacts.xml` file. The `//Title` criterion of the `selectNodes` method looks for the element named `Title` at any level within the tree structure of the nodes.

⊙ Hands-On 20.13   Retrieving Specific Information from Element Nodes

1. In the VBE Code window, in the same module where you entered previous procedures, enter the following `SelectNodesByCriteria` procedure:

```
Sub SelectNodesByCriteria()
   Dim xmldoc As MSXML2.DOMDocument60
   Dim xmlNodeList As MSXML2.IXMLDOMNodeList
   Dim myNode As MSXML2.IXMLDOMNode
   Dim strPath As String

   strPath = "C:\VBAAccess2024_XML\"
   Set xmldoc = New MSXML2.DOMDocument60
   xmldoc.async = False
   xmldoc.Load (strPath & "InternalContacts.xml")
   Set xmlNodeList = xmldoc.selectNodes("//Title")
   If Not (xmlNodeList Is Nothing) Then
```

```
    For Each myNode In xmlNodeList
      Debug.Print myNode.Text
      If myNode.Text = "Sales Representative" Then
        myNode.Text = "Representative"
        xmldoc.Save strPath & "InternalContacts.xml"
      End If
    Next myNode
  End If
  Set xmldoc = Nothing
End Sub
```

The `SelectNodesByCriteria` procedure creates the `IXMLDOMNodeList` object, which represents a collection of child nodes. The `selectNodes` method applies the specified pattern to this node's context and returns the list of matching nodes as `IXMLDOMNodeList`. The expression used by the `selectNodes` method specifies that all the `Title` element nodes should be included in the node list.

> ### Using the Is Nothing Conditional Expression
>
> You can use the `Is Nothing` conditional expression to find out whether a matching element was found in the loaded XML file. If the matching elements were found in the `IXMLDOMNodeList`, the procedure iterates through the node list and prints each element node text to the Immediate window. In addition, if the node element's text value is `Sales Representative`, the procedure replaces this value with `Representative`. The `Save` method of the `DOMDocument` is used to save the changes in the `InternalContacts.xml` file.

2. Position the insertion point anywhere within the code of the `SelectNodesByCriteria` procedure and choose Run | Run Sub/UserForm. Running the `SelectNodesByCriteria` procedure produces the following results:

```
Sales Representative
Vice President, Sales
Sales Representative
Sales Representative
Sales Manager
Sales Representative
Sales Representative
Inside Sales Coordinator
Sales Representative
```

When you run this procedure again, you should see the following output:

```
Representative

Vice President, Sales
Representative
```

```
Representative
Sales Manager
Representative
Representative
Inside Sales Coordinator
Representative
```

Retrieving the First Matching Node

If all you want to do is retrieve the first node that meets the specified criterion, use the `SelectSingleNode` method of the `DOMDocument` object. For this method's argument, specify the string representing the node you'd like to find. For example, the following procedure finds the first node that matches the criterion `//City` in the `InternalContacts.xml` file:

```
Sub SelectSingleNode()
  Dim xmldoc As MSXML2.DOMDocument60
  Dim xmlSingleNode As MSXML2.IXMLDOMNode
  Dim strPath As String

  strPath = "C:\VBAAccess2024_XML\"
  Set xmldoc = New MSXML2.DOMDocument60
  xmldoc.async = False
  xmldoc.Load (strPath & "InternalContacts.xml")
  Set xmlSingleNode = _
    xmldoc.SelectSingleNode("//City")
  If xmlSingleNode Is Nothing Then
    Debug.Print "No nodes selected."
  Else
    Debug.Print xmlSingleNode.Text
  End If
  Set xmldoc = Nothing
End Sub
```

The XML DOM provides a number of other methods that make it possible to programmatically add or delete elements in the XML document tree structure. Covering all of the details of the XML DOM is beyond the scope of this chapter. If you would like more information on this subject, visit *http://www.w3.org/DOM/*

USING ADO WITH XML

Earlier in this book, you learned how to save ADO recordsets to disk using the Advanced Data TableGram (`adPersistADTG`) format. This section expands on what you already know about ADO recordsets by showing you how to use the ADO recordset's `adPersistXML` constant to save all types of recordsets to disk as XML.

Saving an ADO Recordset as XML to Disk

To save an ADO recordset to a disk file as XML, use the `Save` method of the `Recordset` object with the `adPersistXML` constant. Hands-On 20.14 demonstrates how to create an XML file from ADO.

(•) Hands-On 20.14   Creating an XML Document from ADO

1. In the VBE window of the `Chap20.accdb` database, choose Insert | Module to add a new standard module to the current VBA project.
2. Choose Tools | References to open the References dialog box. Check the box next to Microsoft ActiveX Object Library 6.1 (or a lower version, if this one is not available) and click OK.
3. In the module's Code window, enter the following `SaveRst_ToXMLwithADO` procedure:

```
Sub SaveRst_ToXMLwithADO()
  Dim conn As ADODB.Connection
  Dim rst As ADODB.Recordset
  Dim strPath As String
  Dim strDBName As String
  Dim strConn As String
  Dim strSQL As String

  strPath = "C:\VBAAccess2024_XML\"
  strDBName = "Northwind 2007.accdb"
  strConn = "Provider = Microsoft.ACE.OLEDB.12.0;" & _
    "Data Source=" & strPath & strDBName & ";"

  strSQL = "SELECT "
  strSQL = strSQL & "Nz([Supplier IDs], "" "") as SupplierIDs,"
   strSQL = strSQL & "Nz([ID], "" "") as ID, Nz([Product Code],""
                                    "") as ProductCode, "
  strSQL = strSQL & "Nz([Product Name], "" "") as ProductName, "
  strSQL = strSQL & "Nz([Standard Cost], "" "") as StandardCost, "
  strSQL = strSQL & "Nz([List Price], "" "") as ListPrice, "
  strSQL = strSQL & "Nz([Reorder Level], "" "") as ReorderLevel, "
  strSQL = strSQL & "Nz([Target Level], "" "") as TargetLevel, "
  strSQL = strSQL & "Nz([Quantity Per Unit], "" "")
                                    as QuantityPerUnit, "
```

```
strSQL = strSQL & "Nz([Discontinued], "" "") as Discontinued, "
strSQL = strSQL & "Nz([Minimum Reorder Quantity],"" "")
                                        as MinReorderQuantity, "
strSQL = strSQL & "Nz([Category], "" "") as Category "
strSQL = strSQL & "FROM Products;"

Debug.Print strSQL
' open a connection to the database
' execute an SQL SELECT statement
' against the database

  Set conn = New ADODB.Connection
  With conn
      .Open strConn

    Set rst = .Execute(strSQL)

  End With

 ' delete the file if it exists
On Error Resume Next

Kill strPath & "Products_AttribCentric.xml"

' save the recordset as an XML file
rst.Save strPath & "Products_AttribCentric.xml", _
  adPersistXML


  Set rst = Nothing
  Set conn = Nothing

End Sub
```

The `SaveRst_ToXMLwithADO` procedure begins by defining the necessary variables and setting their values. After that, a connection to the `Northwind 2007.accdb` database is established using the ADO `Connection` object and its `Microsoft.ACE.OLEDB.12.0` provider. Next, the procedure executes an SQL `SELECT` statement against the database to retrieve data from the specified fields in the `Products` table. To avoid problems later with the rendering of an HTML page, we use the `Nz` function on each table field to ensure that if there is no value in that field, we get a blank space.

```
strSQL = strSQL & "Nz([Product Name], "" "") as ProductName, "
```

Notice that the blank space is surrounded by double quotation marks. The prior code says, "Take what is already in the variable `strSQL` and add to it the data from the [Product Name] field, replacing it with a blank space if there is no data, and return the result to the `strSQL` variable using `ProductName` (with no spaces) as the new field name." When building a complex select statement in your code, make sure to output it with the `Debug.Print` statement to the Immediate window so you can verify that it is correct. Once the records are placed in a recordset, the `Save` method is called to store the recordset to a disk file using the `adPersistXML` format:

```
Set rst = .Execute(strSQL)

rst.Save strPath & "Products_AttribCentric.xml", adPersistXML
```

If the disk file already exists, the procedure deletes the existing file using the VBA `Kill` statement. The `On Error Resume Next` statement bypasses the `Kill` statement if the file you are going to create does not yet exist.

4. Position the insertion point anywhere within the code of the procedure and choose Run | Run Sub/UserForm.

5. Open the `C:\VBAAccess2024_XML\Products_AttribCentric.xml` file created by the `SaveRst_ToXMLwithADO` procedure and examine its content. The browser displays the raw XML, as shown in Figure 20.26. Notice that the content of this file looks different from other XML files you generated in this chapter. The reason for this is that XML that is persisted from ADO recordsets is created in an attribute-centric XML. Access supports only element-centric XML. Therefore, to import to Access an XML file created from ADO, you must first create and apply an XSLT transformation to the source document. The stylesheet you create should convert the attribute-centric XML to element-centric XML that Access can handle (see Hands-On 20.15).

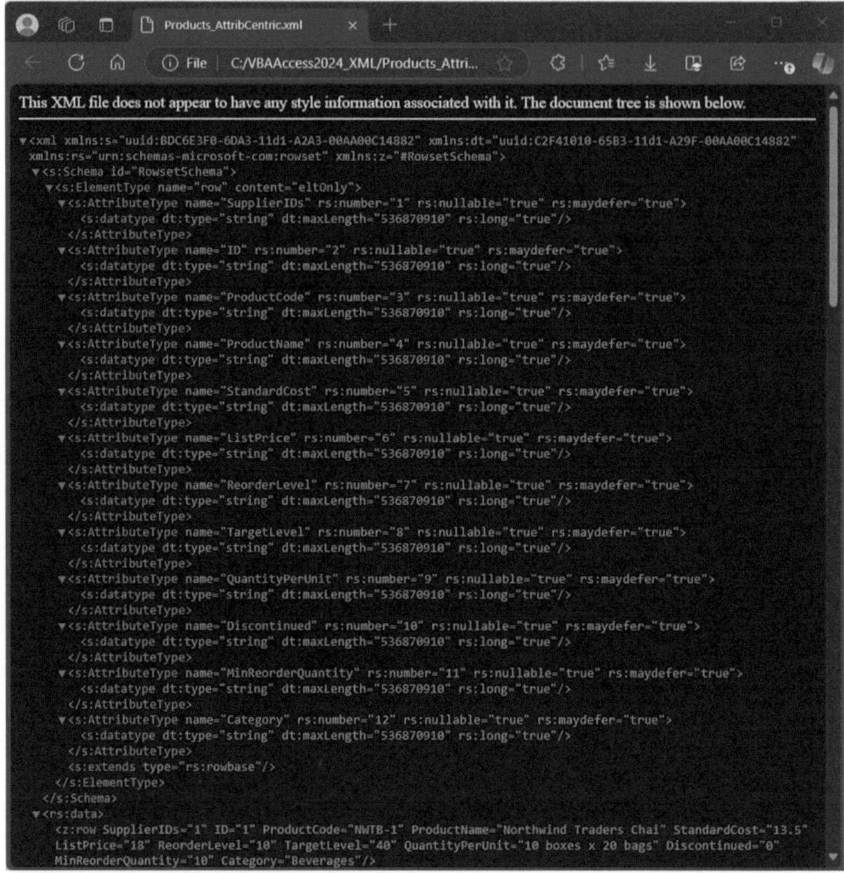

FIGURE 20.26. Saving a recordset to an XML file with ADO produces an attribute-centric XML file.

Attribute-Centric and Element-Centric XML

In the XML file generated in Hands-On 20.14 and shown in Figure 20.26, you can see two child nodes: `<s:Schema>` and `<rs:data>`.

The schema node describes the structure of the recordset, while the data node holds the actual data. Inside the `<s:Schema id="RowsetSchema">` and `</s:Schema>` tags, ADO places information about each column: field name, position, data type and length, nullability, and whether the column is writable. Each field is represented by the `<s:AttributeType>` element. Notice that the value of the name attribute is the field name. The `<s:AttributeType>` element also has a child element, `<s:datatype>`, which holds information about its data type (integer, number, string, etc.) and the maximum field length.

Below the schema definition is the actual data. The ADO schema represents each record using the `<z:row>` tag. The fields in a record are expressed as attributes of the `<z:row>` element. Every XML attribute is assigned a value that is enclosed in a pair of single or double quotation marks; however, if the value of a field in a record is `Null`, the attribute on the `<z:row>` is not created. Notice that each record is written out in the following format:

```
<z:row SupplierIDs="4" ID="1" ProductCode="NWTB-1"
ProductName="Northwind Traders Chai" StandardCost="13.5"
ListPrice="18" ReorderLevel="10" TargetLevel="40"
QuantityPerUnit="10 boxes x 20 bags" Discontinued="False"
MinReorderQuantity="10" Category="Beverages"/>
```

The preceding code fragment is referred to as *attribute-centric XML*. Access will not be able to import it as is. To make the XML file compatible with Access, each record must be written out as follows:

```
<Product>
<SupplierIDs>4</SupplierIDs>
<ID>1</ID>
<ProductCode>NWTB-1</ProductCode>
<ProductName>Northwind Traders Chai</ProductName>
<StandardCost>13.5</StandardCost>
<ListPrice>18</ListPrice>
<ReorderLevel>10</ReorderLevel>
<TargetLevel>40</TargetLevel>
<QuantityPerUnit>10 boxes x 20 bags</QuantityPerUnit>
<Discontinued>False</Discontinued>
<MinReorderQuantity>10</MinReorderQuantity>
<Category>Beverages</Category>
</Product>
```

The code fragment shown above represents *element-centric XML*. Notice that each record is wrapped in a `<Product>` tag, and each field is an element under the `<Product>` tag.

Changing the Type of an XML File

Because it is much easier to work with element-centric XML files (and Access does not support attribute-centric XML), you must write an XSL stylesheet to transform an attribute-centric XML file to an element-centric XML file before you can import to Access an XML file created from an ADO recordset.

The following hands-on exercise demonstrates how to write a stylesheet to perform such a conversion.

> **(◉) Hands-On 20.15   Creating a Stylesheet to Convert Attribute-Centric XML to Element-Centric XML**

1. Open Notepad and type the following stylesheet code:

```
<xsl:stylesheet version="1.0"
   xmlns:xsl="http://www.w3.org/1999/XSL/Transform"
   xmlns:rs="urn:schemas-microsoft-com:rowset">
<xsl:output method="xml" encoding="UTF-8" />

   <xsl:template match="/">

   <!-- root element for the XML output -->
   <Products xmlns:z="#RowsetSchema">

   <xsl:for-each select="/xml/rs:data/z:row">
   <Product>
   <xsl:for-each select="@*">
   <xsl:element name="{name()}">
   <xsl:value-of select="."/>
   </xsl:element>
   </xsl:for-each>
   </Product>
   </xsl:for-each>
   </Products>

   </xsl:template>
</xsl:stylesheet>
```

2. Save this stylesheet as `C:\VBAAccess2024_XML\AttribToElem.xsl`. Be sure to include the `.xsl` extension so the file is not saved as text. You will use this stylesheet for the transformation in the next hands-on exercise.

Notice in the preceding stylesheet that the `"@*"` wildcard matches all attribute nodes. Each time the `<z:row>` tag is encountered, an element named `<Product>` will be created. Also, for each attribute, the attribute name will be converted to the element name using the built-in XPath `name( )` function. Expressions in curly braces are evaluated and converted to strings. `select="."` returns the current value of the attribute being read.

See the next section on how to apply this stylesheet to an XML document.

Applying an XSL Stylesheet

Now that you've created the stylesheet to transform an attribute-centric XML file into an element-centric file, you can use the `transformNodeToObject` method of the `DOMDocument` object to apply the stylesheet to the `Products_AttribCentric.xml` file created in Hands-On 20.14. The hands-on exercise that follows demonstrates how to do this. In addition, the procedure in this exercise will import the converted ADO XML file to Access.

Hands-On 20.16   Applying a Stylesheet to an ADO XML Document and Importing It to Access

1. Enter the following procedure below the procedure code you created in Hands-On 20.14:

```
Sub ApplyStyleSheetAndImport()
  Dim myXMLDoc As New MSXML2.DOMDocument60
  Dim myXSLDoc As New MSXML2.DOMDocument60
  Dim newXMLDoc As New MSXML2.DOMDocument60
  Dim strXMLFile As String
  Dim strPath As String

  strPath = "C:\VBAAccess2024_XML\"

  strXMLFile = "Products_AttribCentric.xml"
  myXMLDoc.Async = False
  If myXMLDoc.Load(strPath & strXMLFile) Then
    myXSLDoc.Load strPath & "AttribToElem.xsl"

    ' apply the transformation
    If Not myXSLDoc Is Nothing Then
      myXMLDoc.transformNodeToObject _
        myXSLDoc, newXMLDoc

      ' save the output in a new file
      newXMLDoc.Save strPath & _
          "Products_Converted.xml"

      ' import to Access
      Application.ImportXML _
      strPath & "Products_Converted.xml"
    End If
  End If
End Sub
```

This procedure begins by loading both the `Products_AttribCentric.xml` file (created in Hands-On 20.14) and the `AttribToElem.xsl` stylesheet (created in Hands-On 20.15) into the `DOMDocument` object. Next, the stylesheet is applied to the source file by using the `transformNodeToObject` method. This method is applied to a node in the source XML document's tree and takes two arguments. The first argument is a stylesheet in the form of a `DOMDocument` node. The second argument is another `DOMDocument` node that will hold the result of the transformation. Next, the result of the transformation is saved to a file (`Products_Converted.xml`) and the file is imported to Access using the `ImportXML` method, which was introduced earlier in this chapter.

2. Run the `ApplyStyleSheetAndImport` procedure.
3. Open the `C:\VBAAccess2024_XML\Products_Converted.xml` file. Notice that the `Products_Converted.xml` file content is now element-centric XML (see Figure 20.27).
4. In the Access window, locate and open the table named `Product`.

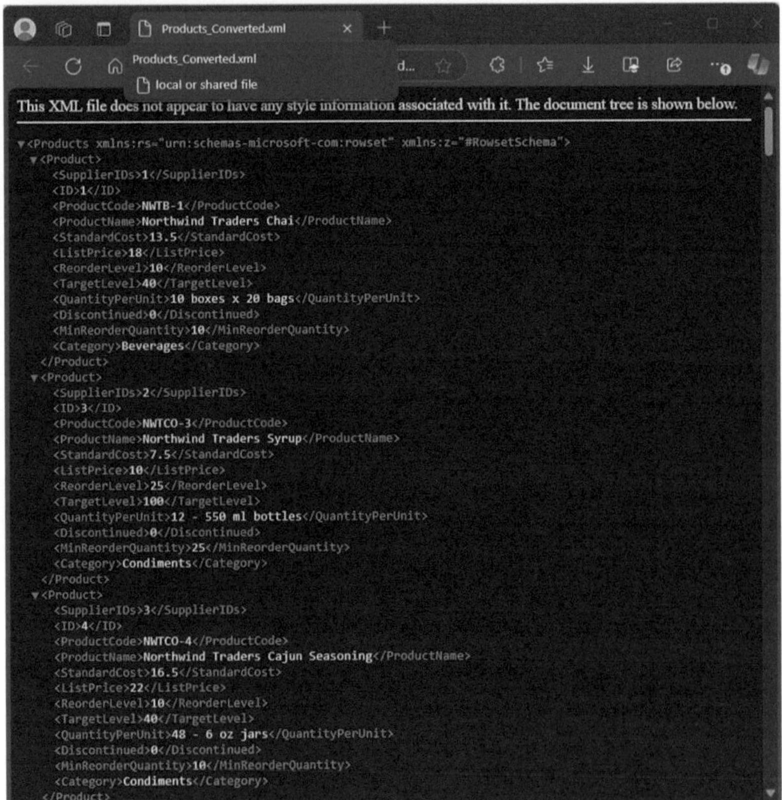

FIGURE 20.27. This element-centric XML file is a result of applying a stylesheet to the attribute-centric ADO recordset that was saved to an XML file.

The `Products` table shown in Figure 20.28 was created by the `ImportXML` method in the `ApplyStyleSheetAndImport` procedure.

SupplierIDs	ID	ProductCode	ProductName	StandardCos	ListPrice	ReorderLevel	TargetLevel	QuantityPer	Discontinue	MinReorder	Category
1	1	NWTB-1	Northwind Tra 13.5	18	10	40		10 boxes x 20 b	0	10	Beverages
2	3	NWTCO-3	Northwind Tra 7.5	10	25	100		12 - 550 ml bot	0	25	Condiments
3	4	NWTCO-4	Northwind Tra 16.5	22	10	40		48 - 6 oz jars	0	10	Condiments
4	5	NWTO-5	Northwind Tra 16.0125	21.35	10	40		36 boxes	0	10	Oil
5	6	NWTJP-6	Northwind Tra 18.75	25	25	100		12 - 8 oz jars	0	25	Jams, Preserve
6	7	NWTDFN-7	Northwind Tra 22.5	30	10	40		12 - 1 lb pkgs.	0	10	Dried Fruit & N
7	8	NWTS-8	Northwind Tra 30	40	10	40		12 - 12 oz jars	0	10	Sauces
8	14	NWTDFN-14	Northwind Tra 17.4375	23.25	10	40		40 - 100 g pkgs.	0	10	Dried Fruit & N
9	17	NWTCFV-17	Northwind Tra 29.25	39	10	40		15.25 OZ	0	10	Canned Fruit &
10	19	NWTBGM-19	Northwind Tra 6.9	9.2	5	20		10 boxes x 12 p	0	5	Baked Goods &
11	20	NWTJP-6	Northwind Tra 60.75	81	10	40		30 gift boxes	0	10	Jams, Preserve
12	21	NWTBGM-21	Northwind Tra 7.5	10	5	20		24 pkgs. x 4 pie	0	5	Baked Goods &

Record: 14 ◄ 1 of 45 ► ►I ►* No Filter Search

FIGURE 20.28.   This table was imported to Access after conversion of an attribute-centric ADO recordset into an element-centric XML file.

Transforming Attribute-Centric XML Data into an HTML Table

As you've seen in earlier examples, creating an XML file from an ADO record-set results in output that contains attribute-centric XML. To import this type of output to Access, you had to create a special stylesheet and apply the transformation to convert the attribute-centric XML to the element-centric XML that Access supports. What if you simply want to display the XML file created from an ADO recordset in a Web browser? To do this, you must create a generic XSL stylesheet that draws a simple HTML table for users when they open the XML attribute-centric file in their browser.

Hands-On 20.17 demonstrates how to create a stylesheet to transform the attribute-centric XML file that we created in Hands-On 20.14 into HTML. Hands-On 20.18 performs the transformation by inserting a reference to the XSL stylesheet into the XML document.

Hands-On 20.17   **Creating a Generic Stylesheet to Transform an Attribute-Centric XML File into HTML**

1. Open Notepad and type the following stylesheet code:

```
<?xml version="1.0"?>
<xsl:stylesheet version="1.0"
xmlns:xsl="http://www.w3.org/1999/XSL/Transform"
xmlns:s='uuid:BDC6E3F0-6DA3-11d1-A2A3-00AA00C14882'
xmlns:dt='uuid:C2F41010-65B3-11d1-A29F-00AA00C14882'
xmlns:rs='urn:schemas-microsoft-com:rowset'
xmlns:z='#RowsetSchema'
xmlns:html="http://www.w3.org/TR/REC-html40">
```

```
<xsl:template match="/">

<html>
<head>
<title>XML to HTML</title>

<style type="text/css">

table {
  font-family: arial, sans-serif;
  font-size:9px;
  border-collapse: collapse;
  width: 100%;
}

td, th {
  border: 1px solid #dddddd;
  text-align: left;
  padding: 8px;
}

th {background-color:#9acd32; color:black}

tr:nth-child(even) {
  background-color: #dddddd;
}
</style>

</head>
<body>
<table width="100%" border="1">

<!-- generate table headings -->
<xsl:for-each
select="xml/s:Schema/s:ElementType/s:AttributeType">
<th>
<xsl:value-of select="@name" />
</th>
</xsl:for-each>

<!-- loop through all data rows and get values for each column -->
<xsl:for-each select="xml/rs:data/z:row">
<tr>
<xsl:for-each select="@*">
<td>
```

```
<xsl:value-of select="."/>

</td>
</xsl:for-each>
</tr>
</xsl:for-each>
</table>
</body>
</html>
</xsl:template>
</xsl:stylesheet>
```

2. Save the stylesheet as `AttribToHTML.xsl`. Be sure to include the `.xsl` extension so the file is not saved as text.

3. Close Notepad.

   The stylesheet uses the feature known as Cascading Stylesheets (CSS) to format the HTML table. A style comprises different properties—bold, italic, font size and font weight, color, etc.—that you want to apply to text (titles, headers, body, etc.). In this stylesheet, we applied simple styles to the following HTML table elements: `table`, `th` (table heading), `td` (table data), and `tr` (table row). Using styles is very convenient. If you don't like the formatting, you can simply change the style definition and get a new look instantly. Each style definition is contained between curly braces, { }.

```
td, th {
   border: 1px solid #dddddd;
   text-align: left;
   padding: 8px;
}
```

For more information about creating HTML styles and an opportunity to try it yourself, check out the following link:

https://www.w3schools.com/html/html_styles.asp

The example stylesheet uses template-based processing, which we discussed earlier.

The code between the opening and closing tags will be processed for all tags whose names match the value of the `match` attribute. In other words, we want the pattern matching to be applied to the entire document (/). Next, a loop is used to write out the table headings. To do this, you must move through all the

`AttributeType` elements of the root element, outputting the name attribute's value like this:

```
<xsl:for-each
select="xml/s:Schema/s:ElementType/s:AttributeType">
<th>
<xsl:value-of select="@name" />
</th>
</xsl:for-each>
```

An attribute's name is always preceded by @. Next, another loop runs through all the `<z:row>` elements representing actual records:

```
<xsl:for-each select="xml/rs:data/z:row">
```

All the attributes of any `<z:row>` element are enumerated:

```
<xsl:for-each select="xml/rs:data/z:row">
<tr>
<xsl:for-each select="@*">
<td>
<xsl:value-of select="."/>
</td>
```

The string `"@*"` denotes any attribute. For each attribute found under the `<z:row>` element, you need to match the attribute name with its corresponding value. Notice the period in the `<xsl:value-of>` tag. The period represents the node that XSLT is currently working with. In summary, the preceding code fragment tells the XSLT processor to display the value of the current node during the iteration of the `<z:row>` attributes.

After completing the stylesheet, the next step is to link the XML and XSL files. You can do this by adding a reference to a stylesheet in your XML document, as shown in Hands-On 20.18.

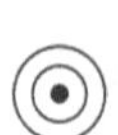

Hands-On 20.18   **Linking the Attribute-Centric XML File with the Generic Stylesheet and Displaying the Transformed File in a Web Browser**

1. Save the `Products_AttribCentric.xml` file as `Products_AttribCentric_2.xml`.
2. Open the `Products_AttribCentric_2.xml` file with Notepad.
3. Type the following definition in the first line of this file:

```
<?xml-stylesheet type="text/xsl" href="AttribToHTML.xsl"?>
```

This instruction establishes a reference to the XSL file.

4. Save the changes made to the `Products_AttribCentric_2.xml` file and close Notepad.
5. Now, let's check the result. Unfortunately, double-clicking the `Products_AttribCentric_2.xml` file produces a blank page. To view the data, you need to access it from the Web server that you set up earlier in this chapter.
6. Open your favorite browser and enter the following URL: *http://localhost/acc_xml/Products_AttribCentric_2.xml*
   You should see the data formatted in a table (see Figure 20.29).

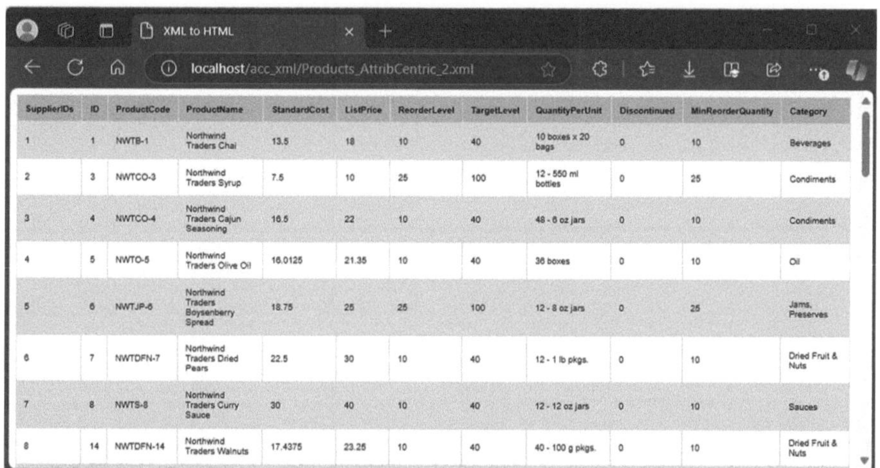

FIGURE 20.29.   You can apply a stylesheet to an XML document generated by ADO to display the data in a nicely formatted HTML table.

Loading an XML Document in Excel

After saving an ADO recordset to an XML file on disk, you can load it into a desired application and read it as if it were a database. To gain access to the records saved in the XML file, use the `Open` method of the `Recordset` object and specify the filename, including its path, and the persisted recordset service provider as `Provider=MSPersist`. The following hands-on exercise demonstrates how to programmatically open in Excel a persisted recordset that was saved in XML files (`Products_AttribCentric.xml` and `Products_AttribCentric_2.xml`).

(⊙) Hands-On 20.19   Loading an XML File into an Excel Workbook

1. In the VBE window, choose Insert | Module to add a new standard module to the current VBA project.
2. Choose Tools | References and click the checkbox next to Microsoft Excel 16.0 Object Library (or its earlier version). Click OK to exit the References dialog box.
3. In the module's Code window, enter the following OpenAdoFile procedure:

```
Sub OpenAdoFile()
  Dim rst As ADODB.Recordset
  Dim objExcel As Excel.Application
  Dim wkb As Excel.Workbook
  Dim wks As Excel.Worksheet
  Dim StartRange As Excel.Range
  Dim h As Integer
  Dim strPath As String

  strPath = "C:\VBAAccess2024_XML\"
  Set rst = New ADODB.Recordset

  ' open your XML file and load it
  rst.Open strPath & "Products_AttribCentric.xml", _
    "Provider=MSPersist"

  ' display the number of records
  MsgBox "There are " & rst.RecordCount & _
    " records in this file."

  Set objExcel = New Excel.Application

  ' create a new Excel workbook
  Set wkb = objExcel.Workbooks.Add

  ' set a reference to the ActiveSheet
  Set wks = wkb.ActiveSheet

  ' make Excel application window visible
  objExcel.Visible = True


  ' copy field names as headings
  ' to the 1st row of the worksheet
  For h = 1 To rst.Fields.Count
```

```
  wks.Cells(1, h).Value = rst.Fields(h - 1).Name
  Next

  ' specify the cell range to
  ' receive the data (A2)
  Set StartRange = wks.Cells(2, 1)

  ' copy the records from the
  ' recordset beginning in cell A2
  StartRange.CopyFromRecordset rst

  ' autofit the columns to make the data fit
  wks.Range("A1").CurrentRegion.Select
  wks.Columns.AutoFit

  ' save the workbook
  wkb.SaveAs strPath & "ExcelReport.xls"

  Set objExcel = Nothing
  Set rst = Nothing
End Sub
```

This procedure is well commented, so we will skip its analysis and proceed to the next step.

4. Run the `OpenAdoFile` procedure.

   When the procedure is complete, the Excel application window should be visible with the `ExcelReport.xls` workbook file displaying products retrieved from the XML file (see Figure 20.30).

5. Close the Excel workbook and exit Excel.

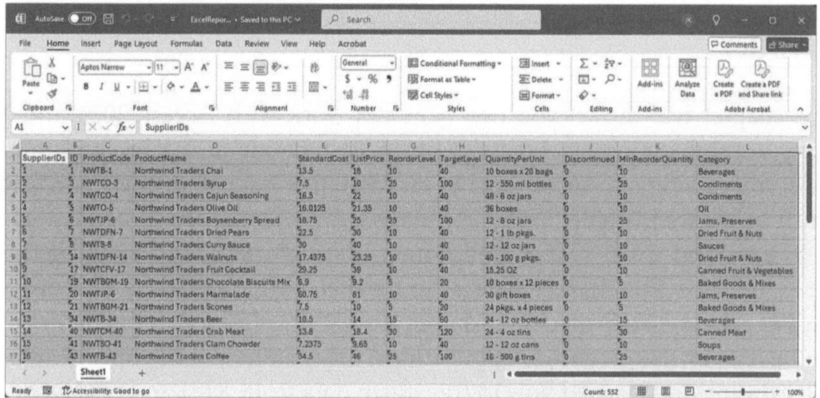

FIGURE 20.30. An ADO recordset persisted to an XML file is now opened in Excel.

USING ChatGPT WITH ACCESS

So far in this book, you've gained lots of practical programming knowledge. It's time to test it out in a complete project. ChatGPT can assist you in outlining the steps of any project you can think of. Let's start with this:

User Prompt: *I have studied the use of XML with Access. Can you provide me with an example project that I could use to test my learning progress?*

ChatGPT/Microsoft Copilot's Response:

That's great to hear! Testing your learning progress with a practical project is a fantastic idea. Here's a simple example project that you can use to practice working with XML in Microsoft Access:

Example Project: Product Inventory Management
Project Overview

Create a database to manage a product inventory, including features to add, update, delete, and list products. The products will be stored in an XML file, and you'll use Access to interact with this file.

The ChatGPT sample project is available in the companion files. See the `Chapter 20 – Using ChatGPT with Access` document. This project includes several user prompts that guide ChatGPT into providing solutions to the issues that were encountered while following the initial ChatGPT guidelines. Please go over the entire document first to understand the problems that were pointed out. The complete project is available in the `ProductInventory.accdb` database in the companion files.

SUMMARY

This chapter has shown you how you can work with Access 2024 and XML. Using a combination of Access' built-in commands and VBA programming code, you can export Access data to an XML file, import an XML file, and display it as an Access table.

You learned what XML is and how it is structured. After working through the examples in this chapter, it's easy to see that XML supplies us with numerous ways to accomplish a specific task. Because XML is stored in plain-text files, it can be read by many types of applications, independent of the operating system or hardware. You learned how to transform data from XML to HTML and from one XML format to another. You explored the ADO recordset methods that are suitable for working with XML programmatically and were introduced to XSL stylesheets and XSLT transformations.

All of the methods and techniques you've discovered here will take time to sink in. XML is not like VBA. It is not very independent; it needs many supporting technologies to assist it in its work. So, don't despair if you don't understand something right away. Learning XML requires learning many other new concepts, such as XSLT, XPath, and schemas. Take XML step by step by experimenting with it. The time that you invest in studying this technology will not be wasted. XML has been around for quite a while and is here to stay. Here are the three main reasons why you should consider using XML:

- XML separates content from presentation.

  If you are planning to design Web pages, you do not need to make changes to your HTML files when the data changes. Because the data is kept in separate files, it's easy to make modifications.

- XML is perfect for sharing and exchanging data.

  You no longer need to worry about whether your data needs to be processed by a system that's not compatible with yours. Because all systems can work with text files (and XML documents are simply text files), you can easily share and exchange your data.

- XML can be used as a database.

  You no longer need a database system to have a database.

Chapter **21**

ACCESS AND REST API

We've almost reached the end of this book. In this last chapter, we will focus on expanding your VBA skillset by covering topics such as working with a VBA Dictionary object, using regular expressions, and calling a new type of Web service, known as REST API.

INTRODUCTION TO VBA DICTIONARY OBJECTS

After you've learned how arrays and collections can help you store values while your program is running, you may be surprised to learn that there is still another way to manipulate your data. An object known as VBA Dictionary operates like a Collection object but offers more flexibility and speed. It works in a similar way to a normal dictionary, allowing you to look up values based on a key you provide. A dictionary is a collection of key-value pairs, and each key must be unique. Unlike an array, its size does not need to be predefined. Its data type is `Variant`, so you can enter any type of data you want to keep track of (text, numbers, dates, arrays, or any other objects).

The Dictionary object is not part of standard VBA. It is a part of the Microsoft Scripting Runtime library (`scrrun.dll`).

Accessing the VBA Dictionary

There are two ways in which you can access VBA Dictionary in your VBA code. One is referred to as *early binding* and the other is called *late binding*.

- Early Binding

  To use early binding, you need to add a reference to the Microsoft Scripting Runtime library, as described in the next section. With early binding, your code is compiled before it runs, so your procedures can run much faster. Once the reference is added to the required library, you can write the following code to define your Dictionary object:

  ```
  Dim myDict As New Scripting.Dictionary
  ```

  With early binding, you can count on *IntelliSense* to help you with syntax and programming.

- Late Binding

  With late binding, your object will be compiled while your code runs, so it will be slower. You are not required to set up a library reference. To define the Dictionary object, specify the `Scripting.Dictionary` using the `CreateObject` method:

  ```
  Dim myDict As Object
  Set myDict = CreateObject("Scripting.Dictionary")
  ```

Adding a Reference to the Microsoft Scripting Runtime Library

You add the reference to the Microsoft Scripting Runtime library in the same way you added references to other libraries that were introduced in this book. Simply select Tools | References on the VBE screen and scroll down in the pop-up window until you locate the library. Select it and click OK. Figure 21.1 shows this selection. After you've added the library reference, it's a good idea to examine the contents of this library by using the Object Browser. On the VBE screen, press F2 or choose View | Object Browser. Choose Scripting from the first drop-down, as shown in Figure 21.2. Notice the available types of objects, one of them being Dictionary. By clicking on each Dictionary member, you can find out the type of the member (method or property) and its function. For example, the `Item` property is the default member of `Scripting.Dictionary` and is used to set or get the item for a given key, while `Add` is a method used to add a new key and item to the dictionary.

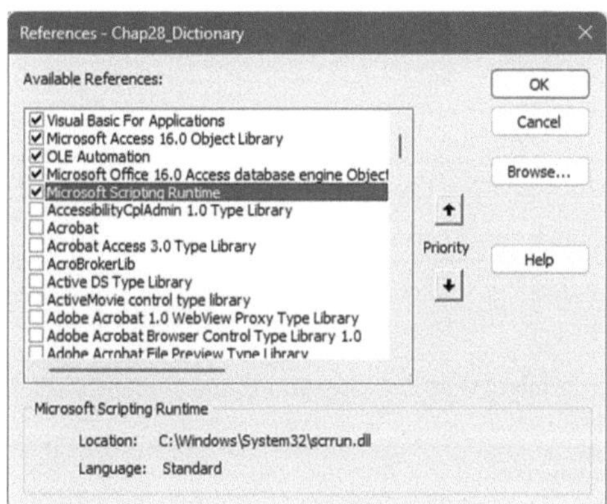

FIGURE 21.1.   Adding a reference to the Microsoft Scripting Runtime library.

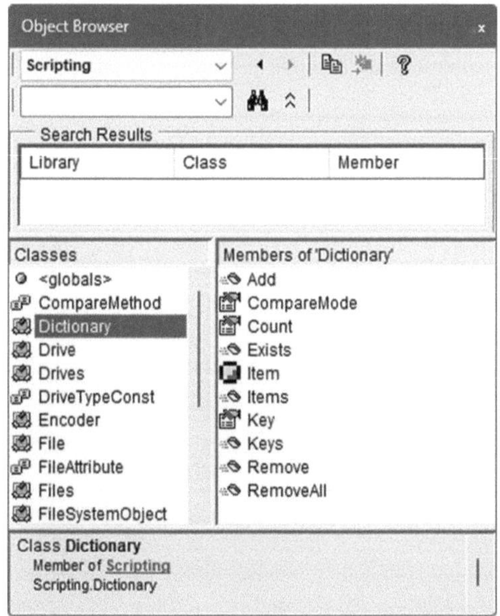

FIGURE 21.2.   Examining the contents of the Microsoft Scripting Runtime library.

Working with the Dictionary Object's Properties and Methods

Table 21.1 lists the methods and properties that are available in `Scripting.Dictionary`.

TABLE 21.1. Scripting.Dictionary's methods and properties.

Methods	
Add	Adds a new key/item pair to a Dictionary object.
Remove	Removes a specified key/item pair from the Dictionary object.
RemoveAll	Removes all the key/item pairs in the Dictionary object.
Items	Returns an array of all the items in a Dictionary object.
Keys	Returns an array of all the keys in a Dictionary object.
Exists	Returns a Boolean value (true/false) that indicates whether a specified key exists in a Dictionary object.
Properties	
Key	Sets a new key value for an existing key value in the Dictionary object.
Item	Sets or returns the value of an item in a Dictionary object.
Count	Returns the number of key/value pairs in a Dictionary object.
CompareMode	Sets or returns the comparison mode for comparing keys in a Dictionary object.

Let's assume that you need to create a dictionary of world capital cities. Using the `Add` method of `Scripting.Dictionary`, you can fill your dictionary like this:

```
Sub FillDictionary()
'declare a dictionary object
'uses early binding
'requires the reference to the Microsoft Scripting Runtime
Library
Dim objDict As New Scripting.Dictionary

'add items to the dictionary
objDict("USA") = "Washington D.C."
objDict("Canada") = "Ottawa"
objDict("France") = "Paris"
objDict("England") = "London"
objDict("Hungary") = "Budapest"
objDict("Italy") = "Rome"
objDict("Japan") = "Tokyo"
objDict.Add "Germany", "Berlin"
objDict.Add key:="China", item:="Beijing"
```

In the code snippet above, you will notice that there are three different ways you can use to add an item to a dictionary. Use whatever method feels most comfortable to you.

After filling in the dictionary, you will want to read its keys/values. You can use the `Keys` method to return an array of all the keys, like this:

```
'iterate through the dictionary to read its keys
Dim i As Long
For i = LBound(objDict.Keys) To UBound(objDict.Keys)
    Debug.Print i & "--> " & objDict.Keys(i)
Next i
```

In the previous code, we utilized the upper- and lower-bound methods (`Ubound` and `LBound`) of an array to list the keys. The following code will retrieve a specific key:

```
'retrieve 3rd key
Debug.Print "3rd key=" & objDict.Keys()(2)
```

Recall that arrays are zero-based. You can place all keys into an array, like this:

```
Dim aKeys() As Variant
aKeys = objDict.Keys
Debug.Print "Dictionary contains " & UBound(aKeys) + 1 & "
keys."
Debug.Print "The first key is " & aKeys(0)
```

It is easy to remove a key from a dictionary, but before removal, always check whether the key exists using the `Exists` method. This method is what makes the Dictionary object easier to manipulate than collections and arrays. Keys are case-sensitive, so pay attention to the case when checking for key existence.

```
'remove the key if it exists
If objDict.Exists("France") Then
    objDict.Remove "France"
Else
    Debug.Print "This key does not exist"
End If
```

The `Count` property returns the total number of items in the dictionary, and the `Item` property is used to set the value of a dictionary item. In the following example, we replace the value of `Germany` with `Frankfurt`:

```
'count the items in the dictionary
Debug.Print "Now the dictionary contains " & objDict.Count & " keys."
objDict.item("Germany") = "Frankfurt"
Debug.Print objDict("Germany") & " is a city in Germany."
```

Using the `For Each` loop, you can list all the items or keys in the dictionary, like this:

```
' list all the items in the dictionary
Dim item As Variant
For Each item In objDict.Items
    Debug.Print item
Next
' List all keys in the dictionary
Dim key As Variant
For Each key In objDict.Keys
    Debug.Print key & " --> " & objDict.item(key)
Next
```

To clear your dictionary of all items, use the `RemoveAll` method:

```
' remove all key/item pairs
objDict.RemoveAll
' verify that dictionary is empty
Debug.Print objDict.Count
End Sub
```

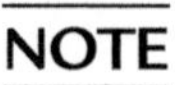

> **NOTE**   *The prior procedure can be found in the* `Chap21.accdb` *database in the companion files.*

Recall that key searches are case-sensitive by default. You can, however, use the `CompareMode` property to change this behavior. The mode change must be specified right after the creation of the Dictionary object, before adding any data to the dictionary. Let's look at some code.

```
Sub CaseNotSensitive()
  Dim objDict As New Scripting.Dictionary
  objDict.CompareMode = TextCompare
  objDict.Add "Math", 89
  objDict.Add "English", 70
  objDict.Add "Chemistry", 90
  Debug.Print objDict.Exists("math")
End Sub
```

In the example above, we set `CompareMode` to `TextCompare` to allow for searches that are not case-sensitive. So, instead of typing `Math` for the key name, we can simply enter `math` in lowercase and the `Exists` method is able to locate the key. The `CompareMode` can also be set to two other settings: `BinaryCompare` and `DatabaseCompare`.

`BinaryCompare` performs binary comparisons; it is case-sensitive, so `Event-Name` is not the same as `eventName` or `eventname`.

`DatabaseCompare` performs a comparison based on information in the database. The latter only exists in Microsoft Access (it's not available in other VBA-capable Office applications).

Dictionary Versus Collection

Table 21.2 shows several advantages of the Dictionary object over the native VBA Collection object. In your programming endeavors, you should always pick the object that is most suitable for a particular task.

TABLE 21.2.   Dictionary versus Collection.

Dictionary	Collection
Retrieving items in a dictionary is faster than in a collection.	Retrieving items is slower than in a dictionary.
Easier to search for a given item.	Harder to search for a given item.
The Item value can be changed directly.	The Item value must first be removed and then the changed item can be added back.
Uses keys to locate a particular item; keys can be checked for existence.	Keys are used to look up data but cannot be retrieved. Uses index values, which are harder to work with.
Offers compare mode for changing case sensitivity.	Collections are case-sensitive, and sensitivity cannot be changed.
Key values can be any data type.	Key values must be strings.
Items can be easily removed using the RemoveAll method.	Removing items from a collection requires re-defining the Collection object.
Cannot store a reference to a custom collection.	Can store a reference to a custom collection.
Requires a reference to the Microsoft Scripting Runtime library or an object created using late binding.	Collection is an object available in the VBA library.

Action Item 21.1

In the companion files, there is an `Order Entry and Lookup` form (see Figure 21.3), which uses the VBA Dictionary object for its various operations. Look for the file called `Chap21_Dictionary.accdb`.

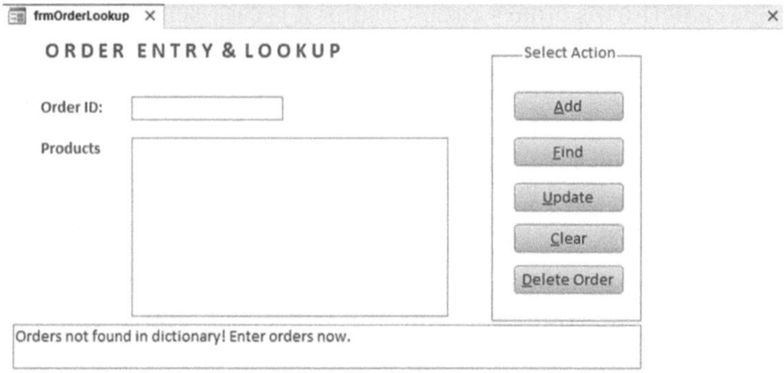

FIGURE 21.3.   This demo form employs the VBA Dictionary object for its order entry and lookup tasks.

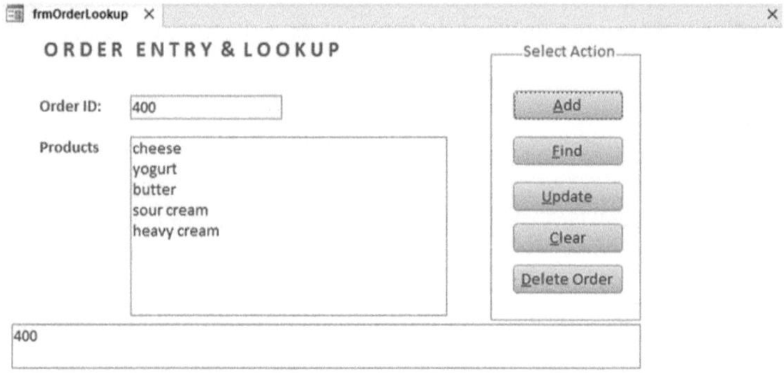

FIGURE 21.4.   Entering an order via the demo form.

INTRODUCTION TO REGULAR EXPRESSIONS

As you know, VBA has many useful functions that can be used to work with strings. For example, the `Len` function returns the number of characters in the provided string expression:

```
?Len("Today is Sunday")
```

You can use the `Left`, `Right`, and `Mid` functions to return a portion of a string. For example:

```
?Left("Today is Sunday", 5)
```

returns the string `Today`. Replace `Left` with `Right`, and you return the five rightmost characters from that string. If you need to return a string starting from a particular character in the string, you can use the `Mid` function to extract the required portion. For example, let's extract `is` from our test string:

```
<Code>

?Mid("Today is Sunday", 7, 2)
```

This returns the string `is`.

To find the position of the first occurrence of one string within another string, call the `InStr` function, like this:

```
? InStr("Today is Sunday and it's a holiday", "Sunday")
```

This will display the number `10`, indicating that the string was found starting at character 10. If you don't need to search from the beginning of the string, specify the position to search from in the first argument, like this:

```
?InStr(5, "Today is Sunday and it's a holiday", "o")
```

This searches for the letter `o`, starting from the fifth character in the specified string. The `o` is found in the twenty-ninth position.

As you can see, using string manipulation functions in VBA is quite straightforward. There will, however, be many situations in your VBA programs where these methods will not be enough. You may need to match a certain pattern of characters in various expressions. A pattern match can involve a character, a word, a group of words, or an entire sentence. This is where a working knowledge of regular expressions can help. Simply put, a *regular expression* (often referred to as *RegEx* or *RegExp*) is a sequence of characters that specifies a search pattern in text. Regular expressions are commonly used in search engines and find/replace dialogs in text editors and word-processing applications. Before you can try out some pattern matching in VBA, let's go over a few basic concepts.

Character Matching in RegExp Patterns

A *pattern* is basically a schema that you put together to match character combinations in strings. Patterns are composed of simple characters, such as `/abc/`, or a combination of simple and special characters, such as `/ab*c/`. The latter indicates that we want to match a single `a` followed by zero or more `b` characters, followed by `c`. The `*` after `b` means zero or more occurrences of the preceding item. Table 21.3 shows some examples of special characters used in regular expression patterns. For more detailed information, you will need to look to other sources. This section supplies just the bare minimum RegExp knowledge for you to complete a specific VBA programming task that will be introduced later in this chapter.

TABLE 21.3. Regular expression patterns.

Pattern	Description	Example	Found Matches
. (a single dot)	Matches any single character except vbNewLine	d.g	deg, dig, dog
[characters]	Matches any single character between brackets, []	[jv]	Would match j and v in "java"
[^characters]	Matches any single character that is not between brackets, []	[^jv]	Would match "a" in "java"
[start-end]	Matches any character that is part of the range in brackets, []	[0-9] [A-Z]	Matches any number in the range 0 to 9 Matches any character in the range "A" to "Z"
\	Escapes special characters so that special characters can be searched for	\[	Escaped character. Matches a [character.
\n	New line	\n	Matches a new line (vbNewLine)
\r	Carriage return	\r	Matches a carriage return (vbCr)
\t	Tab	\t	Matches a tab character (vbTab)
\w	Matches any word character, alphanumeric, and the underscore.	\w	Would match "morning" in "morning"
\W	Matches any non-alphanumeric characters and the underscore	\W	Would match "@" in your email address
\s	Matches any white space character (spaces, tabs, line breaks)	\s	Would match the space in "good morning"
\S	Matches any non-white-space character	\S	Would match "good" and "morning" in "good morning"
\d	Matches any decimal digit	\d	Would match "7" in "7Eleven"
\D	Matches any character that is not a digit character (0–9)	\D	Would match "Eleven" in "7Eleven"

Quantifiers in RegExp Patterns

Regular expression patterns can include quantifiers that allow you to control how many times a match occurs (see Table 21.4).

TABLE 21.4. Quantifiers in RegExp patterns.

Quantifier	Description	Example	Found Matches
*	Matches zero or more of the preceding characters/digits	b\w*	Matches a b character Matches any word character (alphanumeric and underscore) Matches 0 or more of the preceding items
+	Matches one or more of the preceding characters/digits	b\w+	Same as above, but matches one or more
?	Matches zero or one of the preceding characters/digits	colou?r	Matches color, colour
{n}	Matches "n" many times	c{2}	Matches a c character twice. Case-sensitive. Will match the second and third letter c in "Cecilia is sick."
{n,}	Matches at least "n" occurrences of the preceding item	a{3,}	Matches all of the a characters in "baaarber," "baaaarber"
{n,m}	Matches the specified quantity of the previous character/digit	a{1,3}	Will match 1 to 3 of the previous items. Will match the a in barber, the two a's in barber, and the three a's in baaarber.

You can use parentheses, (), to group multiple items in your pattern together. You can also indicate the beginning and ending of lines and words and other patterns indicating that a match is possible. These topics are beyond the scope of this book. Numerous books have been devoted to the subject of regular expression pattern-matching operations. Hundreds of Web sites offer useful tools that will help you decipher an unknown RegExp pattern and understand its building elements. While RegExp can take some time to learn, once mastered, these skills can be reused in many other programming languages for validating, replacing, and extracting data from strings.

Using the RegExp Object in VBA

Many programming languages provide built-in support for working with RegExes. To use RegExes in your VBA programs and take advantage of the built-in programming assistance (IntelliSense), you will need to add a reference to an external library. On your VBE screen, choose Tools | References (see Figure 21.5), scroll down and select Microsoft VBScript Regular Expressions 5.5, and then click OK. Once you've added this library to your VBA project, the Object Browser will display all available properties and methods of the `RegExp` object (see Figure 21.6).

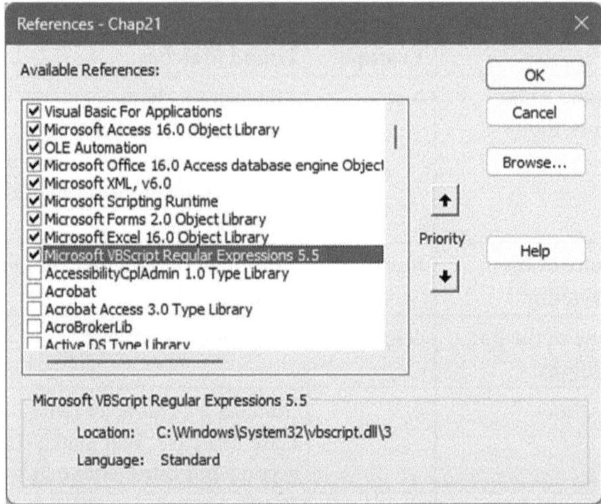

FIGURE 21.5.   Setting a reference to the Microsoft VBScript Regular Expressions 5.5 object library.

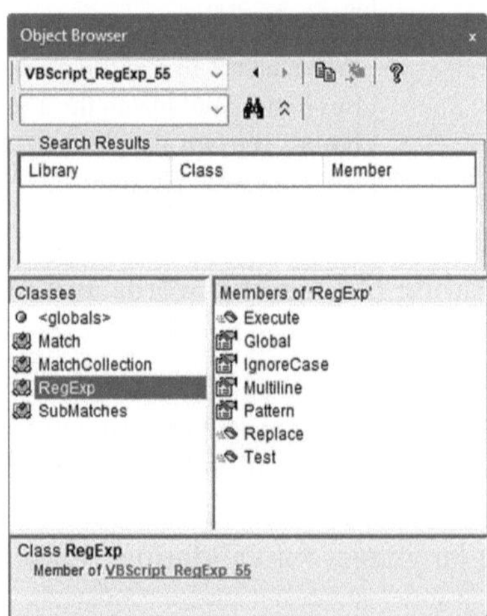

FIGURE 21.6.   Regular expressions can be used via the VBScript Regular Expressions 5.5 library, displayed as VBScript_RegExp_55 in the Object Browser.

The RegExp Object Declaration

If you already set up the reference to the Microsoft VBScript Regular Expressions 5.5 library, you can declare the `RegExp` object using the following early binding syntax:

```
Dim oRegExp As RegExp
Set oRegExp = New RegExp
```

If you don't want to add the reference to the `RegExp` object via the References dialog box, use any of the examples below:

```
Dim oRegExp As Object
Set oRegExp = CreateObject("VBScript.RegExp")
```

Or:

```
Dim oRegExp As Object
Set oRegExp = New VBScript_RegExp_55.RegExp
```

RegExp Properties

The `RegExp` object offers four properties that allow you to specify the pattern to be matched and various options that should be turned on or off. The most important property is `Pattern`. This is where you specify the pattern that you are going to use for matching against the string.

The `Global` property can be set to `True` or `False`. Set it to `True` to find all matches in the pattern. If set to `False`, only the first match will be found.

The `IgnoreCase` property set to `True` will make the matching case insensitive.

The `Multiline` property should be set to `True` if your string consists of multiple lines and you want to run the same pattern through all the lines.

RegExp Methods

To work with the `RegExp` object, you can use the following methods:

- Use the `Test` method to search for a pattern in a string. When a match is found, `True` is returned.
- The `Replace` method allows you to replace the occurrences of the pattern with a replacement string.
- The `Execute` method will return all the matches of the pattern that were found in the provided string.

Writing VBA Programs Using the RegExp Object

Let's create example procedures that use some of the methods and properties of the `RegExp` object. Our first procedure will use the `Test` method to check whether the supplied text string contains a correctly formatted phone number. Assume we want to ensure that phone numbers are in the following US format: (999) 999-9999.

> **NOTE**   *All code files and figures for the hands-on projects may be found in the companion files.*

Hands-On 21.1   Testing for a Pattern Match

1. Create a new database called `Chap21.accdb` in your `C:\VBAAccess2024_ByExample` folder.
2. On the VBE screen, add a new module and rename it `RegExpressions`.
3. Enter the following VBA procedure and run it.

```
Sub RegExp_TestDemo()
Dim oRegExp As RegExp
Dim strToSearch As String
Set oRegExp = New RegExp
strToSearch = "Customer phone number: (201) 234-7899."

' match US Phone numbers in the format: (999) 999-9999
oRegExp.Pattern = "\(\d{3}\) \d{3}-\d{4}"
MsgBox oRegExp.Test(strToSearch)
End Sub
```

When this procedure executes, you should see True in the message box.

4. Remove the parentheses surrounding the area code and run the procedure again.

   The phone number will no longer match the pattern we defined, so the `Test` method will return `False`.

   Let's look at the pattern expression we defined for the phone number:

   `\(\d{3}\) \d{3}-\d{4}`

\(	Escaped character. Matches a (character.
\d	Matches any digit character (0–9).
{3}	Quantifier. Matches three of the preceding digits.
\)	Escaped character. Matches a) character.
	Matches a space character (empty space)
\d	Matches any digit character (0–9).
-	Dash character. Matches a - character.
{4}	Quantifier. Matches four of the preceding digits.

In the next hands-on exercise, we will write a procedure that searches for all occurrences of characters provided in the pattern and replaces them with nothing, meaning that they will be removed from the search string.

(•) Hands-On 21.2   Replacing All Occurrences of the Pattern Match

1. In the VBE window, enter the code of the procedure shown in Figure 21.7.

```
Sub RegExp_ReplaceDemo()
    Dim oRegExp As RegExp
    Dim strToSearch As String

    Set oRegExp = New RegExp
    strToSearch = "{""userId"":1,""title"":""Account Manager"",""taskCompleted"":false}"

    ' Find all matches in the pattern
    oRegExp.Global = True

    ' Match any character in this set
    oRegExp.Pattern = "[\{\}""]"

    MsgBox oRegExp.Replace(strToSearch, "")

End Sub
```

FIGURE 21.7.   This VBA procedure uses the Replace method of the RegExp object to remove characters specified in the pattern from the searched string.

2. Execute the `RegExp_ReplaceDemo` procedure.
Figure 21.8 displays the message box with the resulting string.

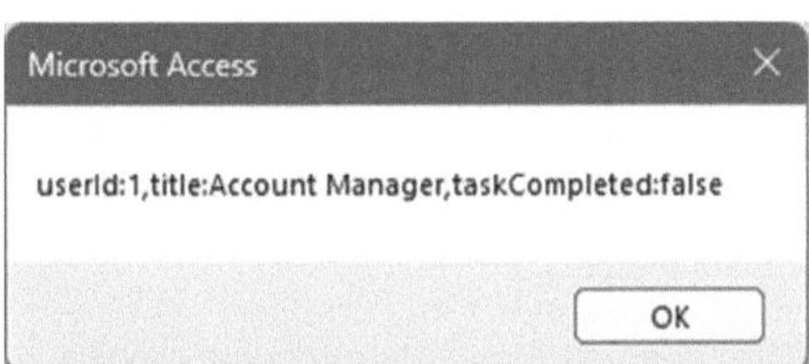

FIGURE 21.8.   The Replace method of the RegExp object has successfully removed all occurrences of the { } "" characters from the original string.

Note that prior to defining the pattern, we used the `Global` property of the `RegExp` object to ensure that all the characters specified in the `Pattern` are removed, not just their first occurrence.

3. Comment out the line of code that sets the `Global` property to `True` and run the procedure again.
This time, the message box should display a partially cleaned-up string; only the first occurrence of each character in the pattern was removed, giving you the following text string:

```
"userId":1,"title":"Account Manager","taskCompleted":false}
```

Let's proceed to create a procedure that uses the `Execute` method of the `RegExp` object to display all the matches for the pattern that was found in the search string. We will use the same pattern and search string as in the previous procedure.

(◉) Hands-On 21.3   Obtaining a List of All the Matches in the Pattern

1. Create a copy of the procedure from Hands-On 21.2 and rename it `RegExp_ExecuteDemo`.

2. Add the following two declaration statements:

```
Dim matches As Object
Dim itm As Variant
```

3. Uncomment the statement that sets the `Global` property to `True`.
4. Comment out the statement that displays the message box. We will not be making any replacements in this procedure.
5. Add the following code before the `End Stub` statement:

```
Set matches = oRegExp.Execute(strToSearch)
For Each itm In matches
    Debug.Print itm
Next
```

6. Run the completed `RegExp_ExecuteDemo` procedure.
   After running the procedure, you should see all the matches that were found, listed on separate lines like this:

```
{
"
"
"
"
"
"
"
"
}
```

Now, you've learned the basics of using the `RegExp` object in your VBA programs. We will revisit this object in a later hands-on project when we need to locate and extract specific strings from a JSON response obtained from an external resource. If you've never heard about JSON, read on. The next section introduces you to communicating with Web servers: sending requests and processing responses.

INTRODUCTION TO REST API

Over the past few years, the method that developers have used to connect to external resources and share information between various computer systems has frequently included a mysterious initialism: API. This vastly popular term is formed from the initial letters of *application programming interface.*

APIs allow programs and scripts to communicate with each other. These programming interfaces expose certain data, services, and functionality of an application so other developers can use them. This allows one product to interact with other products. In other words, APIs are specifically built to be consumed by another application programmatically. APIs allow you to automate many tasks and create user-friendly dashboards and client applications for both mobile and Web use. More than that, they allow you to extend your product functionality by grabbing the required resource from somewhere else. Basically, APIs make things easier. Think of how many times you have seen a Google map embedded in some Web site. That map came from the Google Maps API! Many popular Web sites, such as YouTube, Twitter/X, and Facebook, as well as a multitude of commercial and government Web sites, provide APIs that allow you to get and update their data. To use these APIs, you don't need to know how they were created internally. All you need is to get acquainted with their documentation and find out how to ask for what you need and how to process the response. Some APIs are free, while others require that you pay for the service. Some will ask you to create a developer account to obtain an API key for authentication purposes. This key consists of a set of letters and numbers that uniquely identify you to the application. An API key is like a password; it is important to keep it secure.

There are different types of APIs; the one that is most popular now is called *Representational State Transfer (REST).* The REST API, also referred to as a RESTful API, was created by computer scientist Roy Fielding. REST is a set of rules (also known as an architectural style) that developers must follow to create programs on a server that allow communication with various client applications. In a RESTful system, a client application sends a request to the server usually over the HTTP protocol. This request might be to fetch data (`GET` request), alter the state of the data (`PUT` request), create data (`POST` request), delete some data (`DELETE` request), or modify some details about the resource (`PATCH` request). `POST`, `GET`, `PUT`, and `DELETE` are special verbs that specify a Create, Read, Update, Delete (CRUD) action that needs to be performed on the server. After the server completes the action, it sends a response back to the client application, often in the form of a representation of the requested resource.

A very important fact of the REST API is that all client requests are stateless. This means that each request must contain all the necessary information for the server to process the request. In other words, the client cannot depend on the server to remember prior requests. Server responses can be formatted in plain text/HTML, XML, or JSON.

In this section, you will learn how to use VBA to use a GET method to fetch data from some free APIs that you can access without applying for a developer account or using authentication. There is a lot to know about the REST API and, unfortunately, there isn't enough room in this chapter to cover all methods of using it. Even the simple GET method can get quite complex when you need to pass parameters to the service and authenticate yourself. Thus, for simplicity's sake, we will focus on the basic syntax that should provide you with enough understanding of the topic, so you are ready to learn more about it the next time you encounter it.

Accessing REST APIs with VBA

VBA does not have a special method for accessing REST APIs. There is, however, a special XMLHTTPRequest object that allows you to use an external API from your VBA code. You must declare the XMLHttpRequest object by using early or late binding.

As mentioned earlier in this chapter; to use an early binding, you must set up a reference to an external library. In this case, the library you need is called *Microsoft XML, vb6.0.*

Once the library is selected in the References dialog box, you can view the object's properties and methods (see Figure 21.9) using the Object Browser.

To use this object, first declare it in your VBA code:

```
Dim httpReq As MSXML2.XMLHTTP60
Set httpReq = New MSXML2.XMLHTTP60
```

Or put everything in the declaration line:

```
Dim httpReq As New MSXML2.XMLHTTP60
```

Note that httpReq is the name of the object variable; here, you can specify any name you like. Some people prefer to call it xmlhttp; others use xhr. Use the name that you feel most comfortable with.

With late binding, you can skip selecting a reference. Simply declare the object variable of the generic object type and use the CreateObject function like this:

```
Dim httpReq As Object
Set httpReq = CreateObject("MSXML2.ServerXMLHttp")
```

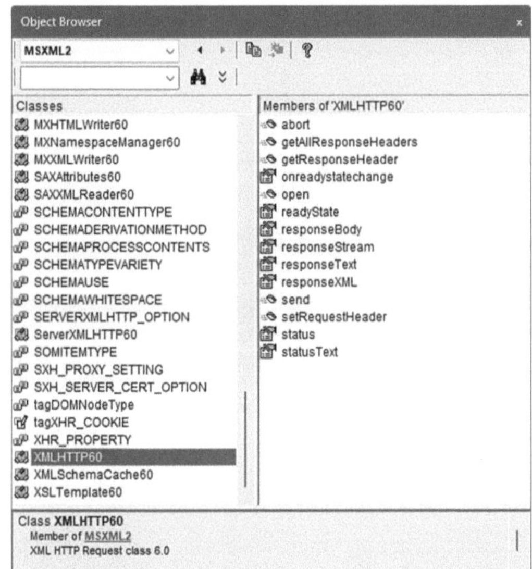

FIGURE 21.9.   Exploring the Microsoft XML vb.60 object library using the Object Browser.

In this chapter's examples, we will be using early binding so we can rely on the built-in programming assistance while writing our code.

Methods and Properties of the XMLHTTPRequest Object

Let's look at the methods and properties that we need to be familiar with to make successful requests to any external API.

The most important methods are `Open` and `Send`. Use the `Open` method to initialize a request. You will need to provide the two required arguments. The first argument is a method, which can be either `GET`, `POST`, or `PUT`. The second argument is the URL of the resource you are calling. You may optionally pass a Boolean value (`TRUE`/`FALSE`) to indicate whether the API call is meant to be asynchronous (`TRUE` is the default) or synchronous (`FALSE`). If you pass `FALSE`, processing waits until the response is returned from the server.

Using the `httpReq` object variable defined earlier, here is how you would set up a basic `GET` request:

```
httpReq.Open "GET","strURL ", False
```

where the `strURL` is the URL address of the server you want to access.

The actual request to the server is made using the `Send` method. If the request was declared asynchronous (`TRUE`), then this method returns immediately; otherwise, it waits until the response is received. You can pass additional optional arguments with the `Send` method. The simple syntax of this method is shown below:

```
httpReq.send
```

The `Send` method will send the request to the resource you indicated in the second parameter of the `Open` method.

The `Abort` method is handy for aborting the current request. You will use it when you want to stop the request.

Any problems and issues with an API can often be resolved by examining the API headers, and we have three methods to deal with headers: `setRequest-Header`, `getResponseHeader`, and `getAllResponseHeaders`. Headers provide extra information about each API call and response. The most common API headers are listed in Table 21.5.

TABLE 21.5.   The most common API headers.

API Header Name	API Header Description
Authorization	This header contains the authentication credentials for HTTP authentication.
WWW-Authenticate	The server may send this header if it needs some form of authentication before sending the response for the requested resource. It may include the error code 401, which means "unauthorized."
Accept_Charset	The client may send this header with a request to let the server know which character sets (UTF-8, ISO-8859-1, Windows-1251, etc.) can be accepted by the client.
Content-Type	This header tells the client what media type (e.g., application/xml or application/json) the response is sent in. This helps the client to correctly process the response received from the server.
Cache-Control	This header contains caching directives (instructions) defined by the server for the response. These directives determine how a resource is cached, where it's cached, and its maximum age before expiring. The no-cache entry in the Cache-Control header indicates that returned responses can't be used for subsequent requests to the same URL before checking whether server responses have changed.

To get all the response headers from the HTTP request, use the `getAllRespon-seHeaders` method. This method must be used after the `Send` method to send the request. For example:

```
httpReq.send
Debug.Print httpReq.getAllResponseHeaders
```

The second statement above should print to the Immediate window the string containing response headers. What you get in the response headers depends on the server. Here is an example of the headers obtained from the resource we'll be querying in Hands-On 21.4:

```
content-type: application/xml
expires: -1
server: Microsoft-IIS/10.0
access-control-expose-headers: Request-Context
request-context: appId=cid-v1:39f1cd0a-de7e-435f-bf7d-
39de930d88c6
x-aspnetmvc-version: 5.2.9
date: Fri, 20 Dec 2024 06:24:30 GMT
strict-transport-security: max-age=31536000 ; includeSubDomains
; preload
x-content-type-options: nosniff
x-frame-options: SAMEORIGIN
```

As you can see from this example, the headers are key/value pairs in text format separated by a colon. To find out a specific header value, use the `getResponseHeader` method, providing it with the argument denoting the specific header value you want.

For example, to get the value of the `content-type` header, use the following line of code:

```
Debug.Print HttpReq.getResponseHeader("content-type")
```

The `setRequestHeader` method is used by the client to provide information to the server about the types of content that are acceptable for the response, the acceptable character sets, a list of acceptable encodings, etc. For a full list of standard request fields see the article at *https://en.wikipedia.org/wiki/List_of_ HTTP_header_fields#Requests*.

It is the responsibility of the server to consider the sent-in client requirements. The `setRequestHeader` method has two required arguments that specify the name of the header and its value. You must call it after calling the `Open` method, but before calling `Send`. Here is an example:

```
httpReq.Open "GET", strURL, False
httpReq.setRequestHeader("Accept", "text/xml")
httpReq.Send
```

The prior example tells the server that the client is looking for a response in `text/xml` format.

<table>
<tr>
<td rowspan="2">NOTE</td>
<td>Before sending a request to the server, you may want to query it to find out whether the server is operational and what server resources are available. By sending a HEAD request, instead of GET or POST, the server will send back its response headers. Here is a short VBA procedure that demonstrates how to query the server:</td>
</tr>
<tr>
<td>

```
Sub GetOnlyHeaders()
Dim xhr As New MSXML2.XMLHTTP60
xhr.Open "HEAD", "https://itunes.apple.com/
search?term=celine+dion", False
xhr.send

If xhr.ReadyState = 4 Then
    Debug.Print xhr.getAllResponseHeaders
End If
End Sub
```

</td>
</tr>
</table>

With the methods covered, let's look at the XMLHTTPRequest object's properties.

The readyState property specifies the state of the request. There are five possible values:

0 = uninitialized
1 = loading
2 = loaded
3 = interactive
4 = complete

Every time readyState changes, the onreadystatechange event is fired. When readyState is 4 and status is 200, the response is ready.

The status property returns the HTTP status code from the server. The most common status is 200, which means "OK," signifying that the request was successful. The 403 status means that the access is forbidden. 404 denotes that the requested page/resource was not found.

For a complete list of statuses, go to *https://en.wikipedia.org/wiki/List_of_HTTP_status_codes*.

The statusText property returns the text version of the HTTP status code. It is useful for programming error messages. You will see an example of using status and statusText in Hands-On 21.4.

Finally, the last four properties, responseText, responseXML, responseStream, and responseBody, specify the form in which the HTTP response can be returned.

Use the `responseXML` property if you know that the response body is XML-formatted text. If you need the response body as a string, use the `responseText` property. The `responseStream` property will return the server response in the form of binary-encoded data (UTF-8, UCS-2, UCS-3, Shift_JIS, and so on). The `responseBody` property is useful when the response body is binary. This property returns the response content as a byte stream.

Making a Basic GET Request

You may be wondering how exactly you can put this newfound knowledge to use. Here, again, the best learning you can benefit from is working through an example.

In the first hands-on example of calling the REST API, we will access the National Highway Traffic Safety Administration (NHTSA) Product Information Catalog and Vehicle Listing (vPIC) API. The following is a direct link: https://vpic.nhtsa.dot.gov/api/.

It describes API methods that can be used to get various types of data in XML, CSV, and JSON format. We will get a list of all the makes available in the vPIC data set. We will get this list in XML format and push it into an Access table. Let's get started.

(◉) Hands-On 21.4   Requesting Data from the REST API

1. On the VBE screen, insert a new standard module into your `Chap21.accdb` database. Use the Properties box to rename the module `APIRequest_XML`.
2. In the `APIRequest_XML` module code window, enter the following procedure:

```
Sub RequestData_XML_toAccessTable()
Dim httpReq As MSXML2.XMLHTTP60
Dim Resp As New MSXML2.DOMDocument60
Dim strURL As String
Dim strFileName As String

strURL = "https://vpic.nhtsa.dot.gov/api/vehicles/getallmakes"

Set httpReq = New MSXML2.XMLHTTP60
httpReq.Open "GET", strURL, False
httpReq.send
Debug.Print httpReq.getAllResponseHeaders
If httpReq.status = 200 Then
    strFileName = "C:\VBAAccess2024_ByExample\AllMakes.xml"
    Debug.Print httpReq.responseText
    Resp.LoadXML httpReq.responseText
    Resp.Save strFileName
```

```
        Application.ImportXML _
          DataSource:=strFileName, _
          ImportOptions:=acStructureAndData
    Else
        Debug.Print "Error " & httpReq.status & "-" & httpReq.
                                                statusText
    End If
    Set httpReq = Nothing
    End Sub
```

3. Click in the selection bar next to the `httpReq.send` statement in the procedure to put a breakpoint on this line of code and press F5 to run the procedure.

4. When break mode is activated and you see the yellow selection in the code window, keep pressing F8 to debug the code line by line. Keep the Immediate window open while debugging the procedure so you can see the output of the `Debug` statements. Activate the Immediate window by pressing Ctrl+G.

   The first `Debug` statement in this procedure should return the contents of the headers, as shown earlier in this chapter. Notice that we are asking for the headers after we have sent the request to the server. This statement is for demonstration purposes only. Most of the time, you don't need to look at headers unless problems arise and you need to troubleshoot some issues.

   After sending the request, the server gives you back a status code. `200` means that the request was successful and the server produced the response. Only then should we proceed with the rest of the code. There is no point in asking for a response when an error code is returned in the server status property. If the status is not `200`, we will output to the Immediate window the status code and the equivalent text error message using the `status` and `statusText` properties discussed earlier. If the request is successful, we use the `responseText` property to get the response and print it to the Immediate window. `Debug` statements help you understand the output from the server.

   Now that we have obtained the output, we also want to save it so we can use it for a specific purpose. In this procedure, we use the `LoadXML` method of the `XMLDocument` object to load the server response into an XML document that we declared at the top of the procedure in the `Resp` object variable. Note that we extensively covered working with XML in Chapter 20. To produce an XML file with the string returned from the server, we use the `Save` method of the `XMLDocument` object. After the XML file is produced (`AllMakes.xml`) we use the `ImportXML` method of the Access `Application` object to import the structure and the data into a new table in the current database.

5. When you have reached the end of the procedure by pressing the F8 key, switch to the main Access application window to view the result. In the

Navigation Pane, you should have two tables, named `AllVehicleMakes` and `Response`. A total of 11,622 records were written to the `AllVehicleMakes` table. The `Response` table is like a control file that provides the total count of records retrieved and the corresponding text message. Figures 21.10 and 21.11 illustrate the contents of these two tables, while Figure 21.12 shows the format of the XML file that provided data for these tables.

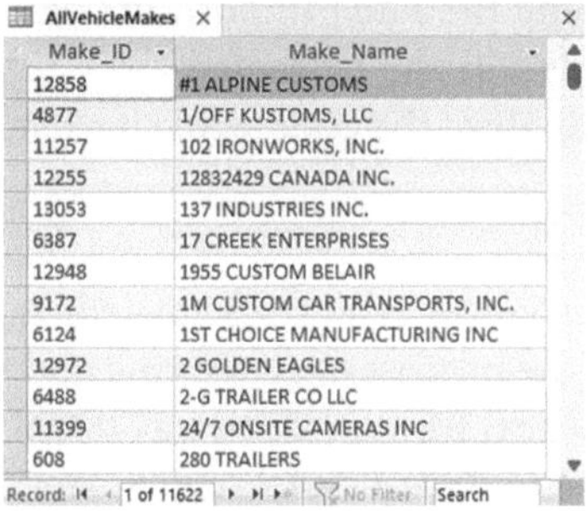

FIGURE 21.10.   The AllVehicleMakes table was created from the REST API response.

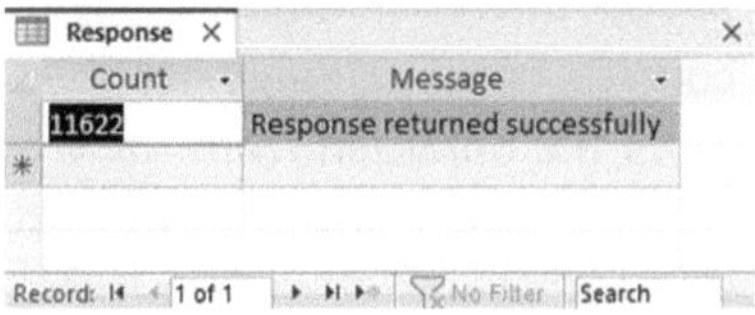

FIGURE 21.11.   The Response table was created from the REST API response.

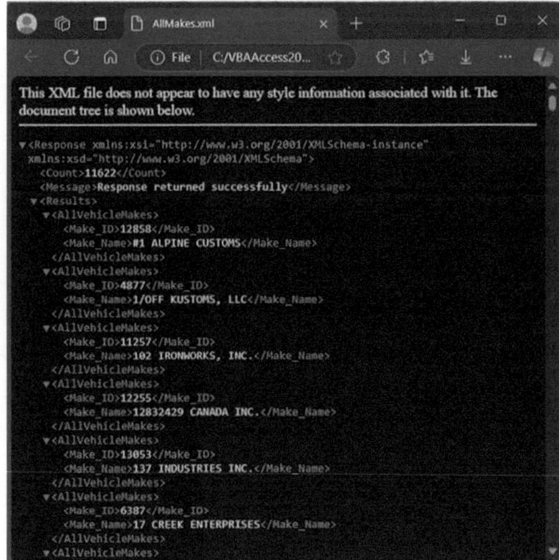

FIGURE 21.12.   The XML data returned from the REST API.

Action Item 21.2

Sometimes it will be useful to read the response from the REST API straight into an Excel spreadsheet so it can be analyzed prior to importing to Access. Included in the companion files is the `APIRequest_XML2Excel.bas` file. It contains the complete VBA procedure that makes the same request to the REST API as we did in the previous hands-on exercise but processes the data to Excel. Bring this code file to your `Chap21.accdb` database using the File | Import File option in the VBE window. Run the procedure provided in the imported module using the Step Into (F8) debug feature so you can analyze the code while it executes.

Overview of JSON

Using XML with REST API requests and responses requires knowledge of the XML language and a good understanding of the process of generating and modifying XML structures. In recent years, a new text format, known as *JSON* (pronounced "Jason"), has become an alternative to XML. JSON, which stands for *JavaScript Object Notation*, is a language-independent data format often used for data interchange between disparate systems due to its lightweight format. JSON format is human-readable text that consists of name/value pairs.

Figure 21.13 displays a sample of the JSON file obtained from the free fake API that is available for testing and prototyping (https://jsonplaceholder.typicode.com/users).

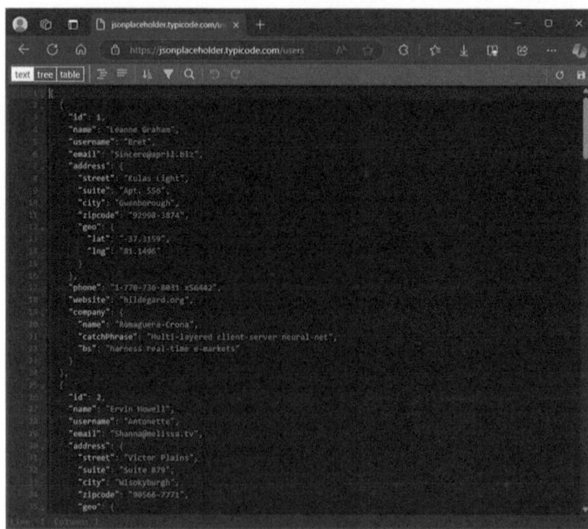

FIGURE 21.13. Example of a JSON file format.

JSON format can include:

- **An Object**

  This is an unordered set of name/value pairs. Objects begin with { (left brace) and end with } (right brace). Each name is followed by a : (colon), and the name/value pairs are separated by , (comma).

- **An Array**

  This is an ordered collection of values. Arrays begin with a [(left bracket) and end with a] (right bracket). Values are separated by a , (comma). A value can be a string enclosed in double quotes, a number, true or false, an object, or an array. Values can be nested, so you can create very elaborate JSON structures to fit all your needs.

- **A String**

  This is a sequence of zero or more Unicode characters, wrapped in double quotes using backslash escapes.

- **A Number**

  For example, digits 1–9, fractions, and exponents.

- **Whitespace**

  For example, space, linefeed, carriage return, and horizontal tab.

In the following example, the following JSON object represents three courses in an array called `courses`. Notice that the array starts and ends with square brackets. Within the array are three objects, one for each course:

```
{
"courses": [
{
"courseID": 1001,
"title": "Access VBA Programming by Example",
"dateOffered": "September 14",
"location": "virtual"
},
{
"courseID": 1002,
"title": "Excel VBA Programming by Example",
"dateOffered": "September 18",
"location": "New York, Hilton"
},
{
"courseID": 1003,
"title": "PowerPoint VBA Programming by Example",
```

```
"dateOffered": "December 5-7",
"location": "Unspecified"
}
]
}
```

Because JSON is a simple text format, you can use Windows Notepad to create, save, and view JSON files. The above snippet can be found in the companion files as `Courses.json`.

The JSON format is supported by virtually all modern browsers, and because of its smaller size than XML encoding, it can provide larger performance gains when sending larger amounts of data over a network. The format you should use for data exchange (plain text /HTML, XML, or JSON) depends on your specific situation and the project requirements.

NOTE	*When working with JSON data, you may come across another term—JSONP, or JSON with **Padding**. JSONP allows you to get JSON data from a server in a different domain. This will help you get around the cross-domain security policy that modern browsers implement.*

A more detailed description and examples of JSON formatting can be found at www.json.org.

Loading JSON Data into Access

In the next hands-on example, we will access another free REST API resource, but this time we will receive the response formatted as JSON. The direct link to that resource is *https://api.zippopotam.us.*

The Web site shows how the API can be used to autocomplete the city and state based on the zip code you enter. We will build a similar form in Access (see Figure 21.14) that obtains the zip code data through that API.

FIGURE 21.14.   Access form used in the zip code demo REST API—JSON.

If you enter `api.zippopotam.us/us/90210` in your favorite browser, you should see the JSON response shown in Figure 21.15.


```
1  {
2    "post code": "90210",
3    "country": "United States",
4    "country abbreviation": "US",
5    "places": [
6      {
7        "place name": "Beverly Hills",
8        "longitude": "-118.4065",
9        "state": "California",
10       "state abbreviation": "CA",
11       "latitude": "34.0901"
12     }
13   ]
14 }
```


FIGURE 21.15.   JSON structure returned from the Zippopotam API.

For the JSON format in VBA, we don't have a method that can help us easily extract individual key values from the JSON string. For simple structures such as the one shown in Figure 21.15, however, we can use the basic string functions discussed earlier in this chapter. Alternatively, we can use what we've learned so far about regular expressions. Let's take the latter route to gain more experience.

Hands-On 21.5   Requesting Data from the REST API (JSON Example)

1. In the `Chap21.accdb` database, create a new Access form, as shown in Figure 21.14. This form should include:

   - Three unbound text boxes with caption properties set to `Zip Code`, `City`, and `State` and name properties set to `txtZip`, `txtCity`, and `txtState`.

   - Two command buttons with caption properties set to `Lookup` and `Clear All`, and name properties set to `cmdRequest` and `cmdClearAll`.

   - One unbound text box without a label. The name property of the text box is `txtStatus`. This box is used to return any errors received during the lookup process.

In addition, set the following form properties:

- ScrollBars: Neither
- Record Selectors: No
- Allow Datasheet View: No
- Popup: Yes

2. Save the form as `ZipLookup`.
3. Open the `ZipLookup` form in design view and right-click the Lookup button. Choose Build Event, select Code Builder from the Choose Builder dialog box, and click OK.
4. In the `form_ZipLookup` code module, enter the following VBA procedure, which will run when the Lookup button is clicked:

```vba
Private Sub cmdRequest_Click()
    ClearFields

    If Me.txtZip = "" Or IsNull(Me.txtZip) Then
        With Me
            .txtStatus.Visible = True
            .txtStatus = "Please enter Zip Code"
            .txtZip.SetFocus
        End With
        Exit Sub
    End If
    If Len(Me.txtZip) <> 5 Or Not IsNumeric(Me.txtZip) Then
        Me.txtStatus.Visible = True
        Me.txtStatus = "Zip code must be 5-digit long."
        Exit Sub
    End If
    RequestData Me.txtZip
End Sub
```

This procedure will make sure that the zip code is not empty and is entered in the correct format. In the first line of this procedure, we will call a `ClearFields` procedure, which will clear the existing entries in the City, State, and Status text boxes and set the visibility of the Status box to `False` when it is empty. In the last procedure statement, we will call the `RequestData` procedure and pass it the current value from the Zip text box.

The `RequestData` procedure will make a call to the REST API. We will enter it later in the standard code module.

5. Enter the following two procedures in the same `Form_ZipLookup` code module.
   The first of these procedures will handle the form's Clear All button click.

```
Private Sub cmdClearAll_Click()
    Me.txtZip = ""
    ClearFields
    Me.txtZip.SetFocus
End Sub
Sub ClearFields()
    With Me
        .txtCity = ""
        .txtState = ""
        .txtStatus = ""
        .txtStatus.Visible = False
    End With
End Sub
```

6. Save the changes you've made in the `Form_ZipLookup` code module.
7. Choose Insert | Module to add a new standard module to your `Chap21` VBA
   project. Use the properties window to rename it `APIRequest_JSON`.
8. In the `APIRequest_JSON` module, enter the code of the `RequestData`
   procedure, as follows:

```
Sub RequestData(ByVal postcode As String)
Dim httpReq As MSXML2.XMLHTTP60
Dim oRegExp As Object
Dim rec As Variant
Dim aRecords As Variant
Dim aRecord As Variant
Dim fld As Variant
Dim fldName As String
Dim fldContent As String
Dim strAObj As String
Dim webResponse As String

Set httpReq = New MSXML2.XMLHTTP60
httpReq.Open "GET", "https://api.zippopotam.us/us/" + postcode, _
False
httpReq.send
If httpReq.status <> "200" Then
    Forms!ZipLookup.txtStatus.Visible = True
    Forms!ZipLookup.txtStatus = "Error Code: " & _
        httpReq.status & " - " & httpReq.statusText
    Exit Sub
End If
```

```
'get the entire JSON string
webResponse = httpReq.responseText

Debug.Print "Below is raw web response json" & vbCrLf
Debug.Print webResponse
'convert json string to an array
Set oRegExp = New RegExp

oRegExp.Global = True
oRegExp.Pattern = "[\[\]\{\}""]+"
strAObj = "[{"

If InStr(1, webResponse, strAObj) > 0 Then
    webResponse = Replace(webResponse, strAObj, ", ")
End If

Debug.Print webResponse
webResponse = oRegExp.Replace(webResponse, "")
Debug.Print webResponse

aRecords = Split(webResponse, ", ")
For Each rec In aRecords
    aRecord = Split(rec, ", ")
        For Each fld In aRecord
            fldName = Split(fld, ":")(0)
                fldContent = Split(fld, ":")(1)
                  If fldName = "place name" Then
                     Forms!ZipLookup.txtCity = fldContent
                  End If
                  If fldName = "state" Then
                     Forms!ZipLookup.txtState = fldContent
                  End If
        Next
    Debug.Print fldName & vbTab & vbTab & fldContent
Next
Set httpReq = Nothing
End Sub
```

 9. Save the changes in the module and return to the main Access application window.
10. Open the `ZipLookup` form in the form view and click the Lookup button. You should see the error message as shown earlier in Figure 21.14.
11. Click the Clear All button. The error message box should disappear.

12. Enter your zip code (or any valid zip code you can recall) and click the Lookup button.

If the zip code exists, you should see both the City and State text boxes populated. If the zip code is invalid, for example, you've entered `11345`, you should see Error Code: 404.

To retrieve the zip code data, we pass the value from the Zip text box to the `RequestData` procedure in the string type variable called `postcode`. Notice how we add this value to the URL string:

```
httpReq.Open "GET", "https://api.zippopotam.us/us/" + postcode,
                                                          False
```

We send the request to the server in the same way we did in the previous hands-on exercise.

Our code will stop executing when the status of the response is not equal to `200`. Any value but successful execution (`200`) will not provide us with a response, so we make the Status box visible on the form and load it with the error message. If the server response code is `200`, our procedure continues, and we store the server response in the `webResponse` string variable. We print the response string to the Immediate window so we can examine its format. To get individual values from the JSON string, we will convert it to an array using the `RegExp` object discussed earlier in this chapter. We define the pattern that we want to match as follows:

```
oRegExp.Pattern = "[\[\]\{\}""]+"
```

The `Global` property of the `oRegExp` object will ensure that all occurrences of the characters specified in our pattern will be removed when we apply the `Remove` method. Prior to that, however, we want to find and replace the character string, `[{`, that follows the `places` key in the returned JSON string. These characters indicate that the next section of JSON is an array containing an object. We clean up the string of characters we don't need by using the VBA `InStr` and `Replace` functions like this:

```
strAObj = "[{"
If InStr(1, webResponse, strAObj) > 0 Then
    webResponse = Replace(webResponse, strAObj, ", ")
End If
```

After this code completes, we print to the Immediate window the revised string:

```
{"post code": "90210", "country": "United States", "country
abbreviation": "US", "places": , "place name": "Beverly Hills",
"longitude": "-118.4065", "state": "California", "state
abbreviation": "CA", "latitude": "34.0901"}]}
```

Notice that `"places":` is now followed by a space and a comma.

Next, we use pattern matching and replace with a comma all the braces and brackets that are remaining in the previous string. As a result, we get the following string:

```
post code: 90210, country: United States, country abbreviation:
US, places: , place name: Beverly Hills, longitude: -118.4065,
state: California, state abbreviation: CA, latitude: 34.0901
```

Now all that's left to do is split the above string into the name/value pairs so we can get access to individual items. We can use the VBA `Split` function to break the string each time we encounter a comma and a space:

```
aRecords = Split(webResponse, ", ")
```

The `aRecords` variable is an array and we can count the number of items we have in it using the `UBound` function. If you enter `?Ubound(aRecords)` in the Immediate window during break mode (while your code is running), you should see `8` as a return value. If you type `? aRecords(0)`, you will get back the first name/value pair, like this:

```
?aRecords(0)
post code: 90210
```

We use the `For Each` loop to iterate through the array. To make the process easier, we split each of the name/value pairs into individual fields using a colon to separate the name from the value. The first (`0`) item is the field name, and the second (`1`) item is the field content (value). We use the `If` statement to find the value for the place name field that we put in the `txtCity` text box on our form and then look for the state to get the state.

The looping process continues until we find the values we are searching for. To gain a better understanding of how this code parses the JSON string using the VBA string functions and regular expressions, set a breakpoint on the first `Debug` statement in the `RequestData` procedure, then go back to your form, enter a valid zip code, and click the Lookup button. When VBA encounters the break statement and the code window appears, you can use Step Into (F8) to step through the entire code line by line, asking questions and checking the responses in the Immediate window.

Parsing JSON with Third-Party Libraries

Parsing REST API responses, especially the complex ones, will not be as straight-forward as the example you've tried here. You may need a custom VBA library written specifically to help you handle the intricate JSON format your response can be returned in. Search the Web for this topic and you're bound to find a great set of VBA-JSON tools created by Tim Hall, available via *https://github. com/VBA-tools.* It contains JSON conversion and parsing for VBA (Windows/ Mac Excel, Access, and other Office applications). (I have successfully used it in several of my own VBA projects and it made the task of dealing with the JSON output so much easier.) There are other tools that you may also like and find useful in your work. These tools may not work 100% of the time, but they are certainly better than having nothing built into VBA to handle all the data-pars-ing issues that you will come across while making REST API requests. Getting a response and not being able to turn it into a format you can work with can be a painful and time-consuming effort. Do your own research; find the tool you like, read its documentation, and be ready to use it in your project.

You now know how to program in VBA; you've learned about classes, dic-tionaries, arrays, and collections, and you can create your own tool or improve one that already exists.

USING ChatGPT WITH ACCESS

It's time for the final chat. I hope the knowledge gained in this chapter will moti-vate you to start integrating REST APIs with Microsoft Access. ChatGPT can guide you in this process and provide you with many additional resources. Just ask:

User Prompt: Can you provide a list of APIs that don't require an account?

ChatGPT/Microsoft Copilot's Response:
Sure! Here are some APIs that don't require an account or API key for access:

General
- **Public APIs Directory:** APIs.guru - A directory of public APIs.

- **Cat Facts:** CatFact.ninja - Get random cat facts.
- **CoinDesk:** CoinDesk - View the Bitcoin Price Index (BPI) in real-time.
- Bored: Bored API - Get suggestions for random activities.
- **ipify:** ipify - Get your public IP address.

Art & Images
- **HTTP Cats:** HTTP Cats - Cat images for HTTP status codes.
- **Lorem Picsum:** Lorem Picsum - Placeholder images.
- **DiceBear:** DiceBear - Generate random SVG avatars.
- **Random Fox:** RandomFox - Random pictures of foxes.

Data
- **Data USA:** Data USA - Get US public data (e.g., population data).
- **Nationalize.io:** Nationalize.io - Predict the nationality of a person based on their name.
- **Genderize.io:** Genderize.io - Predict the gender of a person based on their name.

Entertainment
- **Breaking Bad Quotes:** Breaking Bad Quotes:- Retrieve quotes from Breaking Bad.
- **XKCD Comics:** XKCD Comics - Fetch comics and metadata from XKCD.
- **Disney API:** Disney API - Get information about Disney characters.

These APIs are great for beginners and developers looking to test and integrate APIs without the need for authentication. Do any of these catch your interest?

Yes, I was intrigued by Disney API, so I asked:

***User Prompt:** How can I pull information from Disney API?*

ChatGPT/Microsoft Copilot's Response:
To pull information from the Disney API, you can use the REST endpoints provided by the API. Here's a step-by-step guide to help you get started:

The complete chat is included in the companion files. Refer to the `Chapter 21 - Using ChatGPT with Access` document. Also, the final result of the chat, the `DisneyCharacters` table, and the VBA code that populates this table from the Disney API are provided in the `Chap21.accdb` database.

Nothing happens effortlessly. Programming with ChatGPT requires proficiency in troubleshooting and fine-tuning the code, but the results are well worth it. Your road to mastery of Microsoft Access and related technologies will involve *patience*, *practice*, and *persistence*. Remember, all challenges you encounter are opportunities for growth and learning. As you build your skills, you'll discover new ways of solving problems and enhancing your solutions.

SUMMARY

In this chapter, you explored several external libraries that should help you build more advanced VBA applications. You learned about the Dictionary object and how it compares to the native VBA Collection object. You saw how regular expressions can make it easier to extract information from JSON-formatted data. Finally, you learned the basics of making a REST API request and parsing both XML and JSON response data. Your real-world assignments will be more complex than the examples presented in this chapter, but these simple examples should help you reach higher levels of VBA development quickly and with more confidence. Good luck with your VBA coding!

VBA DATA TYPES

TABLE A.1. VBA data types.

Data Type	Storage Size	Range
Byte	1 byte	A number in the range of 0 to 255.
Boolean	2 bytes	Stores a value of True (0) or False (–1).
Integer	2 bytes	A number in the range of –32,768 to 32,767. The type declaration character for Integer is the percent sign (%).
Long (long integer)	4 bytes	A number in the range of –2,147,483,648 to 2,147,483,647. The type declaration character for Long is the ampersand (&).
LongLong	8 bytes	Stored as a signed 64-bit (8-byte) number ranging in value from –9,223,372,036,854,775,808 to 9,223,372,036,854,775,807. The type declaration character for LongLong is the caret (^). LongLong is a valid declared type only on 64-bit platforms.

(Contd.)

Data Type	Storage Size	Range
LongPtr (long integer on 32-bit systems; long long integer on 64-bit systems)	4 bytes on 32-bit; 8 bytes on 64-bit	Numbers ranging in value from –2,147,483,648 to 2,147,483,647 on 32-bit systems; –9,223,372,036,854,775,808 to 9,223,372,036,854,775,807 on 64-bit systems. Using LongPtr enables writing code that can run in both 32-bit and 64-bit environments.
Single (single-precision floating-point)	4 bytes	Single-precision floating-point real number ranging in value from –3.402823E38 to –1.401298E–45 for negative values and from 1.401298E–45 to 3.402823E38 for positive values. The type declaration character for Single is the exclamation point (!).
Double (double-precision floating-point)	8 bytes	Double-precision floating-point real number in the range of –1.79769313486231E308 to –4.94065645841247E–324 for negative values and 4.94065645841247E–324 to 1.79769313486231E308 for positive values. The type declaration character for Double is the number sign (#).
Currency (scaled integer)	8 bytes	Monetary values used in fixed-point calculations: –922,337,203,685,477.5808 to 922,337,203,685,477.5807. The type declaration character for Currency is the at sign (@).
Decimal	14 bytes	96-bit (12-byte) signed integer scaled by a variable power of 10. The power of 10 scaling factor specifies the number of digits to the right of the decimal point, and ranges from 0 to 28. With no decimal point (scale of 0), the largest value is +/–79,228,162,514,264,337,593,543,950,335. With 28 decimal places, the largest value is +/–7.9228162514264337593543950335. The smallest non-zero value is +/–0.0000000000000000000000000001. You cannot declare a variable to be of type Decimal. You must use the Variant data type. Use the CDec function to convert a value to a decimal number: Dim numDecimal As Variant numDecimal = CDec(0.02 * 15.75 * 0.0006)
Date	8 bytes	Date from January 1, 100, to December 31, 9999, and times from 0:00:00 to 23:59:59. Date literals must be enclosed within number signs (#); for example: #January 1, 2011#
Object	4 bytes	Any Object reference. Use the Set statement to declare a variable as an Object.

Data Type	Storage Size	Range
String (variable-length)	10 bytes + string length	A variable-length string can contain up to approximately 2 billion characters. The type declaration character for String is the dollar sign ($).
String (fixed-length)	Length of string	A fixed-length string can contain 1 to approximately 65,400 characters.
Variant (with numbers)	16 bytes	Any numeric value up to the range of a Double.
Variant (with characters)	22 bytes + string length	Any valid nonnumeric data type in the same range as for a variable-length string.

User-defined (using Type)	One or more elements	A data type you define using the Type statement. User-defined data types can contain one or more elements of a data type, an array, or a previously defined user-defined type. For example:
		
		`Type custInfo`
		
		`    custFullName as String`
		`    custTitle as String`
		`    custBusinessName as String`
		`    custFirstOrderDate as Date`
		`End Type`

In addition to the above data types, Access offers a new `Date/Time Extended` data type. This data type provides a larger date range, higher fractional precision, and compatibility with the SQL Server `datetime2` data type. This data type is not compatible with previous versions of Microsoft Access. The versions of Access that do not include this feature will not be able to open the database. For more information on using the `Date/Time Extended` data type, see the following Microsoft Support link:

https://support.microsoft.com/en-us/office/using-the-date-time-extended-data-type-708c32da-a052-4cc2-9850-9851042e0024#

TABLE A.2. Values returned by the VarType function.

Constant	Value	Description
vbEmpty	0	Empty (uninitialized)
vbNull	1	Null (no valid data)
vbInteger	2	Integer
vbLong	3	Long integer
vbSingle	4	Single-precision floating-point number
vbDouble	5	Double-precision floating-point number
vbCurrency	6	Currency value
vbDate	7	Date value
vbString	8	String
vbObject	9	Object
vbError	10	Error value
vbBoolean	11	Boolean value
vbVariant	12	Variant (used only with arrays of variants)
vbDataObject	13	Data access object
vbDecimal	14	Decimal value
vbByte	17	Byte value
vbLongLong	20	Long long integer (on 64-bit platforms only)
vbUserDefinedType	36	Variants that contain user-defined types
vbArray	8192	Array

ACCESS 2007-2024 FILE FORMATS

TABLE B.1. Access 2007–2024 file formats.

File Format	Description	Additional Notes
.accdb	File format first introduced in Access 2007 (default). This file format is not readable by Access versions prior to 2007. DO NOT use this file format if you need to support: Replication User-level security	***NOTE:*** Access 2013–2024 does not support replicated databases. Use Access 2010–2007 to create a replica of an .mdb database formatted in Access 2000–2003 file format.
.accde	File extension for Access 2007–2024 .accdb files that are in execute-only mode. These files have all VBA source code removed. This file extension replaces the .mde file extension used in earlier versions of Access.	Users can only execute VBA code; they cannot view or modify it. In addition, users do not have permission to make design changes to forms or reports. If you need to save an Access 2024 database in .accde format, open the database and choose File | Save As | Save Database As. Select Make ACCDE and click the Save As button.

(Contd.)

File Format	Description	Additional Notes
.accdt	This is an Access database template file. Access 2007–2024 all come with professionally designed database templates.	Templates provide you with pre-defined tables/table relationships, forms, reports, queries, and macros. To save an Access 2024 database as a template, open the database and choose File | Save As | Save Database As. Select Template (.accdt) and click the Save As button.
.accdr	This file extension denotes an Access 2007–2024 database functioning in runtime mode.	To create a "locked-down" version of your Access 2024 database, simply change the file extension from .accdb to .accdr. To restore the full database functionality, do the reverse: change the file extension from .accdr to .accdb.
.mdb (Access 97, Access 2000, Access 2002, Access 2003)	Access database file format used in versions prior to 2007. NOTE: In Access 2007–2024, you can create files in either the Access 2000 format or the Access 2002–2003 database format. These files will have the extension .mdb.	Use the .mdb file format if the database will be used in earlier versions of Access to: Support replication Support user-level security
.mde (Access 97, Access 2000, Access 2002, Access 2003)	An .mde file is a compiled version of an .mdb database without any VBA code. This change prevents a database user from reading or changing your VBA code. Users cannot edit the design of forms, reports, or modules.	An .accde file is the Access 2007–2024 version of the .mde file in earlier versions of Access.
.adp	This is a file extension for a Microsoft Access Data Project (ADP) file that lets you connect to an SQL Server database or the Microsoft Data Engine (MSDE) on your PC and create client/server applications. A project file does not contain any data or data definition objects such as tables, views, stored procedures, or user-defined functions. All database objects are stored in the SQL Server database. An .adp file stores only database front-end forms, reports, and other application objects (macros, modules).	Access 2013-2024 does not support the .adp file format. If you need to open and edit an existing ADP database that was created in an earlier version of Access or create a new ADP database, use Access 2007–2010.

File Format	Description	Additional Notes
.ade	This is a file format for a Microsoft Access project (.adp) file with all modules compiled and all editable source code removed. Similar to .mde files, projects stored in the .ade file format prevent users from making design changes to the front-end and gaining access to your VBA source code.	Access 2024 does not support the .ade file format. To create an .ade file from your Access Data Project (ADP), use Access 2007–2010.
.mdw (Access 97, Access 2000, Access 2002, Access 2003)	This file format is used by a workgroup information file. The .mdw files store information for secured .mdb databases.	There are no changes to the .mdw file format in Access 2016–2024. The .mdw files created in earlier versions of Access (2000 through 2003) can be used by Access 2016–2024. When an .mdb database is opened, you can choose File | Info | Users & Permissions | User-Level Security Wizard to create a new workgroup information file (.mdw).
.ldb	This is a locking file extension for an .mdb database. This file prevents users from writing data to pages that have been locked by other users and lets you determine which computer/user has a file or record locked. The .ldb file keeps track of usernames/computer names of the people who are currently logged in to the .mdb.	A locking file is created automatically when the database is opened and is deleted automatically when the last user closes a shared database. *NOTE:* You can view the information stored in this file by opening it with Windows Notepad.
.laccdb	This is the file extension for a locking file used by Access 2007–2024 (.accdb file format).	As with the .ldb file, the .laccdb file is created automatically when the database is opened and is deleted automatically when the last user closes a shared database. *NOTE:* Because different locking files are created for .mdb and .accdb databases in Access 2007–2024, .mdb and .accdb files can be opened in Access 2007–2024 without causing conflicts in the locking file.

INSTALLING INTERNET INFORMATION SERVICES (IIS)

Internet Information Services (IIS) is a Web server application developed by Microsoft, designed to host Web sites and applications on the Windows operating system. Both Windows 11 and 10 support IIS 10.0. IIS is not installed by default; however, it is included as an optional feature, which means you can easily enable and install it. You need IIS enabled and configured to get the most out of Chapter 20's hands-on exercises.

⊙ Hands-On C.1   Installing IIS on Windows 11 and Windows 10

1. Press Windows + R, type `Control Panel`, and press Enter.
2. In the Control Panel, click on Programs (see Figure C.1).

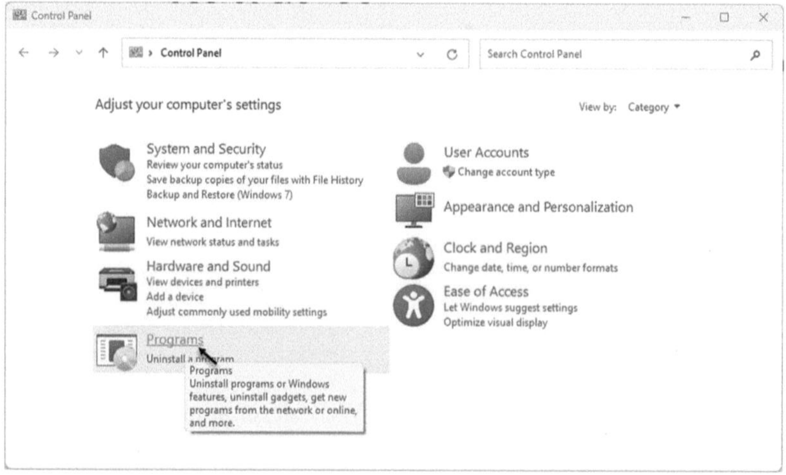

FIGURE C.1.   Installing IIS in Windows.

3. Under Programs and Features, click Turn Windows features on or off, as shown in Figure C.2.
   Wait while Windows retrieves all the features.

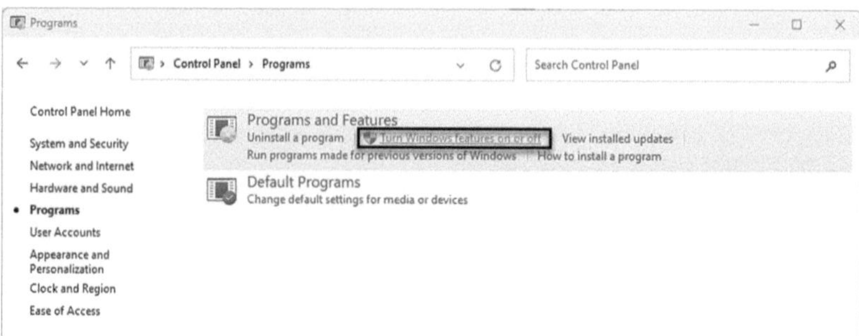

FIGURE C.2.   Installing IIS in Windows.

4. In the Windows Features dialog, scroll down and check the box for Internet Information Services.
5. Expand the World Wide Web Services node and Application Development Features. Check the box next to ASP. Windows will also check ISAPI Extensions (see Figure C.3). When done, click OK to exit.

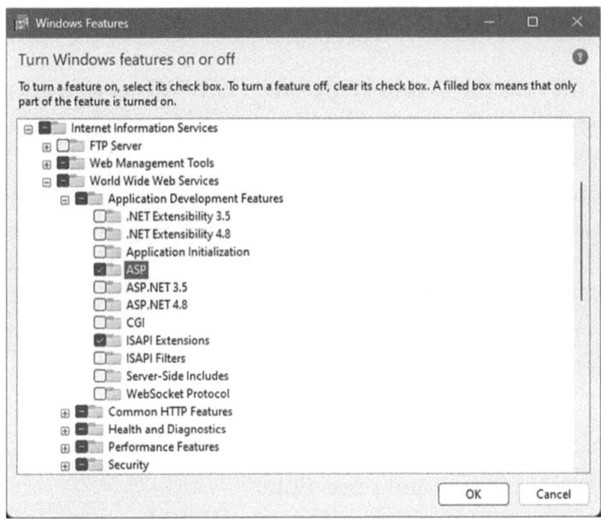

FIGURE C.3.   Installing IIS and enabling Classic ASP in Windows.

6. Once the required features are installed, close the Control Panel.
You should see the folder named `inetpub` on your computer's system drive, as shown in Figure C.4. You can also verify that IIS is installed by opening a Web browser and navigating to *http://localhost*. You should see the default IIS welcome page.

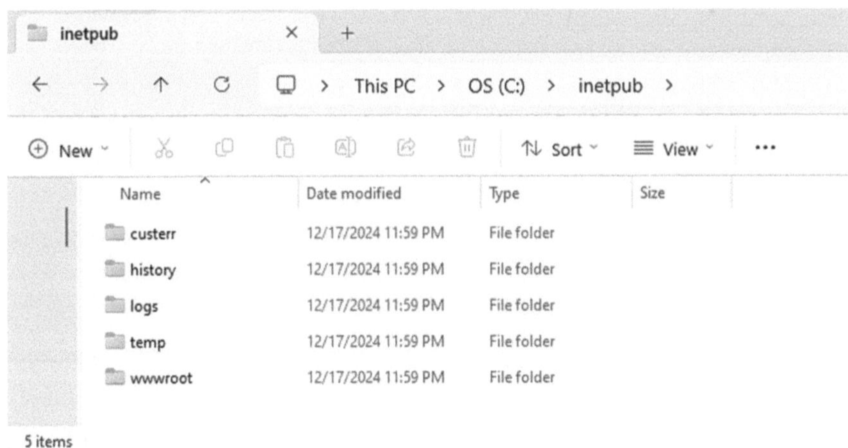

FIGURE C.4.   After installing IIS, a new folder named inetpub should appear on your computer's system drive.

After installing IIS, you can manage its settings by using IIS Manager. Let's continue by creating a virtual directory.

CREATING A VIRTUAL DIRECTORY

The default home directory for the World Wide Web (WWW) service is `\Inet-pub\wwwroot`. Files located in the home directory and its subdirectories are automatically available to visitors to your site. If you have Web pages in other folders on your computer and you'd like to make them available for viewing by your Web site visitors, you can create virtual directories. A virtual directory appears to client browsers as if it were physically contained in the home directory.

In Chapter 20, you created a directory called `VBAAccess2024_XML`. Now you will designate it as a virtual directory.

(◉) Hands-On C.2   Creating a Virtual Directory in Windows

1. Press Windows + R, type `inetmgr`, and press Enter.
   Windows displays the Internet Information Services (IIS) Manager window.

2. Expand the tree nodes in the Connections pane on the left, click Sites, then right-click on Default Web Site and select Add Virtual Directory…, as shown in Figure C.5.

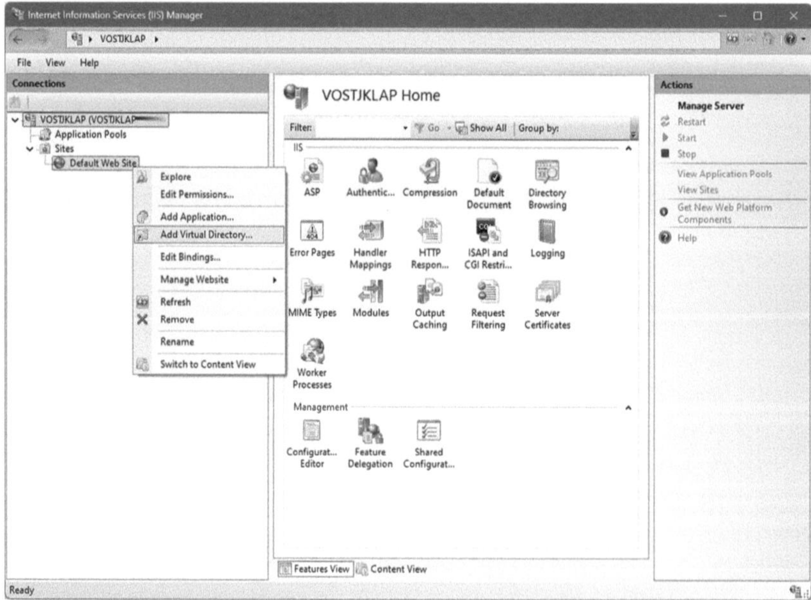

FIGURE C.5.   You can add a virtual directory by right-clicking Default Web Site in the Connections pane of the Internet Information Services (IIS) Manager window.

A virtual directory has an *alias*, that is, a name that client browsers use to access that directory. An alias is often used to shorten a long directory name. In addition, an alias provides increased security. Because users do not know where your files are physically located on the server, they cannot modify them.

3. Type `acc_xml` in the Alias box, as shown in Figure C.6. Set the Physical path to point to the `C:\VBAAccess2024_XML` folder that you created in Chapter 20.

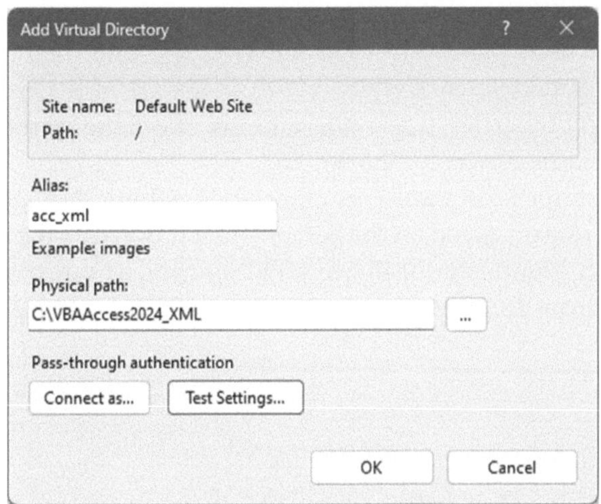

FIGURE C.6.   The Add Virtual Directory dialog box is used to specify the name and path to your Web site folder. The physical folder named VBAAccess2021_XML will be shared over the Web as acc_xml.

4. Click OK to save the changes.

Notice the virtual directory named `acc_xml` now appears under Default Web Site in the Connections pane (Figure C.7). The middle section of Internet Information Services (IIS) Manager displays the acc_xml Home.

5. Do not close the Internet Information Services (IIS) Manager window, as you will continue with it in the next section.

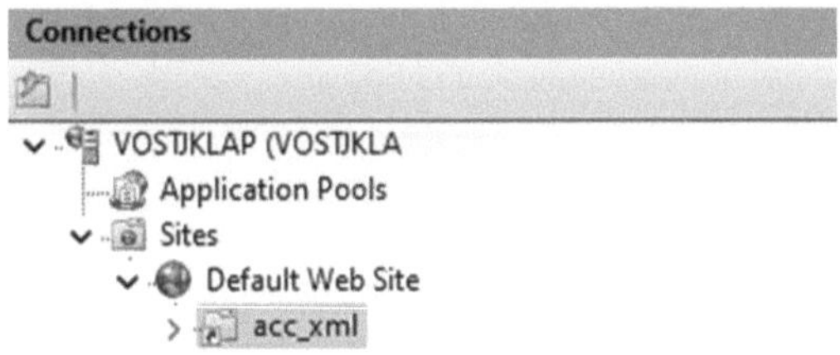

FIGURE C.7.   After creating a virtual directory, you should see it listed under Default Web Site in the Connections pane of the Internet Information Services (IIS) Manager window.

SETTING ASP CONFIGURATION PROPERTIES

To make it easy to debug your code, and to ensure that you can use relative paths in your code, you must change a couple of default configuration properties in IIS Manager.

⊙ Hands-On C.3   Configuring ASP Properties

1. In IIS Manager's Connections pane, select Default Web Site, and then in the middle section, under IIS, double-click ASP.
2. Expand the Debugging Properties tree node and set the Send Errors To Browser property to True, as shown in Figure C.8.

   By default, when ASP script errors are encountered, Windows displays the following message: An error occurred on the Server when processing the URL. Please contact the System Administrator. To prevent this error, be sure to select True next to the Send Errors To Browser property, as shown in Figure C.8.

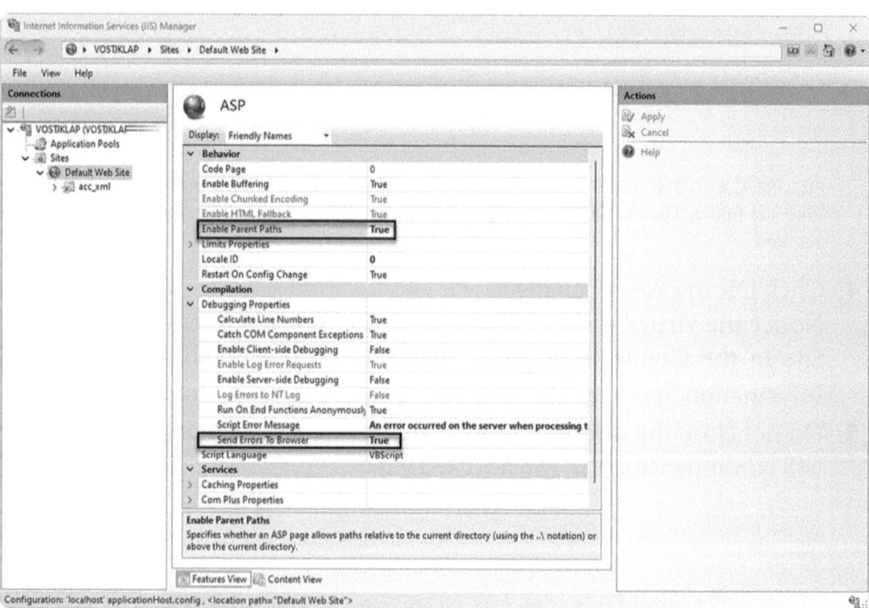

FIGURE C.8.   The highlighted settings have been set to True.

3. In the Behavior section, set Enable Parent Paths to True, as shown in Figure C.8.

Parent paths allow you to use relative addresses that contain .. in the paths of files and folders.

4. In the Actions area on the right, click Apply to save the changes.
   When changes have been successfully saved, you should see a message in the Alerts area in the right pane of the Internet Information Services (IIS) Manager window that the changes have been successfully saved.
5. Close the Internet Information Services (IIS) Manager window.

TURNING OFF FRIENDLY HTTP ERROR MESSAGES

Friendly HTTP error messages don't provide enough information for programmers to effectively troubleshoot script errors. Use the following steps to uncheck the Show friendly HTTP error messages option in your browser so you will get more meaningful error messages that can help you solve your script problems.

Hands-On C.4   Turning Off Friendly HTTP Error Messages

1. Press Windows + R to open the Run dialog.
2. Type `inetcpl.cpl` and press Enter.
   This command will open the Internet Properties window directly. You can also access this window via the Internet Options in Control Panel.
3. In the Internet Properties window, click the Advanced tab.
4. Locate the Browsing settings and uncheck Show friendly HTTP error messages, as shown in Figure C.9.
5. Click Apply to save your changes and then click OK to exit the Internet Properties window.
   Your IIS is now configured to run classic ASP scripts on your computer and provide you with meaningful error messages in case errors are encountered in your scripts at runtime.

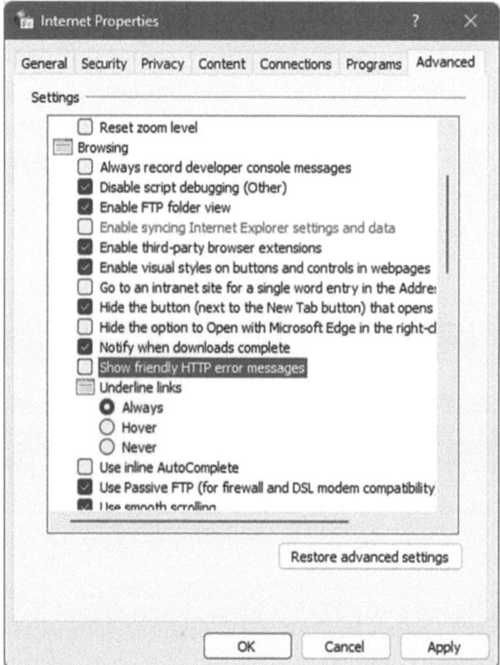

FIGURE C.9. Turn off the Show friendly HTTP error messages option so you can see the actual Windows messages when troubleshooting your ASP scripts.

Your IIS is now configured to run classic ASP scripts on a Windows machine (32-bit system). If you are working with the 64-bit operating system, you will need to take additional steps, as follows:

a. Activate IIS Manager.
b. Expand the tree node in the Connections pane on the left, right-click Application Pools, and choose Add Application Pool.
c. In the name box, enter `MyClassicASP`. For the .NET CRL version, choose No Managed Code. In the Managed Pipeline Mode dropdown, choose Classic. After making these selections, click OK.
d. The MyClassicASP entry should now appear in the Application Pool list in the middle section of the Internet Information Services (IIS) Manager window. Right-click this entry and choose Advanced Settings.
e. In the (General) section of the Advanced Settings dialog, specify True for Enable 32-bit Applications.
f. Click OK to close the Advanced Settings dialog.

g.   In the Connections pane on the left, right-click Default Web Site, and choose Manage Web Site | Advanced Settings.
h.   In the Advanced Settings window, change the Application Pool to MyClassicASP and click OK.
i.   Close the Internet Information Services (IIS) Manager window.

For more information, see the following link:

http://www.iis.net/learn/application-frameworks/running-classic-asp-applications-on-iis-7-and-iis-8

A

.accdb file format, 234, 235, 237, 249, 286, 571, 573, 601, 833, 928, 1101

.ade file format, 1103

.adp file format, 1102

AbsolutePosition property, 306, 418, 428

Accept_Charset header, 1082

Access Connectivity Engine (ACE), 232

Access versions and file formats 2007–2024, 1101–1103

Access Web Database, 959

AcDataErrContinue, 702, 745

AcDataErrDisplay, 702 745

ACE. *See* Access Connectivity Engine (ACE)

Action Catalog in Access 2024, 930

Action queries, 326, 340, 342, 450, 562, 566, 927

Activate event, 695–696, 741

Active procedure call, 211

Active Server Pages (ASP), 1000, 1002

    Configuring ASP Properties, 1110–1111

    Deleting record, 319–320

    Friendly HTTP error messages, turning off, 1111–1113

    Internet Information Services (IIS), 1004, 1105–1113

    Modifying record, 318–319

    Virtual directory, creating, 1108–1109

ActiveConnection parameter, 401

ActiveConnection property, 373, 384, 410, 440, 458, 460

ActiveX controls, 490, 496, 928

ActiveX® Data Objects (ADO), 357, 358, 520

    ADO Classic *versus* ADO.NET, 241

    common data providers, 248, 249, 363

    components of, 240

    differences between ADO and DAO, 432

ActiveX Data Objects, with XML, 1040–1055

AdAsyncExecute, 407

AdAsyncFetch, 407

AdAsyncFetchNonBlocking, 407

AdCmdFile, 406

AdCmdStoredProc, 406, 442

AdCmdTable, 372, 385, 406, 408, 442, 444

AdCmdTableDirect, 406, 408

AdCmdText, 372, 407, 408

AdCmdUnknown, 372, 407

Add method, 40, 170, 325, 434, 497, 498, 875, 894, 895, 897, 1022, 1062

ADD USER statement, 653

Add Watch dialog box, 205–209

AddNew method, 299, 311, 318, 430, 455, 458

AdExecuteNoRecords, 408, 409, 450, 545

AdExecuteRecord, 409

AdExecuteStream, 408

AdKeyForeign, 398

AdLockBatchOptimistic, 460

AdLockOptimistic, 370, 385, 404

AdLockPessimistic, 404

AdLockReadOnly, 372, 404, 444

ADO. *See* ActiveX® Data Objects (ADO)

ADO classic *vs.* ADO.NET, 241

ADO Recordsets, 400–447

    asynchronous fetching, 407

    bookmarks, using, 425–429

    cursor location, 404–405

    cursor types, 402–403

    finding record based on multiple conditions, 424–425

    finding record position, 417–418

    finding records using find method, 421–422

    finding records using seek method, 422–424

    GetRows method to fill the recordset, using, 429–430

    lock types, 403–404

    moving around in Recordset, 416–417

    opening Recordset, 409–416

        based on criteria, 415–416

        based on SQL Statement, 414–415

        based on table or query, 410–412

    Options parameter, 405–409

    returning Recordset as string, 418–420

ADO schema, 1045

ADODB (ActiveX Data Objects), 240

AdOpenDynamic, 402, 414, 444

AdOpenForwardOnly, 402, 403, 426, 444

AdOpenKeyset, 385, 402, 403, 426

AdOpenStatic, 370, 372, 402, 403, 414, 444, 460

AdOptionUnspecified, 409
ADOX (ADO Extensions for DDL and
    Security), 240
ADOX Object Model, 439
AdSchemaColumns, 388
AdSchemaProviderTypes, 389
AdSortAscending, 395
AdSortDescending, 395
Advanced ADO/DAO features
    cloning recordset, 478–483
    creating custom recordset (ADO), 456–459
    data shaping, 485–489
        creating shaped recordset (ADO),
            516–520
        shaped recordsets with
            grandchildren, 524
        shaped recordsets with multiple children
            (ADO), 490
        working with, 485–489
        writing complex SHAPE statement,
            489–499
        writing simple SHAPE statement, 485
    disconnected recordset (ADO), 459–461
    displaying current and previous records by
        using Clone method, 479–483
    fabricating recordset, 455–458
    filling combo box with disconnected
        recordset (ADO), 463–468
    hierarchical recordsets
        creating form with TreeView control,
            490–492
        writing event procedure for form load
            event, 493–499
    saving records to disk (ADO), 461–478
    taking persisted data on road
        creating unbound Access form to view
            and modify data, 465–467
        saving recordset to disk, 465
        viewing and editing data offline, 473–474
        writing procedures to control form and
            data, 467–473
    transaction processing, 501–507
        creating transaction with
            ADO, 501–507
Advanced Data TableGram, 1040

Advanced event programming
    declaring and raising events, 914–916
    responding to control events, 910–914
    sinking events in standalone class module,
        902–909
        cRecordLogger class, creating, 903–906
        cRecordLogger custom class with another
            form, 908–909
        file preparation, 903
        instance of custom class, creating,
            906–908
        Name property, 903, 911, 910, 941,
            1036, 1087
        Object drop-down list, 904
        Procedure drop-down list, 903
        testing clsRecordLogger custom class,
            908–909
    writing event procedure code, 909
AfterDelConfirm event, 694–695
AfterInsert event, 689–690
AfterUpdate event, 691–692
ALL keyword, 331,
ALTER COLUMN clause, 529
ALTER DATABASE PASSWORD statement,
    578, 579
ALTER TABLE statement, 527, 528, 529, 530,
    533, 536
American National Standards Institute
    (ANSI), 515
AND operator, 41, 107, 108, 109, 330
ANSI. *See* American National Standards
    Institute (ANSI)
ANSI SQL-89, 515
ANSI SQL-92 or SQL-2, 515
ANSI SQL query modes, 515
    setting, 516–517
Append method, 279, 283, 292, 374, 394, 398,
    455, 458, 634
Append Only memo fields, 287–288
Append queries, 326–327
Application-defined property, 278
Application Programming Interfaces
    (API), 1075–1093
ApplyFilter event, 704–705
ApplyTransform function, 994, 996

Arguments
optional, 83–85
passing arguments by reference and value, 82–83
Array function, 155–161
Array variable, 143
Array(s), 139–145
Array function, 143–144
Debug button, 162
Declaring, 141–142
Dimensioning, 155
Dynamic, 153–154
Erase function, 157–160
Errors in, 161–162
Fixed-dimension, 153
Functions, 155–161
Initial value of array element, 151
Initializing and filling, 144–145
Array function, 143–144
For…Next loop, 144–145
individual assignment statements, 144
IsArray function, 156–157
LBound and UBound functions, 160–161
Looping statements, 147–151
For Each…Next statement, 133–134
For…Next statement, 134–135
loops in real life and, 150–151
passing elements of array to another procedure, 148–149
One-dimensional array, 139, 140, 142, 144, 145–147, 162, 167
Option Base 1 statement, 140, 143, 179
parameter, 162–163
passing arrays between procedures, 151
passing arrays to function procedures, 163–164
range of, 147
Sorting, 165–166
Static, 152–155
Two-dimensional array, 151–152
Upper and lower bounds, 143
Assert statement, 203–204
Asterisk (*), 309
Async property, 995
Asynchronous record fetching, 407

Attachment data type, 232, 280, 286, 375, 603, 717, 948
Attachment fields, 286–287
Attachments control, in Access forms, 661–725
AttachmentCurrent event procedure, 717
Attachments dialog box, 714
Controlling forms with form properties, 662–682
Current File text box, 718
Forward and Backward buttons, 714
Modules and event programming, 685–687
Referring forms, 682–685
unbound text box, 716
Attribute-based document, 984
Attribute-centric XML, 1043, 1044–1045
Authentication credentials, 1078
AutoExec macro, 810, 928–932
contents of, 929
macro actions, arguments, and program flow, 929–932
OpenForm, 931
AutoNumber, 390–391

B

Backstage View, 853–857
customizing, 857
hiding buttons and tabs, 857
BeforeDelConfirm event, 694
BeforeInsert event, 688–689
BeforeUpdate event, 690
BeginTrans method, 351, 353, 501
BETWEEN…AND operator, 330
BinaryCompare, 1064
BOF (Beginning of file), 300
Bookmark property, 301, 309, 425, 426
Bookmarks, 215, 225, 306
Boolean expressions, 102
Break mode, 185, 193, 198, 201Þ02
Breakpoints, 194–201
removing, 200–201
Bubble sort, 165
Built-in functions, 69, 78, 85–97
ByRef keyword, 83
ByVal keyword, 82, 83, 163

C

Cache-Control header, 1078
Calculated field, 285–286
Call Stack dialog box, 211–212
Callback procedures, 804–805, 816, 826, 830, 832, 846, 847
CancelBatch method, 477
CancelUpdate method, 318
Cascading Stylesheets (CSS), 1051
Case Else clause, 117
Catalog, 358, 372, 377
Categorized tab, 56
Category argument, 791
CData directive, 992
CDate function, 111
ChangePassword method, 634, 648
CHECK constraints, 542–546
ChildNodes property, 1035–1036
Class methods, 874–878
Class modules, 5, 9, 54–55, 170, 663, 724, 737, 864, 865, 866–893
    form, 6
    naming, 868
    report, 6
    standalone, 6
Click event, 469, 472, 585, 591, 671, 685, 686, 697, 710, 878, 888, 893, 941, 970
Client-side cursor (adUseClient), 404
Client-side script, 996
Clone method, 478, 510
Cloning recordset, 478–483
Close event, 741
Close method, 250, 267, 325, 367, 410, 436, 883
Code window
    activate, 58
    Break mode, 201–202
    splitting, 59
    understanding, 58–59
Collection(s) *See also Specific collections*
    custom (*See* Custom collection)
    own, 170–179
Collection class, 896
Collection object, 897, 1059, 1065
Combo box, 15, 195, 200, 283, 463, 482, 692, 693, 710, 721–723

Command Button Wizard, 924
Command object, 401, 406, 410, 439, 441, 447, 449, 451, 506, 545, 563, 651
CommandBars object and Ribbon, 849–852
CommandText property, 409, 441, 506
CommandType property, 406, 442
CommitTrans method, 351, 501
CompactDatabase method, 265, 360
Compacting database
    CompactDatabase (DBEngine), 265, 267, 360
    CompactDatabase (Microsoft Jet and Replication Objects (JRO) Library), 240
CompareMode property, 1064
Concatenation, 28
Conditional expression
    If…Then statement, 102–105
    If…Then…else statement, 109–111
    If…Then…Elseif statement, 112–113
    logical operators, 102
    nested if…then statements, 113–115
    relational operators, 102
    Select Case statement, 116–123
        specifying multiple expressions in Case clause, 122–123
        specifying range of values in Case clause, 120–122
        using Is with Case clause, 119–120
Conditional statements, 41, 101–124
Connection strings, 242–244
    ODBC
        creating and using DSN-less ODBC connections, 250
        creating and using ODBC DSN connections, 245–250
        data sources, 245
    OLE DB, 251–252
    via data link file, 253–254
Constants in VBA procedures, 48–49
    declaring, 48
    intrinsic, 49
    Private constant, 48
    Public constant, 48

Constraints, 513, 520, 526, 527, 514–542
   CHECK, 542–546
   FOREIGN KEY, 541, 546
   NOT NULL, 542
   PRIMARY KEY, 541
   UNIQUE, 542
Constraint clause, 533, 535, 547
Container objects, 267, 647
Content-type header, 1004, 1079
CopyFromRecordset method, 321, 322, 324, 325
Copying database
   with DAO, 265–267
   with FileSystemObject, 360–361
Counter, 131
Count property, 172, 362, 895, 1063
CreateAdditionalData method, 1022
CreateDOM function, 994
CreateField method, 264, 274, 276, 278, 283, 287, 293, 295
CreateIndex method, 278, 292, 295
CREATE INDEX statement, 538
CreateObject function, 325, 360, 367, 436, 1076,
CREATE PROCEDURE (or CREATE PROC) statement, 558
CreateProperty method, 278
CreateQueryDef method, 333
CreateReport method, 737
CreateTableDef method, 263, 274, 276, 292
CREATE TABLE statement, 520, 521, 527
CreateTextFile method, 367, 420, 436
CREATE USER statement, 653
CREATE VIEW statement, 554
CSS, 1051
Current event, 687–688
CurrentDb method, 276, 366
CurrentView property names and values, 742
Cursor, 402–403
CursorLocation parameter, 404–405
CursorType parameter, 402–403
CursorType property, 385
Custom collection
   accessing, 172–173
   adding objects to, 170–171
   creating, 174–176
   number, 172
   removing, 173
   returning, 176
   updating, 174
Custom objects, 866–894
   class variable, 868–869
   creating class methods, 873–878
   creating class module, 867–868
   effective code analysis, 893
   instance of class, 893–894
   property procedures, 869–872
   naming class module, 868
   writing procedures, 878–893

D

DAO. *See* Data Access Objects (DAO)
DAO Recordsets, 295–326
   adding new record, 311
   adding values, multvalue lookup fields, 314—317
   copying records, Excel worksheet, 321–326
   counting records and retrieving field values, 304–307
   deleting attachments, 311–314
   deleting records, 319–320
   filtering records, 320–321
   finding and reading records, 300–301
   finding records in Dynasets and Snapshots, 308–310
   finding records in Table-type recordset, 308
   modifying record, 318–319
   opening recordset and transfering data, 296–300
   retrieving contents of specific field, 304–312
   seek method to find records, 307–308
   types, 296
Data Access Objects (DAO), 452
Data Access technologies
   Access versions and formats, 234
      file formats supported in Access 2007–2024, 1101–1103
   connection to current Access database, 366–367

copying database
   with DAO, 265–267
   with FileSystemObject, 360–361
creating a reference to ADO library,
   241–242
creating new Access database
   with ADO, 358–360
   with DAO, 261–265
database engines: JET/ACE, 231–234
library references, 234–237
Microsoft Access databases, opening
   in read-only mode with DAO, 269
   in read/write mode with ADO,
     363–366
   in read/write mode with DAO, 267–269
   secured with password, 269–270
   with user-level security, 621–623
Object libraries, 237–241
   Microsoft Access 16.0 Object Library,
     238
   Microsoft ActiveX Data Objects 6.1
     Library (ADO), 238–239
   Microsoft DAO 3.6 Object Library, 238
   Microsoft Office 16.0 Access Database
     Engine Object Library, 238
   OLE automation, 238
   VBA object library, 237
opening databases, spreadsheets
   and text files
   connecting to SQL server database, 368
   opening Microsoft Excel workbook,
     368–369
DatabaseCompare, 1064
Data Definition Language (DDL) queries,
   329, 517
Data Definition Query window, 550–552
Data events, 687–695
   AfterDelConfirm, 694–695
   AfterInsert, 689–690
   AfterUpdate, 691–692
   BeforeDelConfirm, 694
   BeforeInsert, 688–689
   BeforeUpdate, 690
   Current, 687–688
   Delete, 693–694
   Dirty, 692–693

   OnUndo, 693
Data Link Properties dialog box, 253, 254
   Advanced tab, 254
   Connection tab, 254
   Provider tab, 254
Data macros, 947–962
   copying, 962
   creating, 955–956
   execution errors, 960–962
   existing named, 958
   named data macro, 958
   ReturnVars, using, 958–960
   using, 948–949
Data Manipulation Language (DML), 450, 517
Data members, 868, 871
Data providers, 239, 248, 249, 363
Dataroot element, 987–988
Data shaping, 483–499
   creating shaped recordset (ADO),
     487–488
   shaped recordsets with multiple children
     and grandchildren, 490
   working with, 485–489
   writing complex SHAPE statement, 489–499
   writing simple SHAPE statement, 485
Data type(s), 22–54
   ADO *vs.* Microsoft Access data types, 375
   converting, 97–99
   listing, 386–387
   user-defined, 1099
   variant, 1099
Database engines
   JET/ACE, 231–233
   versions, 234
Database errors
   On Error GoTo 0, 217
   On Error GoTo Label, 217
   On Error Resume Next, 217
   VBA Err object and ADO Errors collection,
     362–363
Database security
   adding users to groups, 653–654
   changing user password, 649–650
   creating group account, 623–624
   creating user account, 621–622
   deleting group account, 657

deleting user account, 654
granting permissions for object, 654–655
removing database password, 679–580
removing user account from group, 654
revoking security permissions, 655–656
setting database password, 578
Database security, implementing
  opening secured MDB database, 617–620
  securing Access MDB database, 610–617
  share-level security, 269–270
  user and group accounts (ADO)
    creating, 634–638
    deleting, 638–640
    listing, 640–642
    listing users in groups, 642–643
  user and group permissions
    changing user password, 650–651
    object owner, retrieving name of, 644–649
    setting permissions for containers, 647–649
    setting permissions for database, 647
    setting permissions for object, 645–646
  user-level security, 607–620
  workgroup information file, 573, 601, 607–609
    Access versions, 607–608
    creating and joining, 610–617
DblClick event, 697, 706
DblClick (Form section event), 706–707
DDL. *See* Data Definition Language (DDL)
DDL queries, 329, 517
Deactivate event, 696, 743
Debug button, 162
Debugging, 186
Default Value property, 278
Delete event, 693–694
Delete method, 289, 291, 314, 319, 347, 377, 379, 432, 453, 638
Delete query, 339–340
DelimFound function, 710
Dirty event, 692–693
DISALLOW NULL option, 538, 539
Disconnected recordsets, 459–461
  creating, 459–460
DISTINCT keyword, 331, 347

DISTINCTROW keyword, 332
Dictionary object, 1059–1066
Document Object Model (DOM), 994
Document Type Definition (DTD), 982
DOMDocument object, 994, 1003, 1033, 1034, 1040, 1047
DomDocument60, 1033
Do…Until statement, 129–130
Do…While statement, 125–129
DROP COLUMN clause, 530, 536
DROP CONSTRAINT clause, 536
DROP GROUP statement, 657
DROP INDEX statement, 536–537
DROP PROCEDURE (or DROP PROC) statement, 565
DROP USER statement, 654
DROP VIEW statement, 556, 557
DSN (Data Source Name), 245–250
  File, 245
  System, 245
  User, 245
Dynamic array, 142, 152–155
Dynamic link library (DLL), 232, 234
Dynamic-type Recordset, 299
Dynaset-type Recordset, 309, 311, 318, 319

E

Early binding, 1060
Edit method, 303, 318, 432
EditModeEnum constants, 318
Element-centric XML, 1044–1045
ElseIf clause, 112
Embedded macros
  copying, 941–944
  creating, 940
EOF (End of file), 249, 273, 300, 414
Erase function, 157–160
Err object, 217–221
Error, mistake and, 217
Error event, 701–703
  DataErr, 702
  Response, 702
Error handler, 122, 204, 217, 223, 333, 361, 393, 525

Error trapping, 218–221
    Err object, using, 217–221
    On Error statement, 217,
    procedure testing, 221–223
    setting options, 223–224
Event, 866
Event data macros, 948
Event-driven programming, advanced
        concepts in
    declaring and raising events, 914–916
    responding to control events, 910–914
    sinking events in standalone class module,
        902–909
        creating clsRecordLogger class, 903–906
        creating instance of custom class,
            906–908
        file preparation, 903
        testing cRecordLogger custom class,
            908–909
        using cRecordLogger custom class with
            another form, 908–909
    writing event procedure code, 909
Event handler. *See* Event procedures
Event procedures, 6, 9, 39, 469, 472, 591, 659,
        663, 666, 669, 685, 686, 697, 701, 706,
        712, 724, 757, 736, 772, 865, 878, 900,
        902, 910, 916
Event properties, 6, 15–22, 691
Event sink, 866
Event source, 866
Event statement, 866, 914
Event trapping, 686
Event(s), 9, 39, 863–920
    data, 687–695
        AfterDelConfirm, 694–695
        AfterInsert, 689–690
        AfterUpdate, 691–692
        BeforeDelConfirm, 694
        BeforeInsert, 688–689
        BeforeUpdate, 690
        Current, 687–688
        Delete, 693–694
        Dirty, 692–693
        OnUndo, 693
    DblClick, 697

error, 702–703
    DataErr, 702
    Response, 702
filter, 703–705
    ApplyFilter, 704–705
    Filter, 703–704
focus, 695–696
    Activate, 695–696
    Deactivate, 696
    GotFocus, 696
    LostFocus, 696
form section, 706–707
    DblClick, 706
keyboard, 699–714
    KeyDown, 699–701
    KeyPress, 701
    KeyUp, 701
mouse, 696–709
    Click, 697
    DblClick, 697
    MouseDown, 697–698
    MouseMove, 698
    MouseUp, 698
    MouseWheel, 698–699
OpenArgs property, 707–712
sequence of, 686
timing, 705–706
    Timer, 705–706
Exclamation point (!), 331, 1098
Execute method, 340, 341, 354, 375, 407, 409,
        410, 414, 439, 442, 449, 520, 525, 545,
        554, 557, 559, 563, 1071, 1073
ExecuteMso method, 850
Exists method, 889, 1063, 1064
Exiting loops early, 127, 135–136
Exiting procedures, 136
Explicit variable declaration, 24
    advantages of, 24
ExportNavigationPane method, 794
ExportXML method, 1019–1031,
    arguments of, 1031
Expression Builder, 286, 934–935
Extensible Markup Language (XML), 461, 784,
        981–1057
Extensible Stylesheet Language (XSL), 982

F

Fabricating recordset, 455–458
Fast commands, 853
Field Properties Lookup tab, 284
FileDateTime function, 458
FileFormat parameter, 325
file format (in Microsoft Access)
.accdb, 1101
.accde, 1101
.accdt, 1102
.accdr, 1102
.ade, 1103
.adp, 1102
.mdb, 1102
.mde, 1102
.mdw, 1103
.laccdb, 1103
.ldb, 1103
FileLen function, 458
Filter events, 703–705
ApplyFilter, 704–705
Filter, 703–704
Filter property, 320, 424, 436, 760
Find methods, 307, 308–310, 318
Fixed-dimension arrays, 153
Focus events, 695–696
Activate, 695–696
Deactivate, 696
GotFocus, 696
LostFocus, 696
For Each…Next statement, 131–132, 135, 137, 148, 173, 179, 264, 269, 273, 347, 895, 1037
Foreign key, 398, 541, 546
Foreign key constraint, 546, 547
Form(s)
attachments control, 714–178
controlling forms, 662–682
cmdGetform, 670
custom form view, 666
designing and programming custom form, 663–682
formInspector, 681–682
forminspector form, 664–665
Hidden text boxes in, 667
Use cases, 668
Controls, refeering to forms, 682–685
main, 683
Programming in Access, form modules, 685–687
subform, 683
Form module, 5, 6, 493, 591, 663, 669, 685–687, 738, 865, 893, 909
Form section event, 706–707
Format event (Report Section Event), 746–749
Cancel, 746
effect on report sections, 747
FormatCount, 746
Forward-only-type Recordset, 296
Friendly HTTP error messages, turning off, 1111–1113
Function procedures, 6, 8, 12, 77–80
methods of running
from Immediate window, 78–79
from subroutine, 79–80
passing arguments to, 82–83
data types and functions, 80–81
Functions, 77–100
built-in functions, 85
InputBox function, 95–97
IsMissing function, 84
MsgBox function, 85–97
formatting, 86–92
MsgBox buttons argument settings, 89–90
prompt argument, 86
returning values from, 93–94
using functions with arguments, 92–93
passing arguments to function procedures
by reference and value, 82–83
specifying data types, 80–81
using optional arguments, 83–84
running function procedure
from Immediate window, 78–79
from subroutine, 79–80
Writing function procedures, 77–78

G

Galleries, 797
GetAllResponseHeaders, 1078
GetElementsByTagName method, 1036
GetEnabledMso method, 849
GetImageMso method, 850
GET method, 849, 1076
GetObject function, 325
GetObjectOwner method, 644
GetPermissions method, 649
Get request, 1075
GetResponseHeader, 1078–1079
GetRows method, 429–430
GetString method, 418, 420, 432, 434, 436, 442,
    444, 461
Global property, 1071, 1073, 1091
Global variable, 37, 39, 41, 210, 586, 478
GotFocus event, 685, 696, 722
GRANT statement, 653, 655
Group argument, 791
Group auto-scaling, 852–853
GUIDs, 646

H

HasChildNodes method, 1035
Header, 1078, 1080
HTML tags, 992
HTTP GET protocol, 1004
HyperText Markup Language (HTML), 982
Hyphen (-), 331

I

If block instructions, 109
If…Then statement, 102–105
    formats of, 107
    multiline, 105–106
    with AND operator, 108–109
If…Then…else statement, 109–111
If…Then…Elseif statement, 112–113
    ElseIf clause, 112
IgnoreCase property, 1071
IGNORE NULL option, 538, 540
IgnoreNulls property, 293

Immediate window
    in break mode, 201–202
Implicit variable declaration, 24
    disadvantages of, 25
ImportNavigationPane method, 794
ImportXML method, 1019, 1031,
    1048, 1082
ImportXML method, arguments of, 1031
IN operator, 330
Index(es)
    adding multiple-field index to existing table,
        294–295
    creating, 292–293
    creating indexed with restrictions,
        538–541
        DISALLOW NULL option, 539–540
        IGNORE NULL option, 540–541
        PRIMARY option, 538–539
    creating primary key, 391–393
    creating single field index using ADO,
        393–395
    creating table with primary key,
        585–586
    creating tables with indexes, 582–583
    deleting indexes, indexed field, 536–537
    deleting table indexes (ADO),
        396–397
    listing indexes in table (ADO), 395–396
IndexNulls property, 394
Infinite loop, 129
Informal (implicit) variables, 26
InputBox function, 43, 79, 81, 95–97, 99, 150,
    176, 564
InputBox method, 336
Instance, 864, 867
InStr function, 712, 906, 1067
Internet Information Services (IIS), 1004,
    1105–1113
Intrinsic constants, 49, 365, 366, 394, 454, 583
InvalidateControl method, 846, 848
Invalidate method, 848
IRibbonControl properties, 808–809
IRibbonUI object, 846–849
    Invalidate method, 848
    InvalidateControl method, 846, 848

IsArray function, 156–157
IsMissing function, 84
Is Nothing expression, 1039
IS NULL operator, 330
Item property, 1060
Items method, 895
IXMLDOMNodeList method, 1036, 1039
IXMLDOMNode object, 1035–1036

J

JavaScript, 996, 1084
Java*Script* Object Notation (see JSON)
Jet. See Microsoft Jet (Joint Engine Technology (JET)), 231–232
JRO (Jet and Replication Objects), 240
JSON, 1084–1093
JSONP, 1086

K

KeyASCII, 701, 911
Keyboard events, 699–701
    KeyDown, 699
    KeyPress, 701
    KeyUp, 701
KeyCode, 699, 701
KeyDown event, 699–700
    KeyCode, 699
    Shift, 699
KeyPress, 701
Key property, 1061–1062
Keys method, 1061–1062
Keywords, 3, 6, 9, 25, 33, 35, 45, 67, 71, 83, 106, 109, 117, 122, 161, 212, 220, 326, 351, 501, 870, 902, 974
Kill statement, 266, 312, 359, 525, 1043,

L

.laccdb file format, 1103
.ldb file format, 1103
Late binding, 1060
Layout view, 113, 133, 727, 728, 754, 761, 819, 877, 940
LBound function, 160–161

Left function, 1066
Len function, 160, 167, 176, 458, 1066
Library, 69
Library references, 234–237
    default object libraries, 235
    missing library, 236
    References dialog box, 236–237
Lifetime of variables, 38
LIKE operator, 330
List Properties/Methods, 63
Load method, 995
LoadXML method, 1082
Localhost, 1107
Locals Window, 202, 209–210
Local variables. See Procedure-level (local) variables
LockType property, 385, 404
Logic errors, 192, 204
Logical operators, 102
Loop, 125
    infinite, 129
LostFocus event, 696

M

.mdb file format, 243, 249, 573, 601–658, 947, 1102
.mdw file format, 1103
Macro security (Access 2024), 925–928
Macro(s), 923–978
    Access 2024 macro security, 925–928
    AutoExec macro, 928–939
        contents of, 928
        macro actions, arguments, and program flow, 929–932
        OpenForm, 931
    converting macros to VBA code, 967–970
    data macros, 947–948
    embedded macros, creating, 940
    error handling in, 963–966
    generating macros using Command Button Wizard, 947
    Info tab, 926
    Macro Settings options, 925

Microsoft Office Security Options dialog
box, 927
standalone macros, creating, 932–937
submacros, creating, 938–939
temporary variables in, 966–967
VBA and, 967
Make-Table query, 337–338
Method, 873–875
Microsoft Access 16.0 Object Library, 238, 1019
Microsoft Access database
connection to current Access database,
366–367
copying database
with DAO, 265–267
with FileSystemObject, 360
creating new Access database
with ADO, 358–360
with DAO, 261–265
opening database
in read-only mode with DAO, 269
in read/write mode with ADO,
365–366
Microsoft jet read/write mode with ADO,
363–366
secured with password, 269–270
with user-level security, 267, 573,
601, 604
Microsoft Access database field
creating append only memo fields with
DAO, 287–288
creating attachment fields with DAO,
286–287
creating calculated fields with DAO, 285–286
creating multivalue lookup fields with DAO,
284–286
creating rich text memo fields with DAO,
288–289
listing fields, 379–381
removing field from table (ADO/DAO), 379
retrieving field properties, 379–380
Microsoft Access database table
adding new fields to existing tables (ADO/
DAO), 378–379
AutoNumber, changing value of, 390–391
copying table (ADO), 376–377
creating table (DDL/DAO), 520–525

deleting table (ADO), 377
linking Access table, 381–383
linking dBASE table, 292
linking Excel worksheet, 383–386
listing database tables, 386–387
listing tables, 387–388
retrieving table properties, 291
Microsoft Access Jet/ACE database engine,
231–233
opening databases, spreadsheets
and text files, 368–372
connecting to SQL server database, 368
opening Microsoft Excel workbook,
368–369
opening text file using ADO, 371–372
Microsoft Access tables
indexes
adding multiple-field index to existing
table (DAO), 294–295
creating indexes using ADO, 392–393
creating indexes using DAO, 292–293
creating primary key, 391
creating single field index using ADO,
393–395
deleting table indexes (ADO), 396–397
listing indexes in table (ADO), 395–396
primary keys, 391–393
table relationships, using ADO
one-to-many relationship, 398–400
parent-child relationship, 398
Microsoft ActiveX Data Objects 6.1 Library
(ADO), 238–241
ADO classic *vs.* ADO.NET, 241
components of, 240
creating reference to, 241–242
data providers, 249
Microsoft DAO 3.6 Object Library, 238
Errors collection, 242
Parameters collection, 242
Properties collection, 242
Recordsets collection, 242
Workspaces collection, 242
Microsoft Jet (Joint Engine Technology
(JET)), 231–232
Microsoft Jet or Jet database engine,
231–232

Microsoft Office 16.0 Access Database Engine
Object Library, 238
Microsoft XML Object Library, 1032
Mid function, 176, 1010, 1066
Module-level variables, 34–35
Module(s)
class, 5–6, , 54, 170, 224, 585, 663, 668, 737,
863, 865, 866, 894, 900
form, 5–6, 663, 669, 685, 738, 865
renaming, 62
report, 5–6, 737, 772, 865, 909
standalone, 5–6, 902
standard, 5, 10, 13, 38, 53, 170, 509, 712, 894
executing procedures and functions,
13–15
writing procedures in, 10–13
Mouse events, 696–699
Click, 697
DblClick, 697
MouseDown, 697–698
MouseMove, 698
MouseUp, 698
MouseWheel, 698–699
Move methods, 307
MoveLast method, 300, 336, 418
MoveNext method, 300, 319, 417, 432
MovePrevious method, 300
MsgBox function, 7, 9, 79, 85–95
formatting, 86–89
MsgBox buttons argument settings, 89–90
prompt argument, 86
returning values from, 93–94
syntax of, 86
using functions with arguments, 92–93
using parentheses, 95
MSXML parser, 994
Multiline If…Then statement, 105–107
Multiline property, 1071
Multivalue lookup fields, 283–286
data types, 284–285

N

Name property, 62, 373
Named data macros
creating, 955–957
editing, 958
running, 958
Namespace, 987–988
NavigateTo method, 791
Navigating with bookmarks, 215
Navigation pane, 791–796
in Access 2024, 791
adding custom group, 788–789
assigning objects to custom
groups in, 790
with custom groupings, 790
working with, 786–790
controlling display of database objects,
791–792
locking Navigation pane, 791
saving and loading configuration of, 794
setting displayed categories, 793–794
Grouping options, 787
Navigation Options dialog box, 787
Search Bar or navigation options, 787
system objects in, 816
Nested if…then statements, 113–116
Nested loops, 136–138
NewPassword method, 577
NoData event, 743
NodeType property, 1035–1036
Non-row-returning queries, 451
Action queries, 451
DDL queries, 451
NOT NULL constraint, 527
NOT operator, 634
Number sign (#), 331, 1098
NZ function, 680, 1042

O

Object Browser window
intrinsic constants, 49
Object libraries, 237–241
Microsoft Access 16.0 Object Library, 238
Microsoft ActiveX Data Objects 6.1 Library
(ADO), 238–239
Microsoft DAO 3.6 Object Library, 238
Microsoft Office 16.0 Access Database
Engine Object Library, 238
VBA object library, 237

Object variables in VBA procedures, 44–47
  advantages of, 46
  disposing of, 47
ODBC Data Source Administrator, 244–250
  File DSN, 245
  System DSN, 245
  User DSN, 245
OLE DB, 239
One-to-many relationship, between tables,
  398–400
OnError action arguments, 963
On Error GoTo statement, 745
OnUndo event, 693
OOP (Object Oriented Programming), 861
OpenArgs property, 707–712
  of Report object, 758–759
OpenCurrentDatabase method, 1022
Open event, 739–740
OpenForm method, 65, 66, 707
  parameters, 719
Open method, 248, 256, 364, 370, 372, 400, 403,
  406, 410, 415, 444, 458, 478, 1003, 1053,
  1077
OpenQuery method, 555
OpenRecordset method, 273, 296, 299, 318, 319,
  346, 349
OpenReport method, 758
OpenSchema method, 387–389
Option Base 1 statement, 140, 143, 146, 179
Option Explicit statement, 30, 33, 35, 747, 879,
  903, 1022
Option Private Module statement, 38
Optional arguments, 83–85
Options parameter, 405–409
OR operator, 107, 123, 632, 645
ORDER BY clause, 332, 437, 553,
  556, 558

P

.pdf file format, saving reports in, 757
Page event, 743–744
Paired statements, 134
ParamArray keyword, 163
Parameter query

creating Parameter query with ADO,
  446–449
creating Parameter query with DAO,
  334–337
executing Parameter query with ADO,
  448–449
Parameterized stored procedures
  creating, 559–562
  executing, 563–564
Parent-child relationship, between tables,
  398, 484
ParseError object, 996
Parser, 982
Pass-Through query, 341–346
Passing arguments
  ByRef and ByVal, 82–83
  optional arguments, using, 83–84
  by reference and value, 82–83
  specifying data types, 80–81
  subroutines and functions, 81, 82–83
Pattern Match, 204, 1051, 1067, 1069, 1072
Pattern property, 1071
PercentPosition property, 306
Percent sign (%), 331
POST method, 1075, 1077
Predicate, 330
PRIMARY KEY constraint, 542
Primary keys, 391, 533
PRIMARY option, 538
Print event (Report Section Event),
  749–752
  effect on report sections, 750
  PrintCount, 749
Private constant, 48
Private keyword, 868
Procedure-level (local) variables, 34
Procedure testing, 221–223
Procedure(s), 4
  compiling, 16–18
  execution of VBA, 180–186
  in standard modules, 10–13
  stepping through VBA
    running procedure to cursor, 214
    setting Next statement, 214
    showing Next statement, 214

stepping out of procedure, 213–214
stepping over, 212
stopping, 193–194
stopping and resetting VBA, 216
testing VBA, 221–222
types of, 4–9
  event, 9
  function, 8–9
  property, 9–10
  subroutine, 6–7
writing function, 85–86
Project Explorer window
  activate, 55
  buttons, 55
  standard toolbar, 55
Project-level variables, 37–38
Prompt argument, 86
Properties window, 56–57
Property, 869–870
Property Get, 869
Property Let, 871, 872
Property procedures
  Defining, 869–870
  Immediate exit from, 871
  Property Get, 869
  Property Let, 869
  Property Set, 869
Public constant, 48
Public keyword, 37
PUT method, 1075, 1077

Q

Quantifier (in regular expression), 1068–1069
Queries,
  Append query with DAO, running,
    326–327
  Delete query with DAO, running,
    327–328
  Make-Table query with DAO, creating and
    running, 337–338
  non-row-returning, 451
  other operations with
    deleting query from database with
      DAO/ADO, 453–454

listing all queries in database with
    DAO/ADO, 452–453
  performing other operations with
    queries, 346–347
  updatable property, 349–350
Parameter query with ADO/DAO, creating
    and running, 334–337, 446–449
Pass-Through query with ADO/DAO,
    creating and running, 341–346,
    452–453
Queries, introduction, 326–329
  operators used in expressions, 330
  predicates in SQL SELECT statements,
    331–332
  WHERE clause in SQL SELECT
    statements, 333
  wildcard characters used in LIKE
    operator patterns, 333
row-returning, non-parameterized, 441
row-returning, parameterized, 447
Select query with ADO, executing, 441–444
Select query with ADO, modifying, 444–445
Select query with ADO/DAO, creating,
    333–334, 439–441
Update query with ADO, executing,
    449–451
Update query with DAO, creating and
    running, 327
Question mark (?), 331
Quick Access toolbar, 784, 857–858
Quit method, 325

R

RaiseEvent statement, 902, 915
Range of array, 147
ReadyState property, 1080
Record(s)
  adding attachments, 311–314
  adding new record with ADO, 430–431
  adding new record with DAO, 311
  adding values to multivalue lookup field,
    314–318
  copying records to Excel worksheet, 321–326
  copying records to text file (ADO), 434–436

copying records to Word document, 432–434
deleting attachments, 311–312
deleting record with ADO, 432
deleting record with DAO, 319–321
editing multiple records with ADO, 431–432
filtering records using filter property (DAO and ADO), 320–321, 436–438
modifying record with ADO, 430–431
modifying record with DAO, 318–319
sorting records (ADO), 436–438
RecordCount property, 304, 336, 413, 418, 444, 450
Recordset(s)
ADO Recordsets, 400–430
asynchronous fetching, 408
bookmarks, using, 425–429
counting records, 414
cursor location, 404–405
cursor types, 402–403
finding record based on multiple conditions, 424–425
finding record position, 417–418
finding records using find method, 421–422
finding records using seek method, 422–424
GetRows method to fill recordset, 429–430
lock types, 403–404
marking records with bookmark, 427–428
moving around in Recordset, 416–417
opening Recordset, 409–410
opening Recordset based on criteria, 409–410
opening Recordset based on SQL Statement, 414–415
opening Recordset based on table or query, 410–414
opening Recordset directly, 409–410
Options parameter, 405–409
returning Recordset as string, 418–420
DAO Recordsets, 295–326
adding and deleting attachments, 311–314
adding new record, 31
adding values, multivalue lookup fields, 314–317
copying records, excel worksheet, 321–326
counting records and retrieving field values, 304–307
deleting record, 319–320
filtering records, 320–321
finding and reading records, 300–304
modifying record, 318–319
opening recordset and transferring data, 296–300
opening Table-, Dynaset-, and Snapshot-type Recordsets, 308–310
seek methods to find records, 307–308
Recordset objects, 295, 348, 441
RecordStatusEnum constants, 476–477
REFERENCES clause, 547
RefreshDatabaseWindow method, 523
Regular expressions
see also RegExp object, 1066–1067
RegExp (RegExp), 1067
RegExp object
general reference: 1069–1070
patterns: 1068
properties: 1071
Relational operators, 102
RemoveAllTempVar, 966
Remove method, 41, 173, 875, 895, 1062, 1091
RemoveTempVar, 966
Replace method, 1071
Report(s)
creating, 728
events
Activate, 741–742
Close, 741
Deactivate, 743
Error, 745–746
NoData, 743
Open, 739–741
Page, 743
Group, Sort, and Total pane, 755
OpenArgs property, 758–761
report section events, 746–753
Format, 746–749
Print, 749–752

Retreat, 753
Report view, 753–755
saving reports in .pdf or .xps file format, 757
sorting and grouping data, 755–756
ReportML, 984
Report modules, 5, 737
Report section events, 746–753
Format, 746–749
Print, 749–752
Retreat, 753
Report view, 753–755
Representional State Transfer (REST), 1075
Required property, 278, 292, 311
ResponseBody property, 1004, 1081
ResponseStream property, 1081
ResponseText property, 1081, 1082
ResponseXML property, 1081
Rest API, 1059
Restful, 1075
Retreat event (Report Section Event), 753
ReturnVars, 958–960
REVOKE statement, 653
Ribbon extensibility or RibbonX, 799
Ribbon interface, 796–799
contextual tab, 799
Create tab, 797
dialog box launcher button, 798
More Forms button, 801
Ribbon programming, 799–822
Assigning ribbon customizations, forms and
reports, 819–823
callback procedures, 804–805
creating, ribbon customization xml markup,
800–803
embedding ribbon XML markup, 812–813
Loading ribbon customization, external
XML document, 805–812
sorting ribbon customization, XML markup,
813–819
tools for ribbon programming, 800
Ribbon UI customizations
Backstage View, 853–857
CommandBars object and, 849–852
controls in
built-in control, 845
checkboxes, 838–840

combo boxes and drop downs,
841–843
dialog box launcher, 843–844
disabling control, 844–845
edit boxes, 840–841
refreshing Ribbon, 846–849
split buttons, menus, and submenus,
836–838
toggle button, 834–835
images in
attributes and callbacks, 833–834
requesting images via getImage callback,
823–825
requesting images via loadImage
callback, 823–824
Quick Access Toolbar (QAT), 857–858
tab activation and group auto scaling,
852–853
Ribbon user interface (Access 2024), 796–799
contextual tab, 799
Create tab, 797
dialog box launcher button, 798
Rich text memo fields, 288–289
Right function, 273
RollbackTrans method, 350–351, 501–502
Row-returning, non-parameterized queries,
441
Row-returning, parameterized queries, 447
RowSource property, 464, 668, 722
RowSourceType property, 464
Runtime errors, 69, 216

S

Safe expression, 946
Sandbox mode, 946
Save method, 461, 478, 1039, 1041, 1043, 1082
SaveAs method, 325
Saved (persisted) recordset, 461
Saving recordset to disk (ADO), 461–465
Schema file, importing, 1013
Script delimiters and HTML tags, 992, 1009
Scripting Dictionary, 1060
Scripting Runtime Library, 1060–1061
Seek method, 307, 318, 319, 422–423,
Select Case statement, 116–123, 702

specifying multiple expressions in Case clause, 122
specifying range of values in Case clause, 120–122
using Is with Case clause, 119
SELECT INTO statement, 328, 337, 353, 376, 517, 567
Select query, 333–334, 439–441
SELECT statement, 117, 120, 313, 327, 331, 333, 346, 354, 370, 410, 485, 554, 567, 1042
SelectNodes method, 1038
SelectSingleNode method, 1040
Send method, 1004, 1077
Sequence of events, 686
Server-side cursor (adUseServer), 405
Server object, 994
Set Next Statement, 214
SetDisplayedCategories method, 793
SetPermissions method, 645, 647, 649
SetProperty, 1006
setRequestHeader, 1004, 1078–1079
SetTempVar, 42, 966
SHAPE statement, 485, 489, 497
Share-level security, 269
Show Next Statement, 214
Sinking events, in standalone class module, 902–909
  cRecordLogger class, creating, 904–906
  file preparation, 903
  frmCustomers form, 902, 905
  instance of custom class, creating, 906–908
  Object drop-down list, 904
  Procedure drop-down list, 903
  testing cRecordLogger custom class, 908–909
Skipping lines of code, in debugging, 214
Snapshot-type Recordset, 299, 304, 308, 318
Source parameter, 244, 401, 407
Split button, 836–338
Split function, 185, 707, 710, 1092
Spreadsheet constants, 383
SQL. See Structured Query Language (SQL)
SQL JOIN statements, 483–484
SQL Pass-Through Queries, 326, 483, 484
SQL specifications, 515–517
SQL WHERE clause, 415–416

Square brackets [], 331
Standalone class modules, 5, 902–909
Standalone macros
  creating, 932–937
  running, 937–938
Statements, 3
Static array, 152–155
Static variables in VBA procedures, 42–44
Status property, 476, 1080, 1082
StatusText property, 1080, 1082
Stepping through VBA procedure, 212–214
  running procedure to cursor, 214
  setting Next statement, 214
  showing Next statement, 214
  stepping out of procedure, 213–214
  stepping over, 212–213
Stop statement, 207–208
Stopping and resetting, of VBA procedures, 216
Stored procedure(s), 513–570
  changing database records with, 566–567
  contents of, 685–686
  creating, 553–556
  creating parameterized, 559–562
  deleting, 565–566
  enumerating, 557
  executing parameterized, 563–565
Structured Query Language (SQL), 511
Stylesheet, 982
Submacros, creating, 816, 938–940
Subroutine procedures (subroutines), 6, 176
Subscripted variables, 143
Supports method, 423
Syntax errors, 16, 191, 768, 899
SysCmd method, 760
System database (System.mdw), 573, 607, 635
Substring function, 1010

T

Table object, 373
Table relationships, using ADO
  one-to-many relationship, 398–400
  parent-child relationship, 398

Table-type Recordset, 296, 299, 307, 311, 318
TableDef object, 260, 264, 274, 276, 278, 283, 291, 295
Table(s)
  constraints, 541–542
    CHECK, 542
    FOREIGN KEY, 541
    NOT NULL, 542
    PRIMARY KEY, 542
    UNIQUE, 542
  creating, 513–569
    in current database (DDL with ADO), 520–523
    in new database (DDL with ADO/ ADOX), 523–525
  Data Definition Query window, 522–523
  deleting, 525–526
  design data types and Access SQL equivalents, 522–523
  establishing relationship between, 546–550
  modifying with DDL, 527–533
    adding multiple-field index to table, 535–536
    adding new fields to table, 527–528
    adding primary key to table, 533–534
    changing data type of table column, 529
    changing seed and increment values of autonumber columns, 531–533
    changing size of Text column, 530
    deleting column from table, 530
    deleting index, 536–537
    setting default value for table column, 530–531
Templates, 971–976
  .accdt file format, 971–976
  custom blank database template, creating, 971–972
Temporary variables, 38–42
  creating temporary variable with TempVars collection object, 39–40
  removing temporary variable from TempVars collection objects, 41
  retrieving names and values of TempVars objects, 40–41

temporary global variables in expressions, 41
  TempVars collection exposed to macros, 42
Testing and debugging
  Add Watch window, 205–207
  Assert statement, 203–204
  breakpoints, using, 194–200
  Call Stack dialog box, 211–212
  Err object, using, 217–221
  immediate window in break mode, 201–202
  Locals Window, 209–210
  navigating with bookmarks, 215
  quick watch, 208–209
  stepping through VBA procedure, 212–214
  Stop statement, 203
  stopping procedure, 193–194
  trapping errors, 216–224
Test method, 1071
TextCompare, 1064
Text property, 1080
Timer event, 705–706
Toggle button, 834–835
Toggle folders, 55
TOP keyword, 332
Transaction processing, 350–354
  creating transaction with ADO/DAO, 350–354
TransferSpreadsheet method, 383
TransformNode method, 996, 1004
TransformNodeToObject method, 1046–1047
TransformXML method, 1019, 1023
Trapping errors, 216–224
  Err object, using, 217–220
  On Error statement, 217
  procedure testing, 221–223
  setting options in Visual Basic project, 223–224
Troubleshooting errors in arrays, 161–162
Trusted location folder for Access database, 18–22
Type conversion functions (CSng), 44
Type declaration characters, 29
Type mismatch error, 99, 104, 162
Type property, 277

U

UBound function, 160–161
Underscore character (_), 331
Uniform Resource Identifier (URI), 988
Uniform Resource Location (*see* URL)
Uniform Resource Locator (*see* URL), 988
Uniform Resource Name (*see* URN), 988
UNIQUE constraint, 541
UNIQUE keyword, 535
Unique property, 292
Universal data link file (.udl), 253
Update method, 300, 303, 311, 318, 370, 404,
    430, 432, 465, 473, 477
Update query, 326–327
    executing, 449–451
UpdateBatch method, 404, 431, 475, 476, 478
URL, 988
URN, 988
User and group accounts (ADO)
    creating, 635–638
    deleting, 638–640
    listing, 640–641
    listing users in groups, 642–643
User and Group Accounts window, 622–623
User and group permissions
    changing user password, 650–651
    checking permissions for objects, 649
    object owner, determining name of, 644
    setting database password using, 270, 574,
        578, 602–604
    setting database password with DAO,
        576–577
    setting permissions for containers, 647–649
    setting permissions for database, 647
    setting permissions for object, 645–651
User-defined property, 279
User interface (UI)
    Access 2024 Ribbon interface, 796–799
    Backstage view, customizing, 853–857
    CommandBars object and Ribbon, 849–850
    controls in Ribbon customizations
        built-in control, 845
        checkboxes, 838–840
        combo boxes and drop downs, 841–843
        dialog box launcher, 843–844
        disabling control, 844–845
        edit boxes, 840–841
        refreshing Ribbon, 846–849
        split buttons, menus, and submenus,
            836–837
        toggle button, 834–835
    hiding elements of, 803
    images in Ribbon customization
        attributes and callbacks, 833–834
        requesting images via getImage callback,
            828–832
        requesting images via loadImage
            callback, 823–825
    Navigation pane, customizing
        controlling display of database objects,
            791–792
        locking Navigation pane, 791
        saving and loading configuration of,
            794–795
        setting displayed categories, 793–794
    Quick Access Toolbar (QAT), 857–858
    Ribbon programming, 799–823
        assigning Ribbon customizations to
            forms and reports, 819–823
        embedding Ribbon XML markup,
            812–813
        loading Ribbon customizations from
            external XML document,
            805–812
        Ribbon customization XML markup,
            creating, 800–804
        storing Ribbon customization XML
            markup, 813–819
    tab activation and group auto-scaling,
        852–853
    Understanding and exploring the ribbon
        interface, 784–790
User-level security, 267, 573, 601, 604, 607–620
USysApplicationLog table, 960–961
USysRibbons table, 814, 816, 819, 820, 832, 849,
    854

V

Validation Rule property, 278
Validation Text property, 278

Variable type, 27
Variables
    assigning values to, 29–30
    Joining text strings in VBA procedures, 28
    declaring, 25
    declaring typed, 29
    determining data type of, 47–48
    explicit variable declaration, 24
    finding variable definition, 47
    forcing declaration of, 30–31
    global, 37, 38, 39, 40, 41
    implicit variable declaration, 25
    informal, 26
    initialization, 30
    lifetime of, 38
    module-level, 34–35
    names, 24
    object, 44–48
    procedure-level (local), 34
    project-level, 37–38
    scope of, 33
    specifying data type of, 28–29
    static, 42–43
    temporary, 38–39
    type declaration characters, 29
Variant data type, 24, 25, 28, 29, 80, 83, 134, 141,
        148, 758, 1098
VBA. *See* Visual Basic for Applications (VBA)
VBA Array functions
    Array function, 155–161
    Erase function, 157–160
    IsArray function, 156–157
    LBound and UBound functions, 160–161
VBA programs, adding repeating actions
    Do...Until statement, 129–131
    Do...While statement, 125–129
    exiting loops early, 135–136
    For Each...Next statement, 134–135
    For...Next statement, 131–134
    infinite loops, avoiding, 129
    looping statements, 125
    paired statements, 134
    variables and loops, 130
VBA Project, 61
VBE. *See* Visual Basic Editor (VBE)
VBScript, 992, 993, 996, 1003, 1069

View(s)
    creating, 553–556
    deleting, 557–558
    generating list of saved, 558–559
Virtual directory, creating, 1108–1109
Visual Basic Editor (VBE)
    Code window, 58–60
    Immediate window, 72–76
    Object Browser, 68–71
    other windows, 34
    Project Explorer window, 53–55
    Properties window, 56–57
    renaming module, 62
    syntax and programming assistance
        Comment Block button, 68
        Complete Word, 67
        Indent, 67–68
        List Constants, 65–66
        List Properties/Methods option, 63–64
        Outdent, 67–68
        Parameter Info, 64–65
        Quick Info, 66
        Uncomment Block, 68
    VBA object library, using, 71–72
Visual Basic for Applications (VBA), 3
    assigning name to project, 61
    data types, 80–81
    debugging tools of, 186
    object library, 71–72
    procedures
        compiling, 16
        event, 9
        executing, 13–14
        function, 8–9
        property, 9–10
        in standard modules, 5
        subroutine, 6–7
    stopping and resetting, of VBA procedures, 216

W

Watch expressions
    adding, 205–207
    removing, 207
    vs. breakpoint, 204, 206
Well-formed document, 982

WHERE clause, 320, 327, 330, 331, 333, 354, 415, 514, 559
WIF, 573, 601, 607–609
With…End With construct, 203, 283
WithEvents keyword, 866, 902, 910, 911, 916
Workgroup information file (WIF), 573, 601, 607–609
   creating and joining, 610
Write method, 436, 873, 918
WriteLine method, 367, 420
WWW-Authenticate header, 1078

X

.xls, 252, 325
.xlsb, 325
.xlsm, 325
.xlsx, 325
.xps file format, saving reports in, 757
XML (Extensible Markup Language)
   ActiveX data objects with, 1040–1055
      attribute-centric and element-centric XML, 1044–1045
      Changing the type of, 1045–1046
      saving ADO recordset as XML to disk, 1041–1044
   applying XSLT transforms to exported data, 1006–1013
   exporting data, 1011–1013
      advanced XML export options, 997–1006
      data export options, 997–999
      presentation export options, 1000–1006
      schema export options, 999–1000
      XML data, 984–994
      XML documents formatted with stylesheets, 994–997
      XML schema file, 988–990
      XSL transformation files, 990–994
   exporting to and importing from XML, 1019–1031
      ExportXML method, 1020–1023
      ImportXML method, 1031
      TransformXML method, 1023–1030
   importing data, 1013–1019
      XML data to Access database, 1016–1017
      XSD schema file to Access database, 1014–1015
   manipulating XML documents, 1031–1040
      applying XSL stylesheet, 1046–1049
      changing type of XML file, 1045–1046
      loading and retrieving contents of XML file, 1033–1035
      loading XML document in Excel, 1053–1056
      retrieving first matching node, 1040
      retrieving information from element nodes, 1036–1037
      schema file, 1013–1015
      transforming attribute-centric XML data into HTML table, 1049–1053
      XML document nodes, 1040–1041
   XML document, 980–981
XML, 981–1058
XML data file, 984–993
XML data import, 1015–1019
XML data to Access database, 1016–1017
XML document nodes, 1035–1036
XMLDocument object, 1082
XML documents formatted with stylesheets, 994–997
XML Export Options, 997–1006
XML file
      exporting, 1020–1023
      importing, 1015–1019
XMLHTTP object, 1003
XMLHttpRequest object, 1076, 1077–1081
XML nodes, 1035–1040
Xmlns attribute, 802, 988
XML property, 1034
XML schema file, 988–990
XPath, 992
XSD schema, 1000, 1013–1015
XSL (Extensible Stylesheet Language), 982
XSLT (*see* XSL)
XSLT, 982
XSL Transformations (XSLT), 990–994
XSLT transformation, applying 1006–1013